Anthropology in Theory

Anthropology in Theory

Issues in Epistemology

SECOND EDITION

Edited by

Henrietta L. Moore and Todd Sanders

WILEY Blackwell

Library of Congress Cataloging-in-Publication Data is available on request

PB ISBN: 9780470673355

A catalogue record for this book is available from the British Library.

Cover image: Brenda Mayo, *Untitled*. Reproduced by permission of the artist.
Cover design by Simon Levy Associates

Set in 9.5/11.5pt Minion by SPi Publisher Services, Pondicherry, India
Printed in Singapore by Ho Printing Singapore Pte Ltd

1   2014

Contents

Notes on the Editors

Henrietta L. Moore FBA is the William Wyse Chair of Social Anthropology at the University of Cambridge. Her work on gender has developed a distinctive approach to the analysis of the interrelations of material and symbolic gender systems, embodiment and performance, and identity and sexuality. She has worked extensively in Africa, particularly on livelihood strategies, social transformation, and symbolic systems. Recent research has focused on virtual worlds, new technologies, and the relationship between self-imagining and globalization. Her most recent monograph, *Still Life: Hopes, Desires and Satisfactions* (Polity, 2011), argues for a reconsideration of globalization based on ordinary people's capacities for self-making and social transformation.

Todd Sanders is Associate Professor of Anthropology at the University of Toronto, and has worked in Africa for two decades. His projects have had varied foci and share a common theoretical concern with social and scientific knowledge practices. His books include *Those Who Play with Fire: Gender, Fertility and Transformation in East and Southern Africa* (with Henrietta L. Moore and Bwire Kaare; Athlone/Berg, 1999), *Magical Interpretations, Material Realities: Modernity, Witchcraft and the Occult in Postcolonial Africa* (with Henrietta L. Moore; Routledge, 2001), *Transparency and Conspiracy: Ethnographies of Suspicion in the New World Order* (with Harry West; Duke University Press, 2003), and *Beyond Bodies: Rainmaking and Sense Making in Tanzania* (University of Toronto Press, 2008).

General Introduction

Henrietta L. Moore and Todd Sanders

Theory as Practice

This collection attests to the strength and diversity of anthropological theorizing in the twentieth and early twenty-first centuries. We use the term "theorizing" rather than the more usual noun form "theory" because the pieces collected here are intended to reflect the practice of engaging with theory, particular ways of thinking, analyzing, and reflecting that have emerged in the context of writings over this period. Anthropology as a discipline has a number of subdivisions or "traditions." These may be broadly cast as national – as in British, American, Japanese, Brazilian anthropology – and regional – as in the particular theoretical concerns of specific regions, such as "persons," "cross-cousin marriage," "gift exchange," and so on. The boundaries between these different "traditions" are far from fixed, and indeed are being constantly transcended. The writings collected here draw on a variety of perspectives. Our aim is not to provide a representative sample of any – and certainly not all – traditions, but to make available a flavor of the intellectual conversations and debates on specific epistemological issues that formed the practice of theorizing in twentieth- and early twenty-first-century anthropology.

No one collection could ever hope to be representative of anthropological theories per se. The question "What is anthropological theory?" is inextricably tied to the question "What is anthropology?" (Moore 1999: 2; Moore and Sanders, this volume). Anthropology has been variously defined as the study of "other cultures," "cultural difference," "social systems," "world views," "ways of life," and "forms of knowledge." Sometimes these abstractions are given more concrete referents, such as political systems, livelihoods, kinship systems, family structures, and religious beliefs. The only difficulty is that neither the more abstract conceptual categories nor the empirical entities are the exclusive domain of anthropology, which immediately raises the issue of how we would delineate specifically anthropological theories. This is obvious in the practice of anthropology, since most anthropology courses begin by teaching students about Durkheim, Weber, and Marx, whose writings have been formative for the discipline. Contemporary anthropological theorizing also engages in extensive theoretical borrowing, and recent examples would include the work of Bourdieu, Foucault, Gramsci, Bakhtin, Agamben, and many others. We make no attempt in this collection – it would in any case be impossible – to provide examples of all the theories from the humanities, social sciences, and sciences that have influenced anthropological theorizing. Rather, we have integrated extracts from writers outside anthropology where their thinking contributes to particular debates or discussion points within a specific set of epistemological difficulties under discussion within the volume. For example, in section 2 on *structure and system*, we have included an extract from Durkheim (5), not only because his writings had a profound influence, albeit in different ways, on the work of Radcliffe-Brown (6) and Lévi-Strauss (8), but also because it discusses the relationship between the individual and society, which is one of the concerns of section 1. The extract from Durkheim thus provides both a context for readers engaging with the work of Radcliffe-Brown and Lévi-Strauss and an indirect commentary on the vexed question of what distinguishes social structures from social relations. Our intention throughout has been to portray anthropological theorizing as a set of dialogues – dialogues that are not only internal to the discipline, but also engage with writings outside the discipline from which anthropology has often sought inspiration. Thus we have included extracts that not only reflect a writer's theoretical position – or at least one of her or his positions – but can also be maintained in a productive relation with positions taken by other writers elsewhere in the volume. Consequently, individual extracts should not be taken as necessarily representative of an individual's entire oeuvre.

In designing a collection of this kind, it is evident that a plethora of organizational principles proffer themselves, all with strengths and weaknesses. It might have been feasible – if somewhat constraining – to have divided anthropological theorizing into anthropological theories of "kinship," "politics," "economics," and so on. Equally, it might have been appropriate to divide disciplinary endeavor into "schools of thought," such as functionalism, structural-functionalism, and structuralism. Another possible set of categorizations might have been suggested by reference to specialist sub-fields, such as the anthropology of cognition, art, nationalism, psychology, development, gender, the body, medical anthropology, and so on. All these sub-fields borrow extensively from other disciplines and many of them require specialist theoretical knowledge. Every one of these ways of organizing the collection was considered. They were ultimately abandoned not just because as categorizations and principles of organization they can be readily contested, but because we wanted to emphasize what might be distinctive about anthropological theorizing, that is, the *practice* of it.

How This Book is Organized

Anthropology is not anthropology because it studies kinship or cognition or politics or art, or because it has had practitioners who are structuralists or post-structuralists. What is distinctive about anthropology is the way it has created and constructed itself, the particular history of the formation of ideas that have given rise to a distinctive discipline and a set of associated practices. It is this process of theorizing that this volume seeks to capture. Today's conversations are clearly different from those of the past, and while it is difficult to understand contemporary concerns without some knowledge of the origins of the debates, the volume is not organized on a purely historical basis. The aim has been to show the recursive and enduring nature of key questions, principally the lasting search for a more complete understanding of the anthropological object of inquiry; in other words, the extent to which anthropological theorizing has always been driven by the question "What is anthropology?" The volume thus aims to demonstrate both the variations and the continuities in the key questions anthropologists have asked: "what is the relationship between the individual and society"; "what is the difference between society and culture"; "what makes us distinctively human"; "how are we to comprehend cultural difference in the context of a universal humanity"; "what is the relationship between models and reality"; "what is the relationship between the models of the observer and those of the observed"?

The collection as a whole provides an introduction to these questions for readers inside and outside anthropology. It also builds up a dialogue about specific sets of assumptions on which theorizing in anthropology is based, the methods appropriate to address certain questions, and the theoretical frameworks through which they are received. So, for example, in section 2, *structure and system*, we have included extracts from different writers discussing the term "structure" and what it encompasses and entails. A concept such as "structure" not only defines the kinds of questions that can be asked of data, but also determines the methods used to collect data. The aim of each section is to provide a kind of minor "genealogy of knowledge" where the extracts explore through dialogue with each other not only what certain concepts and the pre-theoretical assumptions on which they are based reveal, but also what they remain silent on, the questions that do not get asked. The overall structure of the book is, as we have said, not historically oriented, but is, rather, based on a series of counterpoints or questions, so that issues on which certain sections are silent get picked up later in subsequent sections. The contributions can, of course, be read in any order, but the volume's layout is intended to provide a pathway through a series of interlinked debates for readers less familiar with anthropology. We provide an overview of the theoretical development of anthropology in the twentieth and early twenty-first century and its epistemological concerns in the next chapter (Moore and Sanders, this volume).

In *part I*, the debates are animated by the question of the relationship between society and culture, and indeed the issue which divided British and American anthropology in the first half of the twentieth century: whether it was culture or society that formed the object of anthropological inquiry. Different writers in the sections in *part I* discuss the definition of these terms and how they relate to the individuals who comprise them. One major difficulty here is the fact of cultural difference and how it relates to our common humanity, to the environment in which we live, and to our individual natures. What is crucial is the way that cultural determinism and cultural relativism interact in the thinking of individual authors. While one could characterize the basic trend through the twentieth century as a move from strong forms of cultural determinism (humans are the products of their culture/society and its environment) to a view that emphasizes individual agency in the context of intersubjective relations with others (humans are biologically cultural beings who develop within a cultural world) (see Moore and Sanders, this volume), this would be to ignore the recursive nature of epistemological postulates in anthropological thinking. The extracts in this part demonstrate the differences between writers of similar historical periods, and the continuities and discontinuities between contemporary writers and those at the beginning of the twentieth century, particularly with regard to the mechanisms that link forms of abstraction – concepts such as "structure," for instance – to forms of explanation. A perennial complication in anthropology is that since abstractions are created by the analyst, and they provide the building blocks for anthropological models, there is considerable debate about how such abstractions relate to the empirical data from which they are abstracted, and beyond that, how anthropological models qua models relate to those of informants (see Moore and Sanders, this volume).

Part II takes up these questions in a different guise and focuses on language, meanings, and interpretations, particularly with regard to the relationship of cultural meanings to actors' models. The pre-theoretical assumptions under interrogation in this part are those based on the idea that language is central to social life, that it is what defines us as human, and thus we must analyze social life as the creation and negotiation of meaning within which actors interpret their experience and order their actions. A focus on meaning inevitably raises queries about the degree to which individuals within a culture share meanings, how knowledge may be differentially distributed as a result of power, and how meanings and values get transferred from one generation or group to another. This connects work in this area to older debates about the relationship between culture and thought, not only with regard to the beliefs and thoughts of individuals, but also in relation to the pre-theoretical assumption that language is necessary for thought. Work on bodies, praxis, and phenomenology emphasizes that there are forms of knowledge that are non-linguistic, that the human body, for example, knows the world through its engagement with the world and with others in that world. However, if practical knowledge of the world is the result of engagement with that world, then what scope is there for individual creativity or for social change; how can we negotiate the apparent impasse between objective structures and subjective experience? Thus, *part II* takes up once again, albeit from a very different angle, the question of how to transcend the division between the individual and culture, what might be intended or encompassed by the term "structures" (as in linguistic structures/structures of meaning), and how the models of both observer and observed relate to knowledge and to power (see Moore and Sanders, this volume).

Part III addresses issues of scale and comparison, but more than this, it provides a sustained reflection on a series of models for knowing the world. These models are all derived in one way or another from western philosophical traditions, and the question is the degree to which they are appropriate for knowing the worlds of other people, in other times and places. Underlying this question is a broader concern about whether it is possible to know the world. Is anthropology an objective science or a subjective form of interpretation? What kind of instrument of knowledge is the anthropologist? Anthropology has developed a very clear critique of the relations between power and knowledge that have constituted the domain of anthropology itself and its associated practices. This debate acknowledges that knowledge is always a matter of ethics. Anthropology, like all disciplines, creates a world full of specific kinds of entities – societies, cultures – which is inhabited by particular kinds of agents – persons, individuals, etc. Much critical anthropology has served to work against the power relations that constitute the anthropological field of knowledge, and has criticized the comparative models of anthropology for occluding the perspectives, voices, and lived realities of the people being studied. This raises once again – but in the context of unequal power relations – how adequately anthropological models represent the lived reality of people's lives. However, debates in this area go further than earlier debates because they question the nature of the theoretical itself, including the very project of western knowledge as it underpins anthropology (see Moore 1999; Moore and Sanders, this volume). Hence, the discussion focuses on whether and under what circumstances comparison is possible, appropriate, and powerful. Can we do without models? Can we have objective knowledge of other people's worlds? What do we relinquish – and at what cost to ourselves and others – if we give up on the notion of anthropology as science?

Part IV discusses the shifts in the conditions of production of anthropological research and therefore of anthropological knowledge. Cultures – however they might have been represented in the past – have never been fixed, bounded, or unitary. In the context of globalization, migration, and transnational flows, anthropology has been forced to rethink not only the major concepts of anthropology – society, culture, kinship, and others – but also the very notion of cultural difference itself. This is in part because anthropology has "come home"; "other cultures" are no longer in "other places," and anthropology is much less able to distance itself from the communities it studies. The nature of the academy has also changed profoundly, and it is not just the communities and cultures studied by anthropologists that are transnational and transcultural, but anthropologists themselves. This has had a major impact on both knowledge construction and critical politics within the discipline. Issues of perspective, power, positionality, and hybridity have been largely forced onto the agenda of the discipline by those scholars who most forcefully live hybridity and multiple positionality. Anthropology, like the world itself, is becoming simultaneously globalized and localized. One powerful irony here is that at the very moment anthropology appeared to want to abandon the organizing trope of culture, the rest of the world started to adopt it. International agencies, local civil society groups, management consultants, consumer researchers, and a host of other groups and institutions embraced it as the lens through which to understand difference in a globalized world. It has become a mobilizing concept for many indigenous and civil society groups around the world, and in some cases the explanation for power differentials, exclusions, and even hatreds and acts of violence. The result is that not only have the contexts for anthropological research shifted, but so has the nature of the relationship between observer and observed. Anthropology and anthropologists no longer command the high ground of representation – if indeed they ever did – and have had to recognize that their view on cultural difference is only one among many. New ways of imaging the anthropological object of inquiry have emerged: new images, metaphors, and concepts. This gives rise to new practices, new ways of doing field research, of combining advocacy and research, of imagining the very nature of the social itself (see Moore 1996, 1999; and Moore and Sanders, this volume).

Locating Anthropology

It has often been said that there is no single anthropology, but only a series of anthropologies. The perspective developed in this collection would see that statement as a question of scale, as a matter of position, of what one chooses to foreground, on the one hand, and consign to the background, on the other. The variety, diversity, and richness of contemporary anthropological theorizing are indisputable, as is the existence of the vigorous debates which are its origin. However, when we speak of anthropology we should not lose sight of the fact that it is an intellectual endeavor, a discipline and a profession. In other words, it is not only about ways of thinking, but also about ways of doing in the context of specific institutions and power relations. All ideas are generated and communicated within particular historical, material, social, and political relations and processes. Styles of reasoning, as Hacking argues, create the possibility of truth and falsehood precisely because they are historically situated (Hacking 1982: 56–7). This is not to claim that truth is not the object of our inquiries or that the refinements and careful calibrations of thought, reasoning, and method that make anthropology a social science are unimportant. It is, rather, to draw attention to the circumstances, contexts, and practices within which the effects of truth are produced.

Contemporary anthropology as a discipline and as a set of practices is engaged in multiple ways with the world it reflects upon. This engagement is complex, frequently vexed, but always productive. Theorizing is not only about the nature, limits, and sources of knowledge. It is also about the process of self-reflection that constitutes the practice of theorizing on the grounds and contexts of knowledge production in a way that acknowledges their material and historical constraints and ambitions. This leads to contestation about the very nature of theory and the theoretical. In contemporary anthropology, this has been evident not only in the debate about objects, the question of what constitutes the objects of anthropological inquiry, but also in the parallel discussion about subjects and subject positions – that is to say, who speaks for other cultures, but more than that, who speaks for anthropology itself. These subject positions are geographically and institutionally framed, but they are also epistemological. It seems indisputable that, being a product of western culture and philosophy, anthropology has been constituted historically as much by its subject positions as by its objects of inquiry, as much by who speaks in its name and in what voice as by the question "What is anthropology?" The gaze of the anthropological observer has never been an unmarked one, but the question for the future is whether that gaze can be effectively unmoored not only from the traditions that gave rise to it, but also from the broader imaginary of the west and its relations to others.

References

Hacking, I. 1982 Language, Truth and Reason. In *Rationality and Relativism*. M. Hollis, and S. Lukes, eds. Oxford: Blackwell.

Moore, H. L. 1996 The Changing Nature of Anthropological Knowledge: An Introduction. In *The Future of Anthropological Knowledge*. H. L. Moore, ed. London: Routledge.

Moore, H. L. 1999 Anthropological Theory at the Turn of the Century. In *Anthropological Theory Today*. H. L. Moore, ed. Cambridge: Polity Press.

Acknowledgments

The editors and publisher gratefully acknowledge the permission granted to reproduce the copyright material in this book:

1 Franz Boas, "The Aims of Anthropological Research," pp. 243–59 from *Race, Language and Culture*. Chicago: University of Chicago Press and The Free Press, 1982 [1940]. Originally published in *Science* N.S., vol. 76 (1932), pp. 605–13.

2 A. L. Kroeber, "The Concept of Culture in Science," pp. 118–20, 129–33 from *The Nature of Culture*. Chicago: University of Chicago Press, 1952. Copyright © 1952 by University of Chicago Press. Reprinted by permission of University of Chicago Press.

3 Gregory Bateson, pp. 111–22 from *Naven: A Survey of the Problems Suggested by a Composite Picture of the Culture of a New Guinea Tribe Drawn from Three Points of View*, 2nd edn. Stanford: Stanford University Press, 1958 [1936]. Copyright © 1958 by the Board of Trustees of the Leland Stanford Jr. University. All rights reserved. Used with permission of Stanford University Press, www.sup.org.

4 Ruth Benedict, pp. 251–68, 270–8, 285–6 from *Patterns of Culture*. Boston and New York: Houghton Mifflin Company, 1934. Copyright © 1934 by Ruth Benedict. Copyright renewed 1961 by Ruth Valentine. Reprinted by permission of Houghton Mifflin Company and Taylor and Francis. All rights reserved.

5 Emile Durkheim, pp. 89–12 from George E. G. Caitlin (ed.), *The Rules of Sociological Method*, 8th edn. Sarah A. Solovay and John H. Mueller (trans.). New York: The Free Press, 1938. Copyright © 1938 by George E. G. Catlin. Copyright renewed 1966 by Sarah A. Solovay, John H. Mueller, George E. G. Catlin. Reprinted with the permission of The Free Press, a Division of Simon & Schuster Adult Publishing Group. All rights reserved.

6 A. R. Radcliffe-Brown, "On Social Structure," pp. 189–200 from *Journal of Royal Anthropological Institute* 70(1), 1940. Copyright © 1940 by *Journal of the Royal Anthropological Institute*. Reprinted with permission of John Wiley & Sons UK

7 E. R. Leach, "Introduction," pp. 1–17, 313–18 from *Political Systems of Highland Burma: A Study of Kachin Social Structure*. London: Athlone Press, 1970. Copyright © 1970 by Athlone Press. Reprinted by permission of The Continuum International Publishing Group. First published in 1964.

8 Claude Lévi-Strauss, "Social Structure," pp. 321–8, 333–5, 338–9, 347–50 from *Anthropology Today*. Chicago: University of Chicago Press, 1962 [1952]. Copyright © 1952 by University of Chicago Press. Reprinted by permission of University of Chicago Press.

9   Bronislaw Malinowski, "The Group and the Individual in Functional Analysis," pp. 938–47, 948–62 from *The American Journal of Sociology* 44(6), 1939. Copyright © 1939 by *The American Journal of Sociology*. Reprinted by permission of University of Chicago Press.

10 Julian H. Steward, "The Concept and Method of Cultural Ecology," pp. 31–42, 224, 226–7 from *Theory of Cultural Change: The Methodology of Multilinear Evolution*. Urbana: University of Illinois Press, 1955. Copyright © 1955 by Board of Trustees of the University of Illinois. Copyright renewed 1983 by Jane C. Steward. Used with permission of the University of Illinois Press.

11 Leslie A. White, "Energy and the Evolution of Culture," pp. 363–93, 390–1, 392–3, 423, 427, 431–3 from *The Science of Culture: A Study of Man and Civilization*. New York: Farrar, Straus and Company, 1949. Copyright © 1949 by Leslie White. Reprinted by permission of Robert L. Carneiro, American Museum of Natural History.

12 Andrew P. Vayda and Roy A. Rappaport, "Ecology, Cultural and Noncultural," pp. 476, 479–80, 483– 5, 488–94, 407 from James A. Clifton (ed.), *Introduction to Cultural Anthropology*. Boston: Houghton Mifflin Company, 1968.

13 J. H. M. Beattie, "Understanding and Explanation in Social Anthropology," pp. 45–56, 57–60 from *The British Journal of Sociology* 10(1), 1959. Reprinted with permission of John Wiley & Sons Ltd.

14 Holy Ladislav and Stuchlik Milan, "Anthropological Data and Social Reality," pp. 5–12, 12–19, 122–9 from *Actions, Norms and Representations*. Cambridge: Cambridge University Press, 1983. Copyright © 1983 by Cambridge University Press. Reproduced with permission of Cambridge University Press.

15 Pierre Bourdieu, "Objectification Objectified," pp. 30–41, 287–9, 320, 322–3, 325–9 from *The Logic of Practice*, Richard Nice (trans.). Cambridge: Polity, 1990 [1980]. Copyright © 1990 by Polity Press. Reprinted with permission of Stanford University Press, www.sup.org. All rights reserved and copyright © 1980 by Les Editions de Minuit. Reprinted with permission of Georges Borchardt, Inc. for Les Editions de Minuit, and The Estate of Pierre Bourdieu (Jérôme Bourdieu for ebook rights)

16 Clifford Geertz, "Thick Description: Toward an Interpretive Theory of Culture," pp. 4–7, 9–20 from *The Interpretation of Cultures*. New York: Basic Books, 1973. Copyright © 1973 by Clifford Geertz. Reprinted by permission of Basic Books, a member of the Perseus Books Group.

17 Talal Asad, "Anthropology and the Analysis of Ideology," pp. 609–21, 624–7 from *Man* 14(4), 1979. Copyright © 1979 by *Man*. Reprinted by permission of John Wiley & Sons UK.

18 Sherry B. Ortner, "Subjectivity and Cultural Critique," pp. 31–52 (with cuts) from *Anthropological Theory* 5(1), 2005. Copyright © 2005. Reprinted with permission of SAGE.

19 Claude Lévi-Strauss, "Structural Analysis in Linguistics and in Anthropology," pp. 31–54 from *Structural Anthropology*, Claire Jacobson and Brooke Grundfest Schoepf (trans.). London: Allen Lane, the Penguin Press, 1968. English language translation copyright © 1963 by Basic Books, Inc. Reproduced by permission of Basic Books, a member of the Perseus Book Group.

20 Malcolm Crick, "Ordinary Language and Human Action," pp. 90–8, 173–4, 177, 187, 190–1 from *Explorations in Language and Meaning: Towards a Semantic Anthropology*. New York: John Wiley & Sons, 1976. Copyright © 1976 by John Wiley & Sons.

21 Maurice Bloch, "Language, Anthropology and Cognitive Science," pp. 183–94, 195–8 from *Man* 26, 1991. Copyright © 1991 by *Man*. Reprinted by permission of John Wiley & Sons UK.

22 Harvey Whitehouse, "Towards an Integration of Ethnography, History and the Cognitive Science of Religion," pp. 247–80 (with cuts) from H. Whitehouse and J. Laidlaw (eds.), *Religion, Anthropology and Cognitive Science*. Durham, NC: Carolina Academic Press, 2007, pp. 247–80. Reprinted with permission of Carolina Academic Press.

23 Charles Stafford, "Linguistic and Cultural Variables in the Psychology of Numeracy," pp. S128–S141 from *Journal of the Royal Anthropological Institute* s1, 2008. Reprinted with permission of John Wiley & Sons UK.

24 T. M. Luhrmann, "Subjectivity," pp. 345–61 (with cuts) from *Anthropological Theory* 6(3), 2006. Copyright © 2006. Reprinted with permission of SAGE.

25   Charles Whitehead, "Why the Behavioural Sciences Need the Concept of the Culture-Ready Brain," pp. 43–71 (with cuts) from *Anthropological Theory* 12(1) (2012), pp. 43–71. Copyright © 2012. Reprinted with permission of SAGE.

26   Michael Jackson, "Knowledge of the Body," pp. 327–40, 341–5 from *Man* 18, 1983. Copyright © 1983 by *Man*. Reprinted by permission of John Wiley & Sons UK.

27   Emily Martin, "The End of the Body?," pp. 121–9, 130–40 from *American Ethnologist* 19(1), 1992. All rights reserved. Copyright © 1992 by American Anthropological Association. Reproduced by permission of the American Anthropological Association and the author. Not for sale or further reproduction.

28   Lesley Sharp, "Hybridity: Hybrid Bodies of the Scientific Imaginary," pp. 262–75 from Frances Mascia-Lees (ed.), *Companion to the Anthropology of the Body and Embodiment*. Oxford: Blackwell Publishing Ltd., 2011, Wiley-Blackwell. Reprinted with permission of John Wiley & Sons Ltd.

29   Max Weber, "Puritanism and the Spirit of Capitalism," pp. 25–34 from Sam Whimster (ed.), *The Essential Weber*. London and New York: Routledge, 2004. Reproduced by permission of Taylor & Francis Books.

30   Eric R. Wolf, "Introduction," pp. 3–23, 431, 435, 438–9, 446, 450–1, 456, 460–1, 463, 467–9 from *Europe and the People Without History*, 2nd edn. Berkeley: University of California Press, 1982. Copyright © 1983 The Regents of the University of California. Reprinted by permission of the Regents of the University of California and the University of California Press.

31   Jean Comaroff and John Comaroff, "Introduction," pp. 14–32, 316–18, 353–6, 358–60, 362–70, 372–8, 382–4, 389, 393–4 from *Of Revelation and Revolution: Christianity, Colonialism and Consciousness in South Africa*, Vol. 1. Chicago: University of Chicago Press, 1991. Copyright © 1991 by University of Chicago Press. Reprinted by permission of University of Chicago Press.

32   Donald L. Donham, "Epochal Structures I: Reconstructing Historical Materialism," pp. 52–63, 64–70 (with cuts) from *History, Power, Ideology: Central Issues in Marxism and Anthropology*, 2nd edn. Berkeley: University of California Press, 1999. Copyright © 1999 by Donald L. Donham. Reproduced by permission of University of California Press.

33   Pierre Bourdieu, "Structures and the Habitus," pp. 72–3, 76–84, 85–7, 214–16 from *Outline of a Theory of Practice*, Richard Nice (trans.). Cambridge: Cambridge University Press, 1977. English translation © Cambridge University Press, 1977. Reprinted with permission of Librairie Droz S.A., Genève.

34   Michael Lambek, "Body and Mind in Mind, Body and Mind in Body: Some Anthropological Interventions in a Long Conversation," pp. 103–18, 121–3 (with cuts) from Michael Lambek and Andrew Strathern (eds.), *Bodies and Persons: Comparative Perspectives from Africa and Melanesia*. Cambridge: Cambridge University Press, 1998. Copyright © 1998 by Cambridge University Press. Reprinted with permission of Cambridge University Press.

35   Sherry B. Ortner, "So *Is* Female to Male as Nature Is to Culture?," pp. 173–80, 235, 242–4, 246–8, 250–1 from *Making Gender: The Politics and Erotics of Culture*. Boston: Beacon Press, 1996. Copyright © 1996 by Sherry B. Ortner. Reprinted by permission of Beacon Press, Boston.

36   Henrietta L. Moore, "Global Anxieties: Concept-Metaphors and Pre-theoretical Commitments in Anthropology," pp. 72–88 from *Anthropological Theory* 4(1), 2004. Copyright © 2004 by *Anthropological Theory*. Reproduced by permission of Sage Publications Ltd.

37   Robert J. Thornton, "The Rhetoric of Ethnographic Holism," pp. 285–6, 288–99, 301–3 from *Cultural Anthropology* 3(3), 1988. Copyright © 1988 by *Cultural Anthropology*. Not for sale or further reproduction. Reprinted by permission of the American Anthropological Association.

38   Lila Abu-Lughod, "Writing Against Culture," pp. 137–54, 161–2 from Richard G. Fox (ed.), *Recapturing Anthropology: Working in the Present*. Santa Fe: School of American Research Press, 1991. Copyright © 1991 by the School of American Research Press, Santa Fe, USA. Reproduced by permission of SAR Press.

39   Marilyn Strathern, "Cutting the Network," pp. 517–31, 533–5 from *Journal of the Royal Anthropological Institute* 2(3), 1996. Copyright © 1996 by *Journal of the Royal Anthropological Institute*. Reproduced by permission of John Wiley & Sons UK.

40 Nancy Scheper-Hughes, "The Primacy of the Ethical," pp. 425–20, 438–40 from *Current Anthropology* 36(3), 1995. Copyright © 1995 by *Current Anthropology*. Reprinted by permission of University of Chicago Press.

41 Roy D'Andrade. "Moral Models in Anthropology," pp. 399–406, 438–40 from *Current Anthropology* 36(3), 1995. Copyright © 1995 by *Current Anthropology*. Reprinted by permission of University of Chicago Press.

42 Melford E. Spiro, "Postmodernist Anthropology, Subjectivity, and Science: A Modernist Critique," pp. 759–80 (with cuts) from *Comparative Studies in Society and History* 38(4), 1996. Copyright © 1996 by *Comparative Studies in Society and History*. Reprinted with permission of Cambridge University Press.

43 Didier Fassin, "Beyond Good and Evil? Questioning the Anthropological Discomfort with Morals," pp. 333–44 from *Anthropological Theory* 8(4), 2008. Reprinted with permission of SAGE.

44 Oyèrónké Oyěwùmí, pp. ix–xiii, 7–9, 10–12, 181, 183–4, 210, 213, 215–20 from *The Invention of Women: Making an African Sense of Gender Discourses*. Minneapolis: University of Minnesota Press, 1997. Copyright © 1997 by the Regents of the University of Minnesota. Reprinted by permission of the University of Minnesota Press.

45 Vivek Dhareshwar, "Valorizing the Present: Orientalism, Postcoloniality, and the Human Sciences," pp. 223–31 (with cuts) from *Cultural Dynamics* 10(2), 1998. Copyright © 1998 by *Cultural Dynamics*. Reproduced by permission of SAGE.

46 Eduardo Viveiros de Castro, "Cosmological Deixis and Amerindian Perspectivism," pp. 469–88 from *Journal of the Royal Anthropological Institute* 4(3), 1998. Copyright © 1998 by *Journal of the Royal Anthropological Institute*. Reprinted by permission of John Wiley & Sons UK.

47 Stefan Helmreich, "What Was Life? Answers from Three Limit Biologies," pp. 671–96 (excerpts) from *Critical Inquiry* 37(4), 2011. Reprinted with permission of University of Chicago Press.

48 Marc Augé, "The Near and the Elsewhere," pp. 7–8, 10–41, 121–2 from *Non-places: Introduction to an Anthropology of Supermodernity*, John Howe (trans.). London: Verso, 1995. Copyright © 1995 by Verso. Reprinted by permission of Verso.

49 Bruno Latour, pp. 97–106, 146, 148–53 from *We Have Never Been Modern*, Catherine Porter (trans.). Cambridge, Mass.: Harvard University Press, 1993. Copyright © 1993 by Harvester Wheatsheaf and the President and Fellows of Harvard College.

50 Caitlin Zaloom, "How to Read the Future: The Yield Curve, Affect, and Financial Prediction," pp. 243–66 (with cuts) from *Public Culture* 21(2), 2009. Copyright © 2009 Duke University Press. All rights reserved. Republished by permission of the copyright holder, Duke University Press. www.dukeupress.edu

51 Webb Keane, "Signs Are Not the Garb of Meaning: On the Social Analysis of Material Things," pp. 181–201 (with cuts) from Daniel Miller (ed.), *Materiality*. Durham, NC: Duke University Press, 2005. Copyright © 2005 Duke University Press. Republished by permission of the copyright holder, Duke University Press. www.dukeupress.edu

52 Yael Navaro-Yashin, "Affective Spaces, Melancholic Objects: Ruination and the Production of Anthropological Knowledge," pp. 1–6, 8–18 from *Journal of the Royal Anthropological Institute* 15(1), 2009. (This paper has been significantly shortened for use in our book.) Copyright © 2009 by *Journal of the Royal Anthropological Institute*. Reproduced by permission of John Wiley & Sons UK.

53 Akhil Gupta and James Ferguson, "Beyond 'Culture': Space, Identity, and the Politics of Difference," pp. 6–14, 16–18, 20–3 from *Cultural Anthropology* 7(1), 1992. All rights reserved. Not for sale or further reproduction. Copyright © 1992 by American Anthropological Association. Used by permission.

54 George E. Marcus, "What is at Stake – and is not – in the Idea and Practice of Multi-sited Ethnography," pp. 6–14 (with cuts) from *Canberra Anthropology* 22(2), 1999. Reprinted by kind permission of the author.

55   Arjun Appadurai, "Grassroots Globalization and the Research Imagination," pp. 1–19 from *Public Culture* 12(1), 2000. Copyright © 2000 by Duke University Press. All rights reserved. Republished by permission of the copyright holder, Duke University Press. www.dukeupress.edu

56   John Comaroff, "The End of Anthropology, Again: On the Future of an In/Discipline," pp. 524–32 from *American Anthropologist* 12(4), 2010, pp. 524–32. Reproduced with permission of the American Anthropological Association. Not for sale or further reproduction.

57   Pierre Bourdieu, "Participant Objectivation," pp. 281–8, 291–4 from *Journal of the Royal Anthropological Institute* 9(2), 2003. Reprinted with permission of John Wiley & Sons UK.

58   P. Steven Sangren, "Anthropology of Anthropology? Further Reflections on Reflexivity," pp. 13–16 from *Anthropology Today* 23(4), 2007. Reprinted with permission of John Wiley & Sons UK.

59   Gustavo Lins Ribeiro, "World Anthropologies: Cosmopolitics for a New Global Scenario in Anthropology," pp. 363–86 (with cuts) from *Critique of Anthropology* 26(4), 2006. Copyright © 2006. Reprinted with permission of SAGE.

60   Douglas R. Holmes and George E. Marcus, "Cultures of Expertise and the Management of Globalization: Toward the Re-functioning of Ethnography," pp. 236–41, 243–6, 248–50 from A. Ong and S. Collier (eds.), *Global Assemblages*. New York: Blackwell, 2004. Reprinted with permission of John Wiley & Sons UK.

Every effort has been made to trace copyright holders and to obtain their permission for the use of copyright material. The publisher apologizes for any errors or omissions in the above list and would be grateful if notified of any corrections that should be incorporated in future reprints or editions of this book.

Anthropology and Epistemology

Henrietta L. Moore and Todd Sanders

There are two kinds of question that guide social science inquiry: "What can I know about the world?" and "How can I know the world?" The first is properly the domain of metaphysics – philosophical inquiry into the nature of reality, existence, and being – while the second is the terrain of method. In general terms, however, they are both the stuff of what we term theory in anthropology because they cannot be easily or profitably separated. Anthropological difficulties with knowing the world rest on what we can know about other people, and this is a problem that has several dimensions.

Sameness and Difference

The first issue is whether and to what degree human beings share characteristics and capacities. In anthropology, these reflections on the nature of being have at different times been profoundly influenced by work in biology, psychology, and cognition. At the root of these reflections lies an important question: "Do all humans think in the same way?" This question underlies and forms the presuppositions for two others: "Is it possible to understand other worlds, how other people think?" and if the answer to this is affirmative, then "What is the relationship between culture and thought?" To a very significant extent the answer to these questions depends on the characteristics we assume human beings and indeed cultures to have. One of the factors that has driven change in anthropological theorizing has been variation in our pre-theoretical assumptions about the nature of being human and of being a culture-bearing human.

Twentieth-century anthropology explicitly set itself against nineteenth-century evolutionism, against the idea that all cultures were ranged along a line towards Progress and Civilization set by western values and understandings (Herskovits 1972; Sapir 1985 [1949]). Franz Boas and his students explicitly espoused the notion that cultures had to be understood in their own terms and as wholes (Boas, 1). Their presupposition was that human beings shared a common human condition, but one which expressed itself in diverse forms: underlying cultural difference was an essential human sameness. Boas was interested in using the science of culture to combat racism, but he was also passionately committed to ethnographic particularism, to the idea that cultures could not be understood according to universal standards and values (Boas, 1). In short, Boas was a cultural relativist and he was categorically opposed

Anthropology in Theory: Issues in Epistemology, Second Edition. Edited by Henrietta L. Moore and Todd Sanders.
© 2014 John Wiley & Sons, Inc. Published 2014 by John Wiley & Sons, Inc.

to the analysis of cultural elements outside of their historical and cultural context (Boas 1982 [1940]). Each culture had to be treated as a unique way of life. Each culture had its own "genius" and there was no way that they could be ranked or valued against or in comparison with each other (Bateson, 3; Sapir 1924; Stocking 1968, 1974).[1] The result was that any judgement relating to behavior and behavior patterns must be made relative to the standards of the cultures producing them (Sapir 1985 [1949]). Hence, while the Kwakiutl, for example, may exhibit a constellation of characteristics which appear abnormal by western standards, this judgement is invalid since the behavior is normal by Kwakiutl standards (Benedict, 4).

The notion of "genius" was connected in other writings in the early twentieth century to the concept of *zeitgeist*, or, as it is sometimes glossed, "ethos" or "configuration": the view that cultures had or were to be conceptualized as integrated "systems of thought" or "scales of value" (Bateson, 3). Edward Sapir distinguished between what he termed genuine and spurious culture and in so doing expunged the last of Boas's historicism in favor of the notion of culture as an integrated whole. A genuine culture is one that is both consistent and harmonious; it is not a spiritual hybrid of contradictory patches, made up of a mere accretion of traits (Sapir 1924, 1985 [1949]). However, it was recognized that all thinking and feeling in a culture must be done by individuals, and it followed from this that there must be some way to specify how culture influenced the psychology of individuals, how it affected their thinking. The actual mechanisms through which culture affected individuals were not known, but general propositions were advanced that it "standardized" the potentialities and capacities of the individual, favoring some and suppressing others. The result was a series of behavior patterns characteristic of each society which conditioned the thoughts and emotions of that society's members (Sapir 1985 [1949]). This process was recognized as a fundamentally circular one, since systems of values and thoughts influence not only individuals, but also cultural institutions, and these institutions in their turn shape individuals (Bateson, 3; Benedict, 4). The circularity of argument here depended on a particular pre-theoretical assumption: the idea that while human actions produced culture, human beings are always culturalized. In short, the human beings who make culture are themselves already the product of culture – hence Durkheim's view that society is the origin of social facts (Durkheim, 5).

Different scholars gave different emphases to this process, but a widely accepted view involved a hierarchy of levels based on the assumption that culture presupposes society, society is based on individuals, and individuals have both minds and bodies (Kroeber, 2). The result was a four-"level" approach to the study of human beings based on body, psyche, society, and culture. A biological "level" existing before the operation of culture was assumed, but because of the all-powerful nature of cultural construction it was deemed "remote" from the point of view of the emerging discipline of anthropology. Biopsychological structures were given particular cultural form or content, but in the context of an assumption of the "psychic unity" of humankind, the idea was that culture is itself the product of a uniquely human set of psychological characteristics, and that each culture is a variant upon them. Thus the biological and the psychological were seen as setting constraints or limits on culture (Steward, 10; White, 11). Culture became understood as humanity's unique form of adaptation, a way to meet needs that were simultaneously social and biological (Kroeber, 2; Malinowski, 9).

Among anthropologists in the first half of the twentieth century, there was much debate about the exact emphasis to be given to the relationship between culture and the individual, the social and the psychological. Sapir, for example, was critical of Benedict's treatment of cultures as collective personalities (Benedict, 4). He remained committed to the idea that individuals could exercise independent creative autonomy and thus complete cultural determinism was an impossibility (Bateson, 3; Irvine 1994). These attempts to unravel what linked the development of individuals to the distinctive nature of the culture in which they lived gave rise to what became known as the "culture and personality school" in American anthropology. Nonetheless, while discussion focused on individuals and their psychology, the specific focus on cultures as integrated wholes tended to downplay differences between individuals within the same culture as a consequence of emphasizing the individual distinctiveness of cultures. Theorists were not always consistent in their positions, and circularity of thought was common in the strenuous effort to unravel complex issues. The overall position, however, was a strong form of cultural determinism allied to cultural relativism, but one which was premised on a certain degree of cultural universality. The aim, then, was to understand what specific cultures in their particularity are able to tell us about themselves, but also about universal human capacities.

The question of how values shape lives in the context of the biological and psychic unity of humankind invites a particular rhetorical form. If all humans share certain biological and psychological characteristics, then we should be able to specify what they are. One way to attempt this is to ask what differentiates humans from animals. The standard reply, at least in anthropology, has historically been that it is culture that makes human beings distinctively human, that "the creation of meaning is the distinguishing quality of men" (Sahlins 1976: 102). Humans are ranked over animals by virtue of their culture, and, by extension, their minds (including various arguments about the capacity for language and symbolism that are contentiously debated). Indeed, this ranking is subsumed within the more general hierarchy of mind over body, individual over organism (Ingold 1991). The result is a view of the relation of culture to individuals that depends upon the imposition of cultural meanings on an undifferentiated and underlying biological organism (Malinowski, 9; Ingold 1991; Toren 1999). Culture, in this view, is learnt as a consequence of socialization. Meaning is "dumped into the minds of children" (see Robertson 1996). The idea of humans as clever learners accounts both for the view of cultural diversity as characteristically human, and for the notion of humans as "plastic," infinitely adaptive and innovative (Kroeber, 2; Gibson 2002).

The famous "neural plasticity" of humans which predisposes them to cultural creativity and diversity also shapes and is shaped by a particular notion of culture. There has been a long debate in anthropology about whether culture should be understood as socially patterned behaviors and/or as symbolic systems, values, and meanings. Socially patterned behaviors are common both in non-human primates and in non-primate mammals and depend upon the existence of certain sensorimotor and learning capacities (Gibson 2002). They are certainly not restricted to humans, and thus we cannot simply say that humans are programmed for culture in a way that non-humans are not and/or that culture depends on "neural plasticity" which is also common in non-human mammals. While there are divergent opinions as to whether non-human primates have the capacity for language and symbolism, what is clear is that culture understood as symbolic systems, values, and meanings is not widespread in non-human primates (Gibson 2002). Thus the question of whether or not humanity is premised on culture rather depends on the definition of culture. More crucially, our mental capacities, and those of other mammals, are developed in the context of social interaction and intense sociality. We actually know very little about the evolution of sociality in our own species – it must have taken place long before the evidence for culture in the archaeological record – but what is clear is that sociality and social relations can exist before language and collective representations as they do in non-primate mammals and non-human primates. It logically follows that language and related communicative and symbolic capacities must have evolved in a context of intense sociality, and that sociality is the likely bridge between the non-human primate and human worlds. Thus culture, understood both as social behavior and as symbolic systems involving communication and meanings, is a consequence of our humanity – our sociality – rather than a precondition for it (Ingold 1991; Toren 1999; Gibson 2002).

What this means is that humans are not, strictly speaking, socially constructed in the sense of culture acting upon a pre-given biological entity. But the problem of how culture relates to individuals still needs to be addressed. How does our understanding of our group history, of how we became human, relate to our understanding of individuals, of how we all individually become culture-bearing human beings? Anthropology has traditionally dealt with this by defining human beings as having "capacities." These capacities have not always been very well defined, and have sometimes depended more on linguistic analogy than on empirical facts. Referring to culture as something "hardwired into the brain" is one example (Robertson 1996). The principal difficulty, however, with imagining culture as something "added" to a biological entity and/or imaging that entity as having pre-given modular (often neural) properties is that biology and culture are divorced from their mutual history (Robertson 1996; Toren 1999). For this reason a number of anthropologists are now arguing for a view of the relation between the individual and culture which sees them as ontogenetically related.[2] From this perspective, humans are not biological entities with the capacity to acquire culture, but biologically cultural beings who develop as individuals through intersubjective relations with cultural others (Whitehead, 25; Robertson 1996; Toren 1999). This is a view that not only conceptualizes how the individual human mind develops as a product of ontogenetic growth in a specific cultural context, and signals how culture is reproduced across generations as a consequence of the reproduction of human individuals. It also provides an account of how individual agency – a life lived – is fulfilled within the context of a shared cultural and symbolic world.

Recent work in cognition and psychology has returned to the question of what humans share and what makes them distinctively human. Current thinking emphasizes that these are questions that cannot be answered by anthropology alone, but require interdisciplinary collaboration (Luhrmann, 24; Whitehead, 25). However, psychology, anthropology, and neuroscience construct their objects of inquiry in different ways and seek very different kinds of explanation of the same phenomena (Stafford, 23). Part of the predicament here concerns scale and another concerns method. Anthropology's restless search for context – contexts in which behaviors, values, beliefs, etc., find meaning – drives data collection, analysis and interpretation towards the ideal of wholistic completeness. This is the "we must know everything before we can make sense of it" approach. Psychologists and neuroscientists, by contrast, tend to focus down, concentrating on specific functions and competences. Experimentation and falsifiability are key to the latter approaches, and impossible to apply to the former (Stafford, 23; Whitehead, 25). The key questions here are how do humans think and what drives the way they think? Is it culture or is it the biological structures of the brain? The relationship of culture to the individual mind – and the individual brain – is a contentious one, but psychologists, anthropologists, and neuroscientists alike believe that there are commonalities, universals, in the way humans think, and that these are likely connected to the manner in which we have evolved as biologically social and cultural beings (Whitehouse, 22; Whitehead, 25).

One of the entailments of the term "culture" is the idea that humans share inner lives. Culture is not something external to us, but is part of our phylogenetic and ontogenetic development (Whitehead, 25). It is part of us and we share it with others. How to proceed here is complicated by a number of factors. We know, for example, that the definition, expression, and experience of emotions are culturally variable, and in this sense they must be common to a group of people. However, we also know that different members of that group have different feelings, experiences, and dispositions, both over their lives and in any specific moment (Luhrmann, 24). But, if culture shapes our inner worlds, how could this be possible? The answer to this conundrum is very often historical, in the sense that analysis tries to sort out those factors that are cultural or social from those that are biological. For example, the physiological changes and facial expressions associated with anger appear universal, but the understandings, appropriate manifestations, and cultural discourses concerning anger in any particular historical circumstance are specific. Individual variation within any cultural group or historical epoch comes down to the interaction in the context of the circumstances of a life lived between physiological responses and feelings, and culturally specific constructions and dispositions. This may also explain certain other conundrums, such as why East Asians are better at numbers than Europeans and Americans. Counting systems and number words specific to East Asia have a demonstrable impact on numerical cognition – fewer counting errors, grasp of basic concepts at an earlier age, ability to do mental arithmetic – but so too do schooling and parental pressure (Stafford, 23). Culture is not a simple determinant, but rather a dynamic matrix within which individual lives are lived in interaction with others, institutions, and distributions of resource.

The challenge lies with language and representation. Much recent work in the cognitive sciences has focused on how complex, explicit representations, such as religion, are influenced by implicit and unconscious cognitive processes. These processes are sometimes described as "modules" or "domain-specific" systems, and they are assumed to have evolved in response to evolutionary pressures (Barrett and Kurzban 2006). However, research in this domain does not set out to explain Christianity or religious systems in their totality, but rather focuses on specific aspects of religious behavior amenable to experimentation. The task is to try to determine what effect these unconscious processes have on religious thought and behavior, and its transmission through time. For example, could there be a single underlying cognitive mechanism that produces features of ritualized behavior common to societies around the world? The available evidence suggests that such underlying cognitive processes may account for repeated features of aspects of ritualized behavior, but this is not, of course, the same thing as providing an explanation of a specific ritual or of ritual taken as a feature of human societies in the larger sense (Whitehouse, 22).

Forms of Abstraction and Forms of Explanation

In anthropology, as in all forms of academic inquiry, theories frame questions, and such theories may be both implicit and explicit. They are also embedded in analytic terms, and the degree to which they are so embedded will depend on how deeply those terms have become implanted in everyday usage within the academic discipline, and/or in ordinary life in different parts of the globe (Moore, 36). Two of the most salient terms in this regard are "society" and "culture." Both are widely used inside and outside the academy, and their meanings are assumed to be so generally understood that there is little apparent controversy about their referents. However, terms like these have evident histories (Kroeber, 2), and the frustrating fact from the point of view of social science is that the more generally understood such terms appear to be, the less theoretical purchase they appear to have. Recent discussions in anthropology have suggested that we should abandon the concept of culture altogether, that it has become meaningless as a category of analysis because it is not clear what it refers to (Brightman 1995; Lambek and Boddy 1997). At first glance, this seems curious because from a commonsense perspective it seems clear that cultures self-evidently exist, that there are other cultures, and that anthropology studies them.

In the first half of the twentieth century, the term "culture" was increasingly identified as the object of study in anthropology (see Kuper 1999), but this was not a straightforward process. Nor was it uncontested. Whereas most American anthropologists adhered to the view that the object of study was culture, many of their British colleagues insisted that it was social relations and, later, social structures. One of the major points of disagreement derived from the idea that while social relations based on behavior could be observed and recorded, culture could not because it did not refer to any concrete reality. It was simply an analytical abstraction (Radcliffe-Brown, 6; Holy and Stuchlik, 14). The underlying point of contention here was the difference between behavior that could be observed and values and meanings that could not. Many writers were quick to point out that a simple division or distinction between behavior and ideas was untenable.[3] For instance, one might take social relationships as the object of study. But since this involves looking at behavior between individuals, one has to consider not only what they do, but also who they are. While the first might be directly observable, the second would not, since it would depend on ideas, expectations, and meanings existing in actors' minds about the kind of people these individuals are meant to be and how they should relate to each other (mothers to sons, for example, or chiefs to commoners). Social relations make no sense outside the intentions, ideas, and expectations within which they make sense to historically situated actors (Beattie, 13). It was thus recognized that social relations and culture were mutually determining, although the one could not be reduced to the other. Much depended here on what might be meant by the term "abstraction." Cultural values and beliefs, since they are held to influence social behavior and social relations to varying degrees depending on the theoretical position of the analyst (compare articles 2–4, 9, and 6–8), cannot logically be seen as less material, concrete, or real than social relations, the way people interact with each other. Hence, culture is not more abstract than behavior if by abstraction it is implied that it is more ideal, less material. However, if by "abstraction" we mean the construction of a model or concept or notion that allows us to order, compare, and analyze data, then both culture and social relations are forms of abstraction.

Radcliffe-Brown argued that human beings are connected by a complex web of social relations which he termed "social structure." Societies can be identified as being characterized by certain social structures. Just as anatomy and physiology deal with the structures of organisms, anthropology deals with the structures of society. The social structure of a society would be directly observable as the actually existing relations between people at a given point in time (Radcliffe-Brown, 6). Arguing against this position, Leach pointed out that social structures are things created by the analyst from what she or he observes. They are abstract models that are the product of a particular way of looking at and characterizing social data (Leach, 7). Most often, the purpose of these abstract models is to allow comparison between societies or social institutions; and thus societies or cultures or social institutions are classified into types (Holy and Stuchlik, 14). However, as Beattie points out, anthropologists do not actually study whole societies – nor can they, by extension, study whole cultures or even whole social systems or structures. Instead, they study certain things which they observe and which they abstract or draw out of the data according to some particular interest (Beattie, 13; Thornton, 37). The most evident example of this in anthropology is the study of kinship systems. Leach's criticism was really directed at how anthropological analyses create "entities" by lifting them out of the space and time of real social interaction. When the anthropologist uses a term like "society" or "social system" or "social structure," she or he is effectively describing a model of social reality, a way of understanding how things fit together and work together (Strathern, 39). While this model necessarily forms a coherent whole, social reality itself is never coherent because of its countless inconsistencies and the indeterminate nature of life lived (Leach, 7; Thornton, 37).

As Leach correctly identified, this leaves the rather interesting problem of what, exactly, the relationship is between the anthropologist's model and the empirical reality she or he observes. This question cannot be answered in a single straightforward fashion because it turns out that the relationship of model to data very much depends on what kind of question the analyst is seeking to answer in the first place. Different kinds of questions require different kinds of data, and different kinds of data require different forms of explanation. This is why theory and method remain absolutely intertwined in the social sciences, as in all fields of academic inquiry. This is particularly evident in anthropology in the debates that went on in the first half of the twentieth century about the relative merits of functionalism, structural-functionalism, and structuralism. These theories all had methodological consequences and sought to provide very different forms of explanation.

The functionalism espoused by Malinowski (9) and to a significant extent by American cultural materialists (Steward, 10; White, 11; Vayda and Rappaport, 12) started with the idea of the human being in a natural environment, influenced by it and in turn transforming it in co-operation with others. Culture in this view is seen as an instrumental reality which allows humans to meet their biological and cultural needs, and to transform their environment. Specific cultural traits are thus explained when their function or purpose within the overall system of humans and their environment has been determined. This form of explanation was fundamentally different from that of nineteenth-century evolutionists, for whom explanation was a matter of demonstrating progress and position on a historical chain, and from the sociology of Durkheim, which decried the notion of "function" as valid explanation and sought to show how social facts beget social facts (Durkheim, 5). The notion of function employed in this work depends in large part on a definition of "needs," not just the biological needs of humans, their need for food, and shelter, and so on, but their socially or culturally defined needs, those needs that arise out of the achievements, intentions, and theories of previous generations. Theorists in this framework inevitably hierarchized the different types of needs, and saw "basic" needs as more determining than "social needs," especially in small-scale societies. Discussions of cultural change were therefore focused on how societies progressively met and developed their needs over time, encouraging a view of cultural systems as integrated organic wholes with functionally related component elements (Malinowski, 9; Steward, 10; White, 11; Vayda and Rappaport, 12).

The notion of "function" was crucially dependent on the conceptualization of humans in their environment as a system with interrelated parts. The function of any cultural trait or element was thus demonstrated either when it could be shown that elements in the system were interconnected and affected each other and/or when the existence of certain elements could be demonstrated by reference to their ends or purposes (Beattie, 13). The result was a particular kind of method of data collection and recording which involved amassing huge amounts of empirical data to demonstrate that every-thing was connected to everything else. Consequently, without the idea of the system, "function" as an explanatory concept could not have any analytical purchase. The analogy which linked functionalism to the structural-functionalism of Radcliffe-Brown and the post-1940s school of British anthropology was that of the living organism. The idea was that society and its human members could be seen as a social system which is – like a living organism – constantly being renewed. The notion of function here was restricted to the specific contribution that a particular trait, element, or behavior makes to the existence and continuity of the social system and the social structures from which it is derived. Radcliffe-Brown was heavily influenced in his thinking by the sociology of Durkheim and the idea that societies are orderly and have structures that can be formally analyzed (Radcliffe-Brown, 6).

The notion of "structure" was later developed in the works of Evans-Pritchard, Fortes, Firth, and Schapera.[4] They believed that social structures were abstractions from social behavior (see above) and that the main purpose of their identification was comparison, classification, and generalization bet-ween societies. These scholars did not believe – as they claimed Malinowski had done – in the idea that analytical concepts were inherent in the observed data. Social structures had to be drawn out of obser-vations; organizing principles had to be identified, and comparative frameworks established. Perhaps the most salient of these in British social anthropology was the notion of a "lineage society" (Beattie, 13; Holy and Stuchlik, 14). In this form of analysis, data from observations, informants' reports, recol-lections, and theories were all mined to illustrate the structures devised by the anthropologist. Data were very selectively collected and deployed. In this work, much hinged on what exactly the term "structure" meant and how it related both to the anthropologist's data and to social reality (see above). Evans-Pritchard (1940) and Fortes (1945) both took the view that lineage systems were the basis of informants' models as well as those of the anthropologist. This might have been less problematic if it could be shown that these local models governed behavior, that social relations followed the principles of social structure. Unfortunately this was far from obvious (Holy and Stuchlik, 14). There was thus considerable dispute both about how structures related to the empirical data from which they were abstracted, and about how structures qua anthropological models related to informants' models. This problem was further compounded by a tendency to treat structures as if they were both institutional regularities and underlying principles, both the pattern of relationships between persons and the rela-tions between the logical principles of cultural systems.

As a type of explanation, structural-functionalism focused more on comparisons between societies rather than on the empirical description of a total system that was the object of inquiry in function-alism. Although structures were abstracted from social relations and behavioral data, there was little room analytically for the individual or for any discussion of how culture or society affected individual behavior. The analysis was more firmly settled at the level of the group. It is true that structural-functionalists were interested in beliefs and values, but this was primarily in terms of how they functioned as social systems (the elements of which were systematically interrelated) and the degree to which they could be linked to social relations. It is the idea of the logic behind the system, the underlying struc-tures from which systems are generated, and the rules of transformation which govern how elements will change in relation to each other that links structural-functionalism to structuralism proper in anthropology. Thus, Lévi-Strauss's notion of structure had both continuities and discontinuities with the older concept, and these are in large part due to the influence of Durkheim and Boas on his work (Lévi-Strauss, 8).

If the relationship between norms and actions, between social structures and social relations, had been at the heart of structural-functionalism, the idea of structural analysis that Lévi-Strauss intro-duced was concerned with modes of thought, classification, and symbolic logic. It drew on particular aspects of Durkheim's work, especially on the idea that social facts determine individuals' behaviors and the collective consciousness, and on the axiomatic principle that social facts must be treated as systems where the meaning and purpose of individual elements can only be understood with reference to the total set of relevant social facts. Durkheim used his interest in classification to put forward the view that societies should be studied as moral systems, as systems of thought. Lévi-Strauss also drew on the Boasian school of cultural anthropology and on the belief that cultures form patterned, integrated wholes. These ideas found an easy congruence with his interest in structural linguistics (Lévi-Strauss, 8, 19). Structuralism as it was developed in anthropology was concerned not with the actions of individuals or groups, but with the underlying logic of social and symbolic systems. What it took from structural linguistics was the distinction between speech (*parole*), the medium of day-to-day communication, and language (*langue*), the system of objective elements or underlying structures from which speech is produced (Bourdieu, 15). Structuralism used this distinction to claim that social and symbolic systems should be analyzed with regard to their underlying principles or structures, that they should be treated as systems in which the elements only come to have meaning with reference to their relation with other terms, and that analysis should strive towards the elucidation of general laws (Lévi-Strauss, 8, 19). Thus, in his analysis of kinship systems, Lévi-Strauss showed that the diversity of marriage rules and kinship systems could be explained with reference to a small number of structures or general principles which could then provide the basis for comparative study (Lévi-Strauss, 19). These structures or principles, however, were unconscious; they remained unknown to the people living in those systems (Lévi-Strauss, 8).

Lévi-Strauss was interested in classification, which is to say, in the way humans impose order on their social and environmental worlds. His view was that the categories created were always arbitrary, but that they formed pairs of oppositions grouped together in systems. This was a study of how humans think by creating sets of oppositions with concrete references and then connecting and correlating those oppositions in systems. Radcliffe-Brown had also been interested in classification and how people create patterns, but his assumption was that these patterns and oppositions were present in the environment and that people simply seized upon them (Radcliffe-Brown, 6). Lévi-Strauss took a very different view, seeing classification and opposition as the product of the structures of thought and the mind, as being symbolic systems that operated according to certain formal properties that could be analyzed independently of their elements. Thus, different cultural forms could be compared and analyzed on the basis that they were transformations of the same basic structures. Lévi-Strauss, it might be said, was more interested in *how* people think than in *what* they think. The notion of structure he employed was therefore significantly different from that used by British anthropologists following Malinowski and Radcliffe-Brown. In order to identify and elucidate the "structures" he had in mind it was necessary to ask quite different sorts of questions, and to collect rather different kinds of data. Leach encapsulated the difference by contrasting Lévi-Strauss with contemporary British anthropologists: "His ultimate concern is to establish facts which are true about 'the human mind', rather than about the organization of any particular society or class of societies. The difference is fundamental" (Leach 1970: 7–8).

One of the major critiques of structuralism is its inability to deal with human agency and social change. This is a logical entailment of privileging *langue* (language as system) over *parole* (speech), since analysis focuses on the interrelations between elements in the language system and their relations with each other rather than on how people use language in day-to-day contexts and what they say. When applied to anthropology more generally, this means that analysis focuses on the logic of symbolic systems, their transformations, and the principles underlying cultural forms rather than on what people do and how they use, transform, and manipulate cultural forms in everyday life (Bourdieu, 15). Bourdieu demonstrates most elegantly how the privileging of structures over agency creates a gap between the analyst, who establishes a theoretical relation to language and its underlying structures, and the informant, who speaks the language and uses it as a lived tool of communication. The result is that anthropologists generate an objectified model of the world as outside observers which is quite different from the world as it is lived, and from the model of the world created by the people who live in it. This is what Bourdieu describes as the privileging of logos over praxis (Bourdieu, 15, 33).

The more general point, however, is that particular concepts and theories not only frame the questions to be asked, but actually construct objects of inquiry. What functionalism, structural-functionalism, and structuralism have in common is a concern with how theory relates to data, with how forms of abstraction relate both to the analyst's model and to that of the informant, and with how anthropology constructs its object of inquiry. The solutions to these epistemological difficulties vary according to the emphasis each theory gives to the question it believes it is answering. That said, what remains fairly constant in anthropological theorizing are the fundamental epistemological difficulties themselves: the constant search for a firmer, clearer, and more solid understanding of the nature of the anthropological object of inquiry and of how we should approach it.

Meaning and Interpretation

This is perhaps nowhere more evident than in the rise of semantic and symbolic/interpretive anthropology in the 1970s. Whereas structuralism had created an object of inquiry based on the idea that culture could be studied like a language, as a complex language-like system of signs, semantic and symbolic/interpretive anthropology shifted attention from language models and their validity for cultural analysis to the meaning of what is said in language. The emphasis was on ways of analyzing meanings and their relationship to actors' models (Geertz, 16; Crick, 20; Keesing 1987). Analysts differed from each other in many respects, yet they shared an assumption about the centrality of language to social life, and consequently defined social life as the creation and negotiation of meaning. Many of them owed an implicit or explicit debt to Weber in that they took it as axiomatic that humans endow the world and events in it with meaning and significance, and they therefore viewed beliefs and values as real material forces that have an impact upon the world (Weber, 29).

Clifford Geertz is probably the most famous exponent of interpretive anthropology, and his work sets out a clear link between theory and methodology based on interpretation, both that of the actors and that of the analyst. Geertz wanted to develop culture as an analytic concept and he therefore reformulated it, defining it as an ordered system of meaning and symbols within which actors interpret their experience and order their actions. In his view, cultural meanings and values do more than simply construct a vision of the world, a model of reality. They also provide guidelines for action. In this sense, culture is public and can thus be analyzed by the observer without any need to "get inside actors' heads." Culture can and should be read, translated, and interpreted. Thick description thus becomes a way of understanding what others think they are up to, a way of interpreting their interpretations (Geertz, 16). The view of culture that Geertz espouses is one where social groups are tied together by the expression of shared values, meanings, and symbols. As Asad (17) and others argue, this notion of culture is extremely problematic, not least because culture is not just meaning. It is also power. And to the extent that it is, any effective account of cultural meaning would have to explain why some ideologies become powerful and persuasive, and how they come to serve the interests of some groups over others (Weber, 29; Comaroff and Comaroff, 31; Donham, 32; Keesing 1987). Anthropologists should thus be very wary of creating cultural coherence and consensus when in fact there exists social difference and even discrimination. A truly materialist account of meaning would explain not just how meanings guide action, but how different forms of discourse are actually materially produced and maintained in specific contexts.

The shift from language models to the analysis of meaning in anthropology thus produced various difficulties about the degree to which actors within a single culture could be said to share meanings, and, by extension, values and beliefs. This inevitably raises questions of how language relates to thought and to the individual, and of how shared meanings, values, and representations get transferred between individuals and groups (Sperber 1985). One problematic issue here, as Needham (1972) notes, is the relationship of ordinary English-language terms like "belief" to local actors' understandings and to the analyst's models. Needham suggests that anthropologists often use the word "belief" to indicate an adherence to culturally defined ways of thinking, rather than to indicate anything about an individual's "inner state." This leads to an unsatisfactory situation where it is assumed that all individuals subscribe unproblematically to cultural beliefs, when we know this is simply untrue. The result is that we have very little idea of how values and beliefs actually relate to individual action. Geertz (16) and others suggested that this relationship could be clarified by examining actors' interpretations – that is, folk

10   HENRIETTA L. MOORE AND TODD SANDERS

models (Crick, 20). The pre-theoretical assumption here is that meaning is always contained within action. As Crick (20) argues, one cannot describe an activity as "praying" or "voting" unless the actors involved possess these concepts. In this view of action there is no distinction between systems of ideas and patterns of behavior (Geertz, 16; Crick, 20).

Difficulties arise immediately with strong versions of this theory because it is premised on the assumption that actors are supremely knowledgeable and that they are always able to link belief and action. However, since we know that behavior and belief are not always synonymous, this proposition will not hold. The difficulty is a profound one because human language and human culture (actions, beliefs, values) are not simply empirical facts; they are always conceptual, their structures the consequence of the meaning they have for their actors (Weber, 29). If we neglect this conceptualization (actors' models, understandings, classifications, values), then we will fail to understand what we are trying to investigate (Crick, 20). However, we also know that there are limits to the knowledge of human actors. We do not directly author all of our actions, but neither do we religiously follow rules (Bourdieu, 33; Tyler 1978). While we cannot know the world independently of language and of our interpretations of it, not all knowledge takes the form of verbal propositions (Bloch, 21; Tyler 1978). In fact, much of the knowledge anthropologists study exists in actors' heads in a non-linguistic form. Not only is it not formulated in natural language, but it is not even necessarily language-like in the sense that it does not follow the sentence-logic model of semantics in natural language (Bloch, 21; Jackson, 26). A very strong version of this theory would argue that language is therefore not necessary for conceptual thought (Bloch, 21).

The view that notions of the thinking self are separate from the body, and the idea that the mind controls the body are part of the analytic philosophical traditions of the west (Tyler 1978). They are also one of the major reasons anthropology finds it so difficult to model the relationship between self and soma, culture and biology (Jackson, 26; Ingold 1991). This is compounded by the fact that the western tradition rests on an assumption that knowledge is best articulated in language. However, the work on bodies and phenomenology raises in a particularly dramatic way the question of how adequately language can represent our knowledge of anything, and the kinds of problems that arise when anthropologists have to describe what is non-linguistic through the medium of language. The human body knows the world through its practical engagement with the world, and with others in that world (Lambek, 34). What is built up is a practical understanding, a form of knowledge that is not necessarily conscious and often cannot be brought into language (Mauss 1973 [1935]; Bourdieu 1990). More than this, it is not just that practical knowledge need not – or cannot – be brought into language, but that language-based models and concepts of meaning may be wholly inappropriate for understanding such knowledge. Because body language is not a system of signs in the way that language is, semiotics and semantics cannot stand as the basis for our understanding of embodiment and/or embodied knowledge. Distinctions between the sign and the signified, representation and meaning, are particularly problematic here because embodied knowledge may not stand for or represent something in the way that natural language does. A gesture of dismissal, after all, is not simply a sign of dismissal. It is dismissal (Jackson, 26; cf. Sanders 2008).

However, body movement and experience of the body are grounded in specific social and material environments so that the body becomes both a means for knowing the world and the product of a social and cultural world that pre-exists it (Bourdieu, 33). Thus, an emphasis on practical knowledge may question our analytic reliance on language and meaning, and interrogate what we might mean by the term "belief," but it does not solve the problem of the intentional actor. If body movement, the experience of an embodied self, and practical knowledge of the world are the result of engagement with a socially constructed world, then what scope is there for individual creativity, for innovation, or social change? Actors do not slavishly follow the rules of their embodied cultural worlds any more than their actions are directly determined by their conceptual models of the world. Strong versions of this thesis come perilously close to stating that a change in environment is necessary before change or innovation in embodied understandings is possible. In this context, a parallel critique of that made for the over-determining nature of collective representations (see above) can readily be sustained. However,

Bourdieu's notion of habitus seeks to address this problem – some critics see his attempt as unsuccessful – by focusing on how actors are able to acquire a practical mastery of their world, that is, an ability to act appropriately in a variety of circumstances, without in any sense following a rule-book or being able to discuss or enumerate principles for action (Jackson, 26; Bourdieu, 33). Bourdieu defined the notion of habitus as a system of acquired dispositions functioning on a practical level, a set of classificatory principles acting both as categories of perception and thought, and as the organizing principles of action (Bourdieu, 33). One of his attractions for anthropology was his insistence on the temporality of lived practice, on the way schemes of thought and perception are used in specific historical circumstances. In this sense, his work could be used to resituate anthropological analysis within historical time, the lived reality of social systems. Not all of Bourdieu's critics, though, thought his work successful in this regard, seeing his emphasis on acquired systems of thought and schemes for action reproduced across time as too determining. His focus on practice did nevertheless allow for a situated, temporal understanding of that process of reproduction, and in this his work reveals its indebtedness to marxism.

The problem for all anthropological theories based on language-like models is how to account for forms of knowledge that actors cannot or need not bring into language; and related to this, how to balance in any analysis the emphasis given to innovation and intention on the part of actors as against structural determinants (collective consciousness, social institutions, cultural values, etc.) (Moore 1994: ch. 4). Consequently, Bourdieu's theory of practice had a profound influence on anthropology in the 1970s and 1980s. His emphasis on actors' practical mastery within a socially constructed world was a direct attempt to negotiate the opposition between objective structures (structuralism) and subjective experience (existentialism and phenomenology). Subsequently, it was taken up by those anthropologists who wanted to understand both how individual action shapes social structures and cultural systems and how those systems and structures, in turn, shape social action. The difficulty for many anthropologists was how to transcend the divisions between symbolic and material explanations of culture and agency, and how best to reinsert individual persons and events back into the analysis (Ortner 1984; Abu-Lughod 1986).

In the 1970s, structuralism was emphasizing the determining role of symbolic systems and the structures of the mind, whereas marxism was emphasizing that the relations of production and the structure of economic life were determining in the last instance. Practice theory as it developed in anthropology was never a single coherent theoretical model, but, rather, a series of loosely interlinked attempts to show that both the symbolic and the material were involved in determining social action. Bourdieu's specific contribution was to demonstrate how symbolic systems and material inequalities are linked in the practice of everyday life and are mutually reinforcing. Ultimately, practice theory in anthropology was a further example of a theory attempting to transcend the divisions between culture and the individual, objectivism and subjectivism, structure and agency. The result was an emphasis on structures as both constituted by and constitutive of social action. This was a quite different notion of structure from that developed by Lévi-Strauss or British structural-functionalism. It was directed at quite different sorts of questions and required the collection of different kinds of data.

Structures of Power

In language-based models in anthropology – this includes most versions of semantic and interpretive anthropology – the untheorized relation between structure and agency, culture and intention, raises the question of power. As Emily Martin makes clear, talking about bodies in new ways not only changes our understanding of them, but also changes the way we experience and live them (Martin, 27). New ideas about bodies may arise and be driven by emerging and/or changing sets of values as well as by scientific practices (Sharp, 28). But once these ideas enter public discourse, become part of our lived world and our habits, and pass into the way we think of ourselves as embodied individuals, they are naturalized and fall out of conscious reflection. They become, as it were, the unquestioned world-as-it-is. Over time, established habits, ways of doing and experiencing can become fractured and change, most often as a result of responses to economic and political changes (Weber, 29; Comaroff and Comaroff, 31). However, the naturalized order of the world is powerfully inculcated not just in the human body, but in the human subject (Bourdieu, 33; Foucault 1991 [1977]). Power relations mark, categorize, and invest the body, as well as the subjective understandings of actors and their views of others. These forms of power are powerful, and are particularly so because they can rarely be overtly challenged and because they are central to the way we constitute ourselves as subjects (Foucault 1991 [1977]). Yet the relations between power and knowledge are never complete. There are forms of knowledge – those of women, the colonized, the insane, subaltern groups – that are subordinated or subjugated to dominant understandings and knowledge practices, and they exist on the margins, partially hidden from view, but still active, forming the basis for individual agency and perhaps for group resistance (Wolf, 30; Comaroff and Comaroff, 31; Foucault 1980 [1976]). Foucault's value to anthropology was in allowing analysts to move away from a notion of power as substance or thing, something to be held, towards a notion of power as act, as something that is exercised in the course of social relations, something that requires empirical investigation both at the level of individual practices and at the level of patterns that are institutionalized (Foucault 1980 [1976]).

Foucault's critique of how subjects are created through changing configurations of power and knowledge has been enormously influential in anthropology not only in examining how actors as subjects have been formed in particular historical and ethnographic locations (Comaroff and Comaroff, 31), but also in investigating how the human sciences, including anthropology, constitute the acting subject and classify the world. Foucault's theorizing thus provides a mechanism for exploring how anthropological theories, models, and forms of discourse create specific kinds of entities – societies and cultures – populated by particular kinds of individuals, selves, agents, categories, groups, and persons (Ortner, 35; Moore, 36). In consequence, Foucault has been most often appropriated in anthropological writing as a means to critique the power relations that constitute western epistemology and to unpick anthropology's complicity in those power relations. The emphasis in his work on decentered/ subjugated knowledges and their role in resisting discursive and political power relations was taken up by many anthropologists in the 1980s and 1990s (e.g. Lavie 1990; Taussig 1987; Tsing 1993). The enduring value of Foucault's work for anthropology is his emphasis on the relations between truth and power: who does the classifying, who determines categories of thought, how do those categories and classifications impact on people's understandings of themselves and others, on their actions and aspirations? Foucault's notion of discourse is intended to weld together ideas and classifications with agency, experience, and the process of becoming a subject; it provides a means to transcend the distinction between ideas/values and practice, society and individual which has always been the founding distinction of the social sciences (Abu-Lughod, 38).

The twenty-year period from the 1970s to the 1990s was characterized by a range of loosely associated models that drew on Bourdieu's and Foucault's reworkings of marxism and structuralism, as well as on the work of other theorists and philosophers, including Gramsci, de Certeau, Derrida, and Rorty. The theoretical emphasis in anthropological writing in this period depends very much on whether the author is focusing on the creativity and intentionality of agents at the expense of longer-run structures of domination and power; on displaced, decentered, marginal voices in contrast to dominant ideologies; or on processes of resistance, rebellion, and change as opposed to broader patterns of social, economic, and political control. New analytical concepts such as habitus (Bourdieu), discourse (Foucault), and hegemony (Gramsci) were introduced and selectively employed as a means of dealing with anthropology's increasing disenchantment with the concept of culture (Abu-Lughod, 38).

Starting in the 1980s, voices were increasingly raised against the concept of culture, demanding its redefinition and reformulation (Rabinow 1988; Kahn 1989; Rosaldo 1989; Appadurai 1990). But, it is worth noting that the emphasis on practice and experience and the diversity of voices, as opposed to the homogenizing effect of a coherent culture, was not new in anthropology. Paul Radin argued in 1933 that "The method of describing a culture without any reference to the individual except insofar as he is an expression of rigidly defined cultural forms, manifestly produces a distorted picture" (Radin 1933: 42). Edward Sapir made a similar point in 1931:

> While we often speak of society as though it were a static structure defined by tradition, it is, in the more intimate sense, nothing of the kind, but a highly intricate network of partial or complete understandings.... It is only apparently a static sum of social institutions; actually it is being reanimated or creatively reaffirmed from day to day by particular acts of a communicative nature which obtain among individuals participating in it. (Mandelbaum 1949: 104)

Of course, earlier scholars were not developing a theory of practice or of discourses, not explicitly anyway. Nor were they interrogating the truth claims of anthropology and western epistemology in the way their counterparts in the 1980s were. Nonetheless, what their comments reveal is how theoretical debates in anthropology about how we should define the object of inquiry have continued to oscillate around the problem of culture and individual, psyche and soma, ideas and practices, and that in each generation of scholars, whichever binary they choose to emphasize, the other pole cannot be ignored. It works through the theory uninvited.

It has been argued that the theories of the 1980s were distinctive because they were an attempt to transcend these binary divisions within anthropological theorizing. There is some justification to this claim, but transcending binaries is, by nature, an imperfect and unstable enterprise. True transcendence, if such a thing were possible, would require thinking outside these distinctions. Two immediate kinds of problem arise. The first has to do with the relationship between data, analytical terms, and theoretical propositions. Ortner noted in her 1984 review that an emphasis on practice in some writing had already given way to an analytical preoccupation with actors' strategies, decisions, aspirations, and knowledge at the expense of longer-run structures and values (Ortner 1984: 150). This not only runs the risk of overvaluing agency and change to the detriment of reproduction and the institutionalization of values, but it can potentially seriously misrepresent actors as hyper-agents, overactive strategizers, super-knowledgeable actors. This is not itself problematic except that we know that much of social life is quotidian, unthought, and routine. We don't, after all, spend our whole time asking ourselves whether our actions are reproducing the family or critiquing the dominant ideology (Donham, 32). In addition, we know that aspects of cultural systems, social institutions, and values are durable, long-lived, and buttressed by economic and political resource systems. Some things change fast. Others do not. Some things endure over long periods of time and then change very rapidly. We need to be able to analyze and understand daily practices and routines, as well as to analyze long-running structures and value systems, and the relation between the two (Comaroff and Comaroff, 31; Donham, 32). By focusing on practices or the idea of a practice theory, there is a danger that we will collect data based on quotidian activities and immediate events, and begin to build a picture of strategies, decisions, and cultural knowledge that reinforces a particular view of the acting subject and of the potential instability of systems at the expense of longer-run structures that would require different analytical terms and different kinds of data.

The second problem has to do with the fact that different kinds of theories work at different analytical levels, and that what may be required are composite theories where different kinds of propositions, analytical terms, and data are appropriate to different levels, and indeed to different temporal frames. Human agency is about the flow and flux of life and events. As Marx noted, humans make history – and indeed create themselves – but not under conditions of their own making (Wolf, 30; Donham, 32). This must logically be so because the temporal dimensions of social systems and cultural values are different from those of the biological individual. Yet precisely because humans make social systems, those systems are never stable, never immune from change, no matter how powerful the dominant group that maintains them. No empire has endured or will endure forever. Looking simultaneously at continuity and discontinuity, reproduction and change may require us to deploy more than one theory of culture, more than one theory of power, and more than one theory of agency (Wolf, 30; Comaroff and Comaroff, 31). The kinds of theories we need for understanding social totalities and the way they are structured over time will necessarily differ from those required to analyze daily social activities and how specific discourses become powerful or persuasive. Longer-run patterns of social totalities, and the issue of how certain types of economy go with certain types of polity, are certainly connected to human agency and needs, but exactly how will require specification in each historical context and at each analytical level (Wolf, 30). Marx placed production and the satisfaction of human needs through labor at the heart of his historical materialism in an attempt to specify exactly this linkage (Donham, 32). General theories of this kind are essential to move our thinking on, but they are unlikely to be predictive and/or to account for all empirical instances. More crucially, the value of critical theorizing in anthropology may lie less in attempting to transcend binaries to achieve – we assume – higher-order synthesis, and more in working aspects of the binaries against each other, specifying how they inter-connect and intersect, and examining what kinds of theories and analytical concepts are appropriate to different analytical levels and temporal structures.

The Practice of Criticism

In the 1980s and 1990s, the rise of post-structuralism in anthropology heralded a critique of anthro-pology's modes of analytical classification and representation. Ideas drawn from Foucault and others were used to criticize and re-analyze anthropological concepts and the relationship of forms of knowledge to forms of power. In many ways these critiques formed intelligible links with earlier moments of critique within the discipline. Like those earlier moments, they were not simply the result of auto-genesis, but emerged in response to political movements and economic changes in the world at large: chief amongst which were the black consciousness movement, feminism, postcolonialism, and the gay rights movement. Building on the social activism of the 1960s and 1970s, political changes in the 1980s and 1990s broke down older forms of consensus, but critiques of the world order coincided uneasily with globalization and the growing power of transnational corporations. Technological change and consumer power drove capitalism into a new phase. The anthropological response was diverse, but two important interlinked themes emerged which drew on a critique of the power/knowledge axis. The first focused on representation and anthropology's truth claims, critiquing among other things the idea that the cultures and societies described in anthropological writing mirror exist-ing reality, and thus that the knowing anthropological subject can be distinguished from the known objective other (Clifford and Marcus 1986; Clifford 1988). This part of the critique emphasized the historically situated nature of anthropological constructions, and their relation to western philosophical traditions, theoretical models, and literary conventions. This inevitably raised serious questions about how accounts – and thus facts and truth claims – are constructed (Thornton, 37; Spiro, 42; Weber 2004 [1904]). The second theme focused on the concept of culture and on the analytical constructs of anthropology more generally (Abu-Lughod, 38; Gupta and Ferguson, 53). Drawing on Bourdieu, ana-lysts rejected the notion of culture as a reified abstraction (see above). But rather than simply challeng-ing the ontological status of culture as an abstraction, these critics also argued against the ideas of wholism, determinism, boundedness, totalization, stasis, and constructionism implicit in the concept itself. Culture in this critique was negatively seen as a bounded, timeless entity that determines human agency and occludes real differences, especially those of power (Abu-Lughod, 38).

One element in this latter thread of critique was the recognition of shifts in the conditions of the production of anthropological research and therefore of anthropological knowledge. Cultures, how-ever they had been represented by anthropologists in the past, had likely never been fixed, unitary, and bounded. In the context of globalization, mass migration, and transnational cultural flows, the very notion that cultures represented fixed and bounded populations in specific locales seemed ludicrous (Wolf, 30; Gupta and Ferguson, 53; Appadurai 1990). There was a deeper point to be made because in the context of practice theory and the attempt to rethink how agency and subjectification are connected to larger and longer-run cultural values, discourses, and systems, the idea that different cultures somehow produce distinctively different types of people, subjects, or identities could no longer hold. The dominant emphasis on differences between cultures gave way to a clearer recognition that differences are internal not only to cultures, but also to individuals as subjects (Moore 1994).

The boundedness of cultures in anthropological theorizing was never, however, simply the product of assuming that culture mapped onto society and that both mapped onto a specific place – the basic building block of a discipline concerned with studying "other cultures" (Gupta and Ferguson, 53). It was, rather, the consequence of particular sets of pre-theoretical assumptions about cultures as integrated wholes (Thornton, 37). Social wholes, even if they exist, can never be directly experienced either by anthropologist or by informant. The scope and scale of social systems and cultural forms beyond the level of direct experience must be imagined (Thornton, 37; Strathern, 39). Analytical constructs in anthropology, such as "kinship," "religion," and "exchange systems" are ways of ordering data, not ways of ordering life. They are thus imaginary categories.

In the 1980s and 1990s, anthropology increasingly came to see culture as something constructed, reproduced, and transformed by the activities and ideas of human agents. It was recognized that this is rarely a matter of intentional design, but was most often the consequence of unintended actions. Far from being coherent and systematic, culture is contingent, conflicting, and shot through with power relations (Ortner, 18). As the concept of culture expanded to take account of global flows of images, people, commodities, and capital (Appadurai 1990), the notion of culture itself seemed ever more fragmented, illusive, diverse, and contingent, its purchase enfeebled. The irony, of course, was that at the very moment anthropology looked as though it wished to abandon culture as an organizing principle and analytical category, the rest of the world started to adopt it. And with vigor. From management consultants and international organizations to NGOs and local interest groups it became the prism through which the complexities of a globalized world could be understood (Moore, 36; Appadurai, 55; Jackson 1995). More than this, culture simultaneously became a mobilizing concept for indigenous groups and others seeking to redefine themselves against adjacent or competing groups, or searching to define their distinctiveness within an increasingly global and globalizing world (Moore, 36; Jackson 1995). Suddenly, cultures became self-evident constructs. Everyone had "theirs." Anthropologists, taken by surprise, began dramatically to talk of the authentic and the inauthentic, and of the invention of tradition. Rather mysteriously, local cultures or culture concepts were now criticized for being timeless, bounded, reified, and static: a strange kind of transference, it would seem, between the defects of the anthropologist's analytical construct and the forms of culture that many people wanted to claim for themselves (Sahlins 1999).

What is curious about this theoretical turn is that it is based on two mistaken premises: the first is that anthropologists in the past *did* work exclusively with bounded, fixed, and totalizing views of culture; the second is that people who are making contemporary claims relating to cultural distinctiveness are doing the same thing. The reality, though, as anthropologists are fond of saying, is more complex. Culture as a concept is both stabilizing and negotiable, both about long-run cultural values and systems and about lived daily practice and the determinations of the moment. This tension has always been there in anthropological writings on culture, albeit with particular notes of emphasis at certain historical moments, and indeed at different times in the writings of individual authors. Similarly, many of those who today deploy the culture concept in everyday parlance are hardly naïve about its contested nature.

Postmodernism and post-structuralism in anthropology provided powerful critiques of anthropology's analytical categories, representations, and practices. Yet they often did so by committing the act they so condemned in others: by generalizing and occluding differences. This is clear in the powerful critique that arose concerning the problem of generalization and comparison in anthropological theorizing. Once again, this critique derived from a concern that anthropological categories of analysis create abstract entities (through reification and objectification) and thus erase the particularity of lives lived, smoothing over differences, inconsistencies, and contradictions, in favor of coherence, boundedness, and totalization (Abu-Lughod, 38). This position was particularly powerful either where it could be demonstrated that western philosophical and analytical constructs were being directly imposed on other cultures, and/or where the pre-theoretical assumptions of western philosophical traditions were consistently constructing other cultures/cultural concepts as the "other," reducing the otherness of other cultures to the other of the west (Oyěwùmí, 44; Dhareshwar, 45; Viveiros de Castro, 46; Ingold 1991).

While there were powerful arguments in support of this critique, there were also occlusions. The fact that generalization and comparison can be problematic, and that categories and classifications are linked to differential power relations, is not in itself an argument for abandoning generalization or comparison (Moore, 36; Spiro, 42; Weber 2004 [1904]). Far from it. Generalization and comparison, based on critical use of categories and classifications, are essential to the project of anthropology for two reasons. The first is that longer-run structures of power and domination form patterns in human life, as Marx among others recognized, and those patterns require elucidation and explanation. Gender is a case in point (Ortner, 35). Abandoning generalization and comparison will occlude rather than reveal the workings of power (Weber 2004 [1904]). Second, by assuming that binary classifications, like nature/culture, mind/body, are products of western philosophical traditions and have been imposed on other cultures, we lose sight of the fact that other cultures may deploy similar binaries, albeit in dissimilar ways (Lambek, 34). In our determination to see all analytical constructs as impositions of the west, we run the risk of glossing over the complexities of other peoples' philosophical traditions precisely because we assume that they are completely "other."

Conclusion

Anthropology is changing because the world is changing. This truism is central to anthropological epistemology, to the constant striving to specify its object of inquiry. New ways of imagining the discipline have involved new ways of imaging social relations and social wholes – including imaging the affective role of material objects in producing particular subjectivities and forms of sociality (Zaloom, 50; Keane, 51; Navaro-Yashin, 52). Hybrids, networks, flows, and emergence are now the dominant metaphors (Sharp, 28; Strathern, 39; Navaro-Yashin, 52), but these imaginative constructs are no more mirror images of reality than the earlier ones. The locations and nature of fieldwork are changing, and these too require new forms of imagination (Augé, 48; Latour, 49; Marcus, 54; Appadurai, 55; Sangren, 58; Holmes and Marcus, 60). The exercise of the imagination is not, however, solely anthropological in the sense that it is contained within the discipline. The challenge for anthropology is that its truth claims must be based on the changing nature of others' imaginations, on the way they see the world, their culture, their response to globalization, unequal power relations, and inequalities, as well as the opportunities they perceive for change, for personal and social advancement, for well-being, and for security (Moore, 36; Helmreich, 47; Appadurai, 55). Anthropology has its roots ethically, practically, analytically, and institutionally in its history and in the west (Oyěwùmí, 44; Dhareshwar, 45; Latour, 49; Ribeiro, 59). It can critique that history, to be sure, but it cannot completely disavow it (Bourdieu, 57). To do so would not constitute a moral position, for it would ultimately occlude rather than reveal the relations between truth and power. Anthropological epistemology is ultimately about the way we imagine others as human beings. Thus the question "What can I know about the world?" is always bound up with who I am, for myself and for others.

Notes

1   Boas is famous in anthropology for refusing to theorize explicitly, preferring to locate cultural traits or elements within their specific historical and cultural context. However, Kroeber and Kluckhohn point out that Boas when writing typically vacillated between seeing culture as a specific historical, even accidental, agglomeration of traits and as an integrated "spiritual totality" (Kroeber and Kluckhohn 1952: 214). For a

similar view that cultural phenomena are only intelligible in terms of their history, see Lowie 1937:145.

2 A view first put forward by Geertz in the 1970s (Geertz 1973).

3 See Holy and Stuchlik, 14, for a critique of what happens when anthropologists conflate these two kinds of data.

4 Firth (1936) and Schapera (1940) both wrote early monographs that were functionalist and Malinowskian in style, that is, they were huge empirical studies of how everything in family life was related to everything else, but they lacked a single organizing theory. Their aim was the demonstration of interrelations rather than of organizing principles.

References

Abu-Lughod, L. 1986 *Veiled Sentiments: Honor and Poetry in a Bedouin Society*. Berkeley: University of California Press.

Appadurai, A. 1990 Disjuncture and Difference in the Global Cultural Economy. *Public Culture* 2(2): 1–24.

Barrett, H. C. and Kurzban, R. 2006. Theoretical Note. Modularity in Cognition: Framing the Debate. *Psychological Review* 113(3): 628–47.

Boas, F. 1982 [1940] The Limitations of the Comparative Method of Anthropology. In *Race, Language and Culture*. Chicago: University of Chicago Press and Free Press.

Bourdieu, P. 1990 *The Logic of Practice*. Cambridge: Polity Press.

Brightman, R. 1995 Forget Culture: Replacement, Transcendence, Relexification. *Cultural Anthropology* 10(4): 509–46.

Clifford, J. 1988 *The Predicament of Culture: Twentieth-Century Ethnography, Literature and Art*. Cambridge, MA: Harvard University Press.

Clifford, J. and Marcus, G. E., eds., 1986 *Writing Culture: The Poetics and Politics of Ethnography*. Berkeley: University of California Press.

Evans-Pritchard, E. E. 1940 *The Nuer*. Oxford: Clarendon Press.

Firth, R. 1936 We the Tikopia. Boston: Beacon Press.

Fortes, M. 1945 *The Dynamics of Clanship among the Tallensi*. Oxford: Oxford University Press.

Foucault, M. 1980 [1976] Two Lectures. In C. Gordon, ed., *Power/Knowledge: Selected Interviews and Other Writings 1972–1977*. New York: Harvester Wheatsheaf.

Foucault, M. 1991 [1977] The Body of the Condemned. In *Discipline and Punish: The Birth of the Prison*. London: Penguin Books.

Geertz, C. 1973 The Growth of Culture and the Evolution of Mind. In *The Interpretation of Cultures*. New York: Basic Books.

Gibson, K. R. 2002 Customs and Cultures in Animals and Humans. *Anthropological Theory* 2(3): 323–39.

Herskovits, M. 1972 *Cultural Relativism*. New York: Random House.

Ingold, T. 1991 Becoming Persons: Consciousness and Sociality in Human Evolution. *Cultural Dynamics* 4(3): 355–78.

Irvine, J., ed., 1994 *Edward Sapir: The Psychology of Culture*. Berlin: Mouton de Gruyter.

Jackson, J. 1995 Culture, Genuine or Spurious: The Politics of Indianness in the Vaupés, Colombia. *American Ethnologist* 22(1): 3–27.

Kahn, J., 1989 Culture, Demise or Resurrection? *Critique of Anthropology* 9(2): 5–25.

Keesing, R. 1987 Anthropology as Interpretive Quest. *Current Anthropology* 8(2): 161–76.

Kroeber, A. L. and Kluckhohn, C. 1952 *Culture: A Critical Review of Concepts and Definitions*. Cambridge, MA: Papers of the Peabody Museum, Harvard.

Kuper, A. 1999 *Culture: The Anthropologist's Account*. Cambridge, MA: Harvard University Press.

Lambek, M. and Boddy, J. 1997 Introduction: Culture in Question. In J. Boddy and M. Lambek, eds., Culture at the End of the Boasian Century. *Social Analysis* 41(3): 3–23.

Lavie, S., 1990 *The Poetics of Military Occupation: Mzeina Allegories of Bedouin Identity under Israeli and Egyptian Rule*. Berkeley: University of California Press.

Leach, E., 1970 *Lévi-Strauss*. London: Penguin Books.

Lowie, R. H., 1937 *The History of Ethnological Theory*. New York: Holt, Rinehart and Winston.

Mandelbaum, D., ed., 1949 *Selected Writings of Edward Sapir*. Berkeley: University of California Press.

Mauss, M., 1973 [1935] Techniques of the Body. *Economy and Society* 2: 70–88.

Moore, H. L. 1994 *A Passion for Difference: Essays in Anthropology and Gender*. Cambridge: Polity Press.

Needham, R. 1972 Introduction. In *Belief, Language, and Experience*. Oxford: Blackwell.

Ortner, S. 1984 Theory in Anthropology since the Sixties. *Comparative Studies in Society and History* 26: 126–66.

Rabinow, P. 1988 Beyond Ethnography: Anthropology as Nominalism. *Cultural Anthropology* 3(4): 355–64.

Radin, P. 1933 *The Method and Theory of Ethnology.* New York: McGraw-Hill.

Robertson, A. F. 1996 The Development of Meaning: Ontogeny and Culture. *Journal of the Royal Anthropological Institute* 2(4): 591–610.

Rosaldo, R. 1989 *Culture and Truth: The Remaking of Social Analysis.* Boston: Beacon Press.

Sahlins, M. 1976 *Culture and Practical Reason.* Chicago: University of Chicago Press.

Sahlins, M. 1999 Two or Three Things that I Know about Culture. *Journal of the Royal Anthropological Institute* 5(3): 399–422.

Sanders, T. 2008. *Beyond Bodies: Rainmaking and Sense Making in Tanzania.* Toronto: University of Toronto Press.

Sapir, E. 1924 Culture, Genuine and Spurious. *American Journal of Sociology* 29: 401–29.

Sapir, E., 1985 [1949] Anthropology and Sociology. In D. G. Mandelbaum, ed., *Selected Writings of Edward Sapir in Language, Culture and Personality.* Berkeley: University of California Press.

Schapera, I. 1940 *Married Life in an African Tribe.* London: Faber and Faber Ltd.

Sperber, D. 1985 Anthropology and Psychology: Towards an Epidemiology of Representations. *Man* 20: 73–89.

Stocking, G., 1968 *Race, Culture and Evolution.* New York: Free Press.

Stocking, G. 1974 *The Shaping of American Anthropology, 1883–1911: A Franz Boas Reader.* New York: Basic Books.

Taussig, M. 1987 *Shamanism, Colonialism, and the Wild Man: A Study in Terror and Healing.* Chicago: University of Chicago Press.

Toren, C. 1996 Introduction. In *Mind, Materiality and History: Explorations in Fijian Ethnography.* London and New York: Routledge.

Tsing, A., 1993 *In the Realm of the Diamond Queen: Marginality in an Out-of-the-Way Place.* Princeton, NJ: Princeton University Press.

Tyler, S. A. 1978 The Antinomies. In *The Said and Unsaid: Mind, Meaning, and Culture.* New York: Academic Press.

Weber, M. 2004 [1904] The "Objectivity" of Knowledge in Social Science and Social Policy. In S. Whimster, ed., *The Essential Weber.* London and New York: Routledge.

PART I

PART 1

SECTION 1
Culture and Behavior

1

The Aims of Anthropological Research

Franz Boas

The science of anthropology has grown up from many distinct beginnings. At an early time men were interested in foreign countries and in the lives of their inhabitants. Herodotus reported to the Greeks what he had seen in many lands. Caesar and Tacitus wrote on the customs of the Gauls and Germans. In the Middle Ages Marco Polo, the Venetian, and Ibn Batuta, the Arab, told of the strange peoples of the Far East and of Africa. Later on, Cook's journeys excited the interest of the world. From these reports arose gradually a desire to find a general significance in the multifarious ways of living of strange peoples. In the eighteenth century Rousseau, Schiller and Herder tried to form, out of the reports of travelers, a picture of the history of mankind. More solid attempts were made about the middle of the nineteenth century, when the comprehensive works of Klemm and Waitz were written.

Biologists directed their studies towards an understanding of the varieties of human forms. Linnaeus, Blumenbach, Camper are a few of the names that stand out as early investigators of these problems, which received an entirely new stimulus when Darwin's views of the instability of species were accepted by the scientific world. The problem of man's origin and his place in the animal kingdom became the prime subject of interest. Darwin, Huxley and Haeckel are outstanding names representing this period. Still more recently the intensive study of heredity and mutation has given a new aspect to inquiries into the origin and meaning of race.

The development of psychology led to new problems presented by the diversity of the racial and social groups of mankind. The question of mental characteristics of races, which at an earlier period had become a subject of discussion with entirely inadequate methods – largely stimulated by the desire to justify slavery – was taken up again with the more refined technique of experimental psychology, and particular attention is now being paid to the mental status of primitive man and of mental life under pathological conditions. The methods of comparative psychology are not confined to man alone, and much light may be thrown on human behavior by the study of animals. The attempt is being made to develop a genetic psychology.

Finally sociology, economics, political science, history and philosophy have found it worth while to study conditions found among alien peoples in

From *Race, Language and Culture* (Chicago: University of Chicago Press and The Free Press, 1982 [1940]), pp. 243–59. Originally published in *Science* N.S., vol. 76 (1932), pp. 605–13.

Anthropology in Theory: Issues in Epistemology, Second Edition. Edited by Henrietta L. Moore and Todd Sanders.

order to throw light upon our modern social processes.

With this bewildering variety of approaches, all dealing with racial and cultural forms, it seems necessary to formulate clearly what the objects are that we try to attain by the study of mankind.

We may perhaps best define our objective as the attempt to understand the steps by which man has come to be what he is, biologically, psychologically and culturally. Thus it appears at once that our material must necessarily be historical material, historical in the widest sense of the term. It must include the history of the development of the bodily form of man, his physiological functions, mind and culture. We need a knowledge of the chronological succession of forms and an insight into the conditions under which changes occur. Without such data progress seems impossible and the fundamental question arises as to how such data can be obtained.

Ever since Lamarck's and Darwin's time the biologist has been struggling with this problem. The complete paleontological record of the development of plant and animal forms is not available. Even in favorable cases gaps remain that cannot be filled on account of the lack of intermediate forms. For this reason indirect proofs must be resorted to: These are based partly on similarities revealed by morphology and interpreted as proof of genetic relationship, partly on morphological traits observed in prenatal life, which suggest relationship between forms that as adults appear quite distinct.

Caution in the use of morphological similarities is required, because there are cases in which similar forms develop in genetically unrelated groups, as in the marsupials of Australia, which show remarkable parallelism with higher mammal forms, or in the white-haired forms of the Arctic and of high altitudes, which occur independently in many genera and species, or in the blondness and other abnormal hair forms of domesticated mammals which develop regardless of their genetic relations.

As long as the paleontological record is incomplete we have no way of reconstructing the history of animals and plants except through morphology and embryology.

This is equally true of man, and for this reason the eager search for early human and prehuman forms is justified. The finds of the remains of the Pithecanthropus in Java, the Sinanthropus in China, of the Heidelberg jaw and of the later types of the glacial period are so many steps advancing our knowledge. It requires the labors of the enthusiastic explorer to furnish us with the material that must be interpreted by careful morphological study. The material available at the present time is sadly fragmentary. It is encouraging to see that it is richest in all those countries in which the interest in the paleontology of man has been keenest, so that we may hope that with the increase of interest in new fields the material on which to build the evolutionary history of man will be considerably increased.

It is natural that with our more extended knowledge of the evolutionary history of the higher mammals certain points stand out that will direct the labors of the explorer. Thus on the basis of our knowledge of the distribution of ape forms, nobody would search for the ancestors of humanity in the New World, although the question when the earliest migration of man into America took place is still one of the problems that is prominent in researches on the paleontology of the glacial period of America.

The skeletal material of later periods is more abundant. Still it is difficult to establish definitely the relation of early skeletal remains and of modern races, because many of their most characteristic traits are found in the soft parts of the body that have not been preserved. Furthermore, the transitions from one race to another are so gradual that only extreme forms can be determined with any degree of definiteness.

On account of the absence of material elucidating the history of modern races, it is not surprising that for many years anthropologists have endeavored to classify races, basing their attempts on a variety of traits, and that only too often the results of these classifications have been assumed as expressions of genetic relationship, while actually they have no more than a descriptive value, unless their genetic significance can be established. If the same metric proportions of the head recur in all races they cannot be a significant criterion of fundamental racial types, although they may be valuable indications of the development of local strains within a racial group. If, on the other hand, a particular hair form is a trait well-nigh universal in extensive groups of mankind, and one that does not recur in other groups, it will in all probability represent an ancient hereditary racial trait, the more so, if it occurs in a geographically continuous area. It is the task of the anthropologist to search out these outstanding traits and to remember that the exact measurement of features which are not exclusive racial characteristics will not answer the problems of the evolution of fundamental types, but can be taken only as an indication of independent, special modifications of late origin within the large racial groups.

From this point of view the general question of the occurrence of parallel development in genetically unrelated lines assumes particular importance. We have sufficient evidence to show that morphological form is subject to environmental influences that in some cases will have similar effects upon unrelated forms. Even the most skeptical would admit this for size of the body.

Changes due to environment that occur under our eyes, such as minute changes in size and proportion of the body, are probably not hereditary, but merely expressions of the reaction of the body to external conditions and subject to new adjustments under new conditions.

However, one series of changes, brought about by external conditions, are undoubtedly hereditary. I mean those developing in domestication. No matter whether they are due to survival of aberrant forms or directly conditioned by domestication, they are found in similar ways in all domesticated animals, and because man possesses all these characteristics he proves to be a domesticated form. Eduard Hahn was probably the first to point out that man lives like a domesticated animal; the morphological points were emphasized by Eugen Fischer, B. Klatt and myself.

The solution of the problem of the origin of races must rest not only on classificatory studies and on those of the development of parallel forms, but also on the consideration of the distribution of races, of early migrations and consequent intermingling or isolation.

On account of the occurrence of independent development of parallel forms it seems important to know the range of variant local forms that originate in each race, and it might seem plausible that races producing local variants of similar types are closely related. Thus Mongoloids and Europeans occasionally produce similar forms in regions so wide apart that it would be difficult to interpret them as effects of intermingling.

The biological foundations of conclusions based on this type of evidence are, to a great extent, necessarily speculative. Scientific proof would require a knowledge of the earliest movements of mankind, an intimate acquaintance with the conditions under which racial types may throw off variants and the character and extent of variations that may develop as mutants.

The solution of these problems must extend beyond morphological description of the race as a whole. Since we are dealing to a great extent with forms determined by heredity, it seems indispensable to found the study of the race as a whole on that of the component genetic lines and of their variants, and on inquiries into the influence of environment and selection upon bodily form and function. The race must be studied not as a whole but in its genotypical lines as developing under varying conditions.

In the study of racial forms we are too much inclined to consider the importance of races according to the number of their representatives. This is obviously an error, for the important phenomenon is the occurrence of stable morphological types, not the number of individuals representing each. The numerical strength of races has changed enormously in historic times, and it would be quite erroneous to attribute an undue importance to the White race or to the East Asiatics, merely because they have outgrown in numbers all other racial types. Still, in descriptive classifications the local types of a large race are given undue prominence over the less striking subdivisions of lesser groups. As an example, I might mention Huxley's divisions of the White race as against his divisions of other races.

We are interested not only in the bodily form of races but equally in the functioning of the body, physiologically as well as mentally. The problems presented by this class of phenomena present particular difficulties on account of the adjustability of function to external demands, so that it is an exceedingly precarious task to distinguish between what is determined by the biological make-up of the body and what depends upon external conditions. Observations made on masses of individuals in different localities may be explained equally well by the assumption of hereditary racial characteristics and by that of changes due to environmental influences. A mere description of these phenomena will never lead to a result. Different types, areas, social strata and cultures exhibit marked differences in physiological and mental function. A dogmatic assertion that racial type alone is responsible for these differences is a pseudo-science. An adequate treatment requires a weighing of the diverse factors.

Investigators are easily misled by the fact that the hereditary, biologically determined endowment of an individual is intimately associated with the functioning of his body. This appears most clearly in cases of bodily deficiency or of unusually favorable bodily development. It is quite a different matter to extend this observation over whole populations or racial groups in which are represented a great variety of hereditary lines and individuals, for the many forms of bodily make-up found in each group allow a great variety of functioning. Hereditary characteristics are pronounced in genetic lines, but a population – or to use the technical term, a phenotype – is not a genetic line and the great variety of genotypes within a race forbids the application of results obtained from a single hereditary line to a whole population in which the diversity of the constituent lines is bound to equalize the distribution of diverse genetic types in the populations considered. I have spoken so often on this subject that you will permit me to pass on to other questions.

While paleontological evidence may give us a clue to the evolution of human forms, only the most superficial evidence can be obtained for the development of function. A little may be inferred from size and form of the brain cavity and that of the jaw, in so far as it indicates the possibility of articulate speech. We may obtain some information on the development of erect posture, but the physiological processes that occurred in past generations are not accessible to observation. All the conclusions that we may arrive at are based on very indirect evidence.

The mental life of man also can be studied experimentally only among living races. It is, however, possible to infer some of its aspects by what past generations have done. Historical data permit us to study the culture of past times, in a few localities, as in the eastern Mediterranean area, India, China as far back as a few thousand years – and a limited amount of information on the mental life of man may be obtained from these data. We may even go farther back and extend our studies over the early remains of human activities. Objects of varied character, made by man and belonging to periods as early as the Quaternary, have been found in great quantities, and their study reveals at least certain aspects of what man has been able to do during these times.

The data of prehistoric archeology reveal with progress of time a decided branching out of human activities. While from earliest periods nothing remains but a few simple stone implements, we see an increasing differentiation of form of implements used by man. During the Quaternary the use of fire had been discovered, artistic work of high esthetic value had been achieved, and painted records of human activities had been made. Soon after the beginning of the recent geological period the beginnings of agriculture appear and the products of human labor take on new forms at a rapidly accelerating rate. While in early Quaternary times we do not observe any change for thousands of years, so that the observer might imagine that the products of human hands were made according to an innate instinct, like the cells of a beehive, the rapidity of change becomes the greater the nearer we approach our time, and at an early period we recognize that the arts of man cannot be instinctively determined, but are the cumulative result of experience.

It has often been claimed that the very primitiveness of human handiwork of early times proves organic mental inferiority. This argument is certainly not tenable, for we find in modern times isolated tribes living in a way that may very well be paralleled with early conditions. A comparison of the psychic life of these groups does not justify the belief that their industrial backwardness is due to a difference in the types of organism, for we find numbers of closely related races on the most diverse levels of cultural status. This is perhaps clearest in the Mongoloid race, where by the side of the civilized Chinese are found the most primitive Siberian tribes, or in the American group, where the highly developed Maya of Yucatan and the Aztecs of Mexico may be compared with the primitive tribes of our western plateaus. Evidently historic and prehistoric data give us little or no information on the biological development of the human mind.

How little the biological, organic determinants of culture can be inferred from the state of culture appears clearly if we try to realize how different the judgment of racial ability would have been at various periods of history. When Egypt flourished, northern Europe was in primitive conditions, comparable to those of American Indians or African Negroes, and yet northern Europe of our day has far outdistanced those people, who at an earlier time were the leaders of mankind. An attempt to find biological reasons for these changes would necessitate innumerable unprovable hypotheses regarding changes of the biological make-up of these peoples, hypotheses that could be invented only for the purpose of sustaining an unproved assumption.

A safer mode of approaching the problems at issue would seem to lie in the application of experimental psychology which might enable us to determine the psychophysical and also some of the mental characteristics of various races. As in the case of biological inquiry it would be equally necessary in this study to examine genotypical lines rather than populations, because so many different lines are contained in the mass.

A serious difficulty is presented by the dependence of the results of all psychophysical or mental tests upon the experiences of the individual who is the subject of the tests. His experiences are largely determined by the culture in which he lives. I am of the opinion that no method can be devised by which this all-important element is eliminated, but that we always obtain a result which is a mixed impression of culturally determined influences and of bodily build. For this reason I quite agree with those critical psychologists who acknowledge that for most mental phenomena we know only European psychology and no other.

In the few cases in which the influence of culture upon mental reaction of populations has been investigated it can be shown that culture is a much more important determinant than bodily build. I repeat that in individuals a somewhat close relation between mental reaction and bodily build may be found, which is all but absent in populations. Under these circumstances it is necessary to base the investigation of the mental life of man upon a study of the history of cultural forms and of the interrelations between individual mental life and culture.

This is the subject-matter of cultural anthropology. It is safe to say that the results of the extensive materials amassed during the last fifty years do not justify the assumption of any close relation between biological types and form of culture.

As in the realm of biology our inferences must be based on historical data, so it is in the investigation of cultures. Unless we know how the culture of each group of man came to be what it is, we cannot expect to reach any conclusions in regard to the conditions controlling the general history of culture.

The material needed for the reconstruction of the biological history of mankind is insufficient on account of the paucity of remains and the disappearance of all soft, perishable parts. The material for the reconstruction of culture is ever so much more fragmentary because the largest and most important aspects of culture leave no trace in the soil; language, social organization, religion – in short, everything that is not material – vanishes with the life of each generation. Historical information is available only for the most recent phases of cultural life and is confined to those peoples who had the art of writing and whose records we can read. Even this information is insufficient because many aspects of culture find no expression in literature. Is it then necessary to resign ourselves and to consider the problem as insoluble?

In biology we supplement the fragmentary paleontological record with data obtained from comparative anatomy and embryology. Perhaps an analogous procedure may enable us to unravel some of the threads of cultural history.

There is one fundamental difference between biological and cultural data which makes it impossible to transfer the methods of the one science to the other. Animal forms develop in divergent directions, and an intermingling of species that have once become distinct is negligible in the whole developmental history. It is otherwise in the domain of culture. Human thoughts, institutions, activities may spread from one social unit to another. As soon as two groups come into close contact their cultural traits will be disseminated from the one to the other.

Undoubtedly there are dynamic conditions that mould in similar forms certain aspects of the morphology of social units. Still we may expect that these will be overlaid by extraneous elements that have no organic relation to the dynamics of inner change.

This makes the reconstruction of cultural history easier than that of biological history, but it puts the most serious obstacles in the way of discovering the inner dynamic conditions of change. Before morphological comparison can be attempted the extraneous elements due to cultural diffusion must be eliminated.

When certain traits are diffused over a limited area and absent outside of it, it seems safe to assume that their distribution is due to diffusion. In some rare cases even the direction of diffusion may be determined. If Indian corn is derived from a Mexican wild form and is cultivated over the larger part of the two Americas we must conclude that its cultivation spread from Mexico north and south; if the ancestors of African cattle are not found in Africa, they must have been introduced into that continent. In the majority of cases it is impossible to determine with certainty the direction of diffusion. It would be an error to assume that a cultural trait had its original home in the area in which it is now most strongly developed. Christianity did not originate in Europe or America. The manufacture of iron did not originate in America or northern Europe. It was the same in early times. We may be certain that the use of milk did not originate in Africa, nor the cultivation of wheat in Europe.

For these reasons it is well-nigh impossible to base a chronology of the development of specific cultures on the observed phenomena of diffusion. In a few cases it seems justifiable to infer from the worldwide diffusion of a particular cultural achievement its great antiquity. This is true when we can prove by archeological evidence its early occurrence. Thus, fire was used by man in early Quaternary times. At that period man was already widely scattered over the world and we may infer that either the use of fire was carried along by him when he migrated to new regions or that it spread rapidly from tribe to tribe and soon became the property of mankind. This method cannot be generalized, for we know of other inventions of ideas that spread with incredible rapidity over vast areas. An example is the spread of tobacco over Africa, as soon as it was introduced on the coast.

In smaller areas attempts at chronological reconstruction are much more uncertain. From a cultural center in which complex forms have developed, elements may radiate and impress themselves upon neighboring tribes, or the more complex forms may develop on an old, less differentiated basis. It is seldom possible to decide which one of these alternatives offers the correct interpretation.

Notwithstanding all these difficulties, the study of geographical distribution of cultural phenomena offers a means of determining their diffusion. The outstanding result of these studies has been the proof of the intricate interrelation of people of all parts of the world. Africa, Europe and the greater part of Asia appear to us as a cultural unit in which one area cannot be entirely separated from the rest. America appears as another unit, but even the New World and the Old are not entirely independent of each other, for lines of contact have been discovered that connect northeastern Asia and America.

As in biological investigations the problem of parallel independent development of homologous forms obscures that of genetic relationship, so it is in cultural inquiry. If it is possible that analogous anatomical forms develop independently in genetically distinct lines, it is ever so much more probable that analogous cultural forms develop independently. It may be admitted that it is exceedingly difficult to give absolutely indisputable proof of the independent origin of analogous cultural data. Nevertheless, the distribution of isolated customs in regions far apart hardly admits of the argument that they were transmitted from tribe to tribe and lost in intervening territory. It is well known that in our civilization current scientific ideas give rise to independent and synchronous inventions. In an analogous way primitive social life contains elements that lead to somewhat similar forms in many parts of the world. Thus the dependence of the infant upon the mother necessitates at least a temporary difference in the mode of life of the sexes and makes woman less movable than man. The long dependence of children on their elders leaves also an inevitable impress upon social form. Just what these effects will be depends upon circumstances. Their fundamental cause will be the same in every case.

The number of individuals in a social unit, the necessity or undesirability of communal action for obtaining the necessary food supply constitute dynamic conditions that are active everywhere and that are germs from which analogous cultural behavior may spring.

Besides these, there are individual cases of inventions or ideas in lands far apart that cannot be proved to be historically connected. The fork was used in Fiji and invented comparatively recently in Europe; the spear, projected by a thong wound spirally about the shaft, was used on the Admiralty Islands and in ancient Rome. In some cases the difference in time makes the theory of a transfer all but unthinkable. This is the case, for instance, with the domestication of mammals in Peru, the invention of bronze in Peru and Yucatan and that of the zero in Yucatan.

Some anthropologists assume that, if a number of cultural phenomena agree in regions far apart, these must be due to the presence of an exceedingly ancient substratum that has been preserved notwithstanding all the cultural changes that have occurred. This view is not admissible without proof that the phenomena in question remain stable not only for thousands of years, but even so far back that they have been carried by wandering hordes from Asia to the extreme southern end of South America. Notwithstanding the great tenacity of cultural traits, there is no proof that such extreme conservatism ever existed. The apparent stability of primitive types of culture is due to our lack of historical perspective. They change much more slowly than our modern civilization, but wherever archeological evidence is available we do find changes in time and space. A careful investigation shows that those features that are assumed as almost absolutely stable are constantly undergoing changes. Some details may remain for a long time, but the general complex of culture cannot be assumed to retain its character for a very long span of time. We see people who were agricultural become hunters, others change their mode of life in the opposite direction. People who had totemic organization give it up, while others take it over from their neighbors.

It is not a safe method to assume that all analogous cultural phenomena must be historically related. It is necessary to demand in every case proof of historical relation, which should be the more rigid the less evidence there is of actual recent or early contact.

In the attempt to reconstruct the history of modern races we are trying to discover the earlier forms preceding modern forms. An analogous attempt has been demanded of cultural history. To a limited extent it has succeeded. The history of inventions and the history of science show to us in course of time constant additions to the range of inventions, and a gradual increase of empirical knowledge. On this basis we might be inclined to look for a single line of development of culture, a thought that was pre-eminent in anthropological work of the end of the past century.

The fuller knowledge of to-day makes such a view untenable. Cultures differ like so many species, perhaps genera, of animals, and their common basis is lost forever. It seems impossible, if we disregard invention and knowledge, the two elements just referred to, to bring cultures into any kind of continuous series. Sometimes we find simple, sometimes complex, social organizations associated with crude inventions and knowledge. Moral behavior, except in so far as it is checked by increased understanding of social needs, does not seem to fall into any order.

It is evident that certain social conditions are incompatible. A hunting people, in which every family requires an extended territory to insure the needed food supply, cannot form large communities, although it may have intricate rules governing marriage. Life that requires constant moving about on foot is incompatible with the development of a large amount of personal property. Seasonal food supply requires a mode of life different from a regular, uninterrupted food supply.

The interdependence of cultural phenomena must be one of the objects of anthropological inquiry, for which material may be obtained through the study of existing societies.

Here we are compelled to consider culture as a whole, in all its manifestations, while in the study of diffusion and of parallel development the character and distribution of single traits are more commonly the objects of inquiry. Inventions, economic life, social structure, art, religion, morals are all interrelated. We ask in how far are they determined by environment, by the biological character of the people, by psychological conditions, by historical events or by general laws of interrelation.

It is obvious that we are dealing here with a different problem. This is most clearly seen in our use of language. Even the fullest knowledge of the history of language does not help us to understand how we use language and what influence language has upon our thought. It is the same in other phases of life. The dynamic reactions to cultural environment are not determined by its history, although they are a result of historical development. Historical data do give us certain clues that may not be found in the experience of a single generation. Still, the psychological problem must be studied in living societies.

It would be an error to claim, as some anthropologists do, that for this reason historical study is irrelevant. The two sides of our problem require equal attention, for we desire to know not only the dynamics of existing societies, but also how they came to be what they are. For an intelligent understanding of historical processes a knowledge of living processes is as necessary as the knowledge of life processes for the understanding of the evolution of life forms.

The dynamics of existing societies are one of the most hotly contested fields of anthropological theory. They may be looked at from two points of view, the one, the interrelations between various aspects of cultural form and between culture and natural environment; the other the interrelation between individual and society.

Biologists are liable to insist on a relation between bodily build and culture. We have seen that evidence for such an interrelation has never been established by proofs that will stand serious criticism. It may not be amiss to dwell here again on the difference between races and individuals. The hereditary make-up of an individual has a certain influence upon his mental behavior. Pathological cases are the clearest proof of this. On the other hand, every race contains so many individuals of different hereditary make-up that the average differences between races freed of elements determined by history cannot readily be ascertained, but appear as insignificant. It is more than doubtful whether differences free of these historic elements can ever be established.

Geographers try to derive all forms of human culture from the geographical environment in which man lives. Important though this may be, we have no evidence of a creative force of environment. All we know is that every culture is strongly influenced by its environment, that some elements of culture cannot develop in an unfavorable geographical setting, while others may be advanced. It is sufficient to see the fundamental differences of culture that thrive one after another in the same environment, to make us understand the limitations of environmental influences. The aborigines of Australia live in the same environment in which the White invaders live. The nature and location of Australia have remained the same during human history, but they have influenced different cultures. Environment can affect only an existing culture, and it is worth while to study its influence in detail. This has been clearly recognized by critical geographers, such as Hettner.

Economists believe that economic conditions control cultural forms. Economic determinism is proposed as against geographic determinism. Undoubtedly the interrelation between economics and other aspects of culture is much more immediate than that between geographical environment and culture. Still it is not possible to explain every feature of cultural life as determined by economic status. We do not see how art styles, the form of ritual or the special form of religious belief could possibly be derived from economic forces. On the contrary, we see that economics and the rest of culture interact as cause and effect, as effect and cause.

Every attempt to deduce cultural forms from a single cause is doomed to failure, for the various expressions of culture are closely interrelated and one cannot be altered without having an effect upon all the others. Culture is integrated. It is true that the degree of integration is not always the same. There are cultures which we might describe by a single term, that of modern democracies as individualistic-mechanical; or that of a Melanesian island as individualization by mutual distrust; or that of our Plains Indians as overvaluation of intertribal warfare. Such terms may be misleading, because they overemphasize certain features, still they indicate certain dominating attitudes.

Integration is not often so complete that all contradictory elements are eliminated. We rather find in the same culture curious breaks in the attitudes of different individuals, and, in the case of varying situations, even in the behavior of the same individual.

The lack of necessary correlations between various aspects of culture may be illustrated by the cultural significance of a truly scientific study of the heavenly bodies by the Babylonians, Maya and by Europeans during the Middle Ages. For us the necessary correlation of astronomical observations is with physical and chemical phenomena; for them the essential point was their astrological significance, i.e., their relation to the fate of man, an attitude based on the general historically conditioned culture of their times.

These brief remarks may be sufficient to indicate the complexity of the phenomena we are studying, and it seems justifiable to question whether any generalized conclusions may be expected that will be applicable everywhere and that will reduce the data of anthropology to a formula which may be applied to every case, explaining its past and predicting its future.

I believe that it would be idle to entertain such hopes. The phenomena of our science are so individualized, so exposed to outer accident that no set of laws could explain them. It is as in any other science dealing with the actual world surrounding us. For each individual case we can arrive at an understanding of its determination by inner and outer forces, but we cannot explain its individuality in the form of laws. The astronomer reduces the movement of stars to laws, but unless given an unexplainable original arrangement in space, he cannot account for their present location. The biologist may know all the laws of ontogenesis, but he cannot explain by their means the accidental forms they have taken in an individual species, much less those found in an individual.

Physical and biological laws differ in character on account of the complexity of the objects of their study. Biological laws can refer only to biological forms, as geological laws can refer only to the forms of geological formations. The more complex the phenomena, the more special will be the laws expressed by them.

Cultural phenomena are of such complexity that it seems to me doubtful whether valid cultural laws can be found. The causal conditions of cultural happenings lie always in the interaction between individual and society, and no classificatory study of societies will solve this problem. The morphological classification of societies may call to our attention many problems. It will not solve them. In every case it is reducible to the same source, namely, the interaction between individual and society.

It is true that some valid interrelations between general aspects of cultural life may be found, such as between density and size of the population constituting a community and industrial occupations; or solidarity and isolation of a small population and their conservatism. These are interesting as static descriptions of cultural facts. Dynamic processes also may be recognized, such as the tendency of customs to change their significance according to changes in culture. Their meaning can be understood only by a penetrating analysis of the human elements that enter into each case.

In short, the material of anthropology is such that it needs must be a historical science, one of the sciences the interest of which centers in the attempt to understand the individual phenomena rather than in the establishment of general laws which, on account of the complexity of the material, will be necessarily vague and, we might almost say, so self-evident that they are of little help to a real understanding.

The attempt has been made too often to formulate a genetic problem as defined by a term taken from our own civilization, either based on analogy with forms known to us or contrasted to those with which we are familiar. Thus concepts, like war, the idea of immortality, marriage regulations, have been considered as units and general conclusions have been derived from their forms and distributions. It should be recognized that the subordination of all such forms, under a category with which we are familiar on account of our own cultural experience, does not prove the historical or sociological unity of the phenomenon. The ideas of immortality differ so fundamentally in content and significance that they can hardly be treated as a unit and valid conclusions based on their occurrence cannot be drawn without detailed analysis.

A critical investigation rather shows that forms of thought and action which we are inclined to consider as based on human nature are not generally valid, but characteristic of our specific culture. If this were not so, we could not understand why certain aspects of mental life that are characteristic of the Old World should be entirely or almost entirely absent in aboriginal America. An example is the contrast between the fundamental idea of judicial procedure in Africa and America; the emphasis on oath and ordeal as parts of judicial procedure in the Old World, their absence in the New World.

The problems of the relation of the individual to his culture, to the society in which he lives have received too little attention. The standardized anthropological data that inform us of customary behavior, give no clue to the reaction of the individual to his culture, nor to an understanding of his influence upon it. Still, here lie the sources of a true interpretation of human behavior. It seems a vain effort to search for sociological laws disregarding what should be called social psychology, namely, the reaction of the individual to culture. They can be no more than empty formulas that can be imbued with life only by taking account of individual behavior in cultural settings.

Society embraces many individuals varying in mental character, partly on account of their biological make-up, partly due to the special social conditions under which they have grown up. Nevertheless, many of them react in similar ways, and there are numerous cases in which we can find a definite impress of culture upon the behavior of the great mass of individuals, expressed by the same mentality. Deviations from such a type result in abnormal social behavior and, although throwing light upon the iron hold of culture upon the average individual, are rather subject-matter for the study of individual psychology than of social psychology.

If we once grasp the meaning of foreign cultures in this manner, we shall also be able to see how many of our lines of behavior that we believe to be founded deep in human nature are actually expressions of our culture and subject to modification with changing culture. Not all our standards are categorically determined by our quality as human beings, but may change with changing circumstances. It is our task to discover among all the varieties of human behavior those that are common to all humanity. By a study of the universality and variety of cultures anthropology may help us to shape the future course of mankind.

Note

Address of the president of the American Association for the Advancement of Science, Atlantic City, December 1932.

2

The Concept of Culture in Science

A. L. Kroeber

I propose to discuss the concept of culture – its origin and validity, its use and limitations. Like every concept, this one is a tool; and as a tool the concept of culture is two-edged. It ties some phenomena and interpretations together; it dissimilates and distinguishes others. [...]

Like all important ideas, that of culture was the realization of many minds, and it developed gradually. There are still great civilized nations – the French, for instance – who refuse to admit the word "culture" into their intellectual vocabulary. On the other hand, the ancients knew, and modern primitives are aware of, some of the phenomena of culture – as, for instance, distinctive customs. "We don't do that way, we do like this" – such a statement, which every human being is likely to make at some time, is a recognition of a cultural phenomenon.

Phenomena have a way of occurring composite in nature, intricately blended. Their qualities, still more their conceptualized general aspects, can be extricated only gradually from the welter of appearances. Until well into the nineteenth century and in certain situations and contexts until today, the concept of culture has remained unextricated from that of society. When Comte

founded sociology and coined its name more than a century ago, he stamped on it the impress of the social. But his famous three stages of mythology, metaphysics, and positivism are stages primarily of ideology, and therefore of culture. Only incidentally are they stages of specifically social or interpersonal relations. Still more does this essential reference to culture instead of society hold of Comte's differentiating characterizations of Catholicism and Protestantism and hundreds of other special dicta.

When so original and penetrating a thinker as Durkheim hypostasized society as that by which early groups were impressed, which they worshiped, and thus originated religion, he put forth a view which has generally seemed farfetched and, to many, mystical. But as soon as we substitute for his nondifferentium of "society" the customs and beliefs which hold together primitive societies and seem to help them to survive – in another word, their "culture" – then the Durkheim interpretation begins to assume reasonableness. It seems fair to assume that that is what Durkheim "meant," what he would say today.

That nondifferentiation of the two aspects should continue up to a certain point is expectable,

From *The Nature of Culture* (Chicago: University of Chicago Press, 1952), pp. 118–20, 129–33. Reprinted by permission of University of Chicago Press.

Anthropology in Theory: Issues in Epistemology, Second Edition. Edited by Henrietta L. Moore and Todd Sanders.
© 2014 John Wiley & Sons, Inc. Published 2014 by John Wiley & Sons, Inc.

since culture by definition includes, or at least presupposes, society. As something shared and supraindividual, culture can exist only when a society exists; and conversely every human society is accompanied by a culture. This converse, to be sure, is not complete: it applies only to *human* societies. In principle, however, the limitation is extremely important. The existence of cultureless or essentially cultureless subhuman societies, especially the highly elaborate ones of the social insects, serves as an irrefutable touchstone for the significant discrimination of the concepts of the social and the cultural: they *can* exist separately. At any rate, one of them does exist separately.

The word "social" is itself a relatively late appellation. The Roman term was *civilis, civitas,* from *civis,* a "citizen," corresponding to Aristotle's definition of man as a *zoon politicon* or "political animal" – a civil animal to the Romans, a social animal to us. Of course, institutions were implied in the term "political animal," and therewith culture was implied, but not as a segregated, coagulated concept. These ancient Mediterranean terms are illuminative of how abstract ideas originate in a matrix of the concrete. When Aristotle wanted to talk generically of what we call "society" and "culture," he used the word *polis,* which still carried full implication and imagery of citadel and city wall, of free citizens entitled to vote and to fight.

The word "culture" in its modern scientific sense, as, for instance, any anthropologist would use it with assurance that every other anthropologist would know what he meant, and not something else – this modern meaning of "culture" is still more recent. The first definition of "culture" in this broad but definite sense of its current social science usage – as distinct from cultivation and refinement, from nurture, from agriculture and pearl culture and test-tube cultures – the first definition I have found in an English dictionary dates from the late twenties. The first deliberate usage in a book was by Tylor when in 1871 he published *Primitive Culture* and formulated that mostquoted of definitions of culture which begins: "that complex whole which includes...." It is clear that Tylor was conscious of establishing the term, just as he was aware of using "culture" and "civilization" as synonyms in his discourse. [...]

Let us take a long step back from both culture and its undifferentiated immediate matrix, which we would today call "sociocultural" – a step back to the psychosomatic. Just as culture presupposes society, so society presupposes persons. It is an assemblage of individuals – plus something additional – that something which we and termite societies share. Well, here, then, are three elements or sets of factors: culture, society, persons, each resting upon, or preconditioned by, the next. In fact, we can immediately go one step further and separate persons into bodies and minds as two aspects which in some situations at least it is profitable to deal with separately – in all strictly psychological situations, for instance. That the separation is warranted, when it is useful, is clear not only from the current distinction of biological science from psychology but also from the fact that plants, though possessing somas, are generally conceded as showing no evidence of having psyches.

So now we are already facing four superposed aspects – four "levels," let us call them: body, psyche, society, culture. By now it is obvious where the line of thought is leading us; the next step prefaces the inorganic as underlying the somatic, the psychic, the social, and the cultural. [...]

It has become customary of late to designate these hierarchical planes as "levels of organization" and, alternatively, as "dimensions." The latter term is appropriate in certain contexts, as when it is said that every human situation has environmental, organic, social, and cultural dimensions. The word "dimension" here is equivalent to "aspects" or to "class of impinging factors." It definitely avoids even implication of hierarchy. Dimensions cross-cut one another, levels imply parallelism. In a so-called "field approach" to a limited phenomenal area, such as a personality, where emphasis is on the interaction of factors converging at a single point, it is natural to see cultural, social, organic, and physical factors as so many dimensions "radiating" out from the point under observation. By contrast, as the approach is macroscopic, or even telescopic, as in the tracing of large historic patterns or their interrelations, the dimensions automatically segregate themselves into parallel and superposed layers, and the term "levels" is more appropriate.

However, it is necessary not to confound "levels of organization" with "levels of abstraction." It is true that, while we are focusing on cultural aspects, we are in a technical sense "abstracting" from the organic and physical aspects pertaining to the same phenomena. "Abstracting" here means removing our consideration from, ignoring; it is temporary, shifting, reversible. But cultural phenomena are *not* more abstract than physical or organic phenomena in the sense of being more abstruse, rarefied, unconcrete, or conceptualized. The surge of anger is as concrete a phenomenon as is a contracted eyebrow or a constricted blood vessel. The custom of head-hunting or of catching the bride's bouquet is certainly thoroughly concrete. It is only culture as a generalized concept that is abstract; but so are society, psyche, body, matter, and energy abstract. What is much more significant than abstractness is that cultural phenomena occur organized on different principles from social phenomena, social phenomena from psychic, and so on down the series.

[...]

Cultural values, along with cultural forms and cultural content, surely exist only through men and reside in men. As the products of human bodies and minds and their functionings and as a specialized extension of them, cultural values thus form a wholly "natural" part of nature. Here the concept of the hierarchy of levels helps. Not only are the levels separated into steps; their superposition one on the other also ties them together, though not into an undifferentiated unity.

Values, like all sociocultural manifestations, are largely superpersonal. That is, far more of any individual's values are instilled into him from outside, directly or indirectly from his society, than he produces within and by himself. Hence values participate in what used to be called the "collective" or "mass" origin – what I prefer to call the "essential anonymity" of origin – of phenomena like customs, morals, ideologies, fashions, and speech. Sumner's "folkways" excellently conveys this same quality except for its false implication that there also exists a social intelligentsia exempt from being folk. It is possible to exalt collectivity into something self-containedly mystical, as shown by the example of Jung and perhaps of Durkheim. But it is not necessary to be mystical in dealing with collectivity, and we shall therefore assume that we are concerned with the collective only as something completely in relation with the remainder of nature.

Now the collective or anonymous, being everybody's, is also nobody's: there is a quality of the impersonal about it. The things that are everyone's enter individuality more diffusely than those which a person has sweated out for or by himself. These latter he is likely to prize, almost certain to be well aware of, and to have a conscious history and highlighted reasons for, whether these reasons be true or false. But what he shares with the collectivity is more massive and extensive, often more firmly rooted, and also more obscure; it tends to be less in the focus of consciousness. Hence what has been called the "covertness" of many patterns of culture; they have been set aside from the overt patterns as "configurations" by Kluckhohn. "Covertness" here does not imply intent of concealment, as it does so often in interpersonal motivations, rather only lack of awareness. It is probably a case of cultural forms being relatively more and less in focus of awareness along a sliding scale partly of occasion and partly of generic situation. Thus rules of conduct, which serve as protections to personality, are likely to be formulated with awareness and explicitness, though also subject to attempted warpings by self-interest. At the other end of the scale, rules of grammar in speech, which normally serves to connect personalities when they feel relaxed and in least need of protection, are unformulated, except as a result of the highly sophisticated curiosity of linguists, and can properly be described as having grown up both anonymously and unconsciously. [...]

Allied to this unawareness or unconsciousness of cultural form and organization is the irrationality of much of the collective in culture. "Irrationality" is what it is sometimes called. I have used the term myself. It covers a variety of happenings in culture which have in common a factor of inconsistency. The totality of a situation or way of doing comes out less regular and less coherent than it might have been under rational planning. Daylight saving; the letter *Double-U* after *U* and *V*; mannered mediaeval instead of classic Roman script; ideographs when an alphabet is available; the spellings "ought" and "eight"; the plural "oxen" instead of "oxes," will serve as examples. The point, of course, is that such irregularities and inefficiencies *were* not thought out but are the result of long and complex histories, with quite different factors often impinging successively. Established individual habits, prestige values, change in one part of a system with lag in another, actual economic cost, mere inertia or nostalgia – all sorts of reasons, mostly rational enough in the concrete situation, have been at work; and the resulting system shows the effect of compromises and patches. Any fool could devise a more consistent system than exists, but even a despot rarely can institute one. In one sense the outcome is "irrational" indeed, in that the institution lacks the full reasonableness which its defenders claim for it. Actually, it rather is nonrational, and only partly that. Most strictly, it is that the institutional pattern is irregular, not wholly consistent.

These considerations rather foreshadow what might be said of the integratedness of the cultures of particular societies. Cultures tend toward integration and, in the main, largely achieve some degree of it, though never total integration. This latter is an ideal condition invented by a few anthropologists not well versed in history. It is hard to imagine any historian – other than a propagandist – bringing himself to advance such a claim as the complete integration of any culture, in the face of his professional experience.

That values constitute an essential element of cultures leads to another consideration. A first account of a new culture, having necessarily to seize and portray the values which help to give it organization and orientation, is likely to emerge as a somewhat idealized account, since the values of the culture are reflected in the society's ideals. Ofcourse, no society is ideal in its behavior. The society aims to conform to the value standards; but we are all more or less lazy, mean, self-centered, cowardly, spiteful, motivated by personal interest. There is thus an unavoidable gap between the ideal or "pure" picture of the culture and the actuality of how this ideal is lived out by the average adherent of the culture. The psychologically minded analyst of behavior, the student of personality and culture, for whom culture is less an end than a take-off of interest, will accentuate the actuality; and between personality stresses and strains, traumas and frustrations, the ideal values of conduct which the "culturologist" has built up into such gleaming, streamlined patterns will emerge tarnished and

battered or even cracked. This is a difference to be aware of without worrying too much over it. He who is really interested in the phenomena of culture knows that their ideal values always suffer in actual human living of them. But, at the same time, he knows that in apprehending cultures the most essential thing to apprehend is their values, because without these he will not know either toward what the cultures are slanted or around what they are organized. [...]

Its extraordinary variability or plasticity is one of the most marked properties of culture. Living organisms are also adaptable and modifiable but do repeat their basic plan of structure closely in successive generations of individuals. There is almost nothing in culture to correspond to this organic repetitiveness. Allegations of regular recurrences in culture refer to shadowy, large resemblances which are only dubiously substantiable because they are not precisely definable. Itemized bits of culture content may persist with tenacity for long periods. Functioning organizations of cultural material apparently always change, even if they persist, until it is often difficult to say whether we are still within the original complex, form, or pattern or have slid into a new one. This inherent plasticity is evident as soon as one is in position to follow any one institution in detail through the centuries; or, equally, to follow an institution or custom through its provincial or regional variants, or through its appearances among a series of nonliterate tribes that are geographically contiguous.

The reason for this strong propensity of culture to vary seems to lie in the following fact: All cultural phenomena are invariably related to certain other cultural phenomena to which they are similar and which precede or succeed them or occur near them contemporaneously; and their fullest understanding can be attained only through cognizance of these relations. While these relations are indisputable, they are relations of form, value, and significance. They are not, directly, relations of cause in the ordinary sense of efficient cause. The efficient causes of cultural phenomena are the actions or behavior of men – of psychosomatic individual human beings. A denial of this proposition seems to leave no alternative but admission of a set of insulated, self-contained cultural forces operating in and on a self-sufficient cultural substance. This would be a large assumption and would immediately incur the charge, from scientists, of being a mystical tenet aiming to exclude a particular domain of phenomena from the sway of the remainder of the cosmos as studied by total science.

Now, as soon as the efficient causality of culture is admitted to lie essentially on the psychobiological level, it is evident that cultural phenomena are, in the strict sense, only by-products of organic activities, epiphenomena of primary organic phenomena. This conclusion, in turn, would seem to explain the irregularity, unpredictability, variability, and "plasticity" of cultural phenomena. They may once be the large cultural products of inconsequential subcultural forces or, again, the relatively insignificant side-effects of organic causes whose primary expression is in organic consequences. It cannot be doubted that single individuals occasionally affect the stream of culture perceptibly: Napoleon with his Code, Caesar on the Calendar, Shi Hwang-ti with the Burning of the Books, Copernicus with his revolution – not to mention religious leaders. Even sub-organic influence on culture must be admitted: catastrophes that wipe out one society, obliterating its culture, but spare another, leaving its culture intact; changes in climate favorable to prosperity and increase of particular populations, with consequent dominance of their cultures over those of disadvantaged peoples. It is evident that the greater the number and variety of these subcultural causes, the greater the variability or "plasticity" of cultural phenomena is likely to be.

Of course, the total outcome is not utter cultural randomness but only a high degree of what may properly be called plasticity; and this for the following reason.

Predominantly it will be the psychosomatic actions of human beings that contain the immediate causality of cultural phenomena. But human beings, with their extraordinarily high symbolizing faculties, which means cultural faculties, are always culturalized. That is, they are

culturally determined – and heavily determined – by the time they reach the age at which they become potential causes of culture. What is therefore operative is a powerful system of circular causality. The human beings who influence culture and make new culture are themselves molded; and they are molded through the intervention of other men who are culturalized and thus products of previous culture. So it is clear that, while human beings are always the *immediate* causes of cultural events, these human causes are themselves the result of antecedent culture situations, having been fitted to the existing cultural forms which they encounter. There is thus a continuity of indirect causation from culture event to culture event through the medium of human intermediaries. These intermediaries are concerned, first of all, with relieving their own tensions and achieving their personal gratification; but in so doing they also transmit, and to some degree modify, the culture which they carry because they have been conditioned to it. In a sense, accordingly, a kind of cultural causality is also operative. However, compared with the immediate efficient causality of men on culture, the causation of culture on culture is indirect, remote, and largely a functional relation of form to form. At any rate, as long as one's interest is in what happens in culture, it is the cultural antecedents that become significant. The human transmitters and carriers and modifiers are likely to average pretty much alike. As causes they tend to average uniform and constant, except so far as cultural exposure has differentiated them.

The inquirer, if his interest is really in culture, tends therefore to omit the human agents. He operates *as if* individual personalities did not have a hand in cultural events. In the main he is justified in this procedure. He is certainly justified in proportion as his view is long-range. On telescopic inspection of the greater cultural currents, even the greatest and most influential personalities shrink to minuteness. [...]

3

Problems and Methods of Approach

Gregory Bateson

[...] The historical approach to the cultures of primitive peoples has been frequently abused by students who practise the methods of functional anthropology. It has been said that the historians are solely concerned with the search for origins and with the construction of speculative narrative. This abuse is only justified if the writings of the historians emphasise this aspect of their work at the expense of more scientific aspects. History, in so far as it is a science, is concerned not with narratives and origins but with *generalisations* from narrative, generalisations based upon the comparative study of the processes of cultural and social change. The major achievement of, for example, the heliolithic historians is not their theory that almost all the cultures of the world have been derived from those of Egypt and Sumeria, but the picture which they have given us of the processes of change and degradation in culture. It is indeed high time that some student set to work upon the classification of these processes.

In the description of diachronic process, historians have used many of the same functional and economic concepts as are used in synchronic studies; but they have also elaborated one concept which has only very recently been adopted into the vocabulary of synchronic anthropology. This is the concept of *Zeitgeist*, the spirit of the times, a concept which owes its origin to the Dilthey–Spengler school of philosophical history.

The suggestion of this school is that the occurrence of cultural changes is in part controlled by some abstract property of the culture, which may vary from period to period so that at one time a given change is appropriate and occurs easily though a hundred years earlier the same innovation may have been rejected by the culture because it was in some way inappropriate.

Dr. Benedict[1] has developed a related concept, that of the "configuration" of culture, and has done some very interesting and important work on primitive cultures. She has shown, for instance, that the refusal of the Zuni to adopt either peyote or alcoholic drinks was conditioned by the Apollonian configuration of their culture, while the neighbouring peoples with Dionysian cultures adopted both these stimulants with enthusiasm.

From *Naven: A Survey of the Problems Suggested by a Composite Picture of the Culture of a New Guinea Tribe Drawn from Three Points of View*, 2nd edn. (Stanford: Stanford University Press, 1958 [1936]), pp. 111–22. Copyright © 1958 by the Board of Trustees of the Leland Stanford Jr. University. All rights reserved. Used with permission of Stanford University Press, www.sup.org.

Anthropology in Theory: Issues in Epistemology, Second Edition. Edited by Henrietta L. Moore and Todd Sanders.
© 2014 John Wiley & Sons, Inc. Published 2014 by John Wiley & Sons, Inc.

In European history the same type of concept is invoked in order to explain such curious facts as that Leonardo's mechanical inventions passed unnoticed or were laughed at during his life-time, and their importance was only gradually recognised during the following three centuries; or that the theory of evolution, though stated many times, did not obtain general acceptance until the industrial revolution had made the world "ready" to receive it.

In handling these concepts of *Zeitgeist*, configuration, etc., it is difficult to define their essential meaning without invoking some sort of mysticism. Their exponents have in general taken the wiser course, illustrating the concepts with concrete examples rather than giving abstract definitions of the terms which they use, and it is unfortunate that even this course has led to their being branded as mystics. There are, however, certain generalisations which seem to apply to all these concepts. In the first place the concepts are in all cases based upon an holistic rather than upon a crudely analytic study of the culture. The thesis is that when a culture is considered as a whole certain emphases emerge built up from the juxtaposition of the diverse traits of which the culture is composed.

If we examine the content of these emphases we find that they are conceived to be either *systems of thought* or *scales of values*.

But the two words, *thought* and *value*, are terms which have been snatched from the jargon of individual psychology; we must therefore consider in what sense a culture may be supposed to possess either a system of thought or a scale of values. At the present time, we must follow the opinion of the majority of psychologists in dismissing the theory of the group mind as unnecessary, and therefore regard all the thinking and feeling which occurs in a culture as done by individuals. Thus when we attribute a system of thought or a scale of values to a culture, we must mean that the culture in some way affects the psychology of the individuals, causing whole groups of individuals to think and feel alike.

There are two ways in which culture might do this, either by education, inducing and promoting certain types of psychological process, or by selection, favouring those individuals who have an innate tendency to psychological processes of a certain kind. In the present state of our knowledge of genetics, we cannot pretend to estimate the relative importance of these two methods of changing the psychology of a population. We can only suppose that both the method of selection and the method of education are at work in every community. For convenience, I shall dodge the issue of choosing between the two hypotheses by using a non-committal term which shall subsume them both. Following Dr. Benedict I shall speak of culture as *standardising* the psychology of the individuals. This indeed is probably one of the fundamental axioms of the holistic approach in all sciences: that the object studied – be it an animal, a plant or a community – is composed of units whose properties are in some way *standardised* by their position in the whole organisation. The time is not yet ripe for any detailed analysis of the possible standardising effects which culture may have upon the individuals in the community, but we may say at once that culture will affect their scale of values. It will affect the manner in which their instincts and emotions are organised into sentiments to respond differentially to the various stimuli of life; we may find, for example, that in one culture physical pain, hunger, poverty and asceticism are associated with a heightening of pride, while in another, pride is associated with the possession of property, and in another again, pride may be even gratified by public ridicule.

The effects of the culture upon the system of thought of the individuals are, however, not so clear. That the circumstances of a man's life will affect the *content* of his thought is plain enough, but the whole question of what we mean by a *system* of thought remains to be elucidated. [...]

Psychological Theories and Ethology. With this theory, that a culture may standardise the affective make-up of individuals, we may now turn to the theories of those who have sought to explain social phenomena upon psychological grounds. These theories are based upon broad statements that human beings, men or women or both, in all races and all parts of the world, have certain fixed patterns of emotional reaction. In applying such a theory to our *naven* ceremonies we might for example say that men have *naturally* certain attitudes towards women and that therefore whenever men dress as women their behaviour is exaggerated into buffoonery; while women, on the other hand, are affected in their own special way when they dress up as men and therefore they put on a prodigious amount of swagger. Or again we might say that "human beings are naturally gregarious" and that this fact is a complete and sufficient explanation of the large size of the Iatmul village. When faced with the small size of Mundugumor villages we may say that their smallness is due to the natural hostility which exists between males.

When stated in this way the theories have a slightly ridiculous appearance, but it is worth while to consider the position in which we should find ourselves if we indulged the facile building of these theories to an unlimited extent. We should find that we had attributed to the human race a large number of conflicting tendencies and that we had invoked certain tendencies in the interpretation of one culture and other, perhaps opposite, tendencies in the interpretation of another. Such a position is untenable unless we have some criterion whereby we may justify our choice of a particular psychological potentiality for use in interpreting a particular culture – some criterion whereby we may decide which potentialities may legitimately be invoked in describing a given culture. But, inasmuch as human beings often appear to harbour conflicting tendencies and potentialities, this position, with all its contradictions, may become tenable as soon as a satisfactory criterion is discovered.

Such a criterion may, I believe, be derived from the conclusion [...] that culture standardises the emotional reactions of individuals, and modifies the organisation of their sentiments; in fact, that culture modifies the very same aspects of the individual which are invoked by the rough and ready psychological theories of culture. We must therefore re-phrase the psychological theories in some such terms as these: A human being is born into the world with potentialities and tendencies which may be developed in very various directions, and it may well be that different individuals have different potentialities. The culture into which an individual is born stresses certain of his potentialities and suppresses others, and it acts selectively, favouring the individuals who are best endowed with the potentialities preferred in the culture and discriminating against those with alien tendencies. In this way the culture standardises the organisation of the emotions of individuals.

So long as we bear in mind this process of standardisation, we may safely invoke, in order to explain the culture, the sentiments of the individuals; but we must always verify that the sentiments invoked are actually those which are fostered by the culture in question. In the case of Mundugumor culture, if it can be shown that the hostility between individuals is an aspect of human nature which is as a matter of fact stressed by the culture, then we shall be justified in referring to this hostility as a factor which contributes to cause the people to live in small villages. In the same way, if it could be shown that Iatmul culture stressed man's gregarious tendencies, we should be justified in regarding the gregarious sentiment or instinct as important in the moulding of the culture. As a matter of fact, however, this facet of human nature is *not* specially stressed in Iatmul culture and this explanation must therefore be discarded.

[...] [P]ride is so stressed and [...] is of a sort to be gratified by the big ceremonial houses which require organised labour on a large scale, by great ceremonies and dances which require many performers and by head hunting which prospers when the village is strong in numbers. Thus the large size of the village serves an important function in gratifying pride – an attribute of human nature which is much stressed in Iatmul culture and to which therefore we are justified in referring.

The essence of the method is then that we first determine the system of sentiments which is normal to the culture and emphasised in its institutions; and when this system is identified we are justified in referring to it as a factor which has been active in shaping the institutions. It will be observed that the argument is circular.

In part the circularity is due to a characteristic of all scientific methods – the fact that we must observe a number of comparable phenomena before we can make any theoretical statement about any one phenomenon. But the circularity in the present case is also in part due to the nature of the phenomena which we are studying.

If we are studying jealousy and the institutions which regulate sexual life, we may argue both that the institutions stress jealousy and that jealousy has shaped the institutions. It would seem indeed that circularity is a universal property of functional systems, and that it may be recognised even in such crude and simple systems as the machines devised by man. In the motor-car, for example, the magneto produces electricity because the engine is running and the engine runs because of the sparks provided by the magneto. Each element in the functional system contributes to the activity of the others and each is dependent upon the activity of the others.

As long as we take an external – behaviouristic – view of a functional system we can avoid statements of circularity. We can see a motor-car as a thing into which petrol is poured and which runs along the road producing smoke and killing pedestrians. But the moment we turn from this external view and begin to study the internal workings of the functional system we are forced to accept the fundamental circularity of the phenomena. And this acceptance is demanded not only by ethology but by the whole functional approach to anthropology; and the students who are engaged in working from this point of view have realised this. Thus Malinowski claims that "the functional view avoids the error of attributing priority to one or the other aspect of culture. Material objects, social grouping, traditional and moral values, as well as knowledge are all welded into a functional system."[2]

A further and more compelling argument in favour of the circular or reticulate view of functional systems is to be found in the fact that any other view would drive us to belief either in a "first cause" or in some sort of teleology – in fact we should have to accept some fundamental dualism in nature which is philosophically inadmissible.[3]

Thus, since the phenomena which we are studying are themselves inter-dependent it is certain that our descriptions must contain inter-dependent statements; and since this is so the descriptions must for ever be regarded as "not proven" unless we can devise some method of transcending the limits of the circles. In a functional analysis we subdivide the systems studied into a series of parts or elements and produce theories about the functional relationships between these elements. So long as we study a single system these statements are bound to be circular and therefore not proven. But if we could extract comparable parts from different systems and verify that a given element has the same function in different systems we could finally verify the statements.

The orthodox functional school has adopted the practice of dividing cultures into *institutions*. But since the same institution is liable to have the most various functions in different societies the final verification of the theories is impossible. If we take the institution of marriage we find that it may function variously in the determination of status of offspring, in the regulation of sex life, in the education of offspring, in the regulation of economic life, etc.; and we find that the relative importance of these functions in different cultures varies so widely that it is almost impossible to verify by comparative methods the truth of any statement which we may make about marriage in any one culture.

The ethological approach involves a very different system of subdivision of culture. Its thesis is that we may abstract from a culture a certain systematic aspect called ethos which we may define as the expression of *a culturally standardised system of organisation of the instincts and emotions of the individuals*. The ethos of a given culture is, as we shall see, an abstraction from the whole mass of its institutions and formulations and it might therefore be expected that ethoses would be infinitely various from culture to culture – as various as the institutions themselves. Actually, however, it is possible that in this infinite variousness it is the *content* of affective life which alters from culture to culture, while the underlying systems or ethoses are continually repeating themselves. It seems likely – a more definite statement would be premature – that we may ultimately be able to classify the types of ethos.

The psychologists are already at work on the grading and classification of individuals and already it seems certain that different types of individual are prone to different systems of organisation of their emotions and instincts. If this be so, then there is a strong probability that the types of ethos will fall into the same categories of classification as the individuals and therefore we may expect to find similar ethoses in different cultures and shall be able to verify our conclusions as to the functional effects of any one type of ethos by comparison of its expression in one culture with its expression in another, thus finally transcending the limits of the circular argument.

Examples of Ethos in English Culture

[...] I shall illustrate the ethological approach by some examples taken from our own culture in order to give a clearer impression of what I mean by ethos. When a group of young intellectual English men or women are talking and joking together wittily and with a touch of light cynicism, there is established among them for the time being a definite tone of appropriate behaviour. Such specific tones of behaviour are in all cases indicative of an ethos. They are expressions of a standardised system of emotional attitudes. In this case the men have temporarily adopted a definite set of sentiments towards the rest of the world, a definite attitude towards reality, and they will joke about subjects which at another time they would treat with seriousness. If one of the men suddenly intrudes a sincere or realist remark it will be received with no enthusiasm – perhaps with a moment's silence and a slight feeling that the sincere person has committed a solecism. On another occasion the same group of persons may adopt a different ethos; they may talk realistically and sincerely. Then if the blunderer makes a flippant joke it will fall flat and feel like a solecism.

The point which I wish to stress in this example is that any group of people may establish among themselves an ethos which as soon as it is established becomes a very real factor in determining their conduct. This ethos is expressed in the tone of their behaviour. I have deliberately for my initial example chosen an instance of labile and temporary ethos in order to show that the process of development of ethos, far from being mysterious and rare, is an everyday phenomenon. The same group of intellectuals were at one time serious and at another witty, and if the blunderer had had sufficient force of personality he could have swung the group from one ethos to the other. He could have influenced the evolution of ethos within the group.

But if, instead of such a temporary conversation group, we examine some more formed and permanent group – say an army mess or a college high table – whose members continually meet under the same conditions, we find the ethological position much more stable. In the more casual groups sometimes one sort of remark and sometimes another is inappropriate, but in any formed group we find certain types of remark, certain tones of conversation permanently taboo. The ethoses of the formed groups are still not absolutely fixed. The processes of ethological change are still at work and if we could compare a college high table or an officers' mess of fifty years ago with those groups as they are today we should no doubt find very considerable changes. Such changes are only very much slower in the formed groups, and enormously greater force of character or force of circumstances is required suddenly to shift the ethos.

Correlated with this greater stability of ethos, there is a new phenomenon present in the formed groups which was absent or scarcely recognisable in the unformed. The group has developed its own cultural structure and its own "traditions" which have grown up hand in hand with the ethos. At the high table [...] we find such cultural developments as the Latin Grace, the dons' gowns and the silver presented to the College by former generations of Fellows. All these things have their effect in emphasising and stabilising the ethos of the group; and we cannot in any instance say that a given detail is due exclusively either to tradition or to the present ethos. The dons of St. John's College drink water, beer, claret, sherry and port – but not cocktails; and in their choice they are guided both by tradition and by the ethos of the group. These two factors work together and we may say that the dons drink as they do both because generations of dons have drunk on the same sound system in the past and because actually in the present that system seems to them appropriate to the ethos of their society. Whatever detail of the tradition we examine, the same considerations apply. The Latin Grace, the architecture of the college, the snuff after dinner on Sundays, the loving cup, the rose water, the feasts – all these cultural details constitute an intricate series of channels which express and guide the ethos.[4] The details were in the past selected by the ethos and are still preserved by it. The system is a circular one; and the very attitude which the dons adopt towards the past has been historically formed and is an expression of their present ethos.

This intimate relationship between ethos and cultural structure is especially characteristic of small segregated groups where the ethos is uniform and the "tradition" very much alive. Indeed when we say that a tradition is "alive" what we mean is simply this, that it retains its connection with a persisting ethos. But when we come to consider not isolated groups but whole civilisations we must expect to find much more variety of ethos and more details of culture which have been separated from the ethological contexts in which they were appropriate and retained as discrepant elements in an otherwise harmonious culture. Nevertheless I believe that the concept of ethos may valuably be applied even to such enormous and confused cultures as those of Western Europe. In such cases we must never lose sight of the variations of ethos in different sections of the community and the curious dovetailing of the ethoses of the different sections into an harmonious whole, whereby, for example, peasants with one ethos are enabled to live happily under feudal lords who have a different ethos. Differentiated systems of this kind may persist for generations and only break down when the scales of values are questioned; when the lords begin to doubt the ethics of their position and the serfs to doubt the propriety of submission – phenomena which are liable to occur when the differentiation has proceeded too far.

Notes

1   Ruth Benedict, "Psychological Types in the Cultures of the South-west", *Proc. 23rd Internat. Congress of Americanists*, 1928, pp. 572–81; *Patterns of Culture*, New York, 1934. [. . .]
2   *Encyclopaedia Britannica*, art. Anthropology.
3   Cf. Alfred North Whitehead, *The Concept of Nature*, Cambridge, 1920, especially ch. 11.
4   Such metaphors as this are of course dangerous. Their use encourages us to think of ethos and structure as different "things" instead of realising as we should that they are only different *aspects* of the same behaviour. I have let the metaphor stand *pour encourager les autres*.

4

The Individual and the Pattern of Culture

Ruth Benedict

[…] There is no proper antagonism between the rôle of society and that of the individual. One of the most misleading misconceptions due to this nineteenth-century dualism was the idea that what was subtracted from society was added to the individual and what was subtracted from the individual was added to society. Philosophies of freedom, political creeds of *laissez faire*, revolutions that have unseated dynasties, have been built on this dualism. The quarrel in anthropological theory between the importance of the culture pattern and of the individual is only a small ripple from this fundamental conception of the nature of society.

In reality, society and the individual are not antagonists. His culture provides the raw material of which the individual makes his life. If it is meagre, the individual suffers; if it is rich, the individual has the chance to rise to his opportunity. Every private interest of every man and woman is served by the enrichment of the traditional stores of his civilization. The richest musical sensitivity can operate only within the equipment and standards of its tradition. It will add, perhaps importantly, to that tradition, but its

achievement remains in proportion to the instruments and musical theory which the culture has provided. In the same fashion a talent for observation expends itself in some Melanesian tribe upon the negligible borders of the magico-religious field. For a realization of its potentialities it is dependent upon the development of scientific methodology, and it has no fruition unless the culture has elaborated the necessary concepts and tools.

The man in the street still thinks in terms of a necessary antagonism between society and the individual. In large measure this is because in our civilization the regulative activities of society are singled out, and we tend to identify society with the restrictions the law imposes upon us. The law lays down the number of miles per hour that I may drive an automobile. If it takes this restriction away, I am by that much the freer. This basis for a fundamental antagonism between society and the individual is naïve indeed when it is extended as a basic philosophical and political notion. Society is only incidentally and in certain situations regulative, and law is not equivalent to the social order. In the simpler homogeneous cultures collective habit

Anthropology in Theory: Issues in Epistemology, Second Edition. Edited by Henrietta L. Moore and Todd Sanders.
© 2014 John Wiley & Sons, Inc. Published 2014 by John Wiley & Sons, Inc.

or custom may quite supersede the necessity for any development of formal legal authority. American Indians sometimes say: "In the old days, there were no fights about hunting grounds or fishing territories. There was no law then, so everybody did what was right." The phrasing makes it clear that in their old life they did not think of themselves as submitting to a social control imposed upon them from without. Even in our civilization the law is never more than a crude implement of society, and one it is often enough necessary to check in its arrogant career. It is never to be read off as if it were the equivalent of the social order.

Society in its full sense [...] is never an entity separable from the individuals who compose it. No individual can arrive even at the threshold of his potentialities without a culture in which he participates. Conversely, no civilization has in it any element which in the last analysis is not the contribution of an individual. Where else could any trait come from except from the behaviour of a man or a woman or a child?

It is largely because of the traditional acceptance of a conflict between society and the individual that emphasis upon cultural behaviour is so often interpreted as a denial of the autonomy of the individual. The reading of Sumner's *Folkways* usually rouses a protest at the limitations such an interpretation places upon the scope and initiative of the individual. Anthropology is often believed to be a counsel of despair which makes untenable a beneficent human illusion. But no anthropologist with a background of experience of other cultures has ever believed that individuals were automatons, mechanically carrying out the decrees of their civilization. No culture yet observed has been able to eradicate the differences in the temperaments of the persons who compose it. It is always a give-and-take. The problem of the individual is not clarified by stressing the antagonism between culture and the individual, but by stressing their mutual reinforcement. This rapport is so close that it is not possible to discuss patterns of culture without considering specifically their relation to individual psychology.

We have seen that any society selects some segment of the arc of possible human behaviour, and in so far as it achieves integration its institutions tend to further the expression of its selected segment and to inhibit opposite expressions. But these opposite expressions are the congenial responses, nevertheless, of a certain proportion of the carriers of that culture. We have already discussed the reasons for believing that this selection is primarily cultural and not biological. We cannot, therefore, even on theoretical grounds imagine that all the congenial responses of all its people will be equally served by the institutions of any culture. To understand the behaviour of the individual, it is not merely necessary to relate his personal life-history to his endowments, and to measure these against an arbitrarily selected normality. It is necessary also to relate his congenial responses to the behaviour that is singled out in the institutions of his culture.

The vast proportion of all individuals who are born into any society always, and whatever the idiosyncrasies of its institutions, assume, as we have seen, the behaviour dictated by that society. This fact is always interpreted by the carriers of that culture as being due to the fact that their particular institutions reflect an ultimate and universal sanity. The actual reason is quite different. Most people are shaped to the form of their culture because of the enormous malleability of their original endowment. They are plastic to the moulding force of the society into which they are born. It does not matter whether, with the Northwest Coast, it requires delusions of self-reference, or with our own civilization the amassing of possessions. In any case the great mass of individuals take quite readily the form that is presented to them.

They do not all, however, find it equally congenial, and those are favoured and fortunate whose potentialities most nearly coincide with the type of behaviour selected by their society. Those who, in a situation in which they are frustrated, naturally seek ways of putting the occasion out of sight as expeditiously as possible are well served in Pueblo culture. Southwest institutions [...] minimize the situations in which serious frustration can arise, and when it cannot be avoided, as in death, they provide means to put it behind them with all speed.

On the other hand, those who react to frustration as to an insult and whose first thought is to get even are amply provided for on the Northwest Coast. They may extend their native reaction to situations in which their paddle breaks or their canoe overturns or to the loss of relatives by death. They rise from their first reaction of sulking to thrust back in return, to "fight" with property or with weapons. Those who can assuage despair by the act of bringing shame to others can register freely and without conflict in this society, because their proclivities are deeply channelled in their culture. In Dobu those whose first impulse is to select a victim and project their misery upon him in procedures of punishment are equally fortunate.

It happens that none of the [...] cultures we have described meets frustration in a realistic manner by stressing the resumption of the original and interrupted experience. It might even seem that in the case of death this is impossible. But the institutions of many cultures nevertheless attempt nothing less. Some of the forms the restitution takes are repugnant to us, but that only makes it clearer that in cultures where frustration is handled by giving rein to this potential behaviour, the institutions of that society carry this course to extraordinary lengths. Among the Eskimo, when one man has killed another, the family of the man who has been murdered may take the murderer to replace the loss within its own group. The murderer then becomes the husband of the woman who has been widowed by his act. This is an emphasis upon restitution that ignores all other aspects of the situation – those which seem to us the only important ones; but when tradition selects some such objective it is quite in character that it should disregard all else.

Restitution may be carried out in mourning situations in ways that are less uncongenial to the standards of Western civilization. Among certain of the Central Algonkian Indians south of the Great Lakes the usual procedure was adoption. Upon the death of a child a similar child was put into his place. This similarity was determined in all sorts of ways: often a captive brought in from a raid was taken into the family in the full sense and given all the privileges and the tenderness that had originally been given to the dead child. Or quite as often it was the child's closest playmate, or a child from another related settlement who resembled the dead child in height and features. In such cases the family from which the child was chosen was supposed to be pleased, and indeed in most cases it was by no means the great step that it would be under our institutions. The child had always recognized many "mothers" and many homes where he was on familiar footing. The new allegiance made him thoroughly at home in still another household. From the point of view of the bereaved parents, the situation had been met by a restitution of the *status quo* that existed before the death of their child.

Persons who primarily mourn the situation rather than the lost individual are provided for in these cultures to a degree which is unimaginable under our institutions. We recognize the possibility of such solace, but we are careful to minimize its connection with the original loss. We do not use it as a mourning technique, and individuals who would be well satisfied with such a solution are left unsupported until the difficult crisis is past.

There is another possible attitude toward frustration. It is the precise opposite of the Pueblo attitude, and we have described it among the other Dionysian reactions of the Plains Indians. Instead of trying to get past the experience with the least possible discomfiture, it finds relief in the most extravagant expression of grief. The Indians of the plains capitalized the utmost indulgences and exacted violent demonstrations of emotion as a matter of course.

In any group of individuals we can recognize those to whom these different reactions to frustration and grief are congenial: ignoring it, indulging it by uninhibited expression, getting even, punishing a victim, and seeking restitution of the original situation. In the psychiatric records of our own society, some of these impulses are recognized as bad ways of dealing with the situation, some as good. The bad ones are said to lead to maladjustments and insanities, the good ones to adequate social functioning. It is clear, however, that the correlation does not lie between any one "bad" tendency and abnormality in any absolute sense. The desire to run away from grief, to leave it behind at all costs, does not foster psychotic behaviour where, as among the Pueblos, it is mapped out by institutions and supported by every attitude of the group. The Pueblos are not a neurotic people. Their culture gives the impression of fostering mental health. Similarly, the paranoid attitudes so violently expressed among the Kwakiutl are known in psychiatric theory derived from our own civilization as thoroughly "bad"; that is, they lead in various ways to the breakdown of personality. But it is just those individuals among the Kwakiutl who find it congenial to give the freest expression to these attitudes who nevertheless are the leaders of Kwakiutl society and find greatest personal fulfilment in its culture.

Obviously, adequate personal adjustment does not depend upon following certain motivations and eschewing others. The correlation is in a different direction. Just as those are favoured whose congenial responses are closest to that behaviour which characterizes their society, so those are disoriented whose congenial responses fall in that arc of behaviour which is not capitalized by their culture. These abnormals are those who are not supported by the institutions of their civilization. They are the exceptions who have not easily taken the traditional forms of their culture.

For a valid comparative psychiatry, these disoriented persons who have failed to adapt themselves adequately to their cultures are of first importance. The issue in psychiatry has been too often confused by starting from a fixed list of symptoms instead of from the study of those whose characteristic reactions are denied validity in their society.

The tribes we have described have all of them their non-participating "abnormal" individuals. The individual in Dobu who was thoroughly disoriented was the man who was naturally friendly and found activity an end in itself. He was a pleasant fellow who did not seek to overthrow his fellows or to punish them. He worked for anyone who asked him, and he was tireless in carrying out their commands. He was not filled by a terror of the dark like his fellows, and he did not, as they did, utterly inhibit simple public responses of friendliness toward women closely related, like a wife or sister. He often patted them playfully in public. In any other Dobuan this was scandalous behaviour, but in him it was regarded as merely silly. The village treated him in a kindly enough fashion, not taking advantage of him or making a sport of ridiculing him, but he was definitely regarded as one who was outside the game.

The behaviour congenial to the Dobuan simpleton has been made the ideal in certain periods of our own civilization, and there are still vocations in which his responses are accepted in most Western communities. Especially if a woman is in question, she is well provided for even today in our *mores*, and functions honourably in her family and community. The fact that the Dobuan could not function in his culture was not a consequence of the particular responses that were congenial to him, but of the chasm between them and the cultural pattern.

Most ethnologists have had similar experiences in recognizing that the persons who are put

outside the pale of society with contempt are not those who would be placed there by another culture. Lowie found among the Crow Indians of the plains a man of exceptional knowledge of his cultural forms. He was interested in considering these objectively and in correlating different facets. He had an interest in genealogical facts and was invaluable on points of history. Altogether he was an ideal interpreter of Crow life. These traits, however, were not those which were the password to honour among the Crow. He had a definite shrinking from physical danger, and bravado was the tribal virtue. To make matters worse he had attempted to gain recognition by claiming a war honour which was fraudulent. He was proved not to have brought in, as he claimed, a picketed horse from the enemy's camp. To lay false claim to war honours was a paramount sin among the Crow, and by the general opinion, constantly reiterated, he was regarded as irresponsible and incompetent.

Such situations can be paralleled with the attitude in our civilization toward a man who does not succeed in regarding personal possessions as supremely important. Our hobo population is constantly fed by those to whom the accumulation of property is not a sufficient motivation. In case these individuals ally themselves with the hoboes, public opinion regards them as potentially vicious, as indeed because of the asocial situation into which they are thrust they readily become. In case, however, these men compensate by emphasizing their artistic temperament and become members of expatriated groups of petty artists, opinion regards them not as vicious but as silly. In any case they are unsupported by the forms of their society, and the effort to express themselves satisfactorily is ordinarily a greater task than they can achieve.

The dilemma of such an individual is often most successfully solved by doing violence to his strongest natural impulses and accepting the rôle the culture honours. In case he is a person to whom social recognition is necessary, it is ordinarily his only possible course. One of the most striking individuals in Zuñi had accepted this necessity. In a society that thoroughly distrusts authority of any sort, he had a native personal magnetism that singled him out in any group. In a society that exalts moderation and the easiest way, he was turbulent and could act violently upon occasion. In a society that praises a pliant personality that "talks lots" – that is, that chatters in a friendly fashion – he was scornful and aloof. Zuñi's only reaction to such personalities is to brand them as witches. He was said to have been seen peering through a window from outside, and this is a sure mark of a witch. At any rate, he got drunk one day and boasted that they could not kill him. He was taken before the war priests who hung him by his thumbs from the rafters till he should confess to his witchcraft. This is the usual procedure in a charge of witchcraft. However, he dispatched a messenger to the government troops. When they came, his shoulders were already crippled for life, and the officer of the law was left with no recourse but to imprison the war priests who had been responsible for the enormity. One of these war priests was probably the most respected and important person in recent Zuñi history, and when he returned after imprisonment in the state penitentiary he never resumed his priestly offices. He regarded his power as broken. It was a revenge that is probably unique in Zuñi history. It involved, of course, a challenge to the priesthoods, against whom the witch by his act openly aligned himself.

The course of his life in the forty years that followed this defiance was not, however, what we might easily predict. A witch is not barred from his membership in cult groups because he has been condemned, and the way to recognition lay through such activity. He possessed a remarkable verbal memory and a sweet singing voice. He learned unbelievable stores of mythology, of esoteric ritual, of cult songs. Many hundreds of pages of stories and ritual poetry were taken down from his dictation before he died, and he regarded his songs as much more extensive. He became indispensable in ceremonial life and before he died was the governor of Zuñi. The congenial bent of his personality threw him into irreconcilable conflict with his society, and he solved his dilemma by turning an incidental talent to account. As we might well expect, he was not a happy man. As governor of Zuñi, and high in his cult groups, a marked man in his community, he was obsessed by death. He was a cheated man in the midst of a mildly happy populace.

It is easy to imagine the life he might have lived among the Plains Indians, where every institution favoured the traits that were native to him. The personal authority, the turbulence, the scorn, would all have been honoured in the career he could have made his own. The unhappiness that was inseparable from his temperament as a successful priest and governor of Zuñi would have had no place as a war chief of the Cheyenne; it was not a function of the traits of his native endowment but of the standards of the culture in which he found no outlet for his native responses.

The individuals we have so far discussed are not in any sense psychopathic. They illustrate the dilemma of the individual whose congenial drives are not provided for in the institutions of his culture. This dilemma becomes of psychiatric importance when the behaviour in question is regarded as categorically abnormal in a society. Western civilization tends to regard even a mild homosexual as an abnormal. The clinical picture of homosexuality stresses the neuroses and psychoses to which it gives rise, and emphasizes almost equally the inadequate functioning of the invert and his behaviour. We have only to turn to other cultures, however, to realize that homosexuals have by no means been uniformly inadequate to the social situation. They have not always failed to function. In some societies they have even been especially acclaimed. Plato's *Republic* is, of course, the most convincing statement of the honourable estate of homosexuality. It is presented as a major means to the good life, and Plato's high ethical evaluation of this response was upheld in the customary behaviour of Greece at that period.

The American Indians do not make Plato's high moral claims for homosexuality, but homosexuals are often regarded as exceptionally able. In most of North America there exists the institution of the *berdache*, as the French called them. These men-women were men who at puberty or thereafter took the dress and the occupations of women. Sometimes they married other men and lived with them. Sometimes they were men with no inversion, persons of weak sexual endowment who chose this rôle to avoid the jeers of the women. The berdaches were never regarded as of first-rate supernatural power, as similar men-women were in Siberia, but rather as leaders in women's occupations, good healers in certain diseases, or, among certain tribes, as the genial organizers of social affairs. They were usually, in spite of the manner in which they were accepted, regarded with a certain embarrassment. It was thought slightly ridiculous to address as "she" a person who was known to be a man and who, as in Zuñi, would be buried on the men's side of the cemetery. But they were socially placed. The emphasis in most tribes was upon the fact that men who took over women's occupations excelled by reason of their strength and initiative and were therefore leaders in women's techniques and in the accumulation of those forms of property made by women. One of the best known of all the Zuñis of a generation ago was the man-woman We-wha, who was, in the words of his friend, Mrs. Stevenson, "certainly the strongest person in Zuñi, both mentally and physically." His remarkable memory for ritual made him a chief personage on ceremonial occasions, and his strength and intelligence made him a leader in all kinds of crafts.

The men-women of Zuñi are not all strong, self-reliant personages. Some of them take this refuge to protect themselves against their inability to take part in men's activities. One is almost a simpleton, and one, hardly more than a little boy, has delicate features like a girl's. There are obviously several reasons why a person becomes a berdache in Zuñi, but whatever the reason, men who have chosen openly to assume women's dress have the same chance as any other persons to establish themselves as functioning members of the society. Their response is socially recognized. If they have native ability, they can give it scope; if they are weak creatures, they fail in terms of their weakness of character, not in terms of their inversion.

The Indian institution of the berdache was most strongly developed on the plains. The Dakota had a saying, "fine possessions like a berdache's," and it was the epitome of praise for any woman's household possessions. A berdache had two strings to his bow, he was supreme in women's techniques, and he could also support his *ménage* by the man's activity of hunting. Therefore no one was richer. When especially fine beadwork or dressed skins were desired for ceremonial occasions, the berdache's work was sought in preference to any other's. It was his social adequacy that was stressed above all else. As in Zuñi, the attitude toward him is ambivalent and touched with malaise in the face of a recognized incongruity. Social scorn, however, was visited not upon the berdache but upon the man who

lived with him. The latter was regarded as a weak man who had chosen an easy berth instead of the recognized goals of their culture; he did not contribute to the household, which was already a model for all households through the sole efforts of the berdache. His sexual adjustment was not singled out in the judgment that was passed upon him, but in terms of his economic adjustment he was an outcast.

When the homosexual response is regarded as a perversion, however, the invert is immediately exposed to all the conflicts to which aberrants are always exposed. His guilt, his sense of inadequacy, his failures, are consequences of the disrepute which social tradition visits upon him, and few people can achieve a satisfactory life unsupported by the standards of their society. The adjustments that society demands of them would strain any man's vitality, and the consequences of this conflict we identify with their homosexuality.

Trance is a similar abnormality in our society. Even a very mild mystic is aberrant in Western civilization. In order to study trance or catalepsy within our own social groups, we have to go to the case histories of the abnormal. Therefore the correlation between trance experience and the neurotic and psychotic seems perfect. As in the case of the homosexual, however, it is a local correlation characteristic of our century. Even in our own cultural background other eras give different results. In the Middle Ages when Catholicism made the ecstatic experience the mark of sainthood, the trance experience was greatly valued, and those to whom the response was congenial, instead of being overwhelmed by a catastrophe as in our century, were given confidence in the pursuit of their careers. It was a validation of ambitions, not a stigma of insanity. Individuals who were susceptible to trance, therefore, succeeded or failed in terms of their native capacities, but since trance experience was highly valued, a great leader was very likely to be capable of it.

Among primitive peoples, trance and catalepsy have been honoured in the extreme. Some of the Indian tribes of California accorded prestige principally to those who passed through certain trance experiences. Not all of these tribes believed that it was exclusively women who were so blessed, but among the Shasta this was the convention. Their shamans were women, and they were accorded the greatest prestige in the community. They were chosen because of their

constitutional liability to trance and allied manifestations. One day the woman who was so destined, while she was about her usual work, fell
suddenly to the ground. She had heard a voice
speaking to her in tones of the greatest intensity.
Turning, she had seen a man with drawn bow
and arrow. He commanded her to sing on pain
of being shot through the heart by his arrow,
but under the stress of the experience she fell
senseless. Her family gathered. She was lying
rigid, hardly breathing. They knew that for some
time she had had dreams of a special character
which indicated a shamanistic calling, dreams of
escaping grizzly bears, falling off cliffs or trees, or
of being surrounded by swarms of yellow-jackets.
The community knew therefore what to expect.
After a few hours the woman began to moan
gently and to roll about upon the ground, trem-
bling violently. She was supposed to be repeating
the song which she had been told to sing and
which during the trance had been taught her by
the spirit. As she revived, her moaning became
more and more clearly the spirit's song until at
last she called out the name of the spirit itself, and
immediately blood oozed from her mouth.

When the woman had come to herself after the
first encounter with her spirit, she danced that
night her first initiatory shaman's dance. For three
nights she danced, holding herself by a rope that
was swung from the ceiling. On the third night
she had to receive in her body her power from her
spirit. She was dancing, and as she felt the
approach of the moment she called out, "He will
shoot me, he will shoot me." Her friends stood
close, for when she reeled in a kind of cataleptic
seizure, they had to seize her before she fell or she
would die. From this time on she had in her body
a visible materialization of her spirit's power, an
icicle-like object which in her dances thereafter
she would exhibit, producing it from one part of
her body and returning it to another part. From
this time on she continued to validate her supernatural power by further cataleptic demonstrations, and she was called upon in great
emergencies of life and death, for curing and for
divination and for counsel. She became, in other
words, by this procedure a woman of great power
and importance.

It is clear that, far from regarding cataleptic seizures as blots upon the family escutcheon and as
evidences of dreaded disease, cultural approval
had seized upon them and made of them the

pathway to authority over one's fellows. They
were the outstanding characteristic of the most
respected social type, the type which functioned
with most honour and reward in the community.
It was precisely the cataleptic individuals who in
this culture were singled out for authority and
leadership.

The possible usefulness of "abnormal" types in
a social structure, provided they are types that are
culturally selected by that group, is illustrated
from every part of the world. The shamans of
Siberia dominate their communities. According
to the ideas of these peoples, they are individuals
who by submission to the will of the spirits have
been cured of a grievous illness – the onset of the
seizures – and have acquired by this means great
supernatural power and incomparable vigour and
health. Some, during the period of the call, are
violently insane for several years; others irresponsible to the point where they have to be constantly
watched lest they wander off in the snow and
freeze to death; others ill and emaciated to the
point of death, sometimes with bloody sweat. It is
the shamanistic practice which constitutes their
cure, and the extreme exertion of a Siberian
séance leaves them, they claim, rested and able to
enter immediately upon a similar performance.
Cataleptic seizures are regarded as an essential
part of any shamanistic performance.

[…]

It is clear that culture may value and make
socially available even highly unstable human
types. If it chooses to treat their peculiarities as
the most valued variants of human behaviour, the
individuals in question will rise to the occasion
and perform their social rôles without reference
to our usual ideas of the types who can make
social adjustments and those who cannot. Those
who function inadequately in any society are not
those with certain fixed "abnormal" traits, but
may well be those whose responses have received
no support in the institutions of their culture. The
weakness of these aberrants is in great measure
illusory. It springs, not from the fact that they are
lacking in necessary vigour, but that they are individuals whose native responses are not reaffirmed
by society. They are, as Sapir phrases it, "alienated
from an impossible world."

The person unsupported by the standards of his
time and place and left naked to the winds of ridicule has been unforgettably drawn in European
literature in the figure of Don Quixote. Cervantes

turned upon a tradition still honoured in the abstract the limelight of a changed set of practical standards, and his poor old man, the orthodox upholder of the romantic chivalry of another generation, became a simpleton. The windmills with which he tilted were the serious antagonists of a hardly vanished world, but to tilt with them when the world no longer called them serious was to rave. He loved his Dulcinea in the best traditional manner of chivalry, but another version of love was fashionable for the moment, and his fervour was counted to him for madness. [...]

No society has yet attempted a self-conscious direction of the process by which its new normalities are created in the next generation. Dewey has pointed out how possible and yet how drastic such social engineering would be. For some traditional arrangements it is obvious that very high prices are paid, reckoned in terms of human suffering and frustration. If these arrangements presented themselves to us merely as arrangements and not as categorical imperatives, our reasonable course would be to adapt them by whatever means to rationally selected goals. What we do instead is to ridicule our Don Quixotes, the ludicrous embodiments of an outmoded tradition, and continue to regard our own as final and prescribed in the nature of things.

In the meantime the therapeutic problem of dealing with our psychopaths of this type is often misunderstood. Their alienation from the actual world can often be more intelligently handled than by insisting that they adopt the modes that are alien to them. Two other courses are always possible. In the first place, the misfit individual may cultivate a greater objective interest in his own preferences and learn how to manage with greater equanimity his deviation from the type. If he learns to recognize the extent to which his suffering has been due to his lack of support in a traditional ethos, he may gradually educate himself to accept his degree of difference with less suffering. Both the exaggerated emotional disturbances of the manic depressive and the seclusion of the schizophrenic add certain values to existence which are not open to those differently constituted. The unsupported individual who valiantly accepts his favourite and native virtues may attain a feasible course of behaviour that makes it unnecessary for him to take refuge in a private world he has fashioned for himself. He may gradually achieve a more independent and less tor-

tured attitude toward his deviations and upon this attitude he may be able to build an adequately functioning existence.

In the second place, an increased tolerance in society toward its less usual types must keep pace with the self-education of the patient. The possibilities in this direction are endless. Tradition is as neurotic as any patient; its overgrown fear of deviation from its fortuitous standards conforms to all the usual definitions of the psychopathic. This fear does not depend upon observation of the limits within which conformity is necessary to the social good. Much more deviation is allowed to the individual in some cultures than in others, and those in which much is allowed cannot be shown to suffer from their peculiarity. It is probable that social orders of the future will carry this tolerance and encouragement of individual difference much further than any cultures of which we have experience.

The American tendency at the present time leans so far to the opposite extreme that it is not easy for us to picture the changes that such an attitude would bring about. Middletown is a typical example of our usual urban fear of seeming in however slight an act different from our neighbours. Eccentricity is more feared than parasitism. Every sacrifice of time and tranquillity is made in order that no one in the family may have any taint of nonconformity attached to him. Children in school make their great tragedies out of not wearing a certain kind of stockings, not joining a certain dancing-class, not driving a certain car. The fear of being different is the dominating motivation recorded in Middletown.

The psychopathic toll that such a motivation exacts is evident in every institution for mental diseases in our country. In a society in which it existed only as a minor motive among many others, the psychiatric picture would be a very different one. At all events, there can be no reasonable doubt that one of the most effective ways in which to deal with the staggering burden of psychopathic tragedies in America at the present time is by means of an educational programme which fosters tolerance in society and a kind of self-respect and independence that is foreign to Middletown and our urban traditions. [...]

To a certain extent, therefore, civilization in setting higher and possibly more worth-while goals may increase the number of its abnormals.

But the point may very easily be overemphasized, for very small changes in social attitudes may far outweigh this correlation. On the whole, since the social possibilities of tolerance and recognition of individual difference are so little explored in practice, pessimism seems premature. Certainly other quite different social factors which we have just discussed are more directly responsible for the great proportion of our neurotics and psychotics, and with these other factors civilizations could, if they would, deal without necessary intrinsic loss.

We have been considering individuals from the point of view of their ability to function adequately in their society. This adequate functioning is one of the ways in which normality is clinically defined. It is also defined in terms of fixed symptoms, and the tendency is to identify normality with the statistically average. In practice this average is one arrived at in the laboratory, and deviations from it are defined as abnormal.

From the point of view of a single culture this procedure is very useful. It shows the clinical picture of the civilization and gives considerable information about its socially approved behaviour. To generalize this as an absolute normal, however, is a different matter. As we have seen, the range of normality in different cultures does not coincide. Some, like Zuñi and the Kwakiutl, are so far removed from each other that they overlap only slightly. The statistically determined normal on the Northwest Coast would be far outside the extreme boundaries of abnormality in the Pueblos. The normal Kwakiutl rivalry contest would only be understood as madness in Zuñi, and the traditional Zuñi indifference to dominance and the humiliation of others would be the fatuousness of a simpleton in a man of noble family on the Northwest Coast. Aberrant behaviour in either culture could never be determined in relation to any least common denominator of behaviour. Any society, according to its major preoccupations, may increase and intensify even hysterical, epileptic, or paranoid symptoms, at the same time relying socially in a greater and greater degree upon the very individuals who display them.

This fact is important in psychiatry because it makes clear another group of abnormals which probably exists in every culture: the abnormals who represent the extreme development of the local cultural type. This group is socially in the opposite situation from the group we have discussed, those whose responses are at variance with their cultural standards. Society, instead of exposing the former group at every point, supports them in their furthest aberrations. They have a licence which they may almost endlessly exploit. For this reason these persons almost never fall within the scope of any contemporary psychiatry. They are unlikely to be described even in the most careful manuals of the generation that fosters them. Yet from the point of view of another generation or culture they are ordinarily the most bizarre of the psychopathic types of the period.

The Puritan divines of New England in the eighteenth century were the last persons whom contemporary opinion in the colonies regarded as psychopathic. Few prestige groups in any culture have been allowed such complete intellectual and emotional dictatorship as they were. They were the voice of God. Yet to a modern observer it is they, not the confused and tormented women they put to death as witches, who were the psychoneurotics of Puritan New England. A sense of guilt as extreme as they portrayed and demanded both in their own conversion experiences and in those of their converts is found in a slightly saner civilization only in institutions for mental diseases. They admitted no salvation without a conviction of sin that prostrated the victim, sometimes for years, with remorse and terrible anguish. It was the duty of the minister to put the fear of hell into the heart of even the youngest child, and to exact of every convert emotional acceptance of his damnation if God saw fit to damn him. It does not matter where we turn among the records of New England Puritan churches of this period, whether to those dealing with witches or with unsaved children not yet in their teens or with such themes as damnation and predestination, we are faced with the fact that the group of people who carried out to the greatest extreme and in the fullest honour the cultural doctrine of the moment are by the slightly altered standards of our generation the victims of intolerable aberrations. From the point of view of a comparative psychiatry they fall in the category of the abnormal.

In our own generation extreme forms of ego-gratification are culturally supported in a similar fashion. Arrogant and unbridled egoists as family men, as officers of the law and in business, have been again and again portrayed by novelists and dramatists, and they are familiar in every community. Like the behaviour of Puritan divines, their courses of action are often more asocial than those of the inmates of penitentiaries. In terms of the suffering and frustration that they spread about them there is probably no comparison. There is very possibly at least as great a degree of mental warping. Yet they are entrusted with positions of great influence and importance and are as a rule fathers of families. Their impress both upon their own children and upon the structure of our society is indelible. They are not described in our manuals of psychiatry because they are supported by every tenet of our civilization. They are sure of themselves in real life in a way that is possible only to those who are oriented to the points of the compass laid down in their own culture. Nevertheless a future psychiatry may well ransack our novels and letters and public records for illumination upon a type of abnormality to which it would not otherwise give credence. In every society it is among this very group of the culturally encouraged and fortified that some of the most extreme types of human behaviour are fostered.

Social thinking at the present time has no more important task before it than that of taking adequate account of cultural relativity. In the fields of both sociology and psychology the implications are fundamental, and modern thought about contacts of peoples and about our changing standards is greatly in need of sane and scientific direction. The sophisticated modern temper has made of social relativity, even in the small area which it has recognized, a doctrine of despair. It has pointed out its incongruity with the orthodox dreams of permanence and ideality and with the individual's illusions of autonomy. It has argued that if human experience must give up these, the nutshell of existence is empty. But to interpret our dilemma in these terms is to be guilty of an anachronism. It is only the inevitable cultural lag that makes us insist that the old must be discovered again in the new, that there is no solution but to find the old certainty and stability in the new plasticity. The recognition of cultural relativity carries with it its own values, which need not be those of the absolutist philosophies. It challenges customary opinions and causes those who have been bred to them acute discomfort. It rouses pessimism because it throws old formulas into confusion, not because it contains anything intrinsically difficult. As soon as the new opinion is embraced as customary belief, it will be another trusted bulwark of the good life. We shall arrive then at a more realistic social faith, accepting as grounds of hope and as new bases for tolerance the coexisting and equally valid patterns of life which mankind has created for itself from the raw materials of existence.

Notes

p. 44 Sumner, William Graham. *Folkways*. Boston, 1907.

p. 45 Jones, William. Mortuary Observances and the Adoption Rites of the Algonkin Foxes of Iowa, 271–7. *Quinzième Congrès International des Américanistes*, 273–7. Quebec, 1907.

p. 46 Fortune, R. F. *Sorcerers of Dobu*, 54. New York, 1932.

p. 47 For a native account of this witchcraft incident in Zuñi, see Bunzel, Ruth L. *Publications of the American Ethnological Society*, XV, 44–52. New York, 1933.

p. 48 For description of various Zuñi men-women, see Parsons, Elsie Clews. The Zuñi Lámana. *American Anthropologist*, n.s. 18 (1916), 521–8. For Mrs. Stevenson's description of We-wha, Stevenson, Mathilda C. The Zuñi Indians. *Twenty-Third Annual Report of the Bureau of American Ethnology*, 37(1901–2); 310–31; 374.

p. 48 Deloria, Ella, MS.

pp. 48–9 From Benedict, Ruth. Culture and the Abnormal. *Journal of General Psychology*, I (1934), 60–4.

pp. 48–9 Dixon, Roland B. The Shasta. *Bulletin of the American Museum of Natural History*, XVII, 381–498. New York, 1907.

p. 49 For a convenient summary, Czaplicka, M. A. *Aboriginal Siberia*. Oxford, 1914.

p. 50 Sapir, Edward. Cultural Anthropology and Psychiatry. *Journal of Abnormal and Social Psychology*, XXVII (1932), 241.

p. 50 Dewey, John. *Human Nature and Conduct*. New York, 1922.

p. 50 Lynd, Robert and Helen. *Middletown*. New York, 1929.

p. 52 [Egoistical] individuals are favourite subjects in the novels and short stories of May Sinclair and Chekhov.

SECTION 2
Structure and System

5

Rules for the Explanation of Social Facts

Emile Durkheim

I

[…] Most sociologists think they have accounted for phenomena once they have shown how they are useful, what role they play, reasoning as if facts existed only from the point of view of this role and with no other determining cause than the sentiment, clear or confused, of the services they are called to render. That is why they think they have said all that is necessary, to render them intelligible, when they have established the reality of these services and have shown what social needs they satisfy.

Thus Comte traces the entire progressive force of the human species to this fundamental tendency "which directly impels man constantly to ameliorate his condition, whatever it may be, under all circumstances";[1] and Spencer relates this force to the need for greater happiness. It is in accordance with this principle that Spencer explains the formation of society by the alleged advantages which result from co-operation; the institution of government, by the utility of the regularization of military co-operation;[2] the

transformations through which the family has passed, by the need for reconciling more and more perfectly the interests of parents, children, and society.

But this method confuses two very different questions. To show how a fact is useful is not to explain how it originated or why it is what it is. The uses which it serves presuppose the specific properties characterizing it but do not create them. The need we have of things cannot give them existence, nor can it confer their specific nature upon them. It is to causes of another sort that they owe their existence. The idea we have of their utility may indeed motivate us to put these forces to work and to elicit from them their characteristic effects, but it will not enable us to produce these effects out of nothing. This proposition is evident so long as it is a question only of material, or even psychological, phenomena. It would be equally evident in sociology if social facts, because of their extreme intangibility, did not wrongly appear to us as without all intrinsic reality. Since we usually see them as a product purely of mental effort, it seems to us that they

Anthropology in Theory: Issues in Epistemology, Second Edition. Edited by Henrietta L. Moore and Todd Sanders.
© 2014 John Wiley & Sons, Inc. Published 2014 by John Wiley & Sons, Inc.

may be produced at will whenever we find it necessary. But since each one of them is a force, superior to that of the individual, and since it has a separate existence, it is not true that merely by willing to do so may one call them into being. No force can be engendered except by an antecedent force. To revive the spirit of the family, where it has become weakened, it is not enough that everyone understand its advantages; the causes which alone can engender it must be made to act directly. To give a government the authority necessary for it, it is not enough to feel the need for this authority; we must have recourse to the only sources from which all authority is derived. We must, namely, establish traditions, a common spirit, etc.; and for this it is necessary again to go back along the chain of causes and effects until we find a point where the action of man may be effectively brought to bear.

What shows plainly the dualism of these two orders of research is that a fact can exist without being at all useful, either because it has never been adjusted to any vital end or because, after having been useful, it has lost all utility while continuing to exist by the inertia of habit alone. There are, indeed, more survivals in society than in biological organisms. There are even cases where a practice or a social institution changes its function without thereby changing its nature. The rule, *Is pater quem justae nuptiae declarant*,[3] has remained in our code essentially the same as it was in the old Roman law. While its purpose then was to safeguard the property rights of a father over children born to the legitimate wife, it is rather the rights of children that it protects today. The custom of taking an oath began by being a sort of judiciary test and has become today simply a solemn and imposing formality. The religious dogmas of Christianity have not changed for centuries, but the role which they play is not the same in our modern societies as in the Middle Ages. Thus, the same words may serve to express new ideas. It is, moreover, a proposition true in sociology, as in biology, that the organ is independent of the function – in other words, while remaining the same, it can serve different ends. The causes of its existence are, then, independent of the ends it serves.

Nevertheless, we do not mean to say that the impulses, needs, and desires of men never intervene actively in social evolution. On the contrary,

it is certain that they can hasten or retard its development, according to the circumstances which determine the social phenomena. Apart from the fact that they cannot, in any case, make something out of nothing, their actual intervention, whatever may be its effects, can take place only by means of efficient causes. A deliberate intention can contribute, even in this limited way, to the production of a new phenomenon only if it has itself been newly formed or if it is itself a result of some transformation of a previous intention. For, unless we postulate a truly providential and pre-established harmony, we cannot admit that man has carried with him from the beginning – potentially ready to be awakened at the call of circumstances – all the intentions which conditions were destined to demand in the course of human evolution. It must further be recognized that a deliberate intention is itself something objectively real; it can, then, neither be created nor modified by the mere fact that we judge it useful. It is a force having a nature of its own; for that nature to be given existence or altered, it is not enough that we should find this advantageous. In order to bring about such changes, there must be a sufficient cause.

For example, we have explained the constant development of the division of labor by showing that it is necessary in order that man may maintain himself in the new conditions of existence as he advances in history. We have attributed to this tendency, which is rather improperly named the "instinct of self-preservation," an important role in our explanations. But, in the first place, this instinct alone could not account for even the most rudimentary specialization. It can do nothing if the conditions on which the division of labor depends do not already exist, i.e., if individual differences have not increased sufficiently as a consequence of the progressive disintegration of the common consciousness and of hereditary influences.[4] It was even necessary that division of labor should have already begun to exist for its usefulness to be seen and for the need of it to make itself felt. The very development of individual differences, necessarily accompanied by a greater diversity of tastes and aptitudes, produced this first result. Further, the instinct of self-preservation did not, of itself and without cause, come to fertilize this first germ of specialization. We were started in this new direction, first, because the course we previously followed was now barred and because the greater intensity of the struggle, owing to the more extensive consolidation of societies, made more and more difficult the survival of individuals who continued to devote themselves to unspecialized tasks. For such reasons it became necessary for us to change our mode of living. Moreover, if our activity has been turned toward a constantly more developed division of labor, it is because this was also the direction of least resistance. The other possible solutions were emigration, suicide, and crime. Now, in the average case, the ties attaching us to life and country and the sympathy we have for our fellows are sentiments stronger and more resistant than the habits which could deflect us from narrower specialization. These habits, then, had inevitably to yield to each impulse that arose. Thus the fact that we allow a place for human needs in sociological explanations does not mean that we even partially revert to teleology. These needs can influence social evolution only on condition that they themselves, and the changes they undergo, can be explained solely by causes that are deterministic and not at all purposive.

But what is even more convincing than the preceding considerations is a study of actual social behavior. Where purpose reigns, there reigns also a more or less wide contingency; for there are no ends, and even fewer means, which necessarily control all men, even when it is assumed that they are placed in the same circumstances. Given the same environment, each individual adapts himself to it according to his own disposition and in his own way, which he prefers to all other ways. One person will seek to change it and make it conform to his needs; another will prefer to change himself and moderate his desires. To arrive at the same goal, many different ways can be and actually are followed. If, then, it were true that historic development took place in terms of ends clearly or obscurely felt, social facts should present the most infinite diversity; and all comparison should be almost impossible.

To be sure, the external events which constitute the superficial part of social life vary from one people to another, just as each individual has his own history, although the bases of physical and moral organization are the same for all. But when one comes in contact with social phe-nomena, one is, on the contrary, surprised by the astonishing regularity with which they occur under the same circumstances. Even the most minute and the most trivial practices recur with the most astonishing uniformity. A certain nuptial ceremony, purely symbolical in appearance, such as the carrying-off of the betrothed, is found to be exactly the same wherever a certain family type exists; and again this family type itself is linked to a whole social organization. The most bizarre customs, such as the couvade, the levirate, exogamy, etc., are observed among the most diverse peoples and are symptomatic of a certain social state. The right to make one's will appears at a certain phase of history, and the more or less important restrictions limiting it offer a fairly exact clue to the particular stage of social evolution. It would be easy to multiply examples. This wide diffusion of collective forms would be inexplicable if purpose or final causes had the predominant place in sociology that is attributed to them.

When, then, the explanation of a social phenomenon is undertaken, we must seek separately the efficient cause which produces it and the function it fulfils. We use the word "function," in preference to "end" or "purpose," precisely because social phenomena do not generally exist for the useful results they produce. We must determine whether there is a correspondence between the fact under consideration and the general needs of the social organism, and in what this correspondence consists, without occupying ourselves with whether it has been intentional or not. All these questions of intention are too subjective to allow of scientific treatment.

Not only must these two types of problems be separated, but it is proper, in general, to treat the former before the latter. This sequence, indeed, corresponds to that of experience. It is natural to seek the causes of a phenomenon before trying to determine its effects. This method is all the more logical since the first question, once answered, will often help to answer the second. Indeed, the bond which unites the cause to the effect is reciprocal to an extent which has not been sufficiently recognized. The effect can doubtless not exist without its cause; but the latter, in turn, needs its effect. It is from the cause that the effect draws its energy; but it also restores it to the cause on occasion, and consequently it cannot disappear without the cause showing the effects of its disappearance.[5]

For example, the social reaction that we call "punishment" is due to the intensity of the collective sentiments which the crime offends; but, from another angle, it has the useful function of maintaining these sentiments at the same degree of intensity, for they would soon diminish if offenses against them were not punished.[6] Similarly, in proportion as the social milieu becomes more complex and more unstable, traditions and conventional beliefs are shaken, become more indeterminate and more unsteady, and reflective powers are developed. Such rationality is indispensable to societies and individuals in adapting themselves to a more mobile and more complex environment.[7] And again, in proportion as men are obliged to furnish more highly specialized work, the products of this work are multiplied and are of better quality; but this increase in products and improvement in quality are necessary to compensate for the expense which this more considerable work entails.[8] Thus, instead of the cause of social phenomena consisting of a mental anticipation of the function they are called to fill, this function, on the contrary, at least in a number of cases, serves to maintain the pre-existent cause from which they are derived. We shall, then, find the function more easily if the cause is already known.

If the determination of function is thus to be delayed, it is still no less necessary for the complete explanation of the phenomena. Indeed, if the usefulness of a fact is not the cause of its existence, it is generally necessary that it be useful in order that it may maintain itself. For the fact that it is not useful suffices to make it harmful, since in that case it costs effort without bringing in any returns. If, then, the majority of social phenomena had this parasitic character, the budget of the organism would have a deficit and social life would be impossible. Consequently, to have a satisfactory understanding of the latter, it is necessary to show how the phenomena comprising it combine in such a way as to put society in harmony with itself and with the environment external to it. No doubt, the current formula, which defines social life as a correspondence between the internal and the external milieu, is only an approximation; however, it is in general true. Consequently, to explain a social fact it is not enough to show the cause on which it depends; we must also, at least in most cases, show its function in the establishment of social order.

II

[...] At the same time that it is teleological, the method of explanation generally followed by sociologists is essentially psychological. These two tendencies are interconnected with one another. In fact, if society is only a system of means instituted by men to attain certain ends, these ends can only be individual, for only individuals could have existed before society. From the individual, then, have emanated the needs and desires determining the formation of societies; and, if it is from him that all comes, it is necessarily by him that all must be explained. Moreover, there are in societies only individual consciousnesses; in these, then, is found the source of all social evolution.

Hence, sociological laws can be only a corollary of the more general laws of psychology; the ultimate explanation of collective life will consist in showing how it emanates from human nature in general, whether the collective life be deduced from human nature directly and without previous observation or whether it must be related to human nature after the latter has been analyzed.

These terms are almost literally those used by Auguste Comte to characterize his method. "Since," says he, "the social phenomenon, conceived in its totality, is fundamentally *only a simple development of humanity, without the creation of any special faculties whatsoever,* as I have established above, all the effective dispositions that sociological investigation will successively discover will therefore be found at least in the germ in this primordial type which biology has constructed in advance for sociology."[9] According to him, the predominant fact in social life is progress; and moreover, progress depends on an exclusively psychological factor, namely, the tendency which impels man to perfect his nature more and more. Social facts would then be derived so directly from human nature that during the first phases of history they might be directly deduced from it without the necessity of having recourse to the observation of society.[10] It is true that, as Comte confesses, it is impossible to apply this deductive method to the more advanced periods of evolution. But this impossibility is purely a practical one. It is due to the fact that the distance between the point of departure and the point of arrival becomes so considerable that the human mind risks going astray, if it undertakes to traverse it without a guide.[11] But the relation between the fundamental laws of human nature and the ultimate products of social progress does not cease to be intimate. The most complex forms of civilization are only a development of the psychological life of the individual. Thus, while the theories of psychology are insufficient as premises for sociological reasoning, they are the touchstone which alone can test the validity of propositions inductively established. "A law of social succession," says Comte, "even when indicated with all possible authority by the historical method, ought to be finally admitted only after having been rationally related to the positive theory of human nature, either in a direct or indirect way."[12] Psychology, then, will always have the last word.

Such is likewise the method followed by Spencer. Indeed, according to him, the two primary factors of social phenomena are the external environment and the physical and social constitution of the individual.[13] Now, the former can influence society only through the latter, which thus becomes the essential force of social evolution. If society is formed, it is in order to permit the individual to express his nature; and all the transformations through which this nature has passed have no other object than to make this expression easier and more complete. It is by reason of this principle that, before proceeding to his research in social organization, Spencer thought it necessary to devote almost the entire first volume of his *Principles of Sociology* to the study of the physical, emotional, and intellectual aspects of primitive man. "The science of sociology," he says, "sets out with social units, conditioned as we have seen, constituted physically, emotionally, and intellectually, and possessed of certain early acquired notions and correlative feelings."[14] And it is in two of these feelings – fear of the living and fear of the dead – that he finds the origin of political and religious government.[15]

He admits, it is true, that once it is formed society reacts on individuals.[16] But it does not follow that society itself has the power of directly engendering the smallest social fact; from this point of view it exerts an effect only by the intermediation of the changes it effects in the individual. It is, then, always in human nature, whether original or acquired, that everything is based. Moreover, this action that the social body exercises on its members cannot be at all specific, since political ends have no separate existence but are simply a summary statement of human needs.[17] It can then be only a duplication of private activity. In industrial societies, particularly, we are unable to see where social influence has a place, since the object of these societies is, precisely, to liberate the individual and his natural impulses by ridding him of all social constraint.

This principle is not only at the basis of these great doctrines of general sociology, but it likewise fathers an equally large number of specific theories. Thus, domestic organization is commonly explained by the sentiment parents have for their children, and children for their parents; the institution of marriage, by the advantages it presents for the married pair and their progeny; punishment, by the anger which every grave attack upon his interests causes in the individual. All economic life, as economists of the orthodox school especially conceive and explain it, is definitely dependent upon a purely individual factor, the desire for wealth. In morality, the duty of the individual toward himself is made the basis of all ethics. As for religion, it becomes a product of the impressions which the great forces of nature or of certain eminent personalities awaken in man, etc.

But, if such a method is applied to social phenomena, it changes fundamentally their nature. To prove this, let us recall the definition we have given. Since their essential characteristic is their power of exerting pressure on individual consciousnesses, it follows that they are not derived from the latter and, consequently, that sociology is not a corollary of individual psychology. For this power of constraint is evidence of the fact that social phenomena possess a different nature from ours, since they control us only by force or, at the very least, by weighing upon us more or less heavily. If social life were merely an extension of the individual being, it would not thus ascend toward its source, namely, the individual, and impetuously invade it. If the authority before which the individual bows when he acts, feels, or thinks socially governs him to this extent, it does so because it is a product of social forces which transcend him and for which he, consequently, cannot account. The external impulse to which he submits cannot come from him, nor can it be explained by what happens within him. It is true that we are not incapable of self-control; we can restrain our impulses, habits, and even instincts, and can arrest their development by an act of inhibition. But these inhibitory movements should not be confused with those constituting social constraint. The process of the former is centrifugal; of the latter, centripetal. The former are elaborated in the individual consciousness and then tend to externalize themselves; the latter are at first external to the individual, whom they then tend to fashion in their image from without. Inhibition is, if you like, the means by which social constraint produces its psychological effects; it is not identical with this constraint.

When the individual has been eliminated, society alone remains. We must, then, seek the explanation of social life in the nature of society itself. It is quite evident that, since it infinitely surpasses the individual in time as well as in space, it is in a position to impose upon him ways of acting and thinking which it has consecrated with its prestige. This pressure, which is the distinctive property of social facts, is the pressure which the totality exerts on the individual.

But, it will be said that, since the only elements making up society are individuals, the first origins of sociological phenomena cannot but be psychological. In reasoning thus, it can be established just as easily that organic phenomena may be explained by inorganic phenomena. It is very certain that there are in the living cell only molecules of crude matter. But these molecules are in contact with one another, and this association is the cause of the new phenomena which characterize life, the very germ of which cannot possibly be found in any of the separate elements. A whole is not identical with the sum of its parts. It is something different, and its properties differ from those of its component parts. Association is not, as has sometimes been believed, merely an infertile phenomenon; it is not simply the putting of facts and constituent properties into juxtaposition. On the contrary, it

is the source of all the innovations which have been produced successively in the course of the general evolution of things. What differences are there between the lower and higher organisms, between highly organized living things and protoplasm, between the latter and the inorganic molecules of which it is composed, if not differences in types of association? All these beings, in the last analysis, resolve themselves into the same elements, but these elements are here in mere juxtaposition, there in combination, here associated in one way, there in another. One may even inquire whether this law does not apply in the mineral world and whether the differences separating inorganic bodies are not traceable to this same origin.

By reason of this principle, society is not a mere sum of individuals. Rather, the system formed by their association represents a specific reality which has its own characteristics. Of course, nothing collective can be produced if individual consciousnesses are not assumed; but this necessary condition is by itself insufficient. These consciousnesses must be combined in a certain way; social life results from this combination and is, consequently, explained by it. Individual minds, forming groups by mingling and fusing, give birth to a being, psychological if you will, but constituting a psychic individuality of a new sort.[18] It is, then, in the nature of this collective individuality, not in that of the associated units, that we must seek the immediate and determining causes of the facts appearing therein. The group thinks, feels, and acts quite differently from the way in which its members would were they isolated. If, then, we begin with the individual, we shall be able to understand nothing of what takes place in the group. In a word, there is between psychology and sociology the same break in continuity as between biology and the physicochemical sciences. Consequently, every time that a social phenomenon is directly explained by a psychological phenomenon, we may be sure that the explanation is false.

Our critics will perhaps maintain that although society, once formed, is the proximate cause of social phenomena, the causes determining its formation may still be psychological in nature. They grant that, when individuals are associated, their association can give rise to a new form of life; but they claim that the new form can take place only for reasons inherent in individuals. But, in reality, as far back as one goes in history, the principle of association is the most imperative of all, for it is the source of all other compulsions. As a consequence of my birth, I am obliged to associate with a given group. It may be said that later, as an adult, I acquiesce in this obligation by the very fact that I continue to live in my country. But what difference does that make? This "acquiescence" is still imperative. Pressure accepted and submitted to with good grace is still pressure. Moreover, let us look more closely at the nature of my acquiescence. For the present, it is most certainly imposed upon me, for in the vast majority of cases it is materially and morally impossible for us to strip off our nationality; such a change is generally considered apostasy. Likewise in the past, which determines the present, I could not have given my free consent. I did not desire the education I received, which, more than any other thing, fixes me to my native soil. Finally, for the future, I cannot give my acquiescence, for I cannot know what the future is to be. I do not know all the duties which may be incumbent upon me at some future time in my capacity as a citizen. How could I acquiesce in them in advance?

We have shown, then, that the source of all that is obligatory is outside the individual. So long, then, as we do not desert the facts, the principle of association presents the same character as the others and, consequently, is explained in the same manner.

Moreover, as all societies are born of other societies without a break in continuity, we can be certain that in the entire course of social evolution there has not been a single time when individuals determined by careful deliberation whether or not they would enter into the collective life or into one collective life rather than another. In order for that question to arise, it would be necessary to go back to the first origins of all societies. But the questionable solutions which can be brought to such problems could not, in any case, affect the method by which we must treat the facts given in history. Therefore, we do not need to discuss them.

But one would be strangely mistaken about our thought if, from the foregoing, he drew the conclusion that sociology, according to us, must, or even can, make an abstraction of man and his faculties. It is clear, on the contrary, that the general characteristics of human nature participate in the work of elaboration from which social life results. But they are not the cause of it, nor do they give it its special form; they only make it possible. Collective representations, emotions, and tendencies are caused not by certain states of the consciousnesses of individuals but by the conditions in which the social group in its totality is placed. Such actions can, of course, materialize only if the individual natures are not resistant to them; but these individual natures are merely the indeterminate material that the social factor molds and transforms. Their contribution consists exclusively in very general attitudes, in vague and consequently plastic predispositions which, by themselves, if other agents did not intervene, could not take on the definite and complex forms which characterize social phenomena.

What an abyss, for example, between the sentiments man experiences in the face of forces superior to his own and the present religious institution with its beliefs, its numerous and complicated practices, its material and moral organization! What a contrast between the psychic states of sympathy which two beings of the same blood experience for one another,[19] and the detailed collection of legal and moral regulations that determine the structure of the family, the relations of persons among themselves, of things with persons, etc.! We have seen that, even where society is reduced to an unorganized crowd, the collective sentiments which are formed in it may not only not resemble, but even be opposed to, the sentiments of the average individual. How much greater must be the difference between them when the pressure exerted on the individual is that of a well-organized society, in which the action of the traditions of former generations is added to that of contemporaries! A purely psychological explanation of social facts cannot fail, therefore, to allow all that is characteristic (i.e., social) in them to escape.

What has blinded most sociologists to the inadequacy of this method is that, taking effect for cause, they have very often designated as determining the conditions of social phenomena certain psychological states that are relatively definite and distinctive but which are, after all, only the consequence of these social phenomena. Thus a certain religious sentiment has been considered innate in man, a certain minimum of sexual jealousy, filial piety, paternal love, etc. And it is by these that religion, marriage, and the family have been explained.

History, however, shows that these inclinations, far from being inherent in human nature, are often totally lacking. Or they may present such variations in different societies that the residue obtained after eliminating all these differences – which alone can be considered of psychological origin – is reduced to something vague and rudimentary and far removed from the facts that need explanation. These sentiments, then, *result* from the collective organization and are not its *basis*. It has not been proved at all that the tendency to gregariousness has been an inherited instinct of the human species from its beginnings. It is much more natural to consider it a product of social life, which was slowly developed within us; for it is a fact of observation that animals are or are not gregarious according to whether their habits oblige them to live a common life or to avoid it. We must add that the difference between even the more definite tendencies and social reality remains considerable.

There is, moreover, a way to isolate the psychological factor almost completely in such a manner as to determine precisely the extent of its action, viz., to see how race affects social evolution. Indeed, ethnic characteristics are organico-psychological in type. Social life must, therefore, vary when they vary, if psychological phenomena have on society the effects attributed to them. But no social phenomenon is known which can be placed in indisputable dependence on race. No doubt, we cannot attribute to this proposition the value of a principle; we can merely affirm it as invariably true in practical experience.

The most diverse forms of organization are found in societies of the same race, while striking similarities are observed between societies of different races. The city-state existed among the Phoenicians, as among the Romans and the Greeks; we find it in the process of formation among the Kabyles. The patriarchal family was almost as highly developed among the Jews as among the Hindus; but it is not found among the Slavs, who are, however, of the Aryan race. On the other hand, the family type met among Slavs also exists among the Arabs. The maternal family and the clan are observed everywhere. The detail of legal procedure and of nuptial ceremonies is the same among peoples most dissimilar from the ethnic point of view.

If all these things are true, it is because the psychological factor is too general to predetermine the course of social phenomena. Since it does not call for one social form rather than another, it cannot explain any of them. There are, it is true, a certain number of facts which are customarily attributed to the influence of race. In this manner is explained, notably, the rapid and intensive development of arts and letters in Athens, so slow and mediocre in Rome. But this interpretation of the facts, although classical, has never been scientifically demonstrated; it seems, indeed, to derive all its authority solely from tradition. The possibility of a sociological explanation of the same phenomena has not been explored, but we are convinced that it could be attempted with success. In short, when the artistic character of Athenian civilization is related with such facility to inherited aesthetic faculties, we show as little insight as did scholars in the Middle Ages when they explained fire by phlogiston and the effects of opium by its dormitive property.

Finally, if social evolution really had its origin in the psychological constitution of man, its origin seems to be completely obscure. For we would then have to admit that its motivating force is some inner spring of human nature. But what could this be? Is it the sort of instinct Comte speaks of, which impels man more and more to express his nature? But that is begging the question and explaining progress by an innate "tendency toward progress" – a metaphysical entity of the very existence of which there is no demonstration. Even the highest animal species are not at all activated by the need to progress, and among human societies there are many which are content to remain indefinitely stationary.

Or is this motivating force, as Spencer seems to believe, the urge for greater happiness which the increasingly complex forms of civilization are designed to satisfy more and more completely? We would then have to establish the fact that happiness increases with civilization, and we have elsewhere described all the difficulties to which this hypothesis gives rise.[20] But further, even if one or the other of these two postulates were admissible, historical development would not thereby be rendered intelligible, for the explanation which would result from it would be purely teleological. We have shown above that social facts, like all natural phenomena, are not explained by the simple consideration that they serve some end. When it has been proved satisfactorily that the progressively more intelligent social organizations which have succeeded one another in the course of history have had the effect of satisfying more and more certain of our fundamental desires, we have not shown at all how these social organizations have been produced. The fact that they were useful does not tell us how they originated. Even if we were to explain how we came to imagine them and how we planned them in advance so as to picture to ourselves their services to us – a somewhat difficult problem in itself – the desires which called forth their existence do not have the power of drawing them out of nothing. In a word, admitting that social organizations are the necessary means to attain a desired goal, the whole question remains: From what source and by what means have these been created?

We arrive, therefore, at the following principle: *The determining cause of a social fact should be sought among the social facts preceding it and not among the states of the individual consciousness.* Moreover, we see quite readily that all the foregoing applies to the determination of the function as well as the cause of social phenomena. The function of a social fact cannot but be social, i.e., it consists of the production of socially useful effects. To be sure, it may and does happen that it also serves the individual. But this happy result is not its immediate cause. We can then complete the preceding proposition by saying: *The function of a social fact ought always to be sought in its relation to some social end.*

Since sociologists have often misinterpreted this rule and have considered social phenomena from a too psychological point of view, to many their theories seem too vague and shifting and too far removed from the distinctive nature of the things they are intended to explain. Historians who treat social reality directly and in detail have not failed to remark how powerless these too general interpretations are to show the relation between the facts; and their mistrust of sociology has been, no doubt, partly produced by this circumstance. We do not mean to say, of course, that the study of psychological facts is not indispensable to the sociologist. If collective life is not derived from individual life, the two are nevertheless closely related; if the latter cannot explain the former, it can at least facilitate its explanation. First, as we have shown, it is indisputable that social facts are produced by action on psychological factors. In addition, this very action is similar to that which takes place in each individual consciousness and by which are transformed the primary elements (sensations, reflexes, instincts) of which it is originally constituted. Not without reason has it been said that the self is itself a society, by the same right as the organism, although in another way; and long ago psychologists showed the great importance of the factor of association in the explanation of mental activity.

Psychological training, more than biological training, constitutes, then, a valuable lesson for the sociologist; but it will not be useful to him except on condition that he emancipates himself from it after having received profit from its lessons, and then goes beyond it by special sociological training. He must abandon psychology as the center of his operations, as the point of departure for his excursions into the sociological world to which they must always return. He must establish himself in the very heart of social facts, in order to observe them directly, while asking the science of the individual mind for a general preparation only and, when needed, for useful suggestions.[21] [...]

Notes

1   *Cours de philosophie positive* (Paris: Schleicher, 1893), Vol. IV, 262.

2   *The Principles of Sociology* (New York: D. Appleton & Co., 1897), Vol. II, 247.

3   Legal marriage with the mother establishes the father's rights over the children.

4   *Division du travail social* (Paris: Alcan, 1893), Book II, chs. iii and iv.

5   We do not wish to raise here questions of general philosophy, which would not be in place. Let us say, however, that, if more profoundly analyzed, this reciprocity of cause and effect might furnish a

means of reconciling scientific mechanism with the teleology which the existence, and especially the persistence, of life implies.

6 *Division du travail social*, Book II, ch. ii, notably pp. 105 ff.
7 Ibid., pp. 52–3.
8 Ibid., pp. 301 ff.
9 *Cours de philosophie positive*, Vol. IV, 333.
10 Ibid., p. 345.
11 Ibid., p. 346.
12 Ibid., p. 335.
13 *Principles of Sociology*, Vol. I, Part I, ch. ii.
14 Ibid., p. 437.
15 Ibid., p. 437.
16 Ibid., p. 14.
17 "Society exists for the benefit of its members; not its members for the benefit of society ... the claims of the body politic are nothing in themselves, and become something only in so far as they embody the claims of its component individuals" (ibid., Part II, pp. 461–2).
18 In this sense, and for these reasons, one can, and must, speak of a collective consciousness distinct from individual consciousnesses. In order to justify this distinction, it is not necessary to posit for the former a separate personal existence; it is something special and must be designated by a special term, simply because the states which constitute it differ specifically from those which constitute the individual consciousnesses. This specificity comes from the fact that they are not formed from the same elements. The latter result from the nature of the organicopsychological

being taken in isolation, the former from the combination of a plurality of beings of this kind. The resultants cannot, then, fail to differ, since the components differ to that extent. Our definition of the social fact, moreover, only drew in another way this line of demarcation.

19 We may suppose that this exists in lower social groups. See, on this point, Alfred Espinas, *Sociétés animales* (Paris: Baillière, 1878), p. 474.
20 *Division du travail social*, Book II, ch. i.
21 Psychological phenomena can have only social consequences when they are so intimately united to social phenomena that the action of the psychological and of the social phenomena is necessarily fused. This is the case with certain sociopsychological facts. Thus, a public official is a social force, but he is at the same time an individual. As a result he can turn his social energy in a direction determined by his individual nature, and thereby he can have an influence on the constitution of society. Such is the case with statesmen and, more generally, with men of genius. The latter, even when they do not fill a social function, draw from the collective sentiments of which they are the object an authority which is also a social force, and which they can put, in a certain measure, at the service of personal ideas. But we see that these cases are due to individual accidents and, consequently, cannot affect the constitutive traits of the social species which, alone, is the object of science. The restriction on the principle enunciated above is not, then, of great importance for the sociologist.

6

On Social Structure

A. R. Radcliffe-Brown

[...] I conceive of social anthropology as the theoretical natural science of human society, that is, the investigation of social phenomena by methods essentially similar to those used in the physical and biological sciences. I am quite willing to call the subject "comparative sociology", if anyone so wishes. It is the subject itself, and not the name, that is important. As you know, there are some ethnologists or anthropologists who hold that it is not possible, or at least not profitable, to apply to social phenomena the theoretical methods of natural science. For these persons social anthropology, as I have defined it, is something that does not, and never will, exist. For them, of course, my remarks will have no meaning, or at least not the meaning I intend them to have.

While I have defined social anthropology as the study of human society, there are some who define it as the study of culture. It might perhaps be thought that this difference of definition is of minor importance. Actually it leads to two different kinds of study, between which it is hardly possible to obtain agreement in the formulation of problems.

For a preliminary definition of social phenomena it seems sufficiently clear that what we have to deal with are relations of association between individual organisms. In a hive of bees there are the relations of association of the queen, the workers and the drones. There is the association of animals in a herd, of a mother-cat and her kittens. These are social phenomena; I do not suppose that anyone will call them cultural phenomena. In anthropology, of course, we are only concerned with human beings, and in social anthropology, as I define it, what we have to investigate are the forms of association to be found amongst human beings.

Let us consider what are the concrete, observable facts with which the social anthropologist is concerned. If we set out to study, for example, the aboriginal inhabitants of a part of Australia, we find a certain number of individual human beings in a certain natural environment. We can observe the acts of behaviour of these individuals, including, of course, their acts of speech, and the material products of past actions. We do not observe a "culture", since that word denotes, not any concrete reality, but an abstraction, and as it is commonly used a vague abstraction. But direct observation does reveal to us that these human beings are connected by a complex network of

From *Journal of Royal Anthropological Institute* 70(1) (1940), pp. 189–200. Copyright © 1940 by *Journal of the Royal Anthropological Institute*. Reprinted with permission of John Wiley & Sons UK.

Anthropology in Theory: Issues in Epistemology, Second Edition. Edited by Henrietta L. Moore and Todd Sanders.
© 2014 John Wiley & Sons, Inc. Published 2014 by John Wiley & Sons, Inc.

social relations. I use the term "social structure" to denote this network of actually existing relations. It is this that I regard it as my business to study if I am working, not as an ethnologist or psychologist, but as a social anthropologist. I do not mean that the study of social structure is the whole of social anthropology, but I do regard it as being in a very important sense the most fundamental part of the science.

My view of natural science is that it is the systematic investigation of the structure of the universe as it is revealed to us through our senses. There are certain important separate branches of science, each of which deals with a certain class or kind of structures, the aim being to discover the characteristics of all structures of that kind. So atomic physics deals with the structure of atoms, chemistry with the structure of molecules, crystallography and colloidal chemistry with the structure of crystals and colloids, and anatomy and physiology with the structures of organisms. There is, therefore, I suggest, place for a branch of natural science which will have for its task the discovery of the general characteristics of those social structures of which the component units are human beings.

Social phenomena constitute a distinct class of natural phenomena. They are all, in one way or another, connected with the existence of social structures, either being implied in or resulting from them. Social structures are just as real as are individual organisms. A complex organism is a collection of living cells and interstitial fluids arranged in a certain structure; and a living cell is similarly a structural arrangement of complex molecules. The physiological and psychological phenomena that we observe in the lives of organisms are not simply the result of the nature of the constituent molecules or atoms of which the organism is built up, but are the result of the structure in which they are united. So also the social phenomena which we observe in any human society are not the immediate result of the nature of individual human beings, but are the result of the social structure by which they are united.

It should be noted that to say we are studying social structures is not exactly the same thing as saying that we study social relations, which is how some sociologists define their subject. A particular social relation between two persons

(unless they be Adam and Eve in the Garden of Eden) exists only as part of a wide network of social relations, involving many other persons, and it is this network which I regard as the object of our investigations.

I am aware, of course, that the term "social structure" is used in a number of different senses, some of them very vague. This is unfortunately true of many other terms commonly used by anthropologists. The choice of terms and their definitions is a matter of scientific convenience, but one of the characteristics of a science as soon as it has passed the first formative period is the existence of technical terms which are used in the same precise meaning by all the students of that science. By this test, I regret to say, social anthropology reveals itself as not yet a formed science. One has therefore to select for oneself, for certain terms, definitions which seem to be the most convenient for the purpose of scientific analysis.

There are some anthropologists who use the term social structure to refer only to persistent social groups, such as nations, tribes and clans, which retain their continuity, their identity as individual groups, in spite of changes in their membership. Dr. Evans-Pritchard, in his recent admirable book on the Nuer, prefers to use the term social structure in this sense. Certainly the existence of such persistent social groups is an exceedingly important aspect of structure. But I find it more useful to include under the term social structure a good deal more than this.

In the first place, I regard as a part of the social structure all social relations of person to person. For example, the kinship structure of any society consists of a number of such dyadic relations, as between a father and son, or a mother's brother and his sister's son. In an Australian tribe the whole social structure is based on a network of such relations of person to person, established through genealogical connections.

Secondly, I include under social structure the differentiation of individuals and of classes by their social role. The differential social positions of men and women, of chiefs and commoners, of employers and employees, are just as much determinants of social relations as belonging to different clans or different nations.

In the study of social structure the concrete reality with which we are concerned is the set of actually existing relations, at a given moment of time, which link together certain human beings. It is on this that we can make direct observations. But it is not this that we attempt to describe in its particularity. Science (as distinguished from history or biography) is not concerned with the particular, the unique, but only with the general, with kinds, with events which recur. The actual relations of Tom, Dick and Harry or the behaviour of Jack and Jill may go down in our field note-books and may provide illustrations for a general description. But what we need for scientific purposes is an account of the form of the structure. For example, if in an Australian tribe I observe in a number of instances the behaviour towards one another of persons who stand in the relation of mother's brother and sister's son, it is in order that I may be able to record as precisely as possible the general or normal form of this relationship, abstracted from the variations of particular instances, though taking account of those variations.

This important distinction, between structure as an actually existing concrete reality, to be directly observed, and structural form, as what the field-worker describes, may be made clearer perhaps by a consideration of the continuity of social structure through time, a continuity which is not static like that of a building, but a dynamic continuity, like that of the organic structure of a living body. Throughout the life of an organism its structure is being constantly renewed; and similarly the social life constantly renews the social structure. Thus the actual relations of persons and groups of persons change from year to year, or even from day to day. New members come into a community by birth or immigration; others go out of it by death or emigration. There are marriages and divorces. Friends may become enemies, or enemies may make peace and become friends. But while the actual structure changes in this way, the general structural form may remain relatively constant over a longer or shorter period of time. Thus if I visit a relatively stable community and revisit it after an interval of ten years, I shall find that many of its members have died and others have been born; the members who still survive are now ten years older and their relations to one another may have changed in many ways. Yet I may find that the kinds of relations that I can observe are very little different from those

observed ten years before. The structural form has changed little.

But, on the other hand, the structural form may change, sometimes gradually, sometimes with relative suddenness, as in revolutions and military conquests. But even in the most revolutionary changes some continuity of structure is maintained.

[...]

I have now sufficiently defined, I hope, the subject-matter of what I regard as an extremely important branch of social anthropology. The method to be adopted follows immediately from this definition. It must combine with the intensive study of single societies (i.e. of the structural systems observable in particular communities) the systematic comparison of many societies (or structural systems of different types). The use of comparison is indispensable. The study of a single society may provide materials for comparative study, or it may afford occasion for hypotheses, which then need to be tested by reference to other societies; it cannot give demonstrated results.

Our first task, of course, is to learn as much as we can about the varieties, or diversities, of structural systems. This requires field research. Many writers of ethnographical descriptions do not attempt to give us any systematic account of the social structure. But a few social anthropologists, here and in America, do recognise the importance of such data and their work is providing us with a steadily growing body of material for our study. Moreover, their researches are no longer confined to what are called "primitive" societies, but extend to communities in such regions as Sicily, Ireland, Japan, Canada and the United States.

If we are to have a real comparative morphology of societies, however, we must aim at building up some sort of classification of types of structural systems. That is a complex and difficult task, to which I have myself devoted attention for thirty years. It is the kind of task that needs the cooperation of a number of students and I think I can number on my fingers those who are actively interested in it at the present time. Nevertheless, I believe some progress is being made. Such work, however, does not produce spectacular results and a book on the subject would certainly not be an anthropological best-seller.

We should remember that chemistry and biology did not become fully formed sciences until considerable progress had been made with the systematic classification of the things they were dealing with, substances in the one instance and plants and animals in the other.

Besides this morphological study, consisting in the definition, comparison and classification of diverse structural systems, there is a physiological study. The problem here is: How do structural systems persist? What are the mechanisms which maintain a network of social relations in existence, and how do they work? In using the terms morphology and physiology, I may seem to be returning to the analogy between society and organism which was so popular with medieval philosophers, was taken over and often misused by nineteenth-century sociologists, and is completely rejected by many modern writers. But analogies, properly used, are important aids to scientific thinking and there is a real and significant analogy between organic structure and social structure.

In what I am thus calling social physiology we are concerned not only with social structure, but with every kind of social phenomenon. Morals, law, etiquette, religion, government and education are all parts of the complex mechanism by which a social structure exists and persists. If we take up the structural point of view, we study these things, not in abstraction or isolation, but in their direct and indirect relations to social structure, i.e. with reference to the way in which they depend upon, or affect, the social relations between persons and groups of persons. I cannot do more here than offer a few brief illustrations of what this means.

Let us first consider the study of language. A language is a connected set of speech usages observed within a defined speech-community. The existence of speech-communities and their sizes are features of social structure. There is, therefore, a certain very general relation between social structure and language. But if we consider the special characteristics of a particular language – its phonology, its morphology and even to a great extent its vocabulary – there is no direct connection of either one-sided or mutual determination between these and the special characteristics of the social structure of the community within which the language is spoken. We can easily conceive that two societies might have very similar forms of social structure and very different kinds

of language, or vice versa. The coincidence of a particular form of social structure and a particular language in a given community is always the result of historical accident. There may, of course, be certain indirect, remote interactions between social structure and language, but these would seem to be of minor importance. Thus the general comparative study of languages can be profitably carried out as a relatively independent branch of science, in which the language is considered in abstraction from the social structure of the community in which it is spoken.

But, on the other hand, there are certain features of linguistic history which are specifically connected with social structure. As structural phenomena may be instanced the process by which Latin, from being the language of the small region of Latium, became the language of a considerable part of Europe, displacing the other Italic languages, Etruscan, and many Celtic languages; and the subsequent reverse process by which Latin split up into a number of diverse local forms of speech, which ultimately became the various Romance languages of today.

Thus the spread of language, the unification of a number of separate communities into a single speech-community, and the reverse process of subdivision into different speech-communities, are phenomena of social structure. So also are those instances in which, in societies having a class structure, there are differences of speech usage in different classes.

I have considered language first, because linguistics is, I think, the branch of social anthropology which can be most profitably studied without reference to social structure. There is a reason for this. The set of speech usages which constitute a language does form a system, and systems of this kind can be compared in order to discover their common general, or abstract, characters, the determination of which can give us laws, which will be specifically laws of linguistics.

Let us consider very briefly certain other branches of social anthropology and their relation to the study of social structure. If we take the social life of a local community over a period, let us say a year, we can observe a certain sum total of activities carried out by the persons who compose it. We can also observe a certain apportionment of these activities, one person doing certain things, another doing others. This apportionment of activities, equivalent to what is sometimes called the social division of labour, is an important feature of the social structure. Now activities are carried out because they provide some sort of "gratification", as I propose to call it, and the characteristic feature of social life is that activities of certain persons provide gratifications for other persons. In a simple instance, when an Australian blackfellow goes hunting, he provides meat, not only for himself, but for his wife and children and also for other relatives to whom it is his duty to give meat when he has it. Thus in any society there is not only an apportionment of activities, but also an apportionment of the gratifications resulting therefrom, and some sort of social machinery, relatively simple or, sometimes, highly complex, by which the system works.

It is this machinery, or certain aspects of it, that constitutes the special subject-matter studied by the economists. They concern themselves with what kinds and quantities of goods are produced, how they are distributed (i.e. their flow from person to person, or region to region), and the way in which they are disposed of. Thus what are called economic institutions are extensively studied in more or less complete abstraction from the rest of the social system. This method does undoubtedly provide useful results, particularly in the study of complex modern societies. Its weaknesses become apparent as soon as we attempt to apply it to the exchange of goods in what are called primitive societies.

The economic machinery of a society appears in quite a new light if it is studied in relation to the social structure. The exchange of goods and services is dependent upon, is the result of, and at the same time is a means of maintaining a certain structure, a network of relations between persons and collections of persons. For the economists and politicians of Canada the potlatch of the Indians of the northwest of America was simply wasteful foolishness and it was therefore forbidden. For the anthropologist it was the machinery for maintaining a social structure of lineages, clans and moieties, with which was combined an arrangement of rank defined by privileges.

Any full understanding of the economic institutions of human societies requires that they should be studied from two angles. From one of these the economic system is viewed as the mechanism by which goods of various kinds and in various quantities are produced, transported and transferred, and utilised. From the other the economic system is a set of relations between persons and groups which maintains, and is maintained by, this exchange or circulation of goods and services. From the latter point of view, the study of the economic life of societies takes its place as part of the general study of social structure.

Social relations are only observed, and can only be described, by reference to the reciprocal behaviour of the persons related. The form of a social structure has therefore to be described by the patterns of behaviour to which individuals and groups conform in their dealings with one another. These patterns are partially formulated in rules which, in our own society, we distinguish as rules of etiquette, of morals and of law. Rules, of course, only exist in their recognition by the members of the society; either in their verbal recognition, when they are stated as rules, or in their observance in behaviour. These two modes of recognition, as every field-worker knows, are not the same thing and both have to be taken into account.

If I say that in any society the rules of etiquette, morals and law are part of the mechanism by which a certain set of social relations is maintained in existence, this statement will, I suppose, be greeted as a truism. But it is one of those truisms which many writers on human society verbally accept and yet ignore in theoretical discussions, or in their descriptive analyses. The point is not that rules exist in every society, but that what we need to know for a scientific understanding is just how these things work in general and in particular instances.

Let us consider, for example, the study of law. If you examine the literature on jurisprudence you will find that legal institutions are studied for the most part in more or less complete abstraction from the rest of the social system of which they are a part. This is doubtless the most convenient method for lawyers in their professional studies. But for any scientific investigation of the nature of law it is insufficient. The data with which a scientist must deal are events which occur and can be observed. In the field of law, the events which the social scientist can observe and thus take as his data are the proceedings that take place in courts of justice. These are the reality, and for the social anthropologist they are the mechanism or process by which certain definable social relations between persons and groups are restored, maintained or modified. Law is a part of the machinery by which a certain social structure is maintained. The system of laws of a particular society can only be fully understood if it is studied in relation to the social structure, and inversely the understanding of the social structure requires, amongst other things, a systematic study of the legal institutions.

I have talked about social relations, but I have not so far offered you a precise definition. A social relation exists between two or more individual organisms when there is some adjustment of their respective interests, by convergence of interest, or by limitation of conflicts that might arise from divergence of interests. I use the term "interest" here in the widest possible sense, to refer to all behaviour that we regard as purposive. To speak of an interest implies a subject and an object and a relation between them. Whenever we say that a subject has a certain interest in an object we can state the same thing by saying that the object has a certain value for the subject. Interest and value are correlative terms, which refer to the two sides of an asymmetrical relation.

Thus the study of social structure leads immediately to the study of interests or values as the determinants of social relations. A social relation does not result from similarity of interests, but rests either on the mutual interest of persons in one another, or on one or more common interests, or on a combination of both of these. The simplest form of social solidarity is where two persons are both interested in bringing about a certain result and co-operate to that end. When two or more persons have a *common interest* in an object, that object can be said to have a *social value* for the persons thus associated. If, then, practically all the members of a society have an interest in the observance of the laws, we can say that the law has a social value. The study of social values in this sense is therefore a part of the study of social structure. [...]

7

Introduction to *Political Systems of Highland Burma*

E. R. Leach

[...] Social anthropologists who, following Radcliffe-Brown, use the concept of social structure as a category in terms of which to compare one society with another in fact presuppose that the societies with which they deal exist throughout time in stable equilibrium. Is it then possible to describe at all, by means of ordinary sociological categories, societies which are *not* assumed to be in stable equilibrium?

My conclusion is that while conceptual models of society are necessarily models of equilibrium systems, real societies can never be in equilibrium. The discrepancy is related to the fact that when social structures are expressed in cultural form, the representation is imprecise compared with that given by the exact categories which the sociologist, *qua* scientist, would like to employ. I hold that these inconsistencies in the logic of ritual expression are always necessary for the proper functioning of any social system.

[...] I hold that social structure in practical situations (as contrasted with the sociologist's abstract model) consists of a set of ideas about the distribution of power between persons and groups of persons. Individuals can and do hold contradictory and inconsistent ideas about this system. They are able to do this without embarrassment because of the form in which their ideas are expressed. The form is cultural form; the expression is ritual expression. The latter part of this [...] chapter is an elaboration of this portentous remark.

But first to get back to social structure and unit societies.

Social Structure

At one level of abstraction we may discuss social structure simply in terms of the principles of organisation that unite the component parts of the system. At this level the form of the structure can be considered quite independently of the cultural content.[1] A knowledge of the form of society among the Gilyak hunters of Eastern Siberia[2] and among the Nuer pastoralists of the Sudan[3] helps me to understand the form of Kachin society despite the fact that the latter for the most part are shifting cultivators inhabiting dense monsoon rain forest.

From *Political Systems of Highland Burma: A Study of Kachin Social Structure* (London: Athlone Press, 1970), pp. 1–17, 313–18. Copyright © 1970 by Athlone Press. Reprinted by permission of The Continuum International Publishing Group. First published in 1954.

Anthropology in Theory: Issues in Epistemology, Second Edition. Edited by Henrietta L. Moore and Todd Sanders.
© 2014 John Wiley & Sons, Inc. Published 2014 by John Wiley & Sons, Inc.

At this level of abstraction it is not difficult to distinguish one formal pattern from another. The structures which the anthropologist describes are models which exist only as logical constructions in his own mind. What is much more difficult is to relate such abstraction to the data of empirical field work. How can we really be sure that one particular formal model fits the facts better than any other possible model?

Real societies exist in time and space. The demographic, ecological, economic and external political situation does not build up into a fixed environment, but into a constantly changing environment. Every real society is a process in time. The changes that result from this process may usefully be thought of under two heads.[4] Firstly, there are those which are consistent with a continuity of the existing formal order. For example, when a chief dies and is replaced by his son, or when a lineage segments and we have two lineages where formerly there was only one, the changes are part of the process of continuity. There is no change in the formal structure. Secondly, there are changes which do reflect alterations in the formal structure. If, for example, it can be shown that in a particular locality, over a period of time, a political system composed of equalitarian lineage segments is replaced by a ranked hierarchy of feudal type, we can speak of a change in the formal social structure. [...]

Unit Societies

In the context of the Kachin Hills Area the concept of "a society" presents many difficulties. [...] For the time being I will follow Radcliffe-Brown's unsatisfactory advice and interpret "a society" as meaning "any convenient locality".[5]

Alternatively, I accept Nadel's arguments. By "a society" I really mean any self-contained political unit.[6]

Political units in the Kachin Hills Area vary greatly in size and appear to be intrinsically unstable. At one end of the scale one may encounter a village of four households firmly asserting its right to be considered as a fully independent unit. At the other extreme we have the Shan state of Hsenwi which, prior to 1885, contained 49 sub-states (möng), some of which in turn contained over a hundred separate villages.

Between these two extremes one may distinguish numerous other varieties of "society". These various types of political system differ from one another not only in scale but also in the formal principles in terms of which they are organised. It is here that the crux of our problem lies.

For certain parts of the Kachin Hills Area genuine historical records go back as far as the beginning of the 19th century. These show clearly that during the last 130 years the political organisation of the area has been very unstable. Small autonomous political units have often tended to aggregate into larger systems; large-scale feudal hierarchies have fragmented into smaller units. There have been violent and very rapid shifts in the overall distribution of political power. It is therefore methodologically unsound to treat the different varieties of political system which we now find in the area as independent types; they should clearly be thought of as part of a larger total system in flux. But the essence of my argument is that the process by which the small units grow into larger ones and the large units break down into smaller ones is not simply part of the process of structural continuity; it is not merely a process of segmentation and accretion, it is a process involving structural change. It is with the mechanism of this change process that we are mainly concerned.

There is no doubt that both the study and description of social change in ordinary anthropological contexts presents great difficulties. Field studies are of short duration, historical records seldom contain data of the right kind in adequate detail. Indeed, although anthropologists have frequently declared a special interest in the subject, their theoretical discussion of the problems of social change has so far merited little applause.[7]

Even so it seems to me that at least some of the difficulties arise only as a by-product of the anthropologist's own false assumptions about the nature of his data.

English social anthropologists have tended to borrow their primary concepts from Durkheim rather than from either Pareto or Max Weber. Consequently they are strongly prejudiced in favour of societies which show symptoms of "functional integration", "social solidarity", "cultural uniformity", "structural equilibrium". Such societies, which might well be regarded as moribund by historians or political scientists, are commonly looked upon by social anthropologists as healthy and ideally fortunate. Societies which display symptoms of faction and internal conflict leading to rapid change are on the other hand suspected of "anomie" and pathological decay.[8]

This prejudice in favour of "equilibrium" interpretations arises from the nature of the anthropologist's materials and from the conditions under which he does his work. The social anthropologist normally studies the population of a particular place at a particular point in time and does not concern himself greatly with whether or not the same locality is likely to be studied again by other anthropologists at a later date. In the result we get studies of Trobriand society, Tikopia society, Nuer society, *not* "Trobriand society in 1914", "Tikopia society in 1929", "Nuer society in 1935". When anthropological societies are lifted out of time and space in this way the interpretation that is given to the material is necessarily an equilibrium analysis, for if it were not so, it would certainly appear to the reader that the analysis was incomplete. But more than that, since, in most cases, the research work has been carried out once and for all without any notion of repetition, the presentation is one of *stable* equilibrium; the authors write as if the Trobrianders, the Tikopia, the Nuer are as they are, now and for ever. Indeed the confusion between the concepts of equilibrium and of stability is so deep-rooted in anthropological literature that any use of either of these terms is liable to lead to ambiguity. They are not of course the same thing. My own position is as follows.

Model Systems

When the anthropologist attempts to describe a social system he necessarily describes only a model of the social reality. This model represents in effect the anthropologist's hypothesis about "how the social system works". The different parts of the model system therefore necessarily form a coherent whole – it is a system in equilibrium. But this does not imply that the social reality forms a coherent whole; on the contrary the reality situation is in most cases full of inconsistencies; and it is precisely these inconsistencies which can provide us with an understanding of the processes of social change.

In situations such as we find in the Kachin Hills Area, any particular individual can be thought of as having a status position in several different social systems at one and the same time. To the individual himself such systems present themselves as alternatives or inconsistencies in the scheme of values by which he orders his life. The overall process of structural change comes about through the manipulation of these alternatives as a means of social advancement. Every individual of a society, each in his own interest, endeavours to exploit the situation as he perceives it and in so doing the collectivity of individuals alters the structure of the society itself.

This rather complicated idea [...] may be illustrated by a simple example.

In matters political, Kachins have before them two quite contradictory ideal modes of life. One of these is the Shan system of government, which resembles a feudal hierarchy. The other is that which in this book is referred to as the *gumlao* type organisation; this is essentially anarchistic and equalitarian. It is not uncommon to meet an ambitious Kachin who assumes the names and titles of a Shan prince in order to justify his claim to aristocracy, but who simultaneously appeals to *gumlao* principles of equality in order to escape the liability of paying feudal dues to his own traditional chief.

And just as individual Kachins are frequently presented with a choice as to what is morally right, so also whole Kachin communities may be said to be offered a choice as to the type of political system which shall serve as their ideal. Briefly, my argument is that in terms of political organisation Kachin communities oscillate between two polar types – *gumlao* "democracy" on the one hand, Shan "autocracy" on the other. The majority of actual Kachin communities are neither *gumlao* nor Shan in type, they are organised according to a system described [...] as *gumsa*, which is, in effect, a kind of compromise between *gumlao* and Shan ideals. [...] I describe the *gumsa* system as if it were a third static model intermediate between the *gumlao* and Shan models, but the reader needs clearly to understand that actual *gumsa* communities are not static. Some, under the influence of favourable economic circumstances, tend more and more towards the Shan model, until in the end the Kachin aristocrats feel that they "have become

Shan" (*sam tai sai*) [...]; other *gumsa* communities shift in the opposite direction and become *gumlao*. Kachin social organisation, as it is described in the existing ethnographic accounts, is always the *gumsa* system; but my thesis is that this system considered by itself does not really make sense, it is too full of inherent inconsistencies. Simply as a model scheme it can be represented as an equilibrium system,[9] yet as Lévi-Strauss has perceived the structure thus represented contains elements which are "en contradiction avec le système, et doit donc entraîner sa ruine".[10] In the field of social reality *gumsa* political structures are essentially unstable, and I maintain that they only become fully intelligible in terms of the contrast provided by the polar types of *gumlao* and Shan organisation.

Another way of regarding phenomena of structural change is to say that we are concerned with shifts in the focus of political power within a given system.

The structural description of a social system provides us with an idealised model which states the "correct" status relations existing between groups within the total system and between the social persons who make up particular groups.[11] The position of any social person in any such model system is necessarily fixed, though individuals can be thought of as filling different positions in the performance of different kinds of occupation and at different stages in their career.

When we refer to structural change we have to consider not merely changes in the position of individuals with regard to an ideal system of status relationships, but changes in the ideal system itself: changes, that is, in the power structure.

Power in any system is to be thought of as an attribute of "office holders", that is of social persons who occupy positions to which power attaches. Individuals wield power only in their capacity as social persons. As a general rule I hold that the social anthropologist is never justified in interpreting action as unambiguously directed towards any one particular end. For this reason I am always dissatisfied with functionalist arguments concerning "needs" and "goals" such as those advanced by Malinowski and Talcott Parsons,[12] but I consider it necessary and justifiable to assume that a conscious or unconscious wish to gain power is a very general motive in human affairs. Accordingly I assume that individuals faced with a choice of action will commonly use such choice so as to gain power, that is to say they will seek recognition as social persons who have power; or, to use a different language, they will seek to gain access to office or the esteem of their fellows which may lead them to office.

Esteem is a cultural product. What is admired in one society may be deplored in another. The peculiarity of the Kachin Hills type of situation is that an individual may belong to more than one esteem system, and that these systems may not be consistent. Action which is meritorious according to Shan ideas may be rated as humiliating according to the *gumlao* code. The best way for an individual to gain esteem in any particular situation is therefore seldom clear. This sounds difficult, but the reader need not imagine that such uncertainty is by any means unusual; in our own society the ethically correct action for a Christian business man is often equally ambiguous.

Ritual

In order to elaborate this argument I must first explain my use of the concept *ritual*. Ritual, I assert, "serves to express the individual's status as a social person in the structural system in which he finds himself for the time being". Clearly the significance of such an aphorism must depend upon the meaning that is to be attached to the word *ritual*.

English social anthropologists have mostly followed Durkheim in distinguishing social actions into major classes – namely, religious rites which are *sacred* and technical acts which are *profane*. Of the many difficulties that result from this position one of the most important concerns the definition and classification of magic. Is there a special class of actions which can be described as magical acts and, if so, do they belong to the category "sacred" or to the category "profane", have they more of the nature and function of religious acts or of technical acts?

Various answers have been given to this question. Mauss seems to regard it as profane.[13] But no matter whether the major dichotomy is seen to lie between the magico-religious (sacred) and the technical (profane), or between the religious (sacred) and the magico-technical (profane), the assumption remains that somehow sacred and profane situations are distinct as wholes. Ritual is then a word used to describe the social actions which occur in sacred situations. My own use of the word is different from this.

From the observer's point of view, actions appear as means to ends, and it is quite feasible to follow Malinowski's advice and classify social actions in terms of their ends – i.e. the "basic needs" which they appear to satisfy. But the facts which are thereby revealed are technical facts; the analysis provides no criterion for distinguishing the peculiarities of any one culture or any one society. In fact, of course, very few social actions have this elementary functionally defined form. For example, if it is desired to grow rice, it is certainly essential and functionally necessary to clear a piece of ground and sow seed in it. And it will no doubt improve the prospects of a good yield if the plot is fenced and the growing crop weeded from time to time. Kachins do all these things and, in so far as they do this, they are performing simple technical acts of a functional kind. These actions serve to satisfy "basic needs". But there is much more to it than that. In Kachin "customary procedure", the routines of clearing the ground, planting the seed, fencing the plot and weeding the growing crop are all patterned according to formal conventions and interspersed with all kinds of technically superfluous frills and decorations. It is these frills and decorations which make the performance a *Kachin* performance and not just a simple functional act. And so it is with every kind of technical action; there is always the element which is functionally essential, and another element which is simply the local custom, an æsthetic frill. Such æsthetic frills were referred to by Malinowski as "neutral custom",[14] and in his scheme of functional analysis they are treated as minor irrelevancies. It seems to me, however, that it is precisely these customary frills which provide the social anthropologist with his primary data. Logically, æsthetics and ethics are identical.[15] If we are to understand the ethical rules of a society, it is æsthetics that we must study. In origin the details of custom may be an historical accident; but for the living individuals in a society such details can never be irrelevant, they are part of the total system of interpersonal communication within the group. They are symbolic actions, representations. It is the anthropologist's task to try to discover and to translate into his own technical jargon what it is that is symbolised or represented.

All this of course is very close to Durkheim. But Durkheim and his followers seem to have believed that collective representations were confined to the sphere of the sacred, and since they held that the dichotomy between the sacred and the profane was universal and absolute, it followed that it was only specifically sacred symbols that called for analysis by the anthropologist.

For my part I find Durkheim's emphasis on the absolute dichotomy between the sacred and the profane to be untenable.[16] Rather it is that actions fall into place on a continuous scale. At one extreme we have actions which are entirely profane, entirely functional, technique pure and simple; at the other we have actions which are entirely sacred, strictly æsthetic, technically nonfunctional. Between these two extremes we have the great majority of social actions which partake partly of the one sphere and partly of the other.

From this point of view technique and ritual, profane and sacred, do not denote *types* of action but *aspects* of almost any kind of action. Technique has economic material consequences which are measurable and predictable; ritual on the other hand is a symbolic statement which "says" something about the individuals involved in the action. Thus from certain points of view a Kachin religious sacrifice may be regarded as a purely technical and economic act. It is a procedure for killing livestock and distributing the meat, and I think there can be little doubt that for most Kachins this seems the most important aspect of the matter. A *nat galaw* ("nat making", a sacrifice) is almost a synonym for a good feast. But from the observer's point of view there is a great deal that goes on at a sacrifice that is quite irrelevant as far as butchery, cooking and meat distribution are concerned. It is these other aspects which have meaning as symbols of social status, and it is these other aspects which I describe as ritual whether or not they involve directly any conceptualisation of the supernatural or the metaphysical.[17]

Myth, in my terminology, is the counterpart of ritual; myth implies ritual, ritual implies myth, they are one and the same. This position is slightly different from the textbook theories of Jane Harrison, Durkheim and Malinowski. The classical doctrine in English social anthropology is that myth and ritual are conceptually separate entities which perpetuate one another through functional interdependence – the rite is a dramatisation of the myth, the myth is the sanction or charter for the rite. This approach to the material makes it possible to discuss myths in isolation as constituting a system of belief, and indeed a very large part of the anthropological literature on religion concerns itself almost wholly with a discussion of the content of belief and of the rationality or otherwise of that content. Most such arguments seem to me to be scholastic nonsense. As I see it, myth regarded as a statement in words "says" the same thing as ritual regarded as a statement in action. To ask questions about the content of belief which are not contained in the content of ritual is nonsense.

If I draw a rough diagram of a motor-car on the blackboard and underneath I write "this is a car", both statements – the drawing and the writing – "say" the same thing – neither says more than the other and it would clearly be nonsense to ask: "Is the car a Ford or a Cadillac?" In the same way it seems to me that if I see a Kachin killing a pig and I ask him what he is doing and he says *nat jaw nngai* – "I am giving to the nats" – this statement is simply a description of what he is doing. It is nonsense to ask such questions as: "Do nats have legs? Do they eat flesh? Do they live in the sky?" [...]

Interpretation

In sum then, my view here is that ritual action and belief are alike to be understood as forms of symbolic statement about the social order. Although I do not claim that anthropologists are always in a position to interpret such symbolism, I hold nevertheless that the main task of social anthropology is to attempt such interpretation.[18]

I must admit here to a basic psychological assumption. I assume that all human beings, whatever their culture and whatever their degree of mental sophistication, tend to construct symbols and make mental associations in the same general sort of way. This is a very large assumption, though all anthropologists make it. The situation amounts to this: I assume that with patience I, an Englishman, can learn to speak any other verbal language – e.g. Kachin. Furthermore, I assume that I will then be able to give an *approximate* translation in English of any ordinary verbal statement made by a Kachin. When it comes to statements which, though verbal, are entirely symbolic – e.g. as in poetry – translation becomes very difficult, since a word for word translation probably carries no associations for the ordinary English reader; nevertheless I assume that I can, with patience, come to understand *approximately* even the poetry of a foreign culture and that I can then communicate that understanding to others. In the same way I assume that I can give an approximate interpretation of even *non-verbal* symbolic actions such as items of ritual. It is difficult entirely to justify this kind of assumption, but without it all the activities of anthropologists become meaningless.

From this point we can go back to the problem I raised near the beginning [...] namely the relation between a social structure considered as an abstract model of an ideal society, and the social structure of any actual empirical society.

I am maintaining that wherever I encounter "ritual" (in the sense in which I have defined it) I can, as an anthropologist, interpret that ritual.

Ritual in its cultural context is a pattern of symbols; the words into which I interpret it are another pattern of symbols composed largely of technical terms devised by anthropologists – words like lineage, rank, status, and so on. The two symbol systems have something in common, namely a common *structure*. In the same way, a page of music and its musical performance have a common structure.[19] This is what I mean when I say that ritual makes explicit the social structure.

The structure which is symbolised in ritual is the system of socially approved "proper" relations between individuals and groups. These relations are not formally recognised at all times. When men are engaged in practical activities in satisfaction of what Malinowski called "the basic needs", the implications of structural relationships may be neglected altogether; a Kachin chief works in his field side by side with his meanest serf. Indeed I am prepared to argue that this neglect of formal structure is essential if ordinary informal social activities are to be pursued at all.

Nevertheless if anarchy is to be avoided, the individuals who make up a society must from time to time be reminded, at least in symbol, of the underlying order that is supposed to guide their social activities. Ritual performances have this function for the participating group as a whole; they momentarily make explicit what is otherwise a fiction.

Social Structure and Culture

My view as to the kind of relationship that exists between social structure and culture follows immediately from this. Culture provides the form, the "dress" of the social situation. As far as I am concerned, the cultural situation is a given factor, it is a product and an accident of history. I do not know *why* Kachin women go hatless with bobbed hair before they are married, but assume a turban afterwards, any more than I know *why* English women put a ring on a particular finger to denote the same change in social status; all I am interested in is that in this Kachin context the assumption of a turban by a woman does have this symbolic significance. It is a statement about the status of the woman.

But the structure of the situation is largely independent of its cultural form. The same kind of structural relationship may exist in many different cultures and be symbolised in correspondingly different ways. In the example just given, marriage is a structural relationship which is common to both English and Kachin society; it is symbolised by a ring in the one and a turban in the other. This means that one and the same element of social structure may appear in one cultural dress in locality A and another cultural dress in locality B. But A and B may be adjacent places on the map. In other words there is no intrinsic reason why the significant frontiers of social systems should always coincide with cultural frontiers.

Differences of culture are, I admit, structurally significant, but the mere fact that two groups of people are of different culture does not necessarily imply – as has nearly always been assumed – that they belong to two quite different social systems. [...]

In any geographical area which lacks fundamental natural frontiers, the human beings in adjacent areas of the map are likely to have relations with one another – at least to some extent – no matter what their cultural attributes may be. In so far as these relations are ordered and not wholly haphazard there is implicit in them a social structure. But, it may be asked, if social structures are expressed in cultural symbols, how can the structural relations between groups of different culture be expressed at all? My answer to this is that the maintenance and insistence upon cultural difference can itself become a ritual action expressive of social relations.

In the geographical area considered in this book the cultural variations between one group and another are very numerous and very marked. But persons who speak a different language, wear a different dress, worship different deities and so on are not regarded as foreigners entirely beyond the pale of social recognition. Kachins and Shans are mutually contemptuous of one another, but Kachins and Shans are deemed to have a common ancestor for all that. In this context cultural attributes such as language, dress and ritual procedure are merely symbolic labels denoting the different sectors of a single extensive structural system.

For my purposes it is the underlying structural pattern and not the overt cultural pattern that has real significance. I am concerned not so much with the structural interpretation of a particular culture, but with how particular structures can assume a variety of cultural interpretations, and with how different structures can be represented by the same set of cultural symbols. [...]

Notes

1   Cf. Fortes (1949), pp. 54–60.
2   Lévi-Strauss (1949), ch. XVIII.
3   Evans-Pritchard (1940).
4   Cf. Fortes (1949), pp. 54–5.
5   Radcliffe-Brown (1940).
6   Cf. Nadel (1951), p. 187.
7   E.g. Malinowski (1945); G. and M. Wilson (1945); Herskovits (1949).
8   Homans (1951), pp. 336 ff.
9   Leach (1952), pp. 40–5.

10   Lévi-Strauss (1949), p. 325.

11   For this use of the expression "social person" see especially Radcliffe-Brown (1940), p. 5.

12   Malinowski (1944); Parsons (1949); Parsons and Shils (1951), pt. II.

13   Mauss (1947), p. 207.

14   Malinowski in Hogbin (1934), p. xxvi.

15   Wittgenstein (1922), 6.421.

16   Durkheim (1925), p. 53.

17   Cf. the distinction made by Merton (1951) between *manifest* and *latent* function.

18   The concept of *eidos* as developed by Bateson (1936) has relevance for this part of my argument.

19   Russell (1948), p. 479.

References

Bateson, G., 1936. *Naven* (Cambridge).

Durkheim, E., 1925. *Les Formes élémentaires de la vie religieuse* (2nd edn.) (Paris).

Evans-Pritchard, E. E., 1940. *The Nuer* (London).

Fortes, M., 1949. "Time and Social Structure: An Ashanti Case Study," in *Social Structure: Studies Presented to A. R. Radcliffe-Brown* (Fortes, M., editor) (Oxford).

Herskovits, M. J., 1949. *Man and His Works* (New York).

Hogbin, H. I., 1934. *Law and Order in Polynesia* (Introduction by Malinowski B.) (London).

Homans, G. C., 1951. *The Human Group* (London).

Leach, E. R., 1952. "The Structural Implications of Matrilateral Cross-Cousin Marriage", *JRAI*, LXXXI.

Levi-Strauss, C., 1949. *Les Structures élémentaires de la parenté* (Paris).

Malinowski, B., 1944. *A Scientific Theory of Culture and Other Essays* (Chapel Hill, NC).

Malinowski, B., 1945. *The Dynamics of Culture Change* (New Haven).

Mauss, M., 1947. *Manuel d'Ethnographie* (Paris).

Merton, R. K., 1951. *Social Theory and Social Structure* (Glencoe, Ill.).

Nadel, S. F., 1951. *The Foundations of Social Anthropology* (London).

Parsons, T., 1949. *Essays in Sociological Theory: Pure and Applied* (Cambridge, Mass.).

Parsons, T. and Shils, E. A. (eds.), 1951. *Toward a General Theory of Action* (Cambridge, Mass.).

Radcliffe-Brown, A. R., 1940. "On Social Structure", *JRAI*, LXX.

Russell, B., 1948. *Human Knowledge* (London).

Wilson, G. and M., 1945. *The Analysis of Social Change* (Cambridge).

Wittgenstein, L., 1922. *Tractatus Logico-Philosophicus* (London).

8

Social Structure

Claude Lévi-Strauss

The term "social structure" refers to a group of problems the scope of which appears so wide and the definition so imprecise that it is hardly possible for a paper strictly limited in size to meet them fully.

[...]

Such being the case, it is obvious that the term "social structure" needs first to be defined and that some explanation should be given of the difference which helps to distinguish studies in social structure from the unlimited field of descriptions, analyses, and theories dealing with social relations at large, confounding themselves with the whole scope of social anthropology. This is all the more necessary, since some of those who have contributed toward setting apart social structure as a special field of anthropological studies conceived the former in many different manners and even sometimes, so it seems, came to nurture grave doubts as to the validity of their enterprise. For instance, Kroeber writes in the second edition of his *Anthropology*:

> "Structure" appears to be just a yielding to a word that has a perfectly good meaning but suddenly becomes fashionably attractive for a decade or so – like "streamlining" – and during its vogue tends to be applied indiscriminately because of the pleasurable connotations of its sound. Of course a typical personality can be viewed as having a structure. But so can a physiology, any organism, all societies and all cultures, crystals, machines – in fact everything which is not wholly amorphous has a structure. So what "structure" adds to the meaning of our phrase seems to be nothing, except to provoke a degree of pleasant puzzlement. (Kroeber, 1948, p. 325)[1]

Although this passage concerns more particularly the notion of "basic personality structure," it has devastating implications as regards the generalized use of the notion of structure in anthropology.

Another reason makes a definition of social structure compulsory: from the structuralist point of view which one has to adopt if only to give the problem its meaning, it would be hopeless to try to reach a valid definition of social structure on an inductive basis, by abstracting common elements from the uses and definitions current among all the scholars who claim to have made "social structure" the object of their studies. If these concepts have a meaning at all, they

From *Anthropology Today* (Chicago: University of Chicago Press, 1962 [1952]), pp. 321–8, 333–5, 338–9, 347–50. Copyright © 1952 by University of Chicago Press. Reprinted by permission of University of Chicago Press.

Anthropology in Theory: Issues in Epistemology, Second Edition. Edited by Henrietta L. Moore and Todd Sanders.
© 2014 John Wiley & Sons, Inc. Published 2014 by John Wiley & Sons, Inc.

mean, first, that the notion of structure has a structure. This we shall try to outline from the beginning as a precaution against letting ourselves be submerged by a tedious inventory of books and papers dealing with social relations, the mere listing of which would more than exhaust the limited space at our disposal. In a further stage we will have to see how far and in what directions the term "social structure," as used by the different authors, departs from our definition. This will be done in the section devoted to kinship, since the notion of structure has found in that field its main applications and since anthropologists have generally chosen to express their theoretical views also in that connection.

Definition and Problems of Method

Passing now to the task of defining "social structure," there is a point which should be cleared up immediately. The term "social structure" has nothing to do with empirical reality but with models which are built up after it. This should help one to clarify the difference between two concepts which are so close to each other that they have often been confused, namely, those of *social structure* and of *social relations*. It will be enough to state at this time that social relations consist of the raw materials out of which the models making up the social structure are built, while social structure can, by no means, be reduced to the ensemble of the social relations to be described in a given society. Therefore, social structure cannot claim a field of its own among others in the social studies. It is rather a method to be applied to any kind of social studies, similar to the structural analysis current in other disciplines.

Then the question becomes that of ascertaining what kind of model deserves the name "structure." This is not an anthropological question, but one which belongs to the methodology of science in general. Keeping this in mind, we can say that a structure consists of a model meeting with several requirements.

First, the structure exhibits the characteristics of a system. It is made up of several elements none of which can undergo a change without effecting changes in all the other elements.

In the second place, for any given model there should be a possibility of ordering a series of transformations resulting in a group of models of the same type.

In the third place, the above properties make it possible to predict how the model will react if one or more of its elements are submitted to certain modifications.

And, last, the model should be constituted so as to make immediately intelligible all the observed facts.

These being the requirements for any model with structural value, several consequences follow. These, however, do not pertain to the definition of structure but have to do with the main properties exhibited by, and problems raised by, structural analysis when contemplated in the social and other fields.

Observation and experimentation

Great care should be taken to distinguish between the observation and the experiment levels. To observe facts and elaborate methodological devices permitting of constructing models out of these facts is not at all the same thing as to experiment on the models. By "experimenting on models," we mean the set of procedures aiming at ascertaining how a given model will react when submitted to change and at comparing models of the same or different types. This distinction is all the more necessary, since many discussions on social structure revolve around the apparent contradiction between the concreteness and individuality of ethnological data and the abstract and formal character generally exhibited by structural studies. This contradiction disappears as one comes to realize that these features belong to two entirely different planes, or rather two stages of the same process. On the observational level, the main – one could almost say the only – rule is that all the facts should be carefully observed and described, without allowing any theoretical preconception to decide whether some are more important and others less. This rule implies, in turn, that facts should be studied in relation to themselves (by what kind of concrete process did they come into being?) and in relation to the whole (always aiming to relate each modification which can be observed in a sector to the global situation in which it first appeared).

This rule together with its corollaries has been explicitly formulated by K. Goldstein (1951, pp. 18–25) in relation to psychophysiological studies, and it may be considered valid for any kind of structural analysis. Its immediate consequence is that, far from being contradictory, there is a direct relationship between the detail and concreteness of ethnographical description and the validity and generality of the model which is constructed after it. For, though many models may be used as convenient devices to describe and explain the phenomena, it is obvious that the best model will always be that which is *true*, that is, the simplest possible model which, while being extracted exclusively from the facts under consideration, also makes it possible to account for all of them. Therefore, the first task is to ascertain what those facts are.

Consciousness and unconsciousness

A second distinction has to do with the conscious or unconscious character of the models. In the history of structural thought, Boas may be credited with having introduced this distinction. He made clear that a category of facts can more easily yield to structural analysis when the social group in which they are manifested has not elaborated a conscious model to interpret or justify them (e.g., 1911, p. 67). Some readers may be surprised to find Boas' name quoted in connection with structural theory, since he was often described as one of the main obstacles in its path. But this writer has tried to demonstrate that Boas' shortcomings in matters of structural studies were not in his failure to understand their importance and significance, which he did, as a matter of fact, in the most prophetic way. They rather resulted from the fact that he imposed on structural studies conditions of validity, some of which will remain forever part of their methodology, while some others are so exacting and impossible to meet that they would have withered scientific development in any field (Lévi-Strauss, 1949a).

A structural model may be conscious or unconscious without this difference affecting its nature. It can only be said that when the structure of a certain type of phenomena does not lie at a great depth, it is more likely that some kind of model, standing as a screen to hide it, will exist in the collective consciousness. For conscious models, which are usually known as "norms," are by definition very poor ones, since they are not intended to explain the phenomena but to perpetuate them. Therefore, structural analysis is confronted with a strange paradox well known to the linguist, that is: the more obvious structural organization is, the more difficult it becomes to reach it because of the inaccurate conscious models lying across the path which leads to it.

From the point of view of the degree of consciousness, the anthropologist is confronted with two kinds of situations. He may have to construct a model from phenomena the systematic character of which has evoked no awareness on the part of the culture; this is the kind of simpler situation referred to by Boas as providing the easiest ground for anthropological research. Or else the anthropologist will be dealing, on the one hand, with raw phenomena and, on the other, with the models already constructed by the culture to interpret the former. Though it is likely that, for the reason stated above, these models will prove unsatisfactory, it is by no means necessary that this should always be the case. As a matter of fact, many "primitive" cultures have built models of their marriage regulations which are much more to the point than models built by professional anthropologists.[2] Thus one cannot dispense with studying a culture's "home-made" models for two reasons. First, these models might prove to be accurate or, at least, to provide some insight into the structure of the phenomena; after all, each culture has its own theoreticians whose contributions deserve the same attention as that which the anthropologist gives to colleagues. And, second, even if the models are biased or erroneous, the very bias and types of errors are a part of the facts under study and probably rank among the most significant ones. But even when taking into consideration these culturally produced models, the anthropologist does not forget – as he has sometimes been accused of doing (Firth, 1951, pp. 28–31) – that the cultural norms are not of themselves structures. Rather, they furnish an important contribution to an understanding of the structures, either as factual documents or as theoretical contributions similar to those of the anthropologist himself.

This point has been given great attention by the French sociological school. Durkheim and Mauss, for instance, have always taken care to substitute, as a starting point for the survey of native categories of thought, the conscious representations prevailing among the natives themselves for those grown out of the anthropologist's own culture. This was undoubtedly an important step, which, nevertheless, fell short of its goal because these authors were not sufficiently aware that native conscious representations, important as they are, may be just as remote from the unconscious reality as any other (Lévi-Strauss, 1951).

Structure and measure

It is often believed that one of the main interests of the notion of structure is to permit the introduction of measurement in social anthropology. This view was favored by the frequent appearance of mathematical or semimathematical aids in books or articles dealing with social structure. It is true that in some cases structural analysis has made it possible to attach numerical values to invariants. This was, for instance, the result of Kroeber's studies of women's dress fashions, a landmark in structural research (Richardson and Kroeber, 1940), as well as of a few other studies which will be discussed below.

However, one should keep in mind that there is no necessary connection between *measure* and *structure*. Structural studies are, in the social sciences, the indirect outcome of modern developments in mathematics which have given increasing importance to the qualitative point of view in contradistinction to the quantitative point of view of traditional mathematics. Therefore, it has become possible, in fields such as mathematical logic, set-theory, group-theory, and topology, to develop a rigorous approach to problems which do not admit of a metrical solution. [...]

Mechanical models and statistical models

A last distinction refers to the relation between the scale of the model and that of the phenomena. According to the nature of these phenomena, it becomes possible or impossible to build a model, the elements of which are on the same scale as the phenomena themselves. A model the elements of which are on the same scale as the phenomena will be called a "mechanical model"; when the elements of the model are on a different scale, we will be dealing with a "statistical model." The laws of marriage provide the best illustration of this difference. In primitive societies these laws can be expressed in models calling for actual grouping of the individuals according to kin or clan; these are mechanical models. No such distribution exists in our own society, where types of marriage are determined by the size of the primary and secondary groups to which prospective mates belong, social fluidity, amount of information, and the like. A satisfactory (though yet untried) attempt to formulate the invariants of our marriage system would therefore have to determine average values – thresholds; it would be a statistical model. There may be intermediate forms between these two. Such is the case in societies which (as even our own) have a mechanical model to determine prohibited marriages and rely on a statistical model for those which are permissible. It should also be kept in mind that the same phenomena may admit of different models, some mechanical and some statistical, according to the way in which they are grouped together and with other phenomena. A society which recommends cross-cousin marriage but where this ideal marriage type occurs only with limited frequency needs, in order that the system may be properly explained, both a mechanical and a statistical model, as was well understood by Forde (1941) and Elwin (1947).

It should also be kept in mind that what makes social-structure studies valuable is that structures are models, the formal properties of which can be compared independently of their elements. The structuralist's task is thus to recognize and isolate levels of reality which have strategic value from his point of view, namely, which admit of representation as models, whatever their kind. It often happens that the same data may be considered from different perspectives embodying equal strategic values, though the resulting models will be in some cases mechanical and in others statistical. This situation is well known in the exact and natural sciences; for instance, the theory of a small number of physical bodies belongs to classical mechanics, but if the number of bodies becomes greater, then one should rely on the laws of thermodynamics, that is, use a statistical model instead of a mechanical one, though the nature of the data remains the same in both cases.

The same situation prevails in the human and the social sciences. If one takes a phenomenon like, for instance, suicide, it can be studied on two different levels. First, it is possible by studying individual situations to establish what may be called mechanical models of suicide, taking into account in each case the personality of the victim, his or her life-history, the characteristics of the primary and secondary groups in which he or she developed, and the like; or else one can build models of a statistical nature, by recording suicide frequency over a certain period of time in one or more societies and in different types of primary and secondary groups, etc. These would be levels at which the structural study of suicide carries a strategic value, that is, where it becomes possible to build models which may be compared (1) for different types of suicides, (2) for different societies, and (3) for different types of social phenomena. Scientific progress consists not only in discovering new invariants belonging to those levels but also in discovering new levels where the study of the same phenomena offers the same strategical value. Such a result was achieved, for instance, by psychoanalysis, which discovered the means to lay out models in a new field, that of the psychological life of the patient considered as a whole.

The foregoing should help to make clear the dual (and at first sight almost contradictory) nature of structural studies. On the one hand, they aim at isolating strategic levels, and this can be achieved only by "carving out" a certain family of phenomena. From that point of view, each type of structural study appears autonomous, entirely independent of all the others and even of different methodological approaches to the same field. On the other hand, the essential value of these studies is to construct models the formal properties of which can be compared with, and explained by, the same properties as in models corresponding to other strategic levels. Thus it may be said that their ultimate end is to override traditional boundaries between different disciplines and to promote a true interdisciplinary approach.

An example may be given. A great deal of discussion has taken place lately about the difference between history and anthropology, and Kroeber and others have made clear that the time-dimension has very little importance in this connection. From what has been stated above, one can see exactly where the difference lies, not only between these two disciplines but also between them and others. Ethnography and history differ from social anthropology and sociology, inasmuch as the former two aim at gathering data, while the latter two deal with models constructed from these data. Similarly, ethnography and social anthropology correspond to two different stages in the same research, the ultimate result of which is to construct mechanical models, while history (together with its so-called "auxiliary" disciplines) and sociology end ultimately in statistical models. This is the reason why the social sciences, though having to do – all of them – with the time-dimension, nevertheless deal with two different categories of time. Anthropology uses a "mechanical" time, reversible and non-cumulative. For instance, the model of, let us say, a patrilineal kinship system does not in itself show whether or not the system has always remained patrilineal, or has been preceded by a matrilineal form, or by any number of shifts from patrilineal to matrilineal and vice versa. On the contrary, historical time is "statistical"; it always appears as an oriented and nonreversible process. An evolution which would take back contemporary Italian society to that of the Roman Republic is as impossible to conceive of as is the reversibility of the processes belonging to the second law of thermodynamics.

This discussion helps to clarify Firth's distinction between social structure, which he conceives as outside the time-dimension, and social organization, where time re-enters (1951, p. 40). Also in this connection, the debate which has been going on for the past few years between followers of the Boasian antievolutionist tradition and of Professor Leslie White (1949) may become better understood. The Boasian school has been mainly concerned with models of a mechanical type, and from this point of view the concept of evolution has no operational value. On the other hand, it is certainly legitimate to speak of evolution in a historical and sociological sense, but the elements to be organized into an evolutionary process cannot be borrowed from the level of a cultural typology which consists of mechanical models. They should be sought at a sufficiently deep level to insure that these elements will remain unaffected by different cultural contexts (as, let us say, genes are identical elements combined into different patterns corresponding to the different racial [statistical] models) and can accordingly permit of drawing long statistical runs.

A great deal of inconvenience springs from a situation which obliges the social scientist to "shift" time, according to the kind of study he is contemplating. Natural scientists, who have got used to this difficulty, are making efforts to overcome it. Very important in this connection is Murdock's contention that while a patrilineal system may replace, or grow out of, a matrilineal system, the opposite process cannot take place (1949, pp. 210–20). If this were true, a vectorial factor would for the first time be introduced on an objective basis into social structure. Murdock's demonstration was, however, challenged by Lowie (1948, pp. 44 ff.) on methodological grounds, and for the time being it is impossible to do more than to call attention to a moot problem, the solution of which, when generally accepted, will have a tremendous bearing upon structural studies, not only in the field of anthropology but in other fields as well.

The distinction between mechanical and statistical models has also become fundamental in another respect: it makes it possible to clarify the role of the comparative method in structural studies. This method was greatly emphasized by both Radcliffe-Brown and Lowie. The former writes (1952, p. 14):

> Theoretical sociology is commonly regarded as an inductive science, induction being the logical method of inference by which we arrive at general propositions from the consideration of particular instances. Although Professor Evans-Pritchard ... seems to imply in some of his statements that the logical method of induction, using comparison, classification and generalization, is not applicable to the phenomena of human social life ... I hold that social anthropology must depend on systematic comparative studies of many societies.

Writing about religion, he states (1945, p. 33):

> [T]he experimental method of social anthropology...means that we must study in the light of our hypothesis a sufficient number of diverse particular religions or religious cults in relation to the particular societies in which they are found. This is a task not for one person but for a number.

Similarly, Lowie, after pointing out (1948, p. 38) that "the literature of anthropology is full of alleged correlations which lack empirical support," insists on the need of a "broad inductive basis" for generalization (1948, p. 68). It is interesting to note that by this claim for inductive support these authors dissent not only from Durkheim (1912, p. 593): "when a law has been proved by a well-performed experiment, this law is valid universally," but also from Goldstein, who, as already mentioned, has lucidly expressed what may be called "the rules of structuralist method" in a way general enough to make them valid outside the more limited field in which they were first applied by their author. Goldstein remarks that the need to make a thorough study of each case implies that the amount of cases to be studied should be small; and he proceeds by raising the question whether or not the risk exists that the cases under consideration may be special ones, allowing no general conclusions about the others. He answers (1951, p. 25):

> This objection completely misunderstands the real situation...an accumulation of facts even numerous is of no help if these facts were imperfectly established; it does not lead to the knowledge of things as they really happen.... We must choose only these cases which permit of formulating final judgments. And then, what is true for one case will also be true for any other.

Probably very few anthropologists would be ready to support these bold statements. However, no structuralist study may be undertaken without a clear awareness of Goldstein's dilemma: either to study many cases in a superficial and in the end ineffective way; or to limit one's self to a thorough study of a small number of cases, thus proving that, in the end, one well-done experiment is sufficient to make a demonstration.

Now the reason for so many anthropologists' faithfulness to the comparative method may be sought in some sort of confusion between the procedures used to establish mechanical and statistical models. While Durkheim's and Goldstein's position undoubtedly holds true for the former, it is obvious that no statistical model can be achieved without statistics, i.e., by gathering a large amount of data. But in this case the method is no more comparative than in the other, since the data to be collected will be acceptable only in so far as they are all of the same kind. Therefore, we remain confronted with only one alternative, namely, to make a thorough study of one case. The real difference lies in the selection of the "case," which will be patterned so as to include elements which are either on the same scale as the model to be constructed or on a different scale.

[...]

Social Statics or Communication Structures

A society consists of individuals and groups which communicate with one another. The existence of, or lack of, communication can never be defined in an absolute manner. Communication does not cease at society's borders. These borders, rather, constitute thresholds where the rate and forms of communication, without waning altogether, reach a much lower level. This condition is usually meaningful enough for the population, both inside and outside the borders, to become aware of it. This awareness is not, however, a prerequisite for the definition of a given society. It only accompanies the more precise and stable forms.

In any society, communication operates on three different levels: communication of women, communication of goods and services, communication of messages. Therefore, kinship studies, economics, and linguistics approach the same kinds of problems on different strategic levels and really pertain to the same field. Theoretically at least, it might be said that kinship and marriage rules regulate a fourth type of communication, that of genes between phenotypes. Therefore, it should be kept in mind that culture does not consist exclusively of forms of communication of its own, like language, but also (and perhaps mostly) of *rules* stating how the "games of communication" should be played both on the natural and on the cultural level.

The above comparison between the fields of kinship, economics, and linguistics cannot hide the fact that they refer to forms of communication which are on a different scale. Should one try

to compute the communication rate involved, on the one hand, in the intermarriages and, on the other, in the exchange of messages going on in a given society, one would probably discover the difference to be of about the same magnitude as, let us say, that between the exchange of heavy molecules of two viscous liquids through a not too permeable film, and radio communication. Thus, from marriage to language one passes from low- to high-speed communication; this comes from the fact that what is communicated in marriage is almost of the same nature as those who communicate (women, on the one hand, men, on the other), while speakers of language are not of the same nature as their utterances. The opposition is thus one of *person* to *symbol*, or of *value* to *sign*. This helps to clarify economics' somewhat intermediate position between these two extremes – goods and services are not persons, but they still are values. And, though neither symbols nor signs, they require symbols or signs to succeed in being exchanged when the exchange system reaches a certain degree of complexity.

From this outline of the structure of social communication derive three important sets of considerations.

First, the position of economics in social structure may be precisely defined. Economics in the past has been suspect among anthropologists. Yet, whenever this highly important topic has been broached, a close relationship has been shown to prevail between economic pattern and social structure. Since Mauss's pioneer papers (1904–5, 1923–4) and Malinowski's book on the *kula* (1922) – by far his masterpiece – every attempt in this direction has shown that the economic system provides sociological formulations with some of their more fundamental invariants (Speck, 1915; Richards, 1932, 1936, 1939; Steward, 1938; Evans-Pritchard, 1940; Herskovits, 1940; Wittfogel and Goldfrank, 1943).

The anthropologist's reluctance originated in the condition of economic studies themselves; these were ridden with conflicts between bitterly opposed schools and at the same time bathed in an aura of mystery and conceit. Thus the anthropologist labored under the impression that economics dealt mostly with abstractions and that there was little connection between the actual life of actual groups of people and such notions as value, utility, profit, and the like.

The complete upheaval of economic studies resulting from the publication of Von Neumann and Morgenstern's book (1944) ushers in an era of closer co-operation between the economist and the anthropologist, and for two reasons. First – though economics achieves here a rigorous approach – this book deals not with abstractions such as those just mentioned but with concrete individuals and groups which are represented in their actual and empirical relations of co-operation and competition. Next – and as a consequence it introduces for the first time mechanical models which are of the same type as, and intermediate between, those used in mathematical physics and in social anthropology – especially in the field of kinship. In this connection it is striking that Von Neumann's models are borrowed from the theory of games, a line of thought which was initiated independently by Kroeber when he compared social institutions "to the play of earnest children" (1942, p. 215). There is, true enough, an important difference between games of entertainment and marriage rules: the former are constructed in such a way as to permit each player to extract from statistical regularities maximal differential values, while marriage rules, acting in the opposite direction, aim at establishing statistical regularities in spite of the differential values existing between individuals and generations. In this sense they constitute a special kind of "upturned game." Nevertheless, they can be treated with the same methods. Besides, such being the rules, each individual and group tries to play it in the "normal" way, that is, by maximizing his own advantages at the expense of the others (i.e., to get more wives or better ones, whether from the aesthetic, erotic, or economic point of view). The theory of courtship is thus a part of formal sociology. To those who are afraid that sociology might in this way get hopelessly involved in individual psychology, it will be enough to recall that Von Neumann has succeeded in giving a mathematical demonstration of the nature and strategy of a psychological technique as sophisticated as bluffing at the game of poker (Von Neumann and Morgenstern, 1944, pp. 186–219).

The next advantage of this increasing consolidation of social anthropology, economics, and linguistics into one great field, that of communication, is to make clear that they consist exclusively of the study of *rules* and have little concern with the nature of the partners (either individuals or groups) whose play is being patterned after these rules. As Von Neumann puts it (1944, p. 49): "The game is simply the totality of the rules which describe it." Besides that of game, other operational notions are those of play, move, choice, and strategy. But the nature of the players need not be considered. What is important is to find out when a given player can make a choice and when he cannot.

This outlook should open the study of kinship and marriage to approaches directly derived from the theory of communication.

[...]

The words "social structure" are in many ways linked with the name of A. R. Radcliffe-Brown. Though his contribution does not limit itself to the study of kinship systems, he has stated the goal of these studies in terms which every scholar in the same field would probably be ready to underwrite: the aim of kinship studies, he says, is (1) to make a systematic classification; (2) to understand particular features of particular systems (*a*) by revealing the particular feature as a part of an organized whole and (*b*) by showing that it is a special example of a recognizable class of phenomena; (3) to arrive at valid generalizations about the nature of human societies. And he concludes: "To reduce this diversity (of 2 or 300 kinship systems) to some sort of order is the task of analysis.... We can...find...beneath the diversities, a limited number of general principles applied and combined in various ways" (1941, p. 17). There is nothing to add to this lucid program besides pointing out that this is precisely what Radcliffe-Brown has done in his study of Australian kinship systems. He brought forth a tremendous amount of material; he introduced some kind of order where there was only chaos; he defined the basic operational terms, such as "cycle," "pair," and "couple." Finally, his discovery of the Kariera system in the region and with the characteristics inferred from the study of the available data and before visiting Australia will forever remain one of the great results of sociostructural studies (1930–1). His masterly Introduction to *African Systems of Kinship and Marriage* may be considered a true treatise on kinship; at the same time it takes a step toward integrating kinship systems of the Western world (which are approached in their early forms) into a world-wide theoretical interpretation. [...]

However, it is obvious that, in many respects, Radcliffe-Brown's conception of social structure differs from the postulates which were set up at the outset of the present paper. [...] [T]he notion of structure appears to him as a means to link social anthropology to the biological sciences: "There is a real and significant analogy between organic structure and social structure" (1940, p. 6). Then, instead of "lifting up" kinship studies to put them on the same level as communication theory, as has been suggested by this writer, he has lowered them to the same plane as the phenomena dealt with in descriptive morphology and physiology (1940, p. 10). In that respect, his approach is in line with the naturalistic trend of the British school. In contradistinction to Kroeber (1938, 1942, pp. 205 ff.) and Lowie (1948, chap. iv), who have emphasized the artificiality of kinship, he agrees with Malinowski that biological ties are, at one and the same time, the origin of and the model for every type of kinship tie (Radcliffe-Brown, 1926).

These principles are responsible for two consequences. In the first place, Radcliffe-Brown's empirical approach makes him very reluctant to distinguish between *social structure* and *social relations*. As a matter of fact, social structure appears in his work to be nothing else than the whole network of social relations. It is true that he has sometimes outlined a distinction between *structure* and *structural form*. The latter concept, however, seems to be limited to the diachronic perspective, and its functional role in Radcliffe-Brown's theoretical thought appears quite reduced (1940, p. 4). This distinction was thoroughly discussed by Fortes, who has contributed a great deal to the distinction, quite foreign to Radcliffe-Brown's outlook, between "model" and "reality" (see above): "structure is not immediately visible in the 'concrete reality.'... When we describe structure ... we are, as it were, in the realm of grammar and syntax, not of the spoken word" (Fortes, 1949, p. 56). [...]

Notes

1   Compare with the statement by the same author: "the term 'social structure' which is tending to replace 'social organization' without appearing to add either content or emphasis of meaning" (1943, p. 105).

2   For examples and detailed discussion see Lévi-Strauss (1949b, pp. 558 ff.).

References

Boas, F. (ed.). 1911. *Handbook of American Indian Languages.* (Bureau of American Ethnology Bull. 40 [1908], Part I.) Washington, DC: Government Printing Office.

Durkheim, E. 1912. *Les Formes élémentaires de la vie religieuse.* ("Bibliothèque de philosophie contemporaine.") Paris: F. Alcan.

Elwin, V. 1947. *The Muria and Their Ghotul.* Oxford: Oxford University Press.

Evans-Pritchard, E. E. 1940. *The Nuer.* Oxford: Clarendon Press.

Firth, R. 1951. *Elements of Social Organization.* London: Watts & Co.

Forde, D. 1941. *Marriage and the Family among the Yakö in S.E. Nigeria.* (Monographs in Social Anthropology, no. 5.) London: London School of Economics and Political Science.

Fortes, M. (ed.). 1949. *Social Structure: Studies Presented to A. R. Radcliffe-Brown.* Oxford: Clarendon Press.

Goldstein, K. 1951. *La Structure de l'organisme.* French trans. of *Der Aufbau des Organismus.* Paris: Gallimard.

Herskovits, M. J. 1940. *The Economic Life of Primitive Peoples.* New York: Alfred A. Knopf.

Kroeber, A. L. 1938. "Basic and Secondary Patterns of Social Structure," *Journal of the Royal Anthropological Institute*, LXVIII, 299–309.

Kroeber, A. L. 1942. "The Societies of Primitive Man," *Biological Symposia*, VIII, 205–16.

Kroeber, A. L. 1943. "Structure, Function, and Pattern in Biology and Anthropology," *Scientific Monthly*, LVI, 105–13.

Kroeber, A. L. 1948. *Anthropology.* New ed. New York: Harcourt, Brace & Co.

Lévi-Strauss, C. 1949a. "Histoire et ethnologie," *Revue de métaphysique et de morale*, LIV, Nos. 3–4, 363–91.

Lévi-Strauss, C. 1949b. *Les Structures élémentaires de la parenté.* Paris: Presses universitaires de France.

Lévi-Strauss, C. 1951. "Language and the Analysis of Social Laws," *American Anthropologist*, LIII, No. 2, 155–63.

Lowie, R. H. 1948. *Social Organization*. New York: Rinehart & Co.

Malinowski, B. 1922. *Argonauts of the Western Pacific*. London: George Routledge & Sons, Ltd.

Mauss, M. 1904–5 (1906). "Essai sur les variations saisonnières dan les sociétés Eskimos: Étude de morphologie sociale." *Année sociologique*, IX, 39–132.

Mauss, M. 1923–4. "Essai sur le don, forme archaïque de l'échange," *Année sociologique*, n.s., I, 30–186.

Murdock, G. P. 1949. *Social Structure*. New York: Macmillan Co.

Neumann, J. von, and Morgenstern, O. 1944. *Theory of Games and Economic Behavior*. Princeton, NJ: Princeton University Press.

Radcliffe-Brown, A. R. 1926. "Father, Mother, and Child," *Man*, vol. XXVI, art. 103, pp. 159–61.

Radcliffe-Brown, A. R. 1930–1. "The Social Organization of Australian Tribes," *Oceania*, I, no. 1, 34–63; no. 2, 206–46; No. 3, 322–41; No. 4, 426–56.

Radcliffe-Brown, A. R. 1940. "On Social Structure," *Journal of the Royal Anthropological Institute*, LXX, 1–12.

Radcliffe-Brown, A. R. 1941. "The Study of Kinship Systems," *Journal of the Royal Anthropological Institute*, LXXI, 1–18.

Radcliffe-Brown, A. R. 1945. "Religion and Society (Henry Meyers Lecture)," *Journal of the Royal Anthropological Institute*, LXXV, 33–43.

Radcliffe-Brown, A. R. 1952. "Social Anthropology, Past and Present," *Man*, vol. LII, art. 14, pp. 13–14.

Richards, A. I. 1932. *Hunger and Work in a Savage Tribe*. London: G. Routledge & Sons.

Richards, A. I. 1936. "A Dietary Study in North-eastern Rhodesia," *Africa*, IX, no. 2, 166–96.

Richards, A. I. 1939. *Land, Labour and Diet in Northern Rhodesia*. Oxford: Oxford University Press, for the International Institute of African Languages and Cultures.

Richardson, J., and Kroeber, A. L. 1940. "Three Centuries of Women's Dress Fashions: A Quantitative Analysis," *Anthropological Records*, V, no. 2, 111–54.

Speck, F. G. 1915. *Family Hunting Territories and Social Life of Various Algonkian Bands of the Ottawa Valley*. (Canada Department of Mines, Geological Survey Mem. 70, "Anthropological Series," no. 8.) Ottawa: Government Printing Bureau.

Steward, J. H. 1938. *Basin-Plateau Aboriginal Sociopolitical Groups*. (Bureau of American Ethnology, Smithsonian Institution Bull. 120.) Washington, DC: Government Printing Office.

White, L. A. 1949. *The Science of Culture*. New York: Farrar, Straus & Co.

Wittfogel, K. A., and Goldfrank, E. S. 1943. "Some Aspects of Pueblo Mythology and Society," *Journal of American Folklore*, LVI, 17–30.

SECTION 3

Function and Environment

9

The Group and the Individual in Functional Analysis

Bronislaw Malinowski

Personality, Organization, and Culture

It might seem axiomatic that in any sociological approach the individual, the group, and their relations must remain the constant theme of all observations and argument. The group, after all, is but the assemblage of individuals and must be thus defined – unless we fall into the fallacy of "group mind," "collective sensorium," or the gigantic "Moral Being" which thinks out and improvises all collective events. Nor can such conceptions as individual, personality, self, or mind be described except in terms of membership in a group or groups – unless again we wish to hug the figment of the individual as a detached, self-contained entity. We can, therefore, lay down as an axiom – or better, as an empirical truth – that in field work and theory, in observation and analysis, the *leitmotiv* "individual, group, and their mutual dependence" will run through all the inquiries.

But the exact determination of what we mean by "individual," or how he is related to his "group," the final understanding of the terms "social organization" or "cultural determinism" presents a number of problems to be discussed. I would like to add

that over and above individual mental processes and forms of social organization it is necessary to introduce another factor, which together with the previous ones makes up the totality of cultural processes and phenomena. I mean the material apparatus which is indispensable both for the understanding of how a culturally determined individual comes into being and, also, how he co-operates in group life with other individuals.

In what follows I shall discuss some of these questions from the anthropological point of view. Most of my scientific experiences in culture are derived from work in the field. As an anthropologist I am interested in primitive as well as in developed cultures. The functional approach, moreover, considers the totality of cultural phenomena as the necessary background both of the analysis of man and that of society. Indeed, since in my opinion the relation between individual and group is a universal motive in all problems of sociology and comparative anthropology, a brief survey of the functional theory of culture, with a special emphasis on our specific problem, will be the best method of presentation.

Functionalism differs from other sociological theories more definitely, perhaps, in its conception

From *American Journal of Sociology* 44(6) (1939), pp. 938–47, 948–62. Copyright © 1939 by *The American Journal of Sociology*. Reprinted by permission of University of Chicago Press.

Anthropology in Theory: Issues in Epistemology, Second Edition. Edited by Henrietta L. Moore and Todd Sanders.
© 2014 John Wiley & Sons, Inc. Published 2014 by John Wiley & Sons, Inc.

and definition of the individual than in any other respect. The functionalist includes in his analysis not merely the emotional as well as the intellectual side of mental processes, but also insists that man in his full biological reality has to be drawn into our analysis of culture. The bodily needs and environmental influences, and the cultural reactions to them, have thus to be studied side by side.

The field worker observes human beings acting within an environmental setting, natural and artificial; influenced by it, and in turn transforming it in co-operation with each other. He studies how men and women are motivated in their mutual relations by feelings of attraction and repulsion, by co-operative duties and privileges, by profits drawn and sacrifices made. The invisible network of social bonds, of which the organization of the group is made up, is defined by charters and codes – technological, legal, customary, and moral – to which every individual is differentially submitted, and which integrate the group into a whole. Since all rules and all tribal tradition are expressions in words – that is, symbols – the understanding of social organization implies an analysis of symbolism and language. Empirically speaking the field worker has to collect texts, statements, and opinions, side by side with the observation of behavior and the study of material culture.

In this brief preamble we have already insisted that the individual must be studied as a biological reality. We have indicated that the physical world must be part of our analysis, both as the natural milieu and as the body of tools and commodities produced by man. We have pointed out that individuals never cope with, or move within, their environment in isolation, but in organized groups, and that organization is expressed in traditional charters, which are symbolic in essence.

The Individual Organism under Conditions of Culture

Taking man as a biological entity it is clear that certain minima of conditions can be laid down which are indispensable to the personal welfare of the individual and to the continuation of the group. All human beings have to be nourished, they have to reproduce, and they require the maintenance of certain physical conditions:

ventilation, temperature within a definite range, a sheltered and dry place to rest, and safety from the hostile forces of nature, of animals, and of man. The physiological working of each individual organism implies the intake of food and of oxygen, occasional movement, and relaxation in sleep and recreation. The process of growth in man necessitates protection and guidance in its early stages and, later on, specific training.

We have listed here some of the essential conditions to which cultural activity, whether individual or collective, has instrumentally to conform. It is well to recall that these are only minimum conditions – the very manner in which they are satisfied in culture imposes certain additional requirements. These constitute new needs, which in turn have to be satisfied. The primary – that is, the biological – wants of the human organism are not satisfied naturally by direct contact of the individual organism with the physical environment. Not only does the individual depend on the group in whatever he achieves and whatever he obtains, but the group and all its individual members depend on the development of a material outfit, which in its essence is an addition to the human anatomy, and which entails corresponding modifications of human physiology.

In order to present our argument in a synoptic manner, let us concisely list in Column A of table 9.1 the basic needs of the individual. Thus "Nutrition (metabolism)" indicates not only the need for a supply of food and of oxygen, but also the conditions under which food can be prepared, eaten, digested, and the sanitary arrangements which this implies. "Reproduction" obviously means that the sexual urges of man and woman have to be satisfied, and the continuity of the group maintained. The entry "Bodily comforts" indicates that the human organism can be active and effective only within certain ranges of temperature; that it must be sheltered from dampness and drafts; that it must be given opportunities for rest and sleep. "Safety" again refers to all the dangers lurking in the natural environment, both for civilized and primitive: earthquakes and tidal waves, snowstorms and excessive insolation; it also indicates the need of protection from dangerous animals and human foes. "Relaxation" implies the need of the human organism for a

Table 9.1 Synoptic survey of biological and derived needs and their satisfaction in culture

A Basic needs (Individual)	B Direct responses (Organized, i.e., collective)	C Instrumental needs	D Responses to instrumental needs	E Symbolic and integrative needs	F Systems of thought and faith
Nutrition (metabolism)	Commissariat	Renewal of cultural apparatus	Economics	Transmission of experience by means of precise, consistent principles	Knowledge
Reproduction	Marriage and family				
Bodily comforts	Domicile and dress	Charters of behavior and their sanctions	Social control		
Safety	Protection and defense			Means of intellectual, emotional, and pragmatic control of destiny and chance	Magic Religion
Relaxation	Systems of play and repose	Renewal of personnel	Education		
Movement	Set activities and systems of communication				
Growth	Training and apprenticeship	Organization of force and compulsion	Political organization	Communal rhythm of recreation, exercise, and rest	Art Sports Games Ceremonial

rhythm of work by day and sleep at night, of intensive bodily exercise and rest, of seasons of recreation alternating with periods of practical activity. The entry "Movement" declares that human beings must have regular exercise of muscles and nervous system. "Growth" indicates the fact that the development of the human organism is culturally directed and redefined from infancy into ripe age.

It is clear that the understanding of any one of these entries of Column A brings us down immediately to the analysis of the individual organism. We see that any lack of satisfaction in any one of the basic needs must necessarily imply at least temporary maladjustment. In more pronounced forms, nonsatisfaction entails ill-health and decay through malnutrition, exposure to heat or cold,

to sun or moisture; or destruction by natural forces, animals, or man. Psychologically the basic needs are expressed in drives, desires, or emotions, which move the organism to the satisfaction of each need through systems of linked reflexes.

The science of culture, however, is concerned not with the raw material of anatomical and physiological endowment in the individual, but with the manner in which this endowment is modified by social influences. When we inquire how the bodily needs are satisfied under conditions of culture, we find the systems of direct response to bodily needs which are listed in Column B. And here we can see at once the complete dependence of the individual upon the group: each of these cultural responses is dependent upon organized collective activities, which are carried on according to a traditional scheme, and in which human beings not merely co-operate with one another but continue the achievements, inventions, devices, and theories inherited from previous generations.

In matters of nutrition, the individual human being does not act in isolation; nor does he behave in terms of mere anatomy and unadulterated physiology; we have to deal, instead, with personality, culturally molded. Appetite or even hunger is determined by the social milieu. Nowhere and never will man, however primitive, feed on the fruits of his environment. He always selects and rejects, produces and prepares. He does not depend on the physiological rhythm of hunger and satiety alone; his digestive processes are timed and trained by the daily routine of his tribe, nation, or class. He eats at definite times, and he goes for his food to his table. The table is supplied from the kitchen, the kitchen from the larder, and this again is replenished from the market or from the tribal food-supply system.

The symbolic expressions here used – "table," "kitchen," etc. – refer to the various phases of the process which separates the requirements of the organism from the natural sources of food supply, and which is listed in Column B as "Commissariat." They indicate that at each stage man depends on the group – family, club, or fraternity. And here again we use these expressions in a sense embracing primitive as well as civilized institutions, concerned with the production, preparation, and consumption of nourishment. The raw material of individual physiology is found everywhere refashioned by cultural and social determinism. The group has molded the individual in matters of taste, of tribal taboos, of the nutritive and symbolic value of food, as well as in the manners and modes of commensalism. Above all, the group, through economic co-operation, provides the stream of food supply.

One general point which we will have to make throughout our analysis is that the relation is not of the individual to society or *the* group. Even in matters of commissariat a number of groups make their appearance. In the most primitive society we would have the organization of food-gatherers, some institutions through which the distribution and apportionment of food takes place, and the commensal group of consumers – as a rule, the family. And were we to analyze each

of these groups from the point of view of nutrition, we would find that the place of the individual in each of them is determined by the differentiation as to skill, ability, interest, and appetite.

When we come to the cultural satisfaction of the individual impulses and emotions of sex and of the collective need for reproduction, we would see that human beings do not reproduce by nature alone. The full satisfaction of the impulse, as well as the socially legitimate effect of it, is subject to a whole set of rules defining courtship and marriage, prenuptial and extra-connubial intercourse, as well as the life within the family (Col. B, "Marriage and family"). The individual brings to this, obviously, his or her anatomical equipment, and the corresponding physiological impulses. He also contributes the capacity to develop tastes and interests, emotional attitudes and sentiments. Yet in all this the group not only imposes barriers and presents opportunities, suggests ideals and restrictions, and dictates values, but the community as a whole, through its system of legal rules, ethical and religious principles, and such concepts as honor, virtue, and sin, affects even the physiological attitude of man to woman. Take the most elementary physical impulse, such as the attraction of one sex by another. The very estimate of beauty and the appreciation of the bodily shape is modified by traditional reshaping: lip plugs and nose sticks, scarification and tattooing, the deformation of feet, breasts, waist, and head, and even of the organs of reproduction. In courtship and in selection for marriage such factors as rank, wealth, and economic efficiency enter into the estimate of the integral desirability and value of one mate for the other. And again the fullest expression of the impulse in the desire for children is affected by the systems of legal principle, economic interest, and religious ideology, which profoundly modify the innate substratum of human physiology.

Enough has been said to point out that here once more any empirical study of the reproductive process in a given culture must consider both the individual, the group, and the material apparatus of culture. The individual, in this most personal and subjective concern of human life, is submitted to the influence of tradition which penetrates right down to the processes of internal secretion and physiological response. The selective business of choice and of mating are constantly directed and influenced by the social setting. The most important stages (i.e., marriage and parenthood) have to receive a social hallmark in the contract of marriage. The legitimacy of the fruits of their bodily union depends upon whether they have conformed or not to the systems evolved in the community by traditional dictates.

Yet here once more we do not deal with the group and the individual, but we would have to consider a whole set of human agglomerations: the group of the two principal actors (i.e., marriage), the prospective family, the already developed families of each mate, the local community, and the tribe as the bearer of law, tradition, and their enforcement.

We must survey the other items of Column B more rapidly. The whole cultural system which corresponds to the necessity of keeping the human organism within certain limits of temperature, to the necessity of protecting it from the various inclemencies of wind and weather, obviously implies also the parallel consideration of individual and group. In constructing and maintaining even the simplest habitation, in the keeping of the fire alive, in the upkeep of roads and communications, the individual alone is not enough. He has to be trained for each task in technological and co-operative abilities, and he has to work in conjunction with others.

From the biological point of view the group acts as an indispensable medium for the realization of individual bodily needs. The organism within each culture is trained to accommodate and harden to certain conditions which might prove dangerous or even fatal without this training.

Here, therefore, we have again the two elements: the molding or conditioning of the human anatomy and physiology by collective influences and cultural apparatus, and the production of this apparatus through co-operative activities. Safety is achieved by organized defense, precautionary measures, and calculations based on tribal knowledge and foresight.

The development of the muscular system and the provision of movement are again provided for by the training of the individual organism and by the collective production of means of communication, of vehicles of transport, and of technical rules which define their use. The physical growth as guided by the influence of the group on the individual shows directly the dependence of the organism upon his social milieu. It is also a contribution of the individual to the community in that it supplies in each case an adequate member of one or several social units.

The Instrumental Imperatives of Culture

In glancing at our chart and comparing Columns A and B, we recognize that the first represents the biological needs of the individual organism which must be satisfied in every culture. Column B describes briefly the cultural responses to each of these needs. Culture thus appears first and foremost as a vast instrumental reality – the body of implements and commodities, charters of social organization, ideas and customs, beliefs and values – all of which allow man to satisfy his biological requirements through co-operation and within an environment refashioned and readjusted. The human organism, however, itself becomes modified in the process and readjusted to the type of situation provided by culture. In this sense culture is also a vast conditioning apparatus, which through training, the imparting of skills, the teaching of morals, and the development of tastes amalgamates the raw material of human physiology and anatomy with external elements, and through this supplements the bodily equipment and conditions the physiological processes. Culture thus produces individuals whose behavior cannot be understood by the study of anatomy and physiology alone, but has to be studied through the analysis of cultural determinism – that is, the processes of conditioning and molding. At the same time we see that from the very outset the existence of groups – that is, of individuals organized for co-operation and cultural give and take – is made indispensable by culture.

[...]

Man's anatomical endowment – which obviously includes not only his muscular system and his organs of digestion and reproduction, but also his brain – is an asset which will be developed under any system of culture when the individual is trained into a full tribesman or citizen of his community. The natural endowment of man presents also, we have seen, a system of needs which are, under culture, satisfied by organized and instrumentally adjusted responses. The empirical corollary to our analysis of basic needs has been that, under conditions of culture, the satisfaction of every organic need is achieved in an indirect, complicated, roundabout manner. It is this vast instrumentalism of human culture which has allowed man to master the environment in a manner incomparably more effective than any animal adaptation.

But every achievement and advantage demands its price to be paid. The complex cultural satisfaction of the primary biological needs imposes upon man new secondary or derived imperatives. In Column C of table 9.1 we have briefly listed these new imperatives. It is clear that the use of tools and implements, and the fact that man uses and destroys in the use – that is, consumes – such goods as food produced and prepared, clothing, building materials, and means of transportation, implies the necessity of a constant "Renewal of cultural apparatus."

Every cultural activity again is carried through co-operation. This means that man has to obey rules of conduct: life in common, which is essential to co-operation, means sacrifices and joint effort, the harnessing of individual contributions and work to a common end, and the distribution of the results according to traditional claims. Life in close co-operation – that is, propinquity – offers temptations as regards sex and property. Co-operation implies leadership, authority, and hierarchy, and these, primitive or civilized, introduce the strain of competitive vanity and rivalries in ambition. The rules of conduct which define duty and privilege, harness concupiscences and jealousies, and lay down the charter of family, municipality, tribe, and of every co-operative group, must therefore not only be known in every society, but they must be sanctioned – that is, provided with means of effective enforcement. Thus the need for code and for effective sanction is another derived imperative imposed on every organized group ("Charters of behavior and their sanctions," Col. C).

The members of such groups have to be renewed even as the material objects have to be replaced. Education in the widest sense – that is, the development of the infant into a fully fledged member of his group – is a type of activity which must exist in every culture and which must be

carried out specifically with reference to every type of organization ("Renewal of personnel," Col. C). The need for "Organization of force and compulsion" (Col. C) is universal.

In Column D we find briefly listed the cultural systems to be found in every human group as a response to the instrumental needs imposed by the roundabout type of cultural satisfactions. Thus "Economics," that is, systems of production, of distribution, and of consumption; organized systems of "Social control"; "Education," that is, traditional means by which the individual is brought up from infancy to tribal or national status; and "Political organization" into municipality, tribe, or state are universal aspects of every human society (cf. Col. D).

Let us look at our argument and at our table from the point of view of anthropological field work or that of a sociological student in a modern community – that is, from the angle of empirical observation. Our table indicates that field research on primitive or developed communities will have to be directed upon such aspects of culture as economics, legal institutions, education, and the political organization of the unit. Our inquiries will have to include a specific study of the individual, as well as of the group within which he has to live and work.

It is clear that in economic matters the individual member of a culture must acquire the necessary skills, learn how to work and produce, appreciate the prevalent values, manage his wealth, and regulate his consumption according to the established standard of living. Among primitive peoples there will be in all this a considerable uniformity as regards all individuals. In highly civilized communities, the differentiation of labor and of functions defines the place and the productive value of the individual in society. On the other hand, the collective aspect – that is, the organization of economics – is obviously one of the main factors in defining the level of culture and in determining a great many factors of social structure, hierarchy, rank, and status.

As regards social control, anthropological field work in primitive communities has in my opinion missed two essential points. First of all, the absence of clearly crystallized legal institutions does not mean that mechanisms of enforcement, effective sanctions, and at times complicated systems by which obligations and rights are determined are

BRONISLAW MALINOWSKI

absent. Codes, systems of litigation, and effective sanctions are invariably to be found as a by-product of the action and reaction between individuals within every organized group – that is, institution. The legal aspect is thus in primitive societies a by-product of the influence of organization upon individual psychology.

On the other hand, the study of the legal problem from the individual point of view reveals to us that the submission to tribal order is always a matter of long and effective training. In many primitive communities, the respect for the rule and the command is not inculcated very early in life – that is, parental authority is, as a rule, less rigidly and drastically forced upon children among so-called savages than among civilized peoples. At the same time there are certain tribal taboos, rules of personal decency, and of domestic morality that are impressed not so much by direct castigation as by the strong shock of ostracism and personal indignation which the child receives from parents, siblings, and contemporaries. In many communities we find that the child passes through a period of almost complete detachment from home, running around, playing about, and engaging in early activities with his playmates and contemporaries. In such activities strict teaching in tribal law is enforced more directly and poignantly than in the parental home. The fact remains that in every community the human being grows up into a law-abiding member; and he is acquainted with the tribal code; and that, through the variety of educational influences and considerations of self-interest, reasonable give and take, and balance of sacrifices and advantages, he follows the rulings of his traditional system of laws. Thus the study of how obedience to rules is inculcated in the individual during his life-history and the study of the mutualities of give and take within organized life in institutions constitute the full field for observation and analysis of the legal system in a primitive community. [...]

As regards education, we need only point out that this is the very process through which the total conditioning of the individual is accomplished, and that this always takes place within the organized groups into which the individual enters. He is born into the family, which almost invariably supplies his earliest and most important schooling in the earliest exercise of bodily

functions, in the learning of language, and in the acquisition of the simplest manners of cleanliness, conduct, and polite behavior. He then may, through a system of initiation, enter into a group of adolescents, of young warriors, and then of mature tribesmen. In every one of his technical and economic activities he passes through an apprenticeship in which he acquires the skills as well as the legal code of privilege and obligation of his group.

The Place of the Individual in Organized Groups

So far we have been speaking of the instrumental aspects of culture. Their definition is essentially functional. Since in every community there is the need for the renewal of the material apparatus of tools and implements and the production of goods of consumption, there must exist organized economics at every level of development. All the influences which transform the naked infant into a cultural personality have to be studied and recorded as educational agencies and constitute the aspect which we label "education." Since law and order have to be maintained, there must be a code of rules, a means of their readjustment and re-establishment when broken or infringed. In every community there exists, therefore, a juridical system. This functional approach is based on the empirical summing-up of the theory of derived needs and their relation to individual biology and cultural co-operation alike.

What is the relation between these functional aspects of culture and the organized forms of activities which we have called "institutions"? The aspects define the type of activity; at the same time every one of them is carried out by definite groups. Co-operation implies spatial contiguity. Two human beings of different sex who are engaged in the business of reproduction, and who have to rear, train, and provide for their offspring cannot be separated by a great distance in space. The members of the family are subject to the requirement of physical contiguity in the narrow sense. They form a household, and, since the household needs food, implies shelter, and the whole apparatus of domestic supply, it must not only be a reproductive but also an economic as well as an educational group united by the physical framework of habitation, utensils, and joint wealth.

Thus we find that one of the universal institutions of mankind, the family, is not merely a group of people thrown together into a common nook and shelter of the environment, wielding conjointly the definite apparatus of domicile, of material equipment, and a portion of productive territory, but also bound by a charter of rules defining their mutual relations, their activities, their rights, and their privileges. The charter of the family, moreover, invariably defines the position of the offspring by reference to the marriage contract of the parents. All the rules of legitimacy, of descent, of inheritance, and succession are contained in it.

The territorial principle of integration produces yet another group: the village community, municipal unit, horde, or territorial section. People unite into villages or migratory hordes, roaming together over a joint territory – partly because there are many tasks for which the workers have to unite; partly because they are the natural groups for immediate defense against animals and marauders; partly also because daily contact and co-operation develop the secondary bonds of acquaintance and affection. And here also, apart from the territorial unity with its rules of land tenure, corporate or individual, apart from the joint ownership of certain instruments such as communal buildings, apart from the permanent personnel of which such a group consists, we have also mythological, legal, and legendary charters from which the sentiments that enter into the bonds of membership are largely derived.

Another institution determined by the spatial principle and united through it on a variety of functions is the widest territorial group, the tribe. This unit as a rule is organized on the joint wielding of collective defense and aggression. It presents, even in the most primitive forms, a differentiation and hierarchy in administrative matters, in ceremonial proceedings, and in military or legal leadership.

In many parts of the world political organization on the territorial basis and cultural identity have to be distinguished. We have in our modern world the minority problem; in primitive communities the symbiosis of two races or two culturally different communities under the same political regime. Thus, identity of language, of custom, and of material culture constitutes another principle of differentiation, integrating each component part, and distinguishing it from the other.

We see, thus, that the actual concrete organization of human activities does not follow slavishly or exclusively the functional principles of type activities. This refers more specifically to primitive groups. As civilization develops, we find that law, education, and economics tend more and more to become separated from such forms of organization as the family, the village, or the age-grade. They become institutionalized and bring into being specialized professions, spatially set off, with constructions such as factories, courts, and schools. But even in more primitive groups we find that certain occupations each tend to become incorporated into a definite organization. Such groups as magicians, shamans, potters, blacksmiths, or herdsman fall into natural teams, receiving, at least on certain occasions, a spatial unity – that is, specific rights to portions of the territory and to a material outfit that they have to wield under a differential charter of rules and traditional prerogatives. On occasions they work and act together and in separation from the rest of the community.

The analysis into aspects and the analysis into institutions must be carried out simultaneously, if we want to understand any culture completely. The study of such aspects as economics, education, or social control and political organization defines the type and level of the characteristic activities in a culture. From the point of view of the individual, the study of these aspects discloses to us the totality of motives, interests, and values. From the point of view of the group it gives us an insight into the whole process by which the individual is conditioned or culturally formed and of the group mechanism of this process.

The analysis into institutions, on the other hand, is indispensable because they give us the concrete picture of the social organization within the culture. In each institution the individual obviously has to become cognizant of its charter; he has to learn how to wield the technical apparatus or that part of it with which his activities associate him; he has to develop the social attitudes and personal sentiments in which the bonds of organization consist.

Thus, in either of these analyses the twofold approach through the study of the individual with his innate tendencies and their cultural transformation, and the study of the group as the relationship and co-ordination of individuals, with reference to space, environment, and material equipment, is necessary.

The Cultural Definition of Symbolism

[...] Right through our arguments we have implied the transmission of rules, the development of general principles of conduct and of technique, and the existence of traditional systems of value and sentiment. This brings us to one more component of human culture, symbolism, of which language is the prototype. Symbolism must make its appearance with the earliest appearance of human culture. It is in essence that modification of the human organism which allows it to transform the physiological drive into a cultural value.

Were we to start from the most tangible aspect of culture and try to imagine the first discovery and use of an implement we would see that this already implies the birth of symbolism. Any attempt to reconstruct concretely and substantially the beginnings of culture must remain futile. But we can analyze some of the cultural achievements of early man and see what each of them implies in its essence.

Imagine the transition from subhuman to human management of any environmental factor: the discovery of fire, the use of such a simple unfashioned implement as a stick or a stone. Obviously, the object thus used becomes an effective element in culture only when it is permanently incorporated into collective use, and the use is traditionally transmitted. Thus the recognition of the principle of its utility was necessary, and this principle had to be fixed so as to be communicable from one individual to another and handed on to the next generation. This alone means that culture could not originate without some element of social organization – that is, of permanent relations between individuals and a continuity of generations – for otherwise communication would not be possible. Co-operation was born in the actual carrying-out of any complex task, such as making fire and keeping it, and the use of fire for the preparation of food, but

co-operation was even more necessary in the sharing and transmission even of the simplest principles of serviceability in production or use.

Incorporation and transmission implied one more element – the recognition of value. And it is here that we meet for the first time the mechanism of symbolization. The recognition of value means that a deferred and indirect mechanism for the satisfaction of an urge becomes the object of emotional response. Whether we imagine that the earliest human beings communicated by elementary sounds or by gesture and facial expression, embodied and connected with manual and bodily activity, symbolism was born with the first deferred and indirect satisfaction of any and every bodily need.

The urges of hunger and sex, the desire for personal comfort and security were refocused and transferred onto an object or a process which was the indirect means to the end of satisfying a bodily need. This transference of physiological urge on the secondary reality was in its essence symbolic. Any of the signs, gestures, or sounds which led to the definition of an object, to the reproduction of a process, to the fixation of technique, utility, and value were in essence as fully symbolic as a Chinese pictogram or a letter in our alphabet. For symbolism from its very inception had to be precise, in the sense that it provided a correct formula for the permanent incorporation and transmission of the cultural achievement. It had to be effective in that the drive of the physiological need was transferred and permanently hitched upon the object, which adequately though indirectly subserved the satisfaction of this drive. The sign, sound, or material presentation, the cultural reality to which it referred, and the bodily desire which was indirectly satisfied through it became thus integrated into a unity through the process of conditioned reflex and conditioned stimulus which has become the basis of our understanding of habit, custom, and language through the researches of Pavlov and Bechtyerev.

This analysis proves again that the most important and elementary process – the creation of cultural symbolism and values – cannot be understood without direct reference to individual psychology and physiology. The formation of habits, skills, values, and symbols consists essentially in the conditioning of the human organism to responses which are determined not by nature but by culture.

On the other hand, the social setting is indispensable, because it is the group which maintains and transmits the elements of symbolism, and it is the group which trains each individual and develops in him the knowledge of technique, the understanding of symbols, and the appreciation of values. We have seen also that organization – that is, the personal bonds which relate the members of a group – are based on the psychology and physiology of the individual, because they consist in emotional responses, in the appreciation of mutual services, and in the apprenticeship to the performance of specific tasks by each man within the setting of his group.

The Individual Contributions and Group Activities in Knowledge and Belief

The understanding of the symbolic process allows us to consider another class of necessities imposed upon man by culture. Obviously, the member of any group has to be able to communicate with his fellow-beings. But this communication is never, not even in the highly differentiated groups of today, a matter of detached, abstract transmission of thought. In primitive communities, language is used even more exclusively for pragmatic purposes. Early human beings used language and symbolism primarily as a means of co-ordinating action or of standardizing techniques and imparting prescriptions for industrial, social, and ritual behavior.

Let us look more closely at some of these systems. To every type of standardized technique there corresponds a system of knowledge embodied in principles, which can be imparted to those who learn, and which help to co-operate those who are already trained. Principles of human knowledge based on true experience and on logical reasoning, and embodied in verbal statements, exist even among the lowest primitives. The view that primitive man has no rudiments of science, that he lives in a world of mystical or magical ideas, is not correct. No culture, however simple, could survive unless its techniques and devices, its weapons and economic pursuits, were based on the sound appreciation of experience and on a logical

formulation of its principles. The very first human beings who discovered and incorporated fire-making as a useful art had to appreciate and define the material to be used, its conditions, as well as the technique of friction and of fanning the spark in the tinder. The making of stone implements, and even the selection of useful stones, implied a body of descriptive rules which had to be communicated from one person to another, both in co-operation and in transmission from those who had the experience to those who had to acquire it. Thus we can list in Column E of table 9.1 the necessity of general symbolic principles, which are embodied as a rule not merely in verbal statements but in verbal statements associated with the actual demonstration of technique and material, of physical context, and of utility and value (Col. E, "Transmission of experience by means of precise, consistent principles"). Thus knowledge, or a body of abstract symbols and verbal principles containing the capacity to appear as empirical fact and sound reasoning, is an implication of all cultural behavior even in its earliest beginnings.

In Column F we thus list knowledge as one of the systems of symbolic integration. By knowledge we mean the whole body of experience and of principle embodied in language and action, in techniques and organized pursuits – in food-gathering, with all it implies of natural history, in agriculture, hunting and fishing, sailing and trekking. Knowledge also implies, at every stage of development, the familiarity with the rules of co-operation and with all social obligations and privileges.

But once we realize that even the most primitive human beings developed systems of thought – that is, of foresight, of calculation, and of systematic planning – we are led to another psychological necessity connected with the cultural satisfaction of primary needs. The use of knowledge not only shows man how to achieve certain ends, it also reveals to him the fundamental uncertainties and limitations of his existence. The very fact that man, however primitive, has to think clearly, has to look ahead and also remember the successes and failures of his past experience makes him realize that not every problem can be solved, not every desire satisfied, by his own efforts.

From the point of view of individual psychology we see that reasonable processes and

emotional reactions intertwine. The very calculations, and the fact that the principles of knowledge
have to be built up into systems of thought, subject man to fear as well as to hope. He knows that
his desire is often thwarted and that his expectations are subject to chance.

It is enough to remember that all human beings
are affected by ill-health and have to face death
ultimately, that misfortune and natural catastrophes, and elements disturbing the favorable run
of food-providing activities, always loom on
man's mental horizon. The occurrence of such
acts of destiny engender not merely reflection,
thought, and emotional responses; they force the
human group to take action. Plans have to be
reorganized whenever a natural catastrophe
occurs. The group becomes disintegrated by the
death of one of its members, especially if he is a
leading individual. Calamity or misfortune thus
affects the individual personally, even as it disor-
ganizes the group.

Which is the new, highly derived, yet emotionally founded need or imperative which these considerations entail? We see that acting as he always
does within an atmosphere of uncertainty, with
his hopes raised and fears or anxieties aroused,
man needs certain positive affirmations of stability, success, and continuity. The dogmatic affirmations of religion and magic satisfy these needs.
Whether we take such early beliefs as totemism,
magic, or ancestor worship; or these beliefs more
fully developed into the concept of providence, a
pantheon of gods, or one divinity; we see that
man affirms his convictions that death is not real
nor yet final, that man is endowed with a personality which persists even after death, and that
there are forces in the environment which can be
tuned up and propitiated to the trend of human
hopes and desires.

We can thus realize the dogmatic essence of religion by the analysis of individual mental processes.
But here also the group enters immediately and no
purely physiological or psychological analysis of
the human organism is sufficient. In the first place,
the reaction of man to death and disaster cannot be
understood merely in terms of his concern with
himself. It is the care for those who depend on him,
and the sorrow for those to whom he was attached
and who disappear, that provide as much inspiration to religious belief as does the self-centered
concern for his own welfare.

Religion, however, does not end or even begin
with dogmatic affirmations. It is a system of organized activities, in ritual as well as in ethics. Belief
at no stage, certainly not the primitive levels, is a
mere metaphysical system. It is a mode of ritual
activity which allows man, whether by constraint
or persuasion, to manage the supernatural world
brought into being by his desires, hopes, fears,
and anticipations. All ritual behavior, whether at
burial and mourning, at commemorative ceremony and sacrifice, or even in a magical
performance, is social. It is social in the sense that
often men and women pray, worship, and chant
their magic formula in common. Even when a
magical act is performed in solitude and secrecy,
it invariably has social consequences. Ritual is
also social in the sense that the end to be obtained,
the integration of the group after death, the con-
juring-up of rain and fertility, of a rich haul in
fishing, and hunting, or of a successful sailing
expedition, concerns the interests not of a single
person but of a group. […]

In all this we see once more that a parallel
consideration of individual and organized group
is indispensable in order to give us insight into
the foundations, as well as the forms, of magic
and religion. The structure of these cultural
realities entails dogmatic thought – that is,
positive affirmations about the existence of good
and evil, of benevolent and hostile forces,
residing in the environment and capable of
influencing some of its responses. Such dogmatic
affirmations contain recipes as to how the supernatural forces can be controlled through incan-
tation and prayer, through ritual, sacrifice, and
collective or individual sacrament.

Since religion consists by and large of collective
efforts to achieve ends beneficent to one and all,
we find that every religious system has also its
ethical factors. Even in a magical ceremony, performed for a successful war or sailing expedition,
for the counteracting of sorcery, or for the fertility
of the fields, every participating individual and
the leader of the performance is carrying out a
task in which he subordinates his personal
interest to the communal welfare. Such ceremonies carry with them also taboos and restrictions, duties and obligations. The ethics of a
magical system consist in all these rules and
restrictions to which the individual has to submit
in the interests of the group.

The duties of mourning and burial, of communal sacrifice to ancestor ghosts or to totemic beings, also entail a number of rules, regulations, and principles of conduct which constitute the ethical aspect of such a ritual act. The structure of religion, therefore, consists in a dogmatic system of affirmations, in the technique of ritual, and in the rules and precepts of elementary ethics, which define the subordination of the individual to group welfare. [...]

Summary and Conclusions

This brief outline of the functional approach to anthropological field work and comparative theory of culture shows that at every step we had to study, in a parallel and co-ordinated manner, the individual and the group, as well as their relations. The understanding of both these entities, however, must be supplemented by including the reality of environment and material culture. The problem of the relation between group and individual is so pervading and ubiquitous that it cannot be treated detached from any question of culture and of social or psychological process. A theory which does not present and include at every step the definitions of individual contributions and of their integration into collective action stands condemned. The fact that functionalism implies this problem constantly and consistently may be taken as a proof that, so far as it does, it does not neglect one of the most essential problems of all social science.

Indeed, functionalism is, in its essence, the theory of transformation of organic – that is, individual – needs into derived cultural necessities and imperatives. Society by the collective wielding of the conditioning apparatus molds the individual into a cultural personality. The individual, with his physiological needs and psychological processes, is the ultimate source and aim of all tradition, activities, and organized behavior. [...]

10

The Concept and Method
of Cultural Ecology

Julian H. Steward

[…] Since man is a domesticated animal, he is
affected physically by all his cultural activities.
The evolution of the Hominidae is closely related
to the emergence of culture, while the appearance
of *Homo sapiens* is probably more the result of
cultural causes than of physical causes. The use of
tools, fire, shelter, clothing, new foods, and other
material adjuncts of existence were obviously
important in evolution, but social customs should
not be overlooked. Social groups as determined by
marriage customs as well as by economic activities
in particular environments have undoubtedly
been crucial in the differentiations of local populations and may even have contributed to the
emergence of varieties and subraces of men.

The problem of explaining man's cultural
behavior is of a different order than that of
explaining his biological evolution. Cultural patterns are not genetically derived and, therefore,
cannot be analyzed in the same way as organic
features. Although social ecologists are paying
more and more attention to culture in their
enquiries, an explanation of culture per se has
not, so far as I can see, become their major
objective. Culture has merely acquired greater

emphasis as one of many features of the local web
of life, and the tools of analysis are still predominantly borrowed from biology. Since one of
the principal concepts of biological ecology is
the community – the assemblage of plants and
animals which interact within a locality – social
or human ecology emphasizes the human
community as the unit of study. But "community"
is a very general and meaningless abstraction. If it
is conceived in cultural terms, it may have many
different characteristics depending upon the
purpose for which it is defined. The tendency,
however, has been to conceive of human and
biological communities in terms of the biological
concepts of competition, succession, territorial
organization, migration, gradients, and the like.
All of these derived fundamentally from the fact
that underlying biological ecology is a relentless
and raw struggle for existence both within and
between species – a competition which is ultimately determined by the genetic potentials
for adaptation and survival in particular biotic-
environmental situations. Biological co-operation,
such as in many forms of symbiosis, is strictly
auxiliary to survival of the species.

From *Theory of Culture Change: The Methodology of Multilinear Evolution* (Urbana: University of Illinois Press, 1955),
pp. 31–42, 224, 226–7. Copyright © 1955 by the Board of Trustees of the University of Illinois. Copyright renewed 1983
by Jane C. Steward. Used with permission of the University of Illinois Press.

Anthropology in Theory: Issues in Epistemology, Second Edition. Edited by Henrietta L. Moore and Todd Sanders.
© 2014 John Wiley & Sons, Inc. Published 2014 by John Wiley & Sons, Inc.

Human beings do not react to the web of life solely through their genetically-derived organic equipment. Culture, rather than genetic potential for adaptation, accommodation, and survival, explains the nature of human societies. Moreover, the web of life of any local human society may extend far beyond the immediate physical environment and biotic assemblage. In states, nations, and empires, the nature of the local group is determined by these larger institutions no less than by its local adaptations. Competition of one sort or another may be present, but it is always culturally determined and as often as not co-operation rather than competition may be prescribed. If, therefore, the nature of human communities is the objective of analysis, explanations will be found through use of cultural historical concepts and methods rather than biological concepts, although, as we shall show, historical methods alone are insufficient.

Many writers on social or human ecology have sensed the need to distinguish between biological and cultural phenomena and methods, but they have not yet drawn clear distinctions. Thus, Hollingshead recognizes a difference between an "ecological order [which] is primarily rooted in competition" and "social organization [which] has evolved out of communication" (Hollingshead, 1940; Adams, 1935, 1940). This attempt to conceptualize competition as a category wholly distinct from other aspects of culturally determined behavior is, of course, artificial. Bates (1953), a human biologist, recognizes the importance of culture in determining the nature of communities, but he does not make clear whether he would use human ecology to explain the range of man's biological adaptation under environmental-cultural situations or whether he is interested in man's culture. The so-called Chicago school of Park, Burgess, and their followers were also primarily interested in communities of human beings, especially urban communities. Their methodology as applied to Chicago and other cities treats the components of each as if they were genetically determined species. In analyzing the zoning of a modern city, such categories as retail businesses, wholesale houses, manufacturing firms, and residences of various kinds, and even such additional features as rate of delinquency, are considered as if each were a biological species in competition with one another for zones within the urban area. Such studies are extremely enlightening as descriptive analysis of spacial distributions of kinds of activities within a modern Euro-American city. They do not, however, necessarily throw any light on world-wide ecological urban adaptations, for in other cultures and periods city zoning followed very different culturally prescribed principles. For example, most of the cities of ancient civilizations were rather carefully planned by a central authority for defensive, administrative, and religious functions. Free enterprise, which might have allowed competition for zones between the institutions and sub-societies arising from these functions, was precluded by the culture.

A fundamental scientific problem is involved in these different meanings attached to ecology. Is the objective to find universal laws or processes, or is it to explain special phenomena? In biology, the law of evolution and the auxiliary principles of ecology are applicable to all webs of life regardless of the species and physical environments involved. In social science studies, there is a similar effort to discover universal processes of cultural change. But such processes cannot be conceptualized in biological terms. The social science problem of explaining the origin of unlike behavior patterns found among different societies of the human species is very different from the problems of biological evolution. Analyzing environmental adaptations to show how new cultural patterns arise is a very different matter than seeking universal similarities in such adaptation. Until the processes of cultural ecology are understood in the many particulars exemplified by different cultures in different parts of the world a formulation of universal processes will be impossible.

Hawley, who has given the most recent and comprehensive statement of social ecology (Hawley, 1950), takes cultural phenomena into account far more than his predecessors. He states that man reacts to the web of life as a cultural animal rather than as a biological species. "Each acquisition of a new technique or a new use for an old technique, regardless of the source of its origin, alters man's relations with the organisms about him and changes his position in the biotic community." But, preoccupied with the totality of phenomena within the locale and apparently with a search for universal relationships, Hawley makes the local community the focus of interest (Hawley, 1950:68). The kinds of generalizations which might be found are indicated by the statement: "If we had sufficient knowledge of a preliterate people to enable us to compare the structure of residence groups arranged in order of size from smallest to largest, we should undoubtedly observe the same phenomena – each increment in size is accompanied by an advance in the complexity of organization" (Hawley, 1950:197). This is the kind of self-evident generalization made by the unilinear evolutionists: cultural progress is manifest in increasing populations, internal specialization, over-all state controls, and other general features.

Hawley is uncertain in his position regarding the effect of environmental adaptations on culture. He states: "The weight of evidence forces the conclusion that the physical environment exerts but a permissive and limiting effect" (Hawley, 1950:90), but he also says that "each habitat not only permits but to a certain extent necessitates a distinctive mode of life" (Hawley, 1950:190). The first statement closely conforms with the widely accepted anthropological position that historical factors are more important than environmental factors, which may be permissive or prohibitive of culture change but are never causative. The second is nearer to the thesis of this paper that cultural ecological adaptations constitute creative processes.

Culture, History, and Environment

While the human and social ecologists have seemingly sought universal ecological principles and relegated culture in its local varieties to a secondary place, anthropologists have been so preoccupied with culture and its history that they have accorded environment only a negligible role. Owing in part to reaction against the "environmental determinists," such as Huntington and Semple, and in part to cumulative evidence that any culture increases in complexity to a large extent because of diffused practices, the orthodox view now holds that history, rather than adaptive processes, explains culture. Since historical "explanations" of culture employ the culture area concept, there is an apparent contradiction. The culture area is a construct of behavioral uniformities which occur within an area of environmental uniformities. It is assumed that cultural and natural areas are generally coterminous because the culture represents an adjustment to the particular environment. It is assumed further, however, that various different patterns may exist in any natural area and that unlike cultures may exist in similar environments.

The cultural-historical approach is, however, also one of relativism. Since cultural differences are not directly attributable to environmental differences and most certainly not to organic or racial differences, they are merely said to represent divergences in cultural history, to reflect tendencies of societies to develop in unlike ways. Such tendencies are not explained. A distinctive pattern develops, it is said, and henceforth is the primary determinant of whether innovations are accepted. Environment is relegated to a purely secondary and passive role. It is considered prohibitive or permissive, but not creative. It allows man to carry on some kinds of activities and it prevents others. The origins of these activities are pushed back to a remote point in time or space, but they are not explained. This view has been best expressed by Forde, who writes:

Neither the world distributions of the various economies, nor their development and relative importance among the particular peoples, can be regarded as simple functions of physical conditions and natural resources. Between the physical environment and human activity there is always a middle term, a collection of specific objectives and values, a body of knowledge and belief: in other words, a cultural pattern. That the culture itself is not static, that it is adaptable and modifiable in relation to physical conditions, must not be allowed to obscure the fact that adaptation proceeds by discoveries and inventions which are themselves in no sense inevitable and which are, in any individual community, nearly all of them acquisitions or impositions from without. The peoples of whole continents have failed to make discoveries that might at first blush seem obvious. Equally important are the restrictions placed by social patterns and religious concepts on the utilization of certain resources or on adaptations to physical conditions (Forde, 1949:463).

The habitat at one and the same time circumscribes and affords scope for cultural development in relation to the pre-existing equipment and tendency of a particular society, and to any new concepts and equipment that may reach it from without (Forde, 1949:464).

But if geographical determinism fails to account for the existence and distribution of economies, economic determinism is equally inadequate in accounting for the social and political organizations, the religious beliefs and the psychological attitudes which may be found in the cultures based on those economies. Indeed, the economy may owe as much to the social and ritual pattern as does the character of society to the economy. The possession of particular methods of hunting or cultivating, of certain cultivated plants or domestic animals, in no wise defines the pattern of society. Again, there is interaction and on a new plane. As physical conditions may limit the possibilities of the economy, so the economy may in turn be a limiting or stimulating factor in relation to the size, density and stability of human settlement, and to the scale of the social and political unit. But it is only one such factor, and advantage may not be taken of the opportunities it affords. The tenure and transmission of land and other property, the development and relations of social classes, the nature of government, the religious and ceremonial life – all these are parts of a social superstructure, the development of which is conditioned not only by the foundations of habitat and economy, but by complex interactions within its own fabric and by external contacts, often largely indifferent to both the physical background and to the basic economy alike (Forde, 1949:465).

Cultural Ecology

Cultural ecology differs from human and social ecology in seeking to explain the origin of particular cultural features and patterns which characterize different areas rather than to derive general principles applicable to any cultural-environmental situation. It differs from the relativistic and neo-evolutionist conceptions of culture history in that it introduces the local environment as the extracultural factor in the fruitless assumption that culture comes from culture. Thus, cultural ecology presents both a problem and a method. The problem is to ascertain whether the adjustments of human societies to their environments require particular modes of behavior or whether they permit latitude for a certain range of possible

behavior patterns. Phrased in this way, the problem also distinguishes cultural ecology from "environmental determinism" and its related theory "economic determinism," which are generally understood to contain their conclusions within the problem.

The problem of cultural ecology must be further qualified, however, through use of a supplementary conception of culture. According to the holistic view, all aspects of culture are functionally interdependent upon one another. The degree and kind of interdependency, however, are not the same with all features. Elsewhere, I have offered the concept of *cultural core* – the constellation of features which are most closely related to subsistence activities and economic arrangements. The core includes such social, political, and religious patterns as are empirically determined to be closely connected with these arrangements. Innumerable other features may have great potential variability because they are less strongly tied to the core. These latter, or secondary features, are determined to a greater extent by purely cultural-historical factors – by random innovations or by diffusion – and they give the appearance of outward distinctiveness to cultures with similar cores. Cultural ecology pays primary attention to those features which empirical analysis shows to be most closely involved in the utilization of environment in culturally prescribed ways.

The expression "culturally prescribed ways" must be taken with caution, for its anthropological usage is frequently "loaded." The normative concept, which views culture as a system of mutually reinforcing practices backed by a set of attitudes and values, seems to regard all human behavior as so completely determined by culture that environmental adaptations have no effect. It considers that the entire pattern of technology, land use, land tenure, and social features derive entirely from culture. Classical illustrations of the primacy of cultural attitudes over common sense are that the Chinese do not drink milk nor the Eskimo eat seals in summer.

Cultures do, of course, tend to perpetuate themselves, and change may be slow for such reasons as those cited. But over the millennia cultures in different environments have changed tremendously, and these changes are basically traceable to new adaptations required by changing technology and productive arrangements. Despite occasional cultural barriers, the useful arts have spread extremely widely, and the instances in which they have not been accepted because of pre-existing cultural patterns are insignificant. In pre-agricultural times, which comprised perhaps 99 per cent of cultural history, technical devices for hunting, gathering, and fishing seem to have diffused largely to the limits of their usefulness. Clubs, spears, traps, bows, fire, containers, nets, and many other cultural features spread across many areas, and some of them throughout the world. Later, domesticated plants and animals also spread very rapidly within their environmental limits, being stopped only by formidable ocean barriers.

Whether or not new technologies are valuable is, however, a function of the society's cultural level as well as of environmental potentials. All pre-agricultural societies found hunting and gathering techniques useful. Within the geographical limits of herding and farming, these techniques were adopted. More advanced techniques, such as metallurgy, were acceptable only if certain pre-conditions, such as stable population, leisure time, and internal specialization were present. These conditions could develop only from the cultural ecological adaptations of an agricultural society.

The concept of cultural ecology, however, is less concerned with the origin and diffusion of technologies than with the fact that they may be used differently and entail different social arrangements in each environment. The environment is not only permissive or prohibitive with respect to these technologies, but special local features may require social adaptations which have far-reaching consequences. Thus, societies equipped with bows, spears, surrounds, chutes, brush-burning, deadfalls, pitfalls, and other hunting devices may differ among themselves because of the nature of the terrain and fauna. If the principal game exists in large herds, such as herds of bison or caribou, there is advantage in co-operative hunting, and considerable numbers of peoples may remain together throughout the year. [...] If, however, the game is nonmigratory, occurring in small and scattered groups, it is better hunted by small groups of men who know their territory well [...]. In each case, the cultural repertory of hunting devices may be about the same, but in the first case the society will consist of multifamily or multilineage groups, as among

the Athabaskans and Algonkians of Canada and probably the pre-horse Plains bison hunters, and in the second case it will probably consist of localized patrilineal lineages or bands, as among the Bushmen, Congo Negritoes, Australians, Tasmanians, Fuegians, and others. These latter groups consisting of patrilineal bands are similar, as a matter of fact, not because their total environments are similar – the Bushmen, Australians, and southern Californians live in deserts, the Negritoes in rain forests, and the Fuegians in a cold, rainy area – but because the nature of the game and therefore of their subsistence problem is the same in each case.

Other societies having about the same technological equipment may exhibit other social patterns because the environments differ to the extent that the cultural adaptations must be different. For example, the Eskimo use bows, spears, traps, containers, and other widespread technological devices, but, owing to the limited occurrence of fish and sea mammals, their population is so sparse and co-operative hunting is so relatively unrewarding that they are usually dispersed in family groups. For a different but equally compelling reason the Nevada Shoshoni [...] were also fragmented into family groups. In the latter case, the scarcity of game and the predominance of seeds as the subsistence basis greatly restricted economic co-operation and required dispersal of the society into fairly independent family groups.

In the examples of the primitive hunting, gathering, and fishing societies, it is easy to show that if the local environment is to be exploited by means of the culturally-derived techniques, there are limitations upon the size and social composition of the groups involved. When agricultural techniques are introduced, man is partially freed from the exigencies of hunting and gathering, and it becomes possible for considerable aggregates of people to live together. Larger aggregates, made possible by increased population and settled communities, provide a higher level of sociocultural integration, the nature of which is determined by the local type of sociocultural integration. [...]

The adaptive processes we have described are properly designated ecological. But attention is directed not simply to the human community as part of the total web of life but to such cultural features as are affected by the adaptations. This in turn requires that primary attention be paid only to relevant environmental features rather than to the web of life for its own sake. Only those features to which the local culture ascribes importance need be considered.

The Method of Cultural Ecology

Although the concept of environmental adaptation underlies all cultural ecology, the procedures must take into account the complexity and level of the culture. It makes a great deal of difference whether a community consists of hunters and gatherers who subsist independently by their own efforts or whether it is an outpost of a wealthy nation, which exploits local mineral wealth and is sustained by railroads, ships, or airplanes. In advanced societies, the nature of the culture core will be determined by a complex technology and by productive arrangements which themselves have a long cultural history.

Three fundamental procedures of cultural ecology are as follows:

First, the interrelationship of exploitative or productive technology and environment must be analyzed. This technology includes a considerable part of what is often called "material culture," but all features may not be of equal importance. In primitive societies, subsistence devices are basic: weapons and instruments for hunting and fishing; containers for gathering and storing food; transportational devices used on land and water; sources of water and fuel; and, in some environments, means of counteracting excessive cold (clothing and housing) or heat. In more developed societies, agriculture and herding techniques and manufacturing of crucial implements must be considered. In an industrial world, capital and credit arrangements, trade systems and the like are crucial. Socially-derived needs – special tastes in foods, more ample housing and clothing, and a great variety of appurtenances to living – become increasingly important in the productive arrangement as culture develops; and yet these originally were probably more often effects of basic adaptations than causes.

Relevant environmental features depend upon the culture. The simpler cultures are more directly conditioned by the environment than advanced ones. In general, climate, topography, soils, hydrography, vegetational cover, and fauna are crucial, but some features may be more important

than others. The spacing of water holes in the desert may be vital to a nomadic seed-gathering people, the habits of game will affect the way hunting is done, and the kinds and seasons of fish runs will determine the habits of riverine and coastal tribes.

Second, the behavior patterns involved in the exploitation of a particular area by means of a particular technology must be analyzed. Some subsistence patterns impose very narrow limits on the general mode of life of the people, while others allow considerable latitude. The gathering of wild vegetable products is usually done by women who work alone or in small groups. Nothing is gained by co-operation and in fact women come into competition with one another. Seed-gatherers, therefore, tend to fragment into small groups unless their resources are very abundant. Hunting, on the other hand, may be either an individual or a collective project, and the nature of hunting societies is determined by culturally prescribed devices for collective hunting as well as by the species. When surrounds, grass-firing, corrals, chutes, and other co-operative methods are employed, the take per man may be much greater than what a lone hunter could bag. Similarly, if circumstances permit, fishing may be done by groups of men using dams, weirs, traps, and nets as well as by individuals.

The use of these more complex and frequently co-operative techniques, however, depends not only upon cultural history – i.e., invention and diffusion – which makes the methods available but upon the environment and its flora and fauna. Deer cannot be hunted advantageously by surrounds, whereas antelope and bison may best be hunted in this way. Slash-and-burn farming in tropical rain forests requires comparatively little co-operation in that a few men clear the land after which their wives plant and cultivate the crops. Dry farming may or may not be co-operative; and irrigation farming may run the gamut of enterprises of ever-increasing size based on collective construction of waterworks.

The exploitative patterns not only depend upon the habits concerned in the direct production of food and of goods but upon facilities for transporting the people to the source of supply or the goods to the people. Watercraft have been a major factor in permitting the growth of settlements beyond what would have been possible for a foot people. Among all nomads, the horse has had an almost revolutionary effect in promoting the growth of large bands.

The third procedure is to ascertain the extent to which the behavior patterns entailed in exploiting the environment affect other aspects of culture. Although technology and environment prescribe that certain things must be done in certain ways if they are to be done at all, the extent to which these activities are functionally tied to other aspects of culture is a purely empirical problem. I have shown elsewhere [...] that the occurrence of patrilineal bands among certain hunting peoples and of fragmented families among the Western Shoshoni is closely determined by their subsistence activities, whereas the Carrier Indians are known to have changed from a composite hunting band to a society based upon moieties and inherited statuses without any change in the nature of subsistence. In the irrigation areas of early civilizations [...] the sequence of socio-political forms or cultural cores seems to have been very similar despite variation in many outward details or secondary features of these cultures. If it can be established that the productive arrangements permit great latitude in the sociocultural type, then historical influences may explain the particular type found. The problem is the same in considering modern industrial civilizations. The question is whether industrialization allows such latitude that political democracy, communism, state socialism, and perhaps other forms are equally possible, so that strong historical influences, such as diffused ideology – e.g., propaganda – may supplant one type with another, or whether each type represents an adaptation which is specific to the area.

The third procedure requires a genuinely holistic approach, for if such factors as demography, settlement pattern, kinship structures, land tenure, land use, and other key cultural features are considered separately, their interrelationships to one another and to the environment cannot be grasped. Land use by means of a given technology permits a certain population density. The clustering of this population will depend partly upon where resources occur and upon transportational devices. The composition of these clusters will be a function of their size, of the nature of subsistence activities, and of cultural-historical factors. The ownership of land or resources will reflect subsistence activities on the one hand and the composition of the group on the other. Warfare may be related to the complex of factors just mentioned. In some cases, it may arise out of competition for resources and have a national character. Even when fought for individual honors or religious purposes, it may serve to nucleate settlements in a way that must be related to subsistence activities.

The Methodological Place of Cultural Ecology

Cultural ecology has been described as a methodological tool for ascertaining how the adaptation of a culture to its environment may entail certain changes. In a larger sense, the problem is to determine whether similar adjustments occur in similar environments. Since in any given environment, culture may develop through a succession of very unlike periods, it is sometimes pointed out that environment, the constant, obviously has no relationship to cultural type. This difficulty disappears, however, if the level of sociocultural integration represented by each period is taken into account. Cultural types therefore, must be conceived as constellations of core features which arise out of environmental adaptations and which represent similar levels of integration. [...]

References

Adams, C. C., 1935. "The Relations of General Ecology to Human Ecology," *Ecology*, XVI, 316–35.

Adams, C. C., 1940. "Introductory Note to Symposium on Relation of Ecology to Human Welfare," *Ecological Monographs*, X, 307–11.

Bates, Marston, 1953. "Human Ecology," in *Anthropology Today: An Encyclopedic Inventory*. Ed. A. L. Kroeber. Chicago: University of Chicago Press. Pp. 700–13.

Forde, C. Daryll, 1949. *Habitat, Economy and Society*. London: Methuen and Company.

Hawley, Amos H., 1950. *Human Ecology: A Theory of Community Structure*. New York: The Ronald Press.

Hollingshead, A. B., 1940. "Human Ecology and Human Society," *Ecological Monographs*, X.

11

Energy and the Evolution of Culture

Leslie A. White

The degree of civilization of any epoch, people, or group of peoples, is measured by ability to utilize energy for human advancement or needs.

George Grant MacCurdy,
Human Origins[1]

[T]he history of civilization becomes the history of man's advancing control over energy.
Wilhelm Ostwald, "The Modern
Theory of Energetics"[2]

[...] "[C]ulture" is the name of a distinct order, or class, of phenomena, namely, those things and events that are dependent upon the exercise of a mental ability, peculiar to the human species, that we have termed "symbolling." To be more specific, culture consists of material objects – tools, utensils, ornaments, amulets, etc. – acts, beliefs, and attitudes that function in contexts characterized by symbolling. It is an elaborate mechanism, an organization of exosomatic ways and means employed by a particular animal species, man, in the struggle for existence and survival.

One of the significant attributes of culture is its transmissibility by non-biological means. Culture in all its aspects, material, social, and ideological, is easily and readily transmitted from one individual, one generation, one age, one people, or one region, to another by social mechanisms. Culture is, so to speak, a form of social heredity. We thus view culture as a continuum, a suprabiological, extra-somatic order of things and events, that flows down through time from one age to the next.

We have seen also, in preceding chapters, that since culture constitutes a distinct order of phenomena, it can be described and interpreted in terms of principles and laws of its own. Cultural elements act and react upon one another in their own way. We can discover the principles of behavior of various sub-classes of cultural elements and of cultural systems as a whole; and we can formulate the *laws* of cultural phenomena and systems.

We now propose to sketch the evolution of culture from its beginning upon an anthropoid level to the present time. We may regard the human race – man – as a one. We may likewise think of all of the various cultures, or cultural traditions, as

From *The Science of Culture: A Study of Man and Civilization* (New York: Farrar, Strauss and Company, 1949), pp. 363–93, 423, 427, 431–3. Copyright © 1949 by Leslie White. Reprinted by permission of Robert L. Carneiro, American Museum of Natural History.

Anthropology in Theory: Issues in Epistemology, Second Edition. Edited by Henrietta L. Moore and Todd Sanders.
© 2014 John Wiley & Sons, Inc. Published 2014 by John Wiley & Sons, Inc.

constituting a single entity: the culture of mankind. We may, therefore, address ourselves to the task of tracing the course of the development of this culture from its source to the present day.

Let us return for a moment to a further consideration of the structure and function of the organization of things and processes, the *system*, that we call culture. Culture is an organized, integrated system. But we may distinguish subdivisions within, or aspects of, this system. For our purpose, we shall distinguish three subsystems of culture, namely, technological, sociological, and ideological systems. The technological system is composed of the material, mechanical, physical, and chemical instruments, together with the techniques of their use, by means of which man, as an animal species, is articulated with his natural habitat. Here we find the tools of production, the means of subsistence, the materials of shelter, the instruments of offense and defense. The sociological system is made up of interpersonal relations expressed in patterns of behavior, collective as well as individual. In this category we find social, kinship, economic, ethical, political, military, ecclesiastical, occupational and professional, recreational, etc., systems. The ideological system is composed of ideas, beliefs, knowledge, expressed in articulate speech or other symbolic form. Mythologies and theologies, legend, literature, philosophy, science, folk wisdom, and common-sense knowledge, make up this category.

These three categories comprise the system of culture as a whole. They are, of course, interrelated; each reacts upon the others and is affected by them in turn. But the influence of this mutual interaction is not equal in all directions. The roles played by the several sub-systems in the culture process as a whole are not equal by any means. The primary role is played by the technological system. This is, of course, as we would expect it to be; it could not be otherwise. Man as an animal species, and consequently culture as a whole, is dependent upon the material, mechanical means of adjustment to the natural environment. Man must have food. He must be protected from the elements. And he must defend himself from his enemies. These three things he must do if he is to continue to live, and these objectives are attained only by technological means. The technological system is therefore both primary and basic in

importance; all human life and culture rest and depend upon it.

Social systems are in a very real sense secondary and subsidiary to technological systems. In fact a social system may be defined realistically as the organized effort of human beings in the use of the instruments of subsistence, offense and defense, and protection. A social system is a function of a technological system. A ship, says Childe, "and the tools employed in its production symbolize a whole economic system." The technology is the independent variable, the social system the dependent variable. Social systems are therefore determined by systems of technology; as the latter change, so do the former. "The bronze axe which replaces ... [the stone axe]," again to quote Childe, "is not only a superior implement, it also presupposes a more complex economic and social structure."[3]

Ideological, or philosophical, systems are organizations of beliefs in which human experience finds its interpretation. But experience and interpretations thereof are powerfully conditioned by technologies. There is a type of philosophy proper to every type of technology. The interpretation of a system of experience in which a *coup de poing* is a characteristic feature will, as it must, reflect this kind of experience. It would not be improper to speak of a *coup de poing* type of philosophy as well as of technology. A pastoral, agricultural, metallurgical, industrial, or military technology will each find its corresponding expression in philosophy. One type of technology will find expression in the philosophy of totemism, another in astrology or quantum mechanics.

But experience of the external world is not felt and interpreted merely at the point of technological articulation; it is filtered through the prism of social systems also. The qualities and features of social, political, ecclesiastical, economic, military, etc., systems are therefore reflected in philosophies.

We may view a cultural system as a series of three horizontal strata: the technological layer on the bottom, the philosophical on the top, the sociological stratum in between. These positions express their respective roles in the culture process. The technological system is basic and primary. Social systems are functions of technologies; and philosophies express technological forces and reflect social systems. The technological factor is therefore *the* determinant of a cultural system as a whole. It determines the form of social systems, and technology and society together determine the content and orientation of philosophy. This is not to say, of course, that social systems do not condition the operation of technologies, or that social and technological systems are not affected by philosophies. They do and are. But to condition is one thing; to determine, quite another.

We are now in possession of a key to an understanding of the growth and development of culture: technology. A human being is a material body; the species, a material system. The planet earth is a material body; the cosmos, a material system. Technology is the mechanical means of articulation of these two material systems, man and cosmos. But these systems are dynamic, not static; energy as well as matter is involved. Everything – the cosmos, man, culture – may be described in terms of matter and energy.

The Second Law of Thermodynamics tells us that the cosmos as a whole is breaking down structurally and running down dynamically; matter is becoming less organized and energy more uniformly diffused. But in a tiny sector of the cosmos, namely in living material systems, the direction of the cosmic process is reversed: matter becomes more highly organized and energy more concentrated. Life is a building-up process. But in order to run counter to the cosmic current, biological organisms must draw upon free energy in non-living systems, capture it and put it to work in the maintenance of the vital process. All life is a struggle for free energy. Biological evolution is simply an expression of the thermodynamic process that moves in a direction opposite to that specified for the cosmos as a whole by the Second Law. It is a movement toward greater organization, greater differentiation of structure, increased specialization of function, higher levels of integration, and greater degrees of energy concentration.

From a zoological standpoint, culture is but a means of carrying on the life process of a particular species, Homo sapiens. It is a mechanism for providing man with subsistence, protection, offense and defense, social regulation, cosmic adjustment, and recreation. But to serve these needs of man energy is required. It becomes the primary function of culture, therefore, to harness and control energy so that it may be put

to work in man's service. Culture thus confronts us as an elaborate thermo-dynamic, mechanical system. By means of technological instruments energy is harnessed and put to work. Social and philosophic systems are both adjuncts and expressions of this technologic process. The functioning of culture as a whole therefore rests upon and is determined by the amount of energy harnessed and by the way in which it is put to work.[4]

But "the way in which it is put to work" introduces another factor besides energy. Energy by itself is meaningless. To be significant in cultural systems, energy must be harnessed, directed, and controlled. This is of course accomplished by technological means, by means of tools of one kind or another. The efficiency of technological means varies; some are better than others. The amount of food, clothing, or other goods produced by the expenditure of a given amount of energy will be proportional to the efficiency of the technological means with which the energy is put to work, other factors remaining constant.

We may therefore distinguish three factors in any cultural situation or system: (1) the amount of energy harnessed per capita per year; (2) the efficiency of the technological means with which energy is harnessed and put to work; and (3) the magnitude of human need-serving goods and services produced. Assuming the factor of habitat to be a constant, the degree of cultural development, measured in terms of amount of human need-serving goods and services produced per capita, is determined by the amount of energy harnessed per capita and by the efficiency of the technological means with which it is put to work. We may express this concisely and succinctly with the following formula: $E \times T \rightarrow C$, in which C represents the degree of cultural development, E the amount of energy harnessed per capita per year, and T the quality or efficiency of the tools employed in the expenditure of the energy. We can now formulate the basic law of cultural evolution: Other factors remaining constant, *culture evolves as the amount of energy harnessed per capita per year is increased, or as the efficiency of the instrumental means of putting the energy to work is increased.* Both factors may increase simultaneously of course. We may now sketch the history of cultural development from this standpoint.

If culture is a mechanism for harnessing energy, it must find this energy somewhere; it must lay hold of natural forces in some form or other if they are to be put to work in the service of man's needs. The first source of energy exploited by the earliest cultural systems was, of course, the energy of the human organism itself. The original cultures were activated by human energy and by this source and form alone. The amount of power that an average adult man can generate is small, about 1/10th of one horsepower. When women and children, the sick, aged, and feeble are considered, the average power resources of the earliest cultural systems might be reckoned at about 1/20th horse-power per capita. Since the degree of cultural development – the amount of human need-serving goods and services produced per capita – is proportional to the amount of energy harnessed and put to work per capita per year, other factors remaining constant, these earliest cultures of mankind, dependent as they were upon the meager energy resources of the human body, were simple, meager, and crude, as indeed they had to be. No cultural system, activated by human energy alone, can develop very far. Some progress can of course be made by increasing the efficiency of the technological means of putting energy to work, but there is a limit to the extent of cultural advance on this basis. We can form a realistic picture of cultural development within the limits of human energy resources by looking at such modern cultures as those of the Tasmanians, Fuegians, or Andamanese; or the Paleolithic cultures of Europe.

If culture is to advance beyond the limits of maximum technological efficiency and the energy resources of the human body, it must devise new ways to harness additional amounts of energy by tapping natural resources in some new form. In some preliterate cultural systems, fire, wind, or water was exploited as a source of energy, but only occasionally and to a very insignificant extent. The conquest of fire was a very early cultural achievement, but it was not until the invention of a practical steam engine that fire became important as a form of energy. Fire was important in early cultures in cooking, providing warmth, frightening wild beasts, and as a symbol, but not as a form of energy. In more advanced cultures, fire was important or essential in the ceramic and metallurgical arts, but here also it is not functioning as a form of energy: i.e., we cannot equate, or substitute, muscle power for

fire in any of these contexts. There is one context, however, in which fire functions as energy in some primitive cultures: in hollowing out tree trunks in the manufacture of dugout canoes. Here fire is substituted for muscle power. And there may be a few more similar uses of fire. But, all in all, prior to the invention of the steam engine in modern times, cultural systems made very little use of fire as a form and source of energy which could be substituted for human muscle power.

Primitive peoples could float freight down a flowing stream, but until the invention of the water wheel shortly before the beginning of the Christian era, there was no other way in which moving water could be used as a source of energy for culture building. Wind was not employed as a source of energy until comparatively recent times, and it never has been an important source of power.

Thus, we see that fire, water, and wind were utilized as sources of energy only to a very limited and insignificant extent during the first hundreds of thousands of years of culture history. But there is still another source of energy that was available to primitive man, and eventually we find his cultural systems harnessing it: the energy of plants and animals.

Plants are, of course, forms and magnitudes of energy. Energy from the sun is captured by the process of photosynthesis and stored up in the form of plant tissue. All animal life is dependent, in the last analysis, upon this solar energy stored up in plants. All life, therefore, is dependent upon photosynthesis.

The first men subsisted upon plants and animals as, of course, their pre-human ancestors did before them. The earliest culture systems developed techniques of hunting, fishing, trapping, collecting, gathering, etc., as means of exploiting the plant and animal resources of nature. But merely appropriating natural resources is one thing; harnessing and controlling them is quite another. After some 985,000 years of cultural development, certain plants were brought under the control of domestication and cultivation, and various animal species were brought under control through domestication. The energy resources for culture building were greatly increased as a consequence of this increase in control over the forces of nature. The yield of plant food and other useful plant materials per unit of human labor was greatly increased by the substitution of plant cultivation for wild plant gathering. Improved strains were developed through selective breeding. Cultivation, fertilization, and irrigation served to increase the yield per unit of human energy, or labor. Among the plants brought under cultivation, the cereals have been especially important. Tylor has called them "the great moving power of civilization." All of the great civilizations of antiquity were brought into being by the cultivation of cereals; no great culture has ever been achieved independently of the cultivation of cereals.

The domestication of animals, too, increased the energy resources for culture building as a consequence of the increase in control over these forms of energy. Their yield in food and other useful animal products per unit of human labor was greatly increased by the substitution of domestication for hunting. In a hunting economy animals had to be killed before they could be used, and when they were consumed more had to be found and killed. By means of domestication a people could subsist upon its herds and flocks without diminishing their numbers at all; they could even be increased. Animals, like plants, were improved through selective breeding, and, in addition to supplying milk, meat, wool, and hides, some species could be used as motive power, either to carry burdens or to draw plows or vehicles. The domestication of animals thus greatly increased the amount of energy under cultural control and available for culture building.

A great advance in cultural development would be expected, therefore, as a consequence of the great increase in the amount of energy harnessed and controlled per capita per year by means of the agricultural and pastoral arts. And this is exactly what took place. The archeological record bears out our theory fully at this point. In a few thousand years after the inauguration of the arts of domestication and cultivation, the great civilizations of antiquity, of Egypt, Mesopotamia, India, China, and, in the New World, in Mexico, Middle America, and the Andean Highlands, came quickly into being. After hundreds of thousands of years of relatively slow and meager development during the Old Stone Ages, culture suddenly shot forward under the impetus of augmented energy resources achieved by agriculture and animal husbandry. Great cities, nations, and empires

took the place of villages, tribes, and confederacies as a consequence of the Agricultural Revolution. Rapid progress was made, especially in the Old World, in all of the arts – industrial, esthetic, and intellectual. Great engineering projects were undertaken and executed; huge architectural edifices erected. The ceramic, textile, and metallurgical arts expanded and flourished. Astronomy, writing, and mathematics were developed. Beginnings were made in a rational science of medicine. Impressive works of art were produced, in relief, sculpture, and even in painting. Development and progress took place in all aspects of culture.

But culture did not advance continuously and indefinitely as a consequence of increased energy resources won by the techniques of agriculture and animal husbandry. After a period of rapid growth, the upward curve of progress levelled off onto a plateau. The peaks of cultural development in Egypt, Mesopotamia, India, and China were reached prior to 1000 BC, in some cases considerably earlier, and from that time until the beginning of the Fuel Age, about A.D. 1800, no culture of the Old World surpassed, in any profound and comprehensive way, the highest levels achieved in the Bronze Age. This is not to say, of course, that there was no progress at all from 1,000 BC to AD 1789. There were innovations here and there and many refinements of already existing traits. But, taking cultures as wholes, and measuring them by such yardsticks as size of political unit, size of city, magnitude of architectural edifices and engineering works, density of population, production and accumulation of wealth, etc., the cultures of Europe between the disintegration of the Roman Empire and the rise of the Power Age were in general inferior to those of the ancient oriental civilizations. The reason why cultures did not continue indefinitely to advance under the impetus of an agricultural and stockraising technology is a matter that we shall consider presently.

It appears then that culture had developed about as far as it could on an agricultural and animal husbandry basis before the beginning of the Christian era, at least in the Old World; the New World lagged somewhat behind. And it is reasonable to suppose that culture never would have exceeded the peaks already achieved by this time had not some way been devised to harness additional amounts of energy per capita per year by tapping the forces of nature in a new form. A way was found, however, to do this: energy in the form of coal, and, later, oil and gas, was harnessed by means of steam and internal combustion engines. By tapping the vast deposits of coal, oil, and natural gas, a tremendous increase in the amount of energy available for culture building was quickly effected. The consequences of the Fuel Revolution were in general much like those of the Agricultural Revolution: an increase in population, larger political units, bigger cities, an accumulation of wealth, a rapid development of the arts and sciences, in short, a rapid and extensive advance of culture as a whole.

But, again, after a very rapid rise, the curve of cultural development began to show some signs of levelling off. We do not wish to intimate that culture had already gone as far as it could on a Fuel basis, for we do not believe it had; we merely believe that we can detect signs of a slowing down of the advance. But before the question of how far cultural development *could* advance on a Fuel-Agricultural-Animal-Husbandry-Human-Energy basis could become anything like a matter of immediate concern, a tremendously significant technological event took place: the energy resources of atomic nuclei were harnessed. For the first time in culture history energy in a form other than solar had been harnessed. No cultural advance has as yet been effected by the utilization of this new form of energy as a source of industrial power. And before it becomes significant in this respect, another fateful question will have to be met and answered, namely, the consequences of the use of atomic energy in warfare.

Thus we trace the development of culture from anthropoid levels to the present time as a consequence of periodic increases in the amount of energy harnessed per capita per year effected by tapping new sources of power. There is, however, another technological factor involved which we have merely mentioned incidentally so far; we must now consider it more fully, namely, the role of tools in the culture process.

Energy is of course neither created nor annihilated, at least not within cultural systems; it is merely transformed. It is harnessed and it is put to work or expended. But this requires tools and machines. The amount of energy harnessed may, and the amount of human need-serving goods produced per unit of energy does, depend upon the efficiency of the tools employed. So far, we have been holding the tool factor constant and varying the energy factor. We now hold the energy factor constant and vary that of tools. We get, then, the following generalization: *the degree of cultural development varies directly as the efficiency of the tools employed, other factors remaining constant.* If, for example, one is engaged in chopping wood, the amount chopped per unit of energy expended will vary with the efficiency of the axe; the amount will increase with the improvement of axes from the Old Stone Age, through the Neolithic, Bronze, and Iron ages up to the finest axe of alloyed steel of the present day. And so it is with other instrumental means, such as saws, looms, plows, harnesses, wheeled vehicles, boats, etc. Cultural advance is effected, therefore, by an improvement of tools as well as by increases in the amount of energy harnessed.

But the efficiency of a tool cannot be increased indefinitely; there is a point beyond which improvement of any given tool is impossible. Thus, a canoe paddle can be too long or too short, too narrow or too wide, too heavy or too light, etc. We may therefore both imagine and realize a canoe paddle of such size and shape as to make any alteration of either result in a decrease of efficiency. Similarly, we may improve bows and arrows, hoes, plows, saws, etc., up to but not beyond a certain point. Perfection, as a practical matter, is either reached or at least closely approximated. No significant improvement has been made in violins in decades. The steam locomotive has apparently come close to its limits of size and speed. To be sure, improvements may be continued for a time by the use of new materials or alloys and by the application of new mechanical principles. But even so, the improvement of any tool or machine approaches closely, if it does not reach, a limit. We cannot expect locomotives or ocean liners a mile long; they would fall apart of their own weight.

In the culture process, therefore, we find that progress and development are effected by the improvement of the mechanical means with which energy is harnessed and put to work as well as by increasing the amounts of energy employed. But this does not mean that the tool and energy factors are of equal weight and significance. The energy factor is the primary and basic one; it is the prime mover, the active agent. Tools are merely the means that serve this power. The energy factor may be increased indefinitely; the efficiency of the tool only within limits. With a given amount of energy, cultural development can progress only so far: to the limits of the efficiency of the tools. When these limits have been reached, no further increases in efficiency can make up for a lack of increase in amount of energy harnessed. But increases in the amount of energy harnessed result in technological progress all along the line, in the invention of new tools and in the improvement of old ones should further improvement be possible. We see, therefore, that important though the tool factor may be, it is merely secondary to the primary and basic factor of energy. And, since increases of energy foster improvement of tools, one may say that it is energy that, at bottom, carries the culture process onward and upward. The general statement that, the environmental factor being constant, the degree of cultural development is proportional to the amount of energy harnessed per capita per year is therefore sound and illuminating.

We turn now to a consideration of social systems in the process of cultural development. A social system is, as we have seen it must be, closely related to its underlying technological system. If a people are nomadic hunters – i.e., use certain technological instruments in certain ways in order to obtain food, furs, hides, and other need-serving materials – they will have one type of social system. If they lead a sedentary life, feeding upon rich beds of shellfish, or if they are pastoralists or intensive agriculturalists, or maritime traders, or industrialists, etc., they will have other types of social systems. The process of military offense and defense and the technological means with which it is exercised also acts as a determinant of social organization, sometimes a very powerful one. Thus we see that the social system of a people is at bottom determined by the use of the technological means of subsistence and of offense and defense. Those social institutions not directly related to the technology are related indirectly; they serve to co-ordinate the various sectors of society with one another and to integrate them into a coherent whole.

The social systems of primitive peoples vary tremendously in detail because the specific circumstances of natural habitat and technology

vary. But all social systems resting upon a human energy (i.e., pre-pastoral, pre-agricultural) basis belong to a common type. They are all relatively small and manifest a minimum of structural differentiation and specialization of function. We find no highly developed societies upon the primitive foundation of a technology powered by human energy alone.

The societies of pastoralists and agriculturalists in the early stages of these technological developments are likewise relatively simple, undifferentiated systems. As a matter of fact we may characterize all human social systems up to a certain point in the development of the agricultural, or farming-and-animal-husbandry, technology as *primitive* society: tribes based upon kinship ties, free access to the resources of nature for all, relatively little social differentiation and specialization, and a high degree of social equality. When, however, a certain point in the development of agriculture was reached, a profound change in social systems took place. This was the *social* aspect of the Agricultural Revolution. Let us trace the course of this social revolution in its main outlines at least.

Agriculture and animal husbandry are means of producing more food and other useful materials per unit of human energy than can be obtained by hunting, fishing, or gathering. When agriculture is combined with stock raising, the energy resources for culture building are of course greater than when the cultivation of plants alone is practiced. Not only do flocks and herds supply meat, milk, wool, or hides, but their muscle power may be used to carry burdens, draw plows and carts, etc. All of the great civilizations of the Old World grew up on the basis of agriculture and animal husbandry. Since, however, it is the cultivation of cereals that is the basic factor in the new agriculture-and-animal-husbandry technology, we may for the sake of brevity speak of "the social consequences of a developing agricultural technology."

As the agricultural arts developed and matured, as plants were improved through selective breeding, as new techniques of cultivation, irrigation, drainage, rotation of crops, fertilization, etc., were introduced and improved, the amount of food produced increased. As the food supply was enlarged the population increased. Small tribes grew into large tribes and these into nations and empires; villages grew into towns and towns into cities.

Not only was *more food* produced by agricultural techniques than by hunting, fishing, and gathering, but more food per capita, more per unit of human labor expended. And, as the agricultural arts developed, the productivity of human labor in this field increased. It gradually became possible for a portion of the population to produce food for all. This meant that a portion of the population could be diverted from agriculture and turned into other channels, such as the industrial and esthetic arts. As the agricultural technology advanced, more and more of the population could thus be withdrawn from the fields and put to work at other tasks and occupations. Society thus became divided along occupational lines, differentiated structurally and specialized functionally. This led to further social developments as we shall see in a moment.

The mere increase in population had important consequences in another direction also. Tribes and clans were organized upon a basis of kinship ties; social relations were largely exercised in this form. This mechanism worked very well as long as the social units were relatively small; a clan or tribe could be effective as a mechanism of social organization and intercourse as long as its members were not exceedingly numerous, as long as social relations could be *personal*. But when, under the impetus of a developing agricultural technology and an increasing food supply, clan and tribal units grew to huge size, they tended to fall apart of their own weight. Primitive society tended therefore to disintegrate as a consequence of sheer increase of numbers. A new type of social organization was therefore required if chaos was to be averted. This new organization was found in the State. This was another consequence of the Agricultural Revolution.

The developing agricultural technology brought about a profound change in economic organization, also. In tribal society production, exchange, and consumption of wealth took place upon a personal, kinship basis; the economic organization was virtually identified with the kinship system. This type of economic organization worked well in a small society with a minimum of division of labor and with little differentiation of social structure along occupational lines. But as society became extensively differentiated, as a consequence of the increase in productivity of human labor in agriculture, a new type of economic system was required; a way of relating *classes* economically to one another must be devised. This can be done either in a feudal or a monetary-market system. In either case, however, we have a system in which property relations form the basis of social relations rather than the reverse, as was the case in tribal, kinship, society.

On preliterate cultural levels there was of course some fighting between tribal groups. Competition for favored hunting and fishing grounds or other natural resources, vengeance for real or fancied (e.g., magical) injuries, led to a certain amount of inter-tribal conflict. But the factors necessary for large scale and systematic and sustained warfare were lacking. These were supplied, however, as a consequence of the Agricultural Revolution. A high degree of development of the agricultural, metallurgical, ceramic, and other arts resulted in the production and accumulation of vast amounts of wealth. A rich nation's possessions together with the natural and human resources that made the wealth possible would constitute a rich prize to any people who could conquer it. Warfare became a profitable occupation. Thus we find, especially in Mesopotamia, a condition of almost chronic warfare: nations contending with one another for rich, fertile river valleys, the treasures of palace and temple, one nation conquering and looting another, new empires rising upon the ruins of old.

The social consequences of systematic and chronic warfare are significant: the formation of a professional military class, which in collaboration with political rulers and sometimes even autonomously, may become a powerful political force; the reduction of peoples of conquered nations to the status of slavery or serfdom; and the subordination of the masses at home to the imperatives of prolonged military conflict. Thus warfare tended powerfully to divide society into two major social classes: a relatively small ruling group who organized and directed the campaigns and to whom the overwhelming proportion of the wealth taken as booty went, and a large class who provided the "sinews of war" – the peasants, serfs, the common soldiers, etc. There was often but little difference between the lot of the masses at home and that of the masses of the vanquished nation after conquest and subjugation had been accomplished.

Warfare was not, however, the only means, or social process, that operated to divide societies of the post-Agricultural Revolutionary era into a small, wealthy, powerful, ruling class on the one hand, and a large class of peasants, serfs, or slaves on the other. The peaceful process of commerce, and especially the use of money, operated also to bring about the same end. Trade and commerce are means of concentrating wealth. In this competitive process the big merchants grew at the expense of the small ones. Wealth tended to gravitate into a few hands. Money lending is a particularly rapid and effective means of making the poor poorer and the wealthy richer. When interest rates range from say thirty to one hundred percent or even more, as they did in ancient times, the small borrowers rapidly sink into economic bondage to the money-lenders. It was not at all uncommon in Greece before the reforms of Solon or Kleisthenes for a small farmer to sell his children into slavery in order to pay merely the interest on his loan, let alone the principal. Taxes levied by the ruling class through the mechanism of the state and exorbitant rents levied upon small tenants by large landlords also tended to reduce the masses to a condition of economic bondage and impotence.

Thus we see that the social, political, and economic effects of the technological revolution in agriculture were: the dissolution of the old social system of primitive society, the obsolescence of tribe and clan; the division of society into various occupational groups – guilds of artisans and craftsmen; the division of society horizontally into two major classes: a small, powerful, wealthy, ruling class and a large class, governed and exploited by the ruling class and held in bondage in one form or another by them. Civil society based upon property relations took the place of primitive society based upon kinship; the State replaced tribe and clan. The technological revolution in agriculture precipitated and carried through a revolution in the social, political, and economic sectors of culture. As the amount of energy harnessed and put to work per capita per year was increased by the development of the agricultural technology, society became more and more differentiated structurally and increasingly specialized functionally. Concomitant with this trend was the emergence of a special social mechanism of co-ordination of functions and

correlation of structures, a mechanism of integration and regulation. This political mechanism had two aspects, secular and ecclesiastic, sometimes closely related, sometimes distinct, but always present. We call this special mechanism of co-ordination, integration and regulation the State-Church. The evolution of civil society from the early metallurgical era to the present day, passing through a variety of forms of the state and class relations, is a story that we shall turn to presently. At this point we wish to return to a matter touched upon earlier.

If culture evolves when and as the amount of energy harnessed per capita per year increases, why did not culture continue to advance indefinitely as a consequence of the technological revolution in agriculture? As we have already seen, it did not. On the contrary, after attaining certain levels it ceased to advance and thereafter continued on a plateau until a new and powerful impetus came from the Fuel Revolution. Yet, agriculture as a technological process, as a mechanism of harnessing solar energy, was not developed to its technological limits by any means; it has not even yet reached those limits or even approached them very closely according to agronomists. Why, then, did technological progress in agriculture eventually slow down and virtually stop after so rapid a rise?

The answer seems to lie in the relationship between socioeconomic system and technological system established by the Agricultural Revolution. As we have noted, every social system rests upon and is determined by a technological system. But every technological system functions *within* a social system and is therefore *conditioned* by it. The social system created by the Agricultural Revolution affected the technological process so as eventually to "contain it" and to bring further progress in culture as a whole virtually to a standstill. This is how it was done.

The social system of civil society was, as we have seen, divided into a ruling class and an exploited class. The latter produced the wealth; the former appropriated so large a portion of it as to leave the latter with but minimum means of subsistence. No advantage would accrue to the producing class if they enlarged their production through increased efficiency; the increment would only be appropriated by the ruling class. On the other hand, the ruling class were not likely to resort to a long-range plan to improve the techniques of agricultural production. If they needed more than they were obtaining at the moment the need was immediate and a long-range plan would have been of no use. They would therefore resort to greater exactions from the producing class. But in many, if not most, instances, it would seem, the ruling class had ample for their needs. As a matter of fact, a great deal of evidence indicates that one of the problems they had to contend with was that of overproduction rather than of insufficiency. Thus we see, especially in Egypt but also in Mesopotamia and elsewhere, the ruling class engaging in "conspicuous waste and consumption" and that on a grand scale. Palaces and temples were loaded with wealth and vast treasures were deposited with the dead in tombs. In addition to this, great public works programs – pyramids, monuments, temples, tombs, and palaces – were continually being built. It would appear that the ruling class was frequently confronted with the problem of overproduction and the threat of technological unemployment or a surplus of population among the lower classes. Their great public works programs, the wholesale disposition of wealth in mortuary customs, etc., enabled them to solve both these problems with one stroke. Thus the social system tended to act as a damper on further increase in technological progress once a certain stage of development had been reached. In addition to the factors mentioned above, Childe has pointed out that the social system operated not only to concentrate wealth in the hands of the ruling minority but effectively prevented the fruits of technological progress from being distributed among the masses of the population. There was, consequently, no chance for the technology of production to expand quantitatively or to improve qualitatively.

We see, then, that the new agricultural technology resulted in a tremendous growth of culture in its initial stages. But in effecting this advance a social system was created that eventually curbed and contained the technological system in such a way as to bring progress virtually to a stop, despite the fact that the *technological* limits of agricultural development had not been even closely approximated. We may reasonably conclude, therefore, that human culture would never have gone substantially beyond the peaks

achieved prior to the beginning of the Christian era had not the amount of energy harnessed per capita per year been considerably enlarged by tapping the forces of nature in a new form.

The Fuel Revolution was the culmination and synthesis of a number of streams of cultural elements that had been in progress of development for some time just as the Agricultural Revolution was the organized florescence of trends of earlier ages. And, like its predecessor, the Fuel Revolution brought about great social, political, and economic changes as a consequence of greatly augmenting the energy resources for culture building by harnessing solar energy in a new form, this time in coal, oil, and natural gas.

As in the case of the Agricultural Revolution, the new fuel technology resulted in a great increase in population. The population of Europe prior to the Coal Age grew only from 100,000,000 in 1650 to 187,000,000 in 1800. From 1800 to 1900, however, it increased to over 400,000,000. The population of England, to cite the country in which the Industrial Revolution got under way and in which it developed to a very great extent, increased 50 percent between 1700 and 1800. But during the nineteenth century, it increased 260 percent. In the two centuries prior to 1850, the population of Japan increased by 41 percent. In the fifty years following 1872 – about the time industrialization began – however, the population increased over 80 percent. Urban development was powerfully stimulated and accelerated by the new technology as it had been by the developing agricultural technology in the Bronze Age. The European feudal system – a rural, aristocratic, agricultural production for use economy – was rendered obsolete and replaced by an urban, parliamentary, industrial, production-for-sale-at-a-profit economy. Social structure became ever more differentiated and functions more specialized. The productivity of human labor increased as technology advanced. Farm populations decreased relatively and in some instances absolutely.

Changes occurred in the class structure of society also. The basic dichotomy – a minority ruling class and the majority of the population in a position of subordination and exploitation – remained, but the composition of these classes underwent radical change. Industrial lords and financial barons replaced the landed aristocracy of feudalism as the dominant element in the ruling class, and an urban, industrial proletariat took the place of serfs, peasants, or slaves as the basic element in the subordinate class. Industrial strife took the place of peasant revolts and uprisings of slaves and serfs of earlier days. And, in a new form, the State-Church functioned as a co-ordinative and regulative mechanism to maintain the integrity of society by containing these class antagonisms and by mobilizing the resources of society for offense and defense.

We may pause at this point to take note of an interesting feature of the process of cultural evolution: *as culture evolves the rate of growth is accelerated.* As we have already seen, the rate of growth in late Neolithic and early Bronze times was much greater than in the Paleolithic and Eolithic Ages. The Agricultural Revolution required but a few thousand years to run its course. But the Fuel Revolution is only a century and a half or two centuries old at most, and already greater changes have been effected by it perhaps than by all earlier ages put together. The change is so rapid and we are so much in the midst of it that it is difficult to grasp the situation and to realize the profound and radical nature of the revolution, social and political as well as technological, through which we are passing. Twenty-seven years ago in *New Viewpoints in American History*, Professor A. M. Schlesinger compared the culture of the United States of Lincoln's day with that of Benjamin Franklin's on the one hand, and with the culture of 1922 on the other. He remarked that the daily life with which Lincoln was familiar was in most respects like that known to George Washington and Franklin. But our culture in 1922 would have been strange and bewildering to Lincoln had he returned to the American scene:

Buildings more than three or four stories high would be new. The plate-glass show windows of the stores, the electric street-lighting, the moving-picture theaters, the electric elevators in the buildings and especially the big department stores would be things in his day unknown. The smooth-paved streets and cement sidewalks would be new to him. The fast-moving electric street-cars and motor vehicles would fill him with wonder. Even a boy on a bicycle would be a curiosity. Entering the White House, someone would have to explain to him such commonplaces

of modern life as sanitary plumbing, steam heating, friction matches, telephones, electric lights, the Victrola, and even the fountain pen. In Lincoln's day, plumbing was in its beginnings, coal-oil lamps and gas-jets were coming into use, and the steel pen had only recently superseded the quill pen. The steel rail, the steel bridge, high-powered locomotives, refrigerator cars, artificial ice, the cream separator, the twine binder, the caterpillar tractor, money orders, the parcels post, rural free delivery, the cable, the wireless, gasoline engines, repeating rifles, dynamite, submarines, airplanes – these and hundreds of other inventions now in common use were all alike unknown.[5]

But consider the changes that have taken place – in transportation, medicine, communication, and in technology in general – since Schlesinger wrote in 1922! In warfare perhaps better than in other areas of our culture, is the dizzying rate of technological progress made dramatically apparent. The technology of the First World War looks quaint today, and some of the weapons and techniques introduced for the first time in World War II are already obsolete. One hardly dares to picture the next great military conflict; novelties already unveiled and others only intimated suggest all too vividly the distance that technological progress has gone since the days of Pearl Harbor. And behind the scenes in the theater of Mars are the great research laboratories and proving grounds, working under forced draft to develop and perfect new tools and techniques in all phases of our technology. The rate of cultural advance is now greater than ever before. "Our life," wrote the distinguished physicist, Arthur Holly Compton in 1940, "differs from that of two generations ago more than American life of that day differed from the civilized life at the dawn of written history."[6] And, since Compton wrote these words, a profound and awful revolution – perhaps the most significant in all human history – has taken place: the harnessing of atomic energy.

But, even as in the case of the Agricultural Revolution and its aftermath, so in the Power Age the social system created by the new fuel technology came eventually to act as a brake upon further cultural advance. The price and profit system stimulated production and technological progress as long as the output could find a market.

But, like the socio-economic system of the Bronze Age, the new commercialism of the Fuel era had its inherent limitations. No industrial nation had or could have purchasing power sufficient to keep and absorb its own output; the very basis of the industrial profit system was an excess in value of product over the cost of production in terms of wages paid to the industrial workers. Export of surplus was therefore essential; "we must export or die" is a cry of desperation heard from more than one nation in recent years. For a time new markets could be found abroad. But as the output of industrial nations increased with advances in technology, and as non-European nations such as Japan became industrialized and hence competitors for foreign markets, the international profit system began to bog down. The world market diminished as the industrial output increased. When goods could no longer be sold profitably abroad, production was curtailed at home. Entrepreneurs are disinclined to produce goods that cannot be sold at a profit. Factories, mills, and mines were closed. Millions of workers were thrown out of employment. Surplus goods were destroyed, agricultural production reduced. The awful plague of overproduction and unemployment, "starvation in the midst of plenty," settled upon the land. The social system was strangling the great technological machine of industry and paralyzing the body politic as a whole. The alternatives were stagnation and death or war and revolution. If the social system were able to contain the Fuel technology and the commercial rivalries and class conflicts engendered by it, society would become stabilized in a more or less stagnant form of industrial feudalism. Should, however, the forces inherent in the new technology be able to surmount and overcome the restrictions of the price and parliamentary system, then culture could advance toward higher levels.

There is evidence aplenty that culture, powered by the mighty forces of Fuel technology, is embarking upon the latter course. The first phase of the second great Cultural Revolution – the Industrial Revolution – has run its course and we are now entered upon the second phase, that of social, political, and economic revolution. And, as in the past, war is proving to be an effective means of profound political change. The system of free and individual enterprise in business and commerce is now virtually extinct. The gold standard is merely a memory of an era that is closed. The parliamentary system of government, a device designed to permit the greatest freedom for the growth of industrial and financial enterprise, is practically obsolete also. Private right is no longer significant chiefly as a means of freedom for growth as it was in the early days of commercialism. It now leads toward competitive rivalry, internecine strife, chaos, and paralysis. Concentrations of power without public responsibility among those who own or control vast wealth, or in the ranks of organized labor, are no longer compatible with the degree of unity, integrity, and strength that a nation must have if it is to compete successfully with its rivals in the international arena. The exigencies of national survival require the subordination of private right to general welfare, of part to whole. In short, the State, as the integrative and regulative mechanism of civil society, is destined to acquire ever greater power and to wield more and more control. Social evolution is moving inexorably toward higher levels of integration, toward greater concentrations of political power and control.

On the international level, too, an interesting trend of social evolution can be discerned: movement toward ever larger and larger political units. The Agricultural technology replaced villages with cities, tribes with nations and empires. The modern Fuel technology also is working toward larger political groupings, fewer concentrations of political power. The relatively recent trend toward amalgamation can be seen in the unification of Germany and Italy in the nineteenth century. The Treaty of Versailles attempted, with the "Balkanization of Europe," to oppose the age-old trend of social evolution by breaking the continent up into little pieces. One of the conspicuous and significant aspects of the Second World War in its initial phase was a movement toward the unification of Europe. A half-dozen or so World Powers engaged in the First World War; only two great powers emerged from the second. The competition for power narrows as contestants are eliminated. The logical conclusion is, however, not simply the domination of the world by a single nation – this would be but a transitional stage – but a single political organization that will embrace the entire planet and the whole human race. Toward such a denouement is our mighty Power technology rapidly moving us.

But a new and ominous element has recently entered the picture: nuclear atomic energy for military purposes. Here again the significance of this new factor derives from the fact that a new source of energy has been harnessed and in awful form. Once more we are upon the threshold of a technological revolution. But the consequences of this new technological advance may possibly differ radically from those of the Agricultural and the Fuel Revolutions. New technologies in the past have rendered old social systems obsolete but they have replaced them with new systems. The new nuclear technology however threatens to destroy civilization itself, or at least to cripple it to such an extent that it might require a century, a thousand, or ten thousand, years to regain its present status. At least this is what eminent scientists and military men tell us; as laymen we are in a child's world of ignorance, with almost all the significant facts kept beyond our reach. The destruction of a few score of centers of science and industry in Europe and the United States would just about do for Western civilization, and authorities assure us that this is well within the realm of possibility, not to say probability. The hope of the future, therefore, and the salvation of mankind and civilization would seem to lie in the emergence from the next war of a *victor* – not merely a survivor – and one with sufficient power and resources to organize the whole planet and the entire human species within a single social system.

We have thus presented a sketch of the evolution of the culture of mankind from the horizon of our prehuman forebears to the present time. It is a fascinating story of adventure and progress; of a species lifting itself up by its cultural bootstraps from the status of a mere animal to a radically new way of life, a way destined to win mastery over most other species and to exert a powerful and extensive control over the natural habitat. The origin of culture elevated the evolutionary process to a new plane. No longer was it necessary for the human animal to acquire new powers and techniques through the slow process of biological change; he now had an extra-somatic mechanism of adjustment and control that could grow freely of itself. Moreover, advances in one stream of cultural development could diffuse readily to other traditions so that all might share in the progress of each. Thus the story of man becomes an account of his culture.

Technology is the hero of our piece. This is a world of rocks and rivers, sticks and steel, of sun, air and starlight, of galaxies, atoms and molecules. Man is but a particular kind of material body who must do certain things to maintain his status in a cosmic material system. The means of adjustment and control, of security and survival, are of course technological. Culture thus becomes primarily a mechanism for harnessing energy and of putting it to work in the service of man, and, secondarily, of channelling and regulating his behavior not directly concerned with subsistence and offense and defense. Social systems are therefore determined by technological systems, and philosophies and the arts express experience as it is defined by technology and refracted by social systems. Cultural systems like those of the biological level are capable of growth. That is, the power to capture any energy is also the ability to harness more and still more of it. Thus cultural systems, like biological organisms, develop, multiply, and extend themselves. The sun is the prime mover; culture, a thermodynamic system operated by it. At least, solar energy has activated all cultural systems of history up to now, and it will continue to do so after terrestrial supplies of fissionable fuels have been exhausted – if civilization should survive and reach this point. But technology is still the leading character in our play, even though it may turn out to be a villain instead of the hero. Technology builds but it may also destroy. The belief and faith that civilization, won at such great cost in pain and labor, simply cannot go down in destruction because such an end would be too monstrous and senseless, is but a naive and anthropocentric whimper. The cosmos does little know nor will it long remember what man has done here on this tiny planet. The eventual extinction of the human race – for come it will sometime – will not be the first time that a species has died out. Nor will it be an event of very great terrestrial significance.

But *man* may survive the coming holocaust of radioactivity even though his culture is tumbled to the level of Neolithic times, only to begin the long climb over again, this time perhaps by a somewhat different route; culture too may be able to profit from experience. But culture may *not* destroy or even critically wound itself with its new powers. Destruction is no more inevitable than salvation. Great though the devastation may – and will – be in the next test of strength in the international arena, the creative powers of the new technology may be sufficiently great to rise up from the ruins and to enclose the whole world in a single political embrace. Then and only then will the curse of war be lifted and the way made free and open for a fuller and richer life.

Our sketch of the evolution of culture is, it will be noted, wholly culturological. It does not resort to race, physical type, intelligence, a moral sense, the dignity of man, the spirit of progress or democracy, the individual – genius or otherwise – the rejection of the father, consciousness of kind, a set of instincts or "drives," social interaction, a basic personality structure, toilet training in infancy, or breast *vs.* bottle feeding and weaning, to account for the behavior and growth of this great extra-somatic tradition. We explain it in terms of culture itself. A thunder-shower or a tornado is explained in terms of antecedent and concomitant meteorological events; a clan or a constitution is likewise accounted for by citing its cultural antecedents and concomitants.

   Culture is, as we have pointed out repeatedly, a stream of interacting elements; one trait reacts upon others and is affected by them in return. Some elements become obsolete and are eliminated from the stream; new elements are incorporated into it. New permutations, combinations, and syntheses are continually being formed. Whether we deal with a restricted portion of the cultural continuum such as the evolution of math-

ematics or the genealogy of the steam engine, or whether we encompass culture in its entirety, the principle of interpretation is the same: culture grows out of culture. In our sketch of the evolution of culture as a whole we deal with large categories: technology, social systems, and philosophies. We break technology down into energy and tool factors. We observe the action of each class of elements, their impact upon others, the effect of technology upon social systems, and the influence of economic and political institutions upon agriculture and steam-driven factories. We note the role that war as a culture process has played in the course of political change. And, finally, we see the fate of civilization delicately balanced in a scales to be tipped this way or that, we know not how, by the modern miracles of nuclear technology.

   Culturology is the newest venture of science. After centuries of cultivation in the fields of astronomy, physics, and chemistry; after scores of years of tillage in physiology and psychology, science has at last turned to the most immediate and powerful determinant of man's *human* behavior: his culture. After repeated trials and as many failures it was discovered that culture cannot be explained psychologically; such interpretations are merely anthropomorphisms in scientific clothing. The explanation of culture is and must be culturological. The science of culture is young but full of promise. It is destined to do great things – if only the subject of its study will continue its age-old course: onward and upward.

Notes

1   MacCurdy, II, p. 134.
2   Ostwald, p. 511.
3   Childe, pp. 7, 9.
4   The functioning of any particular culture will of course be conditioned by local environmental conditions. But in a consideration of culture as a whole, we may average all environments together to form a constant factor which may be excluded from our formula of cultural development.
5   Schlesinger, pp. 247–8.
6   Compton, p. 576.

References

Childe, V. Gordon 1936. *Man Makes Himself*. London.
Compton, A. H. 1940. "Science Shaping American Culture," *Proceedings, American Philosophical Society*, 83:573–82.
MacCurdy, Geo. G. 1933. *Human Origins*, 2 vols. New York.
Ostwald, Wilhelm 1907. "The Modern Theory of Energetics," *The Monist*, 17:481–515.
Schlesinger, A. M. 1922. *New Viewpoints in American History*. New York.

12

Ecology, Cultural and Noncultural

Andrew P. Vayda and Roy A. Rappaport

In this chapter our concern will be to indicate the contribution of ecology, or an ecological perspective, towards realization of two major goals of cultural anthropology. One goal is to explain why particular traits or congeries of traits exist at particular times and in particular places: why, for example, do some human groups grow crops and keep domesticated animals while others do not? The other goal is to elucidate how the traits or congeries of traits function or "behave": how, for example, do certain modes of keeping and ritually slaughtering pigs in the New Guinea highlands help to maintain a balance between human populations and their subsistence resources? The two goals are of general interest to cultural anthropologists of various theoretical persuasions, and numerous approaches other than an ecological one have been and can be used both in accounting for the presence and in describing the functioning of particular cultural features. But an ecological approach does have important contributions to make.

[...]

[...] [E]cological work in anthropology has for more than a half-century had a predominantly cultural orientation. There is little indication that

anthropologists during this period have been aware of ongoing developments in animal ecology. Indeed, communication between the two fields has been extremely tenuous.

It is our belief that, while ecological work in anthropology has had some successes, it has suffered from its isolation from developments in the field of general ecology. [...]

Determinists and Possibilists

In the first two decades of [the twentieth] century, two views on environmental influences were distinguished, one labelled "determinism" (or, in some discussions, "environmentalism"), the other, "possibilism." The first, which has antecedents in antiquity (Tatham 1957), held in its most extreme statements that environmental forms dictate cultural ones and therefore cultural phenomena can be explained and should be predictable to a large extent by reference to their contemporary environments. This was denied by adherents of possibilism, some of whom argued that, consistent with what is described as a limiting rather than determining effect of the

From James A. Clifton (ed.), *Introduction to Cultural Anthropology: Essays in the Scope and Method of the Sciences of Man* (Boston: Houghton Mifflin Company, 1968), pp. 476, 479–80, 483–5, 488–94, 497.

environment, only the absence of traits (for instance, "the absence of pineapple plantations in Greenland") could be predicted from characteristics of the environment. With regard to the cultural phenomena the environment permits or makes possible, there are, in the possibilist view, always alternatives, and there is no guarantee that any particular possibility (for instance, food storage rather than seasonal migration as an adjustment to seasonal changes in the amount of food yielded by the local environment) will be the one to materialize. [...]

[...]

The contending points of view are similar to those which long agitated biological science, wherein some students argued for external environmental factors as the determinants of biological traits and other students argued for factors within the organisms themselves as the determinants. The resolution in biology has been the recognition that both classes of factors and the interplay between them are determining (Simpson 1949: 142–3), and today a parallel resolution, emphasizing the interaction of cultural and environmental factors, is possible in cultural anthropology. [...]

[...]

[...] That there are complex interactions with the environment was recognized, and diffusion, specific history, and cultural patterns were seen to be important influences quite apart from the environmental factors. But these other influences were allowed to constitute a dark middle region between man and his physical environment in which almost anything could happen. That is to say, while the complexity of the problems of analysis and explanation were discerned, no models or methods for resolving the problems were put forward. Instead, possibilistic conclusions were reached. Concerning possibilism, we may say that it is neither a theory nor a hypothesis lending itself to empirical test. It is simply a way of saying that causation is not simple.

Steward's Method of Cultural Ecology

To the emphasis placed [...] on unique culture histories and unique cultural patterns, the American anthropologist, Julian Steward, reacted with an emphasis on local environments. Focusing on cultural adjustments and adaptations was to be a way out of the impasse resulting from what Steward described as the "relativistic conception of culture history" and its "fruitless assumption that culture comes from culture" (1955:36). [...]

Steward sees difficulties in dealing with the relation between human societies and the environment when the latter is viewed as the "total web of life wherein all plant and animal species interact with each other and with the physical features in a particular unit of territory" (p. 30). [...] In an attempt to reduce the magnitude of the difficulties, Steward regards the relationship of man, the organism, to environment as separate from the relationship of culture, the "super-organism," to environment. He views the elucidation of biological and of cultural phenomena as different objectives of ecological research, each requiring its own concepts and methods, each to be kept, generally, distinct from the other. He justifies this segregation on the grounds that "cultural patterns are not genetically derived and, therefore, cannot be analyzed in the same way as organic features" (p. 32). He argues that explanations of the presence of cultural phenomena must rely, rather, on culture-historical methods and concepts augmented by the methods and concepts of what he calls cultural ecology. The elucidation of specific histories has, however, only a limited place in Steward's ecological approach despite the fact that he himself has made numerous culture-historical studies. The view is taken that "cultural ecological adaptations" are not merely permitted by the environment but "constitute creative processes" (p. 34), and that there is a "degree of inevitability in cultural adjustments" (p. 89). The implication is that the origins of some (even if not all) particular cultural features can be discovered through the study of relationships between culture and its contemporary environment. The de-emphasizing of the historical influences with which Kroeber and others were preoccupied is indicated clearly in Steward's assertion that the role of cultural diffusion "in explaining culture has been greatly overestimated" (p. 42).

"Three fundamental procedures of cultural ecology" are set forth by Steward. These are analyses of: (1) the relation between environment and exploitative or productive technology; (2) the "behavior patterns involved in the exploitation of a particular area by means of a particular technology"; and (3) the "extent to which the behavior patterns entailed in exploiting the environment affect other aspects of culture" (Steward 1955:40 f.). [...]

[...]

[...] Steward has had recourse to cross-cultural comparisons. These have led to his conclusion that the recurrence of the same interrelations of cultural and environmental variables in cultures not in contact with one another is evidence of "a degree of inevitability" in the association between certain cultural traits [...]. This conclusion may be questioned in a number of ways.

First, we may question the very existence of significant correlations between the cultural traits and ecological adaptations considered by Steward. The procedure does not indicate how many other cases there might be in which there obtain either the adaptations but not the cultural traits in question, or the cultural traits but not the adaptations.

Second, the basis for concluding that the ecological adaptations are "causative" may be questioned. Even if correlations between the adaptations and certain cultural traits were shown to be significant, the task of demonstrating what is cause and what is effect would remain. [...]

Biological aspects of human populations also are given little consideration by Steward. The view stated in his 1955 book is that "culture, rather than genetic potential for adaptation, accommodation, and survival, explains the nature of human societies" (p. 32). But in contrast to this and in light of recent studies, it is possible to see culture and genetics interacting and working together to effect adaptation in human populations much as they do in populations of nonhuman land mammals and birds, which are now recognized to share with human beings a capacity for intra-species transmission of learned behavior (Hockett and Ascher 1964: 136; Scott 1958). [...]

[...]

Despite the exceptions that have been taken to specific aspects of Steward's theory and method of cultural ecology, it must be emphasized that his work has been of signal importance in a number of respects. For one thing, it has made anthropologists realize that the usual textbook refutations of environmental determinism (for instance, that the Pueblo and Navaho Indians had different cultures in purportedly the same environment, [...]) did not constitute an adequate consideration of the relation between cultural phenomena and their environmental settings. Furthermore, his work has pointed to the importance of basing ecological generalizations upon the close examination of particular local groups and their environments. [...]

Ethno-Ecology

Investigations different from Steward's are being advocated by some anthropologists with training in linguistics. Their approach is intended to disclose ecology as seen by the people being studied, and therefore, following Harold Conklin (1954), we will call it the ethno-ecological approach. [...]

The nature and purposes of the ethno-ecological approach have been set forth programmatically by Charles Frake (1962a). [...] Frake proposes that a "successful strategy for writing productive ethnographies must tap the cognitive world of one's informants" (1962a:54). Accordingly, methods drawn mainly from linguistics and systematics are to be brought to bear on the problem of producing descriptions of how the people being studied construe their world. The methods are to be directed first toward the construction of taxonomies of native terms [...] The assumption is made that taxonomies of native terms either comprise in themselves statements of ethno-ecology or provide the information necessary for inferring ethno-ecology. [...]

After the taxonomies of native terms have been constructed, the next step is the formulation of rules of what the native speakers themselves would regard as appropriate behavior towards the environmental phenomena placed by them in one or another category. [...]

[...]

[...] Where Steward's aim is to explain the origins of behavior patterns by reference to aspects of the environments in which the patterns are found, the aim of the ethno-ecological approach is simply to present a people's view of the environmental setting itself and their view of behavior appropriate to that setting.

The aim is an important one. Its relevance to ecological studies lies in the fact that it is reasonable to regard a people's cognition with respect to environmental phenomena as part of the mechanism producing the actual physical behavior through which the people directly effect alterations in their environment. [...]

However, there are some problems in implementing Frake's program [...]. Such rules [...] are claimed by Frake to provide the means not only for predicting the terms native speakers will apply to particular objects but also for understanding what the native speakers' own classificatory concepts are and how the people construe their world. This claim has recently been questioned by Robbins Burling (1964a, 1964b), who has argued that the rules tell us only about verbal behavior and not about what is going on "inside people."

[...] To discover a people's classificatory terms and concepts is to discover what might be designated their "ethno-systematics" or "ethno-taxonomy," and this must be distinguished from ethno-ecology. [...] Taxonomies may of course be based on behavioral characteristics, but they need not be.

[...] Along with any success of the ethno-ecological approach in describing what one of us (Rappaport 1963:159) has elsewhere designated as "cognized environments" (that is, environments as understood by those who act within them) could go a failure to describe ecological processes and environmental relations which affect the people *without* their being aware of them. [...] It is worth noting that long-term advantages may accrue to a people as a result of their using other than ecological considerations in deciding upon courses of action that have ecological functions or consequences. [...] [S]tudies in ethnoscience and cognition might indicate the "nonecological" considerations on which individuals base decisions to act, but for an understanding of the ecological functions and consequences of their actions, the methods of Western biological science are required.

Ecology Rather Than Cultural Ecology

[...] It is now time to make explicit some considerations bearing upon both the possibility and the desirability of a single science of ecology with laws and principles that apply to man as they do to other species.

It must be made clear, first of all, that the development of a unified science of ecology does not require that culture or cultural factors be omitted from consideration. [...]

[...]

[...] [T]he separation of cultural from biological studies may be a result not so much of the nature of the phenomena being investigated as of other influences on the particular courses of intellectual history in the two fields. A new foundation is now being laid for a more unified approach. For one thing, among biologists there has been a general renewal of interest in behavior (Simpson 1958:9, 21). [...]

[...]

The possibility of studying human and non-human behavior in similar ways cannot fail to be enhanced by a new (or renewed) awareness of the broad similarities between the two [...] viz., that both function to effect adaptation to the environment and that both are subject to a kind of selection resulting, *inter alia*, from the fact that individuals or populations behaving in certain different ways have different degrees of success in survival and reproduction and, consequently, in the transmission of their ways of behaving from generation to generation.

There are of course some special problems in studying human behavior. Although it is increasingly appreciated that both human and nonhuman animal behavior are products of a combination of learning and genetically determined capabilities (Lindzey 1964; Scott 1958; Simpson 1962), it is still true that the degree to which behavior is a result of learning rather than genetics is greater in the human species than in other animal species. This contributes to making human behavior relatively complex, varied, variable, and population-specific (cf. Simpson 1962:106 f.). Certainly anthropologists are confronted because of this with formidable tasks in observation and description. But [this] mere fact [...] does not mean that the principles, concepts, or approaches employed by anthropologists studying behavior in interaction with environmental phenomena must be *basically* different from those employed by the other students. [...]

[...]

But [...] do we not thereby sacrifice traditional anthropological concerns? Are we not thereby abandoning the goals stated at the beginning of this chapter, that is, elucidating how particular cultural traits function and why they exist?

The answer is "no." [...] The ecologist is perforce concerned with behavioral as well as morphological attributes of the organisms and populations under study, whether these attributes are the predatory habits of lions, the "troop" deployments of baboons, or the tool-making, tool-using, sociopolitical arrangements, and other cultural traits of human beings. Any number of examples could be given of cultural traits that may, much as any animal behavior, be studied in relation to environmental phenomena.

[...]

[...] In other words, there is [...] a recognition that determinants of cultural traits are to be sought in an *interplay* of factors that include environmental ones and behavioral or cultural ones. Whenever possible, the influence of human biological variations should of course also be considered.

It would seem then that a unified science of ecology has definite contributions to make towards the realization of anthropological goals and does not entail any appreciable sacrifice of traditional anthropological interests. It may, however, entail a somewhat different sacrifice, that is, of the notion of the autonomy of a science of culture, a notion that Leslie White (1949) and others have vigorously defended. But to give this up may be a sacrifice well worth making, for it may make possible generalizations of much broader scope and applicability than have so far been achieved by anthropologists.

References

Burling, Robbins 1964a. Cognition and componential analysis: God's truth or hocus-pocus? *American Anthropologist* 66:20–8.

Burling, Robbins 1964b. Burling's rejoinder [to Hymes and Frake]. *American Anthropologist* 66:120–2.

Conklin, Harold C. 1954. An ethnoecological approach to shifting agriculture. *Transaction of the New York Academy of Sciences*, 2nd series 17:133–42.

Frake, Charles O. 1962a. Cultural ecology and ethnography. *American Anthropologist* 64:53–9.

Frake, Charles O. 1962b. The ethnographic study of cognitive systems. In *Anthropology and Human Behavior*, T. Gladwin and W. C. Sturtevant, eds. Washington, DC: Anthropological Society of Washington.

Hockett, Charles F. and Robert Ascher 1964. The human revolution. *Current Anthropology* 5:135–68.

Lindzey, Gardner 1964. Genetics and the social sciences. *Items* (Social Science Research Council) 18:29–35.

Rappaport, Roy A. 1963. Aspects of man's influence upon island ecosystems: alteration and control. In *Man's Place in the Island Ecosystem*, F. R. Fosberg, ed. Honolulu: Bishop Museum Press.

Scott, John Paul 1958. *Animal Behavior*. Chicago: University of Chicago Press.

Simpson, George Gaylord 1949. *The Meaning of Evolution: A Study of the History of Life and of Its Significance for Man*. New Haven: Yale University Press.

Simpson, George Gaylord 1958. The study of evolution: methods and present status of the theory. In *Behavior and Evolution*, A. Roe and G. G. Simpson, eds. New Haven: Yale University Press.

Simpson, George Gaylord 1962. Comments on cultural evolution. In *Evolution and Man's Progress*, Hudson Hoagland and Ralph W. Burhoe, eds. New York: Columbia University Press.

Steward, Julian 1955. *Theory of Culture Change*. Urbana: University of Illinois Press.

Tatham, George 1957. Environmentalism and possibilism. In *Geography in the Twentieth Century*, 3rd edn., Griffith Taylor, ed. New York: Philosophical Library.

White, Leslie 1949. *The Science of Culture*. New York: Farrar, Straus. Also, Grove Press, Inc.

SECTION 4

Methods and Objects

13

Understanding and Explanation in Social Anthropology

J. H. M. Beattie

I

Any reasoned inquiry seeks to understand its subject-matter, and the kind of understanding appropriate in any particular case will depend both upon the interests of the inquirer and upon the kind of material he is investigating. Social anthropologists have not always been agreed as to exactly what their subject-matter is or as to the nature of their interest in it. It may therefore be useful to see, first of all, what it is that present-day social anthropologists really study and, secondly, to consider how they attempt to make sense of what they study, that is, to understand it. One way of understanding things is to explain them, so I shall undertake a brief review of some of the types of explanation used in, and appropriate to, social anthropology.[1] [...]

First of all, how do present-day social anthropologists conceive their own subject? Here are a few fairly characteristic answers. For Radcliffe-Brown social anthropology was "that branch of sociology which deals with 'primitive' or pre-literate societies", "sociology" being defined as "the study of social systems", and a "social system" as consisting of "individual human beings interacting

with one another within certain continuing associations".[2] [...] According to Evans-Pritchard social anthropology studies

> social behaviour, generally in institutionalized forms, such as the family, kinship systems, political organization, legal procedures, religious cults, and the like, and the relations between such institutions; and it studies them either in contemporaneous societies or in historical societies for which there is adequate information of the kind to make such studies feasible.[3]

For Nadel "the primary object of social anthropology is to understand primitive peoples, the cultures they have created, and the social systems in which they live and act".[4] As a final example, Piddington states simply that "social anthropologists study the cultures of contemporary primitive communities".[5]

Even these few definitions exhibit very varying ideas of what social anthropology is about. Three of them restrict the social anthropologist's field to "primitive" or pre-literate peoples; the other (Evans-Pritchard's) explicitly disavows any such limitation. Radcliffe-Brown affirms that social anthropologists study societies or social systems,

From *British Journal of Sociology* 10(1) (1959), pp. 45–56, 57–60. Copyright © 1959 by *The British Journal of Sociology*. Reprinted by permission of John Wiley & Sons Ltd.

entities which, he implies, are comparable as totalities. Evans-Pritchard speaks of social behaviour and social institutions rather than of social systems. Nadel, though apparently regarding social systems as legitimate objects of study, differs from the other two in admitting culture as a proper theme for social anthropology. And Piddington would have social anthropology concern itself altogether with the latter topic.

We shall do better to consider what social anthropologists actually do. First, what do they not do? To begin with, they do not confine themselves to "primitive" or pre-literate peoples, though it is true that their discipline grew up in the context of the investigation of simpler societies: studies usually regarded as anthropological have been and are being made in European, American and Asian communities which are in no sense primitive. Secondly, and here there lies a more fundamental misunderstanding, social anthropologists do not study or compare "whole" societies, if "society" be taken (as it usually is) to stand for some kind of empirical totality; such a thing would be impossible.[6] What they do, or at least one of the things that they do, is to abstract from the social behaviour which they observe certain enduring or institutionalized[7] aspects or qualities which seem to go together and make sense, in terms of some particular interest of the observer. Thus particular social institutions, such as a kinship relation, a marriage rule, a jural, ritual or economic complex, are identified and defined, and it is these, not whole societies, which may be and are compared.[8] So the subject-matter of social anthropology, or at least of a very important part of it, is more accurately characterized as institutionalized social relations and the systems into which these may be ordered, than as "society" or "societies", considered as totalities somehow given as empirical entities to the observer.

But we must be more explicit. What are these social relations? Briefly, when social anthropologists speak of social relations they have in mind the ways in which people behave when other people are objects of that behaviour. At this preliminary level there are always two basic facts to be ascertained about any social relationship: what it is about, and whom it is between. This distinction is often expressed in the familiar distinction between status and role.[9] Already it is becoming apparent that something more than just observed

behaviour is implied in the notion of a social relationship; for a status is something that is inferred, not observed, and it exists only in so far as it is recognized and acknowledged, that is to say, in somebody's mind. Essential, therefore, to the notion of a social relationship are the kinds of expectations which the parties to it entertain about one another's (and their own) behaviour. It is, of course, this "reciprocity of expectations" (in Parsons' phrase[10]) that makes ordered social interaction possible. It follows that social relations cannot be intelligibly conceived or described apart from the expectations, intentions and ideas which they express or imply; certainly no social anthropologist has ever attempted so to describe them. Behaviour can have no social significance apart from what it means to somebody, and unless such "meanings" are taken into account nothing remotely resembling sociological understanding is possible.[11]

Social anthropologists, then, study both what people do and what they think about what they do. If data of the latter kind be regarded as cultural, then evidently they do and must have regard to some part, at least, of the cultures of the peoples they study.[12] Now the thoughts that people have about what they do are of (at least) two kinds: first, their notions about what they actually do, and, second, their beliefs about what they ought to do, their ethical norms or values. So it may be said that social anthropologists in fact concern themselves with three different kinds or levels of data; (i) "what actually happens",[13] (ii) what people think happens, and (iii) what they think ought to happen, their legal and moral values. Modern anthropological monographs almost always give some account of all of these three different kinds of data, though sometimes one rather than another is emphasized, and they are not always clearly distinguished.

There may be some degree of coincidence between two or even all three of these things, but they differ in important ways. And kinds of explanation appropriate to one may be less so to the others. Thus (to take an obvious example) "what actually happens" is often susceptible of quantitative treatment in a way in which – or at least to an extent to which – data of the other two kinds, beliefs and values, are not. A statement like "in a sample of a thousand marriages bridewealth was paid in seventy-five per cent of the

132   J. H. M. BEATTIE

cases" may be both true and informative. It is at
this factual level that statistical treatment is most
appropriate; it is less feasible to make quantitative
statements of this kind about, say, sorcery beliefs
or ideals of filial piety. Moreover, it should be
noticed that even a statistical assertion demands,
if it is to mean anything, a qualitative statement of
what its terms signify; the statement quoted
above is only sociologically informative when it
is known what "marriage" and "bride-wealth"
mean in the social and cultural context being
investigated.

Social anthropologists, then, study the different kinds of institutionalized social relationships
which they abstract from the observed behaviour
of the peoples they study, and they are also
concerned with the beliefs and values which are
intrinsic to these relationships. It is in terms of
the systematic interrelating of these relationships
that they define and analyse social institutions, as,
for example, such an institution as kingship
implies a complex of (inter alia) ruler–subject
relations, which as it were "hang together" both in
the social field itself and (in terms of his
conceptual interests) in the anthropologist's theoretical interpretation of it.[14] But his interest in
beliefs and values does not end with their implications for systems of social relations. Many, perhaps most, social anthropologists are interested
in such ideal configurations and "meanings", not
only in so far as they are directly relevant to such
systems, but also as constituting systems in their
own right. Thus social anthropologists have written about primitive religions and cosmologies,
and their concern with these themes has not been
restricted to their social significance. Forde
writes, in his Introduction to *African Worlds* (a
collection of essays by social anthropologists),
that "each study seeks to portray and interpret the
dominant beliefs and attitudes of one people
concerning the place of Man *in Nature* [my
italics] and in Society".[15] The essays are studies of
beliefs and attitudes, not of social relations. Of
course it is true that most of the contributors are
interested in social relations, and take note of the
implications for them of the ideas they are investigating, where such implications can be shown.
But they do not abandon their enquiries where
they cannot. Again, in his *Nuer Religion* Evans-
Pritchard defines his inquiry as "a study of what
they [the Nuer] consider to be the nature of Spirit

and of man's relation to it".[16] His book is about
religious ideas and practices, not about social
relations, and this is so notwithstanding that the
author has constantly in mind the social contexts
of the beliefs and rites he is describing. It is plain,
then, that although the central concern of social
anthropologists has been with social relations,
many of them are also interested in systems of
beliefs and values even where these have no direct
relevance to social relations. They are sociologists, but they are also something more.

II

I turn now to my central question: how do social
anthropologists go about explaining the different
kinds of data they deal with? It will be said that
their first task is descriptive, for description must
precede analysis. But although the distinction
between descriptive and analytic studies is indispensable it can be misleading, especially in social
science. It is not one between studies which imply
abstraction and those which do not. It is rather
one between levels and kinds of abstraction, for
even the most matter-of-fact descriptions are shot
through with abstractions, usually unanalysed
"common sense" ones. This must be so, because
all description must use general terms, and general terms are the names of classes, that is, of
abstractions, and not the names of things. So
description does more than merely describe; it is
also in some degree explanatory.[17]

Any account of unfamiliar data, social or otherwise, must begin at this everyday level. To start
with, the appropriateness of any particular framework of explanation must be a hit-or-miss affair,
subject to continuing revision and reformulation.
We must now ask what are the kinds of explanation which are applied, and appropriate, to the
material which social anthropologists study. For
there are different types of explanation, and they
are sometimes confused with one another. But
what every kind of explanation has in common,
what in fact makes it an explanation, is that it
relates what is to be explained to something
else, or to some order of things or events, so that
it no longer appears to hang in the air, as it
were, detached and isolated. Explanation "adds
meaning to 'just so' existence", as Nadel puts it.[18]
What is unintelligible considered in and by itself

becomes meaningful as soon as it is seen as a part or as an exemplification of a wider system or process; that is, as soon as it is placed in an appropriate context.

Now it is an over-simplification to suppose that explanation is simply a process of subsuming the particular under the general, and to leave it at that. For things can be related to other things, and so explained, in a number of different ways. Of these four at least play an important, if rarely explicit, part in social anthropology. These are (i) explanation in terms of antecedent events, or efficient causes; (ii) explanation in terms of mediating factors; (iii) explanation in terms of ends, or purposes, teleological explanation; and (iv) explanation in terms of general laws or principles. It will be worth while to consider separately each of these types.[19]

Explanation in terms of antecedent events is what we commonly call historical explanation. A certain existing state of affairs is supposed to be better understood if it can be shown to have followed from some pre-existing state of affairs, in accordance with certain principles of efficient causation already familiar from other contexts.[20] Thus if it is found that certain social institutions are as they are because of certain historical happenings, the anthropologist takes (or should take) notice of these happenings, provided that there is evidence for them.[21] But there is another and no less important sense in which history is significant for social anthropology, and this is in its aspect not as a record of past events but rather as a body of contemporary ideas about these past events; "incapsulated history", in Collingwood's phrase.[22] These ideas may be potent forces in current social attitudes and relations. We should note, however, that explanation in terms of these ideas is not, strictly speaking, historical explanation at all, but rather explanation in terms of the inter-connectedness of things, the second of the kinds of explanation distinguished above.

This mode of explanation consists simply in the demonstration of connections between things which at first sight appear to be quite separate. If the entities connected are on the "what actually happens" level, these connections will in the last resort be found to be of a causal kind, different events being seen to be linked in a common causal nexus with other events.[23] Thus Durkheim explained the statistical incidence of suicide among persons in certain categories by establishing causal connections with other social factors, such as marital status and church membership.[24] And social anthropologists have added to our understanding of the widespread institution of marriage payment by showing how it is linked with other social institutions such as the system of statuses or the maintenance of inter-group relations. Anthropological literature affords innumerable examples of this kind of explanation. If the entities brought together are mental events, such as the ideas or "collective representations" current in a society, then the connections may be in terms of mutual consistency or inconsistency, moral and intellectual compatibility, and so on, as well as in terms of their implications for social behaviour.

The pointing out of necessary but not always obvious interdependences between things is an integral part of the functionalist approach, as this has been variously understood in social anthropology. But it is not the whole of this approach. For functionalism always implies two quite different kinds of explanation. The second, to which I now turn, involves reference to an end or purpose, which is seen to be achieved by the causal interdependences which have been discovered.[25]

The term "teleological explanation" may itself mean at least two different things. Strictly speaking, it consists in showing that it is a quality of what is being explained to bring about a certain consequence. But not just any consequence; to say, for example, that it is a quality of fire to burn is not to offer a teleological explanation of fire (though certainly it adds to our comprehension of what fire is). For an explanation in terms of consequence to be teleological it is necessary that the consequence should be some sort of meaningful complex, such that when the causal implications for that complex of what is to be explained have been pointed out, it is possible to say of the latter "so *that* is the point of it." Thus the circulation of the blood is teleologically explained in terms of its re-oxygenation and so the maintenance of the life of the organism. What is implied in teleological explanation, then, is not simply reference from a cause to an effect, the simple converse of historical explanation which refers an effect to a cause; what is essential to it is the notion that what is explained has causal implications for some kind of complex, comprehended as a working system, and having some kind of value, such as utility or efficiency, attached to it.[26] What is being explained is teleologically understood when it is shown how it contributes to the maintenance or working of that system.

But just as in explanation by reference to antecedent events the mind cannot rest content with mere correlation in space and time, but demands efficient causation, so in the case of teleological explanation efficient causation is as it were reversed, and the factor to be explained is understood to be as it is *because* it achieves the consequences it does achieve. This provides the second meaning of teleological explanation. The end is thought of as somehow foreseen (by somebody or something), and the thing to be explained is understood when it is seen to be adapted (by somebody or something) to that end.

Now it is plain that this latter kind of explanation is appropriate to much social data. It often enables us to understand the conscious behaviour of human individuals, who do act teleologically (in this sense), at least some of the time.[27] It may even, it seems, help us to understand the behaviour of physical organisms, as the expansions and contractions of the amoeba are understood when they are seen as means to the acquisition of food. But clearly we do not mean quite the same thing in this latter case as we do when we say, for example, that a man is slaughtering a goat with the object of providing a feast. For we can say nothing about the amoeba's intentions, or even know that it has any. Nor can we (as empirical investigators) regard the amoeba's behaviour as due to somebody else's intentions, which provide that amoebae (or a sufficient number of them) will generally do what conduces to their survival.

But we are already on the edge of a confusion, for we are really asking two different questions at once. Not content with observing that a certain kind of event contributes to the working of a certain kind of (already comprehended) system, we are now asking (in terms, it should be noted, of efficient causation) how it comes about that this is so. We are turning, in fact, from teleological explanation to explanation by reference to some antecedent event, for instance somebody's previous act of intelligence or will. So we have two questions here, to one of which a teleological answer is sufficient, and to the other of which it is not. The

first question is: how are we to understand the form of a certain phenomenon (whether this be the behaviour of an amoeba or a marriage regulation)? And the strictly teleological answer is: by seeing that that particular form conduces to the production or maintenance of a particular systematic complex; the maintenance of life through the ingestion of food, for example, or the integration of distinct social groups. Once this is seen the particular form which has been puzzling us is, so far, understood. The second, and quite different, question is: how did it come about that the form of what is to be explained is so conveniently adapted to the consequences by which we explain it? This is clearly a question of another sort: it is an aetiological one and not a teleological one at all, for it does not look forward to an end, but backward to a beginning. And like all historical questions, the usefulness of asking it depends on the likelihood of finding an answer to it.

Now in social anthropology the teleological approach which looks for the social ends served by institutions is a useful one, but that which attempts to provide a historical explanation of existing institutions in terms of somebody's purposes or intentions is much more rarely so. This is so, of course, because social anthropology has, as I have noted, tended on the whole to concentrate on the analysis of social institutions rather than on the study of the human individuals who have these institutions. And these two different approaches are very easily confused.[28] In a social context, the presence of a certain institution and the fact that it contributes to certain socially significant ends may be due historically to any of a number of quite different kinds of factors: perhaps to the conscious intention of past or present members of the society, perhaps to its diffusion from elsewhere, perhaps to some kind of social "natural selection", most likely to a combination of some or all of these factors. Where the answers to historical questions of this kind are ascertainable they are, as we have said, of considerable interest to social anthropologists. But where they are not, understanding in a different if more restricted dimension may be provided by teleological explanation in the narrower sense specified above.

Functional explanation, as it is usually understood, always implies two, sometimes all three, of the kinds of explanation I have so far discussed. It implies, first of all, the second kind of explanation which I distinguished, that in terms of mediating factors. For an essential part of the functional approach is the investigation of the causal links between different institutions. But it also implies the quite different notion (the strictly teleological one) that it is enlightening to regard institutions not simply from the point of view of their effects on some other institution or institutions considered in themselves, but rather in respect of their implications for some kind of enduring and socially significant system, the efficient maintenance of which depends upon (*inter alia*) the institution or institutions being examined. Here the accent is not simply on the causal links between institutions, but rather on the part one institution plays in a systematic and already apprehended complex of inter-locking institutions; on what may in a sense be said to be a part-whole relationship. Thus, for example, the institution of vassalage is explained functionally – and teleologically – when it is shown that it contributes to the maintenance of the particular complex of inter-personal relations which is usually called feudalism.[29] And, thirdly, functional explanation may imply (though it need not) that it is because they bring about certain ends that the institutions studied have the form they do; it may, that is, attempt explanation on the level of effective causality. The ends which are thought of as being brought about may be, and have been, very differently conceived: sometimes they are thought of in terms of particular complexes of institutions localized in the society being studied; sometimes they are conceived as grandiose sociological ends like social equilibrium, integration, or the perpetuation of the social structure; sometimes they are taken to be non-social ends, like biological survival. Evidently the kinds of ends to which a particular institution is seen as conducing will depend to a very large extent on the kinds of interests held by the analyst.

I cannot here undertake a comprehensive analysis of the functional model as it has been developed and used in social anthropology;[30] I simply indicate the parts played in it by the kinds of explanation I have considered. It may be said, however, that since the functional approach derives most of its weight from the analogy with organisms, which are usefully regarded as wholes composed of causally interacting parts or members, this approach is more illuminating where social institutions are being dealt with on the level of systems of social interaction rather than on the level of normative or ideal systems.[31] Such systems may and indeed commonly do have a social dimension, but, as we have seen, it has proved enlightening to examine their interrelations in cultural as well as in social terms. It has, further, often been pointed out that the organic analogy can provide no model for the understanding of social change.

The fourth type of explanation which I distinguished is that which refers to general laws or principles. I might reasonably have put this kind of explanation first instead of last, for very often this reference is classificatory rather than explanatory, and in a sense all other kinds of explanation imply it. As a rule all that this kind of explanation does is to assert that the datum to be explained falls into a particular class or category, and so either possesses the characters by which that class is defined (in which case the "explanation" is tautologous), or else possesses some character or characters with which members of that class have been found invariably to be associated (in which case the association itself demands explanation in some other terms). When, however, there already exists some understanding of the category to which the datum to be explained is referred, then the process of subsuming the particular under the general (as, for example, Mauss referred the institutions known as the *kula* and the *potlatch* to the general class of prestations) certainly adds to our understanding, and so may be called explanatory. But it would not be so unless we already understood the general class of phenomena to which reference is made; that is, unless it were already explicable in other terms. Thus the process of classification really consists in bringing the datum to be explained within the range of some already existing explanation. Of course a great deal depends on what is meant by such very ambiguous terms as "law" and "principle", but in any case what is explanatory is not the generality of the law invoked, nor any kind of regularity in the data which it expresses, but rather the explanatory synthesis which (perhaps implicitly) it entails.

I have been concerned to suggest that the types of explanatory synthesis which we have discussed are among those most used – and most useful – in social anthropology.

III

So far we have been concerned with the ways in which social anthropologists go about understanding particular institutions. But social anthropologists, like others, have sometimes sought to provide understanding not simply of particular institutions, but of societies – or cultures – regarded as wholes, or even of the abstraction "society" itself. I now consider briefly whether such approaches can be said to be explanatory and, if so, in what way.

I consider first those characterizations which are intended to illumine "society" as such; which are, that is, supposed to be valid for all human societies everywhere, and to add to our understanding of what society is. The functional model, which, as we have seen, combines two or more different kinds of explanatory synthesis, provides one such approach. Functionalism, when it is conceived not (as it may most usefully be) as a useful technique for investigating and explaining particular social institutions, but rather as a key to the understanding of society itself, has assumed two main forms. First there is that associated with Malinowski, which holds that society is best understood as an assemblage of contrivances for satisfying the biological and psychological needs of the human organisms which compose it. Few if any social anthropologists nowadays use this approach: though indeed such needs must be met if societies are to survive, it is not instructive to analyse social institutions solely in terms of them. Their satisfaction is a condition of the maintenance of life at all, not only of social life, so they can hardly throw any distinctive light on the latter.

The second type of "total" functionalism, taken over by Radcliffe-Brown from Durkheim, asserts that the function of any social institution is the correspondence between it and some general need (or "necessary condition of existence", to use the term adopted by Radcliffe-Brown)[32] of society. The ultimate value for any society may be said to be its continued existence, and this, so the argument goes, can be achieved only through the maintenance of social solidarity between its members. Cohesion, or social solidarity, is accordingly the end to which social institutions are to be conceived as contributing more or less effectively. Thus for Radcliffe-Brown social function is the contribution made to the functioning of the "total social system", and functional unity is achieved when "all parts of the social system work together with a sufficient degree of harmony or internal consistency; i.e. without producing persistent conflicts which can neither be resolved nor regulated".[33]

I am not concerned here to analyse this approach; in the present context I wish only to point out that it implies the notion that a total social system is some kind of empirical entity to which definite properties can be ascribed. It is, however, now becoming increasingly plain both that this "holistic" view of society is of less analytic value than used to be supposed, and that in any case society or "the social system" is not something given in experience, but is rather an intellectual construct or model. The use of a model of this kind is not to be justified by identifying it with something else that is "really there"; its validity rests simply on its usefulness in helping to order and make sense of data under investigation. Society is not a "thing"; it is rather a way of ordering experience, a working (and in certain contexts indispensable) hypothesis:[34] if we impute to it some kind of substantial reality we saddle ourselves with an entity more embarrassing than useful. When this is realized, the needs or necessary conditions of a society no longer appear to be analogous to the needs of a physical organism; they appear rather as the logical implications of the particular theoretical model which we have constructed. Thus, for example, the American sociologist Levy uses a logical, rather than a teleological, frame of reference; he elaborates a number of "functional requisites of any society", thus in effect saying (though he says a good deal more than this) how he conceives it to be most useful to employ the term "society".[35]

I am not suggesting that attempts to characterize the concept "society" are mistaken or useless; what I am saying is that such exercises, important though they may be for theoretical sociology, have little or nothing to do with the analysis of the kinds of data which are given in field investigation, which is the main business of social anthropologists. It is no part of their task to say what "society" is; their work is cut out for them in explaining the data given to them in fieldwork. But although the concept is of limited usefulness for social anthropologists in its substantive form, the empirical entity to which it sometimes refers being better designated (after Emmet) "social aggregate",[36] it is none the less an indispensable part of the social anthropologist's analytic equipment (as it is of his title) in its adjectival form. So a minimal connotation must be ascribed to it, at least in a relational, if not in a substantive, sense. It is plain, I think, that what the term "social" essentially implies is the idea of bringing together, associating, human beings, and it is simply this relational aspect of human life that we indicate by the terms "social" and "society". "Society" is simply the context in which the social anthropologist carries out his inquiries; as has been said, analysis of the concept itself need form no part of the anthropologist's task, which is simply the understanding of social and cultural institutions.

Anthropologists, then, do not, or at least need not, study "Society". But they can and do study specific societies, or "social aggregates", which is a very different thing. What it usually means is that they study the social institutions in terms of which some at least of the members of a particular social aggregate are interrelated. The people so associated usually share a common territory, and they may – or may not – think of themselves in unitary terms. In this context what terms like "society" or "culture" do is broadly to delimit a particular field of ethnographical or sociological inquiry. My final question, then, must be: is any understanding of particular societies or cultures[37] possible, over and above our understanding of the several institutions which characterize them?

The answer to this question depends, of course, on the way in which it is formulated; but in a certain sense it can, I believe, be answered in the affirmative. It may even, perhaps, be claimed that

this kind of understanding is something which the social anthropologist is peculiarly qualified to provide. For it is to be achieved, if it is achieved at all, by coming to understand the dominant beliefs and values of the people being studied, and the social anthropologist, who lives in the society he studies and as far as possible as a member of it, may with luck achieve, or approximate to, this kind of understanding. When the major values of the people being studied have been apprehended in this way it may fairly be claimed that the society or culture has been "understood", for only then can the investigator represent to himself – and perhaps to others – what it would be like to be a member of that society. Of course this kind of interpretation is extremely hazardous and a particular anthropologist may be mistaken; another anthropologist might conceivably select some other values in terms of which to interpret the same culture, for the student's predilections will affect what he sees and emphasizes. But the last word must be with the people whose society and culture are being studied; no doubt Evans-Pritchard's *Nuer* and Fortune's *Sorcerers of Dobu* (to choose but two examples) would have been very different books if they had been written by other anthropologists, but even if they had been they could hardly have failed to stress the pervasiveness of notions of descent, and the ubiquity of sorcery beliefs, respectively, as they do now. Social anthropology is not wholly hallucinatory. And, as I have noted, the key to this kind of understanding is not to be found simply by watching what people do (which is in any case unintelligible apart from what they think), but through the understanding of their language and familiarity with its idioms and the values it embodies. By these means an anthropologist may be able to give an account of the people he studies which conveys something of how they conceive their own social life, and which may thus possess unity and vitality as a work of art no less than as a scientific record.[38] [...]

Notes

1 Explanation is not, of course, the only means to understanding, at least where the behaviour of human beings is concerned; understanding may also be achieved through imaginative identification with the character described. But social anthropologists, unlike poets and novelists, seek to convey understanding mainly (though not only) by explaining.

2   Radcliffe-Brown (1949), p. 503.

3   Evans-Pritchard (1951), p. 5.

4   Nadel (1956), p. 159.

5   Piddington (1950), p. 3.

6   In the course of a critical discussion of the dangers of the "holistic" approach in the social sciences, Popper (1957, p. 77) points out that, "If we wish to study a thing, we are bound to select certain aspects of it. It is not possible for us to observe or to describe a whole piece of the world, or a whole piece of nature … since all description is necessarily selective."

7   I use the term "institutionalized" simply in the sense of "well established or familiar" (*Shorter Oxford English Dictionary*). Institutionalization is thus a matter of degree; a particular usage or social relationship may be more or less institutionalized.

8   Though even then the usefulness of a comparison will depend on the degree of similarity, in relevant aspects, of the institutional backgrounds of the things compared. On the relevance of this to social anthropology, cf. Schapera (1953).

9   Recently, for example, by Parsons (1952, pp. 25–6), who uses the syncretic concept of status-role. We are not here concerned to relate or analyse these notions, merely to indicate those aspects of social relations which interest social anthropologists.

10 Parsons (1952), p. 39.

11 As Max Weber in particular was concerned to stress (Weber, 1947, p. 80 and *passim*). Cf. also Nadel (1951), pp. 30 ff.

12 Not, most social anthropologists would agree, to the whole of any culture. In most of its usages the term "culture" is far too broad usefully to designate a specific field for systematic study. There is no need in the present context to elaborate the familiar society–culture distinction. It may be said, however, that as the terms are generally used by anthropologists the difference lies rather in the interest of the observer than in what is observed: where the interest is "social" the emphasis is on social relationships; where it is "cultural" it is on configurations of beliefs and values. But the reality which is given to the observer is one, not two. For a clear discussion of the society–culture dichotomy, cf. MacIver (1942), pp. 273 ff.

13 It may be acknowledged at once that "what actually happens" is a construct of the analyst, built up by abstraction and inference from what people do and say. The important point here is that it is the anthropologist's construct, not necessarily that of the people studied. It approximates to Lévi-Strauss's "statistical model", as distinct from his "mechanical model", which is the social system as its members conceive it (Lévi-Strauss, 1953, p. 528). We cannot here examine the ontological status of sociological "facts": for interesting discussions of this and related problems, cf. Lévi-Strauss (1953) and Nadel (1957), especially ch. VII. Here what is important to note is that whatever the level of abstraction involved "what actually happens" is only one of the social anthropologist's concerns.

14 Nadel (1957, p. 155) gives a frank statement of "what the students of social structure really do". According to him what they do is "to describe, still in heavily qualitative terms, types of relationships and groups, their interconnections through activities and recruitment, the believed-in values and norms of the people, and the obtaining sanctioning mechanisms; nor do they exclude the psychological concomitants of relationships ('loyalties', 'sentiments', and other motivations)".

15 Forde (1954), p. vii.

16 Evans-Pritchard (1956), p. vi.

17 Correspondingly, "explanation always spills over into description" (Nadel, 1957, p. 151). Of course this must be so, since abstractions and the "reality" they describe are always inextricably interwoven.

18 Nadel (1951), p. 20.

19 I do not here inquire into the epistemological status of these several types of explanation, nor into the question whether any of them can be reduced to any other, or all to a common type (in a certain sense they certainly can). For practical purposes they can be distinguished, and they can be shown to imply different kinds of interests in the data being examined. Discussions of some of the methodological issues involved may be found in textbooks of scientific method, such as Wolf (1928) and Toulmin (1953).

20 Plainly "historical" explanation implies reference to general principles (the fourth type of explanation distinguished above). None the less it is not explanation in terms of these general principles, but in terms of past events. The principles involved are usually psychological ones of the unanalysed, "common-sense" kind.

21 For a brief reference to the increased interest in history and social change shown by British social anthropologists in recent years, cf. Beattie (1955), pp. 5–7.

22 Collingwood (1944), p. 73 and *passim*.

23 "When the problems concern apparently remote or diverse facts, or events, which, nevertheless, appear to be connected, then an explanation may take the form of discovering, or indicating, intermediate factors or events, which bring the

correlated, but remote, factors or events into closer connection" (Wolf, 1928, p. 122).

24 Durkheim (1951), book II. This kind of explanation evidently implies reference to the first type referred to above, that by reference to antecedent events or "efficient causes". The causal relation may of course be reciprocal, not "one-way" only. It may, and indeed must, imply also reference to a general principle in terms of which the interconnections themselves are understood (for example, in the case quoted, to Durkheim's notion of social cohesion or solidarity).

25 A good account of the manifold ambiguities involved in the notion of functionalism is to be found in Merton (1949), part I. For a discussion of the significance of the concept in contemporary social anthropology, cf. Firth (1955); also Beattie (1955), pp. 3–4.

26 For a most enlightening discussion of the teleological implications of the notion of functionalism, by a philosopher, not a social anthropologist, cf. Emmet (1958), ch. III, an analysis to which I acknowledge particular indebtedness. She writes (p. 289), "We must, I think, say that the notion of function only makes sense where it is possible to talk about a part–whole relation in a context which is in some way a system." This is true also, *a fortiori*, of the notion of teleology.

27 Social anthropologists, as I have noted, tend to be more concerned with social institutions than with the behaviour of particular human individuals. But where they are concerned with the latter, of course the purposes of those individuals must be apprehended if their behaviour is to be "understood". Nadel, in particular, was concerned to stress the pervasiveness of purpose: thus "behaviour is sociologically relevant only if it is aim-controlled or enters into aim-controlled action patterns" (1951, p. 30); and "there must be, somewhere in the task pattern, consciousness, and somewhere in its activation, purpose. Without these two factors there can be no social understanding; more precisely, there can be no material susceptible of such understanding" (1951, p. 33).

28 This is one of the considerations which underlies Hoernlé's criticism of Radcliffe-Brown's "Preface" and Fortes' and Evans-Pritchard's "Introduction" to *African Political Systems* (Hoernlé, 1940).

29 It may be conceded that in the last resort the difference between these two types of explanation (by reference to mediating factors and by reference to ends; teleological explanation) is one of degree rather than of kind; the degree, that is, to which the cause is seen as operative within a system of some kind, and not merely as impacting on some particular institution. For, as we have shown, any institution necessarily implies some degree of systematization of data. But the difference of degree is none the less important, and has significant implications for the kind of sociological analysis undertaken.

30 For contemporary discussions of this theme, cf. Merton (1949), Firth (1955), Nadel (1951), etc.

31 The distinction is precisely made by Firth (1955, p. 241): "Systems of action are functional systems while cultural systems are symbolic systems in which the components have logical or meaningful rather than functional relationships with one another."

32 In an attempt to eliminate teleological content from the notion (Radcliffe-Brown, 1952, p. 178). Since a "necessary condition of existence" is no less an "end" than the satisfaction of a "need" is, the attempt can hardly be said to have succeeded. On this issue, cf. Hoernlé (1940).

33 Radcliffe-Brown (1952), p. 181.

34 Emmet's suggestion that the empirical reality sometimes named "society" ("a number of people are somehow together") should be called "social aggregate", has a great deal to recommend it (Emmet, 1958, p. 23). It means something different from the notion of "community" (Tönnies "*Gemeinschaft*", as developed by MacIver [1942] and others), for the emphasis is on common residence and culture as "given", rather than on any particular kind of interrelationship.

35 Levy (1952).

36 Emmet (1958), p. 23. Elsewhere (p. 15) she writes: "I do not think it is generally helpful … to speak just of 'Society' (with a capital 'S')…. By a 'society' we, generally speaking, mean some alignment between people in virtue of which we can think of them as grouped." In this sense, evidently, the members of any particular social aggregate may be members of a number of different "societies".

37 I have not, here or elsewhere, distinguished "society" from "culture", since the empirical field of ethnographic inquiry which they designate is one. Cf. note 12 above.

38 This process of "translation" from one culture into another has been recognized as one of the most important parts – if not the most important part – of the social anthropologist's task. Cf., for example, Evans-Pritchard (1951), p. 61, also (for a non-anthropological view), Berlin (1954), p. 61: "the modes of thought of the ancients or of any cultures remote from our own are comprehensible to us only in the degree to which we share some, at any rate, of their basic categories."

References

Beattie, J. H. M. "Contemporary Trends in British Social Anthropology". *Sociologus*, vol. V, no. 1 (1955).

Berlin, I. *Historical Inevitability*. August Comte Memorial Trust Lecture, no. 1. London, Oxford University Press (1954).

Collingwood, R. G. *An Autobiography*. London, Pelican Books (1944).

Durkheim, E. *Suicide*. (Translated by Spaulding and Simpson.) Glencoe, Illinois, the Free Press (1951).

Emmet, D. *Function, Purpose and Powers*. London, Macmillan (1958).

Evans-Pritchard, E. E. *Social Anthropology: The Broadcast Lectures*. London, Cohen and West (1951).

Evans-Pritchard, E. E. *Nuer Religion*. Oxford, Clarendon Press (1956).

Firth, R. "Functionalism". In *The Yearbook of Anthropology*. New York, Wenner-Gren Foundation for Anthropological Research (1955).

Forde, D. (ed.). *African Worlds*. Oxford, Oxford University Press (1954).

Hoernlé, W. *Philosophers and Anthropologists. Bantu Studies*, vol. 14, pp. 395–408 (1940).

Lévi-Strauss, C. "Social Structure". In *Anthropology Today*. Chicago, University of Chicago Press (1953).

Levy, M. *The Structure of Society*. Princeton University Press (1952).

MacIver, R. M. *Social Causation*. New York, Ginn (1942).

Merton, R. K. *Social Theory and Social Structure*. Glencoe, Illinois, Free Press (1949).

Nadel, S. F. *The Foundations of Social Anthropology*. London, Cohen and West (1951).

Nadel, S. F. "Understanding Primitive Peoples." *Oceania*, vol. XXVI, no. 3 (1956).

Nadel, S. F. *The Theory of Social Structure*. London, Cohen and West (1957).

Parsons, T. *The Social System*. London, Tavistock Publications in collaboration with Routledge and Kegan Paul (1952).

Piddington, R. *An Introduction to Social Anthropology*, vol. I. Edinburgh, Oliver and Boyd (1950).

Popper, K. R. *The Poverty of Historicism*. London, Routledge and Kegan Paul (1957).

Radcliffe-Brown, A. R. "White's View of a Science of Culture." *American Anthropologist*, vol. 51, no. 3 (1949).

Radcliffe-Brown, A. R. *Structure and Function in Primitive Society*. London, Cohen and West (1952).

Schapera, I. "Some Comments on the Comparative Method in Social Anthropology." *American Anthropologist*, vol. 55, no. 3 (1953).

Toulmin, S. *The Philosophy of Science: An Introduction*. London, Hutchinson's University Library (1953).

Weber, M. *The Theory of Social and Economic Organization*. (Translated by Henderson and Parsons.) London, William Hodge (1947).

Wolf, A. *Essentials of Scientific Method*. London, George Allen and Unwin (1928).

14

Anthropological Data and Social Reality

Ladislav Holy and Milan Stuchlik

"Participant observation" is without doubt one of the most important stock-in-trade terms of social anthropology. It conveys the image of research carried out directly among the people one is studying, usually for a considerable length of time, carefully observing and documenting minutiae of their day-to-day life. "Having been there" and "having seen this and that done" is the ultimate guarantee of the veracity and accuracy of any information divulged about those people. If it were customary to publish, or otherwise make available, not only the papers and monographs resulting from research but also the actual field-notes and the recordings of data, it would soon emerge that "participant observation" is a blanket term for a broad range of ways in which the information comes to the observer. When we read in a monograph that, for example, tribe X subsists on shifting cultivation, we may assume that this information has not been obtained by the researcher participating in any shift of the fields: fieldwork is usually not long enough for that. What it presumably boils down to is that the anthropologist noted the distribution of currently cultivated fields, observed traces of more or less

recent cultivation on other patches of land, was told by the villagers that they had cultivated these patches, and possibly that after some time they would clear and cultivate some hitherto unused land. When an anthropologist describes the family in society Y as having an authoritarian structure with the father at the head, he will again have derived this from a number of more specific data in his fieldnotes: observed instances of fathers behaving in what may be called an authoritarian way, descriptions of what fathers may do or order to be done, and possibly opinions of people on how the family should be or is organized. Some of these data were obtained, undoubtedly, through observations; some of them, equally undoubtedly, came to the anthropologist in the form of expressed opinions, value judgements, etc. Unless we understand "participant observation" in a rather simplistic sense of "being on the spot", these latter forms can hardly be the result of it.

To say that tribe X has shifting cultivation, or that tribe Y has an authoritarian family structure is conveying information, but strictly speaking it is not giving data, unless we can specify to what such information refers. In the first case this can

From *Actions, Norms and Representations: Foundations of Anthropological Inquiry* (Cambridge: Cambridge University Press, 1983), pp. 5–11, 12–19, 122–9. Copyright © 1983 by Cambridge University Press. Reprinted with permission of Cambridge University Press.

Anthropology in Theory: Issues in Epistemology, Second Edition. Edited by Henrietta L. Moore and Todd Sanders.
© 2014 John Wiley & Sons, Inc. Published 2014 by John Wiley & Sons, Inc.

be done: we can say that "shifting cultivation" refers to a pattern, or sequence, of actual observable processes. In the second case the task is more difficult: does authoritarian structure refer to the pattern of observed authoritarian acts of fathers, to the set of orders any father can give, or to a number of expressed opinions? We suggest that in normal anthropological procedure it often refers indiscriminately to all three; it includes all these and other kinds of data, and the differences between them are annulled by putting them all under the same heading, as results of participant observation.

[. . .] [W]e intend to discuss the differences between kinds of data and the question of their reference. More specifically, we wish to argue two main theses. The first is that the differences in data are not merely the consequence of differing data-gathering techniques or ways in which the information comes to the knowledge of the observer, but the consequence of their referring to different levels or domains of social reality. In other words, differences in data often connote the existential difference between levels or domains of reality. Therefore, social reality cannot be conceived of as a unitary system. The second is that the fact that social reality has often been conceived of in this way has led to its misrepresentation and to incorrect formulation of problems and problem-solving procedures. Seemingly simple and non-problematic techniques like participant observation, or even fieldwork, have played quite an important role in this.

The last major discussion of the nature of data and their proper use in social anthropology took place in the 1960s, with the development of situational analysis or the extended-case method (cf. Gluckman 1961, and Van Velsen 1967, for review). The earlier, and at that time still predominant, position can best be characterized by a well-known quote from Radcliffe-Brown, describing the procedure of science as not being

> concerned with the particular, the unique, but only with the general, with kinds, with events which recur. The actual relations of Tom, Dick and Harry or the behaviour of Jack and Jill may go down in our field note-books and may provide illustrations for a general description. But what we need for scientific purposes is an account of the form of the structure. (Radcliffe-Brown 1952:192 [see also chapter 6, this volume, p. 66])

In his view, particular data, of whatever kind, are to be used as bases for generalized description, this description rendered as a structure and eventually illustrated by aptly chosen particular data. On a very small scale, this is exactly the process whereby the family in the above-mentioned society Y comes to be presented as having an authoritarian structure. The practitioners of the extended-case method criticized particularly this way of handling concrete data. They pointed out that in actual fact the data were not used for analysis at all: they were merely illustrations for the structural schemata devised by the anthropologists.

For situational analysts, particular data, actual interactions, the observed cases were something which had to be the subject of analysis. Their regularity or patterning, the structure, should only be elicited directly from these cases and also demonstrated on them (Gluckman 1961:10–11). Thus, the style of analysis this approach proposed was considerably different from that upheld by the preceding approach. However, the criticism, fully justified as it was, did not go far enough and the extended-case style of analysis still did not solve the main problem. The step from structure to actual cases had been an important one, but let us consider what it meant in more practical terms. A particular case analysed by an anthropologist often extends over a considerable period of time, starting long before he comes to the field (cf. Mitchell 1956:95ff, 116ff) and evolving during his stay there. His data about it are thus formed by a rather varied collection of information, consisting of informants' reports of past events, their justifications and explanations of past events, his own observations of present events, informants' reports and justifications of present events, etc. Yet all these data inform him, more or less in the same way, about the case viewed as a pattern of events, and in the last instance about the form of life or social structure. The differences in data are still treated as incidental; in other words, "data" is still a unitary concept, a sum total of information obtained about a particular case and through it about social structure conceived of in an equally unitary way.

Of course, the whole discussion was again about the problem of reference. Addressing anthropological analyses in general, rather than situational analyses in particular, Leach succinctly posed the question of "how far the anthropologist's concept of social structure refers to a set of ideas or to a set of empirical facts" (Leach 1961a:5). Let us examine this question with the help of a concrete example: segmentary lineage structure. The amount of field-work which the concept of segmentary lineage structure has stimulated and the prominence it has attained in theoretical and methodological writings clearly indicate that its formulation has been considered one of the most important achievements of social anthropology. It seems justified, therefore, to use it as a "case study".

So, when an anthropologist concludes that such-and-such a society has a segmentary lineage structure, what does he mean by it? There seems to be a considerable degree of consensus that he is referring to a set of notions held by the members of that society, or, in Leach's terms, to a set of ideas. Evans-Pritchard asserts this when he mentions that the principle of segmentation and opposition between segments "can be stated in hypothetical terms by the Nuer themselves" (Evans-Pritchard 1940:143). Fortes expresses the same view when he states that the paradigm of the lineage system of the Tallensi "is in the mind's eye of every well-informed native when he discusses the structure of his society and takes part in the public affairs" (Fortes 1945:30). Similarly, Southall sees the concept of segmentary lineage structure as a part of the natives' "projective system" (Southall 1952:32). Talking about the Nuer, the Tiv and the Bedouin, Lewis points out that the "political-jural ideology is uncompromisingly one of descent" (Lewis 1965:97). He clarifies what this ideology is meant to be by a quotation from Middleton and Tait: "co-ordinate segments which have come into existence as a result of segmentation are regarded as complementary and as formally equal" (Middleton and Tait 1958:7). The fact that the descent or lineage principle is referred to as ideology indicates that it is taken to be a notion held by the actors; it is a part of their conceptual universe. [...]

So far, there is no problem. The segmentary lineage structure is a set of notions which members of some societies hold about the proper organization of their social relations. They have them in their "mind's eye" and are able to tell the anthropologist that they hold them, even to discuss them in hypothetical terms. However, a considerable number of anthropologists present the segmentary lineage structure, implicitly or explicitly, also as a representation of ongoing social processes, or, in Leach's terms, as referring to a set of empirical facts. The actors not only hold and discuss these notions, but also make them manifest in their behaviour, organize their actual social relations and activities in terms of a segmentary social structure. [...] Some anthropologists, notably Fortes, have gone even further and postulated a direct relationship between the segmentary lineage structure and observable social processes. In reference to the Tallensi, he says that the "Tale society is built up round the lineage system.... It is the skeleton of their social structure, the bony framework which shapes their body politic; it guides their economic life and moulds their ritual ideas and values" (Fortes 1945:30). The Nuer, the Tallensi and the Tiv "may be said to think agnatically about social relations like the Romans and Chinese.... The paradigm of patrilineal descent is not just a means of picturing their social structure; it is their fundamental guide to conduct and belief in all areas of their social life" (Fortes 1969:290–1).

[...]

Thus, we can distinguish two positions as far as the reference of the segmentary lineage structure is concerned. For some of the anthropologists mentioned above, it refers exclusively to a set of ideas, ideology, myth, or simply a set of notions. For others, it refers simultaneously to a set of notions and the pattern of social processes, the way in which the members of a society organize their activities. The first position faces a rather interesting problem: there is no denying that the set of notions called segmentary lineage structure exists; since it exists for the members of a society, it is their social reality. On the other hand, this set of notions is not manifested in social processes, in the organization of their activities. Since social processes, or the activities of the members of a society, exist equally undeniably and are also social reality, it is necessary to distinguish two different kinds of social reality which do not have to be directly related. Unless the observer is prepared to ascribe to both the same degree of facticity or reality, he has to ascribe to one of them ontological priority. This is a problem we will be discussing at considerable length later on; in this context, it would be only a digression. However, it is important to note that the postulation of two levels or domains of social reality is directly necessitated by defining segmentary lineage structure as a set of ideas, ideology or myth.

This problem does not exist for the second position. The segmentary lineage structure is simply a form of society manifested both in actors' notions and in social processes. However, this position runs into considerable problems of its own. On closer inspection, it appears that the view that the segmentary lineage structure is a representation of empirically observable social processes is not all that well founded. For instance, most of the available case histories of hostilities between Nuer tribal sections and their political alliances (Evans-Pritchard 1940:144–5, 229–30; Howell 1954:19–20) indicate that the opposition between tribal sections is not as balanced as Evans-Pritchard's paradigmatic presentation would suggest (cf. Holy 1979 for a more detailed discussion). This has been recognized, to a certain extent, by Evans-Pritchard himself in his admission that the hostilities and alliances between tribal sections were not always as regular and simple as they were explained to him and as he stated them to be (Evans-Pritchard 1940:144); he also admitted that "political actualities are confused and conflicting. They are confused because they are not always, even in a political context, in accord with political values, though they tend to conform to them, and because social ties of a different kind operate in the same field, sometimes strengthening them and sometimes running counter to them" (Evans-Pritchard 1940:138).

There are numerous other cases where a careful reading of the description of actual situations discloses departures from the ideologically asserted balance and opposition of segments, but the Nuer evidence should be sufficient to establish the problem.

It is in this context that Leach's original question acquires its critical strength. However, Leach's criticism is not the only one. Several anthropologists have levelled similar critical comments at the concept of segmentary lineage structure, and at the notion of structure as represented by it in general. The main deficiency is seen specifically in the fact that the distinction between a "set of ideas" and a "set of empirical facts" is not clearly and consistently made. As a consequence of it, the relation between structural forms and actual behaviour is postulated as non-problematic and thus effectively removed from the analysis. [...] The question arises of how it is possible that even the recognition of the above-mentioned discrepancies, i.e. of the fact that activities on the ground are not always structured in terms of the segmentary model, has not detracted from the idea that structure expresses or embodies behaviour. In our view, this is because the ultimate goal of such research has been to formulate a holistic structure of society as its final description and as the explanation of whatever is going on in it. The analysis has not been oriented towards what the members of the society do and why they do it, but towards how the society is structured. The structure has to be, of course, elicited from the data, but, by the same token, the data are seen as indiscriminately referring to the structure. Even a cursory look at any monograph will show us that the data comprise actually observed behaviour, the analyst's generalizations, informants' recollections of past events, their statements of what should be done or what is usually done, etc. The demand for the formulation of the social structure gives the illusion that all these differing data are data about it, that models built on different kinds of data are coincident and that one kind of data is an adequate substitute for another; observed events, events reconstructed by the informants, events reconstructed by the analyst, statements of jural norms are all taken as informing about the same thing.

[...]

It might seem that we are overstressing a point which is obvious and rather trivial. After all, long before he even goes to the field any budding anthropologist knows that he can obtain data in two different ways: by observing what is being done, and by asking people questions or listening to them talking, or, to put it in more general terms, that there are two broad categories of data: the verbal statements of the members of the society and their observed behaviour. He knows also that the information conveyed by one category of data is often quite different from that conveyed by the other, i.e. people often say they do such and such and can be observed actually doing something else. We agree that the point is obvious, but it is hardly trivial: its triviality is the result of the fact that it is denied importance in most analytical procedures in anthropology.

Anthropological literature is full of descriptions of the differences between what people say they do (have done, will do) and what the anthropologist observes as their activities. Such cases are often carefully documented, analysed, and explained. However, the analysis and explanation usually start from the premiss that such differences should not exist, that they constitute a discrepancy, or at least an inconsistency. What is being explained or what is considered as a problem is the discrepancy. Where there is no difference between people's verbal statements and their observed behaviour, no problem exists and no analysis is needed.

What we have in mind can be shown on a study of any given uxorilocal society. A society is classified as uxorilocal on the grounds of verbal statements that such residence is ideal, proper or usual, and of the observation that some, possibly most married couples indeed reside uxorilocally. At the same time, it would be rather difficult to find a uxorilocal society where all married couples were actually uxorilocal; there is always a certain, possibly quite high percentage of couples residing otherwise. Let us imagine a society with 75% of couples residing uxorilocally and 25% of couples residing non-uxorilocally. What is invariably seen as a problem is the existence of these 25% non-uxorilocal marriages, because they constitute a discrepancy between what is said and what is done. The explanation usually consists of finding contingent constraints or influences, either in every single case or in general terms. The important point is that the 75% uxorilocally residing couples do not constitute any problem, simply because in their case there is no difference between what is said and what can be observed. Their residence is counted as explained by the existence of the norm. Thus, though technically the distinction between verbal statements and observed actions is being made, or can be made, it is trivialized by being completely disregarded on the explanatory level: verbal statements are seen as describing what actually happens and the problem arises only when they do not.

Let us overstate the argument and imagine a society whose members profess uxorilocality as a proper form of postmarital residence but never reside uxorilocally: clearly, the verbal statements would then be descriptive of no actual cases at all. Admittedly, it is rather improbable that such a society could be found, but an actual example of the Lapp society will help our argument as well: "I noticed the same discrepancy in statements as to the change of residence upon marriage. The Lapps invariably state that at the marriage, the woman should join her husband's band but an analysis of all marriages shows that about equally often the man joins his wife's band and remains there" (Pehrson 1964:292).

If this is the case, a verbal statement has a more or less equal chance of being descriptive of observed actions and of being discrepant with them. On the basis of this, Pehrson comes to a rather extraordinary conclusion that Lapps have no rule of postmarital residence. What Lapps "invariably say" cannot be considered a rule because it does not sufficiently describe what they can be observed doing. Leaving aside the terminological question of whether their statements should be called a rule or given some other appropriate name, clearly Lapps do say that women should join their husbands. And equally clearly, this is a datum for the anthropologist, regardless of whether all, some or no women actually join their husbands. Obviously, it does not inform him about what Lapp women actually do; [however,] though not necessarily made apparent in observable behaviour, [it is] nevertheless [an] existing social phenomenon.

Since the rule of virilocality is invariably stated by Lapps, it follows that even the husbands who joined their wives state it. If it does not adequately describe or explain their behaviour, it can hardly adequately describe or explain the behaviour of virilocal couples. This can be rephrased in the following way: if the existence of the rule of virilocality can be accompanied by either actual instances of virilocality or actual instances of uxorilocality, then, if we want adequately to account for either, some other elements must be introduced (cf. Holy 1974:112–15). This example alone should be sufficient to show that the premiss of necessary or nonproblematic congruence between what people say and what they do is invalid.

It seems to us that the point about the differences in data is, therefore, not trivial unless made so by the procedures of research. The difference between the verbal statements of the actors (be they spontaneous utterances or answers to the anthropologist's questions) and the anthropologist's own observation of their behaviour is not merely a casual difference in the way in which the information comes to the anthropologist. As we suggested at the beginning of this chapter, it connotes a difference between the areas or domains of the social reality which is being studied. In the simplest possible terms, one of these domains is formed by the notions or ideas people hold, and can verbally state, and the other by the actions they actually perform.

We have tried to show on some examples that a large number of anthropological explanations, by not consistently making the distinction between these categories of data, conflate the domains of reality or treat them as being directly homologous. In other words, a large number of anthropological explanations represent social reality as a unitary system or structure consisting indiscriminately of both notions and observable actions. Explanatory models of social structure, or systems models, are used as "straightforward heuristic devices to 'picture' and organize complex data" (Whyte 1977:77). When such a position is taken, clearly the same informational status is ascribed to qualitatively different data, i.e. they are assumed to inform about the same thing and can therefore quite easily substitute each other.

So far, we have been concerned to show that the difference between the two main categories of data, which can be rather simplifyingly called verbal statements and observed behaviour, embody or connote essential differences between areas or domains of social reality, and that the anthropologists who in their practice disregard these differences are presenting distorted models of social reality and are incorrectly defining problems and procedures for problem-solving. The question now arises of how it is possible, in view of the fact that the differences between the kinds of data are a commonplace knowledge and the discrepancies between verbal statements and observed behaviour both numerous and well documented in anthropological literature, to disregard the whole problem and to maintain, for the purposes of analysis and explanation, the simple dichotomy between undifferentiated data and undifferentiated social reality. It seems to us that this can be traced to three different but interdependent roots.

The first of these is based on a general deterministic conception of man: one of its tenets is that people's behaviour can properly be explained only as the result of some forces external to them. In the social sciences, the most widely accepted version of this is the Durkheimian dictum about social facts being external to individuals and exerting external pressure on them. For example, norms are seen as models which have a direct one-to-one relationship to actions. They are prescriptions of concrete actions with a compelling force of their own to summon actions (for the elaboration of this point cf. Stuchlik 1977: 11ff). However, since they are prescriptions, something which has the force to summon actions, they are also taken to be descriptions of what actually happens. Once we have established, for example, that a society practises descent-group endogamy, on the basis of what we have been told about marriage arrangements (what they are, what they should be, etc.) we treat it as if it were endogamous in the behavioural sense, i.e. as if everybody actually married within his descent group. Even if it is known that the marriages of many people are exogamous, this is an incidental fact which does not weaken the fact that this society is endogamous. In general terms, to conceive of norms (or social facts) in this way leads to consideration of a set of jural ideas as describing a set of patterned actions, or at least as being homologous with it. Since the norms determine actions, they also explain actions: non-conforming behaviour does not really matter because the rest of the social structure is assumed to be interdependent with the rule – and therefore practice – of endogamy. Also, since any particular individual is determined in this way, concrete actions are not problematic. Individual actions are not seen as belonging to the field of the social sciences anyway: the social sciences deal with social wholes. The questions asked are, as we pointed out above, of the type "Why is the society endogamous?", or "What function does endogamy have in that particular society or that type of society?"

The second root lies in the notion that classification, based on comparison, is the ultimate task of social anthropology. The idea that when properly classified, societies, or "the forms of the structure", will also be, somehow, explained lies behind much of the theoretical literature in social anthropology: let us mention as an example *A natural science of society* by Radcliffe-Brown (1957). Despite some quite strongly worded critical comments (cf. Leach 1961b), classificatory zeal, though later often disguised under the notion of comparison, still runs strongly. Let us return to the above-mentioned example of an endogamous society: the category of endogamous societies comprises societies in which some people have been seen to have married within their descent groups, societies in which some members have expressed the view that this is a proper marital arrangement, etc. These are quite obviously different cases. Yet, as a classification the term is meant to refer to the fact that the society as a whole is endogamous and, in the last instance, to the assumed behavioural reality, i.e. to societies where men actually marry women of their own descent groups. The endogamous structure, or model, of such a society is built for the purposes of classification and experimentation, i.e. comparison (or in Leach's terms, butterfly collecting; Leach 1961b:2), and not to account for what people are actually doing. This forces some disagreeable demands:

> For example, ethnography impels us to state that a society has lineages, whereas it may only have certain values for lineages and tendencies to approximate what we conceive to be a lineage organization....The concept is further hardened when this society is compared to other societies that have somewhat different lineage ideologies, but with which they are lumped because of a further reduction of typological criteria and a growing amorphousness of definition....At the very best, the interrelating units in most functional analyses are norms; in comparative analysis, they are models built upon norms. This is an old and familiar problem in anthropology to which we usually doff our hats as we go on doing just this. (Murphy 1972:59–60)

In other words, what we end up with is a model which has no actual reference: social life which is presumably represented has been so generalized and distorted that there is nothing, save possibly a very vague "society", to which we can specifically point and say this is what it is a model of.

The third root is slightly more difficult to name, but it lies in the whole historical–philosophical background of the social sciences. They started to emerge as sciences at a time when the only imaginable idea of a science was that represented by

exact and natural sciences. The "scientificity" of any particular discipline was, therefore, measurable by its similarity or dissimilarity to them. This was so to such a degree that it applied even to philosophy: "…when Austin, Ayer and Ryle were pressed to define their philosophical methodology, in one way or another they all referred to Natural Science. Austin, for instance, emphasised that the way in which one ought to proceed in philosophy is 'comme en Physique ou en sciences naturelles' and even said that: 'Il n'y a pas d'autre manière de procéder'" (Mezaros 1966:319).

For the social sciences, this "natural science of society" approach is not, however, something which belongs to the past. As Giddens has recently pointed out, "The wish to establish a natural science of society, which would possess the same sort of logical structure and pursue the same achievements as the sciences of nature probably remains, in the English-speaking world at least, the dominant standpoint today" (Giddens 1976:13).

However, if social science was to emulate the sciences of nature, or, to be more exact, if it was to be built along the same lines, it also needed a subject matter as real and factual as that of the natural sciences, consisting of empirical phenomena which exist "out there" in the world. Moreover, it had to be available to the observer basically in the same way: participant observation was seen as giving to the researcher something like sense-data, i.e. information about the social world collected through sense experience. Nonobservable relationships were conceived of as nonproblematically following from the proper arrangement of observable phenomena. Or, to put it another way, the observable phenomena, through their proper arrangement, revealed "a form of social life" (Radcliffe-Brown 1952:4). This "jigsaw-puzzle conception of social structure" (Lévi-Strauss 1960:52) made it possible to see social structure as a sort of empirical reality. Since it was so conceived from the beginning, all data gathered by the researcher, regardless of whether they were observed or collected in verbal form, had necessarily to refer to this social structure. How they referred to it was unimportant; what mattered was the reality behind them.

The proposition that the sciences of society are qualitatively different from the sciences of nature has been put forward many times. It is usually argued from the position that social or human phenomena are inherently meaningful while the phenomena of nature are not: consequently, the procedures for the study of the latter are not valid for the study of the former. We are not directly interested in comparing social and natural sciences; however, it seems to us that most of the problems shown in examples in this chapter result from the fact that anthropologists try to follow procedures appropriate to the natural sciences. By denying qualitative differences in data and by considering all information as being about a form of society, or structure, which exists beyond and above individual actors, they are ascribing to this reality an existential status rather similar to that of natural phenomena. The unifying term "observation" covers, as we have tried to show, a broad range of ways in which data are available: these ways indicate the differences in data, and the differences in data are a manifestation of difference in the phenomena they refer to. Let us, therefore, re-examine the concept of observation.

Earlier, we indicated that "observation" in normal anthropological usage designates two different ways of obtaining data: obtaining actors' verbal statements and observing their actual behaviour. For the sake of simplicity, we have treated verbal statements and observable behaviour as two clearly and noncontroversially separate categories of data which refer, one, to the actors' notions, or notional reality, and the other to their actions, or behavioural reality. In doing this, we have provisionally considered observation, in the amended narrow sense, as a nonproblematic procedure and observability as a nonproblematic property of actions. If this were so, normal anthropological procedures would be adequate and our comments on the examples invalid. In actual fact, the two categories of data are not so simply separated: observability is a problematic quality, and "to make a verbal statement" is in a sense an observable action. Consequently, some conceptual clarification is necessary at this point.

Observation in the narrow technical sense means perception through senses; strictly speaking, in the field of social science there is only one phenomenon which can be observed: a specific action of a concrete individual, be it a physical act or a speech act. And even this statement has to be qualified:

what we can directly observe are simple physical movements. A simple physical movement is not, by itself, an action: it is constituted as an action by having a meaning. A hypothetical visitor from Mars can not possibly observe the action of cashing a cheque: what he can observe is one man pushing a piece of paper across the counter in one direction, and another man pushing several pieces of paper in the opposite direction. The same physical movement can have many different meanings attached to it (cf. Anscombe 1957: 40ff) and thus be many different actions. To be able to "observe" an action, people have to know its meaning, and to know the meaning, any "observer" has to possess some pre-existing criteria for ascribing meaning.

To apply such criteria to an observable movement obviously is not an observation but a thought process. Therefore, even a simple action is not available to people only through sensory perception, but through sensory perception and a thought process at the same time (cf. Gorman 1977:60). Thus, observability is not an absolute property of action. However, people do not behave in isolation but with and towards others, which is possible only if others are, by and large, able not only to see the physical movements but also to understand their meaning, on the basis of the criteria they share with the performer. Otherwise it would be impossible for them to behave with and towards others and social life could not exist. Though there may be some misunderstandings and misconstructions, people do understand each other's actions in the course of everyday life, i.e. they ascribe meanings to physical movements more or less automatically and without problems. So, even if "observability" is not an absolute property of action, in the practice of social life actions are considered observable; "observability" becomes a commonsense property. To the extent to which members of a society nonproblematically observe each other's actions, these actions can be considered by the anthropologist as observable.

The meaning of an action consists in the impact the actor makes or tries to make on the physical and/or social world by changing or maintaining the existing state of affairs. The existential status of an action is constituted by three elements: it has a specific location in time and space, i.e. it is unique and unrepeatable and once performed ceases to exist; it is performed by an individual; and at the same time it makes or tries to make an observable impact on the world. These three elements also connote its epistemological status: it is available to the observer directly, as an event, through observation. Clearly, no approach which does not take seriously into account this level of reality, i.e. what the actors really do, in the sense of what impact they make or intend to make on the world, and which does not consistently represent this level of reality in its explanatory models, can claim to give an adequate account of social life.

Since social life exists, which among other things means that people are able to ascribe meaning to each other's actions without any great problem, this presupposes the existence of actions at another level: as models, plans, "blueprints" or schemata (cf. Cheal 1980:40) for actions in the minds of the people. These models exist, i.e. people hold them, regardless of whether or not the corresponding action is at the moment being performed. They are perduring and are not related to any particular action located in space and time, but to a class of action. Such models are in no acceptable sense of the word observable. However, the observer can be told that they exist and what they are. If somebody is getting married, we can observe it as an event; we can also be told how to get married or how people get married, even if we do not at that moment observe the event: this verbal statement does not refer to any particular marriage act but to the model of the marriage act.

The existential status of such models is clearly different from that of the actions. They are held by actors, but by holding them the actors are not making or trying to make an impact on the world: holding a model of action is not "doing" or "intending to do" anything. Moreover, they are perduring over time: they do not lapse after the action has been performed. Such models form part of an individual's knowledge and are part of social life to the extent to which they are shared among individuals. On both existential and epistemic grounds they form an area or domain of reality different from that formed by actions.

However, simple models of actions form only a small part of that area of reality. Not only do people perform actions which have meaning for them and others, they also perform them in concrete conditions, both physical and social. These conditions have to be known. However the knowledge of them is obtained, it again consists of mental constructs and models: not simple descriptions of actions, but more complex notions about relations between actions, representations of parts of the physical and social world, notions of normal, ideal, etc. states of affairs. While a simple model of action may answer the question "How is it known that such an event is marriage?" there are more complex models of how marriage relates to other events of life, why one should marry at all, whom it is proper to marry and why, etc. Again, none of these constructs or notions is observable. However, in the same sense as in the case of actions, no approach can disregard this level of reality and still formulate acceptable accounts of social life.

Thus, it seems that there are good reasons to accept that a seemingly trivial point, i.e. that there are two ways in which the anthropologist obtains his data, through observing what people do and listening to what they say, has considerable methodological importance. What are made available to him in different ways are data referring not to identical but to different areas or domains of social reality, i.e. categories of things which exist in different senses. We will maintain the simplified terminology of notions and actions, or notional reality and behavioural reality, for these two areas. It seems to us that their difference, though recognized, has not been sufficiently taken into account by anthropologists, possibly not so much in the actual process of gathering data, but decidedly in analytical and explanatory procedures and in formulations of explanatory models of social life. [...]

References

Anscombe, G. E. M. 1957. *Intention*. Oxford: Blackwell.

Cheal, D. 1980. Rule-governed behaviour. *Philosophy of Social Sciences* 10: 39–49.

Evans-Pritchard, E. E. 1940. *The Nuer*. Oxford: The Clarendon Press.

Fortes, M. 1945. *The dynamics of clanship among the Tallensi*. Oxford: Oxford University Press.

Fortes, M. 1969. *Kinship and the social order*. Chicago: Aldine Publishers.

Giddens, A. 1976. *New rules of sociological method*. London: Hutchinson.

Gluckman, M. 1961. Ethnographic data in British social anthropology. *Sociological Review* 9: 5–17.

Gorman, R. A. 1977. *The dual vision: Alfred Schutz and the myth of phenomenological social science*. London: Routledge and Kegan Paul.

Holy, L. 1974. *Neighbours and kinsmen: a study of the Berti people of Darfur*. London: C. Hurst.

Holy, L. 1979. Nuer politics. In L. Holy (ed.), *Segmentary lineage systems reconsidered*. The Queen's University Papers in Social Anthropology 3: 83–105. Belfast: Queen's University.

Howell, P. P. 1954. *A manual of Nuer law*. Oxford: Oxford University Press for the International African Institute.

Leach, E. R. 1961a. *Pul Eliya: a village in Ceylon*. Cambridge: Cambridge University Press.

Leach, E. R. 1961b. *Rethinking anthropology*. London School of Economics Monographs on Social Anthropology No. 22. London: The Athlone Press.

Lévi-Strauss, C. 1960. On manipulated sociological models. *Bijdragen tot de Taal-, Land- en Volkenkunde* 112: 45–54.

Lewis, I. M. 1965. Problems in the comparative study of unilineal descent. In *The relevance of models for social anthropology*. ASA Monographs 1: 87–112. London: Tavistock Publications.

Mezaros, I. 1966. The possibility of a dialogue. In B. Williams and A. Montefiore (eds.), *British analytical philosophy*. London: Routledge and Kegan Paul.

Middleton, J. and D. Tait (eds.). 1958. *Tribes without rulers*. London: Routledge and Kegan Paul.

Mitchell, J. C. 1956. *The Yao village*. Manchester: Manchester University Press.

Murphy, R. F. 1972. *The dialectics in social life*. London: Allen and Unwin.

Pehrson, R. 1964. Bilateral kin groupings. In J. Goody (ed.), *Kinship*: 290–5. Penguin Modern Sociology Readings. Harmondsworth: Penguin Books.

Radcliffe-Brown, A. R. 1952. *Structure and function in primitive society*. New York: The Free Press.

Radcliffe-Brown, A. R. 1957. *A natural science of society*. New York: The Free Press.

Southall, A. 1952. *Lineage formation among the Luo*. London: International African Institute, Memorandum 26.

Stuchlik, M. 1977. Goals and behaviour. In M. Stuchlik (ed.), *Goals and behaviour*. The Queen's University Papers in Social Anthropology 2: 7–47. Belfast: Queen's University.

Van Velsen, J. 1967. The extended-case method and situational analysis. In A. L. Epstein (ed.), *The craft of social anthropology*: 129–49. London: Tavistock Publications.

Whyte, A. 1977. Systems as perceived: a discussion of "Maladaptation in social systems". In J. Friedman and M. J. Rowlands (eds.), *The evolution of social systems*: 73–8. London: Duckworth.

15

Objectification Objectified

Pierre Bourdieu

There is perhaps no better way of grasping the epistemological and sociological presuppositions of objectivism than to return to the inaugural operations through which Saussure constructed the specific object of linguistics. These operations, ignored and masked by all the mechanical borrowings from the then dominant discipline and by all the literal translations of an autonomized lexicon on which the new "structural" sciences were hastily founded, have become the epistemological unconscious of structuralism.[1]

To posit, as Saussure does, that the true medium of communication is not speech (*parole*), a datum immediately considered in its observable materiality, but language (*langue*), a system of objective relations which makes possible both the production and the decoding of discourse, is to perform a complete reversal of appearances by subordinating the very substance of communication, which presents itself as the most visible and real aspect, to a pure construct of which there is no sense experience.[2] Conscious of the paradoxical break with doxic experience that is implied in the fundamental thesis of the primacy

of the language (in favour of which he none the less invokes the existence of dead languages or dumbness in old age as proof that one can lose speech while preserving a language, or the linguistic errors that point to the language as the objective norm of speech), Saussure indeed notes that everything tends to suggest that speech is "the precondition of a language": a language cannot be apprehended outside the speech, a language is learned through speech and speech is the origin of innovations and transformations in language. But he immediately observes that the two processes mentioned have only chronological priority and that the relationship is reversed as soon as one leaves the domain of individual or collective history in order to inquire into the logical conditions for decoding. From this point of view, the language, as the medium ensuring the identity of the sound – sense associations performed by the speakers, and therefore their mutual understanding, comes first as the condition of the intelligibility of speech (1974: 17–20). Saussure, who elsewhere proclaims that "the point of view creates the object", here clearly

From *The Logic of Practice*, trans. Richard Nice (Cambridge: Polity, 1990 [1980]), pp. 30–41, 287–9, 320, 322–3, 325–9. Copyright © 1990 by Polity Press. Reprinted with permission of Stanford University Press, www.sup.org. All rights reserved and copyright © 1980 by Les Editions de Minuit. Reprinted with permission of Georges Borchardt, Inc. for Les Editions de Minuit, and The Estate of Pierre Bourdieu (Jérôme Bourdieu for ebook rights).

Anthropology in Theory: Issues in Epistemology, Second Edition. Edited by Henrietta L. Moore and Todd Sanders.
© 2014 John Wiley & Sons, Inc. Published 2014 by John Wiley & Sons, Inc.

indicates the viewpoint one has to adopt in order to produce the "specific object" of the new structural science: to make speech the product of the language one has to situate oneself in the logical order of intelligibility.

It would no doubt be worthwhile to try to set out the whole set of theoretical postulates implied in adopting this viewpoint, such as the primacy of logic and structure, apprehended synchronically, over individual and collective history (that is, the learning of the language and, as Marx might have said, "the historical movement which gave birth to it") or the privilege granted to internal and specific relations, amenable to "tautegorical" (to use Schelling's term) or structural analysis, over external economic and social determinations. However, not only has this already been done, partially at least, but it seems more important to concentrate on the viewpoint itself, the relationship to the object that it asserts and all that follows from this, starting with a particular theory of practice. This presupposes that one momentarily relinquishes, and then tries to objectify, the place designated in advance as that of the objective and objectifying observer who, like a stage manager playing at will with the possibilities offered by the objectifying instruments in order to bring the object closer or move it further away, to enlarge or reduce it, imposes on the object his own norms of construction, as if in a dream of power.

To locate oneself in the order of intelligibility, as Saussure does, is to adopt the viewpoint of an "impartial spectator" who seeks to understand for the sake of understanding and who tends to assign this hermeneutic intention to the agents' practice and to proceed as if they were asking themselves the questions he asks himself about them. Unlike the orator, the grammarian has nothing to do with language except to study it in order to codify it. By the very treatment he applies to it, taking it as an object of analysis instead of using it to think and speak, he constitutes it as a *logos* opposed to *praxis* (and also, of course, to practical language). Does it need to be pointed out that this typically scholastic opposition is a product of the scholastic situation, in the strong sense of *skholè, otium*, inactivity, which is unlikely to be perceived as such by minds shaped by the academic institution? For lack of a theory of the difference between the purely theoretical relation to language of someone who, like himself, has

nothing to do with language except understand it, and the practical relation to language of someone who seeks to understand in order to act and who uses language for practical purposes, just enough for the needs of practice and within the limits allowed by the urgency of practice, the grammarian is tacitly inclined to treat language as an autonomous, self-sufficient object, that is, a purposefulness without purpose – without any other purpose, at any rate, than that of being interpreted, like a work of art. The principle of the grammarians' errors lies therefore not so much in the fact that, as the sociolinguists complain, they take as their object a scholastic or formal language, but rather that they unwittingly adopt a scholastic or formal relation towards all language, whether popular or formal.

The most constant tendencies of the formal grammar which linguistics is and always has been, are inscribed in the scholastic situation which, through the relation to language that it encourages and its neutralization of the functions embedded in the ordinary use of language, governs in many ways the academic treatment of language. One only has to think of the inimitable examples generated by the grammarian's imagination, from bald kings of France to Wittgenstein doing the washing-up, which, like the paradoxes cherished by all formalisms, are able to deploy all their ambiguities and enigmas only because the scholastic *epochè* has isolated them from any practical situation. The "condition of felicity" of scholastic discourse is the scholastic institution and all that it implies, such as the speakers' and the receivers' disposition to accept and indeed believe in what is said. This did not escape Paul Valéry (1960: 696): "*Quia nominor Leo* does not mean *For my name is Lion* but: *I am an example of grammar.*" The chain of commentary unleashed by J. L. Austin's analysis of illocutionary acts has no reason to stop so long as ignorance of the conditions of production and circulation of commentary allows and encourages people to search solely in the discourse in question for the "conditions of felicity" which, though theoretically and practically inseparable from the institutional conditions of the functioning of the discourse, have been assigned to the domain of external linguistics, that is, abandoned to sociology.

Language as conceived by Saussure, an intellectual instrument and an object of analysis, is indeed the dead, written, foreign language referred to by Mikhail Bakhtin, a self-sufficient system, detached from real usage and totally stripped of its functions, inviting a purely passive understanding (the extreme form of which is pure semantics as practised by Fodor and Katz). The illusion of the autonomy of the purely linguistic order that is asserted in the privilege accorded to the internal logic of language at the expense of the social conditions of its opportune use[3] opened the way to all the subsequent research that proceeds as if mastery of the code were sufficient to confer mastery of the appropriate usages, or as if one could infer the usage and meaning of linguistic expressions from analysis of their formal structure, as if grammaticality were the necessary and sufficient condition of the production of meaning, in short, as if it had been forgotten that language is made to be spoken and spoken pertinently. It is not surprising that the aporias of Chomskian linguistics, which have taken the presuppositions of all grammars to their ultimate conclusions, are now forcing linguists to rediscover, as Jacques Bouveresse puts it, that the problem is not the possibility of producing an infinite number of "grammatical" sentences but the possibility of producing an infinite number of sentences really appropriate to an infinite number of situations.

The independence of discourse with respect to the situation in which it functions and the bracketing of all its functions are implied in the initial operation which produces the language by reducing the speech act to a simple execution. And it would not be difficult to show that all the presuppositions, and all the consequent difficulties, of all forms of structuralism derive from this fundamental division between the language and its realization in speech, that is, in practice, and also in history, and from the inability to understand the relationship between these two entities other than as that between the model and its execution, essence and existence – which amounts to placing the linguist, the possessor of the model, in the position of a Leibnizian God possessing *in actu* the objective meaning of practices.

To delimit, within the range of linguistic phenomena, the "terrain of the language", Saussure sets aside "the physical part of communication", that is, speech as a preconstructed object. Then,

within the "speech circuit", he isolates what he calls "the executive side", that is, speech as a constructed object defined in opposition to language as the actualization of a certain sense in a particular combination of sounds, which he also eliminates on the grounds that "execution is never the work of the mass" but "always individual". The word execution, used of an order or a muscial score and more generally of a programme or an artistic project, condenses the whole philosophy of practice and history of semiology, a paradigmatic form of objectivism which, by privileging the constructum over the materiality of the practical realization, reduces individual practice, skill, everything that is determined practically by reference to practical ends, that is, style, manner, and ultimately the agents themselves, to the actualization of a kind of ahistorical essence, in short, nothing.[4]

But it is undoubtedly anthropology which, being predisposed by its identical viewpoint on the object to reckless borrowing of concepts, exhibits in a magnified form all the implications of the question-begging of objectivism. Charles Bally pointed out that linguistic research takes different directions when dealing with the linguist's mother tongue or with a foreign language, and he emphasized in particular the tendency towards intellectualism entailed by apprehending language from the standpoint of the listening rather than the speaking subject, that is, as a means of decoding rather than a "means of action and expression": "The listener is on the side of the language, it is with the language that he interprets speech" (Bally 1965: 58, 78, 102). The practical relation the anthropologist has with his object, that of the outsider, excluded from the real play of social practices by the fact that he has no place (except by choice or by way of a game) in the space observed, is the extreme case and the ultimate truth of the relationship that the observer, willy-nilly, consciously or not, has with his object. The status of an observer who withdraws from the situation to observe implies an epistemological, but also a social break, which most subtly governs scientific activity when it ceases to be seen as such, leading to an implicit theory of practices that is linked to forgetfulness of the social conditions of scientific activity. The anthropologist's situation reminds us of the truth of the relationship that every observer has with the action he states and analyses, namely the insurmountable break with action and the world, with the imminent ends of collective action, with the self-evidence of the familiar world, that is presupposed in the very intention of talking about practice and especially of understanding it and seeking to make it understood other than by producing and reproducing it practically. If words have any meaning, then there cannot be a discourse (or a novel) of action: there is only a discourse which states action and which, unless it is to fall into incoherence or imposture, must never stop stating that it is only stating action. Undue participation of the subject in the object is never more evident than in the case of the primitivist participation of the bewitched or mystic anthropologist, which, like populist immersion, still plays on the objective distance from the object to play the game as a game while waiting to leave it in order to tell it. This means that participant observation is, in a sense, a contradiction in terms (as anyone who has tried to do it will have confirmed in practice); and that the critique of objectivism and its inability to apprehend practice as such in no way implies the rehabilitation of immersion in practice. The participationist option is simply another way of avoiding the question of the real relationship of the observer to the observed and its critical consequences for scientific practice.

In this respect, there is no better example than that of art history, which finds in the sacred character of its object every pretext for a hagiographic hermeneutics more concerned with the *opus operatum* than the *modus operandi*, and treats the work of art as a discourse to be decoded by reference to a transcendent code, analogous to Saussure's *langue*. It forgets that artistic production is also – to various degrees depending on the art and on the historically variable ways of practising it – the product of an "art", as Durkheim (1956: 101) says, or, to put it another way, a *mimesis*, a sort of symbolic gymnastics, like ritual or dance; and that it always contains something "ineffable", not through excess, as the celebrants would have it, but through absence. Here too, the inadequacy of scholarly discourse derives from its ignorance of all that its theory of the object owes to its theoretical relation to the object, as Nietzsche (1969: 103–4) suggested: "Kant, like all philosophers, instead of envisaging the aesthetic problem from the point of view of the artist (the creator), considered art and the beautiful purely

from that of the 'spectator', and unconsciously introduced the 'spectator' into the concept 'beautiful'".

Intellectualism is inscribed in the fact of introducing into the object the intellectual relation to the object, of substituting the observer's relation to practice for the practical relation to practice. Anthropologists would be able to escape from all their metaphysical questioning about the ontological status or even the "site" of culture only if they were to objectify their relation to the object, that of the outsider who has to procure a substitute for practical mastery in the form of an objectified model. Genealogies and other models are to the social orientation which makes possible the relation of immediate immanence to the familiar world, as a map, an abstract model of all possible routes, is to the practical sense of space, a "system of axes linked unalterably to our bodies, which we carry about with us wherever we go", as Poincaré put it.

There are few areas in which the effect of the outsider's situation is so directly visible as in analysis of kinship. Having only cognitive uses for the kinship and the kin of others which he takes for his object, the anthropologist can treat the native terminology of kinship as a closed, coherent system of logically necessary relations, defined once and for all as if by construction in and by the implicit axiomatics of a cultural tradition. Failing to inquire into the epistemological status of his practice and of the neutralization of practical functions which it presupposes and consecrates, he considers only the symbolic effect of collective categorization, which shows and which creates belief, imposing obligations and prohibitions whose intensity varies in inverse ratio to distance in the space arbitrarily produced in this way. In doing so, he unwittingly brackets the different uses which may be made in practice of sociologically identical kinship relations. The logical relations he constructs are to "practical" relations – practical because continuously practised, kept up and cultivated – as the geometrical space of a map, a representation of all possible routes for all possible subjects, is to the network of pathways that are really maintained and used, "beaten tracks" that are really practicable for a particular agent. The family tree, a spatial diagram that can be taken in at a glance, *uno intuitu* and scanned indifferently in any direction from any point, causes the complete network of kinship relations over several generations to exist in the mode of temporal existence which is that of theoretical objects, that is, *tota simul*, as a totality in simultaneity. It puts on the same footing official relationships, which, for lack of regular maintenance, tend to become what they are for the genealogist, that is, theoretical relationships, like abandoned roads on an old map; and practical relationships which really function because they fulfil practical functions. It thereby tends to conceal the fact that the logical relations of kinship, which the structuralist tradition almost completely autonomizes with respect to economic determinants, exist in practice only through and for the official and unofficial uses made of them by agents whose inclination to keep them in working order and to make them work more intensively – hence, through constant use, ever more smoothly – rises with the degree to which they actually or potentially fulfil useful functions, satisfying vital material or symbolic interests.

To make completely explicit the implicit demand which lies behind genealogical inquiry (as in all forms of inquiry), one would first have to establish the social history of the genealogical tool, paying particular attention to the functions which, in the tradition of which anthropologists are the product, have produced and reproduced the need for this instrument, that is, the problems of inheritance and succession and, inseparably from these, the concern to maintain and preserve social capital, understood as effective possession of a network of kinship (or other) relations capable of being mobilized or at least manifested. This social genealogy of genealogy would have to extend into a social history of the relationship between the "scientific" and social uses of the instrument. But the most important thing would be to bring to light the epistemological implications of the mode of investigation which is the precondition for the production of the genealogical diagram. This would aim to determine the full significance of the ontological transmutation that the researcher's questions bring about simply by demanding a quasi-theoretical relationship towards kinship, implying a break with the practical relation directly oriented towards functions.

In fact, projection into the object of a non-objectified objectifying relation produces different effects each time, albeit arising from the same principle, in the different areas of practice. Sometimes the anthropologist presents as the objective principle of practice that which is obtained and constructed through the work of objectification, projecting into reality what only exists on paper; sometimes he interprets actions which, like rites and myths, aim to *act* on the natural world and the social world, as if they were operations designed to interpret them.[5] Here too, the so-called objective relation to the object, which implies distance and externality, comes into contradiction in a quite practical way with the practical relationship which it has to deny in order to constitute itself and by the same token to constitute the objective representation of practice:

"His vision [that of a simple participant in a rite] is circumscribed by his occupancy of a particular position, or even of a set of situationally conflicting positions, both in the persisting structure of his society, and also in the rôle structure of the given ritual. Moreover, the participant is likely to be governed in his actions by a number of interests, purposes, and sentiments, dependent upon his specific position, which impair his understanding of the total situation. An even more serious obstacle against his achieving objectivity is the fact that he tends to regard as axiomatic and primary the ideals, values, and norms that are overtly expressed or symbolized in the ritual.... What is meaningless for an actor playing a specific rôle may well be highly significant for an observer and analyst of the total system" (V. Turner 1967: 67).

Only by means of a break with the theoretical vision, which is experienced as a break with ordinary vision, can the observer take account, in his description of ritual practice, of the fact of *participation* (and consequently of his own separation from this); only a critical awareness of the limits implied in the conditions of production of theory can enable him to include in the complete theory of ritual practice properties as essential to it as the partial, self-interested character of practical knowledge or the discrepancy between the practically experienced reasons and the "objective" reasons of practice. But the triumphalism of theoretical reason is paid for in its inability, from the very beginning, to move beyond simple recording of the duality of the paths of knowledge, the path of appearances and the path of truth, doxa and episteme, common sense and science, and its incapacity to win for science the truth of what science is constructed *against*.

Projecting into the perception of the social world the unthought content inherent in his position in that world, that is, the monopoly of "thought" which he is granted *de facto* by the social division of labour and which leads him to identify the work of thought with an effort of expression and verbalization in speech or writing – "thought and expression are constituted simultaneously", said Merleau-Ponty – the "thinker" betrays his secret conviction that action is fully performed only when it is understood, interpreted, expressed, by identifying the implicit with the unthought and by denying the status of authentic thought to the tacit and practical thought that is inherent in all "sensible" action.[6] Language spontaneously becomes the accomplice of this hermeneutic philosophy which leads one to conceive action as something to be deciphered, when it leads one to say, for example, that a gesture or ritual act *expresses* something, rather than saying, quite simply, that it is "sensible" (*sensé*) or, as in English, that it "makes" sense. No doubt because they know and recognize no other thought than the thought of the "thinker", and cannot grant human dignity without granting what seems to be constitutive of that dignity, anthropologists have never known how to rescue the people they were studying from the barbarism of pre-logic except by identifying them with the most prestigious of their colleagues – logicians or philosophers (I am thinking of the famous title, "The primitive as philosopher"). As Hocart (1970: 32) puts it, "Long ago [man] ceased merely to live and started to think how he lived; he ceased merely to feel life: he conceived it. Out of all the phenomena contributing to life he formed a concept of life, fertility, prosperity, and vitality." Claude Lévi-Strauss does just the same when he confers on myth the task of resolving *logical* problems, of expressing, mediating and masking social contradictions – mainly in some earlier analyses, such "La geste d'Asdiwal" (1958) – or when he makes it one of the sites where, like Reason in history according to Hegel, the universal Mind thinks itself,[7] thereby offering for observation "the universal laws which govern the unconscious activities of the mind" (1951).

The indeterminacy surrounding the relationship between the observer's viewpoint and that of the agents is reflected in the indeterminacy of the relationship between the constructs (diagrams or discourses) that the observer produces to account for practices, and these practices themselves. This uncertainty is intensified by the interferences of the native discourse aimed at expressing or regulating practice – customary rules, official theories, sayings, proverbs, etc. – and by the effects of the mode of thought that is expressed in it. Simply by leaving untouched the question of the principle of production of the regularities that he records and giving free rein to the "mythopoeic" power of language, which, as Wittgenstein pointed out, constantly slips from the substantive to the substance, objectivist discourse tends to constitute the model constructed to account for practices as a power really capable of determining them. Reifying abstractions (in sentences like "culture determines the age of weaning"), it treats its constructions – "culture", "structures", "social classes" or "modes of production" – as realities endowed with a social efficacy. Alternatively, giving concepts the power to act in history as the words that designate them act in the sentences of historical narrative, it personifies collectives and makes them subjects responsible for historical actions (in sentences like "the bourgeoisie thinks that…" or "the working class refuses to accept…").[8] And, when the question cannot be avoided, it preserves appearances by resorting to systematically ambiguous notions, as linguists say of sentences whose representative context varies systematically with the context of use.

Thus the notion of the *rule* which can refer indifferently to the regularity immanent in practices (a statistical correlation, for example), the *model* constructed by science to account for it, or the *norm* consciously posited and respected by the agents, allows a fictitious reconciliation of mutually contradictory theories of action. I am thinking, of course, of Chomsky, who (in different contexts) describes grammatical rules as instruments of description of language; as systems of norms of which speakers have a certain knowledge; and finally as neurophysiological mechanisms ("A person who knows a language has represented in his brain some very abstract system of underlying structures along with an abstract system of rules that determine, by free iteration, an infinite range of sound–meaning correspondences" (1967)). But it is also instructive to re-read a paragraph from the preface to the second edition of *The Elementary Structures of Kinship*, in which one may assume that particular care has been taken with the vocabulary of norms, models or rules, since the passage deals with the distinction between "preferential systems" and "prescriptive systems":

"Conversely, a system which *recommends* marriage with the mother's brother's daughter may be called prescriptive even if the *rule* is seldom observed, since it says what *must* be done. The question of how far and in what proportion the members of a given society *respect the norm* is very interesting, but a different question to that of where this society should properly be placed in a typology. It is sufficient to acknowledge the likelihood that *awareness* of the *rule* inflects *choices* ever so little in the *prescribed* directions, and that the percentage of *conventional* marriages is higher than would be the case if marriages were made *at random*, to be able to recognize what might be called a matrilateral *operator* at work in this society and acting as a pilot: certain alliances at least follow the path which it charts out for them, and this suffices to imprint a specific curve in the genealogical space. No doubt there will be not just one curve but a great number of local curves, merely incipient for the most part, however, and forming closed cycles only in rare and exceptional cases. But the *structural* outlines which emerge here and there will be enough for the system to be used in making a *probabilistic version* of more rigid systems, the *notion* of which is completely *theoretical* and in which marriage would conform rigorously to *any rule the social group pleases to enunciate*" (Lévi-Strauss 1969: 33, my italics).

The dominant tonality in this passage, as in the whole preface, is that of the norm, whereas *Structural Anthropology* is written in the language of the model or structure; not that such terms are entirely absent here, since the metaphors organizing the central passage ("operator", "curve" in "genealogical space", "structural outlines") imply the logic of the theoretical model and the equivalence (which is both professed and repudiated) of the model and the norm: "A preferential system is prescriptive when envisaged at the level of the model, a prescriptive system can only be preferential when envisaged at the level of reality" (1969: 33).

But for the reader who remembers the passages in *Structural Anthropology* on the relationship between language and kinship (for example, "'Kinship systems', like 'phonemic systems', are built up by the mind on the level of unconscious thought" [Lévi-Strauss 1968: 34]) and the imperious way in which "cultural norms" and all the "rationalizations" or "secondary arguments" produced by the natives were rejected in favour of the "unconscious structures", not to mention the texts asserting the universality of the fundamental rule of exogamy, the concessions made here to "awareness of the rule" and the dissociation from rigid systems "the notion of which is entirely theoretical", may come as a surprise, as may this further passage from the same preface: "It is nonetheless true that the empirical reality of so-called prescriptive systems only takes on its full meaning when related to a *theoretical model worked out by the natives themselves* prior to ethnologists" (1969: 32, my italics); or again:

"Those who practise them *know full well* that the spirit of such systems cannot be reduced to the tautological proposition that each group obtains its women from 'givers' and gives its women to 'takers'. They are also *aware* that marriage with the matrilateral cross-cousin (mother's brother's daughter) provides the simplest illustration of the *rule*, the form most likely to *guarantee its survival*. On the other hand, marriage with the patrilateral cross-cousin (father's sister's daughter) would violate it irrevocably" (1969: 32, my italics).

It is tempting to quote in reply a passage in which Wittgenstein effortlessly brings together all the questions evaded by structural anthropology and, no doubt, more generally by all intellectualism, which transfers the objective truth established by science into a practice that by its very essence rules out the theoretical stance which makes it possible to establish that truth:

"What do I call 'the rule by which he proceeds'? – The hypothesis that satifactorily describes his use of words, which we observe; or the rule which he looks up when he uses signs; or the one which he gives us in reply when we ask what his rule is? – But if observation does not enable us to see any clear rule, and the question brings none to light? – For he did indeed give me a definition when I asked him what he understood by 'N', but he was prepared to withdraw and alter it. So how am I to determine the rule according to which he is playing? He does not know it himself. – Or, to ask a better question: What meaning is the expression 'the rule by which he proceeds' supposed to have left to it here?" (1963: 38–9).

To slip from *regularity*, i.e. from what recurs with a certain statistically measurable frequency and from the formula which describes it, to a consciously laid down and consciously respected *ruling* (*règlement*), or to unconscious *regulating* by a mysterious cerebral or social mechanism, are the two commonest ways of sliding from the model of reality to the reality of the model. In the first case, one moves from a rule which, to take up Quine's distinction (1972) between *to fit* and *to guide*, fits the observed regularity in a purely descriptive way, to a rule that governs, directs or orients behaviour – which presupposes that it is known and recognized, and can therefore be stated – thereby succumbing to the most elementary form of legalism, that variety of finalism which is perhaps the most widespread of the spontaneous theories of practice and which consists in proceeding as if practices had as their principle conscious obedience to consciously devised and sanctioned rules. As Ziff puts it:

"Consider the difference between saying 'The train is *regularly* two minutes late' and '*As a rule*, the train is two minutes late'.... There is the suggestion in the latter case that that the train be two minutes late is as it were in accordance with some policy or plan.... Rules connect with plans or policies in a way that regularities do not.... To argue that there must be rules in the natural language is like arguing that roads must be red if they correspond to red lines on a map" (1960: 38).

In the second case, one acquires the means of proceeding as if the principle (if not the end) of the action were the theoretical model one has to construct in order to account for it, without however falling into the most flagrant naiveties of legalism, by setting up as the principle of practices or institutions objectively governed by rules unknown to the agents – significations without a signifying intention, finalities without consciously posited ends, which are so many challenges to the old dilemma of mechanism and finalism – an unconscious defined as a mechanical operator of finality. Thus, discussing Durkheim's

attempts to "explain the genesis of symbolic thought", Lévi-Strauss writes:

"Modern sociologists and psychologists resolve such problems by appealing to the unconscious activity of the mind; but when Durkheim was writing, psychology and modern linguistics had not yet reached their main conclusions. This explains why Durkheim foundered in what he regarded as an irreducible antinomy (in itself a considerable progress over late nineteenth-century thought as exemplified by Spencer): the blindness of history and the finalism of consciousness. Between the two there is *of course the unconscious finality of the mind*" (1947: 527, my italics).

It is easy to imagine how minds trained to reject the naivety of finalist explanations and the triviality of causal explanations (particularly "vulgar" when they invoke economic and social factors) could be fascinated by all the mysterious teleological mechanisms, meaningful and apparently willed products without a producer, which structuralism brought into being by sweeping away the social conditions of production, reproduction and use of symbolic objects in the very process in which it revealed immanent logic. And it is also easy to understand the credit given in advance to Lévi-Strauss's attempt to move beyond the antinomy of action consciously oriented towards rational ends and mechanical reaction to determinations by locating finality in mechanism, with the notion of the unconscious, a kind of *Deus ex machina* which is also a God in the machine. The naturalization of finality implied in forgetting historical action, which leads one to inscribe the ends of history in the mysteries of a Nature, through the notion of the unconscious, no doubt enabled structural anthropology to appear as the most natural of the social sciences and the most scientific of the metaphysics of nature. "As the mind *is* also *a thing*, the functioning of this thing teaches us something about the nature of things; even pure reflexion is in the last analysis an internalization of the cosmos" (Lévi-Strauss 1966: 248, my italics).

One sees the oscillation, in the same sentence, between two contradictory explanations of the postulated identity of mind and nature: an essential identity – the mind is a thing – or an identity acquired through learning – the mind is the internalization of the cosmos. The two theses, which are merged with the help of the ambiguity of another formulation, "an image of the world inscribed in the architecture of the mind" (1964: 346), in any case both exclude individual and collective history. Beneath its air of radical materialism, this philosophy of nature is a philosophy of mind which amounts to a form of idealism. Asserting the universality and eternity of the logical categories that govern "the unconscious activity of the mind", it ignores the dialectic of social structures and structured, structuring dispositions through which schemes of thought are formed and transformed. These schemes – either logical categories, principles of division which, through the principles of the division of labour, correspond to the structure of the social world (and not the natural world), or temporal structures, imperceptibly inculcated by "the dull pressure of economic relations" as Marx puts it, that is, by the system of economic and symbolic sanctions associated with a particular position in the economic structures – are one of the mediations through which the objective structures ultimately structure all experience, starting with economic experience, without following the paths of either mechanical determination or adequate consciousness.

If the dialectic of objective structures and incorporated structures which operates in every practical action is ignored, then one necessarily falls into the canonical dilemma, endlessly recurring in new forms in the history of social thought, which condemns those who seek to reject subjectivism, like the present-day structuralist readers of Marx, to fall into the fetishism of social laws. To make transcendent entities, which are to practices as essence to existence, out of the constructions that science resorts to in order to give an account of the structure and meaningful products of the accumulation of innumerable historical actions, is to reduce history to a "process without a subject", simply replacing the "creative subject" of subjectivism with an automaton driven by the dead laws of a history of nature. This emanatist vision, which makes a structure – Capital or a Mode of production – into an entelechy developing itself in a process of self-realization, reduces historical agents to the role of "supports" (*Träger*) of the structure and reduces their actions to mere epiphenomenal manifestations of the structure's own power to develop itself and to determine and overdetermine other structures.

Notes

1   It is significant, for example, that with the exception of Sapir, who was predisposed by his dual training as linguist and ethnologist to raise the problem of the relationship between culture and language, no anthropologist has tried to bring out all the implications of the homology (which Leslie White is virtually alone in formulating explicitly) between the oppositions which are at the basis of cultural (or structural) anthropology and linguistics: *langue/parole* and culture/conduct.

2   One can extend to the relationship between culture and conduct everything that Saussure says about the relationship between language and speech which is a dimension of it. Just as Saussure posits that the medium of communication is not discourse but language, so cultural anthropology (or iconology, in Panofsky's sense) posits that scientific interpretation treats the sensible properties of practices or works as signs or "cultural symptoms" which yield their full meaning only to a reading armed with a cultural code transcending its actualizations (implying that the "objective meaning" of a work or

a practice is irreducible either to the will and consciousness of the author or to the felt experiences of the observer).

3   It is no accident that the Sophists (I am thinking in particular of Protagoras and Plato's *Gorgias*), who, unlike the pure grammarians, aimed to secure and transmit practical mastery of a language of action, were the first to raise the question of *kairos*, the right moment and the right words for the moment. As rhetoricians they were predisposed to make a philosophy of the practice of language as *strategy*. (It is significant that the original meaning of the word *kairos*, "vital (and therefore deadly) point", and "point aimed at, target", is also present in a number of everyday expressions: to strike home, hit the nail on the head, a shaft of wit, etc.).

4   The social implications of the language of execution become clearer when one knows that the debate over the primacy of meaning or execution, of the idea or the material and the manner ("technique", or as Caravaggio called it, *manifattura*) is at the centre of the history of art and the "emancipation" of the

artist and also at the centre of methodological debates among art historians (cf. Lee 1967; Bologna 1972, 1979).

5   The anthropologist's situation is not so different from that of the philologist and his dead letters. Not only is he forced to rely on quasi-texts – the official discourses of his informants, who are inclined to put forward the most codified aspect of the tradition, but, in his analysis of myths and rites for example, he often has to resort to tests established by others, often in ill-defined conditions. The very fact of recording constitutes a myth or rite as an object of analysis by isolating it from its concrete referents (such as the names of places, groups, land, persons, etc.), from the situations in which it functions and the individuals who make it function in relation to practical functions (e.g. to legitimize hierarchies or distributions of properties or powers). As Bateson (1958) shows, mythological culture can become the tool, and in some cases the object, of extremely complex strategies (and this explains, *inter alia*, why agents undertake the immense mnemonic effort needed to acquire mastery of it), even in societies which do not have a highly developed and differentiated religious apparatus. It follows that it is impossible to account fully for the structure of the mythical corpus and the transformations it undergoes in the course of time, by means of a strictly internal analysis ignoring the functions that the corpus fulfils in the relations of competition or conflict for economic or symbolic power.

6   To show that theoretical or theoreticist triumphalism is part of the very air breathed by all those who claim the status of an intellectual, one would have to cite the innumerable declarations of contempt for the incapacity of the "vulgar" to rise to a thought worthy of the name (and not only those most openly flaunted, such as remarks like "No one meditates!" and "Stupidity isn't my strong point" heard from straw-hatted intellectuals in the style of Valéry's Monsieur Teste) scattered through philosophy and literature.

7   "Mythological analysis has not, and cannot have, as its aim to show how men think.... I therefore claim to show, not how men think in myths, but how myths operate in men's minds without their being aware of the fact" (Lévi-Strauss 1970: 12). Although, taken literally, this text perfectly justifies my reading of Lévi-Strauss's final theory of mythic reason, I have to say – especially at a time when semi-automatic writing, diagonal reading and the critique of suspicion are much in vogue – that in this formulation, which is too elegant to be safe from metaphysical misreadings, one could also find a warning against the temptation of mystical participation and even a valuable contribution to a theory of the practical relation to myth. (Lévi-Strauss is correct in pointing out that, in the production of myth as in the production of discourse, awareness of the rules may be only partial and intermittent because "an individual who conscientiously applied phonological and grammatical rules in his speech, supposing he possessed the necessary knowledge and virtuosity to do so, would nevertheless lose the thread of his ideas almost immediately" [1970: 11].)

8   By postulating the existence of a group or class "collective consciousness" and crediting groups with dispositions which can only be constituted in an individual consciousness, even when they are the product of collective conditions, such as the awakening of consciousness of class interests, the personification of collectives removes the need to analyse these conditions, in particular those determining the degree of objective and subjective homogeneity of the group in question and the degree of consciousness of its members.

References

Bally, C. 1965: *Le Langage et la vie*, Geneva: Droz.

Bateson, G. 1958: *Naven*, Stanford, Calif.: Stanford University Press (1st edn 1936).

Bologna, F. 1972. *Dalle anti Minori all'industrial design*. Storia de una idealogia. Bari: Laterza.

Bologna, F. 1979. I metodi di studio dell'arte italiana e il problema metodologico oggi. In *Storia dell'arte italiana*, I, Rome: Einaudi, 165–273.

Chomsky, N. 1967: General properties of language. In I. L. Daley (ed.), *Brain Mechanisms Underlying Speech and Language*, New York/London: Grune & Straton, 73–88.

Durkheim, E. 1956: *Education and Sociology*. New York: Free Press.

Hocart, A. M. 1970: *Kings and Councillors*. Chicago: University of Chicago Press (first pub. 1936).

Lee, R. W. 1967: *Ut Pictura Poesis*. New York: Norton.

Lévi-Strauss, C. 1947: La sociologie française. In G. Gurvich and W. E. Moore (eds.), *La Sociologie au XXᵉ siècle*, Paris: PUF, vol. II.

Lévi-Strauss, C. 1951: Language and the analysis of social laws. *American Anthropologist*, April–June.

Lévi-Strauss, C. 1958: La geste d'Asdiwal. École pratique des hautes études, Section des sciences religieuses, Annuaire 1958–1959. (Trans. as "The story of Asdiwal", in *Structural Anthropology*, vol. II, London: Allen Lane, 1977, pp. 146–97.)

Lévi-Strauss, C. 1964. *Le Cru et le cuit*. Paris: Plon.

Lévi-Strauss, C. 1966: *The Savage Mind*. London: Weidenfeld & Nicolson. (1st French edn. 1964.)

Lévi-Strauss, C. 1968: *Structural Anthropology*. London: Allen Lane. (1st French edn. 1958.)

Lévi-Strauss, C. 1969: *The Elementary Structures of Kinship*. Revised edition. London: Social Science Paperbacks. (1st French edn. 1967.)

Lévi-Strauss, C. 1970. *The Raw and the Cooked*. Trans J. and D. Weightman. London: Cape. (1st French edn. 1964.)

Nietzsche, F. 1969: *On the Genealogy of Morals*. Trans. W. Kaufmann and R. J. Hollingdale. New York: Vintage Books.

Quine, W. V. 1972: Methodological reflections on current linguistic theory. In D. Harman and G. Davidson (eds.), *Semantics of Natural Language*, Dordrecht: D. Reidel, 442–54.

Saussure, F. de 1974: *Course in General Linguistics*, London: Fontana.

Turner, V. 1967: *The Forest of Symbols*. Ithaca, New York and London: Cornell University Press.

Valéry, P. 1960: Tel Quel. In *Œuvres*, vol. II, Paris: Gallimard.

Wittgenstein, L. 1963: *Philosophical Investigations*. Oxford: Basil Blackwell.

Ziff, P. 1960: *Semantic Analysis*. New York: Cornell University Press.

PART II

SECTION 5
Meanings as Objects of Study

16

Thick Description: Toward an Interpretive Theory of Culture

Clifford Geertz

I

[...] The conceptual morass into which the Tylorean kind of *pot-au-feu* theorizing about culture can lead is evident in what is still one of the better general introductions to anthropology, Clyde Kluckhohn's *Mirror for Man*. In some twenty-seven pages of his chapter on the concept, Kluckhohn managed to define culture in turn as: (1) "the total way of life of a people"; (2) "the social legacy the individual acquires from his group"; (3) "a way of thinking, feeling, and believing"; (4) "an abstraction from behavior"; (5) a theory on the part of the anthropologist about the way in which a group of people in fact behave; (6) a "storehouse of pooled learning"; (7) "a set of standardized orientations to recurrent problems"; (8) "learned behavior"; (9) a mechanism for the normative regulation of behavior; (10) "a set of techniques for adjusting both to the external environment and to other men"; (11) "a precipitate of history"; and turning, perhaps in desperation, to similes, as a map, as a sieve, and as a matrix. In the face of this sort of theoretical diffusion, even a somewhat constricted and not entirely standard concept of culture, which is at least internally coherent and, more important, which has a definable argument to make is (as, to be fair, Kluckhohn himself keenly realized) an improvement. Eclecticism is self-defeating not because there is only one direction in which it is useful to move, but because there are so many: it is necessary to choose.

The concept of culture I espouse [...] is essentially a semiotic one. Believing, with Max Weber, that man is an animal suspended in webs of significance he himself has spun, I take culture to be those webs, and the analysis of it to be therefore not an experimental science in search of law but an interpretive one in search of meaning. It is explication I am after, construing social expressions on their surface enigmatical. But this pronouncement, a doctrine in a clause, demands itself some explication.

II

Operationalism as a methodological dogma never made much sense so far as the social sciences are concerned, and except for a few rather too wellswept corners – Skinnerian behaviorism,

From *The Interpretation of Cultures* (New York: Basic Books, 1973), pp. 4–7, 9–20. Copyright © 1973 by Clifford Geertz. Reprinted by permission of Basic Books, a member of the Perseus Books Group.

Anthropology in Theory: Issues in Epistemology, Second Edition. Edited by Henrietta L. Moore and Todd Sanders. © 2014 John Wiley & Sons, Inc. Published 2014 by John Wiley & Sons, Inc.

intelligence testing, and so on – it is largely dead now. But it had, for all that, an important point to make, which, however we may feel about trying to define charisma or alienation in terms of operations, retains a certain force: if you want to understand what a science is, you should look in the first instance not at its theories or its findings, and certainly not at what its apologists say about it; you should look at what the practitioners of it do.

In anthropology, or anyway social anthropology, what the practioners do is ethnography. And it is in understanding what ethnography is, or more exactly *what doing ethnography is*, that a start can be made toward grasping what anthropological analysis amounts to as a form of knowledge. This, it must immediately be said, is not a matter of methods. From one point of view, that of the textbook, doing ethnography is establishing rapport, selecting informants, transcribing texts, taking genealogies, mapping fields, keeping a diary, and so on. But it is not these things, techniques and received procedures, that define the enterprise. What defines it is the kind of intellectual effort it is: an elaborate venture in to borrow a notion from Gilbert Ryle, "thick description."

Ryle's discussion of "thick description" appears in two recent essays of his [...]: "Thinking and Reflecting" and "The Thinking of Thoughts." Consider, he says, two boys rapidly contracting the eyelids of their right eyes. In one, this is an involuntary twitch; in the other, a conspiratorial signal to a friend. The two movements are, as movements, identical; from an I-am-a-camera, "phenomenalistic" observation of them alone, one could not tell which was twitch and which was wink, or indeed whether both or either was twitch or wink. Yet the difference, however unphotographable, between a twitch and a wink is vast; as anyone unfortunate enough to have had the first taken for the second knows. The winker is communicating, and indeed communicating in a quite precise and special way: (1) deliberately, (2) to someone in particular, (3) to impart a particular message, (4) according to a socially established code, and (5) without cognizance of the rest of the company. As Ryle points out, the winker has not done two things, contracted his eyelids and winked, while the twitcher has done only one, contracted his eyelids. Contracting your eyelids on purpose when there exists a public code in

which so doing counts as a conspiratorial signal *is* winking. That's all there is to it: a speck of behavior, a fleck of culture, and – *voilà!* – a gesture.

That, however, is just the beginning. Suppose, he continues, there is a third boy, who, "to give malicious amusement to his cronies," parodies the first boy's wink, as amateurish, clumsy, obvious, and so on. He, of course, does this in the same way the second boy winked and the first twitched: by contracting his right eyelids. Only this boy is neither winking nor twitching, he is parodying someone else's, as he takes it, laughable, attempt at winking. Here, too, a socially established code exists (he will "wink" laboriously, overobviously, perhaps adding a grimace – the usual artifices of the clown); and so also does a message. Only now it is not conspiracy but ridicule that is in the air. If the others think he is actually winking, his whole project misfires as completely, though with somewhat different results, as if they think he is twitching. One can go further: uncertain of his mimicking abilities, the would-be satirist may practice at home before the mirror, in which case he is not twitching, winking, or parodying, but rehearsing; though so far as what a camera, a radical behaviorist, or a believer in protocol sentences would record he is just rapidly contracting his right eyelids like all the others. Complexities are possible, if not practically without end, at least logically so. The original winker might, for example, actually have been fake-winking, say, to mislead outsiders into imagining there was a conspiracy afoot when there in fact was not, in which case our descriptions of what the parodist is parodying and the rehearser rehearsing of course shift accordingly. But the point is that between what Ryle calls the "thin description" of what the rehearser (parodist, winker, twitcher...) is doing ("rapidly contracting his right eyelids") and the "thick description" of what he is doing ("practicing a burlesque of a friend faking a wink to deceive an innocent into thinking a conspiracy is in motion") lies the object of ethnography: a stratified hierarchy of meaningful structures in terms of which twitches, winks, fake-winks, parodies, rehearsals of parodies are produced, perceived, and interpreted, and without which they would not (not even the zero-form twitches, which, *as a cultural category*, are as much nonwinks as winks are nontwitches) in fact exist, no matter what anyone did or didn't do with his eyelids.

[...]

In finished anthropological writings [...] [the] fact – that what we call our data are really our own constructions of other people's constructions of what they and their compatriots are up to – is obscured because most of what we need to comprehend a particular event, ritual, custom, idea, or whatever is insinuated as background information before the thing itself is directly examined. [...] There is nothing particularly wrong with this, and it is in any case inevitable. But it does lead to a view of anthropological research as rather more of an observational and rather less of an interpretive activity than it really is. Right down at the factual base, the hard rock, insofar as there is any, of the whole enterprise, we are already explicating: and worse, explicating explications. Winks upon winks upon winks.

Analysis, then, is sorting out the structures of signification – what Ryle called established codes, a somewhat misleading expression, for it makes the enterprise sound too much like that of the cipher clerk when it is much more like that of the literary critic – and determining their social ground and import. [...]

The point for now is only that ethnography is thick description. What the ethnographer is in fact faced with – except when (as, of course, he must do) he is pursuing the more automatized routines of data collection – is a multiplicity of complex conceptual structures, many of them superimposed upon or knotted into one another, which are at once strange, irregular, and inexplicit, and which he must contrive somehow first to grasp and then to render. And this is true at the most down-to-earth, jungle field work levels of his activity: interviewing informants, observing rituals, eliciting kin terms, tracing property lines, censusing households... writing his journal. Doing ethnography is like trying to read (in the sense of "construct a reading of") a manuscript – foreign, faded, full of ellipses, incoherencies, suspicious emendations, and tendentious commentaries, but written not in conventionalized graphs of sound but in transient examples of shaped behavior.

III

Culture, this acted document, thus is public, like a burlesqued wink or a mock sheep raid. Though ideational, it does not exist in someone's head; though unphysical, it is not an occult entity. The interminable, because unterminable, debate within anthropology as to whether culture is "subjective" or "objective," together with the mutual exchange of intellectual insults ("idealist!" – "materialist!"; "mentalist!" – "behaviorist!"; "impressionist!" – "positivist!") which accompanies it, is wholly misconceived. Once human behavior is seen as (most of the time; there *are* true twitches) symbolic action – action which, like phonation in speech, pigment in painting, line in writing, or sonance in music, signifies – the question as to whether culture is patterned conduct or a frame of mind, or even the two somehow mixed together, loses sense. The thing to ask about a burlesqued wink or a mock sheep raid is not what their ontological status is. It is the same as that of rocks on the one hand and dreams on the other – they are things of this world. The thing to ask is what their import is: what it is, ridicule or challenge, irony or anger, snobbery or pride, that, in their occurrence and through their agency, is getting said.

This may seem like an obvious truth, but there are a number of ways to obscure it. One is to imagine that culture is a self-contained "superorganic" reality with forces and purposes of its own; that is, to reify it. Another is to claim that it consists in the brute pattern of behavioral events we observe in fact to occur in some identifiable community or other; that is, to reduce it. But though both these confusions still exist, and doubtless will be always with us, the main source of theoretical muddlement in contemporary anthropology is a view which developed in reaction to them and is right now very widely held – namely, that, to quote Ward Goodenough, perhaps its leading proponent, "culture [is located] in the minds and hearts of men."

Variously called ethnoscience, componential analysis, or cognitive anthropology (a terminological wavering which reflects a deeper uncertainty), this school of thought holds that culture is composed of psychological structures by means of which individuals or groups of individuals guide their behavior. "A society's culture," to quote Goodenough again, this time in a passage which has become the *locus classicus* of the whole movement, "consists of whatever it is one has to know or believe in order to operate in a manner acceptable to its members." And from this view of what culture is follows a view, equally assured, of what describing it is – the writing out of systematic rules, an ethnographic algorithm, which, if followed, would make it possible so to operate, to pass (physical appearance aside) for a native. In such a way, extreme subjectivism is married to extreme formalism, with the expected result: an explosion of debate as to whether particular analyses (which come in the form of taxonomies, paradigms, tables, trees, and other ingenuities) reflect what the natives "really" think or are merely clever simulations, logically equivalent but substantively different, of what they think.

As, on first glance, this approach may look close enough to the one being developed here to be mistaken for it, it is useful to be explicit as to what divides them. If, leaving our winks and sheep behind for the moment, we take, say, a Beethoven quartet as an, admittedly rather special but, for these purposes, nicely illustrative, sample of culture, no one would, I think, identify it with its score, with the skills and knowledge needed to play it, with the understanding of it possessed by its performers or auditors, nor, to take care, *en passant*, of the reductionists and reifiers, with a particular performance of it or with some mysterious entity transcending material existence. The "no one" is perhaps too strong here, for there are always incorrigibles. But that a Beethoven quartet is a temporally developed tonal structure, a coherent sequence of modeled sound – in a word, music – and not anybody's knowledge of or belief about anything, including how to play it, is a proposition to which most people are, upon reflection, likely to assent.

To play the violin it is necessary to possess certain habits, skills, knowledge, and talents, to be in the mood to play, and (as the old joke goes) to have a violin. But violin playing is neither the habits, skills, knowledge, and so on, nor the mood, nor (the notion believers in "material culture" apparently embrace) the violin. To make a trade pact in Morocco, you have to do certain things in certain ways (among others, cut, while chanting Quranic Arabic, the throat of a lamb before the assembled, undeformed, adult male members of your tribe) and to be possessed of certain psychological characteristics (among others, a desire for distant things). But a trade pact is neither the throat cutting nor the desire, though it is real enough. […]

Culture is public because meaning is. You can't wink (or burlesque one) without knowing what counts as winking or how, physically, to contract your eyelids, and you can't conduct a sheep raid (or mimic one) without knowing what it is to steal a sheep and how practically to go about it. But to draw from such truths the conclusion that knowing how to wink is winking and knowing how to steal a sheep is sheep raiding is to betray as deep a confusion as, taking thin descriptions for thick, to identify winking with eyelid contractions or sheep raiding with chasing woolly animals out of pastures. The cognitivist fallacy – that culture consists […] of "mental phenomena which can […] be analyzed by formal methods similar to those of mathematics and logic" – is as destructive of an effective use of the concept as are the behaviorist and idealist fallacies to which it is a misdrawn correction. Perhaps, as its errors are more sophisticated and its distortions subtler, it is even more so.

The generalized attack on privacy theories of meaning is, since early Husserl and late Wittgenstein, so much a part of modern thought that it need not be developed once more here. What is necessary is to see to it that the news of it reaches anthropology; and in particular that it is made clear that to say that culture consists of socially established structures of meaning in terms of which people do such things as signal conspiracies and join them or perceive insults and answer them, is no more to say that it is a psychological phenomenon, a characteristic of someone's mind, personality, cognitive structure, or whatever, than to say that Tantrism, genetics, the progressive form of the verb, the classification of wines, the Common Law, or the notion of "a conditional curse" […] is. What, in a place like Morocco, most prevents those of us who grew up winking other winks or attending other sheep from grasping what people are up to is not ignorance as to how cognition works (though, especially as, one assumes, it works the same among them as it does among us, it would greatly help to have less of that too) as a lack of familiarity with the imaginative universe within which their acts are signs. As Wittgenstein has been invoked, he may as well be quoted:

> We … say of some people that they are transparent to us. It is, however, important as regards this observation that one human being can be a

complete enigma to another. We learn this when we come into a strange country with entirely strange traditions; and, what is more, even given a mastery of the country's language. We do not *understand* the people. (And not because of not knowing what they are saying to themselves.) We cannot find our feet with them.

IV

Finding our feet, an unnerving business which never more than distantly succeeds, is what ethnographic research consists of as a personal experience; trying to formulate the basis on which one imagines, always excessively, one has found them is what anthropological writing consists of as a scientific endeavor. We are not, or at least I am not, seeking either to become natives (a compromised word in any case) or to mimic them. Only romantics or spies would seem to find point in that. We are seeking, in the widened sense of the term in which it encompasses very much more than talk, to converse with them, a matter a great deal more difficult, and not only with strangers, than is commonly recognized. "If speaking *for* someone else seems to be a mysterious process," Stanley Cavell has remarked, "that may be because speaking *to* someone does not seem mysterious enough."

Looked at in this way, the aim of anthropology is the enlargement of the universe of human discourse. That is not, of course, its only aim – instruction, amusement, practical counsel, moral advance, and the discovery of natural order in human behavior are others; nor is anthropology the only discipline which pursues it. But it is an aim to which a semiotic concept of culture is peculiarly well adapted. As interworked systems of construable signs (what, ignoring provincial usages, I would call symbols), culture is not a power, something to which social events, behaviors, institutions, or processes can be causally attributed; it is a context, something within which they can be intelligibly – that is, thickly – described.

The famous anthropological absorption with the (to us) exotic [...] is, thus, essentially a device for displacing the dulling sense of familiarity with which the mysteriousness of our own ability to relate perceptively to one another is concealed from us. Looking at the ordinary in places where it takes unaccustomed forms brings out not, as has so often been claimed, the arbitrariness of

human behavior [...], but the degree to which its meaning varies according to the pattern of life by which it is informed. Understanding a people's culture exposes their normalness without reducing their particularity. [...] It renders them accessible: setting them in the frame of their own banalities, it dissolves their opacity.

It is this maneuver, usually too casually referred to as "seeing things from the actor's point of view," too bookishly as "the *verstehen* approach," or too technically as "emic analysis," that so often leads to the notion that anthropology is a variety of either long-distance mind reading or cannibalisle fantasizing, and which, for someone anxious to navigate past the wrecks of a dozen sunken philosophies, must therefore be executed with a great deal of care. Nothing is more necessary to comprehending what anthropological interpretation is, and the degree to which it *is* interpretation, than an exact understanding of what it means – and what it does not mean – to say that our formulations of other peoples' symbol systems must be actor-oriented.[1]

What it means is that descriptions of Berber, Jewish, or French culture must be cast in terms of the constructions we imagine Berbers, Jews, or Frenchmen to place upon what they live through, the formulae they use to define what happens to them. What it does not mean is that such descriptions are themselves Berber, Jewish, or French – that is, part of the reality they are ostensibly describing; they are anthropological – that is, part of a developing system of scientific analysis. They must be cast in terms of the interpretations to which persons of a particular denomination subject their experience, because that is what they profess to be descriptions of; they are anthropological because it is, in fact, anthropologists who profess them. Normally, it is not necessary to point out quite so laboriously that the object of study is one thing and the study of it another. It is clear enough that the physical world is not physics and *A Skeleton Key to Finnegan's Wake* not *Finnegan's Wake*. But, as, in the study of culture, analysis penetrates into the very body of the object – that is, *we begin with our own interpretations of what our informants are up to, or think they are up to, and then systematize those* – the line between [...] culture as a natural fact and [...] culture as a theoretical entity tends to get blurred. All the more so, as the latter is presented in the form of an actor's-eye description of [...] conceptions of everything from violence, honor, divinity, and justice, to tribe, property, patronage, and chiefship.

In short, anthropological writings are themselves interpretations, and second- and third-order ones to boot. (By definition, only a "native" makes first order ones: it's *his* culture.)[2] They are, thus, fictions; fictions, in the sense that they are "something made," "something fashioned" – the original meaning of *fictiō* – not that they are false, unfactual, or merely "as if" thought experiments. To construct actor-oriented descriptions of the involvements of a Berber chieftain, a Jewish merchant, and a French soldier with one another in 1912 Morocco is clearly an imaginative act, not all that different from constructing similar descriptions of, say, the involvements with one another of a provincial French doctor, his silly, adulterous wife, and her feckless lover in nineteenth-century France. In the latter case, the actors are represented as not having existed and the events as not having happened, while in the former they are represented as actual, or as having been so. This is a difference of no mean importance; indeed, precisely the one Madame Bovary had difficulty grasping. But the importance does not lie in the fact that her story was created while Cohen's was only noted. The conditions of their creation, and the point of it (to say nothing of the manner and the quality) differ. But the one is as much a *fictiō* – "a making" – as the other.

Anthropologists have not always been as aware as they might be of this fact: that although culture exists in the trading post, the hill fort, or the sheep run, anthropology exists in the book, the article, the lecture, the museum display, or, sometimes nowadays, the film. To become aware of it is to realize that the line between mode of representation and substantive content is as undrawable in cultural analysis as it is in painting; and that fact in turn seems to threaten the objective status of anthropological knowledge by suggesting that its source is not social reality but scholarly artifice.

It does threaten it, but the threat is hollow. The claim to attention of an ethnographic account does not rest on its author's ability to capture primitive facts in faraway places and carry them home like a mask or a carving, but on the degree to which he is able to clarify what goes on in such places, to reduce the puzzlement – what manner of men are these? – to which unfamiliar acts emerging out of unknown backgrounds naturally give rise. This raises some serious problems of verification, all right – or, if "verification" is too strong a word for so soft a science (I, myself, would prefer "appraisal"), of how you can tell a better account from a worse one. But that is precisely the virtue of it. If ethnography is thick description and ethnographers those who are doing the describing, then the determining question for any given example of it, whether a field journal squib or a Malinowski-sized monograph, is whether it sorts winks from twitches and real winks from mimicked ones. It is not against a body of uninterpreted data, radically thinned descriptions, that we must measure the cogency of our explications, but against the power of the scientific imagination to bring us into touch with the lives of strangers. It is not worth it, as Thoreau said, to go round the world to count the cats in Zanzibar.

V

Now, this proposition, that it is not in our interest to bleach human behavior of the very properties that interest us before we begin to examine it, has sometimes been escalated into a larger claim: namely, that as it is only those properties that interest us, we need not attend, save cursorily, to behavior at all. Culture is most effectively treated, the argument goes, purely as a symbolic system (the catch phrase is, "in its own terms"), by isolating its elements, specifying the internal relationships among those elements, and then characterizing the whole system in some general way – according to the core symbols around which it is organized, the underlying structures of which it is a surface expression, or the ideological principles upon which it is based. Though a distinct improvement over "learned behavior" and "mental phenomena" notions of what culture is, and the source of some of the most powerful theoretical ideas in contemporary anthropology, this hermetical approach to things seems to me to run the danger (and increasingly to have been overtaken by it) of locking cultural analysis away from its proper object, the informal logic of actual life. There is little profit in extricating a concept from the defects of psychologism only to plunge it immediately into those of schematicism.

Behavior must be attended to, and with some exactness, because it is through the flow of behavior – or, more precisely, social action – that cultural forms find articulation. They find it as well, of course, in various sorts of artifacts, and various states of consciousness; but these draw their meaning from the role they play (Wittgenstein would say their "use") in an ongoing pattern of life, not from any intrinsic relationships they bear to one another. [...]

A further implication of this is that coherence cannot be the major test of validity for a cultural description. Cultural systems must have a minimal degree of coherence, else we would not call them systems; and, by observation, they normally have a great deal more. But there is nothing so coherent as a paranoid's delusion or a swindler's story. The force of our interpretations cannot rest, as they are now so often made to do, on the tightness with which they hold together, or the assurance with which they are argued. Nothing has done more, I think, to discredit cultural analysis than the construction of impeccable depictions of formal order in whose actual existence nobody can quite believe.

If anthropological interpretation is constructing a reading of what happens, then to divorce it from what happens – from what, in this time or that place, specific people say, what they do, what is done to them, from the whole vast business of the world – is to divorce it from its applications and render it vacant. A good interpretation of anything – a poem, a person, a history, a ritual, an institution, a society – takes us into the heart of that of which it is the interpretation. When it does not do that, but leads us instead somewhere else – into an admiration of its own elegance, of its author's cleverness, or of the beauties of Euclidean order – it may have its intrinsic charms; but it is something else than what the task at hand [...] calls for.

[...]

The ethnographer "inscribes" social discourse; *he writes it down.* In so doing, he turns it from a passing event, which exists only in its own moment of occurrence, into an account, which exists in its inscriptions and can be reconsulted. [...] "What," Paul Ricoeur, from whom this whole idea of the inscription of action is borrowed and somewhat twisted, asks, "what does writing fix?"

> Not the event of speaking, but the "said" of speaking, where we understand by the "said" of speaking that intentional exteriorization constitutive of the aim of discourse thanks to which the *sagen* – the saying – wants to become *Aus-sage* – the enunciation, the enunciated. In short, what we write is the *noema* ["thought," "content," "gist"] of the speaking. It is the meaning of the speech event, not the event as event.

This is not itself so very "said" – if Oxford philosophers run to little stories, phenomenological ones run to large sentences; but it brings us anyway to a more precise answer to our generative question, "What does the ethnographer do?" – he writes.[3] This, too, may seem a less than startling discovery, and to someone familiar with the current "literature," an implausible one. But as the standard answer to our question has been, "He observes, he records, he analyzes" – a kind of *veni, vidi, vici* conception of the matter – it may have more deepgoing consequences than are at first apparent, not the least of which is that distinguishing these three phases of knowledge-seeking may not, as a matter of fact, normally be possible; and, indeed, as autonomous "operations" they may not in fact exist. [...]

Notes

1 Not only other peoples': anthropology *can* be trained on the culture of which it is itself a part, and it increasingly is; a fact of profound importance, but which, as it raises a few tricky and rather special second-order problems, I shall put to the side for the moment.

2 The order problem is, again, complex. Anthropological works based on other anthropological works (Lévi-Strauss, for example) may, of course, be fourth order or higher, and informants frequently, even habitually, make second-order interpretations – what have come to be known as "native models." In literate cultures, where "native" interpretation can proceed to higher

levels – in connection with the Maghreb, one has only to think of Ibn Khaldun; with the United States, Margaret Mead – these matters become intricate indeed.

3 Or, again, more exactly, "inscribes." Most ethnography is in fact to be found in books and articles, rather than in films, records, museum displays, or whatever; but even in them there are, of course, photographs, drawings, diagrams, tables, and so on. Self-consciousness about modes of representation (not to speak of experiments with them) has been very lacking in anthropology.

17

Anthropology and the Analysis of Ideology

Talal Asad

[...] An emphasis on "meaning" is to be found, whether implicit or explicit, in much recent anthropological writing. A preoccupation with identifying and constituting *a priori* structures of human meaning is shared by a range of writings that are otherwise very different – those dealing with cultural categories, symbolic representations, codes and communication, image management, rational transactions, etc. And the preoccupation is present both in the rationalist perspectives of those concerned to assert the universality and priority of cultural classification systems, and in the empiricist perspectives of those concerned with what they take to be the ultimate datum of flesh-and-bone individuals, interacting intelligently within the real world. This interest in meaning is not itself new, although there is perhaps a new self-consciousness about that interest. Anthropological texts with titles like *Implicit meanings, Rules and meanings, Transaction and meaning, Explorations in language and meaning,* "The management of meaning", "Form and meaning of magical acts", "The politics of meaning", seem to be somewhat more evident today than they were a generation ago – and from authors who might be described as empiricists or as

rationalists, and sometimes even as rationalist and empiricist at one and the same time. It is worth noting that Leach (1976) has recently written about the complementary character of two major perspectives in social anthropology, the rationalist and the empiricist, which he regards not as opposed but as eminently compatible.[1] However it is not my intention to suggest reassuringly, as Leach appears to want to do, that rationalist and empiricist anthropologists are together producing a sum of understanding in which what is lacking on the one side is made up by the achievement of the other. On the contrary, I want to try and indicate some things they have in *common*, and to suggest why and to what extent these things are a source of present theoretical weakness.

One aspect of this weakness can be seen in what is often admitted to be the repeated failure of social anthropologists to produce a viable theory of social change. The reason for this may not be, as it is sometimes proposed, that "real" factors of social change are many and complex, which is a practical difficulty, but rather that the way the object of change is itself conceptualised makes the possibility of such a theory difficult if not impossible.

From *Man* 14(4), 1979, pp. 609–21, 624–7. Copyright © 1979 by *Man*. Reprinted by permission of John Wiley & Sons UK.

Anthropology in Theory: Issues in Epistemology, Second Edition. Edited by Henrietta L. Moore and Todd Sanders.
© 2014 John Wiley & Sons, Inc. Published 2014 by John Wiley & Sons, Inc.

In the writings of both empiricist and rationalist anthropologists, then, human meanings are seen almost everywhere. More precisely, the basic social object (called society, social structure or social order) which is presented in the discourse of such anthropologists is constructed out of essential human meanings. Society as the realm of convention is generally opposed to nature as the realm of necessity. In extreme cases, as in Sahlins's most recent dialogue with Marxism, there is a tendency for even nature to be represented as the product of human action and cognition, as inert raw matter ordered by constitutive human meanings. In a striking passage, which must surely stand as one of the most lyrical expressions of the humanist project in modern anthropology, Sahlins in the conclusion to *Culture and practical reason* writes:

> nature as it exists in itself is only the raw material provided by the hand of God, waiting to be given meaningful shape and content by the mind of man. It is as the block of marble to the finished statue; and of course the genius of the sculptor – in the same way as the technical development of culture – consists of exploiting the lines of defraction within the material to his own ends. That marble is refractory; there are certain things one cannot do with it – such are the facts of nature and the action of selection. But it is the sculptor who decides whether the statue is to be an equestrain knight contemplating his victories [. . .] or a seated Moses contemplating the sins of his people. And if it be objected that it is the composition of the marble which compels the form of the statue, it should not be forgotten that this block of marble was chosen from among all possible ones because the sculptor saw within it the latent image of his own project. (1976: 210)

This bold celebration of man's creative powers, with God complacently occupying the rank of unskilled labourer, may not be to the taste of all anthropologists. However that may be, this passage from Sahlins does raise sharply the question of how the basic social object presented in anthropological texts is constituted in those texts, and the question of what some of the theoretical consequences might be of the fact that the essential defining elements of that object are human meanings and human projects.

My concern is not with the question of whether or not the anthropologist should accept uncritically and reproduce directly in his model the explanations produced by the people he studies. The arguments between so-called symbolists and literalists (sometimes represented as a confrontation between soft, nostalgic liberals on the one hand, and clear-sighted, unsentimental modernists on the other) are still, after all, arguments about the criteria to be used for determining the sense of what people in other societies say and do. On this question one may note in passing that the attempt to make a rigid distinction between symbolic and literal meanings is coming to be seen as a distinction that raises more problems than it solves.[2] Recently, Sperber (1975) and Skorupski (1976) have in their different ways discussed the confusions created by the anthropological addiction to notions of the symbolic. That their own treatments are not free of further difficulties is something I cannot consider now. In any case, my point here has to do not with the proper interpretation of words, gestures, and things in their capacity as signifiers, but with the preoccupation that different kinds of anthropologists have with human meanings as such.

My concern in the first place is with the nature of the basic social object constituted *within* anthropological texts themselves. And I want to argue that in anthropological texts this object is typically constituted with reference to a notion of ideology whose social significance derives from its being the expression of an *a priori* system of essential meanings – an "authentic culture". I shall try to explore briefly this conceptual object constituted of human meanings and to criticise it as I proceed – *not* by pointing to a brute reality which every sensible person must immediately recognise, but by interrogating the texts. In the course of this interrogation I shall try to take note of the very different models that structure the sense of "meaning" – the aim of a speaker/actor, the rules of linguistic (and stylistic) conventions, the content of an experiencing, construing mind, and the process of conceptual unpacking and re-presentation that occurs through objective discourse – because part of my criticism will focus on the troubles that arise from the combination of what are often incompatible models in the anthropological attempt to define authentic cultures.

III

That the central object of anthropological discourse is primarily constituted in terms of human meanings has very recently been reaffirmed by Maurice Bloch in his 1977 paper "The past and the present in the present".

In this paper Bloch is concerned to specify reasons for the perennial difficulty that anthropologists have had in formulating an adequate theory of social change. Bloch points out that the concept of social structure in anthropology refers essentially to an integrated totality of social classifications and meanings, a system of social rules and roles which can, in one widely accepted anthropological sense of the term, be called ritual. Now if this concept of social structure is linked to the doctrine of the social origin of concepts (the social determination of cognition) it becomes impossible to specify how social change can occur. This is because, so Bloch argues, a system of meaningful categories, of shared concepts that makes communication possible (a system which is none other than social structure) cannot explain the creation of new concepts.[3]

Bloch believes that the Marxist theory of determining infrastructure and determined superstructure is no answer to the problem either, because:

the infrastructure is seen as external to the concepts of the actors. [And] for it to be a source of criticism of the social order it means that people must apprehend it in terms available to them and which are different from and incompatible with those of the dominant social theory. This means terms not determined by it. Otherwise the infrastructure, however contradictory to the dominant social theory, is never transformed into action and just carries on in its own sweet way, totally irrelevant to the processes of history. (1977: 281)

Bloch's own solution is to propose that the different conceptions and perceptions required for an effective criticism of the existing social order must be determined by that which is other than society – in other words by nature.[4]

Now Bloch's emphasis on the importance of ideological argument (which has its roots in some fertile suggestions made by Leach in *Political*

systems of highland Burma [1954]) is certainly a move in the right direction – and I will come back to it later. But even in such a discourse "social structure" is presented as a total integrated system of shared subjective meanings and conventions. Even the Marxist notion of infrastructure is declared to be "irrelevant to the processes of history" unless it can be reduced to the experiences and aims of individual actors. The problem of social change is thus presented as being a problem of a change of concepts, the concepts available to "real flesh-and-blood individuals" that can at once define and transform the essence of society.

The main difficulty with Bloch's argument is this: the proposition that universally valid concepts (or new and better forms of understanding) are essentially generated by man's encounter with nature (which is to be thought of as being a kind of "undeceiving" object) and not by his encounter with society (which is to be thought of as being a kind of "mystifying" object) may or may not be acceptable. I would maintain that it is not. But even if it were, it would not explain how people, who are presumably all in direct contact with the same nature, come to have very different concepts within the same society, and how they are able to engage in ideological arguments about the basic transformation of social conditions in which they all live.

In other words, epistemological questions about the ultimate origin or the final guarantee of social concepts and forms of knowledge (so beloved of many anthropologists) are really quite irrelevant to this kind of problem. They cannot tell us anything about the reasons why different kinds of ideological position come to be held in social life, or about the ideological force or effectiveness of particular political arguments. [...] In this respect, Bloch's mistake consists in making the assumption, which is by no means unique to him, that society – and so too social change – is essentially a matter of *structures of meaning*, structures which are at once the collective forms of experience, and the social pre-conditions of communication (culture as language); and that therefore, social criticism is not merely *sometimes* a necessary but *always* a sufficient pre-condition for social change.

Thus anthropologists have presented the basic social objects in their texts ("social structure") in

such a way that they inevitably propose for ideology an essential and determinate function – so
that ideology is not only written in as the basic
organising principle of social life, the integrated
totality of shared meanings which gives that
society its unique identity (its culture), but also
changing ideologies are said to be essential to
basic transformations.

In a recent issue of *Man* (December 1978),
there appears a perceptive comment on Bloch's
paper by Bourdillon. In it he observes quite rightly
that the equation Bloch makes between ritual concepts (or religious languages) on the one hand,
and hierarchy and exploitation (or social structure) on the other is far too simple and therefore
unacceptable.[5] However, Bourdillon has no quarrel with the essentially ideological constitution of
that anthropological object called social structure.
On the contrary, he insists that social structure "is
a way of thinking about society which enables us
to bring together a diverse set of relations into a
manageable system, and which expresses the continuity in any process of social events" (1978: 595).
As against Bloch, Bourdillon maintains that this
integrated system of roles, rules and rituals is
essential for any form of orderly social life, and not
just a source of mystification which can and
should be done away with. Bourdillon is here of
course echoing the argument by Douglas (1970)
that the dissolution of structure, far from being
the rational aim of revolutions is merely the
empirical cause of rebellions. But he does not ask
himself, as he might well have done: is the system
which is supposed to be necessary for thinking
and speaking (whether speculatively, or with
authoritative force) about social life to be identified with what is necessary for living in it?

The ambiguity here is between what is supposed to be the way the anthropologist actually
thinks and speaks *about* social life and the way
the people the anthropologist is studying are supposed actually to think and speak *in* their social
life. In other words, the ambiguity is between
the anthropologist's discourse, and the discourse
of the society (the discourse that is its lived
culture) which is supposed to be reproduced in
the anthropologist's definitive text (an interpretative, reflective discourse). This ambiguity is not
concerned merely with the question mentioned
previously of the degree to which the anthropologist may or must draw on the explanations

provided by the people studied – sometimes
referred to in the anthropological literature as
the problem of the informant's model versus
the anthropologist's model. The question being
raised here is really concerned with the relationship the other way around. And the form which
that question might take is this: to what extent
do anthropological texts construct an *essential*
system of meanings in their attempt to present
the "authentic" structure of social life and of
discourse of the people studied?

Let me first illustrate this point with a familiar
example.

IV

Some years after *Political systems of highland
Burma* was first published, Gellner (1958) wrote a
paper drawing attention to the book as:

> perhaps the most lucid statement of a certain
> kind of Idealism that I know, and teachers of phi-
> losophy could profitably use a selection of his
> statements as a means of explaining to their stu-
> dents what such Idealism is about. (1958: 202)

> Leach in effect sees *other* Functionalists as
> holding a kind of Platonism. Only the static is
> properly knowable, it is merely approximated by
> the empirically real. [...] Leach's own variant to
> this is a kind of Hegelianism: reality changes
> because it is in conflict, the conflict is a conflict of
> embodied ideas, and the change and conflict are
> knowable by means of concepts that are them-
> selves in conflict in a parallel way. (1958: 193)

Gellner's paper contained some useful points of
criticism, but I believe he was mistaken in his
philosophical reading of Leach's text. Besides, the
proposition that *Political systems of highland
Burma* represents a view that is appropriately
described as Hegelian cannot be sustained by a
careful analysis of that text. But that is all by the
way. The interesting thing was Leach's response in
his Introductory Note to the 1964 reprint. There,
you may remember, Leach wrote as follows:

> Incidentally, in a friendly comment, Professor
> Gellner has written off my whole argument as one
> of "idealist error". Truth and error are complicated

matters but it seems to me that in suggesting indirectly that the Kachins have a rather simple minded philosophy which presumes a relationship between "idea" and "reality" not very different from that postulated by Plato, I am not arguing that Plato was correct. The errors of Platonism are very common errors which are shared not only by anthropologists but also by the people whom anthropologists study. (1964: xiv)

This attribution by Leach of the Platonic doctrine of forms to the Kachins is quite astonishing – not because the Kachins are too simple-minded to hold it, but because the doctrine is essentially a metaphysical one, and there is no evidence in the text of Kachin metaphysics in this sense. Whatever the "errors of Platonism" may be, they are not the errors of everyday political and economic life (which is what the book deals with) but the errors of systematic philosophical speculation.

Such is the awe in which philosophy is held by anthropologists, that Leach felt constrained to reply to a philosophical charge in philosophical terms. And yet there was no need for this whatever. Gellner had attributed a particular philosophical theory of meaning to Leach,[6] and it was in this context that he criticised him for assuming that one needed changing concepts to *know* changing reality. But Leach's text is not based on a specific philosophical theory of meaning at all:[7] a basic argument of *Political systems of highland Burma* (like that of Bloch's paper) is that there must *be* changing social concepts for such a thing as social change to occur. Now such an argument could have been countered – by pointing, not to a faulty philosophical theory about the relation between "ideas" and "reality" (as Gellner did), but to an ideological conception of social change. More precisely, it could have been countered by drawing attention to a very questionable theory of culture – the theory which gives logical priority to the system of authentic meaning supposedly shared by an ideologically-defined community, and independent of the political activity and economic conditions of its members.

Political systems of highland Burma is rightly regarded by many anthropologists as a most important text – although its remarkable originality and its failure have rarely been adequately appreciated. But note how arguments about systematic concepts within anthropological discourse can be easily shifted into another key – and thus stopped, by an appeal to the discourse of the natives "out there" which the anthropologist has witnessed and recorded. Since Gellner did not respond, we can perhaps assume that he accepted Leach's authority in this argument. However that may be, on this occasion, as on others in which anthropological discourse seeks to re-present an authentic system of human meanings (the enduring categories which define, from one historical moment to another, who "the Kachin" are), no native was available to contest the system being imputed – if not to him or her individually, then at least to the "society" which was supposed to be authentically his or hers.

Here is one example, then, of the way in which the anthropologist's discursive object comes to be presented as a reproduction of the essential discourse of a whole society. (Although, be it noted, it is not the Kachin but the anthropologist who actually writes.) The example may be unusual in substance but perhaps because of that it serves all the better to raise the question of how anthropological texts construct for a whole society, or even for a group within it, a total, integrated semantic system, which defines for that society what its essential identity is.

Let me pursue this question with further reference to Leach's *Political systems of highland Burma*.

The significance of Leach's text derives not from the fact that it illustrates a simple philosophical error (idealism) which should be replaced by a sounder epistemology but from the fact that it is a rich and complex statement of a particular anthropological problem and its proposed solution. The text is not simply the reflection of an essential philosophy. It is the production of an anthropological object. I cannot here discuss this work in the detail that it deserves, but will draw on an aspect of it which is relevant to my theme.

The starting point of Leach's study, of course, was the question of Kachin identity. The problem was that the so-called hill peoples of the north-eastern Burma frontier region were rather diverse in their culture, lived in contrasting ecological settings, spoke a number of quite distinct (often mutually unintelligible) dialects, and were organised in local communities which apparently held to very different political principles – varying from the comparatively rich, autocratic Shan princedoms to the often rather poor, and relatively egalitarian Kachin *gumlao* village domains. Leach's answer to this basic problem was that Kachin identity was based on a common "ritual language", an ideological system whose primary organising categories were political.

Leach's notion of a common ritual language enabled him to rationalise apparent local divergencies in the Hills Area into conceptual moments of the "same" social structure, and apparent historical changes into elements of the transformational logic of that structure. This rationalist solution to an empirical problem was thus in effect the construction of a system of human meanings (a "grammar of ritual action" Leach called it) which was then identified as the essential language that defined the political economic integrity of the Kachins – and in terms of which the Kachins must speak if they are to remain authentically Kachin. In this way Leach's text defines what can and what cannot be "correctly" said in the political discourse of the Kachins.

Of course Leach allows for and refers in his text to ideological argument among the Kachins. But the arguments described revolve in general around the abstract principles of hierarchy versus equality, and Leach relates the way in which the authoritative Kachin ritual language is used to claim one or other of these two abstract principles, which are at once the principles of prevailing social conditions and the principles of meaningful discourse. The resulting account of social change, as many critics have observed, is thus an account of an eternal cycle – better described as a process of ideological self-reproduction.

The difficulty here is not that there cannot be argument and criticism of social arrangements if there is only one language which is "determined by society". The difficulty is not that Leach should have looked more to "economics and politics" [...] and less to ritual and religion in order to identify the origins of Kachin concepts of Reality. The difficulty resides in the very notion of a "grammar" which is at once the principle that defines the anthropologist's object of discourse and also *the* system of concepts which is held to integrate and define Kachin political and economic life as a whole. This ideological definition of the Kachin system misses the question of

whether there are not specific political economic conditions which make certain rhetorical forms objectively possible, and *authoritative*. For when Kachins become Shan, for example, the process involved is not merely a matter of the mental or behavioural change of subjects, but of the partial undermining of a given form of discourse, and of the production and re-affirmation of another form, within the very different material conditions which Shan political economy articulates. The question that we might ask, therefore, is whether there is a "grammar" that always defines for the population of the entire Hills Area what are the politically correct utterances (or actions), and what are necessarily meaningless ones.

The unsatisfactory state of such anthropological theorising comes, I am arguing, from the fact that the basic social object it presents is constructed out of an integrated system of "shared meaningful ideas", and so from the fact that a closed, definitive status is given to that system (otherwise it would not be "integrated" or "shared" from one generation to the next), and all this in the attempt to reproduce an authentic culture. What makes that system of meanings "authentic" is this very re-presentability from the past[8] (from an original generation to its authorised successors; and from the moment of grasping it in the field to the moment of embodying it in the text). Thus the political discourse of particular societies (as opposed to their knowledge of Reality) is assumed to be self-defining and self-reproducing. Because of this assumption, recent commentators like Bloch cannot see any way out of the Leachean impasse other than by reducing the problem of the authority of political discourse (which defines certain meanings as essential) to the very different problem of the epistemological foundation and growth of objective knowledge ("Man's experience of Nature, direct/indirect"). And in this way an anthropological question is answered in philosophical terms. Neither Leach nor his later critics make any attempt to explore the systematic social connexions between historical forces and relations on the one hand, and the characteristic forms of discourse sustained or undermined by them on the other.

In case it should still be thought that I am merely concerned to criticise structuralist authors for their idealism, let me remind you that Leach's *Political systems of highland Burma* is in its own way as materialist and as actor-oriented as are the more recent texts by self-proclaimed materialists or transactionalists.[9]

V

But perhaps this argument can be made more strongly if we turn to Douglas in her most recent, transactionalist mood – I refer of course to the booklet entitled *Cultural bias*.

Praising Cicourel for his attack on sociology and ethno-science, Douglas comments:

> Everything he writes about our colleagues strikes this anthropologist as good clean fun, but it is a pity that he never writes anything about English social anthropology at all. For we are his natural allies. We also believe that our work is to understand how meanings are generated, caught and transformed. We also assume that meanings are deeply embedded and context-bound. We are also stuck at the same fence that he has baulked. Like him we cannot proceed very far without incorporating real live cultures into our analysis. For the cognitive activity of the real live individual is largely devoted to building the culture, patching it here and trimming it there, according to the exigencies of the day. In his very negotiating activity, each is forcing culture down the throats of his fellow men. When individuals transact, their medium of exchange is in units of culture. (1978: 5–6)

I think we should not be distracted by these vivid images of threatened authority – of horses that will not take the fence, and of prisoners who are forcibly fed. What Douglas wants to know is whether culture is capable of being radically altered, and her conclusion is that it is not. In order to establish this, she attempts a specification of the range of constraints on individual choice and exchange, and this she does by the application of what she calls grid-group analysis – an anthropological offspring of Bernstein's well-known distinction between elaborated and restricted codes. The resulting morphology of four basic types of social context, and their supporting types of cosmology, form the settings within which the "real live individual" makes decisions, experiences his or her environment, and transacts values with others.

Douglas produces ethnographic examples from a wide variety of anthropological studies of non-capitalist societies for each of the four main cultural types. But illustrations for all the types are also provided from industrial capitalist society, such that "individualism", for example, can be inscribed as a basic defining component of "middle class industrial culture", as well as that of highland New Guinea culture. And this is not without significance, for she claims that one of the merits of her approach lies in its ability to "cut across the class structure".

Douglas is quite clear about the futility of what she describes as class analysis.

> Ever since [the eighteenth century] Europe's self-knowledge has considered social change in terms that are based upon stratification, economic and political, and upon occupational categories. For the anthropologist's project, the stratified hierarchical perspective has not lent itself to saying anything very useful about the relation between culture and ideology on the one hand or between culture and forms of social organisation on the other. The present exercise in understanding cosmologies is intended to cut a different kind of slice into social reality. (1978: 54)

For Douglas, culture is represented as a structured field of authentic meanings on which individual experience, social interaction, and collective discourse are all in different ways parasitic. The total culture, which mediates between ideology and social organisation, is at once the collective precondition and the long-term residue of meaningful choice and experience. And because social facts are represented in terms of the shape and content of subjective experience, rationalism and empiricism become, in her text, complementary modes of accounting for the origin of those facts – a typical piece of reductionist reasoning. Furthermore, since the particular pattern of meaningful individual interaction, and the pattern of collective cosmologies, together define the ultimate formation of social conditions in their four contextual variants, the experiencing, transacting individual has really only one of two options: either to adjust to a given integrated context (like learning to use a language correctly) – or to leave it altogether for a more congenial social context (or language). And this is so because, in her own words, "Each position on the [typological] chart is

presented as an integral unit incorporating cosmology and social experience as a single close-
meshed structure" (1978: 41).

Thus for Douglas, the transformation of social
structure is impossible, or impossible to understand, because there is no social object that is
specified independently of a system of human
meanings, and because such a system, like a given
language, has the function of rendering the structure of cultural experience and of political action
isomorphic. As in *Natural symbols*, the cultural
and political pre-conditions for saying and doing
things, as well as the meaningful statements and
actions produced in those conditions, are neatly
fused together. Nothing can be said or done with
meaning if it does not fit into an *a priori* system,
the "authentic" culture which defines the essential
social being of the people concerned. The process
of radical transformation is described quite literally as "an emptying of meaning" – and quite
rightly so if the re-presentation of essential meanings is the mark of an authentic culture.

There is no space in Douglas's text for a concept of forms of social life which have their own
material conditions of existence, their own relations and tendencies – that is to say, conditions,
relations and tendencies which cannot be reduced
to the origins of human meaning, whether
collective cognitive categories or individual social
activity. The concept of mode of production, and
the related concept of class structure, are of course
precisely such concepts. These concepts are not
"slices of social reality". They are not the "true
objects" of human experience. And they are not
the ultimate origin or guarantee of everyday categories or of languages or of ideologies. Such concepts are for theorising the systematic historical
aspects of social forces and relations by which the
material bases of collective life are produced –
forces and relations whose existence is distinct
from that of individual meanings, intentions and
actions. I need not elaborate on this point here
except to note in passing that concepts of forces
and of relations must be historicised, otherwise
theorisation in terms of modes of production is
bound to become legalistic and/or idealistic.[10]
What I want to emphasise is that social life is not
simply a matter of systems of meaning (whether
conventional or intentional), even if it is true
that communication between human beings is
necessarily present in every domain of social

activity – that social life is not identical with
communication, although communication is
necessary to it. The logic of historical structures
based on the forces and relations of production is
quite different from the logic of specific human
intentions, of specific human languages, and of
specific forms of human understanding.[11]

Not only is the logic of ideological structures
different from the logic of modes of production,
but the former is also, in complex ways, dependent
on the latter.[12] Put more concretely: the "individualism" of highland New Guinea societies cannot
be assimilated, as Douglas tries to assimilate it, to
the bourgeois "individualism" of the middle
classes in advanced capitalist society. The parameters of the bourgeois ego are defined by an
authoritative discourse which is rooted in
material conditions profoundly different from
those that sustain the relevant discourses of highland New Guinea. For, to take a crucial aspect of
authoritative discourse: it is only in particular
kinds of social and material conditions that given
forms of performative utterance can be effective.[13] But for these utterances to be effective it is
necessary that they be understood and accepted
in appropriate kinds of situation by appropriate
kinds of person. That is to say, given forms of
effective performatives presuppose certain types
of ego, just as particular kinds of performative
can be effective only in the right material and
social conditions. The difference between the
New Guinea Big Man and the bourgeois ego is
therefore not merely one of degree.

What can be said, in short, about all these
anthropological tendencies which accord a critical priority to systems of human meaning is that
they leave unposed the question of how different
forms of discourse come to be materially produced and maintained as authoritative systems.
And, of course, once this question is seriously
addressed, the theoretical status of such a system
as *a priori*, and its latent function as the organising mode within anthropological discourse, are
also called into question.

VI

Perhaps this is the place to consider very briefly
some popular misunderstandings of Marx's famous
formulation about the relation of ideology to the

material conditions of existence. In this whole area too many different kinds of question are often confounded, by defenders and critics alike of that formulation in anthropology. Let me try, however sketchily, to sort some of them out.

Take first ideology as systematic forms of socially constituted knowledge.

The Marxian proposition that there are specific material conditions for the existence of specific ideologies in this sense does not necessarily imply that the ideologies are simply effects or reflections of those conditions. Thus if we say that the domains of systematic discourse within which specific knowledges are produced, tested and communicated, are *dependent* on specific institutional conditions and relations, this does not require any commitment to the view that the knowledges reflect those institutional conditions – that there is an isomorphic relation between the structure of knowledge and that of institutional conditions. If we say that given social conditions sustain, and at certain stages become obstacles to the development of scholarly understanding, this does not imply that the concept of objective knowledges is nothing but illusion. If we say that particular modes of systematic discourse can be and are used for furthering particular class interests, this does not imply that all such modes of discourse are essentially nothing but an "expression" of the positions that are supposed to define those interests. So much may be familiar enough and acceptable to many of you.

But where the notion of ideology relates to notions of politics and social function it becomes more problematical.

Discourse which seeks to reflect on the nature of social conditions in a systematic way can, in the process of being re-stated, contested, acted upon, have some critical consequences for given conditions of social life. But ideology as such cannot be said *a priori* to have a universal, determinate function, because what verbal discourses (as well as other modes of communication) signify or do can only be determined by analysing the concrete social conditions in which they are produced. It is no accident, for example, that attempts to specify a determinate set of rules for defining performatives in English – let alone in all languages – have not succeeded.[14] Because the developing material conditions of social life always determine the force, if not the occurrence,

of discursive events. And these conditions are not merely those of the face-to-face encounter in which utterances occur (as many speech event theories tend to assume[15]) but those of the political economic structure of society as a whole.

My point is not that we will only have a viable theory of ideology when we can develop a proper science of the symbolic, as some anthropologists have argued.[16] It is that there *cannot* be a general theory of ideology, a theory which will specify the universal pre-conditions, significances and effects of discourse. This is, of course, in itself not a novel argument.[17] But it must be said that it is one that stands opposed to the position not only of many anthropologists but also of many Marxists on this question – although not that of Marx himself.[18]

It is all very well to say, as many Marxists and anthropologists do, that given forms of social organisation (or given relations of production) always require given ideological (or cultural) systems to maintain and reproduce them. But such a statement appears extremely problematical for many reasons. In the first place such a formula is either tautological – as when ideology is said to define relations of property so that what has to be maintained is identical with what is supposed to do the maintaining; or it is reductionist – as when particular utterances are said to have a predetermined impact on the "interpreting minds" of those who uphold basic sets of social relationships, their sense being thereby equated with their effect. What we can deduce, incidentally, from these difficulties is that sometimes ideology is treated as social relation, and sometimes as systematic utterance, and that in both its guises it is sensed as being mediated and structured, in an obscure way, by authorising discourses.

When the question arises of specifying, in concrete cases, what the crucial ideological systems are, the anthropologist responds by postulating the presence of an authentic system of meanings as the key to the discourse noted in the field, and essentially reconstituted in the final text. It is this key that is used to identify particular utterances as mere repetitions of the same discourse, and to determine for them a mental effect as the crucial part of their meaning. In other words, in order to establish the determinate function of a given "meaningful" discourse, the anthropologist isolates what was said from its rhetorical context, and separates tendencies which might support given conditions from those which might contribute to their undermining – taking his theoretical separations for reproductions of the original. In this way, the anthropologist's text suppresses the tensions and ambiguities (conscious as well as unconscious) that obtain within a given field of discourse in specific historical conditions, and thus suppresses also the process by which motives, rhetorical devices and forms of comprehension are constructed and reconstructed. It is of course precisely these ambiguities of discourse, and the elaboration which they call for, that make political argument possible. Yet even when the anthropologist's text presents two or more "competing ideological systems" (official and unofficial, say), actual discourse is generally reduced to something else – something that has a determinate social role which can be definitively established in a neutral fashion by the analyst.

There is another (not unconnected) difficulty with the doctrine of the maintenance function of ideology. When ideology is presented as the culturally inherited lens of a given society by which external reality is filtered and internalised for its members, or as the system of symbols by which their direct experience is rendered uniquely communicable, a well-known paradox is created. For in doing so the anthropologist's text claims for itself the ability to represent that external reality directly, or to reproduce that inner experience through very different symbols which are nevertheless assumed to be appropriate – abilities which the exotic peoples studied necessarily lack. In such an anthropological exercise, historically specific discourses are typically reduced to the status of determinate parts of an integrated social mechanism, and an epistemological paradigm which purports to define the problem of objective knowledge is passed off as a sociological model for analysing ideology.

It may be suggested here that the possibility of such a reduction is located in the absence, in anthropology, of an adequate understanding of authoritative discourse – i.e. of materially founded discourse which seeks continually to preempt the space of radically opposed utterances and so to prevent them from being uttered.[19] For authoritative discourse, we should be careful to note, authorises neither "Reality"

nor "Experience" but other discourse – texts, speech, visual images, etc., which are being structured in terms of given (imposed) concepts, and reproduced in terms of essential meanings. Even when action is authorised, it is as discourse that such action establishes its authority. The action is read as being authorised, but the reading and the action are not identical – that is why it is always logically possible to have an alternative reading.

The problem of understanding ideology is therefore wrongly formulated when it is assumed to be a matter of predicting what "real" or "experiential" social forms are necessarily produced or reproduced by it. And this is so not because forms of utterance never have systematic consequences (performatives do, given that the relevant premisses are understood and accepted) but because the effectiveness of such utterances is dependent on conventions which are viable only within particular material conditions.

[...]

VIII

Let me try to state in a few words the general position which underlies much of what I have been trying to say (a dangerous thing to do, but even so, probably necessary). It is an old position, but one which bears re-stating given the present self-consciousness about ideology and about meaning. However much we might, as professional talkers and writers, wish to affirm the profound importance of systematic discourse, it is difficult to avoid the obvious, but by no means trivial, conclusion that political and economic conditions have developed and changed in ways that are rarely in accord with systematic discourse. Or let me put it another way: it is surely neither the power of social criticism nor the relative strength of competing social ideologies within the societies studied by social anthropologists (in Asia, in Africa and in Latin America) which explains why and how they have become basically transformed, but the historical forces of world industrial capitalism and the way these have impinged upon particular political and economic conditions. Of course political arguments can be important (and especially if they help to mobilise powerful social movements) but perhaps never in the way, nor to the extent, that we flatter ourselves they are important. Given that this is so, the main trouble with much colonial anthropology – and with much contemporary anthropology too – has been not its ideological service in the cause of imperialism, but its ideological conception of social structure and of culture.

Notes

1   Thus, "the two anthropological viewpoints which I have here summarised as 'empiricist' and 'rationalist' are to be regarded as complementary rather than right or wrong" (Leach 1976: 6).

2   See the interesting paper by G. Lakoff and M. Johnson "Toward an experientialist philosophy: the case from literal metaphor" (mimeographed), Linguistics Department, University of California, Berkeley, 1979.

3   "This seems at first sight a strange problem because it is difficult to see why some of the actors at a certain point in the social process cannot say: this system is no good at all, let us take a fresh look at the situation and build up a new system. The reason why they cannot, within the theoretical framework discussed, lies in the unanalysed notion of the social determination of thought. Simply, if all concepts and categories are determined by the social system a fresh look is impossible since all cognition is already moulded to fit what is to be criticised" (Bloch 1977: 281).

4   "It is in contexts where man is in most direct contact with nature that we find universal concepts, [and so] it is something in the world beyond society which constrains at least some of our cognitive categories" (Bloch 1977: 285).

5   Bourdillon is also surely right in criticising Bloch's views on "formal" language – views which are developed at length in his Introduction to *Political language and oratory in traditional society*. But he could have gone much further in his criticism. (See below, my note 19.)

6   "Roughly speaking, Leach believes that language, systems of propositions [sic], describe a reality in virtue of reflecting it in some fairly literal sense, in other words he believes in what might be called the parallelism theory of meaning. This is what we need know of his philosophy. As a matter of anthropology, he believes that ritual reflects the society in which it occurs in a similar way" (Gellner 1958: 189).

7   Gellner's assertion that Leach believes in a parallelist theory of meaning is clearly wrong for the following reasons. (1) In the first place Leach's own discourse claims to present a cultural *grammar*, not a system of propositions which reflects Reality "in some fairly literal sense". As we shall see later, this grammar is presented as authentic, in the sense that it is simply re-presented in his text. This cultural grammar is intended to help us understand the heterogeneous and changing social conditions of the Kachin Hills Area, in the way that a grammar book of a foreign language helps us understand the processes of speech and writing in that language. (2) As for Leach's analysis of the discourse of the Kachins themselves, he argues that their myths, for example, must be seen as "a language in which to maintain controversy" ([1954:] 85–97), and since in his view the truth or untruth of what is uttered in this language "is quite irrelevant" to an understanding of its meaning, it is difficult to see how such a conception of language can be said to be founded on a parallelist theory of meaning. (3) Furthermore, when Leach defines "ritual" as that aspect of almost any behaviour which "serves to express the individual's status as a social person in the structural system in which he finds himself for the time being" ([1954:] 10–11), he is asserting not that ritual "*reflects* society", but that its signifying function is *constitutive* of society. (4) Finally, there are places in the text where Leach seems at first sight to invoke parallelism in his elucidation of the meaning of ritual – as in his analysis of ceremonies of sacrifice (e.g. [1954:] 172–82). Leach's argument here is that such ceremonies have a mnemonic function by virtue of the fact that they represent to the participants what their ideal social structure should be. However, note that what is said to be the meaning here is not "society" or "social reality in some fairly literal sense" – but ideas in the minds of the participants. In other words, what Leach is proposing is *not* that the meaning of ritual is to be found in the way the Idea it embodies reflects Reality (which would be rather like the philosophical theory Gellner alludes to) but in the way the ceremonial evokes certain ideas in the minds of the participants – and that is not a parallelist theory of meaning at all, nor is it necessarily linked to an idealist philosophy.

8   Cf. Walter Benjamin's seminal essay "The work of art in the age of mechanical reproduction" in Benjamin (1970).

9   Marvin Harris (1969) was not mistaken in his reading when he praised that book for its materialist method – Gellner's judgements about its idealism notwithstanding.

10   An a-historical approach to the concept of mode of production has been characteristic of the work of French anthropologists like Godelier, and of English sociologists who follow them. Anthropologists and sociologists who have been strongly influenced by this work are often quite unaware of the strong resemblances between their work and old-fashioned British functional anthropology.

11   Semioticians in France, who have addressed themselves to the task of formulating a Marxist theory of ideology, have sometimes taken up what seems to be a contrary position. Thus Veron writes: "One must understand that semiotic activity is inevitably embodied in every form of social organisation – regardless of whether the order concerned is described as the 'economic', the 'political', the 'cultural', the 'ritual', etc., i.e. when it is treated independently of its signifying aspect. Without this semiotic activity, no form of social organisation is conceivable" (1978: 14). Veron is of course quite right to stress the serious difficulties which the Marxist model of economic base and ideological superstructure engenders for an adequate understanding of ideology, but it is not at all certain that his insistence on the ubiquity of semiotic activity constitutes a resolution of these difficulties – even though he goes on to warn the reader that "This is not to say that this semiotic activity running through society is capable of being described in its entirety in terms of a simple principle of internal coherence – quite the contrary". For in place of the distinction between the discursive and the non-discursive aspects of social life, which the notion of basis/superstructure was intended, however unsatisfactorily, to articulate, he proposes a heterogeneity of discursive principles (distinctive "grammars"), i.e. contradictory principles of discourse which in industrial capitalist societies are situated on the level of class conflict. There is always a danger in tendencies represented by this article (interesting and ingenious though it is) that in the end even Marxists will be left with nothing but "real discourse", and "real people" who produce that discourse, while historical political economies are bracketed on one side as being no more than "abstractions" or "theoretical concepts".

12   Voloshinov's *Marxism and the philosophy of language* [1973], first published fifty years ago, is still one of the most fruitful discussions of this problem, and although it leaves many difficult questions unanswered, it reveals a sensitivity to the complex social foundations of discourse which surpasses much of what is written on this subject today.

13   See Austin (1962), who first coined the term "performative" and then abandoned the concept. In his interesting recent study of Austin, Graham (1977) has forcefully argued that the concept of performative, properly defined, should be retained, and for the very reason that led to the latter's giving it up – namely, the impossibility of establishing, through it, a sharp separation between acting in the world and merely conceiving of it in a particular way.

14   I refer to the attempt that began with Searle "What is a speech act?" (1972). See Coulthard (1977), ch. 2, for some of the problems involved in identifying and classifying performatives (or illocutionary acts) in English. As for other languages, M. K. Foster writes (in Bauman and Sherzer [1974: 468]) that Philip Ravenhill who, more than anyone else, has explored the strengths and weaknesses of this notion for cross-cultural comparison, has "effectively argued against an uncritical application of performative analysis, based on English, to other languages (and cultures)." The work of Ravenhill which is cited by Foster is a mimeographed paper which I have, unfortunately, not been able to secure.

15   Such an assumption is perhaps evident in the following remarks by the editors of that valuable collection, *Explorations in the ethnography of speaking*: "…the ethnography of speaking fills the gap in the anthropological record created by the neglect by anthropological linguists of the social use of language and by the lack of interest of ethnographers in patterns and functions of speaking. The importance of the ethnography of speaking to anthropology cuts far deeper than this, however, for a careful focus on speaking as an instrument for the conduct of social life brings to the fore *the emergent nature of social structures, not rigidly determined by the institutional structure of the society, but rather largely created in performance by the strategic and goal-directed manipulation of resources for speaking*" (Bauman and Sherzer 1974: 8, my emphasis). This notion that it is the level of individual transaction and communication which generates the historical structure of societies is also proposed by Kapferer (1976: 15–16) – and it is one of the things against which I am arguing. In this context, it may be worth stressing that the distinction between the conditions of the political economy and those of discourse does not parallel but cuts across the anthropological distinction between jural and statistical norms.

16   For example Geertz (1973: 208–9).

17   Thus in his more recent work, Roland Barthes has abandoned his early attempts at establishing a

universal science of semiotics. Compare Barthes (1967) with Barthes (1974).

18 It is no accident that Marx did not put forward a general theory of ideology. Contrary to the assumption that he did not find the time to develop such a theory before he died, it can be argued that there is no place for it in his analysis of the capitalist mode of production, and in his commitment to the class struggle.

19 Authoritative discourse should not be confused with "formalised language", which M. Bloch has written about in his Introduction to *Political language and oratory in traditional society*. Bloch (1975: 12) sees formalised speech as "a kind of power" which is employed by traditional leaders to coerce followers ("the extreme formalisation of language with its accompanying exercise of power is characteristic of traditional authority situations as defined by Weber"), and contrasts it with everyday speech which, being flexible, allows for disagreement and opposition. It is not very clear whether Bloch's argument is logical or psychological, and in either case it seems untenable. Is it that certain crucial things cannot be said in "formalised speech acts" even if one wants to say them? In that case, what prevents the speaker from resorting to another style? Or is it perhaps that speakers are lulled into accepting things as they are when they employ "formalised language"? In that case, what gives the initiator an immunity which the respondent lacks? The difficulty with this kind of argument resides in the very vague notion of "formalised language" which might include anything from symbolic logic through legal disputation to authoritative discourse. Strictly speaking, authoritative discourse is not a kind of social power, of one will over another, but a discourse which binds every ego who recognises himself or herself in it – regardless of which is the initiator and which the respondent. (See Arendt [1958], for a provocative discussion of the concept of authority in classical Greek and Roman society.)

References

Arendt, H. 1958. What was authority? In *Authority* (Nomos I) (ed.) C.J. Friedrich. Cambridge, Mass.: Harvard University Press.

Austin, J. L. 1962. *How to do things with words*. Oxford: Clarendon Press.

Barthes, R. 1967. *Elements of semiology*. London: Jonathan Cape.

Barthes, R. 1974. *S/Z*. New York: Hill & Wang.

Bauman, R. and J. Sherzer (eds.) 1974. *Explorations in the ethnography of speaking*. New York: Cambridge University Press.

Benjamin, W. 1970. *Illuminations*. London: Jonathan Cape.

Bloch, M. 1975. *Political language and oratory in traditional society*. London: Academic Press.

Bloch, M. 1977. The past and the present in the present. *Man* (NS) 12, [278–92].

Bourdillon, M. F. C. 1978. Knowing the world or hiding it: a response to Maurice Bloch. *Man* (NS) 13, 591–9.

Coulthard, M. 1977. *An introduction to discourse analysis*. London: Longman.

Douglas, M. 1970. *Natural symbols*. London: Cresset Press.

Douglas, M. 1978. *Cultural bias* (Occ. Pap. R. Anthrop. Inst. 34). London: Royal Anthropological Institute.

Geertz, C. 1973. *The interpretation of cultures*. New York: Basic Books.

Gellner, E. 1958. Time and theory in social anthropology. *Mind* 67, 182–202.

Graham, K. 1977. *J. L. Austin: a critique of ordinary language philosophy*. Hassocks, Sussex: Harvester Press.

Harris, M. 1969. *The rise of anthropological theory*. London: Routledge & Kegan Paul.

Kapferer, B. (ed.) 1976. *Transaction and meaning*. Philadelphia: ISHI.

Leach, E. 1954. *Political systems of highland Burma* (LSE Monogr. social Anthrop. 44). London: Bell.

Leach, E. 1964. *Political systems of highland Burma* (reprint). London: Bell.

Leach, E. 1976. *Culture and communication*. Cambridge: University Press.

Sahlins, M. 1976. *Culture and practical reason*. Chicago: University Press.

Searle, J. 1972. What is a speech act? In *Language and social context* (ed.) P. P. Giglioli. Harmondsworth: Penguin.

Skorupski, J. 1976. *Symbol and theory*. Cambridge: University Press.

Sperber, D. 1975. *Rethinking symbolism*. Cambridge: University Press.

Veron, E. 1978. Sémiosis de l'idéologie et du pouvoir. *Communications* 28, 7–20.

Voloshinov, V. N. 1973. *Marxism and the philosophy of language*. New York: Seminar Press.

18

Subjectivity and Cultural Critique

Sherry B. Ortner

This is an article about the importance of the notion of subjectivity for a critical anthropology. Although there is no necessary link between questions of subjectivity and questions of power and subordination, [...] my particular interest will be in extending those lines of work that do see a close linkage between subjectivity and power. [...]

By subjectivity I will mean the ensemble of modes of perception, affect, thought, desire, fear, and so forth that animate acting subjects. But I always mean as well the cultural and social formations that shape, organize, and provoke those modes of affect, thought and so on. Indeed this article will move back and forth between the examination of such cultural formations and the inner states of acting subjects.

[...]

A Brief History of the Debate over the Subject

One could look at the unfolding of social and cultural theory over the whole 20th century as a struggle over the role of the social being – the person, subject, actor, or agent – in society and history. Although the origins of the struggle over the significance of the subject can be pushed back much further within philosophy, the 20th-century version appears as a debate largely between the newly evolving social sciences on the one hand, and certain lines of philosophic thinking on the other. [...]

[...]

The present landscape of social and cultural theory must be viewed against a backdrop of this history. There are in effect three lines of discussion. The first is so-called post-structuralism [...], which emphatically drops the Durkheimian positivism still present in Lévi-Strauss ("the objective analyses of scientific laws") and which focuses even more actively on "dissolving man". The terms of the critique take another slight turn here as the critique of the concept of "man" begins to emphasize not only its illusory qualities from a philosophical point of view (the self as an originary locus of coherence, intentionality, creativity and so on), but its ideological specificity. In the hands of feminist post-structuralists (e.g. Joan Scott, see Scott, 1988), the issue is its masked gendered nature: what pretends to be man in the universal sense is, literally, man in the gendered sense – men. In the hands of

From *Anthropological Theory* 5(1), 31–52 (with cuts). Copyright © 2005. Reprinted with permission of SAGE.

Anthropology in Theory: Issues in Epistemology, Second Edition. Edited by Henrietta L. Moore and Todd Sanders.
© 2014 John Wiley & Sons, Inc. Published 2014 by John Wiley & Sons, Inc.

post-colonial post-structuralists (e.g. Gayatri Spivak, see Spivak, 1988), the issue is the location of the idea of a supposedly universal man in what is actually a specifically western project of domination: (colonial) white men.

Looked at in these terms, one can understand the continuing appeal of post-structuralism in many academic quarters, including major areas of anthropology. Nonetheless its anti-humanism poses real problems for an anthropology that wishes to understand not just the workings of power, but the attempts of subalterns (in the Gramscian sense) to attain to the privilege of becoming subjects in the first place.

We must turn then to a second important line of post-Lévi-Straussian (but not "post-structuralist") thinking; one that does attempt to restore a subject in some form to the center of social theory, but at the same time seeks to re-theorize the subject in ways that do not reinstate the illusory universalism of "man". Here I would place the various versions of so-called practice theory, as seen in the work of Pierre Bourdieu (e.g. 1977, 1990, 2000), Anthony Giddens (esp. 1979), Marshall Sahlins (esp. 1981), William H. Sewell, Jr. (1992), and several works of my own (e.g. 1984, 1996, 1999). [. . .] For Bourdieu, the subject internalizes the structures of the external world, both culturally defined and objectively real. These internalized structures form a habitus, a system of dispositions that incline actors to act, think, and feel in ways consistent with the limits of the structure. [. . .] [T]he main emphasis of Bourdieu's arguments about habitus is on the ways in which it establishes a range of options and limits for the social actor. [. . .]

For Giddens and Sewell on the other hand, while subjects are understood to be fully culturally and structurally produced, there is also an emphasis on the importance of an element of "agency" in all social subjects. As against Bourdieu's insistence on the deeply internalized and largely unconscious nature of social knowledge in acting subjects, Giddens emphasizes that subjects are always at least partially "knowing", and thus able to act on and sometimes against the structures that made them. [. . .]

All of these thinkers who have in one way or another brought back the acting subject to social theory have significantly inspired my own thinking. [. . .] Having said this let me suggest

that there is a particular lack or area of thinness in all of their work [. . .]: a tendency to slight the question of subjectivity, that is, the view of the subject as existentially complex, a being who feels and thinks and reflects, who makes and seeks meaning.

Why does this matter? Why is it important to restore the question of subjectivity to social theory? [. . .] [I]t is [. . .] important politically [. . .]. In particular I see subjectivity as the basis of "agency", a necessary part of understanding how people (try to) act on the world even as they are acted upon. Agency is not some natural or originary will; it takes shape as specific desires and intentions within a matrix of subjectivity – of (culturally constituted) feelings, thoughts, and meanings.

Let me start with a preliminary definition. By subjectivity I will always mean a specifically cultural and historical consciousness. In using the word consciousness I do not mean to exclude various unconscious dynamics as seen, for example, in a Freudian unconscious or a Bourdieusian habitus. But I do mean that subjectivity is always more than those things, in two senses. At the individual level, I will assume, with Giddens, that actors are always at least partially "knowing subjects", that they have some degree of reflexivity about themselves and their desires, and that they have some "penetration" into the ways in which they are formed by their circumstances. [. . .] At the collective level I use the word consciousness as it is used by both Marx and Durkheim: as the collective sensibility of some set of socially interrelated actors. Consciousness in this sense is always ambiguously part of people's personal subjectivities and part of the public culture [. . .].

The question of complex subjectivities in the more psychological (which is not to say acultural) sense is most often to be seen in studies of dominated groups. Questions not only of "agency" (and "resistance") but of pain or fear or confusion, as well as various modes of overcoming these subjective states, have been central to this kind of work. [. . .]

In addition to this kind of investigation at the level of individual actors or groups of actors, there is also of course a tradition of research and interpretation at a broader cultural (and political) level, concerning the ways in which particular cultural formations shape and provoke subjectivities. At this point I want to shift to that level. I will begin by returning to some of the classic work by Clifford Geertz. Writing over the same period as Lévi-Strauss, Bourdieu, Sahlins, and others [...], Geertz was the only major social and cultural thinker to tackle the question of subjectivity in the sense discussed here, and we must give serious attention to his work.

Another Look at Geertz's Concept of Culture

In a few celebrated essays in the 1960s and 1970s, Geertz drew on philosophy and literary theory to articulate a specifically cultural approach to subjectivity and, one could also say, a specifically subjectivity-oriented theory of culture. The two are so closely interrelated that one cannot discuss one without the other. [...]

There are two identifiable dimensions to Geertz's theory of culture. On the one hand there is the classic American concept of culture, identified with Boas, Mead, Benedict and so on, and defined substantively as the world-view and ethos of a particular group of people. On the other hand there is a philosophical/literary theory of the cultural *process*, inspired particularly by Wittgenstein, which emphasizes the construction of meaning, and of subjectivities, through symbolic processes embedded in the social world. [...]

[C]ulture in the first, American sense, [...] the idea that particular groups "have" particular cultures, each its own, and that this culture is "shared" by all members of the group [...] [has been critiqued as] too undifferentiated, too homogeneous [...] [which] tied it closely to "essentialism", the idea that "the Nuer" or "the Balinese" had some single essence which made them the way they were, and which, moreover, explained much of what they did and how they did it. [...] Geertz of course never subscribed to this kind of thinking. [...]

[...] [B]ut the critique calls for a more articulated defense in terms of the politics involved in using the concept. Thus while recognizing the very real dangers of "culture" in its potential for essentializing and demonizing whole groups of people, one must recognize its critical political value as well, both for understanding the workings

of power, and for understanding the resources of the powerless.

Looked at on the side of power, one can recognize a cultural formation as a relatively coherent body of symbols and meanings, ethos and worldview, and at the same time understand those meanings as ideological, and/or as part of the forces and processes of domination. Perhaps the most important figure in recasting the culture concept in this direction has been Raymond Williams, with his [...] view of culture as hegemony, that is, as an interworking of the American culture concept and the Marxist concept of ideology (Williams, 1977: 108–9). [...]

Looked at from the side of the less powerful, culture in the American anthropological sense, but again with a more critical edge, lives on in studies of "popular culture". These are studies of the local worlds of subjects and groups who, however much they are dominated or marginalized, seek to make meaningful lives for themselves [...]. As in classic American anthropology, culture is here seen as being shared by a group, part of their collective form of life, embodying their shared history and identity, world view and ethos. [...]

In sum, "culture", even in something like the old American sense, is not *inherently* a conservative or dangerous concept; there is a kind of category mistake in seeing it as such. It is a flexible and powerful concept that can be used in many different ways including, most importantly, as part of a political critique.

The American-style culture concept was, however, only one dimension of Geertz's theory. The other was a set of ideas about how cultural processes work and what they do. Geertz argued that culture should be understood as public symbolic forms, forms that both express and shape *meaning for actors* engaged in the ongoing flow of social life. [...] Which brings us back to subjectivity and consciousness.

The Cultural Construction of Subjectivity

In two of his most famous articles, "Person, Time, and Conduct in Bali" (1973b [1966]), and "Deep Play: Notes on the Balinese Cockfight" (1973c [1972]), Geertz provides powerful displays of his method at work, interpreting Balinese cultural forms – person terms, calendrical systems, rules of etiquette, cockfighting events – for the modes of consciousness they embody.

[...]

Geertz makes clear that he traces his ways of thinking about subjectivity back to Max Weber. [For Weber (1958), the] culturally/religiously produced subject is defined not only by a particular position in a social, economic, and religious matrix, but by a complex subjectivity, a complex set of feelings and fears, which are central to the whole argument.

As for Weber, so for Geertz: Cultures are public systems of symbols and meanings, texts and practices, that both represent a world and shape subjects in ways that fit the world as represented. [...]

[...] "Person, Time, and Conduct in Bali" (1973b [1966]), is a reading of multiple Balinese symbolic orders – one could perhaps call them discourses – to try to get at the kind of subjectivity they both reflect and shape. These include Balinese "orders of person-definition" (personal names, birth-order names, kinship terms, status titles, and so on); Balinese discourses of time; and Balinese rules and patterns of social etiquette. Geertz does a detailed interpretation of all these forms [...] with an eye to understanding the kind of consciousness they converge to produce.

[...]

At one level all of this both enacts and induces a certain cultural style, what Geertz calls "playful theatricality" (1973b: 402). But Geertz pushes further into the underlying shape of subjectivity involved, by examining the Balinese emotional category/state of *lek*, which he translates as "stage-fright...a diffuse, usually mild, though in certain situations virtually paralyzing, nervousness before the prospect (and the fact) of social interaction, a chronic, mostly low-grade worry that one will not be able to bring it off with the required finesse" (1973b: 402). [...]

What is interesting about the structure of feeling articulated here is its reflexive complexity. Cultural forms – discourses, practices – produce a certain kind of cultural mind-set [...] and at the same time a set of anxieties about the ability to carry it off. The subjectivity in question has a certain cultural shape, but also a way of inhabiting that shape which is reflexive and anxious concerning the possibilities of one's own failures.

[...] [In] "Deep Play: Notes on the Balinese Cockfight" (1973c [1972]). [Geertz] performs a virtuosic interpretation of the cockfight as a public text. He spends a long time on the social organization of participation and betting, arguing that the cockfight [...] is "fundamentally a dramatization of status concerns" (1973c: 437). But then he asks, what does it mean for Balinese actors that the public dramatization of status rivalry takes the form of "a chicken hacking another mindlessly to bits?" (1973c: 449). His argument follows his model of/model for distinction without explicitly invoking it. On the one hand – the model-of – the cockfight is read as a text, a set of representations and orderings of cultural themes that endow them with particular meanings [...]. At the same time it is more than a text, or rather, texts do more than simply articulate and display meanings. Thus, and this is the model-for aspect, "[a]ttending cockfights and participating in them is, for the Balinese, a kind of sentimental education" (1973c: 449). It is in this context that Geertz presents his most explicit theorization of the formation of subjectivity. He first talks about the ways in which participating in cockfights "opens [a man's] subjectivity to himself" (1973c: 451). But then he moves to the stronger, constructionist position:

> Yet, because...that subjectivity does not properly exist until it is thus organized, art forms generate and regenerate the very subjectivity they pretend only to display. Quartets, still lifes, and cockfights are not merely reflections of a pre-existing sensibility analogically represented; they are positive agents in the creation and maintenance of such a sensibility. (1973c: 451)

At the heart of this sensibility is once again a set of anxieties [...].

[...] Geertz gives [a large] role to anxiety in his theoretical framework [...]; it is one of the central axes not only of particular cultural subjectivities, but of the human condition as a whole, that is, the condition of being a cultural creature. [...]

[...]

These anxieties of interpretation and orientation are seen as part of the generic human condition, grounded in the human dependency on symbolic orders to function within the world. Geertz had argued in an earlier article (1973a) that symbolic systems are not additive to human existence, but constitutive of it. Because human beings are relatively open creatures, vastly unprogrammed compared to most other animals, they literally depend on external symbolic systems – including especially language, but more generally "culture" – to survive.

[...]

Some Very Brief Conclusions

[...] I have argued for the importance of a robust anthropology of subjectivity, both as states of mind of real actors embedded in the social world, and as cultural formations that (at least partially) express, shape, and constitute those states of mind. Clifford Geertz, carrying forward the tremendously important work of Max Weber, has been central here because of what I called earlier his subjectivity-oriented theory of culture. Moving beyond Geertz, however, I have been particularly interested in understanding subjectivity in its relations to (changing) forms of power, and especially [...] the subtle forms of power that saturate everyday life, through experiences of time, space, and work. In short I have been concerned to explore the ways in which such an anthropology of subjectivity can be the basis of cultural critique, allowing us to ask sharp questions about the cultural shaping of subjectivities within a world of wildly unequal power relations, and about the complexities of personal subjectivities within such a world.

References

Bourdieu, Pierre (1977) *Outline of a Theory of Practice* (trans. R. Nice). Cambridge: Cambridge University Press.

Bourdieu, Pierre (1990) *The Logic of Practice* (trans. R. Nice). Stanford, CA: Stanford University Press.

Bourdieu, Pierre (2000) *Pascalian Meditations* (trans. R. Nice). Stanford, CA: Stanford University Press.

Geertz, Clifford (1973a [1962]) "The Growth of Culture and the Evolution of Mind", in Clifford Geertz *The Interpretation of Cultures*, pp. 55–83. New York: Basic Books.

Geertz, Clifford (1973b [1966]) "Person, Time, and Conduct in Bali", in Clifford Geertz *The Interpretation of Cultures*, pp. 360–411. New York: Basic Books.

Geertz, Clifford (1973c [1972]) "Deep Play: Notes on the Balinese Cockfight", in Clifford Geertz *The Interpretation of Cultures*, pp. 412–53. New York: Basic Books.

Giddens, Anthony (1979) *Central Problems in Social Theory: Action, Structure and Contradiction in Social Analysis*. Berkeley: University of California Press.

Ortner, Sherry B. (1984) "Theory in Anthropology Since the Sixties", *Comparative Studies in Society and History* 26(1): 126–66.

Ortner, Sherry B. (1996) "Making Gender: Toward a Feminist, Minority, Postcolonial, Subaltern, etc., Theory of Practice", in Sherry B. Ortner *Making Gender: The Politics and Erotics of Culture*, pp. 1–20. Boston, MA: Beacon Press.

Ortner, Sherry B. (1999) *Life and Death on Mt. Everest: Sherpas and Himalayan Mountaineering*. Princeton, NJ: Princeton University Press.

Sahlins, Marshall (1981) *Historical Metaphors and Mythical Realities: Structure in the History of the Sandwich Islands Kingdoms*. Ann Arbor: University of Michigan Press.

Scott, Joan (1988) *Gender and the Politics of History*. New York: Columbia University Press.

Sewell, William H., Jr (1992) "A Theory of Structure: Duality, Agency, and Transformation", *American Journal of Sociology* 98(1): 1–29.

Spivak, Gayatri Chakravorty (1988) "Can the Subaltern Speak?", in C. Nelson and L. Grossberg (eds) *Marxism and the Interpretation of Culture*, pp. 271–313. Urbana and Chicago: University of Illinois Press.

Weber, Max (1958) *The Protestant Ethic and the Spirit of Capitalism* (trans. T. Parsons). New York: Scribners.

Williams, Raymond (1977) *Marxism and Literature*. Oxford: Oxford University Press.

SECTION 6

Language and Method

19

Structural Analysis in Linguistics and in Anthropology

Claude Lévi-Strauss

Linguistics occupies a special place among the social sciences, to whose ranks it unquestionably belongs. It is not merely a social science like the others, but, rather, the one in which by far the greatest progress has been made. It is probably the only one which can truly claim to be a science and which has achieved both the formulation of an empirical method and an understanding of the nature of the data submitted to its analysis. This privileged position carries with it several obligations. The linguist will often find scientists from related but different disciplines drawing inspiration from his example and trying to follow his lead. *Noblesse oblige.* A linguistic journal like *Word* cannot confine itself to the illustration of strictly linguistic theories and points of view. It must also welcome psychologists, sociologists, and anthropologists eager to learn from modern linguistics the road which leads to the empirical knowledge of social phenomena. As Marcel Mauss wrote already forty years ago: "Sociology would certainly have progressed much further if it had everywhere followed the lead of the linguists...."[1] The close methodological analogy which exists between the two disciplines imposes a special obligation of collaboration upon them.

Ever since the work of Schrader[2] it has been unnecessary to demonstrate the assistance which linguistics can render to the anthropologist in the study of kinship. It was a linguist and a philologist (Schrader and Rose)[3] who showed the improbability of the hypothesis of matrilineal survivals in the family in antiquity, to which so many anthropologists still clung at that time. The linguist provides the anthropologist with etymologies which permit him to establish between certain kinship terms relationships that were not immediately apparent. The anthropologist, on the other hand, can bring to the attention of the linguist customs, prescriptions, and prohibitions that help him to understand the persistence of certain features of language or the instability of terms or groups of terms. At a meeting of the Linguistic Circle of New York, Julien Bonfante once illustrated this point of view by reviewing the etymology of the word for uncle in several Romance languages. The Greek Θεῖος corresponds in Italian, Spanish, and Portuguese to *zio* and *tio*; and he added that in certain regions of Italy the uncle is called *barba*.

Anthropology in Theory: Issues in Epistemology, Second Edition. Edited by Henrietta L. Moore and Todd Sanders.
© 2014 John Wiley & Sons, Inc. Published 2014 by John Wiley & Sons, Inc.

The "beard," the "divine" uncle – what a wealth of suggestions for the anthropologist! The investigations of the late A. M. Hocart into the religious character of the avuncular relationship and the "theft of the sacrifice" by the maternal kinsmen immediately come to mind.[4] Whatever interpretation is given to the data collected by Hocart (and his own interpretation is not entirely satisfactory), there is no doubt that the linguist contributes to the solution of the problem by revealing the tenacious survival in contemporary vocabulary of relationships which have long since disappeared. At the same time, the anthropologist explains to the linguist the bases of etymology and confirms its validity. Paul K. Benedict, in examining, as a linguist, the kinship systems of Southeast Asia, was able to make an important contribution to the anthropology of the family in that area.[5]

But linguists and anthropologists follow their own paths independently. They halt, no doubt, from time to time to communicate to one another certain of their findings; these findings, however, derive from different operations, and no effort is made to enable one group to benefit from the technical and methodological advances of the other. This attitude might have been justified in the era when linguistic research leaned most heavily on historical analysis. In relation to the anthropological research conducted during the same period, the difference was one of degree rather than of kind. The linguists employed a more rigorous method, and their findings were established on more solid grounds; the sociologists could follow their example in "renouncing consideration of the spatial distribution of contemporary types as a basis for their classifications."[6] But, after all, anthropology and sociology were looking to linguistics only for insights; nothing foretold a revelation.[7]

The advent of structural linguistics completely changed this situation. Not only did it renew linguistic perspectives; a transformation of this magnitude is not limited to a single discipline. Structural linguistics will certainly play the same renovating role with respect to the social sciences that nuclear physics, for example, has played for the physical sciences. In what does this revolution consist, as we try to assess its broadest implications? N. Troubetzkoy, the illustrious founder of structural linguistics, himself furnished the answer to this question. In one programmatic statement,[8] he reduced the structural method to four basic operations. First, structural linguistics shifts from the study of *conscious* linguistic phenomena to study of their *unconscious* infrastructure; second, it does not treat *terms* as independent entities, taking instead as its basis of analysis the *relations* between terms; third, it introduces the concept of *system* – "Modern phonemics does not merely proclaim that phonemes are always part of a system; it *shows* concrete phonemic systems and elucidates their structure"[9] –; finally, structural linguistics aims at discovering *general laws*, either by induction "or...by logical deduction, which would give them an absolute character."[10]

Thus, for the first time, a social science is able to formulate necessary relationships. This is the meaning of Troubetzkoy's last point, while the preceding rules show how linguistics must proceed in order to attain this end. It is not for us to show that Troubetzkoy's claims are justified. The vast majority of modern linguists seem sufficiently agreed on this point. But when an event of this importance takes place in one of the sciences of man, it is not only permissible for, but required of, representatives of related disciplines immediately to examine its consequences and its possible application to phenomena of another order.

New perspectives then open up. We are no longer dealing with an occasional collaboration where the linguist and the anthropologist, each working by himself, occasionally communicate those findings which each thinks may interest the other. In the study of kinship problems (and, no doubt, the study of other problems as well), the anthropologist finds himself in a situation which formally resembles that of the structural linguist. Like phonemes, kinship terms are elements of meaning; like phonemes, they acquire meaning only if they are integrated into systems. "Kinship systems," like "phonemic systems," are built by the mind on the level of unconscious thought. Finally, the recurrence of kinship patterns, marriage rules, similar prescribed attitudes between certain types of relatives, and so forth, in scattered regions of the globe and in fundamentally different societies, leads us to believe that, in the case of kinship as well as linguistics, the observable phenomena result from the action of laws which are general but implicit. The problem can therefore be formulated as follows: Although they belong to *another order of reality*, kinship phenomena are *of the same type* as linguistic phenomena. Can the anthropologist, using a method analogous *in form* (if not in content) to the method used in structural linguistics, achieve the same kind of progress in his own science as that which has taken place in linguistics?

We shall be even more strongly inclined to follow this path after an additional observation has been made. The study of kinship problems is today broached in the same terms and seems to be in the throes of the same difficulties as was linguistics on the eve of the structuralist revolution. There is a striking analogy between certain attempts by Rivers and the old linguistics, which sought its explanatory principles first of all in history. In both cases, it is solely (or almost solely) diachronic analysis which must account for synchronic phenomena. Troubetzkoy, comparing structural linguistics and the old linguistics, defines structural linguistics as a "systematic structuralism and universalism," which he contrasts with the individualism and "atomism" of former schools. And when he considers diachronic analysis, his perspective is a profoundly modified one: "The evolution of a phonemic system at any given moment is directed by the *tendency toward a goal....* This evolution thus has a direction, an internal logic, which historical phonemics is called upon to elucidate."[11] The "individualistic" and "atomistic" interpretation, founded exclusively on historical contingency, which is criticized by Troubetzkoy and Jakobson, is actually the same as that which is generally applied to kinship problems.[12] Each detail of terminology and each special marriage rule is associated with a specific custom as either its consequence or its survival. We thus meet with a chaos of discontinuity. No one asks how kinship systems, regarded as synchronic wholes, could be the arbitrary product of a convergence of several heterogeneous institutions (most of which are hypothetical), yet nevertheless function with some sort of regularity and effectiveness.[13]

However, a preliminary difficulty impedes the transposition of the phonemic method to the anthropological study of primitive peoples. The superficial analogy between phonemic systems and kinship systems is so strong that it immediately sets us on the wrong track. It is incorrect to equate kinship terms and linguistic phonemes from the viewpoint of their formal treatment. We

know that to obtain a structural law the linguist analyzes phonemes into "distinctive features," which he can group into one or several "pairs of oppositions."[14] Following an analogous method, the anthropologist might be tempted to break down analytically the kinship terms of any given system into their components. In our own kinship system, for instance, the term *father* has positive connotations with respect to sex, relative age, and generation; but it has a zero value on the dimension of collaterality, and it cannot express an affinal relationship. Thus, for each system, one might ask what relationships are expressed and, for each term of the system, what connotation – positive or negative – it carries regarding each of the following relationships: generation, collaterality, sex, relative age, affinity, etc. It is at this "microsociological" level that one might hope to discover the most general structural laws, just as the linguist discovers his at the infra-phonemic level or the physicist at the infra-molecular or atomic level. One might interpret the interesting attempt of Davis and Warner in these terms.[15]

But a threefold objection immediately arises. A truly scientific analysis must be real, simplifying, and explanatory. Thus the distinctive features which are the product of phonemic analysis have an objective existence from three points of view: psychological, physiological, and even physical; they are fewer in number than the phonemes which result from their combination; and, finally, they allow us to understand and reconstruct the system. Nothing of the kind would emerge from the preceding hypothesis. The treatment of kinship terms which we have just sketched is analytical in appearance only; for, actually, the result is more abstract than the principle; instead of moving toward the concrete, one moves away from it, and the definitive system – if system there is – is only conceptual. Secondly, Davis and Warner's experiment proves that the system achieved through this procedure is infinitely more complex and more difficult to interpret than the empirical data.[16] Finally, the hypothesis has no explanatory value; that is, it does not lead to an understanding of the nature of the system and still less to a reconstruction of its origins.

What is the reason for this failure? A too literal adherence to linguistic method actually betrays its very essence. Kinship terms not only have a sociological existence; they are also elements of speech. In our haste to apply the methods of linguistic analysis, we must not forget that, as a part of vocabulary, kinship terms must be treated with linguistic methods in direct and not analogous fashion. Linguistics teaches us precisely that structural analysis cannot be applied to words directly, but only to words previously broken down into phonemes. *There are no necessary relationships at the vocabulary level.* This applies to all vocabulary elements, including kinship terms. Since this applies to linguistics, it ought to apply *ipso facto* to the sociology of language. An attempt like the one whose possibility we are now discussing would thus consist in extending the method of structural linguistics while ignoring its basic requirements. Kroeber prophetically foresaw this difficulty in an article written many years ago.[17] And if, at that time, he concluded that a structural analysis of kinship terminology was impossible, we must remember that linguistics itself was then restricted to phonetic, psychological, and historical analysis. While it is true that the social sciences must share the limitations of linguistics, they can also benefit from its progress.

Nor should we overlook the profound differences between the phonemic chart of a language and the chart of kinship terms of a society. In the first instance there can be no question as to function; we all know that language serves as a means of communication. On the other hand, what the linguist did not know and what structural linguistics alone has allowed him to discover is the way in which language achieves this end. The function was obvious; the system remained unknown. In this respect, the anthropologist finds himself in the opposite situation. We know, since the work of Lewis H. Morgan, that kinship terms constitute systems; on the other hand, we still do not know their function. The misinterpretation of this initial situation reduces most structural analyses of kinship systems to pure tautologies. They demonstrate the obvious and neglect the unknown.

This does not mean that we must abandon hope of introducing order and discovering meaning in kinship nomenclature. But we should at least recognize the special problems raised by the sociology of vocabulary and the ambiguous character of the relations between its methods and those of linguistics. For this reason it would be preferable to limit the discussion to a case where the analogy can be clearly established. Fortunately, we have just such a case available.

What is generally called a "kinship system" comprises two quite different orders of reality. First, there are terms through which various kinds of family relationships are expressed. But kinship is not expressed solely through nomenclature. The individuals or classes of individuals who employ these terms feel (or do not feel, as the case may be) bound by prescribed behavior in their relations with one another, such as respect or familiarity, rights or obligations, and affection or hostility. Thus, along with what we propose to call the *system of terminology* (which, strictly speaking, constitutes the vocabulary system), there is another system, both psychological and social in nature, which we shall call the *system of attitudes*. Although it is true (as we have shown above) that the study of systems of terminology places us in a situation analogous, but opposite, to the situation in which we are dealing with phonemic systems, this difficulty is "inversed," as it were, when we examine systems of attitudes. We can guess at the role played by systems of attitudes, that is, to insure group cohesion and equilibrium, but we do not understand the nature of the interconnections between the various attitudes, nor do we perceive their necessity.[18] In other words, as in the case of language, we know their function, but the system is unknown.

Thus we find a profound difference between the *system of terminology* and the *system of attitudes*, and we have to disagree with A. R. Radcliffe-Brown if he really believed, as has been said of him, that attitudes are nothing but the expression or transposition of terms on the affective level.[19] The last few years have provided numerous examples of groups whose chart of kinship terms does not accurately reflect family attitudes, and vice versa.[20] It would be incorrect to assume that the kinship system constitutes the principal means of regulating interpersonal relationships in all societies. Even in societies where the kinship system does function as such, it does not fulfill that role everywhere to the same extent. Furthermore, it is always necessary to distinguish between two types of attitudes: first, the diffuse, uncrystallized, and non-institutionalized attitudes, which we may consider as the reflection or transposition of the terminology on the psychological level; and second, along with, or in addition to, the preceding ones, those attitudes which are stylized, prescribed, and sanctioned by taboos or privileges and expressed through a fixed ritual. These attitudes, far from automatically reflecting the nomenclature, often appear as secondary elaborations, which serve to resolve the contradictions and overcome the deficiencies inherent in the terminological system. This synthetic character is strikingly apparent among the Wik Munkan of Australia. In this group, joking privileges sanction a contradiction between the kinship relations which link two unmarried men and the theoretical relationship which must be assumed to exist between them in order to account for their later marriages to two women who do not stand themselves in the corresponding relationship.[21] There is a contradiction between two possible systems of nomenclature, and the emphasis placed on attitudes represents an attempt to integrate or transcend this contradiction. We can easily agree with Radcliffe-Brown and assert the existence of "real relations of interdependence between the terminology and the rest of the system."[22] Some of his critics made the mistake of inferring, from the absence of a rigorous parallelism between attitudes and nomenclature, that the two systems were mutually independent. But this relationship of interdependence does not imply a one-to-one correlation. The system of attitudes constitutes, rather, a dynamic integration of the system of terminology.

Granted the hypothesis (to which we wholeheartedly subscribe) of a functional relationship between the two systems, we are nevertheless entitled, for methodological reasons, to treat independently the problems pertaining to each system. This is what we propose to do here for a problem which is rightly considered the point of departure for any theory of attitudes – that of the maternal uncle. We shall attempt to show how a formal transposition of the method of structural linguistics allows us to shed new light upon this problem. Because the relationship between nephew and maternal uncle appears to have been the focus of significant elaboration in a great many primitive societies, anthropologists have devoted special attention to it. It is not enough to note the frequency of this theme; we must also account for it.

Let us briefly review the principal stages in the development of this problem. During the entire nineteenth century and until the writings of Sydney Hartland,[23] the importance of the mother's brother was interpreted as a survival of matrilineal descent. This interpretation was based purely on speculation, and, indeed, it was highly improbable in the light of European examples. Furthermore, Rivers' attempt[24] to explain the importance of the mother's brother in southern India as a residue of cross-cousin marriage led to particularly deplorable results. Rivers himself was forced to recognize that this interpretation could not account for all aspects of the problem. He resigned himself to the hypothesis that *several* heterogeneous customs which have since disappeared (cross-cousin marriage being only one of them) were needed to explain the existence of a *single* institution.[25] Thus, atomism and mechanism triumphed. It was Lowie's crucial article on the matrilineal complex[26] which opened what we should like to call the "modern phase" of the problem of the avunculate. Lowie showed that the correlation drawn or postulated between the prominent position of the maternal uncle and matrilineal descent cannot withstand rigorous analysis. In fact, the avunculate is found associated with patrilineal, as well as matrilineal, descent. The role of the maternal uncle cannot be explained as either a consequence or a survival of matrilineal kinship; it is only a specific application "of a very general tendency to associate definite social relations with definite forms of kinship regardless of maternal or paternal side." In accordance with this principle, introduced for the first time by Lowie in 1919, there exists a general tendency to *qualify attitudes*, which constitutes the only empirical foundation for a theory of kinship systems. But, at the same time, Lowie left certain questions unanswered. What exactly do we call an avunculate? Do we not merge different customs and attitudes under this single term? And, if it is true that there is a tendency to qualify all attitudes, why are only certain attitudes associated with the avuncular relationship, rather than just any possible attitudes, depending upon the group considered?

A few further remarks here may underline the striking analogy between the development of this problem and certain stages in the evolution of linguistic theory. The variety of possible attitudes in the area of interpersonal relationships is almost unlimited; the same holds true for the variety of sounds which can be articulated by the vocal apparatus – and which are actually produced during the first months of human life. Each language, however, retains only a very small number among all the possible sounds, and in this respect linguistics raises two questions: Why are certain sounds selected? What relationships exist between one or several of the sounds chosen and all the others?[27] Our sketch of the historical development of the avuncular problem is at precisely the same stage. Like language, the social group has a great wealth of psychophysiological material at its disposal. Like language too, it retains only certain elements, at least some of which remain the same throughout the most varied cultures and are combined into structures which are always diversified. Thus we may wonder about the reason for this choice and the laws of combination.

For insight into the specific problem of the avunculate we should turn to Radcliffe-Brown. His well-known article on the maternal uncle in South Africa[28] was the first attempt to grasp and analyze the modalities of what we might call the "general principle of attitude qualification." We shall briefly review the fundamental ideas of that now-classic study.

According to Radcliffe-Brown, the term *avunculate* covers two antithetical systems of attitudes. In one case, the maternal uncle represents family authority; he is feared and obeyed, and possesses certain rights over his nephew. In the other case, the nephew holds privileges of familiarity in relation to his uncle and can treat him more or less as his victim. Second, there is a correlation between the boy's attitude toward his maternal uncle and his attitude toward his father. We find the two systems of attitudes in both cases, but they are inversely correlated. In groups where familiarity characterizes the relationship between father and son, the relationship between maternal uncle and nephew is one of respect; and where the father stands as the austere representative of family authority, it is the uncle who is treated with familiarity. Thus the two sets of attitudes constitute (as the structural linguist would say) two pairs of oppositions. Radcliffe-Brown concluded his article by proposing the following interpretation: In the final analysis, it is descent that determines the choice of oppositions. In patrilineal societies, where the father and the father's descent group represent traditional authority, the maternal uncle is considered a "male mother." He is generally treated in the same fashion, and sometimes even called by the same name, as the mother. In matrilineal societies, the opposite occurs. Here, authority is vested in the maternal uncle, while relationships of tenderness and familiarity revolve about the father and his descent group.

It would indeed be difficult to exaggerate the importance of Radcliffe-Brown's contribution, which was the first attempt at synthesis on an empirical basis following Lowie's authoritative and merciless criticism of evolutionist metaphysics. To say that this effort did not entirely succeed does not in any way diminish the homage due this great British anthropologist; but we should certainly recognize that Radcliffe-Brown's article leaves unanswered some fundamental questions. First, the avunculate does not occur in all matrilineal or all patrilineal systems, and we find it present in some systems which are neither matrilineal nor patrilineal.[29] Further, the avuncular relationship is not limited to two terms, but presupposes four, namely, brother, sister, brother-in-law, and nephew. An interpretation such as Radcliffe-Brown's arbitrarily isolates particular elements of a global structure which must be treated as a whole. A few simple examples will illustrate this twofold difficulty.

The social organization of the Trobriand Islanders of Melanesia is characterized by matrilineal descent, free and familiar relations between father and son, and a marked antagonism between maternal uncle and nephew.[30] On the other hand, the patrilineal Cherkess of the Caucasus place the hostility between father and son, while the maternal uncle assists his nephew and gives him a horse when he marries.[31] Up to this point we are still within the limits of Radcliffe-Brown's scheme. But let us consider the other family relationships involved. Malinowski showed that in the Trobriands husband and wife live in an atmosphere of tender intimacy and that their relationship is characterized by reciprocity. The relations between brother and sister, on the other hand, are dominated by an extremely rigid taboo. Let us now compare the situation in the Caucasus. There, it is the brother–sister relationship which is tender – to such an extent that among the Pschav an only daughter "adopts" a "brother" who will play the customary brother's role as her chaste bed companion.[32] But the relationship between spouses is entirely different. A Cherkess will not appear in public with his wife and visits her only in secret. According to Malinowski, there is no greater insult in the Trobriands than to tell a man that he resembles his sister. In the Caucasus there is an analogous prohibition: It is forbidden to ask a man about his wife's health.

When we consider societies of the Cherkess and Trobriand types it is not enough to study the correlation of attitudes between *father/son* and *uncle/sister's son*. This correlation is only one aspect of a global system containing four types of relationships which are organically linked, namely: *brother/sister, husband/wife, father/son,* and *mother's brother/sister's son*. The two groups in our example illustrate a law which can be formulated as follows: In both groups, the relation between maternal uncle and nephew is to the relation between brother and sister as the relation between father and son is to that between husband and wife. Thus if we know one pair of relations, it is always possible to infer the other.

Let us now examine some other cases. On Tonga, in Polynesia, descent is patrilineal, as among the Cherkess. Relations between husband and wife appear to be public and harmonious. Domestic quarrels are rare, and although the wife is often of superior rank the husband "is nevertheless of higher authority in all domestic matters, and no woman entertains the least idea of rebelling against that authority."[33] At the same time there is great freedom between nephew and maternal uncle. The nephew is *fahu*, or above the law, in relation to his uncle, toward whom extreme familiarity is permitted. This freedom strongly contrasts with the father-son relationship. The father is *tapu*; the son cannot touch his father's head or hair; he cannot touch him while he eats, sleep in his bed or on his pillow, share his food or drink, or play with his possessions. However, the strongest *tapu* of all is the one between brother and sister, who must never be together under the same roof.

Although they are also patrilineal and patrilocal, the natives of Lake Kutubu in New Guinea offer an example of the opposite type of structure. F. E. Williams writes: "I have never seen such a close and apparently affectionate association between father and son...."[34] Relations between husband and wife are characterized by the very low status ascribed to women and "the marked separation of masculine and feminine interests...."[35] The women, according to Williams, "are expected to work hard for their masters...they occasionally protest, and protest may be met with a beating."[36] The wife can always call upon her brother for protection against her husband, and it is with him that she seeks refuge. As for the relationship between nephew and maternal uncle, it is "best summed up in the word 'respect'...tinged with apprehensiveness,"[37] for the maternal uncle has the power to curse his nephew and inflict serious illness upon him (just as among the Kipsigi of Africa).

Although patrilineal, the society described by Williams is structurally of the same type as that of the Siuai of Bougainville, who have matrilineal descent. Between brother and sister there is "friendly interaction and mutual generosity...."[38] As regards the father–son relationship, Oliver writes, "I could discover little evidence that the word 'father' evokes images of hostility or stern authority or awed respect."[39] But the relationship between the nephew and his mother's brother "appears to range between stern discipline and genial mutual dependence...." However, "most of the informants agreed that all boys stand in some awe of their mother's brothers, and are more likely to obey them than their own fathers...."[40] Between husband and wife harmonious understanding is rare: "...there are few young wives who remain altogether faithful...most young husbands are continually suspicious and often give vent to jealous anger...marriages involve a number of adjustments, some of them apparently difficult...."[41]

The same picture, but sharper still, characterizes the Dobuans, who are matrilineal and neighbors of the equally matrilineal Trobrianders, while their structure is very different. Dobuan marriages are unstable, adultery is widespread, and husband and wife constantly fear death induced by their spouse's witchcraft. Actually, Fortune's remark, "It is a most serious insult to refer to a woman's witchcraft so that her husband will hear of it"[42] appears to be a variant of the Trobriand and Caucasian taboos cited above.

In Dobu, the mother's brother is held to be the harshest of all the relatives. "The mother's brother may beat children long after their parents have ceased to do so," and they are forbidden to utter his name. There is a tender relationship with the "navel," the mother's sister's husband, who is the father's double, rather than with the father himself. Nevertheless, the father is considered "less harsh" than the mother's brother and will always seek, contrary to the laws of inheritance, to favor his son at the expense of his uterine nephew. And, finally, "the strongest of all social bonds" is the one between brother and sister.[43]

What can we conclude from these examples? The correlation between types of descent and forms of avunculate does not exhaust the problem. Different forms of avunculate can coexist with the same type of descent, whether patrilineal or matrilineal. But we constantly find the same fundamental relationship between the four pairs of oppositions required to construct the system. This will emerge more clearly from the diagrams which illustrate our examples. The sign + indicates free and familiar relations, and the sign − stands for relations characterized by hostility, antagonism, or reserve (figure 19.1). This is an oversimplification, but we can tentatively make use of it. We shall describe some of the indispensable refinements farther on.

The synchronic law of correlation thus suggested may be validated diachronically. If we summarize, after Howard, the evolution of family relationships during the Middle Ages, we find approximately this pattern: The brother's authority over his sister wanes, and that of the prospective husband increases. Simultaneously, the bond between father and son is weakened and that between maternal uncle and nephew is reinforced.[44]

This evolution seems to be confirmed by the documents gathered by Léon Gautier, for in the "conservative" texts (Raoul de Cambrai, Geste des Loherains, etc.),[45] the positive relationship is

established chiefly between father and son and is only gradually displaced toward the maternal uncle and nephew.[46]

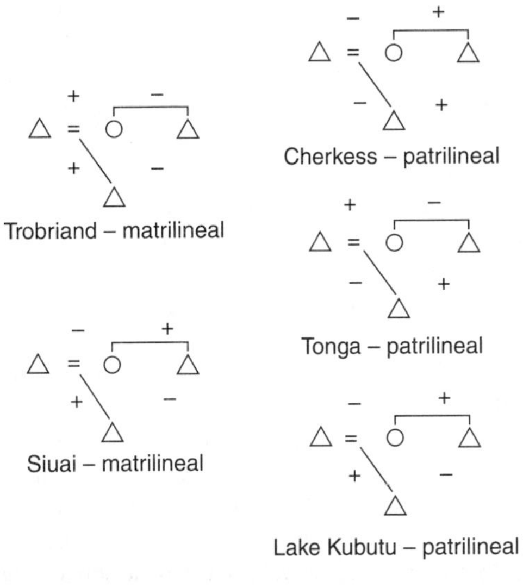

Thus we see[47] that in order to understand the avunculate we must treat it as one relationship within a system, while the system itself must be considered as a whole in order to grasp its structure. This structure rests upon four terms (brother, sister, father, and son), which are linked by two pairs of correlative oppositions in such a way that in each of the two generations there is always a positive relationship and a negative one. Now, what is the nature of this structure, and what is its function? The answer is as follows. This structure is the most elementary form of kinship that can exist. It is, properly speaking, *the unit of kinship*.

One may give a logical argument to support this statement. In order for a kinship structure to exist, three types of family relations must always be present: a relation of consanguinity, a relation of affinity, and a relation of descent – in other words, a relation between siblings, a relation between spouses, and a relation between parent and child. It is evident that the structure given here satisfies this threefold requirement, in accordance with the scientific principle of parsimony. But these considerations are abstract, and we can present a more direct proof for our thesis.

The primitive and irreducible character of the basic unit of kinship, as we have defined it, is actually a direct result of the universal presence of an incest taboo. This is really saying that in human society a man must obtain a woman from another man who gives him a daughter or a sister. Thus we do not need to explain how the maternal uncle emerged in the kinship structure: He does not emerge – he is present initially. Indeed, the presence of the maternal uncle is a necessary precondition for the structure to exist. The error of traditional anthropology, like that of traditional linguistics, was to consider the terms, and not the relations between the terms.

Before proceeding further, let us briefly answer some objections which might be raised. First, if the relationship between "brothers-in-law" is the necessary axis around which the kinship structure is built, why need we bring in the child of the marriage when considering the elementary structure? Of course the child here may be either born or yet unborn. But, granting this, we must understand that the child is indispensable in validating

Figure 19.1

the dynamic and teleological character of the initial step, which establishes kinship on the basis of and through marriage. Kinship is not a static phenomenon; it exists only in self-perpetuation. Here we are not thinking of the desire to perpetuate the race, but rather of the fact that in most kinship systems the initial disequilibrium produced in one generation between the group that gives the woman and the group that receives her can be stabilized only by counter-prestations in following generations. Thus, even the most elementary kinship structure exists both synchronically and diachronically.

Second, could we not conceive of a symmetrical structure, equally simple, where the sexes would be reversed? Such a structure would involve a sister, her brother, brother's wife, and brother's daughter. This is certainly a theoretical possibility. But it is immediately eliminated on empirical grounds. In human society, it is the men who exchange the women, and not vice versa. It remains for further research to determine whether certain cultures have not tended to create a kind of fictitious image of this symmetrical structure. Such cases would surely be uncommon.

We come now to a more serious objection. Possibly we have only inverted the problem. Traditional anthropologists painstakingly endeavored to explain the origin of the avunculate, and we have brushed aside that research by treating the mother's brother not as an extrinsic element, but as an immediate *given* of the simplest family structure. How is it then that we do not find the avunculate at all times and in all places? For although the avunculate has a wide distribution, it is by no means universal. It would be futile to explain the instances where it is present and then fail to explain its absence in other instances.

Let us point out, first, that the kinship system does not have the same importance in all cultures. For some cultures it provides the active principle regulating all or most of the social relationships. In other groups, as in our own society, this function is either absent altogether or greatly reduced. In still others, as in the societies of the Plains Indians, it is only partially fulfilled. The kinship system is a language; but it is not a universal language, and a society may prefer other modes of expression and action. From the viewpoint of the anthropologist this means that

in dealing with a specific culture we must always ask a preliminary question: Is the system systematic? Such a question, which seems absurd at first, is absurd only in relation to language; for language is the semantic system par excellence; it cannot but signify, and exists only through signification. On the contrary, this question must be rigorously examined as we move from the study of language to the consideration of other systems which also claim to have semantic functions, but whose fulfillment remains partial, fragmentary, or subjective, like, for example, social organization, art, and so forth.

Furthermore, we have interpreted the avunculate as a characteristic trait of elementary structure. This elementary structure, which is the product of defined relations involving four terms, is, in our view, the true *atom of kinship*.[48] Nothing can be conceived or given beyond the fundamental requirements of its structure, and, in addition, it is the sole building block of more complex systems. For there are more complex systems; or, more accurately speaking, all kinship systems are constructed on the basis of this elementary structure, expanded or developed through the integration of new elements. Thus we must entertain two hypotheses: first, one in which the kinship system under consideration operates through the simple juxtaposition of elementary structures, and where the avuncular relationship therefore remains constantly apparent; second, a hypothesis in which the building blocks of the system are already of a more complex order. In the latter case, the avuncular relationship, while present, may be submerged within a differentiated context. For instance, we can conceive of a system whose point of departure lies in the elementary structure but which adds, at the right of the maternal uncle, his wife, and, at the left of the father, first the father's sister and then her husband. We could easily demonstrate that a development of this order leads to a parallel splitting in the following generation. The child must then be distinguished according to sex – a boy or a girl, linked by a relation which is symmetrical and inverse to the terms occupying the other peripheral positions in the structure (for example, the dominant position of the father's sister in Polynesia, the South African *nhlampsa*, and inheritance by the mother's brother's wife). In this type of structure the avuncular relationship continues to prevail, but it is no longer the predominant one. In structures of still greater complexity, the avunculate may be obliterated or may merge with other relationships. But precisely because it is part of the elementary structure, the avuncular relationship re-emerges unmistakably and tends to become reinforced each time the system under consideration reaches a crisis – either because it is undergoing rapid transformation (as on the Northwest Coast), or because it is a focus of contact and conflict between radically different cultures (as in Fiji and southern India), or, finally, because it is in the throes of a mortal crisis (as was Europe in the Middle Ages).

We must also add that the positive and negative symbols which we have employed in the above diagrams represent an oversimplification, useful only as a part of the demonstration. Actually, the system of basic attitudes comprises at least four terms: an attitude of affection, tenderness, and spontaneity; an attitude which results from the reciprocal exchange of prestations and counter-prestations; and, in addition to these bilateral relationships, two unilateral relationships, one which corresponds to the attitude of the creditor, the other to that of the debtor. In other words there are: mutuality (=), reciprocity (±), rights (+), and obligations (−). These four fundamental attitudes are represented in their reciprocal relationships in figure 19.2.

In many systems the relationship between two individuals is often expressed not by a single attitude, but by several attitudes which together form, as it were, a "bundle" of attitudes (as in the Trobriands, where we find both mutuality *and* reciprocity between husband and wife). This is an additional reason behind the difficulty in uncovering the basic structure.

We have tried to show the extent to which the preceding analysis is indebted to outstanding contemporary exponents of the sociology of

primitive peoples. We must stress, however, that in its most fundamental principle this analysis departs from their teachings. Let us cite as an example Radcliffe-Brown:

> The unit of structure from which a kinship is built up is the group which I call an "elementary family," consisting of a man and his wife and their child or children.... The existence of the elementary family creates three special kinds of social relationship, that between parent and child, that between children of the same parents (siblings), and that between husband and wife as parents of the same child or children.... The three relationships that exist within the elementary family constitute what I call the first order. Relationships of the second order are those which depend on the connection of two elementary families through a common member, and are such as father's father, mother's brother, wife's sister, and so on. In the third order are such as father's brother's son and mother's brother's wife. Thus we can trace, if we have genealogical information, relationships of the fourth, fifth or n^{th} order.[49]

The idea expressed in the above passage, that the biological family constitutes the point of departure from which all societies elaborate their kinship systems, has not been voiced solely by Radcliffe-Brown. There is scarcely an idea which would today elicit greater consensus. Nor is there one more dangerous, in our opinion. Of course, the biological family is ubiquitous in human society. But what confers upon kinship its socio-cultural character is not what it retains from nature, but, rather, the essential way in which it diverges from nature. A kinship system does not consist in the objective ties of descent or consanguinity between individuals. It exists only in human consciousness; it is an arbitrary system of representations, not the spontaneous development of a real situation. This certainly does not mean that the real situation is automatically contradicted, or that it is to be simply ignored. Radcliffe-Brown has shown, in studies that are now classic, that even systems which are apparently extremely rigid and artificial, such as the Australian systems of marriage-classes, take biological parenthood carefully into account. But while this observation is irrefutable, still the fact (in our view decisive) remains that, in

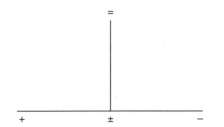

Figure 19.2

human society, kinship is allowed to establish and perpetuate itself only through specific forms of marriage. In other words, the relationships which Radcliffe-Brown calls "relationships of the first order" are a function of, and depend upon, those which he considers secondary and derived. The essence of human kinship is to require the establishment of relations among what Radcliffe-Brown calls "elementary families." Thus, it is not the families (isolated terms) which are truly "elementary," but, rather, the relations between those terms. No other interpretation can account for the universality of the incest taboo; and the avuncular relationship, in its most general form, is nothing but a corollary, now covert, now explicit, of this taboo.

Because they are symbolic systems, kinship systems offer the anthropologist a rich field, where his efforts can almost (and we emphasize the "almost") converge with those of the most highly developed of the social sciences, namely, linguistics. But to achieve this convergence, from which it is hoped a better understanding of man will result, we must never lose sight of the fact that, in both anthropological and linguistic research, we are dealing strictly with symbolism. And although it may be legitimate or even inevitable to fall back upon a naturalistic interpretation in order to understand the emergence of symbolic thinking, once the latter is given, the nature of the explanation must change as radically as the newly appeared phenomenon differs from those which have preceded and prepared it. Hence, any concession to naturalism might jeopardize the immense progress already made in linguistics, which is also beginning to characterize the study of family structure, and might drive the sociology of the family toward a sterile empiricism, devoid of inspiration.

Notes

1   Marcel Mauss, "Rapports réels et pratiques de la psychologie et de la sociologie," *Journal de Psychologie Normale et Pathologique* (1924); reprinted in *Sociologie et Anthropologie* (Paris: 1951), p. 299.

2   O. Schrader, *Prehistoric Antiquities of the Aryan Peoples*, trans. F. B. Jevons (London: 1890), ch. XII, part 4.

3   Ibid. See also H. J. Rose, "On the Alleged Evidence for Mother-Right in Early Greece," *Folklore*, XXII (1911), and the more recent studies by George Thomson, which support the hypothesis of matrilineal survivals.

4   A. M. Hocart, "Chieftainship and the Sister's Son in the Pacific," *American Anthropologist*, n.s., XVII (1915); "The Uterine Nephew," *Man*, XXIII, no. 4 (1923); "The Cousin in Vedic Ritual," *Indian Antiquary*, LIV (1925); etc.

5   Paul K. Benedict, "Tibetan and Chinese Kinship Terms," *Harvard Journal of Asiatic Studies*, VI (1942); "Studies in Thai Kinship Terminology," *Journal of the American Oriental Society*, LXIII (1943).

6   L. Brunschvicg, *Le Progrès de la conscience dans la philosophie occidentale* (Paris: 1927), II, p. 562.

7   Between 1900 and 1920 Ferdinand de Saussure and Antoine Meillet, the founders of modern linguistics, placed themselves determinedly under the wing of the anthropologists. Not until the 1920s did Marcel Mauss begin – to borrow a phrase from economics – to reverse this tendency.

8   N. Troubetzkoy, "La Phonologie actuelle," in *Psychologie du langage* (Paris: 1933).

9   Ibid., p. 243.

10 Ibid.

11 Ibid., p. 245; Roman Jakobson, "Principien der historischen Phonologie," *Travaux du Cercle linguistique de Prague*, IV (1931); and also Jakobson, "Remarques sur l'évolution phonologique du russe," ibid., II (1929).

12 W. H. R. Rivers, *The History of Melanesian Society* (London: 1914), *passim*; *Social Organization*, ed. W. J. Perry (London: 1924), ch. IV.

13 In the same vein, see Sol Tax, "Some Problems of Social Organization," in Fred Eggan (ed.), *Social Anthropology of North American Tribes* (Chicago: 1937).

14 Roman Jakobson, "Observations sur le classement phonologique des consonnes," *Proceedings of the Third International Congress of Phonetic Sciences* (Ghent: 1938).

15 K. Davis and W. L. Warner, "Structural Analysis of Kinship," *American Anthropologist*, n.s., XXXVII (1935).

16 Thus at the end of the analysis carried out by these authors, the term *husband* is replaced by the formula:

$$C^{2a/2d/0} S U^{1a \ 8}/Ego \text{(ibid.)}$$

There are now available two works which employ a much more refined logical apparatus and offer greater interest in terms both of method and of results. See F. G. Lounsbury, "A Semantic Analysis of the Pawnee Kinship Usage," *Language*, XXXII, no. 1 (1956), and W. H. Goodenough, "The Componential Analysis of Kinship," ibid.

17 A. L. Kroeber, "Classificatory Systems of Relationship," *Journal of the Royal Anthropological Institute*, XXXIX (1909).

18 We must except the remarkable work of W. L. Warner, "Morphology and Functions of the Australian Murngin Type of Kinship," *American Anthropologist*, n.s., XXXII–XXXIII (1930–1), in which his analysis of the system of attitudes, although fundamentally debatable, nevertheless initiates a new phase in the study of problems of kinship.

19 A. R. Radcliffe-Brown, "Kinship Terminology in California," *American Anthropologist*, n.s., XXX-VII (1935); "The Study of Kinship Systems," *Journal of the Royal Anthropological Institute*, LXXI (1941).

20 M. E. Opler, "Apache Data Concerning the Relationship of Kinship Terminology to Social Classification," *American Anthropologist*, n.s., XXX-IX (1937); A. M. Halpern, "Yuma Kinship Terms," *American Anthropologist*, n.s., XLIV (1942).

21 D. F. Thomson, "The Joking Relationship and Organized Obscenity in North Queensland," *American Anthropologist*, n.s., XXXVII (1935).

22 Radcliffe-Brown, "The Study of Kinship Systems," p. 8. This later formulation seems to us more satisfactory than his 1935 statement that attitudes present "a fairly high degree of correlation with the terminological classification" (*American Anthropologist*, n.s., XXXVII [1935], p. 53).

23 Sydney Hartland, "Matrilineal Kinship and the Question of its Priority," *Memoirs of the American Anthropological Association*, No. 4 (1917).

24 W. H. R. Rivers, "The Marriage of Cousins in India," *Journal of the Royal Asiatic Society* (July, 1907).

25 Ibid., p. 624.

26 R. H. Lowie, "The Matrilineal Complex," *University of California Publications in American Archaeology and Ethnology*, XVI, no. 2 (1919).

27 Roman Jakobson, *Kindersprache, Aphasie und allgemeine Lautgesetze* (Uppsala: 1941).

28 A. R. Radcliffe-Brown, "The Mother's Brother in South Africa," *South African Journal of Science*, XXI (1924).

29 As among the Mundugomor of New Guinea, where the relationship between maternal uncle and nephew is always familiar, although descent is alternately patrilineal or matrilineal. See Margaret Mead, *Sex and Temperament in Three Primitive Societies* (New York: 1935), pp. 176–85.

30 B. Malinowski, *The Sexual Life of Savages in Northwestern Melanesia* (London: 1929), 2 vols.

31 Dubois de Monpereux (1839), cited in M. Kovalevski, "La Famille matriarcale au Caucase," *L'Anthropologie*, IV (1893).

32 Ibid.

33 E. W. Gifford, "Tonga Society," *Bernice P. Bishop Museum Bulletin*, No. 61 (Honolulu: 1929), pp. 16–22.

34 F. E. Williams, "Group Sentiment and Primitive Justice," *American Anthropologist*, n.s., XLIII, no. 4, part 1 (1941), p. 523.

35 F. E. Williams, "Natives of Lake Kutubu, Papua," *Oceania*, XI (1940–1), p. 266.

36 Ibid., p. 268.

37 Ibid., p. 280. See also *Oceania*, XII (1941–2).

38 Douglas L. Oliver, *A Solomon Island Society: Kinship and Leadership among the Siuai of Bougainville* (Cambridge, Mass.: 1955), p. 255.

39 Ibid., p. 251.

40 Ibid., p. 257.

41 Ibid., pp. 168–9.

42 R. F. Fortune, *The Sorcerers of Dobu* (New York: 1932), p. 45.

43 Ibid., pp. 8, 10, 62–4.

44 G. E. Howard, *A History of Matrimonial Institutions*, 3 vols. (Chicago: 1904).

45 [*Translator's note*: The "Chansons de Geste," which survive in manuscript versions of the twelfth to the fifteenth century, are considered to be remodelings of much earlier originals, dating back to the age of Charlemagne. These poems of heroic and often legendary exploits also constitute a source of information on the family life of that period.]

46 Léon Gautier, *La Chevalerie* (Paris: 1890). See also: F. B. Gummere, "The Sister's Son," in *An English Miscellany Presented to Dr. Furnivall* (London: 1901); W. O. Farnsworth, *Uncle and Nephew in the Old French Chanson de Geste* (New York: 1913).

47 The preceding paragraphs were written in 1957 and substituted for the original text, in response to the judicious remark by my colleague Luc de Heusch of the Université Libre of Brussels that one of my examples was incorrect. I take this opportunity to thank him.

48 It is no doubt superfluous to emphasize that the atomism which we have criticized in Rivers refers to classical philosophy and has nothing to do with the structural conception of the atom developed in modern physics.

49 Radcliffe-Brown, "The Study of Kinship Systems," p. 2.

20

Ordinary Language and Human Action

Malcolm Crick

The Durkheimian premiss that social facts must be regarded as "things" was one way of stating that science requires one to adopt a certain attitude towards one's objects of study. Such a premiss does not entail that restrictive method and positivist outlook which virtually regards human beings as if they were themselves things – an outlook which merely caricatures science. The subject matter of social studies are persons who use language, construct meanings, follow rules, give accounts of their actions – beings, in short, who have considerable insight into their own nature. Such powers[1] cannot justifiably be excluded from any adequate science of social life.

It is because human agents are able to use language, and because their knowledge about their own action is substantially contained in ordinary language, that the work of the linguistic philosophers has such a value for social inquiry. Austin, for instance, has shown what an immensely rich stock of subtle distinctions ordinary English contains relating to human responsibility (1956). In natural languages, as he emphasized, are embedded those associations and discriminations which generations of speakers have found it important to make (ibid.:46). This does not mean that ordinary language should always have the last word. Our everyday concepts might prove deficient in certain areas – Freud, for instance, drew our attention to hitherto little noticed episodes for which the ordinary resources of language did not make adequate provision. Technical terms may be quite legitimate additions to the stock of ordinary notions, but inventions are far more likely to be inadequate than the readily available terms which are already a part of the social institutions which the investigator has to describe. As psychology deals with the same phenomena that Jane Austen wrote about, ordinary language should at least have the first word. This at least is a more realistic beginning for studying human action than that chosen by those favouring a "physicalist" discourse who, embarrassed by the elaborateness of ordinary language, so often expressed pride in the number of terms they had avoided using (Neurath 1966:51).

A social inquiry which exploits ordinary concepts will not depart totally from our ordinary understanding of ourselves. If this seems unscientific, then we should recall that this ordinary understanding constitutes a great part of what we are. And the elaborateness of ordinary language is

From *Explorations in Language and Meaning: Towards a Semantic Anthropology* (New York: John Wiley & Sons, 1976) pp. 90–8, 173–4, 177, 187, 190–1. Copyright © 1976 by John Wiley & Sons.

Anthropology in Theory: Issues in Epistemology, Second Edition. Edited by Henrietta L. Moore and Todd Sanders.
© 2014 John Wiley & Sons, Inc. Published 2014 by John Wiley & Sons, Inc.

simply a scientific fact about human beings, not a matter to be disregarded. The new kind of social science is first and foremost a conceptual study of an intrinsically semantic subject matter – a fact obscured and often obliterated by the old scientistic desire for quantification. To depart from the conceptual system involved in a set of moral and evaluative notions by breaking actions down into quantifiable physical units of behaviour does not promote a more precise study of social or psychological facts, since the new units completely destroy the nature of the facts one is investigating (Louch 1966: 18, 54–5). No doubt, for some, the very familiarity of this "anthropomorphic" approach will make it unacceptable, yet clearly scientific realism demands that an anthropomorphic model be used when a science actually is about human beings. It is hardly an adequate framework which excludes whole dimensions of what it is to be a human being and which discounts powers which the social scientist like everyone else knows he possesses. A social scientist has no more basic capacity to understand human action than the people whom he is studying, but it is clearly absurd that he should proceed as if he had far less. To dispense with the semantic resources of ordinary language can only produce nonsense descriptions of human activity [...]

Thought, Action and the Nature of Human Studies

We have seen that while a particular view of the nature of physical science produces nonsense when employed in the study of social action, this gives no grounds for thinking that there can be no scientific study of a phenomenon which is so much bound up with notions like meaning and rule. Since Winch has argued forcibly that human action is a subject matter to which the sorts of explanations given in the physical sciences are inapplicable (1958: 72), we can use his work to discuss in the most general terms what is involved in the study of such a phenomenon. Certainly his book omits a great deal that is a part of social science, but he states very clearly the basic logical features that an account of human action must have if it is to be reckoned appropriate.

Even if Winch is concerned only with a starting point, it is vital to see how important it is to begin social inquiry in the right framework. If such inquiry rests on mistaken assumptions, no amount of actual empirical research or quantification will rectify the initial mistake so as to produce meaningful results. No statistical flair, for instance, can possibly relieve the investigator of the necessary prior semantic inquiry: statistical significance can well be without significance in a significant sense. Even when one is dealing with so seemingly countable a phenomenon as a tribal population, in fact one is speaking of a conceptual entity with boundaries constituted by definitions (Ardener 1974). Numbers here are the "surface structure" of systems whose deep structures are necessarily classificatory in nature. Failure to identify these underlying conceptual parameters is to miss the significant generative units, after which no study could be either exact or even empirical in the true sense of the word. There is no general form of precision at which all sciences should aim. With a conceptual subject matter, to be exact may just involve close attention to a semantic structure. Since social interaction is so much a matter of exchanging meaning, the precision of measurement of the physical sciences corresponds in the social sciences to a more minute conceptual delineation (Harré and Secord 1972: 132).

[...]

The crucial fact which Winch conveys by contrasting social and physical science is that, as social phenomena are meaningful, social action is a species of "internal" relations, because the relations between ideas are of a logical kind (1958: 123). This could be a potentially misleading way of expressing the point, but much of its power can be grasped by recalling the deep conceptual gulf in our language between "reason concepts" and "cause concepts". Even if the gulf can be bridged conceptually, we are talking of two very different semantic fields. We can speak of a causal sequence as a matter of external links, but the connection between a reason and an action is not of this contingent sort: meaning is contained within action, since action expresses a conceptual schema. So, mental terms like "motive" or "intention" do not refer to causal forces (Ryle 1966: 113) because their relation to any action is internal – they are a part of the action.

This important separation of two semantic fields is maintained in our ordinary everyday discourse, and is clearly embedded in legal proceedings, for instance. Normally, to call something an "action" invites an explanation of a very different sort from that we give of a "bodily movement" (MacIntyre 1966: 108). Obviously, therefore, the gulf between "action" and "behaviour" risks being obliterated by those social scientists who see their work as concerned with "human behaviour",[2] and who view their task as giving causes of behaviour and setting out causal consequences of behaviour. We ordinarily only invoke causal factors when a human being is in some way less than a person – when his agency is destroyed by drunkenness or the compulsion of others, for example. When we are dealing with an "agent", a causal account can never be adequate and may be totally inappropriate. By now it is patently clear how hopelessly a causal theory of language use fails us. It reads like a mythical description of a matter which we as speakers can already explain in more adequate ways. This failure with language is stark; and it is of the very widest significance, because speaking is a paradigm case of a human rule-governed activity. Gross deficiency in causal explanation here necessarily implies similar failure with other types of social activity.

This basic conceptual problem concerning the description and explanation of human action can be usefully stated by employing the distinction between "transcription" and "transliteration" from the theory of translation. Of course, the relationship between model and reality is not simple in the physical sciences; nonetheless the contrast between these terms well suggests the extra dimension involved in theorizing in the social sciences. We can say that theoretical statements in the physical sciences point to regularities in phenomena: such propositions register conceptually connections between occurrences. With social phenomena, however, such conceptual links already exist, because they are structured by virtue of the meaning they have for their actors. The physical sciences have to transcribe, in that they must devise a graphological set to systematize the sounds of a "language" previously unrecorded. By contrast, the language which the social sciences investigate is already a system possessing a conventional orthography composed of human meanings. In such a case, one must transliterate – that is, descriptions in social science must preserve this structure as an important part of the facts being dealt with. When inquiring into human phenomena, we are not dealing only with our technical language but with the discourse of others too. Our facts are not only already classified, they are classifications. Human data are of a conceptual order, so they are destroyed if this pre-existing order is disrespected. In social science, one can explain only if one can describe, and this one can do only if one has grasped the concepts embodied in human action. If the investigator fails to understand the conceptual structures which compose the subject matter of his science, he does not have the right to speak of human action at all. Thus, he must build upon this semantic foundation, not violate it.[3]

We can elaborate the difference between human studies and the physical sciences by using the opposition "internality"/"externality". The social sciences deal with conceptual facts, so we can speak of "events" and "rules", and liken the procedure of investigation to a communication exchange. By contrast, we can say that the physical sciences are concerned with regularities in occurrences, and that they are observationalist in method. Social science cannot be observationalist in this latter sense because of the internal dimension of its subject matter. The grammar of action is not external in a simple sense: it is semantic, existing in language and other shared conceptual reservoirs. Discovering the structure of social phenomena therefore entails symbolic dialogue between investigator and other human beings.

This internal aspect of rule-governed phenomena has been well illustrated by Hart in his discussion of the activities of drivers at traffic lights. It would not take an observer long to notice regularities in the motion of vehicles, related to the colour of the lights. But the lights are not the causes of these patterns. The lights are part of a convention structure and do not have to be obeyed. They are quite literally signs – that is they have meaning for drivers. What one is witnessing is rule-following activity, not causal regularities. If one describes this situation in only external observational terms, a whole dimension of social life would be omitted (1961: 55–7, 86–7).

This sort of consideration is not of a mere abstract philosophical relevance, for the semantic nature of social events must intrude in all sociological descriptions. It is internal considerations, for instance, which determine whether two events are of the same kind, and even whether something is an event at all. We could imagine a Christian ceremony in which one of the participants sneezed, for instance. As far as the meaning of the situation was concerned this would literally be noise – a non-event. On the other hand, in a culture where there was a belief in disease caused by indwelling spirits, the same physical occurrence of a sneeze during a healing rite might well be the most central and significant event of the proceedings, indicating that the spirit had been expelled. Although a physical scientist has to formulate the theory he uses, he is not under the same semantic constraints as the social investigator. The anthropological failing of ethnocentrism – thoughtlessly imposing our own cultural categories on another society – is thus just one instance of a general epistemological difficulty in inquiries into social facts. Because an action has an internal connection with the meaning embedded in it, one cannot describe an activity as "praying" or "voting", for instance, unless the actor possesses these concepts or ones which substantially overlap with them. Voting does not bear the same relation to a specific human action as does gravity to the fall of a physical object, because the concept of "voting" is part of the action itself (Winch 1958:51).

As semantics and not observation determine the nature and boundaries of events, so we should remember that a rule can create a phenomenon. In some cases rules merely regulate an activity which exists independently of them. But there are also "constitutive" rules where rule and phenomenon are not at all separable. For instance, the act of mating in chess is the expression of the rule which actually establishes the move itself. The move did not exist first and then have a rule added to regulate it: it has no existence apart from the rule, and this rule no existence apart from the others which make up the game of chess as a whole. Thus, to return to the notions of externality and internality, an observer at a football match unfamiliar with the game could easily note patterns of behaviour on the field, but such regularities could not reveal to him the point of the game, nor could he understand what fouls or offside were or even that they were separate events. Lacking the conceptual system in which these notions have their place he might not have registered them at all. Because rules can create events, the observational ideology of the sciences

of human behaviour is clearly logically inadequate. Just as an occurrence may be a non-event, so a non-occurrence may well be an event. For instance, saying or doing nothing can constitute a positive act of politeness if there is a rule that silence is a sign of respect in certain circumstances. Such a fact could well be exposed by a process of communication, but it would remain undetected by any purely observationalist method of inquiry.

In recent anthropology, some of the general dualisms upon which the discussion of this chapter has been based have appeared in Ardener's richly suggestive distinction between paradigmatic and syntagmatic structures (1971).[4] His stress on the conceptual dimension of human facts involved in the analytical separation of a generative programme and a sequence of events (1973a) in effect inverts the structure of the functionalist ideology. For functionalists, the prime data to be recorded during field-work were the "real" observable phenomena like economic, political and kinship behaviour. Values, beliefs and symbolic usages were also noted, and interpreted as elaborations of this primary social reality. They were located by reducing them to the needs of the social system, that is explained away as elements which served to make the society work better by integrating the diverse parts of the social structure, and so on. The general argument of this chapter should make it clear why the order of priorities enshrined in this positivistic scheme must be rejected. It is precisely the conceptual structures which contain the syntax of those events which the investigator can actually observe. It is the semantic structures which are generative, behaviour merely being the linear physical realization of these constitutive programmes.

Such a view does not mean that functional work was not valuable. Actions have consequences, and no doubt there are bonds between different social institutions. The deficiency has been that functionalism was coupled with a devaluation of semantic concerns. Clearly this has impeded the development of semantic anthropology; but the point also needs to be made that this prejudice cuts away the ground from underneath functionalism too. As it is a semantic foundation which constitutes the events the fieldworker detects, he cannot scientifically speak about the functional links between institutions until his data have been understood. Even functionalists, therefore, must admit the priority of conceptual structures. If they do not, they simply have no basis from which to pass on to their more sociological interests. Human action is a semantic fabric, so any social investigation must be a conceptual inquiry. Any other starting-point will make a nonsense of scientific method. Human beings are meaning-makers, and this directly determines what general form a science of social action must assume. Functionalism (just like the extreme case of behaviourism in psychology) was part of an observationalist ideology which rested on a fundamental epistemological error about the nature of human action. For those who fail to see the intrinsically conceptual nature of human social facts, real scientific empiricism would prove impossible.

Of course it is often said that what is "internal" necessarily falls outside the domain of science, that science can only deal with the publicly observable. Hence, if sociological inquiries are to deserve the label "scientific", they too must restrict their scope to what is external. This argument is perhaps the major factor lying behind the sad state of so much psychology today. Haunted by the problem of "other minds", equating mentalism with non-science, psychologists in many fields retreated into a behaviourism which has left out some of the most basic characteristics of human beings. In so doing, psychology cut itself off from that conceptual system out of which a realistic account of human action could have been built. Such a strategy, moreover, was based on a series of profound conceptual errors, as recent linguistic philosophy has made very clear. When we speak of the "internality" of social activity, we are not talking of a private realm – the concepts of "meaning" and "rule", in fact, only make sense given a public context.[5] The internal aspect is not observable in a gross sense, but it exists in language and can be located by communication – a shared method which is the basis not only of social life but also of social inquiry.

Wittgenstein constantly stressed this need for public criteria in semantic issues, and he used it against the ego-centric standpoint which lay at the root of so many classical philosophical problems. Language was not just a social institution, it was an *essentially* shared possession. The impossibility of a "private" language thus establishes the strongest conceptual affinities between the notions of publicity, meaning and rule. There have to be other human beings if we are to follow a rule; and we could not speak at all if we could not speak to each other. This refutation of linguistic privacy, and the demolition of Cartesian privacy in general, is not only of philosophical import, but of the very widest significance to investigators of social life. Ryle's analysis of mental concepts, for instance, fully exposes the absurdity of regarding human action as if a person were composed of distinct mental and physical sequences (1966). But the crucial point to grasp is that the destruction of this dualism not only eliminates a certain concept of mind but also liquidates the corresponding concept of the human body. This is why the Rylean concept of action is not behaviourist. In the same way that internality is not synonymous with privacy, so publicity is not the equivalent of physical behaviour. When watching a human being in the course of a social interaction, one is not witnessing a body behaving and failing to witness a mind thinking, one is seeing a person in action.

While an "inner" life is a basic part of a human being, we well know in daily life that for all ordinary people this internality in no way means inaccessibility.[6] Social life would not just be very different, it could not possibly exist were this not so. That we normally understand other persons is essential to their being persons and to our being a person. We cannot think of language, mind and meaning in an individual context, and then try to fit others into the scheme: they all three can only exist in a shared context. It is basic to everyday life that we can understand one another. We can do this even when we try to give misleading information about our motives. Concepts like "bluff" or "pretend" would not exist in our language otherwise. It is even a familiar situation for someone else to know one's mind better than one knows it oneself, as for example when one accepts another person's account of one's action which conflicts with the explanation one had originally given oneself. These are not mystical occurrences, they simply register basic powers possessed by human beings, and they give social life fundamental logical characteristics which any adequate account should accept as data. Some provision should be made for such phenomena in building a conceptual system to describe social interaction. To leave them out in an effort to be more objective leads to a scientistic metaphysics which is quite the reverse of true science. Those who wish to deny that we have these powers merely validate our contentions; for to challenge our position they must utilize their semantic powers even to frame an argument, let alone engage in dispute. [. . .]

Notes

1 On the importance of the concept of "powers" in the realist philosophy of science, see Harré and Secord (1972: 78–82). It is worth recalling in this context the similar way Chomsky has granted scientific import to speakers' knowledge.

2 In fact, the notion of "behaviour" – seemingly such an easily identifiable and universal phenomenon – was picked up by the infant social sciences from chemistry, where its history is still little more than a century long (Ardener 1973b).

3 It does not follow from this viewpoint that a scientific account is concerned only with noting the forms of events which ordinary language traces. One has also to account for the nature of these forms; and to express their deep structures it will often be necessary to go beyond the resources of ordinary concepts, even to systems like non-metrical mathematics, for instance.

4 The term "paradigmatic" is taken from Saussure, but as the notion of paradigm now has such a diversity of uses – particularly after the work of Kuhn – to free his terminology from these associations, Ardener now prefers to talk simply of p- and s-structures.

5 The *verstehen* literature is often very confusing, since it sometimes makes the act of understanding another human being seem like an unverifiable and intuitive fathoming, rather than that exchange of meanings with which people are perfectly familiar.

6 Of course, while rules and meanings are public, we are all ultimately individuals with unique histories and with very different experiences of our language. But if we therefore all speak slightly differing tongues, these idiolects are nonetheless not private languages. There is an inevitable interpretative act which is quite rightly regarded as translation (Steiner 1975: 45, 47), even for communication in one language. And, as with interlingual translation, the negotiation over semantic issues lacks finality in that interpretations are always further negotiable. But disagreements are possible only because people can understand each other: if other minds were inaccessible there could be no negotiation at all.

References

Ardener, E. W. 1971. The new anthropology and its critics. *Man* (NS) 6: 449–67.

Ardener, E. W. 1973a. Some Outstanding Problems in the Analysis of Events. ASA Conference Paper.

Ardener, E. W. 1973b. Behaviour: A social anthropological criticism. *Journal of the Anthropological Society of Oxford* 4: 152–4.

Ardener, E. W. 1974. Social Anthropology and Population. In H. B. Parry (ed.), *Population and Its Problems*. Clarendon Press, Oxford: 25–50.

Austin, J. L. 1956. A Plea for Excuses. In V. C. Chappell (ed.), *Ordinary Language*. Prentice-Hall, Englewood Cliffs, NJ, 1964: 41–63.

Harré, R. H. and Secord, P. 1972. *The Explanation of Social Behaviour*. Blackwell, Oxford.

Hart, H. L. A. 1961. *The Concept of Law*. Clarendon Press, Oxford.

Louch, A. R. 1966. *Explanation and Human Action*. Blackwell, Oxford.

Macintyre, A. C. 1966. The Antecedents of Action. In *Against the Self-Images of the Age: Essay on Ideology and Philosophy*. Duckworth, London, 1971.

Neurath, O. 1966. *Foundations of the Social Sciences*. University of Chicago Press, Chicago.

Ryle, G. 1966. *The Concept of Mind*. Hutchinson & Co., London.

Steiner, G. 1975. *After Babel: Aspects of Language and Translation*, OUP, Oxford.

Winch, P. 1958. *The Idea of a Social Science and Its Relations to Philosophy*. Routledge & Kegan Paul, London.

21

Language, Anthropology and Cognitive Science

Maurice Bloch

[...] Cultural anthropologists study culture. This can be defined as that which needs to be known in order to operate reasonably effectively in a specific human environment.[1] Social anthropologists traditionally study social organisation and the behaviour by means of which people relate to each other. Both cultural and social anthropologists, however, are well aware that the distinction between the two branches of the discipline is not absolute. Cultural anthropologists know that they cannot get at culture directly, but only through the observation of communicative activity, verbal or otherwise, natural or artificially simulated. Social anthropologists are aware that they cannot understand action, verbal or otherwise, if they do not construct, probably in imagination, a representation of the culture of the people they study, since this is the only way to make sense of their activities (Winch 1958).

Some concept of culture is therefore essential to all social and cultural anthropologists. However, a further assumption of anthropology, sometimes stated and sometimes unstated, is that this culture is inseparably linked to language, on the grounds either that culture is thought and transmitted as a text through language, or that culture is ultimately "language like", consisting of

linked linear propositions. It is these two assumptions about culture that I want to challenge here.

If culture is the whole or a part of what people must know in a particular social environment in order to operate efficiently, it follows first, that people must have acquired this knowledge, either through the development of innate potentials, or from external sources, or from a combination of both, and secondly that this acquired knowledge is being continually stored in a manner that makes it relatively easily accessible when necessary.[2] These obvious inferences have in turn a further implication which is that anthropologists' concerns place them right in the middle of the cognitive sciences, whether they like it or not, since it is cognitive scientists who have something to say about learning, memory and retrieval. Anthropologists cannot, therefore, avoid the attempt to make their theories about social life *compatible* with what other cognitive scientists have to say about the processes of learning and storage.

Perhaps all this may seem commonplace but it is striking how often anthropologists' theories of learning, memory and retrieval have *not* been compatible with those of other cognitive scientists. The exception is the small group of cognitive

From *Man* 26 (1991), pp. 183–94, 195–8. Copyright © 1991 by *Man*. Reprinted by permission of John Wiley & Sons UK.

Anthropology in Theory: Issues in Epistemology, Second Edition. Edited by Henrietta L. Moore and Todd Sanders.
© 2014 John Wiley & Sons, Inc. Published 2014 by John Wiley & Sons, Inc.

anthropologists, largely confined to the United States,[3] who have paid serious attention to recent developments in cognitive science. Things are nevertheless beginning to change, and I hope that in this article I am swimming with the tide, but a tide which has only just started to flow and which has not reached, especially in Europe, the heartland of anthropological theory where it is perhaps most needed.[4]

Of course I do not claim that other cognitive scientists have figured out how the mind works, and that anthropologists have only to slot culture into this well-advanced model. Cognitive scientists' understanding of the mind-brain is dramatically incomplete and tentative. Nonetheless, some findings are fairly clear and we should take these into account. Moreover, the hypotheses of cognitive scientists, however speculative, fundamentally challenge many unexamined anthropological assumptions in a way that should not be ignored.

II

As noted above, my main concern is with only one aspect of the broad topic of the relation between cognitive science and anthropology, namely the importance or otherwise of language, or language-like phenomena, for cultural knowledge. A good place to start is with a consideration of concept formation, particularly classificatory concept formation, a topic about which much has been written, and which is often recognised as of relevance to anthropology.

In discussing this topic I am not concerned with the traditional anthropological issue, recently reviewed by Atran, of the extent to which classificatory concepts have an innate basis (Atran 1990), though it is quite clear that in the past, anthropologists have grossly exaggerated cultural variation, and that the traditional questions of cultural anthropologists concerning very broad areas of knowledge should be rephrased from "How are these things learned?" to "How is culturally specific knowledge produced out of universal predispositions?". Such rephrasing is too easily obscured in anthropological references to "cultural models" (Holland and Quinn 1987).

Leaving this fundamental question aside, it is nonetheless clear that all classificatory concepts are at least partially learned, and recent work in this area has brought about certain fundamental changes in the way we envisage the process. The old idea that the child learns classificatory concepts as minimal and necessary definitions, an idea taken for granted in most of anthropology and which was more particularly implied in structuralism and ethnoscience, was shown to be untenable some time ago (Fillmore 1975; Rosch 1977; 1978; Smith 1988). The more generally accepted position now is that such concepts are formed through reference back to rather vague and provisional "prototypes" which anchor loosely-formed "families" of specific instances. For example, the concept of a house is not a list of essential features (roof, door, walls, and so on) which have to be checked off before deciding whether or not the thing is a house. If that were so we would have no idea that a house which has lost its roof is still a house. It is rather that we consider something as "a house" by comparing it to a loosely associated group of "houselike" features, no one of which is essential, but which are linked by a general idea of what a typical house is.

Thus, as suggested by Markham and Seibert (1976), classificatory concepts are in fact based on an appraisal of their referents in the world, on how we think of the construction and make-up of these referents, or on our understanding of the way they are constituted. It therefore seems that the mental form of classificatory concepts, essential building blocks of culture, involves loose and implicit practical-cum-theoretical pattern networks of knowledge, based on the experience of physical instances sometimes called "best exemplars" (Smith et al. 1988: 372). A significant aspect of looking at classificatory concepts in this way is that it makes them isomorphic with what are known as "scripts" and "schemata", although these latter may be on a much larger and more elaborate scale. These "scripts" and "schemata" are, in effect, chunked networks of loose procedures and understandings which enable us to deal with standard and recurring situations, for example "getting the breakfast ready", that are clearly culturally created (Abelson 1981; Holland and Quinn 1987; D'Andrade 1990).[5]

If classificatory concepts such as "scripts" and "schemata" are not like dictionary entries, but are instead small networks of typical understandings and practices concerning the world, then the question of their relation to words becomes more problematic than it was with the old "checklist of necessary and sufficient conditions" view. That there is no inevitable connexion between concepts and words is shown by the now well-established fact that concepts can and do exist independently of language. This is made clear in the many examples of conceptual thinking in pre-linguistic children, first presented by Brown (1973). Children have the concept "house" before they can say the word. We also have studies which show that the acquisition of lexical semantics by children is very largely a matter of trying to match words to already formed concepts. This is the so called "concept first" theory.

Contrary to earlier views in cognitive anthropology (Tyler 1969), therefore, language is not essential for conceptual thought.[6] It is possible to go beyond this initial distancing between the lexicon and mental concepts, however, thanks to work on semantic acquisition by Bowerman (1977). This demonstrates a continual back and forth movement between aspects of classification which are introduced through language and mental concepts, as the child learns to express these concepts through words. This dialectical movement is not only interesting in itself but also suggests a much more general process, to which I shall return, by which originally non-linguistic knowledge is partly transformed as it becomes linguistic, thereby taking on a form which much more closely resembles what structuralists, among other anthropologists, had assumed to characterise the organisation of all human knowledge (Keil and Batterman 1984).

This brief review of concept formation enables us to reach the following provisional conclusions: (1) that much of knowledge is fundamentally non-linguistic; (2) that concepts involve implicit networks of meanings which are formed through the experience of, and practice in, the external world; and (3) that, under certain circumstances, this non-linguistic knowledge can be rendered into language and thus take the form of explicit discourse, but changing its character in the process.

III

Another area of joint concern to anthropology and cognitive psychology also reveals the importance of non-linguistic knowledge. This is the study of the way we learn practical, everyday tasks. It is clear that we do not usually go through a point-by-point explanation of the process when we teach our children how to negotiate their way around the house or to close doors. Much culturally transmitted knowledge seems to be passed on in ways unknown to us. Perhaps in highly schooled societies this fact is misleadingly obscured by the prominence of explicit instruction, but in non-industrialised societies most of what takes people's time and energy – including such practices as how to wash both the body and clothes, how to cook, how to cultivate, etc. – are learned very gradually through imitation and tentative participation.

The cultural specificity, complexity and embeddedness of such tasks, and their character as not linguistically explicit, have often been commented upon by anthropologists, for example by Mauss (1936), Leroi-Gourhan (1943) and Haudricourt (1968), but have rarely been studied satisfactorily. The few studies we do have tend to deal with unusual tasks necessary for specialised crafts which require formal apprenticeships. In these cases, also, anthropologists have noted that language seems to play a surprisingly small role in the transmission of knowledge. For example, in her study of weavers in Ghana, Goody (1978) was amazed at the small part played by questioning and speaking in teaching apprentices. Similarly, Lave, in her study of Liberian tailors, notes that what she calls "apprenticeship learning", which relies on the "assumptions that knowing, thinking, and understanding are generated in practice" (Lave 1988; 1990: 310), is more effective than formal teaching based on linguistic, socratic forms. If this is so for these relatively specialised tasks there is no doubt that the same conclusions would be reached even more emphatically in studies of learning more common, though not necessarily less skilled, everyday tasks.

The significance of such findings is much more important than we might at first suppose. This is because the fact that the transmission of knowledge in West African weaving or tailoring is largely non-linguistic may have less to do with the culture of education in these places than with a general feature of the kind of knowledge that underlies the performance of complex practical tasks, which *requires* that it be non-linguistic.

That this is so is suggested by various studies of learning in which, by contrast to the examples just mentioned, the original teaching is received through language, or at least in propositional form, but in which the process of becoming an expert seems to involve the transformation of the propositions of the teacher into fundamentally non-linguistic knowledge (Dreyfus and Dreyfus 1986: ch. 1).[7] Thus Anderson [1976] points out how people who are taught driving through a series of propositions have to transform this knowledge into non-linguistic, integrated procedures before the task can be effected rapidly, efficiently and automatically – one might say properly. Only when they do not think about what they are doing in words are drivers truly experts.[8] Probably some teaching needs to be done verbally, but there are also advantages in the non-linguistic transmission of practical skills typical of non-industrial societies since such transmission by-passes the double transformation from implicit to linguistically explicit knowledge made by the teacher and from linguistically explicit to implicit knowledge made by the learner.

It could be objected that my stress on the non-linguistic side of practical activities is somewhat exaggerated. After all, language also plays a role in the performance of many familiar practical actions, though not necessarily driving. Even this fact, however, may bear less on the extent to which knowledge is linguistic than might appear at first sight.

Let me take an example which is in part derived from the semantic work of Johnson-Laird (1988: ch. 18; see also Johnson-Laird 1983: 396–447), modified by Sperber and Wilson's (1986) theory of relevance and which is also indirectly inspired by Malinowski's (1935) study of the role of language in Trobriand agriculture. Imagine a Malagasy shifting cultivator with a fairly clear, yet supple mental model, perhaps we could say a script, stored in long-term memory, of what a "good swidden" is like; and that this model, like that of a roundabout in the mind of the expert driver, is partly visual, partly analytical (though not necessarily in a sentential logical way), partly welded to a series of procedures about what you should do to make and maintain a swidden. This Malagasy is going through the forest with a friend who says to him "Look over there at that bit of

forest, that would make a good swidden". What happens then is that, after a rapid conceptualisation of the bit of forest, the model of "the good swidden" is mentally matched with the conceptualised area of forest, and then a new but related model, "this particular place as a potential swidden" is established and stored in long-term memory. This stored mental model, however, although partly created by the linguistic event and understood in terms of the relevance of the statement to both the mental model of the "good swidden" and to that of the area of forest, is not likely to include the linguistic statement tagged onto it. The intrusion of language has therefore not made the mental model any more linguistic.

To return to the example of car driving: we have seen that driving expertly seems to require that the information be stored non-linguistically if it is to be accessible in an efficient way. Why should this be so?

In order to begin to answer this question we need to turn again to the process involved in becoming an expert. It is not surprising that practice in performing a complex task makes the practitioner more efficient, but studies of expertise show that the increase in efficiency is more puzzling than might at first appear. For example, when people are repeatedly asked to read a page of text upside down they gradually do this faster and faster, but the increase in speed is not continuous, nor does it go on for ever. At first there is a rapid increase in efficiency which continues for a while, then it begins to slow down, until eventually there is no further increase. The shape of the curve of increased efficiency suggests (Johnson-Laird 1988: 170, citing Newell and Rosenbloom 1981) that the process of learning involves the construction of a cognitive apparatus dedicated to cope with this sort of task. The establishment of that apparatus is slow, and while it is in construction there is significant improvement; however once it has been set up no further improvement becomes possible. A chunk or apparatus concerned with a familiar activity has thus come into existence in the brain as a result of repeated practice (Simon 1979: 386 sqq.).

A more complex and much discussed example of what happens when someone becomes an expert comes from studies of master chess players. It has been convincingly argued that expert chess players do not differ from novices (who are not complete beginners) in knowing the rules of chess or in performing such motor tasks as moving one piece without knocking the others down. What seems to distinguish the expert from the novice is not so much an ability to handle complex strategic logico-mathematical rules, but rather the possession, in memory, of an amazingly comprehensive and organised store of total or partial chessboard configurations, which allows the expert to recognise the situation *in an instant* so as to know what should be done next (Dreyfus and Dreyfus 1986: 32–5). However, bearing in mind the example of driving, what is surely happening is that the expert is not just remembering many games but that she has developed through long practice a specific apparatus which *enables her to remember* many games and configurations much more easily and quickly than the non-expert. She has learned how to learn this kind of information. This would explain how the expert can cope, not only with situations which she recognises, but also with situations which are new, so long as they fall within the domain which she has learned to cope with efficiently.

Learning to become an expert would therefore be a matter not simply of remembering many instances, but of constructing a dedicated cognitive mechanism for dealing with instances of a particular kind. Such a mechanism, because it is concerned only with a specific domain of activity, can cope with information relating to that domain of activity remarkably quickly and efficiently, whether this be information about chess-piece configurations, motorway scenarios, or potentially useful areas of forest, and even though the specific cases of chess, motorway or forest have not been previously encountered in exactly that way (Dreyfus and Dreyfus 1986: ch. 1).

If becoming an expert does involve the creation of apparatuses dedicated to handle families of related tasks, then this is surely something which an anthropologist must bear in mind. For what she studies is precisely people coping with familiar yet ever novel situations (Hutchins 1980). It seems reasonable to assume that the construction of dedicated apparatuses for dealing expertly with certain areas of activity is going on in the process of cultural learning of all common practical tasks. Indeed some recent work suggests that learning to become an expert in familiar areas is a necessary preliminary to other types of learning and to being able to cope with the less familiar and less predictable. The reason seems to be partly neurological.

In the case of car driving, it seems that as a person becomes an expert, not only does she drive better, not only does she transform what was once linguistic propositional information into something else, she also seems to employ much less neurological potential in doing the necessary tasks (Schneider and Shiffrin 1977), thereby freeing her for other mental tasks, such as talking on a car phone. Similarly, the extraordinary feats of memory of the chess master seem to be made possible by the efficient packing of information through the use of the expert apparatus for coping with novel situations of play.

Such observations suggest the general conclusion that the ability to learn more is largely a matter of organising what one has already learned in packed chunks so that one has room for the new. Some cognitive scientists have therefore argued that the problems young children have in doing the tasks which, as Piaget showed, only adults can do, stem not from the immaturity of the children's brains, but from the fact that this "packing" has not yet taken place. Once the essential preliminary procedures have been sufficiently organised, their implementation will only require limited neurological capacity, leaving enough "room" for the child to perform further supplementary tasks. These are the tasks which the child had earlier seemed unable to perform; but really the problem was that they could not normally be performed simultaneously with their necessary preliminaries (Smith et al. 1988).

There is therefore considerable evidence that learning is not just a matter of storing received knowledge, as most anthropologists implicitly assume when they equate cultural and individual representations, but that it is a matter of constructing apparatuses for the efficient handling and packing of specific domains of knowledge and practice. Furthermore, as suggested by the case of learning to drive, evidence shows that once these apparatuses are constructed, the operations connected with these specific domains not only *are* non-linguistic but also *must* be non-linguistic if they are to be efficient.[9] It follows that much of the knowledge which anthropologists study necessarily exists in people's heads in a non-linguistic form.

Before proceeding further, an ambiguity in what has been argued so far must be removed. To say that knowledge concerned with the familiar must be non-linguistic could mean one of two things. It could mean simply that this knowledge is not formulated in natural language. On the other hand it could mean something much stronger. It could mean that this knowledge is in no way "language like", that it is not governed by the characteristic sentential logic of natural and computer languages.[10] Here I adopt the stronger of the two alternatives because I believe that the studies on expertise discussed above suggest that the knowledge organised for efficiency in day-to-day practice is not only non-linguistic, but also not language like in that it does not take a sentential logical form. To argue this and to make my argument less negative I now turn to the admittedly controversial assumptions of what has been called "connectionism".

IV

What is particularly interesting for anthropology in connectionism is not so much connectionism itself, but the reasons why a theory like it is necessary. Simply put, a theory such as connectionism is necessary because a sentential linear model of the mind-brain, sometimes called the sentence-logic model (Churchland and Sejnowski 1989), which is broadly similar in form to the semantics of natural language, cannot account for the speed and efficiency with which we perform daily tasks and cope with familiar situations.

The sentence-logic or sentential linear model is intuitively attractive for a number of reasons, and these explain why it is implicit in anthropological theory and was accepted unchallenged for a long time in cognitive psychology. First of all, and probably most significantly, it is *the* model of folk psychology, as anthropologists have nicely demonstrated (D'Andrade 1987). Sentential logical forms are how we think we think. Secondly, sentential logical models work well for the semantics of natural language; and thirdly, they worked well for those metaphors for the mind – the von Neumann or digital computers.

However, these three arguments in favour of the sentence-logic model are very weak. First, folk psychology, whatever the majority of anthropologists

may say, need not, as Churchland and Churchland (1983) point out, be any more valid than folk physics as a basis for scientific accounts. Secondly, what applies to language need not apply to other forms of mental activity. Thirdly, digital computers come nowhere near to doing the jobs we humans can do, and so they must be, in some way, inappropriate as metaphors for the mind-brain.

The case for connectionism is best made by considering an example, and by using this type of example we can see the relevance of the theory for anthropology. Remember the Malagasy peasant. When the man said to his friend, "look over there...that piece of forest would make a good swidden", an unbelievable mental feat seems to have then been achieved by the man addressed. He recalled from long-term memory the complex yet highly flexible mental model or schema "the good swidden", then he conceptualised the piece of forest indicated, taking in information about the vegetation, the slope, the surrounding countryside, the hydrology, the soil, etc., then he matched the two intricate conceptualisations in what could not be just a simple comparison but a highly complex set of transformations. When put in this way, the total task seems Herculean, but in reality even the moderately talented Malagasy farmer would come to some assessment in just a few seconds. Furthermore, this computational feat is no more difficult than many other similar tasks which human beings perform all the time. Why then does such a task appear so impossibly complicated when we think about what it entails? The reason is that we are explaining the behaviour of the Malagasy farmer in terms of our own folk psychology, including a model of language-like semantics. This makes an easy task, which we know the farmer can perform in an instant or two, seem absolutely awesome. There must, indeed, be something wrong about how we think we think.

Connectionism is an alternative theory of thought which makes such commonplace feats as that of our Malagasy farmer possible to envisage. It suggests that we go about the whole process of thought in a quite different way from what we had previously and loosely assumed. The problem with the folk way of describing thought procedures, for example of how a decision is reached, is that we tend to see the activity as a serial process of analysis carried on along a single line by a single processor. For complex yet familiar tasks such processing would be impossibly clumsy and lengthy. Instead, connectionism suggests that we access knowledge, either from memory or as it is conceptualised from perception of the external world, through a number of processing units which work in parallel and feed in information simultaneously. It suggests, too, that the information received from these multiple parallel processors is analysed simultaneously through already existing networks connecting the processors. Only with this multiple parallel processing could complex understandings and operations, like those about the swidden, be achieved as fast as they are. Otherwise, given the conduction velocities and synaptic delays in neurons, it is a physical-cum-biological impossibility for the number of steps required by a logical-sentential model of the mind-brain to be carried out in the time within which even the simplest mental tasks are ordinarily performed. A connectionist brain, on the other hand, could (at least hypothetically) work sufficiently fast (Feldman and Ballard 1982).

It is much too early to say whether connectionism will prove to be an accurate analysis of the working of the brain and, in any case, I am not in a position to be able to evaluate its neurological validity. What matters here, above all, is that the theory offers the kind of challenge to sentential logical models which anthropology requires, and it offers the kind of answers which would cope with the situations we seek to understand.

Support for connectionism does not, however, all come from first principles. Some psychological experimental work seems to confirm the theory (Rumelhart et al. 1986). The fact that computer programs which enable digital computers to work on something like parallel processing seem to be able to get them to do tasks which ordinary digital computers working with classical programs are unable to do, such as reading and reproducing in three dimensions grey shaded images, is also encouraging. There are, however, two other aspects of the theory which make it particularly attractive to the anthropologist.

The first is that connectionism can cope well with what Johnson-Laird (1983: 438–47) called the "provisional" character of mental models, while sentential logical models imply a much greater rigidity which is quite unlike what we find in natural situations. The mental model of "the good swidden" cannot be a checklist of characteristics to be found in a particular configuration or even an example of the kind of "fuzzy" digital models recently proposed. With such fundamentally fixed models the Malagasy farmer would never find the right plot. The model cannot require absolutely any particular characteristic or configuration; just a general flexible theoretical-practical hypothesis. Connectionism can handle this type of "fairly loose" practical-theoretical thinking, which as we saw is also implied in prototype theory, while other theories cannot.

Secondly, a connectionist model can account for the length of the process of becoming an expert at a particular task, a fact which itself is quite a puzzle. With such a model we can understand what would be happening when a person is learning to handle a family of related tasks, such as learning how to learn chess configurations. The person would be creating connected networks dedicated to specific domains of cognition, and procedures which, once set up, could be accessed quickly and efficiently by multiple parallel processing. Such a process for complex tasks, such as becoming a car driver or a chess expert, would require a good deal of packing and quite a bit of connecting, but once the job was done it would be highly efficient.

Since much of culture consists of the performance of these familiar procedures and understandings, connectionism may explain what a great deal of culture in the mind-brain is like. It also explains why this type of culture cannot be either linguistic or "language like". Making the culture efficient requires the construction of connected domain-relevant networks, which by their very nature cannot be stored or accessed through sentential logical forms such as govern natural language. Furthermore, as the discussion of apprenticeship learning shows, it is not even necessary for this type of knowledge ever to be put into words for it to be transmitted from one member of the community to another. The highly efficient non-linear packing in purpose-dedicated domains, formed through the practice of closely related activities, also explains why the transfer of one type of knowledge from one specific domain to another is so difficult. Lave's (1988) observation that there is no carry-over between school maths and coping with mathematical problems in a supermarket may well be due to the fact that the latter are dealt with in such a well-chunked and connected domain that it cannot easily admit knowledge of such a different kind as sentential-logically organised school maths.[11]

V

To claim that much of culture is neither linguistic nor "language like" does not imply that language is unimportant. Nevertheless, contrary to what anthropologists tend to assume, we should see linguistic phenomena as a *part* of culture, most of which is non-linguistic. Instead of taking language for granted, we should see its presence as requiring explanation. I cannot, in the space of this article, review all the circumstances and reasons for the occurrence of language in cultural life. Nonetheless, even here, cognitive science can offer provocative suggestions.

As we have seen, everyday practical actions and knowledge are probably packaged fairly hermetically into networks that take the form presumed by connectionist models. This packaging works very well for quick and efficient operations in familiar domains, but occasionally these networks can also be unpacked into linear sentential sequences which can then be put into words. If such transformations are commonplace, as I believe they are, we should then see culture as partly organised by connectionist networks and partly consisting of information organised by sentential logic, with a fluid transformative boundary between the two.[12]

The process of putting knowledge into words must require such a transformation in the nature of knowledge that the words will then have only a distant relationship to the knowledge referred to. But the process may also involve gains in different areas, as suggested by work, cited earlier in this article, on the transformation of prototype concepts into classical concepts (concepts which can be defined by a checklist of necessary and sufficient features).

For example, the extension of aspects of knowledge, normally chunked in a particular domain, into another domain may be one of the processes that require verbalisation, and such extension may well be linked with the process of innovation, as some of the work on the significance of analogical thinking for creativity suggests

(Sternberg 1985). Indeed, we should perhaps see culture as always balanced between the need for chunking for efficiency, on the one hand, and, on the other, linguistic explicitness which allows, *inter alia*, for innovation and for ideology. With such a perspective we might be able to envisage a kind of general "economy" of knowledge, which social anthropologists could then place in specific social and historical situations.

VI

In mentioning one of the possible reasons for explicitness I am suggesting a direction which would take me far from the limited concerns of this article. But even without going into these issues our discussion of the ways in which knowledge is organized has fundamental implications for anthropology. The first point is that culture is probably a different kind of phenomenon from what it has previously been thought to be, with the result that our understanding of culture has remained partial and superficial. Up to now, anthropology has tried to analyse culture through folk models of thought applicable only to sentential logical knowledge which, as noted, is but a small part of all knowledge. Dreyfus and Dreyfus (1986: 28) point out how social scientists use a "Hamlet model" of decision making where the actor is assumed to weigh up and analyse alternatives in a self-conscious, logical fashion. In this respect it is interesting to note that unlike most of our informants doing familiar tasks, when Hamlet was trying to decide what to do next he was putting his thoughts into words. It is striking how many of the theories which have been popular in anthropology, such as transactionalist theories and other forms of methodological individualism, fall foul of Dreyfus and Dreyfus's strictures.

Then there are methodological implications. If the anthropologist is often attempting to give an account of chunked and non-sentential knowledge in a linguistic medium (writing), and she has no alternative, she must be aware that in so doing she is not reproducing the organisation of the knowledge of the people she studies but is transmuting it into an entirely different logical form. To effect such a transmutation is not impossible – after all we can describe things which are not linguistic. But in the attempt to evoke such knowledge we should avoid stylistic devices which turn attempts at description into "quasi-theory", as was the case with structuralism and transactionalism. Perhaps we should make much more use of description of the way things look, sound, feel, smell, taste and so on – drawing on the realm of bodily experience – simply for heuristic purposes, to remind readers that most of our material is taken from the world of non-explicit expert practice and does not only come from linear, linguistic thought. Above all we should beware the temptations of folk psychology. Folk psychology is indeed a form of competence employed in certain limited circumstances by the people we study, and it is therefore an object of research for anthropologists, but it is not something we want, or need, to carry over into anthropological explanation.

Thus, when our informants honestly say "this is why we do such things", or "this is what this means", or "this is how we do such things", instead of being pleased we should be suspicious and ask what kind of *peculiar* knowledge is this which can take such an explicit, linguistic form?[13] Indeed, we should treat all explicit knowledge as problematic, as a type of knowledge probably remote from that employed in practical activities under normal circumstances.

Of course such conclusions raise the question of how we are ever going to get at this connected, chunked knowledge. But here I believe anthropologists have an advantage over other cognitive scientists in that they already do have a technique advocated by Malinowski but perhaps never followed by him: participant observation. [...]

Notes

1 I do not want to imply that all members of a community need possess all cultural knowledge. Discussions of "distributed cognition" by Cicourel and others suggest that this may not be so.
2 See Sperber (1985) to find this point fully argued.
3 Among American anthropologists who have discussed connectionism are Quinn and Strauss (1989), Hutchins (1988) and D'Andrade (1990).
4 It is true that structuralism, at least in its Lévi-Straussian form, paid attention to memory in that it assumed that the source of structuration was the need to encode information so that it could be kept and retrieved. In retrospect, however, as was shown by Sperber, the structuralist's view of memory was much too simple. In particular it assumed, with other types of cognitive anthropology, that what an individual received from others was stored in the same form as it had been communicated and that all information was equally memorable (Sperber 1985).

The theories of learning implicit in structuralism are even more problematic since they cannot account for the inevitably gradual construction of structured knowledge, a criticism which has been made in a variety of ways by Piaget (1968), Turner (1973), Sperber (1985) and myself (1985). Admittedly, such writers as Bourdieu (1972) have tried to remedy this situation, but in his case with a theory of learning *habitus* which is psychologically vague and which, because of its reintroduction of the notion of individual "rational" choice, runs into some of the difficulties which I go on to discuss.

5 Holland and Quinn (1987: 19) draw attention to the significance of these for our understanding of culture.
6 Work on deaf and dumb children also seems to show that advanced conceptual thought does not require language (Petitto 1987; 1988). I am grateful to L. Hirschfeld for pointing out the significance of this work for my argument.
7 Although I am relying extensively on Dreyfus and Dreyfus's characterisation of expertise (1986), I do this to reach quite different conclusions.
8 I am told that in Norway, although the normal driving test involves both a practical section and a question and answer section, some people seem totally unable to do the language part of the test, and so a more difficult practical test has been devised for them which eliminates the need to do the language part. There is apparently no evidence that people who have obtained their test in this way are worse drivers than the others.
9 The point has already been made by Schank and Abelson (1977).
10 After all, it is possible to argue, as Fodor does, that although thought is not a matter of speaking to oneself silently, it still is ultimately "language like" and involves series of "grammatically" (though not the grammar of the surface structure of natural languages) linked representations and propositions. This suggestion enables Fodor to talk of a "language of thought", though it might be better to say a "quasi-language" of thought" (Fodor 1987).

11   The fact that people who are unable to perform Wason's task (a logical test performed under laboratory conditions with two-sided cards) when faced by his cards can do it when it is reproduced in a context familiar to them points to similar conclusions (Johnson-Laird and Wason 1977). See the discussion of this point in Dreyfus and Dreyfus (1986: 19).

12   Such a reconciliation of rule and representation models with connectionist ones has been proposed by Bechtel (1990).

13   These explicitly linguistic forms may have different relations to knowledge (see Barth 1990).

References

Abelson, R. 1981. Psychological status of the script concept. *American Psychologist* 36, 715–29.

Anderson, J.R. 1976. *The architecture of memory.* Cambridge, MA: Harvard University Press.

Atran, S. 1990. *Cognitive foundations of natural history.* Cambridge: University Press.

Barth, F. 1990. The guru and the conjurer: transactions in knowledge and the shaping of culture in Southeast Asia and Melanesia. *Man* (N.S.) 25, 640–53.

Bechtel, W. 1990. Connectionism and the philosophy of mind: an overview. In *Mind and cognition* (ed.) W. Lycan. Oxford: Blackwell.

Bloch, M. 1985. From cognition to ideology. In *Power and knowledge: anthropological and sociological approaches* (ed.) R. Fardon. Edinburgh: Scottish Academic Press.

Bourdieu, P. 1972. *Esquisse d'une théorie de la pratique.* Paris: Droz.

Bowerman, M. 1977. The acquisition of word meaning: an investigation in some current concepts. In *Thinking: readings in cognitive science* (eds.) P. Johnson-Laird and P. Wason. Cambridge: University Press.

Brown, R. 1973. *A first language: the early stages.* Harmondsworth: Penguin.

Churchland, P. M. and P. S. Churchland 1983. Stalking the wild episteme. *Nous* 17, 5–18 (reprinted in *Mind and cognition* (ed.) W. L. Lycan. Oxford: Blackwell, 1990).

Churchland, P.S. and T. Sejnowski 1989. Neural representation and neural computation. In *Neural connections, mental computations* (eds.) L. Nadel et al. Cambridge, Mass.: MIT Press.

D'Andrade, R. 1987. A folk model of the mind. In *Cultural models in language and thought* (eds.) D. Holland and N. Quinn. Cambridge: University Press.

D'Andrade, R. 1990. Some propositions about the relations between culture and cognition. In *Cultural psychology* (eds.) J. Stigler et al. Cambridge: University Press.

Dreyfus, H. and S. Dreyfus 1986. *Mind over machine: the power of intuition and expertise in the era of the computer.* Oxford: Blackwell.

Feldman, J. and D. Ballard 1982. Connectionist models and their properties. *Cognitive Science* 6, 205–54.

Fillmore, C. 1975. An alternative to checklist theories of meaning. In *Proceedings of the First Annual Meeting of the Berkeley Linguistic Society,* 123–31.

Fodor, J.A. 1987. *Psychosemantics.* Cambridge, MA: MIT Press.

Goody, E. 1978. Towards a theory of questions. In *Questions and politeness: strategies in social interaction* (ed.) E. Goody. Cambridge: University Press.

Haudricourt, A.-G. 1968. La technologie culturelle: essai de méthodologie. In *Ethnologie générale* (ed.) J. Poirier. Paris: Pléiade.

Holland, D. and N. Quinn (eds.) 1987. *Cultural models in language and thought.* Cambridge: University Press.

Hutchins, E. 1980. *Culture and inference: a Trobriand case study.* Cambridge, MA: Harvard University Press.

Hutchins, E. 1988. Where's the expertise in expert navigation? Paper delivered at the annual meeting of the American Anthropological Association at Phoenix, Arizona.

Johnson-Laird, P. 1983. *Mental models: towards a cognitive science of language, inference and consciousness.* Cambridge: University Press.

Johnson-Laird, P. 1988. *The computer and the mind: an introduction to cognitive science.* London: Fontana.

Johnson-Laird and P. Wason 1977. A theoretical analysis of insight into a reasoning task. In *Thinking: readings in cognitive science* (eds.) P. Johnson-Laird and P. Wason. Cambridge: University Press.

Keil, F.C. and N. Batterman 1984. A characteristic-to-defining shift in the development of word meaning. *Journal of Verbal Learning and Verbal Behavior.* 23, 221–36.

Lave, J. 1988. *Cognition in practice.* Cambridge: University Press.

Lave, J. 1990. The culture of acquisition and the practice of understanding. In *Cultural psychology* (eds.) J. Stigler et al. Cambridge: University Press.

Leroi-Gourhan, A. 1943. *Evolution et techniques.* Paris: PUF.

Malinowski, B. 1935. *The language of magic and gardening (Coral Gardens and Their Magic vol. 2).* London: Allen & Unwin.

Markham, E. M. and J. Seibert 1976. Classes and collections: internal organisation and resulting holistic properties. *Cognitive Psychology* 8, 561–77.

Mauss, M. 1936. Les techniques du corps. *Journal de Psychologie* 32, nos. 3–4.

Newell, A. and P. S. Rosenbloom 1981. Mechanisms of skill acquisition and the law of practice. In *Cognitive skills and their acquisition* (ed.) J. R. Anderson. Hillsdale, NJ: Erlbaum.

Petitto, L. A. 1987. On the autonomy of language and gesture: evidence from the acquisition of personal pronouns in American sign language. *Cognition* 27, 1–52.

Petitto, L. A. 1988. Language and the prelinguistic child. In *The development of language and language researchers: essays in honor of Roger Brown* (ed.) F. S. Kessel. Hillsdale, NJ: Erlbaum.

Piaget, J. 1968. *Le structuralisme.* Paris: PUF.

Quinn, N. and C. Strauss 1989. A cognitive cultural anthropology. Paper prepared for the session on "Assessing Developments in Anthropology" of the American Anthropological Association Annual Meetings, 1989.

Rosch, E. 1977. Classification of real world objects: origins and representations in cognition. In *Thinking: readings in cognitive science* (eds.) P. Johnson-Laird and P. Wason. Cambridge: University Press.

Rosch, E. 1978. Cognitive representations of semantic categories. *Journal of Experimental Psychology* 104, 192–223.

Rumelhart, D., G. Hinton and J. McClelland 1986. A general framework for parallel distributed processing. In *Explorations in the microstructure of cognition*, vol. 1. (eds.) D. Rumelhart and J. McClelland. Cambridge, MA: MIT Press.

Schank, R. and R. Abelson 1977. *Scripts, plans, goals and understanding.* Hillsdale, NJ: Erlbaum.

Schneider, W. and R. Shiffrin 1977. Controlled and automatic human information processing, 1: detection, search and attention. *Psychological Review* 84, 1–66.

Simon, H. 1979. *Models of thought.* New Haven: Yale University Press.

Smith, E. E. 1988. Concepts and thought. In *The psychology of human thought* (eds.) R. J. Sternberg and E. E. Smith. Cambridge: University Press.

Smith, L., M. Sera and B. Gattuso 1988. The development of thinking. In *The psychology of human thought* (eds.) R. J. Sternberg and E. E. Smith. Cambridge: University Press.

Sperber, D. 1985. Anthropology and psychology: towards an epidemiology of representations. *Man* (NS) 20, 73–89.

Sperber, D. and D. Wilson 1986. *Relevance: communication and cognition.* Oxford: Blackwell.

Sternberg, R. J. 1985. *Beyond IQ: a triadic theory of human intelligence.* Cambridge: University Press.

Turner, T. 1973. Piaget's structuralism. *American Anthropologist* 75, 351–73.

Tyler, S. (ed.) 1969. *Cognitive anthropology.* New York: Holt, Rinehart & Winston.

Winch, P. 1958. *The idea of a social science.* London: Routledge & Kegan Paul.

SECTION 7

Cognition, Psychology, and Neuroanthropology

22

Towards an Integration of Ethnography, History and the Cognitive Science of Religion

Harvey Whitehouse

Scientific explanations and interpretive accounts of human behaviour, including religious behaviour, are different kinds of enterprise. It is tempting to think that although the questions asked by both scientists and humanist scholars look similar, they are actually incommensurate. [...] Nothing could be further from the truth.

Cognitive scientists are typically interested in fundamentally the same problems that perplex interpretive anthropologists, as well as historians and others. In the scenario involving a professor caught in a girls' dormitory, all would be eager to know about the professor's motivations and intentions. The ethnographer or historian might seek to contextualize the professor's own account of his intentions within a web of locally and temporally variable values (e.g. whether this event occurred on a California campus in the 1960s or in a twenty-first century theological seminary). The question of how the professor's behaviour is judged in the prevailing cultural context (e.g. one that celebrates free love or one that counsels moral censure or litigation), is unquestionably relevant to understanding his predicament. But the cognitive scientist urges us to heed an *additional* set of questions. For instance (and this is

only an example), what kinds of evolved human capacities govern processes of reputation management? How are these brought to bear when a transgression occurs?

[...] [H]umans have to make immensely subtle calculations about such matters, resulting in a glorious repertoire of strategies for managing their reputations. Recent studies suggest, for example, that confession is widely used as a means of damage limitation in circumstances when exposure is a serious risk, based on the intuition that punishment will be less severe if the transgressor displays remorse. The greater the risk of exposure and the more serious its consequences the stronger the urge to confess becomes (at least by the statistical measures used in these kinds of studies). Consequently, meaning and context *matter*, even for cognitive scientists—in fact, *especially* for cognitive scientists. [...]

If cognitive and interpretive anthropologists are really studying the same things, as I think they are, then the crunch question is whether the kinds of answers they provide could be *integrated*. Two extreme views on this matter may be distinguished. Hardline cognitivists maintain that conscious thought is merely a surface expression of

From H. Whitehouse and J. Laidlaw (eds.), *Religion, Anthropology and Cognitive Science*. Durham, NC: Carolina Academic Press, 2007, pp. 247–80 (with cuts). Reprinted with permission of Carolina Academic Press.

Anthropology in Theory: Issues in Epistemology, Second Edition. Edited by Henrietta L. Moore and Todd Sanders.
© 2014 John Wiley & Sons, Inc. Published 2014 by John Wiley & Sons, Inc.

processes outside our awareness, and that the latter processes shape and constrain our consciousness whereas it seldom (if ever) happens the other way around [...]. For this reason asking people about their intentions or the meanings of their experiences and observations elicits no more than cryptic clues to the real causes of their behaviour. We ignore these clues at our peril, to be sure, but they do not constitute explanations in themselves. Hardline interpretivists insist that meanings and reasons are only explainable in terms of other meanings and reasons, whether those of informants (the ethnographic gambit) or of the interpreter (the hermeneutic gambit). Both forms of hardline interpretivism constitute a circular strategy (amusingly dubbed "the hermeneutic vortex") that accomplishes ever more elaborate stories but forecloses the possibility of ever explaining anything. An alternative to both extremes is available, based on a certain amount of compromise but also a large dose of messy-world empirical enquiry.

There is now a mounting body of evidence that explicit representations, including many (if not all) the things go to make a religious tradition, are influenced by implicit cognition, about which we can only learn indirectly, through experimental research (both laboratory-based and naturalistic). Such findings have opened up the possibility of two major types of contribution to core anthropological problems. The first type seeks to contribute to an explanation for cross-culturally recurrent features of religious thinking and behaviour, regardless of the specificities of local contexts and histories. Such a strategy proceeds on the basis that, all else being equal, certain kinds of religious concepts (for instance) will be more widespread in human societies than others. Such claims pertain to statistical patterns of recurrence in the ethnographic record as a whole rather than to individual cases. The second potential contribution from this quarter, however, considers how specified environmental conditions bias the activation of different types and configurations of cognitive mechanisms in predictable ways. How does the presence of a particular institutional system trigger or inhibit implicit thinking, overt behaviour and consequent patterns of cultural transmission? The latter question (which of course could be fractionated in a wide range of narrower variants), encompasses our

concerns about Putnam's unfortunate Professor, whose individual mental states and behaviour can only be fully understood in its wider context. While a generalizing approach may accurately quantify the likelihood of intended sexual transgressions on the part of half-naked men in girls' dormitories, the more detail we provide about the context in which such escapades occur the more precisely we can predict the psychological states and behavioural choices of particular would-be transgressors. Lawyers do it. So do anthropologists. But on the whole they do it by appeal to more or less implicit assumptions, stereotypes, or fashionable interpretive frameworks rather than with reference to testable theories of the way people actually think.

Implicit cognitive biases, even if situated in richly specified sociocultural contexts, may turn out to be only part of the story, however. Contrary to some cognitivist hardliners, I would argue that conscious reasoning and reflection also influence the way we behave, in turn shaping and constraining processes of cultural innovation and transmission. Experimental psychology provides just a fraction of the evidence needed to understand such processes. We must look also to the data commanded by ethnographers and historians, among others who catalogue the statements and deeds of our fellow human beings in their historically specific cultural habitats. For this reason, anthropologists must be part of the explanatory endeavour, in on the ground floor. Although we cannot (yet) measure the relative importance of implicit and explicit cognition in patterns of social behaviour and cultural efflorescence that is the direction in which I believe we need to go. [...]

Implicit Cognitive Constraints on Religious Transmission

A substantial and growing literature in the cognitive science of religion argues that religious transmission is shaped and constrained by implicit (unconscious) cognitive processes. A central feature of this approach is that it seeks to fractionate religious thinking and behaviour into myriad different components that are explainable in terms of a finite array of relatively discrete cognitive mechanisms. Sometimes construed as "modules", or at least as "domain-specific" systems, [...] the main evidence [...] comes from experimental research by developmental and cognitive psychologists (and to some extent also from neuroscientists and clinical psychologists). The strategy is to ask what effect these implicit mechanisms have on the transmission of culture, for instance in the area of religious thinking and behaviour. And what this requires, in practice, is a piecemeal approach to the phenomena of interest.

Religious behaviour is extremely complex, involving a huge diversity of cognitive systems. Nobody could study all of those things at once. [...] Rather than asking, for instance, "how are rituals in general transmitted?" cognitive scientists home in on some strikingly recurrent features of ritual behaviour around the world (e.g. the tendency to repeat nonsensical verbal formulae) and try to explain each component more or less in isolation, before moving on to explain other aspects of the same ritual behaviour [...]. Scholars trained in the grand theoretical traditions of Marxism, psychoanalysis, semiotics, or phenomenology may assume that theories of religion must always take the form of *general theories of religion as a whole*. Indeed, it may seem absurd to reduce religion to one puny little mechanism in the mind. But such reactions belie a basic misunderstanding. The aim is to build up a picture of the multiple causes of a huge variety of different components of, for instance, ritual behaviour *before* attempting to declare that we have something approaching a "theory of ritual" as such.

[...]

It might be argued that if we were to persist in this type of exercise for long enough we would end up with an explanation for the ritual of the Pomio Kivung religious movement in 1980s Papua New Guinea, and all other rituals that exhibit similar features. I have my doubts about that, however. Although we could certainly do a great deal more to explain our Kivung ritual [...] by pursuing this strategy to its limits, we will eventually discover that there are important features of the observed behaviour that cannot be understood in that way, either because the approach is too narrow to encompass all the relevant facts (a problem of lack of comprehensiveness of the approach) or because the approach

excludes more creative aspects of cognition responsible for the variability of thinking and behaviour from one cultural tradition to the next (a problem of lack of particularity of the approach). Both problems have always haunted the hardline cognitivist approach to explaining culture. But I will argue that they can also be overcome if we expand our conception of cognition to encompass processes that are often *conscious* and always *historically constituted*. [...]

Cognition and Religious Variation: Where Ethnography, History, and Science Meet

Hardline *interpretivism* envisages culture as an unstable (continuously contested, mediated, disrupted) network of meanings and inter-subjective states that hovers somewhat mysteriously above (or at least beyond) all other ontological levels of reality (e.g. the psychological or the biological) and is certainly irreducible to them. But I favour an alternative view of culture. We learn about other people's thoughts and feelings through empathetic dialogue and observation. Over time, we can build up such a rich understanding of other people's construals of the world that they seem to assume a systemic quality more or less tentatively generalizable to others in their community, marking the group off from others living in different places or historical periods. The challenge for ethnographers and historians, it seems to me, is to characterize accurately such patterns among individuals and populations, present and past. Explaining how the patterns came into being certainly entails close tracking of the way they change over time or are spread through the movement of people and things across space. But [...] for people to invent or spread their ways of thinking to others [...] requires tools – not just physical artefacts, like books and buildings, but also mental tools, such as the ability to acquire new concepts and to recognize their potential applications. Such abilities certainly include the kinds of domain-specific cognitive mechanisms discussed in the last section and understanding such mechanisms takes us a long way in explaining the behaviour of most mammals, ourselves included. But the case of humans is complicated by the fact that we have an extraordinary capacity for innovation and learning and therefore for the transmission of cumulative bodies of *acquired knowledge*. Only some of our psychological mechanisms confer this advantage, as we shall see, but they do so in ways that have consequences for the operation of all the kinds of mechanisms discussed above.

[...]

Conclusion

Social and cultural anthropologists who are interested in explaining religion have much to learn from cognitive approaches. The evidence that our minds are composed of numerous specialized tools for handling different types of information is supporting increasingly plausible claims about the shaping and constraining effects of cognition on the invention and spread of culture in general, and religion in particular. So far, the contributions of cognitive scientists have focused rather heavily on a small set of domain-specific cognitive specializations [...] in generating *universal* features of religious thinking and behaviour. Children, it now seems, cannot be raised to believe just anything; nor can adults be converted to any type of ideological system. Religions must exploit certain fundamental universal human intuitive biases and predilections if they are to get a foothold. The cognitivist project has certainly been valuable in explaining why many features of religious thinking and behaviour are much the same everywhere.

But religions also *vary* significantly from one place to the next. They differ not only their myriad details but also at the level of what we might call a "middle range" of generalization. For instance, patterns of communication and exchange with putative supernatural beings are readily grouped into loose families of similar types of acts (prayers, rites of passage, sacrificial rituals, and so on) that receive strikingly different emphasis from one religious tradition to the next. Likewise, systems of belief exhibit highly contrasting cosmological, theological, ethical, and aesthetic predilections and biases. [...] This kind of variation, which has been the traditional focus of *interpretive* approaches to the study of religion, is salient for the very obvious practical reason that apparent differences between religious traditions provide a basis for coalitional thinking and contestations of identity. But it may also be salient theoretically, insofar as we are able to devise plausible explanations for varying patterns of practice, belief, scale, and structure in the world's diverse religions.

I have argued that the most promising explanatory strategies will be those that combine cognitivist, ethnographic, and historiographical perspectives on religion. The theory of modes of religiosity is one such approach. According to this theory, any universal tendencies towards certain types of religious thinking and behaviour are heavily shaped and constrained by socially and historically constituted prior patterns of innovation and transmission. But, at the same time, those patterns of innovation and transmission depend upon the presence of cognitive systems capable of forging novel ideas (and networks of ideas) and of "fixing" those ideas in collective memory. Such processes are clearly influenced by the extent to which knowledge can be distributed and combined among specialists and by the ways in which external mnemonics (such as inscribing practices or commemorative artefacts and *aides memoires*) are used and elaborated. The theory of modes of religiosity focuses on just some (arguably significant) variables influencing the creation and storage of religious ideas, specifically such factors as frequency of transmission and level of arousal in the area of ritualized behaviour. But we are (or should be) witnessing only the beginning, and not the end, of a new synthesis of perspectives.

Reference

Bering, J. M. and Shackelford, T. K. (in press). "Consciousness, intentionality, and human psychological adaptations" in *Theoria et Historia Scientiarum*.

23

Linguistic and Cultural Variables in the Psychology of Numeracy

Charles Stafford

It is sometimes said that anthropologists specialize in looking at human experience in very fine, even "microscopic", detail. Perhaps this is true in some poetic sense or by comparison with, say, macroeconomists. Anthropologists do, of course, sometimes focus on the tiny details of rituals, language use, everyday life, and so on. [...]

When I started reading the literature on numerical cognition a few years ago (as background for a project on numeracy and economic agency in China), it struck me that experimental psychologists are the ones who *really* do fine-grained research. For instance, an article by Starkey, Spelke, and Gelman [...] (1990) rests largely on evidence about the reactions of 6- to 9-month old infants to displays of either two or three objects. The key question is whether or not their staring time [...] will increase when the number of objects is changed from two to three, and back again. Would it ever occur to an anthropologist to consider *infant staring time* in such meticulous detail? Such things are surely well below our radar. [...]

Needless to say, if experimental psychology seems fine-grained and rigorous by comparison with anthropology, it is partly because it is exper-

imental. Unlike social and cultural anthropologists, psychologists spend much of their time and energy devising experimental protocols in order – eventually – to gather evidence related to tightly defined hypotheses (e.g. about the ability of human infants, at specific stages of cognitive development, to take in and process numerical information). This lends a precise and exacting nature to their work. But they are also prepared, more prosaically, to consider human life and thought in terms of manageable chunks. Instead of asking questions such as "How do Chinese children learn to be good sons and daughters?" [...] they might ask questions such as "How do Chinese children learn to count to three?" This scaling down (which does *not* mean that the questions at stake are any less important) makes it possible for them to be more precise about the evidence needed to sustain particular types of psychological claims; or perhaps one should say that the drive to sustain particular types of psychological claims is what leads, in the first place, to the scaling down. [...] [A]s a general rule, psychologists seem quite happy – for better or worse – to eliminate variables and/or control them out of the analytical/experimental frame in

From *Journal of the Royal Anthropological Institute* s1 (2008), S128–S141. Reprinted with permission of John Wiley & Sons UK.

order to have a manageable topic of research. [...] By contrast, anthropologists seem preternaturally inclined – for better or worse – to try to take "everything" into account.

In spite of these marked differences in outlook and approach towards evidence and scale (which, of course, are far from the only differences between anthropologists and psychologists [...]), there have been a growing number of calls in recent years for increased co-operation between the two disciplines (e.g. Astuti, Solomon & Carey 2004; Bloch 1998; Cole 1996; Hirschfeld 2000; Shore 1996). In simple terms, it has been suggested that psychologists can no longer ignore, or gently side-step, the historical and socio-cultural foundations of human knowledge, while anthropologists must surely now accept (*pace* Durkheim) that many of their most cherished topics of research – emotion, memory, identity, and so on – are intrinsically psychological in nature. Calls for co-operation are presumably a good thing, but will our basic orientations towards research scale and selectivity stand in the way? Are practitioners of either discipline actually going to cede methodological (as opposed to conceptual) ground in order to achieve a *rapprochement*? [...]

Here I want to consider these questions with reference to work on human numeracy. This is an area of individual cognitive development in which, after all, the significance of cultural and linguistic variables is beyond doubt (cf. Butterworth 1999; Dehaene 1999). Lacking expertise in the variety of human cultures and languages, psychologists of numeracy might reasonably turn to anthropologists for help. But the psychology of numeracy is also a field of study in which, to a large extent, the most relevant data turn out to be very micro indeed, at least when seen from an anthropological perspective. [...] I want to ask how much cultural evidence psychologists are prepared to take on board, and also to what extent anthropologists are prepared – or even able – to provide psychologists with the types of (stripped-down) evidence they want or need. My sense is that practitioners in both disciplines are committed, for the most part without even thinking about it, to their customary scales of research. In turn, this may make it difficult (good intentions notwithstanding) for them to engage seriously with evidence from the other side – which probably seems, respectively, either

much too "big" to be useful or much too "small" to be interesting. I will suggest, however, that even relatively minor concessions in either direction can pay dividends.

In a fascinating article in *Science*, the psychologist Peter Gordon (2004) has recently discussed experiments he conducted amongst an Amazonian people, the Pirahã, who have an unusually limited vocabulary for numbers. To be more precise, they have terms which *can* be used to mean "one" and "two", but even these are not used very consistently by them. Beyond "two", there is simply an expression for "many". [...] In the absence of counting words, how well will these people perform on non-verbal numerical tasks, such as matching up sets of objects? In some respects, it is not very difficult to find out – although Gordon did have to spend a significant amount of time in Amazonia in order to do so. The results suggest, in brief, that the Pirahã are reasonably good at dealing with tasks involving very small numbers – one, two, sometimes three – whereas beyond this they lose the ability to be precise. However, if imprecision is allowed, they can also deal fairly well with larger quantities by drawing, Gordon claims, on the innate human ability to make "analog magnitude representations" of a rather fuzzy kind. Language, he concludes, is what you need in order to represent large numerical values exactly (2004: 498).

However, Gordon's data are already being used to support very different theories about the role of language in the development of numeracy. Gelman and Butterworth cite the Pirahã case along with material from another Amazonian people, the Mundurukú, to support their claim (contra Gordon) that "numerical concepts have an ontogenetic origin and a neural basis that are *independent of language*" (2005: 6, emphasis added [...]). They stress that the peoples in question, in spite of having very restricted number vocabularies, are able to cope surprisingly well with large numerical approximations.

At stake in this debate, of course, are fundamental questions about the role of language and culture in human thought, and about our ability to think, if you like, without words. But in spite of these grand themes it might be noted [...] the crucial experimental evidence (e.g. "The amazing result was that both groups succeeded on non-verbal number tasks that used displays representing values...as large as 80") and the crucial descriptive evidence (e.g. "The Pirahã do not even use the words for 1 and 2 consistently") are cited by Gelman and Butterworth in a bracingly stripped-down fashion that would rarely be encountered in reading anthropology (2005: 8–9). Of course, this is partly a matter of writing and publishing conventions – after all, how much can one say about language or culture in an article restricted to four or five pages, in which details of experimental protocols and results are meant to be the principal focus? But it is also surely a matter of intellectual priorities. At least on the surface, it seems that, for experimental psychologists, one does not need to know and/or say very much about Pirahã life – even about the bits of their life that relate directly to numeracy and numerical practices – in order to debate their numerical cognition. More specifically, although everyone (including Gordon, Gelman, and Butterworth) appears to be in no doubt that culture and language may sometimes matter a great deal, cultural and linguistic *evidence* typically enters these scientific debates in highly circumscribed form.

[...] Gordon, for his part, provides brief descriptions of everyday numeracy practices among the Pirahã (such as their rather incompetent use of fingers as an enumeration aid), and his experiments were certainly intended to have ecological validity – that is, to take serious account of Pirahã culture and the flow of ordinary life amongst the people with whom he lived for some weeks.

But again: how much scope is there, within psychology, genuinely to incorporate evidence about the "innumerable differences" between cultures, or indeed non-experimental evidence of any kind? In an on-line discussion which followed the publication of his *Science* article, Gordon complains about the difficulty of doing precisely this. He says that his original manuscript contained some potentially very important information about Pirahã numeracy, more specifically about their ability/inability to learn numbers in a *different* (i.e. non-Pirahã) language when presented with the opportunity. In brief, another scholar reported to him that a few years ago an attempt had been made to teach Portuguese numbers to Pirahã villagers. It seems that "[t]he adults had a horrible time with it, the children had no

problems (but were later told not to continue [learning/using the numbers] by adults)". Gordon points out that he had originally included this information in a footnote to his paper, but was "rebuked by a reviewer who said that such anecdotal evidence does not belong in the pages of *Science*". (Note that what is rejected here is not "macro" evidence, as such, but rather non-experimental evidence. [...]).

[...]

However, given Gordon's reliance, in the end, on standard research protocols, does this background noise about cultural particularities, the perils of real life, and so forth, really make any difference? He certainly stresses that his conclusions are informed not only by the experiments but also by his direct experience of the Pirahã way of life. Significantly, they are further informed by the "background of continuous and extensive immersion in the Pirahã culture" of the two scholars who made the project possible in the first place: Daniel and Keren Everett (Gordon 2004: 496). After all, Daniel Everett, a linguistic anthropologist, has been living and working with the tribe for over twenty years. Who better to give the imprimatur of holistic cultural understanding to Gordon's tightly focused experimental work?

But while Gordon must have anticipated criticisms from fellow psychologists, recent comments from Everett – the man who introduced him to the Pirahã – will perhaps have been more surprising. Everett says that Gordon's very general conclusions about Pirahã numeracy are "likely correct", but he also says, rather confusingly, that he disagrees with them – pointing out that Gordon's experimental design was culturally insensitive, making the Pirahã do precisely the kinds of things they hate to do.

[...]

[...] He claims not only that they lack number terms but also that, among other things, they lack colour terms, that they have "the simplest pronoun inventory known", that they lack creation myths and fiction, that they have "the simplest kinship system yet documented", that they have no "individual or collective memory of more than two generations past", that they do not draw or produce art of any kind, and that they have "one of the simplest material cultures documented" (Everett 2005: 621–34). These extremely surprising features of Pirahã life, Everett suggests, are all the product of one thing: a culture that makes Pirahã talk only about "nonabstract subjects which fall within the immediate experience of interlocutors" (2005: 621). It is this – according to Everett – that constrains the development or adoption by them of linguistic or cultural features (such as telling stories about the past or using relative tenses) that are found in most human societies.

[...]

[...] [L]ike a true anthropologist, he also says that language (including the language of number) must be studied in the context of its use; that one should be extremely cautious about "testing" people through procedures which are alien to their way of life; and, perhaps most importantly, that human societies and human thought are highly synthetic – everything is embedded in, and connected to, everything else. [...] [I]f you really want to understand Pirahã numeracy, Everett seems to be saying to Gordon, you need to visit them over the course of twenty years and collect evidence about kinship, whisky-buying, trading, sexual relations, and so on: that is, you need to collect evidence about "everything". [...] By contrast, Gordon, of course, simply wanted to know if the Pirahã, lacking number words, could or could not do some simple non-verbal numerical tasks such as matching two objects to two objects. This is an empirical question, and Gordon (to his everlasting credit) went to a great deal of trouble to generate what is, in fact, a rather minimal and tightly focused data set in order to try to answer it. It is presumably this evidence which will be taken up and debated by other psychologists – not the fine details of Pirahã social life, and certainly not Everett's radical holism.

[...]

[...] I would like to conclude this discussion by noting two rather common sins, as I see it, on the anthropological side – sins which relate very directly to the overarching topics of evidence and scale addressed in this collection. The first is the use of anthropological holism as an excuse for avoiding detail, and therefore avoiding saying anything falsifiable. By holding that all things are interconnected, we tend to make falsification of our claims (e.g. via experimentation) more or less impossible. The second is the romanticization of anthropological research, and more specifically

the idea that it has an ecological validity unmatched by other disciplines – this in spite of the fact that fieldwork is, of course, a dramatic intervention in the lives of our informants. Would it really be such an unnatural imposition for anthropologists to examine the micro, as psychologists do, using experimental techniques?

Bearing this in mind, and inspired by my reading in (micro) cognitive psychology, during a recent period of fieldwork in rural Taiwan I carried out a pilot project [...]. Very briefly: I showed subjects a drawing of a street scene in which certain types of information was embedded: colour (e.g. the colour of a girl's dress), written language (e.g. words on a street sign), explicit number (by which I mean numbers written out, e.g. numbers on a licence plate), and implicit number (by which I mean objects that could be counted, e.g. birds in the sky). Subjects were given fifteen seconds to look at the drawing, after which it was taken away and they were asked a series of questions about the content – such as "What colour is the dog?", "What is the number on the house?", "How many trees are there?", and so on. A sample of respondents from the UK, approximately matched in terms of age and educational level, provided a control group for the research.

My hypothesis was that the Taiwanese subjects – having been enculturated into the Chinese way of thinking of numerical information as having an intrinsic relevance, regardless of context – would be more likely than UK subjects to notice and recall correctly the numbers embedded in the drawing. In fact, the results (based on this very limited pilot project) showed no such thing: the UK subjects were marginally more likely to get the numbers right. Of course, this outcome might be explained in many ways, including the possibility that my research design was completely wrong, or – just as likely – that my hypothesis was an implausible one to start with.

And yet, the simple fact of attempting to prove, through quantification, a general claim I was making about Chinese numeracy was extremely productive for me in a range of ways. One rather simple point is that the drawings proved to be a good prompt for general discussions. The task facing my friends in the village was a completely unexpected one, and it provoked them into saying interesting, sometimes very telling, things about numbers and numerical skills. [...] [It also] forced me to think – in ways which anthropologists are often *not* forced to think – about exactly what I was trying to say or claim about numbers in China. For instance, the task called on subjects to remember numbers, and from this I would infer whether or not they think that numerical information is, by default, important. But this raises the complex question of whether *remembering* something is the same thing as attributing *relevance* to it. Also, although my hypothesis was that numbers would be shown to have "intrinsic relevance", a more likely scenario (as I suspected from the outset) is that numerical relevance is highly context-specific. This raises the question of which contextual effects would elicit more attention to numbers, and whether or not these effects, which are very hard to reproduce artificially, could be tested in an ecologically valid way.

In short, simply using the pilot project as a heuristic device had the effect of improving my thinking, as an anthropologist, about Chinese numerical culture and how it is learned and used. This involved scaling down – giving up a little bit on anthropological holism, and trying to be more precise about how my claims and observations could, or could not, be supported.

[...] To be an expert in social and cultural anthropology is, for the most part, to possess a kind of encyclopaedic store of evidence – historical, ethnographic, anecdotal – about a particular group of people. The risk for psychologists is that, caught up in the activity of eliminating variables and restricting scale, they might not see the forest for the trees. [...] The risk for anthropologists, caught up in the activity of accumulating variables and expanding scale, is that they might not understand any of the trees very well, and simply wander around the forest making claims that can never be falsified.

References

Astuti, R., G. Solomon & S. Carey 2004. *Constraints on conceptual development: a case study of the acquisition of folkbiological and folksociological knowledge in Madagascar.* (Monographs of the Society for Research in Child Development **69: 3**, vii–135).

Bloch, M. 1998. *How we think they think.* Boulder, Colo.: Westview Press.

Butterworth, B. 1999. *The mathematical brain.* London: Macmillan.

Cole, M. 1996. *Cultural psychology: a once and future discipline.* Cambridge, Mass.: Harvard University Press.

Dehaene, S. 1999. *The number sense: how the mind creates mathematics.* London: Penguin.

Everett, D. L. 2005. Cultural constraints on grammar and cognition in Pirahã. *Current Anthropology* **46**, 621–46.

Gelman, R. & B. Butterworth 2005. Number and language: how are they related? *Trends in Cognitive Science* **9**, 6–10.

Gordon, P. 2004. Numerical cognition without words: evidence from Amazonia. *Science* **306**, 496–9.

Hirschfeld, L. 2000. The inside story. *American Anthropologist* **102**, 620–9.

Shore, B. 1996. *Culture in mind.* New York: Oxford University Press.

Starkey, P., E. Spelke & R. Gelman 1990. Numerical abstraction by human infants. *Cognition* **36**, 97–127.

24

Subjectivity

T. M. Luhrmann

[...] "Subjectivity" is a term loosely used by anthropologists to refer to the shared inner life of the subject, to the way subjects feel, respond, experience. In some general sense, everyone agrees with the definition Holland and Leander use to open a special issue of *Ethos*: "we think about subjectivities as actors' thoughts, sentiments and embodied sensibilities, and, especially, their sense of self and self-world relations" (2004: 127). The term evokes the psychological dimension of human life. But that is not all it evokes for many anthropologists, and this something more is the reason they use the term in preference to the drier, more empirical "psychology", collective or otherwise. [...]

[...] [I]n her [...] thoughtful attempt to grapple with the concept, in "Subjectivity and Cultural Critique", recently published in *Anthropological Theory* (2005), Sherry Ortner [chapter 18, this volume, p. 186] begins with the basic psychology-and-culture definition: "by subjectivity I will mean the ensemble of modes of perception, affect, thought, desire, fear, and so forth that animate acting subjects. But I will always mean as well the cultural and social formations that shape, organize, and provoke those modes of affect, thought and so on" (2005: 31). Then she makes it clear that her interest

in the psychology, and the interest of the other anthropologists she cites who use the term "subjectivity", lies in the subject's emotional experience in political struggle.

> The question of complex subjectivities in the more psychological (which is not to say acultural) sense is most often to be seen in studies of dominated groups. Questions not only of "agency" (and "resistance") but of pain and fear and confusion, as well as various modes of overcoming these subjective states, have been central to this kind of work. (2005: 34)

[...]

Why does subjectivity matter? For her in this essay, as throughout her work, the knotty problem is that of domination and freedom, between the subjection of the subject, and the subject's agency. "I see subjectivity as the basis of 'agency', a necessary part of understanding how people (try to) act on the world even as they are acted upon" (2005: 34). Ortner – a committed feminist – wants more room in these theories for agency. But she does not want (as she put it in the talk on which the essay is based) a backwards swing, theoretically, to the imagined unfettered

Anthropology in Theory: Issues in Epistemology, Second Edition. Edited by Henrietta L. Moore and Todd Sanders.
© 2014 John Wiley & Sons, Inc. Published 2014 by John Wiley & Sons, Inc.

independence of a freely acting person: no doubt a man, certainly a white man, bushwhacking his way through social complexity. Her own theoretical image is that of a serious game (1996): actors bound but choosing, constrained but transforming, both strategically manipulating and unconscious of the frames within which they move.

[...]

[...] But what would a psychological perspective – an argument from universal mechanism – add to a subtle theorization of the way individuals emotionally experience their movement within dense webs of meaning spun by someone else? To critics, of course, Ortner's theories are not subtle. To critics, it is a crude error to talk about the "structure of feeling" without invoking data and models and theories produced by academicians called scientists located properly in psychology departments, who have a kind of usufruct to assert what is important and true about the mind. Ortner would be unimpressed by the critique. She is not talking about mechanism. She is talking about politics and power, and the way the local shapes our lives so deeply that we have no sense of being caught within its net.

[...]

[...] The anthropological interest in a concept of "subjectivity" arises from our desire to describe something like an emotional tone or mood common to a group of people. And yet each of us knows that individual members of that group have different feelings, different personalities, different dispositions, both over the course of time and at any one moment. To use Ortner's metaphor, some are bewildered by the game, some delighted, some conniving, some depressed. How are we to understand the social shaping of the inner world when individual agents are so different from each other?

A psychological model of emotion can help us to solve this problem. [...] This is because a psychological model of emotion can help us to sort out the role of the social in an individual's experience of emotion. And that is what anthropologists are deeply interested in, and what I believe they use the word "subjectivity" to describe. Whether we are anthropologists or not, we use the word subjectivity to refer to the way the subject thinks and feels – but above all to the way to the subject feels, often about what he or she thinks. To sort out the social part of emotion helps us to sort out the shared inner life anthropologists seek to understand. A *psychological* model of emotion, that is, can deliver to us an *anthropological* model of subjectivity.

Many of the debates about emotion in the anthropological literature take the form of arguments over whether emotions are universal or not, as if there were a yes–no answer to that question. But we know that emotion is more complicated than that. We know that our feelings are private, but we read them off each other's faces. We know that we know what we feel better than any observer, and yet we know that observers can see on our faces emotions we did not feel. We go to therapists to learn about the unacknowledged feelings that trip us up, and we believe in an honest, authentic emotional life. We also know full well that unfettered emotions get us fired, friendless and abandoned in love. We know that emotions are deeply structured by the local culture – yet when we go thousands of miles away, none of us has a problem recognizing anger, fear and joy. Emotion is profoundly sculpted, and also uncontrollable. Understanding that sculpting is at the heart of understanding the way individuals experience being caught within larger social worlds that structure even the way they feel. To do so, we need to sort out the distinctive features that psychological research identifies for us in the emotions. There are several versions of a componential model of the emotions (Shweder, 1991; Mesquita and Frijda, 1992; Scherer, 2000). I call this one the six-factor model of emotion.

What is an emotion, anyway? The word that springs to mind is "feeling", and yet, I submit that "feeling" is the least part of emotion. Certainly it is the least researchable. You cannot study feeling without words; you cannot judge it physiologically; you cannot map its contours independently of crude tools which really measure something else. [...] If I see that you are angry, I see that your cheeks are flushed, that your muscles are tensed, and that your face is contorted in a threat. I might even smell your fury. But I cannot know exactly what you feel. Still, feeling is the first factor in the six-factor model.

When Darwin studied the emotions, he studied the face. *Expression of the Emotions* was published in 1872, 13 years after the *Origin of the Species* (1859). He claimed that the expression of emotion is universal, and that those expressions are shared with animals at least to some degree. The book makes three major arguments: that the human expression of emotion is universal and innate; that emotional expression is not unique to humans; and that there are three general principles which explain those expressions – that expressions reflect either a goal or that goal's opposite, and the direct action of the excited nervous system on the body. Anger is expressed by the impulse to fight, and the angry dog, like the furious human, becomes stiff, erect, teeth bared, prepared to spring. [...]

In the great sprawling literature that is the psychological study of emotions, Darwin's successors have made two points clearly. First, there is a physiology of emotion, and in some crude, biological form, there are basic emotions. When we are angry, blood goes to our face, our nostrils dilate and quiver, our teeth clench, our voices change, our whole body trembles. In fear, blood rushes to the legs, so that we can run. The heart beats quickly, the muscles tremble, the mouth goes dry, small arteries in the skin contract, the hands grow cold. [...] [It is not] clear that there is always a physiology to every feeling, for the body may be active below the thresholds of our instruments. But that physiology is important is clear. That is the second factor in the six-factor model of the emotions.

The second point is that there are universal facial expressions. Paul Ekman has devoted his considerable career to demonstrating that Darwin was right about faces; that the emotional expressions of the face are in some broad sense invariant. [...]

Ekman carried out his first study in 1966, when he took six pictures of white people expressing strong emotions – happiness, disgust, surprise, anger, fear and sadness – and showed them to adults in Chile, Argentina, Japan and America. He gave his subjects a list of local emotion terms and asked them to match the expressions to the words. They did. He expanded the work to [further countries and societies]. [...] Ekman concluded that people express the same emotion the same way the world over. He acknowledged a significant caveat. "Our evidence, and that of others, shows only that when people are experiencing certain strong emotions, and are not making any attempt to mask their expressions (display rules) the expression will be the same regardless

of age, race, culture, sex or education" (Ekman, 1998: 391). It is a powerful finding. Facial expression must be the third of our six factors.

There are, then, two emotion factors that seem in some crude way universal, common to all human bodies: physiology and facial expressions. And there is elusive, unknowable feeling. The final three factors are social.

Ekman's caveat is important. [...] [P]eople are good at masking what they feel, and most of us rapidly alter our faces to comply with social demands that we be a certain sort of person, feeling some emotions and not others. These are "display rules", social rules about who can show what feeling to whom, and they are a clear domain in which the social shapes the emotional. This is the fourth of the six factors in the model of emotion. And this is what anthropologists are good at describing.

[...]

Appraisal is the fifth of the six factors, and emerges in the psychological literature most fully in the famous debate between Zajonc and Lazarus over whether cognition is necessarily a significant part of the emotion experience. In a series of experiments, Zajonc and others exposed subjects to unfamiliar letters (Turkish-like words, Japanese ideographs), images that had no meaning for them and which they quickly confused with other images. But when re-exposed to those images in a line-up with new, similar images, they preferred the ones that were familiar to them – and yet had no cognitive recall of having seen them before. In "Feeling and Thinking" (1980) Zajonc draws on a wide swath of such data to argue that emotions are primary, and not secondary, to cognition. It was a time in psychological research dominated by research on cognition – "contemporary psychology regards feelings as last" (1980: 151) – and the essay and the debate it initiated changed the direction of the field.

[...]

[...] Zajonc's combatant was a psychotherapist turned scientist called Richard Lazarus [...]. Lazarus retaliated that the experiments Zajonc detailed singularly failed to capture everyday life. In the real world, he pointed out, we encounter very few ideographs. Instead, he argued, almost all emotional experience depends on a cognitive appraisal which is a judgment on the relationship between a person and the environment. A person has goals at stake in every encounter: status, esteem, attachment, and so on (Lazarus, 1991). Emotions, he argued, are reactions to the fate of these goals. [...]

[...]

Lazarus (1991) went on to argue that there were really two kinds of appraisals at work in any one emotional experience. There was a primary appraisal of goal achievement (did she like what I said? Did he insult me?). Then there was a secondary appraisal of the available coping option, habits of managing felt emotion or, as he sometimes described them, defenses. [...]

The anthropological point, of course, is that the same events can trigger different appraisals, and thus different emotional responses, in different individuals and in different settings. [...]

The sixth factor in the six-factor model of the emotions is the representation of emotion in a culture, and in particular the words which a culture has available to identify and describe emotional states. From one perspective, there are many similarities in the way societies categorize emotions even across great variations of time and culture. [Yet the] psychologist James Russell [...] found that basic emotion concepts seemed to be missing from many groups. "Happiness" was not found among the Malaysian Chewong; "surprise" was missing among the Dani, the Fore and the Ifaluk; "fear" was missing from Ifaluk; "disgust" was missing in Polish, among the Ifaluk, and from the Chewong. "What", Anna Wierzbicka grumpily asks, "if the psychologists working on 'fundamental human emotions' happened to be native speakers of Polish rather than of English? Would it still have occurred to them to include 'disgust' on their list?" (1986: 584; also cited in Russell, 1991; see also Wierzbicka, 1999).

[...]

Six factors: feeling, physiology, facial expression, display rules, appraisals (primary and secondary) and representations. The point of delineating each of these six factors is that all of them are present in the experience of an emotion, and yet none of them determine that emotional experience. To disaggregate them is to underscore that we are both deeply embedded within, and created through, the social, and in some sense free of it as well. There are basic emotions, in that the body responds reliably and predictably to insults, loss, and threat. Indeed, from that

perspective, as Paul Ekman (1994) has said, all emotions are basic. And yet that very basic, physiological, gut-based automatic judgment means that an emotional experience is a moral judgment [...]. Emotions are our most basic moral reactions. We feel disgust; we feel rage; we feel joy; we feel these responses to the way others behave and events unfold. That insight makes our politics physical and fundamental. Our opinions are not airy cognitive ideas, but core to the very physical experiences of our body. Emotions, Richard Shweder tells us, become "complex narrative structures" that give shape and meaning to our lives (1994: 37). Emotions are the way we make fundamental judgments on the rightness or wrongness of social acts.

And yet at the same time, to disaggregate these different factors in emotional experience enables us to see just how powerfully the social controls our basic, physiological responsiveness. [...] Social expectations reach deep within our bodies. Socially regulated words identify the feelings we are thought to feel, the events which trigger them, the display which governs what a good and proper man should do under provocation or in dread. [...]

[...]

We began with the observation that anthropologists used the word "subjectivity" to refer to the shared inner life of the subject and particularly to the emotional experience of a political subject, the subject caught up in a world of violence, struggle and oppression. Ortner calls for an attention to subjectivity as the means to understand both the capitulation to authority, the way we are formed by power pressing down, and the resistance to that authority. [...] How does a psychologically attentive model of emotion help to answer her call?

The six-feature model of emotions helps us to understand that Ortner is attending to the socially shared elements of the six factors of emotion – appraisal, display, and representation. That is not all of subjectivity, but it is the part of subjectivity that lies squarely in the anthropological domain and that the anthropological method is uniquely good at assessing. Moreover, we can use that attention to the social by shared and shaped elements of emotion to suggest a theoretical solution to Ortner's puzzle: that the complex subjectivity of dominated groups arises from the emotional experience of negotiating contradictory emotional codes. Often, these contradictory codes will be the code for correct emotional response to the dominant authority, and the code for correct emotional response to peers. The emotional vise arises not only out of there being two codes – different appraisals, different appropriate displays, different representations – but a recognition that in being responsive to each, one fails both. [...]

References

Darwin, C. (1998 [1872]) *The Expression of the Emotions in Man and Animals*. Oxford: Oxford University Press.

Ekman, P. (1994) "All Emotions are Basic", in P. Ekman and R. Davidson (eds) *The Nature of Emotion*, pp. 15–19. Oxford: Oxford University Press.

Ekman, P. (1998) "Introduction", "Afterword", "Commentary", in Charles Darwin *The Expression of the Emotions in Man and Animals*, pp. xiii–xvii; xxi–xxxvi; 363–94. Oxford: Oxford University Press.

Holland, D. and K. Leander (2004) "Ethnographic Studies of Positioning and Subjectivity: An Introduction", *Ethos* 32: 127–39.

Lazarus, R. (1991) *Emotion and Adaptation*. Oxford: Oxford University Press.

Mesquita, B. and N. Frijda (1992) "Cultural Variations in Emotions: A Review", *Psychological Bulletin* 112: 179–204.

Ortner, S. (1996) *Making Gender*. Boston, MA: Beacon.

Ortner, S. (2005) "Subjectivity and Cultural Critique", *Anthropological Theory* 5: 31–52.

Russell, J. (1991) "Culture and the Categorization of Emotions", *Psychological Bulletin* 110: 426–50.

Scherer, K. (2000) "Psychological Models of Emotion", in J. Borod (ed.) *The Neuropsychology of Emotion*, pp. 137–62. Oxford: Oxford University Press.

Shweder, R. (1991) *Thinking Through Cultures*. Cambridge, MA: Harvard University Press.

Shweder, R. (1994) "'You're Not Sick, You're Just In Love': Emotion as an Interpretive System", in P. Ekman and R. Davidson (eds) *The Nature of Emotion*, pp. 32–44. Oxford: Oxford University Press.

Wierzbicka, A. (1986) "Human Emotions: Universal or Culture-Specific?", *American Anthropologist* 88: 584–94.

Wierzbicka, A. (1999) *Emotions Across Languages and Cultures*. Cambridge: Cambridge University Press.

Zajonc, R. (1980) "Feeling and Thinking: Preferences Need No Inferences", *American Psychologist* 35: 151–75.

25

Why the Behavioural Sciences Need the Concept of the Culture-Ready Brain

Charles Whitehead

The Trouble with Anthropology

Anthropology could be defined as the study of the human condition in the broadest possible sense. As such, and in view of the daunting consequences of human activity in terms of violence, deprivation, and destruction, one might imagine that anthropology is the most important of all the sciences and that other human disciplines – such as psychology and neuroscience – should be sub-disciplines within anthropology. The trouble is, in actuality, few psychologists or neuroscientists think of themselves as engaged in "anthropology", and (in my experience) few believe that anthropologists have much to say that would be interesting or relevant to their work. […]

The uninterest in anthropology extends beyond science. Governments do not routinely consult anthropologists before taking decisions with potentially momentous consequences, and until recently, there was very little interest in teaching anthropology below university level. Good citizenship, apparently, is not widely thought to require anthropological insight. And when it comes to research funding, governments generally have non-anthropological priorities.

So why isn't anthropology more influential?

Part of the problem may lie in anthropologists themselves, many of whom would rather talk to each other than engage in cross-disciplinary dialogue. This, however, is a symptom rather than a cause. […]

I suggest a deeper issue is involved. One of the first things I learned as a student at University College London is that social and biological anthropologists can barely talk to each other without lapsing into polemic. […]

The conceptual gulf dividing social from biological anthropology indicates that something is amiss. This is more than a simple conflict between two anthropologies – it divides social anthropology from the rest of science as a whole (cf. Perry and Mace 2010). Biologists have no special difficulty talking to and persuading psychologists, neuroscientists, and others. It is the more esoteric musings of social anthropologists that rouse incomprehension, disbelief, or – more commonly – uninterest. There seems to be an impenetrable mental block separating those who have studied the "anthropological other" from those who have not. It appears that the beliefs and ideology of western science do not survive unscathed following deep involvement with cultural "otherness".

From *Anthropological Theory* 12(1) (2012), pp. 43–71 (with cuts). Copyright © 2012. Reprinted with permission of SAGE.

Anthropology in Theory: Issues in Epistemology, Second Edition. Edited by Henrietta L. Moore and Todd Sanders.
© 2014 John Wiley & Sons, Inc. Published 2014 by John Wiley & Sons, Inc.

[...] Bourdieu (1977 [1972]) pointed out the political conditions on which scientific practice depends, and the taken-for-granted way in which cultural fictions, which serve to validate privilege, are never critically examined however logically incoherent they may be. A more systematic critique of western science and scholarship is required – and is beginning to receive attention from anthropologists (e.g. Jackson 2009), psychologists (e.g. Baruss 2008, 2010) and neuroscientists (e.g. Turner [2012]).

One might expect that, if social anthropology has the potential to resolve deep errors at the heart of the western "scientific" worldview, then social anthropologists should feel a surge of confidence and a determination to set about this all-important task. With few exceptions, however, the opposite has occurred. The bathetic "Finale" to the fourth volume of *Mythologiques*, which led to the collapse of structuralism, may have been the critical factor provoking a crisis of self-doubt in (mainly European) anthropology. "Grand theories" became virtually taboo and the discipline focused on increasingly local studies with increasingly modest aims. [...]

Cognitive and cultural anthropologists commonly duck the problem by defecting to the biological camp. Forgetting Durkheim's injunction to "treat social facts as things" irreducible to lower orders of explanation such as biology or psychology, and denying the "anti-biological" character of cultural phenomena, they favour naturalistic explanations. Religion, for example, is explained by a genetically-evolved "symbolic module" (Sperber 1994), "neurognostic processes" (Laughlin et al. 1992) or a hominid "mimetic controller" (Winkelman 2002). [...] Such approaches make cultural phenomena arbitrary, disembodied, and of dubious (if any) functionality.

What social anthropologists could be doing is exposing the political origins and self-contradictory character of "collective deceptions" in western science (Whitehead 2002, 2006). This is not to deny the utility of science within its zone of applicability. The power of science, however, is the result of its empirical method, and not its institutional self-legitimation [...].

[...]

Culture and Biology

The specific issue dividing biological from social anthropology is the question of whether enculturated human behaviour is "biological" or "anti-biological". But are these mutually exclusive or even meaningful alternatives? Is there any utility in separating "nature" from "nurture", other than academic convenience? A genotype ("nature") specifies nothing unless there is an appropriate environment ("nurture") to read out the code and translate it into a chicken or a banana plant. Further, every major transition in biological evolution is "anti-biological" relative to what went before. [...] All major transitions create *sui generis* emergent orders, so human culture is not unique in this respect. Other examples include the genetic code, chimerical modern cells, sexual reproduction, multi-cellular organisms, brains, and animal societies.

A common error in current Darwinian thinking [...] is the assumption that "selfish genes" are the prime mover in evolution. In strict Darwinism the prime mover is environmental threat. In the absence of threat, natural selection tends to *resist* change. It is un-biological to "explain" behavioural change as *resulting from* genetic change or the *ex vacuo* emergence of domain-specific brain modules. Evolutionary psychologists surely know why brains evolved: as Cosmides and Tooby (1997) point out, brains are found only in animals that move. Brains are behavioural organs, and behavioural adaptation, being immediate and non-random, is vastly more efficient than genetic adaptation. So, in animals with brains, behavioural change is the usual first response to environmental threat. If the change is successful, genetic adaptation to the new behaviour will follow more gradually. Animals do not evolve carnivore teeth and then decide it might be a good idea to eat meat.

[...]

A striking feature of biological and quasi-biological approaches in anthropology is a tendency to ignore proximate mechanisms (primarily the brain). Where biological anthropologists have investigated the brain, their research has been ethnographically naïve [...]. Social anthropologists are also not commonly interested in brains, but in this respect are following a reasonable precedent set by Simmel and Durkheim. There is no such precedent in biology. On the contrary, there is a well established respect for Tinbergen's (1963) "four whys". That is, to fully account for a behavioural trait, four independent explanations are required: how it evolved (phylogeny), how it develops (ontogeny), how it is adaptive (ultimate mechanism), and how it is accomplished (proximate mechanism).

In order to resolve the conceptual differences dividing biological from social anthropology I think we need to take these four questions seriously. If we accept that major transitions in evolution lead to the emergence of *sui generis* systems which are "anti-biological" relative to what went before, then this affects the answers we give to all four of Tinbergen's questions. Purely genetic explanations will no longer suffice. Emergent orders have their own internal logic and top-down causality. They create collaborative societies of individuals who must sacrifice some of their biological "selfishness" to the larger interests of the collective whole. The chastity of priests may serve the land-owning interests and spiritual authority of the Catholic church, just as cell death serves the interests of a well-formed multicellular body. New levels of cooperation create larger "selfish collectivities" which in turn introduce new levels of competition where collective interests collide.

Some of the questions we need to answer have been neglected or virtually outlawed in social and biological anthropology [...].

We further need to define in what specific sense human culture might be considered "anti-biological" (i.e. discontinuous with ape cultures). Lévi-Strauss (1969 [1949]) distinguished human biological from cultural behaviour by noting that the former is universal whereas the latter is governed by culturally variable rules. [...] Marshall Sahlins (1960) further observed that in apes, sex controls society, whereas in humans, society controls sex. He inferred that human culture must have begun with a revolutionary inversion of a primordial ape-like social order. There has been a great deal of research on apes since Sahlins wrote, but this hardly detracts from the pertinence of his observation, or the fact that sexual modesty appears to be a uniquely human universal. Sahlins hit the "anti-

biological" nail squarely on the head, which is more than can be said for many behavioural scientists today.

[...]

Cultural Distortions of Perception

[...] Individualism, thankfully, is in decline in the behavioural sciences, although the concept of the "social brain" is still somewhat individualistic. In his 1999 discussion of the social brain, Adolphs does not mention music, song, or dance. Non-representational art is described as "non-social", and his list of social brain structures does not include the massively expanded inferior parietal lobule or classical language areas. He even asks "Is it possible that language evolved primarily to subserve social behaviour?" Such thinking persists despite widespread acceptance of the "social intelligence" hypothesis, which holds that brain expansion in primates is an adaptation to the complexities of social life. [...]

In reacting against behaviourism, cognitive science emphasized the brain as a thinking rather than a doing organ. Although the computer metaphor for mind and brain is now thankfully in decline, the associated notion of "information processing" remains dominant. This implicitly assumes an input-processing-output model of cognition which, however, represents only one half of a circular process (Cisek 1999). Neglect of output-first brain functions partly accounts for the relative lack of neuroscientific studies of social displays such as dance and pretend play (see below). If brains only evolve in animals that move, then behaviour (output) must be phylogenetically prior to cognition (processing) and sensation (input). This is equally true ontogenetically – the foetal brain puts out efferents to muscles before it receives afferents from sense organs (Trevarthen 1985). As the great educator Maria Montessori (cited in Lillard 2001), observed: "The mind will follow the hand", which was her way of saying that doing comes before thinking. A child learns to count on her fingers before she can do so in her head, and plays with toys before she can internalize pretence in role-play. [...]

The central belief of the cognopardigm, however, is older than computing – namely, that human beings are set apart from the rest of the animal kingdom by a single quality known as "general intelligence", and that this is the major reason for our relatively large brains. [...] [T]he Protestant work ethic and the industrial revolution have given us a world in which work is valued over play, logic over imagination, and science and technology over the arts. Hence brains are conceived to be specialized for linear reasoning, "executive control", and planning goal-directed instrumental actions. As Gazzaniga (2000) observes: "The human brain is a bizarre device, set in place through natural selection for one main purpose – to make decisions that enhance reproductive success." What is being denied here is just about everything that makes us human. [...]

Intelligence is notoriously as difficult to define as the "human difference", and for the same reason. [...] The "Flynn effect" – the discovery that, since IQ testing began, scores have been rising at an average rate of three points per decade, and faster than that in "developing" populations (Flynn 2007) – suggests that what these tests measure is culturally acquired skills, though this inference is still contested.

There may be no such single ability as "general intelligence" – commonly referred to as "g" – which IQ tests are presumed to measure. [...] It may well be that "g" is a [...] side-effect [...] of our evolved social abilities.

The belief that big brains are mainly an adaptation for non-social reasoning, however, persists with little empirical encouragement. [...]
[...]
[...] IQ rating scales were not designed to assess factors of likely relevance to human brain expansion, but rather reflect the idiosyncratic educational needs of post-industrial nation-states. [...]
[...]

The Culture-Ready Brain

So far I have discussed a number of problems affecting the behavioural sciences, and suggested actions which social anthropologists could take to resolve them. [...] This section addresses one of them, namely anthropological neuroscience.

The social brain concept (Brothers 1990), if rather long in coming, has proved fruitful, having led to important advances in theory and knowledge, as well as several new subdisciplines as brain scientists began to collaborate with social scientists. [...]
[...]
[...] [T]here has been a veritable tsunami of brain studies by social neuroscientists [...]. Biological anthropologists have contributed to this research, many of them comparing human with ape brains. [However, s]uch studies have often focused on micro-architectural details [...]. Such research is of course interesting and potentially useful, but the problem remains that no one is joining up the dots or providing a big picture of the brain or of human behaviour. As one refreshingly honest review explains, the basic aim of social neuroscience is to map social functions onto the brain, but the problem is that no one knows just which brain structures to investigate or which functions need to be mapped (Adolphs 2010). Because of the cognitive/social intelligence paradigm, what is being universally ignored is output-first behaviours which, I submit, constitute the essence of our humanity. [...]
[...]
There were two main reasons why, in 1999, I thought that anthropological brain research might help to bridge the gulf dividing social from biological anthropology. Firstly, at that time, both biological and social anthropologists generally ignored proximate mechanisms at the neurological level. As the brain is crucially involved at the interface between biology and culture, I felt this could provide a nexus of common interest and convergent theorizing. Secondly, I was dissatisfied by individualistic and cognocentric accounts of brain expansion during human evolution. Even the social intelligence hypothesis did not seem sufficient to explain hominid encephalization: in part because it applies to all primates, and in part because there is a lot more to human behaviour than just intelligence. A more culturally-relevant hypothesis of brain expansion might help to allay the suspicions of social anthropologists [...] while raising awareness of ethnographically-validated issues in biological anthropology, psychology, and neuroscience – in other words, identifying true cross-cultural universals of behaviour, and defining what needs to be explained.

I had no doubt about the kind of imaging studies that were needed. I took my cue from social mirror theory and the work of Victor Turner, who himself advocated anthropological brain research (Turner 1983). Social mirror theory holds that "mirrors in the mind depend on mirrors in society" (Whitehead 2001) – that is, reflective awareness of one's own experiences, and those of others, depends on social displays which make experiences public. [...]

In the context of output-first behaviours, one conspicuous difference between humans and apes is that humans possess a formidable armamentarium of social displays – unprecedented in any other animal (Whitehead 2001). Furthermore, we have three distinct kinds of display, two of which – play and performance – are functionally distinct from communication. Whereas communication is goal-directed and manipulative (Krebs and Dawkins 1984), play is autotelic (Turner 1982) – pursued "just for fun". Play has exploratory and developmental functions, but no instrumental goal or manipulative intent. Performance [...] is both playful and manipulative, and has functions additional to communication – namely, social grooming and entrainment. [...]

According to social mirror theory, it is this extraordinary range of highly elaborated displays that accounts for human self- and other-consciousness. If the social intelligence hypothesis can only partially account for brain expansion in hominids, and bearing in mind that social intelligence must in part be dependent on social displays, then it is conceivable that social displays themselves may have been a factor contributing to human encephalization. Displays variously involve multi-modal integration, timing precision, skill, and – in the case of role-play – modelling more than one mind in parallel. So the execution as well as the perception and interpretation of displays must make demands on the brain, and the selection pressures responsible for the proliferation of human displays (Whitehead 2003, 2008, 2010) would promote increasing size and/or connective complexity in relevant brain areas.

The "play and display" hypothesis holds that song-and-dance display had already emerged by 2.7 million years ago (mya), when the first unequivocal stone tools were being used for butchering meat. This triggered the first "grade shift" during which the genus *Homo* appeared

and, by 2 mya, cranial capacity had doubled from around 400 to 800 cm³. Song-and-dance display pre-adapted the brain, and provided the requisite levels of social insight and social trust, for the later expansion of mimetic and pretend play abilities. However, further expansion of the brain required dietary change (probably provided by cooking meat) to lift the metabolic and nutritional "lid" on brain expansion (Aiello and Wheeler 1995). This change triggered the second grade shift, from 0.5 mya (0.7 mya in Asia), when cranial capacity again doubled to around 1500 cm³. Following the agricultural revolution around 10,000 years ago, there was a third grade shift in which cranial capacity was reduced by around 12 per cent. If the "play and display" hypothesis is correct, then this decline suggests a diminished need for some aspects of display behaviour – perhaps timing precision – in a strongly hierarchical society where social integration is imposed from above.

To compare the play and display hypothesis with other hypotheses of hominid brain expansion requires a detailed examination of archaeological and fossil data. I have reviewed this evidence elsewhere (Whitehead 2003, 2008, 2010) [...].

[...]

Imaging research

The role of neuroimaging in my own research is to establish how social display behaviours map onto the brain regions expanded during the first two grade shifts. I judged that role-play (introjective play) would be the most revealing and should be investigated first. Subsequent studies would include investigations of projective pretence (using objects as representations), song, dance, decorative art, and representational image-making.

[...]

At the time of our experiment, mirror neurons in monkeys (Rizzolatti et al. 1996) were a relatively recent discovery. Mirror neurons fire when a monkey performs an action – such as grasping a nut to eat it – and also when the monkey sees another individual – monkey or human – perform the same action. This important discovery was hailed as having the potential to explain human sociality (Knoblich and Sebanz 2006), including theory of mind (Gallese and Goldman 1998) and

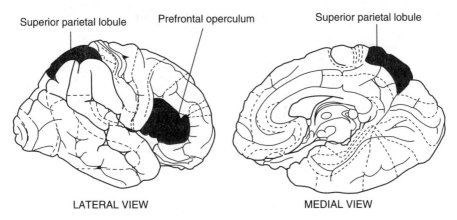

Figure 25.1 Right cerebral hemisphere showing sensorimotor mirroring areas. Praxic actions such as tool use activate this system mainly in the left hemisphere.

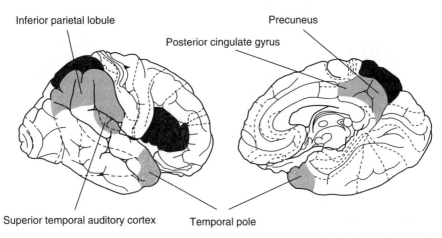

Figure 25.2 Major cortical areas in which activation loci were associated with dance. These include the sensorimotor mirror system.

language (Gallese 1998; Rizzolatti and Arbib 1998). Of course mirror neurons – common to monkeys as well as humans – cannot be sufficient to explain uniquely human abilities.

[...] Since then there have been over 40 imaging studies of manual action and tool-use [...], but only four of dance [...], two of pretence [...], and one of role-play. [...]

What this imaging research shows is, firstly, that tool-use and object manipulation involve the presumed sensorimotor mirror system in opercular prefrontal (including Broca's area) and superior parietal cortices (see Figure 25.1). [This]

area is [...] clearly involved in many kinds of motor action. The superior parietal lobule is a navigational area which coordinates body-part movements in visually mapped space. [...]

Secondly, dance – as would be expected – also activates the sensorimotor mirror system, and does so more bilaterally than tool-use. [...] In addition, there were bilateral activations in the temporal pole, precuneus/posterior cingulate, and inferior parietal lobule (see Figure 25.2). The latter, a multimodal integration area, is known to have expanded during the first grade shift.

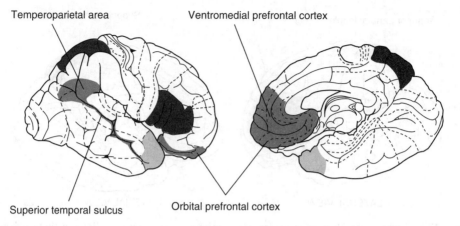

Figure 25.3   Major cortical areas in which activation loci were associated with projective pretence include some common to dance.

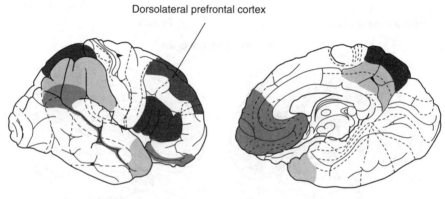

Figure 25.4   Major cortical areas in which activation loci were associated with narrative and role-play include all major dance and pretend-play areas.

Thirdly, the activation pattern associated with projective pretence included areas that were the same as or close to those implicated by dance, though with no significant activity in the precuneus/posterior cingulate. In addition, pretence activated areas of major social importance – ventromedial and orbital prefrontal cortex (see Figure 25.3). […] [T]his finding is equally consistent with social mirror theory, according to which pretend play scaffolds the development of mental insight, suggesting that ToM "theory of mind" may "piggy-back" on brain structures originally dedicated to pretence.

Our pilot study of role-play was problematic in that it showed less brain activity in role than control tasks, possibly because the latter involved

implicit role-play. However, many authors have assumed continuity between role-play, narrative, and daydreaming (or "theatre of mind") (review: Mar 2004). As we identify with characters in a story this presumably involves mental role-play. In our role-play study, major areas common to narrative were activated when participants switched from role to control tasks, perhaps indicating increased activity due to dissociation during the shift from explicit to implicit role-play. Figure 25.4 shows major areas activated in studies of narrative, in the expectation that a more definitive study of role-play will show similar neural responses.

[…]

The findings […] are consistent with an evolutionary sequence from song-and-dance display to role-play, as assumed by the "play and display" hypothesis, suggesting that increasingly sophisticated forms of display evolve by extension or proliferation and re-adaptation of older mirror systems (as proposed by Arbib 2002). The "play and display" hypothesis clearly needs – and justifies – further research into the neural correlates of social displays. The imaging evidence I have reviewed also illustrates one area where anthropologists and neuroscientists can usefully collaborate.

Closing Remarks

I began this essay by asking why social anthropology is not accorded the respect that one would expect for a science of culture. From the treatment of human culture in other disciplines, it is clear that many scientists reduce human culture to something continuous with ape behaviour, denying the several Rubicons that separate us from non-humans. We live in a culture-denying culture, one which is largely antipathetic to social anthropology. Reductionist, deterministic, mechanistic, cognocentric, logocentric, and/or genocentric accounts are supported by faulty Darwinian arguments. However, it is equally true to say that social anthropologists have not been entirely effective in refuting such arguments.
[…]

I have suggested a number of actions which (at least some) social anthropologists could take to resolve the problems affecting the behavioural sciences, viz:

1   We need a systematic anthropological critique of western scientific ideology. What social anthropologists could be doing is exposing the political origins and self-contradictory character of collective deceptions in western science.
2   We need greater collaboration between social anthropology and other disciplines, both by engaging in cross-disciplinary debates (as in consciousness studies, for example), and multi-disciplinary research. Anthropological neuroscience and developmental psychology are promising options, since both address the interface between biology and culture. Since the advent of the social brain concept, brain scientists have become increasingly interested in the social sciences, and this is an opportune time for interdisciplinary collaboration.
3   All the behavioural disciplines need to pay more systematic attention to Tinbergen's four questions.
4   We need to define in what specific sense human culture might be considered "anti-biological". […]

References

Adolphs R (1999) Social cognition and the human brain. *Trends in Cognitive Sciences* 3(12): 469–79.

Adolphs R (2010) Conceptual challenges and directions for social neuroscience. *Neuron* 65: 752–67.

Aiello LC and Wheeler P (1995) The expensive tissue hypothesis: The brain and the digestive system in human and primate evolution. *Current Anthropology* 36(2): 199–221.

Arbib MA (2002) The mirror system, imitation, and the evolution of language. In: Nehaniv C and Dautenhahn K (eds) *Imitation in Animals and Artefacts*. Cambridge, MA: MIT Press, 229–80.

Baruss I (2008) Beliefs about consciousness and reality: Clarification of the confusion concerning consciousness. *Journal of Consciousness Studies* 15(10–11): 277–92.

Baruss I (2010) Beyond scientific materialism: Toward a transcendent theory of consciousness. *Journal of Consciousness Studies* 17(7): 213–31.

Bourdieu P (1977 [1972]) *Outline of a Theory of Practice*, trans. Nice R. Cambridge: Cambridge University Press.

Brothers L (1990) The social brain: A project for integrating primate behavior and neurophysiology in a new domain. *Concepts in Neuroscience* 1: 27–51.

Cisek P (1999) Beyond the computer metaphor: Behaviour as interaction. *Journal of Consciousness Studies* 6(11–12): 125–42.

Cosmides L and Tooby J (1997) Evolutionary psychology: A primer. Center for Evolutionary Psychology: www.psych.ucsb.edu/research/cep/primer.html.

Flynn JR (2007) *What Is Intelligence? Beyond the Flynn Effect.* Cambridge: Cambridge University Press.

Gallese V (1998) Mirror neurons: From grasping to language. *Journal of Consciousness Studies: Consciousness Research Abstract* 129.

Gallese V and Goldman A (1998) Mirror neurons and the simulation theory of mind-reading. *Trends in Cognitive Sciences* 2: 493–501.

Gazzaniga MS (2000) Cerebral specialization and inter-hemispheric communication: Does the corpus callosum enable the human condition? *Brain* 123(7): 1293–326.

Jackson MD (2009) Where thought belongs: An anthropological critique of the project of philosophy. *Anthropological Theory* 9(3): 235–51.

Knoblich G and Sebanz N (2006) The social nature of perception and action. *Current Directions in Psychological Science* 15: 99–104.

Krebs JR and Dawkins R (1984) Animal signals: Mind-reading and manipulation. In: *Behavioural Ecology: An Evolutionary Approach*, 2nd edn. Oxford: Blackwell, 380–403.

Laughlin CD, McManus J and d'Aquili EG (1992) *Brain, Symbol and Experience: Toward a Neurophenomenology of Human Consciousness.* New York: Columbia University Press.

Lévi-Strauss C (1969 [1949]) *The Elementary Structures of Kinship.* London: Eyre & Spottiswoode.

Lillard AS (2001) Pretend play as twin earth: A social-cognitive analysis. *Developmental Review* 21(4): 495–531.

Mar RA (2004) The neuropsychology of narrative: Story comprehension, story production and their interrelation. *Neuropsychologia* 42: 1414–34.

Perry G and Mace R (2010) The lack of acceptance of evolutionary approaches to human behaviour. *Journal of Evolutionary Psychology* 8(2): 105–25.

Rizzolatti G and Arbib MA (1998) Language within our grasp. *Trends in Neuroscience* 21(5): 188–94.

Rizzolatti G, Fadiga L, Gallesi V and Fogassi L (1996) Premotor cortex and the recognition of motor actions. *Brain Research and Cognitive Brain Research* 3(2): 131–41.

Sahlins MD (1960) The origin of society. *Scientific American* 203(3): 76–87.

Sperber D (1994) The modularity of thought and the epidemiology of representations. In: Hirschfeld LA and Gelman SA (eds) *Mapping the Mind: Domain Specificity in Cognition and Culture.* Cambridge: Cambridge University Press, 39–67.

Tinbergen N (1963) On aims and methods in ethology. *Zeitschrift für Tierpsychologie* 20: 410–33.

Trevarthen C (1985) Neuroembryology and the development of perceptual mechanisms. In: Falkner F and Tanner JM (eds) *Human Growth*, 2nd edn. New York: Plenum, 301–83.

Turner R (2012) The need for systematic ethnopsychology: The ontological status of mentalistic terminology. *Anthropological Theory* 12(1): 29–42.

Turner V (1982) *From Ritual to Theatre: The Human Seriousness of Play.* New York: PAJ Publications.

Turner V (1983) *On the Edge of the Bush: Anthropology as Experience* (ed. Turner ELB). Tucson: University of Arizona Press.

Whitehead C (2001) Social mirrors and shared experiential worlds. *Journal of Consciousness Studies* 8(4): 3–36.

Whitehead C (2002) Political origins of the hard problem. Toward a Science of Consciousness: Tucson 2002, Center for Consciousness Studies, University of Arizona, Tucson, USA, 6–13 April.

Whitehead C (2003) Social mirrors and the brain: Including a functional imaging study of role play and verse. PhD thesis, Department of Anthropology, University College London.

Whitehead C (2006) Collective deceptions in western science. Toward a Science of Consciousness: Tucson 2006, Center for Consciousness Studies, University of Arizona, Tucson, USA, 4–8 April.

Whitehead C (2008) The neural correlates of work and play. *Journal of Consciousness Studies* 15(10–11): 93–121.

Whitehead C (2010) The culture ready brain. Invited submission to a special issue on Cultural Neuroscience, J.Y. Chiao (ed.) *Social Cognitive and Affective Neuroscience.* DOI: 10.1093/scan/nsq036.

Winkelman M (2002) Shamanism and cognitive evolution. *Cambridge Archaeological Journal* 12(1): 71–101.

SECTION 8

Bodies of Knowledges

26

Knowledge of the Body

Michael Jackson

Whether one considers the idealist traditions of the eighteenth and nineteenth centuries which "etherealised"[1] the body or anthropological conceptions of culture which play up the intellectual and linguistic characteristics of human social existence to the exclusion of somatic and biological processes, one finds that science since the Enlightenment has always been pervaded by a popular bourgeois notion of culture as something "superorganic".[2] It refers to a self-contained world of unique qualities and manners divorced from the world of materiality and biology.[3] Culture has thus served as a token to demarcate, separate, exclude and deny;[4] and although at different epochs the excluded "natural" category shifts about among peasants, barbarians, workers, primitive people, women,[5] children, animals and material artefacts,[6] a persistent theme is the denial of the somatic, a turning of blind eyes on the physical aspects of Being where our sense of separateness and distinctiveness is most readily blurred.[7]

Throughout the 1970s studies of body movement and body meaning appeared in increasing numbers, but analysis tended to be either too symbolic and semiotic or, in the case of ethological studies, heavily mechanistic.[8] Since it is the semiotic model which has dominated anthropological studies of the body I intend to focus on this mode. My main contention will be that the "anthropology of the body" has been vitiated by a tendency to interpret embodied experience in terms of cognitive and linguistic models of meaning.

The Language of Representation

The first problem arises from the intellectualist tendency to regard body praxis as secondary to verbal praxis. For example, while critical of the "logo-centric" bias in many studies of so-called "non-verbal communication" (cf. Polhemus 1975: 14) whereby "speech has been over-emphasised as the privileged means of human communication, and the body neglected", Douglas (1978: 85) still asserts that "normally the physical channel supports and agrees with the spoken one". This subjugation of the bodily to the semantic is empirically untenable. In the first place, from both phylogenetic and ontogenetic points of view, thinking and communicating through the body precede and to a great extent always remain beyond speech.[9] This may be recognised in the

From *Man* 18 (1983), pp. 327–40, 341–5. Copyright © 1983 by *Man*. Reprinted by permission of John Wiley & Sons UK.

Anthropology in Theory: Issues in Epistemology, Second Edition. Edited by Henrietta L. Moore and Todd Sanders.
© 2014 John Wiley & Sons, Inc. Published 2014 by John Wiley & Sons, Inc.

way our earliest memories are usually sensations or direct impressions rather than words or ideas, and refer to situated yet not spoken events.[10] It is, moreover, often the case that gestures and bodily habits belie what we put into words, and give away our unconscious dispositions, betraying character traits of which our verbal and conceptual habits keep us in ignorance.[11] In therapies which focus on the embodied personality and the bodily unconscious, such as hypnotherapy and Reichian bioenergetic analysis, the "somatic mind" mediates understandings and changes in which verbal consciousness plays little part.[12] In the second place, as Binswanger and Merleau-Ponty have argued, meaning should not be reduced to a sign which, as it were, lies on a separate plane outside the immediate domain of an act. For instance, when our familiar environment is suddenly disrupted we feel uprooted, we lose our footing, we are thrown, we collapse, we fall. But such falling, Binswanger says, is not "something metaphorical derived from physical falling", a mere manner of speaking; it is a shock and disorientation which occurs simultaneously in body and mind, and refers to a basic ontological structure of our Being-in-the-world (Binswanger 1963: 222–5, cf. Reich 1949: 435). In this sense, uprightness of posture may be said to define a psychophysical relationship with the world, so that to lose this position, this "standing", is simultaneously a bodily and intellectual loss of balance, a disturbance at the very centre and ground of our Being.[13] Metaphors of falling and disequilibrium disclose this integral connexion of the psychic and the physical; they do not express a concept *in terms of* a bodily image.

The meaning of body praxis is not always reducible to cognitive and semantic operations: body movements often make sense without being intentional in the linguistic sense, as communicating, codifying, symbolising, signifying thoughts or things that lie outside or anterior to speech.[14] Thus an understanding of a body movement does not invariably depend on an elucidation of what the movement "stands for." As Best (1978: 137) puts it, "Human movement does not symbolise reality, it *is* reality."[15] To treat body praxis as necessarily being an effect of semiotic causes is to treat the body as a diminished version of itself.[16]

The second problem in the anthropology of the body is a corollary of the first. In so far as the body tends to be defined as a medium of expression or communication,[17] it is not only reduced to the status of a sign; it is also made into an object of purely mental operations, a "thing" onto which social patterns are projected. Thus, Douglas (1978: 87) speaks of the body as an "it"[18] and examines how "In its role as an image of society, the body's main scope is to express the relation of the individual to the group". As a result a Cartesian split is made which detaches the knowing and speaking subject from the unknowing inert body. At the same time, through a reification of the knowing subject, which is made synonymous with "society" or "the social body", *society* is made to assume the active role of governing, utilising and charging with significance the physical bodies of individuals.[19] In this view the human body is simply an object of understanding, or an instrument of the rational mind, a kind of vehicle for the expression of a reified social rationality.[20] This view is fallacious on epistemological grounds, as well as contradicting our experience of the body as lived reality, wherein no sense of the mind as causally prior can be sustained, and wherein any notion of the body as an instrument of mind or of society is absurd. Dewey dismisses this kind of dualism by drawing attention to the "natural medium" in which bodies and minds exist equally:

> In ultimate analysis the mystery that mind should use a body, or that a body should have a mind, is like the mystery that a man cultivating plants should use the soil; or that the soil which grows plants at all should grow those adapted to its own physico-chemical properties …
>
> Every "mind" that we are empirically acquainted with is found in connection with some organized body. Every such body exists in a natural medium to which it sustains some adaptive connection: plants to air, water, sun, and animals to these things and also to plants. Without such connections, animals die; the "purest" mind would not continue without them. (1929: 277–8)[21]

A third problem arises from the dualistic and reified views on which I have commented. In many anthropological studies of the body, the body is regarded as inert, passive and static. Either the body is shown to be a neutral and ideographic means of embodying ideas, or is dismembered so that the symbolic value of its various parts in indigenous discourse can be enumerated. There seems to be a dearth of studies on the body-as-subject, of a phenomenology of embodied experience, of studies of interactions and exchanges occurring within the field of bodily existence rather than resulting from mechanical rules or innate preprogramming.

My aim in the following pages is to outline a phenomenological approach to body praxis which avoids naive subjectivism by showing how human experience is grounded in bodily movement within a social and material environment, and examining at the level of event the interplay between habitual patterns of body use and conventional ideas about the world.

Initiations and Imitations

In the dry season of 1970 in northern Sierra Leone, not long after I had begun fieldwork in the Kuranko village of Firawa, I was lucky enough to see the public festivities associated with girls' initiation rites (*dimusu biriye*). Each night I would watch the girls performing the graceful and energetic *yatuiye* and *yamayili* dances which presaged the end of their childhood. Their hair specially braided and adorned with snail-shell toggles, and wearing brightly-coloured beaded head-bands, groups of girls passed from house to house around the village, dancing, clapping and singing that their girlhood days were almost over. The days too were crowded with activities. Visitors poured into the village, diviners were consulted to see what dangers might lie in store for the girls during the operations, sacrifices were made to avert such dangers, gifts were given to help defray expenses for those families whose daughters were being initiated, and all the while the neophytes continued to circulate around the village in the company of indefatigable drummers. Then, at dusk on the day before the operations, the girls were led down to the river by older women to be washed and dressed in long white gowns. That night they were sequestered in a special house and we did not see them. Nor in the morning, for they were ushered away into the bush at first light by the women to be made ready for the operations. They remained in the bush, lodged in a makeshift house, for three weeks, all the time

receiving instruction from older women in domestic, sexual and moral matters, and waiting for the clitoridectomy scars to heal.

On the day the girls left the village, I sat about with the other men, talking and being entertained by groups of performers, mostly women and young girls, who came by the house just as the neophytes had done in the days before. These performers fascinated me. A young girl, her body daubed with red and white ochres and charcoal, stood before us with an immobile face. Another, wearing a man's hat and gown, and carrying a cutlass hilt-down, held a pad of cloth clamped over her mouth. When she and her companions moved on another group took their place: small boys who pranced around a comical figure trussed in grass, dancing in mimicry of a chimpanzee, falling to the ground from time to time to be "revived" by his friends' urgent drumming. Then women performers danced before us. One was dressed in men's clothes with a wild fruit hung from a cord across her forehead. She imitated the maladroit dance movements of men, her face expressionless, while other women surrounded her, clapping, singing and laughing. Other women had daubed their bodies with red and white clay and charcoal, and painted symmetrical black lines under their eyes. They too danced awkwardly with deadpan faces, some holding red flowers clenched between tight lips.

[...]

In my notebooks, among detailed descriptions of what I saw, I listed searching questions which could not be phrased in Kuranko, let alone answered, and the following self-interrogations now remind me of the fervour with which I sought clues to hidden meanings:[22]

These mask-like expressions – are they a way in which these girls strive to sympathetically induce in their older sisters some measure of self-control? Is this impassivity a way in which they seek magically to countermand or neutralise the emotional turmoil in the hearts of the neophytes? These songs the women sing, assuaging fear and urging calm – are they ways in which the village tries to cool "the bush"? These girls in men's clothes – do they want to assimilate something of men's fortitude and fearlessness, or is this muddling of quotidian roles simply an expression of the confusion surrounding this moment of mid-passage?

And the chimpanzee boy, falling to the ground and lying there utterly still before being roused by the drumming and resuming his dance – is this an image of death and rebirth?

Some years later when I published an account of the initiations I tried to answer these questions by making inordinate use of the slight exegesis which informants had given me, decoding the ritual activities as if they were symbolic representations of unconscious concerns. Determined, however, to be faithful to at least one aspect of the ritual form – its non-lineal, mosaic-like character – I borrowed my interpretative model from the structural study of myth, claiming that the initiations could be seen as "a myth staged rather than spoken, acted out rather than voiced". Noting that "ritual meanings are not often verbalised and perhaps cannot be because they surpass and confound language", I nevertheless applied a method of analysis that reduced "acts to words and gives objects a specific vocabulary." And while admitting that "ritual often makes language redundant" and makes questions superfluous, I proceeded to paraphrase the ritual movements and translate its actions into words (Jackson 1977: 181–2).

With hindsight I now realise the absurdity of this analytical procedure. In the first place I failed to take Kuranko comments at their face value and accept that the performances I witnessed were "just for entertainment", or as my field assistant put it, "for no other reason but to have everyone take part". In the second place I failed to accept that human beings do not necessarily act from opinions or employ epistemological criteria in finding meaning for their actions. In his "Remarks on Frazer's *Golden Bough*", Wittgenstein (1979: 7) argues that Frazer was not warranted in assuming that primitive rituals are informed by erroneous conceptions about the world, since "What makes the character of ritual action is not any view or opinion, either right or wrong",[23] though opinions and beliefs may of course "belong to a rite". In as much as Kuranko ritual actions make sense to them at the level of immediate experience, and do not purport to be true in terms of some systematic theory of knowledge, who are we to deny their emphasis on use-value and ask impertinent questions about veracity? It is probably the separateness of the observer from the ritual acts which makes him think that the acts refer to, or require

justification in, a domain beyond their actual compass.

For these reasons it is imperative to explore further what Wittgenstein called "the environment of a way of acting" and accept that understanding may be gained through seeing and drawing attention to connexions or "intermediary links" within such an environment, rather than by explaining acts in terms of preceding events, projected aims, unconscious concerns or precepts and rules.[24] After all, I never thought to ask Kuranko farmers why they hoed the earth or broadcast grain; neither did I interrogate women about the meaning of lighting a fire or the significance of cooking or raising children. In my approach to initiation I was clearly applying a distinction which Kuranko themselves do not recognise: between pragmatic "work" and "ritual" activity. Or, rather, I regarded the ludic elements in the ritual performances as exactly comparable to theatrical and stage performances in my own society where actions are scripted, deliberately directed and variously interpreted. My bourgeois conception of culture as something "superorganic", something separable from the quotidian world of bodily movements and practical tasks, had led me to seek the script, the director, and the interpretation in a rite which had none. This quest for semiotic truths also explained my inability to participate in the spirit of the performances, and why I spent my time asking people to tell me what was going on, what it all meant, as if the painted bodies and mimetic dances were only the insipid remnants of what had perhaps once been a symbolically coherent structure of myths and masks.

But to hold that every act signifies something is an extravagant form of abstraction, so long as this implies that the action stands for something other than itself, beyond the here and now. In anthropology this "something other" is usually a reified category designated by such verbal tokens as "social solidarity", "functional equilibrium", "adaptive integration" or "unconscious structure".[25]

Many of these notions enter into customary explanations given for the kinds of imitative practices I saw during the Kuranko initiations. Gluckman's (1963, 1970) account of ritualised role reversals in the Zulu first fruits ceremony (*umkhosi wokweshwama*) and *Nomkhulbulwana* ("Heavenly princess") cult stresses the psychological value of having a ritual safety-valve for women's grievances and resentments against men in a society where men control political and jural processes. The periodic catharsis afforded by the Zulu "rituals of rebellion" helps maintain social solidarity and functional equilibrium.[26] Leach (1961: 132–6) emphasises the relationship between role reversals and the ambiguous, liminal period during calendrical rites when, so to speak, time stands still and behaviour is not constrained by conventional structure. Giving less emphasis to cathartic and Saturnalian aspects of sex role reversal, Rigby has shown that among the Ugogo of Tanzania, calamities such as drought, barrenness in women, crop failure and cattle disease are considered to be reversals in fortune which can be mitigated by the manipulation of gender categories. Thus, women dress as men, mimic male demeanour, and perform male tasks in order to induce a re-reversal in correlative domains of natural ecology (1968: 172–3).

These studies convey invaluable insights, and in writing my original account of role reversals in Kuranko initiation I felt I had enough support from native exegesis to advance a similar interpretation. But I have always had serious misgivings about the way this sort of interpretation tends to exclude, because of its focus on oblique aims, semantic meanings and abstract functions, those very particularities of body use which are the most conspicuous elements in the rites, and which refer not to a domain of discourse or belief but to an environment of practical activity. What I now propose to do is work from an account of *how* these mimetic performances arise towards an account of *what* they mean and *why* they occur, without any a priori references to precepts, rules or symbols.

The Environment of a Way of Acting

Let us first take up a problem posed by Franziska Boas in 1944: "What is the relationship between the movements characteristic of a given dance, and the typical gestures and postures in daily life of the very people who perform it?" (1944: 55).

In the case of the mimetic performances I have described, every bodily element can be seen in other fields of Kuranko social life. Thus the women's uncanny imitations of male comportment are

mingled with elements which are conspicuous "borrowings" from mortuary ritual, such as the miming, the deadpan faces and the cutlass held hilt-down.[27] Still other elements refer us to the bush: the boy's imitation of the chimpanzee, the young men who pierce their cheeks with porcupine quills, the music of the praise-singer of the hunters (*serewayili*), the women's mimicry of hunters, the bush ochres daubed on the body and the wild fruit worn by the *Sewulan*.[28] The following transpositions can therefore be recognised:

Male domain	→	Female domain
Mortuary rites	→	Initiation rites
Bush	→	Village

The second crucial observation is that mimetic performers are women *not* immediately related to the neophytes. In this way, they are like the women who, with flat and doleful faces, perform at a man's funeral, and mimic the way he walked, danced, spoke and moved (Jackson 1978). Often wives of the dead man's sons, they simulate grief and repining *on behalf of* the immediate bereaved who play no part at all in the public rites. We cannot, therefore, explain the mimetic performances at initiations or funerals in terms of individual interest or affect. Indeed, when I put Gluckman's thesis to Kuranko women – that acting as men was a way of venting their resentments at men's power over them in everyday life – the women were bemused. "Was the 'mad *Kamban*' (*Kamban Yuwe*) really insane (*yuwe*) just because she behaved in a crazy way?" I was asked, and referred to another woman performer who, with distracted gestures, deadpan face and male attire, joined the *Sewulan* in the final stages of the ritual.

These patterns of body use are thus in a sense neutral, and are transposable from one domain to another. Moreover, the regular or conventional character of these bodily practices is not necessarily the result of obedience to rules or conscious intentions, but rather a consequence of ways people's bodies are informed by habits instilled within a shared environment and articulated as movements which are, to use Bourdieu's phrase, "collectively orchestrated without being the product of the orchestrating action of a conductor" (1977: 72).

These "transposable dispositions" arise in an environment of everyday practical activities which Bourdieu calls the *habitus*. As Mauss

(1973: 73) and Dewey (1929: 277–8) have also stressed, habits are interactional and tied to an environment of objects and others.[29] Forms of body use ("techniques du corps") are conditioned by our relationships with others, such as the way bodily dispositions which we come to regard as "masculine" or "feminine" are by our parents and peers encouraged and reinforced in us as mutually exclusive patterns. Or, patterns of body use are ingrained through our interactions with objects, such as the way that working at a desk or with a machine imposes and reinforces postural sets which we come to regard as belonging to sedentary white-collar workers and factory workers respectively. According to this view, collective representations such as those of gender and class are always correlated with patterns of body use generated within the habitus (see Bourdieu 1979). Moreover, both stereotypical ideas and bodily habits tend to reinforce each other in ways which remain "set" so long as the environment in which these attitudes are grounded itself remains stable.

Nevertheless, the habitual or "set" relations between ideas, experiences and body practices may be broken. Thus altered patterns of body use may induce new experiences and provoke new ideas, as when a regulation and steadying of the breath induces tranquillity of mind, or a balanced pose bodies forth a sense of equanimity. Likewise, emotional and mental turmoil may induce corresponding changes in bodily attitude, as when depression registers in a slumped posture or grief is manifest in an absolute loss of muscle tonus. But it is the disruption of the environment which mainly concerns me here, and the way such disruption triggers changes in bodily and mental disposition.

Kuranko initiation is first and foremost a disruption in the habitus, and it is this, rather than any precept, rule or stage management, that sets in train the social and personal alterations whose visible bodily aspect is role reversal. My argument is that this disruption in the habitus, wherein women enjoy a free run of the village and men must fend for themselves (even cooking their own meals) or stay indoors like cowed women (when the women's cult object is paraded through the village), lays people open to possibilities of behaviour which they embody but ordinarily are not inclined to express. Furthermore, I believe that it is on the strength of these extraordinary

possibilities that people control and recreate their world, their habitus.[30]

What then are these embodied yet latent possibilities which are realised during initiations? Some, like the grieving behaviours, are phylogenetically given. Others, like the entranced and dissociated rocking of the mimetic dancers, suggest a hypnotic element, the basis of which is a conditioned reflex whose origins are probably intra-uterine.[31] As for the basis of the sexual mimesis, it is important to point out that Kuranko children enjoy a free run of house and village space, unconfined by the conventional rules that strictly separate male and female domains. At the level of bodily knowledge, manifest in sexually amorphous modes of comportment, hairstyle and dress, pre-pubescent children are, as Kuranko themselves say, sexually indeterminate and "dirty". The transformed habitus during initiation simply reactivates these modes of comportment and opposite sex patterns deeply instilled in the somatic unconscious.

Now to the question why these particular possibilities are socially implemented and publicly played out. Let us first consider the transposition of bodily practices from domain to domain: bush to village, male to female, funeral to initiation. Here we find a parallel with those remarkable transpositions in nature whereby various organisms assume or mimic features of other organisms in the same habitat.[32] Just as this natural mimicry has survival value for a species, so it may be supposed that the survival of Kuranko society depends on the creation of responsible adults through initiatory ordeals as much as it depends upon the physical birth of children. To create adults requires a concerted application of information from *throughout the environment*, tapping the vital energies of the natural world,[33] "capturing" such "male" virtues as fortitude and bravery, and imitating the chimpanzee mother's alleged rejection of her offspring or the public mourners at a funeral whose feigned indifference to death also reminds women of how they must endure their daughters' separation in order for the girls to become independent women themselves.[34] We can therefore postulate that initiation ritual maximises the information available in the total environment in order to ensure the accomplishment of its vital task: creating adults and thereby recreating the social order. This process does not necessarily involve verbal or conceptual knowledge; rather, we might say that people are informed by and give form to a habitus which only an uninformed outside observer would take to be an object of knowledge.[35] Kuranko intentionality is thus less of a conceptual willing than a bodily in-tension, a stretching out, a habitual disposition towards the world.[36] Initiation rites involve a "practical mimesis"[37] in which are bodied forth and recombined elements from several domains, yet without script, sayings, promptings, conscious purposes or even emotions. No notion of "copying" can explain the naturalness with which the mimetic features appear. Women performers do not, as it were, observe men's behaviour in piecemeal fashion and then self-consciously put these observations together in an "act"; rather, this behaviour is generated by an innate and embodied principle which only requires an altered environment to "catch on" and come into play. This innate principle is, of course, the mimetic faculty itself,[38] though, as we have seen, it is always an environment of *cultural* practices which endows it with its specific expression.

The way in which initiation opens up and allows the enactment of possibilities which would not normally be entertained has also to be seen from an existential viewpoint since, as Sarles (1975: 30) notes, it is through attunement "and interaction with other bodies [that] one gains a sense of oneself and the external world". Although everybody is informed by common predispositions, it is the individual alone who embodies these predispositions as mimetic plays.[39] In so far as they permit each individual to play an active part in a project which effectively recreates the world, initiation rites maximise participation as well as information, allowing each person to discover in his or her own personality a way of producing, out of the momentary chaos, something which will contribute to a renewal of the *social* order. In this process, each person makes the world himself or herself out of elements which ordinarily are not considered appropriate; for example, women wearing the clothes and carrying the weapons of men. Yet, curiously enough, the principle of sexual complementarity in Kuranko society can be viable only if Kuranko men and women periodically recognise the other in themselves and see themselves in the other. Mimesis, which is based upon a bodily awareness of the

other in oneself, thus assists in bringing into relief a reciprocity of viewpoints.[40] As to the question why it is the same social order which is created over and over again, we must remember that the Kuranko habitus constrains behaviour, and that when the bodily unconscious is addressed openly it answers with forms and features which reflect a closed social universe. Thus the creative freedom and interpretative licence in mimetic play is always circumscribed by the habitus in which people have been raised. Freedom must therefore be seen as a matter of realising and experiencing one's potential within this given universe, not above or beyond it.

Let us now turn to a second kind of transposition, in which patterns of body use engender mental images and instill moral qualities. We are all familiar with the way decontraction of muscular "sets" and the freeing of energies bound up in habitual deformations of posture or movement produce an altered sense of self, in particular a dissolution of those conceptual "sets" such as role, gender and status which customarily define our social identity.[41] My argument is that the distinctive modes of body use during initiation tend to throw up images in the mind whose form is most immediately determined by the pattern of body use. This is not to say that all mental forms should be reduced to bodily practices; rather, that within the unitary field of body-mind-habitus it is possible to intervene and effect changes from any one of these points. By approaching cognition in this manner we are able to enter the domain of words and symbols by the back door, so to speak, and show that what the Kuranko themselves say about initiation can be correlated at every turn with what is done with the body.

Apart from the examples in which facial impassivity is correlated with such moral qualities as the control of emotion and the acceptance of separation, other instances can be cited of bodily praxis inducing or suggesting ethical ideas. Thus, the value of moderation is inculcated through taboos on calling for food or referring to food whilst in the initiation lodge. The interdiction on the neophytes speaking out of turn, moving or crying out during the operations is directly connected to the virtues of keeping secrets, promises and oaths, and of forbearance and circumspection.[42] Similarly, the importance placed on listening to elders during the period of sequestration in the bush is correlated with the virtue of respecting elders whose counsels guarantee social as well as physical life – a correlation pointed up by such adages as *sie tole l to* ("long life comes from attending") and *si ban tol sa* ("short life ear has not"). Again, the sleepless night (*kinyale*) which initiates must endure in a smoke-filled house on the eve of their return from the bush after initiation is a way of instilling in them the virtues of withstanding hardship and being alert; enforced confinement is connected to the value placed on self-restraint and self-containment. Other senses are developed too, so that keenness of smell is correlated with the quality of discrimination (newly-initiated boys often quite literally "turn up their noses" at the sight of uninitiated kids, remarking on their crude smell), and control of the eyes is connected with sexual proprieties, most notably mindfulness of those domains and secret objects associated with the other sex which one may not see except on pain of death. Finally, the donning of new clothes suggests in the initiate's mind the assumption of a new status, while the women's imitations of men are sometimes explained similarly as a way women take on "male" virtues of fortitude and bravery which they feel they sorely lack.[43]

These examples indicate how, in Kuranko initiation, what is done with the body is the ground of what is thought and said. From an existential point of view we could say that the bodily practices mediate a personal realisation of social values, an immediate grasp of general precepts as sensible truths. Such a view is consistent with the tendency to effect understanding through bodily techniques, to proceed through bodily awareness to verbal skills and ethical views.[44] Bodily self-mastery is thus everywhere the basis for social and intellectual mastery. The primacy given to embodied over verbal understanding is readily seen in the following excerpt from a conversation I once had with a Kuranko elder, Saran Salia Sano,

ss: Even when they are cutting the foreskin you must not flinch. You have to stand stock still. You must not make a sound from the mouth. Better to die than to wince or blink or cry out!

MJ: But what kind of instruction is given?

ss: To respect your elders... not to be arrogant ... that is all. Disrespectful boys are beaten. A pliable stick is flicked against the side of your face or ear if you begin to doze. In the *fafei* (initiation lodge) you get tamed properly.

It is not surprising to find such an emphasis on bodily praxis in a preliterate society where most practical learning is a matter of direct observation and "prestigious imitation".[45] It is this emphasis on embodied knowledge and "kinaesthetic learning"[46] which may explain why failures to uphold ethical expectations are usually seen by the Kuranko in bodily terms: as leading to physical weakening, disease or death. Furthermore, it is because bodily praxis in initiation imparts knowledge directly that the Kuranko do not need to formulate the meaning of the rite in terms of verbal elaborations or moral concepts.[47] The fact is that knowledge is directly linked to the production of food and community, and the relationship between thought, language and activity is intrinsically closer in a preliterate subsistence society than in a modern literate society where knowledge is often abstracted and held aloof from the domains of bodily skills and material processes of production. It is noteworthy that when the Kuranko *do* supply verbal exegesis it tends to centre on root metaphors which refer to bodily and practical activity in the habitus. Thus, initiation is said to be a process of taming (unruly emotions and bodies), of moulding (clay), of making dry or cool (as in cooking, smoking and curing), of ripening (as of grain and fruit), of strengthening (the heart), hardening or straightening (the body), of getting "new sense" (*hankili kura*).[48] These allusions to domestic and agricultural life are not mere figures of speech, for they disclose real connexions between personal maturity and the ability to provide food for and give support to others. Bodily and moral domains are fused, and, as Kuranko say, maturity is a matter of common sense (*communis sententia*) which is achieved when inner thoughts are consistent with spoken words and external actions.

Why should ritual action accord such primacy to bodily techniques? In the first place, bodily movements can do more than words can say. In this sense techniques of the body may be compared with musical techniques since both transport us from the quotidian world of verbal distinctions and categorical separations into a world where boundaries are blurred and experience transformed. Dance and music move us to participate in a world beyond our accustomed roles, and to recognise ourselves as members of a community, a common body. This is not to say that music and bodily practices are never means of making social distinctions;[49] only that, within the context of communal rites, music and movement often take the form of oppositional practices which eclipse speech and nullify the divisions which dominate everyday life. Kuranko say that music and dance are "sweet"; they loosen and lighten, by contrast with normal behaviour which is contractual, binding, and constrained.[50] In this way, movement and music promote a sense of levity and openness in both body and mind, and make possible an empathic understanding of others, a fellow-feeling, which verbal and cognitive forms ordinarily inhibit.[51] But such a reciprocity of viewpoints is often experienced bodily before it is apprehended in the mind, as in the case of mimetic practices in which one literally adopts the position or dons the clothing of another. Merleau-Ponty puts it in this way:

> The communication or comprehension of gestures comes about through the reciprocity of my intentions and the gestures of others, of my gestures and intentions discernible in the conduct of other people. It is as if the other person's intention inhabited my body and mine his...There is a mutual confirmation between myself and others...The act by which I lend myself to the spectacle must be recognized as irreducible to anything else. I join it in a kind of blind recognition which precedes the intellectual working out and clarification of the meaning. (1962: 185)

In Kuranko initiation, women's imitations of men presumably promote a sense of what it is to be a man. Yet, inasmuch as these body practices are not preceded by any verbal definition of intention, they are ambiguous. The imitations are therefore open to interpretation, and the meaning they may assume for either performer or observer is indeterminate. This indeterminacy is of the essence, and it is perfectly possible that the imitations will be experienced or seen variously as a way of "borrowing" male virtue, a kind of mockery of men, an inept copying that only goes to show that women could

never really occupy the roles of men, a rebellious expropriation of male privileges, or even as a marker that men are temporarily "dead". It is this ambiguity, and the fact that the interpretations which do arise tend to confound everyday proprieties of gender and role, which may account for Kuranko women's silence on the question of meaning: the imitations mean everything and nothing. By the same token, the anthropologist who seeks to reduce bodily praxis to the terms of verbal discourse runs the risk of falsifying both (cf. Bourdieu 1977: 120; 223 n. 40). Practical understanding can do without concepts, and as Bourdieu points out "the language of the body...is incomparably more ambiguous and overdetermined than the most overdetermined uses of ordinary language...Words, however charged with connotation, limit the range of choices and render difficult or impossible, and in any case explicit and therefore 'falsifiable', the relations which the language of the body suggests" (1977: 120).

It is because actions speak louder *and* more ambiguously than words that they are more likely to lead us to common truths; not semantic truths, established by others at other times, but experiential truths which seem to issue from within our own Being when we break the momentum of the discursive mind or throw ourselves into some collective activity in which we each find our own meaning yet sustain the impression of having a common cause and giving common consent.

My main argument has been against undue abstraction in ethnographical analysis. Against the tendencies to explain human behaviour in terms of linguistic models, patterns of social organisation, institutions or roles, structures of the mind or symbolic meaning, I have endeavoured to advance a grounded view which begins with interactions and movements of people in an organised environment, and considers in detail the patterns of body praxis which arise therein.

My focus on the embodied character of lived experience in the habitus also reflects a conviction that anthropological analysis should be consonant with indigenous understandings which, in preliterate societies, are frequently embedded in practices (doings) rather than spelled out in ideas (sayings). Although such a consonance is, for me, a fundamental measure of adequacy in ethnographical interpretation, I do not think that interpretation necessarily consists in finding *agreement* between our verbal reactions to observed practices and the exegesis which may be provided by the practitioners. Inasmuch as bodily praxis cannot be reduced to a semiotic, bodily practices are always open to interpretation; they are not in themselves interpretations of anything.

If we construe anthropological understanding as principally a language game in which semiotic values are assigned to bodily practices, then we can be sure that to the extent that the people we

study make nothing of their practices outside of a living, we will make anything of them within reason. But if we take anthropological understanding to be first and foremost a way of acquiring social and practical skills without any *a priori* assumptions about their significance or function, then a different kind of knowledge follows. That is to say that, by avoiding the solipsism and ethnocentrism that pervade much symbolic analysis, an empathic understanding may be found. [...]

Notes

1 I have borrowed this term from Russell Keat (per. comm. 1982) who argues that the body has been excluded from social scientific discourse through a twofold process of "etherealisation" and "materialisation". While the first gives the body to the humanities, the second assigns it to the biological sciences.

2 The term is introduced by Kroeber in his seminal 1917 paper, *The superorganic*; his definition of culture remains largely unrevised in his 1952 review of the concept of culture (Kroeber and Kluckhohn 1963: 284).

3 Such a view can be traced back even further to the Aristotelian metaphysical doctrine that nature is an ordered series from lower to higher potentialities and actualisations in which the organic body was "the highest term in a physical series and the lowest term in a psychical series" (Dewey 1929: 250).

4 Cf. Brown's thesis that "culture originates in the denial of life and the body" and "the recovery of life in the body is the hidden aim of history" (1959: 297).

5 Here one should note the male bias in anthropology towards uncritically adopting the male emphasis in many preliterate worldviews, defining women as subservient, passive and low in status, and assuming that women are logically if not biologically closer to nature than men are (MacCormack 1980; Etienne and Leacock 1980: 3). It is interesting that feminism has played a significant role in bringing the body back into discourse by making issues such as rape and abortion crucial to an understanding of social inequality.

6 Studies of "material culture" have come to occupy an increasingly marginal place in anthropology, artefacts being defined as insignificant unless, like masks, they can be assimilated into the field of cognitive and symbolic analysis.

7 It is really only since the 1960s that studies of bodily movement and dance have begun to assume a significant place in anthropological inquiry.

Hitherto, Morgan's dismissive view of music and dance seemed to prevail: "These amusements of our primitive inhabitants are not, in themselves, devoid of interest, although they indicate a tendency of mind unbefitting rational men" (cited in Royce 1977: 190).

8 For an excellent critique of such ethological approaches to "non-verbal communication" and the problem of objective meaning see Poole 1975: 74–106.

9 "Whereas the conscious ego speaks through the rational verbal language, the observable behavior of the body speaks an expressive language of its own. It may even say 'no' when the verbal language asserts 'yes'. We understand this language of facial expression, posture, gesture, or involuntary bodily changes first and best. The small child understands the facial expression of his mother long before he understands the verbal language" (Thass-Thienemann 1968: 38–9). On the phylogenetic and ontogenetic primacy of non-linguistic thinking see Vygotsky 1962: 42–4; Hewes 1973: 5–12; Reich 1949: 361, 381; Blacking 1977: 21.

10 Cf. Bachelard's notion of the "housed" unconscious, and of the way memories are housed. He suggests that the systematic exploration of the "sites of our intimate lives" would be a topoanalysis rather than a psychoanalysis (1964: 8).

11 Reich: "The living not only functions before and beyond word language; more than that, it has *its own specific forms of expression which cannot be put into words at all...the biopathy, with its disturbed expression of life, is outside the realm of language and concepts*" (1949: 361, 363, original emphasis).

12 Cf. Black on the background of hypnotherapy: "There is thus a 'somatic mind' which is unconscious and presumably without any means of verbalisation of experience – and a 'cerebral mind' which is conscious. But since the brain and nervous system are

also part of the body...the dividing line between the two is not always clearly defined" (1969: 133). On the background to activity therapies (including ritual) see d'Aquili et al. 1979: 143; Lowen 1971: xii; Reich 1949; Ferenczi 1955.

13   See Straus 1966: 137–65, cf. Jantsch 1975: 28–32. It is worth noting that the root *sta* is found in terms for physical, conceptual *and* social Being: standing, estate, understanding, status, institution, constitution, statute (Straus 1966: 143).

14   Best 1978: 139–45. In a similar vein, referring to dance studies that relate dance to language categories such as syntax and grammer, Royce notes: "It may be, in fact, that we are distoring the phenomenon of dance by forcing it into a taxonomic system designed for a qualitatively different kind of phenomenon. This type of comparison may ultimately tell us that we have to deal with dance on its own terms" (1977: 201).

15   Speaking of an angry or threatening gesture, Merleau-Ponty makes a similar point: "The gesture *does not make me think* of anger, it is anger itself...The sense of the gestures is not given, but understood, that is, seized upon by an act on the spectator's part. The whole difficulty is to conceive this act clearly without confusing it with a cognitive operation" (1962: 184–5, original emphasis).

16   This view is elaborated in Wittgenstein 1953.

17   This is at once evident in the titles of books and essays which have proliferated such phrases as "body language", "body symbolism", "body syntax", "body semiotics".

18   See for instance the second part of the introductory paragraph in chapter 5 of *Natural symbols* ("The two bodies"), 1970: 93.

19   Polhemus comments on the dual preoccupation of the anthropology of the body with problems of communication and with a Durkheimian model of society "as a holistic beast" (1975: 30).

20   In so far as Western notions of culture have alienated us from the body, the reduction of the body to mere instrumentality is an expression of a long-standing historical bias (see May 1969: 239).

21   Hubert Benoit speaks of mind and body at "the point at which they are born...the central unconscious cross-roads of my 'being'", and notes that the physical and psychic "reveal the same principle and...are not obliged to react one against the other" (1955: 57–8).

22   The ethnographical data to which the following account refers are published elsewhere (Jackson 1977) and detailed description is, in this essay, kept to a minimum.

23   "A religious symbol does not rest on any *opinion*. And error belongs only with opinion" (Wittgenstein 1979: 3). Cf. Leenhardt's comment on

Canaque (New Caledonia) myth: "What is lived cannot be disputed" (1979: 19).

24   Cf. Oakeshott's arguments against the notion that activity springs from "premeditated propositions about the activity" such as the grammar of a language, rules of research, canons of good workmanship (1962: 91). His example of the cookery book succinctly summarises his view: "The cookery book is not an independently generated beginning from which cookery can spring; it is nothing more than an abstract of somebody's knowledge of how to cook; it is the stepchild, not the parent of the activity" and already presupposes a knowledge of cooking and a capable cook (1962: 119).

25   See Elster 1979: 28–35 for a critique of such theories of meaning.

26   Gluckman 1970: ch. 5; 1963: ch. 3. See Rigby 1968: 166–74 and Ngubane 1977: 151–5 for critiques.

27   See Jackson 1978 for detailed account.

28   For exact descriptions see Jackson 1977: 188–95.

29   Jones (1976: 100–3) has pointed out that Dewey's account of habit draws closely on Alexander's theory and practice of "use", and I also acknowledge an indebtedness to Alexander's work in this essay, especially his book *The use of self* (1931).

30   In *Allegories of the wilderness* (1982) I argue that folk narratives similarly provoke in people a realisation of possibilities which are regarded as being extra-social and belonging to the "bush" yet are vitally essential to the recreation and continuity of the social order.

31   Hypnotic induction depends on rhythmic stimulation and some kind of constriction. Swaddling of infants may condition hypnotic responsiveness, but Black (1969: 161–3) argues that the intrauterine environment is probably the basis for the hypnotic patterning.

32   Black 1969: 280–1 discusses specific examples.

33   Such as when men draw their strength from stones and from mountains in the *Konke* ("stone mountain") cult or from bush spirits in other cults (e.g. *Kome*).

34   Control of emotions at funerals is considered essential to the separation of the deceased's shade from the living community (Jackson 1978).

35   Cf. May: "in the process of knowing, we are *informed* by the thing understood, and in the same act, our intellect simultaneously *gives form* to the thing we understand" (1969: 225, original emphasis).

36   This notion of "embodied will" is conveyed in the etymology of the word "intentionality". The Latin stem *intendere* consists of *in* plus *tendere, tensum*, the latter meaning "to stretch." "This tells us immediately that intention is a 'stretching' toward something" (May 1969: 228; also 240–2).

37 See Bourdieu on the difference between "practical mimesis" and verbal analogy or metaphor (1977: 116).

38 For an account of the anatomical basis of mimetic behaviour and the mimetic faculty see Goss (1959) and Sarles (1975: 25–6).

39 This means that imitative practices have both a passive and an active aspect; the performer both discovers in himself things already there *and* makes those things happen or come alive, as well as charging them with meaning. This ambiguous sense of the concept of "imitation" is clearly present in Aristotle's account of mimesis in the *Poetics* (see Else 1957: 321).

40 Body praxis thus reinforces emotional *and* cognitive attitudes (ethos *and* eidos). Cf. Bateson's arguments concerning the periodic offsetting of complementary schizmogenetic tendencies with ritualised forms of symmetrical schizmogenesis (1958: 289–90).

41 Cf. Reich (1949) on the relation between character and specific patterns of muscular spasm and "armouring", and Benoit on the relation between sense of self and forms of muscular contraction (1955: 85–6).

42 A complete account of these moral precepts and the keeping of secrets is given in Jackson 1982: ch. I.

43 A comparable explanation has been offered for female imitations of male behaviour in the Zulu *nomkhulbulwana* rites. When Zulu girls dress in their lovers' clothes they say it is a way of inducing thoughts of and exerting influence over their lovers who are often living away in the mines. "The ones we are thinking of when we do this thing are the men who love us. We wish to think of them... If we wear the dress of our lovers then *Nomkhulbulwana* sees that we want her to assist us in marrying them" (Berglund 1976: 68).

44 "One thing becomes remarkably clear as soon as we begin to look at initiation. This is that, first and foremost, initiation constitutes a progressive course of instruction designed to familiarize the person with the significations of his own body and with the meaning he gives to the environment. Moreover, each of these is in a sense a function of the other: the human body and the world constitute two inseparable entities conceived in relation to each other" (Zahan 1970: 56).

45 The phrase is used by Mauss to designate a person's imitation of actions which he has seen successfully performed "by people in whom he has confidence and who have authority over him" (1973: 73).

46 An excellent account of this mode of learning is Bateson and Mead's account of Balinese learning: "Balinese learn virtually nothing from verbal instruction" (1942: 15).

47 Cf. "Words must be captured and repeated to have meaning for action, but there is no need at all to translate action into words" (Bateson and Mead 1942: 15).

48 The Kuranko word for intelligence, *hankilimaiye*, designates common sense and savoir faire, a mode of being in-formed, of having social *and* practical skills. As one informant defined it, "intelligence is the way you do things".

49 As Blacking has pointed out, musicality and musical production in European societies have increasingly come to define distinctions at the levels of ability, taste and class, and generate the illusion that musicality is not a universal faculty. Comparing the European with the African situation where musicality is a common property and musicians choose musical forms that enable participation, Blacking asks: "Must the majority be made 'unmusical' [in European societies] so that the few may become more 'musical'?" (1973: 4).

50 See Jackson 1982 for detailed discussion in the context of folk narratives.

51 I share Blacking's view here when he writes that his "concern for an anthropology of the body rests on a conviction that feelings, and particularly fellow-feeling, expressed as movements of bodies in space and time and *often without verbal connotations*, are the basis of mental life" (1977: 21, my emphasis).

References

Alexander, F. Matthias 1931. *The use of self.* London: Methuen.

Bachelard, Gaston 1964. *The poetics of space* trans. Maria Jolas. New York: Orion Press.

Bateson, Gregory 1958. *Naven.* Stanford: University Press.

Bateson, Gregory and Margaret Mead 1942. *Balinese character: a photographic analysis.* Special publications of the New York Academy of Sciences vol. 2.

Benoit, Hubert 1955. *The supreme doctrine.* London: Routledge & Kegan Paul.

Berglund, Axel-Ivar 1976. *Zulu thought-patterns and symbolism.* London: C. Hurst.

Best, David 1978. *Philosophy and human movement.* London: George Allen & Unwin.

Binswanger, Ludwig 1963. *Being-in-the-world: selected papers* trans. Jacob Needleman. New York: Basic Books.

Black, Stephen 1969. *Mind and body*. London: William Kimber.

Blacking, John 1973. *How musical is man?* Seattle: University of Washington Press.

Blacking, John 1977. Towards an anthropology of the body. In *The anthropology of the body* ed. John Blacking, London: Academic Press.

Boas, Franziksa 1944. *The function of dance in human society*. New York: Dance Horizons.

Bourdieu, Pierre 1977: *Outline of a theory of practice* trans. Richard Nice. Cambridge: University Press.

Bourdieu, Pierre 1979. *La distinction: critique sociale du jugement*. Paris: Editions de Minuit.

Brown, Norman O. 1959. *Life against death: the psycho-analytical meaning of history*. London: Routledge & Kegan Paul.

d'Aquili, E. G., C. D. Laughlin and John McManus 1979. *The spectrum of ritual, a biogenetic structural analysis*. New York: Columbia University Press.

Dewey, John 1929. *Experience and nature*. London: George Allen & Unwin.

Douglas, Mary 1970. *Natural symbols*. London: Barrie & Jenkins.

Douglas, Mary 1978. *Implicit meanings: essays in anthropology*. London: Routledge & Kegan Paul.

Else, Gerald F. 1957. *Aristotle's poetics: the argument*. Cambridge, Mass.: Harvard University Press.

Elster, Jon 1979. *Ulysses and the sirens: studies in rationality and irrationality*. Cambridge: University Press.

Etienne, Mona and Eleanor Leacock 1980. Introduction. In *Women and colonization: anthropological perspectives* (eds.) Mona Etienne and Eleanor Leacock. New York: Praeger.

Ferenczi, Sándor 1955. *Final contributions to the problems and methods of psychoanalysis*. London: Hogarth Press.

Gluckman, Max 1963. *Order and rebellion in tribal Africa*. London: Cohen & West.

Gluckman, Max 1970. *Custom and conflict in Africa*. Oxford: Basil Blackwell.

Goss, Charles Mayo (ed.) 1959. [Gray's] *Anatomy of the human body*. Philadelphia: Lea & Febiger.

Hewes, Gordon W. 1973. Primate communication and the gestural origin of language. *Current Anthropology* 14, 5–24.

Jackson, Michael 1977. *The Kuranko: dimensions of social reality in a West African society*. London: C. Hurst.

Jackson, Michael 1978. The identity of the dead. *Cah. Étud. Afr.* 66–7 (2–3), 271–97.

Jackson, Michael 1982. *Allegories of the wilderness: ethics and ambiguity in Kuranko narratives*. Bloomington: Indiana University Press.

Jantsch, Erich 1975. *Design for evolution: self-organization and planning in the life of human systems*. New York: George Braziller.

Jones, Frank Pierce 1976. *Body awareness in action: a study of the Alexander technique*. New York: Schocken Books.

Kroeber, A. L. 1917. The superorganic. *American Anthropologist* 10, 163–213.

Kroeber, A. L. and Clyde Kluckhohn 1963. *Culture: a critical review of concepts and definitions*. New York: Vintage Books.

Leach, Edmund 1961. *Rethinking anthropology*. London: Athlone Press.

Leenhardt, Maurice 1979. *Do Kamo: person and myth in the Melanesian world* trans. Basia Miller-Gulati. Chicago: University Press.

Lowen, Alexander 1971. *The language of the body*. London: Collier-Macmillan.

MacCormack, Carol P. 1980. Nature, culture and gender: a critique. In *Nature, culture and gender* (eds.) Carol P. McCormack and Marilyn Strathern. Cambridge: University Press.

Mauss, Marcel 1973. Techniques of the body. Translated from the French by Ben Brewster. *Economy and Society* 2, 70–88.

May, Rollo 1969. *Love and will*. New York: W. W. Norton.

Merleau-Ponty, Maurice. 1962. *The phenomenology of perception* trans. Colin Smith. London: Routledge & Kegan Paul.

Ngubane, Harriet 1977. *Body and mind in Zulu medicine*. London: Academic Press.

Oakeshott, Michael 1962. *Rationalism in politics and other essays*. London: Methuen.

Polhemus, Ted 1975. Social bodies. In *The body as a medium of expression* (eds.) Jonathan Benthall and Ted Polhemus. London: Allen Lane.

Poole, Roger 1975. Objective sign and subjective meaning, in *The body as a medium of expression* (eds.) Jonathan Benthall and Ted Polhemus. London: Allen Lane.

Reich, Wilhelm 1949. *Character analysis*. New York: Noonday Press.

Rigby, Peter 1968. Some Gogo rituals of "purification": an essay on social and moral categories. In *Dialectic in practical religion* ed. E. R. Leach. Cambridge: University Press.

Royce, Anya Peterson 1977. *The anthropology of dance*. Bloomington: Indiana University Press.

Sarles, Harvey B. 1975. A human ethological approach to communication: ideas in transit around the Cartesian impasse. In *Organization of behavior in face-to-face interaction*. (eds.) Adam Kendon, Richard M. Harris and Mary Ritchie Key. The Hague: Mouton.

Straus, Erwin W. 1966. *Phenomenological psychology*. New York: Basic Books.

Thass-Thienemann, Theodore 1968. *Symbolic behavior.* New York: Washington Square Press.

Vygotsky, L. S. 1962. *Thought and language* (eds.) and trans. Eugenia Hanfmann and Gertrude Vakar. New York: John Wiley.

Wittgenstein, Ludwig 1953. *Philosophical investigations* trans. G. E. M. Anscombe. Oxford: Basil Blackwell.

Wittgenstein, Ludwig 1979. *Remarks on Frazer's Golden Bough* trans. A. C. Miles ed. Rush Rhees. Atlantic Highlands, NJ: Humanities Press.

Zahan, Dominique 1970. *The religion, spirituality, and thought of traditional Africa* trans. Kate Ezra Martin and Lawrence M. Martin. Chicago: University Press.

27

The End of the Body?

Emily Martin

Why is the body such an intense focus of attention in the academy today? New books rain down on us: *The Body in the Mind* (Johnson 1987), *The Body and the French Revolution* (Outram 1989), *Body Invaders* (Kroker and Kroker 1987), *Bodies* (Glassner 1988), *Gender/Body/Knowledge* (Jaggar and Bordo 1989), and so on. Perhaps all this attention has come about simply because the body is now a central feature of contemporary Western social forms. Certainly, numerous historical forces could be said to have played a role in producing the current salience of the body. European state formation, creating and protecting individual rights, produced citizens who, one per body, voted, fought, paid taxes, and sowed their seed (Corrigan and Sayer 1985). Industrialization, which incorporated workers into factory structures separated from family and community, controlled and harnessed individual bodies in new ways. Modern forms of power, deployed in the normalizing discourses of sciences such as psychiatry and biology, lead us to spill the contents of our inner lives into the waiting arms of new disciplines of knowledge. This power "seeps into the very grain of individuals, reaches right into their bodies, permeates their gestures, their posture, what they say, how they learn to live and work with other people" (Foucault, quoted in Sheridan 1980:217).

Given all this, it is no wonder that the body is so often a focus of social and cultural analysis. However, I would argue that there is another way of explaining why the body is such an intense focus of academic attention today. In *Tristes Tropiques* (1967) Lévi-Strauss described how phenomena become the focus of attention in the academy precisely when they are ending; he was speaking of the "primitive," which was in the process of disappearing for the last time. Is one reason so many of us are energetically studying the body precisely that we are undergoing fundamental changes in how our bodies are organized and experienced? Some have claimed that the body as a bounded entity is in fact ending under the impact of commodification, fragmentation, and the proliferation of images of body parts (Kroker and Kroker 1987:20). Without discounting these claims, I would argue they need to be seen in a particular context. In the following I will suggest that people in the United States (and perhaps elsewhere) are now experiencing a

Anthropology in Theory: Issues in Epistemology, Second Edition. Edited by Henrietta L. Moore and Todd Sanders.
© 2014 John Wiley & Sons, Inc. Published 2014 by John Wiley & Sons, Inc.

dramatic transition in body percept and practice, from bodies suited for and conceived in the terms of the era of Fordist mass production to bodies suited for and conceived in the terms of the era of flexible accumulation. We are seeing not the end of the body, but rather the end of one kind of body and the beginning of another kind of body.

The Fordist Body

Imagery in reproductive biology exemplifies what I mean by the Fordist body. In reproductive biology, bodies are organized around principles of centralized control and factory-based production. Men continuously produce wonderfully astonishing quantities of highly valued sperm, women produce eggs and babies (though neither efficiently) and, when they are not doing this, either produce scrap (menstruation) or undergo a complete breakdown of central control (menopause). The models that confer order are hierarchical pyramids with the brain firmly located at the top and the other organs ranged below. The body's products all flow out over the edge of the body, through one orifice or another, into the outside world. Steady, regular output is prized above all, preferably over the entire life span, as exemplified by the production of sperm (Martin 1987, 1991).

In contemporary cell biology similar motifs are present. Inside the cell, the nucleus with its genetic material is seen as the privileged head of the cell "family":

> The master-molecule has become, in DNA, the unmoved mover of the changing cytoplasm. In this cellular version of the Aristotelian cosmos, the nucleus is the efficient cause (as Aristotle posited the sperm to be) while the cytoplasm (like Aristotle's conception of the female substrate) is merely the *material* cause. The nuclear DNA is the essence of domination and control. Macromolecule as machomolecule. (Beldecos et al. 1988:70)

These models of the body seem related in form and function to early 20th-century Fordist mass-production systems. Such systems sought efficiency by means of economies of scale in production; they were geared to producing large quantities of standardized products put together from standardized components.

During the establishment of Fordist forms of organization in the United States, Antonio Gramsci wrote that Fordism implied "the biggest collective effort to date to create, with unprecedented speed, and with a consciousness of purpose unmatched in history, a new type of worker and a new type of man" (quoted in Harvey 1989a:126).[1] The success of Fordist production would rely on new constructions of sexuality, reproduction, family life, moral ideals, masculinity, and femininity. New habits would preserve, "outside of work, a certain psychophysical equilibrium which [would] prevent the physiological collapse of the worker, exhausted by the new method of production." This equilibrium could become internalized "if it [were] proposed by a new form of society, with appropriate and original methods" (Gramsci 1971:303). Some means by which a new form of society was "proposed" involved coercion. Henry Ford sent investigators into workers' homes to intervene in their private lives. One hundred fifty investigators admonished workers to practice thrifty and hygienic habits and to avoid smoking, gambling, and drinking. These early social workers decided which workers "because of unsatisfactory personal habits or home conditions" were not eligible to receive the full five-dollar wage Ford offered (Gelderman 1981:56–7). Other means, we might speculate, could operate at a less obvious level. Perhaps scientific body imagery, capturing the essential features of Fordist production, was one "appropriate and original method" that could lead people to internalize a new form of society. Perhaps the two sets of interrelated imageries in the body and in society were used to think thoughts and organize practice about time, space, substance, productivity, efficiency, and so on.

The Body in Late Capitalism

In the course of my fieldwork on contemporary concepts of the immune system, I began to wonder whether the Fordist body was being transformed.[2] Far from being reminiscent of Fordist production, talk about the immune system seems to share its logic with a different social formation, one that began to coalesce sometime in the 1970s. Are new modes of "living and thinking and feeling life" (Gramsci, quoted in Harvey 1989a:126) coming into being alongside wrenching new forms of social organization? Could the writing of these new modes into the body, via what we think of as scientific "truth," be a particularly powerful way in which certain principles are literally being internalized, making an important contribution to creating a "new type of worker and a new type of man [and woman]," a new "shape of life" (Flax 1990:39)?

Called variously late capitalism (Ernst Mandel) or the regime of flexible accumulation (David Harvey), the new formation has as its hallmarks technological innovation, specificity, and rapid, flexible change. It entails "flexible system production with [an] emphasis upon problem solving, rapid and often highly specialized responses, and adaptability of skills to special purposes"; "an increasing capacity to manufacture a variety of goods cheaply in small batches" (Harvey 1989a:155); "an acceleration in the pace of product innovation together with the exploration of highly specialized and small-scale market niches"; and "new organizational forms (such as the 'just-in-time' inventory-flows delivery system, which cuts down radically on stocks required to keep production flow going)" (Harvey 1989a:156).[3]

Laborers experience a speed-up in the processes of labor and an intensification in the deskilling and re-skilling that are constantly required. New technologies in production reduce turnover time dramatically, entailing similar accelerations in exchange and consumption. "Improved systems of communication and information flow, coupled with rationalizations in techniques of distribution (packaging, inventory control, containerization, market feed-back, etc.), make it possible to circulate commodities through the market system with greater speed" (Harvey 1989a:285). Time and space are compressed, as the time horizons of decision making shrink and instantaneous communications and cheaper transport costs allow decisions to be effected over a global space (Harvey 1989a:147).[4] Multinational capital operates in a globally integrated environment: ideally, capital flows unimpeded across all borders, all points are connected by instantaneous communications, and products are made as needed for the momentary and continuously changing market.[5]

The imagery used to describe the immune system in the body strongly evokes these descriptions of the operation of global capital.[6] In the scientific discipline of immunology, the body is depicted as a whole, interconnected system complete unto itself. The body is seen as "an

engineered communications system, ordered by a fluid and dispersed command-control-intelligence network" (Haraway 1989:12). One example of this is a line drawing from a college textbook showing the complex communications among three types of immune system cells: macro-phages, T cells, and B cells. The macrophage has taken the foreign bacterium, the antigen, inside itself, processed it, and put it back on the surface along with a protein called MHC, which marks cells in this particular body as "self." This allows a T cell to "recognize" the foreign antigen as something to be dealt with, and it sends the first activation "signal" to a B cell. At the same time the B cell recognizes the foreign material directly. Meanwhile the macrophage is sending signals to both T and B cells. Then other T cells send further signals to the B cell, leading it to differentiate and start producing antibody, which will eliminate the foreign matter that the macrophage ingested in the first place. This is only a tiny portion of the total system of communication and control involved. One further element is crucial: at a later stage, another kind of T cell is activated; called the T suppressor cell, it is a "controlling mechanism that turn[s] off the proliferation of reactive cells and limit[s] the extent of the response" (Sell 1987:224).

The classroom version of this tends to be elaborate chalkboard sketches with countless arrows showing signals from one cell to another in the system, accompanied by frequent statements that all functions are interrelated. This is a homeostatic, self-regulating system, complete unto itself. This way of seeing the immune system is far from limited to an esoteric scientific community. As part of a three-year research project, several graduate students and I have done over 100 extensive interviews on health concepts and practices with residents of several urban neighborhoods.[7] We have found that people convey the systemic character of the immune system in various ways:[8]

BILL WALTERS (SERVICE WORKER IN HIS TWENTIES): I don't even think about the heart anymore; I think about the immune system as being the major thing that's keeping the heart going in the first place, and now that I think about it I would have to say yeah, the immune system is really…important…and the immune system isn't even a vital organ, it's just an act, you know? […]

STEVEN BAKER (TEACHER IN HIS SIXTIES): The immune system is the whole body, it's not just the lungs or the abdomen, it's, I mean if I cut myself, doesn't my immune system start to work right away to prevent infection? So it's in your finger; I mean it's everywhere.

Next, consider what kind of production is associated with the immune system. The essence of contemporary scientific descriptions of the immune system is careful regulation of production in orientation to specific needs, not efficient production on a mass scale as in the Fordist model. When I was taking my first course in immunology, I was struck by the repeated emphasis on the "specificity" of immune system cells, both T cells and B cells. For example, as a B cell matures, it develops surface receptors that will be "committed to a single specificity…a specificity to a single antigen." One of the first lectures in the course, on immunoglobulins (also called antibodies), started out with "immuno-globulin facts to amaze you":

> There are 6×10^{16} immunoglobulin molecules per ml of blood, 5 liters of blood in the body, or 3×10^{20} molecules of immunoglobulin in the body. A visiting lecturer will say there are 10^6 or 10^8 different specificities possible. In theory it is possible to have 6×10^{10} molecules of different specificity in each ml of serum. Potentially there are a lot of preformed specificities for an organism to encounter. There are a lot of these little suckers running around.

The visiting lecturer later called them "tailor-made specificities."

But this specificity is not a mechanical sort of specificity. Referring to a diagram of the immunoglobulin molecule, depicted as a Y-shaped molecule whose forked end can lock into antigens (foreign material), the lecturer went on: "Exquisite specificity was a term used earlier, but it is not clear now how exquisite the specificity is because of the flexibility at the hinge region…. They can move and lock in." What is emphasized is specificity *and* flexibility, so that any possible foreign molecule or protein can be matched from the body's store of specific/flexible antibodies.

In flexible accumulation, the stress is on constant innovation, which is the basis for flexible response to new markets.[9] […]

In the immune system the basis for all the "tailor-made specificities" in the body is genetic mutation, which produces a constant flow of new specificities in certain immune system cells, B

cells. These new specificities wait in the body like bits of potentially useful information until (if it ever happens) a match is made with a foreign antigen. Then antibodies are produced, in just the right amount needed.

In our interviews, people have many ways of depicting the immune system as a flexible, specific response system. Here is one example:

INTERVIEWER: You mentioned antibodies. What do you see them doing?

JIM BARTLETT (SOCIAL WORKER IN HIS FORTIES): Protect your body from anything that's going to do you harm, you know, that's going to make you sick. Like an army, I guess,…that keeps some sort of balance in your body, and keeps and controls things that enter your body that shouldn't be there or that [might]… upset the equilibrium in your body…. The sense I've always had is that antibodies,…you aren't just born with a certain set of them and that's what you have the rest of your life, but that they're very much shaped and changed by what they respond to and what they deal with, so that if you're exposed to hepatitis, for instance, then you are going to have hepatitis antibodies for the rest of your life, because your antibodies dealt with that particular disease, and if you're still alive, that means that they got rid of it somehow or other, or got it under control, so that they'll [have] that particular imprint on your immune system…. That's how… they maintain that identity of that recognition…. That's just like people, you know, we're very much become a part of what we confront and it changes us, you know, changes our ideas and the way we think and the way we act…. If…every morning when you get up and walk out your front door, somebody smacks you in the face, you're going to develop a certain reaction to that, you know, hopefully very quickly, like use the back door.

Finally, consider how time and space are depicted in descriptions of the immune system. With the transition from Fordism to flexible accumulation, we experience

> an intense phase of time-space compression that has had a disorienting and disruptive impact upon political-economic practices…. Spaces of very different worlds seem to collapse upon each other, much as the world's commodities are

assembled in the supermarket and all manner of sub-cultures get juxtaposed in the contemporary city. (Harvey 1989a:284, 301–2)

In Harvey's view, time/space compression is a phenomenon that "so revolutionize[s] the objective qualities of space and time that we are forced to alter, sometimes in quite radical ways, how we represent the world to ourselves" (Harvey 1989a:240).

When, in our interviews about the immune system, people are asked to move in imagination to the world inside the body, they often find the experience spatially dislocating. After people have talked at length about their conceptions of the immune system, immunity, health, and illness, we then show them micrographs of greatly magnified immune system cells, such as macrophages or T cells. Many people have seen these before in popular magazines or educational movies. Here is a typical response:

DAVE POTTER (ACCOUNTANT IN HIS TWENTIES, LOOKING AT A MICROGRAPH OF CELLS): That's, see to me, that's what's incredible.... I mean that one cell is unto its own. It doesn't have a brain, your brain isn't connected to it, and it's got its own....God! it's so incredible, I mean it's phenomenal!...It's like being in two different worlds.

INTERVIEWER: Really?

DAVE POTTER: Yeah, I mean, even though I've seen all these kinds of things before and I realize that these are the exact same kinds of things that are in my body, it's still distanced somehow. I mean *these cells act on their own, you know, there's no connection between being a human and having, there's no connection between me being a conscious human being and this cell that's inside me.*

The self has retreated inside the body, is a witness to itself, a tiny figure in a cosmic landscape, which is the body. This scene is one that is both greatly exciting and greatly bewildering.

Dramatic forms of spatial disorientation are particularly apparent in the large numbers of people who interpret scientific images as visions of something colossal and distant inside us: these images look, as Nancy Harris puts it, "like star wars," "like space sharks," "like the sun and the moon." Consider the remarks of John Marcellino, a community organizer in his forties:

It's funny,...when you think about the inside of your body, I think about outer space. It's like those are the only things that look like this, you know, they're that far away from you. It's weird because outer space is like, way out there, and your body is just right here, but it's about the same, it's the same thing.

No wonder it is disconcerting: the unimaginably small and the unimaginably large coalesced in the same image, agency residing in cells, the person becoming an observer of the agency of others inside him or herself. The "I" who used to wear the body like a closely fitting set of clothes is now miniaturized, and is dwarfed by its body. The "I" is made a passive and powerless witness to the doings of the components of the body. Somewhere in the system lies agency; the "I" can only watch.[10]

It is much less clear to me what is happening with representations of time. In popular texts about the immune system it is striking how many different historical periods are "plundered" to depict the workings of this postmodern instantaneous information deployment system. Here are some typical images: an ancient city (Jewler 1989), an ancient walled castle (Kobren 1989), ancient Japanese warriors (Schindler 1988), conventional contemporary arms (Brownlee 1990; Lertola 1984).[11]

Describing the immune system in our interviews, people not infrequently juxtapose images taken from different time periods. This person, for example, switches from a current pastoral scene to an ancient city:

INTERVIEWER: Can you describe to me what you think's going on in the body of someone with AIDS?

JIM BARTLETT: Well, I guess, I usually think of it as like a huge barn...that's got big doors on either end, and this barn is in fire, rain, you know, tornados, wild animals, you know, whatever. That there's nothing to stop, nothing to stop it, you know, anything can come in.... [Description of a friend of a friend who has AIDS.] So AIDS [it] would seem just renders you helpless to things that, in the past you had, like maybe, if you think of a big medieval city that all of a sudden doesn't have any walls or any moat or any, anything, can come along and just knock you out.

Perhaps these images convey a sense of being unmoored in time, unable to unify past, present, and future, a disorientation in time to match a disorientation in space.[12]

I am suggesting that the science of immunology is helping to render a kind of aesthetic or architecture for our bodies that captures some of the essential features of flexible accumulation. Presumably these images in science developed in complex interaction with many changing social forms and practices. Here I have space only to point out that the era of flexible accumulation is usually said to have begun in the early 1970s (with some seeds present in the 1960s) (Harvey 1989a:141–72). The ideas in immunology that I have discussed emerged at roughly the same time. It was not until the late 1960s that the concept of an immune *system* as such existed (Moulin 1989), and it was not until the early 1970s that departments of immunology existed in American or other universities. Knowledge of how specificity in antibodies works came at this time too: Edelman and Porter shared the Nobel prize for studies of the structural basis of immunological specificity in 1972 (Silverstein 1989:134–5).[13]

To see further complexities of the late 20th-century body, we must turn to a different picture, one that exists alongside the flexible response system I have outlined. This is a portrait of the body as a nation-state, organized around a hidden discourse of gender, race, and class, the "hierarchical, localized organic body" (Haraway 1989:14).[14] In this picture, which is taught in biology classes and conveyed in the popular media, the boundary between the body ("self") and the external world ("nonself") is rigid and absolute: "At the heart of the immune system is the ability to distinguish between self and nonself. Virtually every body cell carries distinctive molecules that identify it as self" (Schindler 1988:1). These molecules are class 1 MHC proteins, present on every nucleated cell in an individual's body and different from every other individual's. One popular book calls these our "trademarks" (Dwyer 1988:37). The maintenance of the purity of self within the borders of the body is seen as tantamount to the maintenance of the self: a chapter called "The Body under Siege," in the popular book on the immune system *In Self Defense*, begins with an epigraph, " 'To be or not to be, that is the question' (William Shakespeare)" (Mizel and Jaret 1985:1).[15]

As one of the interviews I quoted hints, talk about the immune system's maintenance of a clear boundary between self and nonself is often accompanied by a conception of the nonself world as foreign and hostile.[16] Our bodies are faced with masses of cells bent on our destruction: "to fend off the threatening horde, the body has devised astonishingly intricate defenses" (Schindler 1988:13). As a measure of the extent of this threat, contemporary popular publications[17] depict the body as the scene of all-out war between ruthless invaders and determined defenders: "Besieged by a vast array of invisible enemies, the human body enlists a remarkably complex corps of internal bodyguards to battle the invaders" (Jaret 1986: 702). A site of injury is "transformed into a battle field on which the body's armed forces, hurling themselves repeatedly at the encroaching microorganisms, crush and annihilate them" (Nilsson 1985:20).

Small white blood cells called granulocytes are "kept permanently at the ready for a blitzkrieg against microorganisms" and constitute the "infantry" of the immune system: "multitudes fall in battle, and together with their vanquished foes, they form the pus which collects in wounds" (Nilsson 1985:24). Larger macrophages are another type of white blood cell, the "armoured unit" of the defense system: "These roll forth through the tissues,... devouring everything that has no useful role to play there" (Nilsson 1985:25). Another part of the immune system, the complement system, can "perforate hostile organisms so that their lives trickle to a halt" (Nilsson 1985:24). The components of the complement system function as " 'magnetic mines.' They are sucked toward the bacterium and perforate it, causing it to explode" (Nilsson 1985:72). When the system "comes together in the right sequence, it detonates like a bomb, blasting through the invader's cell membrane" (Jaret 1986:720). Certain T lymphocytes, whose technical scientific name is the "killer cells," are the "immune system's special combat units in the war against cancer"; killer cells "strike," "attack," and "assault" (Nilsson 1985:96, 98, 100). "The killer T cells are relentless. Docking with infected cells, they shoot lethal proteins at the cell membrane. Holes form where the protein molecules hit, and the cell, dying, leaks out its insides" (Jaroff 1988:59).

Not surprisingly, identities involving gender, race, and class are present in this war scene. Compare two categories of immune system cells, macrophages, which surround and digest foreign organisms, and T cells, which kill by transferring toxin to them. The macrophages are a lower form of cell, evolutionarily, and are even found in such primitive organisms as worms (Roitt, Brostoff, and Male 1985:2.1); they are called a "primeval tank corps" (Michaud, Feinstein, and Editors 1989:3). T cells are more evolutionarily advanced and have higher functions such as memory (Jaroff 1988:60; Roitt, Brostoff, and Male 1985:2.5). It is only these advanced cells which "attend the technical colleges of the immune system" (Nilsson 1985:26).

There is clearly a hierarchical division of labor here, one that is to some extent overlaid with our gender categories. Specifically, there are obvious female associations with the engulfing and surrounding that macrophages do and obvious male associations with the penetrating or injecting that killer T cells do. In addition, many scholars have pointed out the frequent symbolic association of the female with lower functions, and especially with a lack of or lesser degree of mental functions.

Beyond this, macrophages are the cells that are the "housekeepers" (Jaret 1986) of the body, cleaning up the dirt and debris, including the "dead bodies" of both self and foreign cells (one immunologist called them "little drudges"):[18]

> The first defenders to arrive would be the phagocytes [a category of "eating" cells that includes macrophages] – the scavengers of the system. Phagocytes constantly scour the territories of our bodies, alert to anything that seems out of place. What they find, they engulf and consume. Phagocytes are not choosy. They will eat anything suspicious that they find in the bloodstream, tissues, or lymphatic system. (Jaret 1986:715)

Given their uncultivated origins, it should not be surprising that after eating, macrophages "burp": "After [a macrophage] finishes its meal, it burps out pieces of the enemy and puts them out on its surface" (Michaud, Feinstein, and Editors 1989:6). As macrophages feed, they may be described as "angry" or in a "feeding fury,"[19] an image combining uncontrolled emotions with an obliterating, engulfing presence, both common cultural ascriptions of females. In addition, as is often the case with the lower orders of human females, the macrophage harbors disease. It is the macrophage that is the reservoir of HIV. "Unlike T 4 cells, the macrophage is not killed by HIV. It may serve as a reservoir for the virus" (Gallo and Montagnier 1989).

Gender might not be the only overlay on this division of labor. Racial overtones could be there as well, although I have less convincing evidence for them. Macrophages are the cells that actually eat other cells belonging to the category "self," and so engage in a form of "cannibalism." Cannibalism is often associated with the attribution of a lower animal nature to those who engage in it (Arens 1979). In immunology, macrophages are seen as feminized in some ways but as simply "uncivilized" in other ways. These "cannibals" are indiscriminate eaters, barbaric and savage in their willingness to eat any manner of thing at all. Sometimes macrophages are feminized "housekeepers," and sometimes they seem to be racially marked, as when they are described as "roving garbage collectors" (Brownlee 1990:50).

A more certain reason for the lowliness of macrophages is that they lack the highly valued characteristic (given a regime of flexible accumulation) of specificity. In a class lecture, I heard that macrophages are "the dumb cells of the immune system. They don't have any specificity, while T cells do have specificity."

To explore the hierarchy of cells further, we need to look at another immune system cell, the B cell. B cells are clearly ranked far above the lowly macrophage. They are not educated in the college of the thymus, but they are "educated" in the bone marrow (Dwyer 1988:47) and they have enormous specificity. However, they rank below the T cell, which is consistently termed the "orchestrator" of the immune response and which activates B cells. In one popular book, the T cell is said to give the B cell "permission" to attack invading organisms (Dwyer 1988:47). (This assertion is frequently made in spite of the interlocking nature of all the elements of the system.) B cells exist in two stages, virgin or immature B cells and, when stimulated by antigen of the right specificity, mature B cells. Mature B cells are the cells that, with T cell "permission," rapidly produce antibodies against invading antigen. A B cell starts out a virgin, is stimulated by the right nonself antigen and the T cell, and thereupon starts to produce antibodies like mad.

In one lecture I heard, T cells were said to "sidle up" to B cells as a part of their orchestration of B cell responses to antigen. I think that in most American courtship behavior, it would be the man who sidled up to the woman. So this suggests that

B cells are sometimes feminized but rank much higher in the hierarchy than the lowly macrophage.[20] In the B cell, then, we may have a kind of upper-class female, a suitable partner for the top-ranked T cell. Far below her in terms of class and race is the macrophage, angry, scavenging, engulfing, housekeeping, and harboring disease.

The cartoon on a recent cover of the technical journal *Immunology Today* provides clear evidence for the picture I am drawing. This cartoon depicts a B cell with long eyelashes and high heels, silently taking orders from a T cell called a gamma/delta cell, drawn as a doctor with a stethoscope and a hypodermic needle. The gamma/delta T cell is kicking the B cell. In the next frame the gamma/delta T cell kicks another kind of T cell, one unmarked by any adornments, but this T cell registers a verbal protest, "Ouch!" In the final frame, two gamma/delta T cells are shown standing on top of a macrophage, while one of them shouts into a megaphone, "Come on – the action's here!!" (Born et al. 1990).

So we have T cells, masculine and high-ranking; B cells, feminine and high-ranking; and macrophages, feminine, perhaps racially marked, and low-ranking on all counts. What is missing? Low-ranking males, revealing by their invisibility in this system (even as they seem to be "invisible" in the US social structure) how salient a system of race and class is to the understanding of relationships among these cells.[21]

In this system, gendered distinctions are not limited to male and female, they also encompass the distinction heterosexual and homosexual. T cells convey aspects of male potency, cast as heterosexual potency. There is evidence that T cells are for many researchers the virile heroes of the immune system, highly trained commandos who have been selected for and then educated in the technical college of the thymus gland. T cells are referred to as the "master regulators of the immune system" (Sell 1987:26). Some T cells, killer cells, are masculine in the old-fashioned mold of a brawny, brutal he-man: in a mail advertisement for a book on the immune system, we are told, "You owe your life to this little guy, the Rambo of your body's immune system." Other T cells, T 4 cells, have a different kind of masculinity, one focused on abilities required in the contemporary world of global corporations, especially strategic planning and corporate team participation.[22] The T 4 cell is often called the quarterback of the immune system, because he orchestrates everything else and

because he is the brains and memory of the team. As it is put in one popular source, "besides killer T-cells...there are also helper [T 4] and suppressor T-cells. *Somebody* has to make strategic decisions" (Michaud, Feinstein, and Editors 1989:10). A popular manual on the immune system, *Fighting Disease*, clinches the heterosexuality of the T cell:

> In order to slip inside a cell, a virus has to remove its protein coat, which it leaves outside on the cell membrane. The viral coat hanging outside signals the passing T cell that viral hanky panky is going on inside. Like the jealous husband who spots a strange jacket in the hall closet and *knows* what's going on in the upstairs bedroom, the T cell takes swift action. It bumps against the body cell with the virus inside and perforates it. (Michaud, Feinstein, and Editors 1989:8)

[...]

Sexuality, Family, and Disposable People

When Fordism was becoming established in the United States, deliberate efforts were made to transform workers' concepts of sexuality and domestic life. Are similar processes occurring today? Earlier I described both the virile, heterosexualized T cell and the dominance hierarchy among immune system cells. These descriptions take on a stark significance in light of the fact that HIV is killing off precisely the high-ranking cells, the masculinized T cells, in gay men and minority drug users (the demographic groups now most affected by HIV in Baltimore). HIV especially depletes the T 4 cell, the particular cell that is compared to that most masculine of figures, the quarterback in football, because it directs and orchestrates the other T cells (Redfield and Burke 1989:64).[23] After all, as one popular book on the immune system puts it, "We are not all born equal when it comes to the T cell system" (Dwyer 1988:46).

The way HIV is seen as destroying the virile T cell made me wonder whether the men at the hospice where I volunteer as an AIDS "buddy" experienced the weakening of the body as a defeat on several different fronts. My buddy training manual explains, "Think of lots of rebels and a government dictatorship protected by the army. As soon as your immune system gets impaired (your army dies) all the diseases which you have been carrying for years can run amok (the rebels seize power)" (*Washington HIV News* 1988, quoted in Health Education Resource Organization 1989). It seemed possible that the weakening of the body these men experienced was being linked in scientific language to a loss of heterosexual potency. It was not simply that you were no longer a "man" but that your body as a centralized nation-state had lost its virility.

I had these thoughts in mind before my buddy, Mark Scott, was presented at grand rounds. Grand rounds are elaborate, formal presentations of cases, held in a large lecture hall. Although Mark was extremely ill, recovering from a serious toxoplasmosis infection, he was elated at the prospect of being presented at grand rounds. He told me the week before that he was the one and only patient his doctor, John Aubrey, wanted to present. He said that he was going to try to get across the patient's need to be responsible for his own illness, no matter how sick. He wanted to convey the importance of not taking a doctor's word for it and of learning as much as possible by asking questions. He was planning to start off with a funny but risqué joke, the panda joke, so that the audience could see he had a sense of humor.[24] When he told me this, he was in the hospital, unable to walk or even sit up. Three days later – by dint of incredible determination – he was shaved, with a fresh haircut, dressed in a dark double-breasted suit, leaning on the arm of Aubrey as they walked across the stage at grand rounds.

Far from beginning with the panda joke, Mark was asked a series of detailed questions in which the various stages of his disease were constructed entirely in terms of the progressive elimination of T 4 cells:

> DR. AUBREY: Mr. Scott has an identical twin, and he underwent a series of leukocyte infusions from the identical twin, followed by bone marrow transplantation. Before the bone marrow transplantation, do you know what the status of your immune system was?
> MARK SCOTT: Yes I do.
> DR. AUBREY: What was it?
> MARK SCOTT: My T 4 count was 60.
> DR. AUBREY: 60. OK. The normal value at that laboratory was 600, 800? So you had less than 10 percent of the normal number of helper T cells. Had you had that test done before?
> [Mark Scott looks puzzled.]

> DR. AUBREY: The T cell count, before you went to NIH.
> MARK SCOTT: In 1984 it was normal.
> DR. AUBREY: So over a period of three or four years, the helper T cells, the primary target of HIV, had fallen from near normal, a near normal range, down to a very low range of a T 4 count of 60. What happened with bone marrow transplantation?
> MARK SCOTT: I believe to this day that I got a boost. I was very strong for a while after the bone marrow. I went back to college and studied word processing, and was making a 4 point while working a full-time job. Only in the last six months was I ill.
> DR. AUBREY: And in terms of the laboratory evaluations that they did...clearly functionally you did extremely well. You were working full-time, functioning entirely normally. The laboratory tests that they did to monitor you, what did that show?
> [Mark Scott shakes his head uncomprehendingly.]
> DR. AUBREY: The T cells, did they change?
> MARK SCOTT: My T cells went up after the bone marrow to about 180 and stayed there for about three months before coming back down to 60.
> DR. AUBREY: So there was a *transient* increase in your helper T cells, but functionally you felt fine.

Mark's condition was relentlessly defined by his T 4 cell count, and in the process, given the significance of T 4 cells in the armamentarium of the body, Mark was defined as impotent and feeble. The force of this drama could not have struck deeper when later many doctors came down onto the stage to congratulate Mark and his doctor: they said that Mark's presence had "given AIDS a human face."

Could this scientific imaging of the body be seen as an aspect of secular opposition to homosexuality?[25] There are broad social currents in the United States today, especially in the New Right, that seek to "restore heterosexual patriarchy, the control of men over their wives and children":

> Homosexuality is characterized by "pro-family" representatives as "unnatural," "evil," and psychologically "perverse"; but male homosexuality is even more dangerous than female, in the "pro-family" view, because it signals a breakdown of "masculinity" itself – or what one right-wing ideologue calls the "male spirit," or the "male principle." (Petchesky 1981:231)

Or this diminishment of the homosexual body might be related to ideas brought to life with the weakening of the liberal state and of the state's responsibility to provide for social welfare needs. Withdrawal of government support from social services of all kinds makes the nuclear family seem to be the only source of these glues to the social fabric, and conservative efforts to buttress the heterosexual family ideologically may reflect this perception. The depiction of body cells that privileges some as heterosexually potent has a part to play here and operates at a particularly subtle, invisible, and therefore insidious level.

It may be that while flexibility in adjusting to retraining, deskilling, part-time work, home-based work, periodic unemployment, relocation, changing product lines, downward mobility, and all the other ways restructuring bears on wage earners is desirable, flexibility in domestic arrangements is threatening to this very restructuring.[26] Part-time work, home-based work, service sector work without health benefits or retirement benefits, and unemployment themselves seem to entail dependence on the family to fill in the gaps in order to enable the workforce to reproduce itself.[27] Contemporary conservative publications are filled with exactly this logic:[28]

Teachers at urban schools speak of chaotic, scattered families, of gross parental irresponsibility, of small schoolchildren who witness open sexual activity at home. The cycle perpetuates itself across generations: a teenage mother, abused as a child, cannot read, write, add or subtract. She is pregnant with her third child and living on welfare. She has zero skills, zero work habits, zero future. Work at a fast food restaurant seems beyond her capacity. She is neglecting her 3-year-old, who is often sick and ill-fed. She shunts the child off to relatives as often as she can.

These poor neighborhoods and families are radically different from their counterparts of two decades ago. People talk now of an inability to cope with life's most rudimentary demands, such simple things as getting up in the morning to go to work. Idleness and irresponsibility pave the tragic road to self-destruction: teenage pregnancy, long-term welfare dependence, drugs, crime, prison and death. (Lochhead 1989:10, 11)

If restructuring makes the heterosexual family seem to some a necessary prop to the social fabric,

restructuring also makes some people seem superfluous. Flexible accumulation goes along with high levels of "structural unemployment" and an increase in a labor market periphery that lacks job security (Harvey 1989a:149–50). These conditions affect disadvantaged groups disproportionately: not all groups seem equally superfluous. A growing sense that some groups of people are superfluous must surely be related to the recent increase in intolerance in the United States, a willingness to openly express racist, classist, homophobic, or misogynistic sentiments and act on them. The poor are said to have become "American untouchables" (Kozol 1990). Young black males are said to have become an "endangered species" (Corey 1990). We read in the paper of a student "hospitalized speechless after racial threats": "A [black] freshman at Emory University was found in her dormitory room curled in the fetal position and unable to speak...following the latest episode in a reported campaign of racial terror against her" (Smith 1990).[29] Here is how this climate feels to John Marcellino, a community leader in a chronically poor, mostly white neighborhood in Baltimore:

[The person in charge of commercial redevelopment in this area] says the area, the problems in this area, will not improve until this community changes, until the people who live here are no longer here. And so you won't get rid of the drug abuse or the prostitution or the crime or stuff until the people who live here are no longer here. And that to me is the same as the underclass thing, disposable people....As soon as they can't figure out a need for us, they'll get rid of us.

INTERVIEWER: What's the need for you right now?
JOHN MARCELLINO: We still make money for somebody or another. They still need us some, like they needed people to come up out of the south to work in the mills, so they attract them all up. Now there's not as much need for the people to work in the mills; they need some people in the service economy, they try to retrain...but if not they're no use, they'll put you in jail,...they'll choke you off so that you can't make a living doing anything else, so they get rid of you, or you know, hopefully you'll go back to Virginia or somewhere else, right? You know, you'll crawl in a crack or you won't have children or something.

As with secular opposition to homosexuality, scientific imagery has a role to play here too. We know that 19th-century anthropology had a view of the natural order of the world which could be used to justify denying women the privileges of citizenship in the Enlightenment project and to justify the colonization, enslavement, and exploitation of people of color. If women and people of color were simply lower on the evolutionary scale, doing them harm became less bothersome (Stocking 1987:230–7). In present-day circumstances – with poor whites as "disposable people," poor blacks as an "endangered species," the Secretary of Health and Human Services comparing the calamitous situation of blacks in the United States today to slavery (Corey 1990) – the popularization of the notion of a world within the body with cells ranked by gender, race, and class is not trivial. Learning that our bodies are made up of hierarchically ranked kinds of cells, with dumb, uncouth, barbaric "females" at the bottom and smart, educated, civilized, executive "males" at the top, has its part to play in showing us why it is all right to think some kinds of people are not as worthy of life in human society as others.[30]

In describing a "collective effort" that is pushing us toward new modes of living, thinking, and feeling, I have only hinted at how these modes actually get instantiated in our lives. Part of the full story would obviously involve the "media" in Raymond Williams' social sense (1977). Many of the images I have discussed are from newspapers, magazines, or mass market books, and it would be easy to add images from films such as The Miracle of Life and The Fighting Edge, episodes of "L.A. Law,"[31] innumerable television specials or talk shows, and amusements such as the "Wonder of Life" ride at Epcot Center near Disney World.[32]

Another part of the story would involve individuals or groups who are explicit advocates of links between biological knowledge of the body and social control. For example, James D. Watkins, who was the head of Ronald Reagan's AIDS commission, said in an interview:

> We have an opportunity to restructure what a healthy lifestyle is all about.... [T]oo often we assume a child in our society will be healthy.... [This] may have been true years ago, but society is changing. One third of youngsters today are born into poverty. Now we are hardening an

underclass and there is a strong overlay between that underclass and AIDS. It is mainly Hispanic and Black Americans. AIDS brings into focus a variety of flaws in our system.... [T]he job of educators then is to help people learn in a fundamental way about human biology and their own bodies so they can possess lifelong strategies for healthy wholesome lifestyles.

The interviewer broke in: "You are talking about trying to get at health care problems by getting students to understand the nature of human biology!?" And Watkins answered, "Absolutely" (Newman 1988). Watkins put it all together: the social control entailed in disseminating biological knowledge of the body; the fear and threat of AIDS, linked to "flaws in our system," among them homosexuals, people of color, and people living in poverty.

I have emphasized the wrenching effects of a new mode of being. Hence my focus has been on how people stretch and are stretched to adjust, rather than on the other side of this process, always potentially present: how people revise and bend ideas and events to fit their circumstances. Mark Scott used grand rounds to flatter and please a doctor whose experimental protocol he wanted to join; AIDS activists have produced films and publications, among them Ecstatic Antibodies: Resisting the AIDS Mythology (Boffin and Gupta 1990), which create more enabling body imagery.[33] [...] These actions might well turn out to be examples of the kinds of political resistance, based on reimaging, relocation, and rearrangement of alliances, that are possible and efficacious in a regime of flexible accumulation (Harvey 1989b:274).[34]

I have sketched a transformation in embodiment, from Fordist bodies held by disciplined order in time and space and organized for efficient mass production, to late capitalist bodies learning flexible response in rapidly collapsing time and space, bodies which nonetheless contain (contradictorily) increasingly sharp and terrible internal divisions. I am suggesting that there are changes afoot in our embodied dispositions, changes that will surely take importantly different forms among different people and groups. We are experiencing not so much the end of the body as the ending of one organizational scheme for bodies and persons and the beginning of another.

The depth of the transformations that are entailed accounts for at least some of the academy's justifiable fascination with the subject of the body, even as the body's borders waver, its internal parts become invested with agency, and its responses become ever more flexibly specific.

Notes

1 The concern of American industrialists was to

> maintain the continuity of the physical and muscular-nervous efficiency of the worker. It [was] in their interests to have a stable, skilled labour force, a permanently well-adjusted complex, because the human complex (the collective worker) of an enterprise is also a machine which cannot, without considerable loss, be taken to pieces too often and renewed with single new parts. (Gramsci 1971:303)

2 The fieldwork I refer to involves participant observation in a university department of immunology, an immunology research lab, several urban neighborhoods, several community organizations dedicated to the AIDS crisis, an AIDS hospice, and the AIDS ward of an inner-city nursing home. The argument below draws on a limited segment of the ongoing research. Other work in progress will describe the impact of the AIDS crisis on immunology and the impact of grass-roots political organizations dealing with HIV infection on scientific research.

3 See Schoenberger (1987:207) on just-in-time inventories. Silver and Peterson 1985 is a handbook for making decisions on what kind of inventory system to adopt.

4 As the barriers of time and space collapse, they crash down with terrific violence upon the bodies of women, as depicted in films such as David Lynch's Blue Velvet.

5 See Piore and Sabel (1984) for a different analysis of the relationship between the global division of labor and flexible specialization.

6 Jameson (1984) and Harvey (1989a) have a variety of ways of understanding how the social formation of late capitalism can relate to such things as architecture, art, and literature. According to Jameson, postmodern forms reveal the "cultural logic" of late capitalism; they are the "internal and superstructural expression of a whole new wave of American military and economic domination throughout the world"; they instantiate a "cultural dominant," a "new systemic cultural norm," a "dominant cultural logic or hegemonic norm" (1984:57). They are a "figuration of . . . the whole world system of present-day multinational capitalism" (1984:79), and they are an approach to a representation of a new reality, a peculiar new form of realism, a kind of mimesis of reality (1984:88). For Harvey these forms are also mimetic. "In the last instance" they are produced by the experience of time-space compression, itself the product of processes in flexible accumulation (1989a:336–44).

In the following section I am obviously indebted to the kinds of patterns Jameson and Harvey have seen in architecture and other forms, even though I prefer not to see the economic realm as so simply determinant of cultural forms.

7 The neighborhoods embrace differences of class, ethnicity, gender, and age. Monica Schoch-Spana, Bjorn Claeson, Karen-Sue Taussig, and Wendy Richardson are the graduate assistants doing these interviews. The discussions focus on people's concepts of health and illness, understanding of immunity, reactions to HIV disease, and responses to a variety of community and urban issues. Neighborhood interviews are not, except by happenstance, with people directly involved in the AIDS epidemic, personally or professionally.

8 The names attached to the quotations from interviews are pseudonyms; they are followed by an indication of the person's age and occupation.

9 Kash's Perpetual Innovation (1989) is a "clear and tough minded look" (jacket flap) at the necessity for the United States to move beyond industrial society, with its standardized products manufactured on a massive scale by the dividing of production of the whole into production of the parts, and the components of the parts, all designed for maximum efficiency. The book urges the United States to become a "synthetic society," organized so as to

> combine components into previously nonexistent wholes, be they products, processes, or projects. The goal of the synthetic society is innovation. That is, its goal is to create newer, higher-performance products or to achieve higher quality in existing products more cheaply by integrating components in the production process in new ways. (1989:17)

Harvey points out that in flexible accumulation, where production can be standardized, it has "proved hard to stop its moving to take advantage of low-paid labour power in the third world, creating there what Lipietz (1986) calls 'peripheral Fordism' " (1989a:155).

10 These sensations are often evoked by other postmodern aesthetic forms. Jameson points out that although the Bonaventure Hotel suggests an all-encompassing whole, once a person actually goes inside, the experience of space and volume is profoundly disorienting. The hotel "gives the feeling that emptiness here is absolutely packed, that it is an element within which you yourself are immersed, without any of that distance that formerly enabled the perception of perspective or volume" (1984:83). What is lost is the perspective of a human observer. Calling Philip Johnson's AT&T building "the manifesto of the postmodern movement in American architecture," a sympathetic critic points out that its architect has achieved a similar effect by putting the shape of a Chippendale chest in elephantine scale on top of a skyscraper (Hardison 1989:115). The dramatic disjunction of scale between the chest/building and the observer is as disorienting as it is funny: if that is a chest, then who puts his or her clothes in there?

11 Other postmodern aesthetic forms also depict dislocation in time. "Postmodernist architecture, for example, takes bits and pieces from the past quite eclectically and mixes them together at will" (Harvey 1989a:54); it is a "random cannibalization of all the styles of the past" (Jameson 1984:65–6). Experience is reduced to a "series of pure and unrelated presents in time" (Harvey 1989a:53). Postmodernism "abandon[s] all sense of historical continuity and memory, while simultaneously developing an incredible ability to plunder history and absorb whatever it finds there as some aspect of the present" (Harvey 1989a:54).

12 See Harvey (1989a:53) for a description of the inability to unify past, present, and future, which is a common characteristic of postmodern aesthetics and literature.

13 Elsewhere I plan to examine a change from the body/person as an agent of productive processes (the worker on a Fordist assembly line) to the body as itself a resource, whose parts can be stored, cloned, and marketed. A California man, for example, is contesting the right of scientists at the University of California to own, patent, and profit from a clone of a malignant T cell taken from his spleen. The cell line was named the "Mo" cell line, presumably after the man's name, Moore. A newspaper account remarks that "the tendency of the medical profession to regard people as products is growing, especially once that tissue leaves a person's body" (Ferrell 1990). A lawyer who, acting on behalf of the nation's largest consumer health group, filed a brief in support of Moore's rights to his cell line comments, "We didn't want physicians viewing patients as potential treasure troves." But then, as if realizing that granting people legal rights to their body tissue hardly ends the problem, she adds, "Perhaps it should be a limited form of property.... [W]e don't want hospitals holding people hostage for their valuable organs if they didn't pay their bills" (Ferrell 1990).

14 In her work Haraway eloquently stresses the displacement of the hierarchical, localized body by a new kind of body: "a highly mobile field of strategic differences,...a semiotic system, a complex meaning-producing field" (1989:15). No one could improve on her characterization of these new elements; I would only add that there may be strategic reasons why a kind of remnant of the old body is carried forward with the new.

15 I think that the emphasis on the purity of the self is related to what Petchesky calls the ideology of "privatism" (1981:208).

16 For lack of space, I cannot deal with the subtleties of how this "old body discourse" appears in interviews. Suffice it to say that military metaphors are extremely widespread.

17 These include mass media magazines, such as Time and Newsweek, as well as The National Geographic. They also include more expensive items, such as Lennart Nilsson's popular coffee-table book, The Body Victorious (1985).

18 Overheard by Paula Treichler (personal communication).

19 Heard in a department guest lecture.

20 B cells are not always feminized: in Fighting Disease, for example, they are described as admirals and supermen (Michaud, Feinstein, and Editors 1989:7, 13).

21 Gibbs discusses the literal and figurative invisibility of black males in the United States:

> Two hundred years after blacks were first counted as only three-fifths of a person by the framers of the US Constitution in 1787, young black men are still being discounted by the US Census Bureau in 1987 with the same effect of denying their existence and disenfranchising them as citizens. (1988:27)

A contrast that may help make my point can be drawn with 19th-century paintings that show black men cleaning bones for anatomical skeletons. Jordanova analyzes these paintings as showing the association of black men with otherness, with death, evil, and the profane, even with cannibalism, which is conveyed by the apron and pots that could well be used for cooking. They represent that which must be kept apart from the (white, male) science in whose service they work. Instead of paintings, we now have widely disseminated micrographs. We see only molecules, molecules that everyone, regardless of race, gender, or class, possesses, molecules shown in technicolor, every color of the rainbow. Macrophages, T cells, and B cells do not usually appear to have the phenotypic markers of race or gender; but because of the cultural life they are given as cells, they are carrying inside our bodies a hierarchy of distinctions based on race, class, and gender, a hierarchy that 19th-century paintings carried, more obviously, on their surfaces (Jordanova 1989).

22 See Kash (1989) for a lengthy discussion of why teamwork is required in the economic world of today.

23 As Redfield and Burke explain, "At some point the T 4 cells that orchestrate the immune response become so depleted that the balance of power switches. HIV then replicates wildly, killing the remaining T 4 cells and hence any vestiges of immune defense" (1989:72).

24 A panda goes off with a woman of the streets to a hotel room, where they make love. Afterward the panda starts to leave and the prostitute stops him, saying, "Don't you know you have to pay? That is the meaning of a prostitute." The panda refuses. So the prostitute says, "Look here in this dictionary – you'll see the definition of a prostitute: a lady who gives sex in return for money." The panda says, "Well, look at the definition of a panda." They turn to "panda." The definition reads: "Panda: eats bush, shoots, and leaves."

25 See Sylvia Law (1988:218) on the meaning of secular opposition to homosexuality and its instantiation in the law.

26 Haraway (1985) discusses the importance of the home-work economy and its links with race and gender in a time of international capital.

27 The concept of social reproduction is crucial here, and not yet well developed. Lipuma and Meltzoff (1989:322) give a useful definition: "not only material reproduction but the reproducing of embodied dispositions, from regional dialects and educational horizon to senses of religious duty, self-worth, and manners."

28 Gibbs analyzes how neoconservatism has

> shifted the emphasis from the goal of providing all citizens with a decent standard of living through federally subsidized health and welfare programs to the need to blame the poor and disadvantaged for their perceived lack of motivation, their "dysfunctional" family systems, and their dependency on welfare programs. (1988:21).

29 See Gibbs (1988:3–4) for a discussion of recent racist incidents in the United States.

30 There are echoes of this line of thought in domains that I have no space to explore here. For example, deep ecology sometimes implies that the demise of certain people would help preserve the ecosystem. Statements such as the following are highly ambiguous on this point: "The fate of the fortunate is immutably bonded to the fate of the dispossessed through the land, water, and air: in an ecologically endangered world, poverty is a luxury we can no longer afford" (Durning 1990:153).

31 An episode on 15 March 1990 showed a doctor who had refused to operate on an AIDS patient and was being sued by the patient's wife. Speaking on the stand in his own defense, the doctor said that the patient's immune system had broken down anyway and that he could not have lived for more than a few months.

32 A part of this description would show how the conflict between the body as a self-regulating system for flexibly specific response and the body as something internally fragmented along the lines of hierarchical power relationships is inherent in particular representations in the media or in the way people talk about the immune system. For example, one man objected strenuously to a picture on the cover of *Time* magazine that showed a white blood cell boxing a germ in a cutaway view of a person. He said that the picture was misleading because it didn't depict a system:

> STEVEN BAKER: The immune system is the whole body, it's not just the lungs or the abdomen, it's, I mean if I cut myself, doesn't my immune system start to work right away to prevent infection? So it's in your finger; I mean it's everywhere. So that would be my criticism to *Time* magazine.

Stromberg suggests that systems of symbols (for religious conversion) can function to help people "express and come to terms with persisting emotional ambivalence" (1990:42). I am interested in whether systems of symbols for thinking about the body's immunity are sometimes used to express and work on persisting social and psychological contradictions related to the existence of a global system of flexible accumulation and, in the United States, dramatic industrial restructuring.

33 See also Crimp 1988, Crimp and Ralston 1990, and Treichler 1987.

34 In other work in progress I am exploring the remarkable political successes of AIDS activist groups even in a homophobic climate.

References

Arens, W. 1979 *The Man-Eating Myth: Anthropology and Anthropophagy*. Oxford: Oxford University Press.

Beldecos, Athena, et al. 1988 The Importance of Feminist Critique for Contemporary Cell Biology. *Hypatia* 3(1): 61–76.

Boffin, Tessa, and Sunil Gupta, eds., 1990 *Ecstatic Antibodies: Resisting the AIDS Mythology*. London: Unwin Hyman.

Born, Willi, et al. 1990 Recognition of Heat Shock Proteins and Gamma Delta Cell Function. *Immunology Today* 11(2):40–3.

Brownlee, Sharon 1990 The Body at War. *US News and World Report*, 2 July: 48–54.

Corey, Mary 1990 Endangered Species: Officials Look for Ways to Reduce Risks in Being Young, Black and Male. *The Sun (Baltimore)*, 4 April: 1E.

Corrigan, Philip, and Derek Sayer 1985 *The Great Arch: English State Formation as Cultural Revolution*. Oxford: Blackwell.

Crimp, Douglas, ed., 1988 *AIDS: Cultural Analysis, Cultural Activism*. Cambridge, MA: MIT Press.

Crimp, Douglas, and Adam Ralston, eds., 1990 *AIDS Demo Graphics*. Seattle: Bay Press.

Durning, Alan B. 1990 Ending Poverty. In *State of the World 1990*. Lester R. Brown et al., eds., pp. 135–53. New York: Norton.

Dwyer, John M. 1988 *The Body at War: The Miracle of the Immune System*. New York: New American Library.

Ferrell, J. E. 1990 Surgeons Removed and Sold His Spleen Cells: Should He Get a Cut? *The Sun (Baltimore)*, 21 January:5E.

Flax, Jane 1990 Postmodernism and Gender Relations in Feminist Theory. In *Feminism/Postmodernism*. Linda J. Nicholson, ed., pp. 39–62. New York: Routledge.

Gallo, Robert C., and Luc Montagnier 1989 The AIDS Epidemic. In *The Science of AIDS: Readings from Scientific American Magazine*. pp. 1–11. New York: W. H. Freeman.

Gelderman, Carol 1981 *Henry Ford: The Wayward Capitalist*. New York: St. Martin's Press.

Gibbs, Jewelle 1988 Young Black Males in America: Endangered, Embittered, and Embattled. In *Young, Black, and Male in America: An Endangered Species*. Jewelle Gibbs et al., eds., pp. 1–36. Dover, MA: Auburn House.

Glassner, Barry 1988 *Bodies: Why We Look the Way We Do and How We Feel about it*. New York: G. P. Putnam's Sons.

Gramsci, Antonio 1971 *Selections from the Prison Notebooks of Antonio Gramsci*. Q. Hoare and G. N. Smith, eds., New York: International Publishers.

Haraway, Donna 1985 A Manifesto for Cyborgs: Science, Technology, and Socialist Feminism in the 1980s. *Socialist Review* 80:65–108.

Haraway, Donna 1989 The Biopolitics of Postmodern Bodies: Determinations of Self in Immune System Discourse. *Differences* 1(1):3–43.

Hardison, O. B. 1989 *Disappearing through the Skylight*. New York: Viking.

Harvey, David 1989a *The Condition of Postmodernity: An Enquiry into the Origins of Cultural Change*. Oxford: Basil Blackwell.

Harvey, David 1989b *The Urban Experience*. Baltimore, MD: Johns Hopkins University Press.

Health Education Resource Organization 1989 *Health Education Resource Organization Buddy Training Manual*. Baltimore, MD: Health Education Resource Organization.

Jaggar, Alison M., and Susan R. Bordo 1989 *Gender/Body/Knowledge: Feminist Reconstructions of Being and Knowing*. New Brunswick, NJ: Rutgers University Press.

Jameson, Fredric 1984 Postmodernism, or the Cultural Logic of Late Capitalism. *New Left Review* 146:53–92.

Jaret, Peter 1986 Our Immune System: The Wars Within. *National Geographic* 169(6):702–35.

Jaroff, Leon 1988 Stop That Germ! *Time* 131(21):56–64.

Jewler, Donald 1989 Diabetes and the Immune System. *Diabetes Forecast*, August:32–40.

Johnson, Mark 1987 *The Body in the Mind: The Bodily Basis of Meaning, Imagination, and Reason*. Chicago: University of Chicago Press.

Jordanova, L. J. 1989 *Sexual Visions: Images of Gender in Science and Medicine between the Eighteenth and Twentieth Centuries*. Madison: University of Wisconsin Press.

Kash, Don E. 1989 *Perpetual Innovation: The New World of Competition*. New York: Basic Books.

Kobren, Gerri 1989 A Body on the Fritz. To Your Health. *The Sun (Baltimore)*, 3 October:4–6.

Kozol, Jonathan 1990 The New Untouchables. *Newsweek* (winter/spring special issue) 114(27):48–53.

Kroker, Arthur, and Marilouise Kroker 1987 *Body Invaders: Panic Sex in America*. New York: St. Martin's Press.

Law, Sylvia 1988 Homosexuality and the Social Meaning of Gender. *Wisconsin Law Review* 2:187–235.

Lertola, Joe 1984 The Virus Invasion. *Time* 123(18):67.

Lévi-Strauss, Claude 1967 *Tristes Tropiques: An Anthropological Study of Primitive Societies in Brazil*. John Russel, trans. New York: Atheneum.

Lipietz, Alain 1986 New Tendencies in the International Division of Labour: Regimes of Accumulation and Modes of Regulation. In *Production, Work, Territory: The Geographical Anatomy of Industrial Capitalism*.

Allen Scott and Michael Storper, eds., pp. 16–40. London: Allen & Unwin.

Lipuma, Edward, and Sarah Keene Meltzoff 1989 Toward a Theory of Culture and Class: An Iberian Example. *American Ethnologist* 16:313–34.

Lochhead, Carolyn 1989 Poor Neighborhoods Fall to a Widening Decay. *Insight* 5(14):10–12.

Martin, Emily 1987 *The Woman in the Body: A Cultural Analysis of Reproduction*. Boston: Beacon Press.

Martin, Emily 1991 The Egg and the Sperm: How Science Has Constructed a Romance Based on Stereotypical Male–Female Roles. *Signs* 16(3):1–18.

Michaud, Ellen, Alice Feinstein, and the Editors of Prevention Magazine 1989 *Fighting Disease: The Complete Guide to Natural Immune Power*. Emmaus, PA: Rodale Press.

Mizel, Steven B., and Peter Jaret 1985 *In Self Defense*. San Diego, CA: Harcourt Brace Jovanovich.

Moulin, Anne Marie 1989 The Immune System: A Key Concept for the History of Immunology. *History and Philosophy of the Life Sciences* 11: 221–36.

Newman, Frank 1988 AIDS, Youth and the University: An Interview with Admiral Watkins. *Change* 20(5):39–44.

Nilsson, Lennart 1985 *The Body Victorious*. New York: Delacorte Press.

Outram, Dorinda 1989 *The Body and the French Revolution: Sex, Class, and Political Culture*. New Haven, CT: Yale University Press.

Petchesky, Rosalind Pollack 1981 Antiabortion, Antifeminism and the Rise of the New Right. *Feminist Studies* 7(2):206–46.

Piore, Michael J., and Charles F. Sabel 1984 *The Second Industrial Divide: Possibilities for Prosperity*. New York: Basic Books.

Redfield, Robert, and Donald S. Burke 1989 HIV Infection: The Clinical Picture. In *The Science of AIDS: Readings from Scientific American Magazine*. pp. 64–73. New York: W. H. Freeman.

Roitt, Ivan, Jonathan Brostoff, and David Male 1985 *Immunology*. St. Louis, MO: C. V. Mosby.

Schindler, Lydia Woods 1988 *Understanding the Immune System*. Washington, DC: US Department of Health and Human Services.

Schoenberger, Erica 1987 Technological and Organizational Change in Automobile Production: Spatial Implications. *Regional Studies* 21(3):199–214.

Sell, Stewart 1987 *Basic Immunology: Immune Mechanisms in Health and Disease*. New York: Elsevier.

Sheridan, Alan 1980 *Michel Foucault: The Will to Truth*. London: Tavistock.

Silver, Edward A., and Rein Peterson 1985 *Decision Systems for Inventory Management and Production Planning*. New York: Wiley.

Silverstein, Arthur M. 1989 *A History of Immunology*. San Diego, CA: Academic Press.

Smith, Ben 1990 Ga. Student Hospitalized Speechless after Racial Threats. *The Sun (Baltimore)*, 14 April:1A, 3A.

Stocking, George 1987 *Victorian Anthropology*. New York: Free Press.

Stromberg, Peter G. 1990 Ideological Language in the Transformation of Identity. *American Anthropologist* 92:42–56.

Treichler, Paula 1987 Aids, Homophobia, and Biomedical Discourse: An Epidemic of Signification. *Cultural Studies* 1(3):263–305.

Washington HIV News 1988 A Layman's Guide to HIV. *Washington HIV News* 1(1):5.

Williams, Raymond 1977 *Marxism and Literature*. Oxford: Oxford University Press.

28

Hybridity: Hybrid Bodies of the Scientific Imaginary

Lesley Sharp

In the wake of Paul Rabinow's now often cited essay "Artificiality and Enlightenment" (Rabinow 1992), those working at the intersection of anthropology and science studies have revitalized scholarly interest in categories of relatedness, offering compelling works intent on deciphering the moral parameters of embodied hybridity. Human bodies are now regularly reformed by the presumed promises of interspeciality (Haraway 1992). Such efforts help insure that the human form may no longer stand apart as discrete and clearly bounded, but, rather, as simultaneously flexible, permeable (Martin 1994), and capable of sharing biological substance with other individuals or creatures. These sorts of blended bodies inspire newly configured forms of intimacy. This trend is especially pronounced in contexts circumscribed by reproductive technologies, molecular science, genomics, genetics, transplant medicine, and soon, I predict, nanoscience and robotic surgery. [...]

Hybrid renderings of bodies are inherently moral projects, as is evident on several fronts. For one, hybridity raises thorny bioethical questions about scientific tampering and the associated insecure nature of the body's boundaries.

This remaking of bodies by science engenders significant consequences for sociality and subjectivity, inevitably "surfacing" (Taylor 2005) particular meanings otherwise concealed by a scientific longing to transform, alter, shift, or enhance bodies formerly imagined as distinct, stable, and predictable. [...] Deliberate efforts to generate hybrids, then, are simultaneously moral and imaginative projects.

Of particular concern to me is how hybridity insists on reconfigured meanings and values, and how these affect, on the one hand, public perceptions of bodies remade by science and, on the other, the scientific logic that drives and, more importantly, legitimates experimental efforts to merge disparate forms. [...]

[...] Today, a wide swath of authors interrogates how users, consumers, laity, or the afflicted imagine hybridity and associated technologies as social processes [...].

However intriguing, when hybridity flags biosociality, this analytical strategy nevertheless risks generating imprecise readings of values and meanings. Biosociality is commonly evoked to demonstrate only rough approximations of "kinship," commonly glossed as a generalized

From Frances Mascia-Lees (ed.), *Companion to the Anthropology of the Body and Embodiment* (Oxford: Blackwell Publishing Ltd., 2011), pp. 262–75, Wiley-Blackwell. Reprinted with permission of John Wiley & Sons Ltd.

Anthropology in Theory: Issues in Epistemology, Second Edition. Edited by Henrietta L. Moore and Todd Sanders.
© 2014 John Wiley & Sons, Inc. Published 2014 by John Wiley & Sons, Inc.

statement about newly imagined configurations of sameness and difference. Absent are references to the more intricate workings – and conflicts – that older kinship studies provided. In this light, I argue that anthropology could profit from a reopening of kinship and its associated categories of analysis as a compelling methodological tool (Franklin and McKinnon 2001: 7–11). [...]

When set alongside the contemporary category of biosociality, reinvigorated understandings of kinship may in fact offer a far more complex – albeit woefully underutilized – means to probe what Beidelman (1993) once referenced as the "moral imagination," a framework interpreted more recently by Livingston as encompassing efforts to respond creatively (and, even, strategically) to unusual, stigmatized, or debilitated bodies where no clear resolution is in sight (Livingston 2005). A central idea at work here is that social responses to the strange or uncanny (Douglas 1966; Kristeva 1982) are inescapably complex and problematic affairs that foreground the dilemmas and enigmatic character of everyday life. As moral projects, then, imaginative efforts are less about distinguishing right from wrong, or recognizing clear solutions, as they are about emergent struggles during moments of uncertainty. Whereas Beidelman's and Livingston's respective labors are set within small and mid-range African communities, I argue that a similar problematic pervades scientific action and thought during efforts to transform human bodies into hybrids. Whereas formalized, bioethical codes might clearly dictate the proper treatment of human and animal subjects, still other dilemmas surface when humans and/or particular animal species generate complicated and ambiguous meanings that inescapably reference sociality and subjectivity. It is at these very moments when scientists themselves – and not simply the lay public – may activate the logic of kinship.

One way to approach this, then, is to ask, how are meanings reinscribed onto bodies after they have been removed from their social contexts, altered by science, and then reintroduced within specific social milieux? Or, phrased yet another way, how are bodies that are subjected to scientific reasoning then reenculturated by scientists themselves? [...]

The Moral Parameters of Embodied Hybridity

Currently, biosociality most frequently glosses newly configured ways to think about how science provokes (and, even, empowers) emergent understandings of similarity, belonging, and selfhood among previously unrelated persons in contexts involving shared, embodied substance (be it transfused blood, genetic markers, or implanted organs or tissues). What, though, of more intricate and intimate categories of relatedness and difference within the very science that enables such imaginings? [...]

Kinship has long been understood by anthropologists as an inherently moral and temporal project: as Maurice Bloch [1973] once asserted, the moral "character" of kinship unfolds over the "long and the short term." Kinship is simultaneously about sameness, reliability, trust, and, ultimately, morality, where those who fail in the end to fulfill kinship obligations stand outside that moral order. [...] Marriage, for instance, transforms outsiders into insiders; lines of descent may convert enemies into allies; and shared origins can foster cooperation over competition. Kinship reconfigures sociality and subjectivity by transforming "strange" into "same" within particular sociomoral worlds. Finally, whereas kinship is most certainly about relationality, it is also about sentimental structures (Wilson 1971), the latter all too frequently overlooked in those instances where biosociality is invoked (Sharp 2006: 193).

I offer xenotransplantation as a field within which to probe the limitations of biosociality by drawing upon kinship idioms in contexts that specifically involve the creation of human/animal hybrids. Perhaps no other field of science exemplifies hybridity more profoundly than xenotransplantation (henceforth *xeno*), a highly experimental realm driven by the determination to overcome significant immunological hurdles so that the failed organs of human patients might be replaced with those derived from various animal species. [...] [X]eno researchers most frequently describe their efforts as spurred on by a health crisis of grave significance [...] transplant medicine is plagued by a scarcity in donated human organs and tissues, and the gap between demand and supply increases annually as more patients join waiting lists for hearts, livers, kidneys, and other transplantable parts. Against this backdrop, xeno is framed as an inherently moral project. Involved scientists are determined to alleviate human suffering by overcoming immunological hurdles that impede the successful implantation of xenografts within dying patients. Thus, the answer to human organ scarcity lies with a reliable, alternative market and, potentially, unlimited supply of parts derived from expendable "donor" animals.

Of particular interest to me are the specific categories of animals deemed the most appropriate candidates for such hybrid meldings. Throughout much of the 20th century, scientific desire has focused intently on a range of simian species (most notably chimpanzees, baboons, and macaques); within the last two decades or so, however, nonhuman primates have been sidelined in response to a very recent shift in preference for developing porcine xenografts. These various embodied human/ simian and human/swine pairings, when staged as moral projects, are regularly framed [. . .] by drawing on idioms of kinship.

[. . .] [W]ithin xeno research, primates and pigs share a joint position as compatible, albeit unusual, companion species (Haraway 2003) to humans and, as such, they stand neatly alongside us within the imposing framework of biosociality. In this broad sense, the trope of "compatibility" – at times imagined as immunological, at others, social – pervades xeno scientists' discourse on interspecies hybridity. Closer inspection reveals, however, that scientific desire reads compatibility differently vis-à-vis these two categories of animals, such that primates begin to resemble consanguinal or blood relatives, whereas pigs are more akin, so to speak, to distant albeit promising future affines. Furthermore, when, by the late 20th century, scientific desire within xeno science shifted its focus from primates to pigs, hybrid pairings of humans with apes and monkeys were reconfigured as inappropriate and even incestuous unions, paving the way for a new sort of "match" – or simultaneously immunological and social marriage – with swine.

Xeno experts thus (re)frame hybrid experimentation as a legitimate and inherently moral project by invoking the sentimental qualities of kinship. This process, however, is contingent on several epistemological shifts that reference biocapital, monsters, and embodied intimacy. First, xeno's success (or peril) is driven unquestionably by the marketplace; nevertheless, the moral imperative to alleviate human suffering squelches discussions of experimental animals as rarified sources of futuristic biocapital. Second, whereas hybrid bodies are viewed as inherently unnatural within general social contexts, their potentially monstrous qualities are resocialized by involved researchers as sites of intensified scientific desire. Third, as xeno scientists struggle tirelessly to overcome the instability of hybrid meldings, immunological "compatibility" informs ways in which to reimagine "donor" primates and, most recently, pigs as bearing the promises of newfound interspecies kith and kin.

[. . .]

The Intimacy of Interspeciality

Xeno research is by very definition an anticipatory branch of experimental science, thus marking especially fertile ground for exploring emergent categories of sociality and subjectivity. [. . .]

[. . .]

Primates and pigs each have their own particular cultural histories that render them simultaneously adaptable to human use and morally compatible mates for us in science (Bartkowski 2008; Franklin 2007; Haraway 1989; Papagaroufali 1996). [. . .] Their appropriateness as research subjects has always been framed in terms of their evolutionary and, even, social proximity to us. As close cousins related to us by our sharing of primordial ancestors, chimpanzees, baboons, macaques, and other primates made a relatively effortless transition to being the animals most desired by xeno researchers, who have long imagined them as bearing the promises of compatibility and, thus, embodied intimacy. If immunological rejection could indeed be overcome, simians would ultimately master the shift from being similar to us to being the same as us.

[. . .]

Deeper meanings and values surface, however, if we shift the register to the more intricate (and intimate) analyses fostered by kinship studies. Attention to older categories of belonging foreground not simply the transfer of substance, but the sentimental structures associated with desired intimacy. This merging of shared substance within xeno is dependent on a very particular sort of narrative, one whose veracity hinges on the ability to spin convincing stories about evolutionary proximity, shared origins, and blood relatedness (Bartkowski 2008). When, in the recent past, xeno experts spoke of nonhuman primates, they regularly referenced apes and monkeys as the closest of cousins and, thus, the most desired of immunological mates. [...] Xenografting thus emerged as a rather uncanny sort of arranged interspecies marriage between chimps, baboons, and macaques with human beings.

When read within the analytical framework of kinship, these seemingly scientific narratives read as morality tales about desired kin relations – and, perhaps, even, subsequent obligations – as they unfold over time. In temporal terms, primates as a broad category of stranger species have been viewed, first, as ideal mates, later as newfound kin, and, eventually, should xenografts prove successful, fully integrated as equivalents to or even as the same as self. In other words, xeno is not merely about shared substance, but about coterminous meanings and associated dilemmas activated by scientific desire. [...] Just as marriage transforms human strangers into kin, xeno science bears the promise of converting cousin species immunologically and socially into "same" or "self." When viewed as such, chimps, baboons, and macaques indeed stand out as an extraordinary category of consanguinal or blood kin.

By the late 20th century, however, xeno experts' desires for primates had begun to wither, and eventually these creatures reemerged as potential pariahs in the face of several insurmountable hurdles. These included the AIDS pandemic in the wake of theories that the HIV virus could have originated in colonies of African primates; associated fears that still other pathogens could jump the species barrier; and several recent xenograft surgeries that proved fatal to human patients. [...]

Currently, swine shoulder hybridity's promises [...] [W]hen xeno experts abandoned primates in preference for pigs, they activated narratives of practicality and, thus, the marketplace, that featured both categories of animals as sources of biocapital. As xeno experts now regularly explain, pigs mature rapidly, and sows more particularly are prolific breeders, producing large litters with ease. Furthermore, the genetic makeup of pigs can be altered fairly easily, and they present fewer challenges where their care is concerned [...]. In contrast, monkeys and even more so, chimps, generate significant problems in terms of their upkeep. [...]

The vagaries of biocapital thus (re)surface at those moments when xeno experts (re)imagine the promises of hybridity as embodied by competing animal species; once a particular animal is in place (be it primate or pig), the register shifts yet again to foreground xeno as a sociomoral project intent on saving human lives. As this shift in register occurs, kinship idioms are (re)activated. [...] Xeno experts now speak of pigs as a superior match that stands against archaic understandings of primates.

I am often told today by xeno experts that pigs are so similar anatomically to humans as to be indistinguishable from us [...]. [T]hese imagined notions of similarity and sameness are rooted in the human ability to manipulate pigs genetically and, thus, transform "difference" into "sameness" or a "foreign species" into "self." Because generations of pigs can be bred in fairly rapid succession, genetically altered pigs emerge as "evolutionarily close" to us because we can potentially manipulate genetic lines of succession, thus creating creatures tailored to scientific needs. [...]

The grammar of kinship aids us in disentangling this emergent preference for pigs [...]: whereas primates, as true evolutionary cousins, are regarded as blood kin, pigs represent an altogether different sort of match [...] because primates are genetically and evolutionarily *too* close to humans they harbored significant dangers. That is, they could easily transmit species-specific life-pathogens in ways that pigs, presumably, would not. [...] [This reconfigured] the union between humans and primates as an unproductive and, ultimately, incestuous one. In the end, primates are no longer desired as mates, but have been reconfigured as pariahs, standing outside the social imaginary of xeno science. [...]

Conclusion: Hybrids and the Scientific Imaginary

[...] These newly imagined bonds of interspecies kinship are thus simultaneously utilitarian and sentimental in character. If kinship is an inherently moral process whose character unfolds over time, then intimate bonds do indeed insist on complex, enduring social responses. As Bloch reminds us, the failure to act appropriately may eventually place one outside the moral order (again, see Bloch 1973). These sorts of moral dilemmas emerge not simply within small-scale communities, but within contexts framed by experimental science, too. [...] The presumed intimate bonds of interspecies matching inevitably oblige primate "donors" to give quite literally of themselves to humans. When they later proved to be incompatible matches, they reemerged as a newly conceived category of failed, albeit serviceable, outcasts. [...]

In response to such failures, the pig has now displaced our primate "cousins," standing in as the new darling of xeno research. Pigs are currently imagined as robust, easily altered genetically, marvelously prolific, and fertile creatures. As such, transgenic pigs now bear the promises of a newly fashioned category of hybrid vigor. The sentimental musings focused specifically on the transgenic breed sow reveal that, within a newly imagined species hierarchy, she far surpasses the temperamental and less productive ape or monkey. Simians proved too close for comfort, embodying the dangers of proximity assigned to incestuous unions and so now, today, xeno science is wed to the pig as its perfect, future partner.

Unquestionably, the consequences of hybridity should concern anthropologists working at the intersection of science studies. [...] The scientific imagination is characterized by deeply embedded sentiments that reorder contradictions and legitimate laboratory work (and subsequent social consequences). More specifically within xeno, the values assigned to monstrous couplings, interspecies compatibility, evolutionary proximity, anatomical equivalence, and the obligations imposed on donor species expose the complex workings of scientific desire to reconfigure bodies and social boundaries. [...]

References

Bartkowski, Frances, 2008 Kissing Cousins: A New Kinship Bestiary. New York: Columbia University Press.

Beidelman, T. O., 1993 Moral Imagination in Kaguru Modes of Thought. Washington, DC: Smithsonian Institution Press.

Bloch, Maurice, 1973 The Long Term and the Short Term: The Economic and Political Significance of the Morality of Kinship. In The Character of Kinship. J. Goody, ed. pp. 75–87. Cambridge: Cambridge University Press.

Douglas, Mary, 1966 Purity and Danger: An Analysis of Concepts of Pollution and Taboo. New York: Praeger.

Franklin, Sarah, 2007 Dolly Mixtures: The Remaking of Genealogy. Durham, NC: Duke University Press.

Franklin, Sarah and Susan McKinnon, eds., 2001 Relative Values: Reconfiguring Kinship Studies. Durham, NC: Duke University Press.

Haraway, Donna J., 1989 Primate Visions: Gender, Race, and Nature in the World of Modern Science. New York: Routledge.

Haraway, Donna J., 1992 The Promises of Monsters: A Regenerative Politics for Inappropriate/d Others. In Cultural Studies. L. Grossberg, C. Nelson, and P. Treichler, eds. pp. 295–337. New York: Routledge.

Haraway, Donna J., 2003 The Companion Species Manifesto: Dogs, People, and Significant Otherness. Chicago: Prickly Paradigm Press.

Kristeva, Julia, 1982 Powers of Horror: An Essay on Abjection. New York: Columbia University Press.

Livingston, Julie, 2005 Debility and the Moral Imagination in Botswana. Bloomington, IN: Indiana University Press.

Martin, E., 1994 Flexible Bodies: Tracking Immunity in American Culture From the Days of Polio to the Age of AIDS. Boston: Beacon Press.

Papagaroufali, Eleni, 1996 Xenotransplantation and Transgenesis: Immoral Stories about Human–Animal Relations in the West. *In* Nature and Society: Anthropological Perspectives. P. Descola and G. Pálsson, eds. pp. 240–55. New York: Routledge.

Rabinow, Paul, 1992 Artificiality and Enlightenment: From Sociobiology to Biosociality. *In* Incorporations: Zone 6. J. Crary and S. Kwinter, eds. pp. 234–52. New York: Urzone.

Sharp, Lesley A., 2006 Strange Harvest: Organ Transplants, Denatured Bodies, and the Transformed Self. Berkeley: University of California Press.

Taylor, Janelle S., 2005 Surfacing the Body's Interior. Annual Review of Anthropology 34: 741–56.

Wilson, Peter J., 1971 Sentimental Structure: Tsimihety Migration and Descent. American Anthropologist 73(1): 193–208.

PART III

SECTION 9
Coherence and Contingency

29

Puritanism and the Spirit of Capitalism

Max Weber

Let us now try to clarify the points in which the Puritan idea of the calling and the requirement it placed upon the ascetic conduct of life was bound to have a direct influence on the development of a capitalistic way of life. As we have seen, asceticism turns with all its force against one thing: the *spontaneous enjoyment* of life and the pleasure existence has to offer. This is perhaps most characteristically brought out in the struggle over the *Book of Sports* which James I and Charles I made into law expressly as a means of counteracting Puritanism, and which the latter ordered to be read from all the pulpits. The fanatical opposition of the Puritans to the ordinances of the King, permitting certain popular amusements on Sunday outside of Church hours by law, was not only explained by the disturbance of the Sabbath rest, but also by resentment against the intentional diversion from the ordered life of the saint, which it caused. And, on his side, the King's threats of severe punishment for every attack on the legality of those sports were motivated by his purpose of breaking the *anti-authoritarian ascetic* tendency of Puritanism, which was so dangerous to the State. The feudal and monarchical forces protected the pleasure seekers against the emergent middle-class morality and the anti-authoritarian ascetic conventicles, just as to-day capitalistic society tends to protect those willing to work against the class morality of the proletariat and the anti-authoritarian trade union.

As against this the Puritans upheld their most decisive characteristic, the principle of the ascetic conduct of life. Apart from this, though, the Puritan aversion to sport, even for the Quakers, was by no means simply one of principle. Sport was accepted if it served a rational purpose, that of recreation necessary for physical efficiency. But as a means for the spontaneous expression of undisciplined impulses, it was under suspicion; and in so far as it became purely a means of enjoyment, or awakened competitive ambition, raw instincts or the irrational gambling instinct, it was of course strictly condemned. Impulsive enjoyment of life, which leads away both from work in a calling and from religious devotion, was as such the enemy of rational asceticism, whether in the form of "seigneurial" sports, or the enjoyment of the dance-hall or the public-house of the common man.

Its attitude was thus suspicious and often hostile to the aspects of culture without any immediate

From Sam Whimster, (ed.) *The Essential Weber* (London and New York: Routledge, 2004), pp. 25–34. Reprinted with permission of Taylor & Francis Books.

Anthropology in Theory: Issues in Epistemology, Second Edition. Edited by Henrietta L. Moore and Todd Sanders.
© 2014 John Wiley & Sons, Inc. Published 2014 by John Wiley & Sons, Inc.

religious value. It is not, however, true that the ideals of Puritanism implied a solemn, narrow-minded contempt of culture. Quite the contrary is the case at least for science, with the exception of the hatred of Scholasticism. Moreover, the great men of the Puritan movement were thoroughly steeped in the culture of the Renaissance. The sermons of the Presbyterian wing of the movement abound with classical allusions, and even the Radicals, although they objected to it, were not ashamed to display that kind of learning in theological polemics. Perhaps no country was ever so full of graduates as New England in the first generation of its existence. The satire of their opponents, such as, for instance, Butler's *Hudibras*, attacks directly the pedantry and highly trained dialectics of the Puritans. This is partially due to the religious valuation of knowledge which followed from their attitude to the Catholic confusion of faith (*fides implicita*).

But the situation is quite different when one looks at non-scientific literature, and especially the arts that appeal to the senses. Here asceticism descended like a frost on the life of "Merrie old England". And not only worldly merriment felt its effect. The Puritan's ferocious hatred of everything which smacked of superstition, of all survivals of magical or ritualistic means of grace, applied to the Christmas festivities and the May Pole and the uninhibited use of art in churches. That there was room in Holland for a great, often uncouthly realistic art proves only how far from completely the authoritarian moral discipline of that country was able to counteract the influence of the court and the regents (a class of *rentiers*). It also shows the joy in life of the parvenu bourgeoisie after the short supremacy of the Calvinistic theocracy had been transformed into a moderate national Church, and with it Calvinism had perceptibly lost in its power of ascetic influence.

The theatre was obnoxious to the Puritans, and with the strict exclusion of the erotic and of nudity from the realm of toleration, a radical view of either literature or art could not exist. The conceptions of idle talk, of superfluities, and of vain ostentation, all designations of an irrational attitude without objective purpose, thus not ascetic, and especially not serving the glory of God, but of man, were always at hand to serve in deciding in favour of sober utility as against any artistic tendencies. This was especially true in the case of decoration of the person, for instance clothing. That powerful tendency toward uniformity of style of life, which to-day so immensely aids the capitalistic interest in the standardization of production, had its ideal foundations in the repudiation of all "idolatry of the flesh".

Of course we must not forget that Puritanism included a world of contradictions, and that the instinctive sense of eternal greatness in art was certainly stronger among its leaders than in the atmosphere of the Cavaliers. Moreover, a unique genius like Rembrandt, however little his conduct may have been acceptable to God in the eyes of the Puritans, was very strongly influenced in the character of his work by his religious environment. But that does not alter the picture as a whole. In so far as the development of the Puritan tradition could, and in part did, lead to a powerful spiritualization (*Verinnerlichung*) of personality, it was a decided benefit to literature. But for the most part that benefit only accrued to later generations.

Although we cannot here enter upon a discussion of the influence of Puritanism in all these directions, we should call attention to the fact that the toleration of pleasure in cultural goods, which contributed to purely æsthetic or athletic enjoyment, certainly always ran up against one characteristic limitation: *they must not cost anything*. Man is only a trustee of the goods which have come to him through God's grace. He must, like the servant in the parable, give an account of every penny entrusted to him, and it is at least hazardous to spend any of it for a purpose which does not serve the glory of God but only one's own enjoyment. What person, who keeps his eyes open, has not met representatives of this view-point even in the present? The idea of a man's *duty* to his possessions, to which he subordinates himself as an obedient steward, or even as an acquisitive machine, bears with chilling weight on his life. The greater the possessions the heavier, if the ascetic attitude toward life stands the test, the feeling of responsibility for them, for holding them undiminished for the glory of God and increasing them by restless effort. The origin of this style of life also extends in certain roots, like so many aspects of the spirit of capitalism, back into the Middle Ages. But it was in the ethic of ascetic Protestantism that it first found a consistent ethical foundation. Its significance for the development of capitalism is obvious.

This worldly Protestant asceticism, as we may recapitulate up to this point, acted powerfully against the spontaneous *enjoyment* of possessions; it restricted *consumption*, especially of luxuries. On the other hand, it had the psychological effect of *freeing* the acquisition of goods from the inhibitions of traditionalistic ethics. It broke the bonds of the search for gain in that it not only legalized it, but (in the sense discussed) looked upon it as directly willed by God. The campaign against the temptations of the flesh, and the dependence on external things, was, as besides the Puritans the great Quaker apologist Barclay expressly says, not a struggle against the rational *acquisition*, but against the irrational use of wealth.

But this irrational use was exemplified in the outward forms of luxury which their code condemned as "idolatry of the flesh", however natural they had appeared to the feudal mind. On the other hand, they approved the rational and utilitarian uses of wealth which were willed by God for the needs of the individual and the community. They did not wish to impose *mortification* on the man of wealth, but the use of his means for necessary and *practical* things. The idea of comfort characteristically limits the extent of ethically permissible expenditures. It is naturally no accident that the development of a manner of living (*Lebensstil*) consistent with that idea may be observed earliest and most clearly among the most consistent representatives of this whole attitude toward life: the Quakers. Over against the glitter and ostentation of feudal magnificence which, resting on an unsound economic basis, prefers a sordid elegance to a sober simplicity, they set the clean and solid comfort of the middle-class home as an ideal.

On the side of the *production* of private wealth, asceticism condemned both dishonesty and impulsive avarice. What was condemned as covetousness, Mammonism, etc., was the pursuit of riches for their own sake. For wealth in itself was a temptation. But here asceticism was the power "which ever seeks the good but ever creates evil"; what was evil in its sense was possession and its temptations. For, in conformity with the Old Testament and in analogy to the ethical valuation of "good works", asceticism looked upon the pursuit of wealth as an *end* in itself as highly reprehensible; but the attainment of it as a *fruit* of labour in a calling (*Berufsarbeit*) was a sign of God's blessing. And even more important: the religious valuation of restless, continuous, systematic work in a worldly calling, as the highest means to asceticism, and at the same time the surest and most evident proof of rebirth and genuine faith, must have been the most powerful conceivable lever for the expansion of that attitude toward life which we have here called the "spirit" of capitalism.

When the limitation of consumption is combined with this release of acquisitive activity, the inevitable practical result is obvious: *accumulation of capital* through *ascetic compulsion to save*. The restraints which were imposed upon the consumption of wealth naturally served to increase it by making possible the productive *investment* of capital. How strong this influence was is not, unfortunately, susceptible to exact statistical demonstration. In New England the connection is so evident that it did not escape the eye of so discerning a historian as Doyle. But also in Holland, which was really only dominated by strict Calvinism for seven years, the greater simplicity of life in the more seriously religious circles, in combination with great wealth, led to an excessive propensity to capital accumulation.

It is further evident that the tendency which has existed everywhere and at all times, and is quite strong in Germany to-day, for middle-class fortunes to be absorbed into the nobility was necessarily checked by the Puritan antipathy to the feudal way of life. English Mercantilist writers of the seventeenth century attributed the superiority of Dutch capital to English to the circumstance that newly acquired wealth there did not regularly seek investment in land. Also, since it is not simply a question of the purchase of land, the Dutch did not seek to acquire feudal habits of life, and thereby to forgo the possibility of capitalistic investment. The high esteem for *agriculture* as a particularly important branch of activity, which the Puritans held and one also consistent with piety, applied (for instance in Baxter) not to the traditional landlord (*Junker*) but to the yeoman and farmer; and in the eighteenth century not to the squire, but the "rational" cultivator. Through the whole of English society in the time since the seventeenth century goes the conflict between the squirearchy, the representatives of "Merrie old England", and the Puritan circles of widely varying social influence. Both elements, that of an unspoiled naïve joy of life, and of a strictly regulated, reserved self-control, and conventional ethical conduct are even to-day combined to form the English "national character". Similarly, the early history of the North American Colonies is dominated by the sharp contrast of the adventurers who wanted to set up plantations with the labour of indentured servants, and live as feudal lords, and the specifically middle-class outlook of the Puritans.

As far as the influence of the Puritan outlook extended, under all circumstances – and this is, of course, much more important than the mere encouragement of capital accumulation – it favoured the development of a bourgeois, economically *rational* way of life; it was the most important, and above all the only consistent support for the development of that life. It stood at the cradle of the modern economic man.

To be sure, these Puritanical ideals tended to give way under excessive pressure from the temptations of wealth, as the Puritans themselves knew very well. With great regularity we find the most genuine adherents of Puritanism among the classes which were rising from a lowly status, the small bourgeois and farmers, while the *beati possidentes*, even among Quakers, are often found tending to repudiate the old ideals. It was the same fate which again and again befell the predecessor of innerworldly asceticism, the monastic asceticism of the Middle Ages. In the latter case, when rational economic activity had worked out its full effects by strict regulation of conduct and limitation of consumption, the wealth accumulated either succumbed directly to the nobility, as in the time before the Reformation, or monastic discipline threatened to break down, and one of the numerous reformations became necessary.

In fact the whole history of monasticism is in a certain sense the history of a continual struggle with the problem of the secularizing influence of wealth. The same is true on a grand scale of the innerworldly asceticism of Puritanism. The great revival of Methodism, which preceded the expansion of English industry toward the end of the eighteenth century, may well be compared with such a monastic reform. We may hence quote here a passage from John Wesley himself which

might well serve as a motto for everything which has been said above. For it shows that the leaders of these ascetic movements understood the seemingly paradoxical relationships which we have here analysed perfectly well, and in the same sense that we have given them. He wrote:

I fear, wherever riches have increased, the essence of religion has decreased in the same proportion. Therefore I do not see how it is possible, in the nature of things, for any revival of true religion to continue long. For religion *must necessarily* produce both industry and frugality, and these cannot but produce riches. But as riches increase, so will pride, anger, and love of the world in all its branches. How then is it possible that Methodism, that is, a religion of the heart, though it flourishes now as a green bay tree, should continue in this state? For the Methodists in every place grow diligent and frugal; consequently they increase in goods. Hence they proportionately increase in pride, in anger, in the desire of the flesh, the desire of the eyes, and the pride of life. So, although the form of religion remains, the spirit is swiftly vanishing away. Is there no way to prevent this – this continual decay of pure religion? We ought not to prevent people from being diligent and frugal; *we must exhort all Christians to gain all they can, and to save all they can; that is, in effect, to grow rich.*[1]

There follows the advice that those who gain all they can and save all they can should also give all they can, so that they will grow in grace and lay up a treasure in heaven. It is clear that Wesley here expresses, even in detail, just what we have been trying to point out.

As Wesley says, the full economic effect of those great religious movements, whose significance for economic development lay above all in their ascetic *educative* influence, generally came only after the peak of the purely religious enthusiasm was past. Then the intensity of the search for the Kingdom of God commenced gradually to pass over into sober vocational virtue; the religious roots died out slowly, giving way to utilitarian worldliness. Then, as Dowden puts it, the place occupied in the popular imagination by Bunyan's pilgrim, hurrying through "Vanity Fair" in a lonely spiritual search for the Kingdom of Heaven, was taken by "Robinson Crusoe" – the *isolated economic man* who carries on missionary activities on the side.

When later the principle "to make the most of both worlds" became dominant in the end, as Dowden has remarked, a good conscience simply became one of the means of enjoying a comfortable bourgeois life, as is well expressed in the German proverb about the "soft pillow". What the great religious epoch of the seventeenth century bequeathed to its utilitarian successor was, however, above all an amazingly good, we may even say a pharisaically good, conscience in the acquisition of money, so long as it took place legally. Every trace of the *Deo placere vix potest* [it is scarcely pleasing to God] has disappeared.

A specifically *bourgeois vocational ethic* had grown up. With the consciousness of standing in the fullness of God's grace and being visibly blessed by Him, the bourgeois business man, as long as he remained within the bounds of formal correctness, as long as his moral conduct was spotless and the use to which he put his wealth was not objectionable, could follow his pecuniary interests as he would, and feel that he was fulfilling a duty in doing so. In addition, the power of religious asceticism placed at his disposal sober, conscientious, and unusually industrious workmen, who clung to their work as to a life purpose willed by God.

Finally, it gave him the comforting assurance that the unequal distribution of the goods of this world was a special dispensation of Divine Providence, which in these differences, as in particular grace, pursued secret ends unknown to men. Calvin himself had made the much-quoted statement that only when the people, i.e. the mass of labourers and craftsmen, were poor did they remain obedient to God. In the Netherlands (Pieter de la Court and others), that had been "secularized" to the effect that the mass of men only *labour* when necessity forces them to do so. This formulation of a leading idea of capitalistic economy later entered into the current theories of the "productivity" of low wages. Here also, with the dying out of the religious root, the utilitarian interpretation crept in unnoticed, in the line of development which we have again and again observed.

Mediæval ethics not only tolerated begging but actually glorified it in the mendicant orders. Even secular beggars, since they gave the person of means opportunity for good works through giving alms, were sometimes considered an "estate" and treated as such. Even the Anglican social ethic of the Stuarts was very close to this attitude. It remained for Puritan asceticism to take part in the severe English Poor Relief Legislation which fundamentally changed the situation. And it could do that, because the Protestant sects and the strict Puritan communities actually *did not know* any begging in their own midst.

On the other hand, seen from the side of the workers, the Zinzendorf branch of Pietism, for instance, glorified the loyal worker who did not seek acquisition, but lived according to the apostolic model, and was thus endowed with the charisma of the disciples. Similar ideas had originally been prevalent among the Baptists in an even more radical form.

Now naturally the whole ascetic literature of almost *all* denominations is saturated with the idea that faithful labour, even at low wages, on the part of those whom life offers no other opportunities, is highly pleasing to God. In *this* respect Protestant asceticism added in itself nothing new. But it not only deepened this idea most powerfully, it also created the force which was alone decisive for its effectiveness: the psychological sanction (*Antrieb*) of it through the conception of this labour as a *calling*, as the best, often in the last analysis the only means of attaining certainty of grace. And on the other hand it legalized the exploitation of this specific willingness to work, in that it also interpreted the employer's business activity as a "calling". It is obvious how powerfully the *exclusive* search for the Kingdom of God only through the fulfilment of duty in the calling, and the strict asceticism which Church discipline naturally imposed, especially on the propertyless classes, was bound to affect the productivity of labour in the capitalistic sense of the word. The treatment of labour as a "calling" became as characteristic of the modern worker as the corresponding attitude toward acquisition of the business man. It was a perception of this situation, new at his time, which caused so able an observer as Sir William Petty to attribute the economic power of Holland in the seventeenth century to the fact that the very numerous dissenters in that country (Calvinists and Baptists) "are for the most part thinking, sober men, and such as believe that Labour and Industry is their duty towards God".

Calvinism opposed "organic" social organization in the fiscal-monopolistic form which it assumed in Anglicanism under the Stuarts, especially in the conceptions of Laud, this alliance of Church and State with the monopolists on the basis of a Christian-social ethical foundation. The Puritan leaders were universally among the most passionate opponents of this type of politically privileged commercial, putting-out, and colonial capitalism. Over against it they placed the individualistic motives of rational legal acquisition by virtue of one's own ability and initiative. And, while the politically privileged monopoly industries in England all disappeared in short order, this attitude played a large and decisive part in the development of the industries which grew up in spite of and against the authority of the State. The Puritans (Prynne, Parker) repudiated all connection with the large-scale capitalistic "courtiers and projectors" as an ethically suspicious class. On the other hand, they took pride in their own superior middle-class business morality, which formed the true reason for the persecutions to which they were subjected on the part of those circles. Defoe proposed to win the battle against dissent by boycotting bank credit and withdrawing deposits. The difference of the two types of capitalistic attitude went to a very large extent hand in hand with religious differences. The opponents of the Nonconformists, even in the eighteenth century, again and again ridiculed them for personifying the spirit of shopkeepers, and for having ruined the ideals of old England. Here also lay the difference of the Puritan economic ethic from the Jewish; and contemporaries (Prynne) knew well that the former and not the latter was the *bourgeois* capitalistic ethic.

One of the fundamental elements of the spirit of modern capitalism, and not only of that but of all modern culture: rational conduct on the basis of the idea of the calling, was born – that is what this discussion has sought to demonstrate – from the spirit of *Christian asceticism*. [...] [T]he essential elements of the attitude [...] called the "spirit of capitalism" are the same as what we have just shown to be the content of the Puritan worldly asceticism, only without the religious basis [...]. The idea that modern labour has an *ascetic* character is of course not new. Limitation to specialized work, with a renunciation of the Faustian universality of man which it involves, is

a condition of any valuable work in the modern world; hence deeds and renunciation inevitably condition each other today. This fundamentally ascetic trait of middle-class life, if it attempts to be a style of life at all, and not simply the absence of any, was what Goethe wanted to teach, at the height of his wisdom, in the *Wanderjahren*, and in the end which he gave to the life of his *Faust*. For him the realization meant a renunciation, a departure from an age of full and beautiful humanity, which can no more be repeated in the course of our cultural development than can the flower of the Athenian culture of Antiquity.

The Puritan *wanted* to work in a calling; we are *forced* to do so. For when asceticism was carried out of monastic cells into everyday life, and began to dominate innerworldly morality, it did its part in building the tremendous cosmos of the modern economic order. This order is now bound to the technical and economic conditions of machine production which to-day determine the style of life of all the individuals who are born into this mechanism, not only those directly concerned with economic acquisition, with irresistible force. Perhaps it will so determine them until the last ton of fossilized coal is burnt. In Baxter's view the concern for external goods should only lie on the shoulders of the "saint like a light cloak, which can be thrown aside at any moment". But fate decreed that the cloak should become an iron cage.[2]

Since asceticism undertook to remodel the world and to work out its ideals in the world, material goods have gained an increasing and finally an inexorable power over the lives of men as at no previous period in history. To-day the spirit of religious asceticism – whether finally, who knows? – has escaped from the cage. But victorious capitalism, since it rests on mechanical foundations, needs its support no longer. The rosy blush of its laughing heir, the Enlightenment seems also to be irretrievably fading, and the idea of "duty in one's calling" prowls about in our lives like the ghost of dead religious beliefs. Where the fulfilment of the calling cannot directly be related to the highest spiritual and cultural values, or when, on the other hand, it need not be felt simply as economic compulsion, the individual generally abandons the attempt to justify it at all. In the field of its highest development, in the United States, the pursuit of wealth, stripped of its religious and ethical meaning, tends to become associated with purely competitive passions, which often actually give it the character of sport.

No one knows who will live in this cage in the future, or whether at the end of this tremendous development entirely new prophets will arise, or there will be a great rebirth of old ideas and ideals, or, if neither, mechanized petrification, embellished with a sort of convulsive self-importance. For of the "last men" of this cultural development, it might well be truly said: "Specialists without spirit, sensualists without heart; this nullity imagines that it has attained a level of civilization (*Menschentum*) never before achieved."

But this brings us to the world of judgments of value and of faith, with which this purely historical discussion need not be burdened. The next task would be rather to show the significance of ascetic rationalism, which has only been touched in the foregoing sketch, for the content of socio-political ethics, thus for the types of organization and the functions of social groups from the conventicle to the State. Then ascetic rationalism's relations to humanistic rationalism and its ideals of life and cultural influence; further to the development of philosophical and scientific empiricism, to technical development and to spiritual ideals of culture would have to be analysed. Then its past development from the mediæval beginnings of innerworldly asceticism to its dissolution into pure utilitarianism would have to be traced out historically through all the areas of ascetic religion. Only then could the extent of the cultural significance of ascetic Protestantism in its relation to the other plastic elements of modern culture be estimated.

Here we have only attempted to trace the fact and the nature of the effect of ascetic Protestantism back to the motives of that influence in one, though a very important point. But it would also further be necessary to investigate how Protestant asceticism was in turn influenced in its development and its character by the totality of social conditions, especially *economic*. The modern man is in general, even with the best will, unable to give religious ideas a significance for conduct of life, culture and national character which they deserve. But it is, of course, not my aim to substitute for a one-sided "materialistic" an equally one-sided spiritualistic causal interpretation of culture and of history. *Each is equally possible*,[3] but each, if it does not serve as the preparation, but as the conclusion of an investigation, accomplishes equally little in the interest of historical truth.

Notes

1   Quoted in Robert Southey, *Life of Wesley*, 2nd edn., vol. 2, New York, Harper & Brothers, 1847, ch. 29.
2   Talcott Parsons' translation – the iron cage – has now become iconic as an image of the inflexibility of the modern economic order. The original German is slightly different – a casing as hard as steel (*stahlhartes Gehäuse*).
3   [Weber] For the above sketch has deliberately taken up only the relations in which an influence of religious ideas on the material culture is beyond doubt. It would have been easy to proceed beyond that to a regular construction which logically deduced everything characteristic of modern culture from Protestant rationalism, but that sort of thing may be left to the type of dilettante who believes in the "unity" of the "group mind" and its reducibility to a single formula. Let it be remarked only that the period of capitalistic development lying before that which we have studied was everywhere co-determined (*mitbedingt*) by religious influences, both hindering and helping. [...]

30

Introduction to *Europe and the People Without History*

Eric R. Wolf

The central assertion of this book is that the world of humankind constitutes a manifold, a totality of interconnected processes, and inquiries that disassemble this totality into bits and then fail to reassemble it falsify reality. Concepts like "nation," "society," and "culture" name bits and threaten to turn names into things. Only by understanding these names as bundles of relationships, and by placing them back into the field from which they were abstracted, can we hope to avoid misleading inferences and increase our share of understanding

On one level it has become a commonplace to say that we all inhabit "one world." There are ecological connections: New York suffers from the Hong Kong flu; the grapevines of Europe are destroyed by American plant lice. There are demographic connections: Jamaicans migrate to London; Chinese migrate to Singapore. There are economic connections: a shutdown of oil wells on the Persian Gulf halts generating plants in Ohio; a balance of payments unfavorable to the United States drains American dollars into bank accounts in Frankfurt or Yokohama; Italians produce Fiat automobiles in the Soviet Union;

Japanese build a hydro-electric system in Ceylon. There are political connections: wars begun in Europe unleash reverberations around the globe; American troops intervene on the rim of Asia; Finns guard the border between Israel and Egypt.

This holds true not only of the present but also of the past. Diseases from Eurasia devastated the native population of America and Oceania. Syphilis moved from the New World to the Old. Europeans and their plants and animals invaded the Americas; the American potato, maize plant, and manioc spread throughout the Old World. Large numbers of Africans were transported forcibly to the New World; Chinese and Indian indentured laborers were shipped to Southeast Asia and the West Indies. Portugal created a Portuguese settlement in Macao off the coast of China. Dutchmen, using labor obtained in Bengal, constructed Batavia. Irish children were sold into servitude in the West Indies. Fugitive African slaves found sanctuary in the hills of Surinam. Europe learned to copy Indian textiles and Chinese porcelain, to drink native American chocolate, to smoke native American tobacco, to use Arabic numerals.

From *Europe and the People Without History*, 2nd edn. (Berkeley: University of California Press, 1982), pp. 3–23, 431, 435, 438–9, 446, 450–1, 456, 460–1, 463, 467–9. Copyright © 1983 the Regents of the University of California. Reprinted by permission of the Regents of the University of California and the University of California Press.

Anthropology in Theory: Issues in Epistemology, Second Edition. Edited by Henrietta L. Moore and Todd Sanders.
© 2014 John Wiley & Sons, Inc. Published 2014 by John Wiley & Sons, Inc.

These are familiar facts. They indicate contact and connections, linkages and interrelationships. Yet the scholars to whom we turn in order to understand what we see largely persist in ignoring them. Historians, economists, and political scientists take separate nations as their basic framework of inquiry. Sociology continues to divide the world into separate societies. Even anthropology, once greatly concerned with how culture traits diffused around the world, divides its subject matter into distinctive cases: each society with its characteristic culture, conceived as an integrated and bounded system, set off against other equally bounded systems.

If social and cultural distinctiveness and mutual separation were a hallmark of humankind, one would expect to find it most easily among the so-called primitives, people "without history," supposedly isolated from the external world and from one another. On this presupposition, what would we make of the archaeological findings that European trade goods appear in sites on the Niagara frontier as early as 1570, and that by 1670 sites of the Onondaga subgroup of the Iroquois reveal almost no items of native manufacture except pipes? On the other side of the Atlantic, the organization and orientations of large African populations were transformed in major ways by the trade in slaves. Since the European slavers only moved the slaves from the African coast to their destination in the Americas, the supply side of the trade was entirely in African hands. This was the "African foundation" upon which was built, in the words of the British mercantilist Malachy Postlethwayt, "the magnificent superstructure of American commerce and naval power." From Senegambia in West Africa to Angola, population after population was drawn into this trade, which ramified far inland and affected people who had never even seen a European trader on the coast. Any account of Kru, Fanti, Asante, Ijaw, Igbo, Kongo, Luba, Lunda, or Ngola that treats each group as a "tribe" sufficient unto itself thus misreads the African past and the African present. Furthermore, trade with Iroquois and West Africa affected Europe in turn. Between 1670 and 1760 the Iroquois demanded dyed scarlet and blue cloth made in the Stroudwater Valley of Gloucestershire. This was also one of the first areas in which English weavers lost their autonomy and became hired factory hands. Perhaps there

was an interconnection between the American trade and the onset of the industrial revolution in the valley of the Stroud. Conversely, the more than 5,500 muskets supplied to the Gold Coast in only three years (1658–61) enriched the gunsmiths of Birmingham, where they were made (Jennings 1976: 99–100; Daaku 1970: 150–1).

If there are connections everywhere, why do we persist in turning dynamic, interconnected phenomena into static, disconnected things? Some of this is owing, perhaps, to the way we have learned our own history. We have been taught, inside the classroom and outside of it, that there exists an entity called the West, and that one can think of this West as a society and civilization independent of and in opposition to other societies and civilizations. Many of us even grew up believing that this West has a genealogy, according to which ancient Greece begat Rome, Rome begat Christian Europe, Christian Europe begat the Renaissance, the Renaissance the Enlightenment, the Enlightenment political democracy and the industrial revolution. Industry, crossed with democracy, in turn yielded the United States, embodying the rights to life, liberty, and the pursuit of happiness.

Such a developmental scheme is misleading. It is misleading, first, because it turns history into a moral success story, a race in time in which each runner of the race passes on the torch of liberty to the next relay. History is thus converted into a tale about the furtherance of virtue, about how the virtuous win out over the bad guys. Frequently, this turns into a story of how the winners prove that they are virtuous and good by winning. If history is the working out of a moral purpose in time, then those who lay claim to that purpose are by that fact the predilect agents of history.

The scheme misleads in a second sense as well. If history is but a tale of unfolding moral purpose, then each link in the genealogy, each runner in the race, is only a precursor of the final apotheosis and not a manifold of social and cultural processes at work in their own time and place. Yet what would we learn of ancient Greece, for example, if we interpreted it only as a prehistoric Miss Liberty, holding aloft the torch of moral purpose in the barbarian night? We would gain little sense of the class conflicts racking the Greek cities, or of the relation between freemen and their slaves. We would have no reason to ask why there were more Greeks fighting in the ranks of the Persian kings than in the ranks of the Hellenic Alliance against the Persians. It would be of no interest to us to know that more Greeks lived in southern Italy and Sicily, then called Magna Graecia, than in Greece proper. Nor would we have any reason to ask why there were soon more Greek mercenaries in foreign armies than in the military bodies of their home cities. Greek settlers outside of Greece, Greek mercenaries in foreign armies, and slaves from Thrace, Phrygia, or Paphalagonia in Greek households all imply Hellenic relations with Greeks and non-Greeks outside of Greece. Yet our guiding scheme would not invite us to ask questions about these relationships

Nowhere is this myth-making scheme more apparent than in school-book versions of the history of the United States. There, a complex orchestration of antagonistic forces is celebrated instead as the unfolding of a timeless essence. In this perspective, the ever-changing boundaries of the United States and the repeated involvements of the polity in internal and external wars, declared and undeclared, are telescoped together by the teleological understanding that thirteen colonies clinging to the eastern rim of the continent would, in less than a century, plant the American flag on the shores of the Pacific. Yet this final result was itself only the contested outcome of many contradictory relationships. The colonies declared their independence, even though a majority of their population - European settlers, native Americans, and African slaves - favored the Tories. The new republic nearly foundered on the issue of slavery, dealing with it, in a series of problematic compromises, by creating two federated countries, each with its own zone of expansion. There was surely land for the taking on the new continent, but it had to be taken first from the native Americans who inhabited it, and then converted into flamboyant real estate. Jefferson bought the Louisiana territory cheaply, but only after the revolt of the Haitian slaves against their French slave masters robbed the area of its importance in the French scheme of things as a source of food supply for the Caribbean plantations. The occupation of Florida closed off one of the main escape hatches from southern slavery. The war with Mexico made the Southwest safe for slavery and cotton. The Hispanic landowners who stood in the way of the American drive to the Pacific became "bandits" when they defended their own against the Anglophone newcomers. Then North and South – one country importing its working force from Europe, the other from Africa – fought one of the bloodiest wars in history. For a time the defeated South became a colony of the victorious North. Later, the alignment between regions changed, the "sunbelt" rising to predominance as the influence of the industrial Northeast declined. Clearly the republic was neither indivisible nor endowed with God-given boundaries.

It is conceivable that things might have been different. There could have arisen a polyglot Floridian Republic, a Francophone Mississippian America, a Hispanic New Biscay, a Republic of the Great Lakes, a Columbia – comprising the present Oregon, Washington, and British Columbia. Only if we assume a God-given drive toward geopolitical unity on the North American continent would this retrojection be meaningless. Instead, it invites us to account in material terms for what happened at each juncture, to account for how some relationships gained ascendancy over others. Thus neither ancient Greece, Rome, Christian Europe, the Renaissance, the Enlightenment, the industrial revolution, democracy, nor even the United States was ever a thing propelled toward its unfolding goal by some immanent driving spring, but rather a temporally and spatially changing and changeable set of relationships, or relationships among sets of relationships.

The point is more than academic. By turning names into things we create false models of reality. By endowing nations, societies, or cultures with the qualities of internally homogeneous and externally distinctive and bounded objects, we create a model of the world as a global pool hall in which the entities spin off each other like so many hard and round billiard balls. Thus it becomes easy to sort the world into differently colored balls, to declare that "East is East, and West is West, and never the twain shall meet." In this way a quintessential West is counterposed to an equally quintessential East, where life was cheap and slavish multitudes groveled under a variety of despotisms. Later, as peoples in other climes began to assert their political and economic independence from both West and East, we assigned these new applicants for historical status to a Third World of underdevelopment – a residual category of conceptual billiard balls – as contrasted with the developed West and the developing East. Inevitably, perhaps, these reified categories became intellectual instruments in the prosecution of the Cold War. There was the "modern" world of the West. There was the world of the East, which had fallen prey to communism, a "disease of modernization" (Rostow 1960). There was, finally, the Third World, still bound up in "tradition" and strangled in its efforts toward modernization. If the West could only find ways of breaking that grip, it could perhaps save the victim from the infection incubated and spread by the East, and set that Third World upon the road to modernization – the road to life, liberty, and the pursuit of happiness of the West. The ghastly offspring of this way of thinking about the world was the theory of "forced draft urbanization" (Huntington 1968: 655), which held that the Vietnamese could be propelled toward modernization by driving them into the cities through aerial bombardment and defoliation of the countryside. Names thus become things, and things marked with an X can become targets of war.

The Rise of the Social Sciences

The habit of treating named entities such as Iroquois, Greece, Persia, or the United States as fixed entities opposed to one another by stable internal architecture and external boundaries interferes with our ability to understand their mutual encounter and confrontation. In fact, this tendency has made it difficult to understand all such encounters and confrontations. Arranging imaginary building blocks into pyramids called East and West, or First, Second, and Third Worlds, merely compounds that difficulty. It is thus likely that we are dealing with some conceptual shortcomings in our ways of looking at social and political phenomena, and not just a temporary aberration. We seem to have taken a wrong turn in understanding at some critical point in the past, a false choice that bedevils our thinking in the present.

That critical turning point is identifiable. It occurred in the middle of the nineteenth century, when inquiry into the nature and varieties of humankind split into separate (and unequal) specialties and disciplines. This split was fateful. It led not only forward into the intensive and specialized study of particular aspects of human

existence, but turned the ideological reasons for that split into an intellectual justification for the specialties themselves. Nowhere is this more obvious than in the case of sociology. Before sociology we had political economy, a field of inquiry concerned with "the wealth of nations," the production and distribution of wealth within and between political entities and the classes composing them. With the acceleration of capitalist enterprise in the eighteenth century, that structure of state and classes came under increasing pressure from new and "rising" social groups and categories that clamored for the enactment of their rights against those groups defended and represented by the state. Intellectually, this challenge took the form of asserting the validity of new social, economic, political, and ideological ties, now conceptualized as "society," against the state. The rising tide of discontent pitting "society" against the political and ideological order erupted in disorder, rebellion, and revolution. The specter of disorder and revolution raised the question of how social order could be restored and maintained, indeed, how social order was possible at all. Sociology hoped to answer the "social question." It had, as Rudolph Heberle noted, "an eminently political origin.... Saint Simon, Auguste Comte, and Lorenz Stein conceived the new science of society as an antidote against the poison of social disintegration" (quoted in Bramson 1961: 12, n. 2).

These early sociologists did this by severing the field of social relations from political economy. They pointed to observable and as yet poorly studied ties which bind people to people as individuals, as groups and associations, or as members of institutions. They then took this field of social relations to be the subject matter of their intensive concern. They and their successors expanded this concern into a number of theoretical postulates, using these to mark off sociology from political science and economics. I would summarize these common postulates as follows:

1   In the course of social life, individuals enter into relations with one another. Such relations can be abstracted from the economic, political, or ideological context in which they are found, and treated sui generis. They are autonomous, constituting a realm of their own, the realm of the social.

2 Social order depends on the growth and extension of social relations among individuals. The greater the density of such ties and the wider their scope, the greater the orderliness of society. Maximization of ties of kinship and neighborhood, of group and association, is therefore conducive to social order. Conversely, if these ties are not maximized, social order is called into question. Development of many and varied ties also diminishes the danger of polarization into classes.

3 The formation and maintenance of such ties is strongly related to the existence and propagation of common beliefs and customs among the individuals participating in them. Moral consensus, especially when based on unexamined belief and on nonrational acceptance of custom, furthers the maximization of social ties; expectations of mere utility and the exercise of merely technical reason tend to weaken them.

4 The development of social relations and the spread of associated custom and belief create a society conceived as a totality of social relations between individuals. Social relations constitute society; society, in turn, is the seat of cohesion, the unit to which predictability and orderliness can be ascribed. If social relations are orderly and recurrent, society has a stable internal structure. The extent of that structure is coterminous with the intensity and range of social relations. Where these grow markedly less intense and less frequent, society encounters its boundary.

What is the flaw in these postulates? They predispose one to think of social relations not merely as autonomous but as causal in their own right, apart from their economic, political, or ideological context. Since social relations are conceived as relations between individuals, interaction between individuals becomes the prime cause of social life. Since social disorder has been related to the quantity and quality of social relations, attention is diverted from consideration of economics, politics, or ideology as possible sources of social disorder, into a search for the causes of disorder in family and community, and hence toward the engineering of a proper family and community life. Since, moreover, disorder has been located in the divergence of custom and belief from common norms, convergence in custom and consensus in belief are converted into the touchstone of society in proper working order. And, finally, the postulates make it easy to identify Society in general with a society in particular. Society in need of order becomes a particular society to be ordered. In the context of the tangible present, that society to be ordered is then easily identified with a given nation-state, be that nation-state Ghana, Mexico, or the United States. Since social relations have been severed from their economic, political, or ideological context, it is easy to conceive of the nation-state as a structure of social ties informed by moral consensus rather than as a nexus of economic, political, and ideological relationships connected to other nexuses. Contentless social relations, rather than economic, political, or ideological forces, thus become the prime movers of sociological theory. Since these social relations take place within the charmed circle of the single nation-state, the significant actors in history are seen as nation-states, each driven by its internal social relations. Each society is then a thing, moving in response to an inner clockwork.

Economics and political science

This severance of social relations from the economic, political, and ideological contexts in which they are embedded and which they activate was accompanied by the assignment of the economic and political aspects of human life to separate disciplines. Economics abandoned its concern with how socially organized populations produce to supply their polities and became instead a study of how demand creates markets. The guiding theory of this new economics was

a theory of markets and market interdependence. It is a theory of general equilibrium in *exchange*, extended almost as an afterthought, to cover production and distribution. It is not a theory of a social system, still less of economic power and social class. Households and firms are considered only as market agents, never as parts of a social structure. Their "initial endowments," wealth, skills, and property, are taken as *given*. Moreover, the object of the theory is to demonstrate the tendency towards equilibrium; class and sectoral conflict is therefore ruled out almost by assumption. (Nell 1973: 77–8)

Stated in another form, this new economics is not about the real world at all (Lekachman 1976). It is an abstract model of the workings out of subjective individual choices in relation to one another.

A similar fate befell the study of politics. A new political science severed the sphere of the political from economics and turned to consideration of power in relation to government. By relegating economic, social, and ideological aspects of human life to the status of the "environment," the study of politics divorced itself from a study of how the organization of this environment constrains or directs politics, and moved instead to an inquiry into decision making. The political process is one in which demands are aggregated and translated into decisions, much as in the market model of economics the interplay of demands issues in the production of supplies. As in the market model, such an approach easily slips into the assumption

> that the organized private power forces of the society balance one another so as to preclude concentrated irresponsible rule....wise public policy is assumed to prevail, explained by a mystique not unlike Adam Smith's invisible hand. (Engler 1968: 199)

Ultimately, in such a model, the willingness to abide by the rules of the political market is necessarily determined not by the market itself but by the orientation and values of the participants, aspects of what political scientists have come to call their "political culture." Much of political science thus focused on the study of decisions, on the one hand, and the study of orientations, understood as constituting together the autonomous political system of a given society, on the other.

Underlying all these specialties is the concept of an aggregate of individuals, engaged in a contract to maximize social order, to truck and barter in the marketplace, and to provide inputs for the formulation of political decisions. Ostensibly engaged in the study of human *behavior*, the various disciplines parcel out the subject among themselves. Each then proceeds to

set up a model, seemingly a means to explain "hard," observable facts, yet actually an ideologically loaded scheme geared to a narrow definition of subject matter. Such schemes provide self-fulfilling answers, since phenomena other than those covered by the model are ruled out of the court of specialized discourse. If the models leak like sieves, it is then argued that this is either because they are merely abstract constructs and not expected to hold empirical water, or because troublemakers have poked holes into them. The specialized social sciences, having abandoned a holistic perspective, thus come to resemble the Danae sisters of classical Greek legend, ever condemned to pour water into their separate bottomless containers.

The development of sociological theory

We have seen how sociology stemmed from an attempt to counteract social disorder by creating a theory of social order, by locating order and disorder in the quantity and quality of social relations. An important implication of this approach is that it issues in a polarity between two types of society: one in which social order is maximized because social relations are densely knit and suffused with value consensus; and another in which social disorder predominates over order because social relations are atomized and deranged by dissensus over values. It is only a short step from drawing such a polarity to envisioning social process as a change from one type of society to the other. This seemed consistent with the common view that modern life entails a progressive disintegration of the lifeways that marked the "good old days" of our forebears. In nineteenth-century Europe, where older social ties in fact disintegrated under the twin impact of capitalism and industrialization, such a temporal interpretation of the sociological polarity carried the conviction of experience. Ferdinand Tonnies saw this movement as one from "community," or Gemeinschaft, to "society," or Gesellschaft. Sir Henry Maine phrased it as a shift from social relations based on status to social relations based on contract. Emile Durkheim conceived it as a movement from a kind of social solidarity based on the similarity of all members to a social solidarity based on an "organic" complementarity of differences. The Chicago school of urban sociology saw it as the contrast between a cohesive society and the atomized, heterogeneous, disorganized city. Finally, Robert Redfield drew the various formulations together into a polar model of progression from Folk to Urban Society. In this model the quantity and quality of social relations again were the primary, independent variables. Isolation or paucity of social interaction, coupled with homogeneity or similarity of social ties, generated the dependent variables: orientation toward the group, or "collectivization"; commitment to belief, or "sanctity"; and "organization," the knitting together of understandings in the minds of men. In contrast, contact, or high frequency of contact, coupled with heterogeneity or dissimilarity of social ties, was seen as producing the dependent variables of "individualization," "secularization," and "disorganization." In sum, increases in the quantity and diversity of social interaction caused "the moral order" of the folk to give way to "the technical order" of civilization.

Sociology thus took its departure from a sense that social order was threatened by the atrophy of community. As the twentieth century wore on, however, it gradually came to be taken for granted that society was headed toward increased size and differentiation, and hence also toward the growth of utilitarian and technical relations at the expense of sacred and moral ties. Society was evidently moving toward what Max Weber, using Tonnies's terms, had called *Vergesellschaftung*. By this he meant the expansion of relations resting on

> rationally motivated adjustment of interests or a similarly motivated agreement, whether the basis of rational judgement be absolute values or reasons of expediency. It is especially common, though by no means inevitable, for the associative type of relationship to rest on a rational agreement by mutual consent. (1968: 10)

Although Weber himself used the term with ambivalence and misgivings, his latter-day followers embraced the prognosis with enthusiasm. Whereas "traditional society" had fitted people narrowly into inherited positions, and then bound them together tightly in particularistic positions, "modern society" would sever people from inherited ties and allocate the newly mobile population to specialized and differentiated roles responding to the changing needs of an over-

arching universal society. Such an emerging society would also require a mechanism for setting social goals and a machinery for implementing them. The way the modernizers saw it, goal setting would come out of enlarged popular participation. Implementation of the goals, such as economic development, in turn would require the creation of bureaucracy, defined as organizations capable of marshalling resources rationally and efficiently toward stated goals. Finally, public participation in setting and meeting goals would require a psychic reorientation that could sustain the enactment of such technical and rational norms. Those capable of generating such new arrangements would find themselves launched into modernity. Those incapable of doing so would find their society arrested at the point of transition or mired in traditionalism. In the succession from Max Weber to Talcott Parsons, therefore, *Vergesellschaftung* was transfigured into "modernization" through a simple change of signs. If Gesellschaft had once seemed problematical, after the mid-twentieth century it came to be seen as desirable and forward-looking. The negative pole of the polarity was now allocated to "traditional society," slow to change, inflexible, and lacking in psychic drive toward rational and secular achievement.

Thus, in a reversal of sociology's original critical stance toward the workings of nineteenth-century society, "modernization theory" became an instrument for bestowing praise on societies deemed to be modern and casting a critical eye on those that had yet to attain that achievement. The political leaders of the United States had pronounced themselves in favor of aiding the development of the Third World, and modernization theorists seconded that pronouncement. Yet modernization theory effectively foreclosed any but the most ideologically charged understanding of that world. It used the term *modern*, but meant by that term the United States, or rather an ideal of a democratic, pluralistic, rational, and secular United States. It said *traditional*, but meant all those others that would have to adopt that ideal to qualify for assistance. As theory it was misleading. It imparted a false view of American history, substituting self-satisfaction for analysis. By casting such different entities as China, Albania, Paraguay, Cuba, and Tanzania into the hopper of traditional society, it simultaneously precluded any study of their significant differences. By equating tradition with stasis and lack of development, it denied societies marked off as traditional any significant history of their own. Above all, by dividing the world into modern, transitional, and traditional societies, it blocked effective understanding of relationships among them. Once again each society was defined as an autonomous and bounded structure of social relations, thus discouraging analysis of intersocietal or intergroup interchanges, including internal social strife, colonialism, imperialism, and societal dependency. The theory thus effectively precluded the serious study of issues demonstrably agitating the real world.

Anthropology

If these social sciences have not led to an adequate understanding of the interconnected world, what of anthropology? Anthropology, ambitiously entitled The Science of Man, did lay special claims to the study of non-Western and "primitive" peoples. Indeed, cultural anthropology began as world anthropology. In its evolutionist phase it was concerned with the evolution of culture on a global scale. In its diffusionist phase it was interested in the spread and clustering of cultural forms over the entire face of the globe. The diffusionists also saw relations between populations exhibiting the same cultural forms – matriliny, blackening of teeth, or tailored clothing – as the outcome of intergroup communication by migration or by copying and learning. They were not much concerned with people, but they did have a sense of global interconnections. They did not believe in the concept of "primitive isolates."

Such interests and understandings were set aside, however, as anthropologists turned from a primary concern with cultural forms to the study of "living cultures," of specified populations and their life-ways in locally delimited habitats. Fieldwork – direct communication with people and participant observation of their ongoing activities in situ – became a hallmark of anthropological method. Fieldwork has proved enormously fruitful in laying bare and correcting false assumptions and erroneous descriptions. It has also revealed hitherto unsuspected connections among sets of social activities and cultural forms.

Yet the very success of the method lulled its users into a false confidence. It became easy for them to convert merely heuristic considerations of method into theoretical postulates about society and culture.

Limitations of time and energy in the field dictate limitations in the number and locations of possible observations and interviews, demanding concentration of effort on an observable place and on a corps of specifiable "informants." The resulting observations and communications are then made to stand for a larger universe of unrealized observations and communications, and used to construct a model of the social and cultural entity under study. Such a model is no more than an account of "descriptive integration," a theoretical halfway house, and not yet explanation. Functionalist anthropology, however, attempted to derive explanations from the study of the microcosm alone, treating it as a hypothetical isolate. Its features were explained in terms of the contribution each made to the maintenance of this putatively isolated whole. Thus, a methodological unit of inquiry was turned into a theoretical construct by assertion, a priori. The outcome was series of analyses of wholly separate cases.

There were three major attempts to transcend the boundaries of the microcosm. One of these, that of Robert Redfield, had recourse to sociological theory. It applied the polarity of Gemeinschaft and Gesellschaft to anthropological cases by using "communities" as representations or exemplifications of such "imagined types of societies." Thus the communities of X-Cacal and Chan Kom in Yucatan were made to exemplify the folk end of a universal folk–urban continuum of social relations and cultural understandings. The two locations illuminated the theory, but the theory could not explicate the political and economic processes that shaped the communities: X-Cacal as a settlement set up by Maya-speaking rebels during the Caste Wars of the nineteenth century; Chan Kom as a village of cultivators released from the hacienda system by the Mexican Revolution, settling as newcomers in a frontier area with the support of the Yucatecan Socialist Party. Thus, like Gemeinschaft–Gesellschaft theory in general, Redfield's concepts led only in one direction, up to the theory but not back down from it.

A second attempt to generate a theoretical construct for understanding the microcosm studied in a larger context was Julian Steward's concept of levels of sociocultural integration. The concept, derived from the philosophy of "emergent evolution," was meant to suggest that units of the same kind, when subjected to integrative processes, could yield novel units that not only subsumed those of the lower level but also exhibited qualitatively different characteristics at the higher, emergent level. Steward initially used the concept to counter arguments that treated "the community" as a small replica of "the nation," as if these were qualitatively identical structural phenomena. He then proceeded, however, to construct a conceptual edifice in which units at the family level became parts of a community level, units at the community level became parts of a regional level, and units at the regional level became parts of the level of the nation.

Although the term *integration* suggests a process, the concept is not processual but structural. It suggests an architecture of a whole and its parts, which remain to be specified substantively only after the fact. The model is thus a "hollow" representation of societal complexity, theoretically applicable to all complex sociocultural wholes. Yet it makes no statement about any processes generating the structure, or about the specific features that integrate it, or about the content of any of its parts. Knowledge about processes does not flow from the model but must be added to it. Thus, when Steward turned to the study of "contemporary change in traditional societies," the model remained silent about the penetration of capitalism, the growth of a worldwide specialization and division of labor, and the development of domination by some populations over others. Steward was forced back, unhappily, to the comparative study of separate cases and the unsatisfactory concepts of tradition and modernization.

The third attempt to go beyond the microscopic study of populations in specified locations took the form of a revival of evolutionism. Evolutionary thinking in anthropology, so prominent in the nineteenth century, had been halted by the assertion that "the extensive occurrence of diffusion ... lays the axe to the root of any theory of historical laws" (Lowie 1920: 434). Evolutionists and diffusionists were not so much opposed as interested in quite different phenomena. The evolutionists had recognized the facts of diffusion, but had felt justified in abstracting from these facts to their model of successive stages of social and cultural development. The diffusionists, in turn, sidestepped the problem posed by major inequalities in the technology and organization of different populations to focus instead on the transmission of cultural forms from group to group. Whereas the evolutionists disclaimed an interest in the history of particular societies and cultures, the diffusionists disclaimed any interest in the ecological, economic, social, political, and ideological matrix within which the cultural forms were being transmitted in time and space. The two schools of thought thus effectively talked past each other. The functionalists, in turn, rejected altogether the "conjectural history" of the diffusionists in favor of the analysis of internal functioning in putatively isolated wholes.

When Leslie White reintroduced the evolutionary perspective into American anthropology in the forties and fifties, he did so by reasserting the validity of the earlier model proposed by Tylor, Morgan, and Spencer. To this model of universal or unilineal evolution, Julian Steward opposed a multilineal model that depicted evolution as a process of successive branching. Subsequently Sahlins and Service sought to unify the two approaches by counterposing general and specific evolution as dual aspects of the same evolutionary process. General evolution was defined by them as "passage from less to greater energy exploitation, lower to higher levels of integration, and less to greater all-round adaptability" (Sahlins and Service 1960: 22–3). Specific evolution they defined as "the phylogenetic, ramifying, historic passage of culture along its many lines, the adaptive modification of particular cultures" (1960: 38). Though cognizant of convergence as an aspect of cultural as opposed to biological phylogeny, they defined it in old-fashioned diffusionist terms as the diffusion of culture traits, and not as the outcome of multifaceted relationships between interacting culture-bearing populations. When they turned to the detailed analysis of specific evolution, they thus emphasized adaptation as "specialization for the exploitation of particular facets of the environment" (1960: 50). They understood that environment included both the physical and the sociocultural matrices of human life, but they laid primary stress on adaptation to different physical environments. In the sixties and seventies, the study of particular ecological "systems" became increasingly sophisticated, without, however, ever transcending the functional analysis of the single case, now hypothesized as an integral, self-regulating ecological whole. Thus, despite its theoretical effort, evolutionary anthropology turned all too easily into the study of ecological adaptation, conducting anthropology back to the comparative study of single cases.

The ecological concentration on the single case is paralleled by the recent fascination with the study and unraveling of what is "in the heads" of single culture-bearing populations. Such studies turn their back on functionalism, including what was most viable in it, the concern with how people cope with the material and organizational problems of their lives. They also disregard material relationships linking the people with others outside. Instead, their interest lies in the investigation of local microcosms of meaning, conceived as autonomous systems.

This turn toward the study of meaning has been influenced strongly by the development of linguistics, notably by de Saussure's structural theory of language as a superindividual social system of linguistic forms that remain normatively identical in all utterances. Such a view relates linguistic sign to linguistic sign without reference to who is speaking to whom, when, and about what. It was originally put forward to oppose the position that a language consisted of an ever-changing historical stream of individually generated utterances, a perspective associated with the names of Humboldt and Vossler. De Saussure, instead, wholly divorced language (langue) from utterance (parole), defining signs by their mutual relation to one another, without reference to any context external to them. In the same way, meanings were defined in terms of other meanings, without reference to the practical contexts in which they appear.

Clearly, the opposition between the two views requires for its resolution a relational, dialectical perspective, as Vološinov noted in the 1930s. He called into question de Saussure's view of the static linguistic system carried by a faceless and passive collectivity, noting instead that in reality such a collectivity consisted of a population of speakers with diverse "accents" or interests, participating in a historical stream of verbal utterances about diverse, concrete contexts. Contexts should not be thought of as internally homogeneous and externally segregated. For Vološinov, they constituted instead intersections between "differently oriented accents...in a state of constant tension, of incessant interaction and conflict" (1973: 80). Neither sign nor meaning could be understood without reference to what they are about, their theme in a given situation. The trend within anthropology to treat systems of meaning as wholly autonomous systems threatens to reverse this insight by substituting for it the study of solipsistic discourses generated *in vacuo* by the human mind.

While some anthropologists thus narrow their focus to the ever more intensive study of the single case, others hope to turn anthropology into a science by embarking on the statistical cross-cultural comparisons of coded features drawn from large samples of ethnographically known cases. A good deal of attention has been paid to the methodological problems of how to isolate discrete cases for comparison and how to define the variables to be coded and compared. Are the hundreds of Eskimo local groups separate cases? Are they instances of larger, self-identified clusters such as Copper, Netsilik, and Iglulik? Or do they constitute a single Eskimo case? Other questions deal with the nature of the sample. Can one be sure that the cases are sufficiently separated historically and geographically to constitute distinct cases? Or is the sample contaminated by spatial or temporal propinquity and communication? All the answers to these questions nevertheless assume the autonomy and boundedness of the cases that are selected in the end. Whatever sample is finally chosen, it is interpreted as an aggregate of separate units. These, it is held, either generate cultural traits independently through invention, or borrow them from one another through diffusion. We are back in a world of sociocultural billiard balls, coursing on a global billiard table.

What, however, if we take cognizance of *processes* that transcend separable cases, moving through and beyond them and transforming them as they proceed? Such processes were, for example, the North American fur trade and the trade in native American and African slaves.

What of the localized Algonkin-speaking patri-lineages, for example, which in the course of the fur trade moved into large nonkin villages and became known as the ethnographic Ojibwa? What of the Chipeweyans, some of whose bands gave up hunting to become fur trappers, or "carriers," while others continued to hunt for game as "caribou eaters," with people continuously changing from caribou eating to carrying and back? What of the multilingual, multiethnic, intermarrying groups of Cree and Assiniboin that grew up in the far northern Plains of North America in response to the stimulus of the fur trade, until the units "graded into one another" (Sharrock 1974: 96)? What of the Mundurucú in Amazonia who changed from patrilocality and patriliny to adopt the unusual combination of matrilocality and patrilineal reckoning in response to their new role as hunters of slaves and suppliers of manioc flour to slave-hunting expeditions? What, moreover, of Africa, where the slave trade created an unlimited demand for slaves, and where quite unrelated populations met that demand by severing people from their kin groups through warfare, kidnapping, pawning, or judicial procedures, in order to have slaves to sell to the Europeans? In all such cases, to attempt to specify separate cultural wholes and distinct boundaries would create a false sample. These cases exemplify spatially and temporally shifting relationships, prompted in all instances by the effects of European expansion. If we consider, furthermore, that this expansion has for nearly 500 years affected case after case, then the search for a world sample of distinct cases is illusory.

One need have no quarrel with a denotative use of the term *society* to designate an empirically verifiable cluster of interconnections among people, as long as no evaluative prejudgments are added about its state of internal cohesion or boundedness in relation to the external world. Indeed, I shall continue to use the term in this way [. . .], in preference to other clumsier formulations. Similarly, it would be an error to discard the anthropological insight that human existence entails the creation of cultural forms, themselves predicated on the human capacity to symbol.

Yet the concept of the autonomous, self-regulating and self-justifying society and culture has trapped anthropology inside the bounds of its own definitions. Within the halls of science, the compass of observation and thought has narrowed, while outside the inhabitants of the world are increasingly caught up in continent-wide and global change. Indeed, has there ever been a time when human populations have existed in independence of larger encompassing relationships, unaffected by larger fields of force? Just as the sociologists pursue the will-o'-the-wisp of social order and integration in a world of upheaval and change, so anthropologists look for pristine replicas of the precapitalist, preindustrial past in the sinks and margins of the capitalist, industrial world. But Europeans and Americans would never have encountered these supposed bearers of a pristine past if they had not encountered one another, in bloody fact, as Europe reached out to seize the resources and populations of the other continents. Thus, it has been rightly said that anthropology is an offspring of imperialism. Without imperialism there would be no anthropologists, but there would also be no Dené, Baluba, or Malay fishermen to be studied. The tacit anthropological supposition that people like these are people without history amounts to the erasure of 500 years of confrontation, killing, resurrection, and accommodation. If sociology operates with its mythology of Gemeinschaft and Gesellschaft, anthropology all too frequently operates with its mythology of the pristine primitive. Both perpetuate fictions that deny the facts of ongoing relationships and involvements.

These facts clearly emerge in the work of anthropologists and historians who have specialized in what has come to be known as ethnohistory. Perhaps "ethnohistory" has been so called to separate it from "real" history, the study of the supposedly civilized. Yet what is clear from the study of ethno-history is that the subjects of the two kinds of history are the same. The more ethnohistory we know, the more clearly "their" history and "our" history emerge as part of the same history. Thus, there can be no "Black history" apart from "White history," only a component of a common history suppressed or omitted from conventional studies for economic, political, or ideological reasons.

These remarks echo those made by the anthropologist Alexander Lesser who, in a different context, asked years ago that "we adopt as a working hypothesis the universality of human contact and influence"; that we think "of human societies – prehistoric, primitive, or modern – not as closed systems, but as open systems"; that we see them "as inextricably involved with other aggregates, near and far, in weblike, netlike connections" (1961: 42). The labors of the ethnohistorians have demonstrated the validity of this advice in case after case. Yet it remains merely programmatic until we can move from a consideration of connections at work in separate cases to a wider perspective, one that will allow us to connect the connections in theory as well as in empirical study.

In such a perspective, it becomes difficult to view any given culture as a bounded system or as a self-perpetuating "design for living." We thus stand in need of a new theory of cultural forms. The anthropologists have shown us that cultural forms – as "determinate orderings" of things, behavior, and ideas – do play a demonstrable role in the management of human interaction. What will be required of us in the future is not to deny that role, but to understand more precisely how cultural forms work to mediate social relationships among particular populations.

The Uses of Marx

If we grant the existence of such connections, how are we to conceive of them? Can we grasp a common process that generates and organizes them? Is it possible to envision such a common dynamic and yet maintain a sense of its distinctive unfolding in time and space as it involves and engulfs now this population, now that other?

Such an approach is possible, but only if we can face theoretical possibilities that transcend our specialized disciplines. It is not enough to become multidisciplinary in the hope that an addition of all the disciplines will lead to a new vision. A major obstacle to the development of a new perspective lies in the very fact of specialization itself. That fact has a history and that history is significant, because the several academic disciplines owe their existence to a common rebellion against political economy, their parent discipline. That discipline strove to lay bare the laws or regularities surrounding the production of wealth. It entailed a concern with how wealth was generated in production, with the role of classes in the genesis of wealth, and with the role of the state in

relation to the different classes. These concerns were common to conservatives and socialists alike. (Marx addressed himself to them when he criticized political economists for taking as universals what he saw as the characteristics of historically particular systems of production.) Yet these concerns have been expunged so completely from the repertory of the social sciences that the latest *International Encyclopedia of the Social Sciences* does not even include entries under "political economy" and "class." Today, concern with such matters is usually ascribed only to Marxists, even though Marx himself wrote in a letter to a friend (Joseph Weydemeyer, March 5, 1852):

> no credit is due me for discovering the existence of classes in society nor yet the struggle between them. Long before me bourgeois historians had described the historical development of this class struggle and bourgeois economists the economic anatomy of the classes. (quoted in Venable 1945: 6, n. 3)

It is likely that it was precisely the conception of political economy as a structure of *classes* that led the nascent social sciences to turn against the concept of class. If social, economic, and political relations were seen to involve a division into antagonistic classes, endowed by the structure of the political economy itself with opposing interests and capabilities, then the pursuit of order would indeed be haunted forever by the specter of discord. This was what led James Madison, in his tough-minded *Federalist Papers*, to define the function of government as the regulation of relations among antagonistic classes. The several social science disciplines, in contrast, turned their back on political economy, shifting instead to the intensive study of interaction among individuals – in primary and secondary groups, in the market, in the processes of government. They thus turned away also from concern with crucial questions about the nature of production, class, and power: If production is the condition of being human, how is production to be understood and analyzed? Under what conditions does production entail the rise of classes? What are the implications of class division for the allocation of resources and the exercise of power? What is the nature of the state?

Although these questions were abandoned by the social sciences, they persist as their hidden agenda. Because Marx raised these questions most persistently and systematically, he remains a hidden interlocutor in much social science discourse. It has been said, with reason, that the social sciences constitute one long dialogue with the ghost of Marx. If we are to transcend the present limits and limitations of the specialized disciplines, we must return to these unanswered questions and reconsider them.

Marx is important for this reconsideration in several ways. He was one of the last major figures to aim at a holistic human science, capable of integrating the varied specializations. Contrary to what is all too often said about him, he was by no means an economic determinist. He was a materialist, believing in the primacy of material relationships as against the primacy of "spirit." Indeed, his concept of production (*Produktion*) was conceived in opposition to Hegel's concept of *Geist*, manifesting itself in successive incarnations of spirit. For him, production embraced at once the changing relations of humankind to nature, the social relations into which humans enter in the course of transforming nature, and the consequent transformations of human symbolic capability. The concept is thus not merely economic in the strict sense but also ecological, social, political, and social-psychological. It is relational in character.

Marx further argued – against those who wanted to universalize Society, or the Market, or the Political Process – the existence of different modes of production in human history. Each mode represented a different combination of elements. What was true of one mode was not true of another: there was therefore no universal history. But Marx was profoundly historical. Both the elements constituting a mode of production and their characteristic combination had for him a definable history of origin, unfolding, and disintegration. He was neither a universal historian nor a historian of events, but a historian of configurations or syndromes of material relationships. Most of his energy was, of course, spent on efforts to understand the history and workings of one particular mode, capitalism, and this not to defend it but to effect its revolutionary transformation. Since our specialized disciplinary discourse developed as an antidote to revolution and disorder, it is understandable that this ghostly interrogator should have been made unwelcome in the halls of academe.

Yet the specter has vital lessons for us. First, we shall not understand the present world unless we trace the growth of the world market and the course of capitalist development. Second, we must have a theory of that growth and development. Third, we must be able to relate both the history and theory of that unfolding development to processes that affect and change the lives of local populations. That theory must be able to delineate the significant elements at work in these processes and their systemic combinations in historical time. At the same time, it ought to cut finely enough to explain the significant differences marking off each such combination from all the others – say, capitalism from other historically known combinations. Finally, theoretically informed history and historically informed theory must be joined together to account for populations specifiable in time and space, both as outcomes of significant processes and as their carriers.

Among those who have contributed to a theoretically informed history of the world to which capitalism has given rise, two names stand out, both for the trenchancy of their formulations and the scope of their research effort. One of these is Andre Gunder Frank, an economist, who began to question the modernization approach to economic development in the early 1960s. Frank clearly articulated the heretical proposition that development and under-development were not separate phenomena, but were closely bound up with each other (1966, 1967). Over the past centuries, capitalism had spread outward from its original center to all parts of the globe. Everywhere it penetrated, it turned other areas into dependent satellites of the metropolitan center. Extracting the surpluses produced in the satellites to meet the requirements of the metropolis, capitalism distorted and thwarted the development of the satellites to its own benefit. This phenomenon Frank called "the development of underdevelopment." The exploitative relation between metropolis and satellite was, moreover, repeated within each satellite itself, with the classes and regions in closer contact with the external metropolis drawing surplus from the hinterland and distorting and thwarting its development. Under-development in the satellites was therefore not a phenomenon sui generis, but the outcome of relations between satellite and metropolis, ever renewed in the process of surplus transfer and ever reinforced by the

306 ERIC R. WOLF

continued dependency of the satellite on the metropolis.

Similar to Frank's approach is Immanuel Wallerstein's explicitly historical account of capitalist origins and the development of the "European world-economy." This world-economy, originating in the late fifteenth and early sixteenth centuries, constitutes a global market, characterized by a global division of labor. Firms (be they individuals, enterprises, or regions) meet in this market to exchange the goods they have produced in the hope of realizing a profit. The search for profit guides both production in general and specialization in production. Profits are generated by primary producers, whom Wallerstein calls proletarians, no matter how their labor is mobilized. Those profits are appropriated through legal sanctions by capitalists, whom Wallerstein classifies as bourgeois, no matter what the source of their capital. The growth of the market and the resulting worldwide division of labor generate a basic distinction between the core countries (Frank's metropolis) and the periphery (Frank's satellites). The two are linked by "unequal exchange," whereby "high-wage (but low-supervision), high-profit, high-capital intensive" goods produced the core are exchanged for "low-wage (but high-supervision), low-profit, low-capital intensive goods" produced in the periphery (see Wallerstein 1974: 351). In the core, goods are produced mainly by "free" wage-remunerated labor; in the periphery goods are produced mainly by one kind or another of coerced labor. Although he adduces various factors to explain this difference, Wallerstein has recourse to what is basically a demographic explanation. He argues that the growth of free wage labor in the core area arose in response to the high densities of population that made workers competitive with one another and hence willing to submit to market discipline, while in the periphery low population densities favored the growth of labor coercion. We shall have occasion to look critically at some of these propositions. Yet what is important about both Frank's and Wallerstein's work is that they have replaced the fruitless debates about modernization with a sophisticated and theoretically oriented acount of how capitalism evolved and spread, an evolution and spread of intertwined and yet differentiated relationships.

Both Frank and Wallerstein focused their attention on the capitalist world system and the arrangements of its parts. Although they utilized the findings of anthropologists and regional historians, for both the principal aim was to understand how the core subjugated the periphery, and not to study the reactions of the micro-populations habitually investigated by anthropologists. Their choice of focus thus leads them to omit consideration of the range and variety of such populations, of their modes of existence before European expansion and the advent of capitalism, and of the manner in which these modes were penetrated, subordinated, destroyed, or absorbed, first by the growing market and subsequently by industrial capitalism. Without such an examination, however, the concept of the "periphery" remains as much of a cover term as "traditional society." Its advantage over the older term lies chiefly in its implications: it points to wider linkages that must be investigated if the processes at work in the periphery are to be understood. Yet this examination still lies before us if we wish to understand how Mundurucú or Meo were drawn into the larger system to suffer its impact and to become its agents. [...]

References

Bramson, Leon 1961. *The Political Context of Sociology.* Princeton, NJ: Princeton University Press.

Daaku, Kwame Yeboa 1970. *Trade and Politics on the Gold Coast 1600-1720: A Study of the African Reaction to European Trade.* Oxford: Clarendon Press.

Engler, Robert 1968. Social Science and Social Consciousness: The Shame of the Universities. In *The Dissenting Academy.* Theodore Roszak, ed. Pp. 182–207. New York: Vintage Books.

Frank, Andre Gunder 1966. The Development of Underdevelopment. *Monthly Review* 18: 17–31.

Frank, Andre Gunder 1967. Sociology of Development and Underdevelopment of Sociology. *Catalyst* (Buffalo) no. 3: 20–73.

Huntington, Samuel P. 1968. The Bases of Accommodation. *Foreign Affairs* 46: 642–56.

Jennings, Francis 1976. *The Invasion of America: Indians, Colonialism, and the Cant of Conquest.* New York: W. W. Norton.

Lekachman, Robert 1976. *Economists at Bay*. New York: McGraw-Hill.

Lesser, Alexander 1961. Social Fields and the Evolution of Society. *South-western Journal of Anthropology* 17: 40–8.

Lowie, Robert H. 1920. *Primitive Society*. New York: Boni and Liveright.

Nell, Edward 1973. Economics: The Revival of Political Economy. In *Ideology in Social Science: Readings in Critical Social Theory*. Robin Blackburn, ed. Pp. 76–95. New York: Vintage Books/Random House.

Rostow, Walt Whitman 1960. *The Stages of Economic Growth: A Non-Communist Manifesto*. Cambridge: Cambridge University Press.

Sahlins, Marshall D., and Elman R. Service, eds. 1960. *Evolution and Culture*. Ann Arbor: University of Michigan Press.

Sharrock, Susan R. 1974. Crees, Cree-Assiniboines, and Assiniboines: Inter-ethnic Social Organization on the Far Northern Plains. *Ethnohistory* 21: 95–122.

Venable, Vernon 1945. *Human Nature: The Marxian View*. New York: Knopf.

Vološinov, Valentin N. 1973. *Marxism and the Philosophy of Language*. New York and London: Seminar Press. (First pub. in Russian 1930.)

Wallerstein, Immanuel 1974. *The Modern World-System: Capitalist Agriculture and the Origins of the European World-Economy in the Sixteenth Century*. New York: Academic Press.

Weber, Max 1968. *On Charisma and Institution Building: Selected Papers*. Shmuel N. Eisenstadt, ed. Chicago: University of Chicago Press.

31

Introduction to *Of Revelation and Revolution*

Jean Comaroff and John Comaroff

[…] Our objective is to understand a particular historical process: an encounter in which a (self-elected group of Britons sought, *methodically*, to "make history" for people whom, they thought, lacked it; to induct those people into an *order* of activities and values; to impart *form* to an Africa that was seen as formless; to reduce the chaos of savage life to the *rational* structures and techniques that, for the Europeans, were both the vehicle and the proof of their own civilization. To anticipate one of our usages below, the italics here are ours, but the emphasis was theirs. This colonial encounter was not a contingent set of events, a cosmic coincidence in which some human beings happened arbitrarily into a foreign text. It was, as has been said many times, an integral part of the cultural and social revolution that accompanied the rise of industrial capitalism, an expression of the expansive universalism that marked the dawn of modernity.

It also marked the dawn of modernism: the new age of science and economics; of realism and rationalization; of the "master narrative" and, in both senses of the term, the novel; of heroic, imperious humanism; and of knowledge-as-discovery

(cf. Bakhtin 1981). Put them together and they add up to a worldview that bred not only colonialism but also, in the longer run, the social sciences. If our missionaries and their other colonizing compatriots were the self-conscious agents of an heroic imperial history, the social historians and ethnographers who followed them stand accused of having also been unwitting colonialists.[1] De Certeau (1988:72) captures nicely the parallel between the civilizing mission and historiography: "[historians] 'civilize' nature," he says, "which has always meant that they 'colonize' and change it." The point, now commonplace, is that the essence of colonization inheres less in political overrule than in seizing and transforming "others" by the very act of conceptualizing, inscribing, and interacting with them on terms not of their choosing; in making them into the pliant objects and silenced subjects of our scripts and scenarios; in assuming the capacity to "represent" them, the active verb itself conflating politics and poetics. But is it true that the modern historical anthropologist does this in a way no different from the nineteenth-century missionary, military man, merchant, or minister of state? Are we

From *Of Revelation and Revolution: Christianity, Colonialism, and Consciousness in South Africa*, 1 (Chicago: University of Chicago Press, 1991), pp. 14–32, 316–18, 353–6, 358–60, 362–70, 372–8, 382–4, 389, 393–4. Copyright © 1991 by University of Chicago Press. Reprinted by permission of University of Chicago Press.

Anthropology in Theory: Issues in Epistemology, Second Edition. Edited by Henrietta L. Moore and Todd Sanders.
© 2014 John Wiley & Sons, Inc. Published 2014 by John Wiley & Sons, Inc.

merely manufacturers of texts that convert difference into sameness through the Midas touch of western universalism, just as evangelists sought to convert the savage by removing the differences which excluded him from God's *universe* – and from the master narratives of European culture? Some of our interlocutors would certainly answer in the affirmative. And yet there is an obvious irony in the accusation. Anthropologists have long been taken to task for exactly the opposite sin: for fetishizing difference in a global order of political and economic continuities (Said 1978; Fabian 1983).

But ironies aside, whether we make difference out of sameness or vice versa – each, in any case, is a condition of the other – the underlying point remains. Ethnography and social history are alike, and like nineteenth-century colonial evangelism, the undeniable progeny of modernism. As such they cannot escape the epistemological horizons that continue to enclose mainstream western social thought. Even those "interpretive" anthropologists who eschew most forcefully our positivist heritage appear to be stranded halfway along the road to postmodernism. On the one hand, as Rabinow and Sullivan (1987:9) explain, they reject the existence of a material "reality before and behind the cultural world," a world lacking clarity and characterized by alienation. And they regard the analysis of social action as "analogous to textual interpretation," in which any text is "open to several [if not infinite] readings" (1987:14). And yet, despite being extremely wary of the reification of culture – of totality and teleology, formalism and functionalism – they rarely end up disputing the existence of, say, "Balinese culture." Nor, in analytic practice, do they deny that culture a good deal of closure; and, notwithstanding the language of phenomenology, speak readily of "cultural *systems*" (Geertz 1973). As Evans-Pritchard (1937) long ago realized, the very nature of translation at the core of anthropology – the act of "doing ethnography" itself – makes anything else almost impossible (cf. Leach 1954:ch. 1).[2] No wonder, then, as Hebdige (1988:186) reminds us, that postmodernist critiques of the social sciences make

> no real distinctions ... between positivist/nonpositivist; qualitative/quantitative; marxist/pluralist/ interpretative/functionalist, etc. sociologies:[3]

all are seen as strategies embedded in institutions themselves irrefragably implicated in and productive of particular configurations of power and knowledge.

If this is true, none of us – not the most reflexive interpretive anthropologist or the most critical humanist Marxist – can be a little bit postmodern. Of course, critical postmodernism is itself largely a western *endo*cultural enterprise. As such it has by and large been able to ignore the task of cultural translation – or the problems of dealing with, for instance, the semantic and material politics of colonialism. Of having, in other words, to be a little bit anthropological.

This is especially apparent in the manner in which those philosophers and literary theorists who live in hyphenated states of ironic detachment – poststructuralism, post-Marxism and so on – cast their cynical gaze upon the nature of meaning and power. Meaning, some of them tell us, is "polymorphously perverse," the polysemic, amorphous solvent of everyday discourses: since we live in a world of unfixed signifiers, meaning cannot inhere in enduring schemes of signs and relations. As this suggests, poststructuralisms, in their various guises, begin with a revisionist reading of the basic principles of structural linguistics – in particular, of the arbitrariness of the sign and of the concept of language as a system of distinctions. Granted the ambiguities of his original formulations (Benveniste 1971:ch. 4), Saussure did not, in asserting the arbitrary connection of sign to referent, deny that conventional ties are established between them in culture and history (see Sahlins 1981). But in the poststructuralist reading, the focus is on absences rather than presences. Arbitrariness and difference are taken to imply the fundamental instability of all meaning in the world, its lack of any order or consistent social determination – and, therefore, of any teleology or totality whatsoever in society and history. Negation is the dominant analytic trope here. Anything may turn out to mean anything else and, hence, nothing at all (Hebdige 1988:192). Similarly, in the wake of Foucault, power has long left the formal bounds of "political" institutions and has diffused and proliferated into hitherto uncharted terrains. Inscribed in the mind and on the body of the person – the subject who imagines herself or himself free and who yet bears the terms of sub-jection within – it saturates all the planes of human existence. Now everywhere, it is nowhere in particular.

It is here that we wish to intervene in the name of a historical anthropology. On the one hand, we believe, some of the lessons of critical postmod-ernism have to be taken very seriously: among them, (1) the need to address the *in*determinacies of meaning and action, events and processes in history; (2) the admonition to regard culture not as an *over*determining, closed system of signs but as a set of polyvalent practices, texts, and images that may, at any time, be contested; (3) the invita-tion to see power as a many-sided, often elusive and diffuse force which is always implicated in culture, consciousness, and representation; and (4) the importance of treating the writing of his-tories as a generic mode of making both the past and the present.

On the other hand, we have our own questions to counterpose. How is it that – if *all* meaning were potentially open to contest, *all* power poten-tially unfixed – history keeps generating hege-monies that, for long periods, seem able to impose a degree of order and stability on the world? How come relatively small groups of people – class fractions, ethnic minorities, or whatever – often succeed in gaining and sustaining control over large populations and in drawing them into a consensus with dominant values? How do we explain the fact that, at any moment, at any place, some meanings appear meaningless, some prac-tices impracticable, some conceptions of the past and present inconceivable? All histories may or may not be texts; that depends on what we under-stand by history, what we take to be a text (see e.g., Jameson 1981:296–7, 100 ff.; Hanks 1989). But nowhere can anything or everything be thought or written or done or told. Most people live in worlds in which many signs, and often the ones that count most, look as though they are eternally fixed.

This is where our particular story, with all its italics and emphases, becomes salient – and why we insist on situating methodological discussion in analytic practice. [...] [C]olonial evangelism in South Africa hinged upon the effort of a few men, with closely shared social origins, to impose an entire worldview upon their would-be sub-jects; that is, to contrive reality for them as a coherent and closed, uniform and universalistic order. In the long conversation to which this gave rise – a conversation full of arguments of words and images – many of the signifiers of the colo-nizing culture became unfixed. They were seized by the Africans and, sometimes refashioned, put to symbolic and practical ends previously unfore-seen, certainly unintended. Conversely, some of the ways of the Africans interpolated themselves, again detached and transformed, into the habitus of the missionaries. Here, then, was a process in which signifiers were set afloat, fought over, and recaptured on both sides of the colonial encounter. What is more, this encounter led to the objectifi-cation of "the" culture of the colonized in opposi-tion to that of the whites. The "natives," that is, began to conceive of their own conventions as an integrated, closed "system" to which they could and did attach an abstract noun (*setswana*). The most curious feature of the process, however, is that, notwithstanding the rejection and transfor-mation of many elements of "the" European worldview, its *forms* became authoritatively inscribed on the African landscape. Not only did colonialism produce reified cultural *orders;* it gave rise to a new hegemony amidst – and despite – cultural contestation. But how can that be?

We shall try to answer this question in the course of our account. For now, the more impor-tant implication is this. While signs, social rela-tions, and material practices are constantly open to transformation – and while meaning may indeed *become* unfixed, resisted, and recon-structed – history everywhere is actively made in a dialectic of order and disorder, consensus and contest. At any particular moment, in any marked event, *a* meaning or *a* social arrangement may appear freefloating, underdetermined, ambig-uous. But it is often the very attempt to harness that indeterminacy, the seemingly unfixed signi-fier, that animates both the exercise of power and the resistance to which it may give rise. Such arguments and struggles, though, are seldom equal. They have, *pace* postmodernism, a political sociology that emerges from their place in a system of relations. And so, as the moment gives way to the medium-term, and some people and practices emerge as (or remain) dominant, their authority expresses itself in the apparently established *order* of things – again, in the dual sense of an edifice of command and a condition of being. What might once have seemed eventful and contingent now looks to have been part of a more regular pattern – indeed, ofa structured history, a historical structure. As Stuart Hall (1988:44) reminds us, following Gramsci:

> Ruling or dominant conceptions of the world [may] not directly prescribe the mental content of…the heads of the dominated classes. But the circle of dominant ideas *does* accumulate the symbolic power to map or classify the world for others; its classifications do acquire not only the constraining power of dominance over other modes of thought but also the inertial authority of habit and instinct. It becomes the horizon of the taken-for-granted: what the world is and how it works, for all practical purposes. Ruling ideas may dominate other conceptions of the social world by setting the limit to what will appear as rational, reasonable, credible, indeed sayable or thinkable, within the given vocabularies of motive and action available to us.

This would serve well as a description of hegemony *sui generis*, at least as the term has come widely to be understood.[4] Hall is concerned here to account for the rise of the new right in modern Britain. And, finding postmodernist approaches suggestive yet unequal to the task – for the same reasons we do in South Africa – he spins a fine methodological web between the poles of Marxism and structuralism, relying mainly on the concepts of hegemony and ideology. We should also like to appeal to these two concepts, although we locate them in an analytic lexicon broadened to include culture and consciousness, power and representation. Taken together, this array of terms provides a cogent framework within which to capture the story, the history, which we have to tell.

Culture, Hegemony, Ideology

The difficulties of establishing what Gramsci may have meant by hegemony are by now notorious. For reasons to do, perhaps, with the conditions of their production, *The Prison Notebooks* do not help us much. Nowhere in them is there a clear or precise definition (Lears 1985:568). Nowhere do we find, say, the widely cited characterization offered by Williams (1977:108 f.; see n.14): that is, of "the hegemonic" as a dominant system of lived meanings and values, relations and practices, which shapes experienced reality (cf. Hall 1988:44; quoted above). Only in a few places, in fact, does Gramsci come even close to speaking in such terms – and then not about hegemony per se.[5] Moreover, the definition quoted most often in recent commentaries – "the 'spontaneous' consent given by the great masses of the population to the general direction imposed on social life by the dominant fundamental group" (Gramsci 1971:12) – is actually a description of one of "the subaltern functions of social hegemony and political government" exercised by intellectuals. Not only does it raise more problems than it resolves, but it is a far cry from the concept as it has come to be used in much contemporary theoretical writing.

The very fact that Gramsci's notion of hegemony was so unsystematically stated has made it good to think with; as a relatively empty sign, it has been able to serve diverse analytical purposes and positions (see e.g., Genovese 1971; Hebdige 1979; Gaventa 1980; Hall 1986; Laitin 1986). Among poststructuralists its sustained popularity is due in part to the fact that it appears to offer a ready rapprochement between theory and practice, thought and action, ideology and power. But it is also because, as Hebdige (1988:206) explains, for Gramsci "nothing is anchored to…master narratives, to stable (positive) identities, to fixed and certain meanings: all social and semantic relations are contestable, hence mutable." Always uncertain, hegemony is realized through the balancing of competing forces, not the crushing calculus of class domination. Thus Laclau and Mouffe (1985), for example, find it possible to use the term to connote a kind of Foucaultian discourse, cut loose from any objective notion of society or culture – although they have been accused by Geras (1987) of robbing the concept of any principle of historical constraint whatsoever. Among post-Marxists, too, Gramsci has become "the Marxist you can take home to mother" (Romano 1983), providing an appealing escape from vulgar materialism and essentialism by speaking of production as a continuous ideological, social, and economic process (Hall 1988:53 ff.). And yet, notwithstanding a great deal of discussion and elaboration in recent years,[6] the construct remains underspecified and inadequately situated in its conceptual context. Often used as no more than a trendy buzzword, it is frequently invoked in the name of unreconciled and unreconcilable theoretical approaches.

For our own part, we do not seek to enter into contemporary debates over the notion of hegemony itself, let alone to offer a reading of Gramsci; the textual pursuit of the "real" meaning of an inherently equivocal concept is an exercise in futility. Nonetheless, given suitable specification, the term remains useful for our analytic purposes, since it may be made to illuminate some of the vital connections between power and culture, ideology and consciousness. This having been said, we have no alternative but to spell out our own usage amidst all the ambiguity. We do so, as we have said, by situating it in a more embracing set of analytic terms – and in a particular historical and ethnographic problem.

Some theorists have tried, directly (Williams 1977:108 ff.) or indirectly (e.g., Lears 1985:572 ff.), to assert the superiority of the notion of hegemony over culture and/or ideology; as if one might subsume and replace the others. Concealed in this argument is the idea that culture *plus* power *equals* hegemony, an equation that simplifies all three terms. Not that the reasoning behind it is surprising. As we have noted elsewhere (1987), the anthropological conception of culture has long been criticized, especially by Marxists, for overstressing the implicit, systemic, and consensual, for treating symbols and meanings as if they were neutral and above history, and for ignoring their empowering, authoritative dimensions. Conversely, Marxist theories of ideology and consciousness have been taken to task, by anthropologists, for neglecting the complex ways in which meaning inhabits consciousness and ideology. Neither ideology nor consciousness, goes the argument, is merely culture in the active voice. They are alike products of a process in which human beings deploy salient signs and relations to make their lives and worlds; signs and relations drawn from a structured, largely implicit repertoire of forms that lie below the surfaces of everyday experience. If culture seems to require power to make it complete, then, ideology and consciousness seem to require a good dose of semantics. Add all this together and the sum of the parts may appear to be "hegemony." But there

is a problem with both the arithmetic of authority and the mathematics of meaning. Since it is possible, indeed inevitable, for some symbols and meanings *not* to be hegemonic – and impossible that any hegemony can claim all the signs in the world for its own – culture cannot be subsumed within hegemony,[7] however the terms may be conceived. Meaning may never be innocent, but it is also not merely reducible to the postures of power.

Gramsci clearly realized this himself. Rather than posit "hegemony" as a replacement for "culture" or "ideology," he treated the three as quite distinct. At times, furthermore, "culture" was described in a manner to which many anthropologists would not object: as an order of values, norms, beliefs, and institutions that, being "reflected in...language" and being also profoundly historical, express a "common conception of the world" embodied in a "cultural-social unity" (1971:349). This "common conception" was composed of a stock of shared "dispositions," a "popular 'mentality'," which any hegemony had to capture (1971:348 ff., 26 ff.). But there is yet more. Gramsci went on to make an explicit chain of associations in which "common conceptions of the world" were equated with "cultural movements" and, by turn, with "philosophies" (1971:328). Significantly, a few pages before (1971:323), "spontaneous philosophy" – i.e. practical, "everyman" philosophy – was said to be contained in (1) language, itself an order "of determined notions and concepts"; (2) common and good sense; and (3) the "entire system of beliefs, superstitions, ways of seeing things and of acting."

Here, the circle closed, we appear to have Gramsci's image of culture as totality. It is the shared repertoire of practices, symbols, and meanings from which hegemonic forms are cast – and, by extension, resisted. Or, in other words, it is the historically situated field of signifiers, at once material and symbolic, in which occur the dialectics of domination and resistance, the making and breaking of consensus. Of course, not all signifiers are drawn upon at all times in such processes: some may come to be implicated unintentionally; others may become unfixed and remain, at least for a while, freefloating; yet others, more susceptible to the appropriations of authority, may be woven into tightly integrated worldviews, ideologies. We shall have more to say about these things in due course. For now, however, following the *Geist* of Gramsci, let us take culture to be the space of signifying practice, the semantic ground on which human beings seek to construct and represent themselves and others – and, hence, society and history. As this suggests, it is not merely a pot of messages, a repertoire of signs to be flashed across a neutral mental screen. It has form as well as content; is born in action as well as thought; is a product of human creativity as well as mimesis; and, above all, is empowered. But it is not all empowered in the same way, or all of the time.

This is where hegemony and ideology become salient again. They are the two dominant forms in which power enters – or, more accurately, is entailed in – culture. It is through them, therefore, that the relationship between power and culture is finally to be grasped, although a further caveat is necessary: that power itself is Janus-faced. Sometimes it appears as the (relative) capacity of human beings to shape the actions and perceptions of others by exercising control over the production, circulation, and consumption of signs and objects, over the making of both subjectivities and realities. This is power in its *agentive* mode: it refers to the command wielded by human beings in specific historical contexts. But power also presents, or rather hides, itself in the forms of everyday life. Sometimes ascribed to transcendental, suprahistorical forces (gods or ancestors, nature or physics, biological instinct or probability), these forms are not easily questioned. Being "natural" and "ineffable," they seem to be beyond human agency, notwithstanding the fact that the interests they serve may be all too human. This kind of *nonagentive* power proliferates outside the realm of institutional politics, saturating such things as aesthetics and ethics, built form and bodily representation, medical knowledge and mundane usage. What is more, it may not be experienced as power at all, since its effects are rarely wrought by overt compulsion. They are internalized, in their negative guise, as constraints; in their neutral guise, as conventions; and, in their positive guise, as values. Yet the silent power of the sign, the unspoken authority of habit, may be as effective as the most violent coercion in shaping, directing, even dominating social thought and action.

None of this is new, of course: identifying technologies and typologies of power, albeit in very diverse terms, has become a growth industry in modern social theory (see e.g., Lukes 1974; Bourdieu 1977; Wrong 1979; Mann 1986; also Foucault 1978, 1979, 1980). The point, though, goes back a long way. For Marx, to take one instance, the power of the capitalist was clearly different from the power of the commodity, the contrast corresponding broadly to the way in which ideology is portrayed in *The German Ideology* and *Capital* respectively (see e.g., Larrain 1979, 1983; Lichtheim 1967; J. Comaroff 1985:ch. 1). In the former it comes across primarily as a set of ideas that reflect the interests of the ruling class; ideas which, inverted through a camera obscura, are impressed upon the (false) consciousness of the proletariat (Marx and Engels 1970:64 f.). It is a function, in other words, of the capacity of the dominant to impose their will and their worldview on others. In *Capital*, by contrast, ideology is not named as such, and it is not said to arise mechanically from the politics of class domination. It is held, instead, to reside unseen in the commodity form itself. For commodity production, the dominant mode of value creation in modern capitalism, makes a whole world of social relations in its own image, a world that appears to be governed by natural laws above and beyond human intervention. Indeed, it is the inversion by which relations between people seem to be determined by relations among objects, and not vice versa, that makes commodity fetishism; and in this ontological moment a historically specific set of inequalities take root in subjective and collective experience, determining the way in which the social order is perceived and acted upon (Marx 1967:71 ff.; Giddens 1979:183). The contrast between the two images of ideation, in short, goes together with that between the two forms of power. The first is directly supported by, in fact hinges on, the agency of dominant social groups; the second derives, as if naturally, from the very construction of economy and society. As it happens, Marx decided to call the one "ideology." The other, to which he applied no term, lays the ground for a characterization of hegemony.

Until now we also have used both of these terms without specification. Significantly, there is a passage in *The Prison Notebooks* in which

Gramsci speaks of "ideology" – in quote marks – in its "highest sense." It is here that he comes closest to defining "hegemony," in the spirit of *Capital*, as Williams and others have characterized it (above, n. 5) – and as theorists like Bourdieu (1977) have transposed and redeployed it. In his own words, it is "a conception of the world that is implicitly manifest in art, in law, in economic activity and in all manifestations of individual and collective life" (1971:328). This, however, is not just *any* conception of the world. It is the *dominant* conception, an orthodoxy that has established itself as "historically true" and concretely "universal" (1971:348). Building upon this and upon its conceptual roots, we take hegemony to refer to that order of signs and practices, relations and distinctions, images and epistemologies – drawn from a historically situated cultural field – that come to be taken-for-granted as the natural and received shape of the world and everything that inhabits it. It consists, to paraphrase Bourdieu (1977:167), of things that go without saying because, being axiomatic, they come without saying; things that, being presumptively shared, are not normally the subject of explication or argument (Bourdieu 1977:94). This is why its power has so often been seen to lie in what it silences, what it prevents people from thinking and saying, what it puts beyond the limits of the rational and the credible. In a quite literal sense, hegemony is habit forming. For these reasons, it is rarely contested directly, save perhaps in the roseate dreams of revolutionaries. For once its internal contradictions are revealed, when what seemed natural comes to be negotiable, when the ineffable is put into words – then hegemony becomes something other than itself. It turns into ideology and counterideology, into the "orthodoxy" and "heterodoxy" of Bourdieu's (1977) formulation. More commonly, however, such struggles remain clashes of symbols, the practical iconoclasm that is produced when tensions within the hegemonic – or between the grains of habit and habitat – chafe for immediate resolution.

Ideology in less than the "highest sense," we suggest, is ideology more conventionally understood. Following Raymond Williams (1977:109), who seems here to have *The German Ideology* in mind, we use it to describe "an articulated system of meanings, values, and beliefs of a kind that can be abstracted as [the] 'worldview'" of any social grouping. Borne in explicit manifestos and everyday practices, self-conscious texts and spontaneous images, popular styles and political platforms, this worldview may be more or less internally systematic, more or less assertively coherent in its outward forms. But, as long as it exists, it provides an organizing scheme (a master narrative?) for collective symbolic production. Obviously, to invoke Marx and Engels (1970) once again, the regnant ideology of any period or place will be that of the dominant group. And, while the nature and degree of its preeminence may vary a good deal, it is likely to be protected, even enforced, to the full extent of the power of those who claim it for their own.

But other, subordinate populations, at least those with communal identities, also have ideologies. And, inasmuch as they try to assert themselves against a dominant order or group, perhaps even to reverse existing relations of inequality, they too must call actively upon those ideologies. To be sure, if it is joined in the name of a collective identity, any such struggle, whether or not it is seen to be specifically "political," is an ideological struggle; for it necessarily involves an effort to control the cultural terms in which the world is ordered and, within it, power legitimized. Here, then, is the basic difference between hegemony and ideology. Whereas the first consists of constructs and conventions that have come to be shared and naturalized throughout a political community, the second is the expression and ultimately the possession of a particular social group, although it may be widely peddled beyond. The first is nonnegotiable and therefore beyond direct argument; the second is more susceptible to being perceived as a matter of inimical opinion and interest and therefore is open to contestation. Hegemony homogenizes, ideology articulates. Hegemony, at its most effective, is mute; by contrast, says de Certeau (1984:46), "all the while, ideology babbles on."

There are other differences, to which we shall return in a moment. But first, a more immediate question: What is the relationship between hegemony and ideology, either dominant or dissenting? This is a crucial issue, and one on which we depart from much current – and, we believe, currently confused – thinking. Indeed, the unusual, triangular manner in which we have chosen to define culture, hegemony, and ideology is meant not merely to find a way out of the thicket of ambiguity surrounding these concepts in modern anthropology; it is also to arrive at a set of terms with which to address both this question and the many problems about the nature of power, consciousness, and representation to which it points.

Hegemony, we suggest, exists in reciprocal interdependence with ideology: it is that part of a dominant worldview which has been naturalized and, having hidden itself in orthodoxy, no more appears as ideology at all. Inversely, the ideologies of the subordinate may give expression to discordant but hitherto voiceless experience of contradictions that a prevailing hegemony can no longer conceal. Self-evidently, the hegemonic proportion of any dominant ideology may be greater or lesser. It will never be total, save perhaps in the fanciful dreams of fascists, and only rarely will it shrink away to nothing. The manner in which some of the acts and axioms of a sectarian worldview actually come to be naturalized, or how critical reactions grow from the invisible roots that anchor inequality, is always a historically specific issue; we shall address it in detail in our account. Typically, however, the making of hegemony involves the assertion of control over various modes of symbolic production: over such things as educational and ritual processes, patterns of socialization, political and legal procedures, canons of style and self-representation, public communication, health and bodily discipline, and so on. That control, however – as Foucault understood about the generic nature of surveillance – must be sustained over time and in such a way that it becomes, to all intents and purposes, invisible. For it is only by repetition that signs and practices cease to be perceived or remarked; that they are so habituated, so deeply inscribed in everyday routine, that they may no longer be seen as forms of control – or seen at all. It is then that they come to be (un)spoken of as custom, (dis)regarded as convention – and only disinterred, if at all, on ceremonial occasions, when they are symbolically invoked as eternal verities.

Yet the seeds of hegemony are never scattered on barren ground. They might establish themselves at the expense of prior forms, but they seldom succeed in totally supplanting what was there before. Not only is hegemony never total, as

Williams (1977: 109) has insisted. It is always threatened by the vitality that remains in the forms of life it thwarts. It follows, then, that the hegemonic is constantly being made – and, by the same token, may be unmade. That is why it has been described as a process as much as a thing: "a process of continuous creation," says Adamson (1980:174), which "is bound to be uneven...and to leave some room for antagonistic cultural expressions...." Nor is its perpetuation a mechanical consequence of politicoeconomic control: ruling regimes can never rest on their material laurels. Even the most repressive ones tend to be highly evangelical, constantly "seek[ing] to win the consent of subordinate groups to the existing social order" (Lears 1985:569). As we have said, the more successful they are, the more of their ideology will disappear into the domain of the hegemonic; the less successful, the more that unremarked truths and unspoken conventions will become remarked, reopened for debate. This, as we shall see, is ever more likely to occur as the contradictions between the world as represented and the world as experienced become ever more palpable, ever more insupportable; although the human capacity to tolerate and rationalize cognitive dissonance is notoriously variable. It is this form of dissonance that Gramsci (1971:333) himself, again following Marx and Engels (1970:51 ff.), took to be the basis of "contradictory consciousness"; that is, the discontinuity between (1) the world as hegemonically constituted and (2) the world as practically apprehended, and ideologically represented, by subordinated people (the "man-in-the-mass").[8]

It is also with reference to this form of contradictory consciousness that some historians – most notably, perhaps, Genovese (1974) – have accounted for the reactions of oppressed peoples to their experience of subordination and dehumanization (see Lears 1985:569 ff.). Those reactions, it is said, consisted in a complex admixture of tacit (even uncomprehending) accommodation to the hegemonic order at one level and diverse expressions of symbolic and practical resistance at another, although the latter might have reinforced the former by displacing attention away from, or by actively reproducing, the hidden signs and structures of domination. The point may be extended to colonialism at large: a critical feature of the colonization of consciousness among the Tswana, and others like them, was the process by which they were drawn unwittingly into the dominion of European "civilization" while at the same time often contesting its presence and the explicit content of its worldview. A new hegemonic order, as we said earlier, was established amidst ideological struggle along an expanding, imploding cultural frontier. However, there is also a counterpoint to be anticipated here. "Contradictory consciousness" may be one key to the creation and perpetuation of relations of domination. But as it gives way to an ever more acute, articulate consciousness of contradictions, it may also be a source of ever more acute, articulate resistance. Of course, dominant groups usually seek to paper over such contradictions and to suppress their revelation by means both symbolic and violent; it is, more often than not, a very long road from the dawning of an antihegemonic consciousness to an ideological struggle won. That is why the history of colonialism, even in the most remote backwaters of the modern world, is such a drawn out affair, such an intricate fugue of challenge and riposte, mastery and misery.

Hegemony, then, is always intrinsically unstable, always vulnerable. For Gramsci (1971:12, 168) the ascendancy of a particular group, class, or whatever, was founded on its "position and function in the world of production," with the qualification that "production" ought not to be understood in narrow economistic terms. Quite the opposite: its material bases notwithstanding, effective domination was held to depend on cultural imperialism – on the ceaseless effort to forge alliances never simply given by existing structures of class and society (cf. Hall 1988:53–4), on the constant attempt to convert sectarian ideas into universal truths. Even in the face of such exertions, though, changes in the content and extent of hegemonies can occur fairly rapidly.

In the societies of the modern West, for instance, there have been significant shifts, in the late twentieth century, in the degree to which discrimination based on gender and race is naturalized. Distinctions of sex and color are obviously still inscribed in common linguistic usage, in aesthetic values and scientific knowledge; they continue to be a matter of widespread consensus and silent complicity; they also remain inscribed in everyday activity. Yet ever more articulate political and social protest has forced these issues on the collective conscience and into ideological debate. Formerly taken-for-granted discriminatory usages have been thrust before the public eye. As a result, the premises of racial and sexual inequality are no longer acceptable, at least in the official rhetoric of most modern states – although, in the world of mundane practice, the battle to control key signs and ostensibly neutral values rages on. This follows a very common pattern: once something leaves the domain of the hegemonic, it frequently becomes a major site of ideological struggle. Even when there is no well-formed opposing ideology, no clearly articulated collective consciousness among subordinate populations, such struggles may still occur. But they are liable to be heard in the genre of negation – refusal, reversal, the smashing of idols and icons – and not in the narrative voice of political argument. Which, finally, brings us to the relationship between culture, hegemony, and ideology and their human vehicles, consciousness and representation.

Consciousness and Representation

Thus far we have portrayed hegemony and ideology as two modalities, each associated with a characteristic form of empowerment, within any cultural field. We use "cultural field" here for two reasons: first, to reiterate that, far from being reducible to a closed system of signs and relations, the meaningful world always presents itself as a fluid, often contested, and only partially integrated mosaic of narratives, images, and signifying practices; and, second, to mark the fact that, in colonial (and many other) contexts, the semantic scape contains a plurality of "cultures" – that is, of "systems" of symbols, values, and meanings which are reified and objectified in the course of colonization itself (see [...] Comaroff and Comaroff 1989). In these circumstances ideological struggles come often to be clothed in the rhetoric of cultural difference, although the field of signifiers in which they occur necessarily expands to take in the very possibility of "intercultural" discourse and its primary textual act, translation.

If hegemony and ideology are two modalities within a cultural field – two tendencies whose relative proportions and substance are constantly liable to shift – it follows that they are best visualized as the ends of a continuum. So too are the forms of power associated with them. Indeed, just as the hegemonic and the ideological may alter in relation to one another, so may the nature of empowerment inscribed in any regime of signs and values. Take the case of modern South Africa, for example: between 1950 and 1990, black campaigns of defiance repeatedly contested the everyday vehicles – such things as segregated trains and buses, hospitals and schools – that naturalized racial inequality. The hidden bases of domination were repeatedly brought into the light of scrutiny. With each crack in, each diminution of, the axiomatic foundations of apartheid, the resort to state power in its brute, agentive form became more palpable, more pervasive. Conversely, as hegemonies insinuate themselves into a political community and spread, the perceived need to protect them by the visible exercise of force recedes; their authority is internalized through habitual practice, suffusing everyday life and the conventions that regulate it.

But this continuum is still missing a crucial element. For what differentiates hegemony from ideology, one face of power from the other, is not some existential essence. It is, as we have implied throughout, the factor of human consciousness and the modes of representation that bear it. The post-enlightenment western tradition has left the human sciences – except maybe psychology – with a binary image of social consciousness. This is not merely an extension into the collective realm of theories of the individual psyche. The founders of modern sociology and anthropology were vehemently opposed, in principle if not always in practice, to psychological reductionism and to any idea of a collective unconscious; recall Malinowski's (1954) denunciation of what he misread as the notion of a "group mind" in Durkheim's writings on religion (see 1947). It is rather a matter of the unspecified Cartesian assumptions about personhood, cognition, and social being that persist in mainstream western thought, both orthodox and critical. In this tradition consciousness is all or none, true or false, present or absent. It is moreover the stuff of contemplative rather than practical understanding – though, as we have noted, theorists in the Gramscian tradition have long challenged the

dichotomy. Whether it be seen as the mere reflection of social facts or the actual source of common action, consciousness itself is rarely treated as a problem. It is understood as content not form, as knowledge not modes of knowing. For all our sophisticated analyses of subjectivity and experience, we social scientists continue to speak as if it stands in a simple opposition to *unconsciousness*, as if these were the only collective states of mind and being in the world.

Yet few anthropologists should be able to accept this; it runs counter to much of what we presume when we interpret cultures and the meaningful practices that animate them. Much more plausible is the notion that social knowledge and experience situate themselves along a *chain of consciousness* – once again a continuum whose two extremes are the unseen and the seen, the submerged and the apprehended, the unrecognized and the cognized. It hardly needs pointing out that the one extreme corresponds to the hegemonic pole of culture, the other to the ideological. And just as hegemonies and ideologies shift over time and space, so the contents of consciousness are not fixed. On the one hand, the submerged, the unseen, the unrecognized may under certain conditions be called to awareness; on the other, things once perceived and explicitly marked may slip below the level of discourse into the unremarked recesses of the collective unconscious. The latter is emphatically *not* some form of group mind. It is the implicit structure of shared meaning that human beings absorb as they learn to be members of particular social worlds.

Between the conscious and the unconscious lies the most critical domain of all for historical anthropology and especially for the analysis of colonialism and resistance. It is the realm of partial recognition, of inchoate awareness, of ambiguous perception, and, sometimes, of creative tension: that liminal space of human experience in which people discern acts and facts but cannot or do not order them into narrative descriptions or even into articulate conceptions of the world; in which signs and events are observed, but in a hazy, translucent light; in which individuals or groups know that something is happening to them but find it difficult to put their fingers on quite what it is. It is from this realm, we suggest, that silent signifiers and unmarked practices may rise to the level of explicit consciousness, of ideological assertion, and become the subject of overt political and social contestation – or from which they may recede into the hegemonic, to languish there unremarked for the time being. As we shall see, it is also the realm from which emanate the poetics of history, the innovative impulses of the bricoleur and the organic intellectual, the novel imagery called upon to bear the content of symbolic struggles.

The space between consciousness and unconsciousness is significant for another reason. In the course of our account we shall argue that hegemony stands to ideology, broadly speaking, as form to content – with the qualification that the distinction is self-evidently one of degree. The hegemonic, in short, is inscribed largely in what we take to be enduring forms (or "structures") – the commodity form, linguistic forms, epistemological forms, and so on – in relation to which substantive differences of social value and political ideology are given voice (*form*ulated?). As long as they last, these forms lay down the implicit ground – the authoritative frame of reference – within which the content of the meaningful world may be subjectively constructed, negotiated, actively empowered. The obvious analogy here is with language, which is commonly described, like culture, in such a way as to suggest that it plies the chain of consciousness between the unsaid and the said, code and message, grammatical form and the content of speech. The journey along the chain, patently, is envisaged as dialectical (Barthes 1967:15 ff.): if grammatical forms were not a ("deeper" structural) distillate of substance, they could not generate meaningful new utterances, new moments of content; conversely, if the latter were not expressions of those underlying grammatical forms, it would be difficult to account for their production, let alone their comprehensibility. So it is with culture, hegemony, and ideology: hegemony is a product of the dialectic whereby the content of dominant ideologies is distilled into the shared forms that seem to have such historical longevity as to be above history – and, hence, to have the capacity to generate new substantive practices along the surfaces of economy and society. Like formal semantic oppositions in culture – with their putative arbitrariness – they do not themselves appear to have any ideological content. They belong to the

domain of fact, not value. They are just there, ineffably.

Because the liminal space between the hegemonic and the ideological, consciousness and unconsciousness, is also an area in which new relations are forged between form and content, it is likely to be the source of the poetic imagination, the creative, the innovative. The latter, after all, *depend* on the play of form and content, on experimentations in expressive technique, on conjuring with ambiguity. Ideology may, of course, take many guises, narrative and nonnarrative, realistic or whimsical; it may be heavily symbolic, deeply coded; but at root its messages must be communicable. Hegemony, as we have said, represents itself everywhere in its saturating silences or its ritual repetitions. It is on the middle ground between such silences and repetitions that human beings often seek new ways to test out and give voice to their evolving perceptions of, and dispositions toward, the world. The analytic implication is both clear and complex: modes of representation, and the diverse forms they take, are *part* of culture and consciousness, hegemony and ideology, not merely their vehicles. "Reading" them, then, is the primary methodological act of any historical anthropology. [...]

One last, closely related issue remains: the nature of protest and symbolic struggle. [...] [W]e believe that the present debate among historians and anthropologists over the conception and definition of resistance boils down to the problem of consciousness and motivation. As we put it in a recent paper (Comaroff and Comaroff 1989), much of that debate hinges on two matters: Does an act require explicit consciousness and articulation to be properly called "resistance?" Should the term apply only to the intentions behind social and political acts, or may it refer equally to their consequences? When a people can be shown to express some measure of awareness of their predicament as victims of domination – and, better yet, can state the terms of their response – the matter is clear. Where they do not, characterizing their reactions becomes an altogether more murky business. We will suggest, however, that there is an analytic lesson to be taken from the evident fact that most historical situations are extremely murky in just this respect.

Just as technologies of control run the gamut from overt coercion to implicit persuasion, so modes of resistance may extend across a similarly wide spectrum. At one end is organized protest, explicit moments and movements of dissent that are easily recognizable as "political" by western lights. At the other are gestures of tacit refusal and iconoclasm, gestures that sullenly and silently contest the forms of an existing hegemony. For the most part, however, the ripostes of the colonized hover in the space between the tacit and the articulate, the direct and the indirect. And far from being a mere reflection – or a reflex expression – of historical consciousness, these acts are a practical means of *producing* it. If anything will become evident in our study, it is that much of the Tswana response to the mission encounter was an effort to fashion an understanding of, and gain conceptual mastery over, a changing world. This, it seems, is a very general phenomenon. Early on in the colonizing process, wherever it occurs, the assault on local societies and cultures is the subject of neither "consciousness" nor "unconsciousness" on the part of the victim, but of recognition – recognition that occurs with varying degrees of inchoateness and clarity. Out of that recognition, and the creative tensions to which it may lead, there typically arise forms of *experimental practice* that are at once techniques of empowerment and the signs of collective representation.

Through such reactions "native peoples" seek to plumb the depths of the colonizing process. They search for the coherence – and, sometimes, the *deus ex machina* – that lies behind its visible face. For the recently colonized, or those who feel the vibrations of the imperial presence just over the horizon, generally believe that there *is* something invisible, something profound, happening to them – and that their future may well depend on gaining control over its "magic." Thus, for instance, many "Christianized" peoples the world over are, or once were, convinced that whites have a second, secret bible or set of rites (cricket? telegraphs? tea parties?) on which their power depends. The whimsical "unreason" of such movements as cargo cults stems from precisely this conviction. These movements, as is now well known, are early efforts to capture and redeploy the colonialist's ability to produce value. And they are often seen as enough of a threat to elicit a punitive response.

With time and historical experience, the colonized show greater discrimination, greater subtlety in interpreting the European embrace and its implications. Attempts to come to terms with the latter grow more diverse and are ever more closely tied to processes of social stratification. Among those drawn most fully into the forms of "modernity" – the petite bourgeoisies and "new elites" scattered across the Third World – there occurs a gradual appropriation of the images, ideologies, and aesthetics of the postenlightenment West, and, not least, its orthodox styles of political discourse and protest. But for the rest modernity and its modes of resistance are by no means the inevitable or even the likely consequences of the colonization of consciousness – or of the consciousness of colonization that follows. Indeed, as we have said several times already, the dynamics of cultural imperialism are such that, while the power structure of colonialism is everywhere clearly drawn, the colonizing process itself is rarely a simple dialectic of domination and resistance. [...]

Notes

1 Some of the earliest ethnographies and histories of Africa, as is well known, were written by evangelists with a "scientific" interest in their would-be subjects. Here colonial evangelism merged into a scholarly colonialism that foreshadowed and paved the way for modern anthropology. But this is quite another topic; we do not it address here.

2 Note, again, that we are speaking here of the *practice* of anthropology. As every anthropologist knows, there has recently been much programmatic and prescriptive discussion about "writing culture" – discussion that has called, at times very suggestively, for new, experimental forms of ethnography. The intentions are undeniably worthy, as are the efforts to overcome the epistemological problems and limitations of older anthropological genres. However, it is always a far cry from program to production, prescription to practice; until we have a body of work to assess, the exercise remains little more than an interesting stimulant for the theoretical imagination. Thus far, there is, in our view, only one monograph that may claim to be postmodernist, *sensu strictu*: Taussig's *Shamanism, Colonialism, and the Wild Man* (1987). For a very thoughtful review of the

theoretical, methodological, and ideological issues raised by the book, see Kapferer (1988). Kapferer also voices a number of general worries about post-modernist ethnography: (1) that, for all its radical stance - and accusations of fascism in others – it may conceal both political neoconservatism and method-ological neopositivism; (2) that, despite its repudia-tion of order and totality, it is founded on a hidden sys- tematicity of its own; (3) that its new rhetoric obscures unacknowledged continuities and similar-ities with older theoretical perspectives; and (4) that it is no less prone to appropriate the "other" than are its more orthodox predecessors. Inasmuch as these con-cerns are valid – and they appear to be – the problems raised by critical postmodernism seem not to be resolvable by postmodernist ethnography, at least as presently conceived.

3   The term "sociologies" is used here as a synonym for "social sciences." Hebdige's observations throughout the essay are clearly meant to include anthropology and history.

4   For reasons to which we shall return, this conven-tional understanding of hegemony owes less to Gramsci's own definition than it does to Raymond Williams (1977), whose commentary on the con-cept has insinuated itself into popular scholarly usage – and this in spite of the curious fact that it is written without a single page reference to, or quotation from, The Prison Notebooks.

5   See, for example, the passages on (1) the creation of a new culture (1971:325); (2) the self-conception of a social group (1971:327); (3) contradictory con-sciousness (1971:333); (4) the "realisation of a [new] hegemonic apparatus" (1971:365); (5) ideology as "a conception of the world that is implicitly manifest in art, in law, in economic activity and in all manifestations of individual and collective life" (1971:328); (6) the nature of philoso-phy (e.g., 1971:348, 370); and, in particular, of (7) "spontaneous philosophy" (1971:323), which is to be read in light of the association elsewhere in the text between (a) "spontaneity" and "social hege-mony" (1971:12) and (b) philosophy, political action, and ideology (e.g., 1971:326). We shall return to (5), (6), and (7) in our discussion below.

6   The potential list of citations is huge. See, for just a small sample, Kraditor (1972); Femia (1975, 1981); Anderson (1976–7); Williams (1977); Adamson (1980); Laclau and Mouffe (1985); Lears (1985); and Hall (1986).

7   It follows that we find the term "cultural hegemony," which is used by some Gramscian commentators, a misguided conflation of two quite distinct (albeit the-oretically related) concepts. The same, for reasons that will become clear, applies to "ideological hegemony."

8   Being less concerned with textual exposition than with the development of a conceptual framework, we have transposed the characterization of "contradictory con-sciousness" into our own conceptual terms; although, as it happens, we do not depart very far from the spirit of the original. For a brief summary of the precise terms in which Marx and Engels (1970:52 ff.) and Gramsci (1971:326 f., 333), respectively, characterized this contradiction, see Cheal (1979:110 f.).

References

Adamson, Walter L. 1980 Hegemony and Revolution: A Study of Antonio Gramsci's Political and Cultural Theory. Berkeley and Los Angeles: University of California Press.

Anderson, Perry 1976–7 The Antinomies of Antonio Gramsci. New Left Review 100:5–78.

Bakhtin, Mikhail M. 1981 The Dialogic Imagination: Four Essays. Ed. M. Holquist. Trans. C. Emerson and M. Holquist. Austin: University of Texas Press.

Barthes, Roland 1967 Elements of Semiology. Trans. A. Lavers and C. Smith. London: Jonathan Cape.

Benveniste, Emile 1971 Problems in General Linguistics. Trans. M. E. Meek. Coral Gables, Fla.: University of Miami Press.

Bourdieu, Pierre 1977 Outline of a Theory of Practice. Trans. R. Nice. Cambridge: Cambridge University Press.

Cheal, David J. 1979 Hegemony, Ideology and Contradictory Consciousness. The Sociological Quarterly 20: 109–17.

Comaroff, Jean 1985 Body of Power, Spirit of Resistance: The Culture and History of a South African People. Chicago: University of Chicago Press.

Comaroff, Jean and John L. Comaroff 1989 The Colonization of Consciousness in South Africa. Economy and Society 18:267–96.

Comaroff, John L., and Jean Comaroff 1987 The Madman and the Migrant: Work and Labor in the Historical Consciousness of a South African People. American Ethnologist 14:191–209.

de Certeau, Michel 1984 The Practice of Everyday Life. Trans. S. F. Rendall. Berkeley and Los Angeles: University of California Press.

de Certeau Michel 1988 The Writing of History. New York: Columbia University Press.

Durkheim, Emile 1947 The Elementary Forms of the Religious Life: A Study in Religious Sociology. Trans. J. W. Swain. Glencoe: The Free Press.

Evans-Pritchard, Edward E. 1937 Witchcraft, Oracles and Magic among the Azande. Oxford: Clarendon Press.

Fabian, Johannes 1983 *Time and the Other: How Anthropology Makes Its Object*. New York: Columbia University Press.

Femia, Joseph V. 1975 Hegemony and Consciousness in the Thought of Antonio Gramsci. *Political Studies* 23:29–48.

Femia, Joseph V. 1981 *Gramsci's Political Thought: Hegemony, Consciousness, and the Revolutionary Process*. Oxford: Clarendon Press.

Foucault, Michel 1978 *The History of Sexuality*. Trans. R. Hurley. New York: Pantheon Books.

Foucault, Michel 1979 *Discipline and Punish: The Birth of the Prison*. Trans. A. Sheridan. New York: Vintage Books.

Foucault, Michel 1980 *Power/Knowledge: Selected Interviews and Other Writings, 1972–77*. Ed. C. Gordon; trans. C. Gordon et al. New York: Pantheon Books.

Gaventa, John 1980 *Power and Powerlessness: Quiescence and Rebellion in an Appalachian Valley*. Urbana: University of Illinois Press.

Geertz, Clifford 1973 *The Interpretation of Cultures: Selected Essays*. New York: Basic Books.

Genovese, Eugene D. 1971 *In Red and Black: Marxian Explorations in Southern and Afro-American History*. New York: Pantheon Books.

Genovese, Eugene D. 1974 *Roll, Jordan, Roll: The World the Slaves Made*. New York: Pantheon Books.

Geras, Norman 1987 Post-Marxism? *New Left Review* 163:40–82.

Giddens, Anthony 1979 *Central Problems in Social Theory: Action, Structure, and Contradiction in Social Analysis*. Berkeley and Los Angeles: University of California Press.

Gramsci, Antonio 1971 *Selections from the Prison Notebooks*. Ed. and trans. Q. Hoare and G. Nowell Smith. New York: International Publishers.

Hall, Stuart 1986 Gramsci's Relevance for the Study of Race and Ethnicity. *Journal of Communication Inquiries* 10:5–27.

Hall, Stuart 1988 The Toad in the Garden: Thatcherism among the Theorists. In *Marxism and the Interpretation of Culture*. Ed. C. Nelson and L. Grossberg. Urbana and Chicago: University of Illinois Press.

Hanks, William F. 1989 Text and Textuality. *Annual Review of Anthropology* 18:95–127.

Hebdige, Dick 1979 *Subculture: The Meaning of Style*. New York: Methuen.

Hebdige, Dick 1988 *Hiding in the Light: On Images and Things*. London and New York: Routledge (Comedia Books).

Jameson, Fredric 1981 *The Political Unconscious: Narrative as a Socially Symbolic Act*. Ithaca: Cornell University Press.

Kapferer, Bruce 1988 The Anthropologist as Hero: Three Exponents of Post-Modernist Anthropology. *Critique of Anthropology* 8:77–104.

Kraditor, Aileen S. 1972 American Radical Historians on their Heritage. *Past and Present* 56:136–53.

Laclau, Ernesto, and Chantal Mouffe 1985 *Hegemony and Socialist Strategy: Towards a Radical Democratic Politics*. Trans. W. Moore and P. Cammack. London: Verso.

Laitin, David D. 1986 *Hegemony and Culture: Politics and Religious Change among the Yoruba*. Chicago: University of Chicago Press.

Larrain, Jorge 1979 *The Concept of Ideology*. Athens: University of Georgia Press.

Larrain, Jorge 1983 *Marxism and Ideology*. London: Macmillan.

Leach, Edmund R. 1954 *Political Systems of Highland Burma*. London: Bell.

Lears, T. J. Jackson 1985 The Concept of Cultural Hegemony: Problems and Possibilities. *American Historical Review* 9:567–93.

Lichtheim, George 1967 *The Concept of Ideology, and Other Essays*. New York: Random House.

Lukes, Steven 1974 *Power: A Radical View*. London: Macmillan.

Malinowski, Bronislaw 1954 *Magic, Science and Religion and Other Essays*. Garden City, NY: Doubleday.

Mann, Michael 1986 *The Sources of Social Power*. Vol. 1, *A History of Power from the Beginning to AD 1760*. Cambridge: Cambridge University Press.

Marx, Karl 1967 *Capital: A Critique of Political Economy*. 3 vols. Ed. F. Engels; trans. from the third German edition by S. Moore and E. Aveling. New York: International Publishers.

Marx, Karl and Friedrich Engels 1970 *The German Ideology*. Ed. with an Introduction by C. J. Arthur. New York: International Publishers.

Rabinow, Paul, and William M. Sullivan 1987 The Interpretive Turn: A Second Look. In *Interpretive Social Science: A Second Look*. Ed. P. Rabinow and W. M. Sullivan. Berkeley and Los Angeles: University of California Press.

Romano, Carlin 1983 But Was He A Marxist? Review of *Approaches to Gramsci*, ed. A. S. Sassoon, 1982. *Village Voice*, 29 March, 41.

Sahlins, Marshall D. 1981 *Historical Metaphors and Mythical Realities: Structure in the Early History of the Sandwich Islands Kingdom*. Ann Arbor: University of Michigan Press.

Said, Edward W. 1978 *Orientalism*. New York: Pantheon Books.

Taussig, Michael 1987 *Shamanism, Colonialism, and the Wild Man: A Study in Terror and Healing*. Chicago: University of Chicago Press.

Williams, Raymond 1977 *Marxism and Literature*. London: Oxford University Press.

Wrong, Dennis H. 1979 *Power: Its Forms, Bases and Uses*. Oxford: Basil Blackwell; New York: Harper & Row.

32

Epochal Structures I: Reconstructing Historical Materialism

Donald L. Donham

[...]I am going to argue that historical materialism requires both a notion of stuctural determination and one of human agency:

> Men make their own history, but they do not make it just as they please; do not make it under circumstances chosen by themselves, but under circumstances directly encountered, given and transmitted from the past.[1]

The problem will be to move beyond an easy eclecticism (a little of this, a little of that) to show exactly how analyses of structural determination are incomplete and in what senses a comprehensive understanding of history actually requires a theory of human agency.[2] [...]

Marx's concept of essential human nature is, as a number of recent commentators have argued, a touchstone for his entire system of thought.[3] In order to define Marx's ideas by contrast, one can imagine a range of possible positions from one extreme (human needs are everywhere the same – the same, that is, as in capitalist society) to its opposite (humans are so formed by their milieux

that their needs and aspirations are fundamentally different). Not surprisingly, the first extreme often gets associated with notions of biology and natural givens, whereas the second is usually expressed in terms of cultural relativity.

Marx rejected both of these positions. The first idea, that humans are everywhere the same, would not be defended by many social scientists these days (with perhaps the exception of extreme sociobiologists or vulgar neoclassical economists). Still, it is a powerful popular notion and one that Marx attacked again and again in his own day. Its political commitments are clear. Humanity is capitalist man writ large; it is foolhardy to dream of other ways of organizing society, for capitalist inequalities are the result of natural qualities of human beings.

The opposite extreme, that human nature offers no constraints on social arrangements, is a considerably stronger position within current social science. [...] [N]eoclassical economic theory in its most attractive form – the kind of social theory that underpins much of Max Weber's work, for example – depends on such a view. Humans make choices, particular choices with a view toward

From *History, Power, Ideology: Central Issues in Marxism and Anthropology*, 2nd edn. (Berkeley: University of California Press, 1999), pp. 52–63, 64–70 (with cuts). Copyright © 1999 by Donald L. Donham. Reprinted by permission of University of California Press.

Anthropology in Theory: Issues in Epistemology, Second Edition. Edited by Henrietta L. Moore and Todd Sanders.
© 2014 John Wiley & Sons, Inc. Published 2014 by John Wiley & Sons, Inc.

attaining certain ends. But those ends vary from place to place, and all that an analysis can posit is a more-or-less stable hierarchy of *some* ends. What unites mankind is, at best, a capacity, a generic potential for "culture." But particular cultures vary, as Clifford Geertz would have it, from that of "transformed Aztecs lifting pulsing hearts torn live from the chest of human sacrifices" to that of "stolid Zuni dancing their great mass supplications to the benevolent gods of rain."[4]

This second view has important consequences that also contrast with Marxist theory, for it sees humanity as essentially plastic and therefore in need of culture – *any* culture, apparently. According to Geertz, cultural patterns provide the terms in which "we give form, order, point, and direction to our lives" and without which we would be "unworkable monstrosities," "mental basket cases." To summarize briefly, to provide a foil against which Marx will stand out, this image of humankind promotes a view of cultural analysis as a (bookish) sort of "translation" of one symbolic system to another, encourages a primarily aesthetic attitude toward other cultures, and perhaps most important in relation to Marxism, limits the analyst's political commitments to a respect for diversity. "The essential vocation of interpretive anthropology is not to answer our deepest questions, but to make available to us answers that others, guarding other sheep in other valleys, have given, and thus to include them in the consultable record of what man has said."[5] Capitalism in this view is not universal; instead, it is only one of a thousand cultural systems, among which it is impossible rationally to choose.

Marx's social theory is different. Whether one is convinced or not, it is impossible to deny that Marxism *is* aimed at answering our deepest questions. At the base of historical materialism is a notion of human nature and of essential human needs as both socially conditioned (and therefore different from epoch to epoch) and, in some respects, universally the same. The aspect of socially conditioned (and therefore varying) human needs will perhaps be clear enough. By contrast, Marx's concept of universal human nature requires further explanation, for this idea is intimately connected both with Marx's commitment to socialism and with how he locates tensions and impulses for change in other economic formations.

For Marx, free and creative labor is *the* fundamental and universal human need. To forestall confusion, it is necessary to point out that Marx's concept of labor is not confined to the narrow one that has come to dominate our thought in capitalist societies. Rather, "labor," social activity in the material world, potentially comprises notions of self-expression, rational development, and aesthetic enjoyment. As Allen Wood points out, "...science and art seem to serve as his [Marx's] chief models for the forms which production will take in the post-capitalist 'realm of freedom.'"[6] Nor does Marx's notion of labor depend on a simplified opposition between "material" and "cultural" (and hence an exclusion of the latter from consideration). For Marx, just as for modern cultural anthropology, man is a symbolic animal:

> A spider conducts operations which resemble those of weaver, and a bee would put many a human architect to shame by the construction of its honeycomb cells. But what distinguishes the worst architect from the best of bees is that the architect builds the cell in his mind before he constructs it in wax. At the end of every labour process, a result emerges which had already been conceived by the worker in the beginning, hence already existed ideally.[7]

What is distinctive about humans, according to Marx, is not simply that we depend on symbols but that we, in a sense, create ourselves through symbolically formed action in the world – "labor." At the beginning of every labor process, a person begins with a certain symbolic project and a certain set of needs. In association with others and through action in the world, such a person not only satisfies those needs; he or she also produces new needs. This self-creation is what distinguishes human beings from animals. It is our "species-being."[8] And it is this aspect of our being human that creates an objective need for a kind of society in which individuals in association with others can maximally reach their powers of creativity and expression.[9]

> free conscious activity constitutes the species–character of man. ... conscious life activity directly distinguishes man from animal life activity. ... It is true that animals also produce.

They build nests and dwellings, like the bee, the beaver, the ant, etc. But they produce only their own immediate needs or those of their young; they produce one-sidedly, while man produces universally; they produce only when immediate physical need compels them to do so, while man produces even when he is free from physical need and truly produces only in freedom from such need. ... It is therefore in his fashioning of the objective that man really proves himself to be a *species being*. Such production is his active species-life. ... man reproduces himself not only intellectually, in his consciousness, but actively and actually, and he can therefore contemplate himself in a world he himself has created.[10]

Quite literally, we produce, transform, and create ourselves through labor. Thought and action continually interact to produce new thought and new action. Marx's vision is one of what might be called humankind in the active voice.

To revert to either of the positions on human nature discussed above – humanity as everywhere the same or everywhere different – is to translate Marx's vision into the passive voice. Either biology creates men and women or culture creates them, and we are left with no internally-generated dynamism or tension. Notice the subtle switch from active to passive voice, as it were, in a passage by Clifford Geertz that echoes Marx:

Beavers build dams, birds build nests, bees locate food, baboons organize social groups, and mice mate on the basis of forms of learning that rest predominantly on the instructions encoded in their genes and evoked by appropriate patterns of external stimuli: physical keys inserted into organic locks. But men build dams and shelters, locate food, organize their social groups, or find sexual partners under the guidance of instructions encoded in flow charts and blueprints, hunting lore, moral systems and aesthetic judgments: conceptual structures molding formless talents.[11]

Culture, here, replaces biology. Culture molds and creates a formless humanity, culture in the active voice and mankind in the passive. It is not that such a view is simply wrong. Indeed, Geertz's insistence on the centrality of interpretation in the human sciences has much to offer, particularly to Marxism. But compared to historical materialism, modern cultural anthropology

lacks the key notions of radical human needs and of humanity's self-creation through labor in response to those needs. No doubt, culture as intersubjectively produced meaning creates socially-formed persons, but surely people create and produce culture. It is only by neglecting the second half of this dialectic that anthropologists have turned cultural systems into reified texts, waiting to be interpreted and translated.[12]

It is no accident that almost all of Marx's concepts to be explicated next – "forces of production," "relations of production," and "mode of production" – build on the root "to produce." Production is the privileged point of entry for understanding social totalities, for understanding how people make their own history but not exactly as they choose.

[...] In regard to the concept of structure, at basic issue is the simple notion that societies have some degree of internal consistency, that certain types of economy "go with" certain types of polity, "go with" certain types of religion. Social totalities, in other words, have "structures," more-or-less consistent arrangements of parts that stamp a character on the whole – despite variation. These structures can take only a limited number of forms, since not everything goes with everything else. As a consequence, world history unfolds as a discontinuous succession of epochs. The broad patterns that hold across epochs, the basic ways of producing human social life, are what makes it possible to talk of capitalist or feudal societies, indeed, what makes it possible to talk more generally of modes or ways of producing.

[...]

[...] [P]roductive powers are anything that can be *used* in productive interaction with nature. To qualify as a productive power, "a facility must be capable of use by a producing agent in such a way that production occurs (partly) as a result of its use, and it is someone's purpose that the facility so contribute to production."[13] Notice what this definition presupposes: First, an objective knowledge of what contributes to production in any place at any time; second, a hermeneutic understanding of culturally relative systems of meaning, so that a person's intention to produce can be adequately interpreted. It is the intersection of these two considerations that defines productive powers according to Cohen's definition.

On this reading, productive powers are not simply raw materials or tools; more inclusively, they are human skills, productive knowledge, and even technical aspects of cooperation in the labor process, all of these being intentionally used to produce.[14] These factors Marx considered equally "material" in that they can be used to produce materially. But most modern readers and even some "materialists" would probably classify objects, knowledge, and the technical aspects of cooperation as variously material, ideal, and social.

This unusual way of defining the category of the material is related to Marx's central notion of human nature, of human beings creating themselves through productive action in the world. Productive powers are the resources that people use in that process. Marx's focus is on persons acting, using ideas and objects to change nature. Notice the difference it would make if the category of the material were confined to objects outside human beings, outside human consciousness. Then, if one were a materialist, one would see human society only as it is conditioned by its environment, the "objective" material world. This point of view, it must be emphasized, is different from Marx's materialism; it translates an active vision of humankind into the passive voice.[15]

It might be objected that the preceding definition of productive powers is altogether too broad, that it includes almost everything social. After all, do not all social arrangements, in some sense, contribute to production? Marx himself wrote, "...*all* human relations and functions, however and in whatever form they appear, influence material production and have a more or less decisive influence upon it."[16] Consider an example [...] of a group of farmers who, in order to work their fields, must be protected by soldiers.[17] Is protection, then, a productive power? Not according to the definition above. Soldiers' protection is not directly used in productive interaction with nature; it is not required by the production process itself. This is not to say, of course, that in some wider social sense, soldiers' services do not make production possible, and, as I shall point out directly, Marx was centrally concerned with just such sorts of contingent connections between productive powers and their social integuments.

Having outlined a definition of productive powers, I should note their outstanding characteristic for Marx's theoretical scheme as a whole:

that productive powers tend to expand in world history. At least two aspects of this assertion should be clarified. First, no evolutionary teleology is implied. Instead, in the most general sense, the anterior cause of this tendency is located in human nature itself. Humans everywhere have felt a need to actualize themselves through labor. And through labor, people have developed their powers and skills in a continuous dialectic with nature. Increase in productive knowledge is, then, a critical part of what makes human beings human.

But more specifically, the expansion of productive powers has to be seen relative to different kinds of societies. [...] Different relations of production give variously placed social groups different (and sometimes opposed) interests in technological improvement. But no revolutionary group in any society, it seems, has ever had direct interests in reducing labor productivity. This means that, given *any* socially conditioned impulse toward technological improvement, the development of productive powers is, in Eric Olin Wright's phrase, "sticky downwards."[18] That is, societal transformations tend to preserve the level of productive powers already achieved.

This image of technical progress as a variously paced, fitful climb upward must be understood in relation to the second point I wish to emphasize: The tendency for powers to expand can be seen only at a world level. Particular societies may and indeed have stagnated; some have even experienced local declines in the level of productive powers. As I shall point out below, relations of production can prevent technical development beyond a certain point. For any particular society in stasis, there is no reason to believe that new social relations compatible with the further expansion of powers *must* develop. In fact, what has happened most often in world history is that technical knowledge diffuses from place to place, and typically the most "advanced" societies are not the ones that give rise to the next evolutionary development. Rather, peripheral groups that are the recipient of the productive knowledge of their more "advanced" neighbors often leap-frog ahead.[19]

I have referred to the level of development of productive powers. Just what this notion entails should be considered. A society's mass of productive powers is determined by two factors: first, average labor productivity, and second, population.

The product of these two factors yields the level of productive powers. In this formulation, population itself is not a productive power, yet it enters into the determination of the level of productive powers.[20]

To return to Marx's argument, the next step is famous but not well understood: The level of productive powers "determines" the Produktionsverhältnisse, so-called relations of production.

> The general conclusion at which I arrived and which once reached, became the guiding principle of my studies can be summarized as follows. In the social production of their existence, men inevitably enter into definite relations, which are independent of their will, namely relations of production [Produktionsverhältnisse] appropriate to a given stage in the development of their material forces of production [Produktivkräfte]. The totality of these relations of production constitutes the economic structure of society, the real foundation, on which arises a legal and political superstructure [Überbau] and to which correspond definite forms of social consciousness.[21]

What are Produktionsverhältnisse? Once again, Marx's language confounds our expectations, for Produktionsverhältnisse are not just social relationships formed in production but, more centrally, the basic structure of power that determines differential control over the division of the fruits of society's labor. Otherwise put, Produktionsverhältnisse are "productive inequalities," and it is this phrase I shall use in translating Marx's term rather than the more literal "relations of production."[22]

Productive inequalities are, then, relationships among groups that place some in materially superordinate positions in relation to others. Moreover, superordination depends precisely on subordination. [...] [I]f there are "poor" people, there must be "rich" people.[23] The labor of the first supports the existence of the second. *How* this difference is instituted, it must be emphasized, is not specified. To qualify, productive inequalities must delineate differences in power over society's total product. But productive inequalities do not have to be constituted in relation to immediate control over productive powers themselves.

[...]

Why do productive inqualities occupy such a central place in Marx's thought? The answer is that they locate the basic divisions within any society, the lines of potential opposition – of contradiction. Marx saw these as the potential fault lines along which tensions tend to build up, are routinely dissipated by small readjustments, and are sometimes violently resolved by radical realignments. These fault lines are structural; they do not necessarily lead to actual struggle and conflict (indeed, the function of the superstructure is precisely to prevent such occurrences). Nevertheless, contradictions always exist as potentialities; they lie just below the surface.[24]

The concept of productive inequality has to be related, finally, to Marx's view of human nature. Every person needs to realize himself or herself in free, creative activity in the world. Productive inequalities set up social obstacles to that process; they alienate groups from the social product that is required for human self-realization at any particular technological level. Different sets of productive inequalities institute different degrees of alienation, different depths of inequality, that vary from relatively shallow and easily contained ones to those that can be resolved only by revolutionary transformations.[25] In this sense, contradictions in technologically simple societies are less dynamic, less tense, than those in capitalist ones.

It is precisely Marx's concept of essential human nature that makes his theory different from orthodox functionalist theories of social integration. In functionalism, there is no notion that particular social and cultural orders can come into conflict with human nature. Instead, societies must be organized somehow, and complex societies can only be organized hierarchically. Social hierarchies, in turn, must be legitimated, and the systems of values and beliefs that seem to be best at this task are evolutionarily selected. One expects a certain amount of conflict at all levels of the system inasmuch as common values are not perfectly inculcated into each new generation. But conflicts do not sum into a pattern, nor do they propel social change; they are merely the friction that must be overcome in all forms of social integration.

Contrast Marx's point of view expressed in this well-known passage from *Capital*:

> The specific economic form in which unpaid surplus labor is pumped out of direct producers determines the relationship of domination and

servitude, as this grows directly out of production itself and reacts back on it in turn as a determinant. On this is based the entire configuration of the economic community arising from the actual relations of production, and hence also its specific political form. It is in each case the direct relationship of the owners of the conditions of production to the immediate producers – a relationship whose particular form naturally corresponds always to a certain level of development of the type and manner of labor, and hence to its social productive power – in which we find the innermost secret, the hidden basis of the entire social edifice.[26]

If productive inequalities are the "hidden basis of the entire social edifice," how are they regularly reproduced? How is a system of power that limits the actualization of what Marx took to be universal human needs able to persist? Nothing we have said so far provides a satisfactory answer.

Let me outline a response to this question for capitalist society, one made famous by Marx's analysis in *Capital*. At the start of any production process, capitalist society is divided by productive inequalities into two opposed classes: capitalists who control the great mass of productive powers versus workers who control no such powers, except their own capacities for labor. Capitalists, therefore, have the means to set up enterprises; they have the money to buy machines and to hire workers. Workers, by contrast, own nothing but their own labor power. Without access to other powers, workers cannot initiate production on their own. They have only two options: to sell their labor power to capitalists or to starve. Because workers control their own labor power, they can choose *which* capitalist to work for. But the structure of the economy requires them to work for *some* capitalist.

So capitalists buy labor power and workers sell it. At this point, production proper commences, and we begin to see, for the first time, how control over productive powers is translated into power over workers in the production process – what William Shaw aptly calls "work" relations of production.[27] It is, by and large, the capitalist who organizes and directs production; it is he who appoints managers who oversee and maintain the pace of work. And the constant imperative is always the production of

more in less time. Workers, of course, are not helpless; they can resist in various ways, organize into unions, and so forth. But the capitalist retains the upper hand. And retaining the upper hand, he appropriates the product at the end of the production process. By virtue of the fundamental power asymmetry established in production, the capitalist is typically left with a surplus after selling the product and paying his costs – a surplus created by the labor of workers. This surplus labor can then be turned into yet more capital, and the circle is completed. The contradiction between workers and capitalists has not only been reproduced; it has been deepened and augmented, for the capitalist is relatively richer and workers relatively poorer (relative, that is, to each other).

This circular movement – from an original pattern of control over productive powers to control over people in production to a restoration (and perhaps augmentation) of the original pattern of control over productive powers – is what Marx called a reproduction schema. Notice particularly that the story told above is directly dependent on a whole array of particular legal institutions – contracts defined and backed by the power of the state – and cultural concepts – not the least of which is that labor is a commodity to be bought and sold just like any other thing. In other words, in constructing this story of reproduction, we have left the realm of de facto powers specified in the notion of productive inequalities and have entered a socially and culturally specific world of particular practices with particular meanings: the superstructure.

We are forced to the conclusion that (1) Marx's own reproduction schemata for capitalism include what he called the Überbau or superstructure, and more generally (2) it is precisely the superstructure that allows for and that explains the reproduction of productive inequalities.

For a last time, we are misled by Marx's language. Ordinarily, if something is described as having a base and a superstructure, we think of the base as a foundation. It supports the superstructure; without the foundation, the superstructure would fall to the ground. Yet, if the argument presented here is correct, the truth of historical materialism is closer to the opposite. Superstructures provide one of the keys to historical materialism; they explain how productive inequalities are reproduced.

What, then, can be said about superstructures, about reproduction schemata? Perhaps the first point to make is a negative one. Not all legal and political arrangements nor all systems of ideas can be counted as part of what Marx called the superstructure. Such a course would lead to innumerable difficulties. Science, for example, would have to be placed in the superstructure (when we have already placed aspects of it in the productive powers). And if *all* forms of law, politics, and ideas were seen as maintaining productive inequalities, then we would have disposed of Marx's key concept of contradiction – that is, we would have deprived the dominated groups of society of any impulse to resist. In a phrase, we would have functionalized Marx's social theory.

E. P. Thompson, in a study of law in eighteenth-century England, sums up the role of contradiction in the legal order this way:

> We reach, then, not a simple conclusion (law = class power) but a complex and contradictory one. On the one hand, it is true that the law did mediate existent class relations to the advantage of the rulers.... On the other hand, the law mediated these class relations through legal forms, which imposed, again and again, inhibitions upon the actions of the rulers.... There were even occasions (one recalls John Wilkes and several of the trials of the 1790s) when the Government itself retired from the courts defeated. Such occasions served, paradoxically, to consolidate power, to enhance its legitimacy, and to inhibit revolutionary movements. But, to turn the paradox around, these same occasions served to bring power even further within constitutional control.[28]

Without compromising the existence of contradiction, the notion of reproduction schemata requires only three things: (1) The existence of systems of ideas in public discourse that culturally construct the power of superior groups by predominantly (but not totally) naturalizing productive relations. (2) The organization of institutions that will adjudicate social conflicts (including those arising out of economic contradictions) so as, by and large, to allow contradictions to be reproduced anew. (3) The institutionalization of coercive force that can be used to protect the superior positions of dominant groups whenever

(1) or (2) fails. These three aspects of reproduction schemata, which combine variously the functions of "mask" and "weapon," relate respectively to (1) ideology, (2) law, and (3) political organization.[29] I shall take up each in turn.

(1) In the formulation above, I spoke of ideology as constructing and naturalizing power. In doing so, I deliberately avoided any formulation that might suggest that power may stably exist apart from ideology. In this sense, it would be misleading to say that ideology "legitimates" power, as if power could exist on its own. The second part of my definition, naturalization, means first of all that the great majority of the group in power will see their positions as so clothed in an aura of factuality, so meaningfully given that they naturally act to preserve their power. (This does not prevent individuals from, as Marx said, "going to the other side.") And, second, naturalization requires that a large enough section of the exploited group live within dominant values and beliefs a large enough portion of the time so that opposition is at least divided.

[...] [T]he extent to which exploited groups accept dominant values is a complex problem. In any case, it would be a mistake to see ideology as simple trickery or false consciousness. As E. P. Thompson argued in relation to law, "people are not as stupid as some structuralist philosophers suppose them to be. They will not be mystified by the first man who puts on a wig."[30] Most ideologies contain partial truths, and their "falseness" is due not to blanket error but to unwarranted generalization across contexts. Part of the exercise of constructing reproduction schemata is, then, to understand the particular productive contexts in which ideologies "make sense." Within those contexts, ideologies contain their truths. But what makes ideologies ideologies is precisely a lack of recognition of the context that renders their claims persuasive.[31]

(2) Even if ideology played its role perfectly (it never does), there would still be a need for socially recognized ways of resolving conflict. Not every society has specifically legal institutions such as courts and professional judges, yet all have regularized ways of settling, or at least dampening, social conflicts. Conflicts can perhaps be grouped into two kinds: those that coincide with economic contradictions as defined by productive inequalities, and those that crosscut such contradictions.

Conflicts that coincide with contradictions are, obviously, the most dangerous for social reproduction. For those cases, *if* societies are to persist in the same mode of production, methods of resolution must exist that will uphold the power of dominant groups. Exactly how this is accomplished is often a complex matter and varies from outright denial of rights to certain categories of persons (slaves in slave-based societies), to the formal exclusion of categories of persons from participation in legal procedures (women, even those directly involved, are not allowed to participate in divorce cases in some technologically simple societies), and finally to the de facto exclusion of still other groups from recourse to the law (workers in capitalist societies are generally too poor to fight certain legal matters).

Conflicts that crosscut contradictions are a good deal less threatening and may even contribute to social stability. For example, lords (allied with peasants) fighting other lords (allied with other peasants) can do much to prevent the contradiction between all lords and peasants from becoming too visible, from erupting into overt conflict. Accordingly, such kinds of conflicts may resist methods for settling them longer than those discussed above.

(3) Finally, neither ideology nor law is enough. Both are usually backed by coercive force. The "amount" of institutionalized coercive force varies with the depth of material contradictions. For example, the power differences between husbands and wives in relatively egalitarian hunting and gathering societies are slight. Still, the power of men over women in such societies is sometimes reinforced by gang rape. Whatever the amount, organized coercion typically reinforces and depends on both ideology and forms of conflict resolution. All are parts of the reproduction of productive inequalities.

To recapitulate the concepts discussed so far, productive powers are anything that can be used in the material process of production – tools, raw materials, scientific ideas, the technical aspects of organizing labor. Productive inequalities, the next category Marx introduced, are patterns of effective power over the production process and over the total social product. Reproduction schemata, finally, are the set of superstructural discourses and practices within which productive inequalities are constructed and reproduced.

Through conscious action, people (unconsciously) reproduce the whole mode of production in which they live – their way of life. Social reproduction does not occur entirely behind the backs of actors. It is probable that people in all societies have some understanding of the inequalities that order their lives, some insight into the oppression that limits their being. This knowledge remains, however, typically partial and unclarified, hard to dredge up to the light of day, difficult to systematize in public discourse. It remains repressed – a part of what Fredric Jameson has called the political unconscious.[32] [...]

Notes

1   Marx, "The Eighteenth Brumaire of Louis Bonaparte," in Marx and Engels, *Collected Works*, vol. 11 (London: Lawrence & Wishart, [1852] 1979), p. 103.

2   The notion of agency is not well defined in recent discussions in social theory. I use it in two senses, the first of which [...] might be called epochal agency: that is, patterns of individual action, motivated by particular meanings and practices, the result of which is the reproduction of certain broad structures of inequality. This sense of agency is hardly opposed to the idea of structure; exactly the opposite, it is required in order to understand how structures are reproduced. The second kind of agency, what might be called historical agency, is different; it involves struggles between groups of various kinds, set in specific space-time, that put into question the continuance of inequalities. This "questioning" may or may not result in fundamental transformations. See E. P. Thompson, *The Poverty of Theory and Other Essays* (New York: Monthly Review Press, 1978); Perry Anderson, *Arguments Within English Marxism* (London: Verso, 1980); Anthony Giddens, *Central Problems in Social Theory: Action, Structure and Contradiction in Social Analysis* (Berkeley: University of California Press, 1979).

3   John Plamenatz, *Karl Marx's Philosophy of Man* (Oxford: Clarendon Press, 1975), chs. 2–3; Bertell Ollman, *Alienation: Marx's Conception of Man in Capitalist Society*, 2nd edn. (Cambridge: Cambridge University Press, 1976), chs. 7–17; John McMurtry, *The Structure of Marx's World-View* (Princeton:

Princeton University Press, 1978), ch. 1; Norman
Geras, *Marx and Human Nature: Refutation of a
Legend* (London: New Left Books, 1983); Jon Elster, *Making Sense of Marx* (Cambridge: Cambridge University Press, 1985), ch. 2.

4   Clifford Geertz, *The Interpretation of Cultures*
(New York: Basic Books, 1973), p. 40.

5   Ibid., p. 30.

6   Allen W. Wood, *Karl Marx* (London: Routledge &
Kegan Paul, 1981), p. 28.

7   Marx, *Capital*, vol. 1, tr. Ben Fowkes (New York:
Vintage, [1867] 1976), p. 284.

8   Marx's arguments about the "species-being" of
humanity play the role of an assumption in his
theories about society. They can be defended philosophically and politically, but considered as part
of a scientific attempt to understand human societies, these arguments are assumptions that
cannot be tested in themselves. They allow "testable" propositions to be formed.

9   Whether this need is subjectively felt in any
particular society is another question. Jon Elster
defines objective alienation as the situation that
occurs when satisfiable needs are large compared
to actual and to satisfied needs. This definition
contrasts with subjective alienation, in which
actual needs are large but satisfied ones small. See
Making Sense of Marx, pp. 74–8. In general,
epochal analyses [...] correlate with the notion of
objective alienation, but historical analyses [...]
depend upon the degree of subjective alienation.

I believe that Elster is wrong when he writes,
"In precapitalist society men were not objectively alienated, since even with a reorganization
of the production it would not have been possible to satisfy needs much wider than those
actually satisfied" (p. 77). Nonetheless, it is true
that the distance between what is and what could
be has been enormously expanded by technological progress, particularly by capitalist production. As a correlate, revolution – a process in
which men and women more or less consciously
attempt to reshape society – is a relatively recent
phenomenon in world history.

10 Marx, "Economic and Philosophical Manuscripts,"
Early Writings, tr. Rodney Livingstone and Gregor
Benton (New York: Vintage, [1934] 1975), pp. 328–9.

11 Geertz, *Interpretation of Cultures*, p. 50.

12 See William Roseberry, "Balinese Cockfights and
the Seduction of Anthropology," *Anthropologies
and Histories: Essays in Culture, History, and
Political Economy* (New Brunswick: Rutgers University Press, 1929), pp. 17–29.

13 G. A. Cohen, *Karl Marx's Theory of History: A
Defence* (Oxford: Clarendon, 1978), p. 32. See Jon
Elster's extended commentary on Cohen's definition

in *Making Sense of Marx* (Cambridge: Cambridge
University Press, 1985), pp. 243–53, particularly
his discussion of the difference between extensive
and intensive notions of development of powers.

14 Cohen argues that work relations themselves are not
productive powers, but that knowledge of ways of
organizing labor is *(Karl Marx's Theory of History*,
pp. 113–4). For a critique of Cohen, see Richard
W. Miller, *Analyzing Marx: Morality, Power and History*
(Princeton: Princeton University Press, 1984),
p. 194. Finally, William Shaw has argued that work
relations should be counted as a subtype of "relations of production" (*Marx's Theory of History*,
Stanford: Stanford University Press, 1978, pp. 32–6).

15 Marxism's definition of the material gives it a different theoretical cast from, for example, strands of
North American anthropology such as evolutionism and cultural ecology. Anthropologists in the
latter traditions tend to view the "hard" realities of
environment, technology, and population as basic.
Human beings have to adapt their culture to them.
But notice the peculiar one-sidedness in this point
of view: Technology, population, and even environment are to some extent created and shaped by men
and women. The concept of adaptation, by itself,
cannot capture the active side of human history.

16 Marx, *Theories of Surplus Value*, Part I, trans.
Emile Burns, S. Ryazanskaya, ed. (Moscow:
Progress Publishers, [1905–10] 1963), p. 288.

17 Cohen, *Karl Marx's Theory of History*, pp. 33–4.

18 Eric Olin Wright, "Giddens's Critique of Marxism," *New Left Review* 138 (1983): 27–9.

19 Yuri I. Semenov, "The Theory of Socio-Economic
Formations and World History," and Ernest Gellner,
"A Russian Marxist Philosophy of History," in Er-
nest Gellner, ed., *Soviet and Western Anthropology*
(London: Duckworth, 1980), pp. 29–82.

20 This is a different formulation from Cohen's and
is inspired by Elster's discussion in *Making Sense
of Marx*, pp. 249–53.

21 Marx, *A Contribution to the Critique of Political
Economy*, trans. S. W. Ryazanskaya (Moscow:
Progress Publishers, [1859] 1970), p. 20.

22 One difficulty with the phrase "productive
inequality" is that it may suggest that inequality is a
required aspect of production in any form. Although
there is good reason to believe that all societies to
date have been organized around material inequalities, I do not assume that this outcome is inevitable.
Productive inequalities can theoretically take a
number of values – including zero.

23 Sidney W. Mintz, "American Anthropology in the
Marxist Tradition," in Sidney W. Mintz et al., eds.,
*On Marxian Perspectives in Anthropology: Essays
in Honor of Harry Hoijer, 1981* (Malibu: Undena
Publications, 1984), pp. 18–19.

24 For a review of the notion of contradiction and an exposition of its central place in social – not merely logical – analysis, see Giddens, *Central Problems*, ch. 4.

25 As Allen Wood, *Karl Marx*, p. 36, argues, "The degree to which people are alienated is a function of the extent to which their lives fall short of actualizing the human essence, of exercising their essential human powers. These powers, however, are not fixed but historically varying and on the whole expanding. Oppressed people will therefore become more and more alienated the greater the gap becomes between the essential powers belonging to the human species and the degree to which their own lives participate in the development and exercise of these powers."

26 Marx, *Capital*, vol. 3, trans. David Fernbach (New York: Vintage, [1894] 1981), p. 927.

27 Shaw, *Marx's Theory of History*, pp. 32–6.

28 E. P. Thompson, *Whigs and Hunters: The Origin of the Black Act* (Harmondsworth: Penguin, 1977), pp. 264–5.

29 McMurtry, *The Structure of Marx's World-View*, p. 120.

30 Thompson, *Whigs and Hunters*, p. 262.

31 See Pierre Bourdieu, *Outline of a Theory of Practice*, trans. R. Nice (Cambridge: Cambridge University Press, [1972] 1977), pp. 159–71.

32 Fredric Jameson, *The Political Unconscious: Narrative as a Socially Symbolic Act* (Ithaca: Cornell University Press, 1981).

33

Structures and the Habitus

Pierre Bourdieu

Methodological objectivism, a necessary moment in all research, by the break with primary experience and the construction of objective relations which it accomplishes, demands its own supersession. In order to escape the *realism of the structure*, which hypostatizes systems of objective relations by converting them into totalities already constituted outside of individual history and group history, it is necessary to pass from the *opus operatum* to the *modus operandi*, from statistical regularity or algebraic structure to the principle of the production of this observed order, and to construct the theory of practice, or, more precisely, the theory of the mode of generation of practices, which is the precondition for establishing an experimental science of the *dialectic of the internalization of externality and the externalization of internality*, or, more simply, of incorporation and objectification.

A False Dilemma: Mechanism and Finalism

The structures constitutive of a particular type of environment (e.g. the material conditions of existence characteristic of a class condition)

produce *habitus*, systems of durable, transposable *dispositions*,[1] structured structures predisposed to function as structuring structures, that is, as principles of the generation and structuring of practices and representations which can be objectively "regulated" and "regular" without in any way being the product of obedience to rules, objectively adapted to their goals without presupposing a conscious aiming at ends or an express mastery of the operations necessary to attain them and, being all this, collectively orchestrated without being the product of the orchestrating action of a conductor.

Even when they appear as the realization of the explicit, and explicitly stated, purposes of a project or plan, the practices produced by the habitus, as the strategy-generating principle enabling agents to cope with unforeseen and everchanging situations, are only apparently determined by the future. If they seem determined by anticipation of their own consequences, thereby encouraging the finalist illusion, the fact is that, always tending to reproduce the objective structures of which they are the product, they are determined by the past conditions which have produced the principle of their production, that

From *Outline of a Theory of Practice*, trans. Richard Nice (Cambridge: Cambridge University Press, 1977), pp. 72–3, 76–84 , 85–7, 214–16. English translation © Cambridge University Press, 1977. Reprinted with permission of Librairie Droz S.A., Genève.

Anthropology in Theory: Issues in Epistemology, Second Edition. Edited by Henrietta L. Moore and Todd Sanders.
© 2014 John Wiley & Sons, Inc. Published 2014 by John Wiley & Sons, Inc.

is, by the actual outcome of identical or inter-changeable past practices, which coincides with their own outcome to the extent (*and only to the extent*) that the objective structures of which they are the product are prolonged in the structures within which they function. Thus, for example, in the interaction between two agents or groups of agents endowed with the same habitus (say A and B), everything takes place as if the actions of each of them (say, a_1 for A) were organized in relation to the reactions they call forth from any agent possessing the same habitus (say, b_1, B's reaction to a_1) so that they objectively imply anticipation of the reaction which these reactions in turn call forth (say a_2, the reaction to b_1). But the teleolog-ical description according to which each action has the purpose of making possible the reaction to the reaction it arouses (individual A performing action a_1, e.g. a gift or challenge, in order to make individual B produce action b_1, a counter-gift or riposte, so as to be able to perform action a_2, a stepped-up gift or challenge) is quite as naive as the mechanistic description which presents the action and the riposte as moments in a sequence of programmed actions produced by a mechanical apparatus. The habitus is the source of these series of moves which are objectively organized as strategies without being the product of a genuine strategic intention – which would presuppose at least that they are perceived as one strategy among other possible strategies.[2]

It is necessary to abandon all theories which explicitly or implicitly treat practice as a mechanical reaction, directly determined by the antecedent conditions and entirely reducible to the mechanical functioning of pre-established assemblies, "models" or "rôles" – which one would, moreover, have to postulate in infinite number, like the chance configurations of stimuli capable of triggering them from outside, thereby con-demning oneself to the grandiose and desperate undertaking of the anthropologist, armed with fine positivist courage, who recorded 480 ele-mentary units of behaviour in twenty minutes' observation of his wife in the kitchen.[3] But rejection of mechanistic theories in no way implies that, in accordance with another obliga-tory option, we should bestow on some creative free will the free and wilful power to constitute, on the instant, the meaning of the situation by projecting the ends aiming at its transformation,

and that we should reduce the objective inten-tions and constituted significations of actions and works to the conscious and deliberate intentions of their authors. [...]

It is, of course, never ruled out that the responses of the habitus may be accompanied by a strategic calculation tending to carry on quasi-consciously the operation the habitus carries on in a quite different way, namely an estimation of chances which assumes the transformation of the past effect into the expected objective. But the fact remains that these responses are defined first in relation to a system of objective potenti-alities, immediately inscribed in the present, things to do or not to do, to say or not to say, in relation to a *forthcoming* reality which – in contrast to the future conceived as "absolute possibility" (*absolute Möglichkeit*), in Hegel's sense, projected by the pure project of a "negative freedom" – puts itself forward with an urgency and a claim to existence excluding all deliberation. To eliminate the need to resort to "rules", it would be necessary to establish in each case a complete description (which invocation of rules allows one to dispense with) of the relation between the habitus, as a socially constituted system of cognitive and moti-vating structures, and the socially structured situation in which the agents' *interests* are defined, and with them the objective functions and subjective motivations of their practices. It would then become clear that as Weber indicated, the juridical or customary rule is never more than a *secondary principle* of the determination of prac-tices, intervening when the primary principle, interest, fails.[4]

Symbolic – that is, *conventional* and *conditional* – stimulations, which act only on condition they encounter agents conditioned to perceive them, tend to impose themselves unconditionally and necessarily when inculcation of the arbitrary abolishes the arbitrariness of both the inculcation and the significations inculcated. The world of urgencies and of goals already achieved, of uses to be made and paths to be taken, of objects endowed with a "permanent teleological character", in Husserl's phrase, tools, instruments and institu-tions, the world of practicality, can grant only a conditional freedom – *liberesi liceret* – rather like that of the magnetic needle which Leibniz imag-ined actually enjoyed turning northwards. If one regularly observes a very close correlation between the scientifically constructed *objective probabilities* (e.g. the chances of access to a particular good) and *subjective aspirations* ("motivations" or "needs") or, in other terms, between the *a posteriori* or *ex post* probability known from past experience and the *a priori* or *ex ante* probability attributed to it, this is not because agents consciously adjust their aspirations to an exact evaluation of their chances of success, like a player regulating his bets as a function of perfect information as to his chances of winning, as one implicitly presupposes whenever, forgetting the "everything takes place as if", one *proceeds as if* game theory or the calculation of probabilities, each constructed *against* spontaneous dispositions, amounted to anthropological descriptions of practice.

Completely reversing the tendency of objectivism, we can, on the contrary, seek in the scientific theory of probabilities (or strategies) not an anthropological model of practice, but the elements of a *negative description* of the implicit logic of the *spontaneous interpretation of statistics* (e.g. the prospensity to privilege early experiences) which the scientific theory necessarily contains because it is explicitly constructed against that logic. Unlike the estimation of probabilities which science constructs methodically on the basis of controlled experiments from data established according to precise rules, practical evaluation of the likelihood of the success of a given action in a given situation brings into play a whole body of wisdom, sayings, commonplaces, ethical precepts ("that's not for the likes of us") and, at a deeper level, the unconscious principles of the *ethos* which, being the product of a learning process dominated by a determinate type of objective regularities, determines "reasonable" and "unreasonable" conduct for every agent subjected to those regularities.[5] "We are no sooner acquainted with the impossibility of satisfying any desire", says Hume in *A Treatise of Human Nature*, "than the desire itself vanishes." And Marx in the *Economic and Philosophical Manuscripts*: "If I have no money for travel, I have no *need*, i.e. no real and self-realizing need, to travel. If I have a vocation to study, but no money for it, I have *no* vocation to study, i.e. no *real, true* vocation."

Because the dispositions durably inculcated by objective conditions (which science apprehends through statistical regularities as the probabilities objectively attached to a group or class) engender aspirations and practices objectively compatible with those objective requirements, the most improbable practices are excluded, either totally without examination, as *unthinkable*, or at the cost of the *double negation* which inclines agents to make a virtue of necessity, that is, to refuse what is anyway refused and to love the inevitable. The very conditions of production of the ethos, *necessity made into a virtue*, are such that the expectations to which it gives rise tend to ignore the restriction to which the validity of any calculus of probabilities is subordinated, namely that the conditions of the experiments should not have been modified. Unlike scientific estimations, which are corrected after each experiment in accordance with rigorous rules of calculation, practical estimates give disproportionate weight to early experiences: the structures characteristic of a determinate type of conditions of existence, through the economic and social necessity which they bring to bear on the relatively autonomous universe of family relationships, or more precisely, through the mediation of the specifically familial manifestations of this external necessity (sexual division of labour, domestic morality, cares, strife, tastes, etc.), produce the structures of the habitus which become in turn the basis of perception and appreciation of all subsequent experience. Thus, as a result of the *hysteresis effect* necessarily implied in the logic of the constitution of habitus, practices are always liable to incur negative sanctions when the environment with which they are actually confronted is too distant from that to which they are objectively fitted. This is why generation conflicts oppose not age-classes separated by natural properties, but habitus which have been produced by different *modes of generation*, that is, by conditions of existence which, in imposing different definitions of the impossible, the possible, and the probable, cause one group to experience as natural or reasonable practices or aspirations which another group finds unthinkable or scandalous, and vice versa.

Structures, Habitus and Practices

The habitus, the durably installed generative principle of regulated improvisations, produces practices which tend to reproduce the regularities immanent in the objective conditions of the production of their generative principle, while adjusting to the demands inscribed as objective potentialities in the situation, as defined by the cognitive and motivating structures making up the habitus. It follows that these practices cannot be directly deduced either from the objective conditions, defined as the instantaneous sum of the stimuli which may appear to have directly triggered them, or from the conditions which produced the durable principle of their production. These practices can be accounted for only by relating the objective *structure* defining the social conditions of the production of the habitus which engendered them to the conditions in which this habitus is operating, that is, to the *conjuncture* which, short of a radical transformation, represents a particular state of this structure. In practice, it is the habitus, history turned into nature, i.e. denied as such, which accomplishes practically the relating of these two systems of relations in and through the production of practice. The "unconscious" is never anything other than the forgetting of history which history itself produces by incorporating the objective structures it produces in the second natures of habitus:

> ...in each of us, in varying proportions, there is part of yesterday's man; it is yesterday's man who inevitably predominates in us, since the present amounts to little compared with the long past in the course of which we were formed and from which we result. Yet we do not sense this man of the past, because he is inveterate in us; he makes up the unconscious part of ourselves. Consequently we are led to take no account of him, any more than we take account of his legitimate demands. Conversely, we are very much aware of the most recent attainments of civilization, because, being recent, they have not yet had time to settle into our unconscious.[6]

Genesis amnesia is also encouraged (if not entailed) by the objectivist apprehension which, grasping the product of history as an *opus operatum*, a *fait accompli*, can only invoke the mysteries of pre-established harmony or the prodigies of conscious orchestration to account for what, apprehended in pure synchrony, appears as objective meaning, whether it be the internal coherence of works or institutions such as myths, rites, or bodies of law, or the objective co-ordination which the concordant or conflicting practices of the members of the same group or class at once manifest and presuppose (inasmuch as they imply a community of dispositions).

Each agent, wittingly or unwittingly, willy nilly, is a producer and reproducer of objective meaning. Because his actions and works are the product of a *modus operandi* of which he is not the producer and has no conscious mastery, they contain an "objective intention", as the Scholastics put it, which always outruns his conscious intentions. The schemes of thought and expression he has acquired are the basis for the *intentionless invention* of regulated improvisation. Endlessly overtaken by his own words, with which he maintains a relation of "carry and be carried", as Nicolaï Hartmann put it, the virtuoso finds in the *opus operatum* new triggers and new supports for the *modus operandi* from which they arise, so that his discourse continuously feeds off itself like a train bringing along its own rails.[7] If witticisms surprise their author no less than their audience, and impress as much by their retrospective necessity as by their novelty, the reason is that the *trouvaille* appears as the simple unearthing, at once accidental and irresistible, of a buried possibility. It is because subjects do not, strictly speaking, know what they are doing that what they do has more meaning than they know. The habitus is the universalizing mediation which causes an individual agent's practices, without either explicit reason or signifying intent, to be none the less "sensible" and "reasonable". That part of practices which remains obscure in the eyes of their own producers is the aspect by which they are objectively adjusted to other practices and to the structures of which the principle of their production is itself the product.[8]

One of the fundamental effects of the orchestration of habitus is the production of a common-sense world endowed with the *objectivity* secured by consensus on the meaning (*sens*) of practices and the world, in other words the harmonization of agents' experiences and the continuous reinforcement that each of them receives from the expression, individual or collective (in festivals, for example), improvised or programmed (commonplaces, sayings), of similar or identical experiences. The homogeneity of habitus is what – within the limits of the group of agents possessing the schemes (of production and interpretation) implied in their production – causes practices and works to be immediately intelligible and foreseeable, and hence taken for granted. This practical comprehension obviates the "intention" and "intentional transfer into the Other" dear to the phenomenologists, by dispensing, for the ordinary occasions of life, with close analysis of the nuances of another's practice and tacit or explicit inquiry ("What do you *mean*?") into his intentions. Automatic and impersonal, significant without intending to signify, ordinary practices lend themselves to an understanding no less automatic and impersonal: the picking up of the objective intention they express in no way implies "reactivation" of the "lived" intention of the agent who performs them.[9] "Communication of consciousnesses" presupposes community of "unconsciouses" (i.e. of linguistic and cultural competences). The deciphering of the objective intention of practices and works has nothing to do with the "reproduction" (*Nachbildung*, as the early Dilthey puts it) of lived experiences and the reconstitution, unnecessary and uncertain, of the personal singularities of an "intention" which is not their true origin.

The objective homogenizing of group or class habitus which results from the homogeneity of the conditions of existence is what enables practices to be objectively harmonized without any intentional calculation or conscious reference to a norm and mutually adjusted *in the absence of any direct interaction* or *a fortiori*, explicit co-ordination. "Imagine", Leibniz suggests,

> two clocks or watches in perfect agreement as to the time. This may occur in one of three ways. The first consists in mutual influence; the second is to appoint a skilful workman to correct them and synchronize them at all times; the third is to construct these clocks with such art and precision that one can be assured of their subsequent agreement.[10]

So long as, retaining only the first or at a pinch the second hypothesis, one ignores the true principle of the conductorless orchestration which gives regularity, unity, and systematicity to the practices of a group or class, and this even in the absence of any spontaneous or externally imposed organization of individual projects, one is condemned to the naive artificialism which recognizes no other principle unifying a group's or class's ordinary or extraordinary action than the conscious co-ordination of a conspiracy.[11] If the practices of the members of the same group or class are more and better harmonized than the agents know or wish, it is because, as Leibniz puts it, "following only [his] own laws", each "nonetheless agrees with the other".[12] The habitus is precisely this immanent law, *lex insita*, laid down in each agent by his earliest upbringing, which is the precondition not only for the co-ordination of practices but also for practices of co-ordination, since the corrections and adjustments the agents themselves consciously carry out presuppose their mastery of a common code and since undertakings of collective mobilization cannot succeed without a minimum of concordance between the habitus of the mobilizing agents (e.g. prophet, party leader, etc.) and the dispositions of those whose aspirations and world-view they express.

So it is because they are the product of dispositions which, being the internalization of the same objective structures, are objectively concerted that the practices of the members of the same group or, in a differentiated society, the same class are endowed with an objective meaning that is at once unitary and systematic, transcending subjective intentions and conscious projects whether individual or collective.[13] To describe the process of objectification and orchestration in the language of *interaction* and mutual adjustment is to forget that the interaction itself owes its form to the objective structures which have produced the dispositions of the interacting agents and which allot them their relative positions in the interaction and elsewhere. Every confrontation between agents in fact brings together, in an *interaction* defined by the *objective structure* of the relation between the groups they belong to (e.g. a boss giving orders to a subordinate, colleagues discussing their pupils, academics taking part in a symposium), systems of dispositions (carried by "natural persons") such as a linguistic competence and a cultural competence and, through these habitus, all the objective structures of which they are the product, structures which are active only when *embodied* in a competence acquired in the course of a particular history (with the different types of bilingualism or pronunciation, for example, stemming from different modes of acquisition).[14]

Thus, when we speak of class habitus, we are insisting, against all forms of the occasionalist illusion which consists in directly relating practices to properties inscribed in the situation, that "interpersonal" relations are never, except in appearance, *individual-to-individual* relationships and that the truth of the interaction is never entirely contained in the interaction. This is what social psychology and interactionism or ethnomethodology forget when, reducing the objective structure of the relationship between the assembled individuals to the conjunctural structure of their interaction in a particular situation and group, they seek to explain everything that occurs in an experimental or observed interaction in terms of the experimentally controlled characteristics of the situation, such as the relative spatial positions of the participants or the nature of the channels used. In fact it is their present and past positions in the social structure that biological individuals carry with them, at all times and in all places, in the form of dispositions which are so many marks of *social position* and hence of the social distance between objective positions, that is, between social persons conjuncturally brought together (in physical space, which is not the same thing as social space) and correlatively, so many reminders of this distance and of the conduct required in order to "keep one's distance" or to manipulate it strategically, whether symbolically or actually, to reduce it (easier for the dominant than for the dominated), increase it, or simply maintain it (by not "letting oneself go", not "becoming familiar", in short, "standing on one's dignity", or on the other hand, refusing to "take liberties" and "put oneself forward", in short "knowing one's place" and staying there).

Even those forms of interaction seemingly most amenable to description in terms of "intentional transfer into the Other", such as sympathy, friendship, or love, are dominated (as class homogamy attests), through the harmony of habitus, that is to say, more precisely, the harmony of ethos and tastes – doubtless sensed in the imperceptible cues of body *hexis* – by the objective structure of the relations between social conditions. The illusion of mutual election or predestination arises from ignorance of the social conditions for the harmony of aesthetic tastes or ethical leanings, which is thereby perceived as evidence of the ineffable affinities which spring from it.

In short, the habitus, the product of history, produces individual and collective practices, and hence history, in accordance with the schemes engendered by history. The system of dispositions – a past which survives in the present and tends to perpetuate itself into the future by making itself present in practices structured according to its principles, an internal law relaying the continuous exercise of the law of external necessities (irreducible to immediate conjunctural constraints) – is the principle of the continuity and regularity which objectivism discerns in the social world without being able to give them a rational basis. And it is at the same time the principle of the transformations and regulated revolutions which neither the extrinsic and instantaneous determinisms of a mechanistic sociologism nor the purely internal but equally punctual determination of voluntarist or spontaneist subjectivism are capable of accounting for.

It is just as true and just as untrue to say that collective actions produce the event or that they are its product. The conjuncture capable of transforming practices objectively co-ordinated because subordinated to partially or wholly identical objective necessities, into *collective action* (e.g. revolutionary action) is constituted in the dialectical relationship between, on the one hand a *habitus*, understood as a system of lasting, transposable dispositions which, integrating past experiences, functions at every moment as a *matrix of perceptions, appreciations, and actions* and makes possible the achievement of infinitely diversified tasks, thanks to analogical transfers of schemes permitting the solution of similarly shaped problems, and thanks to the unceasing corrections of the results obtained, dialectically produced by those results, and on the other hand, an *objective event* which exerts its action of conditional stimulation calling for or demanding a determinate response, only on those who are disposed to constitute it as such because they are endowed with a determinate type of dispositions (which are amenable to reduplication and reinforcement by the "awakening of class consciousness", that is, by the direct or indirect possession of a discourse capable of securing symbolic mastery of the practically mastered principles of the class habitus). Without ever being totally co-ordinated, since they are the product of "causal series" characterized by different structural durations, the dispositions and the situations which combine synchronically to constitute a determinate conjuncture are never wholly independent, since they are engendered by the objective structures, that is, in the last analysis, by the economic bases of the social formation in question. The hysteresis of habitus, which is inherent in the social conditions of the reproduction of the structures in habitus, is doubtless one of the foundations of the structural lag between opportunities and the dispositions to grasp them which is the cause of missed opportunities and, in particular, of the frequently observed incapacity to think historical crises in categories of perception and thought other than those of the past, albeit a revolutionary past.

If one ignores the dialectical relationship between the objective structures and the cognitive and motivating structures which they produce and which tend to reproduce them, if one forgets that these objective structures are themselves products of historical practices and are constantly reproduced and transformed by historical practices whose productive principle is itself the product of the structures which it consequently tends to reproduce, then one is condemned to reduce the relationship between the different social agencies (*instances*), treated as "different translations of the same sentence" – in a Spinozist metaphor which contains the truth of the objectivist language of "articulation" – to the logical formula enabling any one of them to be derived from any other. The unifying principle of practices in different domains which objectivist analysis would assign to separate "sub-systems", such as matrimonial strategies, fertility strategies, or economic choices, is nothing other than the habitus, the locus of practical realization of the "articulation" of fields which objectivism (from Parsons to the structuralist readers of Marx) lays out side by side without securing the means of discovering the real principle of the structural homologies or relations of transformation objectively established between them (which is not to deny that the structures are objectivities irreducible to their manifestation in the habitus which they produce and which tend to reproduce them). So long as one accepts the canonic opposition which, endlessly reappearing in new forms throughout the history of social thought, nowadays pits "humanist" against "structuralist" readings of Marx, to declare diametrical

opposition to subjectivism is not genuinely to *break* with it, but to fall into the fetishism of social laws to which objectivism consigns itself when in establishing between structure and practice the relation of the virtual to the actual, of the score to the performance, of essence to existence, it merely substitutes for the creative man of subjectivism a man subjugated to the dead laws of a natural history. And how could one underestimate the strength of the ideological couple subjectivism/ objectivism when one sees that the critique of the *individual* considered as *ens realissimum* only leads to his being made an epiphenomenon of hypostatized structure, and that the well-founded assertion of the primacy of objective relations results in products of human action, the structures, being credited with the power to develop in accordance with their own laws and to determine and overdetermine other structures?

Just as the opposition of language to speech as mere execution or even as a preconstructed object masks the opposition between the objective relations of the language and the dispositions making up linguistic competence, so the opposition between the structure and the individual against whom the structure has to be won and endlessly rewon stands in the way of construction of the dialectical relationship between the structure and the dispositions making up the habitus.

[...]

The habitus is the product of the work of inculcation and appropriation necessary in order for those products of collective history, the objective structures (e.g. of language, economy, etc.) to succeed in reproducing themselves more or less completely, in the form of durable dispositions, in the organisms (which one can, if one wishes, call individuals) lastingly subjected to the same conditionings, and hence placed in the same material conditions of existence. Therefore sociology treats as identical all the biological individuals who, being the product of the same objective conditions, are the supports of the same habitus: social class, understood as a system of objective determinations, must be brought into relation not with the individual or with the "class" as a *population*, i.e. as an aggregate of enumerable, measurable biological individuals, but with the class habitus, the system of dispositions (partially) common to all products of the same structures. Though it is impossible for *all* members of the same class (or even two of them) to have had the same experiences, in the same order, it is certain that each member of the same class is more likely than any member of another class to have been confronted with the situations most frequent for the members of that class. The objective structures which science apprehends in the form of statistical regularities (e.g. employment rates, income curves, probabilities of access to secondary education, frequency of holidays, etc.) inculcate, through the direct or indirect but always convergent experiences which give a social environment its *physiognomy*, with its "closed doors", "dead ends", and limited "prospects", that "art of assessing likelihoods", as Leibniz put it, of anticipating the objective future, in short, the sense of reality or realities which is perhaps the best-concealed principle of their efficacy.

In order to define the relations between class, habitus and the organic individuality which can never entirely be removed from sociological discourse inasmuch as, being given immediately to immediate perception (*intuitus personae*), it is also socially designated and recognized (name, legal identity, etc.) and is defined by a *social trajectory* strictly speaking irreducible to any other, the habitus could be considered as a subjective but not individual system of internalized structures, schemes of perception, conception, and action common to all members of the same group or class and constituting the precondition for all objectification and apperception: and the objective coordination of practices and the sharing of a world-view could be founded on the perfect impersonality and inter-changeability of singular practices and views. But this would amount to regarding all the practices or representations produced in accordance with identical schemes as impersonal and substitutable, like singular intuitions of space which, according to Kant, reflect none of the peculiarities of the individual ego. In fact, it is in a relation of homology, of diversity within homogeneity reflecting the diversity within homogeneity characteristic of their social conditions of production, that the singular habitus of the different members of the same class are united; the homology of world-views implies the systematic differences which separate singular world-views, adopted from singular but concerted standpoints. Since the history of the individual is never anything other than a certain specification of the collective history of his group or class, *each*

individual system of dispositions may be seen as a *structural variant* of all the other group or class habitus, expressing the difference between trajectories and positions inside or outside the class. "Personal" style, the particular stamp marking all the products of the same habitus, whether practices or works, is never more than a *deviation* in relation to the *style* of a period or class so that it relates back to the common style not only by its conformity – like Phidias, who, according to Hegel, had no "manner" – but also by the difference which makes the whole "manner".

The principle of these individual differences lies in the fact that, being the product of a chronologically ordered series of structuring determinations, the habitus, which at every moment structures in terms of the structuring experiences which produced it the structuring experiences which affect its structure, brings about a unique integration, dominated by the earliest experiences, of the experiences statistically common to the members of the same class. Thus, for example, the habitus acquired in the family underlies the structuring of school experiences (in particular the reception and assimilation of the specifically pedagogic message), and the habitus transformed by schooling, itself diversified, in turn underlies the structuring of all subsequent experiences (e.g. the reception and assimilation of the messages of the culture industry or work experiences), and so on, from restructuring to restructuring.

Springing from the encounter in an integrative organism of relatively independent causal series, such as biological and social determinisms, the habitus makes coherence and necessity out of accident and contingency: for example, the equivalences it establishes between positions in the division of labour and positions in the division between the sexes are doubtless not peculiar to societies in which the division of labour and the division between the sexes coincide almost perfectly. In a class society, all the products of a given agent, by an essential *overdetermination*, speak inseparably and simultaneously of his class - or, more precisely, his position in the social structure and his rising or falling trajectory – and of his (or her) body – or, more precisely, all the properties, always socially qualified, of which he or she is the bearer – sexual properties of course, but also physical properties, praised, like strength or beauty, or stigmatized. [...]

Notes

1 The word *disposition* seems particularly suited to express what is covered by the concept of habitus (defined as a system of dispositions). It expresses first the *result of an organizing action*, with a meaning close to that of words such as structure; it also designates a *way of being, a habitual state* (especially of the body) and, in particular, a *predisposition, tendency, propensity*, or *inclination*. [The semantic cluster of "disposition" is rather wider in French than in English, but as this note – translated literally – shows, the equivalence is adequate. Translator.]

2 The most profitable strategies are usually those produced, on the hither side of all calculation and in the illusion of the most "authentic" sincerity, by a habitus objectively fitted to the objective structures. These strategies without strategic calculation procure an important secondary advantage for those who can scarcely be called their authors – the social approval accruing from apparent disinterestedness.

3 "Here we confront the distressing fact that the sample episode chain under analysis is a fragment of a larger segment of behavior which in the complete record contains some 480 separate episodes. Moreover, it took only twenty minutes for these 480 behavior stream events to occur. If my wife's rate of behavior is roughly representative of that of other actors, we must be prepared to deal with an inventory of episodes produced at the rate of some 20,000 per sixteen-hour day per actor... In a population consisting of several hundred actor-types, the number of different episodes in the total repertory must amount to many millions during the course of an annual cycle" (M. Harris, *The Nature of Cultural Things* (New York: Random House, 1964), pp. 74–5).

4 See the whole chapter entitled "Rechtsordnung, Konvention und Sitte", in which Max Weber analyses the differences and transitions between custom, convention, and law (*Wirtschaft und Gesellschaft* (Cologne and Berlin: Kiepenhauer und Witsch, 1964), vol. I, pp. 240–50, esp. pp. 246–9; English trans. "Law, Convention and Custom", *Economy and Society*, ed. G. Roth and C. Wittich (New York: Bedminster Press, 1968), I, pp. 319–33).

5 "We call this subjective, variable probability – which sometimes excludes doubt and engenders a certainty *sui generis* and which at other times appears as no more than a vague glimmer - *philosophical probability*, because it refers to the exercise of the higher faculty whereby we comprehend the order and the rationality of things. All reasonable men have a confused notion of similar probabilities; this then determines, or at least justifies, those unshakable beliefs we call *common sense*" (A. Cournot, *Essai sur les fondements de la connaissance et sur les caractères de la critique philosophique* (Paris: Hachette, 1922; 1st edn., 1851), p. 70).

6 E. Durkheim, *L'évolution pedagogique en France* (Paris: Alcan, 1938), p. 16.

7 R. Ruyer, *Paradoxes de la conscience et limites de l'automatisme* (Paris: Albin Michel, 1966), p. 136.

8 This universalization has the same limits as the objective conditions of which the principle generating practices and works is the product. The objective conditions exercise simultaneously a universalizing effect and a particularizing effect, because they cannot homogenize the agents whom they determine and whom they constitute into an objective group, without distinguishing them from all the agents produced in different conditions.

9 One of the merits of subjectivism and moralism is that the analyses in which it condemns, as inauthentic, actions subject to the objective solicitations of the world (e.g. Heidegger on everyday existence and "*das Man*" or Sartre on the "spirit of seriousness") demonstrate, *per absurdum*, the impossibility of the authentic existence that would gather up all pregiven significations and objective determinations into a project of freedom. The *purely ethical* pursuit of authenticity is the privilege of the leisured thinker who can afford to dispense with the economy of thought which "inauthentic" conduct allows.

10 G. W. Leibniz, "Second éclaircissement du système de la communication des substances" (1696), in *Oeuvres philosophiques*, ed. P. Janet (Paris: de Lagrange, 1866), vol. II, p. 548.

11 Thus, ignorance of the surest but best-hidden foundation of group or class integration leads some (e.g. Aron, Dahl, etc.) to deny the unity of the dominant class with no other proof than the impossibility of establishing empirically that the members of the dominant class have an explicit *policy*, expressly imposed by explicit co-ordination, and others (Sartre, for example) to see the awakening of class consciousness – a sort of revolutionary cogito bringing the class into existence by constituting it as a "class for itself" – as the only possible foundation of the unity of the dominated class.

12 Leibniz, "Second éclaircissement", p. 548.

13 Were such language not dangerous in another way, one would be tempted to say, against all forms of subjectivist voluntarism, that class unity rests fundamentally on the "class unconscious". The awakening of "class consciousness" is not a

primal act constituting the class in a blaze of freedom; its sole efficacy, as with all actions of symbolic reduplication, lies in the extent to which it brings to consciousness all that is implicitly assumed in the unconscious mode in the class habitus.

14 This takes us beyond the false opposition in which the theories of acculturation have allowed themselves to be trapped, with, on the one hand, the *realism of the structure* which represents cultural or linguistic contacts as contacts between cultures or languages, subject to generic laws (e.g. the law of the restructuring of borrowings) and specific laws (those established by analysis of the structures specific to the languages or cultures in contact) and on the other hand the *realism of the element*, which emphasizes the contacts between the *societies* (regarded as populations) involved or, at best, the structures of the relations between those societies (domination, etc.).

SECTION 10

Universalisms and Domain Terms

34

Body and Mind in Mind, Body and Mind in Body: Some Anthropological Interventions in a Long Conversation

Michael Lambek

It is with some trepidation that I enter the long conversation on mind and body, a conversation that has included many more strong and subtle positions than I can possibly encompass. This [...] is not an intervention in philosophical arguments so much as an exercise in anthropological ground-clearing; I have no pretensions about resolving philosophical debates between monism and dualism. I take these debates to be constitutive of our philosophical tradition rather than assuming that one position must be foundational and others wrong. What is of equal interest is to start with the philosophical problems – not solutions – of our tradition and then to extend the horizons of these debates to include, in a Gadamerian sense, the philosophical conversations, explicit and implicit, of other societies. It is my suspicion that both monistic and dualistic experiences are inherent in the human condition and hence that mind/body and perhaps even monism/dualism are oppositions like nature/culture and male/female which all cultures, hence all anthropologists, must encounter. In sum, my position is very much like the famous wit who claimed that there are two kinds of thinkers in the world, those who divide the world into two and those who do not. To raise the paradox is perhaps already to take sides. Less comfortably, the position might be described as having my cake and eating it too.

Since the reflections that follow are ethnographic in inspiration, it may help to provide some background. Much of my fieldwork has been concerned with spirit possession as I encountered it among Malagasy speakers on the French-controlled island of Mayotte in the Mozambique Channel and among Sakalava in north-west Madagascar. Spirit possession has to do with intimate relationships that, in Malagasy understanding, particular spirits engage in with particular human hosts. At some times, while the host is in a state of dissociation, the spirit speaks and acts through the host's body, temporarily taking it over, in a manner that one spirit medium, seeking the means to make me understand, described as a *coup d'état*. But between such moments of manifest possession, a long-term relationship between host and spirit continues to be recognized and is marked by such things as the attribution of particular dreams or illnesses to the

From Michael Lambek and Andrew Strathern (eds.), *Bodies and Persons: Comparative Perspectives from Africa and Melanesia* (Cambridge: Cambridge University Press, 1998), pp. 103–18, 121–3 (with cuts). Copyright © 1998 by Cambridge University Press. Reprinted with permission of Cambridge University Press.

Anthropology in Theory: Issues in Epistemology, Second Edition. Edited by Henrietta L. Moore and Todd Sanders.
© 2014 John Wiley & Sons, Inc. Published 2014 by John Wiley & Sons, Inc.

spirit and by certain actions, notably adherence to specific taboos, on the part of the host. On-going social obligations are acknowledged between host and spirit and with other parties.

Spirit possession is widespread, across not only most of Africa but the globe, although the Malagasy are perhaps at one end of a continuum in emphasizing the distinctiveness of host and spirit as discrete, alternate voices and persons. Spirit possession is a complex phenomenon, integrally related to many other aspects of society and culture in Mayotte and Madagascar and it is of great interest to local people themselves. Much intellectual, creative, and emotional energy is invested in it and generated by it. But spirit possession is also, I think, intrinsically interesting – it raises questions that are provocative for all of us as human beings, questions pertaining to such things as the sources of human agency, or the relationship between action and passion, or autonomy and connection, in selfhood. One of the questions it inevitably touches on has to do with the relationships between mind and body.

[…] I explore the directions to which my thinking on mind and body via spirit possession has led me. The attempt is to clarify the bases on which references in the anthropological literature to mind and body arguments rest. I am responding to a general trend in contemporary anthropology and to some degree going against it, but I hope the direction of my arguments will also reveal some of the kinds of connections that can be made between anthropology and philosophy. To put this more specifically, how anthropology might continue to bring cultural difference to the attention of philosophy without advocating a simplistic relativism.

The body is currently a topic of great interest. But, it is anthropologically relevant only in its relationship to other significant categories: body and person, body and self, body and mind, body and memory (and so on). Anything less is simply biology. In question is, first, the relations through which the body helps constitute, express, and ground such things as experience, meaning, reason, identity, value, vitality, continuity, transformation, relationship, agency, and intentionality; and second, how these relations are configured in local thought (including, naturally, our own).

We tend sometimes to suggest that mind/body dualism is peculiarly Western and that we can turn to other cultures for the solution of our "mind–body problem." It is my contention that body/mind or body/person distinctions are widespread, and probably universal, although obviously they need not take the same form, divide the terrain in the same manner, or reach the same proportions or significance as the Cartesian version. My argument is that mind/body dualism is at once everywhere transcended in practice yet everywhere present, in some form or other, in thought.

In other words, we have to attend to body and mind in body (embodiment), and also to body and mind in mind (imagination). I note in passing that this distinction may be a way to characterize the shift of emphasis between the phenomenologists, like Csordas (1990) or Jackson (1989), who are interested in mindful bodies, and the cognitivists, like Lakoff and Johnson (1980), who are interested in embodied minds.

Whether these propositions – that mind/body dualism is at once everywhere transcended in practice and yet everywhere present, in some form or other, in thought – prove true or not, I believe they provide an interesting space for comparative work. They alert us to the fact that in making cross-cultural comparisons we ought not to be comparing embodied practice in one society with concepts or theories in another, but practice with practice and thought with thought, or moving up a level of abstraction, their suitably historicized mutual constitution and interrelationships in the societies in question. Moreover, insofar as the mind/body contrasts we find in different societies do not map directly onto one another, but leave problems of translation, these discrepancies should themselves open up new avenues for investigation.

More generally, my discussion speaks to the fact that philosophy supplies interesting questions for anthropological investigation. And if anthropology can intervene in philosophical debate that is surely to the good as well. Such intervention was a matter of course for writers such as Durkheim and Lévi-Strauss. It is all the more critical today that we contribute to the task of widening the horizons of academic philosophy, providing diverse cultural material to think about and with. At the same time, philosophy can help reduce anthropologists' naiveté and both refine and expand the questions we ask of our material. Together we ought to be able to move beyond both ethnographic particularism and academic philosophy's arguably ethnocentric embeddedness in Western concepts. Despite the long-standing existence of Asian philosophies and the recent emergence of a vigorous professional African philosophy (e.g. Kwame 1995), the questions – can there be a transcultural or pluralist philosophy (not to speak of a global one) and, if so, what would it look like? – have hardly begun to be addressed.

Body and Mind in Mind

In a recent article on taboo as cultural practice (Lambek 1992) I attempted to demonstrate a dialectic of embodiment and objectification in which the body serves to substantiate and legitimate certain cultural ideals, identities, and relationships. I congratulated myself for showing how taboos, identifiable by means of both explicit, objectified rules and embodied practices – avoiding certain foods or sexual engagements – as well as visceral reactions to their violation – nausea, rashes, and so on – transcend the mind/body opposition. But by the time I had completed the paper I was disconcerted to realize that my analysis had, in fact, proceeded by means of a discussion of similar dual oppositions salient among speakers of Kibushy, the northern Malagasy dialect spoken in Mayotte. Thus, although spirit possession in Mayotte, as over much of Africa and parts of Asia and Oceania, is a highly embodied cultural phenomenon, it is equally grounded in a conceptual distinction – and quite a radical one at that – between particular minds and bodies. Simply put (and over-simply glossed), possession is constituted by the occupation of one body (*nênin*) by more than one person (*ulu*) or mind (*rohu, fânahy*).

Thus I discovered that while I had attempted to deploy theoretical vehicles that would transcend Western dualism, I was actually making use of the dualistic categories of the people I was studying. That such dualism is present in the semantic area of mind/body, even if the Kibushy terms do not correspond exactly to Western ones, and in fact differ from them in interesting ways (Lambek 1992), suggests that dual or possibly multiple categories might be common or even necessary for apprehending this area of human experience. In

other words, while "mind" and "body" may not be universal categories, it is striking that people seem to need more than one term to talk about the domains covered by their referent/s. I am not making the strong cognitivist claim that the inferences people make distinguishing what pertains to mind and what pertains to body will be the same everywhere; research on this question is under way (Bloch, pers. comm.). I am saying that what we call the "mind/ body problem" (at its most general level, whether a valid distinction can be made between the mind and body[1]) may be but one particular historical expression of what are universal existential conundra rooted in the human capacity for self-reflection. I emphasize that the point of cross-cultural comparison is not to seek solutions to a reified "mind/ body problem," but to contextualize a component of Western thought and hence to clarify its very constitution *as* a problem. The assumption is emphatically not that others have "solved" a problem.[2]

The body is good to think with, as we know from countless studies of symbolic dualism or the work of Mary Douglas (1966) on boundaries and transgressions. Indeed, bodily registers have long been prevalent in Western European culture to represent social distinctions (Stallybrass and White 1986). Lakoff and Johnson go further: the body is *necessary* to think with. They appear to suggest that the body (via image schemata) underlies all metaphor and that metaphor, in turn, underlies many of our basic concepts (Lakoff and Johnson 1980; Johnson 1987). For example, to speak of a moral person as upright, or a clever argument as insightful, makes use of prevalent metaphors – so prevalent that they are largely unremarked – metaphors that draw upon sensory or proprioceptive aspects of our embodied condition. But studies of metaphor or of bodily symbolism rarely move beyond the corporeal to examine the way the contrast between the body and something "other" to it (whether glossed as "soul," "spirit," or "mind") is expressed. I suggest that some kind of a mind/body dichotomy marks, and indeed helps constitute, such pervasive oppositions as those between animation and inertion, choice and necessity, "consciousness" and "unconsciousness," and even the transcendental and the mundane (cf. Bloch 1992), as well as providing an idiom in which to address questions of accountability. Of course, the particular ways in which the dichotomy is expressed, the kinds of relations posited between mind and body, the places where boundaries are drawn, even which terms will appear on which sides of the analogies posited above, will vary from place to place and over time. This is the case if only because there is no single or final exclusive, comprehensive, and parsimonious way available for humans to comprehend the human situation.

"Mind" and "body" speak to fundamental tensions of human experience: connection to and separation from others, the boundary between the subjective and the objective, the relation of concepts to objects, or reason to sensation, experiences of the voluntary and the involuntary, morality and desire, being and becoming, active and passive, male and female, the transient and the enduring, culture and nature, life and death. Phrased as "mind" and "body," the opposition and the concerns just listed may appear specific to Western metaphysics. However there are roughly equivalent sets of terms, such as Kibushy *rohu* and *nênin*, addressing roughly similar oppositions, though not necessarily all of them at once, characteristic of the thought of other traditions (cf. Gyekye 1995). These terms and oppositions will not be identical to each other, any more than Plato's mind/body dualism is identical to that of Descartes. In Mayotte, as I elaborated in the earlier article, the body substantiates socially significant distinctions and relationships, for example between kin, manifest in the maintenance of specific taboos or the effects of ignoring them, thereby serving as a primary means to articulate personhood. Individual preferences that are socially insignificant, or indeed antisocial, are attributed to mind. This is in contrast to the Western picture as articulated by Durkheim, in which "Passion individualizes, yet it also enslaves. Our sensations are essentially individual; yet we are more personal the more we are freed from our senses and able to think and act with concepts". Durkheim associates the universal with reason and the individual with the body whereas the ideology I heard expressed in Mayotte did something different (Lambek 1992:258; cf. Parry 1989).

I do not mean to suggest that usage in Mayotte is fully consistent. Although the mind/body distinction is evident from spirit possession, the fact that two persons are thought to share the same body complicates the way the body personalizes. Thus the partition of particular attributes, such as skill at dancing, or sensations, such as hunger, pain, exhaustion, or too much liquor, to one person or the other, is not entirely straightforward, any more than we ourselves are fully clear whether to attribute these traits, or others, such as emotions, to body or to mind.

Although in each case, Mayotte and the West, the distinctions premised on mind and body are relative rather than absolute, the lack of identity between cultural models creates a translation problem. There are two things about this problem that may look contradictory but in fact, I will argue, are not. The first point is that the translation problem is not radical; it is possible to see that both inheritors of the Western tradition and the Malagasy speakers are addressing similar kinds of problems or issues even if their phrasing means that they are not identical; they can be placed within the same horizon. The second point is that translation problems may be intrinsic to the subject matter, that is to say that the very irresolution of mind/body issues within any given tradition is part and parcel of what makes full and complete translation impossible between traditions.

The argument that "mind"/"body" distinctions address basic dimensions of human experience has some affinities with structuralism, specifically Lévi-Strauss's understanding of culture (myth) as the unending attempts to resolve conceptual "irritations" and the displacement of abstract oppositions by sets of concrete signifiers. My argument about analogy owes much to him. However I do not suggest that the categories function in the formal way some followers of Lévi-Strauss have sought to understand binary oppositions of the left/right, hot/cold variety. The more interesting sets of terms are those that are composed not of logical opposites (good and evil) or empirical contraries (life and death) but of *incommensurables*. These provide genuine conundra. Mind and body, I claim, refer not to contraries or opposites, but to fundamental incommensurables in human experience. Incommensurables (by definition) are not susceptible to measurement by a common yardstick. In this way they are radically different from binary oppositions whose very definition, in the phonological prototype, is relational and constituted by their commensurability.[3]

For this reason, transposition of their terms into the register of the concrete does not provide a very satisfying or neat form of resolution. Moreover, what is at issue is in part the relationship between the concrete and something different from it. The field that the terms cover is inherently messy and complex. Incommensurables do not exclude each other, but by the same token they cannot readily be mediated since they share no common measure along which an intermediary position could be staked out. There is no place half-way between mind and body. Similarly, neither suffices, neither can cover the ground alone. Water may be hot or cold and food raw or cooked, but what could it mean to say of a living human being that they were all body or all mind? Robert Murphy (1987) may have come close, but one of the points of his story of his paralysis is surely how he could never escape the limits of his embodied, albeit bodily silent, condition. Neither "body" nor "mind" is sufficient to describe human experience yet they are not simply additive either, since each is somehow implicated in the other.[4]

Incommensurables are not logical or empirical opposites; in fact, there is no single way in which their connection can be definitively and parsimoniously described. They simply fail, in Kuhn's words, "to make *complete* contact."[5] Mind/body is our expression for one such area of fundamental incommensurability, with no possibility for "resolution." Mind is not simply the absence of body, nor body the absence of mind, though this is one coordinate along which their relationship might, to a degree, be fruitfully explored. Some attempts to mediate the terms, some conversations, may mistakenly assume or try to establish an exclusive, foundational logic. To the degree that we can be said to have a mind/ body *problem*, it is precisely this. I mean first, the assumption that we can clearly establish, as Descartes may have asserted, a real distinction between two essential, stable phenomena. Second, then, are the attempts to establish whether there are definitive relations between such discrete substances.[6] Similar pairs or sets of pairs can be found in other traditions, but without the sense of urgency regarding precise clarification of the points of separation or connection.[7]

In sum, the mistake of Cartesianism lies not in its dualism, not in distinguishing mind from body, but in assuming that the relationship between them is one that can be definitively and unilaterally established. The mistake lies in trying to reach conclusion; in Weberian terms, in trying to rationalize the boundary.

In suggesting that mind and body are incommensurable I am extending the understanding which Kuhn (1970) applied to successive paradigms in science and Feyerabend (1975) to distinctive art styles and societies (as studied by anthropologists) to outlooks and even individual sets of terms that are found within a single society or language. Hence my point about body and mind is part of a broader argument about culture. Culture does not rest exclusively on a unitary bedrock of axioms or a primary set of logical oppositions. Rather than being built entirely from logically related categories, systematic propositions, or relationally constituted terms in a structural set, culture is equally constituted from incommensurables and the diverse series of tropes, statements, practices, and interpretations to which they give rise, situated in local "conversations" in which the participants inevitably talk not only to each other but past each other, and which in turn shape experience, although never fully systematically or conclusively.[8] Mind and body must be located in such long, indeed, interminable conversations.

My argument is heavily indebted to Bernstein's discussion of the distinction between incommensurability and both incompatibility (logical contradiction) and incomparability (Bernstein 1983, esp. 79 ff.). The incommensurability argument claims neither that there is an overarching framework in terms of which mind and body can be measured against each other point by point such that contradictions can be established, nor that each is encased in a radically different framework such that no communication between them is possible. It is thus neither objectivist nor relativist. Instead, Bernstein emphasizes the open-endedness of incommensurability. Rather than ruling out comparison, it implies that the forms of comparison (or interpretation) will be multiple and not anchored along some fixed grid.[9] A good illustration is the comparison of art styles; just as there is no single or final axis of comparison between two styles of representing the body artistically, so too with thinking about the human condition by means of "body" and by means of "mind." Hence, the lack of resolution between mind and body is not a negative thing but generative of potentially lively cultural production and debate. Indeed, the very incommensurability between mind and body suggests that both monist and dualist ideas will be produced.

I have been arguing that real incommensurables of human experience (including, in this case, the very incommensurability between representational language and experience itself) elicit the production and use of incommensurable categories. Rather than the cross-cultural evidence suggesting that the Cartesian form of conceptualizing the opposition is simply false, it suggests that it is one contingent way of thinking about an issue that does not permit a single "true" representation.[10] Not only is any local formulation likely to be composed of terms incommensurable with each other, but we can expect this to be the case in any comparison of terms drawn from different cultural loci. The different ways in which the primary incommensurability is phrased may have distinctive local consequences which we will want to pursue. However, it follows from my argument that once we have passed the first round of describing local concepts (African, Melanesian, etc.) and of demonstrating that they fail to make "complete contact" with Occidental "mind" and "body," as they surely will fail, we will nevertheless find ourselves within a common horizon of ideas, enabling multiple forms of comparison and directions for conversation. Comparing the alternative formulations should raise many questions and, at the very least, speak to the broader significance of the Western constructions.[11]

In other words, cultural comparison serves to enlarge the discussion of mind and body that is carried on within any given culture or tradition. The discrepancies between some of the terms used in one tradition and those used in another are of the same order (though not the same degree) as the discrepancies between some of the terms used in any given tradition.

It is worth mentioning in passing a problem which my argument raises, namely why, if "mind" and "body" do not emerge from a logical discrimination or a relational paradigm, they are represented by pairs of concepts rather than any other number above one. The empirical question is whether the terms genuinely appear in pairs

cross-culturally. [...] Strathern suggests (1996) that we often encounter a triad of mind, spirit, and body. Among another Highlands group, the Paiela, the distinction between a working, active body and a stationary, vegetative one is extremely significant, although the ethnographer (Biersack 1996) provides no specific lexical terms for the contrast. Thus it may be that the collapse of "more-than-two" into "two" in my presentation is simply a rhetorical product of cultural bias, a distortion produced by centuries of attempting to argue within a framework in which the terms are assumed to be commensurable. The alternative, of course, is that human *experience* does have something genuinely dual about it, a matter which comparative work can surely address. If the roots of mind/body *dualism* lie in our embodied existential condition rather than more narrowly within human language there is all the more reason that the terms to express it be incommensurable.[12] A compromise position would be to suggest that the terrain is transected by multiple incommensurable pairs. Indeed, I think it likely that the domain for "mind" will be constituted by multiple terms which arise in different historical circumstances (viz. the Arabic origins of Kibushy *rohu*) but which, since they are not commensurable, never quite displace each other. Thus body may be opposed to soul in some contexts and to mind in others. The foreign anthropologist who attempted to organize the English terms "mind," "soul," "spirit," "self," "ego," etc. into a paradigmatic set would have a difficult time of it.

Body and Mind in Body

I now turn, in equally condensed fashion, to practice, that is, to body and mind in body. If, from the perspective of mind, body and mind are incommensurable, from the perspective of body they are integrally related. The view that I present here is not (I hope) in contradiction to the previous discussion, but rather incommensurable with it.

Bodies serve as icons, indices, and symbols of society and also of individuals and of the relationships between them. But they are also something more. At the most basic level, in posture, adornment, and so on – but also in touching, in relative positioning, in gathering together, in coitus, in feeding and being fed, in working cooperatively and in consuming together, and again in refusal of engagement or consumption, in the maintenance of taboos, in all these situated practices – persons and ongoing social relationships are not simply signified but actively constituted. Their development is simultaneously established, enacted, charted – and naturalized or challenged, celebrated or mourned as well. If sociality is embodied, conversely human bodily activities are culturally mediated, hence infused with "mind."[13] At the same time, bodily action is critical to the constitution of the perceiving and thinking person.

In one of his formative essays, Mauss (1985) derived Western notions of the person from two sources, the dramatistic or performative and the jural. Unlike Mauss, we can take these to represent less distinct traditions, successive historical phases, or discrete types (status and contract; oral and literate; cold and hot; pre-modern and modern) than two poles of an ongoing dialectical relationship between embodiment and objectification which is operative in any society. In saying this I am drawing on the model so memorably developed by Berger and Luckmann (1966) but with a greater emphasis, deriving largely from Bourdieu, on the embodied, performative, mimetic nature of the internalization pole (1990). Too often the person (and culture itself) has been identified uniquely with the objectifications, especially the mental ones encoded in language. Yet to have a social identity, as Fortes (1983) argued, requires embodying it in actions, putting your body where your mouth is, so to speak. Being a person requires in Bourdieu's phrase, a "feel for the game";

> the values given body, *made* body, by the hidden persuasions of an implicit pedagogy which can instil a whole cosmology, through injunctions as insignificant as "sit up straight" or "don't hold your knife in your left hand", and inscribe the most fundamental principles of the arbitrary content of a culture in seemingly innocuous details of bearing or physical and verbal manners, so putting them beyond the reach of consciousness and explicit statement. (Bourdieu 1990: 69)

The habitus, Bourdieu tells us, is "embodied history, internalized as a second nature and so forgotten as history" (p. 56). At the same time, he makes a different point: this habitus is a locus of "dispositions...predisposed to function as structuring structures, that is, as principles which generate and organize practices and representations" (p. 53).

Elsewhere I have examined the way in which cultural rules, values, and social relations are embodied and thereby ostensibly naturalized by means of spirit possession (1992, 1993). Following the lead of van Gennep, I argued for the centrality of practicing and internalizing taboos in delimiting, differentiating, and thus ultimately constituting social 'persons, as selected aspects of the context are alternately incorporated or repulsed. As Alfred Gell put it: "outside the specific acts, observances – and taboos – which specify a self as *my* self, there is nothing for an emblem of the self to be an emblem of." And further: "To observe a taboo is to establish an identifiable self by establishing a relationship... with an external reality such that the 'self' only comes into existence in and through this relationship" (1979:136). Moreover, if such acts constitute selfhood, they also, as Rappaport saw (1979), instantiate morality.

These arguments refer to the embodiment of selfhood and society. Here I want to turn to the other swing of the dialectic, the way embodied dispositions may "generate and organize" objectified representations, or as Jackson puts it, how "persons actively body forth the world" (1989:136). As Merleau-Ponty, from whose inspiration this position is derived, is a good deal more opaque to me than Malagasy spirit possession, I turn to an anecdote, drawn from my fieldnotes, to illustrate.

However in arguing that embodiment entails the conjunction of mind and body, I want to resist a completely smooth picture. Embodied practices are carried out by agents who can still think contemplatively; nothing "goes without saying" forever. The relation between conceptual objectification and embodied practices is always dynamic; there is always something that escapes or exceeds what is given from either side. The body provides objective limits to what can be embodied, and embodied performance provides more than the thought alone would. Yet as my vignette indicates, thought, too, pushes beyond the limits of the embodied performance, linking alternate embodiments.

French or Creole sailors from the pre-colonial period form one of the kinds of characters manifest in spirit possession by means of which the northern Sakalava of Madagascar imaginatively re-present and quite literally re-embody their history. The sailors are neither the most common nor the most important type of spirits in the city of Mahajanga, but in some mediums they serve as popular diviners and consultants, characters with whom one can chat more comfortably than the complex and powerful deceased Sakalava monarchs who comprise the main spirits.[14] In 1994 I visited a male medium whom I will call Ali who has a sailor spirit among the many spirits who possess him. Through his performance Ali brilliantly embodies the French sailor or bodies forth his world. When possessed by the Sailor (as I will refer to the spirit) he switches from Malagasy to a pungent, idiomatic, properly accented French. He changes into a blue and white striped sailor's shirt and jaunty blue hat with a red pompom. In contrast to the older Sakalava spirits who chew tobacco and drink rhum from the bottle, the Sailor chain-smokes cigarettes (sometimes he asks for menthol), and drinks his rhum from a glass. His bearing shifts as does his whole demeanor. The mimetic performance engages the entire body of the medium, drawing upon and transforming the senses, and constituting a new habitus. The bodily habitus in turn generates thought.

Let me quote an edited excerpt from my field-notes (July 27, 1994).

A young man accompanied me to the medium's house, ostensibly to show me the way, but also, it turned out, in order to pose his own question. The Sailor spirit lit up a cigarette and addressed my friend, Richar', in French. Thereafter their conversation was largely in French; Richar' indicated he was able to follow, but his own contribution was limited to monosyllables.

The Sailor began by remarking that we can only pray to God for what we want. He added that while religions are many, there is only the one God, le Bon Dieu. [Both Ali and Richar' are nominally Muslim.]

Richar' explained that he was having difficulty finding work on one of the small transport boats that ply the west coast of Madagascar.

The Sailor inquired whether he had his work papers, then picked up a deck of playing cards in order to perform divination.[15] "*Votre nom, monsieur?*" he asked politely.

"Richar'."

"Nothing more?"

"Théophile."

"*Ah, vous avez un joli nom* [You have a nice name]," opined the Sailor. He shuffled the cards, asked Richar' to cut, and then laid them out in a pattern. After a few more comments and questions he concluded, "You have luck. Wait a little and you'll have work." He added, "You think too much about your future, but one of these days it will come."

After a pause the Sailor suggested, this time in Malagasy, "You have a child out of wedlock (*bitiky an tany*)?"

"No. ... Well, I might, but I don't know," said Richar' somewhat lamely.

"You must use a condom," responded the Sailor. "It's the fashion in Réunion."

"Corn silk (*volovolo n'tsakotsako*) worked as a medicine for syphilis," the Sailor went on, "but it won't work for AIDS (*SIDA*)." Offering us another drink of rhum and another cigarette, he began reminiscing about his ostensible experiences in the good old days. "Working in the boats, you travel. I have visited Singapore and Johannesburg when I was a sailor. Single men ... one knows the malady ..." But the Sailor's point was the radically changed implications of sexually transmitted diseases and the necessity today for proper protection against AIDS.

The Sailor made these observations in a droll French accent, but seriously, a little world weary. He continued that he was young himself [spirits remain the age at which they died, in his case around 35], but that he saw how young people today tend to forget the customs of their ancestors. "One must respect the ancestors. People here disrespect the [Malagasy] spirits, yet look at all the Comorians who come to them for advice."

Somewhat nonplussed by the direction of the conversation and hampered by his lack of facility in French, Richar' kept replying, "*Ah oui, c'est vrai.*"

The Sailor said, "I am more intelligent than my medium. (*Je suis plus intelligent que saha nakahy*)." He explained that the senior spirits [i.e. those from earlier times] could never understand about *SIDA* and condoms, whereas he warns people to stay with their spouses due to the spread of AIDS. Most people in Madagascar now use condoms, he observed. The other "sailors" also spread the warning.

Richar' then said he had been sick. At night he feels something moving up and down inside his body.

"You can't just eat anything or with anybody... Your stomach cannot support every kind of liquor. People can't drink like spirits. *Nous, c'est autre chose*; we drink and don't get drunk. The odor lingers but the effects disappear... [This is a salient means for expressing the local distinction between the host and spirit, hence between mind and body, while also illustrating for us their connection such that the meaning imposed on the context of drinking can offset the hangover.] *Rapellez les ancêtres. C'est eux qui étaient içi avant nous* (remember the ancestors; it is they who were here before us)."

Richar' brought the conversation back to his main concern, entreating that he might find work on a boat and that things would turn out well for him.

The Sailor replied, still in French, that this depended on "*la volonté de la personne, la volonté de Dieu* (the will of the person, the will of God). If you strive with your force, aim toward your goal, God will help you. You must not be jealous of other people. Do your own work, and you can succeed with the force that God has given you."

Warming to his subject and broadening the argument, the Sailor continued, "Malagasy shouldn't think they are better than each other. Malagasy tend to be competitive." He turned to me. "It's not like that between Toronto and Montreal... or Paris and Marseilles. That's why this country is in trouble."

"You young Malagasy are lucky; this is a good country (*vous avez [de] la chance; c'est un bon pays*)." He compared it with Kenya where people don't understand each other's languages and have to use English or Swahili. "But here in Madagascar, everyone can understand each other ..."

Before we left the Sailor provided Richar' with more specific assurances about his future and further warnings about his behavior. Richar' having drunk several glasses of the rhum that was offered freely during the interview (and that, as was customary, we had provided to the spirit at the outset), the Sailor observed that he should watch his drinking.

Although a surprise to both of us, the lecture to Richar' embedded in the consultation appeared to be a natural pronouncement from the person of the worldly spirit. Indeed, a discussion of sexually transmitted diseases could have found no more appropriate spokesperson since, as his conversation made explicit, the Sailor was someone once associated with promiscuous sexual exploits himself. It is striking that this discourse was pronounced specifically by a sailor spirit rather than any other kind. The representation of AIDS appears to emerge directly from the habitus of the Sailor, the embodied condition or pre-objective giving rise spontaneously to the objectified discourse or at least having tremendous affinity with it. Yet at the same time, the Sailor's own experience is of a maritime culture that has largely passed. It is remarkable that any of the Sakalava spirits have begun talking about AIDS, keeping up with the times despite being voices from the past.

In a similar vein one can note how the embodiment of the Sailor's persona enables him to speak about "Madagascar," to construct "the Malagasy" as an object; he speaks of the nation from the perspective of a partial outsider. The Sailor also reflects on race (at one point he remarked "God created us all the same except the colour of our skins"); on ethnic politics (in his view the critical problem in Madagascar, despite the fact that people are closer linguistically than in many African countries); on religion (every religion has its forms of worship, its own sacred day, etc., but God is really One); and formulates a work ethic. It is ironic that his discussion of the fact that the Malagasy, unlike the Kenyans, do not need a lingua franca was conducted in French. [...] Regarding religion, the Muslim spirit medium can take on the voice of Christianity from within the Sakalava idiom of possession. His ecumenical point is prefigured in his practice.

The Sailor's ability to objectify was also apparent in a conversation we held the year before. On that occasion he explained how the Sailor spirits were all pro-French in their politics and had helped ensure the victory of the pro-French forces in neighbouring Mayotte.[16] "But then," he said, "I'm only a sailor (*un marin*) and don't mix in politics ..." He went on to mention the malagasization policy in national education with reference to a female client who had come for assistance in passing her *bac*.

There is a wonderfully imaginative weaving of politics, positionality, and French culture in the Sailor's talk. To my ear he seemed to have the tone exactly right and he is also extremely charming in the role, exuding a confidence and a sparkle that are absent from Ali's ordinary speech. Indeed, the Sailor went on to apply his insights to the medium, saying that he [the Sailor] had taught Ali some French. Ali had been an art student in Antananarivo in his youth. The Sailor took down Ali's portfolio. As we looked over the rather mediocre drawings, the Sailor said of Ali, "*Il n'avait pas de talent, peut-être, mais il s'amusait . . .* (He had no talent, perhaps, but he enjoyed himself)."

We see in the performance a unity of mind and body, exactly the sort of *savoir faire* and feel for the rules of the game that Bourdieu describes or the bodying forth that Jackson makes claims for. The spirit's speech seems intrinsically connected to the embodied comportment, emerging from the habitus established by the state of possession. Yet there are several qualifications. First, it is not trance *per se*, trance viewed as an abstract physiological state, but meaningful possession by a particular kind of spirit, a garrulous French one, that establishes the spirit's discourse. Had Ali been possessed by one of his other spirits, the politics expressed would have been of a rather different order.[17] Second, whatever may be pre-objective *vis-à-vis* what is enunciated is at the same time post-objective, as it were, *vis-à-vis* the cultural model of the sailor that Ali embodies. What bodies forth is in relation to what has been embodied – the persona of the Sailor himself. Moreover, the body from which the Sailor speaks is not the body that slept with prostitutes across the ports of the Indian Ocean. The mimesis of alterity, to recombine Taussig's terms (1993), is not a quality of the "mindful body" (Lock and Scheper-Hughes 1987) alone. While mimesis, in Plato's formulation, is opposed to contemplative reason (Havelock 1963) and, in arguments like Stoller's (1995) or Taussig's, to purely discursive reason, we see here that possession enables Ali to take a more distanciated position *vis-à-vis* society and the self. To put this in Weberian language, it is from the very position of enchantment, that the rationalized discourse of modernity emerges. The

Sailor declares himself more intelligent than his medium and in commenting on Ali's art career engages in remarkable self-objectification; he comments reflectively on contemporary politics and religion; with the cosmopolitanism of a French sailor he can refer with ease to the anthropologist's home in Canada; and he makes a specific and quite deliberate intervention with regard to his client's sexual practice.

It is quite right that it should be the sailor spirit who propagates AIDS prevention, even though "in our day the problem was only syphilis and there is medicine for that." The worldly cosmopolitanism of the Sailor contrasts with the fear and chauvinism of several of the older Sakalava spirits. Yet Ali also embodies some of these other spirits and thus at times speaks in different voices. Possessed by a spirit from an earlier epoch I once heard him stumble playfully over the word for a cigarette lighter. Each voice emerges from its habitus and is closely connected to it. But too great an emphasis on the smooth unfolding of embodied dispositions would be to underplay the agency, acuity, and artistry of the particular virtuoso.

Stepping back from this case, and even from the entire subject of spirit possession, it is the particular constitution of the dialectic of body and mind in practice, the means, performative obligations and possibilities, and the particular dynamic trajectories they establish in a given society that are of interest; the ways in which they shape experience, model personhood and social connection, and underpin political, moral, religious, and therapeutic agency and institutions and their changing relations. Persons, and ultimately society itself, are the product (even as they are also the producers). But embodied personhood always leaves open the possibility, via one cultural medium or another, for self-reflection and for grasping the implications of such possibility. [. . .]

Notes

1 The depiction is from Shaffer (1967) who provides a useful overview of Western philosophical thought on the issue.
2 We need also to allow for multiple formulations within any given society and the effects of their

institutionalization in domains such as medicine. Likewise, we have to distinguish, at the very least, between the formulations of people when they are thinking more reflectively and when they are simply trying to get something done. The debate between Gyekye (1995) and Appiah (1992) on the presence of dualism among the Akan is relevant here (cf. Kwame 1995).

3 Commensurability lies at the heart of what Lévi-Strauss means by a structure. We can argue about *what* the common measure is – in the case of death, cessation of breathing, heart beat, brain waves, etc. – without doubting that there is a binary distinction. It is possible that nature/culture provides another example of an incommensurable pair.

4 What Murphy's account illustrates is neither the exclusion of mind from body nor a fundamental opposition between them, but rather the breakdown of the socially relevant dialectic of embodiment and objectification.

5 Kuhn (1970:148) as cited by Bernstein (1983:81), Bernstein's italics.

6 For Descartes mind and body are nonidentical and the content of each might be described as incommensurable with one another. But the tendency in post-Cartesian thought to emphasize the exclusive properties of each presupposes incompatibility (rather than incommensurability), while attempts to characterize the boundary between them in positive and unilateral terms, whether to shore it up or to conflate or substantively mediate it, assume commensurability. However, it is not my intention here to depict the bulk of Western philosophy since Descartes is mistaken or naive on this matter. Shaffer ends his review of the philosophical literature with the remarkable comment that: "It may well be that the relation between mind and body is an ultimate, unique, and unanalyzable one. If so, philosophical wisdom would consist in giving up the attempt to understand the relation in terms of other, more familiar ones and accepting it as the anomaly it is" (1967:v, 344).

7 The urgency derives, of course, from the culture of Occidental science with its assumptions about nature. "Mind" presents an unstable category for science. Claims that the objects of science are all reducible to number or measure – commensurability in the most literal sense – transform the study of soul or mind into "behaviour." My thanks to Paul Antze for this point.

8 This view is elaborated in the conclusion to Lambek (1993).

9 Hence the criticism of "comparing apples and oranges" is misphrased; we compare them all the time (for example, when we choose what to eat). What is invalid, however, is submitting them to a single common measure (cf. Lambek 1991).

10 This point can also be made by comparison of the historical transformations of the issue within Western philosophy (cf. Taylor 1989).

11 There is a parallel with "nature/culture" (and also, as Astuti suggests in her chapter, with sex/gender) although the debate about these terms foundered in relativism when, in response to Ortner's formulation (1974), it was discovered that the terms did not fit precisely onto each other in other cultures (Mac-Cormack and Strathern 1980). It is only from an objectivist perspective that one would ever have expected them to.

12 Conversely, if mind/body dualism is rooted in language I am more likely to be wrong in claiming incommensurability. Here my position is doubly removed from that of Lévi-Strauss since he begins with dualism as a property of mind or language, rooted in binary oppositions, rather than of the phenomenal world (1963), and since he then assumes, at least in some places in his work (1972), a parallelism or consistency between the structure of language and the world of which it speaks. I assume an initial and fundamental incommensurability between language and world.

13 See Geertz (1973) for an evolutionary argument establishing that the human brain is culturally mediated and Sahlins (1976) for the demonstration that practice is culturally mediated.

14 The sailors appear to be from Ste. Marie, an island that long saw the intermixing of French and Malagasy, producing a sort of Creole culture. According to an account that Ali gave me on another occasion they were under the employ of a nineteenth-century Sakalava king (Ndramânavaka) when their boat was wrecked and they drowned between Madagascar and Mayotte. The sailors are also found on Mayotte as the *changizy* spirits (Lambek 1981).

15 Divination by means of playing cards is a common practice, not limited to the sailor spirits.

16 This refers to struggles over three decades in Mayotte to ensure special status with France rather than incorporation in the independent republic of the Comores (cf. Lambek 1995).

17 There is a kind of spirit for virtually every political persuasion, though the spirits are not the direct product of political interest. That possession does not merely enumerate ethnic or historical types, but appropriates their voices and their perspectives on politics and history thereby constructing a complex heteroglossia and multi-levelled historical consciousness, is the subject of my ongoing work in Madagascar (Lambek 1998).

References

Appiah, Kwame Anthony 1992. *In My Father's House: Africa in the Philosophy of Culture*. Oxford: Oxford University Press.

Berger, Peter and Thomas Luckmann 1966. *The Social Construction of Reality*. Garden City, NY: Doubleday.

Bernstein, Richard 1983. *Beyond Objectivism and Relativism: Science, Hermeneutics, and Praxis*. Philadelphia: University of Pennsylvania Press.

Biersack, Aletta 1996. Word made flesh: religion, the economy, and the body in the Papua New Guinea Highlands. *History of Religions* 36(2):85–111.

Bloch, Maurice 1992. *Prey into Hunter: The Politics of Religious Experience*. Cambridge: Cambridge University Press.

Bourdieu, Pierre 1990. *The Logic of Practice*, trans. Richard Nice. Cambridge: Polity Press.

Csordas, T. J. 1990. Embodiment as a paradigm for anthropology. *Ethos* 18:5–47.

Douglas, Mary 1966. *Purity and Danger: An Analysis of Concepts of Pollution and Taboo*. London: Routledge and Kegan Paul.

Feyerabend, Paul 1975. *Against Method: Outline of an Anarchistic Theory of Knowledge*. London: NLB.

Fortes, M. 1983. Problems of identity and person. In Anita Jacobson-Widding, ed., *Identity: Personal and Socio-Cultural*. Stockholm: Almqvist and Wiksell, pp. 389–401.

Geertz, Clifford 1973. The growth of culture and the evolution of mind. In C. Geertz, ed., *The Interpretation of Cultures*. New York: Basic Books, pp. 55–84.

Gell, A. 1979. Reflections on a cut finger: taboo in the Umeda conception of the self. In R. H. Hook, ed., *Fantasy and Symbol: Studies in Anthropological Interpretation*. London: Academic Press, pp. 133–48.

Gyekye, Kwame 1995. *An Essay on African Philosophical Thought: The Akan Conceptual Scheme*. Revised edition. Philadelphia: Temple University Press.

Havelock, Eric A. 1963. *Preface to Plato*. Oxford: Basil Blackwell.

Jackson, Michael 1989. *Paths toward a Clearing: Radical Empiricism and Ethnographic Inquiry*. Bloomington: Indiana University Press.

Johnson, Mark 1987. *The Body in the Mind: The Bodily Basis of Meaning, Imagination, and Reason*. Chicago: University of Chicago Press.

Kuhn, Thomas 1970. *The Structure of Scientific Revolutions*. Chicago: University of Chicago Press.

Kwame, Safro, ed., 1995. *Readings in African Philosophy: An Akan Collection*. Lanham, MD: University Press of America.

Lakoff, George and Mark Johnson 1980. *Metaphors We Live By*. Chicago: University of Chicago Press.

Lambek, Michael 1981. *Human Spirits: A Cultural Account of Trance in Mayotte*. Cambridge: Cambridge University Press.

Lambek, Michael 1991. Tryin' to make it real, but compared to what? In M. Lambek, ed., *From Method to Modesty: Essays on Thinking and Making Ethnography Now*. Special section of *Culture* 11 (1–2): 43–52.

Lambek, Michael 1992. Taboo as cultural practice among Malagasy speakers. *Man* 27(2):245–66.

Lambek, Michael 1993. *Knowledge and Practice in Mayotte: Local Discourse of Islam, Sorcery, and Spirit Possession*. Toronto: University of Toronto Press.

Lambek, Michael 1995. Choking on the Quran and other consuming parables from the western Indian Ocean front. In Wendy James, ed., *The Pursuit of Certainty: Religious and Cultural Formulations*. London: Routledge, pp. 258–81.

Lambek, Michael 1998. The Sakalava poiesis of history: realizing the past through spirit possession in Madagascar. *American Ethnologist* 25(2): 106–27.

Lévi-Strauss, Claude 1963 [1962]. *Totemism*, trans. R. Needham. Boston: Beacon Press.

Lévi-Strauss, Claude 1963 [1958]. *Structural Anthropology*, trans. Clare Jacobson and Brooke Grundfest Schoepf. New York: Basic Books.

Lévi-Strauss, Claude 1972. Structuralism and ecology. *Barnard Alumnae* (Spring 1972), pp. 6–14.

Lock, Margaret and Nancy Scheper-Hughes 1987. The mindful body. *Medical Anthropology Quarterly* 1(1): 6–41.

MacCormack, Carol and Marilyn Strathern, eds. 1980. *Nature, Culture and Gender*. Cambridge: Cambridge University Press.

Mauss, Marcel 1985. A category of the human mind: the notion of person, the notion of self. In M. Carrithers, S. Collins and S. Lukes, eds., *The Category of the Person*. Cambridge: Cambridge University Press, pp. 1–25.

Murphy, Robert 1987. *The Body Silent*. New York: Henry Holt.

Ortner, Sherry B. 1974. Is female to male as nature is to culture? In Michelle Rosaldo and Louise Lamphere, eds., *Woman, Culture, and Society*. Stanford: Stanford University Press, pp. 67–87.

Parry, Jonathan 1989. The end of the body. In Michel Feher, ed., *Fragments for a History of the Human Body*, Vol. 2. New York: Zone Books, pp. 490–517.

Rappaport, Roy A. 1979. The obvious aspects of ritual. In R. Rappaport, ed., *Ecology, Meaning, and Religion*. Richmond: North Atlantic Books, pp. 173–221.

Sahlins, Marshall 1976. *Culture and Practical Reason*. Chicago: University of Chicago Press.

Shaffer, Jerome 1967. Mind–body problem. *The Encyclopedia of Philosophy*. New York: Macmillan.

Stallybrass, Peter and Allon White 1986. *The Politics and Poetics of Transgression*. London: Methuen.

Stoller, Paul 1995. *Embodying Colonial Memories: Spirit Possession, Power, and the Hauka in West Africa*. New York and London: Routledge.

Strathern, Andrew 1996. *Body Thoughts*. Ann Arbor: University of Michigan Press.

Taussig, Michael 1993. *Mimesis and Alterity: A Particular History of the Senses*. New York: Routledge.

Taylor, Charles 1989. *Sources of the Self: The Making of Modern Identity*. Cambridge, MA: Harvard University Press.

35

So *Is* Female to Male as Nature Is to Culture?

Sherry B. Ortner

The paper "Is Female to Male as Nature Is to Culture?" [1972] was my first piece of feminist writing, and my second professional publication. It was written for the Rosaldo and Lamphere (1974) collection, *Woman, Culture and Society*. The first three papers of the volume – Michelle Rosaldo's, Nancy Chodorow's, and mine – received a lot of attention, in good part because they all took the position that "male dominance" was universal, and then tried to offer some kind of (universal) explanation for that "fact." The idea that male dominance was universal was (meant to be) somewhat shocking to many non-anthropologists, who seemed to think that although our own Western society is patriarchal, "the anthropologists" would have some little stock of more reassuring cases of matriarchy and egalitarianism to bring forth. The universal male dominance position also went up against the intellectual assumptions of a certain "Marxist" wing within anthropology, and thus played into some preexisting – and already quite heated – intellectual politics within the discipline.

"Is Female to Male..." has continued to have a life of its own, well into the present. On the one

hand many people seemed to have found it persuasive. On the other hand it attracted – and still seems to attract – a great deal of very intense criticism. I do not know whether I would write the same paper today, but I assume not, both because the questions have changed (universals are of less compelling interest), and because what would seem satisfactory as answers to those questions has changed (exposing an underlying logic seems less satisfying than exposing the politics of representation in play). Yet the paper's role as theoretical lightning rod over time remains interesting. To borrow a phrase from Lévi-Strauss, the paper has been good to think (Lévi Strauss 1963b). A brief tour through some of the criticism of this paper will allow me then to reflect on some aspects of both feminism and anthropology as these have (and have not) evolved over the past twenty or so years.

Is Male Dominance Universal?

This seemingly simple question can be constructed in a variety of ways. It may take the form of an empirical question: let us look around the

From *Making Gender: The Politics and Erotics of Culture* (Boston: Beacon Press, 1996), pp. 173–80, 235, 242–4, 246–8, 250–1, 253. Copyright © 1996 by Sherry B. Ortner. Reprinted by permission of Beacon Press, Boston.

Anthropology in Theory: Issues in Epistemology, Second Edition. Edited by Henrietta L. Moore and Todd Sanders.
© 2014 John Wiley & Sons, Inc. Published 2014 by John Wiley & Sons, Inc.

world and see if all cases have this quality. This, I think, is how Rosaldo, Chodorow, and I treated it initially. We looked around and the answer seemed to be yes.

But the first round of reactions, as noted above, came from people commited to a certain Marxist evolutionary paradigm, especially Eleanor Leacock (1981) working from Engels's *The Origin of the Family, Private Property and the State.*[1] Within this paradigm, early human societies were presumed to have been egalitarian, and factors of inequality were introduced in conjunction with the emergence of private property. Thus if examples of egalitarian cases in the contemporary world could not be found, it is not because, in their pristine state, they did not exist. It is because all societies have already been touched in one way or another by capitalism, and/or because anthropology has been theoretically blinded by capitalist culture.

Even granting Leacock's points about both capitalist penetration and bourgeois blinders, there were simply too many cases that could not be worked into Leacock's picture. Nonetheless at another level what she and others were saying is that recognizing egalitarianism is not as easy as it appears, that it is a matter of interpretation. I came to agree with this position, and in a recent paper (1996a) I argued that if one looks at certain cases from a certain theoretical angle, they look more egalitarian than not. It is not that these societies lack traces of "male dominance," but the elements of "male dominance" are fragmentary – they are not woven into a hegemonic order, are not central to some larger and more coherent discourse of male superiority, and are not central to some larger network of male-only or male-superior practices.

My point, in other words, was to look again at some cultures at the relatively egalitarian end of the spectrum. I wanted to try to rethink the significance of culturally unmarked elements of "male dominance" in such cases, to try to get a better feel for their relative weight within a culture's gender patterns. I felt that my mistake earlier had been to play up such items too much, to seize upon any indicator of male superiority, female "pollution," etc., and label a whole culture "male dominant." Behind my rethinking are larger shifts in the conceptualization of "culture" in the field of anthropology as a whole, in the

direction of seeing "cultures" as more disjunctive, contradictory, and inconsistent than I had been trained to think.[2]

The case I focused on was the Andaman Islanders, and I concluded that it was fair to view them as "egalitarian," despite the presence of certain items of special male privilege and authority. I argued that, since these items were not woven into a hegemonic order, they could not be treated as pervasively redefining the dominant egalitarianism. Interestingly enough, Jane Atkinson and Anna Tsing published papers at virtually the same time as "Gender Hegemonies," taking up similar kinds of materials in similar kinds of ways. Atkinson examined gender relations among the Wana of Central Sulawesi, and Tsing considered material from the Meratus of Kalimantan, both within Indonesia. Their cases are both very similar to the Andaman example I had discussed. In all three cases there is a lack of formal ideology about male superiority; in all three cases there are extensive patterns of gender equivalence and equality; in all three cases there is a tendency not to use gender as a conceptual or social organizational principle at all.[3] Very few things are limited to men simply because they are men, or to women simply because they are women. But in both cases some people nonetheless come to occupy, and/or to create for themselves, positions of influence and authority, and those people tend predominantly to be men.

We three authors wind up in slightly different places with respect to the egalitarianism question, although this seems largely a function of the way each author posed the problem in the first place. My agenda had been to try to learn to "see egalitarianism" – to see how some kinds of de facto male dominance might remain isolated and, at a given moment in time at least, not basically challenge a prevailing egalitarianism in a culture. Atkinson and Tsing, on the other hand, were interested in seeing how male dominance gets produced and reproduced, largely in an unmarked way, in societies that represent themselves as basically egalitarian. Together, however, the papers convey a suggestion that you can call such societies "gender-egalitarian" if you want, and you would not exactly be wrong, but the egalitarianism is complex, inconsistent, and – to some extent – fragile.

Picturing the Emergence of Male Dominance

These papers also raise another point about the male dominance issue, one that was not much debated at the time of the publication of the Rosaldo and Lamphere volume, but that nonetheless seems to me important: how shall we imagine the process of the emergence of male dominance in human societies? Should we think of it as the product of male intentionality, some sort of "will to power" emerging from a "natural" aggressiveness? Or should we think of it – as I did in "Is Female to Male..." – as a kind of side effect, an unintended consequence of social arrangements designed for other purposes?

The cases just discussed show how tricky this question is. On the one hand they can be read as supporting my original contention. Whether we call them "egalitarian" or not, these cases show that certain kinds of male privilege emerge in a de facto way from certain relatively functionally defined arrangements. Men emerge as "leaders" and as figures of authority, vis-à-vis both women and other men, as a function of engaging in a variety of practices, only some of which are predicated on power, including trade, exchange, kinship networking, ritual participation, dispute resolution, and so forth. That is, male dominance does not in fact seem to arise from some aggressive "will to power," but from the fact that – as Simone de Beauvoir first suggested in 1949 – men as it were lucked out: their domestic responsibilities can be constructed as more episodic than women's, and they are more free to travel, congregate, hang out, etc., and thus to do the work of "culture."

In a subsequent paper, Collier and Rosaldo criticized the functionality of this argument (1981; see also Rosaldo 1980). Although they did not argue that men "naturally" sought to dominate women, they nonetheless emphasized that male power relations, often grounded in violence and threats of violence, had to be at the heart of understanding gender inequality. In general I shifted over to a more political perspective in my own work as well. Yet I retained a certain commitment to the "functionalist" argument in the context of the nature/culture paper, that is, in the context of the origin-of-male-dominance story that is embedded in that paper. We seemed to

have two choices: either to imagine that male dominance came about as, in Engels's famous phrase, "the world historical defeat of women" by men (1972), or alternatively that it came about as the unintended consequence of certain functional arrangements and other paths of least resistance.

I preferred the latter interpretation, in part because the will to power position presumed, even if it did not clearly declare, some kind of essentialized male aggression, and I thought essentialized characteristics were exactly what feminists (at least some of us) were trying to get away from. Yet it is clear from cross-cultural data (Sanday 1981, 1990) that issues of greater male physical size and strength, and perhaps greater male "aggressiveness" in some form, do matter in many cases, although in a wide variety of not entirely predictable ways. The issue haunts contemporary feminist politics as well, where one finds a fairly deep split between what I think of as the "body feminists," who focus on rape and other forms of violence against women (e.g., Brownmiller 1975; MacKinnon 1987), as against the more socially and culturally oriented thinkers and activists. I would more fully acknowledge today, then, the challenge to capture bodily issues in our understandings of gender asymmetry, but without essentializing either women or men.

Is Nature/Culture Universal?

The second bundle of arguments against "Is Female to Male as Nature Is to Culture?" concerned its use of the nature/culture opposition to explain (universal) male dominance. Again there were several sets of issues here: Is the nature/culture opposition truly universal? Does it have more or less the same meanings cross-culturally? Does an alignment between gender on the one hand and nature/culture on the other in fact explain universal male dominance? And even if it does not, is there still some significant sense in which female is to male as nature is to culture?

Beneath these various questions, there seems to me to be one large question that is of continuing relevance today: in this era of poststructuralism, does it still make sense to talk about "structures," and if so what do we mean by them? In order to get to this question, I will first yield and set aside those parts of the argument in "Is Female to

Male..." that now seem to me probably wrong, or at the least, not very useful. And then I will defend what still seems to me right, partly in the spirit of defending myself, but largely – I hope – in the spirit of learning something from all this.

The biggest substantive "error" in the paper may be the main point, that is, the point that a linkage between female and nature, male and culture "explains" male dominance, whether universal or not. Rather, an explanation of universal or near-universal male dominance seems to me largely explicable in ways just discussed: as a result of some complex interaction of functional arrangements, power dynamics, and bodily effects.

The other big problem surrounding the use of the nature/culture opposition concerns the seeming attribution of universality to certain meanings of "nature" and "culture." Here I think it was more a matter of too casual an exposition in the paper than gross "error," but the point is well taken. Thus, for example, even if the nature/culture relationship is a universal structure across cultures, it is not always constructed – as the paper may seem to imply – as a relationship of cultural "dominance" or even "superiority" over nature. Moreover, "nature" can be a category of peace and beauty, or of violence and destruction, or of inertia and unresponsiveness, and so on and so forth, and of course "culture" will have concomitant variations. Such variation at the level of explicit cultural meanings – unemphasized in the paper – is indeed crucial to variation in the construction of gender and sexuality cross-culturally; the argument from the universality of the nature/culture opposition was in no way meant to suggest a similar universality at the level of "sexual meanings."[4]

As these points suggest, however, there is still some sense in which I would argue, first, that the nature/culture opposition is a widespread (if not universal) "structure," and second, that it is generally (if not universally) the case that female is indeed related to male as nature is to culture. This needs to be elaborated here.

Probably the most consistently articulated charge against "Is Female to Male..." is that an opposition between nature and culture is simply not a universal opposition, that it therefore could not be assumed to underlie either "universal male dominance" or – a priori – any given ethnographic case. As with the first takes on the universal male dominance question, the question

of the universality of some sort of nature/culture opposition was at first taken to be an empirical issue: does the opposition appear in all cultures? to which the contributors to Nature, Culture and Gender, looking at both non-Western examples and pre-nineteenth-century Western cultural history, answered, pretty much, no (MacCormack and Strathern 1980).

The problem here, as a number of observers quickly pointed out, was that may of the contributors to the Nature, Culture and Gender volume fundamentally sidestepped the notion of "structure," which I had used in a Lévi-Straussian (e.g., 1963a) semse, and which has only a complex relationship to empirical cultural terminologies and ideologies. That is, nature/culture as used in my essay (or throughout Lévi-Strauss's work) is not an empirical object that can be found through ethnographic scrutiny; it is an assumption of a relationship that underlies a variety of ethnographic "surfaces." An early review by Beverley Brown (1983) took the volume to task for this confusion, as did more recent essays by Valeri (1990), Hoskins (1990), and Peletz (1996). Simply finding an absence of terminological categories in a particular cultural case does not mean that the structure is not there; the structure is a patterning of relations that may exist without cultural labeling.[5]

But what shall we mean by structure? There have been many definitions of the term, and this is not the place to review the state of structural theory in general. Part of the problem, I think, was Lévi-Strauss's tendency to picture structures as binary oppositions,[6] and also in fact – despite disclaimers – to picture them as sets of terms, words. My own way of thinking about structures, however, is to think of them as existential questions, even riddles, which humanity everywhere must face. Of these, one of the most central is how to think about the confrontation between humanity and nature, that is, between humanity and "what happens without the agency, or without the voluntary and intentional agency, of man" (Mill 1874, quoted in Valeri 1990: 266), or between humanity and, in Marilyn Strathern's terms, those processes that proceed autonomously in the world, and "that limit the possible" of human action (quoted in Valeri 1990: 266).

Nature/culture in one or another specifically Western sense – as a "struggle" in which "man" tries to "dominate" nature, as a confrontation with a system that obeys "natural laws," and so forth – is certainly not universal. Even the idea that "nature" and "culture" are two relatively distinct kinds of objects is probably not universal. But the *problem of the relationship* between what humanity can do, and that which sets limits upon those possibilities, must be a universal problem – to which of course the solutions will vary enormously, both cross-culturally and historically.

Now add gender into the equation. Gender difference, along with nature/culture, is a powerful question. And the gender relationship is always at least in part situated on one nature/culture border – the body. What I think tends to happen in most if not all cultures is that the two oppositions easily move into a relationship of mutual metaphorization: gender becomes a powerful language for talking about the great existential questions of nature and culture, while a language of nature and culture, when and if it is articulated, can become a powerful language for talking about gender, sexuality, and reproduction, not to mention power and helplessness, activity and passivity, and so forth. The particular articulations of the relationship will vary greatly across cultures, with surprising and unexpected shifts and alignments. But the chances that the two sets of issues will be interconnected in specific cultural and historical contexts still seem to me fairly high.

The chances seem to me high, further, although less so perhaps than the chance of sheer interconnection, that the relationship between the terms will be asymmetrical, and that both women and nature will be in some sense the more problematic categories. The logic that de Beauvoir first put her finger on – that men get to be in the business of trying to transcend species-being, while women, seen as mired in species-being, tend to drag men down – still seems to me enormously widespread,

and hardly an invention of "Western culture." From a range of tribal societies with male-only rituals and practices that would be spoiled by women's gaze, to so-called high religions, both Western and non-Western, that exclude women from their higher practices, the basic logic shows up. And it is a logic grounded in a particular construction of the relationship between nature and culture, the idea that culture must at least in part be about the transcendence of nature.

I think the final question for this paper is probably, "so what?" While I do think there are such things as structures in the sense just discussed, large existential questions that all human beings everywhere must cope with, I also think that the *linkage* between such structures and any set of social categories – like female/male – is a culturally and politically constructed phenomenon. From early on after the publication of "Is Female to Male…," my interests lay much more in understanding the politics of the construction of such linkages, than in the static parallelism of the categories.[7]

In conclusion, then, I must say first that it is very odd to have written what has evidently become a "classic"; I certainly did not set out to write one in advance. I and all the other authors in the two founding volumes of feminist anthropology – *Woman, Culture and Society* (Rosaldo and Lamphere 1974) and *Toward an Anthropology of Women* (Reiter 1975) – benefited enormously from the fact that the feminist movement as a political movement had created a virtually ready-made audience for the books. And the argument in "Is Female to Male…," written from the position of a young, white, middle-class female academic, trying to figure out how to live a life as an embodied woman while launching a career as a disembodied mind, evidently touched something in many others similarly positioned in that era.

Notes

1   There was another line of argument against the universal male dominance position, represented in part by Sanday (1981). The various positions are discussed relatively fully in "Gender Hegemonics" (Ortner 1996a).

2   When I was in graduate school at the University of Chicago, for example, the introductory graduate core course was called "Systems." I think it still is, but in the 1960s the title was genuinely descriptive of the content of the course.

3   Maria Lepowsky (1993) has published a full-length monographic study of the people of Vanatinai, whom she shows to have a very similar configuration.

4   These points of cultural variation were at the heart of Ortner and Whitehead 1981.

5   Marilyn Strathern's brilliant essay, "No Nature, No Culture. . ." (1980), was a major exception to these charges against *Nature, Culture and Gender* as a whole. Among other things, Strathern specifically recognized that the structure could be present without cultural labeling, and interrogated a range of cultural data for this kind of indirect structural presence. Her conclusion that the linkage did not hold for the Hagen case was quite persuasive.

6   The problem of binary oppositions in relation to the nature, culture, and gender debate has been discussed by Rosaldo (1980) and more recently by Tsing (1990). Both argue that analysis based on binary oppositions produces essentialized views of the categories; both use this argument to launch an alternative, politics-of-meaning, kind of approach.

7   See again *Sexual Meanings* (Ortner and Whitehead 1981), as well as the papers in Ortner 1996b.

References

Brown, Beverley. 1983. "Displacing the Difference." *m/f* 8:79–89.

Brownmiller, Susan. 1975. *Against Our Will: Men, Women, and Rape*. New York: Simon and Schuster.

Collier, Jane F. and Michelle Z. Rosaldo. 1981. "Politics and Gender in Simple Societies." In Sherry B. Ortner and Harriet Whitehead, eds., *Sexual Meanings: The Cultural Construction of Gender and Sexuality*. Cambridge and New York: Cambridge University Press.

Engels, Friedrich. 1972. *The Origin of the Family, Private Property and the State*. New York: International Publishers.

Hoskins, Janet. 1990. "Doubling Deities, Descent, and Personhood: An Exploration of Kodi Gender Categories." In Jane Atkinson and Shelly Errington, eds., *Power and Difference: Gender in Island Southeast Asia*. Stanford: Stanford University Press.

Leacock, Eleanor. 1981. *Myths of Male Dominance: Collected Articles on Women Cross-Culturally*. New York: Monthly Review Press.

Lepowsky, Maria. 1993. *Fruit of the Motherland: Gender in an Egalitarian Society*. New York: Columbia University Press.

Lévi-Strauss, Claude. 1963a. *Structural Anthropology*. Translated by C. Jacobson and B. G. Schoepf. New York: Basic Books.

Lévi-Strauss, Claude. 1963b. *Totemism*. Translated by R. Needham. Boston: Beacon Press.

MacCormack, Carol, and Marilyn Strathern, eds. 1980. *Nature, Culture and Gender*. Cambridge: Cambridge University Press.

MacKinnon, Catharine A. 1987. *Feminism Unmodified: Discourses on Life and Law*. Cambridge, Mass.: Harvard University Press.

Mill, John Stuart. 1874. *Nature, the Utility of Religion and Theism*. London: Longmans, Green, Reeder and Dyer.

Ortner, Sherry B. 1972. "Is Female to Male as Nature Is to Culture?" *Feminist Studies* 1(2):5–31. Revised and reprinted in Michelle Z. Rosaldo and Louise Lamphere, eds., *Women Culture and Society*. Stanford: Stanford University Press, 1974.

Ortner. Sherry B. 1996a. "Gender Hegemonies." In Sherry B. Ortner, *Making Gender: The Politics and Erotics of Culture*. Boston: Beacon Press.

Ortner, Sherry B. 1996b. *Making Gender: The Politics and Erotics of Culture*. Boston: Beacon Press.

Ortner, Sherry B., and Harriet Whitehead, eds. 1981. *Sexual Meanings: The Cultural Construction of Gender and Sexuality*. Cambridge and New York: Cambridge University Press.

Peletz, Michael. 1996. *Reason and Passion: Representations of Gender in a Malay Society*. Berkeley: University of California Press.

Reiter, Rayna R., ed. 1975. *Toward an Anthropology of Women*. New York: Monthly Review Press.

Rosaldo, Michelle Z. 1980. "The Use and Abuse of Anthropology: Reflections on Feminism and Cross-Cultural Understanding." *Signs* 5(3) (Spring): 389–417.

Rosaldo, Michelle Z., and Louise Lamphere, eds. 1974. *Woman, Culture and Society*. Stanford: Stanford University Press.

Sanday, Peggy Reeves. 1981. *Female Power and Male Dominance: On the Origins of Sexual Inequality*. New York: Cambridge University Press.

Sanday, Peggy Reeves. 1990. *Fraternity Gang Rape: Sex, Brotherhood and Privilege on Campus*. New York: New York University Press.

Strathern, Marilyn. 1980. "No Nature, No Culture: The Hagen Case." In Carol MacCormack and Marilyn Strathern, eds., *Nature, Culture and Gender*. Cambridge: Cambridge University Press.

Tsing, Anna Lowenhaupt. 1990. "Gender and Performance in Meratus Dispute Settlement." In Jane Atkinson and Shelly Errington, eds., *Power and Difference: Gender in Island Southeast Asia*. Stanford: Stanford University Press.

Valeri, Valerio. 1990. "Both Nature and Culture: Reflections on Menstrual and Parturitional Taboos in Huaulu (Seram)." In Jane Atkinson and Shelly Errington, eds., *Power and Difference: Gender in Island Southeast Asia*. Stanford: Stanford University Press.

36

Global Anxieties: Concept-Metaphors and Pre-theoretical Commitments in Anthropology

Henrietta L. Moore

History, Methodology and Comparison

[...] Problems with conceptualizing the relationship between the local and the global may appear new, and seem to require new reflections on methodology and theory. To a considerable extent, this is true, but it is equally the case that any reflection on these matters is beset with issues relating to the history of anthropology, the historicity of anthropological data, and problems of comparison and methodology – all of which are familiar problems in the discipline. One area in which this is particularly clear concerns the question of the imaginary project of anthropology itself. As has often been remarked, anthropology works through a continuous process of contextualization – things and people make sense in their contexts – and the result is both an implicit and explicit categorization of space and time (see also Fabian, 1983; Gupta and Ferguson, 1992 [see chapter 53, this volume]). Anthropology is, of course, not unique in this regard. In the history of western social science, data have only had relevance in relation to objects of study, and objects of study have become entities through subsequent processes of reification. In simple terms, we might say that

intellectually in order to foreground something it is necessary to have a background, so that smaller things are revealed only in relation to and as part of larger ones. Robert Thornton has made the point well:

> Reference to some ulterior entity is always implicit in holism: we merely choose between the moral imperative of society, the "spirit" of history, the textile-like "text" which is no text in particular, or the "nature" of Man. Like the imaginary "frictionless space" in Newtonian mechanics, these ulterior images of wholes are not directly accessible to either the author's nor his subject's experience. They can only exist in the imaginations of the author, her informants, and her readers. This is the "essential fiction" of the ethnographic text. (Thornton, 1988: 287 [see chapter 37, this volume, p. 378])

This point is well taken in contemporary anthropology, as in all the other social sciences, where scholars no longer imagine themselves as studying bounded entities, but none the less recognize the essential intellectual and cognitive value of concepts like society, nation and the self.

From *Anthropological Theory* 4(1) (2004), pp. 72–88. Copyright © 2004 by *Anthropological Theory*. Reproduced by permission of Sage Publications Ltd.

Anthropology in Theory: Issues in Epistemology, Second Edition. Edited by Henrietta L. Moore and Todd Sanders.
© 2014 John Wiley & Sons, Inc. Published 2014 by John Wiley & Sons, Inc.

It is impossible to delineate or describe a society in its entirety, but without such a notion it is impossible to make sense of the ethnography of people's lives and social relations. It is on this basis that various scholars have argued that the global and the local are no more than heuristic devices, and as such they do not exist as empirical realities; they are contexts for making sense of data, experiences, and processes – both for social scientists and for their subjects. This point is a good one, as far as it takes us. One version of this argument is that the global is no more than a trope, an expansive metaphor that adumbrates a conceptual domain, but has no explanatory power. The critical point seems to be that one should not refer to the global, use it lightly, without being able to specify what it means in concrete terms (Comaroff and Comaroff, 1999: 294). In anthropological terms, this would clearly mean to provide some sort of ethnographic facts or details. There is nothing wrong with such an aspiration – this is after all what the intellectual activity of anthropology demands – but it fails to capture the complex nature of concept-metaphors within the discipline, and within the daily practice of people's lives (see Moore, 1997: 139–42, 1999).

Concept-metaphors like global, gender, the self and the body are a kind of conceptual shorthand, both for anthropologists and for others. They are domain terms that orient us towards areas of shared exchange, which is sometimes academically based. Concept-metaphors are examples of catachresis, i.e. they are metaphors that have no adequate referent. Their exact meanings can never be specified in advance – although they can be defined in practice and in context – and there is a part of them that remains outside or exceeds representation. Concept-metaphors are, of course, as important to science as they are to social science: think, for example, of the notion of the mind. One of their very important roles is to act as a stimulus for thought – precisely because they do exceed representation – and to act as domains within which apparently new facts, connections or relationships can be imagined. At such a stage, their existence is posited and not proven. The problem with concept-metaphors – or at least some of them – is that by their nature they continue to have a shifting and unspecified tie to physical objects or relationships in the

world. It is, for example, impossible to argue that bodies have nothing to do with physiological entities, that gender is completely independent of the sexed body, and that selves are unrelated to individuals (Moore, 1997: 140). It is constantly being asserted in contemporary feminist writing that the sex/gender distinction cannot hold, just as it is now asseverated that the global/local distinction cannot be maintained, or that if it is then it must be concretely specified.

However, the role of concept-metaphors, like gender or the global, is not to resolve ambiguity, but to maintain it. Their purpose is to maintain a tension between pretentious universal claims and particular contexts and specifics. They are the "spaces" in which details, facts, and connections make sense (cf. Strathern, 1991). More than this, the role of concept-metaphors is to open up spaces for future thinking. What has a discussion of gender done for all the social sciences and humanities, and indeed for many hundreds of thousands of people not concerned with academic debate? It has opened up a space between sex and gender for contestation, debate and action. Whatever happens to gender in feminist theory, sex and gender will never be together again (Moore, 1997: 140). This is what has happened also to the distinction between the global and the local. The distinction between them has opened up a space for future thinking and practical action, and this is true not just for social scientists but for millions of others. As social scientists, it therefore makes sense to argue that what the global means or is in any context should be concretely specified, but it is foolish to rue the fact that it is a metaphor.

The global, like other concept-metaphors in the discipline, has an indeterminate status both as a theoretical abstraction and as a set of processes, experiences and connections in the world; and, as such, its use requires rigorous critical practice. The need for such rigour comes not just from what we might think of as the standards of intellectual activity, but from the fact that the relationship between an imaginary or hypothetical construct and a concrete set of processes and connections in the world is important to ordinary individuals. A notion of the global is now part of most people's imagined and engaged worlds. This is one of the consequences of the processes and experiences of mass migration, mass media, the electronic economy, flexible capital, global consumerism, diasporic identities and transnational communities.

It is a feature of the social sciences that concept-metaphors are shared – to greater or lesser extents – between practising academics and the individuals who are the subject of academic enquiry. Obvious examples include the notions of society and the unconscious. In order to understand how these concept-metaphors inform the imagination and the practice of both academics and non-academics, and the degree to which understandings are shared, diverge and differ, it is necessary to subject these concept-metaphors to critical scrutiny. The result, of course, is that not only do ideas from the academy enter the popular domain, but that theoretical concepts developed in the academy are directly influenced by ideas and assumptions prevalent outside it. There is no purely academic space or theory. This is manifestly true in anthropology where it is impossible, for example, to have an academic theory of society that is uncontaminated by other people's views of what a society is. Part of the process then of subjecting both academic and popular concept-metaphors to critical scrutiny involves examining not just the concepts or theories themselves, but their pre-theoretical commitments.

Pre-theoretical commitments are underlying assumptions and principles. Principles are, of course, linked to methods. However, examinations of anthropological methodology are often reduced to a discussion or reassertion of the importance of participant observation. For some anthropologists, participant observation is the defining feature of anthropology, and its easy elision with the ethnographic accounts for much of the anthropological commitment to the "local". In some sense then, participant observation, the ethnographic and the local make up a methodologism: a procedure that is a theory. What this suggests is that the notion of the "local" is a pretheoretical commitment, and one that, in spite of recent experimental ethnographies (cf. Marcus, 1998: Ch. 2) and the critiques of bounded entities, takes much of its analytical and emotive value from earlier pre-theoretical commitments to "wholism" (society, community, ethnography). The local exists in so far as it is defined in contradistinction to something that is not local, now commonly referred to as the global. The term

global – sometimes refigured as globalization, globality, globalism – replaces earlier grounding figures, such as world system and centre/periphery. The mutual imbrication of the global and the local are subject to debate within the discipline, both conceptually and empirically. However, in most of the theoretical writing to date, the problematic term is assumed to be the global. An ethnography of the local is by definition possible – otherwise how could anthropology exist as a discipline and a practice – but an ethnography of the global remains in doubt.

There are, of course, many good reasons for this assumption, not least the problem of scale, and the fact that many of the processes, experiences and connections that make up the global do not involve face-to-face interactions, and are extended over space and time; for example, flows of capital and financial transactions. None the less, the fact remains that the concept-metaphor of the local is under-examined in terms of its pretheoretical commitments. While assumptions about wholism have come under scrutiny within the discipline starting with the critique of representation and authority in the "writing culture debate", the contemporary use of the term local is elided with participant observation and ethnography in a way that effectively suggests that we know what the local is. The local is thus presented as permanently and naturally linked both to empirical detail and the ethnographic perspective in a way that makes it difficult to examine its pretheoretical commitments.

One issue here is the way that methodology itself is reduced to participant observation as method. The term methodology actually has two meanings, the first being the system of methods as used in a particular discipline. This is essentially the definition that is used in practice in anthropology. The second is a branch of philosophy that analyses the principles and procedures of inquiry in a particular discipline. This last, properly speaking, defines methodology as an analysis of the underlying principles and assumptions of ways of thinking. Both meanings are frequently elided in contemporary uses of the term methodology in anthropological writing. However, more attention to the second definition would have the advantage of denaturalizing and subjecting to critical scrutiny the notion of participant observation as the defining method of anthropology and its connection to an unproblematic notion of the local.

What this points to is the idea that rather than simply seek, as many authors do, to conceptualize the relation between the local and the global, we should perhaps begin by "methodologizing" their relation: in other words, examining the pre-theoretical commitments that underpin their putative connections and interrelations. Of interest here is the implicit view of the world contained in the local/ global distinction, where the local is associated with the empirical and the concrete, while the global is seen as more abstract. In point of fact, both are abstractions, in the sense that they are models. As concept-metaphors they act as framing devices, and as such they are perspectival. The fact of perspective is evidently intrinsic to their definition since they are viewed as acting at different scales. One of the purposes of concept-metaphors in the social and natural sciences is to facilitate comparison, to frame contexts, levels or domains within which data – however defined – can be compared for similarities and differences. But, the nature of comparisons alters with changes in the types of models of the world used and kinds of explanation sought: comparison is extrinsic rather than intrinsic (Holy, 1987; Howe, 1987).

It is almost a truism of contemporary anthropology – and certainly part of its ethical commitment – that perspectives and voices are partial, and that phenomena can only ever be partially described by analytical models. This is a view that finds favour in many parts of the social sciences, and is evidenced, amongst other things, by the breakdown of barriers and disciplinary boundaries between the social sciences themselves. However, reflection on the pre-theoretical commitments of the local/global debate suggests that partiality may not always be truly partial! In other words, for every scholar who emphasizes that partiality and perspective do not presuppose a totalized and totalizing vista just out of view (cf. Appadurai, 1996; Marcus, 1998; Strathern, 1991), there are others seeking to understand what is happening to the "new economy", the "new feudalism", and the "new political economy". In other words, partiality becomes part of a part/whole relationship, where comparison will reveal how local situations fit into larger wholes, how new structures are taking particular shape in

specific contexts, and how the global connects to the local. In anthropology, this form of pre-theoretical commitment is most evident in the "resistance and accommodation" theorists who emphasize how the local either resists or adapts to the global (cf. Miller, 1995). In such writing, the implicit image is of a system, and of parts that together make sense within a whole. The global is the result of many local exemplifications, and by the same extension, the global only makes sense in the context of its local appropriation, as it becomes part of a local system (cf. Englund and Leach, 2000).

However, the picture is much more complex than this because the local is imaged both as a context – perhaps culture, less often society – just out of view or off the analytical scanner, and as a non-bounded entity, a fictive construct. This ambivalence gives rise to a dominant image, one of fragmentation. It is a commonplace now to read that the world we live in is fragmented; that our lives, and even our selves, are fragmented: this holographic imagery suggests that our selves are now modelled on our world. It's fragmentation turtles all the way down. The holographic in this context is another version of the part/whole relation. The actuality of fragmentation could be the result of translocal lives, time/space compression and the complexity of knowledge working, consumer choice and interest group politics, but is this really the case? It seems unlikely that what is imagined as fragmentation actually comes from a world of fragments, any more than the traditional notion of culture or society came from a world that was already a totality (Strathern, 1991: 22). The notion of fragmentation – and the imaginative work it performs within the contemporary social sciences – is intrinsically connected to pretheoretical assumptions about wholism and the associated notion of the local. In this view, what globalization has done is to break the whole down into parts, but without us being able to tell how the parts could be fitted back together again. The fact that we are no longer sure how parts fit into the whole probably accounts for the current popularity of the notion of disjuncture in anthropology and elsewhere, as it slowly shades into the associated sentiment of dysfunction (see also Appadurai, 1996; Comaroff and Comaroff, 2000; Derrida, 1994; Lash and Urry, 1987).

Alternative Images of the Global

George Marcus (1998: chs. 1–3) has suggested a way forward beyond a notion of the local/global based on a pre-theoretical commitment to wholism towards an ethnography of the global:

> I want to consider an individual project of eth-nography whose main ambition is to represent something of the operation of the system itself rather than to demonstrate continually and habitually in the spirit of pluralism the power of local culture over global forces of apparent homogenization. The point is to reconceptualize through ethnography such forces themselves, to efface the macro–micro dichotomy itself as a framing rhetoric for ethnography that seriously limits ethnography's possibilities and applica-tions in the context of so-called postmodern conditions of knowledge. (Marcus, 1998: 34–5)

Marcus draws his own inspiration from the work of social scientists who are trying both to make sense of global cultural diversity and to imagine and model the complex, pluralistic, multifaceted and labile nature of contemporary capitalism (Comaroff and Comaroff, 2000; Lash and Urry, 1987). Models based on pre-theoretical commit-ments to wholism are simply not appropriate for the task which, broadly defined, is one of under-standing how commonalities are built upon asymmetries, how processes and connections that are not part of a totality can be conceived and how their function and future development can be modelled. One of the key problems is that globalization builds on diversification, and yet global processes and structures can be identified. Broadly speaking, key processes include the refig-uring of temporal and spatial relations through technology and new forms of communication and production; growing inequality within and between nations; the increasing power of trans-national networks and connections; the mount-ing pressure on nation states and the increasingly international nature of national economies; the cultural transformation of the economy and the increasing commodification of culture; the explosion of identity politics and the ethniciza-tion of civil society. These processes are under-pinned by key structural changes, including the enormous growth in service industries; the

relative decline of factory industrialism; the importance of knowledge as a form of wealth creation; flexible accumulation and the enormous increase in the speed and volume of capital flows; mass migration; the feminization and ethniciza-tion of the labour force; and the growth of mass media and consumerism.

The pressing question is what kind of concept-metaphors do we have at our disposal to provide a context for thought and action? The local and the global remain the foundational tropes, but in seeking to explain how they are interconnected authors have developed alternative concept-metaphors. Some scholars, for example, have moved towards trying to characterize the nature of contemporary or "late" capitalism, and to look at the specific ways in which it differs from earlier forms of capitalism: for example, disorga-nized capitalism (Lash and Urry, 1987), millennial capitalism (Comaroff and Comaroff, 2000), the global economy (Greider, 1997), the new capitalism (Sennett, 1998), and virtualism (Carrier and Miller, 1998). Others are concerned with the effects of globalization on the nation state, and views differ as to whether the state will survive or wither (Hirst and Thompson, 1996; Sassen, 1996). These debates are about how the local and the global are interacting, and how we can under-stand the process of simultaneous integration and diversification that seems to be at the core of their interaction.

Part of the underlying argument here is about the dominance of the "market" or the "economy". Views differ: some scholars have argued that capitalism was never the sole influence on global-ization (Giddens, 1994; Robertson, 1992), while others have seen the economy as a "cultural dom-inant" under neoliberal capitalism (Jameson, 1991). These debates are an attempt to come to terms with what drives the processes of integration and diversification, and to understand exactly what the interconnections are between the local and the global. One very dominant view that is widely shared across academic disciplines is that cultural production and issues of identity are now at the core of a new political economy. Culture has become increasingly commodified, and it has also become the means through which diversification is replicated through globalized processes, experi-ences and interconnections. As workplaces and organizations become less relevant to identity formation and a sense of place, processes of subjectivity and subjectification become increasingly cultural, bound up with images, aspirations, identifications, lifestyles and forms of consumerism that are not based on locale, but on interconnection, and forms of time-space compression. Homogenization and fragmentation are the products of the transnationalization of production and the global economy (cf. Dirlik, 1994), because difference itself has become a commodity. Economic profit is gained through the commodification of difference, and through the active and conscious production of that difference, hence the importance of culture. As Jameson argues, cultural production and innovation are at the basis of the expansion of the economic system, and suddenly what is for sale is the production of everyday life (Jameson, 1998: 67).

The peculiar interpenetration of the cultural and the economic is the site of the interconnection between the local and the global, and it presents anthropology with both a challenge and an opportunity: the production of the global is the production of everyday life. However, the challenge lies in the fact that in this new political economy, the economic, the cultural and the political interconnect, but do not coincide in fixed structural fashion(s). The result is a complex set of interconnections and processes through which meanings, goods and people flow, coalesce and diverge. Recognizing this not only transforms our notion of the global, but our notion of the local. The local is not about taxonomies, bounded cultures and social units, but about contested fields of social signification and interconnection, flows of people, ideas, images and goods. Both Marcus (1998: chs. 1–3) and Appadurai (1996: chs. 2–4) have tried to capture these sets of shifting interconnections between the local and the global, the former by developing a notion of multi-locale/multi-sited ethnography and the latter by advancing the notion of "scapes". In both cases, the authors had to proceed by problematizing the notion of the local, and prying it away from a pre-theoretical commitment to wholism.

Appadurai characterizes the "new global cultural economy" as a complex, overlapping, disjunctive order, and identifies five dimensions of global cultural flows: ethnoscapes, mediascapes, technoscapes, financescapes and ideoscapes. The suffix "scape" indicates the pre-theoretical commitments underpinning his vision of the relationship between the local and the global. He sees them as fluid, irregular landscapes that far from providing a rigid taxonomy look different from every angle of vision, and are perspectival constructs, inflected by context, and experience and aspiration. The notion of "scape" as a concept-metaphor explicitly moves away from part/whole relationships to focus on flows, processes, interconnections and experiences. It provides a space for action and thought not only for anthropologists, but also for nation states, multinationals, diasporic communities, interest groups, villages, neighbourhoods, families and individuals. "Indeed, the individual actor is the last locus of this perspectival set of landscapes, for these landscapes are eventually navigated by agents who both experience and constitute larger formations, in part from their own sense of what these landscapes offer" (Appadurai, 1996: 32–3). Appadurai does not see these "scapes" as the parts of the global system. He emphasizes that the relationship between them is "deeply disjunctive and unpredictable" because each is subject to its own constraints and incentives (Appadurai, 1996: 35). This point is a good one although much rests on what is actually meant by the term disjuncture and how we might be able to operationalize it in relation to understanding how the local and the global are interconnected. Appadurai points out that what he is attempting to characterize is a set of global flows – images, people, goods, money, ideas – that occur in and through the disjunctures between ethnoscapes, technoscapes, financescapes, mediascapes and ideoscapes. In other words, people, money, images, technology and so on now follow increasingly isomorphic paths, and thus their interconnections cannot be predicted. Underpinning such interconnections is a mutual contest and cannibalization of sameness and difference (Appadurai, 1996: 37, 43).

One of the great strengths of Appadurai's new concept-metaphor of "scape" is its pretheoretical commitment to the idea of processes, interconnections, experiences and imagination at the expense of units, entities, systems and sub-systems – although there are moments in his writing when systemic, part/whole thinking appears to reassert itself. This may be inevitable since in the social sciences however processual our models of the global economy might be there is always a little bit of Marxism struggling to get out – or perhaps in. Appadurai emphasizes in his work the importance of the imagination and the imaginary: the fact that people and groups around the world live in an imagined relation to the global and the local. It is not just academics who use these concept-metaphors, and part of any anthropological study should surely be to investigate how people themselves live in relation to these grounding tropes.

Imagined Worlds

An emphasis on imagined worlds and/or the social imaginary is hardly new in the social sciences, but what is characteristic of contemporary global/local relations is the degree to which issues of individual and collective identity – of persons, groups, nations – are at the core of the new cultural political economy. Individual and collective identities can no longer be understood as produced within defined locations, and their study can no longer be confined to observable activities and ideas within one locale. The identity of any one person or group or nation is produced simultaneously in several locales or contexts, and connected to many that are not physically present, and to others that have never been directly experienced or engaged with. In this sense, the methodological interconnections between the local and the global are already evident in the way that such subjects as ethnicity, gender, race, nationality and postcolonialism have become key topics of anthropological analysis. Kinship systems, family structures, communities, rituals, cosmologies and political structures are all studied still, minutely observed and recorded, but they no longer provide the key conceptual frameworks of the discipline. "Cultural difference or diversity arises here not from some local struggle for identity, but as a function of a complex process among all the sites in which the identity of someone or a group anywhere is defined in simultaneity. It is the burden of the modernist ethnography to capture distinctive identity formations in all their migrations and dispersions" (Marcus, 1998: 63). Diversity arises from engagement with a set of simultaneous processes – as, in fact, does homogenization or integration – and not from a defined cultural tradition or given community or social

location. Thus it is in beginning to transform the local that we come to terms with the global. Anthropology's commitment to a reformed and renewed understanding of the local is ultimately what qualifies it for the study of the global. This does not mean the global in all its dimensions and ramifications, just as anthropology has never been able to study gender, the body, the self, economics and politics in all their dimensions either.

The local and the global as concept-metaphors are not just important in the social sciences, but also in the practice of people's everyday lives. But, if concept-metaphors are to be relevant in a disciplinary context then they must connect to the construction of composite theories. Composite theories are those that contain ontological, epistemological and empirical claims. Concept-metaphors that merely act as a descriptive gloss or posit causal forces that remain unexamined are essentially suffering – at the very least – from under-theorization. The local and the global are important social realities that call for comprehension and detailed specification. In order to understand how the local and the global are interconnected through processes, structures and aspirations, it is necessary to produce detailed and careful analysis of such things as economic and technological change, language usage, shifting understandings of terms and identities, forms of communication and connections between images, among many other things. What results is a view of the local and the global that is modified through a process of critical reflection based on empirical data. This is in effect a description of scientific method, and at earlier moments in its own development anthropology used such methods – arguments about subjectivity/objectivity, emic/etic, qualitative/quantitative notwithstanding – to investigate the nature of "the social", "the person", "the family" and so on. Such procedures are at the basis of a comparative method to which anthropology is committed, and underpin a modernist conception of science.

However, as many social scientists – notably feminist, postmodernist and postcolonial theorists – have pointed out, the comparative dimension in an earlier anthropology was between cultures, and more specifically between "the west and the rest". At the basis of this was a dichotomy based on a set of particular differences between the context of the anthropologist and the context of Others. Contemporary work on the local and the global breaks with this dichotomy, hence the importance of the radical questioning of the notion of the local. But much contemporary work continues to maintain the fiction that concept-metaphors such as the local and the global are academic categories of analysis. There is insufficient direct engagement with the fact that the people studied by anthropologists now make use of the global/local distinction, or other sets of concept-metaphors that organize thought and action around similar sets of processes, structures and aspirations. Social scientists and their subjects are now part of one world, a coeval world. This is not the same thing as saying that the worlds of anthropologists and subjects are exactly the same world or that they share identical views, circumstances, and opportunities. This would be idiotic. It is simply to argue that the self/other, academic/popular dichotomies, which were at the basis of earlier views of the local, and of the academic as the expert in theoretical comparison, are no longer valid (Moore, 1996, 1999).

It is this very fact that makes the question – "is it possible to do a study of the global?" – a misplaced one. The global/local distinction and the vocabulary of globalization are found not only in the discourse of academics, but in that of politicians, corporate executives, journalists and media workers, advertisers, and civil society activists. These groups still receive remarkably little attention from anthropologists, possibly an historical legacy of the discipline's commitment to non-elite groups and localized communities. When one writes of the global being part of the everyday, some sceptics still view this as referring primarily to elite groups of individuals, whose lifestyles or circumstances are necessarily globalized and who, for whatever reason, already cross boundaries, cultures, and contexts. To take this view is to misunderstand the nature of what the global is. Of course, there are individuals, groups and communities who are more directly engaged with global flows and information technology, with media images and communication strategies, and with travel and consumption than others. However, the notion of "home" was as transformed, for example, for those members of the Bangladeshi community who remain in Bangladesh as it was for those who went to London to settle and work. The key point here is

that the global is not just about how globalization operates as an alien and inexorable force, but it is also about how people – individuals and groups – engage with the global and make themselves both global and local. Globalization, like modernization with which it is inextricably intertwined, is a discourse about the present and about possible futures (Gaonkar, 1999).

People in Focus

How can we as anthropologists study the process, structures and aspirations that form the interconnections between the local and the global? One way is to study how people themselves form those interconnections and to understand that process within specific contexts – economic, political, technological, symbolic. Recent work on sexuality and identity provides a very good example of exactly how an ethnography of local/global interconnections is possible. For example, Mark Johnson's work on the Southern Philippines shows how the notion of America and ideas about American love relations provide the conceptual space and the vocabulary for the articulation of local Philippine gay transgendered identities (Johnson, 1997, 1998). This vision of America is not about a shared homosexual identity and solidarity with American gays, but about the possibility of true-love relations that would transcend the relations of exchange on which sexual encounters for transgendered gays in the Philippines are based. It is also about how the association of Philippine gays with America in the local community defines them as sexually and ethnically deviant: not real Muslim men or real Muslim women (Johnson, 1998: 707). The America referred to here is an imaginary one, a constructed one, and is not directly experienced as such. The distinction between the local Muslim world and that of America works in various ways to express distinctions between Christians and Muslims, normal and deviant sexualities, commoditization and true love. These distinctions form the basis for a set of locales in which identities, personal and collective, are formed. Identities and identifications are thus both global and local in character.

Much has been made in recent years of what Dennis Altman (1996) called the invention of gay as a global category, but comparison of Johnson's work with that of Jackson (1999) on Thailand and

Donham (1998) on South Africa shows how an understanding of what the emergent category "gay" means requires detailed historical, political and ethnographic analysis, and how each situation shares similarities, but is also very different. Altman has misleadingly implied that in analysing the global category gay, one is permanently caught between political economy – universalizing tendencies – and anthropology – cultural specificities (Altman, 1996: 87). This is not the case. What ethnographic analysis is about is how and in what form this newly imagined community becomes available to people across the globe, and part of that analysis will include such things as economic circumstances, legal rights, political support, technological provision, and the impact of print and mass media, as well as detailed symbolic and cultural analysis. In other words, the local and the global are not separate from one another, tied into a system of part/whole relations, or linked through simple differences of scale. Altman, like the anthropological authors criticized earlier in this article, posits an incommensurability between political economy and anthropology because he mistakenly assumes that the analyst's and the informant's grasp of cultural specificities is more secure than their understanding of the larger context.

The formation of the global gay community does not necessarily involve travel or direct contact between individuals, although tourism, media and information technologies clearly play an important role. But in the commodification of the everyday and of cultural authenticity that is increasingly part of the phenomenon of globalization, more direct forms of contact and mediation are also taking place. These situations provide key contexts within which individuals and groups construct themselves as both global and local, as both having authentic cultures, and knowing how to cross cultural boundaries. Some of the most dramatic examples come from work on tourism, material culture and the arts (Marcus and Myers, 1995; Nash, 1993). Ecological and cultural tourism is on the increase, and tourists not only want to buy cultural artefacts, but to experience local – tribal, exotic – life in all its details. This form of consumption is a key part of identity formation for the tourists concerned and may be linked to other ideological commitments and involvement in activism in their home locale – political or religious. On the part of the cultural producers themselves, they are extending their culture into the global market, and may be using this process of extension to make the global flows of people, income and knowledge work towards their own social and cultural reproduction (cf. Phillips and Steiner, 1999). Little (2000) describes how Kaqchikel women in the Mayan site of San Antonio Aguas Calientes have adapted to the tourist market by putting on performances of daily living for tourists, and Krystal (2000) describes how the revitalization of ritual performances for tourists in San Miguel Totonicapán is stimulating artisanal production. In many cases, the forms of cultural production entered into cannot easily be glossed or dismissed as the destruction of traditional culture by commodification. There are many examples where production for tourists and indeed for international art markets has extended ways of reflecting on core values and symbols, allowing artists to imaginatively broaden and rework cosmological and symbolic understandings and forms of representation (cf. Marcus and Myers, 1995; Phillips and Steiner, 1999). This process of cultural extension, which remains deeply implicated in unequal power relations and access to resources, is none the less part of a process of reimagining the local and its value in a global context. It is part of a process through which people make themselves simultaneously global and local. In understanding this process, it is important, however, not to fall back on originary categories. The local that is reimagined is always already global; it has no originary starting point.

At first sight, this process of creative extension can be contrasted to what appears to be an emerging process of cultural reappropriation. There have been requests and declarations by a number of Native North American tribes, Australian Aboriginal, South American and Pacific groups, as well as others, for museums to restrict access to anthropological field data and cultural property – including all field notes, drawings, photographs, music, songs, stories, and representations of the culture or cultural knowledge – to those with written authority from the group concerned. In some cases, requests to repatriate materials to the group have been made, and in more recent developments attempts have been made to have cultural material treated as a form of intellectual property (cf. Brown, 1998). These requests could be seen unreflectively as a form of "relocalization" of culture, the opposite of participation in a global world. In point of fact, they are a reasoned response to the reality of the local/global relation, and very much part of that relation. They are a clear recognition of the importance of flows of people, information and technology, and the ways those flows are part of broader economic and political power structures. The debate here is a clear extension of attempts by native people to extend rights to land and resources in many contexts around the world, but it is also a way of rethinking and seeking to act upon the interconnections between the local and the global. Cultural activism itself also provides forms of collective identification at another level, as groups around the world unite in recognition of common struggles, and is therefore another example of simultaneous diversification and integration as a product of the global.

One of the key issues in the processes of rei-magining identities within global/local relations is the use of language, concepts and images. The very same language, concepts, and images that are used by activists to try to preserve the ozone layer and prevent environmental catastrophe are employed by multinational corporations to pro-mote images of global responsibility. One of the more frustrating problems faced by advocacy groups, like Oxfam and Greenpeace, is that the language and concepts they deploy in their work are rapidly recolonized by others with quite dif-ferent aims and political agendas. The language of the political right and left converges and diverges, exploiting images, brands and associations, and mixing them with political agendas that can seem frustratingly similar. Hilary Cunningham's study of the Sanctuary Movement in the United States, a church-based activist group concerned with illegal immigrants and US government policy on Central America in the 1980s and 1990s, demon-strates how an interest group defined itself as transnational (Cunningham, 2000). She shows how members of the group deployed the Christian imagery of brotherhood to redefine their senses of self, and their relations to family, Church, State and citizenship. Cunningham also documents how over time the increasing use of information technology and the internet transformed access to information and allowed members to redefine contexts for action as well as knowledge.

Two very important points emerge from Cunningham's work. The first is that in studying

an activist group that is self-consciously part of a global civil society, the global is both about struc-tures and technology, and about symbols, iden-tities, mindsets and beliefs. In other words, her work demonstrates very clearly the particular nature of the new cultural political economy. However, such a demonstration is dependent upon detailed ethnographic work. The second impor-tant point to emerge is the mingling of academic and popular language and concepts. Cunningham bravely describes her own unease when on return-ing into the field in the 1990s, she suddenly found her informants talking like her: "there were times during this phase of research when I experienced fieldwork as indoctrination into my own cate-gories of analysis" (Cunningham, 2000: 585).

As Cunningham points out, contemporary anthropology finds itself working in a world where the lines between theoretical analysis and cultural production are now blurred. Social sci-ence concepts and language are no longer, if they ever were, confined to the academy, and are rou-tinely used by civil rights and environmental activists, political lobbyists, journalists and media workers, business leaders and analysts, and a whole variety of individuals. University students trained in anthropology and the other social sci-ences become involved in all areas of commercial and cultural production, political and economic activism: many of them are from indigenous and minority communities themselves. New forms of conjuncture between academic, professional and popular discourses mean that social scientists are studying worlds created, to a certain extent, in their own image. It also means that academics are only one of many "expert" elites, and that the analysis of cultural productions and their engage-ments with political economy based on detailed empirical data for comparative purposes are not confined to the academy. Ironically, where anthropology might once have been a local discourse, it is now definitively a global one, and professional anthropologists are far from the only "native speakers" to be involved.

Getting a Grip

Although one's grip on a tool is no less secure because on an infinitesimal scale skin and wood do not touch, the knowledge creates the sensation of there being something else to explain. Certainty itself appears partial, information intermittent. An answer is another question, a connection a gap, a similarity a difference, and vice versa. Wherever we look we are left with the further knowledge that surface understanding conceals gaps and bumps. (Strathern, 1991: xxiv)

Anthropology, like the other social sciences, is being reconstituted as it reworks its relationship with the world it studies. Part of studying the interconnections between the global and the local is the study of this process itself: the social sciences in the world, as players in a modernizing global project. What then is the problem about anthropologists studying the global? Why does the question "is an ethnography of the global possible" cause so much unease? The anxiety seems to arise from the notion that there is nothing – no theory, no appropriate method – between a micro and a macro anthropology, between the local and the global: the difficulty appears to be one of scale. But this perception is itself a consequence of particular pre-theoretical commitments, which posit the idea that the local and the global are linked as parts to wholes, as internal divisions to a single holistic entity. There are two types of pre-theoretical commitment that haunt much of the current work on the interconnections between the global and the local, including many contemporary accounts that emphasize fragmentation and disjuncture. The first is the notion of a system, and the related possibility of a worldview. This idea comes into anthropology through, amongst other things, organic metaphors drawn from the biological sciences and from early cybernetics. The paradox is that recent commitments to fragmentation, positionality and perspective all reinvoke this notion even as they appear to work against it. The very notion of perspective implies the idea of a totalizing view, even if it is one that is constantly substituted for by others – other people's views, other voices, other ways of looking (cf. Strathern, 1991). When we can no longer adequately specify how parts link to wholes, then we produce ideas about fragmentation and disjuncture: perspectives multiply and there is no one way to characterize the system.

This argument may appear strange given anthropology's current pre-theoretical commitments to doing away with bounded entities and wholes, but

the very idea of globalization invokes an idea of different parts becoming part of some larger whole or process. This idea itself is, of course, much reinforced by discussion of capitalism, even though we now speak not of the capitalist system, but of capitalisms, just as we now talk of multiple modernities. Marx may have been proved to be prescient or finally shown to be irrelevant depending on one's perspective, but in current work on global relations the spectre of Marx flits in and out of the picture. This links to the second type of pre-theoretical commitment that haunts much contemporary work on the interconnections between the global and the local. This pre-theoretical commitment is to the notion of dialectics: the unavoidable push and pull of convergence and divergence, integration and diversification. Dialectical thinking contains an ultimate implication of synthesis – via thesis and antithesis – and thus connects intellectually to notions of resolution and holism. It also relates to the notion of contradiction: where a contradiction between conflicting forces or ideas serves as a determining factor in their continuing interaction. This particular idea seems to capture the process that drives globalization forward. However, perhaps the time has come to ask ourselves more forcefully than we have to date whether our current models and their pre-theoretical commitments – fragmentation, disjuncture, positionality, perspective, and dialectics – serve us appropriately. Do they provide sufficient purchase to understand the complex and rapid set of interconnections, processes and aspirations through which meanings, goods and people flow, coalesce and diverge? Are we looking for some sort of structural-causal order? Both Appadurai (1996: ch. 2) and Marcus (1998: ch. 2) seem to suggest not, or rather that we need to move beyond historical determinism and take more account of contingency, improvisation, and non-isomorphism.

If this is true then new concept-metaphors might be to hand, and interestingly they are emerging through ethnography: through ethnographic work on physics, biotechnologies, computer technologies, biomedical sciences, engineering, mathematics, and simulation technologies. These ethnographies are exposing social scientists in a variety of disciplines to new imaginaries: ways of imagining the world and its connections. Biotechnological work produces images of replication rather than reproduction;

computer technologies provide images of interacting and learning that break down the boundary between mind and machine; quantum mechanics deploys notions of undecidability; and fractal mathematics breaks down ideas about binaries. All these models are based on pre-theoretical commitments quite different from those currently employed in thinking about global/local interconnections in anthropology. These models are, however, already rapidly entering the domain of the social and transforming it. This occurs sometimes through direct interaction, as in multinationals' attempts to exploit bioinformation for profit or in people's engagement with virtual reality and its impact on notions of self and sociality, and sometimes indirectly as immunology, scanning technology and informatics provide images through which to construct new versions of inner worlds and social lives. It seems likely that our current concept-metaphors and models may be inadequate for understanding the interconnections, processes and aspirations of global/local relations, non-isomorphic patterns of change, and flows that coalesce and diverge along constantly changing lines of fracture. New concept-metaphors and models may emerge from the bio, medical, and information sciences, and as they do they will entail new pre-theoretical commitments: they cannot be maintained or even thought on the basis of the existing ones in the social sciences. However, when these new concept-metaphors, models and pre-theoretical commitments do emerge, we will subject them to critical reflection in the way we have always done, by looking at how people themselves deploy them in their imagined and engaged worlds: that is, ethnographically.

References

Altman, D. (1996) "Rupture or Continuity? The Internationalization of Gay Identities", *Social Text* 14(3): 77–94.

Appadurai, A. (1996) *Modernity at Large: Cultural Dimensions of Globalization.* Minneapolis: University of Minnesota Press.

Brown, M. (1998) "Can Culture Be Copyrighted?", *Current Anthropology* 39(2): 193–222.

Carrier, J. and D. Miller, eds. (1998) *Virtualism: A New Political Economy.* Oxford: Berg.

Comaroff, J. and J.L. Comaroff (1999) "Occult Economies and the Violence of Abstraction: Notes from the South African Postcolony", *American Ethnologist* 26(2): 279–303.

Comaroff, J. and J.L. Comaroff (2000) "Millennial Capitalism: First Thoughts on a Second Coming", *Public Culture* 12(2): 291–343.

Cunningham, H. (2000) "The Ethnography of Transnational Social Activism: Understanding the Global as Local Practice", *American Ethnologist* 26(3): 583–604.

Derrida, J. (1994) *Specters of Marx: The State of Debt, the Work of Mourning, and the New International.* London: Routledge.

Dirlik, A. (1994) *After the Revolution: Waking to Global Capitalism.* Hanover, NH: Wesleyan University Press.

Donham, D. (1998) "Freeing South Africa: The 'Modernization' of Male–Male Sexuality in Soweto", *Cultural Anthropology* 13(1): 3–21.

Englund, H. and J. Leach (2000) "Ethnography and the Meta-narratives of Modernity", *Current Anthropology* 41(2): 225–48.

Fabian, J. (1983) *Time and the Other: How Anthropology Makes Its Object.* New York: Columbia University Press.

Gaonkar, D.P. (1999) "On Alternative Modernities", *Public Culture* 11(1): 1–18.

Giddens, A. (1994) *Beyond Left and Right: The Future of Radical Politics.* Cambridge: Polity Press.

Greider, W. (1997) *One World, Ready Or Not: The Manic Logic of Global Capitalism.* New York: Simon and Schuster.

Gupta, A. and J. Ferguson (1992) "Beyond 'Culture': Space, Identity and the Politics of Difference", *Cultural Anthropology* 7: 6–23.

Hirst, P. and G. Thompson (1996) *Globalization in Question: The International Economy and the Possibilities of Governance.* Cambridge: Polity Press.

Holy, L. (1987) *Comparative Anthropology.* Oxford: Basil Blackwell.

Howe, L., ed. (1987) "Caste in Bali and India: Levels of Comparison", in L. Holy (ed.) *Comparative Anthropology.* Oxford: Basil Blackwell.

Jackson, P. (1999) "Kathoey Gay Man: The Historical Emergence of Gay Male Identity in Thailand", in L. Manderson and M. Jolly (eds.) *Sites of Desire, Economies of Pleasure: Sexualities in Asia and the Pacific.* Chicago, IL: University of Chicago Press.

Jameson, F. (1991) *Postmodernism, Or the Cultural Logic of Late Capitalism*. Durham, NC: Duke University Press.

Jameson, F. (1998) "Notes on Globalization as a Philosophical Issue", in F. Jameson and M. Miyoshi (eds.) *The Cultures of Globalization*. Durham, NC: Duke University Press.

Johnson, M. (1997) *Beauty and Power: Transgendering and Cultural Transformation in the Southern Philippines*. Oxford: Berg.

Johnson, M. (1998) "Global Desirings and Translocal Loves: Transgendering and Same-Sex Sexualities in the Southern Philippines", *American Ethnologist* 25(4): 695–711.

Krystal, M. (2000) "Cultural Revitalization and Tourism at the Moreria Nima" K'iche', *Ethnology* 39(2): 149–62.

Lash, S. and J. Urry (1987) *The End of Organized Capitalism*. Madison: University of Wisconsin Press.

Little, W. (2000) "Home as a Place of Exhibition and Performance: Mayan Household Transformations in Guatemala", *Ethnology* 39(2): 163–81.

Marcus, G. (1998) *Ethnography Through Thick and Thin*. Princeton, NJ: Princeton University Press.

Marcus, G. and F. Myers, eds. (1995) *The Traffic in Culture: Refiguring Art and Anthropology*. Berkeley: University of California Press.

Miller, D. (1995) "Introduction: Anthropology, Modernity and Consumption", in D. Miller (ed.) *Worlds Apart: Modernity Through the Prism of the Local*. London: Routledge.

Moore, H. L. ed. (1996) *The Future of Anthropological Knowledge*. London: Routledge.

Moore, H. L. (1997) "Interior Landscapes and External Worlds: The Return of Grand Theory in Anthropology", *Australian Journal of Anthropology* 8(2): 125–44.

Moore, H. L. ed. (1999) *Anthropological Theory Today*. Cambridge: Polity Press.

Nash, J., ed. (1993) *Crafts in the World Market: The Impact of the Global Exchange on Middle American Artisans*. Albany: State University of New York Press.

Phillips, R. and C. Steiner, eds. (1999) *Unpacking Culture: Art and Commodity in Colonial and Postcolonial Worlds*. Berkeley: University of California Press.

Robertson, R. (1992) *Globalization: Social Theory and Global Culture*. London: Sage.

Sassen, S. (1996) *Losing Control? Sovereignty in an Age of Globalization*. New York: Columbia University Press.

Sennett, R. (1998) *The Corrosion of Character: The Personal Consequences of Work in the New Capitalism*. New York: W. W. Norton.

Strathern, M. (1991) *Partial Connections*. Savage, MD: Rowman and Littlefield.

Thornton, R. (1988) "The Rhetoric of Ethnographic Holism", *Cultural Anthropology* 3(3): 285–303.

SECTION 11

Perspectives and Their Logics

37

The Rhetoric of Ethnographic Holism

Robert J. Thornton

The fundamental and motivating problem of ethnography is how to use writing to bring the "everyday" into relation with "history" and "environment." Since writing is a work of the imagination, it is in the imagination that the crucial synthesis between the microcosm and the macrocosm takes place. Unlike the zoologist who describes the mollusc before him, the ethnographer must imagine the "whole" that is society, and convey this imagination of wholeness to his reader along with the descriptions of places seen, speech heard, persons met. The description of wholes, however, is "description without place ... a sight indifferent to the eye." For this, the ethnography needs a special kind of rhetorical technique. Both the rhetoric and the imagination essential to it are founded on classification employed as rhetorical figure. The ethnography's use of classification constitutes a use of language outside of its normal syntactic and semantic sense that point to or suggest other levels of meaning – that is, it functions as a trope that I shall call the rhetoric of classification.

[...]

Imagination of Wholeness and Rhetorical Necessity

Social wholes can not be directly experienced by a single human observer. The vision of the scope and scale of social life that extends beyond what we can experience must be imagined. But this imagination of social wholes never includes *only* that one which is being described. The ethnographic imagination inevitably includes those realities that are or have been realized in historical or present time, and those that exist as possibilities, dreams or nightmares. For European thought since the time of the Eleatics, the possible, the imagined, and the future have been treated as though they possessed the same status in reason as the realized, the observed and the past. There are historical as well as rhetorical reasons for this, but most important perhaps is the fact that anthropology – indeed any science that attempts to say what man "really is," what he is "in essence" – must necessarily be a moral science. Some have called anthropology a "reformer's science," as did E. B. Tylor (1871) or Henri-Alexandre Junod (1927 vol. 1:9). For others it has

Anthropology in Theory: Issues in Epistemology, Second Edition. Edited by Henrietta L. Moore and Todd Sanders.
© 2014 John Wiley & Sons, Inc. Published 2014 by John Wiley & Sons, Inc.

been the choice between "being history or being nothing," as the constitutional historian F. W. Maitland once claimed. It has been defined as a "natural science of society" by Radcliffe-Brown (1925), or as many contemporary ethnographers seem to agree, as a never-ending unraveling of textile-like meanings, morals, and messages through hermeneutic interpretation of texts.

In other words, reference to some ulterior entity is always implicit in holism: we merely choose between the moral imperative of society, the "spirit" of history, the textile-like "text" which is no text in particular, or the "nature" of Man. Like the imaginary "frictionless space" in Newtonian mechanics, these ulterior images of wholes are not directly accessible to either the author's nor his subject's experience. They can only exist in the imaginations of the author, his informants, and his readers. This is the "essential fiction" of the ethnographic text.

The fiction of wholes, however, guarantees the facticity of "fact." The imagination is an essential part of this rhetorical process for several reasons. Inhabiting the minds of all writers of ethnography is an ideal vision of society – existing in states of utopic grace or absolute horror, positive harmony or debasement and negation of all value – or the vision of the imagined past of the classics, the images of distant, different lands of travelers.[1] These images, scenarios, or counterfactuals have served as the templates against which reality, and the description of reality, has been compared and judged. In fact, these images may well be archetypes, the sort of thing a possible pidgin sociology would constantly resort to, or which exist framed in some deep-structure of the human mind.

Indeed, it may be that it is impossible to conceptualize society,[2] except in terms of holistic images. But, while we can experience social relationships in which we are involved, and witness a few of those in which others are involved, it is manifestly impossible to witness or experience society. We may only experience parts of what we today call "society," and somehow bring these experiences into relation with a larger entity that we can not directly experience. Phrased in this way, the question about the relationship of ethnography to social reality becomes a more general one about the role of the image and the imagination and the cognitive process by which such images come into being. The rhetoric of ethnography presents these

ulterior images against which description makes sense, and within which microcosm may be wedded to macrocosm.

All explanations eventually make reference to these ulterior images. The scientific, or nomothetic-deductive method achieves explanation through appeal to formulae that are regarded as "established" through either empirical or logical means. As Kuhn (1970) has shown, this appeal to truth is only effective within scientific communities who share certain beliefs and formulae whose proof is beyond the range of "ordinary science." The laws of nature serve as one such ulterior whole. Similarly, a moral understanding consists of making a connection between a moral problem and the universe of absolute and ultimate values. A theoretical understanding connects the description with the partition of the universe into discrete but related parts and assigns it a place in this world. The scientific understanding depends on the existence of natural order, the moral understanding depends on the cosmological image of ultimate moral truth, and the theoretical account acquires its truth-value from the belief that such connectivity must exist. As the quasi-religious speculation of contemporary astronomers and physical cosmologists demonstrates, an absolute dissolution of the universe into mystery or indeterminacy is intolerable (Toulmin 1982).

An ethnographic description, then, is a work, in the sense of an effort, *un travail* as opposed to *un oeuvre*, because it cannot offer in itself the understanding that it seeks. Ethnography cannot be replicated as a test of its validity or truth precisely because it is always in the process of achieving an understanding of an object that can never be completely understood. Description conveys its understanding through multiple levels of analogy, and, for ethnography, the classificatory mode of description does this best.

Social Wholes, Social Parts and Classification

Today, after McLuhan (1962), Foucault (1974) and Derrida (1976), the text itself is not longer taken to be just a medium for communicating what is discovered elsewhere by other means. We see it now as an object, a practice and a form that communicates ideas in its own right, independent of whatever its "content" might be. In anthropology (and social sciences generally) this content – social or cultural wholes – is nevertheless still taken to be constituted elsewhere and by other means. Is ethnography "just description" of these objective wholes? Or, does such description merely "resemble reason" as Leibniz claims memory does? It seems to me that the heart of the problem may be the very *concept of wholes themselves.*

Indeed, "social wholes" may be seen as an artifact of rhetoric. The notion of "social wholes" and the doctrine of "holism" has long been taken to be the hallmark of anthropology, and the broadly classificatory or "classified" way in which ethnographic monographs are presented is central to the idea of "wholes." By understanding classification as itself a kind of trope, attention is directed to the problematic nature of the idea of "holism" or "social wholes" for the entire ethnographic project.

Social wholes are conceptualized against a background of other possible "wholes" within which, and compared with which, the ethnographic doctrine of holism makes sense. In fact, the notion of the whole is heavily overdetermined in anthropology and in other social sciences as well. The history of the Judeo-Christian religion, philosophy, modern politics, biology, and psychology all contribute to the notion of "the whole." The Kingdom of God, Eden, the concept of truth, the nation-state, language, ecology, and mind are all thought of as wholes, chiefly as a consequence of a particular intellectual history. It could scarcely be different for anthropology, which has interacted closely with the other disciplines of the sciences, and with literature and politics, and ever since Tylor spoke of "culture or civilization as that complex whole," anthropology has taken it for granted. The classification, however, provides a rhetorical means for bringing any number of "wholes" into play at one time. In doing so, however, it may have confused us somewhat about how these wholes actually "work."

Parts and Wholes

An anatomy of ethnography's essential fiction reveals that the "social whole" consists of parts, and it is in terms of the part–whole relationship (formally called the mereological relation) that

many theoretical arguments within ethnographic writing are phrased. Whether the parts are taken to be persons, groups, institutions, symbols, combinations of these or something else entirely, it is usually asserted that the "social whole" is made up of just these parts. Furthermore, the ethnographic text is made up of parts or "chapters" that are compilations of many disparate observations of behavior, language, ritual, dance, art and other aspects of expressive culture, spatial dispositions, reports of these, and so on. These small fragments of patterned, usually formalized behavior and thought are the elements of the fieldwork record, that is, they are "real" (given to experience), and more importantly here, necessarily shared by the ethnographer and his interlocutors. But once we have begun to collect and combine these records they are no longer given to experience in quite the same way. The "experience of fieldwork" is both the experience of social life and the experience of the textual fragments in which it is recorded.

Chapters and divisions of books reflect an idea of society as a "sum of parts." As the social whole is held to be composed of mutually determining parts, the textual whole is composed of these textual fragments. The apparent wholeness of society, then, emerges from this process of collection and combination, and may have more to do with the manifest and concrete wholeness of the book that is itself constructed from parts.

But, this assumed relationship between social wholes and what are taken to be their parts – namely, social entities such as individuals, clans, age-grades, hospitals, nations, factories, etc. – is founded on a mistaken analogy with the text whose parts – namely chapters, titles, subheadings, paragraphs and so on – are truly constitutive of the textual whole. This relation of constituency does not hold true of "social wholes": they are not composed of parts in this way at all; they do not "add up." Again, the elusive "replicability" of ethnographic data demonstrates this pervasive but mistaken analogy: replicability is only elusive at the level of text. Individual events observed, stories heard, phrases remembered, formulae recited, artifacts seen, etc. are repeated again and again, often monotonously across epochs and cultures. It is the writing, collection, and compilation of these into books that cannot be replicated.

There is a further difficulty arising from the fact that there are two types of wholes. On the one hand a whole may be conceptualized mereologically, as a relationship between a concrete whole and its parts, as a cake and its slices, the Leviathan and its organs, a graph and its bars. On the other hand, the social whole may be held to be constituted by a rule of class-inclusion or it may be defined as the class of instances of specific attributes. E. B. Tylor's famous definition of culture as "that complex whole," is just such a set of elements selected according to some more or less specific criteria of which there are many possibilities (e.g., all human behaviors, all thoughts, all customs). The problem is that these two logically distinguishable holisms are almost always confused in sociological thought.

First of all, all organic and mechanistic metaphors of society imply that there is a mereological relationship between the parts of society and the whole that they are said to constitute. These images of social wholes are usually framed in terms of metaphorical images of organic bodies (function, functionalism), texts (signs and symbols, hermeneutics), trees (branches, evolution), rivers (flow, history), geological and architectural formations (strata, structuralism and Marxism) or machines (process, economics). Since the mereological relationship holds for the metaphorical image (i.e., an arm or head is clearly a part of the whole body, the branch a part of the whole tree, and so on), it is accepted that the same relationship holds for the social whole and its parts. That is simply the way good metaphors work. The matter is further complicated by the fact that class-inclusion relationships are often represented in graphic images. When the analysis is developed and elaborated in writing, it is done by recourse to terms for these images of branches, organs, strata, links and nodes, bodies and flow, that is, in terms of the same spatial or graphic images that are employed as metaphors for society. And finally, the words category, kind, class, genus, type are all used more or less interchangeably, and all conceived as parts of a classification (Manley Thompson 1983:342). But the class-inclusion rules that make categories members of classifications must be carefully distinguished from the mereological part-to-whole relationship.

In ethnography, this distinction is usually confused, especially since the material text is composed of (true mereological) parts and since

the image-like metaphors of body/text/tree/river etc. are rarely far from the surface.

In fact, it appears that the confusion is almost essential to the achievement of what must be one of the chief aims of ethnography: to convince the reader of the existence of an initially unperceived coherence, a surprising meaningfulness, a covert rationality, or (merely) a history. This aim could not be carried out were it not for the writer's appeal to an ulterior image of wholeness or individuality, of organic or mechanical orderliness that transcends both the Author and the Other.

Inasmuch as classification functions as rhetorical trope, it is the chief means for evoking the imagination of wholeness. Roughly speaking, the tropes of synecdoche and classification are two sides of the same coin. On the one side, synecdoche suggests the whole through reference to one of its parts; on the other, a classificatory trope refers to an imagined whole in order to assert that the parts compose it. In writing, this takes the form of an assertion that if the whole (society, culture, *conscience collectif*, etc.) exists, then the evidence presented must constitute it.

Rhetorical Wholes Are Not Social Entities

The problem lies, in part, in the confusion of the different kinds of wholes that can be imagined. It should be clear that in a *logic* of classification we may distinguish between a class and a class that contains itself as its only member, or we may specify a class and then derive from this a class that contains all subsets of its members. *No such relations hold for a material or spatial (mereological) whole and its parts.* In the first case, the (mereological) whole and the whole that contains only itself must be identical. In the second case, a mereological whole cannot be itself and all subsets of itself. These propositions are intuitively obvious but can also be rigorously proved. Furthermore, we may conceive of an empty class, a class that has no instances of a given attribute, or for which no items satisfying a given criterion could be found. An empty mereological whole is a transparent contradiction (Korner 1983:355). Arguing along these lines, Ruben (1983) has claimed that any social philosophy is seriously misconceived if it holds that the relations between "at least some social entities and the human beings who are their members is the relation of the whole to its parts." This belief, however, appears to underlie much social philosophy since ancient times.

Ruben argues that either social wholes have parts that are not people, or they do not exist as such, and if people are parts of something then these entities cannot be social wholes conceived in mereological terms. His arguments rest on the material and spatial properties of the mereological relation of being parts of wholes, and the differences between this relationship and the class-inclusion relation holding between members of social wholes. An example illustrates his argument.

> If the queue waiting for the 38 bus forms itself into local branch 38 of the bus-users' association, the individuals in the queue are parts, not the members, of the queue, and the members, not the parts, of the local branch of the bus-users' association. Each of the individuals in the queue is a material entity and so is the queue that they make up. No material entity can completely occupy the same total spatial position occupied by the queue at the same time unless it is just identical with the queue. On the other hand, the local association of bus-users is a social entity, and if it did have parts, perhaps committees, they would also be social entities. Some other entity can completely occupy precisely the same total spatial position at the same time, if indeed an association of this sort has any spatial position at all, for the same individuals might form themselves into any number of analogous associations they care to create. (Ruben 1983:237)

Rhetorical wholes, then, are not social entities. They are cognitive constructs that are relative to the scale and scope of the observer's view and to the rhetoric that constitutes them in the imagination. Some fondly held images of social wholes may be little more than a property of the argument that social wholes exist. Emile Durkheim, for instance, says in effect that the social wholes *must* exist because the text that describes them does.

> There can be no sociology unless societies exist, and societies cannot exist if there are only individuals.... [There will] emerge ... from every page of this book, so to speak, the impression that the individual is dominated by a moral reality greater than himself. (Durkheim 1966:38)

Durkheim's "so to speak" seems ingenuous, but it directs attention away from "every page of this book," where the force he speaks of clearly lies, to the social whole that he endeavors to construct. He ignores the differences in scale between the observer, the analytical "individual," and the rhetorically constructed concepts of "societies" and "moral reality." These concepts are essential to the Durkheimian imagination that lives in so much 20th-century ethnography, but an argument for their *validity as concepts* does not prove the existence of their ostensible object.

The parts of texts – of books and articles – achieve their reality not from correspondence to reality but from coherence with the rest of their text and the rest of texts in general. We may see the problem in a different light when the rhetorical whole is dissected into its "parts," which achieve their reality not from their bearing on experience, but rather from the degree to which they are consistent with the image of the whole. Henri Bergson's commentary on religion, for instance, which is closely tied to Durkheim's own notion of the collective, illustrates this by unself-consciously confusing textual and social "parts":

> The future of a science depends on the way it first dissects its object. If it has the luck to cut along the lines of the natural joints, like Plato's good cook, the number of "cuts" is of little importance; as the cutting up into pieces will have prepared the way for the analysis into elements, we shall be finally in possession of a simplified representation of the whole. (Bergson 1935:96)

Here an image of a simple "cutting" of the whole is asserted to be identical with analysis, and the parts are not the elements of experience, but the decomposition of the imagined whole. Textual parts are confused with social "parts." [...]

From Rhetoric to Social Structure

One of the most characteristic differences between narrative and ethnographic description is that the ethnography is compiled over a relatively long period and from a range of discrete, disparate, and fundamentally incommensurate experiences, and expressed in terms of a classificatory schema or image. It is in terms of this schematization, rather than in terms of a discursive argument, plot or narrative flow, that the ethnographic (more generally: social) description achieves a closure that is intellectually satisfying. Chapters have special rhetorical significance in this regard since it is under their "headings" that data are classified. This format alone suggests another level or kind of meaningfulness that is not given by the facts themselves.

A monograph classified in chapters and subheadings must convey to the reader, by virtue of the classified discontinuity of chapters, citations, quoted discourse, case studies, and so on, that a connectedness does exist on another level. Simply a numbering of chapters and subheadings suggests a rationalized and higher-order logic than that which exists in the continuous narrative itself. [...]

Unlike discourse, and unlike narrative, the ethnography is compiled from "items" – notes, observations, texts, commentary (themselves compiled from items) – that are all subordinate to an encompassing classifying framework. The ethnographic text never really escapes from this "item-level." There are two related classificatory procedures: the practical, technical classification that takes place "in the field" and the intellectual (rhetorical) classifications that emerge most clearly in chapter and subheadings, and in textual keywords. While these are related processes, they differ in their conceptualization as "technique" on the one hand, and as "format" or "style" on the other. Both conceptualizations, however, disguise the rhetorical nature of the classificatory mode of exposition.

Meyer Fortes expressed this clearly in *The Web of Kinship among the Tallensi*:

I was fortunate in that both my chief teachers on [the subject of kinship], the late Professor Bronislaw Malinowski and Professor Radcliffe-Brown, approached it with working hypotheses founded on the realities of field observation. Their theories have the merit of being adapted to the methods of observation available to the anthropologist in the field, and to the kind of data within his reach. (Fortes 1949:1)

[...]

Thus, the items of the field notebook, the so-called units of description appear to be prefigured by the technical practice of data collection in the field. The person met on the path that morning was simply a contingent event – contingent on a trip to the shop for salt, or being *en route* to the next interview. The mask described, among all possible masks, was the one that just happened to be seen while pencil and paper were ready to hand, one that belonged to a "best informant." But mere contingency cannot account for the text that eventually results. Reflection shows that even merely counting implies a rhetorical project. By counting, listing, summing, averaging, and other numerical manipulations we begin to construct macrocosmic entities (volume of petroleum shipped, total population of China, the average distance traveled by a Bushman hunting party) that are representative of some aspects of social reality, but only insofar as those aspects are part of a textual argument. The same is true of measurement. The "rate of suicides" is an example of one such measure (Durkheim 1966) that makes sense only in the context of Durkheim's moral project, and could be realized only through textual methods of compilation, analysis, graphical display, and exposition. Total yam yields compared with total pig yields in a New Guinea village is another such example. The derived ratio (yams to pigs), moreover, when considered as a changing quantity over time, exhibits a periodic rise and fall characteristic of "ideal" market economies or of population trends arising from predator–prey interactions in closed, near-equilibrium ecologies (Rappaport 1968: 153–67ff; Michael Thompson 1979: 184ff).

Numerical regularities such as these, and the arguments that depend on them, are types of holism that are critically dependent on textual argument. A "rate of suicide" or a pig-to-yam ratio are conceptually distant and even irrelevant to the experience of a suicidal depression or feeding pigs. Nevertheless, within an appropriate numerically constructed holism both suicide and pig-raising can be encompassed. Incommensurate experiences become commensurate within the domain of a rhetorical project through which they are defined, isolated, and rendered discrete.

Numerical methods in ethnography achieve their rhetorical effectiveness in sociological writing by permitting one to itemize and classify in order to relate small-scale entities to macrocosmic entities. Experienced reality is immediately translated, first of all, into a domain of symbolic tokens such as numbers, or ratios or formulae. These formalisms may translate or express a sense of coherence, but not meaning. By isolating specific interactions from the ramifying complexities of social life, they focus attention, and permit reductive propositions to be stated. There is also an undoubted appeal to physical-scientific methods that contributes an aura of legitimacy. But most important, any such sociology relies on the assumption that the entities it counts are both discrete and finite, an assumption that must be made in order to begin counting at all. Thus, it is not surprising that any statistical sociology easily achieves a sense of "finiteness" or "closure" which discursive and narrative methods must achieve by other rhetorical means.

The classificatory rhetoric may also subsume many other rhetorics, and thus encompass a range of expressive forms that are otherwise incommensurate. The classificatory rhetoric is a "macro-structure," which because it subsumes other rhetorics within an imagined or image-like "whole" is able to transcend the requirements of linguistic or propositional logics. Such "macro-structure must be accorded as much cognitive and grammatical reality as other aspects of grammatical structure in linguistic analysis if larger-scale (i.e., larger than the sentences, phrases, words, and morphemes) features of discourse, tone, anaphoresis, etc. are to be comprehended linguistically (van Dijk 1983). Unlike most common narrative tropes that are closely tied to signs, simple reference, sentence-level syntax, poetics and prosody, the classification, as rhetorical trope, relies on macro-structures, comprehensive images, and a commitment to inclusivity and analogy.

Similarly, an outline order of chapters, heads, subheads, and paragraphs imparts an architectural pattern that may be rhetorically useful in legitimizing the text as reasoned or scientific, or which may serve to frame it in order to hold the reader's attention, or, may suggest the part-to-whole rela-

tionship that is crucial to the satisfactory closure of this kind of discourse. In fact the vocabulary of the classification of the physical book is nothing more than extended metaphors of the body ("chapter,"[3] "heading," "footnote," "spine"), of the landscape ("verse,"[4] "strophe") of trees ("leaves," "page"[5] buildings ("tables"), and streets ("margin").

[...]

The ethnography relies on the fact that it is an object, a text, radically removed from the initial experiences and perceptions on which it is based. The representation of reality, whether on note cards or in chapter headings is confused with reality and manipulated as objects in ways that culture or society can not be. The text itself is the object of knowledge.

[...]

The ethnographic monograph presents us with an analogy between the text itself and the "society" or "culture," that it describes. The sense of a discrete social or cultural entity that is conveyed by an ethnography is founded on the sense of closure or completeness of both the physical text and its rhetorical format. In this it shares features with the novel or the travelogue. The novel rounds out a plot by bringing events to expected conclusions, a rhetorical method that is shared by prophecy in religious and epic narratives. The travelogue achieves closure as a result of an actual itinerary with a definite start and finish: The traveler comes home in the end to write of his journeys. (Otherwise, it is an "origin myth" – a travelogue without a return sequence – or a "Roots" type of narrative, told from the other end, as it were, with only the expectation of an imaginary or emotional "return") The ethnographic monograph, however, presents "society" through the order of its chapters which do not unfold temporally but spatially and logically. [...]

Notes

1 Naturally, I mean here travelers who *write*, who travel as such, ultimately in service of the texts they create.
2 Here society as the object of ethnographic and sociological description, must not be confused with the social, the experience of other people and our relationships with them.
3 "Chapter," from *caput* (Latin), "head," via Old French *chapitre*.
4 "Verse," from Old English *vers*, from Latin *versus*, "furrow," literally "a turning," from *vertere*, "to turn."
5 "Page," from Latin *fagus*, "tree," "wood."

References

Bergson, Henri 1935 *The Two Sources of Morality and Religion*. R. A. Audra and C. Brereton, trans. New York: Doubleday.

Derrida, Jacques 1976 *Of Grammatology*. G. C. Spivak, trans. Baltimore: Johns Hopkins University Press.

Durkheim, Emile 1966 [1897] *Suicide: A Study in Sociology*. J. A. Spaulding and George Simpson, trans. New York: The Free Press.

Fortes, Meyer 1949 *The Web of Kinship among the Tallensi*. Oxford: Oxford University Press.

Foucault, Michel 1974 *The Archaeology of Knowledge*. Sheridan Smith, trans. London: Tavistock.

Junod, Henri-Alexandre 1927 *The Life of a South African Tribe*. 2 volumes. London: Macmillan.

Korner, Stephen 1983 Thinking, Thought and Categories. *The Monist* 66(3):353–66.

Kuhn, Thomas 1970 *The Structure of Scientific Revolutions*. Chicago: University of Chicago Press.

McLuhan, Marshall 1962 *The Guttenburg Galaxy: The Making of Typographic Man*. London: Routledge & Kegan Paul.

Radcliffe-Brown, A. R. 1925 *Structure and Function in Primitive Society*. New York: The Free Press.

Rappaport, Roy A. 1968 *Pigs for the Ancestors: Ritual in the Ecology of a New Guinea People*. New Haven: Yale University Press.

Ruben, David-Hillel 1983 Social Wholes and Parts. *Mind* 92:219–38.

Thompson, Manley 1983 Philosophical Approaches to Categories. *The Monist* 66(3):336–52.

Thompson, Michael 1979 *Rubbish Theory: The Creation and Destruction of Value*. Oxford: Oxford University Press.

Toulmin, Stephen 1982 *The Return to Cosmology: Postmodern Science and the Theology of Nature*. Berkeley: University of California Press.

Tylor, Edward B. 1871 *Primitive Culture*. 2 volumes. London.

van Dijk, Teun A. 1983 *Macrostructures: An Interdisciplinary Study of Global Structures in Discourse*. Hillsdale, NJ: Erlbaum.

38

Writing Against Culture

Lila Abu-Lughod

Writing Culture (Clifford and Marcus 1986), the collection that marked a major new form of critique of cultural anthropology's premises, more or less excluded two critical groups whose situations neatly expose and challenge the most basic of those premises: feminists and "halfies" – people whose national or cultural identity is mixed by virtue of migration, overseas education, or parentage.[1] In his introduction, Clifford (1986a) apologizes for the feminist absence; no one mentions halfies or the indigenous anthropologists to whom they are related. Perhaps they are not yet numerous enough or sufficiently self-defined as a group.[2] The importance of these two groups lies not in any superior moral claim or advantage they might have in doing anthropology, but in the special dilemmas they face, dilemmas that reveal starkly the problems with cultural anthropology's assumption of a fundamental distinction between self and other.

In this essay I explore how feminists and halfies, by the way their anthropological practice unsettles the boundary between self and other, enable us to reflect on the conventional nature and political effects of this distinction and

ultimately to reconsider the value of the concept of culture on which it depends. I will argue that "culture" operates in anthropological discourse to enforce separations that inevitably carry a sense of hierarchy. Therefore, anthropologists should now pursue, without exaggerated hopes for the power of their texts to change the world, a variety of strategies for writing *against* culture. For those interested in textual strategies, I explore the advantages of what I call "ethnographies of the particular" as instruments of a tactical humanism.

Selves and Others

The notion of culture (especially as it functions to distinguish "cultures"), despite a long usefulness, may now have become something anthropologists would want to work against in their theories, their ethnographic practice, and their ethnographic writing. A helpful way to begin to grasp why is to consider what the shared elements of feminist and halfie anthropology clarify about the self/other distinction central to the paradigm of anthropology. Marilyn Strathern (1985, 1987)

From Richard G. Fox (ed.), *Recapturing Anthropology: Working in the Present* (Santa Fe: School of American Research Press, 1991), pp. 137–54, 161–2. Copyright © 1991 by the School of American Research, Santa Fe, USA. Reprinted by permission of SAR Press.

Anthropology in Theory: Issues in Epistemology, Second Edition. Edited by Henrietta L. Moore and Todd Sanders.
© 2014 John Wiley & Sons, Inc. Published 2014 by John Wiley & Sons, Inc.

raises some of the issues regarding feminism in essays that both Clifford and Rabinow cited in *Writing Culture*. Her thesis is that the relationship between anthropology and feminism is awkward. This thesis leads her to try to understand why feminist scholarship, in spite of its rhetoric of radicalism, has failed to fundamentally alter anthropology, and why feminism has gained even less from anthropology than vice versa.

The awkwardness, she argues, arises from the fact that despite a common interest in differences, the scholarly practices of feminists and anthropologists are "differently structured in the way they organize knowledge and draw boundaries" (Strathern 1987: 289) and especially in "the nature of the investigators' *relationship to* their subject matter" (1987: 284). Feminist scholars, united by their common opposition to men or to patriarchy, produce a discourse composed of many voices; they "discover the self by becoming conscious of oppression from the Other" (1987: 289). Anthropologists, whose goal is "to make sense of differences" (1987: 286), also constitute their "selves" in relation to an other, but do not view this other as "under attack" (1987: 289).

In highlighting the self/other relationship, Strathern takes us to the heart of the problem. Yet she retreats from the problematic of power (granted as formative in feminism) in her strangely uncritical depiction of anthropology. When she defines anthropology as a discipline that "continues to know itself as the study of social behavior or society in terms of systems and collective representations" (1987: 281), she underplays the self/other distinction. In characterizing the relationship between anthropological self and other as nonadversarial, she ignores its most fundamental aspect. Anthropology's avowed goal may be "the study of man [sic]," but it is a discipline built on the historically constructed divide between the West and the non-West. It has been and continues to be primarily the study of the non-Western other by the Western self, even if in its new guise it seeks explicitly to give voice to the Other or to present a dialogue between the self and other, either textually or through an explication of the fieldwork encounter (as in such works as Crapanzano 1980; Dumont 1978; Dwyer 1982; Rabinow 1977; Riesman 1977; Tedlock 1983; and Tyler 1986). And the relationship between the West and the non-West, at least since the birth of anthropology, has been constituted by Western domination. This suggests that the awkwardness Strathern senses in the relationship between feminism and anthropology might better be understood as the result of diametrically opposed processes of self-construction through opposition to others – processes that begin from different sides of a power divide.

The enduring strength of what Morsy (1988: 70) has called "the hegemony of the distinctive-other tradition" in anthropology is betrayed by the defensiveness of partial exceptions. Anthropologists [...] conducting fieldwork in the United States or Europe wonder whether they have not blurred the disciplinary boundaries between anthropology and other fields such as sociology or history. One way to retain their identities as anthropologists is to make the communities they study seem "other." Studying ethnic communities and the powerless assures this.[3] So does concentrating on "culture" [...], for reasons I will discuss later. There are two issues here. One is the conviction that one cannot be objective about one's own society, something that affects indigenous anthropologists (Western or non-Western). The second is a tacit understanding that anthropologists study the non-West; halfies who study their own or related non-Western communities are still more easily recognizable as anthropologists than Americans who study Americans.

If anthropology continues to be practiced as the study by an unproblematic and unmarked Western self of found "others" out there, feminist theory, an academic practice that also traffics in selves and others, has in its relatively short history come to realize the danger of treating selves and others as givens. It is instructive for the development of a critique of anthropology to consider the trajectory that has led, within two decades, to what some might call a crisis in feminist theory, and others, the development of postfeminism.

From Simone de Beauvoir on, it has been accepted that, at least in the modern West, women have been the other to men's self. Feminism has been a movement devoted to helping women become selves and subjects rather than objects and men's others.[4] The crisis in feminist theory (related to a crisis in the women's movement) that followed on the heels of feminist attempts to turn those who had been constituted as other into selves – or, to use the popular metaphor, to let women speak – was the problem of "difference." For whom did feminists speak? Within the women's movement, the objections of lesbians, African-American women, and other "women of color" that their experiences as women were different from those of white, middle-class, heterosexual women problematized the identity of women as selves. Cross-cultural work on women also made it clear that masculine and feminine did not have, as we say, the same meanings in other cultures, nor did Third World women's lives resemble Western women's lives. As Harding (1986: 246) puts it, the problem is that "once 'woman' is deconstructed into 'women' and 'gender' is recognized to have no fixed referents, feminism itself dissolves as a theory that can reflect the voice of a naturalized or essentialized speaker."[5]

From its experience with this crisis of selfhood or subjecthood, feminist theory can offer anthropology two useful reminders. First, the self is always a construction, never a natural or found entity, even if it has that appearance. Second, the process of creating a self through opposition to an other always entails the violence of repressing or ignoring other forms of difference. Feminist theorists have been forced to explore the implications for the formation of identity and the possibilities for political action of the ways in which gender as a system of difference is intersected by other systems of difference, including, in the modern capitalist world, race and class.

Where does this leave the feminist anthropologist? Strathern (1987: 286) characterizes her as experiencing a tension – "caught between structures… faced with two different ways of relating to her or his subject matter." The more interesting aspect of the feminist's situation, though, is what she shares with the halfie: a blocked ability to comfortably assume the self of anthropology. For both, although in different ways, the self is split, caught at the intersection of systems of difference. I am less concerned with the existential consequences of this split (these have been eloquently explored elsewhere [e.g., Joseph 1988; Kondo 1986; Narayan 1989]) than with the awareness such splits generate about three crucial issues: positionality, audience, and the power inherent in distinctions of self and

other. What happens when the "other" that the anthropologist is studying is simultaneously constructed as, at least partially, a self?

Feminists and halfie anthropologists cannot easily avoid the issue of positionality. Standing on shifting ground makes it clear that every view is a view from somewhere and every act of speaking a speaking from somewhere. Cultural anthropologists have never been fully convinced of the ideology of science and have long questioned the value, possibility, and definition of objectivity.[6] But they still seem reluctant to examine the implications of the actual situatedness of their knowledge.[7]

Two common, intertwined objections to the work of feminist or native or semi-native anthropologists, both related to partiality, betray the persistence of ideals of objectivity. The first has to do with the partiality (as bias or position) of the observer. The second has to do with the partial (incomplete) nature of the picture presented. Halfies are more associated with the first problem, feminists the second. The problem with studying one's own society is alleged to be the problem of gaining enough distance. Since for halfies, the Other is in certain ways the self, there is said to be the danger shared with indigenous anthropologists of identification and the easy slide into subjectivity.[8] These worries suggest that the anthropologist is still defined as a being who must stand apart from the Other, even when he or she seeks explicitly to bridge the gap. Even Bourdieu (1977: 1–2), who perceptively analyzed the effects this outsider stance has on the anthropologist's (mis)understanding of social life, fails to break with this doxa. The obvious point he misses is that the outsider self never simply stands outside. He or she stands in a definite relation with the Other of the study, not just as a Westerner, but as a Frenchman in Algeria during the war of independence, an American in Morocco during the 1967 Arab–Israeli war, or an Englishwoman in postcolonial India. What we call the outside is a position within a larger political-historical complex. No less than the halfie, the "wholie" is in a specific position vis-à-vis the community being studied.

The debates about feminist anthropologists suggest a second source of uneasiness about positionality. Even when they present themselves as studying gender, feminist anthropologists are dismissed as presenting only a partial picture of the societies they study because they are assumed to be studying only women. Anthropologists study society, the unmarked form. The study of women is the marked form, too readily sectioned off, as Strathern (1985) notes.[9] Yet it could easily be argued that most studies of society have been equally partial. As restudies like Weiner's (1976) of Malinowski's Trobriand Islanders or Bell's (1983) of the well-studied Australian aborigines indicate, they have been the study of men.[10] This does not make such studies any less valuable; it merely reminds us that we must constantly attend to the positionality of the anthropological self and its representations of others. James Clifford (1986a: 6), among others, has convincingly argued that ethnographic representations are always "partial truths." What is needed is a recognition that they are also positioned truths.

Split selfhood creates for the two groups being discussed a second problem that is illuminating for anthropology generally: multiple audiences. Although all anthropologists are beginning to feel what might be called the Rushdie effect – the effects of living in a global age when the subjects of their studies begin to read their works and the governments of the countries they work in ban books and deny visas – feminist and halfie anthropologists struggle in poignant ways with multiple accountability. Rather than having one primary audience, that of other anthropologists, feminist anthropologists write for anthropologists and for feminists, two groups whose relationship to their subject matter is at odds and who hold ethnographers accountable in different ways.[11] Furthermore, feminist circles include non-Western feminists, often from the societies feminist anthropologists have studied, who call them to account in new ways.[12]

Halfies' dilemmas are even more extreme. As anthropologists, they write for other anthropologists, mostly Western. Identified also with communities outside the West, or subcultures within it, they are called to account by educated members of those communities. More importantly, not just because they position themselves with reference to two communities but because when they present the Other they are presenting themselves, they speak with a complex awareness of and investment in reception. Both halfie and feminist anthropologists are forced to confront

squarely the politics and ethics of their representations. There are no easy solutions to their dilemmas.

The third issue that feminist and halfie anthropologists, unlike anthropologists who work in Western societies (another group for whom self and other are somewhat tangled), force us to confront is the dubiousness of maintaining that relationships between self and other are innocent of power. Because of sexism and racial or ethnic discrimination, they may have experienced – as women, as individuals of mixed parentage, or as foreigners – being other to a dominant self, whether in everyday life in the US, Britain, or France, or in the Western academy. This is not simply an experience of difference, but of inequality. My argument, however, is structural, not experiential. Women, blacks, and people of most of the non-West have been historically constituted as others in the major political systems of difference on which the unequal world of modern capitalism has depended. Feminist studies and black studies have made sufficient progress within the academy to have exposed the way that being studied by "white men" (to use a shorthand for a complex and historically constituted subject-position) turns into being spoken for by them. It becomes a sign and instrument of their power.

Within anthropology, despite a long history of self-conscious opposition to racism, a fast-growing, self-critical literature on anthropology's links to colonialism (for example, Asad 1973; Clifford 1983; Fabian 1983; Hymes 1969; Kuper 1988), and experimentation with techniques of ethnography to relieve a discomfort with the power of anthropologist over anthropological subject, the fundamental issues of domination keep being skirted. Even attempts to refigure informants as consultants and to "let the other speak" in dialogic (Tedlock 1987) or polyvocal texts – decolonizations on the level of the text – leave intact the basic configuration of global power on which anthropology, as linked to other institutions of the world, is based. To see the strangeness of this enterprise, all that is needed is to consider an analogous case. What would our reaction be if male scholars stated their desire to "let women speak" in their texts while they continued to dominate all knowledge about them by controlling writing and other academic practices, supported in their positions by a particular organization of economic, social, and political life?

Because of their split selves, feminist and halfie anthropologists travel uneasily between speaking "for" and speaking "from." Their situation enables us to see more clearly that dividing practices, whether they naturalize differences, as in gender or race, or simply elaborate them, as I will argue the concept of culture does, are fundamental methods of enforcing inequality.

Culture and Difference

The concept of culture is the hidden term in all that has just been said about anthropology. Most American anthropologists believe or act as if "culture," notoriously resistant to definition and ambiguous of referent, is nevertheless the true object of anthropological inquiry. Yet it could also be argued that culture is important to anthropology because the anthropological distinction between self and other rests on it. Culture is the essential tool for making other. As a professional discourse that elaborates on the meaning of culture in order to account for, explain, and understand cultural difference, anthropology also helps construct, produce, and maintain it. Anthropological discourse gives cultural difference (and the separation between groups of people it implies) the air of the self-evident.

In this regard, the concept of culture operates much like its predecessor – race – even though in its twentieth-century form it has some important political advantages. Unlike race, and unlike even the nineteenth-century sense of culture as a synonym for civilization (contrasted to barbarism), the current concept allows for multiple rather than binary differences. This immediately checks the easy move to hierarchizing; the shift to "culture" ("lower case c with the possibility of a final s," as Clifford [1988a: 234] puts it) has a relativizing effect. The most important of culture's advantages, however, is that it removes difference from the realm of the natural and the innate. Whether conceived of as a set of behaviors, customs, traditions, rules, plans, recipes, instructions, or programs (to list the range of definitions Geertz [1973: 44] furnishes), culture is learned and can change.

Despite its anti-essentialist intent, however, the culture concept retains some of the tendencies to freeze difference possessed by concepts like race. This is easier to see if we consider a field in which there has been a shift from one to the other. Orientalism as a scholarly discourse (among other things) is, according to Said (1978: 2), "a style of thought based upon an ontological and epistemological distinction made between 'the Orient' and (most of the time) 'the Occident.'" What he shows is that in mapping geography, race, and culture onto one another, Orientalism fixes differences between people of "the West" and people of "the East" in ways so rigid that they might as well be considered innate. In the twentieth century, cultural difference, not race, has been the basic subject of Orientalist scholarship devoted now to interpreting the "culture" phenomena (primarily religion and language) to which basic differences in development, economic performance, government, character, and so forth are attributed.

Some anticolonial movements and present-day struggles have worked by what could be labelled reverse Orientalism, where attempts to reverse the power relationship proceed by seeking to valorize for the self what in the former system had been devalued as other. A Gandhian appeal to the greater spirituality of a Hindu India, compared with the materialism and violence of the West, and an Islamicist appeal to a greater faith in God, compared with the immorality and corruption of the West, both accept the essentialist terms of Orientalist constructions. While turning them on their heads, they preserve the rigid sense of difference based on culture.

A parallel can be drawn with feminism. It is a basic tenet of feminism that "women are made, not born." It has been important for most feminists to locate sex differences in culture, not biology or nature. While this has inspired some feminist theorists to attend to the social and personal effects of gender as a system of difference, for many others it has led to explorations of and strategies built on the notion of a women's culture. Cultural feminism (cf. Echols 1984) takes many forms, but it has many of the qualities of reverse Orientalism just discussed. For French feminists like Irigaray (1985a, 1985b), Cixous (1983), and Kristeva (1981), masculine and feminine, if not actually male and female, represent essentially different modes of being. Anglo-American feminists take a different tack.

Some attempt to "describe" the cultural differences between men and women – Gilligan (1982) and her followers (e.g., Belenky et al. 1986) who elaborate the notion of "a different voice" are popular examples. Others try to "explain" the differences, whether through a socially informed psychoanalytic theory (e.g., Chodorow 1978), a Marxist-derived theory of the effects of the division of labor and women's role in social reproduction (Hartsock 1985), an analysis of maternal practice (Ruddick 1980), or even a theory of sexual exploitation (MacKinnon 1982). Much feminist theorizing and practice seeks to build or reform social life in line with this "women's culture."[13] There have been proposals for a woman-centered university (Rich 1979), a feminist science, a feminist methodology in the sciences and social sciences (Meis 1983; Reinharz 1983; Smith 1987; Stanley and Wise 1983; see Harding 1987 for a sensible critique), and even a feminist spirituality and ecology. These proposals nearly always build on values traditionally associated in the West with women – a sense of care and connectedness, maternal nurturing, immediacy of experience, involvement in the bodily (versus the abstract), and so forth.

This valorization by cultural feminists, like reverse Orientalists, of the previously devalued qualities attributed to them may be provisionally useful in forging a sense of unity and in waging struggles of empowerment. Yet because it leaves in place the divide that structured the experiences of selfhood and oppression on which it builds, it perpetuates some dangerous tendencies. First, cultural feminists overlook the connections between those on each side of the divide, and the ways in which they define each other. Second, they overlook differences within each category constructed by the dividing practices, differences like those of class, race, and sexuality (to repeat the feminist litany of problematically abstract categories), but also ethnic origin, personal experience, age, mode of livelihood, health, living situation (rural or urban), and historical experience. Third, and perhaps most important, they ignore the ways in which experiences have been constructed historically and have changed over time. Both cultural feminism and revivalist movements tend to rely on notions of authenticity and the return to positive values not represented by the dominant other. As becomes obvious in the

most extreme cases, these moves erase history. Invocations of Cretan goddesses in some cultural-feminist circles and, in a more complex and serious way, the powerful invocation of the seventh-century community of the Prophet in some Islamic movements are good examples.

The point is that the notion of culture which both types of movements use does not seem to guarantee an escape from the tendency toward essentialism. It could be argued that anthropologists use "culture" in more sophisticated and consistent ways and that their commitment to it as an analytical tool is firmer. Yet even many of them are now concerned about the ways it tends to freeze differences. Appadurai (1988), for example, in his compelling argument that "natives" are a figment of the anthropological imagination, shows the complicity of the anthropological concept of culture in a continuing "incarceration" of non-Western peoples in time and place. Denied the same capacity for movement, travel, and geographical interaction that Westerners take for granted, the cultures studied by anthropologists have tended to be denied history as well.

Others, including myself (1990b), have argued that cultural theories also tend to overemphasize coherence. Clifford notes both that "the discipline of fieldwork-based anthropology, in constituting its authority, constructs and reconstructs coherent cultural others and interpreting selves" (Clifford 1988b: 112) and that ethnography is a form of culture collecting (like art collecting) in which "diverse experiences and facts are selected, gathered, detached from their original temporal occasions, and given enduring value in a new arrangement" (Clifford 1988a: 231). Organic metaphors of wholeness and the methodology of holism that characterizes anthropology both favor coherence, which in turn contributes to the perception of communities as bounded and discrete.

Certainly discreteness does not have to imply value; the hallmark of twentieth-century anthropology has been its promotion of cultural relativism over evaluation and judgment. If anthropology has always to some extent been a form of cultural (self-) critique (Marcus and Fischer 1986), that too was an aspect of a refusal to hierarchize difference. Yet neither position would be possible without difference. It would be worth thinking about the implications of the high stakes anthropology has in sustaining and perpetuating a belief in the existence of cultures that are identifiable as discrete, different, and separate from our own.[14] Does difference always smuggle in hierarchy?

In *Orientalism*, Said (1978: 28) argues for the elimination of "the Orient" and "the Occident" altogether. By this he means not the erasure of all differences but the recognition of more of them and of the complex ways in which they crosscut. More important, his analysis of one field seeks to show how and when certain differences, in this case of places and the people attached to them, become implicated in the domination of one by the other. Should anthropologists treat with similar suspicion "culture" and "cultures" as the key terms in a discourse in which otherness and difference have come to have, as Said (1989: 213) points out, "talismanic qualities"?

Three Modes of Writing Against Culture

If "culture," shadowed by coherence, timelessness, and discreteness, is the prime anthropological tool for making "other," and difference, as feminists and halfies reveal, tends to be a relationship of power, then perhaps anthropologists should consider strategies for writing against culture. I will discuss three that I find promising. Although they by no means exhaust the possibilities, the sorts of projects I will describe – theoretical, substantive, and textual – make sense for anthropologists sensitive to issues of positionality and accountability and interested in making anthropological practice something that does not simply shore up global inequalities. I will conclude, however, by considering the limitations of all anthropological reform.

Discourse and practice

Theoretical discussion, because it is one of the modes in which anthropologists engage each other, provides an important site for contesting "culture." It seems to me that current discussions and deployments of two increasingly popular terms – practice and discourse – do signal a shift away from culture. Although there is always the danger that these terms will come to be used simply as synonyms for culture, they were

intended to enable us to analyze social life without presuming the degree of coherence that the culture concept has come to carry.

Practice is associated, in anthropology, with Bourdieu (1977; also see Ortner 1984), whose theoretical approach is built around problems of contradiction, misunderstanding, and misrecognition, and favors strategies, interests, and improvisations over the more static and homogenizing cultural tropes of rules, models, and texts. Discourse (whose uses I discuss in L. Abu-Lughod 1989 and Abu-Lughod and Lutz 1990) has more diverse sources and meanings in anthropology. In its Foucauldian derivation, as it relates to notions of discursive formations, apparatuses, and technologies, it is meant to refuse the distinction between ideas and practices or text and world that the culture concept too readily encourages. In its more sociolinguistic sense, it draws attention to the social uses by individuals of verbal resources. In either case, it allows for the possibility of recognizing within a social group the play of multiple, shifting, and competing statements with practical effects. Both practice and discourse are useful because they work against the assumption of boundedness, not to mention the idealism (Asad 1983), of the culture concept.[15]

Connections

Another strategy of writing against culture is to reorient the problems or subject matter anthropologists address. An important focus should be the various connections and interconnections, historical and contemporary, between a community and the anthropologist working there and writing about it, not to mention the world to which he or she belongs and which enables him or her to be in that particular place studying that group. This is more of a political project than an existential one, although the reflexive anthropologists who have taught us to focus on the fieldwork encounter as a site for the construction of the ethnographic "facts" have alerted us to one important dimension of the connection. Other significant sorts of connections have received less attention. Pratt (1986: 42) notes a regular mystification in ethnographic writing of "the larger agenda of European expansion in which the ethnographer, regardless of his or her own attitudes to it, is caught up, and that determines the ethnographer's own material relationship to the group under study." We need to ask questions about the historical processes by which it came to pass that people like ourselves could be engaged in anthropological studies of people like those, about the current world situation that enables us to engage in this sort of work in this particular place, and about who has preceded us and is even now there with us (tourists, travelers, missionaries, AID consultants, Peace Corps workers). We need to ask what this "will to knowledge" about the Other is connected to in the world.

These questions cannot be asked in general; they should be asked about and answered by tracing through specific situations, configurations, and histories. Even though they do not address directly the place of the ethnographer, and even though they engage in an oversystemization that threatens to erase local interactions, studies like those of Wolf (1982 [see chapter 30, this volume]) on the long history of interaction between particular Western societies and communities in what is now called the Third World represent important means of answering such questions. So do studies like Mintz's (1985) that trace the complex processes of transformation and exploitation in which, in Europe and other parts of the world, sugar was involved. The anthropological turn to history, tracing connections between the present and the past of particular communities, is also an important development.

Not all projects about connections need be historical. Anthropologists are increasingly concerned with national and transnational connections of people, cultural forms, media, techniques, and commodities.[16] They study the articulation of world capitalism and international politics with the situations of people living in particular communities. All these projects, which involve a shift in gaze to include phenomena of connection, expose the inadequacies of the concept of culture and the elusiveness of the entities designated by the term *cultures*. Although there may be a tendency in the new work merely to widen the object, shifting from culture to nation as locus, ideally there would be attention to the shifting groupings, identities, and interactions within and across such borders as well. If there was ever a time when anthropologists could

consider without too much violence at least some communities as isolated units, certainly the nature of global interactions in the present makes that now impossible.[17]

Ethnographies of the particular

The third strategy for writing against culture depends on accepting the one insight of Geertz's about anthropology that has been built upon by everyone in this "experimental moment" (Marcus and Fischer 1986) who takes textuality seriously. Geertz (1975, 1988) has argued that one of the main things anthropologists do is write, and what they write are fictions (which does not mean they are fictitious).[18] Certainly the practice of ethnographic writing has received an inordinate amount of attention from those involved in *Writing Culture* and an increasing number of others who were not involved. Much of the hostility toward their project arises from the suspicion that in their literary leanings they have too readily collapsed the politics of ethnography into its poetics. And yet they have raised an issue that cannot be ignored. Insofar as anthropologists are in the business of representing others through their ethnographic writing, then surely the degree to which people in the communities they study appear "other" must also be partly a function of how anthropologists write about them. Are there ways to write about lives so as to constitute others as less other?

I would argue that one powerful tool for unsettling the culture concept and subverting the process of "othering" it entails is to write "ethnographies of the particular." Generalization, the characteristic mode of operation and style of writing of the social sciences, can no longer be regarded as neutral description (Foucault 1978; Said 1978; Smith 1987). It has two unfortunate effects in anthropology that make it worth eschewing. I will explore these before presenting some examples from my own work of what one could hope to accomplish through ethnographies of the particular.

I will not be concerned with several issues frequently raised about generalization. For example, it has often been pointed out that the generalizing mode of social scientific discourse facilitates abstraction and reification. Feminist sociologist Dorothy Smith (1987: 130) put the problem vividly in her critique of sociological discourse by noting that

> the complex organization of activities of actual individuals and their actual relations is entered into the discourse through concepts such as class, modernization, formal organization. A realm of theoretically constituted objects is created, freeing the discursive realm from its ground in the lives and work of actual individuals and liberating sociological inquiry to graze on a field of conceptual entities.

Other critics have fixed on different flaws. Interpretive anthropology, for example, in its critique of the search for general laws in positivistic social science, notes a failure to take account of the centrality of meaning to human experience. Yet the result has been to substitute generalization about meanings for generalizations about behavior.

I also want to make clear what the argument for particularity is not: it is not to be mistaken for arguments for privileging micro over macro processes. Ethnomethodologists [...] and other students of everyday life seek ways to generalize about microinteractions, while historians might be said to be tracing the particulars of macroprocesses. Nor need a concern with the particulars of individuals' lives imply disregard for forces and dynamics that are not locally based. On the contrary, the effects of extralocal and long-term processes are only manifested locally and specifically, produced in the actions of individuals living their particular lives, inscribed in their bodies and their words. What I am arguing for is a form of writing that might better convey that.

There are two reasons for anthropologists to be wary of generalization. The first is that, as part of a professional discourse of "objectivity" and expertise, it is inevitably a language of power. On the one hand, it is the language of those who seem to stand apart from and outside of what they are describing. Again, Smith's critique of sociological discourse is relevant. She has argued (1987: 62) that this seemingly detached mode of reflecting on social life is actually located: it represents the perspective of those involved in professional, managerial, and administrative structures and is thus part of "the ruling apparatus of this society." This critique applies as well to anthropology with

its inter-rather than intrasocietal perspective and its origins in the exploration and colonization of the non-European world rather than the management of internal social groups like workers, women, blacks, the poor, or prisoners.

On the other hand, even if we withhold judgment on how closely the social sciences can be associated with the apparatuses of management, we have to recognize how all professionalized discourses by nature assert hierarchy. The very gap between the professional and authoritative discourses of generalization and the languages of everyday life (our own and others') establishes a fundamental separation between the anthropologist and the people being written about that facilitates the construction of anthropological objects as simultaneously different and inferior.

Thus, to the degree that anthropologists can bring closer the language of everyday life and the language of the text, this mode of making other is reversed. The problem is, as a reflection on the situation of feminist anthropologists suggest, that there may be professional risks for ethnographers who want to pursue this strategy. I have argued elsewhere (1990a) that Rabinow's refreshingly sensible observation about the politics of ethnographic writing – that they are to be found closer to home, in academia, than in the colonial and neocolonial world – helps us understand a few things about feminist anthropology and the uneasiness about it that even someone like Clifford betrays in his introductory essay for *Writing Culture*.[19] His excuse for excluding feminist anthropologists was that they were not involved in textual innovation. If we were to grant the dubious distinction he presumes between textual innovation and transformations of content and theory, we might concede that feminist anthropologists have contributed little to the new wave of experimentation in form.

But then a moment's thought would provide us with clues about why. Without even asking the basic questions about individuals, institutions, patrons, and tenure, we can turn to the politics of the feminist project itself. Dedicated to making sure that women's lives are represented in descriptions of societies and women's experiences and gender itself theorized in accounts of how societies work, feminist scholars have been interested in the old political sense of representation. Conservatism of form may have been helpful because the goal was to persuade colleagues that an anthropology taking gender into account was not just good anthropology but better anthropology.

The second pressure on feminist anthropology is the need to assert professionalism. Contrary to what Clifford writes (1986: 21), women *have* produced "unconventional forms of writing." He just ignored them, neglecting a few professional anthropologists like Bowen (Bohannon) (1954), Briggs (1970), and Cesara (Poewe) (1982) who have experimented with form.[20] More significantly, there is also what might be considered a separate "woman's tradition" within ethnographic writing. Because it is not professional, however, it might only reluctantly be claimed and explored by feminist anthropologists uncertain of their standing. I am referring to the often excellent and popular ethnographies written by the "untrained" wives of anthropologists, books like Elizabeth Fernea's *Guests of the Sheik* (1965), Marjorie Shostak's *Nisa* (1981), Edith Turner's *The Spirit and the Drum* (1987), and Margery Wolf's *The House of Lim* (1968). Directing their works to audiences slightly different from those of the professional writers of standard ethnographies, they have also followed different conventions: they are more open about their positionality, less assertive of their scientific authority, and more focused on particular individuals and families.

[...]

The second problem with generalization derives not from its participation in the authoritative discourses of professionalism but from the effects of homogeneity, coherence, and timelessness it tends to produce. When one generalizes from experiences and conversations with a number of specific people in a community, one tends to flatten out differences among them and to homogenize them. The appearance of an absence of internal differentiation makes it easier to conceive of a group of people as a discrete, bounded entity, like the "the Nuer," "the Balinese," and "the Awlad 'Ali Bedouin'" who do this or that and believe such-and-such. The effort to produce general ethnographic descriptions of people's beliefs or actions tends to smooth over contradictions, conflicts of interest, and doubts and arguments, not to mention changing motivations and circumstances. The erasure of time and conflict make what is inside the boundary set up by homogenization something essential and fixed. These effects are of special moment to anthropologists because they contribute to the fiction of essentially different and discrete others who can be separated from some sort of equally essential self. Insofar as difference is, as I have argued, hierarchical, and assertions of separation a way of denying responsibility, generalization itself must be treated with suspicion.

For these reasons I propose that we experiment with narrative ethnographies of the particular in a continuing tradition of fieldwork-based writing.[21] In telling stories about particular individuals in time and place, such ethnographies would share elements with the alternative "women's tradition" discussed above. I would expect them to complement rather than replace a range of other types of anthropological projects, from theoretical discussions to the exploration of new topics within anthropology [...]

Anthropologists commonly generalize about communities by saying that they are characterized by certain institutions, rules, or ways of doing things. For example, we can and often do say things like "The Bongo-Bongo are polygynous." Yet one could refuse to generalize in this way, instead asking how a particular set of individuals – for instance, a man and his three wives in a Bedouin community in Egypt whom I have known for a decade – live the "institution" that we call polygyny. Stressing the particularity of this marriage and building a picture of it through the participants' discussions, recollections, disagreements, and actions would make several theoretical points.

First, refusing to generalize would highlight the constructed quality of that typicality so regularly produced in conventional social scientific accounts. Second, showing the actual circumstances and detailed histories of individuals and their relationships would suggest that such particulars, which are always present (as we know from our own personal experiences), are also always crucial to the constitution of experience. Third, reconstructing people's arguments about, justifications for, and interpretations of what they and others are doing would explain how social life proceeds. It would show that although the terms of their discourses may be set (and, as in any society, include several sometimes contradictory and often historically changing discourses), within

these limits, people contest interpretations of
what is happening, strategize, feel pain, and live
their lives. In one sense this is not so new.
Bourdieu (1977), for example, theorizes about
social practice in a similar way. But the difference
here would be that one would be seeking textual
means of representing how this happens rather

than simply making theoretical assertions that
it does.

By focusing closely on particular individuals
and their changing relationships, one would necessarily subvert the most problematic connotations of culture: homogeneity, coherence, and
timelessness. [...]

Notes

1 *Halfies* is a term I borrowed from Kirin Narayan
   (personal communication).
2 Likewise, Marcus and Clifford (1985) and Marcus
   and Fischer (1986) gesture toward feminists as
   important sources of cultural and anthropological
   critique but do not discuss their work. Fischer
   (1984, 1986, 1988), however, has long been interested in the phenomenon of biculturality.
3 It is still rare for anthropologists in this society or
   others to do what Laura Nader (1969) advocated
   many years ago – to "study up."
4 Its various strategies are based on this division and
   the series of oppositions (culture/nature, public/
   private, work/home, transcendence/immediacies,
   abstract/particular, objectivity/subjectivity, auton-
   omy/connectedness, etc.) associated with it:
   (a) women should be allowed to join the valued
   men's world, to become like men or have their
   privileges, (b) women's values and work, even if different, should be as valued as men's, or (c) women
   and men should both change and enter each other's
   spheres so that gender differences are erased.
5 It does not, Harding adds, dissolve feminism as a
   political identity, but the most pressing issue in
   feminist circles now is how to develop a politics of
   solidarity, coalition, or affinity built on the recognition of difference rather than the solidarity of a unitary self defined by its opposition to an other which
   had formerly defined it as other. The most interesting thinking on this subject has been Haraway's
   (1985).
6 For a discussion of the convergence of anthropological and feminist critiques of objectivity, see
   Abu-Lughod (1990a).
7 In his 1988 address to the American Anthropological
   Association, Edward Said's central point was that
   anthropologists had to attend not just to "the
   anthropological site" but to the "cultural situation
   in which anthropological work is in fact done"
   (1989: 212).
8 Much of the literature on indigenous anthropology
   is taken up with the advantages and disadvantages
   of this identification. See Fahim (1982) and Altorki
   and El-Solh (1988).

9 See also my discussion of the study of gender in
   Middle East anthropology (L. Abu-Lughod 1989).
10 In parallel fashion, those who study the black
   experience are thought of as studying a marked
   form of experience. It could be pointed out, and
   has been by such figures as Adrienne Rich, that
   the universal unmarked form of experience from
   which it differs is itself partial. It is the experience
   of whiteness.
11 Crapanzano (1977) has written insightfully about
   the regular process of distancing from the fieldwork experience and building identifications with
   the anthropological audience that all anthropologists go through when they return from the field.
12 This is happening, for example, in heated debates
   in the field of Middle East women's studies about
   who has the right to speak for Middle Eastern
   women.
13 Some would like to make distinctions between
   "womanism" and "feminism," but in much of
   literature they blur together.
14 Arens (1979), for example, has asked the provocative question of why anthropologists cling so
   tenaciously to the belief that in some cultures cannibalism is an accepted ritual practice, when the
   evidence (in the form of eye witness accounts) is
   so meager (if not, as he argues, absent).
15 In my own work on an Egyptian Bedouin
   community I began to think in terms of discourses rather than culture simply because I had
   to find ways to make sense of the fact that there
   seemed to be two contradictory discourses on
   interpersonal relations – the discourse of honor
   and modesty and the poetic discourse of vulnera-
   bility and attachment – which informed and were
   used by the same individuals in differing contexts
   (Abu-Lughod 1986). In a recent reflection on
   Bedouin responses to death (Abu-Lughod n.d.),
   I also had to make sense of the fact that there were
   multiple discourses on death in this community.
   Not only did people play with contradictory
   explanations of particular deaths (invoking, in
   one case of an accidental killing, stupidity, certain
   actions on the part of family members, the [evil]

eye, fate, and God's will), but the two primary discourses – ritual funerary laments and the Islamic discourse of God's will – were attached to different social groups, men and women, and worked to sustain and justify the power differences between them.

16 Two new journals, *Public Culture: Bulletin of the Center for Transnational Cultural Studies* and *Diaspora: A Journal of Transnational Studies*, provide forums for discussion of these transnational issues.

17 For evidence of a "world system" in the thirteenth century, see J. Abu-Lughod (1989).

18 Dumont (1986) has recently reiterated this, declaring changes in social theory to be merely methodological changes.

19 For a more detailed and interesting discussion of Clifford's unease with feminism, see Gordon (1988).

20 To this list could be added many others, including most recently Friedl (1989).

21 My own experiment in this sort of narrative ethnography is [Abu-Lughod 1993].

References

Abu-Lughod, Janet 1989 *Before European Hegemony*. New York: Oxford University Press.

Abu-Lughod, Lila 1986 *Veiled Sentiments: Honor and Poetry in a Bedouin Society*. New York: Oxford University Press.

Abu-Lughod, Lila 1989 Zones of theory in the anthropology of the Arab world. *Annual Review of Anthropology* 18:276–306.

Abu-Lughod, Lila 1990a Can there be feminist ethnography? *Women and Performance: A Journal of Feminist Theory* 5:7–27.

Abu-Lughod, Lila 1990b Shifting politics in Bedouin love poetry. In *Language and the Politics of Emotion*. C. Lutz and L. Abu-Lughod, eds., pp. 24–45. New York: Cambridge University Press.

Abu-Lughod, Lila 1993 *Writing Women's Worlds*. Berkeley: University of California Press.

Abu-Lughod, Lila n.d. Islam and the discourses of death. Unpublished manuscript.

Abu-Lughod, Lila, and Catherine Lutz 1990 Introduction: discourse, emotion, and the politics of everyday life. In *Language and the Politics of Emotion*. C. Lutz and L. Abu-Lughod, eds., pp. 1–23. New York: Cambridge University Press.

Altorki, Soraya, and Camillia El-Solh 1988 *Arab Women in the Field: Studying Your Own Society*. Syracuse, NY: Syracuse University Press.

Appadurai, Arjun 1988 Putting hierarchy in its place. *Cultural Anthropology* 3: 36–49.

Arens, William 1979 *The Man-Eating Myth: Anthropology and Anthropophagy*. New York OUP.

Asad, Talal 1973 *Anthropology and the Colonial Encounter*. London: Ithaca Press.

Asad, Talal 1983 Anthropological conceptions of religion: reflections on Geertz. *Man* 18: 237 59.

Belenky, Mary, Blithe Clinchy, Nancy Goldberger, and Jill Tarule 1986 *Women's Ways of Knowing*. New York: Basic Books.

Bell, Diane 1983 *Daughters of the Dreaming*. Melbourne: McPhee Gribble/N. Sydney: George Allen & Unwin.

Bowen, Elenore S. 1954 *Return to Laughter*. Reprint edition, 1964. Garden City, NY: Anchor Books.

Bourdieu, Pierre 1977 *Outline of a Theory of Practice*. Trans. R. Nice. Cambridge: Cambridge University Press.

Briggs, Jean 1970 *Never in Anger*. Cambridge, MA: Harvard University Press.

Cesara, Manda 1982 *Reflections of a Woman Anthropologist: No Hiding Place*. London and New York: Academic Press.

Chodorow, Nancy 1978 *The Reproduction of Mothering*. Berkeley: University of California Press.

Cixous, Hélène 1983 The laugh of the Medusa. In *The Signs Reader*. K. Cohen and P. Cohen, trans., E. Abel and E. Abe, eds., pp. 279–97. Chicago: University of Chicago Press.

Clifford, James 1983 Power in dialogue in ethnography. In *Observers Observed: Essays on Ethnographic Fieldwork*. G. W. Stocking, Jr., ed., pp. 121–56. Madison: University of Wisconsin Press.

Clifford, James 1986 Introduction: partial truths. In *Writing Culture: The Poetics and Politics of Ethnography*. J. Clifford and G. Marcus, eds., pp. 1–26. Berkeley: University of California Press.

Clifford, James 1988a On collecting art and culture. In *The Predicament of Culture: Twentieth-Century Ethnography, Literature, and Art*. James Clifford, pp. 215–51. Cambridge, MA: Harvard University Press.

Clifford, James 1988b On ethnographic self fashioning. In *The Predicament of Culture: Twentieth-Century Ethnography, Literature, and Art*. James Clifford, pp. 92–113. Cambridge, MA: Harvard University Press.

Clifford, James, and George E. Marcus, eds. 1986 *Writing Culture: The Poetics and Politics of Ethnography*. Berkeley University of California Press.

Crapanzano, Vincent 1977 On the writing of ethnography. *Dialectical Anthropology* 2:69–73.

Crapanzano, Vincent 1980 *Tuhami: Portrait of a Moroccan*. Chicago: University of Chicago Press.

Dumont, Jean-Paul 1978 *The Headman and I*. Austin: University of Texas Press.

Dumont, Jean-Paul 1986 Prologue to ethnography or prolegomena to anthropology. *Ethos* 14:344–67.

Dwyer, Kevin 1982 *Moroccan Dialogues: Anthropology in Question*. Baltimore: The Johns Hopkins University Press.

Echols, Alice 1984 The taming of the id: feminist sexual politics 1968–83. In Pleasure and Danger. C. Vance, ed., pp. 50–72. Boston: Routledge and Kegan Paul.

Fabian, Johannes 1983 *Time and the Other: How Anthropology Makes Its Object*. New York: Columbia University Press.

Fahim, Hussein, ed. 1982 *Indigenous Anthropology in Non-Western Countries*. Durham, NC: North Carolina Academic Press.

Fernea, Elizabeth W. 1965 *Guests of the Sheik: An Ethnography of an Iraqi Village*. Reprint edition, 1969. Garden City, NY: Anchor Books.

Fischer, Michael M. J. 1984 Towards a third world poetics: seeing through short stories and films in the Iranian culture area. *Knowledge and Society* 5: 171–241.

Fischer, Michael M. J. 1986 Ethnicity and the post-modern arts of memory. In *Writing Culture: The Poetics and Politics of Ethnography*. J. Clifford and G. Marcus, eds., pp. 194–233. Berkeley: University of California Press.

Fischer, Michael M. J. 1988 Aestheticized emotions and critical hermeneutics. *Culture, Medicine and Psychiatry* 12:31–42.

Foucault, Michel 1978 *Discipline and Punish*. A. Sheridan, trans. New York. Partheon.

Friedl, Erika 1989 *Women of Deh Koh: Lives in an Iranian Village*. Washington, DC: Smithsonian Institution Press.

Geertz, Clifford 1973 The impact of the concept of culture on the concept of man. In *The Interpretation of Cultures*. Clifford Geertz, pp. 33–54. New York: Basic Books.

Geertz, Clifford 1975 Thick description: toward an interpretive theory of culture. In *The Interpretation of Cultures*. Clifford Geertz, pp. 3–30. London: Hutchinson.

Geertz, Clifford 1988 *Works and Lives: The Anthropologist as Author*. Stanford: Stanford University Press.

Gilligan, Carol 1982 *In a Different Voice*. Cambridge, MA: Harvard University Press.

Gordon, Deborah 1988 Writing culture, writing feminism: the poetics and politics of experimental ethnography. *Inscriptions* 3/4:7–24.

Haraway, Donna 1985 A manifesto for cyborgs: science technology and socialist feminism in the 1980s. *Socialist Review* 80:65–107.

Harding, Sandra 1986 *The Science Question in Feminism*. Ithaca: Cornell University Press.

Harding, Sandra 1987 The method question. *Hypatia* 2:19–35.

Hartsock, Nancy 1985 *Money, Sex, and Power: Toward a Feminist Historical Materialism*. Boston: Northeastern University Press.

Hymes, Dell, ed. 1969 *Reinventing Anthropology*. New York: Pantheon.

Irigaray, Luce 1985a *Speculum of the Other Woman*. G. C. Gill, trans. Ithaca: Cornell University Press.

Irigaray, Luce 1985b *This Sex Which Is Not One*. C. Porter with C. Burks, trans. Ithaca: Cornell University Press.

Joseph, Suad 1988 Feminization, familism, self, and politics: research as a *Mughtaribi*. In *Arab Women in the Field: Studying Your Own Society*. S. Altorki and C. El-Solh, eds., pp. 25–47. Syracuse, NY: Syracuse University Press.

Kondo, Dorinne 1986 Dissolution and reconstitution of self: implications for anthropological episte-mology. *Cultural Anthropology* 1:74–88.

Kristeva, Julia 1981 Women's time. A. Jardine and H. Blake, trans. *Signs* 7:13–35.

Kuper, Adam 1988 *The Invention of Primitive Society: Transformation of an Illusion*. Boston and London: Routledge and Kegan Paul.

MacKinnon, Catherine 1982 Feminism, Marxism, method, and the state: an agenda for theory. *Signs* 7: 515–44.

Marcus, George E. and James Clifford 1985 The making of ethnographic texts: preliminary report. *Current Anthropology* 26:267–71.

Marcus, George, and Michael M. J. Fischer 1986 *Anthropology as Cultural Critique: An Experimental Moment in the Human Sciences*. Chicago: University of Chicago Press.

Meis, Maria 1983 Towards a methodology for feminist research. In *Theories of Women's Studies*. G. Bowles and R. D. Klein, eds., pp. 117–39. London and Boston: Routledge and Kegan Paul.

Mintz, Sidney 1985 *Sweetness and Power: The Place of Sugar in Modern History*. New York: Viking.

Morsy, Soheir 1988 Fieldwork in my Egyptian homeland: toward the demise of anthropology's distinctive-other hegemonic tradition. In *Arab Women in the Field: Studying Your Own Society*. S. Altorki and C. El-Solh, eds., pp. 69–90. Syracuse: Syracuse University Press.

Nader, Laura 1969 "Up the anthropologist" – perspectives gained from studying up. In *Reinventing Anthropology*. D. Hymes, ed., pp. 284–311. New York: Pantheon.

Narayan, Kirin 1989 *Saints, Scoundrels, and Storytellers*. Philadelphia: University of Pennsylvania Press.

Ortner, Sherry B. 1984 Theory in anthropology since the sixties. *Comparative Studies in Society and History* 26: 126–66.

Pratt, Mary Louise 1986 Fieldwork in common places. In *Writing Culture: The Poetics and Politics of Ethnography*. J. Clifford and G. Marcus, eds., pp. 27–50. Berkeley: University of California Press.

Rabinow, Paul 1977 *Reflections on Fieldwork in Morocco*. Berkeley: University of California Press.

Reinharz, Shulamit 1983 Experimental analysis: a contribution to feminist research. In *Theories of Women's Studies*. G. Bowles and R. D. Klein, eds., pp. 162–91. London and Boston: Routledge and Kegan Paul.

Rich, Adrienne 1979 Toward a woman-centered university. In *On Lies, Secrets and Silence*, pp. 125–56. New York: W. W. Norton & Co.

Riesman, Paul 1977 *Freedom in Fulani Social Life*. Chicago: University of Chicago Press.

Ruddick, Sara 1980 Maternal thinking. *Feminist Studies* 6(2):342–67.

Said, Edward 1978 *Orientalism*. New York: Pantheon.

Said, Edward 1989 Representing the colonized: anthropology's interlocuters. *Critical Inquiry* 15:205–25.

Shostak, Marjorie 1981 *Nisa: The Life and Words of a !Kung Woman*. Cambridge, MA: Harvard University Press.

Smith, Dorothy 1987 *The Everyday World as Problematic*. Boston: Northeastern University Press.

Stanley, Liz, and Sue Wise 1983 *Breaking Out: Feminist Consciousness and Feminist Research*. London: Routledge and Kegan Paul.

Strathern, Marilyn 1985 Dislodging a worldview: challenge and counter-challenge in the relationship between feminism and anthropology. *Australian Feminist Studies* 1:1–25.

Strathern, Marilyn 1987 An awkward relationship: the case of feminism and anthropology. *Signs* 12:276–92.

Tedlock, Dennis 1983 *The Spoken Word and the Work of Interpretation*. Philadelphia: University of Pennsylvania Press.

Tedlock, Dennis 1987 Questions concerning dialogical anthropology. *Journal of Anthropological Research* 43:325–37.

Turner, Edith 1987 *The Spirit and the Drum: A Memoir of Africa*. Tucson: University of Arizona Press.

Tyler, Stephen 1986 Post-modern ethnography: from document of the occult to occult document. In *Writing Culture: The Poetics and Politics of Ethnography*. J. Clifford and G. Marcus, eds., pp. 122–40. Berkeley: University of California Press.

Weiner, Annette 1976 *Women of Value, Men of Renown*. Austin: University of Texas Press.

Wolf, Eric R. 1982 *Europe and the People without History*. Berkeley: University of California Press.

Wolf, Margery 1968 *The House of Lim*. New York: Appelton-Century-Crofts.

39

Cutting the Network

Marilyn Strathern

The owner of the Shell petrol distribution licence for West Cameroon lives for part of the year in London, has children taking courses in Britain, France and the United States, and keeps houses in both capital and country (Rowlands 1995). The extent of his network is shown in a sumptuous lifestyle. The business on which it is based is run along hierarchical principles; unmarried youths are sent to work for him in the hopes that he will set them up on their own. Rowlands finds an apt description in an image the Bamiléké people offered to Warnier: "A notable [chef de famille] is a living piggy bank for the whole descent group: in him is contained the plenitude of blood received since the creation, through a chain of ancestors" (translated by Rowlands 1995: 33, after Warnier 1993: 126). Blood is a metonym for transmissible life essence, but only when channelled through those who take the title of "father", ensuring that the contents of the bank are not dissipated. An heir undergoes an "installation ritual [that] transforms his body into the piggy bank of the descent group, containing its blood and semen, which together with camwood and oil, also his possession, forms the corporate estate of the lineage" (Rowlands 1995: 33). He must guard that container. The businessman emphasizes the importance of containment to his commercial operations, for this allows him to refuse the claims of close kin while retaining their support, since it is from him that future prosperity will flow. Consider Rowlands's deliberate phrasing: it is the man's body which is transformed into the piggy bank.

When Hageners, from the Highlands of Papua New Guinea, remarked that women were like trade-stores (M. Strathern 1972: 99, 120), the analogy was with the flow of money through the store: as the repository of nurture from her kin which she contains, a bride is also a "store" or "bank" of the wealth due her kin in return. Elsewhere Melanesians translate terms for bridewealth into the English idioms of buying and selling (cf. Thomas 1991: 194–6). Indeed monetary metaphors would seem to flow like money itself, and like money act as condensed symbols of power. In turn, these persons imagined as repositories, Cameroonian businessman and Highlands bride alike, would seem both to carry the flow *and* to stop it. That is, they hold it within themselves.

The monetary idioms through which Melanesians speak of transactions such as bridewealth

From *Journal of the Royal Anthropological Institute* 2(3) (1996), pp. 517–31, 533–5. Copyright © 1996 by *Journal of the Royal Anthropological Institute*. Reprinted by permission of John Wiley & Sons UK.

Anthropology in Theory: Issues in Epistemology, Second Edition. Edited by Henrietta L. Moore and Todd Sanders.
© 2014 John Wiley & Sons, Inc. Published 2014 by John Wiley & Sons, Inc.

are often taken as a sign of commodity relations, whether of an indigenous kind (Gell 1992) or as the effect of exposure to wage labour and the world economy (Carrier 1995: 95). It is not buying and selling as such, of course, that are at the heart of anthropological understandings of commoditization, but the quality of relationships. The Hagen husband who speaks of his wife as a purchase, like something from a tradestore, awards himself new freedoms. But in some formulations, the bride is also the tradestore itself. If so, then she is a store of wealth for others who benefit from their relations through her, and it seems to be the *person* of the bride who, like the Cameroonian notable, contains the possibility of converting the fertile essence or nurture of others into wealth. Twentieth-century Euro-Americans, by contrast, do not like to imagine themselves as commoditizing people and do not, at least in the English vernacular, talk of bodies as piggy banks. Persons may have property, be propertied, but are not property themselves. On the contrary, recognizing the agency of the owner, and thus keeping "persons" separate from what may be owned as "property", was a hard-won project of their modernism. It was until recently, that is.

Some of the transactions in persons that characterize Papua New Guinea societies offer interesting theoretical resources for thinking about recent Euro-American experiments with relationships. One issue is the incursion of commodities, especially money, into kin relations, as in anxieties voiced over commercializing surrogacy agreements (see, for instance, Wolfram 1989; Ragoné 1994: 124). The reverse is also pertinent, although not pursued here. Euro-American debates over transactions in human tissue (see, for instance, Nuffield Council on Bioethics 1995) offer interesting theoretical resources for thinking about recent Melanesian experiments with commodities. In the 1960s and 1970s New Guinea Highlanders were forever commenting on money. By all accounts "money" (shell valuables) had been present for a long time, but at that period "money" (pounds and dollars) had also come on them as a new thing, an object of overt speculation about social change, an omen of a new era. Outsiders also worried about the incursion of kinship into commodity relations, how those tradestores would actually be run, since notions about obligations to kin supposedly interfered with the development of commerce.

Parallels cannot be taken too far. The Cameroonian piggy bank and the tradestore bride suggest mixes of person and property that Euro-Americans find unacceptable. Indeed, anthropologists have traditionally dissipated such strong images by talking of bundles of rights, or by referring to "bridewealth" rather than "brideprice", and analysing the ownership of persons in terms of governance. Thus was the authority system of the Maasai of Kenya translated by Llewelyn-Davies (1981). However, she makes it perfectly clear that Maasai ownership also involved rights of alienation, exercised over human and nonhuman resources alike, and that it was therefore appropriate to refer to property in women. Jolly (1994) reports that on South Pentecost, Vanuatu, women have a "price" (for which there is an indigenous term) just as goods in tradestores do; men nowadays prefer to pay this in cash rather than with the traditional valuables they reserve for transactions among themselves (such as the purchase of rank).

Now the benefits and evils of money (Bloch and Parry 1989) have been supplemented by a further subject for Euro-American anxiety and speculation: technology. By all accounts "technology" (the machine age) has been present for a long time, but in the 1980s and 1990s "technology" (hitech and micro) seems to strike people anew. It is ubiquitous, threatening, enabling, empowering, an omen of a new era. And if Hagen anxieties were about how to *control the flow* of money (A. J. Strathern 1979), these Euro-American anxieties are about where to *put limits* on technological inventions that promise to run away with all the old categorical divisions (Warnock 1985). These include the division between human and nonhuman. That division was ordinarily upheld (rendered durable) by a host of others, including distinctions between person and property, and between kinship and commerce. Across diverse areas of life, they seemingly threaten to fold in on one another, and notions about humanity and visions of technological development threaten newly to interfere with each other.

This mutual interference is more interesting than it might seem; I shall suggest that it bears comparison with gathering, stopping or containing flows of wealth or fertility. More generally, if increasing awareness of the role of technology in human affairs newly links human and nonhuman phenomena, does it invite us to re-think the kinds of flows of persons and things anthropologists have described elsewhere?

I

Mixed narratives

At the same time as anthropologists have made explicit the artificial or ethnocentric nature of many of their analytical divisions, they find themselves living in a cultural world increasingly tolerant of narratives that display a mixed nature. I refer to the combination of human and nonhuman phenomena that, in the 1980s and early 1990s, produced the imagery of cyborgs and hybrids. This imagery has been fed by the late twentieth-century Euro-American discovery of science as a source of cultural discourse (Franklin 1995). Neither culture nor science is outside the other.

In the case of the hybrid, combinations have been pressed into interpretative service to the point of surfeit. Narayan (1993: 29) was moved to identify an "enactment of hybridity" in anthropological writings, citing nine works appearing between 1987–92. What is true inside anthropology is also true outside. Cultures are everywhere interpreted as hybrid amalgams, whether of an indigenous kind or as the effect of exposure to one another: "almost every discussion on cultural identity is now an evocation of the hybrid state" (Papastergiadis 1995: 9). The Cameroonian businessman's biography seems another example. However, Rowland's source on the Bamiléké, Warnier, draws attention to a very particular kind of hybrid object, using the term hybrid in the sense given it by Latour (1993) and to which I shall return. The object was the heterogeneous knowledge created by a research team investigating a company's business networks (Warnier 1995: 107). The research team comprised a network of different competences. Their knowledge, a mix of technique cum social relationship, could be used to throw light on actual business operations, although Warnier doubted its legitimacy in the eyes of experts. They were likely to be proprietorial over certain components of this knowledge to whose pure form they could lay claim as "pure technicalities".

Warnier's comment takes the tension between pure and hybrid forms to be part of the construction of claims between different experts. The interpretation of cultures has led to similar competition; in the hands of the hybridizers, however, the very concept of the hybrid signals a critique of separations, of categorical divisions, encompassing that between the pure and the hybrid itself. "Hybridity" is invoked as a force in the world. This applies to the world created by certain forms of critical narrative in which the target is interpretation as such, and the concept of the hybrid a political move to make some kinds of representations impossible (Bhabha 1994). Now, imagining the impossibility of representation is often rendered concrete through the excoriation of boundaries (artificial divides) or the celebration of margins (deterritorialized, decentralized spaces). Such conceptualizations have in turn been criticized as re-enacting the old inversions of an us/them divide when one should be attending the processes of mutual translation (Papastergiadis 1995: 15; Purdom 1995). The huge critical onslaught against how to think the way different "identities" impact on one another has yielded a multitude of hybridizing concepts such as amalgamation, co-optation and conjuncture.

Yet despite the surfeit of terms, there are constant appeals to what this or that writer leaves out; most regularly, appeals to power relations. It is as though the politics that lies within the image of hybridity does not do sufficient analytical work – politics is re-created as though it were also "outside" the analysis of representations. Hence, too, the frequent appeals to categories such as race and gender which are presented, uninflected, prior to the work that the concept of the hybrid is supposed to do in undermining them ("power must be thought in the hybridity of race and sexuality" [Bhabha 1994: 251]). One reason may be that the language of boundaries and cultural translation raises inappropriate expectations of social analysis. Such expectations are both superfluous and insufficient: the complexity of people's interactions as they might be apprehended sociologically does not find a simple substitute in the subtlety with which categorical boundaries may be re-thought. For a start, the concept of boundary is one of the least subtle in the social science repertoire.

It is therefore interesting to consider a recent sociological approach which hybridizes its tools of social analysis, and devises a new term: network. This is of course an old term newly inflected. "Networks" (conventional network analysis) have long been present, but now we have "networks" (in actor-network theory) of a new kind. I deployed the latter in referring to the mix of technical and social competences in Warnier's research team, while juxtaposing the older usage in regard to the company's range of contacts. But what do the new networks convey about hybrids?

Actor-network theorists set up narrational fields in order to show how effects are produced out of alliances between human and nonhuman entities. The body, as a "network" of materials, is one such narrative for it gives off diverse signals, revealing skill, charisma and pathology (Law 1994: 183). Thus Pasteur's discovery of the microbe for anthrax depended on a whole series of statistical, rhetorical and operational factors that had to be held together in order to sustain, within a continuous network of effects, the crucially demonstrative links between bacillus, disease, laboratory, field experiment and the life and death of individual animals (Latour 1988: 84–92). The concept of network summons the tracery of heterogeneous elements that constitute such an object or event, or string of circumstances, held together by social interactions: it is, in short, a hybrid imagined in a socially extended state. The concept of network gives analytical purchase on those interactions. Latour (1993: 10–11) is explicit: the networking activity of interpretations that "link in one continuous chain" representations, politics and the world of the scientific discovery creates mixed narratives. The theorist's interpretations are as much networks as any other combination of elements.

For Latour, the rhetorical power of the hybrid rests on its critique of pure form, of which the archetype is the critique of the separation of technology from society, culture from nature, and human from nonhuman. And this is indeed critique: in his terms, the work of "translation" depends on the work of purification, and vice versa. At the same time, the hybridized form appeals to a reality that pure forms would conceal. Euro-Americans have always mixed their categories. It is (modernist) academic disciplines that have tried to pretend otherwise, and Latour castigates anthropology as condemned to territories and unable to follow networks (1993: 116). Now, anthropologists are perfectly capable of following such networks, that is, of tracking between the Achuar and Arapesh (his examples) and, in the organization of knowledge, between science and technology. Indeed, in the spirit of his account (Euro-Americans have always had hybrids), anthropologists have always done so in their "translations" of "other cultures". As students of comparative inquiry, however, they will not necessarily end up with a critique of the same pure forms that bother Euro-Americans, such as technology and society. That is, their accounts will not necessarily look like anything that could be applied to the social analysis of science and technology. In fact, we know that anthropologists are often diverted by kinship, and may attend instead to matters such as the flow of substance or the application of marriage rules.

In anthropologizing some of these issues, however, I do not make appeals to other cultural realities simply because I wish to dismiss the power of the Euro-American concepts of hybrid and network. The point is, rather, to extend them with social imagination. That includes seeing how they are put to work in their indigenous context, as well as how they might work in an exogenous one. It also includes attention to the way they become operationalized as manipulable or usable artefacts in people's pursuit of interests and their construction of relationships. In the home culture, part of their power will lie in their analogizing effect, in their resonance with other concepts and other people's usages; outside the home culture, anthropologists must make their own interpretative decisions as to their utility. I propose to utilize one characteristic of the hybrid, its apparent ubiquity, and to consider how this is supplemented by the concept of network.

Can networks have lengths?

Latour refers to the modern proliferation of hybrids as an *outcome* of purificatory practice. The more hybrids are suppressed – the more categorical divisions are made – the more they secretly breed. Their present visibility is just that: the outcome of present awareness of this process. Yet the capacity of hybrids to proliferate is also contained within them. For the very concept of the hybrid lends itself to endless narratives of (about, containing) mixture, including the constant splicing of cultural data in what a geneticist might call recombinant culturology. In fact, the concept can conjoin anything, a ubiquity consonant with the perceived ubiquity of culture itself. I see the apprehension of surfeit, then, as a moment of interpretative pause. Interpretation must hold objects of reflection stable long enough to be of use. That holding stable may be imagined as stopping a flow or cutting into an expanse, and perhaps some of the Euro-Americans' voiced concern over limits re-runs Derrida's question of how to "stop" interpretation. How are we to bring to rest expandable narratives, not to speak of the cultural anthropologist's endless production of cultural meanings [...]? "Cutting" is used as a metaphor by Derrida himself [...] for the way one phenomenon stops the flow of others. Thus the force of "law" cuts into a limitless expanse of "justice", reducing it and rendering it expressible, creating in the legal judgment a manipulable object of use; justice is operationalized so as to produce social effects.

If I see in the network of some actor-network theorists a socially expanded hybrid, it is because they have captured a concept with similar properties of auto-limitlessness; that is, a concept which works indigenously as a metaphor for the endless extension and intermeshing of phenomena.

A network is an apt image for describing the way one can link or enumerate disparate entities without making assumptions about level or hierarchy. Points in a narrative can be of any material or form, and network seems a neutral phrase for interconnectedness. Latour's own symmetrical vision brings together not only human and non-human in the ordering of social life, but also insights from both modern and premodern societies. And that is the purpose of his democratizing negative, *We have never been modern* (1993). Moderns divide society from technology, culture from nature, human from nonhuman, except that they do not – Euro-American moderns are like anyone else in the hybrids they make, even though they are rarely as explicit. Before he castigates anthropology for not going far enough, he praises the discipline both for creating hybrid accounts (mixing natural and supernatural in their ethnographies, politics and economics, demons and ecology) *and* for uncovering the thinking of those who make such hybrids explicit (in dwelling on them, he says, such people in fact keep them in

check). The divides of modern people's thinking do not correspond to the methods they actually deploy, and this is what people such as Papua New Guineans can tell them. There are similarities, he implies, in the way everyone puts hybrids together: "Is Boyle's air pump any less strange than the Arapesh spirit houses?" (1993: 115).

For Euro-Americans, technological development offers a vision of the mixed forms implied by technique (nonhuman materials modified by human ingenuity, or human disposition moulded by tools). Network imagery offers a vision of a social analysis that will treat social and technological items alike; any entity or material can qualify for attention. Thus instead of asking questions about the relationship of "science" and "society" in Pasteur's development of the anthrax vaccine, Latour (1988: 91) suggests we follow what Pasteur did and what his invention depended on. However, the power of such analytical networks is also their problem: theoretically, they are without limit. If *diverse* elements make up a description, they seem as extensible or involuted as the analysis is extensible or involuted. Analysis appears able to take into account, and thus create, any number of new forms. And one can always discover networks within networks; this is the fractal logic that renders any length a multiple of other lengths, or a link in a chain a chain of further links. Yet analysis, like interpretation, must have a point; it must be enacted as a stopping place.

Now if networks had lengths they would stop themselves. One kind of length is imagined by Latour: networks in action are longer the more powerful the "allies" or technological mediators that can be drawn in. (Technology has a lengthening effect and, in his view, premoderns tend to have limited networks.) We may also say that a network is as long as its different elements can be enumerated. This presupposes a summation; that is, enumeration coming to rest in an identifiable object (the sum). In coming to rest, the network would be "cut" at a point, "stopped" from further extension. How might that be done? It is worth consulting some of the actors who put such images to use in their dealings with one another.

Cutting networks

Actor-network theorists, and their allies and critics, are interested in the diverse props, to use Law's (1994) phrasing, that sustain people's actions and in the way the props are held in place long enough to do so. Networks rendered contingent on people's interactions turn out to have a fragile temporality. They do not last for ever; on the contrary, the question becomes how they are sustained and made durable. They may seem to depend on continuities of identity (that is, on homogeneity). But heterogeneous networks also have their limits. I shall argue that if we take certain kinds of networks as socially expanded hybrids then we can take hybrids as condensed networks. That condensation works as a summation or stop. The Euro-American hybrid, as an image of dissolved boundaries, indeed displaces the image of boundary when it takes boundary's place.

I give two very brief illustrations, the first an instance in which the actors involved might well have recognized themselves as a network in the conventional social sense, and the second a case in which the social scientist might think of the chain of elements as a "network" in Latour's sense and of the resultant artefact as a hybrid. The perceivable network in the first, and the analytical hybrid in the second, both bring potential extensions to a halt. In both cases these images of network or hybrid serve the furtherance of claims to ownership.

In 1987 a Californian corporation discovered the hepatitis C virus. The virus was a discovery in the sense of an unearthing of fresh knowledge about the world. But the means of detecting the virus led to the invention of a blood test for which the corporation applied for, and was granted, a patent. Patents are claims to inventions; that is, to applications of someone's inventiveness which others technically could, but are forbidden to, utilize without acknowledgement. This test met all the modern criteria for a patent. It was novel, produced by human intervention and, in the interests of simultaneously protecting and promoting competition, capable of industrial application. As a result, the British National Health Service will reportedly be paying more than £2 for every hepatitis C test it administers – some 3 million a year. Apparently, the technology for the blood test is standard. What the inventors added was the genetic sequence of the virus, making identification of the DNA an integral part of the test.

Hepatitis C had been under investigation for twelve years before the virus was isolated. The patent counsel for the company that developed the test was reported as saying: "We don't claim we did all the research, but we did the research that solved the problem" (*The Independent*, Dec. 1 1994). Any one invention is only made possible by the field of knowledge which defines a scientific community. The social networks here are long; patenting truncates them. So it matters very much over *which* segment or fragment of a network rights of ownership can be exercised. In another case, forty names to a scientific article became six names to a patent application; the rest did not join in. The long network of scientists that was formerly such an aid to knowledge becomes hastily cut. Ownership thereby curtails relations between persons; owners exclude those who do not belong.

Scientists working with reference to one another would no doubt recognize themselves as a social network, along the lines of conventional social analysis ("network analysis"). In this sense, the interests linking the several investigators of the virus were comparable: at the outset, any one of them was a potential claimant. The network as string of obligations, a chain of colleagues, a history of co-operation, would be sustained by continuities of identity. However diverse their roles, participants replicated one another in the fact of their participation. The patent introduced the question over what area the network spread; who participated in the final spurt.

The extent of a homogeneous network, such as this one, appears to be bounded by the definition of who belongs to it. However, the divide, created for the purposes of the patent, between those who did and those who did not belong, was established not by some cessation of the flow of continuity but by a quite extraneous factor: the commercial potential of the work that turned a discovery into a patentable invention. We could say that the prospect of ownership cut into the network. The claim to have done the research that solved "the problem" justified a deliberate act of hybridization: co-operative or competitive, the scientists' prior work could now be evaluated by criteria from a different world altogether: that of commerce.

Now, while we might expect our (not quite hypothetical) scientists to talk of networks, we would be surprised if they talked of hybrids. However, an actor-network theorist might well observe that the act of hybridization was doubly accomplished in this instance, for it also involved a classic form of Latourian hybrid: the invention.

An invention implies by definition that culture has been added to nature. The ingenuity of the inventor is held to change the character of an entity; intellectual activity confers property in it, as does the application of skill or labour which gives people (the possibility of) property in products. Hence a person from whom the original tissue comes finds it difficult to claim ownership of cell lines subsequently produced in the laboratory. Property rights cannot be claimed over an unaltered nature; they apply only to an altered one. The inventor's claim is that human tissue has been demonstrably modified by ingenuity, including ingenuity embodied in technological process. An American commentary on immortal cell lines, that is, cells infinitely reproducible in the laboratory, is explicit. "Many human cells have already been granted patents in the US on the basis that they would not exist but for the intervention of the "inventor", who extracted and manipulated them" (*New Scientist*, January 12, 1991).

In the famous Moore litigation, the man who tried to claim property rights in cells developed from tissue removed from his body during an operation lost the case. It was the claim to the heterogeneous hybrid, the fact that these cells had been immortalized through human ingenuity, that was upheld. In fact Moore was castigated by one judge (see Rabinow 1992) for *his* commercial motives, unseemly in relation to one's body but appropriate for those developing technology with commercial application in mind. Between Moore and his opponents, the claims could be constructed as of different orders; one claimed a body part as part of his person, the other an intellectual product as a result of certain activities. The hybrid object, then, the modified cell, gathered a network into itself; that is, it condensed into a single item diverse elements from technology, science and society, enumerated together as an invention and available for ownership as property. In fact there is a good case for seeing property as a hybridizing artefact in itself, although I do not develop the point here.

Ownership cuts both kinds of network, homogeneous and heterogeneous. First, it can truncate a chain of several claimants, otherwise identifiable through their social relationships with one another, dividing those who belong from those who do not. Belonging is thus given a boundary. Second, it can bring together a network of disparate elements

summated in an artefact (such as the invention) that holds or contains them all. If it is the perceived addition of human enterprise that bestows property rights, the human element added to the nonhuman one, then the proof of that hybridity curtails other interests. As at once the thing that has become the object of a right, and the right of a person in it, property is, so to speak, a network in manipulable form.

The structure of these entailments and curtailments holds an interest beyond the specific applications noted here. It is thus necessary to spell out the fact that there is a cultural predisposition among Euro-Americans to imagine that social relationships concern commonalities of identity before they concern difference, and that heterogeneity is inevitable in combining the human with the nonhuman. I turn now to networks that are homogeneous in so far as they presuppose a continuity of identities between human and nonhuman forms, and heterogeneous in so far as persons are distinguished from one another by their social relationships.

II

Stopping flow

Coppet's account of 'Are'are of the Solomon Islands shows the power of making objects which can be manipulated. 'Are'are divide living creatures into three kinds. Cultivated plants have body, domesticated pigs have both body and breath, while human beings also hold a name or "image". At death, the once living person is disaggregated or decomposed into these different elements: the body, a product of nurture received from others, is eaten as taro and vegetable food; breath is taken away in the breath of slaughtered pigs, while the image becomes an ancestor (Coppet 1994: 42, 53, referring, it would seem, primarily to men). This ancestral image is revealed as an enduring entity, as the person is stripped of body, breath and relations with all other persons bar ancestors and descendants. Interpersonal debts are settled (Coppett 1994: 53), as elsewhere the memory of the deceased is "finished" (Battaglia 1992).

The living human being thus appears to be a hybrid. But we would be mistaken to see this in the "addition" of breath to body or in the "modification" of breathing body by ancestral image. Each of the three components has its own manifestation, and if the amalgamated human being is a person, so too we may think of each component as a person (a person is made up of persons), in continuities facilitated by flows of money. I use the term "person" since the human being is also conceived as an aggregation of relations; it can take the form of an object available for consumption by those others who compose it. In these acts of consumption, the person is, so to speak, hybridized, dispersed among a network of others.

Nonhuman substitutes exist, then, for each of the forms (body, breath and image) that the human person takes. Through body and breath persons are interchangeable with taro and pigs, both of which are living beings like themselves; in the case of their distinctive image, however, they become interchangeable with non-living things. Ancestral image appears in the form of money; that is, strings of shell beads of varying lengths. The image is composed of strands presented at earlier funeral feasts and destined for future ones. Shell money travels from one funeral platform to another, gathering and dispersing as one might imagine a shadowy throng of ancestors doing; the fragmentation and recombination of different strands in the dealings of everyday life, Coppet notes, anticipate the money's appearance as an entirety at death. Every transaction assists the circulation of fragments or segments of an image. This image is the deceased made present as an ancestor; for shell money is, in effect, an "ancestor-image" (1994: 42), one of a person's persons, so to speak, in nonhuman form.

What is this money? Money is divisible into standarized portions, measured by the fathom containing twenty-four units of fifty shells. It thus "serves as a measuring rod, situating on a single scale events as different as the purchase of ten taros or of a canoe, a marriage or a murder, the amount of a funeral prestation, the payment for a ritual service or for an ensemble of musicians" (Coppet 1994: 40). Marking an event in monetary terms gives it an official seal. It also builds up the person as a composite of past transactions with diverse others. There is a further dimension to money. This stimulator of flows can stop flow. Shell money has circulatory power precisely because other entities, events and products can be

converted into it: past encounters and relationships circulate in condensed form in its "body" (my metaphor). Now, at death there is a finalizing sequence of exchanges in which the living being's two other components become money; in one sequence taro is converted into money, in another pigs (Coppet 1994: 53–4). The ancestor-image encompasses both, and the sequences stop at that point. Money thus becomes the repository or container of prior interchanges. It is as an anticipation of the final cessation of flow at death that money at other points in life can stop other flows, most significantly in homicide payments (Coppet 1994: 10–11). Where there has been a series of deaths, money alone stems the flow of revenge.

'Are'are are explicit about this finalizing sequence: they refer to it as a "stop" or "break", imagined as a fall, as at sunset, or as the sinking of a stone. Such stops can only be effected by means of shell money. In other types of exchange, by contrast, money is merely a contributory element; these include tied exchanges ("linked succession") which connect events leading inexorably from one to another so that the giver's repayment of a debt constitutes a new debt for the recipient. Any one prestation is also composed of "returns", the smallest sequence in a cycle of exchanges; exchanges are thus made up of exchanges. Together, these activities bring about networks of different lengths: 'Are'are measure the length of debt in an enlarging series of acts, from "return" to "linked succession" to "stop", the last gathering up all preceding flows into one moment. Like strands of shell money itself, these flows are simultaneously divisible and indivisible. In short, networks are composed of both human and nonhuman entities; they differ in how they are absorbed or consumed.

The mortuary ceremony that makes the deceased's networks visible also blocks their future effect. Old networks are cut by being gathered up at a point (in the deceased), whose socially hybrid form is dispersed and thereby brings new networks into play. The relationships that once sustained the deceased become recombined in the persons of others.

Bringing flow back

If the 'Are'are person emerges from such transactions as hybrid, then its heterogeneity comes from the way differences are sustained between the social relations that sustain it; the hybrid is an amalgam of social relations. In this Melanesian case, it is made visible as a network via funerary, bridewealth and similar prestations, transactions that lay out the person in terms of the claims diverse others have. And vice versa: the same transactions condense claims into socially manipulable objects of consumption (things). What are, in a manner of speaking, homogeneous, implying continuities of identity, are the forms – human and nonhuman – that these objects of consumption take (the body *is* the taro). With reference to similar transactions on Tanga, Foster (1995: 166 ff.) reminds us that it is an illusion to imagine that differences of value lie in the intrinsic nature of things: values are the outcome of relational practices. Thus "identical" products may have "different" values (cf. Piot 1991).

Coppet analyses exchanges in terms of a hierarchy of encompassment: from the tiniest interchange that carries an expectation of a return, to the ritual compulsion by which people are linked through making payments requiring further payments, to the capacity to gather such exchanges up in a mortuary prestation that caps them all. Here they are condensed into money. Money can, in turn, be spread out and disaggregated. What is true of a man's death is also true of a woman's marriage. Bride-givers bestow on the husband's kin the potential for growth in their sister whom they have grown, and they receive back, and thus consume, evidence of growth already accomplished in the form of valuables. Here are objects with different values: reproductive wealth (a future wife) in return for a non-reproductive sister. Now a non-returnable portion of money ("money to stop the woman") is said to stop the woman's image; her kinsmen's identity will no longer flow through her. In addition, her kin receive further money which they return to the husband's side in separate lots as money, taro and pigs. Her kin thereby re-create, as separate components, the body, breath and image of the woman from the single gift of money.

'Are'are ancestor-money is thus a condensed objectification of the person who can be disaggregated into various manifestations of relations with others. The (homogeneous) network of elements that make up the person – human and nonhuman – is also a (heterogeneous) network of social relationships. In turn, the person acts as both container and channel, blocking flow and bodying it forth.

Kinship systems, as anthropologists model them, have long provided analogies to this kind of process. Consider those curtailments of claims that come with exogamy, sister-exchange or cross-cousin marriage. If we imagine these protocols as creating networks of varying lengths, then they have different capacities for sustaining flow or stopping it. Many kinship systems certainly presuppose measurements for tracing the extent of substance. Indeed we may take this as diagnostic of "lineal" modes of kinship reckoning. Extensiveness of claims may be reckoned in terms of continuity of identity, as when a descent group whose members share common substance truncates claims over its members at the exogamic boundary; making new relations through marriage stops the flow. Or old relations may have to be cancelled before new ones are produced. Or, again, the kind of marriage rule that invites persons to think of themselves as marrying cousins or exchanging siblings invites them to think of substance as turning back on itself. Here networks are stopped in the persons of relatives who become the turning point for directing the flow of fertility back.

[...]

III

One class of kinship systems in the anthropological repertoire is notorious for having no internal stops. Bilateral or cognatic (nonunilineal) kinship reckoning allows that substance flows, and evinces itself, in individual persons but it does not stop in them or turn back. Indeed, indigenes may tell themselves that they are all related – trace far enough back and everyone shares substance with everyone else. As a response to such systems, there was, in the 1950s and 1960s, much anthropological debate about cutting networks. These debates addressed the problem of potentially endless networks of relations that seemingly did not cut themselves. One could trace forever outwards. From this came the presumption that there was no measure beyond the dictates of contingency: bilateral kinship appeared to have no inbuilt boundaries of its own. It was argued that in order to create groups, for example, ramifying kin ties had to be cut through other principles of social organization.

I would argue that what was applied to analysing group formation in such societies were the very mechanisms that do in fact give bilateral kin networks of the English kind a self-limiting character (Edwards and Strathern n.d.). One kind of reckoning never operates alone; it *always operates in conjunction with* factors of a different order. From the anthropologist's comparative viewpoint, "kinship" has to lie in the combination.

Here we have the Euro-American hybrid: not just an expanse "cut into" by other phenomena but a specific abridgement of nature and culture. Social relations depend on multitudinous factors that truncate the potential of forever-ramifying biological relations. Biological relatedness – "blood ties" – can thus be cut by failure to accord social recognition (someone is forgotten), just as social relationships can be cut by appeal to biological principles (dividing "real" kin from others). So in practice one does not trace connexions for ever; conversely the most intimate group is also open to discovering contacts they never knew existed. Factors from diverse domains can affect the reach of an otherwise homogeneous network based on "blood" or "family".

What is interesting about English bilateralism, then, is that the basis on which everyone might say they are related (biological and genetic connexion) can be reckoned separately from the traffic of social relations. This gives us both continuities and discontinuities of identity. In so far as biology and society are taken as distinct domains, we can see why the users of English culture presume an identity of interests in social relations and why they presume heterogeneity in mixes of human and nonhuman. In Melanesian terms I might want to say that these Euro-Americans imagine a boundary to the person that makes internal flows of substance radically different from external ones (interactions with others). That also gives a tenacity to their ideas about race and sexuality: continuities are somehow within and discontinuities somehow outside.

While my arguments have been pitched very generally, I would assert that such generalizations lie "within" the specificities of social life as well as "outside" them. Consider Steve, in Simpson's account of the "unclear family" constituted through parental divorce.

Steve's narration of his "family life" places him at the centre of a network of relationships which carry varying loads in terms of affect and commitment. For example, he sees himself as a "father" to six children. However, the way in which fatherhood is expressed and experienced by Steve in relation to each of his children is variable. The label "father" condenses and conceals varying levels of financial and emotional commitment, different residential arrangements and variable quantities of contact. (1994: 834)

Steve is at once a (singular) father and contains within his fatherhood a range of elements. They comprise connexions with persons, different social practices, resources and materials, heterogeneous elements from which, in this passage, Simpson has selected a few.

Disaggregated into its components, it would seem that the figure of the father expands to bring in a range of reference points; yet it also contracts in so far as only a small set of components is singled out: what Steve means by "father" is likely to encompass more than can ever be specified. When the specification is reduced to distinguishable elements, as in commitments defined as both financial and emotional, then we can refer to the resultant construct, the father who shows both, as a hybrid. As a kinsperson, then, this figure constitutes a condensed image whose dispersed, network version is distributed between separable orders of fact (money, emotion).

English and other Euro-American bilateral systems of kinship join together disparate reasons for relatedness. They are premised on conserving ontological difference between domains: on imagining that the affective relations of kinship are materially different from the flux of economic life, or that the transmission of substance operates under laws of biology separate from social laws, or that individual persons are natural beings modified by society. Here the earlier examples of invention have a particular point in my narrative. The inventor is a kind of enhanced agent. All human agents are inventors (creators) in a modern, Euro-American sense: the person is substance plus the animating self-inventiveness of agency, a combination of distinct elements. The elements may be regarded as "added" together, "modifying" one another in the same way as culture modifies nature. If, in Melanesian terms, Euro-Americans sometimes seek to sustain a difference between internal and external flows (body and intellect versus biology and culture, and so forth), it is because each can be presented as having its own impetus or logic. For they can be turned to use separately as well as in conjunction, as I have indicated in respect of concepts of ownership. Belonging marks relations based on continuities of identity, and thus the separation of pure forms, while property presupposes discontinuity, and the conjunction of human enterprise with nonhuman resources. [...]

References

Battaglia, D. 1992. The body in the gift: memory and forgetting in Sabarl mortuary exchange. *American Ethnologist* 9, 3–18.

Bhabha, H.K. 1994. *The location of culture*. London: Routledge.

Bloch, M. and J. Parry (eds.) 1989. *Money and the morality of exchange*. Cambridge: University Press.

Carrier, J. 1995. Maussian occidentalism: gift and commodity systems. In *Occidentalism: images of the West* (ed.) J. Carrier. Oxford: Clarendon Press.

Coppet, D. de 1994. 'Are'are. In *Of relations and the dead: four societies viewed from the angle of their exchanges* (eds.) C. Barraud, D. de Coppet, A. Iteanu and R. Jamous (trans.) S. Suffern. Oxford: Berg.

Edwards, J. and M. Strathern n.d. Including our own. Paper for conference, Boundaries and Identities, Edinburgh, 1996.

Foster, R.J. 1995. *Social reproduction and history in Melanesia: mortuary ritual, gift exchange and custom in the Tanga Islands*. Cambridge: University Press.

Franklin, S. 1995. Science as culture, cultures of science. *Annual Review of Anthropology* 24, 163–84.

Gell, A. 1992. Inter-tribal commodity barter and reproductive gift exchange in old Melanesia. In *Barter, exchange and value: an anthropological approach* (eds.) C. Humphrey and S. Hugh-Jones. Cambridge: University Press.

Jolly, M. 1994. *Women of the place: kastom, colonialism and gender in Vanuatu*. Chur, Switzerland: Harwood Academic.

Latour, B. 1988. *The Pasteurization of France* (trans.) A. Sheridan and J. Law. Cambridge, MA: Harvard University Press.

Latour, B. 1993. *We have never been modern* (trans.) C. Porter. London: Harvester Wheatsheaf.

Law, J. 1994. *Organizing modernity*. Oxford: Blackwell.

Llewelyn-Davies, M. 1981. Women, warriors and patriarchs. In *Sexual meanings: the cultural construction of gender and sexuality* (eds.) S. Ortner and H. Whitehead. Cambridge: University Press.

Narayan, K. 1993. How native is a "native" anthropologist? *American Anthropologist* 95, 19–34.

Nuffield Council on Bioethics 1995. *Human tissue: ethical and legal issues*. London.

Papastergiadis, N. 1995. Restless hybrids. *Third Text* 32, 9–18.

Piot, C.D. 1991. Of persons and things: some reflections on African spheres of exchange. *Man* (NS) 26, 405–24.

Purdom, J. 1995. Mapping difference. *Third Text* 32, 19–32.

Rabinow, P. 1992. Severing the ties: fragmentation and dignity in late modernity In *Knowledge and society: Vol. 9: the anthropology of science and technology* (eds.) D. Hess and L. Layne. 169–87.

Ragoné, H. 1994. *Surrogate motherhood: conception in the heart*. Boulder: Westview Press.

Rowlands, M. 1995, Prestige of presence: negotiating modernisation through tradition. In *Worlds apart: modernity through the prism of the local* (ed.) D. Miller (ASA Dec. Conf. Ser.). London: Routledge.

Simpson, R. 1994. Bringing the "unclear" family into focus: divorce and re-marriage in contemporary Britain. *Man* (NS) 29, 831–51.

Strathern, A.J. 1979. Gender, ideology and money in Mount Hagen. *Man* (NS), 14, 530–48.

Strathern, M. 1972. *Women in between: female roles in male world*. London: Seminar (Academic) Press.

Thomas, N. 1991. *Entangled objects: exchange, material culture, and colonialism in the Pacific*. Cambridge, MA: Harvard University Press.

Warnier, J.-P. 1993. *L'esprit d'enterprise au Cameroun*. Paris: Karthala.

Warnier, J.-P. 1995. Around a plantation: the ethnography of business in Cameroon. In *Worlds apart: modernity through the prism of the local* (ed.) D. Miller (ASA Dec. Conf. Ser.). London: Routledge.

Warnock, M. 1985. *A question of life: the Warnock Report on Human Fertilisation and Embryology*. Oxford: Blackwell.

Wolfram, S. 1989. Surrogacy in the United Kingdom. In *New approaches to human reproduction: social and ethical dimensions* (eds.) L. M. Whiteford and M. L. Poland. London: Westview Press.

SECTION 12
Objectivity, Morality, and Truth

40

The Primacy of the Ethical: Propositions for a Militant Anthropology

Nancy Scheper-Hughes

Moral Accountability and Anthropology in Extreme Situations

[...] The idea of an active, politically committed, morally engaged anthropology strikes many anthropologists as unsavory, tainted, even frightening. This is less so in parts of Latin America, India, and Europe (Italy and France, for example), where the anthropological project is at once ethnographic, epistemologic, and political and where anthropologists do communicate broadly with "the polis" and "the public."

Many colleagues reacted with anger when I first began to speak and to write about the routinization and medicalization of hunger among Brazilian sugarcane cutters and about the mortal selective neglect and unnecessary deaths of their young children, in which layers of bad faith and complicity joined the oppressed and their oppressors in a macabre dance of death. The bad faith existed on many levels: among doctors and pharmacists who allowed their knowledge and skills to be abused; among local politicians who presented themselves as community benefactors while knowing full well what they were doing in distributing tranquilizers and appetite stimulants to hungry people from the overstocked drawers of municipal file cabinets; among the sick poor themselves, who even while critical of the medical mistreatment they received continued to hold out for a medical-technical solution to their political and economic troubles; and, finally, among medical anthropologists whose fascination with metaphors, signs, and symbols can blind us to the banal materiality of human suffering and prevent us from developing a political discourse on those hungry populations of the Third World that generously provide us with our livelihoods.

What was I after, after all? Chronic hunger, of the sort that I was describing in rural Brazil, was not unusual, I was told at a faculty seminar at the University of North Carolina, Chapel Hill, in 1983. Many, perhaps the majority, of Indonesian villagers the critic had been studying were surviving on a similarly meager and deficient diet as the Northeast Brazilian cane cutters. Why had I made *that* – the mundane concreteness of chronic hunger and its eroding effects on the human spirit – the driving force and focus of my Brazilian work? "Is this an anthropology of evil?" asked the late Paul Riesman as a formal discussant in a

From *Current Anthropology* 36(3) (1995), pp. 415–20, 438–40. Copyright © 1995 by *Current Anthropology*. Reprinted by permission of University of Chicago Press.

Anthropology in Theory: Issues in Epistemology, Second Edition. Edited by Henrietta L. Moore and Todd Sanders.
© 2014 John Wiley & Sons, Inc. Published 2014 by John Wiley & Sons, Inc.

AAA-sponsored symposium in response to my analysis of the "bad faith" which allowed clinic doctors, as well as rural workers themselves, to overlook the starvation that lay just beneath the skin of their own and their babies' "nervousness," "irritability," and "delirium" and permitted the doctors to medicate even the smallest toddler's hunger with painkillers, phenobarbital, antibiotics, and sleeping pills. Riesman (cited in Scheper-Hughes 1988:456 n. 4) concluded:

It seems to me that when we act in critical situations of the sort that Scheper-Hughes describes for Northeast Brazil, *we leave anthropology behind*. We leave it behind because we abandon what I believe to be a fundamental axiom of the creed we share, namely that all humans are equal in the sight of anthropology. Though Scheper-Hughes does not put it this way, the struggle she is urging anthropologists to join is a struggle against evil. Once we identify an evil, I think we give up trying to understand the situation as a human reality. Instead we see it as in some sense inhuman, and all we then try to understand is how best to combat it. At this point we [leave anthropology behind] and we enter the political process.

But why is it assumed that when anthropologists enter the struggle we must inevitably bow out of anthropology? Since when is *evil* exempt from human reality? Why do anthropologists so steadfastly refuse to stare back at it, to speak truth to its power? What are we passively *waiting* for? One listener threw up his hands in mock confusion in response to a paper on the political economy of mother love and infant death in the Brazilian shantytown that I delivered at the University of Chicago in 1987. "Why are we being served this?" he asked. "How are we supposed to *feel*? ... And what in the world are we supposed to do?"

The Politics of Representation

As writers and producers of demanding images and texts, what *do* we want from our readers? To shock? To evoke pity? To create new forms of narrative, an "aesthetic" of misery, an anthropology of suffering, an anthropological theodicy? And what of the people whose suffering and fearful accommodations to it are transformed into a public spectacle? What is our obligation to them?

Those of us who make our living observing and recording the misery of the world have a particular obligation to reflect critically on the impact of the harsh images of human suffering that we foist on the public. I think of the brutal images of fleeing Haitian boat people and the emotionally devastated family around the bedside of a dying AIDS patient with which the business magnate Benetton has assaulted us, for reasons that remain altogether unclear, and of the daily media images of horror in Bosnia, Somalia, the Middle East, and the townships of South Africa and of Sebastião Salgado's images of hunger and death in the Brazilian Northeast. To what end are we given and do we represent these images as long as the misery and the suffering continue unabated? The experience of Northeast Brazil and South Africa indicates that the more frequent and ubiquitous the images of sickness, political terror, starvation and death, burnings and hangings, the more people living the terror accept the brutality as routine, normal, even expected. The shock reaction is readily extinguished, and people everywhere seem to have an enormous capacity to absorb the hideous and go on with life and with the terror, violence, and misery as usual.

As Michael Taussig (1992) has noted, citing Walter Benjamin's analysis of the history of European fascism, it is almost impossible to be continually conscious of the state of emergency in which one lives. Sooner or later one makes one's accommodations to it. The images meant to evoke shock and panic evoke only blank stares, a shrug of the shoulders, a nod – acceptance as routine and *normal* of the extraordinary state of siege under which so many live. Humans have any uncanny ability to hold terror and misery at arm's length, especially when they occur in their own community and are right before their eyes. Anthropologists do so themselves when they apply their theoretical abstractions and rhetorical figures of speech to the horrors of political violence – both wars of repression and wars of liberation – so that the suffering is aestheticized (turned into theater, viewed as "performance") and thereby minimized and denied. The new cadre of "barefoot anthropologists" that I envision must become alarmists and shock troopers – the producers of politically complicated and morally demanding texts and images capable of sinking through the layers of acceptance, complicity, and bad faith that allow the suffering and the deaths to continue without even the pained cry of recognition of Conrad's evil protagonist, Kurtz: "*The horror! the horror!*"

Anthropology without Borders: The Postmodern Critique

Ethnography has had a rough time of it lately. In the brave new world of reflexive postmodernists, when anthropologists arrive in the field everything local is said to dissolve into merged media images, transgressed boundaries, promiscuously mobile multinational industry and workers, and transnational-corporate desires and commodity fetishism. This imagined postmodern, borderless world (Appadurai 1991) is, in fact, a Camelot of free trade that echoes the marketplace rhetoric of global capitalism, a making of the world and social science safe for "low-intensity democracy" backed by World Bank capital. The flight from the local in hot pursuit of a transnational, borderless anthropology implies a parallel flight from local engagements, local commitments, and local accountability. Once the circuits of power are seen as capillary, diffuse, global, and difficult to trace to their sources, the idea of resistance becomes meaningless. It can be either nothing or anything at all. (Have we lost our senses altogether?)

The idea of an anthropology without borders, although it has a progressive ring to it, ignores the reality of the very real borders that confront and oppress "our" anthropological subjects and encroach on our liberty as well. (The obstacles that the US government puts in the way of North Americans wishing to conduct research in Cuba or establish ties with Cuban scholars are just one case in point.) These borders are as real as the passports and passbooks, the sandbagged bunkers, the armed roadblocks and barricades, and the "no-go zones" that separate hostile peoples, territories, and states. The borders confront us with the indisputable reality of electric fences, razor wire, nail-studded hand grenades, AK47's; where these are lacking, as in South African townships and squatter camps, stones and torches will do.

Having recently returned from South Africa, where both black and white tribes, Zulus and Afrikaners, were demanding enclosed and militarily defended homelands, it is difficult to relate to the whimsical postmodernist language extolling borderless worlds. The anthropology that most Cape Town Xhosa, Venda, Zulu, Afrikaner, and Moslem students want is *not* the anthropology of deconstruction and the social imaginary but the anthropology of the *really real*, in which the stakes are high, values are certain, and ethnicity (if not essentialized) is certainly essential. Here, writing against culture[1] would be writing against them, against *their* grain, against their emergent need, in a newly forming and, one hopes, democratic state, for collective self-definition and historical legitimacy – for a place the sun.

Anthropology, it seems to me, must be there to provide the kind of deeply textured, fine-tuned narratives describing the specificity of lives lived in small and isolated places in distant homelands, in the "native yards" of sprawling townships, or in the Afrikaner farm communities of the Stellenbosch and the Boland. And we need, more than ever, to locate and train indigenous local anthropologists and organic intellectuals to work with us and to help us redefine and transform ourselves and our vexed craft.

Many younger anthropologists today, sensitized by the writings of Michel Foucault on power/knowledge, have come to think of anthropological fieldwork as a kind of invasive, disciplinary "panopticon" and the anthropological interview as similar to the medieval inquisitional confession through which church examiners extracted "truth" from their native and "heretical" peasant parishioners. One hears of anthropological observation as a hostile act that reduces our "subjects" to mere "objects" of our discriminating, incriminating, scientific gaze. Consequently, some postmodern anthropologists have given up the practice of descriptive ethnography altogether.

I am weary of these postmodernist critiques, and, given the perilous times in which we and our subjects live, I am inclined toward compromise, the practice of a "good enough" ethnography (1992:28). While the anthropologist is always a necessarily flawed and biased instrument of cultural translation, like every other craftsperson we can do the best we can with the limited resources we have at hand: our ability to listen and to observe carefully and with empathy and compassion. I still believe that we are best doing what we do best as ethnographers, as natural historians of people until very recently thought to have no history. And so I think of some of my anthropological subjects – in Brazil Biu, Dona Amor, little Mercea, little angel-baby that she is now; in South Africa, Sidney Kumalo and the three boys rescued in the nick of time from a mortal flogging – for whom anthropology is not a "hostile gaze" but rather an opportunity for self-expression. Seeing, listening, touching, recording can be, if done with care and sensitivity, acts of solidarity. Above all, they are the work of recognition. Not to look, not to touch, not to record can be the hostile act, an act of indifference and of turning away.

If I did not believe that ethnography could be used as a tool for critical reflection and for human liberation, what kind of perverse cynicism would keep me returning again and again to disturb the waters of Bom Jesus da Mata or to study the contradictory medical and political detention of Cubans in the Havana AIDS sanatorium? Or, more recently, to study the underbelly of political violence and terror in the makeshift mortuary chapels of Chris Hani squatter camp (Scheper-Hughes 1994)? What draws me back to these people and places is not their exoticism and their "otherness" but the pursuit of those small spaces of convergence, recognition, and empathy that we share. Not everything dissolves into the vapor of absolute cultural difference and radical otherness. There are ways in which my Brazilian, Cuban, Irish, and South African interlocutors and I are not so radically "other" to each other. Like the peasants of Ireland and Northeast Brazil, I too instinctively make the sign of the cross when I sense danger or misfortune approaching. And like Mrs. Kumalo and so many other middle-aged women of Chris Hani squatter camp, I too wait up (till dawn if necessary) for the scrape-scrape sound of my son and daughters as, one by one, following their own life plans, they turn their keys in the latch and announce their arrival one more day from an unsafe and booby-trapped outside world.

The Primacy of the Ethical

The work of anthropology demands an explicit ethical orientation to "the other." In the past – and with good reason – this was interpreted as a

respectful distance, a hesitancy, and a reluctance to name wrongs, to judge, to intervene, or to prescribe change, even in the face of considerable human misery. In existential philosophical terms, anthropology, like theology, implied a leap of faith to an unknown, opaque other-than-myself, before whom a kind of reverence and awe was required. The practice of anthropology was guided by a complex form of modern pessimism rooted in anthropology's tortured relationship to the colonial world and its ruthless destruction of native lands and peoples. Because of its origins as a mediator in the clash of colonial cultures and civilizations, anthropological thinking was, in a sense, radically "conservative" with respect to its "natural" suspiciousness of all projects promoting change, development, modernization, and the like. We knew how often such interventions were used against traditional, nonsecular, and communal people who stood in the way of Western cultural and economic expansion. Therefore, it was understood that anthropological work, if it was to be in the nature of an ethical project, had to be primarily transformative of the self, while putting few or no demands on "the other." The artificial and (at times) counterintuitive notion of cultural (and moral and political) relativism evolved as the sacred oath of anthropological fieldwork. As the physicians' injunction was to "do no harm," the anthropologists' injunction was (like the three monkeys of ancient China) to "see no evil, hear no evil, speak no evil" in reporting from the field.

While the first generations of cultural anthropologists were concerned with relativizing thought and reason, I have suggested that a more "womanly" anthropology might be concerned not only with how humans think but with how they behave toward each other. This would engage anthropology directly with questions of ethics. The problem remains in searching for a standard or divergent ethical standards that take into account (but do not privilege) our own "Western" cultural presuppositions.

In the shantytown of Alto do Cruzeiro in Northeast Brazil I encountered a situation in which some mothers appear to have "suspended the ethical" – compassion, empathic love, and care – in relation to some of their weak and sickly children, allowing them to die of neglect in the face of overwhelming difficulties. In the South

African squatter camps of the Western Cape I stumbled upon another instance: the expressed sentiment that one less young thief or police "collaborator" makes good sense in terms of social and community hygiene. At times the shantytown or the squatter camp resembles nothing so much as a battlefield, a prison camp, or an emergency room in a crowded inner-city hospital, where an ethic of triage replaces an ethical regard for the equal value of every life. The survivor's "logic" that guides shantytown mothers' actions toward some of their weak babies is understandable. The fragility and "dangerousness" of the mother–infant relationship is an immediate and visible index of chronic scarcity, hunger, and other unmet needs. And the revolutionary logic that sees in the pressured but self-serving acts of a young police collaborator the sorcery of a scarcely human witch or devil is also understandable. But the moral and ethical issues must still give reason to pause and to doubt. How often the oppressed turn into their own oppressors or, worse still, into the oppressors of others!

Anthropologists who are privileged to witness human events close up and over time, who are privy to community secrets that are generally hidden from the view of outsiders or from historical scrutiny until much later – after the collective graves have been discovered and the body counts made – have, I believe, an ethical obligation to identify the ills in a spirit of solidarity and to follow what Gilligan (1982) has called a "womanly" ethic of care and responsibility. If anthropologists deny themselves the power (because it implies a privileged position) to identify an ill or a wrong and choose to ignore (because it is not pretty) the extent to which dominated people sometimes play the role of their own executioners, they collaborate with the relations of power and silence that allow the destruction to continue.

To speak of the "primacy of the ethical" is to suggest certain transcendent, transparent, and essential, if not "precultural," first principles. Historically anthropologists have understood morality as contingent on and embedded within specific cultural assumptions about human life. But there is another philosophical position that posits "the ethical" as existing prior to culture because, as Emmanuel Levinas (1987:100) writes, in presupposing all meaning, ethics makes culture

possible: "Mortality does not belong to culture: [it] enables one to judge it." Here I will tentatively and hesitantly suggest that responsibility, accountability, answerability to "the other" – the ethical as I would define it – is precultural to the extent that our human existence as social beings presupposes the presence of the other. The extreme relativist position assumes that thought, emotion, and reflexivity come into existence with words and words come into being with culture. But the generative prestructure of language presupposes, as Sartre (1956) has written, a given relationship with another subject, one that exists prior to words in the silent, preverbal "taking stock" of each other's existence. Though I veer dangerously toward what some might construe as a latent sociobiology, I cannot escape the following observation: that we are thrown into existence at all presupposes a given, implicit moral relationship to an original (m)other and she to me. "Basic strangeness" – as the psychoanalyst Maria Piers labeled the profound shock of mis-recognition reported by a great many mothers in their first encounters with a newborn – is perhaps the prototype of all other alienated self–other relations, including that of the anthropologist and her overly exoticized others. Just as many women may fail to recognize a human kinship with the newborn and see it as a strange, exotic, other – a bird, a crocodile, a changeling, one to be returned to sky or water rather than adopted or claimed – so the anthropologist can view her subjects as unspeakably other, belonging to another time, another world altogether. If it is to be in the nature of an ethical project, the work of anthropology requires a different set of relationships. In minimalist terms this might be described as the difference between the anthropologist as "spectator" and the anthropologist as "witness."

Witnessing: Toward a Barefoot Anthropology

In the act of writing culture what emerges is always a highly subjective, partial, and fragmentary but also deeply personal record of human lives based on eyewitness accounts and testimony. If "observation" links anthropology to the natural sciences, "witnessing" links anthropology to moral philosophy. Observation, the anthropologist as "fearless spectator," is a passive act which positions the anthropologist above and outside human events as a "neutral" and "objective" (i.e., uncommitted) seeing I/eye. Witnessing, the anthropologist as *companheira*, is in the active voice, and it positions the anthropologist inside human events as a responsive, reflexive, and morally committed being, one who will "take sides" and make judgments, though this flies in the face of the anthropological nonengagement with either ethics or politics. Of course, noninvolvement was, in itself, an "ethical" and moral position.

The fearless spectator is accountable to "science"; the witness is accountable to history. Anthropologists as witnesses are accountable for what they see and what they fail to see, how they act and how they fail to act in critical situations. In this regard, Orin Starn's poignant essay "Missing the Revolution: Anthropologists and the War in Peru" (1992) indirectly makes "my" case. Anthropologists, no less than any other professionals, should be held accountable for how we have used and how we have failed to use anthropology as a critical tool at crucial historical moments. It is the act of "witnessing" that lends our work its moral, at times almost theological, character. In *Death without Weeping* I observed how participant-observation has a way of drawing ethnographers into spaces of human life where they might really prefer not to go at all and, once there, do not know how to escape except through writing, which willy-nilly draws others there as well, making them party to the witnessing.

I have an image, taken from John Berger (1967), of the ethnographer/witness as the "clerk of the records." The village clerk listens, observes, and records the minutiae of human lives. The clerk can be counted on to remember key events in the personal lives and in the life history of the community and to keep confidences, knowing when to speak and when to keep silent. The ethnographer/witness as clerk is a minor historian of the ordinary lives of people often presumed to have no history. Privileged to be present at births and deaths and other life cycle events, the clerk can readily call to mind the fragile web of human relations that bind people together into a collectivity and identify those external and internal relations that destroy them as a community. In the shantytowns and squatter camps of Brazil and South Africa there are a great many lives and even more deaths to keep track of, numbering the bones of a people often thought of as hardly worth counting at all. The answer to the critique of anthropology is not a retreat from ethnography but rather an ethnography that is personally engaged and politically committed. If my writings have promoted a certain malaise or discomfort with respect to their sometimes counterintuitive claims, then they have done the work of anthropology, "the difficult science": to afflict our comfortable assumptions about what it means to be human, a woman, a mother.

I want to ask what anthropology might become if it existed on two fronts: as a field of knowledge (as a "discipline") and as a field of action, a force field, or a site of struggle. Anthropological writing can be a site of resistance. This resembles what the radical Italian psychiatrist Franco Basaglia (1987) called becoming a "negative worker." The negative worker is a species of class traitor – a doctor, a teacher, a lawyer, psychologist, a social worker, a manager, a social scientist, even – who colludes with the powerless to identify their needs against the interests of the bourgeois institution: the university, the hospital, the factory. Negative workers are hospital-based psychiatrists who side with their resistant or "noncompliant" mental patients, grade-school teachers who side with their "hyperactive" students, social workers who side with their welfare "cheats," and so forth.

Anthropologists, too, can be negative workers. We can practice an anthropology-with-one's-feet-on-the-ground, a committed, grounded, even a "barefoot" anthropology. We can write books that go against the grain by avoiding impenetrable prose (whether postmodernist or Lacanian) so as to be accessible to the people we say we represent. We can disrupt *expected* academic roles and statuses in the spirit of the Brazilian "carnavalesque." We can make ourselves available not just as friends or as "patrons" in the old colonialist sense but as *comrades* (with all the demands and responsibilities that this word implies) to the people who are the subjects of our writings, whose lives and miseries provide us with a livelihood. We can – as Michel De Certeau suggests – exchange gifts based on our labors, use book royalties to support radical actions, and seek to avoid the deadening treadmill of academic achievement and in this way subvert the process that puts our work at the service of the scientific, academic factory.

We can distance ourselves from old and unreal loyalties, as Virginia Woolf (1938) described them: loyalties to old schools, old churches, old ceremonies, and old countries. Freedom from unreal loyalties means ridding oneself of pride of family, nation, religion, pride of sex and gender, and all the other dangerous loyalties that spring from them. In doing so we can position ourselves, as Robert Redfield once put it, squarely on the side of humanity. We can be anthropologists, comrades, and *companheiras*.

Note

1 Here I have taken Lila Abu-Lughod's "writing against culture" notion [see chapter 38, this volume] out of context, and I want to suggest that her reflections on the "abuses" of the culture concept are not incompatible with the views put forward in this paper. Culture has been invoked in many inappropriate contexts as a kind of fetish. Paul Farmer (1994) notes in his recent reflections on the structure of violence that the idea of culture has often been used to obscure the social relations, political economy, and formal institutions of violence that promote and produce human suffering. Cultures do not, of course, only generate meaning in the Geertzian sense but produce legitimations for institutionalized inequality and justifications for exploitation and domination.

The culture concept has been used to exaggerate and to mystify the differences between anthropologists and their subjects, as in the implicit suggestion that because they are "from different *cultures*, they are [also therefore] of different *worlds*, and of different *times*" (Farmer 1994:24). This "denial of coevalness" is deeply ingrained in our discipline, exemplified each time we speak with awe of the impenetrable opacity of culture or of the incommensurability of cultural systems of thought, meaning, and practice. Here culture may actually be a disguise for an incipient or an underlying racism, a pseudo-speciation of humans into discrete types, orders, and kinds – the bell jar rather than the bell curve approach to reifying difference.

References

Appadurai, Arjun. 1991. "Global ethnoscapes: Notes and queries for a transnational anthropology," in *Recapturing anthropology*. Ed. Richard G. Fox, pp. 191–210. Santa Fe: School of American Research Press.

Basaglia, Franco. 1987. "Peacetime crimes," in *Psychiatry inside out: Selected writings of Franco Basaglia*. Ed. Nancy Scheper-Hughes and Anne M. Lovell, pp. 143–223. New York: Columbia University Press.

Berger, John. 1967. *A fortunate man*. London: Writers and Readers Cooperative.

De Certeau, Michel. 1984. *The practice of everyday life*. Berkeley: University of California Press.

Farmer, Paul. 1994. Conflating structural violence and cultural difference. Lecture given at the Department of Anthropology, University of California, Berkeley, November 10.

Gilligan, Carol. 1982. *In a different voice: Psychological theory and women's development*. Cambridge, MA: Harvard University Press.

Levinas, Emmanuel. 1987. "Meaning and sense," in *Collected philosophical papers*, pp. 75–107. Dordrecht: Martinus Nijhoff.

Sartre, Jean-Paul. 1956. *Being and nothingness*. London: Methuen.

Scheper-Hughes, Nancy. 1988. The madness of hunger: Sickness, delirium, and human needs. *Culture, Medicine, and Psychiatry* 12:429–58.

Scheper-Hughes, Nancy. 1992. *Death without weeping: The violence of everyday life in Brazil*. Berkeley: University of California Press.

Scheper-Hughes, Nancy. 1994. Unpopular justice: The case for people's courts. *Democracy in Action* 8(4):16–20.

Starn, Orin. 1992. "Missing the revolution: Anthropologists and the war in Peru," in *Rereading cultural anthropology*. Ed. George Marcus, pp. 152–80. Durham, NC: Duke University Press.

Taussig, Michael. 1992. *The nervous system*. New York: Routledge.

Woolf, Virginia. 1938. *Three guineas*. New York: Harcourt Brace, Jovanovich.

41

Moral Models in Anthropology

Roy D'Andrade

For over a decade there have been concerted attacks in anthropology on objectivity (Rosaldo 1989), science (Scheper-Hughes 1990), the notion of truth (Tyler 1986), making generalizations of any kind (Abu-Lughod 1991 [see chapter 38, this volume]), doing ethnography (Dwyer 1982), and anthropology itself as a type of Western colonialism (Asad 1973). These attacks come not from some fringe group but from well-known and established anthropologists. Why should so many anthropologists attack the very foundations of their discipline? Originally, I thought these attacks came from people who had the same agenda I did, just different assumptions about how to accomplish that agenda. I now realize that an entirely different agenda is being proposed – that anthropology be transformed from a discipline based upon an *objective* model of the world to a discipline based upon a *moral* model of the world.

By a "model" I mean a set of cognitive elements used to understand and reason about something. The term "moral" is used here to refer to the primary *purpose* of this model, which is to identify what is *good* and what is *bad* and to allocate *reward* and *punishment*. In the usual language of philosophy, goodness and badness, like beauty and taste, are considered subjective, not objective things; the beauty of a human baby may not be beauty to an ostrich and the badness of killing one's lover may not be badness to a praying mantis. An objective description tells about the thing described, not about the agent doing the description, while a subjective description tells how the agent doing the description *reacts* to the object. "He is a good guy" is a subjective description of someone; "He helps his friends" would be a more objective description of the same person.

The distinction between object and subject is one of the basic human cognitive accomplishments. Normal people are expected to be able to recognize the difference between their response to an object and the object itself. Despite the cognitive salience of the objective/subjective distinction, in ordinary talk the two are often blended. To say someone is a "crook" is to refer to more than the objective fact that something was intentionally taken by someone who had no legal right to it; part of the meaning of "crook" is that the person who did this did something *bad* and is a *bad person*. Many of the terms of natural language blend the way the world is and our reaction

From *Current Anthropology* 36(3) (1995), pp. 399–406, 438–40. Copyright © 1995 by *Current Anthropology*. Reprinted by permission of University of Chicago Press.

Anthropology in Theory: Issues in Epistemology, Second Edition. Edited by Henrietta L. Moore and Todd Sanders.
© 2014 John Wiley & Sons, Inc. Published 2014 by John Wiley & Sons, Inc.

420 ROY D'ANDRADE

to it, perhaps because in this way we can tell others how we want them to respond also ("respond as *I* do"). Although it may be impossible to present an entirely objective account, when we want to understand something outside ourselves we use terms that, so far as possible, tell about *that thing* so we can understand *that thing*, rather than our *response* to that thing. One tries to be objective if one wants to tell others about the *object*, not about oneself.

It should be noted that an objective account is not necessarily value-free. For example, the statement "X cures cancer" is not free of positive value for most people. Nor are objective accounts necessarily unbiased. One well-known way of producing a biased account is to report only those facts which reflect badly on something. As used here, *objectivity* refers just to the degree to which an account gives information about the object being described. Finally, it should be noted that trying to be objective does not preclude investigating other people's subjective worlds. One can be as objective about what people think as one can be about the crops they grow.

One result of the attempt to be objective – to talk about the thing, not oneself – is that it is more likely that what one says can be tested to see if it is true or false. And because it is more likely that an objective account can be tested, an objective account can be attempted again by someone else and the replicability of the account assessed. For knowledge to accumulate, accounts must be objective, but they must also be testable and replicable. What Pons and Fleischman said about cold fusion was objective enough, but unfortunately what they described seems to be unreplicable.

In contrast to an objective model, which tries to describe the object, the aim of a moral model is to identify what is good and bad, to allocate praise and blame, and also to explain how things not in themselves good or bad come to be so. Typically, this is done using words that Kenneth Burke (1945) calls "god" terms, words that stand for things that are an *ultimate* good or an *ultimate* evil and which are the source of further good or evil. Thus, in the current moral model in anthropology, *oppression* is an ultimate evil; nothing can make oppression good, and it is assumed that most of the bad things in the world are the result of oppression. The truth of the badness of *oppression* is not an empirical matter. If you lack moral sense, no recounting of

the facts can explain it to you. And given the ultimate badness of oppression, anything that creates or maintains oppression must also be bad. Thus colonialism is bad because it necessarily involves the use of oppression. Power is bad because it is an instrument of oppression. The hegemony of Western culture is bad because it supports and maintains Western colonialist oppression. Silencing and violence are bad because they are typical means of oppression. And so on.

Every moral model must contain at least partially objective terms if it is to apply to things in the world. Thus "oppression" is not totally subjective; like the term "crook," it refers to something objective – the use of power by some individuals or groups to affect other individuals or groups in ways not to their liking. The subjective part of the term "oppression" is the evaluation built into it that defines this use of power as something bad and as something that brings about things that are bad.

In most moral models there is some way to correct evil. In the current moral model in anthropology this is done by unmasking the symbolic hegemony that hides and legitimates oppression. The morally corrective act is *denunciation*. One can also act morally by giving voice to those who resist oppression; this at least identifies the oppression and the oppressors. Nowadays, one can have a moral career in anthropology; having a moral career in anthropology is being known for what one has denounced.

[...]

According to Scheper-Hughes (1992:229):

The essential insight, derived from European critical theory, is that the given world or the "commonsense reality" may be false, illusory, and oppressive. It is an insight shared with all contemporary critical epistemologies including modern psychoanalysis, feminism and Marxism. All variants of modern critical theory work at the essential task of stripping away the surface forms of reality in order to expose concealed and buried truths. Their aim, then, is to "speak truth" to power and domination, both in individuals and submerged social groups or classes.

Demystification – "exposing concealed and buried truths" – is thus seen as a necessary remedy for the domination of individuals, groups, and classes. And the "critical theories" which do this are different from "objective" theories.

> [Critical theories] are reflexive rather than objective epistemologies. Critical theories differ radically in their epistemology from positivist theories derived from the natural sciences. All theories in the "natural" sciences presuppose an "objective" structure of reality knowable by minds that are likewise understood as sharing a uniform cognitive structure. Critical theories assert the subjectivity of knowable phenomena and propose "reflection" as a valid category and method of discovery.

The problem Scheper-Hughes is addressing here, I think, involves the term "truth." Immediately before, she has said that the goal is to "speak truth to power." But isn't finding out the truth what science – old-fashioned anthropology – does? She claims that "critical theories" do something else – they know in a "subjective" way, not just an "objective" way, by "reflection." Scheper-Hughes is not explicit about how reflection works as a method of discovery, but she is clear that it is different from "positivism" and "natural science." In her view, "The objectivity of science and of medicine is always a phantom objectivity, a mask that conceals more than it reveals" (p. 229). Thus, positivistic natural science is a *bad* way to find out about the world because it is part of the process of mystification. Objectivity turns out to be a mask for domination. One of the most salient characteristics of the current moral model is exactly this attack on objectivity.

Scheper-Hughes continues (p. 229):

> At the heart of all critical theories and methods is a critique of ideology and power. Ideologies (whether political, economic, or religious) can mystify reality, obscure relations of power and domination, and prevent people from grasping their situation in the world. Specific forms of consciousness may be called ideological when they are invoked to sustain or legitimate particular institutions or social practices. When these institutional arrangements reproduce inequality, domination, and human suffering, the aims of critical theory are broadly emancipatory.

This repeats some of the ideas already presented: reality gets mystified to obscure relations of

domination; the goal is to emancipate by revealing the ideologies which mystify such relations (pp. 229–30):

> The process of liberation is complicated, however, by the unreflexive complicity and identification of people with the very ideologies and practices that are their own undoing. Here is where Antonio Gramsci's notion of hegemony is useful. Gramsci...recognized that the dominant classes exercised power both directly and forcefully through the state, and also indirectly by merging with the civil society and identifying their own class-based interests with broad cultural ideas and aims, making them appear indistinguishable from each other.

Here Scheper-Hughes begins to specify how mystification works – by the identification of the interests of the dominant classes with "broad" cultural ideas and aims. The state is the power that acts to create this mystification (p. 230):

> Increasingly in modern bureaucratic states technicians and professionals – laboratory scientists, geneticists, doctors, psychologists, teachers, social workers, sociologists, criminologists and so forth – come to play the role of the "traditional intellectuals" in sustaining "commonsense" definitions of reality through their highly specialized and validating forms of discourse. Gramsci anticipated Foucault (see Foucault 1972) in his understanding of the diffuse power circuits in modern states and of the role of "expert" forms of power/knowledge in sustaining the "common sense" order of things.

Scheper-Hughes makes the case that in Northeast Brazil people suffer from a disorder called *nervos* that involves weakness, sleeplessness, heart palpitations, shaking, headache, fainting, etc., and that this disorder "is a primary idiom through which hunger and hunger-anxiety are expressed" (1992:231). For this disorder, minor tranquilizers are considered by the Brazilian medical establishment to be an appropriate treatment. This treatment, according to Scheper-Hughes, by *not* recognizing the problems of hunger that underlie *nervos*, deflects the underlying rage against domination and mystifies the source of the problem (p. 230):

In the context of this discussion, doctors occupy the pivotal role of "traditional" intellectuals whose function is, in part, to fail to see the secret indignation of the hungry poor expressed in their inchoate folk idiom of "*nervos*." But anthropologists, too, often play the role of the "traditional" intellectual in their unconscious collusions with hegemonic interpretations of social reality fostered by powerful local interests.

The specification of the immoral agents moves from the state to bureaucratic technicians to doctors to teachers and social workers and finally to anthropologists. All are in complicity with oppression, although they may not know it. So – "What is to be done?" According to Scheper-Hughes (p. 229),

> As social scientists (and not social revolutionaries) critical practice implies an epistemological struggle in which the contested domain is anthropology itself. The struggle concerns the way knowledge is generated, the class interests that it serves, and the challenge is to make our discipline more relevant and non-oppressive to the people we study. Finally, it is addressed to clinical practitioners as a challenge to reintegrate the social and political dimension in their practice so as to put themselves squarely on the side of human suffering.

The call to action is clear. Anthropology has been part of the process of mystification, serving interests that oppress others. The moral thing to do is to denounce those who maintain this mystification and transform anthropology from an objective natural science, which is just a charade and a means of continuing oppression, into a *critical anthropology* which will help change the world.

It is important to keep in mind that one can also use an objective model for moral purposes, as for example, in investigating the biochemical basis of schizophrenia in order to make possible better medicine for schizophrenics. The separation between moral models and objective models is not based on the motives or biases of the investigator. In most scientific fields which aim to help people, there are both moral and objective models, linked together. For example, in medicine, there is an objective language of physiology and biochemistry that describes what various

pathogens do and how the body reacts to them. This biological model describes how things work, not whether viruses or antibodies are good or bad. Linked to this objective model is a less formal model concerning what is healthy, what is safe, what is medically ethical, etc., in which, for example, melanoma is considered a *bad* cancer while warts are usually considered *benign*. This language of health and ethics is carefully kept separate from the objective language of biological processes. One of my colleagues calls this the "separation of church and state." You can have both, but they should be kept separate and distinct.

The separation of moral models and objective models is a crucial issue. It is exactly this separation that is explicitly attacked by anthropology's current moralists. For example, Rabinow (1983:68–70, emphasis added) offers what he calls a "schematization of relations of truth and power" as follows:

> In the first position, that represented by Boas, the role of the anthropologist as scientist was to speak truth to power. Boas was a profoundly political man: a typical secular, emancipated, German, Jewish liberal with a strong faith in the force of reason as a functional tool of political emancipation and as an absolute value in its own right. The calling of the intellectual, for Boas, consisted of the advancement of reason through science and the conquest of tradition, irrationality, and injustice.
>
> The dignity and achievements of Boas and his students are not in question – they were centrally responsible for making antiracism an accepted part of the American academic agenda – but neither are their limits and contradictions. The position of speaking truth to power, opposing humanism to nihilism, is still with us; and it is by no means the worst alternative. But ultimately *this position has not proved sufficiently hardy*, either intellectually or politically, to have spawned a science or politics which lives up to the standards of coherence and efficacy by which these individuals wished to be judged.
>
> In an important sense, the second position, that represented by Geertz, *has no politics at all*. The ascetic imperative of Boas or Weber, who sought to separate truth and politics, still entailed an active vigilance lest these two realms fuse. It never occurred to these European intellectuals that political concerns were not central to the life

of an intellectual – they saw them as so central they had to be kept in check. The sacrifice demanded of the scientist was not the loss of political passions but only that they be kept clearly distinct from scientific activities qua science. Over the time of two generations, the tension between these two callings, and hence the potential threat they posed for each other's autonomy, was gradually dissipated. In its place an ethics of scientific comportment became a code of civility. As this code took center stage, the more directly political concerns were weakened.

I am not advocating that we jettison the moral and intellectual achievements of the aggressively antiracist anthropology of Boas, nor that we discard what has been constructed and made to function as a civility which allows for dispute within a community of shared discourse. The main conclusion I draw from the analysis presented in this paper is that *it is the dogged separation of truth and power in order to construct a science which has had the most deleterious effects on anthropology*; it is the conception of a humanist activity which has unwittingly pushed these anthropologists into a kind of nihilism which is the exact opposite of their intent.

Rabinow is clear that in his opinion the separation of moral models from objective models is a mistake resulting in an anthropology without morality ("politics" is a code word for "morality"). He presumes that anthropology *should* be moral and that the failure of anthropologists to maintain Boas's moral passion condemns the idea of separating moral and objective models; Geertz has failed us because he has no politics.

Rabinow asserts that all anthropologists must have Boas's moral passion. I do not agree. In my moral universe, one can be an anthropologist simply because one is interested in human life and still be a good person. However, whether or not one has politics, or believes that all anthropologists should have politics, I argue that anthropology's claim to moral authority rests on knowing *empirical* truths about the world and that moral models should be kept separate from objective models because moral models are counterproductive in discovering how the world works. This is not an argument that anthropologists should have no politics; it is an argument that they should keep their politics separate from the way they do their science.

Without attempting to meet all attacks, I will first take up some of the most egregious arguments against objectivity.

1 *Objective models are dehumanizing*. According to Rorty (1983:164), "Foucault is doubtless right that the social sciences have coarsened the moral fiber of our rulers. Something happens to politicians who are exposed to endless tabulations of income levels, rates of recidivism, cost-effectiveness of artillery fire, and the like – something like what happens to concentration camp guards." Here is complete fantasy. No evidence besides a mention of Foucault is cited. Certainly I know of no research that shows that social science research findings have a dehumanizing effect on people. What seem to be operating here are the assumptions of the current moral model; objectivity is part of science, science is used in the domination of others, domination is the inhuman treatment of others, hence objectivity is dehumanizing. All this follows from first principles and need not be proved.

2 *The distinctions between objectivity and subjectivity, fact and language, knowledge and opinion, depend on a realist conception of the world and the correspondence theory of truth. This theory is flawed, and therefore the distinctions which grow out of it are confusing and unnecessary*. The realist conception of science argues that science "works" because it corresponds in some degree and in some manner to the "way the world really is." That is, science tries to find out the "truth," and "truth" consists of statements that correspond to "reality." It is this correspondence to reality that explains why science is successful at prediction and control. The argument of Rorty (1991) and others, who call themselves "relativists," or "antirealists" or "antirationalists," is that the "correspondence" between statements and the world is not an obvious matter. Various conventions about what counts as evidence are needed in order to decide the truth or falsity of statements; in a mature science these conventions are quite complex. For example, in psychology, the value of experimental evidence depends on a variety of statistical considerations involving reliability, control cases, proportion of the variance accounted for, type 1 and type 2 errors, etc. But where do these conventions come from? They are conventions agreed upon by a community. Thus truth depends on the consensus of the community, and

objectivity reduces to social solidarity (Rorty 1991:22).

[...]

There is probably no "knock-down" argument from first principles to demonstrate that the correspondence theory of truth is right (or wrong) or that scientific knowledge has advanced (or not advanced). Whether the correspondence theory of truth is right and whether scientific knowledge has advanced are empirical questions, and I think that the empirical answers are reasonably clear. As Gellner (1992:60–1) has said:

> One particular style of knowledge [scientific knowledge] has proved so overwhelmingly powerful, economically, militarily, administratively, that all societies have had to make their peace with it and adopt it. Some have done it more successfully than others, and some more willing or more quickly than others; but all of them have had to do it, or perish. Some have retained more, and some less, of their previous culture.

That is, the empirical support for the hypothesis that science advances is simply the strong evidence that scientific knowledge about the world *has* advanced. Whether, on balance, scientific knowledge has been used for good or evil is another question. My own unoriginal conclusion is that, on balance, the world is considerably better off because of science. However, those who disagree on this point would, I believe, still have to agree that scientific *knowledge* has advanced. Given the obvious success of science as a way of finding out about the world, it is remarkable that many anthropologists are attracted to philosophers and historians who flirt with the idea that there is no true progress in scientific knowledge and no way of knowing what is true.[1]

The antirationalists further argue that there are no independent criteria for explaining the success of science (Rorty 1991). My own opinion is that the success of science is due primarily both to the norm of presenting generalizations in a form that makes it possible to dispute them with evidence and to the norm of carrying out extensive tests of other people's generalizations. The testability of statements and the constant testing of statements ward off the very strong tendency of humans to believe what they *want*

to believe. It is these two norms that give the scientific enterprise its power.

Finally, there is something inconsistent about the statements made by Rorty and others about the badness of the subject/object, language/fact, and knowledge/opinion distinctions. For example, according to Rorty (1991:41, emphasis added),

> On the pragmatist view, the contrast between "relations of ideas" and "matters of fact" is a special case of the bad seventeenth-century contrasts between being "in us" and being "out there," between subject and object, between our beliefs and what those beliefs (moral, scientific, theological, etc.) are trying to get right.... [The pragmatist] is suggesting that instead of invoking anything like the idea–fact, or language–fact, or mind–world, or subject–object distinctions to explicate our intuition that *there is something out there to be responsible to*, we just drop the intuition.

Imagine a lazy student in one of Rorty's classes who complains that he only got a D. Professor Rorty says, "That is what you deserve." The student replies, "You are invoking the intuition that there is something out there (my performance, objectively viewed) *to be responsible to*. You should drop that intuition. Subjectively, I *feel* I did quite well, and although I said that I would turn in a paper, the *fact* that I did not simply reinvokes the language/fact distinction, which depends on the flawed correspondence theory of truth." Of course, Rorty would explain that he bases his judgments on the normal consensus about what counts as true (the professor's judgment) rather than some ultimate correspondence of the professor's judgment with reality. What Rorty means by "objectivity" and "truth" is not what the student means; Rorty is talking about ultimate truth and complete objectivity, not ordinary judgments about course performance and broken promises. Rorty does not mean (I think) that in ordinary life the distinctions between object and subject, mind and world, idea and fact, etc., should be dispensed with (that would make an odd world). It is only in certain kinds of philosophic discourse that these distinctions are not to be made. However, in my opinion this speaks badly for such kinds of philosophic discourse.

3 *The idea that people can be objective is illusory; people construct the reality that suits them best. Hence an objective model is impossible, and*

any pretense that such a model can be achieved is simply hegemonic mystification. Scheper-Hughes's statement "The objectivity of science and of medicine is always a phantom objectivity, a mask that conceals more than it reveals" (1992:229) is one example of this position. It should be noted that the meaning of "objective" in these arguments is shifted from "an account which describes the object, not the describer" to "an account given without bias or self-interest." This is a secondary sense of the term, literally, "objective" glosses as "pertaining to the object." The secondary sense of the term "unbiased" is an extension based on the notion that those who have no axe to grind give a more objective account. By shifting from the primary sense to the secondary sense one can make the case that, since people are always biased to some degree, an "objective" account is impossible. Then, since "objectivity" (not having any interests) is impossible, any claim to objectivity must be a "mask," a mystification. However, the accusation depends on the trick of substituting a secondary for a primary meaning. Besides, who ever claimed that scientists are unbiased? A brief acquaintanceship with the history of science would certainly disabuse anyone of that notion. Science works not because it produces unbiased accounts but because its accounts are objective enough to be proved or disproved no matter what anyone wants to be true.

While I am objecting to the rhetorical tricks that are used to identify objectivity and science with badness, I should also note that similar tricks are used to identify objectivity and science with goodness. The methods of science and the use of objective accounts are the best way to find out about the world (I would argue), but the method has no *guarantee* of working. Employment of the term "science" as an honorific to give weight to unreplicated and often unsound generalizations, sometimes constructed with considerable bias, is a continuing abuse. One could even argue that there is so much positive mystification around the term "science" that some negative mystification is needed as a balance. Fine, if the result is intellectual balance – the recognition that, on both sides, rhetoric is not evidence and that "fact" is always a probability, not an absolute.

It might be thought that I am claiming that science should be value-free and outside politics. This is not the case. Science is an institutionalized activity – a means, not an end. It can be used for all

sorts of ends – to create engines of war, to make new products, to cure physical and mental ills, and even just to discover things. The determination of the ends of scientific activity in the United States has long been a political matter in which Congress and a variety of interest groups, including those who want to do science just for the sake of enlightenment, contend for the money. Science demystified is not intrinsically good *or* bad.

4 *Objectivity is part of the general hegemony of Western culture, and is authoritarian and oppressive.* Abu-Lughod (1991:150–1) writes:

> Generalization, the characteristic model of operation and style of writing of the social sciences, can no longer be regarded as neutral description.... There are two reasons for anthropology to be wary of generalization. The first is that, as part of a professional discourse of "objectivity" and expertise, it is inevitably a language of power. On the one hand, it is the language of those who seem to stand apart from and outside of what they are describing.... On the other hand, even if we withhold judgment on how closely the social sciences can be associated with the apparatuses of management, we have to recognize how all professional discourses by nature assert hierarchy. [see chapter 38, this volume, p. 386]

Here the contagious badness-of-oppression continues to spread like a plague; oppression's badness infects power, power's badness infects objectivity ("standing apart"), and objectivity's badness infects generalizations. Again, the badness is asserted on the basis of first principles, not demonstrated. In opposition to Abu-Lughod, I claim that it is *not* bad to make generalizations about people and that ethnographic generalizations do *not* damage people. *Nor* does objectivity. *Nor* do power differences. This is another fantasy. What damages people is the way power is *used* and the way generalizations are *used*. And what *helps* people is the way power is *used* and the way generalizations are *used*. It is irrational to hold that power as such is bad. The result is a spreading pollution that makes it bad to say that the Bedouin are polygynous (Abu-Lughod 1991:153 [see chapter 38, this volume, p. 386]).

One effect of the current ban on objectivity is the substitution of stories and narratives for generalizations. Abu-Lughod says, "For these reasons I propose that we experiment with *narrative*

426

ethnographies of the particular in a continuing tradition of fieldwork-based writing" (1991:153, emphasis added [see chapter 38, this volume, p. 386]). By telling a story about someone, the ethnographer does not have to make any generalizations and thereby appears to avoid the danger of hegemonic discourse. However, the appearance is deceptive; quite the reverse happens in fact. It is a natural assumption of the reader that any narrative is, in some important sense, typical of what happens in that place, unless told otherwise. Kenneth Burke (1945) calls this rhetorical strategy that of the "reductive anecdote" – the world is "summarized by" and "reduces to" the story one tells about it. *Presenting an anecdote is just as essentializing and totalizing as stating a generalization.* Consider, for example, the well-known anecdote about George Washington and the cherry tree: it acts just like the generalization "Washington was honest" but hides the claim. Hence Burke's comment on the rhetorical use of anecdotes: beware of people just telling stories.

It is striking that these attacks on objective models do not present any evidence of the damage done by objectivity. In the same vein, evidence about the good done by science is ignored. A major reason for the unimportance of evidence, I believe, is what is being asserted is not a set of empirical facts but whether one's first allegiance is to morality or to truth. My hypothesis that what is being expressed is allegiance to a set of moral principles explains another rather odd aspect of many of the attacks – their loose adherence to the laws of logic. A number of scholars who have critiqued various postmodernist positions (e.g., Spiro 1986, Bailey 1991, Gellner 1992) have commented on the internal contradictions, principle begging, and appeals to authority found in much of this writing. These objections have not been answered; the usual response I have heard is that they are "beside the point." And, if the point is that relativism is the correct *moral* response to cultural differences, then, indeed, logic and evidence are not relevant.

One might say, "Well, some of these moral concerns may be overdone, but why not use the current moral model? Isn't it a reasonable model of reality as well as a model which shows what is right? Can't one blend together objectivity and morality in a single model?" So far as I know, a mixed model would not violate any principle of logic. However, there are reasonably well-understood

problems with trying to graft moral and objective models together if one wants to find out about the world. It may need to be repeated that the argument here is not against anthropologists' having moral models. Indeed, I believe that anthropologists should work to develop more coherent, clearly articulated moral models. These moral models should, I think, describe both the anthropologist's responsibilities and a vision of what the good society and the good culture would look like. The point has often been made that if anthropologists do not try to influence the ends to which the knowledge they produce is used, others will do it for them. But – the point I am arguing – these moral models should be kept separate from the objective models with which we debate what is.

The first problem with blended models is *identification*. To use the current moral model, with its emphasis on the badness of oppression, to understand the world, one must be able to identify when something is or is not oppression. But what makes something oppression? Is taking away the freedom of serial murderers oppression? Most people would say that it is not – that they deserve to have their freedom taken away, and that it is prudent to do so as well. It is not oppression, then, if the people being dominated deserve to be dominated or need to be dominated for the common good. But who is to say who deserves to be dominated? And who is to say what the common good is? Serbs believe that Croats should be dominated for a variety of reasons. Badness and goodness are not simple properties of things but complex interactions between events and human intentions and welfare. It becomes very difficult to define what oppression is except by one's *reaction* to the situation – whenever it seems to be a bad use of power call it "oppression," and whenever it is a good use call it "justice" or something else. This is a central doctrine of subjectivity; what one truly feels is bad *is* bad. Of course, one can say that this is just quibbling, and that everyone – or almost everyone – can tell a good from a bad use of power. However, because of the complexity of human life we often find ourselves vehemently disagreeing even with people we respect about exactly this. The experience of people trying to find out about how the world works is that you find out more when you avoid the use of evaluative terms – otherwise you spend all your time arguing about the use of these terms, trying to make the bad things get the bad words and the good things get the good words.

A second problem in trying to meld together moral and objective models is that the objective world comes in many shades of grey but the moral world tends toward black and white. Oppression, for example, is not an all-or-none state; it varies in degree. Not every use of power is equally bad. To make a model account for what happens in the world, one usually needs to distinguish *more* from *less*. But morality does not seem to like to do this; each case of oppression must be treated as an equal horror because they all are *wrong*. Sin is sin, and if one sets up a scale of greater and lesser sins one quickly finds out that lesser sins are no longer considered *real* sins. Thus the pragmatics of morality and the pragmatics of finding out about the world pull in different directions.

A third problem is the powerful tendency to believe that good things produce good results and bad things produce bad results: "By their fruits ye shall know them." But the complexities of causality do not respect our human wish for the good to produce good and the bad to produce bad. Furthermore, the pragmatics of morality tend strongly toward a uni-causal view of events; for every bad event there is a single bad thing that caused it. This makes assignment of blame much easier. But the world tends to be strongly multicausal. When a fire burns down a building, who is to blame? Why, the man who threw the match in the wastepaper basket. But for a physicist the match would not have lit the material in the wastepaper basket if it had a higher combustion point or if there had been no oxygen in the air or if the building had been made entirely of stone. We *blame* a knowing and intentional agent, but almost always what happens is the result not *just* of a knowing intentional act but of a complex web of causes. Use of the notion that "bad causes bad" results in the kind of conclusion that Abu-Lughod reaches about generalizations: power brings about oppression, therefore power is bad. Science gives people power, therefore science is bad. Objectivity is part of science, therefore objectivity is bad. Generalizations are produced by objective science, therefore generalizations are bad. And some would take it further: generalizations are based on fieldwork, therefore fieldwork is, if not bad, at least a situation that places one in very grave moral jeopardy.

A fourth pragmatic problem in trying to meld moral and objective models is that whereas an objective model can – at least sometimes – be changed by new data, new arguments, new theories, moral models are very hard to change. [. . .]

Note

1 Bruno Latour (1993) appears to have moved to a realist position not substantially different from that of Kitcher. For example, in discussing Shapin and Schaffer's account of the controversy between Boyle and Hobbes about vacuum pumps and the role of experimentation, Latour (1993:28 emphasis added) says,

> Boyle . . . invents the laboratory within which artificial machines create phenomena out of whole cloth. Even though they are artificial, costly, and hard to reproduce, and despite the small number of trained reliable witnesses, *these facts indeed represent nature as it is. . . . Scientists are scrupulous representatives of the facts.* Who is speaking when they speak? The facts themselves beyond all question, but also their authorized spokespersons.

References

Abu-Lughod, Lila. 1991. "Writing against culture," in *Recapturing anthropology.* Edited by Richard G. Fox, pp. 137–62. Santa Fe: School of American Research Press.

Asad, Talal. 1973. *Anthropology and the colonial encounter.* London: Ithaca Press.

Bailey, F. G. 1991. *The prevalence of deceit.* Ithaca: Cornell University Press.

Burke, Kenneth. 1945. *A grammar of motives.* New York: Prentice-Hall.

Dwyer, Kevin. 1982. *Moroccan dialogues: Anthropology in question.* Baltimore: Johns Hopkins University Press.

Foucault, Michel. 1972. *The archaeology of knowledge.* Tr. A. M. Sheridan Smith. New York: HarperCollins.

Gellner, Ernest. 1992. *Postmodernism, reason, and religion.* New York: Routledge.

Latour, Bruno. 1993. *We have never been modern.* Cambridge, MA: Harvard University Press.

Rabinow, Paul. 1983. "Humanism as nihilism: The bracketing of truth and seriousness in American cultural anthropology," in *Social science as moral inquiry.* Edited by R. Bellah, P. Rabinow, and W. Sullivan, pp. 33–51. New York: Columbia University Press.

Rorty, Richard. 1983. "Method and morality," in *Social science as moral inquiry.* Ed. R. Bellah, P. Rabinow, and W. Sullivan, pp. 52–75. New York: Columbia University Press.

Rorty, Richard. 1991. *Objectivity, relativism, and truth: Philosophical papers,* vol. I. Cambridge: Cambridge University Press.

Rosaldo, Renato. 1989. *Culture and truth: The remaking of social analysis.* Boston: Beacon Press.

Scheper-Hughes, Nancy. 1990. Three propositions for a critically applied medical anthropology. *Social Science and Medicine* 30:189–97.

Scheper-Hughes, Nancy. 1992. "Hungry bodies, medicine, and the state: Toward a critical psychological anthropology," in *New directions in psychological anthropology.* Ed. T. Schwartz, G. White, and C. Lutz, pp. 221–47. New York: Cambridge University Press.

Spiro, Melford E. 1986. Cultural relativism and the future of anthropology. *Cultural Anthropology* 1:259–86.

Tyler, Stephen A. 1986. "Post-modern ethnography: From the document of the occult to occult document," in *Writing cultures.* Ed. J. Clifford and G. Marcus, pp. 122–40. Berkeley: University of California Press.

42

Postmodernist Anthropology, Subjectivity, and Science: A Modernist Critique

Melford E. Spiro

[...] The postmodernist critique of science consists of two interrelated arguments, epistemological and ideological. Both are based, however, on the central postmodern notion of subjectivity. First, because of the subjectivity of the human object, anthropology, according to the epistemological argument, cannot be a science; and in any event the subjectivity of the human subject precludes the possibility of science discovering objective truth. Second, since its much-vaunted objectivity is an illusion, science, according to the ideological argument, serves the interests of dominant social groups (males, whites, Westerners), thereby subverting those of oppressed groups (females, ethnics, third-world peoples).

Since both of these arguments stem from the central emphasis that postmodernists place on subjectivity, my primary concern in this essay is to assess the postmodernist interpretation and use of that critical concept. Hence, in what follows I shall do three things. First, I shall summarize those claims of the postmodernist view of subjectivity which, in my view, are valid. Second, I shall argue that although valid, these claims are not new, having been innovated many years ago by the founders of the Culture and Personality

movement. Third, I shall argue that the postmodernist innovations have unfortunate consequences for anthropological scholarship.

The Importance of Subjectivity

Postmodernists (like symbolists and interpretivists) stress that the understanding of persons and groups requires an understanding of their meanings – and I agree with them. Moreover, since the anthropological investigator is an actor in a social field that includes both himself and the natives, postmodernists also stress, correctly in my view, that field work is dialogical; that the anthropologist not only observes the natives but is also observed by them; and that anthropological data are not produced by the anthropologist's action alone nor consist of the natives' actions alone but, rather, are produced by, and consist of, the interaction between the anthropologist and the natives.

But if the anthropologist, among other things, investigates meanings and if meanings are found in the psyches of persons, then it follows, postmodernists correctly stress, that the anthropologist must attend to subjectivity. Moreover, since field

From *Comparative Studies in Society and History* 38(4) (1996), pp. 759–80 (with cuts). Copyright © 1996 by *Comparative Studies in Society and History*. Reprinted with permission of Cambridge University Press.

Anthropology in Theory: Issues in Epistemology, Second Edition. Edited by Henrietta L. Moore and Todd Sanders.
© 2014 John Wiley & Sons, Inc. Published 2014 by John Wiley & Sons, Inc.

work is a two-directional, not a one-directional enterprise, it also follows, they emphasize, that the anthropologist must attend to the subjectivity not only of the natives (the human object), but also his own (the human subject). Once again I agree with them.

I agree with all of the above propositions not, however, because like Kant, who claimed to have been awakened from his philosophical slumber by reading Hume, I was awakened from my anthropological slumber by reading the post-modernists. Rather, it is because much before the advent of postmodernism, I had read Freud and Sapir, Mead and Benedict, DuBois and Kardiner, Hallowell and Devereux, Erikson and Kluckhohn, and the other founders of the Culture and Personality movement for whom the subjectivity both of object and subject was a truism. [. . .]

Culture and Personality

The subjectivity of the object

Arguably, Freud was the inspiration for the founders of the Culture and Personality movement. That inspiration, however, came not from his anthropological but his psychological work, which consistently emphasized that what was critical to the elucidation of actors' ideas, beliefs, and values is an understanding of their intentions, desires, and wishes, in short, their meanings (unconscious as well as conscious). Indeed, one of Freud's revolutionary innovations is his claim, first published one hundred years ago (Breuer and Freud [1893–5]), that even seemingly meaningless phenomena (such as neurotic symptoms, dreams, and parapraxes) are meaningful and that the task of the analyst is to discover their meanings.

[. . .]

If Freud was the grandfather of Culture and Personality, then Edward Sapir was clearly its father. Like Freud, whose psychology he took as his model, Sapir emphasized that the individual and his subjectivity – he used the term personality – was absent from the anthropology of his time. Thus, as early as 1932, Sapir emphasized that culture patterns "cannot be realistically disconnected from those organizations of ideas and feelings which constitute the individual" because

the true locus of culture is in the interactions of specific individuals and, on the subjective side, in the world of meanings which each one of these individuals may unconsciously abstract for himself from his participation in these interactions. (Sapir 1932, in Mandelbaum 1957:151)

To offer only one more example, as early as 1938 A. I. Hallowell, who acknowledged the influence of both Freud and Sapir, began to publish a series of articles on Ojibwa subjectivity (Hallowell 1938). Nevertheless, Hallowell's influence was not felt beyond the small circle of Culture and Personality specialists until the 1980s, when his pathbreaking article on the self (though published three decades earlier) was discovered by a new generation of anthropologists. In this article, Hallowell argued *inter alia* that while "culture-centered" ethnographies were valuable for both "comparative and analytic" purposes, still

of necessity the material is presented from the stand-point of an outside observer. Presented to us in this form, these cultural data do not permit us to apprehend, in an integral fashion, the most significant and meaningful aspects of the world of the individual as experienced by him and in terms of which he thinks, is motivated to act, and satisfies his needs. (Hallowell 1954:79)

It should be noted, moreover, that Hallowell was not content to rely on empathy and insight alone for elucidating the "meaningful aspects of the world" of individual actors. Consequently, he pioneered the anthropological use of the Rorschach test as a means for obtaining an objective assessment of their subjectivity, one that could make possible more precise cross-group comparisons. In this regard, however, he influenced only a few of his contemporaries, the others arguing that projective tests were culture-bound, and hence not suitable for the investigation of non-Western groups.

The subjectivity of the subject

Freud, who once again is the pioneer figure, first emphasized the importance of the subjectivity of the subject – in this case, the analyst – in his concept of "countertransference" (1910). Viewing the analyst's countertransference as a formidable obstacle to objectivity, he stressed the paramount importance of self-reflexivity as a means for dealing with this obstacle. (Since he believed it highly unlikely, however, that anyone is capable of the kind of self understanding with the honesty that genuine self-reflexivity requires, Freud [1937] recommended that every analyst undergo a personal analysis as well as a periodic self-reflexive reexamination.)

Beginning, however, in the 1950s, psycho-analysis came to view countertransference not only as an obstacle to objective understanding but also (if properly understood and dealt with) as an important instrument for such understanding (Tyson 1984). In this regard, the psychoanalysts' stress on self-reflexivity, like that of the psychological anthropologists discussed below, is very different from that of many postmodernists who also stress its importance (for example, Ruby 1982). For while the former two deploy their countertransferential experience in the service of understanding the object (patients and non-Western peoples, respectively), the latter – or at least some of them – deploy it instead in the service of their own "self-growth" (for example, Marcus and Fischer 1986:ix–x; Rabinow 1977).

Despite the influence of Freud, early Culture and Personality researchers seem not to have attended to the role of countertransference in anthropological field work, at least not explicitly. Indeed, so far as I can tell, the first ethnographic investigation to attend explicitly to countertransference is Gladwin and Sarason's nuanced study of Trukese personality (Gladwin and Sarason 1953). Unfortunately, this admirable study was still-born, perhaps because of its heavy use of projective tests, and has been neglected ever since. This was not the fate, however, of another early, but highly influential, work which (though not explicitly psychological nor even, in the strict sense of the term, ethnographic) dealt even more extensively with the anthropologist's counter-transference. I am referring, of course, to *Tristes Tropiques* (Lévi-Strauss 1955).

More recently, a variety of anthropologists have discussed their own countertransferential reactions in field work with admirable honesty and courage. Here, I would mention especially the studies of L. Bohannan [Bowen] (1964), Briggs (1970), Crapanzano (1980), Kracke (1987), Read (1967) and R. Rosaldo (1984). From the evidence

of all these works, as well as my own fieldwork experience, I would suggest that the counter-transferential reactions of field anthropologists, like those of clinical analysts, stem from their anxieties, inner conflicts, loneliness, investment in favorite theories, personal values, professional ambition, and so forth.

It was Devereux who, in a brilliant if exasperating *tour de force* (1967), provided the theoretical rationale for the importance of countertransference, not only in anthropology but also in the other social sciences as well. It is worth noting that in a preface to this book La Barre commented that with its publication "the un-self-examined anthropologist henceforth has no right or business anthropologizing" (La Barre 1967:ix). As in the case of the recent views of psychoanalysis mentioned above, Devereux not only addressed the distorting effects of countertransference but also emphasized its use "as an important and even indispensable source of relevant supplementary social science data" (Devereux 1967:30). As he saw it, "it is *not* countertransference *per se*, but the *ignoring* and *mismanagement* of countertransference [that] is the real source of sterile error" (Devereux 1967:202, italics in original).

Although aside from psychological anthropology, anthropologists have typically not attended to the countertransferential dimension of the anthropologist's subjectivity, nevertheless virtually all of them have persistently emphasized others of its dimensions, which are usually subsumed under the concept of ethnocentrism. Beginning with Boas, novice field workers have been warned of the distorting influence of their cultural biases; and anthropological training has attempted to minimize such biases by requiring that graduate students acquire ethnographic competence in a wide range of non-Western societies and cultures.

Despite such training, cultural bias, so post-modernists claim, is an inescapable characteristic of all Western ethnographers, as are the other biases (such as racial, gender, social class) that comprise part of their subjectivity; and these biases, together with those engendered by colonialism and imperialism, produce serious distortions in the collection and reporting of ethnographic data.

While these claims, though often exaggerated, cannot be disregarded, postmodernists tend to disregard other biases inherent in the Western ethnographer's subjectivity which are the reverse of those which they emphasize. I have in mind, for example, the liberal political ideology of most Western anthropologists, their lingering noble savagism, and their alienation from, if not hostility to, Western culture (Lévi-Strauss [1955]:381, 388), which arguably account for the idealization of non-Western cultures that characterizes more than a few ethnographies. Having now examined my contention that many of the postmodernist claims concerning subjectivity, though true, are not new – as is also the case, according to Eysteinsson (1990), with postmodernist thought more generally – we may now turn to my contention that in some critical respects its innovative claims are invalid.

Postmodernist Innovations Regarding Subjectivity

Before assessing the postmodernist innovations, I wish to register two caveats – the first related to my representation of the postmodernist position and the second to the representation of my own. First, since postmodernist anthropologists are as diverse a group as any other, the following generalized and schematic summary of their views applies to most, but not all, of them. That being so, some of my postmodernist friends will no doubt feel that I have misrepresented their views; and although I regret that, I trust they will appreciate that an essay of limited space must confine itself to central tendencies. Second, since any theoretical position, as postmodernists rightly stress, stems from a particular point of view, it is important to note that my assessment of their innovations is offered from the point of view of what John Searle calls the "Western Rationalist Tradition" and its epistemological and metaphysical postulates. Because the postmodernist project takes the repudiation of this tradition as one of its central aims, it is perhaps useful to briefly summarize these postulates which, following Searle (1993b:60–8), I shall explicate in a set of six, interrelated, propositions:

First, reality exists independently of human representations; and any true statement about the world refers to "actual situations" in the world which correspond to such a statement. In short,

contrary to postmodernism, this postulate holds that there is a "mind-independent external reality" which (in the language of philosophy) is referred to as "metaphysical realism."

Second, language serves not only to communicate meanings but also to refer to objects and situations in the world that exist independently of language. In short, this postulate holds that language, contrary to postmodernism, has referential, and not merely communicative, functions.

Third, statements are true or false depending on whether the objects and situations to which they refer correspond to a greater or lesser degree to these statements. This, of course, is the "correspondence theory" of truth, which, to the extent that postmodernists hold a theory of truth – many of them, of course, reject this concept as "essentialist" – stands in sharp contrast to their "coherence" or "narrative" theory, as it is variously called.

Fourth, knowledge is objective, which signifies, contrary to postmodernism, that the truth of any knowledge claim is independent of the motive, culture, ethnicity, race, social class, or gender of the person(s) who make such a claim. Rather, its truth depends on the empirical support adduced on its behalf.

Fifth, logic and rationality provide a set of procedures, methods, and standards (of proof, validity, or reasonableness) which, contrary to postmodernism, enables one to assess competing knowledge claims.

Sixth, there exist valid criteria (both objective and intersubjective) for judging the relative merit of statements, theories, explanations, interpretations, and other kinds of accounts. According to this postulate, it is not the case that Creationism, for example, is as true as Darwinism, that the geocentric view is as correct as the heliocentric, that shamanistic explanations of dissociative states are as veridical as those of clinical psychiatry.

Postmodernists repudiate these six postulates of the Western Rationalist Tradition because of what they take to be two epistemological entailments of their conception of subjectivity. First, the subjectivity of the human object entails that the human sciences cannot – indeed ought not – be a science. Second, the subjectivity of the human subject entails that it is impossible to discover (what might be termed) objective or intersubjective truth. Beginning with the first, I now wish to assess these claims insofar as they relate to anthropology. (The following assessment is taken in part from Spiro [1994: ch. 1]).

The rejection of anthropology as science

Anthropology cannot (and should not) aspire to scientific status, postmodernists argue (for example, Rabinow and Sullivan 1987; Rosaldo 1989; Tyler 1987) because science is in the business of discovering causes; whereas if the subjectivity of the human object is taken seriously, then anthropology can only be in the business of discovering meanings. Although the term meaning is the black box of the anthropological lexicon, still since postmodernists believe (as I do) that culture and mind can be understood only by reference to intentions, purposes, desires, and the like, I take it that they are indicating these subjective entities when they refer to meaning. If that is so, then their opposing of meaning to cause only makes sense, however, in the hermeneutic view that the scientific concept of cause refers to material conditions alone (Habermas 1971; Ricoeur 1981; Vendler 1984). Thus, on that view a causal account of culture refers to ecological niches, modes of production, subsistence techniques, and so forth, just as a causal account of mind refers to the firing of neurons, the secretion of hormones, the action of neurotransmitters, and so on.

I would submit, however, that this materialist conception of cause represents an older view that is hardly credible today. To be sure, psychological behaviorists persist in denying that non-material things like intentions, purposes, and desires serve as causes of action, just as cultural materialists deny that these mental events have causal relevance for the creation and persistence of culture; but these views, which reflect what the philosopher Adolf Grünbaum (1984:3) has characterized as the "ontologically reductive notion of scientific status," are dead as a dodo bird. As construed by even the most tough-minded philosophers of science, intentions, purposes, and desires, for all their being subjective, are no less causal than hormonal secretions and subsistence techniques (Grünbaum 1984:69–94; Hempel 1965:225–58).

Indeed, it is precisely because they hold that such subjective events are causal that most psychological anthropologists, beginning with the Culture and Personality movement, have insisted that they are critically important for the understanding of mind and culture. Since postmodernists, however, do not believe that intentions, desires, and so forth, have causal (explanatory) relevance, then why do they insist that such subjective events are critical for anthropological inquiry? 'Tis a paradox. That paradox aside, if causal explanation is central to the scientific enterprise and if these subjective events do have causal relevance, then, contrary to postmodernism, there are no valid grounds (in this regard at any rate) for denying that anthropology is, or at least in principle might be, a science.

If now the scientific method consists both of the formulation of explanatory theories in respect to some subject-matter and the employment of empirical and logical procedures by which, at least in principle, they can be verified or falsified, then the remaining question regarding the scientific status of anthropology is whether its modes of inquiry conform to this paradigm. Writing more than half a century ago, John Dewey put it this way.

> The question is not whether the subject-matter of human relations [including anthropology] is or can ever become a science in the sense in which physics is now a science, but whether it is such as to permit...the development of methods which, as far as they go, satisfy the logical conditions that have to be satisfied in other branches of inquiry. (Dewey 1938:487)

Notice that Dewey refers to methods, not techniques, for whereas techniques refer to the empirical procedures employed for obtaining or eliciting data, methods refer to the logical conditions that must be satisfied if the data are to be judged evidentially relevant for the acceptance or rejection of an explanation or interpretation. Now with the exception of a few remaining scientistic (not scientific) diehards among us, I dare say that virtually every one else (postmodernist and modernist alike) agrees that the study of the human world requires very different techniques from those employed for the study of the physical world. Thus, while subjective techniques, such as insight, *Verstehen*, and empathy are critical in the study of mind and culture, that is not the case, for example, in the study of atoms, molecules, and galaxies.[1]

This consensus, however, does not obtain in respect to methods. Thus, postmodernists (and others who follow in the hermeneutic tradition) maintain that, whereas the physical sciences employ objective methods, such methods are not appropriate in the human sciences. In short, the subjectivity of the human object requires that subjective procedures of empathy, insight, Verstehen) be used not only as techniques but also as methods of inquiry. But if "method," as I have already observed, refers to the logical conditions that must be satisfied if data are to be judged evidentially relevant for the acceptance or rejection of an explanation or interpretation, then this view is hard to credit. As the philosopher Richard Rudner (echoing Dewey) put it:

> To hold that the social sciences are methodologically distinct from the other sciences is to hold not merely (or perhaps not at all) the banal view that the social sciences employ different techniques of inquiry, but rather the startling view that the social sciences require a different *logic* of inquiry. (Rudner 1966:5, added emphasis)

Such a view is "startling," I would suggest, because if empathy, Verstehen, and so forth, are employed not only as techniques for generating data, explanations, and interpretations (the context of discovery) but also as methods for assessing their truth value (the context of justification), then this subjective methodology suffers from critical logical and empirical problems (Rudner 1966:5–6). Logically, it is of course hopelessly circular, the "hermeneutic circle," as hermeneutists themselves recognize. Empirically, especially in those all-too frequent instances in which the interpretations of different investigators disagree, it is useless: It provides no objective or intersubjective criteria by which conflicting interpretations can be adjudicated. As the psychologist Morris Eagle puts it, "If my interpretation or deciphered meaning or empathic grasp is radically different from and even contradicts yours, on whose empathy of interpretation does one rely for knowledge?" (Eagle 1984:164).

Although it might now seem evident that, in the context of justification, intellectually responsible inquiry requires objective (that is, scientific) methods not only in the physical but also in the human sciences, postmodernists reject this argument on two grounds, empirical and logical. As for the former, virtually all postmodernists dismiss the empirical procedures of the scientific method (when used in the human sciences) as positivistic, a highly pejorative term in their lexicon. In addition, many (but not all) of them also reject (Western) logic as a "logocentric" and "linear" discourse invented by "hegemonic" Western males and used by them to dominate non-Westerners and females; hence, to "privilege" such a "phallocentric" discourse only serves to perpetuate their "patriarchal" interests. [...]

It should be noted that both arguments are reasoned, not capricious. For consistent with the post-modernist view that the concept of objective truth is "essentialist" (another pejorative term in their lexicon), their primary intellectual worries relate not to ethnographic research but ethnographic writing (Clifford and Marcus 1986); and in the latter regard the critical issue, as they see it, is not so much the truth of ethnographic findings, as the "authority" of ethnographic texts. Thus, for Clifford, the problem (mentioned above) is primarily a problem of textual authority (1983:142), of which he distinguishes four "modes" (experiential, interpretive, dialogical, and polyphonic); and how one chooses among them depends on one's taste. It is only in a footnote that Clifford mentions "modes of authority based on natural-scientific epistemologies," and then only to say that he does not intend to discuss them (1983: n. 1).

In my view this cavalier dismissal of "natural-scientific epistemologies" would, if taken seriously, have disastrous consequences, not only, however, for scholarship but also for civil society itself. Commenting on a similar attitude prevalent in his time, Dewey observed that it

> encourages obscurantism; it promotes acceptance of beliefs formed before methods of inquiry had reached their present state; and it tends to relegate scientific (that is, competent) methods of inquiry to a specialized technical field. Since scientific methods simply exhibit free intelligence operating in the best manner available at a given time, the

cultural waste, confusion and distortion that results from the failure to use these methods, in all fields in connection with all problems, is incalculable. (Dewey 1938:535)

The rejection of objective truth

Having examined the postmodernists' contention that the subjectivity of the human object entails that anthropology cannot (and ought not) aspire to scientific status, I now wish to examine their contention that the subjectivity of the human subject precludes the discovery of objective knowledge. This contention takes two forms: a restricted form, which denies that there can be objective knowledge of the non-Western human object, and an unrestricted one, which denies that there can be objective knowledge of any object. [...]

The restricted form
The contention that anthropology cannot discover objective truths about the non-Western human object is a conclusion derived from two postmodernist premises. First, human intentions, purposes, and desires – that is, meanings – are wholly culturally constructed; and, seeing that cultures differ one from another, meanings are culturally relative. Second, since cultures not only are different but radically different, their meanings are incommensurate one with another. From this postmodernists argue that the meanings of Western anthropologists are thus incommensurate with those of the non-Western peoples they study and that for Western anthropology non-Western peoples are wholly Other, that is, their minds and cultures opaque to objective understanding, which precludes the possibility of a comparative study of cultural meaning systems.

Although these conclusions follow validly from their premises, in my view (Spiro 1986, 1994: ch.1) both the premises and the conclusions are false. Rather, however, than reiterate my reasons for rejecting the premises, here I only wish to observe that the conclusions are both paradoxical and self-defeating for the postmodernist project itself. If (as postmodernists contend) anthropological inquiry is concerned with the study of meanings and if (as they also contend) non-Western peoples are Other, then how can a Western anthropologist comprehend

their meanings when, *ex hypothesi*, they cannot be known? Moreover, if their Otherness precludes the possibility of a comparative study of cultural meaning systems, then the very foundational claims of postmodernism – that meanings are wholly culturally constructed and culturally relative and that cultures are radically different and incommensurable – can only remain unfounded speculations with no empirical warrant (see, in this regard, Wikan [1993]).

Although many non-postmodernist anthropologists also view the elucidation of meanings as one of their central tasks, since they do not view cultures as incommensurable, they retain the traditional conception of anthropology as a comparative discipline. For while they too are impressed by the extraordinary range of cultural diversity, they recognize (or at least many of them do) that there are important constraints (for example, biological, psychological, ecological) on that diversity; consequently, cross-cultural differences in meaning systems are not so radical as to preclude anthropologists from understanding non-Western peoples. In short, for them cultural diversity does not entail that the non-Western object is *Other*. This, at least, is the testimony of many seasoned field workers, including, for example, Bourguignon ("The differences between human groups are not so radical that we cannot recognize ourselves as we are, or as we might be, in others" [1979:79]), E. Bruner ("We understand other people and their expressions on the basis of our own experience and self-understanding" [1986:6]), Erikson ("You will not see in another what you have not learned to recognize in yourself" [1964:29]), and R. Paul (We should be wary of social science theories that do not come "close to corresponding to what one's own actual experience of being alive is like" [1990:433]).

The unrestricted form
This form of the contention that the subjectivity of the human subject precludes the discovery of objective knowledge applies, unlike the first, not to the non-Western human object uniquely but to all objects (non-human as well as human, Western as well as non-Western); and it is grounded not in the postmodernist conception of culture but in its metaphysics and epistemology. (For an important discussion, see Reyna [1994]. For an illuminating,

mostly postmodernist, examination of the concept of objectivity itself, see the collection of essays in Megill [1994].)

In opposition to the metaphysical realism of the Western Rationalist Tradition, postmodernism is committed to metaphysical idealism. Although some metaphysical idealists reject the very notion of an objective reality, this is not the case for most postmodernist anthropologists; rather, they reject the notion that such a reality exists independently of human representations (for example, Rabinow 1986). To put it differently, they deny the existence of a mind-independent reality. Since here, however, I am concerned not with metaphysical idealism as such but with the epistemological implications that postmodernists derive from it, my evaluation of this philosophical position can be expressed by a single passage in Searle (1993a:38–9) which, in my opinion, is decisive.

> When [metaphysical idealists] present us with an argument they claim to do so in a language that is publicly intelligible. But, I wish to argue, public intelligibility presupposes the existence of a publicly accessible world.... Whenever we use a language that purports to have public objects of reference, we commit ourselves to realism. The commitment is not a specific theory as to *how* the world is, but rather *that* there is a way that it is. Thus, it is self-refuting for someone to claim in a public language that metaphysical realism is false, because a public language presupposes a public world, and that presupposition is metaphysical realism.

Let us now turn, then, from metaphysical idealism, as such, to the epistemological implications that postmodernists draw from it, especially as they relate to science. Since the external world, they argue, is perceived and understood by means of one or another cultural "discourse," all knowledge-claims (whether of the physical or the human world) are "culturally constructed," hence necessarily subjective; moreover, since every cultural discourse is arbitrary, all knowledge-claims are also necessarily relative. That being so, then as Nietzsche (to whom postmodernism is profoundly indebted) argued, "There are not facts, but only interpretations."[2]

If, now, there are only interpretations – hence, if knowledge-claims do not correspond to any facts, none at any rate that can be agreed upon – then objective knowledge, postmodernists argue, is impossible, and science is only a particular kind of "story telling." Moreover, since scientific stories are derived from one or another discourse, the criteria for their assessment, like those for any other story, can only be subjective. Given this view, it requires but a short step to conclude that to "privilege" the knowledge claims of Western science is hopelessly ethnocentric. As Feyerabend (who both influenced and was influenced by postmodernist anthropologists) put it, "There exist no 'objective' reasons for preferring science and Western rationalism to other traditions" (quoted in Rorty 1995:34).

But if science is just another kind of story telling, then scientific theories rest not so much on objective knowledge and an objective logic as on the "interests" (racial, ethnic, sexual, gender, economic) of the story tellers. Since, then, its truth claims are not so much empirically as ideologically grounded, science is a form of domination which, in the case of anthropology, is evident in the asymmetries of power that characterize ethnographic field work and writing (see Fabian 1983, 1991; Haraway 1989; Lutz 1990; Rosaldo 1986; Said 1989; and the critique by Spencer 1989).

Since, however, hardly any one would deny that science is influenced by ideology and interests, what makes the postmodernists' view exceptional is that, for them, they are not one aspect of science but the whole of it: Ideology and interests do more than influence the conduct of science, they dominate it. In short, if warfare, according to Clausewitz, is diplomacy by other means, then for postmodernists, science – to borrow an expression from Haraway (1986) – is politics by other means.

Thus, Bruno Latour, whose studies of the laboratory sciences are widely cited by postmodernists, holds that scientific laboratories are entirely shaped by political agendas and that "*nothing* of any cognitive quality" takes place in them (1983:161, my added emphasis). Again, for Bob Scholte the concern of the physical sciences with discovering lawful relations and order – his example is the concept of biological constants – is primarily ideologically motivated. "Law and order in 'nature,'" he writes (1984:964), "become scientific means to rationalize law and order in society." Or consider Catherine Lutz on the scientific study of emotion. Since Western students of emotion, she claims, view emotions as "irrational," "chaotic," "uncontrollable," and "dangerous" and since moreover these are the very qualities by which they "define women," it is then evident – never mind that both claims are false (Spiro 1993) – that "the academic literature on emotion can be considered a form of political discourse on gender relations.... That literature arises out of and reenters a field of power struggles for the definition of true womanhood" (Lutz 1990:78).

Consider, finally, Rosaldo's critique of *The Nuer* which, rather than addressing Evans-Pritchard's methods or the accuracy of his findings – what one would normally expect of a critique of an ethnographic monograph – addresses only Evans-Pritchard's allegedly "close links to contexts of domination" and his putative attempt "to deny the connections between power and knowledge ... and to bracket the purity of [the] data...from the contaminating contexts through which they are extracted" (1986:88). In that attempt, Rosaldo continues, Evans-Pritchard implicitly "asks his readers to set aside the context of colonial domination and view his study as [an]...objective scientific account" (1986:93). Just in case, however, we mistake Evans-Pritchard's "persona...of the detached ironic observer" from the real thing, Rosaldo asks us to consider two rhetorical questions: "Why did the government of the Anglo-Egyptian Sudan request his report?" and "How much did it pay for the research and the publication of its results?" (1986:88).

If now science is ideologically motivated story telling whose function is domination, then what makes one scientific story better than another is not, so postmodernists contend, that one is true and the other false but that one is good and the other bad, the latter qualities being taken here not as cognitive but as moral and political predicates. Hence, given their moral and political commitments, a scientific story is "good" insofar as it "empowers" subjugated groups (ethnic and racial minorities, women, third-world peoples) and "bad" insofar as it perpetuates their subjugation (see Abu-Lughod and Lutz 1990; Lutz 1990; Scheper-Hughes 1992, 1994. For an important analysis of this "moral model" of science, as he calls it, see D'Andrade [1995]).

It is now perhaps evident that this conception of science is far removed from – indeed it is an explicit critique of – the Western Rationalist Tradition, according to which science is the disinterested pursuit of reliable knowledge, or (more grandiosely) Truth. That this Enlightenment conception, however, has been honored more often in the breach than in the practice is, of course, a truism. Anyone acquainted with the conduct of science, whether as participant or observer, knows that scientists are motivated not only by the Holy Grail of knowledge – nor only, I would add, by the political and power motives stressed by postmodernists – but also by ambition and envy, fame and power, wealth and prestige, and an assortment of other, all too human motives. It is also well-known that the influence of such non-cognitive motives on the conduct of science (but also on every other type of knowledge production) can be disastrous, ranging from unwitting distortions and misinterpretations to the willful cooking of data and the falsifying of reports.

It is precisely, however, because of these non-cognitive motives that science (and, I would add, any disciplined search for knowledge) needs an objective method as a means for counteracting their influence. Moreover, it is because scientific norms, uniquely, require such a method that science, post-modernist claims to the contrary notwithstanding, has been capable of discovering objective knowledge. (Indeed, in view of its extraordinary intellectual achievements, I would suggest that the cavalier dismissal of science by postmodernists is stunning.)

Lest, however, I be misunderstood, let me stress that non-cognitive motives are never, in my view, absent from scientific (or any other type of) inquiry, and no method, however objective, can eliminate them. Nor, I might add, is the influence of these motives necessarily negative. Thus, in the context of discovery, as I emphasized in a previous section, they may generate important ideas, interpretations, and findings. In order, however, for the truth-value of these (and all other) ideas, interpretations, and findings to be established, they must be tested; and it is in this phase of scientific (or any other) inquiry that it is critical that the influence of non-cognitive motives be counteracted.

In short, it is here, in the context of justification, that the objective procedures of the scientific method – procedures which assess the truth of an idea or the validity of an interpretation by testing its predictive or retrodictive consequences – are indispensable if objective knowledge is to be discovered. Not only indispensable, but also efficacious. For if, in order to gain acceptance by the scientific community, the ideas, interpretations, and findings of the individual scientist must first pass through the crucible of the scientific method, then sooner or later – more often later than sooner – the distortions and misinterpretations engendered by the biases and interests of the individual scientist are discovered (and usually rectified), if not by the individual scientist him- or herself, then by the community of scientists. In sum, if science has discovered objective knowledge, it is not because scientists, unlike the rest of mankind, are capable of transcending their subjectivity but because the latter's baneful effects on the conduct of science are, more often than not, neutralized by the norms of science as a social institution.

I would now contend that, in the context of justification, the need for objective procedures is arguably more important in the human than in the physical sciences. For if subjective interests are formidable obstacles to objectivity, for example in physics, then surely they are even more so, for example in anthropology, in which the potentiality for ideologically motivated distortion – imperialist and anti-imperialist, racist and anti-racist, ethnocentric and multicultural, sexist and feminist – is much the greater. Thus, if ethnography, as postmodernists (and others) insist, is an interpretive enterprise and if the ethnographer's interpretations are processed (as they surely are) through all those and other ideological filters, then without objective assessment procedures, how much credence can be placed in any interpretation, no matter how empathic or insightful the ethnographer?

Hence, just as it is a genetic fallacy for scientific materalists to contend that because interpretations are subjective, ethnographers must employ objective techniques even in the context of discovery, so also it is a logical fallacy for interpretive postmodernists to insist that they can only employ a subjective method even in the context of justification. It is not only fallacious but irresponsible. For if, on principle, ethnographers will not employ an objective method for assessing the validity of their interpretations – and, consequently, conflicting interpretations are merely different stories to be accepted or rejected because one is morally or politically better than another – then anything goes, in which case the ethnographic enterprise is not only empirically dubious but intellectually irresponsible.

Although I have done so before (Spiro 1986), it is perhaps useful to emphasize once again that, although the scientific method is applicable no less in the human than in the physical sciences, this does not entail that the empirical procedures they employ in compliance with that method must be the same. For while methods, as I indicated earlier, refer to the logical conditions that must be satisfied for assessing the validity of an interpretation (or explanation), nonetheless the empirical procedures employed in physics, for example, for achieving such a valid assessment may be inappropriate in anthropology.

Hence, while I have no principled objection to laboratory experimentation, quantification, mathematical modeling, and so forth, for assessing the validity of ethnographic interpretations – on the contrary, I believe Chairman Mao's dictum that 100 flowers should bloom – nevertheless, I believe that in practice these procedures are only rarely appropriate (or efficacious) for that purpose. But though holding that in regard to its assessment procedures, the scientific method is pluralistic (not only across disciplines, but also within them), I do not believe, however, that this is the case in regard to that method itself. If the aim of responsible inquiry is objective knowledge, then regardless of discipline, the most reliable method (so far at least) for achieving that aim is the scientific method. [...]

Notes

1   This, however, is not always the case. Although empathy, for example, is usually regarded as a technique unique to the human sciences, still it is not entirely absent from the physical sciences. Thus, in his biography of the brilliant physicist and nobel laureate, Richard Feynman, Gleick

(1992:142) writes that Feynman's colleagues suspected that if he wanted to know what an electron would do under given circumstances, he merely asked himself, "If I were an electron, what would I do?"

2 Since such a stance, Gellner observes, "means in effect the abandonment of any serious attempt to

give a reasonable precise, documented, and testable account of anything…[it is unclear] why, given that universities already employ people to explain why knowledge is impossible (in philosophy departments), anthropology should reduplicate this task, in somewhat amateurish fashion" (1992:29).

References

Abu-Lughod, Lila and Catherine Lutz. 1990. "Introduction," in Catherine Lutz and Lila Abu-Lughod, eds., *Language and the Politics of Emotion*. Cambridge: Cambridge University Press.

Bourguignon, Erika. 1979. *Psychological Anthropology: An Introduction to Human Nature and Cultural Differences*. New York: Holt, Rinehart and Winston.

Bowen, Elenore Smith (Laura Bohannan). 1964. *Return to Laughter*. New York: Doubleday.

Breuer, Josef and Sigmund Freud. 1893–5 [1955]. *Studies on Hysteria*, vol. 2 of *The Standard Edition of the Complete Psychological Works of Sigmund Freud*. London: Hogarth Press.

Briggs, Jean L. 1970. *Never in Anger: Portrait of an Eskimo Family*. Cambridge, MA: Harvard University Press.

Bruner, Edward M. 1986. "Experience and Its Expression," in Victor W. Turner and Edward M. Bruner, eds., *The Anthropology of Experience*. Urbana: University of Illinois Press.

Clifford, James. 1983. "On Ethnographic Authority." *Representations*, 1:118–46.

Clifford, James and George E. Marcus, eds. 1986. *Writing Culture: The Poetics and Politics of Ethnography*. Berkeley: University of California Press.

Crapanzano, Vincent. 1980. *Tuhami: Portrait of a Moroccan*. Chicago: University of Chicago Press.

D'Andrade, Roy. 1995. "Moral Models in Anthropology." *Current Anthropology*, 36:399–408.

Devereux, George, 1967. *From Anxiety to Method in the Behavioral Sciences*. The Hague: Mouton.

Dewey, John. 1938. *Logic: The Theory of Inquiry*. New York: Henry Holt.

Eagle, Morris N. 1984. *Recent Developments in Psychoanalysis*. New York: McGraw-Hill.

Erikson, Erik H. 1964. *Insight and Responsibility*. New York: Norton.

Eysteinsson, Astradur. 1990. *The Concept of Modernism*. Ithaca: Cornell University Press.

Fabian, Johannes. 1983. *Time and the Other: How Anthropology Makes its Object*. New York: Columbia University Press.

Fabian, Johannes. 1991. "Dilemmas of Critical Anthropology," in Lorraine Nencel and Peter Pels, eds., *Constructing Knowledge: Authority and Critique in Social Science*. London: Sage Publications.

Freud, Sigmund. 1910. [1958]. *The Future Prospects of Psychoanalytic Therapy*, vol. 11 of *The Standard Edition of the Complete Psychological Works of Sigmund Freud*. London: Hogarth Press.

Freud, Sigmund. 1937. [1964]. *Analysis Terminable and Interminable*, vol. 23 of *The Standard Edition of the Complete Psychological Works of Sigmund Freud*. London: Hogarth Press.

Gellner, Ernest. 1992. *Postmodernism, Reason and Religion*. London: Routledge.

Gladwin, Thomas and Seymour B. Sarason. 1953. *Truk: Man in Paradise*. New York: Wenner-Gren Foundation for Anthropological Research.

Gleick, James. 1992. *Genius: The Life and Science of Richard Feynman*. New York: Pantheon.

Grünbaum, Adolf. 1984. *The Foundations of Psychoanalysis: A Philosophical Critique*. Berkeley: University of California Press.

Habermas, Jurgen. 1971. *Knowledge and Human Nature*. Boston: Beacon Press.

Hallowell, A. Irving. 1938. [1955]. "Fear and Anxiety as Cultural and Individual Variables in a Primitive Society." *Journal of Social Psychology*, 9:25–47. Reprinted in *Culture and Experience*. Philadelphia: University of Pennsylvania Press.

Hallowell, A. Irving. 1954. [1955]. *The Self and its Behavioral Environment Explorations*, II (April). Reprinted in *Culture and Experience*. Philadelphia, PA: University of Pennsylvania Press.

Haraway, Donna Jean. 1986. "Primatology is Politics by Other Means," in Ruth Bleier, ed., *Feminist Approaches to Science*. New York: Routledge.

Haraway, Donna Jean. 1989. *Primate Visions*. New York: Routledge.

Hempel, Carl. 1965. *Aspects of Scientific Explanation*. New York: The Free Press.

Kracke, Waud. 1987. "Encounter with Other Cultures: Psychological and Epistemological Aspects." *Ethos*, 15:58–81.

La Barre, Weston. 1967. "Preface," in George Devereux, *From Anxiety to Method in the Behavioral Sciences*. The Hague: Mouton.

Latour, Bruno. 1983. "Give Me a Laboratory and I Will Raise the World," in Karin D. Knorr-Cetina and Michael Mulkay, eds., *Science Observed: Perspectives on the Social Study of Science*. London; Beverly Hills: Sage Publications.

Lévi-Strauss, Claude. 1955 [1964]. *Tristes Tropiques*. New York: Antheneum.

Lutz, Catherine. 1990. "Engendered Emotion: Gender, Power, and the Rhetoric of Emotional Control in American Discourse," in Catherine Lutz and Lila Abu-Lughod, eds., *Language and the Politics of Emotion*. Cambridge: Cambridge University Press.

Mandelbaum, David G., ed. 1957. *Edward Sapir: Culture, Language and Personality*. Berkeley: University of California Press.

Marcus, George E. and Michael M. Fischer. 1986. *Anthropology as Cultural Critique: An Experimental Moment in the Human Sciences*. Chicago: University of Chicago Press.

Megill, Allan, ed. 1994. *Rethinking Objectivity*. London: Duke University Press.

Paul, Robert A. 1990. "What Does Anybody Want? Desire, Purpose, and the Acting Subject in the Study of Culture." *Cultural Anthropology*, 5:431–51.

Rabinow, Paul. 1977. *Reflections on Fieldwork in Morocco*. Berkeley: University of California Press.

Rabinow, Paul 1986. "Representations are Social Facts: Modernity and Postmodernity in Anthropology," in James Clifford and George E. Marcus, eds., *Writing Culture: The Poetics and Politics of Ethnography*. Berkeley: University of California Press.

Rabinow, Paul and William Sullivan. 1987. *Interpretive Social Science: A Second Look*. Los Angeles: University of California Press.

Read, Kenneth E. 1967. *The High Valley*. London: George Allen and Unwin.

Reyna, S. P. 1994. "Literary Anthropology and the Case Against Science." *Man*, 29:55–81.

Ricoeur, Paul. 1981. *Hermeneutics and the Human Sciences*. New York: Cambridge University Press.

Rorty, Richard. 1995. "Untruth and Consequences." *New Republic*, July 31, 32–6.

Rosaldo, Renato. 1984. "Grief and a Headhunter's Rage: On the Cultural Force of Emotions," in Edward Brunner, ed., *Text, Play and Story*. Washington, DC: Proceedings of the American Ethnological Society.

Rosaldo, Renato. 1986. "From the Door of His Tent: The Fieldworker and the Inquisitor," in James Clifford and George E. Marcus, eds., *Writing Culture: The Poetics and Politics of Ethnography*. Berkeley: University of California Press.

Rosaldo, Renato. 1989. *Culture and Truth: The Remaking of Social Analysis*. Boston: Beacon.

Ruby, Jay, ed. 1982. *A Crack in the Mirror: Reflexive Perspectives in Anthropology*. Philadelphia: University of Pennsylvania Press.

Rudner, Richard. 1966. *Philosophy of Social Science*. Englewood Cliffs, NJ: Prentice Hall.

Said, Edward W. 1989. "Representing the Colonized: Anthropology's Interlocutors." *Critical Inquiry*, 15: 205–25.

Scheper-Hughes, Nancy. 1992. "Hungry Bodies, Medicine, and the State: Toward a Critical Psychological Anthropology," in Theodore Schwartz, Geoffrey M. White, and Catherine A. Lutz, eds., *New Directions in Psychological Anthropology*. Cambridge: Cambridge University Press.

Scheper-Hughes, Nancy 1994. "The Violence of Everyday Life: In Search of a Critical and Politically Engaged Psychological Anthropology," in Marcelo M. Suarez-Orozco and George and Louise Spindler, eds., *The Making of Psychological Anthropology*, II. Fort Worth: Harcourt Brace College Publishers.

Scholte, Bob. 1984. "Reason and Culture: The Universal and the Particular Revisited." *American Anthropologist*, 86:960–5.

Searle, John R. 1993a. "Is There a Crisis in American Higher Education?" *Bulletin of the American Academy of Arts and Sciences*, 56:24–47.

Searle, John R. 1993b. "Rationality and Realism, What is at Stake?" *Daedalus*, 122:55–84.

Spencer, Jonathan. 1989. "Anthropology as a Kind of Writing." *Man*, 24:145–64.

Spiro, Melford E. 1986 [1992]. "Cultural Relativism and the Future of Anthropology." *Cultural Anthropology*, 1:259–86. Reprinted and expanded in *Anthropological Other or Burmese Brother?: Studies in Cultural Analysis*. New Brunswick: Transaction Publishers.

Spiro, Melford E. 1993. "On a Feminist/Constructionist View of Emotions," Manuscript.

Spiro, Melford E. 1994. *Culture and Human Nature*, 2nd edn., B. Kilborne and L. L. Languess, eds., New Brunswick: Transaction Publishers.

Tyler, Steven. 1987. *The Unspeakable: Discourse, Dialogue, and Rhetoric in the Postmodern World*. Madison: University of Wisconsin Press.

Tyson, Robert L. 1984. "Countertransference: Evolution in Theory and Practice." *Journal of the American Psychoanalytic Association*, 34:251–74.

Vendler, Zeno. 1984. "Understanding People," in Richard Shweder and Robert Levine, eds., *Culture Theory*. Cambridge: Cambridge University Press.

Wikan, Unni. 1993. "Beyond the Words: The Power of Resonance," in Gisli Palsson, ed., *Beyond Boundaries: Understanding Translation and Anthropological Discourse*. Berg: Oxford/Providence.

43

Beyond Good and Evil?
Questioning the Anthropological
Discomfort with Morals

Didier Fassin

The moral sentiment in Europe at present is perhaps as subtle, belated, diverse, sensitive, and refined, as the "science of morals" belonging thereto is recent, initial, awkward, and coarse-fingered: an interesting contrast, which sometimes becomes incarnate and obvious in the very person of the moralist.
Friedrich Nietzsche, *Beyond Good and Evil* (1886)

The classical act of duettists which turned into an intellectual joust between the detractor of "moral models in anthropology" (D'Andrade, 1995 [see chapter 41, this volume]) and the champion of "the primacy of the ethical" (Scheper-Hughes, 1995 [see chapter 40, this volume]) has given birth to a rhetorical paradigm based on a radical opposition between the pros and the cons of moral engagements and ethical implications in the social sciences. However, each article used these terms in a rather loose sense. On the one hand, the "moral" also meant critical anthropology denounced for its post-modern nihilism with regards to knowledge and power (anthropology representing both). On the other hand, the "ethical" signified political involvement through field activism

as well as academic militancy (anthropology allowing both). Roy D'Andrade called for anthropological objectivity, thus indicating that "moral" was generously and paradoxically associated with both cognitive relativism and value judgement. Nancy Scheper-Hughes proclaimed the anthropologist's responsibility, thus implying in a broad sense her rejection of cultural relativism and her adhesion to political commitment. The show certainly gained in dramatic intensity what the debate sometimes lost in conceptual clarity.

[...]

Plea for a Moral Anthropology

My point here is not to defend any kind of moral obligation for anthropologists but to underline the need for a moral anthropology. In Nietzsche's words, it is not to call for "moral sentiments" as a moralist would do, but for a "science of morals" as social scientists should do. By "morals" I do not mean any kind of norms and values, of certainties about truth or knowledge (often written with a capital letter), of denunciation of power or authority (clearly separating the two):

From *Anthropological Theory* 8(4) (2008), pp. 333–44. Reprinted with permission of SAGE.

Anthropology in Theory: Issues in Epistemology, Second Edition. Edited by Henrietta L. Moore and Todd Sanders.
© 2014 John Wiley & Sons, Inc. Published 2014 by John Wiley & Sons, Inc.

I simply refer to the human belief in the possibility of telling right from wrong and in the necessity of acting in favour of the good and against the evil. [...]

When I talk of "moral anthropology", [...] I do not mean that I want anthropology to act for the good of humanity [...] and anthropologists to become moralists [...]: I merely plead for an anthropology which has morals for its object – in other words, which explores how societies ideologically and emotionally found their cultural distinction between good and evil, and how social agents concretely work out this separation in their everyday life. A medical anthropology does not cure – it is interested in local knowledge and practice about illness. A religious anthropology does not proselytize – even if researchers sometimes get converted to the doctrine or mystique they study. A political anthropology does not tell whom to vote for – although some might let their audience know where their preference lies. Similarly, a moral anthropology does not propose a code of good conduct or a guide towards a better society. It helps understand the evaluative principles and practices operating in the social world, the debates they arouse, the processes through which they become implemented, the justifications that are given to account for discrepancies observed between what should be and what is actually.

Let me give a brief illustration [...] based on my own research. A few years ago I taught a course entitled "The Politics of Suffering". My point was not to arouse a compassionate feeling in my audience about the misfortunes and afflictions of the unemployed and immigrants but to analyse the sort of moral engagement French society had with these populations at a particular time in its history, that is, in the 1990s. [...]

[...] [W]hat I was interested in is how the "social question" has been turned into a "moral question" in France during this period; how the poor received money not in relation to their resources but according to their capacity to exhibit their misfortune and merit; how the clandestine immigrants were granted residence permits with medical aid because they were affected by severe diseases, and also how drug-users previously seen as delinquents were henceforth considered with empathy because of the lethal infections they were exposed to and how clinics of listening were opened in the impoverished suburbs with psychologists to consult the marginalized youth.

The sort of anthropology I tried to implement around this historical reconfiguration of moral sentiments and values within politics was thus a critical anthropology in the sense that it made visible and significant what had been taken for granted – the exclusion and suffering of unemployed and immigrants, drug-users and marginalized youth. My intention was to account for the changes that had occurred in our perception of the poor and the "other", and to apprehend what it meant to display compassion rather than justice. It is clear that this moral anthropology is closely related to political anthropology.

Who's Afraid of Morals?

Thus exposed and illustrated, the project of a moral anthropology might not seem scandalous, and at this stage of my argument the reader may wonder if it is really necessary to make a case of it. Should not any anthropologist agree on the idea of studying morals just as one studies kinship, rituals, religious institutions, representations of nature or categories of knowledge? Can we not assume the fact that anthropology should contribute to a science of morals as it did for the science of politics since Evans-Pritchard and Meyer Fortes? [...]

In fact, were it true, moral anthropology would be an entry in social science dictionaries and encyclopaedias, it would be presented in student textbooks and taught in humanities courses – which it is not. Moral philosophy is a traditional intellectual domain, and moral sociology has recently gained an academic space. But in spite of Kant's enthusiastic claim (Louden, 2000) – or maybe because of it since it had clearly a normative orientation – there is no such thing as a moral anthropology [...].

The question is, then, why should anthropologists be afraid of morals? In other words, why is there not a moral anthropology? I suggest that anthropologists' reluctance with respect to morals has two principal explanations, epistemological and historical.

On the one hand, anthropology constructed its intellectual autonomy, at least since Franz Boas and his followers, on a principle of cultural relativism, opposed to evolutionist as well as universalist para-digms. Cultures were ethically incommensurable. The analysis of their values would risk surrepti-tiously reintroducing value judgements and moral hierarchies. [...] However, a response to this legiti-mate epistemological anxiety may be given through case-studies in the "ethnography of moralities", to use Signe Howell's words (1997), which reveal the local systems of moral values within specific soci-eties [...]. Here the anthropologist does what he usually does, that is to say he provides a culturally situated account of a particular dimension of social reality, in this case the local sense of right and wrong.

On the other hand, anthropology has a long history of erring in the name of morality. There is no need to return to the well-known past of col-laboration between anthropologists and colonial administrations to provide evidence of the [...]. In a different historical context, David Price's research (2004) on "Cold War anthropology" highlights not only the courageous resistance of anthropologists to surveillance and repression under McCarthyism but also the ambivalent and often conniving relationships between the Central Intelligence Agency and the American Anthropological Association. [...]

[...]

Portrait of the Anthropologist as a Moralist

A significant proportion of contemporary anthro-pological studies deals with inequalities and violence, refugee camps and military conflicts, human rights and sustainable development, ethnic groups in danger and social resistance to domination. To put it bluntly, this trend demon-strates the generalization of moral concern within the discipline. [...] [B]y referring to this ten-dency I do not mean to suggest that moral engagements were absent in the past [...]. I merely want to underline the fact that moral indignation has become a major resource in the choice of topics to be studied, in particular among younger researchers or students, with the obvious risk of confusion between anthropological inter-pretation and moral evaluation. The consequence is a need for an even more demanding method-ology and ethics. The more we are conscious and

critical of our own moral presuppositions or certainties – instead of keeping them in the black box of self-contentment – the more we are capable of respecting the epistemological grounds and of preserving the political engagements of our scientific work.

[...]

[...] [I wish] to underline the difference I con-sider crucial in theory, although difficult to estab-lish in practice, between a moral discourse (what doctors should do and what the president should not say, in these particular cases) and a critical analysis of a moral topic (what are the issues at stake in relation to the question of telling the truth to one's patient or of taking care of one's people). The moral discourse evaluates, judges, sanctions. Critical analysis proposes a possible intelligibility by considering the sense that words and acts have for social agents but also by inscrib-ing them in their broader historical and political context. Moral discourse simplifies for the purpose of its cause (which we can consider as just) whereas critical analysis renders the com-plexity of issues and positions (which can be taken into account by social agents themselves). Moral discourse is enunciated a priori (it knows where good and evil are located) on the basis of intangible principles: it does not need ethno-graphic validation. Critical analysis is formulated a posteriori (it is interested in where and why social agents locate the good and the bad) as a result of an investigation: it requires an empirical exploration as well as a theoretical discussion.

The Politics of a Moral Anthropology

[...] Leaving morals – and politics – aside does not guarantee a rigorous epistemology or ethics, and there is a sort of "unbearable lightness of anthropological being", to paraphrase Kundera, sometimes displayed in our disciplinary arenas: avoiding moral issues may be seen as a moral position as well.

A few years ago, Orin Starn (1991) wondered how anthropologists working in Peru had been "missing the Revolution" that the Shining Path was preparing in the rural areas of the country. [...] [T]heir intellectual indifference to these issues had certainly spared them the sort of moral engagement of which we saw the limits, but it had also blinded them to what was about to happen. After the outbursts of urban violence which occurred in the autumn of 2005 in the French "banlieues", I suggested (Fassin, 2006) that anthropologists had similarly missed the riots. The ethnography which had been carried out in France focused primarily either on traditional beliefs and practices, especially in rural areas, or on strictly symbolic dimensions of political and social life. It had clearly prevented most anthropologists from pronouncing moral judgements on their own society, or had got those pronouncements seriously wrong in relation to what was really transpiring in the country.

[...]

Conclusion

Returning to the introduction, I will conclude with the following interrogation: What are the conditions of possibility of a moral anthropology? To answer this question I will resort to a rhetorical presentation borrowed from Spinoza's *Ethics* – my topic being a good excuse for it – with two propositions and their corollaries.

First proposition: Anthropology is always confronted in field situations with a series of moral issues which it often crystallizes by its mere presence. Since value judgement is the most commonly shared attitude toward the social world, the anthropologist cannot avoid and should not

elude the moral position he or she adopts, either explicitly or implicitly, either by excess or by omission.

First corollary: It is thus epistemologically but also politically crucial to consider moral reflexivity as part of our research activity, in other words to question the values and judgements that underlie our work.

Second proposition: Moral anthropology is an anthropology which has as its object the study of moral issues posed to societies or which societies pose to themselves – an important distinction since it implies that one should explore questions overtly present but also questions which remain covert or unformulated.

Second corollary: It is then obvious that moral anthropology is not an anthropology which proposes its own morality – that of the anthropologist. Even if it cannot completely escape an evaluative perspective, it remains a critical approach just as any domain of social anthropology and as such it attempts to render visible and intelligible moral issues in a cultural, and consequently historical, context.

This formulation, which advances general principles rather than specific methods, may suggest certainties more than doubts. In fact my main conclusion is, on the contrary, that moral anthropology, that is to say a science of morals based on ethnographic work, should always remain problematic, in the sense that it should always pose problems to the researcher both epistemologically and ethically. [...]

References

D'Andrade, Roy (1995) "Moral Models in Anthropology", *Current Anthropology* 36(3): 399–408.
Fassin, Didier (2006) "Riots in France and Silent Anthropologists" (editorial), *Anthropology Today. Journal of the Royal Anthropological Institute* 22(1): 1–3.
Howell, Signe (1997) "Introduction", in Signe Howell (ed.) *The Ethnography of Moralities*, pp. 1–22. London: Routledge.
Louden, Robert (2000) *Kant's Impure Ethics: From Rational Beings to Human Beings.* New York: Oxford University Press.
Nietzsche, Friedrich (1989 [1886]) *Beyond Good and Evil: Prelude to a Philosophy of the Future* (trans. Helen Zimmern). New York: Prometheus Books.
Price, David (2004) *Threatening Anthropology: McCarthyism and the FBI's Surveillance of Activist Anthropologists.* Durham, NC: Duke University Press.
Scheper-Hughes, Nancy (1995) "The Primacy of the Ethical: Propositions for a Militant Anthropology", *Current Anthropology* 36(3): 409–20.
Starn, Orin (1991) "Missing the Revolution: Anthropologists and the War in Peru", *Cultural Anthropology* 6(1): 63–91.

PART IV

SECTION 13

The Anthropology of Western Modes of Thought

44

The Invention of Women

Oyèrónké Oyĕwùmí

[…] As the work and my thinking progressed, I came to realize that the fundamental category "woman" – which is foundational in Western gender discourses – simply did not exist in Yorùbáland prior to its sustained contact with the West. There was no such preexisting group characterized by shared interests, desires, or social position. The cultural logic of Western social categories is based on an ideology of biological determinism: the conception that biology provides the rationale for the organization of the social world. Thus this cultural logic is actually a "bio-logic." Social categories like "woman" are based on body-type and are elaborated in relation to and in opposition to another category: man; the presence or absence of certain organs determines social position. It is not surprising, then, that feminist sociologist Dorothy Smith notes that in Western societies "a man's body gives credibility to his utterance, whereas a woman's body takes it away from hers."[1] Judith Lorber also notes the depth and ubiquity of notions of biology in the social realm when she writes that "gender is so pervasive in our [Western] society we assume it is bred into our genes."[2] Given this, it is obvious that if one wanted to apply this Western

"bio-logic" to the Yorùbá social world (i.e., use biology as an ideology for organizing that social world), one would have first to invent the category "woman" in Yorùbá discourse.

The assertion that "woman" as a social category did not exist in Yorùbá communities should not be read as antimaterialist hermeneutics, a kind of post-structuralist deconstructing of the body into dissolution. Far from it – the body was (and still is) very corporeal in Yorùbá communities. But, prior to the infusion of Western notions into Yorùbá culture, the body was not the basis of social roles, inclusions, or exclusions; it was not the foundation of social thought and identity. Most academic studies on the Yorùbá have, however, assumed that "body-reasoning" was present in the Yorùbá indigenous culture. They have assumed the Western constructions as universal, which has led to the uncritical usage of these body-based categories for interpreting Yorùbá society historically and in the contemporary period.

Consequently, in order to analyze how and why gender is constructed in Yorùbá society (and indeed in other contemporary African societies), the role and impact of the West are of utmost

From The Invention of Women: Making an African Sense of Western Gender Discourses (Minneapolis: University of Minnesota Press, 1997), pp. ix–xiii, 7–9, 10–12, 181, 183–4, 210, 213, 215–20. Copyright © 1997 the Regents of the University of Minnesota. Reprinted by permission of the University of Minnesota Press.

importance, not only because most African societies came under European rule by the end of the nineteenth century but also because of the continued dominance of the West in the production of knowledge. In African studies, historically and currently, the creation, constitution, and production of knowledge have remained the privilege of the West. Therefore, body-reasoning and the bio-logic that derives from the biological determinism inherent in Western thought have been imposed on African societies. The presence of gender constructs cannot be separated from the ideology of biological determinism. Western conceptual schemes and theories have become so widespread that almost all scholarship, even by Africans, utilizes them unquestioningly.

[...]

I interrogate the ways in which Western assumptions about sex differences are used to interpret Yorùbá society and, in the process, create a local gender system. My analysis challenges a number of ideas, some mentioned above, common in many Western feminist writings:

1 Gender categories are universal and timeless and have been present in every society at all times. This idea is often expressed in a biblical tone, as if to suggest that "in the beginning there was gender."
2 Gender is a fundamental organizing principle in all societies and is therefore always salient. In any given society, gender is everywhere.
3 There is an essential, universal category "woman" that is characterized by the social uniformity of its members.
4 The subordination of women is a universal.
5 The category "woman" is precultural, fixed in historical time and cultural space in antithesis to another fixed category – "man."

I posit that these assumptions are a result of the fact that in Western societies, physical bodies are *always* social bodies. As a consequence, there is really no distinction between sex and gender, despite the many attempts by feminists to distinguish the two. In the West, social categories have a long history of being embodied and therefore gendered. According to anthropologist Shelly Errington, "Sex (with a capital 'S') is the gender system of the West." She continues: "But Sex is not the only way to sort out human bodies, not the

only way to make sense of sex. One can easily imagine different cultural classifications and rationales for gender categories, different scenarios that equally take into account the evidence our bodies provide."[3]

The Yorùbá case provides one such different scenario; and more than that, it shows that the human body need not be constituted as gendered or be seen as evidence for social classification at all times. In precolonial Yorùbá society, body-type was not the basis of social hierarchy: males and females were not ranked according to anatomic distinction. The social order required a different kind of map, not a gender map that assumed biology as the foundation for social ranking.

I use the concepts "sex" and "gender" as synonyms. With regard to Yorùbá society in the precolonial period, however, I have coined the terms "anatomic sex," "anatomic male," and "anatomic female" to emphasize the nongendered attitude toward the relation between the human body and social roles, positions, and hierarchies. In some places I have shortened those terms to "anasex," "anamale," and "anafemale." My purpose in qualifying these terms with "anatomic" (or "ana-") is to show that the Yorùbá distinctions were superficial and did not assume any social hierarchical dimensions, as they do in the West (Western social categories derive essentially from a perceived sexual dimorphism of the human body). Gender was simply not inherent in human social organization.

Although precolonial Yorùbá cultural logic did not use the human body as the basis for social ranking (in no situation in Yorùbá society was a male, by virtue of his body-type, inherently superior to a female), Yorùbá society was hierarchically organized, from slaves to rulers. The ranking of individuals depended first and foremost on seniority, which was usually defined by relative age. Another fundamental difference between Yorùbá and Western social categories involves the highly situational nature of Yorùbá social identity. In Yorùbá society before the sustained infusion of Western categories, social positions of people shifted constantly in relation to those with whom they were interacting; consequently, social identity was relational and was not essentialized. In many European societies, in contrast, males and females have gender identities deriving from the elaboration of anatomic types; therefore, man and woman are essentialized.

These essential gender identities in Western cultures attach to all social engagements no matter how far from the issues of reproduction such undertakings may be. The classic example is that for many years women could not vote solely because they were women. Another example is the genderization of professions to the extent that professional lexicons contain phrases such as "woman pilot," "woman president," and "professor emerita," as if whatever these women do in these occupations is different from what men do in the same professions.

In light of the foregoing, I will argue that the concentration of feminist scholars on the status of women – an emphasis that presupposes the existence of "woman" as a social category always understood to be powerless, disadvantaged, and controlled and defined by men – can lead to serious misconceptions when applied Òyó-Yorùbá society.[4] In fact, my central argument is that there were no *women* – defined in strictly gendered terms – in that society. Again, the concept "woman" as it is used and as it is invoked in the scholarship is derived from Western experience and history, a history rooted in philosophical discourses about the distinctions among body, mind, and soul and in ideas about biological determinism and the linkages between the body and the "social."[5]

[…]

Visualizing the Body: Western Theories and African Subjects

[…] From the ancients to the moderns, gender has been a foundational category upon which social categories have been erected. Hence, gender has been ontologically conceptualized. The category of the citizen, which has been the cornerstone of much of Western political theory, was male, despite the much-acclaimed Western democratic traditions.[6] Elucidating Aristotle's categorization of the sexes, Elizabeth Spelman writes: "A woman is a female who is free; a man is a male who is a citizen."[7] Women were excluded from the category of citizens because "penis possession"[8] was one of the qualifications for citizenship. Lorna Schiebinger notes in a study of the origins of modern science and women's

exclusion from European scientific institutions that "differences between the two sexes were reflections of a set of dualistic principles that penetrated the cosmos as well as the bodies of men and women."[9] Differences and hierarchy, then, are enshrined on bodies; and bodies enshrine differences and hierarchy. Hence, dualisms like nature/culture, public/private, and visible/invisible are variations on the theme of male/female bodies hierarchically ordered, differentially placed in relation to power, and spatially distanced one from the other.[10]

In the span of Western history, the justifications for the making of the categories "man" and "woman" have not remained the same. On the contrary, they have been dynamic. Although the boundaries are shifting and the content of each category may change, the two categories have remained hierarchical and in binary opposition. For Stephen Gould, "the justification for ranking groups by inborn worth has varied with the tide of Western history. Plato relied on dialectic, the church upon dogma. For the past two centuries, scientific claims have become the primary agent of validating Plato's myth."[11] The constant in this Western narrative is the centrality of the body: two bodies on display, two sexes, two categories persistently viewed – one in relation to the other. That narrative is about the unwavering elaboration of the body as the site and cause of differences and hierarchies in society. In the West, so long as the issue is difference and social hierarchy, then the body is constantly positioned, posed, exposed, and reexposed as their cause. Society, then, is seen as an accurate reflection of genetic endowment – those with a superior biology inevitably are those in superior social positions. No difference is elaborated without bodies that are positioned hierarchically. In his book *Making Sex*,[12] Thomas Laqueur gives a richly textured history of the construction of sex from classical Greece to the contemporary period, noting the changes in symbols and the shifts in meanings. The point, however, is the centrality and persistence of the body in the construction of social categories. In view of this history, Freud's dictum that anatomy is destiny was not original or exceptional; he was just more explicit than many of his predecessors.

Social orders and biology: natural or constructed?

The idea that gender is socially constructed – that differences between males and female are to be located in social practices, not in biological facts – was one important insight that emerged early in second-wave feminist scholarship. This finding was understandably taken to be radical in a culture in which difference, particularly gender difference, had always been articulated as natural and, therefore, biologically determined. Gender as a social construction became the cornerstone of much feminist discourse. The notion was particularly attractive because it was interpreted to mean that gender differences were not ordained by nature; they were mutable and therefore changeable. This in turn led to the opposition between social constructionism and biological determinism, as if they were mutually exclusive.

Such a dichotomous presentation is unwarranted, however, because the ubiquity of biologically rooted explanations for difference in Western social thought and practices is a reflection of the extent to which biological explanations are found compelling.[13] In other words, so long as the issue is difference (whether the issue is why women breast-feed babies or why they could not vote), old biologies will be found or new biologies will be constructed to explain women's disadvantage. The Western preoccupation with biology continues to generate constructions of "new biologies" even as some of the old biological assumptions are being dislodged. In fact, in the Western experience, social construction and biological determinism have been two sides of the same coin, since both ideas continue to reinforce each other. When social categories like gender are constructed, new biologies of difference can be invented. When biological interpretations are found to be compelling, social categories do derive their legitimacy and power from biology. In short, the social and the biological feed on each other.

The biologization inherent in the Western articulation of social difference is, however, by no means universal. The debate in feminism about what roles and which identities are natural and what aspects are constructed only has meaning in a culture where social categories are conceived as having no independent logic of their own. This debate, of course, developed out of certain problems; therefore, it is logical that in societies where such problems do not exist, there should be no such debate. But then, due to imperialism, this debate has been universalized to other cultures, and its immediate effect is to inject Western problems where such issues originally did not exist. Even then, this debate does not take us very far in societies where social roles and identities are not conceived to be rooted in biology. By the same token, in cultures where the visual sense is not privileged, and the body is not read as a blueprint of society, invocations of biology are less likely to occur because such explanations do not carry much weight in the social realm. That many categories of difference are socially constructed in the West may well suggest the mutability of categories, but it is also an invitation to endless constructions of biology – in that there is no limit to what can be explained by the body-appeal. Thus biology is hardly mutable; it is much more a combination of the Hydra and the Phoenix of Greek mythology. Biology is forever mutating, not mutable. Ultimately, the most important point is not that gender is socially constructed but the extent to which biology itself is socially constructed and therefore inseparable from the social.

The way in which the conceptual categories sex and gender functioned in feminist discourse was based on the assumption that biological and social conceptions could be separated and applied universally. Thus sex was presented as the natural category and gender as the social construction of the natural. But, subsequently, it became apparent that even sex has elements of construction. In many feminist writings thereafter, sex has served as the base and gender as the superstructure.[14] In spite of all efforts to separate the two, the distinction between sex and gender is a red herring. In Western conceptualization, gender cannot exist without sex since the body sits squarely at the base of both categories. Despite the preeminence of feminist social constructionism, which claims a social deterministic approach to society, biological foundationalism,[15] if not reductionism, is still at the center of gender discourses, just as it is at the center of all other discussions of society in the West.

[...]

From a cross-cultural perspective, the significance of this observation is that one cannot assume the social organization of one culture (the dominant West included) as universal or the interpretations of the experiences of one culture as explaining another one. On the one hand, at a general, global level, the constructedness of gender does suggest its mutability. On the other hand, at the local level – that is, within the bounds of any particular culture – gender is mutable only if it is socially constructed as such. Because, in Western societies, gender categories, like all other social categories, are constructed with biological building blocks, their mutability is questionable. The cultural logic of Western social categories is founded on an ideology of biological determinism: the conception that biology provides the rationale for the organization of the social world. Thus, as pointed out earlier, this cultural logic is actually a "bio-logic."

The "sisterarchy": feminism and its "other"

From a cross-cultural perspective, the implications of Western bio-logic are far-reaching when one considers the fact that gender constructs in feminist theory originated in the West, where men and women are conceived oppositionally and projected as embodied, genetically derived social categories.[16] The question, then, is this: On what basis are Western conceptual categories exportable or transferable to other cultures that have a different cultural logic? This question is raised because despite the wonderful insight about the social construction of gender, the way cross-cultural data have been used by many feminist writers undermines the notion that differing cultures may construct social categories differently. For one thing, if different cultures necessarily always construct gender as feminism proposes that they *do and must*, then the idea that gender is socially constructed is not sustainable.

The potential value of Western feminist social constructionism remains, therefore,

largely unfulfilled, because feminism, like most other Western theoretical frameworks for interpreting the social world, cannot get away from the prism of biology that necessarily perceives social hierarchies as natural. Consequently, in cross-cultural gender studies, theorists impose Western categories on non-Western cultures and then project such categories as natural. The way in which dissimilar constructions of the social world in other cultures are used as "evidence" for the constructedness of gender and the insistence that these cross-cultural constructions are gender categories as they operate in the West nullify the alternatives offered by the non-Western cultures and undermine the claim that gender is a social construction.

Western ideas are imposed when non-Western social categories are assimilated into the gender framework that emerged from a specific sociohistorical and philosophical tradition. An example is the "discovery" of what has been labeled "third gender"[17] or "alternative genders"[18] in a number of non-Western cultures. The fact that the African "woman marriage,"[19] the Native American "berdache,"[20] and the South Asian "hijra"[21] are presented as gender categories incorporates them into the Western bio-logic and gendered framework without explication of their own sociocultural histories and constructions. A number of questions are pertinent here. Are these social categories seen as gendered in the cultures in question? From whose perspective are they gendered? In fact, even the appropriateness of naming them "third gender" is questionable since the Western cultural system, which uses biology to map the social world, precludes the possibility of more than two genders because gender is the elaboration of the perceived sexual dimorphism of the human body into the social realm. The trajectory of feminist discourse in the last twenty-five years has been determined by the Western cultural environment of its founding and development. [. . .]

Notes

1 Dorothy E. Smith, *The Everyday World as Problematic: A Feminist Sociology* (Boston: Northeastern University Press, 1987), 30.

2 Judith Lorber, *Paradoxes of Gender* (New Haven: Yale University Press, 1994), 13.

3 Shelly Errington, "Recasting Sex, Gender, and Power," in *Power and Difference: Gender in Island Southeast Asia*, ed. Jane Atkinson and Shelly Errington (Stanford, Calif.: Stanford University Press, 1990), 33.

4 For a history of the emergence of and shifts in the category "women" in Britain, see Denise Riley, *Am I That Name? Feminism and the Category of Women in History* (Minneapolis: University of Minnesota Press, 1988).

5 Standard Yorùbá as it is spoken today derives mostly from the Ọ̀yọ́- dialect.

6 Susan Okin, *Women in Western Political Thought* Princeton, NJ: Princeton University Press, 1979); Elizabeth Sperman, *Inessential Woman: Problems of Exclusion in Feminist Thought* (Boston: Beacon Press, 1988).

7 Quoted in Thomas Laqueur, *Making Sex: Body and Gender from the Greeks to Freud* (Cambridge, Mass.: Harvard University Press, 1990), 54.

8 Ibid.

9 Lorna Schiebinger, *The Mind Has No Sex? Women in the origins of Modern Science* (Cambridge, Mass.: Harvard University Press, 1989), 162.

10 For an account of some of these dualisms, see "Hélène Cixous," in *New French Feminisms: An Anthology*, ed. Elaine Marks and Isabelle de Courtivron (Amherst, Mass.: University of Massachusetts Press, 1980).

11 Stephen Gould, *The Mismeasure of Man* (New York: Norton, 1981), 20.

12 Laqueur, *Making Sex*.

13 See Suzanne J. Kessler and Wendy McKenna, *Gender: An Ethnomethodological Approach* (New York: John Wiley and Sons, 1978)

14 For elucidation, see Jane F. Collier and Sylvia J. Yanagisako, eds., *Gender and Kinship: Essays toward a Unified Analysis* (Stanford, Calif.: Stanford University Press, 1987).

15 Linda Nicholson has also explicated the pervasiveness of biological foundationalism in feminist thought. See "Interpreting Gender," in *Signs* 20 (1994): 79–104.

16 In the title of this section, I use the term "sisterarchy." In using the term, I am referring to the well-founded allegations against Western feminists by a number of African, Asian, and Latin American feminists that despite the notion that the "sisterhood is global," Western women are at the top of the hierarchy of the sisterhood; hence it is actually a "sisterarchy." Nkiru Nzegwu uses the concept in her essay "O Africa: Gender Imperialism in Academia," in *African Women and Feminism: Reflecting on the Politics of Sisterhood*, edited by Oyèrónkẹ́ Oyěwùmí (Trenton, N.J.: African World Press, 2003).

17 Lorber, *Paradoxes of Gender*, 17–18.

18 Ibid.

19 See Ifi Amadiume, *Male Daughters, Female Husbands: Gender and Sex in an African Society* (London: Zed Books, 1987), for an account of this institution in Igboland of southeastern Nigeria. See also Melville J. Herskovitz, "A Note on 'Woman Marriage' in Dahomey," *Africa* 10 (1937): 335–41, for an earlier allusion to its wide occurrence in Africa.

20 Kessler and McKenna, *Gender*, 24–36.

21 Serena Nanda, "Neither Man Nor Woman: The Hijras of India," in *Gender in Cross-cultural Perspective* edited by Caroline Brettell and Carolyn Sargent (Englewood Cliffs, N.J.: Prentice Hall, 1993).

References

Amadiume, Ifi. *Male Daughters, Female Husbands: Gender and Sex in an African Society*. London: Zed Books, 1987.

Collier, Jane F., and Sylvia J. Yanagisako, eds. *Gender and Kinship: Essays toward a Unified Analysis*. Stanford, Calif.: Stanford University Press, 1987.

Errington, Shelly. "Recasting Sex, Gender, and Power." In *Power and Difference: Gender in Island Southeast Asia*, edited by Jane Atkinson and Shelly Errington. Stanford, Calif.: Stanford University Press, 1990.

Gould, Stephen. *The Mismeasure of Man*. New York: Norton, 1981.

Herskovitz, Melville. J. "A Note on 'Woman Marriage' in Dahomey." *Africa* 10 (1937): 335–41.

Kessler, Suzanne J., and Wendy McKenna. *Gender: An Ethnomethodological Approach*. New York: John Wiley and Sons, 1978.

Laqueur, Thomas. *Making Sex: Body and Gender from the Greeks to Freud*. Cambridge, Mass.: Harvard University Press, 1990.

Lorber, Judith. *Paradoxes of Gender*. New Haven: Yale University Press, 1994.

Marks, Elaine, and Isabelle de Courtivron, eds. *New French Feminisms: An Anthology*. Amherst, Mass.: University of Massachusetts Press, 1980.

Nanda, Serena. "Neither Man nor Woman: The Hijras of India." In *Gender in Cross-cultural Perspective*, edited by Caroline Brettell and Carolyn Sargent. Englewood Cliffs, NJ: Prentice Hall, 1993.

Nicholson, Linda. "Interpreting Gender." *Signs* 20 (1994): 79–104.

Nzegwu, Nkiru. "O Africa: Gender Imperialism in Academia," in *African Women and Feminism:*

Reflecting on the Politics of Sisterhood, ed. Oyèrónké Oyěwùmí (Trenton, NJ: African World Press, 2003).

Okin, Susan. *Women in Western Political Thought*. Princeton, NJ: Princeton University Press, 1979.

Riley, Denise. *Am I That Name? Feminism and the Category of Women in History*. Minneapolis: University of Minnesota Press, 1988.

Schiebinger, Londa. *The Mind Has No Sex? Women in the Origins of Modem Science*. Cambridge, Mass.: Harvard University Press, 1989.

Smith, Dorothy E. *The Everyday World as Problematic: A Feminist Sociology*. Boston: Northeastern University Press, 1987.

Spelman, Elizabeth. *Inessential Woman: Problems of Exclusion in Feminist Thought*. Boston: Beacon Press, 1988.

45

Valorizing the Present: Orientalism, Postcoloniality and the Human Sciences

Vivek Dhareshwar

Sketches for a Metatheory of Western Theories

[...] If the West's attempt to understand the otherness of another culture ends up transforming latter into a variation of itself, and if the same attitude underlies its attempt to understand itself, how do we make sense of its theories about the domains it regards as essential to itself? With this question I now turn to the moral and political domain theorized by the West. [...]

I am [...] talking about theories – say moral or political – which emerged as a result of the West's attempt to understand its own experience but which impinge on us. This distinction between western theories about us and western theories about its own experiences that nevertheless impinge on us is a matter partly of expositional convenience rather than of any epistemic or qualitative importance (apart, of course, from helping to highlight the scope and ambition of the project), but only partly. The distinction can be used to provide a check or a constraint on how we go about constructing a metatheory of a theory by specifying its particular domain of problems.

For instance, theories about Indian culture will, as we have seen, typically use or presuppose notions of tradition/practice, action, belief, etc. Now turn to philosophical theories of action, belief, propositional attitudes, practice, truth, etc. Our problem now is not the rather easy one of showing how the ideas from the latter are used in the former (as they indeed are, sometimes consciously). We should be able to show how a set of problems persist in and motivate the theories so far apart otherwise, temporally, methodologically and substantively. Consider this sample list: tradition/practice is embodiment of beliefs; action is execution of belief (intention, desire); the problem of specifying what is involved in understanding another language (culture, action) is resolved by specifying the requirements of a theory of translation/interpretation, which involves attributing (largely) truths to the alien sentences and true and rational beliefs to aliens "natives") uttering those sentences. The philosophical tradition takes specific features and problems and constructs theories that are supposed to apply universally; the sector that busies itself with other cultures finds/attributes (unwittingly validating the philosophical theory of translation/interpretation) the same

From *Cultural Dynamics* 10(2) (1998), pp. 223–31 (with cuts). Copyright © 1998 by *Cultural Dynamics* Reproduced by permission of SAGE.

Anthropology in Theory: Issues in Epistemology, Second Edition. Edited by Henrietta L. Moore and Todd Sanders.
© 2014 John Wiley & Sons, Inc. Published 2014 by John Wiley & Sons, Inc.

features and problems in other cultures. No wonder then that the philosophical tradition cannot formulate a theory of cultural difference (think of the arid debates on relativism, the recent debate on multiculturalism) and the anthropological tradition cannot give an account of what it is to understand the other. I do not wish to enter into a discussion of the specific items in the sample; it is sufficient for now if they clarify the distinction between the western theories of ourselves and the western theories of its own experience that impinge on us, and the methodological purpose or use of that distinction.

The West has generated theories about itself, theories about what it means to be a moral person, to be a citizen, what it is to have moral and political conflicts and how to go about resolving them, and so forth. These theories have generated concepts – rights, sovereignty, autonomy, rationality – which in turn have generated further problems. These theories have been in conflict with one another about the way to formulate the problems, as well as about the interpretation of the concepts used in the formulation and resolution of the problems. Thus the Kantians and the utilitarians disagree about morality and rationality; the liberals and communitarians disagree about political values; the hermeneuticians and the deconstructionists disagree about interpretation itself (about what it means to interpret a text or an action) and both of them disagree with the positivists. Our task is not to join in these disputes or to choose what seems to suit us (although that is what we have been doing during our long apprenticeship); instead, I am suggesting that we ask what these theories tell us about the West, about, to put it in the words of Wittgenstein, how it goes on.

If after the long apprenticeship with the West we now feel that what we say and experience are two different things, it is important to say whether we are asserting (a) it is *something in our experience* that makes the theories we have used to describe ourselves unintelligible, or (b) *something in the nature of western theories* renders our experience unintelligible or prevents them from speaking about "ourselves" and "our experience". It is worth spending some time clarifying these two formulations since they lead in radically different directions (the first one in fact leads very quickly to an impasse). Let me explicate the first

formulation by recalling what I said about the denial or rejection of our experience. A clear and simple way of understanding what that rejection involved would be this: something in our experience prevents the application or whatever of western theories, hence the "something" in our experience, if not the experience as a whole, must be changed, reformed, modified or rejected. If this sounds bizarre, that is because some of our projects are bizarre! Take for instance, the project of secularism. The above formulation captures it very well, including its inability to say both what secularism in the Indian context would mean and what that "something" is that needs to be secularized. This was however a negative evaluation of our experience (and, correspondingly, a positive evaluation of the normativity of western theories). But (a) could also be seen (and has been seen) as an attempt to describe our experience of the world. In answering the question "what is it in our experience that makes the western theories unintelligible?", the focus is on "our experience" and "something" in it. The attempt quickly leads to "despair" because it cannot say what to look for and how to look without using "theory" which turns out to be western and unintelligible. (It is also possible to interpret [a] as a celebration of the "something", whatever it may be, that always resists western theories.)

Turning now to formulation (b), let us note that by focusing on theories, it already specifies, to some extent, the unintelligibility of theories. They are unintelligible because they fail to do what they are supposed to: as theories they are supposed to enable us to describe and conceptualize our experience and they fail to do this. Hence their unintelligibility. This way of putting the matter immediately raises the question: to whom are these theories unintelligible? The only possible answer is: they are (or, more cautiously, must be) unintelligible to whoever uses them to conceptualize our experience and describe ourselves. I suggest that we have plenty of evidence that this is indeed the case: we need only look at the theories of "caste system", "Hinduism", Indian morality, and so forth. None of them can be said to describe "our experience". Why, then, talk about western theories? Why make them the object our investigations?

The thought is this: the West claims to have theories of the social/cultural world; what we do is study these theories in order to infer about western culture as part of the process of describing ourselves. Their theory of "other cultures" is a component of their existing theories of their own world. Our metatheory should tell us why this culture looks at us the way it does. At the moment, however, there are only western theories (of themselves and ourselves). How do we then go about saying what in the western theories makes them unintelligible? We may have intuitions, even a sense of the practices, which allow us an initial distance; by themselves, however, they do not give us reasons for regarding western theories as inapplicable. Our intuitions could be misleading, or entirely wrong. We need to begin to theorize those intuitions in order to generate concepts that can organize those intuitions into problematics to be developed, investigated and argued about. Because our apprenticeship has been both an obstacle and an enabling condition, our attempt to describe ourselves has to follow a two-fold movement: on the one hand, we must pick out the western theory that impinges on our conflicting intuitions and interrogate it not for what it says or could be made to say about our experience but by specifying the intelligibility condition of the problems which generated these theories in the relevant experiential domain in the West; on the other hand, that interrogation will be undertaken in order to clarify our experiential context, a clarification that should supply the heuristics for the theorization of that context.

An example or two might help. Consider the phenomenon or the institution called morality which by all accounts the West regards as central to its self-understanding. Whenever the West has turned to other cultures – be they the cultures of classical antiquity (Greece and Rome) or of the Indian subcontinent – it has claimed to distinguish itself from, and assert its superiority over, them by claiming that it alone possesses what they lack, namely morality. This thing or institution involves a cluster of concepts: the concept of moral law and a certain concept of the self as prior to experience, a concept of action as expression of the will, an absolute distinction between moral and non-moral motives and the related notion of autonomy and heteronomy, a concept of moral obligation as unconditional, a peculiar moral feeling called guilt, a special set of difficulties created by conflict of duties, a conception of blame and its correlative voluntary action. This cluster of concepts does impinge on us, sometimes directly but often indirectly. They are, however, not particularly intelligible to us (in this of course the western writers who noted its absence in our culture got something right, whatever one may say about the conclusions they drew from it): in most cases, we have neither the words nor, more importantly, the concepts to capture this domain of morality. It would be hard to find in any of the Indian languages a word to translate "guilt". Of course, the absence of a word itself does not show that the concept does not obtain, but it is an important clue, nonetheless. What we have is a much more complex experience which can only be described by using a combination of honour, pride, shame and humiliation. That, however, is a domain of practical action firmly embedded in multiple (and multiply ordered) contexts and unintelligible outside of that context. In contrast, moral theories deal with a dozen or so moral rules, laws or injunctions. Or, they set about answering the question: "Why should I be moral?", "Is it rational to be moral?" (Rawls's *A Theory of Justice* [1971], for example, tries to justify two principles of justice, and has a hard time doing so). The sheer quantity of literature on this domain, even if we restrict ourselves to the last few decades, is truly astonishing. This is an extremely rich problematic that needs to be developed at length. The point, however, is or should be clear.

What we now need to do is to initiate the double movement I spoke of above: interrogate the western theories of morality to construct a metatheory which specifies the intelligibility conditions of the claims and problems of those theories. This involves, it bears repeating, explaining in terms intelligible to the West how, if at all, they make sense of notions such as moral law or the concept of self prior to experience. We need to construct a theory precisely because we could not make sense of their theories; because they did not capture any significant feature of our experience. But the question that the metatheory of moral theories has to clarify is: what must be the nature of this domain of western experience such that theorizing of it produces impoverished and uniluminating reflections on a handful of laws or rules? In constructing such a metatheory we will be bringing to bear the range of our experiences which now includes not only our intuitive sense of our own practices but also what we have learned of/from the West itself. Hence the act of this construction is at the same time a reflexive grasp of our own experiential context. The theory that we construct must not only be cognitively productive for us but it should at the same time say something cognitively interesting about the West too. It is important to notice that this is not a relativizing move, that is, the claim is not that the western moral theories capture or adequately conceptualize (some specific kind of features of) western experience.

If all this seems a bit abstract, if not abstruse, consider the problem of rights: what makes these rights fundamental? The western moral and political theories try to answer by mobilizing a cluster of concepts such as sovereignty, freedom, dominion, duty, moral law and so forth. Since we regard the question of rights as important for us, but cannot really make sense of the justification of those rights, we have no option but to undertake the project I have been outlining. What the taste calls for is neither intellectual in political history natural rights (of the type to be found in, say, Skinner, Finnis, Berman or Tuck), nor an exegesis of, say, Aquinas, Grotius, Kant, Rawls and Dworkin, but the construction of a domain of problems that *persists* not only from Aquinas to Rawls, but also appears in very different theories or fields. But instead of asking *what sense* these problems have, we ask what kind of an audience it must be for the problems to make sense to it. The idea is to delineate hypothetically the possible structure of an audience and the structure of its experience that can make sense of these problems. Consider in this context Rawls's doctrine of political liberalism (Rawls, 1993). Rawls presents this doctrine as a framework for resolving the question of how liberal society can accommodate/tolerate multiculturalism. Consequently, he says that this doctrine does not claim truth itself (if it did, it would be one more "comprehensive doctrine" imposing its own conception of the good on others with different conceptions of the good). He cannot however present it merely as a modus vivendi, for then its appeal would be weakened. He therefore claims that it is a *moral* conception, though it denies truth to itself. This is strange and incomprehensible, indeed. It would be a mistake, however, to see this as a problem local to Rawls's theory (its inconsistency, or lack of rigour, or whatever). It is the problem inherited by any conception of natural rights which does not or cannot use the theological resolution of the problem (moral law is divine and hence true). So Rawls not only has a problem in conceptualizing multiculturalism, his attempted framework looks unintelligible. Multiculturalism, cultural difference, theorizing otherness, turn up as unresolved problems in very different places. Therefore, our inference about the limiting structures of an audience and its experience must help us generate the problems which those different theories in some particular domain try to resolve.

Perhaps the point can be made with regard to secularism, which continues to generate much passion and rhetoric but little clarity. Addressing this issue will also enable me to tie up the two aspects of the project I have discussed so far and to show how such a project renders intelligible the links between abstract theoretical problems and pressing political issues. To begin, consider some of the consequences of Balagangadhara's metatheory of Christianity. Secularization (along with proselytization) is the dynamic of religion; the political doctrine of secularism makes sense in the context of a culture that exhibits that dynamic. That Hinduism is a religion was the hypothesis of western theorists who sought to explain Indian culture. As Balagangadhara demonstrates, that hypothesis and the theories used to prove it tell us more about western culture than about Indian culture. They fail to show that Hinduism is an identifiable domain individuated by religion. It may seem as though we are now confronted with the question: "What is Hinduism, if it is not a religion?". Actually though, we do not need to address that question at all, at least not in that form, for that hypothesis makes sense only as the attempt of one culture to theorize another culture. Outside of that hypothesis and the theories generated by it, "Hinduism" does not capture anything. If that is indeed the case, what are our social scientists saying when they claim that Indian culture is insufficiently or weakly secular or that the state must be thoroughly secular?

When pressed, the social scientists come up with utterly confused statements such as the following: "Secularism is more than laws, concessions and special considerations. It is a state of mind, almost an instinctive feeling..." (Gopal, 1991). This hardly distinguishes secularism from, say, mysticism or, indeed, from what social scientists have often said about religion. The point is not the vacuousness, however well-meaning, of this particular statement; most pronouncements on secularism tend to be garbled and cliché-ridden. It would be nothing short of a miracle if it were to turn out that this ill-defined doctrine and process were the only thing preventing our slide into "medieval barbarism". Once we begin to free ourselves from the grip of a doctrine and its authority, we can set about the task of redescribing the problem. For the garbled discussion of secularism is indeed an attempt to name a problem. What is the nature of this problem?

The secularists often accuse the Hindu nationalists of being revivalists, indigenists, and so forth (thus the constant invocation of medieval barbarity to characterize the Bharatiya Janata Party). The idea (or perhaps the fear) is that they are anti-modern (anti-western); hence the recourse to the authority of a western doctrine (and hence also the suspicion of any criticism of secularism). The secularists have got this completely wrong. The Hindu nationalists' programme attempts to forge a tight link between territory, sovereignty and/or ethnie. In this they are very close to the West, for that indeed was/is the project of the nation-states in Europe. Will the Hindu right succeed in its programme of linking territory, sovereignty and ethnie? I doubt it, for the simple reason that "Hindu" does not individuate anything, which does not, of course, mean that the attempt will have no consequences. On the other hand, the secularist narrative, which has been telling the story of our incomplete modernization or secularization, is also committed to the sovereignty project, except that in place of the ethnicization politics they propose a secularization politics. That the sovereignty project based on ethnicization is dangerous by itself does not validate the sovereignty project based on secularization. Do we have another political language in which to address or reformulate the problem? The truth is that we do not. All I have suggested is that such a language can only emerge when we actually begin the process of (re)describing ourselves.

Does it mean that we have to wait till that process is complete (whenever that is and whatever that may mean) or at least well on its way before we can address political questions? Although this is not an answer, it might, I think, help to think of the relationship between theory and politics in what I have said so far in the following way: theory is doing politics in (relatively) ideal circumstances; politics is doing theory in (again, relatively) non-ideal situations.

We are back to the question of valorizing the present. In the process of outlining that project, I hope I have persuaded you that to describe or theorize our present we have to undertake the construction of a metatheory of western theories, a description of the West, which initiates at the same time a politics of self-description, a narrative epistemology (to give the project a name) of our experience.

What I have called our apprenticeship has been an experience of detour; narrative epistemology initiates the project of retour or return. The narrative of that detour is at the same time a metatheory of western culture. The hope is that the narrative epistemological account will be experience-preserving because the success of the project depends on making our experience constitutive of it. The valorization of the present then is nothing other than the construction of a language – using the resources of theoretical, practical, practical-political reasoning that are at our disposal – which, unlike the existing social sciences, will be both knowledge-preserving and experience-preserving. Finally, a word or two about the possible bearing a project so conceived might have on "rethinking the Third-World". Earlier, comparative work undertaken by, say, Asian and African scholars took the form of comparing the results of either sociological or economic investigations (the problem of growth, the effect of structural adjustment programmes, ethnicity and class) to which comparison itself did not contribute much, and consequently, the results had no significance for one another. In contrast, the project I have outlined, even in the abstract form I have presented it, is *essentially* comparative. If the construction of a metatheory of western theories is a prelude or an inseparable part of theorizing our (Asian, African ... and, yes, European) own experience, the latter can

be enriched by learning from and making available to one another forms of knowledge in the

form of theories in the very process of their
construction.

References

Gopal, S. (1991) "Introduction" in S. Gopal
(ed.) *Anatomy of a Confrontation: The Babri:
Masjlid-Ranjanbhumi Issue*, p. 19. New Delhi:
Viking.

Rawls, John (1971) *A Theory of Justice*. Cambridge,
MA: Harvard University Press.

Rawls, John (1993) *Political Liberalism*. New York:
Columbia University Press.

46

Cosmological Deixis and Amerindian Perspectivism

Eduardo Viveiros de Castro

Introduction

This article deals with that aspect of Amerindian thought which has been called its "perspectival quality" (Århem 1993): the conception, common to many peoples of the continent, according to which the world is inhabited by different sorts of subjects or persons, human and non-human, which apprehend reality from distinct points of view. This idea cannot be reduced to our current concept of relativism (Lima 1995; 1996), which at first it seems to call to mind. In fact, it is at right angles, so to speak, to the opposition between relativism and universalism. Such resistance by Amerindian perspectivism to the terms of our epistemological debates casts suspicion on the robustness and transportability of the ontological partitions which they presuppose. In particular, as many anthropologists have already concluded (albeit for other reasons), the classic distinction between Nature and Culture cannot be used to describe domains internal to non-Western cosmologies without first undergoing a rigorous ethnographic critique.

Such a critique, in the present case, implies a redistribution of the predicates subsumed within the two paradigmatic sets that traditionally oppose one another under the headings of "Nature" and "Culture": universal and particular, objective and subjective, physical and social, fact and value, the given and the instituted, necessity and spontaneity, immanence and transcendence, body and mind, animality and humanity, among many more. Such an ethnographically-based reshuffling of our conceptual schemes leads me to suggest the expression, "multinaturalism", to designate one of the contrastive features of Amerindian thought in relation to Western "multiculturalist" cosmologies. Where the latter are founded on the mutual implication of the unity of nature and the plurality of cultures – the first guaranteed by the objective universality of body and substance, the second generated by the subjective particularity of spirit and meaning – the Amerindian conception would suppose a spiritual unity and a corporeal diversity. Here, culture or the subject would be the form of the universal, whilst nature or the object would be the form of the particular.

[...]

From *Journal of the Royal Anthropological Institute* 4(3) (1998), pp. 469–88. Copyright © 1998 by *Journal of the Royal Anthropological Institute*. Reprinted by permission of John Wiley & Sons UK.

Perspectivism

The initial stimulus for the present reflections were the numerous references in Amazonian ethnography to an indigenous theory according to which the way humans perceive animals and other subjectivities that inhabit the world – gods, spirits, the dead, inhabitants of other cosmic levels, meteorological phenomena, plants, occasionally even objects and artefacts – differs profoundly from the way in which these beings see humans and see themselves.

Typically, in normal conditions, humans see humans as humans, animals as animals and spirits (if they see them) as spirits; however animals (predators) and spirits see humans as animals (as prey) to the same extent that animals (as prey) see humans as spirits or as animals (predators). By the same token, animals and spirits see themselves as humans: they perceive themselves as (or become) anthropomorphic beings when they are in their own houses or villages and they experience their own habits and characteristics in the form of culture – they see their food as human food (jaguars see blood as manioc beer, vultures see the maggots in rotting meat as grilled fish, etc.), they see their bodily attributes (fur, feathers, claws, beaks etc.) as body decorations or cultural instruments, they see their social system as organized in the same way as human institutions are (with chiefs, shamans, ceremonies, exogamous moieties, etc.). This "to see as" refers literally to percepts and not analogically to concepts, although in some cases the emphasis is placed more on the categorical rather than on the sensory aspect of the phenomenon.

In sum, animals are people, or see themselves as persons. Such a notion is virtually always associated with the idea that the manifest form of each species is a mere envelop (a "clothing") which conceals an internal human form, usually only visible to the eyes of the particular species or to certain trans-specific beings such as shamans. This internal form is the "soul" or "spirit" of the animal: an intentionality or subjectivity formally identical to human consciousness, materializable, let us say, in a human bodily schema concealed behind an animal mask. At first sight then, we would have a distinction between an anthropomorphic essence of a spiritual type, common to animate beings, and a variable bodily appearance,

characteristic of each individual species but which rather than being a fixed attribute is instead a changeable and removable clothing. This notion of "clothing" is one of the privileged expressions of metamorphosis – spirits, the dead and shamans who assume animal form, beasts that turn into other beasts, humans that are inadvertently turned into animals – an omnipresent process in the "highly transformational world" (Rivière 1994: 256) proposed by Amazonian ontologies.[1]

[...]

Some general observations are necessary. Perspectivism does not usually involve all animal species (besides covering other beings); the emphasis seems to be on those species which perform a key symbolic and practical role such as the great predators and the principal species of prey for humans – one of the central dimensions, possibly even the fundamental dimension, of perspectival inversions refers to the relative and relational statuses of predator and prey (Århem 1993: 11–12; Vilaça 1992: 49–51). On the other hand, however, it is not always clear whether spirits or subjectivities are being attributed to each individual animal, and there are examples of cosmologies which deny consciousness to post-mythical animals (Overing 1985: 249 ff.; 1986: 245–6) or some other spiritual distinctiveness (Baer 1994: 89; Viveiros de Castro 1992a: 73–4). Nonetheless, as is well known, the notion of animal spirit "masters" ("mothers of the game animals", "masters of the white-lipped peccaries", etc.) is widespread throughout the continent. These spirit masters, clearly endowed with intentionality analogous to that of humans, function as hypostases of the animal species with which they are associated, thereby creating an intersubjective field for human–animal relations even where empirical animals are not spiritualized.

We must remember, above all, that if there is a virtually universal Amerindian notion, it is that of an original state of undifferentiation between humans and animals, described in mythology. Myths are filled with beings whose form, name and behaviour inextricably mix human and animal attributes in a common context of intercommunicability, identical to that which defines the present-day intra-human world. The differentiation between "culture" and "nature", which Lévi-Strauss showed to be the central theme of Amerindian mythology, is not a process of differentiating the human from the animal, as in our own evolutionist mythology. The original common condition of both humans and animals is not animality but rather humanity. The great mythical separation reveals not so much culture distinguishing itself from nature but rather nature distancing itself from culture: the myths tell how animals lost the qualities inherited or retained by humans (Brightman 1993: 40, 160; Lévi-Strauss 1985: 14, 190; Weiss 1972: 169–70). Humans are those who continue as they have always been: animals are ex-humans, not humans ex-animals. In sum, "the common point of reference for all beings of nature is not humans as a species but rather humanity as a condition" (Descola 1986: 120).

This is a distinction – between the human species and the human condition – which should be retained. It has an evident connexion with the idea of animal clothing hiding a common spiritual "essence" and with the issue of the general meaning of perspectivism. For the moment, we may simply note one of its main corollaries: the past humanity of animals is added to their present-day spirituality hidden by their visible form in order to produce that extended set of food restrictions or precautions which either declare inedible certain animals that were mythically co-substantial with humans, or demand their desubjectivization by shamanistic means before they can be consumed (neutralizing the spirit, transubstantiating the meat into plant food, semantically reducing it to other animals less proximate to humans), under the threat of illness, conceived of as a cannibal counter-predation undertaken by the spirit of the prey turned predator, in a lethal inversion of perspectives which transforms the human into animal.[2]

[…]

Animism

The reader will have noticed that my "perspectivism" is reminiscent of the notion of "animism" recently recuperated by Descola (1992 […]). Stating that all conceptualizations of non-humans always refer to the social domain, Descola distinguishes three modes of objectifying nature: totemism, where the differences between natural species are used as a model for social distinctions;

that is, where the relationship between nature and culture is metaphorical in character and marked by discontinuity (both within and between series); animism, where the "elementary categories structuring social life" organize the relations *between* humans and natural species, thus defining a social continuity between nature and culture, founded on the attribution of human dispositions and social characteristics to "natural beings" […] and naturalism, typical of Western cosmologies, which supposes an ontological duality between nature, the domain of necessity, and culture, the domain of spontaneity, areas separated by metonymic discontinuity. The "animic mode" is characteristic of societies in which animals are the "strategic focus of the objectification of nature and of its socialization" (1992: 115), as is the case amongst indigenous peoples of America, reigning supreme over those social morphologies lacking in elaborate internal segmentations. […]

Animism could be defined as an ontology which postulates the social character of relations between humans and non-humans: the space between nature and society is itself social. Naturalism is founded on the inverted axiom: relations between society and nature are themselves natural. Indeed, if in the animic mode the distinction "nature/culture" is internal to the social world, humans and animals being immersed in the same socio-cosmic medium (and in this sense "nature" is a part of an encompassing sociality), then in naturalist ontology, the distinction "nature/culture" is internal to nature (and in this sense, human society is one natural phenomenon amongst others). Animism has "society" as the unmarked pole, naturalism has "nature": these poles function, respectively and contrastively, as the universal dimension of each mode. Thus animism and naturalism are hierarchical and metonymical structures (this distinguishes them from totemism, which is based on a metaphoric correlation between equipollent opposites).

In Western naturalist ontology, the nature/society interface is natural: humans are organisms like the rest, body-objects in "ecological" interaction with other bodies and forces, all of them ruled by the necessary laws of biology and physics; "productive forces" harness, and thereby express, natural forces. Social relations, that is, contractual or instituted relations between subjects, can only exist internal to human society. But how alien to nature – this would be the problem of naturalism – are these relations? Given the universality of nature, the status of the human and social world is unstable and, as the history of Western thought shows, it perpetually oscillates between a naturalistic monism ("socio-biology" being one of its current avatars) and an ontological dualism of nature/culture ("culturalism" being its contemporary expression). The assertion of this latter dualism, for all that, only reinforces the final referential character of the notion of nature, by revealing itself to be the direct descendant of the opposition between Nature and Super*nature*. Culture is the modern name of Spirit – let us recall the distinction between *Naturwissenschaften* and *Geisteswissenschaften* – or at the least it is the name of the compromise between Nature and Grace. Of animism, we would be tempted to say that the instability is located in the opposite pole: there the problem is how to administer the mixture of humanity and animality constituting animals, and not, as is the case amongst ourselves, the combination of culture and nature which characterize humans; the point is to differentiate a "nature" out of the universal sociality.

However, can animism be defined as a projection of differences and qualities internal to the human world onto non-human worlds, as a "sociocentric" model in which categories and social relations are used to map the universe? This interpretation by analogy is explicit in some glosses on the theory: "if totemic systems model society after nature, then animic systems model nature after society" (Århem 1996: 185). The problem here, obviously, is to avoid any undesirable proximity with the traditional sense of "animism", or with the reduction of "primitive classifications" to emanations of social morphology; but equally the problem is to go beyond other classical characterizations of the relation between society and nature such as Radcliffe-Brown's.[3]

Ingold (1991; 1996) showed how schemes of analogical projection or social modelling of nature escape naturalist reductionism only to fall into a nature/culture dualism which by distinguishing "really natural" nature from "culturally constructed" nature reveals itself to be a typical cosmological antinomy faced with infinite regression. The notion of model or metaphor supposes a previous distinction between a domain wherein social relations are constitutive and literal and another where they are representational and metaphorical. Animism, interpreted as human sociality projected onto the non-human world, would be nothing but the metaphor of a metonymy.

Amongst the questions remaining to be resolved, therefore, is that of knowing whether animism can be described as a figurative use of categories pertaining to the human-social domain to conceptualize the domain of non-humans and their relations with the former. Another question: if animism depends on the attribution of human cognitive and sensory faculties to animals, and the same form of subjectivity, then what in the end is the difference between humans and animals? If animals are people, then why do they not see us as people? Why, to be precise, the perspectivism? Finally, if animism is a way of objectifying nature in which the dualism of nature/culture does not hold, then what is to be done with the abundant indications regarding the centrality of this opposition to South American cosmologies? Are we dealing with just another "totemic illusion", if not with an ingenuous projection of our Western dualism?

Ethnocentrism

In a well-known essay, Lévi-Strauss observed that for "savages" humanity ceases at the boundary of the group, a notion which is exemplified by the widespread auto-ethnonym meaning "real humans", which, in turn, implies a definition of strangers as somehow pertaining to the domain of the extra-human. Therefore, ethnocentrism would not be the privilege of the West but a natural ideological attitude, inherent to human collective life. Lévi-Strauss illustrates the universal reciprocity of this attitude with an anecdote:

> In the Greater Antilles, some years after the discovery of America, whilst the Spanish were dispatching inquisitional commissions to investigate whether the natives had a soul or not, these very natives were busy drowning the white people they had captured in order to find out, after lengthy observation, whether or not the corpses were subject to putrefaction. (1973: 384)

The general point of this parable [...] is quite simple: the Indians, like the European invaders, considered that only the group to which they belong incarnates humanity; strangers are on the other side of the border which separates humans from animals and spirits, culture from nature and supernature. As matrix and condition for the existence of ethnocentrism, the nature/culture opposition appears to be a universal of social apperception.

At the time when Lévi-Strauss was writing these lines, the strategy of vindicating the full humanity of savages was to demonstrate that they made the same distinctions as we do: the proof that they were true humans is that they considered that they alone were the true humans. Like us, they distinguished culture from nature and they too believed that *Naturvölker* are always the others. The universality of the cultural distinction between Nature and Culture bore witness to the universality of culture as human nature. In sum, the answer to the question of the Spanish investigators (which can be read as a sixteenth-century version of the "problem of other minds") was positive: savages do have souls.

Now, everything has changed. The savages are no longer ethnocentric but rather cosmocentric; instead of having to prove that they are humans because they distinguish themselves from animals, we now have to recognize how *inhuman we* are for opposing humans to animals in a way they never did: for them nature and culture are part of the same sociocosmic field. Not only would Amerindians put a wide berth between themselves and the Great Cartesian Divide which separated humanity from animality, but their views anticipate the fundamental lessons of ecology which we are only now in a position to assimilate (Reichel-Dolmatoff 1976). Before, the Indians' refusal to concede predicates of humanity to other men was of note; now we stress that they extend such predicates far beyond the frontiers of their own species in a demonstration of "ecosophic" knowledge (Århem 1993) which we should emulate in as far as the limits of our objectivism permit. Formerly, it had been necessary to combat the assimilation of the savage mind to narcissistic animism, the infantile stage of naturalism, showing that totemism affirmed the cognitive distinction between culture and nature; now, neo-animism reveals itself as the recognition of the universal admixture of subjects and objects, humans and non-humans against modern

hubris, the primitive and post-modern "hybrids", to borrow a term from Latour (1991).

Two antinomies then, which are, in fact, only one: either Amerindians are ethnocentrically "stingy" in the extension of their concept of humanity and they "totemically" oppose nature and culture; or they are cosmocentric and "animic" and do not profess to such a distinction, being models of relativist tolerance, postulating a multiplicity of points of view on the world.

I believe that the solution to these antinomies[4] lies not in favouring one branch over the other, sustaining, for example, the argument that the most recent characterization of American attitudes is the correct one and relegating the other to the outer darkness of pre-post-modernity. Rather, the point is to show that the "thesis" as well as the "antithesis" are true (both correspond to solid ethnographic intuitions), but that they apprehend the same phenomena from different angles; and also it is to show that both are false in that they refer to a substantivist conceptualization of the categories of Nature and Culture (whether it be to affirm or negate them) which is not applicable to Amerindian cosmologies.

The first point to be considered is that the Amerindian words which are usually translated as "human being" and which figure in those supposedly ethnocentric self-designations do not denote humanity as a natural species. They refer rather to the social condition of personhood, and they function (pragmatically when not syntactically) less as nouns than as pronouns. They indicate the position of the subject; they are enunciative markers, not names. Far from manifesting a semantic shrinking of a common name to a proper name (taking "people" to be the name of the tribe), these words move in the opposite direction, going from substantive to perspective (using "people" as a collective pronoun "we people/us"). For this very reason, indigenous categories of identity have that enormous contextual variability of scope that characterizes pronouns, marking contrastively Ego's immediate kin, his/her local group, all humans, or even all beings endowed with subjectivity: their coagulation as "eth-nonyms" seems largely to be an artefact of interactions with ethnographers. Nor is it by chance that the majority of Amerindian ethnonyms which enter the literature are not self-designations, but rather names (frequently pejorative) conferred by other groups:

ethnonymic objectivation is primordially applied to others, not to the ones in the position of subject. Ethnonyms are names of third parties; they belong to the category of "*they*" not to the category of "*we*". This, by the way, is consistent with a widespread avoidance of self-reference on the level of personal onomastics: names are not spoken by the bearers nor in their presence; to name is to externalize, to separate (from) the subject.

Thus self-references such as "people" mean "person", not "member of the human species", and they are personal pronouns registering the point of view of the subject talking, not proper names. To say, then, that animals and spirits are people is to say that they are persons, and to attribute to non-humans the capacities of conscious intentionality and agency which define the position of the subject. Such capacities are objectified as the soul or spirit with which these non-humans are endowed. Whatever possesses a soul is a subject, and whatever has a soul is capable of having a point of view. Amerindian souls, be they human or animal, are thus indexical categories, cosmological deictics whose analysis calls not so much for an animist psychology or substantialist ontology as for a theory of the sign or a perspectival pragmatics (Taylor 1993a, 1993b; Viveiros de Castro 1992b).

Thus, every being to whom a point of view is attributed would be a subject; or better, wherever there is a point of view there is a subject position. Whilst our constructionist epistemology can be summed up in the Saussurean formula: *the point of view creates the object* – the subject being the original, fixed condition whence the point of view emanates – Amerindian ontological perspectivism proceeds along the lines that the *point of view creates the subject*; whatever is activated or "agented" by the point of view will be a subject.[5] This is why terms such as *wari'* (Vilaça 1992), *dene* (McDonnell 1984) or *masa* (Århem 1993) mean "people", but they can be used for – and therefore used by – very different classes of beings: used by humans they denote human beings; but used by peccaries, howler monkeys or beavers they self-refer to peccaries, howler monkeys or beavers.

As it happens, however, these non-humans placed in the subject perspective do not merely "call" themselves "people"; they see themselves anatomically and culturally as *humans*. The symbolic spiritualization of animals would imply their imaginary hominization and culturalization; thus the anthropomorphic-anthropocentric character of indigenous thought would seem to be unquestionable. However, I believe that something totally different is at issue. Any being which vicariously occupies the point of view of reference, being in the position of subject, sees itself as a member of the human species. The human bodily form and human culture – the schemata of perception and action "embodied" in specific dispositions – are deictics of the same type as the self-designations discussed above. They are reflexive or apperceptive schematisms by which all subjects apprehend themselves, and not literal and constitutive human predicates projected metaphorically (i.e. improperly) onto non-humans. Such deictic "attributes" are immanent in the viewpoint, and move with it (Brightman 1993: 47). Human beings – naturally – enjoy the same prerogative and therefore see themselves as such.[6] It is not that animals are subjects because they are humans in disguise, but rather that they are human because they are potential subjects. This is to say *Culture is the Subject's nature*; it is the form in which every subject experiences its own nature. Animism is not a projection of substantive human *qualities* cast onto animals, but rather expresses the logical equivalence of the reflexive *relations* that humans and animals each have to themselves: salmon are to (see) salmon as humans are to (see) humans, namely, (as) human.[7] If, as we have observed, the common condition of humans and animals is humanity not animality, this is because "humanity" is the name for the general form taken by the Subject.

Multinaturalism

With this we may have discarded analogical anthro-pocentrism, but only apparently to adopt relativism.[8] For would this cosmology of multiple viewpoints not imply that "every perspective is equally valid and true" and that "a correct and true representation of the world does not exist" (Århem 1993: 124)?

But this is exactly the question: is the Amerindian perspectivist theory in fact asserting a multiplicity of representations of the same world? It is sufficient to consider ethnographic evidence to perceive that the opposite applies: all beings see ("represent") the world in the same way – what changes is the world that they see. Animals impose the same categories and values on reality as humans do: their worlds, like ours, revolve around hunting and fishing, cooking and fermented drinks, cross-cousins and war, initiation rituals, shamans, chiefs, spirits. "Everybody is involved in fishing and hunting; everybody is involved in feasts, social hierarchy, chiefs, war, and disease, all the way up and down" (Guédon 1984: 142). If the moon, snakes and jaguars see humans as tapirs or white-lipped preccaries (Baer 1994: 224), it is because they, like us, eat tapirs and peccaries, people's food. It could only be this way, since, being people in their own sphere, non-humans see things *as* "people" do. But the things *that* they see are different: what to us is blood, is maize beer to the jaguar; what to the souls of the dead is a rotting corpse, to us is soaking manioc; what we see as a muddy waterhole, the tapirs see as a great ceremonial house.

(Multi)cultural relativism supposes a diversity of subjective and partial representations, each striving to grasp an external and unified nature, which remains perfectly indifferent to those representations. Amerindian thought proposes the opposite: a representational or phenomenological unity which is purely pronominal or deictic, indifferently applied to a radically objective diversity. One single "culture", multiple "natures" – perspectivism is multinaturalist, for a perspective is not a representation.

A perspective is not a representation because representations are a property of the mind or spirit, whereas the point of view is located in the body.[9] The ability to adopt a point of view is undoubtedly a power of the soul, and non-humans are subjects in so far as they have (or are) spirit; but the differences between viewpoints (and a viewpoint is nothing if not a difference) lies not in the soul. Since the soul is formally identical in all species, it can only see the same things everywhere – the difference is given in the specificity of bodies. This permits answers to be found for our questions: if non-humans are persons and have souls, then what distinguishes them from humans? And why, being people, do they not see us as people?

Animals see in the *same* way as we do *different* things because their bodies are different

from ours. I am not referring to physiological differences – as far as that is concerned, Amerindians recognize a basic uniformity of bodies – but rather to affects, dispositions or capacities which render the body of every species unique: what it eats, how it communicates, where it lives, whether it is gregarious or solitary, and so forth. The visible shape of the body is a powerful sign of these differences in affect, although it can be deceptive since a human appearance could, for example, be concealing a jaguar-affect. Thus, what I call "body" is not a synonym for distinctive substance or fixed shape; it is an assemblage of affects or ways of being that constitute a *habitus*. Between the formal subjectivity of souls and the substantial materiality of organisms there is an intermediate plane which is occupied by the body as a bundle of affects and capacities and which is the origin of perspectives.

The difference between bodies, however, is only apprehendable from an exterior viewpoint, by an other, since, for itself, every type of being has the same form (the generic form of a human being): bodies are the way in which alterity is apprehended as such. In normal conditions we do not see animals as people, and vice-versa, because our respective bodies (and the perspectives which they allow) are different. Thus, if "culture" is a reflexive perspective of the subject, objectified through the concept of soul, it can be said that "nature" is the viewpoint which the subject takes of other body-affects; if Culture is the Subject's nature, then *Nature is the form of the Other as body*, that is, as the object for a subject. Culture takes the self-referential form of the pronoun "I"; nature is the form of the non-person or the object, indicated by the impersonal pronoun "it" (Benveniste 1966a: 256).

If, in the eyes of Amerindians, the body makes the difference, then it is easily understood why, in the anecdote told by Lévi-Strauss, the methods of investigation into the humanity of the other, employed by the Spanish and the inhabitants of the Antilles, showed such asymmetry. For the Europeans, the issue was to decide whether the others possessed a soul; for the Indians, the aim was to find out what kind of body the others had. For the Europeans the great diacritic, the marker of difference in perspective, is the soul (are Indians humans or animals?); for the Indians it is the body (are Europeans humans or spirits?).

The Europeans never doubted that the Indians had bodies; the Indians never doubted that the Europeans had souls (animals and spirits have them too). What the Indians wanted to know was whether the bodies of those "souls" were capable of the same affects as their own – whether they had the bodies of humans or the bodies of spirits, non-putrescible and protean. In sum: European ethno-centrism consisted in doubting whether other bodies have the same souls as they themselves; Amerindian ethnocentrism in doubting whether other souls had the same bodies.

As Ingold has stressed (1994; 1996), the status of humans in Western thought is essentially ambiguous: on the one hand, humankind is an animal species amongst others, and animality is a domain that includes humans; on the other hand, humanity is a moral condition which excludes animals. These two statuses co-exist in the problematic and disjunctive notion of "human nature". In other words, our cosmology postulates a physical continuity and a metaphysical discontinuity between humans and animals, the former making of man an object for the natural sciences, the latter an object for the "humanities". Spirit or mind is our great differentiator: it raises us above animals and matter in general, it distinguishes cultures, it makes each person unique before his or her fellow beings. The body, in contrast, is the major integrator: it connects us to the rest of the living, united by a universal substrate (DNA, carbon chemistry) which, in turn, links up with the ultimate nature of all material bodies.[10] In contrast to this, Amerindians postulate a metaphysical continuity and a physical discontinuity between the beings of the cosmos, the former resulting in animism, the latter in perspectivism: the spirit or soul (here not an immaterial substance but rather a reflexive form) integrates, while the body (not a material organism but a system of active affects) differentiates.

The Spirit's Many Bodies

The idea that the body appears to be the great differentiator in Amazonian cosmologies – that is, as that which unites beings of the same type, to the extent that it differentiates them from others – allows us to reconsider some of the classic questions of the ethnology of the region in a new light.

Thus, the now old theme of the importance of corporeality in Amazonian societies (a theme that much predates the current "embodiment" craze [...] acquires firmer foundations. For example, it becomes possible to gain a better understanding of why the categories of identity – be they personal, social or cosmological – are so frequently expressed through bodily idioms, particularly through food practices and body decoration. The universal symbolic importance of food and cooking regimes in Amazonia – from the mythological "raw and the cooked" of Lévi-Strauss, to the Piro idea that what literally (i.e. naturally) makes them different from white people is "real food" (Gow 1991); from the food avoidances which define "groups of substance" in Central Brazil (Seeger 1980) to the basic classification of beings according to their eating habits (Baer 1994: 88); from the ontological productivity of commensality, similarity of diet and relative condition of prey-object and predator-subject (Vilaça 1992) to the omnipresence of cannibalism as the "predicative" horizon of all relations with the other, be they matrimonial, alimentary or bellicose (Viveiros de Castro 1993) – this universality demonstrates that the set of habits and processes that constitute bodies is precisely the location from which identity and difference emerge.

The same can be said of the intense semiotic use of the body in the definition of personal identities and in the circulation of social values (Mentore 1993; Turner 1995). The connexion between this overdetermination of the body (particularly of its visible surface) and the restricted recourse in the Amazonian socius to objects capable of supporting relations – that is, a situation wherein social exchange is not mediated by material objectifications such as those characteristic of gift and commodity economies – has been shrewdly pinpointed by Turner, who has shown how the human body therefore must appear as the prototypical social object. However, the Amerindian emphasis on the social construction of the body cannot be taken as the culturalization of a natural substrate but rather as the production of a distinctly human body, meaning *naturally* human. Such a process seems to be expressing not so much a wish to "deanimalize" the body through its cultural marking, but rather to particularize a body still too generic, differentiating it from the bodies of other human collectivities as well as from those of other species. The body, as the site of differentiating perspective, must be differentiated to the highest degree in order completely to express it.

The human body can be seen as the locus of the confrontation between humanity and animality, but not because it is essentially animal by nature and needs to be veiled and controlled by culture (Rivière 1994). The body is the subject's fundamental expressive instrument and at the same time the object *par excellence*, that which is presented to the sight of the other. It is no coincidence, then, that the maximum social objectification of bodies, their maximal particularization expressed in decoration and ritual exhibition is at the same time the moment of maximum animalization (Goldman 1975: 178; Turner 1991; 1995), when bodies are covered by feathers, colours, designs, masks and other animal prostheses. Man ritually clothed as an animal is the counterpart to the animal supernaturally naked. The former, transformed into an animal, reveals to himself the "natural" distinctiveness of his body; the latter, free of its exterior form and revealing itself as human, shows the "supernatural" similarity of spirit. The model of spirit is the human spirit, but the model of body is the bodies of animals; and if from the point of view of the subject culture takes the generic form of "I" and nature of "it/they", then the objectification of the subject to itself demands a singularization of bodies – which naturalizes culture, i.e. embodies it – whilst the subjectification of the object implies communication at the level of spirit – which culturalizes nature, i.e. supernaturalizes it. Put in these terms, the Amerindian distinction of Nature/Culture, before it is dissolved in the name of a common animic human–animal sociality, must be reread in the light of somatic perspectivism.

It is important to note that these Amerindian bodies are not thought of as given but rather as made. Therefore, an emphasis on the methods for the continuous fabrication of the body (Viveiros de Castro 1979); a notion of kinship as a process of active assimilation of individuals (Gow 1989; 1991) through the sharing of bodily substances, sexual and alimentary – and not as a passive inheritance of some substantial essence; the theory of memory which inscribes it in the flesh (Viveiros de Castro 1992a: 201–7), and more

generally the theory which situates knowledge in the body (Kensinger 1995: ch. 22; McCallum 1996). The Amerindian *Bildung* happens in the body more than in the spirit: there is no "spiritual" change which is not a bodily transformation, a redefinition of its affects and capacities. Furthermore, while the distinction between body and soul is obviously pertinent to these cosmologies, it cannot be interpreted as an ontological discontinuity (Townsley 1993: 454–5). As bundles of affects and sites of perspective, rather than material organisms, bodies "are" souls, just, incidentally, as souls and spirits "are" bodies. The dual (or plural) conception of the human soul, widespread in indigenous Amazonia, distinguishes between the soul (or souls) of the body, reified register of an individual's history, site of memory and affect, and a "true soul", pure, formal subjective singularity, the abstract mark of a person (e.g. McCallum 1996; Viveiros de Castro 1992a: 201–14). On the other hand, the souls of the dead and the spirits which inhabit the universe are not immaterial entities, but equally types of bodies, endowed with properties – affects – *sui generis*. Indeed, body and soul, just like nature and culture, do not correspond to substantives, self-subsistent entities or ontological provinces, but rather to pronouns or phenomenological perspectives.

The performative rather than given character of the body, a conception that requires it to differentiate itself "culturally" in order for it to be "naturally" different, has an obvious connexion with inter-specific metamorphosis, a possibility suggested by Amerindian cosmologies. We need not be surprised by a way of thinking which posits bodies as the great differentiators yet at the same time states their transformability. Our cosmology supposes a singular distinctiveness of minds, but not even for this reason does it declare communication (albeit solipsism is a constant problem) to be impossible, or deny the mental/spiritual transformations induced by processes such as education and religious conversion; in truth, it is precisely because the spiritual is the locus of difference that conversion becomes necessary (the Europeans wanted to know whether Indians had souls in order to modify them). Bodily metamorphosis is the Amerindian counterpart to the European theme of spiritual conversion.[11] In the same way, if solipsism is the phantom that continuously threatens our cosmology – raising the fear of not recognizing ourselves in our "own kind" because they are not like us, given the potentially absolute singularity of minds – then the possibility of metamorphosis expresses the opposite fear, of no longer being able to differentiate between the human and the animal, and, in particular, the fear of seeing the human who lurks within the body of the animal one eats[12] – hence the importance of food prohibitions and precautions linked to the spiritual potency of animals, mentioned above. The phantom of cannibalism is the Amerindian equivalent to the problem of solipsism: if the latter derives from the uncertainty as to whether the natural similarity of bodies guarantees a real community of spirit, then the former suspects that the similarity of souls might prevail over the real differences of body and that all animals that are eaten might, despite the shamanistic efforts to de-subjectivize them, remain human. This, of course, does not prevent us having amongst ourselves more or less radical solipsists, such as the relativists, nor that various Amerindian societies be purposefully and more or less literally cannibalistic.[13]

The notion of metamorphosis is directly linked to the doctrine of animal "clothing", to which I have referred. How are we to reconcile the idea that the body is the site of differentiating perspectives with the theme of the "appearance" and "essence" which is always evoked to interpret animism and perspectivism (Århem 1993: 122; Descola 1986: 120; Hugh-Jones 1996; Rivière 1994)? Here seems to me to lie an important mistake, which is that of taking bodily "appearance" to be inert and false, whereas spiritual "essence" is active and real (see the definitive observations of Goldman 1975: 63). I argue that nothing could be further from the Indians' minds when they speak of bodies in terms of "clothing". It is not so much that the body is a clothing but rather that clothing is a body. We are dealing with societies which inscribe efficacious meanings onto the skin, and which use animal masks (or at least know their principle) endowed with the power metaphysically to transform the identities of those who wear them, if used in the appropriate ritual context. To put on mask-clothing is not so much to conceal a human essence beneath an animal appearance, but rather to activate the powers of a different body.[14] The animal clothes that shamans use to travel the cosmos are not fantasies but

instruments: they are akin to diving equipment, or space suits, and not to carnival masks. The intention when donning a wet suit is to be able to function like a fish, to breathe underwater, not to conceal oneself under a strange covering. In the same way, the "clothing" which, amongst animals, covers an internal "essence" of a human type, is not a mere disguise but their distinctive equipment, endowed with the affects and capacities which define each animal.[15] It is true that appearances can be deceptive (Hallowell 1960; Rivière 1994); but my impression is that in Amerindian narratives which take as a theme animal "clothing" the interest lies more in what these clothes do rather than what they hide. Besides this, between a being and its appearance is its body, which is more than just that – and the very same narratives relate how appearances are always "unmasked" by bodily behaviour which is inconsistent with them. In short: there is no doubt that bodies are discardable and exchangeable and that "behind" them lie subjectivities which are formally identical to humans. But the idea is not similar to our opposition between appearance and essence; it merely manifests the objective permutability of bodies which is based in the subjective equivalence of souls.

Another classic theme in South American ethnology which could be interpreted within this framework is that of the sociological discontinuity between the living and the dead (Carneiro da Cunha 1978). The fundamental distinction between the living and the dead is made by the body and precisely not by the spirit; death is a bodily catastrophe which prevails as differentiator over the common "animation" of the living and the dead. Amerindian cosmologies dedicate equal or greater interest to the way in which the dead see reality as they do to the vision of animals, and as is the case for the latter, they underline the radical differences vis-à-vis the world of the living. To be precise, being definitively separated from their bodies, the dead are not human. As spirits defined by their disjunction from a human body, the dead are logically attracted to the bodies of animals; this is why to die is to transform into an animal (Pollock 1985: 95; Schwartzman 1988: 268; Turner 1995: 152; Vilaça 1992: 247–55), as it is to transform into other figures of bodily alterity, such as affines and enemies. In this manner, if animism affirms a subjective and social continuity between humans and animals, its somatic complement, perspectivism, establishes an objective discontinuity, equally social, between live humans and dead humans.[16]

Having examined the differentiating component of Amerindian perspectivism, it remains for me to attribute a cosmological "function" to the transpecific unity of the spirit. This is the point at which, I believe, a relational definition could be given for a category, Supernature, which nowadays has fallen into disrepute (actually, ever since Durkheim), but whose pertinence seems to me to be unquestionable. Apart from its use in labelling cosmographic domains of a "hyper-uranian" type, or in defining a third type of intentional beings occurring in indigenous cosmologies, which are neither human nor animal (I refer to "spirits"), the notion of supernature may serve to designate a specific relational context and particular phenomenological quality, which is as distinct from the intersubjective relations that define the social world as from the "inter-objective" relations with the bodies of animals.

Following the analogy with the pronominal set (Benveniste 1966a; 1966b) we can see that between the reflexive "I" of culture (the generator of the concepts of soul or spirit) and the impersonal "it" of nature (definer of the relation with somatic alterity), there is a position missing, the "you", the *second person*, or the other taken as other subject, whose point of view is the latent echo of that of the "I". I believe that this concept can aid in determining the supernatural context. An abnormal context wherein a subject is captured by another cosmologically dominant point of view, wherein he is the "you" of a non-human perspective, *Supernature is the form of the Other as Subject*, implying an objectification of the human I as a "you" for this Other. The typical "supernatural" situation in an Amerindian world is the meeting in the forest between a man –

always on his own – and a being which is seen at first merely as an animal or a person, then reveals itself as a spirit or a dead person and speaks to the man (the dynamics of this communication are well analysed by Taylor 1993a).[17] These encounters can be lethal for the interlocutor who, overpowered by the non-human subjectivity, passes over to its side, transforming himself into a being of the same species as the speaker: dead, spirit or animal. He who responds to a "you" spoken by a non-human accepts the condition of being its "second person", and when assuming in his turn the position of "I" does so already as a non-human. The canonical form of these supernatural encounters, then, consists in suddenly finding out that the other is "human", that is, that *it* is the human, which automatically dehumanizes and alienates the interlocutor and transforms him into a prey object, that is, an animal. Only shamans, multi-natural beings by definition and office, are always capable of transiting the various perspectives, calling and being called "you" by the animal subjectivities and spirits without losing their condition as human subjects.[18]

I would conclude by observing that Amerindian perspectivism has a vanishing point, as it were, where the differences between points of view are at the same time annulled and exacerbated: myth, which thus takes on the character of an absolute discourse. In myth, every species of being appears to others as it appears to itself (as human), while acting as if already showing its distinctive and definitive nature (as animal, plant or spirit). In a certain sense, all the beings which people mythology are shamans, which indeed is explicitly affirmed by some Amazonian cultures (Guss 1989: 52). Myth speaks of a state of being where bodies and names, souls and affects, the I and the Other interpenetrate, submerged in the same pre-subjective and pre-objective milieu – a milieu whose end is precisely what the mythology sets out to tell.

Notes

1 This notion of the body as a "clothing" can be found amongst the Makuna (Århem 1993), the Yagua (Chaumeil 1983: 125–7), the Piro (Gow, pers. comm.), the Trio (Rivière 1994) the Upper Xingu societies (Gregor 1977: 322). The notion is very likely pan-American, having considerable symbolic yield for example in North-west Coast cosmologies (see Goldman 1975 and Boelscher 1989), if not of much wider distribution, a question I cannot consider here.

2 See Århem 1993; Crocker 1985; Hugh-Jones 1996; Overing 1985; 1986; Vilaça 1992.

3 See Radcliffe-Brown 1952: 130–1, who, amongst other interesting arguments, distinguishes *processes of personification* of species and natural phenomena (which "permits nature to be thought of as if it were a society of persons, and so makes of it a social or moral order"), like those found amongst the Eskimos and Andaman Islanders, from *systems of classification* of natural species, like those found in Australia and which compose a "system of social solidarities" between man and nature – this obviously calls to mind Descola's distinction of animism/totemism as well as the contrast of *manido/totem* explored by Lévi-Strauss.

4 The uncomfortable tension inherent in such antinomies can be gauged in Howell's article (1996) on Chewong cosmology, where the Chewong are described as being both "relativist" and "anthropocentric" – a double mischaracterization, I believe.

5 "Such is the foundation of perspectivism. It does not express a dependency on a predefined subject; on the contrary, whatever accedes to the point of view will be subject…" (Deleuze 1988: 27).

6 "Human beings see themselves as such; the Moon, the snakes, the jaguars and the Mother of Smallpox, however, see them as tapirs or peccaries, which they kill" (Baer 1994: 224).

7 If salmon look to salmon as humans to humans – and this is "animism" – salmon do not look human to humans (they look like salmon), and neither do humans to salmon (they look like spirits, or maybe bears; see Guédon 1984: 141) – and this is "perspectivism". Ultimately, then, animism and perspectivism may have a deeper relationship to totemism than Descola's model allows for.

8 The attribution of human-like consciousness and intentionality (to say nothing of human bodily form and cultural habits) to non-human beings has been indifferently denominated "anthropocentrism" or "anthropomorphism". However, these two labels can be taken to denote radically opposed cosmological outlooks. Western popular evolutionism is very anthropocentric, but not particularly anthropomorphic. On the other hand, "primitive animism" may be characterized as anthropomorphic, but it is definitely not anthropocentric: if sundry other beings besides humans are "human", then we humans are not a special lot.

9 "The point of view is located in the body, says Leibniz" (Deleuze 1988: 16).

10 The counterproof of the singularity of the spirit in our cosmologies lies in the fact that when we try to universalize it, we are obliged – now that supernature is out of bounds – to identify it with the structure and function of the brain. The spirit can only be universal (natural) if it is (in) the body.

11 The rarity of unequivocal examples of spirit possession in the complex of Amerindian shamanism may derive from the prevalence of the theme of bodily metamorphosis. The classical problem of the religious conversion of Amerindians could also be further illuminated from this angle; indigenous conceptions of "acculturation" seem to focus more on the incorporation and embodiment of Western bodily practices (food, clothing, interethnic sex) rather than on spiritual assimilation (language, religion etc.).

12 The traditional problem of Western mainstream epistemology is how to connect and universalize (individual substances are given, relations have to be made); the problem in Amazonia is how to separate and particularize (relations are given, substances must be defined). See Brightman (1993: 177–85) and Fienup-Riordan (1994: 46–50) – both inspired by Wagner's (1977) ideas about the "innate" and the "constructed" – on this contrast.

13 In Amazonian cannibalism, what is intended is precisely the incorporation of the subject-aspect of the enemy (who is accordingly hyper-subjectivized, in very much the same way as that described by Harrison [1993: 121] for Melanesian warfare), not its desubjectivization as is the case with game animals. See Viveiros de Castro 1992*a*: 290–3; 1996: 98–102; Fausto 1997.

14 Peter Gow (pers. comm.) tells me that the Piro conceive of the act of putting on clothes as an animating of clothes. See also Goldman (1975: 183) on Kwakiutl masks: "Masks get 'excited' during Winter dances".

15 "'Clothing' in this sense does not mean merely a body covering but also refers to the skill and ability to carryout certain tasks" (Rivière in Koelewijn 1987: 306).

16 Religions based on the cult of the ancestors seem to postulate the inverse: spiritual identity goes beyond the bodily barrier of death, the living and the dead are similar in so far as they manifest the same spirit. We would accordingly have superhuman ancestrality and spiritual possession on one side, animalization of the dead and bodily metamorphosis on the other.

17 This would be the true significance of the "deceptiveness of appearances" theme: appearances deceive because one is never certain whose point of view is dominant, that is, which world is in force when one interacts with other beings. The

similarity of this idea to the familiar injunction not to "trust your senses" of Western epistemologies is, I fear, just another deceitful appearance.

18 As we have remarked, a good part of shamanistic work consists in de-subjectivizing animals, that is in transforming them into pure, natural bodies capable of being consumed without danger. In contrast, what defines spirits is precisely the fact that they are inedible; this transforms them into eaters *par excellence*, i.e. into anthropophagous

beings. In this way, it is common for the great predators to be the preferred forms in which spirits manifest themselves, and it is understandable that game animals should see humans as spirits, that spirits and predator animals should see us as game animals and that animals taken to be inedible should be assimilated to spirits (Viveiros de Castro 1978). The scales of edibility of indigenous Amazonia (Hugh-Jones 1996) should therefore include spirits at their negative pole.

References

Århem, K. 1993. Ecosofia makuna. In *La selva humanizada: ecologia alternativa en el trópico húmedo colombiano* (ed.) F. Correa. Bogotá: Instituto Colombiano de Antropologia, Fondo FEN Colombia, Fondo Editorial CEREC.

Århem, K. 1996. The cosmic food web: human–nature relatedness in the northwest Amazon. In *Nature and society: anthropological perspectives* (ed.) P. Descola and G. Pálsson. London: Routledge.

Baer, G. 1994. *Cosmología y shamanismo de los Matsiguenga*. Quito: Abya-Yala.

Benveniste, E. 1966a. La nature des pronoms. In *Problèmes de linguistique générale*. Paris: Gallimard.

Benveniste, E. 1996b. De la subjectivité dans le langage. In *Problèmes de linguistique générale*. Paris: Gallimard.

Boelscher, M. 1989. *The curtain within: Haida social and mythical discourse*. Vancouver: University of British Columbia Press.

Brightman, R. 1993. *Grateful prey: Rock Cree human–animal relationships*. Berkeley: University of California Press.

Carneiro da Cunha, M. M. 1978. *Os mortos e os outros*. São Paulo: Hucitec.

Chaumeil, J.-P. 1983. *Voir, savoir, pouvoir: le chamanisme chez les Yagua du nord-est péruvien*. Paris: Ecole des Hautes Etudes en Sciences Sociales.

Crocker, J. C. 1985. *Vital souls: Bororo cosmology, natural symbolism, and shamanism*. Tucson: University of Arizona Press.

Deleuze, G. 1988. *Le pli: Leibniz et le baroque*. Paris: Minuit.

Descola, P. 1986. *La nature domestique: symbolisme et praxis dans l'écologie des Achuar*. Paris: Maison des Sciences de l'Homme.

Descola, P. 1992. Societies of nature and the nature of society. In *Conceptualizing society* (ed.) A. Kuper. London: Routledge.

Fausto, C. 1997. A dialética da predação e familiarização entre os Parakanã da Amazônia oriental. Thesis, Museu Nacional, University of Rio de Janeiro.

Fienup-Riordan, A. 1994. *Boundaries and passages: rule and ritual in Yup'ik Eskimo oral tradition*. Norman: University of Oklahoma Press.

Goldman, I. 1975. *The mouth of heaven: an introduction to Kwakiutl religious thought*. New York: Wiley-Interscience.

Gow, P. 1989. The perverse child: desire in a native Amazonian subsistence economy. *Man (NS)* 24, 567–82.

Gow, P. 1991. *Of mixed blood: kinship and history in Peruvian Amazonia*. Oxford: Clarendon Press.

Gregor, T. 1977. *Mehinaku: the drama of daily life in a Brazilian Indian village*. Chicago: University of Chicago Press.

Guédon, M.-F. 1984. An introduction to the Tsimshian world view and its practitioners. In *The Tsimshian: images of the past, views for the present* (ed.) M. Seguin. Vancouver: University of British Columbia Press.

Guss, D. 1989. *To weave and to sing: art, symbol and narrative in the South American rain forest*. Berkeley: University of California Press.

Hallowell, A. I. 1960. Ojibwa ontology, behavior, and world view. In *Culture in history: essays in honor of Paul Radin* (ed.) S. Diamond. New York: Columbia University Press.

Harrison, S. 1993. *The mask of war: violence, ritual and the self in Melanesia*. Manchester: University Press.

Howell, S. 1996. Nature in culture or culture in nature? Chewong ideas of "humans" and other species. In *Nature and society: anthropological perspectives* (eds.) P. Descola and G. Pálsson. London: Routledge.

Hugh-Jones, S. 1996. Bonnes raisons ou mauvaise conscience? De l'ambivalence de certains Amazoniens envers la consommation de viande. *Terrain* 26, 123–48.

Ingold, T. 1991. Becoming persons: consciousness and sociality in human evolution. *Cultural Dynamics*. 4, 355–78.

Ingold T. 1994. Humanity and animality. In *Companion encyclopedia of anthropology: humanity, culture and social life* (ed.) T. Ingold. London: Routledge.

Ingold, T. 1996. Hunting and gathering as ways of perceiving the environment. In *Redefining nature: ecology, culture and domestication* (eds.) R. F. Ellen and K. Fukui. London: Berg.

Kensinger, K. 1995. *How real people ought to live: the Cashinahua of eastern Peru*. Prospect Heights: Waveland Press.

Koelewijn, C. with P. Rivière 1987. *Oral literature of the Trio Indians of Surinam*. Dordrecht: Foris.

Latour, B. 1991. *Noun n'avons jamais été modernes*. Paris: Editions La Découverte.

Lévi-Strauss, C. 1973 [1952]. Race et histoire. In his *Anthropologie structurale deux*. Paris: Plon.

Lévi-Strauss, C. 1985. *La potière jalouse*. Paris: Plon.

Lima, T. S. 1995. A parte do cauim: etnografia juruna. Thesis, Museu Nacional, University of Rio de Janeiro.

Lima, T. S. 1996. O dois e seu múltiplo: reflexões sobre o per-spectivismo em uma cosmologia tupi. *Mana* 2:2, 21–47.

McCallum, C. 1996. The body that knows: from Cashinahua epistemology to a medical anthropology of lowland South America. *Medical. Anthropology Quarterly* 10:3, 1–26.

McDonnell, R. 1984. Symbolic orientations and systematic turmoil: centering on the Kaska symbol of *dene*. *Canadian Journal of Anthropology* 4, 39–56.

Mentore, G. 1993. Tempering the social self: body adornment, vital substance, and knowledge among the Wai-wai. *Journal of Archaeology and Anthropology* 9, 22–34.

Overing, J. 1985. There is no end of evil: the guilty innocents and their fallible god. In *The anthropology of evil* (ed.) D. Parkin. London: Basil Blackwell.

Overing, J. 1986. Images of cannibalism, death and domination in a "non-violent" society. *Journal de Société des Americanistes* 72, 133–56.

Pollock, D. 1985. Personhood and illness among the Culina of western Brazil. Thesis, University of Rochester.

Radcliffe-Brown, A.R. 1952 [1929]. The sociological theory of totemism. In *Structure and function in primitive society*. London: Routledge & Kegan Paul.

Reichel-Dolmatoff, G. 1976. Cosmology as ecological analysis: a view from the rain forest. *Man (NS)* 12, 307–18.

Rivière, P. 1994. WYSINWYG in Amazonia. *JASO* 25, 255–62.

Schwartzman, S. 1988. The Panara of the Xingu National park. Thesis, University of Chicago.

Seeger, A. 1980. Corporação e corporalidade: ideologia de concepção e descendência. In his *Os índios e nós*. Rio de Janeiro: Campus.

Taylor, A.-C. 1993a. Des fantômes stupéfiants: langage et croyance dans la pensée achuar. *L'Homme* 126–8, 33/2–4, 429–47.

Taylor, A.-C. 1993b. Remembering to forget: identity, mourning and memory among the Jivaro. *Man (NS)* 28, 653–78.

Townsley, G. 1993. Song paths: the ways and means of Yaminahua shamanic knowledge. *L'Homme* 126–8, 33:2–4, 449–68.

Turner, T. 1991. "We are parrots, twins are birds": play of tropes as operational structure. In *Beyond metaphor: the theory of tropes in anthropology* (ed.) J. Fernandez. Stanford: University Press.

Turner, T. 1995. Social body and embodied subject: bodiliness, subjectivity, and sociality among the Kayapó. *Cultural. Anthropology* 10, 143–70.

Vilaça, A. 1992. *Comendo comogente: formas do canibalismo Wari" (Pakaa-Nova)*. Rio de Janeiro: Editora da UFRJ.

Viveiros de Castro, E. 1978. Alguns aspectos do pensamento yawalpíti (Alto Xingu): classificações e transformações. *Boletim do Museu nacional* 26, 1–41.

Viveiros de Castro, E. 1979. A fabricação do corpo na sociedade xinguana. *Boletim do Museu nacional* 32, 2–19.

Viveiros de Castro, E. 1992a. *From the enemy's point of view: humanity and divinity in an Amazonian society*. Chicago: University of Chicago Press.

Viveiros de Castro, E. 1992b. Apresentação to A. Vilaça. In *Comendo como gente: formas do canibalismo Wari'*. Rio de Janeiro: Editoral da UFRJ.

Viveiros de Castro, E. 1993. Alguns aspectos da afinidade no dravidianato amazônico. In *Amazônia: etnologia e história indígena* (eds.) E. Viveiros de Castro and M. Carneiro da Cunha. São Paulo: Núcleo de História Indígena e do Indigenismo (USP/FAPESP).

Vivieros de Castro, E. 1996. Le meurtrier et son double chez les Araweté: un exemple de fusion rituelle. *Systèmes de Pensée en Afrique Noire* 14, 77–104.

Wagner, R. 1977. Scientific and indigenous Papuan conceptualizations of the innate: a semiotic critique of the ecological perspective. In *Subsistence and survival: rural ecology in the Pacific* (eds.) T. Bayliss-Smith and R. G. Feachem. London: Academic Press.

Weiss, G. 1972. Campa cosmology. *Ethnology* 11, 157–72.

SECTION 14

(Re)defining Objects of Inquiry

47

What Was Life? Answers from Three Limit Biologies

Stefan Helmreich

What was life? No one knew.
            Thomas Mann, *The Magic Mountain*

What is life? A gathering consensus in anthropology, science studies, and philosophy of biology suggests that the theoretical object of biology, "life," is today in transformation, if not dissolution. Proliferating reproductive technologies, along with genomic reshufflings of biomatter in such practices as cloning, have unwound the facts of life. Biotechnology, biodiversity, bioprospecting, biosecurity, biotransfer, and molecularized biopolitics draw novel lines of property and protection around organisms and their elements. From cultural theorists and historians of science we learn that life itself, consolidated as the object of biology around 1800, has morphed as material components of living things – cells and genes – that are rearranged and dispersed, and frozen, amplified, and exchanged within and across laboratories. Writers in philosophy, rhetoric, and cultural studies, meanwhile, claim that, as life has become the target of digital simulation and bioinformatic representation, it has become virtual, mediated, and multiple.

All these transformations destabilize any naturalistic or ontological foundation that life forms – embodied bits of vitality like organisms and species – might provide for forms of life – social, symbolic, and pragmatic ways of thinking and acting that organize human communities. In the language of my own professional guild, anthropology, these changes unsettle the nature so often imagined to ground culture. Life moves out of the domain of the given into the contingent, into quotation marks, appearing not as a thing-in-itself but as something in the making in discourse and practice. "Life" becomes a trace of the scientific and cultural practices that have asked after it, a shadow of the biological and social theories meant to capture it.

[…]

But if it is now possible to think of "life" as having a plurality of futures – as a 2007 conference, "Futures of Life," held in the Department of Science and Technology Studies at Cornell University had it – it is also possible, in the face of a seemingly endless multiplication of forms, to inquire, as did a 2007 conference at Berkeley, "What's Left of Life?" That question posed by scholars in the humanities and social sciences asked whether what Michel Foucault in 1966 identified as "life itself," the epistemic object of biology that Foucault claimed first manifested in

From *Critical Inquiry* 37(4)(2011), pp. 671–96 (excerpts). Reprinted with permission of University of Chicago Press.

Anthropology in Theory: Issues in Epistemology, Second Edition. Edited by Henrietta L. Moore and Todd Sanders.
© 2014 John Wiley & Sons, Inc. Published 2014 by John Wiley & Sons, Inc.

the early nineteenth century, still retains its force to organize matters of fact and concern – life forms and forms of life – arrayed around the life sciences. It is a question about limits, a worry about ends. *What was life?*

[...]

Introducing Three Limit Biologies

[...][M]y three ethnographic examples [...] suggest that biologies in which "life" is conceptually stretched to a limit calibrate to uncertainties about what kinds of sociocultural forms of life biology might now anchor. Limit biologies like Artificial Life, extreme marine microbiology, and astrobiology also point to larger instabilities in concepts of nature – organic, earthly, cosmic. Such instabilities can be fruitfully mapped by attending to how scientists of extreme biologies test the limits of *form* in life forms. [...] I am equally interested in how biologists think about limits – and I think that the very notion of the *limit*, as an object of study and fascination in biology and in interpretative social science, also requires analytic scrutiny. [...]

Artificial Life: Life Forms at Limits of Abstraction

The late 1980s and early 1990s saw the rise of Artificial Life, a hybrid of computer science, theoretical biology, and digital gaming devoted to mimicking the logic of biology in the virtual worlds of computer simulation and in the hardware realm of robotics. [...] [R]esearchers claimed that life would be "a property of the organization of matter, rather than a property of matter itself." Some found this claim so persuasive that they held that life forms could exist in the digital medium of cyberspace; they hoped the creation of such life could expand biology's purview to include not just *life-as-we-know-it* but also *life-as-it-could-be* – life as it might exist in other materials or elsewhere in the universe. On the initiate's view, Artificial Life's extreme abstraction leverages biology into the realm of universal science, like physics, with a formalism applicable anywhere in the cosmos.

Chris Langton characterized the ethos behind Artificial Life as animated by "the attempt to abstract the logical form of life in different material forms." This definition of life holds that formal and material properties can be partitioned and that what matters is form. What was *form* for Artificial Life scientists? Two things: information and performance.

Information

Artificial Life founded its reputation on computational models of evolutionary dynamics. One of the most popular models during my fieldwork was Tom Ray's [...]. For Ray, trained as a topical ecologist and self-taught as a programmer, Tierra is not so much a *model* of evolution as it is "an *instantiation* of evolution by natural selection in the computational medium." [...] Ray understands life to be a process of information replication and, like many of his Artificial Life colleagues, interprets genetic code on an analogy to computer code; in fact, the analogy is almost as close as identity. "The 'body' of a digital organism," he urges, "is the information pattern in memory that constitutes its machine language program."

[...]

Performance

The other side of form for Artificial Life has been performance [as seen in Karl Sims'] video of simulated creatures with boxes for arms, legs, torsos, and heads. These creatures were not animations but "evolved" pieces of software in a simulated universe [...]. Using a technique called genetic programming, Sims treats the software running his programs as genetic code and assays the phenotypic performance of the code by running the programs. [...] Sims's graphics allowed his audience to watch these creatures attempt various tasks in artificial worlds.

Sims's brilliance in explicating his work was to show video of his virtual organisms' performances, calibrated so they would run in what looked like real time. As they passed or flunked their Darwinian fitness tests, Sims's boxy critters elicited laughter. [...] What made the images funny was a sense that Sims was not fully in control; he had programmed a three-dimensional artificial world – and a visual representation of it – that simulated Newtonian physics, gravity, and fluid dynamics, and he had introduced creatures that could interact with this world. Because simulated physics and creatures were programmed together, behaviors looked realistic, even purposeful. By playing with the boundary between simulation and animation and by explaining the genetic program back end of the model, Sims bolstered his viewership's faith in the lifelike character of the simulations. The persuasive force of Sims's presentation is visual; watching a stream of computer code text would not have produced the same life-effect. Life becomes a formal effect.

[...]

But, as Marilyn Strathern saw as early as 1992, the putatively oxymoronic "artificial life" hints at an undoing of the self-evidence of "life" as a natural kind. As Jean Baudrillard would have had it, simulation reveals there was never an original. When form is decoupled from life, we are left with free-floating form. In the bargain, "nature" becomes everywhere and nowhere, both completely given and thoroughly constructed; we are left in a zone that Strathern calls "after nature," referring both to being postnature and enduringly in pursuit of it. Artificial Life can be read as a sign of the instability, the limits, of nature as an ontological category. [...]

Marine Microbiology: Life Forms at Limits of Materiality and Relationality

At the same time, one could argue that "extreme nature" is the new "after nature." Such certainly seemed plausible to me when I switched gears after Artificial Life to examine the work of biologists studying microbes living at deep-sea hydrothermal vents [...]; these creatures made their living through chemosynthesis, the production of organic materials using energy from chemicals, such as hydrogen sulfide – a mode of life not discovered in the wild until the 1970s. If Artificial Life scripted life as detachable from particular substrates, the marine biology of extremophilic microbes construes life as possessed of an as-yet-unmapped elasticity – though one still anchored in organic chemistry. This is not abstract form, then, as in Artificial Life, but

form plastic to extreme conditions, to limits. This angle is appropriate to the form of life known as environmentalism, concerned about material, embodied limits and flexibility in the biosphere [...].

[...] Trying to get a fix on how these people made microbial life legible, I spoke with them about their difficulties pinning down that most elementary of biological forms: the species. The categorical stability of species has been troublesome for at least a century in microbiology but has become a central worry in recent debates about how to place marine microbes with respect to the origin of life on Earth. [...]

[...] [L]ateral gene transfer in microbes – the travel of genes not just down generations, but rather across, within, among contemporaries – places treelike representations at risk. [...]

Gene transfer interrupts what Darwin called the "natural classification" that would follow from following lines of descent. In a microbiological restaging of those personalized, family genetic history tests that suggest that people's "racial" and "ethnic" ancestries are more polyglot than they may have imagined, *species*, like the "pure" racial type, falls apart, denatures. In part, this is because sex – the generative center of classical biopolitics, joining together individuals and populations – is supplanted by transfer, which undoes the genealogical stability of the categories it brings into juxtaposition. It makes clear that there is no natural classification – that biology is bound up with human social purposes. Life forms are always described with respect to some form of life.

[...]

Categories – genetic, metabolic – proliferate. Some marine microbiologists I spoke with reveled in the complexity, making clear what this rearrangement of life forms might mean for forms of life. Some saw it underwriting a bioengineering form of life: "Natural genetic engineering," one biotech booster told me, "is very common." [...] Still others thought microbial webworks endorsed a thrillingly relational vision of the planet [...].

What does all this mean for the form that life takes? It is multiple; even when reduced to genes, it flows all over the place. Marine microbiologists are clear that classifications are matters of framing. The form in "life forms" changes with scale and context. These scientists understand microbes with respect simultaneously to their genes, metabolisms, and interaction with one another in communities, ecologies, and global biogeochemical processes like the carbon cycle. Many of their theoretical and classificatory conundrums are about how to link, as they phrase it, genomes to biomes. The question, how to think about the forms life might take depends on which properties are relevant to the unit of description in question and on how sociopolitical frames – biotechnological, environmentalist – condition these choices [...]. A dramatic effect on the category of "life" is that it oscillates between being located at the level of the gene and emergent at the level of the globe. Penny Chisholm said about *Prochlorococcus*, the world's most abundant photosynthetic marine bacterium: "I consider this the minimal life form – having the smallest number of genes that can make life from light and only inorganic compounds. It is the essence of life." But [...] she concluded by offering that *Prochlorococcus* should guide biologists to "think of life as something with properties similar at all scales, a system of self-stabilizing networks. Life is a hierarchy of living systems." [...]

What are life forms here – in this realm of extreme metabolisms, jumbled genealogies, shifting scales? They are the result of how phenomena are contextualized [...]. The form in a life form is a sign of one's methodological and theoretical approach; in many ways it is an abstraction [...]

[...]

Astrobiology: Life Forms at Limits of Definition

In 1998, NASA founded the Astrobiology Institute, distributed across a number of universities and research facilities. [...] They [...] look to other planets for what they call [...] a "biosignature," [or] a "fingerprint of life." [...] Direct signatures include measurements that show evidence (in extraterrestrial rock samples, for example) of the production of organic molecules. Remote signatures include such items as the spectral signature of other worlds' atmospheres, which can point toward such bioproducts as ozone or methane. Astrobiologists often zero in on the spectral trace of water as an indication of

the possibility of vitality. A founding challenge, according to David Des Marais, is that "our definitions are based upon life on Earth" and that, "accordingly, we must distinguish between attributes of life that are truly universal versus those that solely reflect the particular history of our own biosphere." This is no simple task, since knowing what is universal is precisely what is to be discovered.

[...]

What are life forms for astrobiology, then? Things that leave *traces* of their form. And astrobiologists are adamant that they do not yet know what all these forms could be, that they will always be operating at the limits of their knowledge. [...] Astrobiologists live firmly in the domain of Strathern's "after nature." But they also live in the time of "extreme nature," nature imagined as host to entities that push its own limits. This extreme nature is a secularized supernatural because its orbit extends beyond and embraces our planet, but also because the "natural," encountered elsewhere, intimates its own incompleteness as a source of explanation.

[...]

What Was Life?

[...] The three limit biologies I have examined here indicate instabilities in the nature supposed to ground life. And they all do so through a wiggling of what is meant by the form that life takes, a loosening that suggests epistemic shifts in the biological sciences generally; in the age of synthetic biology, biologists know full well that their knowledge is, in addition to an attempt to describe the organic world, a thick epistemological construction. This puts biology as a universalizing science at risk, one reason these limit biologies come with the promise to reboot the life sciences. [...]

[...]

What is a limit? It is the point at which an identity uncouples from itself, shades or snaps into something else. [...] In the examples I have offered here, form becomes the shadow of life, only to outgrow it – at the same time as biologists continue to try to recapture it; no surprise that astrobiologists now explicitly discuss shadow life.

What is the shadow of life? The first-draft answer would of course be death – and a good case could be made that today's biopolitics are ever more entangled with necropolitics. But this is not quite right, since the better question is: what can we see in the shadow of life's limit? Answer: the absence of a theory for biology; reaching the limit of life reveals what was there all along, that there is no once and for all theoretical grounding for life. [...]

48

The Near and the Elsewhere

Marc Augé

More and more is being said about the anthropology of the near. A seminar held in 1987 at the Musée des Arts et Traditions populaires ("Social anthropology and ethnology of France"), whose papers were published in 1989 under the title *L' Autre et le semblable*, noted a convergence in the concerns of ethnologists working elsewhere and those working here. Both the seminar and the book are explicitly placed in the aftermath of the reflections started at the Toulouse seminar of 1982 ("New paths in the ethnology of France") and developed in a few books and special issues of reviews.

That said, it is by no means certain that (as is so often the case) the recognition of new interests and fields for research, of hitherto unsuspected convergences, is not based at least partly on misunderstandings, or responsible for causing them. A few preliminary remarks may help to clarify this reflection on the anthropology of the near.

Anthropology has always dealt with the here and now. The practising ethnologist is a person situated somewhere (his "here" of the moment) who describes what he is observing or what he is hearing at this very moment. It will always be possible afterwards to wonder about the quality of his observation and about the aims, prejudices or other factors that condition the production of his text: but the fact remains that all ethnology presupposes the existence of a direct witness to a present actuality. [...]

Certainly the European, Western "here" assumes its full meaning in relation to the distant elsewhere – formerly "colonial", now "underdeveloped" – favoured in the past by British and French anthropology. But the opposition of here and elsewhere (a sort of gross division – Europe, rest of the world – reminiscent of the football matches organized by England in the days when it still had great football: England vs Rest of the World) can serve as a starting point for the opposition of the two anthropologies only by presupposing the very thing that is in question: that they are indeed two distinct anthropologies.

The assertion that ethnologists are turning to Europe as overseas fieldwork becomes more difficult to arrange is an arguable one. In the first place, there are still ample opportunities to work abroad, in Africa, Asia and the Americas.[...] In the second place, the reasons for doing anthropological work in Europe are positive ones. It is not a matter of second best, an anthropology by

From *Non-places: Introduction to an Anthropology of Supermodernity*, trans. John Howe (London: Verso, 1995), pp. 7–8, 10–41, 121–2. Copyright © 1995 by Verso. Reprinted by permission of Verso.

Anthropology in Theory: Issues in Epistemology, Second Edition. Edited by Henrietta L. Moore and Todd Sanders.
© 2014 John Wiley & Sons, Inc. Published 2014 by John Wiley & Sons, Inc.

default. And it is precisely by examining these positive reasons that we may come to question the Europe/elsewhere opposition that lies behind some of the more modernist definitions of Europeanist ethnology.

The whole idea of an ethnology of the near raises a double question. In the first place, can an ethnology of Europe lay claim to the same level of sophistication, of conceptual complexity, as the ethnology of remote societies? The answer to this question is generally affirmative, at least on the part of Europeanist ethnologists in a forward-looking context. Thus Martine Segalen, in the collection mentioned above, is able to note with satisfaction that two kinship ethnologists who have worked on the same European region should henceforth be able to talk to one another "like specialists in the same African ethnic group"; while Anthony P. Cohen points out that kinship studies carried out by Robin Fox on Tory Island and Marilyn Strathern at Elmdon show, on the one hand, the central role of kinship and the strategies based on it in "our" societies; and, on the other, the plurality of cultures coexisting in a country like present-day Britain.

It must be admitted, though, that in this form the question is baffling. What, one wonders, is being suggested: a possible weakness in the capacity of European societies for symbolization, or the limited ability of Europeanist ethnologists to analyse it?

The second question has an entirely different significance: are the facts, institutions, modes of assembly (work, leisure, residential), modes of circulation specific to the contemporary world, amenable to anthropological scrutiny? For a start, this question does not arise solely – far from it – in relation to Europe. Anyone with experience of Africa (for example) is well aware that any attempt at an overall anthropological approach must take account of a multitude of interacting elements that arise from immediate reality, but are not readily divisible into "traditional" and "modern" categories. It is well known that all the institutional forms that have to be recognized in order to grasp social life (salaried labour, business, spectator sports, the media...) play a role, on all the continents, that grows more important by the day. Secondly, it displaces the original question completely: it is not Europe that is under scrutiny but contemporaneity itself, in all the aggressive

and disturbing aspects of reality at its most immediate.

It is therefore essential not to confuse the question of method with that of object. It has often been said (not least, on several occasions, by Lévi-Strauss himself) that the modern world lends itself to ethnological observation, however bad we may be at defining areas of observation within reach of our investigative methods. And we know what importance Gérard Althabe (who cannot have realized at the time that he was supplying grist to the mills of our politicians) gave to stairwells, to staircase life, in his studies of big housing estates in Saint-Denis and the Nantes periphery.

It is obvious to anyone who has done fieldwork that ethnological inquiry has limitations which are also assets, and that the ethnologist needs to delineate the approximate limits of a group that he will study, and that will acknowledge him. But there are various aspects. The aspect of method, the need for effective contact with interlocutors, is one thing. The representativeness of the chosen group is another: in effect, it is a matter of being able to assess what the people we see and speak to tell us about the people we do not see and speak to. The field ethnologist's activity throughout is the activity of a social surveyor, a manipulator of scales, a low-level comparative language expert: he cobbles together a significant universe by exploring intermediate universes at need, in rapid surveys; or by consulting relevant documents as a historian. He tries to work out, for himself and others, whom he can claim to be talking about when he talks about the people he has talked to. There is nothing to suggest that the case of some great African kingdom is any different from that of an industrial concern in the Paris suburbs, where this problem of the empirical real object – of representativeness – is concerned.

Two things can be said here, one touching on history and the other on anthropology. Both concern the care that the ethnologist takes to locate the empirical object of his research, to evaluate its qualitative representativeness – for here, strictly speaking, the aim is not to select statistically representative samples but to establish whether what is valid for one lineage, or one village, is valid for others [...]: the difficulty of defining notions like "tribe" or "ethnic group" can be seen in this perspective. This concern of ethnologists brings them together with, and at the same time distances them from, historians of microhistory; or – to put it the other way round (for it is ethnologists we are concerned with here) – microhistorians find themselves in the ethnologist's shoes when they are themselves obliged to question the representativeness of the cases they analyse; for example, the life of a fifteenth-century Frioul miller. But in support of this representativeness they have to fall back on notions like "traces" and "indications", or resort to exemplary exceptionality; while the field ethnologist, if he is conscientious, can always cast his net a little wider and make sure that what he thought he observed in the first place still holds good. This is the advantage of working on the present, in truth a modest compensation for the essential advantage possessed by all historians: they know what happens afterwards.

The second remark also touches on the object of anthropology, but this time its intellectual object or, if you prefer, the ethnologist's capacity for generalization. It is quite obvious that there is a considerable step between the minute observation of part of a village or the collection of a range of myths from a given population, and the elaboration of a theory on "elementary kinship structures" or "*mythologiques*". Structuralism is not the only thing at issue here. All the main anthropological approaches have tended at the very least to generate a range of general hypotheses which may have been inspired initially by examination of a particular case, but have a bearing on the elaboration of problematic configurations going well beyond this case alone: theories of witchcraft, matrimonial alliance, power or relations of production.

Without saying anything here about the validity of these efforts at generalization, we can note their existence as a constituent part of the ethnological literature to point out that the size argument, when it is mentioned in connection with non-exotic societies, concerns only a particular aspect of the research, thus of the method and not the object: neither the empirical object nor, *a fortiori*, the intellectual, theoretical object, which presupposes comparison as well as generalization.

The question of method could not be confused with that of object, for the object of anthropology has never been the exhaustive description of, say,

a village or part of a village. When they are produced, monographs of this type are always presented as contributions to a still-incomplete inventory, and usually outline, at least on an empirical level, generalizations more or less based on the research, but applicable to a whole ethnic group. The first question that arises in connection with near-contemporaneity is not whether, or how, it is possible to do fieldwork in a big housing estate, a factory or a holiday camp: that will be managed, either well or badly. The question is whether there are any aspects of contemporary social life that seem to be accessible to anthropological investigation, in the same way that questions of kinship, marriage, bequest, exchange, and so on, came to the attention of anthropologists of the elsewhere, initially as empirical objects, then as objects of reflection (intellectual objects). In this connection, and in the context of the (perfectly legitimate) concerns about method, it is appropriate to refer to what we will call the premiss of the object.

This premiss of the object may raise doubts about the legitimacy of an anthropology of near contemporaneity. Louis Dumont, in his preface to the revised edition of *La Tarasque*, points out (in a passage quoted in Martine Segalen's introduction to *L'Autre et le semblable*) that the "shifting of centres of interest" and the change of "problematics" (what we will call here the changes to empirical and intellectual objects) prevent our disciplines from being simply cumulative "and may even undermine their continuity". As an example of the shifting of centres of interest he cites in particular, in contrast to the study of popular tradition, a "way of looking at French social life which is both broader and more finely differentiated, which no longer makes an absolute distinction between the non-modern and the modern, for example between the artisanate and industry".

I am not convinced that the continuity of a discipline is proportional to that of its objects. The proposition is certainly dubious when it is applied to the life sciences, nor am I sure that these are cumulative in the sense implied by Dumont's phrase: the outcome of research, surely, is new objects of research. It seems to me even more arguable in the case of the social sciences; for when there is change in the modes of grouping and hierarchy it is always social life that is affected, offering the researcher new objects which – like those discovered by the researcher in the life sciences – do not supersede the ones he worked on earlier, but complicate them. That said, however, Louis Dumont's anxiety is not without echoes among those committed to an anthropology of the here and now. An example is the amusing comment in *L'Autre et le semblable* by Gérard Althabe, Jacques Cheyronnaud and Béatrix Le Wita to the effect that the Bretons "are a lot more worried about their loans from the Crédit Agricole than they are about their genealogies…". Behind this throwaway formulation, the question of the object is outlined once again: why should anthropology attribute more importance to the Bretons' genealogies than they do themselves (although it is hard to imagine Bretons being totally indifferent to them)? If the anthropology of near contemporaneity had to be based exclusively on the categories already registered, if it were not allowed to formulate new objects, then the act of moving into new empirical terrain would not answer a need, merely the researcher's idle curiosity.

These premises call for a positive definition of anthropological research. We will try to formulate one here, starting with two observations.

The first of these concerns anthropological research: anthropological research deals in the present with the question of the other. The question of the other is not just a theme that anthropology encounters from time to time; it is its sole intellectual object, the basis on which different fields of investigation may be defined. It deals with the other in the present; that is sufficient to distinguish it from history. And it deals with it simultaneously in several senses, thus distinguishing itself from the other social sciences.

It deals with all forms of other: the exotic other defined in relation to a supposedly identical "we" (we French, we Europeans, we Westerners); the other of others, the ethnic or cultural other, defined in relation to a supposedly identical "they" usually embodied in the name of an ethnic group; the social other, the internal other used as the reference for a system of differences, starting with the division of the sexes but also defining everyone's situation in political, economic and family terms, so that it is not possible to mention

a position in the system (elder, younger, next-born, boss, client, captive…) without referring to one or more others; and finally the private other – not to be confused with the last – which is present at the heart of all systems of thought and whose (universal) representation is a response to the fact that absolute individuality is unthinkable: heredity, heritage, lineage, resemblance, influence, are all categories through which we may discern an otherness that contributes to, and complements, all individuality. All the literature devoted to the notion of the self, interpretation of sickness and sorcery bears witness to the fact that one of the major questions posed by ethnology is also posed by those it studies: the question concerning what one might call essential or private otherness. Representations of private otherness, in the systems studied by ethnology, place the need for it at the very heart of individuality, at a stroke making it impossible to dissociate the question of collective identity from that of individual identity. This is a remarkable example of what the very content of the beliefs studied by the ethnologist can impose on the approach devised to register it: representation of the individual interests anthropology not just because it is a social construction, but also because any representation of the individual is also a representation of the social link consubstantial with him. By the same token, we are indebted to the anthropology of remote societies – and still more to the individuals it studies – for this discovery: the social begins with the individual; and the individual is the object of ethnological scrutiny. The concrete in anthropology is the opposite of the definition of the concrete accepted by certain schools of sociological thought: something to be seen in terms of orders of magnitude from which all individual variables are eliminated.

Marcel Mauss, discussing the relationship between psychology and sociology, nevertheless makes a definition of individuality amenable to ethnological scrutiny which has serious limitations. In a curious passage, he says in effect that the individual studied by sociologists is not the man typical of the modern elite, divided, controlled and conditioned, but the ordinary or obsolete man who can be defined as a totality:

The average man today – this is especially true of women – along with almost all men in archaic or backward societies, is a whole; his entire being is affected by the smallest of his perceptions or by the slightest mental shock. The study of this "totality" is therefore crucial in dealing with all but the elite of our modern societies. (Mauss, p. 306)

But the idea of totality – well known to be important to Mauss, who sees the concrete as the complete – restricts and, in a sense, mutilates the idea of individuality. More precisely, the individuality he considers is one that represents the culture, a typical individuality. This is confirmed in his analysis of the total social phenomenon, whose interpretation (Lévi-Strauss notes in his "Introduction to the Work of Marcel Mauss") must include not only all the discontinuous aspects, anyone of which (family, technical, economic) could serve as an exclusive basis for the analysis, but also the image that any of its indigenous members has or may have of it. Experience of the total social fact is doubly concrete (and doubly complete): experience of a society precisely located in time and space, but also experience of some individual belonging to that society. But this individual is not just anybody: he is identified with the society of which he is an expression. It is significant that to give an idea of what he means by "an" individual, Mauss resorts to the definite article: "*the* Melanesian from Island X or Y". The text quoted above further clarifies this point. The Melanesian is not total only because we perceive him in his different individual dimensions, "physical, physiological, psychic and sociological", but because his individuality is a synthesis, the expression of a culture which itself is regarded as a whole.

Much could be said (indeed, a fair amount has been said here and there) about this conception of culture and individuality. The fact that in some ways and in some contexts culture and individuality might be defined as reciprocal expressions of one another is a triviality, or anyway a commonplace, which we use when we say, for example, that so-and-so is a "real" Breton, Briton, Auvergnat or German. The fact that the responses of supposedly free individuals can be assessed or even predicted from those of a statistically significant sample does not surprise us either. It is just that in the meantime we have learned to distrust absolute, simple and substantive identities, on the collective as well as the individual level. Cultures "work" like green timber, and (for extrinsic and intrinsic reasons) never constitute finished totalities; while individuals, however simple we imagine them to be, are never quite simple enough to become detached from the order that assigns them a position: they express its totality only from a certain angle. Apart from this, the problematic character of all established order would perhaps never manifest itself as such – through wars, revolts, conflicts, tensions – without the triggering flick of an individual initiative. Neither the culture located in time and space, nor the individuals in which it is embodied, defines a base level of identity above which any otherness would become unthinkable. Of course, the culture's "working" around its fringes, or individual strategies inside its institutional systems, do not always have to be taken into account in defining (intellectual) research objects. Discussion and polemic on this point have sometimes been afflicted by bad faith, or myopia: let us simply note, for example, that whether or not a rule is observed – the fact that it might possibly be evaded or transgressed – has nothing whatever to do with the examination of all its logical implications, which constitute a genuine research object. But there are other, different research objects, which do require attention to be given to procedures of transformation or change, to gaps, initiatives, transgressions, and so forth.

It is important at least to know what one is talking about; and it is enough for us here to note that, whatever the level at which anthropological research is applied, its object is to interpret the interpretation others make of the category of other on the different levels that define its place and impose the need for it: ethnic group, tribe, village, lineage, right down to the elementary particle of kinship, which is known to subject the identity of the bloodline to the need for alliance; and finally the individual, defined by all ritual systems as a composite steeped in otherness, a figure who is literally unthinkable (as, in different ways, are those of the monarch and the sorcerer).

The second observation is not about anthropology but about the world in which it finds its objects, and more especially the contemporary world. It is not that anthropology has become bored with foreign fields and turned to more familiar terrain, thus risking (as Louis Dumont fears) loss of its continuity; it is that the contemporary world itself, with its accelerated transformations, is attracting anthropological scrutiny: in other words, a renewed methodical reflection on the category of otherness. We will examine three of these transformations more closely.

The first is concerned with time, our perception of time but also the use we make of it, the way we dispose of it. For a number of intellectuals, time today is no longer a principle of intelligibility. The idea of progress, which implied an afterwards explainable in terms of what had gone before, has run aground, so to speak, on the shoals of the twentieth century, following the departure of the hopes or illusions that had accompanied the ocean crossing of the nineteenth. To tell the truth, this reassessment refers to several observations that are distinct from one another: the atrocities of the world wars, totalitarianisms and genocidal policies, which (to say the very least) do not indicate much moral progress on the part of humanity; the end of the grand narratives, the great systems of interpretation that aspired to map the evolution of the whole of humanity, but did not succeed, along with the deviation or obliteration of the political systems officially based on some of them; in sum, a doubt as to whether history carries any meaning. Perhaps we should say a renewed doubt, strangely reminiscent of the one in which Paul Hazard thought he could discern, at the turn of the seventeenth and eighteenth centuries, the root of the quarrel between the Ancients and Moderns and the crisis of European consciousness. But Fontenelle's doubts about history were focused essentially on its method (anecdotal and not very reliable), its object (the past speaks to us only of human folly) and its usefulness (surely young people really need to know about the period in which they are going to have to live). When today's historians – especially in France – have doubts about history, it is not for technical reasons or reasons concerned with method (for history has made progress as a science) but, more fundamentally, because they find it very difficult to make time into a principle of intelligibility, let alone a principle of identity.

Moreover, we now see them paying attention to a number of major themes normally considered "anthropological" (the family, private life, "places of memory"). These researches meet halfway the public's interest in obsolete forms, which seem to tell our contemporaries what they are by showing them what they are no longer. Nobody expresses this point of view better than Pierre Nora, in his preface to the first volume of *Lieux de mémoire*: what we are seeking, he says in substance, through our religious accumulation of personal accounts, documents, images and all the "visible signs of what used to be", is what is different about us now; and "within the spectacle of this difference the sudden flash of an unfindable identity. No longer a genesis, but the deciphering of what we are in the light of what we are no longer."

This general finding also corresponds to the decline of the Sartrean and Marxist references of the early postwar period, which held that in the final analysis the universal was the truth of the specific; and to the rise of what (along with many others) we might call the postmodern sensibility, the belief that one mode is worth the same as another, the patchwork of modes signifying the erasure of modernity as the end product of an evolution resembling progress.

This theme is inexhaustible, but the question of time can be looked at from another point of view, starting with something very commonplace with which we are confronted every day: the acceleration of history. We barely have time to reach maturity before our past has become history, our individual histories belong to history writ large. People of my age witnessed in their childhood and adolescence the tight-lipped nostalgia of men who had fought in the 1914–18 war: it seemed to be telling us that they had lived through some history (and what history!) but we would never really be able to understand what it meant. Nowadays the recent past – "the sixties", "the seventies", now "the eighties" – becomes history as soon as it has been lived. History is on our heels, following us like our shadows, like death. History meaning a series of events recognized as events by large numbers of people (the Beatles, '68, Algeria, Vietnam, Mitterrand's victory in '81, Berlin Wall, democratization of East Europe, Gulf War, disintegration of USSR) – events we believe will count in the eyes of future historians and to which each of us, while fully aware that our part in them is as insignificant as Fabrice's at Waterloo, can attach some circumstance or image of a personal, particular nature; as if it were becoming daily less true that men (who else?) make history without knowing it. Surely this very overabundance (in a planet growing smaller by the day – see below) is a problem to the historian of the contemporary?

Let us define this point more precisely. The event or occurrence has always been a problem to those historians who wished to submerge it in the grand sweep of history, who saw it as a pure pleonasm between a before and an after conceived as the development of that before. Behind the polemics, this is the meaning of the analysis of the Revolution (an event if ever there was one) suggested by François Furet. What does he tell us in *Penser la Révolution?* That from the day the Revolution breaks out, the revolutionary event "institutes a new modality of historic action, one that is not inscribed in the inventory of the situation". The revolutionary event (and in this sense the Revolution is exemplary as an event) cannot be reduced to the sum of the factors that make it possible and, after the event, understandable. We would be quite wrong to limit this analysis to the case of the Revolution alone.

The "acceleration" of history corresponds, in fact, to a multiplication of events very few of which are predicted by economists, historians or sociologists. The problem is the overabundance of events, not the horrors of the twentieth century (whose only new feature – their unprecedented scale – is a by-product of technology), nor its political upheavals and intellectual mutations, of which history offers many other examples. This overabundance, which can be properly appreciated only by bearing in mind both our overabundant information and the growing tangle of interdependences in what some already call the "world system", causes undeniable difficulties to historians, especially historians of the contemporary – a denomination which the density of events over the last few decades threatens to rob of all meaning. But this problem is precisely anthropological in nature.

Listen to Furet defining the dynamic of the Revolution as an event. It is, he tells us, a dynamic "that might be called political, ideological or cultural, whose amplified power of mobilizing men and acting on things arises from an overinvestment of meaning" (p. 39). This overinvestment of meaning, exemplarily accessible to anthropological scrutiny, is also apparent in a number of contemporary events (resulting in contradictions whose full scale has yet to be measured); one of these, obviously, is the sudden dissolution of regimes whose fall nobody had dared to predict; but a better example, perhaps, would be the latent crises affecting the political, social and economic life of liberal countries, which we have fallen unconsciously into the habit of discussing in terms of meaning. What is new is not that the world lacks meaning, or has little meaning, or less than it used to have; it is that we seem to feel an explicit and intense daily need to give it meaning: to give meaning to the world, not just some village or lineage. This need to give a meaning to the present, if not the past, is the price we pay for the overabundance of events corresponding to a situation we could call "supermodern" to express its essential quality: excess.

For each of us has – or thinks he has – the use of it, of this time overloaded with events that encumber the present along with the recent past. This can only – please note – make us even more avid for meaning. The extension of life expectancy, the passage from the normal coexistence of three generations to four, are bringing about gradual, practical changes in the order of social life. By the same token they are expanding the collective, genealogical and historical memory, multiplying the occasions on which an individual can feel his own history intersecting with History, can imagine that the two are somehow connected. The individual's demands and disappointments are linked to the strengthening of this feeling.

So it is with an image of excess – excess of time – that we can start defining the situation of supermodernity, while suggesting that, by the very fact of its contradictions, it offers a magnificent field for observation and, in the full sense of the term, an object of anthropological research. We could say of supermodernity that it is the face of a coin whose obverse represents postmodernity: the positive of a negative. From the viewpoint of supermodernity, the difficulty of thinking about time stems from the overabundance of events in the contemporary world, not from the collapse of an idea of progress which – at least in the caricatured forms that make its dismissal so very easy – has been in a bad way for a long time; the theme of imminent history, of history snapping at our heels (almost immanent in each of our day-to-day existences) seems like a premiss of the theme of the meaning or non-meaning of history.

For it is our need to understand the whole of the present that makes it difficult for us to give meaning to the recent past; the appearance, among individuals in contemporary societies, of a positive demand for meaning (of which the democratic ideal is doubtless an essential aspect) may offer a paradoxical explanation of phenomena which are sometimes interpreted as the signs of a crisis of meaning; for example, the disappointments of all the world's disappointed: disappointment with socialism, with liberalism, and (before long) with post-communism too.

The second accelerated transformation specific to the contemporary world, and the second figure of excess characteristic of supermodernity, concerns space. We could start by saying – again somewhat paradoxically – that the excess of space is correlative with the shrinking of the planet: with the distancing from ourselves embodied in the feats of our astronauts and the endless circling of our satellites. In a sense, our first steps in outer space reduce our own space to an infinitesimal point, of which satellite photographs appropriately give us the exact measure. But at the same time the world is becoming open to us. We are in an era characterized by changes of scale – of course in the context of space exploration, but also on earth: rapid means of transport have brought any capital within a few hours' travel of any other. And in the privacy of our homes, finally, images of all sorts, relayed by satellites and caught by the aerials that bristle on the roofs of our remotest hamlets, can give us an instant, sometimes simultaneous vision of an event taking place on the other side of the planet. Of course we anticipate perverse effects, or possible distortions, from information whose images are selected in this way: not only can they be (as we say) manipulated, but the broadcast image (which is only one among countless possible others) exercises an influence, possesses a power far in excess of any objective information it carries. It should be noted, too, that the screens of the planet daily carry a mixture of images (news, advertising and fiction) of which neither the presentation nor the purpose is identical, at least in principle, but which assemble before our eyes a universe that is relatively homogeneous in its diversity. What could be more realistic and, in a sense, more informative about life in the United States than a good American TV series? Nor should we forget the sort of false familiarity the small screen establishes between the viewers and the actors of big-scale history, whose profiles become as well known to us as those of soap-opera heroes and international artistic or sporting stars. They are like the landscapes in which we regularly watch them playing out their moves: Texas, California, Washington, Moscow, the Elysée, Twickenham, the gruelling stages of the Tour de France or the Arabian desert; we may not know them personally, but we recognize them.

This spatial overabundance works like a decoy, but a decoy whose manipulator would be very hard to identify (there is nobody pulling the strings). In very large part, it serves as a substitute for the universes which ethnology has traditionally made its own. We can say of these universes, which are themselves broadly fictional, that they are essentially universes of recognition. The property of symbolic universes is that they constitute a means of recognition, rather than knowledge, for those who have inherited them: closed universes where everything is a sign; collections of codes to which only some hold the key but whose existence everyone accepts; totalities which are partially fictional but effective; cosmologies one might think had been invented for the benefit of ethnologists. For this is the point where the ethnologist's fantasies meet those of the indigenous people he studies. One of the major concerns of ethnology has been to delineate signifying spaces in the world, societies identified with cultures conceived as complete wholes: universes of meaning, of which the individuals and groups inside them are just an expression, defining themselves in terms of the same criteria, the same values and the same interpretation procedures.

We will not return to the concepts of culture and individuality criticized above. Suffice it to say that this ideological conception reflects the ethnologists' ideology as much as that of the people they study, and that experience of the supermodern world may help ethnologists to rid themselves of it – or, more precisely, to measure its import. For it rests (among other things) on an organization of space that the space of modernity overwhelms and relativizes. Here too we should make certain things clear: just as the intelligence of time, it seems to us, is more complicated by the overabundance of events in the present than undermined by the radical subversion of prevailing modes of historical interpretation, so the intelligence of space is less subverted by current upheavals (for soils and territories still exist, not just in the reality of facts on the ground, but even more in that of individual and collective awareness and imagination) than complicated by the spatial overabundance of the present. This, as we have seen, is expressed in changes of scale, in the proliferation of imaged and imaginary references, and in the spectacular acceleration of means of transport. Its concrete outcome involves considerable physical modifications: urban concentrations, movements of population and the multiplication of what we call "non-places", in opposition to the sociological notion of place, associated by Mauss and a whole ethnological tradition with the idea of a culture localized in time and space. The installations needed for the accelerated circulation of passengers and goods (high-speed roads and railways, interchanges, airports) are just as much non-places as the means of transport themselves, or the great commercial centres, or the extended transit camps where the planet's refugees are parked. For the time we live in is paradoxical in this aspect, too: at the very same moment when it becomes possible to think in terms of the unity of terrestrial space, and the big multinational networks grow strong, the clamour of particularisms rises; clamour from those who want to stay at home in peace, clamour from those who want to find a mother country. As if the conservatism of the former and the messianism of the latter were condemned to speak the same language: that of the land and roots.

One might think that the shifting of spatial parameters (spatial overabundance) would confront the ethnologist with difficulties of the same order as those encountered by historians faced with overabundance of events. They may well be of the same order, but where anthropological research is concerned these difficulties are particularly stimulating. Changes of scale, changes of parameter: as in the nineteenth century, we are poised to undertake the study of new civilizations and new cultures.

It matters little that to some extent we may be involved in these as interested parties, for as individuals we are far – very far indeed – from knowing them in all their aspects. Conversely, exotic cultures seemed so different to early Western observers only when they succumbed to the temptation to read them through the ethnocentric grille of their own customary behaviour. Experience of the remote has taught us to de-centre our way of looking, and we should make use of the lesson. The world of supermodernity does not exactly match the one in which we believe we live, for we live in a world that we have not yet learned to look at. We have to relearn to think about space.

The third figure of excess in relation to which the situation of supermodernity might be defined is well known to us. It is the figure of the ego, the individual, who is making a comeback (as they say) in anthropological thought itself, as ethnologists, or some of them, at a loss for new fields in a universe without territories and theoretically breathless in a world without grand narratives, having attempted to deal with cultures (localized cultures, cultures à la Mauss) as if they were texts, have reached the point of being interested only in ethnographic description as text; text expressive, naturally, of its author, so that (if we are to believe James Clifford) the Nuer, in the end, teach us more about Evans-Pritchard than he teaches us about them. Without questioning here the spirit of hermeneutic research, whose interpreters construct themselves through the study they make of others, we will suggest that when it is applied to ethnology and ethnological literature, a narrowly based hermeneutics runs the risk of triviality. It is by no means certain that the application of deconstructivist literary criticism to the ethnographic corpus can tell us much that is not banal or obvious (for example, that Evans-Pritchard lived during the colonial era). On the other hand, it is quite possible that ethnology will be straying from the true path if it replaces its fields of study with the study of those who have done fieldwork.

But postmodern anthropology (to give the devil his due) does seem to depend on an analysis of supermodernity, of which its reductivist method (field to text, text to author) is in fact just a particular expression.

In Western societies, at least, the individual wants to be a world in himself; he intends to interpret the information delivered to him by himself and for himself. Sociologists of religion have revealed the singular character even of Catholic practice: practising Catholics intend to practise in their own fashion. Similarly, the question of relations between the sexes can be settled only in the name of the undifferentiated value of the individual. Note, though, that this individualization of approaches seems less surprising when it is referred to the analyses outlined above: never before have individual histories been so explicitly affected by collective history, but never before, either, have the reference points for collective identification been so unstable. The individual production of meaning is thus more necessary than ever. Naturally, sociology is perfectly placed to expose the illusions on which this individualization of approaches is based, and the effects of reproduction and stereotyping which wholly or partly escape the notice of the players. But the singular character of the production of meaning, backed by a whole advertising apparatus (which talks of the body, the senses, the freshness of living) and a whole political language (hinged on the theme of individual freedoms), is interesting in itself. It relates to what ethnologists have studied among foreigners under various headings: what might be called local anthropologies (rather than cosmologies), the systems of representation in which the categories of identity and otherness are given shape.

So anthropologists are today facing, in new terms, a problem that raises the same difficulties that Mauss, and after him the culturalist school, confronted in their day: how to think about and situate the individual. Michel de Certeau, in *L'Invention du quotidien*, talks about "tricks in the arts of doing" that enable individuals subjected to the global constraints of modern – especially urban – society to deflect them, to make use of them, to contrive through a sort of everyday tinkering to establish their own decor and trace their own personal itineraries. But, as Michel de Certeau was aware, these tricks and these arts of doing refer sometimes to the multiplicity of average individuals (the ultimate in concreteness), sometimes to the average of individuals (an abstraction). Similarly Freud, in his "sociological" works *Civilization and its Discontents* and *The Future of an Illusion*, uses the expression "ordinary man" – *der gemeine Mann* – to contrast, rather as Mauss does, the general run of individuals with the enlightened elite: those human individuals capable of making themselves the object of a reflective approach.

Freud is perfectly well aware, however, that the alienated man of whom he writes – alienated from various institutions: religion for example – is also all mankind or Everyman, starting with Freud himself or anyone else in a position to observe at first hand the mechanisms and effects of alienation. This necessary alienation is clearly the one Lévi-Strauss means when he writes in his "Introduction to the Work of Marcel Mauss" that, strictly speaking, it is the person we consider healthy in mind who is alienated, since he agrees to exist in a world defined by relations with others.

Freud, as we know, practised self-analysis. The question facing anthropologists today is how best to integrate the subjectivity of those they observe into their analysis: in other words, how to redefine the conditions of representativeness to take account of the renewed status of the individual in our societies. We cannot rule out the possibility that the anthropologist, following Freud's example, might care to consider himself as indigenous to his own culture – a privileged informant, so to speak – and risk a few attempts at ethno-self-analysis.

Beyond the heavy emphasis placed today on the individual reference (or, if you prefer, the individualization of references), attention should really be given to factors of singularity: singularity of objects, of groups or memberships, the reconstruction of places; the singularities of all sorts that constitute a paradoxical counterpoint to the procedures of interrelation, acceleration and de-localization sometimes carelessly reduced and summarized in expressions like "homogenization of culture" or "world culture".

The question of the conditions for practising an anthropology of contemporaneity should be transferred from the method to the object. This is not to suggest that questions of method do not have decisive importance, or that they can be entirely dissociated from the question of object. But the question of object comes first. It can even be said to constitute a double premiss, because before taking an interest in the new social forms, modes of sensibility or institutions that may seem characteristic of present contemporaneity we need to pay some attention to the changes affecting the major categories people use when they think about their identity and their reciprocal relations. The three figures of excess which we have employed to characterize the situation of supermodernity – overabundance of events, spatial overabundance, the individualization of references – make it possible to grasp the idea of supermodernity without ignoring its complexities and contradictions, but also without treating it as the uncrossable horizon of a lost modernity with which nothing remains to be done except to map its traces, list its isolates and index its files. The twenty-first century will be anthropological, not only because the three figures of excess are just the current form of a perennial raw material which is the very ore of anthropology, but also because in situations of supermodernity (as in the situations anthropology has analysed under the name of "acculturation") the components pile up without destroying one another. So we can reassure in advance those passionately devoted to the phenomena studied by anthropology (from marriage to religion, from exchange to power, from possession to witchcraft): they are not about to disappear from Africa, or from Europe either. But they will make sense again (they will remake meaning), along with all the rest, in a different world, whose reasons and unreasons the anthropologists of tomorrow, just like those of today, will have to try to understand.

References

Certeau, Michel de, *L'Invention du quotidien. 1. Arts de faire* (1990 edn.), Gallimard, "Folio-Essais".

Furet, François, *Penser la Révolution*, Gallimard, 1978.

Mauss, Marcel, *Sociologie et anthropologie*, PUF, 1966.

L'Autre et le semblable. Regards sur l'ethnologie des sociétés contemporaines, collected and edited by Martine Segalen, Presses du CNRS, 1989.

49

Relativism

Bruno Latour

The Import–Export System of the Two Great Divides

[…] "We Westerners are absolutely different from others!" – such is the moderns' victory cry, or protracted lament. The Great Divide between Us – Occidentals – and Them – everyone else, from the China seas to the Yucatan, from the Inuit to the Tasmanian aborigines – has not ceased to obsess us. Whatever they do, Westerners bring history along with them in the hulls of their caravels and their gunboats, in the cylinders of their telescopes and the pistons of their immunizing syringes. They bear this white man's burden sometimes as an exalting challenge, sometimes as a tragedy, but always as a destiny. They do not claim merely that they differ from others as the Sioux differ from the Algonquins, or the Baoules from the Lapps, but that they differ radically, absolutely, to the extent that Westerners can be lined up on one side and all the cultures on the other, since the latter all have in common the fact that they are precisely cultures among others. In Westerners' eyes the West, and the West alone, is not a culture, not merely a culture.

Why does the West see itself this way? Why would the West and only the West not be a culture? In order to understand the Great Divide between Us and Them, we have to go back to that other Great Divide between humans and nonhumans […]. In effect, *the first is the exportation of the second*. We Westerners cannot be one culture among others, since we also mobilize Nature. We do not mobilize an image or a symbolic representation of Nature, the way the other societies do, but Nature as it is, or at least as it is known to the sciences – which remain in the background, unstudied, unstudiable, miraculously conflated with Nature itself. Thus at the heart of the question of relativism we find the question of science. If Westerners had been content with trading and conquering, looting and dominating, they would not distinguish themselves radically from other tradespeople and conquerors. But no, they invented science, an activity totally distinct from conquest and trade, politics and morality.

Even those who have tried, in the name of cultural relativism, to defend the continuity of cultures without ordering them in a progressive series, and without isolating them in their separate

From *We Have Never Been Modern*, trans. Catherine Porter (Cambridge, Mass.: Harvard University Press, 1993), pp. 97–106, 146, 148–53. Copyright © 1993 by Harvester Wheatsheaf and the President and Fellows of Harvard College.

Anthropology in Theory: Issues in Epistemology, Second Edition. Edited by Henrietta L. Moore and Todd Sanders.
© 2014 John Wiley & Sons, Inc. Published 2014 by John Wiley & Sons, Inc.

prisons (Lévi-Strauss, [1952] 1987), think they can do this only by bringing them as close as possible to the sciences.

"We have had to wait until the middle of this century", writes Lévi-Strauss in *The Savage Mind*, "for the crossing of long separated paths: that which arrives at the physical world by the detour of communication [the savage mind], and that which, as we have recently come to know, arrives at the world of communication by the detour of the physical [modern science]" (Lévi-Strauss, [1962] 1966, p. 269).

> The false antinomy between logical and prelogical mentality was surmounted at the same time. The savage mind is as logical in the same sense and the same fashion as ours, though as our own is only when it is applied to knowledge of a universe in which it recognizes physical and semantic properties simultaneously...It will be objected that there remains a major difference between the thought of primitives and our own: Information Theory is concerned with genuine messages whereas primitives mistake mere manifestations of physical determinism for messages...In treating the sensible properties of the animal and plant kingdoms as if they were the elements of a message, and in discovering "signatures" – and so signs – in them, men [those with savage minds] have made mistakes of identification: the meaningful element was not always the one they supposed. But, without perfected instruments which would have permitted them to place it where it most often is – namely, at the microscopic level – they already discerned "as through a glass darkly" principles of interpretation whose heuristic value and accordance with reality have been revealed to us only through very recent inventions: telecommunications, computers and electron microscopes. (Lévi-Strauss, [1962] 1966, p. 268)

Lévi-Strauss, a generous defence lawyer, imagines no mitigating circumstances other than making his clients look as much like scientists as possible! If primitive peoples do not differ from us as much as we think, it is because they anticipate the newest conquests of information theory, molecular biology and physics, but with inadequate instruments and "errors of identification". The very sciences that are used for this promotion are now off limits. Conceived in the fashion of epistemology,

these sciences remain objective and external, quasi-objects purged of their networks. Give the primitives a microscope, and they will think exactly as we do. Is there a better way to finish off those one wants to save from condemnation? For Lévi-Strauss (as for Canguilhem, Lyotard, Girard, Derrida, and the majority of French intellectuals), this new scientific knowledge lies entirely outside culture. It is the transcendence of science – conflated with Nature – that makes it possible to relativize all cultures, theirs and ours alike – with the one caveat, of course, that it is precisely our culture, not theirs, that is constructed through biology, electronic microscopes and telecommunication networks....The abyss that was to supposed to be narrowing opens up again.

Somewhere in our societies, and in ours alone, an unheard-of transcendence has manifested itself: Nature as it is, ahuman, sometimes inhuman, always extrahuman. Since this event occurred – whether one situates it in Greek mathematics, Italian physics, German chemistry, American nuclear engineering or Belgian thermodynamics – there has been a total asymmetry between the cultures that took Nature into account and those that took into account only their own culture or the distorted versions that they might have of matter. Those who invent sciences and discover physical determinisms never deal exclusively with human beings, except by accident. The others have only representations of Nature that are more or less disturbed or coded by the cultural preoccupations of the humans that occupy them fully and fall only by chance – "as through a glass darkly" – on things as they are.

So the Internal Great Divide accounts for the External Great Divide: we are the only ones who differentiate absolutely between Nature and Culture, between Science and Society, whereas in our eyes all the others – whether they are Chinese or Amerindian, Azande or Barouya – cannot really separate what is knowledge from what is Society, what is sign from what is thing, what comes from Nature as it is from what their cultures require. Whatever they do, however adapted, regulated and functional they may be, they will always remain blinded by this confusion; they are prisoners of the social and of language alike. Whatever we do, however criminal, however imperialistic we may be, we escape from the prison of the social or of language to gain access to things themselves

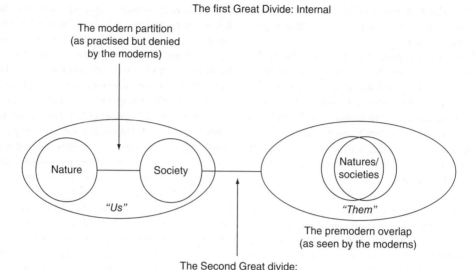

The first Great Divide: Internal

The modern partition
(as practised but denied
by the moderns)

Nature — Society

"Us"

Natures/
societies

"Them"

The premodern overlap
(as seen by the moderns)

The Second Great divide:
external

Figure 49.1   The two Great Divides

through a providential exit gate, that of scientific knowledge. The internal partition between humans and nonhumans defines a second partition – an external one this time – through which the moderns have set themselves apart from the premoderns. For Them, Nature and Society, signs and things, are virtually coextensive. For Us they should never be. Even though we might still recognize in our own societies some fuzzy areas in madness, children, animals, popular culture and women's bodies (Haraway, 1989), we believe our duty is to extirpate ourselves from those horrible mixtures as forcibly as possible by no longer confusing what pertains to mere social preoccupations and what pertains to the real nature of things.

Anthropology Comes Home from the Tropics

When anthropology comes home from the tropics in order to rejoin the anthropology of the modern world that is ready and waiting, it does so at first with caution, not to say with pusillanimity. At first, it thinks it can apply its methods only when Westerners mix up signs and things the way savage thought does. It will therefore look for what most resembles its traditional terrains as defined by the External Great Divide. To be sure,

it has to sacrifice exoticism, but not at great cost, since anthropology maintains its critical distance by studying only the margins and fractures of rationality, or the realms beyond rationality. Popular medicine, witchcraft in the Bocage (Favret-Saada, 1980), peasant life in the shadow of nuclear power plants (Zonabend, 1989), the representations ordinary people have of technical risks (Douglas, 1983) – all these can be excellent field study topics, because the question of Nature – that is, of science – is not yet raised.

However, the great repatriation cannot stop there. In fact, by sacrificing exoticism, the ethnologist loses what constituted the very originality of her research as opposed to the scattered studies of sociologists, economists, psychologists or historians. In the tropics, the anthropologist did not settle for studying the margins of other cultures (Geertz, 1971). If she remained marginal by vocation and method, and out of necessity, she nevertheless claimed to be reconstituting the centre of those cultures: their belief system, their technologies, their ethno-sciences, their power plays, their economies – in short, the totality of their existence (Mauss, [1923] 1967). If she comes back home but limits herself to studying the marginal aspects of her own culture, she loses all the hard-won advantages of anthropology. For example Marc Augé when he resided among the lagoon-dwellers of the

Ivory Coast, sought to understand the entire social phenomenon revealed by sorcery (Augé, 1975). His marginality did not hinder him from grasping the full social fabric of Alladian culture. But back at home he has limited himself to studying the most superficial aspects of the metro (Augé, 1986), interpreting some graffiti on the walls of subway corridors, intimidated this time by the evidence of his own marginality in the face of Western economics, technologies and science. A symmetrical Marc Augé would have studied the sociotechnological network of the metro itself: its engineers as well as its drivers, its directors and its clients, the employer-State, the whole shebang – simply doing at home what he had always done elsewhere. Western ethnologists cannot limit themselves to the periphery; otherwise, still asymmetrical, they would show boldness toward others, timidity toward themselves. Back home anthropology need not become the marginal discipline of the margins, picking up the crumbs that fall from the other disciplines' banquet table.

In order to achieve such freedom of movement and tone, however, one has to be able to view the two Great Divides in the same way, and consider them both as one particular definition of our world and its relationships with the others. Now these Divides do not define us any better than they define others; they are no more an instrument of knowledge than is the Constitution alone, or modern temporality alone [...]. To become symmetrical, anthropology needs a complete overhaul and intellectual retooling so that it can get around both Divides at once by believing neither in the radical distinction between humans and nonhumans at home, nor in the total overlap of knowledge and society elsewhere.

Let us imagine an ethnologist who goes out to the tropics and takes along with her the Internal Great Divide. In her eyes, the people she studies continually confuse knowledge of the world – which the investigator, as a good scientistic Westerner, possesses as her birthright – and the requirements of social functioning. The tribe that greets her thus has only one vision of the world, only one representation of Nature. To go back to the expression Marcel Mauss and Emile Durkheim made famous, this tribe projects its own social categories on to Nature (Durkheim and Mauss, [1903] 1967; Haudricourt, 1962). When our ethnologist explains to her informers

that they must be more careful to separate the world as it is from the social representation they provide for it, they are scandalized or nonplussed. The ethnologist sees in their rage and their misunderstanding the very proof of their premodern obsession. The dualism in which she lives – humans on one side, nonhumans on the other, signs over here, things over there – is intolerable to them. For social reasons, our ethnologist concludes, this culture requires a monist attitude. "We traffic in ideas; [the savage mind] hoards them up" (Lévi-Strauss, [1962] 1966, p. 267).

But let us suppose now that our ethnologist returns to her homeland and tries to dissolve the Internal Great Divide. And let us suppose that through a series of happy accidents she sets out to analyze one tribe among others – for example, scientific researchers or engineers (Knorr-Cetina, 1992). The situation turns out to be reversed, because now she applies the lessons of monism she thinks she has learned from her earlier experience. Her tribe of scientists claims that in the end they are completely separating their knowledge of the world from the necessities of politics and morality (Traweek, 1988). In the observer's eyes, however, this separation is never very visible, or is itself only the by-product of a much more mixed activity, some tinkering in and out of the laboratory. Her informers claim that they have access to Nature, but the ethnographer sees perfectly well that they have access only to a vision, a representation of Nature that she herself cannot distinguish neatly from politics and social interests (Pickering, 1980). This tribe, like the earlier one, projects its own social categories on to Nature; what is new is that it pretends it has not done so. When the ethnologist explains to her informers that they cannot separate Nature from the social representation they have formed of it, they are scandalized or nonplussed. Our ethnologist sees in their rage and incomprehension the very proof of their modern obsession. The monism in which she now lives – humans are always mixed up with nonhumans – is intolerable to them. For social reasons, our ethnologist concludes, Western scientists require a dualist attitude.

However, her double conclusion is incorrect, for she has not really heard what her informers were saying. The goal of anthropology is not to scandalize twice over, or to provoke incomprehension

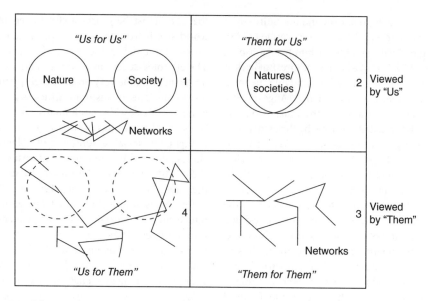

Figure 49.2   Them and Us

twice in a row: the first time by exporting the Internal Great Divide and imposing dualism on cultures that reject it; the second time by cancelling the External Great Divide and imposing monism on a culture, our own – that rejects it absolutely. Symmetrical anthropology must realize that the two Great Divides do not describe reality – our own as well as that of others – but define the particular way Westerners had of establishing their relations with others as long as they felt modern. "We", however, do not distinguish between Nature and Society more than "They" make them overlap. If we take into account the networks that we allow to proliferate beneath the official part of our Constitution they look a lot like the networks in which "They" say they live. Premoderns are said never to distinguish beween signs and things, but neither do "We" (figure 49.2.3 and the bottom of 49.2.1 look very much alike). If, through an acrobatic thought experiment, we could go further and ask "Them" to try to map on to their own networks our strange obsession with dichotomies and to try to imagine, in their own terms, what it could mean to have a pure Nature and a pure Society they would draw, with extreme difficulty, a provisional map in which Nature and Society would barely escape from the networks (figure 49.2.4). But what does this picture represent, this picture in

which Nature and Culture appear to be redistributed among the networks and to escape from them only fuzzily as if in dotted lines? It is exactly our world as we now see it through nonmodern eyes! It is exactly the picture I have tried to offer from the beginning, in which the upper and lower halves of the Constitution gradually merge. Premoderns are like us. Once they are considered symmetrically, they might offer a better analysis of the Westerners than the modernist anthropology offered of the premoderns! Or, more exactly, we can now drop entirely the "Us" and "Them" dichotomy, and even the distinction between moderns and premoderns. We have both always built communities of natures and societies. There is only one, symmetrical, anthropology.

There Are No Cultures

Let us suppose that anthropology, having come home from the tropics, sets out to retool itself by occupying a triply symmetrical position. It uses the same terms to explain truths and errors (this is the first principle of symmetry); it studies the production of humans and nonhumans simultaneously (this is the principle of generalized symmetry); finally, it refrains from making any *a priori* declarations as to what might distinguish Westerners from Others. To be sure, it loses exoticism, but it gains new fields of study that allow it to analyze the central mechanism of all collectives, including the ones to which Westerners belong. It loses its exclusive attachment to cultures alone – or to cultural dimensions alone – but it gains a priceless acquisition, natures. The two positions I have been staking out since the beginning of this essay – the one the ethnologist is now occupying effortlessly, and the one the analyst of the sciences was striving toward with great difficulty – can now be superimposed. Network analysis extends a hand to anthropology, and offers it the job that has been ready and waiting.

The question of relativism is already becoming less difficult. If science as conceived along the epistemologists' lines made the problem insoluble, it suffices, as is often the case, to change the conception of scientific practices in order to dispel the artificial difficulties. What reason complicates, networks explicate. It is the peculiar trait of Westerners that they have imposed, by their official Constitution, the total separation of humans and nonhumans – the Internal Great Divide – and have thereby artificially created the scandal of the others. "How can one be a Persian?" How can one not establish a radical difference between universal Nature and relative culture? But *the very notion of culture is an artifact created by bracketing Nature off*. Cultures – different or universal – do not exist, any more than Nature does. There are only natures-cultures, and these offer the only possible basis for comparison. As soon as we take practices of mediation as well as practices of purification into account, we discover that the moderns do not separate humans from nonhumans any more than the "others" totally superimpose signs and things.

I can now compare the forms of relativism according to whether they do or do not take into account the construction of natures as well. Absolute relativism presupposes cultures that are separate and incommensurable and cannot be ordered in any hierarchy; there is no use

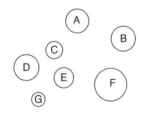

Absolute relativism

Culture without hierarchy
and without contacts,
all incommensurable;
Nature is bracketed

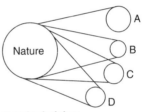

Cultural relativism

Nature is present but outside cultures;
cultures all have a more or less precise
point of view toward Nature

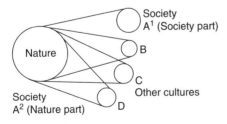

Particular universalism

One of the cultures (A) has
a privileged access to Nature
which sets it apart from the others

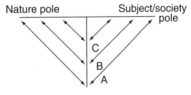

Symmetrical anthropology

All the collectives similarly constitute
natures and cultures; only the
scale of the mobilization varies

Figure 49.3   Relativism and universalism

talking about it, since it brackets off Nature. As for cultural relativism, which is more subtle, Nature comes into play, but in order to exist it does not presuppose any scientific work, any society, any construction, any mobilization, any network. It is Nature revisited and corrected by epistemology, for which scientific practice still remains off camera, *hors champ*. Within this tradition, the cultures are thus distributed as so many more or less accurate viewpoints on that unique Nature. Certain societies see it "as through a glass darkly", others see it through thick fog, still others under clear skies. Rationalists will insist on the common aspects of all these viewpoints; relativists will insist on the irresistible distortion that social structures impose on all perception. The former will be undone if it can be shown that cultures do not superimpose their categories; the latter will lose ground if it can be proved that the categories are superimposed (Hollis and Lukes, 1982; Wilson, 1970).

In practice, however, as soon as Nature comes into play without being attached to a particular culture, a third model is always secretly used: a type of universalism that I would call "particular". One society – and it is always the Western one – defines the general framework of Nature with respect to which the others are situated. This is Lévi-Strauss's solution: he distinguishes Western society, which has a specific interpretation of Nature, from that Nature itself, miraculously known to our society. The first half of the argument allows for modest relativism (we are just one interpretation among others), but the second permits the surreptitious return of arrogant universalism – we remain absolutely different. In Lévi-Strauss's eyes, however, there is no contradiction between the two halves, precisely because our Constitution, and it alone, allows us to distinguish society A^1, made up of humans, from society A^2, composed of nonhumans but forever removed from the first one! The contradiction stands out today only in the eyes of symmetrical anthropology. This latter model is the common stock of the other two, whatever the relativists (who never relativize anything but cultures) may say.

The relativists have never been convincing on the subject of the equality of cultures, since they limit their consideration precisely to cultures. And Nature? According to them, it is the same for all, since universal science defines it. In order to get out of this contradiction, they then either have to limit all peoples to a representation of the world by locking them up for ever in the prison of their own societies or, conversely, they have to reduce all scientific results to products of local and contingent social constructions in order to deny science any universality. But to imagine billions of people imprisoned in distorted views of the world since the beginning of time is as difficult as it is to imagine neutrinos and quasars, DNA and universal gravitation, as Texan, British or Burgundian social productions. The two responses are equally absurd, and that is why the great debates over relativism never lead anywhere. *It is as impossible to universalize nature as it is to reduce it to the narrow framework of cultural relativism alone.*

The solution appears along with the dissolution of the artifact of cultures. All natures-cultures are similar in that they simultaneously construct humans, divinities and nonhumans. None of them inhabits a world of signs or symbols arbitrarily imposed on an external Nature known to us alone. None of them – and especially not our own – lives in a world of things. All of them sort out what will bear signs and what will not. If there is one thing we all do, it is surely that we construct both our human collectives and the nonhumans that surround them. In constituting their collectives, some mobilize ancestors, lions, fixed stars, and the coagulated blood of sacrifice; in constructing ours, we mobilize genetics, zoology, cosmology and hæmatology. "But those are sciences!" the moderns will exclaim, horrified at this confusion. "They have to escape the representations of society to the greatest possible extent!" Yet the presence of the sciences does not suffice to break the symmetry; such is the discovery of comparative anthropology. From cultural relativism we move on to "natural" relativism. The first led to absurdities; the second will allow us to fall back on common sense. [...]

References

Augé, Marc (1975), *Théorie des pouvoirs et idéologie*, Paris: Hermann.

Augé, Marc (1986), *Un ethnologue dans le métro*, Paris: Hachette.

Douglas, Mary (1983), *Risk and Culture: An essay in the selection of technical and environmental dangers*, Berkeley: University of California Press.

Durkheim, Emile and Marcel Mauss ([1903] 1967), *Primitive Classifications*, Chicago: University of Chicago Press.

Favret-Saada, Jeanne (1980), *Deadly Words: Witchcraft in the Bocage*, trans. Catherine Cullen, Cambridge: Cambridge University Press.

Geertz, Clifford (1971), *The Interpretation of Cultures: Selected essays*, New York: Basic Books.

Haraway, Donna (1989), *Primate Visions: Gender, race and nature in the world*, London: Routledge & Kegan Paul.

Haudricourt, A.G. (1962), "Domestication des animaux, culture des plantes et traitement d'autrui", *L'Homme* 2:40–50.

Hollis, Martin and Stephen Lukes, eds. (1982), *Rationality and Relativism*, Oxford: Blackwell.

Knorr-Cetina, Karin (1992) "The couch, the cathedral and the laboratory: on the relationships between experiment and laboratory in science", in *Science as Practice and Culture*, ed. Andrew Pickering, pp. 113–38, Chicago: University of Chicago Press.

Lévi-Strauss, Claude ([1952] 1987), *Race and History*, Paris: UNESCO.

Lévi-Strauss, Claude ([1962] 1966), *The Savage Mind*, Chicago: University of Chicago Press.

Mauss, Marcel ([1923] 1967), *The Gift: Forms and functions of exchange in archaic societies (with a foreword by E. Evans-Pritchard)*, New York: W. W. Norton.

Pickering, Andrew (1980), "The role of interests in high-energy physics: the choice between charm and colour", *Sociology of the Sciences* 4: 107–38.

Traweek, Sharon (1988), *Beam Times and Life Times: The world of high energy physicists*, Cambridge, MA: Harvard University Press.

Wilson, Bryan R., ed. (1970), *Rationality*, Oxford: Blackwell.

Zonabend, Françoise (1989), *La presqu'île au nucléaire*, Paris: Odile Jacob.

SECTION 15

Subjects, Objects, and Affect

50

How to Read the Future: The Yield Curve, Affect, and Financial Prediction

Caitlin Zaloom

The future is unknowable. Yet in global financial markets, profits and protection of wealth depend on actions taken under this necessarily uncertain condition. Several decades ago John Maynard Keynes pointed to the modern desire for clear knowledge in economic activity. Statistical data promise certainty. Affect arises when knowledge has no solid ground. The future, for him, defined the limits of reason most powerfully. "Whim," "sentiment," and "chance" enter at the edges of calculation. The twin poles of reason and affect define certainty and uncertainty, two key sets of modern divisions, as unattainable as they are powerful. [...] [But j]udgements regarding the future, even those based on statistical assessment, easily entwine with sentiments. [...] [Keynes's] clear distinction between calculation and feeling tenders a modern fantasy (see Keynes 2008). The affects that Keynes assigns to the limits of reason accrue even as calculation proceeds.

I argue here that contemporary financial knowledge is organized around the interplay of reason and affect. The composition and use of common financial tools provide a window onto this process. The devices that should create grounds for calculating future profits and

opportunities also open avenues for affective discomfort. [...] Predictive instruments flag economic risks by consolidating the individual assessments of market participants regarding the future. At the same time, their signals feed back into professionals' affects and decisions in striking ways.

The reflexive character of financial devices provides fertile ground for emotions. In this, these tools share characteristics with the shaky knowledge that undergirds "reflexive modernity" as Anthony Giddens (1990) describes it. [...] As practitioners of reflexive modernity, financial professionals design and act within the expert systems that create and monitor risk in contemporary markets. Yet even such direct technical understanding and experience do not provide the certainty that modern knowledge promises. Financial actors share the puzzlement to which Giddens points. Experts, too, are caught up in the play of reason and affect around the systems of their own creation. But why? How might the particulars of financial prediction help to characterize reflexive, modern knowledge systems?

The yield curve of the US Treasury, a widely used indicator of economic strength, offers a compelling example. The curve is a graphic

Anthropology in Theory: Issues in Epistemology, Second Edition. Edited by Henrietta L. Moore and Todd Sanders.
© 2014 John Wiley & Sons, Inc. Published 2014 by John Wiley & Sons, Inc.

representation of US bonds' future value. A powerful model of the future, it points to the health of America's economy and therefore reflects global economic stability. Financial participants are knitted in a loosely entangled economic public through recursive loops of feeling, reading, interpreting, and acting around this tool. The yield curve unifies a field of market action, reflection, and emotion, bringing together the dispersed and disparate actors who make up the credit market. [...] For these actors, both internationally and in the United States, the curve's shape crystallizes particular uncertainties about the future under the specific conditions of the present. However, the fundamental indeterminacy of the future does not fully explain the power of the affects that the curve's movements elicit.

The design of the yield curve, like many predictive tools, embodies contradictions that disturb even as they offer knowledge. The curve was constructed as a device for understanding risk and time in the US Treasury market. An image of the relationship between bond yields of varied durations, the curve offers a way to understand the market's collective assessment of the future (i.e., whether the economy is weak or strong). At the same time, it shows savvy investors where profit potential lies if they can outsmart the dealers whose trades make up the curve. It is a terrain of future knowledge and intervention. It is also an affective lightning rod. As an indicator, the yield curve points to the particular uncertainties of the economy to come. But the curve does not merely indicate; like all indicators, it also produces its own uncertainties.

[...] If the participants are rational, then the yield curve's signals about the future should be valid. Bank traders and hedge fund managers assume their counterparts act as they do [...]. However, the market may include traders whose intentions or "irrational" judgments distort the picture. The bond market cannot be assumed to be composed of only judicious experts. Yet participants can never know who exactly does what in the market.

[...] Inevitably, anxiety, fear, and suspicion creep into the most calculating financial minds. A lack of faith in the rational actions of others renders the yield curve a useful but not fully reliable tool. Speculative questions arise: Can the yield curve and its predictions be trusted?

Who, exactly, is making it move? What does its image really reveal about the future?

In the following pages I develop a picture of the yield curve as a simultaneously epistemic and affective object that financial professionals place at the heart of their planning and trading practices. [...] I illustrate how predictive tools shape visions of the future in the practice of financial capitalism and, in the process, form their own locus of doubt and disturbance.

[...]

What Is the Yield Curve?

The yield curve provides a picture of the emerging economy. Fund managers, traders, and bank-based economists attempt to exploit the curve's fluctuations. Academic economists consult the curve for information that they use in planning reports and public policy. [...] In December 2005 one hedge fund manager told me of its centrality in the financial universe, offering celestial reverence as he called it "the sun around which everything else revolves." Throughout the workday its [...] shape [shifts] at a dizzying pace. Longer-term twists in the curve are also meaningful. An "inverted" curve has preceded each recession since the mid-1960s (with one exception), a record that some use to orient their strategies, while others question its salience. Traders and investors read, reflect, and nervously anticipate movements in the curve, a robust yet controversial predictor of economic health or weakness. Their future profits could depend on it.

The yield curve is also widely used for understanding investors' collective sentiments about the future conditions in the US economy and for orienting financial planning and policy. Interest rates are the major monetary tools of the US government [...]. The curve graphically depicts today's Treasury "yields," or the relationship between the interest rate and the time to maturity of a bond. [...] US instruments of debt – bills, notes, and bonds – come in different "maturities" or durations, from a few days to thirty years. The yield curve visually describes the relationship between the yields of these different bonds. [...] Movement in the slope of the curve is affected mainly by two actions: the monetary policy of the Federal Reserve as it raises or lowers short-term interest rates, and the buying and selling of US Treasury bonds. Financial professionals read these fluctuations carefully and dissect them with focused consideration.

[...]

A New Epistemic Terrain

[...][T]he curve itself arises from a specific past. The yield curve's significance emerged in the 1970s and 1980s, times of transformation in global finance. [...]

In the 1970s the US government introduced a new relationship between time and money. [...] [A]s petrodollars amassed in the Middle East and the Vietnam War wore on, the rise of rival economic powers to US hegemony brought the Bretton Woods agreement to an end. American currencies and interest rates would "float" on the open market.

[...] Investors, not the US government, began to set the prices of dollars and America's debt. Bank traders now bought and sold on the shifting and unsteady prospects of the American economy going forward. [...]

As the US government allowed the market to set values for American bonds, key players in the bond markets and in bond theory built the significance of the yield curve with their novel trading strategies and writings. Before this shift, bonds had been dealt as distinct packages of time; traders were assigned to separate markets in two-, five-, and ten-year bonds. During the 1970s traders conceived of these bonds instead as a continuum of moments. Traders' deals embodied their assessments of risk along the curve, connecting the formerly independent packages of time and money. [...] In the process, the yield curve became an important topic of debate both among financial professionals and in the popular press. [...]

[...]

The 1970s introduced an interconnection among global currencies, government bonds, and the technological systems that would link traders in real time across vast distances [...]. Markets had always operated through distant connections, but the yield curve added something crucial: an object with which market players could both participate in and reflect on the economy.

[...] Once bond yields recorded primarily collective buying and selling, the curve could be read as an aggregate opinion to which individual players added their voice. The curve could stand in for the feelings of the market about the future of the US economy, about current federal policy in shaping it, and about the potential of economic and political events to alter financial plans. [...]

It took a few years for traders' vision of the yield curve to filter into more general use. The Economist (1976) provided its readers with a tutorial on the economic elements that shape the yield curve. The New York Times first mentioned the yield curve in 1978, noting that President Jimmy Carter's new Federal Reserve chairman was responding to the credit market's "gloomy" demeanor with an intention to reshape the yield curve (Allan 1978). [...]

What had begun in the 1970s continued with the expansion of fixed-income trading in the 1980s and 1990s. Traders, policy makers, and the public turned to the yield curve to reflect on the market's judgment of the economic future. The yield curve established a new relationship between money and time. [...] In theory and in practice, financial professionals had built the yield curve into an object for interpreting the contours of a possible future. The curve also gained power as an object with which traders and planners intervened to draw profit and to manage the economy. As new techniques for trading thrived and analytic talk flowered, the curve became a powerful connection among investors around the world. This new terrain of trading on credit risk and, at the same time, monitoring it solidified the reflexive character of the yield curve.

[...]

The Yield Curve Today

Today two groups of finance professionals are especially interested in the yield curve: fund managers, traders, and bank-based economists, whose profit-seeking strategies draw on the curve's fluctuations, and academic economists, who read the curve for information that they use in planning reports and public policy. [...]

The yield curve is an uncertain model for an uncertain future. Both the strengths and the weaknesses of models like the yield curve develop from their reflexive uses: the rationality of monitoring risk clashes with the heterogeneous intentions and rationalities of the traders who make up the market. [...]

Through the prism of the yield curve, the market shows two faces to those who assess its expressions: it is an emergent entity composed of the simultaneous and coordinated actions of individuals making separate decisions and an aggregation, a consolidation of their opinions (marked in buying and selling) into a single number – price. Each feature figures into its participants' conscious experience and strategies, requiring constant monitoring and revision of opinions and plans.

In particular, financial professionals develop a reflexive relationship with their devices, asking questions and constantly revising opinions. Most important is to understand who is making the judgments that shape the yield curve. The conflict between the curve as a monitoring system and its constantly changing makeup creates hot debate, rendering the yield curve a lightning rod. Assessments of collective market feelings lead, then, to a cascade of affects and arguments related to the composition of the market itself.

Market sentiments

[...] The market's emergent nature is responsible for this dual life: it is made up of individuals but apprehended in aggregate. Collectively, the shifts in price and therefore in mood can seem like the vagaries of a sentient being. Traders describe interactions with the market as interpersonal engagements. For instance, futures traders speak of the market's swift and painful judgments, of its striking down those who exhibit hubris or rewarding humility in their deals (Zaloom 2006). Currency traders, Karin Knorr Cetina and Urs Breugger (2000) argue, engage the market as an "object of attachment" in the Lacanian sense. Attachment to the yield curve compels close readings of its moods. At the same time, this attention elicits the reader's own affective relationships to it. Anxiety, concern, or confidence about the economic future hinges on the reading of the curve and the commentary around it. Sentiments, both the market's and their own, orient financial experts and policy makers in their plans for profit and governance.

A disturbing shape

In the fall of 2005 that judgment seemed grave. The financial world began to buzz about an impending and portentous event. The yield curve had taken on an odd shape. Its normal winglike sweep had flattened. [...] The price for selling US government debt rose as the market registered increasing risks in the near future. For consumers, rising interest rates portend a sharp increase in their mortgage rates and a tightening of credit. For corporations, higher debt costs gnaw away at profits, slowing hiring and investment in new infrastructure. Though few people outside the financial professions might link a twist of their economic fate to the arc of the yield curve, the two are intricately entwined.

Later that year, in the normally sleepy period after Christmas when traders depart for vacations, the slope slumped again. The curve wilted to a positively pessimistic half frown. Fund managers, bond traders, economists, and market analysts chattered about what that inverted yield curve might herald. Recession was surely in the cards, many conjectured. Others argued that financial professionals should not take this seemingly gloomy sign to heart. Across the financial public – in news sites, in newsletters, and on specialist blogs – an impassioned discussion emerged about the significance of this twist.

[...]

As an aggregate image of myriad decisions, the yield curve drives, perhaps paradoxically, constant reflection on others' choices, thoughts, and strategies. As an image of a defined but elusive collective, the yield curve does not say who is doing and thinking what about the state of the economy. Instead, financial professionals create a virtual social world around its image. Their speculations about who is making the yield curve move provide provisional definition to an unexplainable contour. In informal settings such as blogs, speculations abound about the players and the affects that make the yield curve move. Whose actions can explain the shape of the curve – duplicitous Chinese bankers, reckless hedge fund managers, or rational private equity giants? The virtual players loop around the figure of the curve and provide narrative purchase for policy makers and bond traders alike to weave their strategies and to orient their own actions. Such guesses and assertions mesh with formal explanations of the yield curve found in textbooks and in formal presentations.

Formal theory

Economic theories codify the yield curve as the habitat of the rational investor whose actions explain the shape of the curve. These technical models provide traders and policy makers with conceptual frameworks that draw their actions in line with those that dwell in the theories. Economists have elaborated four approaches to the behavior of the yield curve. Now incorporated into the textbooks that traders and practicing economists consult, these four hypotheses summarize assumptions about investors' behavior and in particular their preferences for investing in time, which can be detected by the shape of the yield curve.

[...]

In the temporal structure of academic approaches to the yield curve, history also has a role to play. The past enters as a set of former predictions. A yield curve inversion has preceded each recession since the mid-1960s (with the exception of one inversion). This record has led to economic studies assessing the yield curve's predictive abilities. [...]

Professional spheres, like academic economics, impose their own time requirements and also their own affects. The rational investor of economic theory's yield curve is matched by the detached affect of academic writing. More informal sites of communication offer the possibility of bringing together professionals with distinct institutional, temporal, and affective demands. Blogs in particular offer financial professionals forums to go beyond their workplace constraints of feeling and time. Online, the financial public reflects on the power of the yield curve and speculates about the reasons for the curve's shape.

[...]

Conclusion: Reflexive Troubles

Powerful models like the yield curve focus investors' attentions around the globe, even as they pursue their varied financial goals and interests. [...] But the day's traders are not the only actors placing pressure on the curve's bend. Both formal economic theory and impressionistic, provisional explanations contribute to the yield curve's ability to speak the market's verdict. [...] As the

yield curve crystallizes theoretical positions, it also defines a topography for trading. Dealers buy and sell with the yield curve's signals about the future in mind, weaving together theory and action.

[...] Thus far the depiction hews closely to Giddens's (1990: 41) observations on economic reflexivity: formal knowledge, informal translations, and lay appropriation of economic concepts all contribute to the economy by shaping behavior, "creating a situation of continual mutual involvement between economic discourse and the activities to which it refers." [...] The yield curve, however, poses some challenges to this model of contemporary knowledge and its relation to affect.

In the yield curve and other models of the economic future, reflexive knowledge couples with the emergent organization of the market. The power of predictive instruments to provide a contour of the future relies on the constant involvement of a global trading collective. These inhabitants of the trading space bring the market into being moment by moment through their concerns, judgments, and deals. The yield curve describes this market in the continuously shifting price activity of US debt offerings. Financial professionals experience this emergent character of markets as an integral part of their work. However, the anonymity it entails leaves them constantly guessing. Who is populating the market right now? What is compelling the strategies that are shifting the curve's shape?

Some answers might lie in textbook explanations of yield curve movements that infer investors' intentions and time frames for action. However, these historically based readings cannot take into account the most current composition of the market, a makeup that continually changes. Experts hotly debate who is making the curve move and why. [...] Who they believe is making the curve move shapes opinion, not only about the market but also about the condition of their own knowledge. The reflexive emergence of financial models opens the corridor of doubt.

The interplay between reason and affect is productive: of market activity, of financial liquidity, and of the changing vision of the future around which financial professionals trade and plan. The importance of emotion is not that it enters at the limits of reason, as Keynes suggested, or as the complement to incomplete knowledge, as Giddens proposes. Rather, the high affects around the yield curve point to a conflict in the very composition of financial understanding and to an intractable problem of modern knowledge more generally. Professionals' engagements with the yield curve proceed through the uncertainties sustained in it, uncertainties about both the market players and the quality of the signal the curve offers.

The ability of the instrument to predict is always under question. Constant market changes transform the tool itself. Its meaning and effectiveness shift as financial and political conditions develop and as market participants move in and out. [...] Financial understanding and activity work through these affects, not in opposition to them. The rationality of the market model is troubling because it depends on the rationality of its participants, provoking an urgent financial problem: how to read the future.

References

Allan, John H. 1978. Credit market analysts turn gloomy. *New York Times*, January 3.

Economist. 1976. Finance and the marketplace. November 6.

Giddens, Anthony. 1990. *Consequences of modernity.* Stanford, Calif.: Stanford University Press.

Keynes, John Maynard. 2008. *The general theory of employment, interest, and money.* Israel: Beta Nu.

Knorr Cetina, Karin, and Urs Breugger. 2000. The market as an object of attachment. *Canadian Journal of Sociology* 25: 141–68.

Zaloom, Caitlin. 2006. *Out of the pits: Traders and technology from Chicago to London.* Chicago: University of Chicago Press.

51

Signs Are Not the Garb of Meaning: On the Social Analysis of Material Things

Webb Keane

How can we both understand things and do full justice to their materiality? The effort seems still to be haunted and confounded by such ancient dichotomies as form and substance, essence and accident, matter and spirit. [...]

Materiality as a Semiotic Problem

[C]onsider a more specific arena: the lingering effects of certain models of the sign. Here efforts to rethink materiality are still commonly hampered by certain assumptions built into the lineage that runs from Ferdinand de Saussure to poststructuralism. Guided by these assumptions, we tend to divide our attention between things and ideas. Those whose attention centers on things may be tempted to relegate ideas to an epiphenomenal domain, subordinated to real, tangible, stuff. Conversely, attention to ideas often seems to render material forms into little more than transparent expressions of meaning. And the more social analysis stresses the intentions, agency, and self-understandings of humans (following, for instance, Weber 1978), the more it tends to reproduce the very dichotomy between subject and object it might better be putting under critical scrutiny (Keane 2003).

This chapter aims to develop an approach to signs for which the practical and contingent character of things is neither subordinated to, nor isolated from, communication and thought. It aims to shake off what has been described as "one of [Saussure's] most durable legacies" (Irvine 1996: 258), the radical separation of the sign from the material world. The result should be a better understanding of the historicity *inherent* to signs *in their very materiality*.

Objects as a Problem for Subjects

Throughout this chapter I will return to the example of clothing, which has an indisputably intimate relationship to persons – not just their appearance and social identities, but even their gestures and smell (Stallybrass 1996). Given this intimacy, we should perhaps wonder why anyone would think of clothes as superficial. Or worse: in 1854 the American Transcendentalist Henry

Anthropology in Theory: Issues in Epistemology, Second Edition. Edited by Henrietta L. Moore and Todd Sanders.
© 2014 John Wiley & Sons, Inc. Published 2014 by John Wiley & Sons, Inc.

David Thoreau famously wrote, "I say, beware of all enterprises that require new clothes, and not rather a new wearer of clothes" (1971: 23). What's to fear? Beneath Thoreau's moralizing of things lie implicit and, today, widespread assumptions about signs. Thoreau's moralism dwells on the ways in which clothing marks social distinctions, subjects us to the vagaries of fashion, and displaces our proper concern with the immaterial. [...] Clothes form a material outside that distracts us from the spiritual inside [...].

But there is more. Caring about clothing gives us over too much to the opinion of others. [...] It leads us to invert our values, imputing life to the lifeless and thereby losing ourselves. The proper understanding of material signs has moral implications. These hinge both on a particular understanding of the subject's fundamental interiority and on the subject's relations to other people, to the extent that they are mediated by signs. Signs are viewed, like other people, as thoroughly external to, or even at odds with, that interiority.

[...]

Why should materiality be a moral question? Part of the answer involves the historical fate of a particular ontology that defines subjects in opposition to objects (Keane 1996, 2002). But there is a more specific manifestation of this ontology, in background assumptions about the sign common to much Western social theory. If social and cultural analysts still find it difficult to treat objects as no more than illustrations of something else, as, say, communicating meanings or identities, it is because we remain heirs of a tradition that treats signs as if they were merely the garb of meaning – meaning that, it would seem, must be stripped bare. As this tradition dematerializes signs, it privileges meaning over actions, consequences, and possibilities. Yet we must be wary of merely reversing this privilege and thereby inadvertently reproducing the same dichotomy. Drawing on semiotic concepts such as iconicity and indexicality, and the ideologies that organize them in representational economies, I'd like to suggest some alternatives.

Signs in Their Causal Relations

[...] Saussurean "semiology" (not "semiotics") also makes it hard to perceive the role that language does play vis-à-vis material things. First, it treats language as something that exists in a plane of reality quite distinct from that in which any nonlinguistic things (material or conceptual) are found. It connects to those things only as objects of reference and denotation. Second, by seeing language only as coded meaning, Saussurean semiology fails to see the role linguistic practices play in the objectification of things, a point to which I will return at the end of this chapter. The problem is, semiotics has too often been treated, especially in cultural studies, as merely about the communication of meanings. [...]

In contrast to those who treat signs as coded messages, Peirce located signs within a material world of consequences. He insisted that concrete circumstances were essential to the very possibility of signification. [...]

The Peircean model of the sign has two features I want to bring out here. First, it is processual: signs give rise to new signs, in an unending process of signification. This point is important because it entails sociability, struggle, historicity, and contingency. This interpretation of the model offers a challenge to the facile but commonplace claim that to take things as signs is to reduce the world to discourse and its interpretation, to give in to the totalizing imperative to render all things meaningful. Second, the Peircean model devotes considerable attention to the complex range of possible relationships among signs, interpretations, and objects. For purposes of material analysis, I will be concerned with relations between signs and their possible objects of signification, which can be one of resemblance (*iconicity*), actual connection (*indexicality*), or rule (*symbolism*).

[...]

Bundling and the Openness of Objects

"She likes red," said the little girl.
"Red," said Mr. Rabbit. "You can't give her red."
"Something red, maybe," said the little girl.
"Oh, something red," said Mr. Rabbit.
Charlotte Zolotow, *Mr. Rabbit and
the Lovely Present*

One of the most sophisticated and far-reaching uses of iconicity in ethnographic analysis is Nancy Munn's (1986) account of a Melanesian system of production, consumption, and exchange. Her analysis gives a special role to those sensuous qualities of objects which have a privileged role within a larger system of value. [...] As Mr. Rabbit observes, redness must be embodied in something red. But the little girl's intuition is right too: for someone who likes red, in theory any number of quite different objectifications will do. Similarly for Gawans, according to Munn, "lightness," for instance, can pertain to canoes, garden plots, decorations, bodies, and so forth.

Mr. Rabbit reminds us that qualities must be embodied in something in particular. But as soon as they do, they are actually, and often contingently (rather than by logical necessity), bound up with other qualities – redness in an apple comes along with spherical shape, light weight, sweet flavor, a tendency to rot, and so forth. In practice, there is no way entirely to eliminate that factor of copresence, or what we might call *bundling*. This points to one of the obvious, but important, effects of materiality: redness cannot be manifest without some embodiment that inescapably binds it to some other qualities as well, which can become contingent but real factors in its social life. [...]

[...]

If the properties of a material thing exist even if never taken as iconic elements of a sign, the reverse is also the case. An icon can resemble an object that doesn't exist – a map, say, of a fantastic land, or a cloud that looks like a unicorn. Since all objects have qualities, *any* given object potentially resembles *something*. This means any object can suggest possible future uses or interpretations. The artist's preliminary sketch for a sculpture makes use of this characteristic openness of iconicity as a means of discovery[...]. The object in this case plays a role in the creation of something new that is not reducible to the acting subject's intentions. Rather, the interaction between the possibilities suggested by form and the taking up of that suggestion by the sculptor are a version of what Bruno Latour (1993) calls hybrids. Moreover, since resemblance is underdetermined, icons require some further guidance to determine how exactly they are similar to their objects. After all, even an ordinary portrait photograph is normally flat, immobile, and much smaller than its subject (see Pinney 1997). This guidance is thoroughly enmeshed with the

dynamics of social value and authority – they are not merely external and supplementary to the force of iconicity.

[...]

Iconicity is only a matter of potential. The realization or suppression of that potential cannot be ascribed simply to the qualities of the object in themselves. There must always be other social processes involved. These processes may involve varying degrees of self-consciousness and control. [...]

Semiotic Ideology

[...] By *semiotic ideology* I mean people's background assumptions about what signs are and how they function in the world. Such assumptions help determine, for instance, what people will consider the likely role that intentions play in signification to be, what kinds of possible agent (humans only? animals? spirits?) exist to which acts of signification might be imputed, whether signs are arbitrary or necessarily linked to their objects, and so forth. Thorstein Veblen's (1912) notion of conspicious consumption, for instance, seems on the face of it to be a clear-cut example of indexicality. One appreciates the value of a classical education or high-heeled shoes by recognizing their lack of utility, and from that draws the inference that someone who can afford to dispense with utility must hold a certain status. But this recognition is mediated by what you assume about the world. Knowing Latin or wearing high heels are not useful, for example, only if you believe Latin doesn't have magical power or that height is immaterial to selfhood. Semiotic ideologies are thus concerned not just with signs per se but with what kinds of agentive subjects and acted-upon objects might be found in the world. [...]

The Openness of Things Is Inherently Historical

What do material things make possible? What is their futurity? How might they change the person? [...] [T]here are times when these questions become urgent. For example, missionary history across the colonial world shows a persistent and troubling tension between the hope that clothing will change people, and the danger that people once clad will invest their clothing with too great a significance (Comaroff and Comaroff 1997: 223; Hansen 2000: 26, 30–2; Spyer 1998). On the one hand, proper dress is essential to the inculcation of modesty, propriety, and civility. Yet how much should one hope clothing will transform people? Not so much that they forget it is but a surface that can be removed. [...] Morality thus depends on the correct understanding of the materiality of things and the immateriality of persons, a balancing act that invites perpetual anxiety.

[...]

[...] If we are to treat things "in their own right," and not just as the tangible garments draped on otherwise invisible and immaterial ideas, we must consider their forms, qualities, practical capacities, and, thus, their place within causal relations. [...] If things mediate our historicity, we cannot be content to ask only what meanings people attribute to them now. And even of those meanings, we must be attentive to the ways in which they are (for the time being) regimented and brought into relation to other things – much of this being the task of social power.

Clothing Taken to Be Meaningful

[...] [T]he semiotic character of material things means that outcome is not, in principle, settled. It is not simply that their meanings are underdetermined, but also that their semiotic orientation is, in part, toward unrealized futures. Take the most ordinary of things. George Herbert Mead remarked, "The chair is what it is in terms of its invitation to sit down" (1934: 279). What interests us as embodied actors rather than, say, spectators, is the chair's instigation (by virtue of its form, that is, iconic suggestion) to certain sorts of action – and, thus, its futurity. [...] And as instigation, the chair can only invite actions, not determine them [...]. To realize some of the potentials of things, and not others, is the stuff of historical struggles and contingencies. The reason this seemingly obvious point is worth stressing is that it points us beyond the retrospective character of common ways of understanding signs, seeking to read them in terms only of what they presuppose and express.

[...]

Semiotic ideologies are vulnerable, not least by their exposure to the openness of things. Consider the effects of what I have called bundling. Necessarily embodied in some particular objectual form, a given quality is contingently (rather than by logical necessity or social convention) bound up with other qualities – redness on a cloth comes along with light weight, flat surface, flexibility, warmth, combustability, and so forth. There is no way to eliminate (nor, entirely, to regiment) that factor of co-presence or bundling. This points to one of the obvious, but important, effects of materiality: redness cannot be manifest without some embodiment that inescapably binds it to some other qualities as well, which remain available, ready to emerge as real factors, as it crosses contexts. Western slacks treat the legs independently of one another. This permits a longer gait than does a Javanese sarong, inviting (but not determining) athleticism and giving them the potential for becoming socially realized conventions, that is, symbols understood as icons, of, say, "freedom." In Indonesia they have tended to be more expensive than the sarong as well, and thus indexical of relative wealth and, by extension, urban life. But now that the sarong has come to be purposefully deployed as a conventional symbol of Islam (indexical, but only by decree), slacks also threaten to be indexical of the not-wearing of sarong.

[...]

Words and the Objectualization of Things

I have been arguing against approaches to material things that privilege language, or even received notions of meaningfulness, as their model. [...] I want briefly to sketch out one illustration of historical transformation and objectualization in which language *does* play a critical role.

[...]

I have suggested (Keane 1995) that the concreteness of the house as a cultural object, that is, as a repeatable, relatively stable, and intertextually rich representation (see, for instance, Bourdieu 1979), derives in part from certain features of the ways of speaking that purportedly refer to it. In Sumba, these features include an emphasis on canonical poetic forms such as parallelistic couplets and schematic list-making [...]. The various discursive possibilities afforded by the house take as their authorizing foundation, interpretative content, and structural guide verbal performances that seem to trace a pathway through the house, naming its parts one by one. [...]

How does this help us understand the consolidation of material things as social objects? I argue that the significance of the material qualities of the house [...] changes when the conditions for ritual speech change. For self-consciously modern Christians, the spirits cease to be real addressees [...]. Yet ritual speech persists, increasingly as a text understood as carrying traditional wisdom and Sumbanese ethnic identity. The materiality of its poetic form reproduces the structure of the house, but now as the object of reference, rather than as the sequence for a potential real-time unfolding of an encounter with invisible agents. [...]

This is part of a general shift in semiotic ideology distinguishing and linking words and things. [...] [A]s Protestants, [contemporary Sumbanese] are learning that verbal prayers are merely the outward expression of sincere inner thoughts that are, in essence, wholly immaterial, like the soul who intends them (Keane 1997, 2002). They deny any significance to the material form that their words take. Language, like sacrificial goods, has become "merely symbolic" and thus ideologically dematerialized. In short, an explicit ontological claim, reinforced by new liturgical speech practices, along with a host of other mundane practices of modernity, underwrites the transformation of the dominant semiotic ideologies within which the objectivity of material things comes to play its emergent social roles. Whereas language should not be the privileged theoretical model for a semiotics of material things, discursive practices *do* play a crucial role in ideological *consolidation* or semiotic regimentation (Silverstein 1996) in rendering objects legible, full of stabilized "meaning."
[...]

Objects and the Possibilities of Subjects

[...] It is a historically specific semiotic ideology that determines what will count for the interpreter and actor as objects and in contrast to what subjects. A yam prestation that falls short of expectations, or a telephone call not returned, may index malevolent human intentions, an individual's forgetfulness, the disfavor of spirits, abstract social forces, one's own fate, mere happenstance, or something else altogether, only with reference to a specific ideological context that makes these plausible and relevant inferences. [...] A semiotic analysis of the social power of things would thus demand an account of the semiotic ideologies and their discursive regimentation that enter into or are excluded from the processes by which things become objects, for these are the same processes that configure the borders and the possibilities of subjects.

References

Bourdieu, P. 1979/1970. "The Kabyle House, or the World Reversed." In *Algeria 1960*. Trans. R. Nice. Cambridge: Cambridge University Press.

Comaroff, John L., and Jean Comaroff. 1997. *Of Revelation and Revolution*, vol. 2: *The Dialectics of Modernity on a South African Frontier*. Chicago: University of Chicago Press.

Hansen, Karen Tranberg. 2000. *Salaula: The World of Secondhand Clothing and Zambia*. Chicago: University of Chicago Press.

Irvine, J. T. 1996/1989. "When Talk Isn't Cheap: Language and Political Economy." In D. Brenneis and R. K. S. Macaulay, eds., *The Matrix of Language: Contemporary Linguistic Anthropology*, Boulder, Colo.: Westview.

Keane, Webb. 1995. "The Spoken House: Text, Act, and Object in Eastern Indonesia." *American Ethnologist* 22:102–24.

Keane, Webb. 1996. "Materialism, Missionaries, and Modern Subjects in Colonial Indonesia." In Peter van der Veer, ed., *Conversion to Modernities: The Globalization of Christianity*, 137–70. New York and London: Routledge.

Keane, Webb. 1997. "From Fetishism to Sincerity: Agency, the Speaking Subject, and Their Historicity in the Context of Religious Conversion." *Comparative Studies in Society and History* 39:674–93.

Keane, Webb. 2002. "Sincerity, 'Modernity', and the Protestants." *Cultural Anthropology* 17:65–92.

Keane, Webb. 2003. "Self-Interpretation, Agency, and the Objects of Anthropology: Reflections on a Genealogy." *Comparative Studies in Society and History* 45:222–48.

Latour, Bruno. 1993. *We Have Never Been Modern.* Trans. C. Porter. Cambridge: Harvard University Press.

Mead, George Herbert. 1934. *Mind, Self, and Society from the Standpoint of a Social Behaviorist,* Chicago: University of Chicago Press.

Munn, Nancy. 1986. *The Fame of Gawa: A Symbolic Study of Value Transformation in a Massim (Papua New Guinea) Society.* Cambridge: Cambridge University Press.

Pinney, Christopher. 1997. *Camera Indica: The Social Life of Indian Photographs.* Chicago: University of Chicago Press.

Saussure, Ferdinand de. 1959. *Course in General Linguistics.* New York: Philosophical Library.

Silverstein, Michael. 1996. *Indexical Order and the Dialectics of Sociolinguistic Life.* Austin: Texas Linguistic Forum (SALSA III).

Spyer, Patricia. 1998. "The Tooth of Time, or Taking a Look at the 'Look' of Clothing in Late Nineteenth-Century Aru." In Patricia Spyer, ed., *Border Fetishisms: Material Objects in Unstable Places,* 150–82. New York: Routledge.

Stallybrass, Peter. 1996. "Worn Worlds: Cloth and Identity on the Renaissance Stage." In Margreta de Grazia, Maureen Quilligan, and Peter Stallybrass, eds., *Subject and Object in Renaissance Culture.* Cambridge: Cambridge University Press.

Thoreau, Henry D. 1971/1854. *Walden.* Ed. Lyndon Shanley. Princeton, NJ: Princeton University Press.

Veblen, Thorstein. 1912. *The Theory of the Leisure Class: An Economic Study of Institutions.* New York: Macmillan.

Weber, Max. 1978. *Economy and Society: An Outline of Interpretive Sociology.* Trans. E. Fischer et al. Berkeley: University of California Press.

52

Affective Spaces, Melancholic Objects: Ruination and the Production of Anthropological Knowledge

Yael Navaro-Yashin

Consider an island space, not too distant from Western Europe, where communities that had coexisted for centuries, if with tension, have begun to assume distinctly separate national identities, entering armed conflict with one another. [...] Imagine these two communities, now already defined as distinct "political communities", further divided from one another with the arrival of an external army which invades the northern part of the island, declaring that it does so in the interest of the minority.

I am referring to 1974, the date of the partition of Cyprus in the aftermath of the invasion of the north of the island by the Turkish army. [...] Turkish-Cypriots who happened to live in southern towns and villages escaped to the north, now under Turkish sovereignty, to protect themselves from Greek nationalist reprisals. Greek-Cypriots who lived in the north moved in great numbers to the south, experiencing and fleeing major brutalities during the war.

[...] Turkish-Cypriot refugees were mostly allocated Greek-Cypriot houses, land, and belongings by the Turkish-Cypriot administration in the north. Consider these refugees using, inhabiting, employing, and interacting with spaces and properties left behind by the former community (Greek-Cypriots) during the war. Living in the village of members of the other community officially construed as "the enemy". What is left of social relations with the other community is the other community's objects. [...]

[...]

A local moral discourse exists in relation to the use of properties, land, and belongings owned by the Greek-Cypriots. [...] Turkish-Cypriots refer to properties which they appropriated from the Greek-Cypriots as "loot". The word they use to refer to "loot" in the Turkish-Cypriot idiomatic sense is "*ganimet*". [...] In its contemporary Turkish-Cypriot usage, *ganimet* is evoked [...] to refer, specifically and in a self-reprimanding mode, to Greek property and objects which were appropriated by the Turkish-Cypriots in the aftermath of war. This is no neutral or apolitical term for an "object" or "thing". [...]

[...] [I]n the arena of such conflictual politics and symbolic language, what interests me is the affect that is generated in a community that has re-created its life and livelihood significantly on the

From *Journal of the Royal Anthropological Institute* 15(1) (2009), pp. 1–6, 8–18 (this paper has been significantly shortened for use in our book). Copyright © 2009 by *Journal of the Royal Anthropological Institute*. Reprinted with permission of John Wiley & Sons UK.

basis of objects and properties belonging to another community which was officially coined as "the enemy". [...] What sort of affect is exuded by dwellings, objects, and spaces left behind by another community after a cataclysmic war? [...] Here, I am interested in two things at once: one, the subjectivity of Turkish-Cypriots inhabiting expropriated dwellings [...]; and, two, the affect generated by the assumed objects, appropriated dwellings, and the broader post-war environment itself.

Turkish-Cypriots reflected a melancholic interiority during the period when I did intensive, long-term fieldwork in Northern Cyprus (in 2001 and 2002). The notion that they widely employed to describe their condition, feeling, or inner state of being was "*maraz*". [...] [This] refers to a state of mental depression, deep and unrecoverable sadness, and dis-ease, which I explore, in English, through the concept of melancholia. [...] What, I ask, is the role of the outer environment in engendering subjective feeling? Or, how are subjective feeling and environmentally produced affect intertwined? More specifically, what is the intersection between subjectivity and affect?

[...] Here, I follow Malinowski in centring affectivity in an exploration of sociality.

[...]

[...] [T]he psychoanalytic work of Julia Kristeva [...] studies "the abject" not only as that which contradicts the social order, but also as the negative counterpart to the ego. For Kristeva, abjection is an othering process through which the individual attempts to maintain and protect her psychical integrity. [...] Here, subjectivity is considered to be constituted in necessary opposition to the abject. "The abject is that which is not me". [...]

In contrast, [...] [i]n the Cypriot context I have described, the abject, or "the ruin", is not that against which the social order or political system was defined. [...] Rather, the abject is right there, in one's vicinity, environment, and domestic space [...]. The abject has become not a negative counterpart ("the other") to the subjective realm or the social order, but intrinsically constitutive of it. Therefore, I argue that the abject is not an exteriority against which subjectivity and sociality are to be defined (challenging the order from without), but fundamentally an interiority [...]. So, in place of Kristeva's proposition "the abject is that which is not me", [...] I would change this as follows: "The abject is so much inside me now that I don't know who I would be without it".

[...]

Ruination, Abject and Social Theory

[...] This is a story of ruination at the foundation of a new political system. By "ruination", I refer to the material remains or artefacts of destruction and violation, but also to the subjectivities and residual affects that linger, like a hangover, in the aftermath of war or violence. [...] What emerges from my ethnographic explorations of living with and among ruins of war in Northern Cyprus is the abject quality of ruination, as distinct from its aesthetics. [...] Abject matter, in this case, refers to things assumed through an act of violation. [...] I speak of a context where abjected material has been recycled, domesticated, and incorporated, quite creatively in fact, if self-consciously, into the social order. A new political system has been formed by way of assuming the abject. Such a merging of the self with abjected matter, the wearing and donning of the ruins of another community, should push us towards a new conceptualization of abjection.

[...]

Objects of Violence

[...] I am interested in exploring the limitations of ethnographic works that would privilege one theoretical framework or methodology to the detriment of another. My core question here is: Is the affect of melancholy experienced in relation to looted objects and properties a projection of their users' subjectivities onto the objects or an energy discharged out of these objects themselves?

Here, I find it helpful to think my material through the exercises proposed by Actor Network Theory. I will refer specifically to the work of Bruno Latour. I read Latour's work as a contribution to Foucault's critique of humanist philosophy or the philosophy of the subject. Latour has written against the privileged ascription of agency to human beings, arguing that, as "actants" of sorts, "non-human entities" too may be interpreted as effecting "agency" (Latour 1993). [...] The point [...] is to effect a shift from a subject- to an "object-oriented" philosophy (2005; also see Henare *et al.* 2007).

[...] I agree with Latour that there is a need to attend to the centrality of objects in the making of politics. [...] [A]s I have argued above, a new body politic has been fashioned in Northern Cyprus out of appropriating, using, and exchanging objects captured by violation from other people. I am therefore interested in the thingliness of politics.

And yet, I find that Latour's work is limited in its *qualification* of objects and their politics. Latour argues, without ethnographic specification or historicization, that subjects and objects are always and already engaged with and entangled in one another, imagining a flat or horizontal "network" of assemblages between human and non-human entities transcendentally and at all times, without qualification or interpretation. [...] I shall argue differently. The relation which people forge with objects must be studied in historical contingency and political specificity. If persons and objects are assembled in a certain manner, I would argue that this is not because they always, already, or anyway would do so. Rather, "assemblages" of subjects and objects must be read as specific in their politics and history. [...] [T]he Turkish-Cypriots' relations with looted objects is an assemblage of sorts forged in the aftermath of an act of sovereignty [...]. This [...] is no neutral assembly. [...] Therefore, the "network" cannot be theorized as an all-inclusive or pervasive, transcendental phenomenon. [...] Latour's horizontal and two-dimensional imaginary of "the network", then, has to be complemented with a theory of sovereignty and history which introduces qualified verticality and multiple dimensionality.

[...]

Objects are not involved in relations with human beings in a linguistically or symbolically neutral arena. Objects are, rather, qualified through language. They could be neither pre- nor post-linguistic. Nor could they be non-symbolic. Remember what my Turkish-Cypriot informants call the objects which they use: "Greek property", "*ganimet*", or "loot". Likewise, recall the moral discourses and ideologies that battle over the representation of objects in Northern Cyprus. Latour would like to situate the political in things. But with his attack on the linguistic turn in the social sciences, he "mops up" (or "ruins") theoretical vantage-points that suggest that objects are discursively qualified as well.

As welcome as its emphasis is on the agency of "non-human actants", [...] ANT has so much tilted the see-saw towards studying "non-human" entities that all methodologies for studying "the human" (including non-essentialist theoretical approaches) are deemed antithetical to its efforts. Or, if "the human" has not altogether disappeared in ANT frameworks, accounts of it have become extremely impoverished. Here, I certainly do not mean to call for a return to the philosophy of the subject or to humanist philosophy by reinstating the highly problematic notion of "the human". [...] [But as] they ardently keep any inferences to "the human" (or anything associated with human subjectivity or interiority) fearfully at bay, so do actor-network theorists limit themselves in their imagination of any agency that is also or especially "human" in its associations, like the imagination or the emotions (see also Thrift 2000: 215). If we were to limit ourselves to an ANT framework or methodology, we would have to call off any query into "affect" as referring to "human" factors too.

[...]

Affective Spaces

[...] [T]he British geographer Nigel Thrift (2000) has developed what is called "non-representational theory" along these lines. Thrift correctly argues that much of cultural theory in the last couple of decades has been dominated by an interest in texts, semiotics, and discourse, what he identifies as approaches centred on studies of "representation". [...] Instead and in place of the primacy of language in such approaches, Thrift would like to open researchers' imagination to a study of non- or pre-linguistic registers of experience, which he studies via the work of Gilles Deleuze, through the rubric of "affect". But what is affect?

"Affect is not simply emotion", writes Thrift, "nor is it reducible to the affections or perceptions of an individual subject" (2000: 219). [...] The point with which I very much agree is that most theoretical work on affectivity, before this particular "affective turn", has focused on the inner world or interiority of the human subject, coined "subjectivity". In the psychoanalytic tradition, for example, affect has been synonymous with subjectivity [...]. Emergent theories of affect hijack the traditional subject matter of psychoanalysis and illustrate that affectivity can be studied in sites and spaces beyond the scope of the "human subject", his or her "subjectivity", or "psyche".

Thrift's spatial theory of affect goes straight to Gilles Deleuze for its inspiration. [...]

Deleuze's own theory of affect follows [a] post-subjective trajectory. [...] The reference-point for affect (which used to be, singularly, subjectivity) has been radically altered and multiplied in this approach, making it possible to read many other things, such as space and the environment, as affective (Massumi 2002). [...]

Just as ANT could be read as a critique of the "linguistic turn" in the human sciences, as I argued before, so is the Deleuzian turn to affect a reaction to the centrality of discursivity in the human sciences. In fact, as Deleuze and Guattari's works can be read as a direct attack on psychoanalysis, so are they as explicitly critical of linguistics (see 2004: 13). Guattari has specifically argued that "affect is non-discursive" (1996: 159). Not about language, affect is pre- or extra-linguistic. Guattari speaks of a sensation which is "scenic or territorializing [in its] dispositions" (1996: 160). Affect, in his terms, is "hazy and atmospheric" (1996: 158). It is the non-discursive sensation which a space or environment generates.

Deleuze and Guattari's notion of affect is as open in orientation as is their theory of spatiality. In *A thousand plateaus* (2004), the two philosophers differentiate the "root" from their preferred notion, the "rhizome". Their metaphor for what they call "the root book" is the tree, which, well installed downwards into the ground, sets out branches upwards and vertically (2004: 5). For Deleuze and Guattari, the "root book" emblematizes Western modes of thinking. [...] The root traces, it locates, it creates a grid, defines structures, in this reading. Instead, Deleuze and Guattari propose the imaginary of the "rhizome" (2004: 7). Above all, rhizomes are about multiplicity; they cannot be sited, cornered, controlled, curbed, or located. Nor can they be given any shape, structure, or hierarchy. [...] Deleuze and

Guattari conceptualize affect as rhizomatic, or see affect as the rhizome itself which is everywhere, in constant motion, and unsitable. This is a distinctly different imagination about affectivity from that of the psychoanalytic notion of "the unconscious", for which the two authors' metaphor would be "the root".

So, Deleuze and Guattari are asking us to reverse the orientation of our thinking, from a verticalist imaginary where things are grounded and rooted to the metaphor of the endless and limitless "plateau". [...]

I used the metaphor of "the plateau" intentionally when I described the landscape of my ethnographic field of prickly bushes, thorns, and thistles growing over an appropriated and unkempt plain. [...] Now, in Deleuze and Guattari "the plateau", like "nomadology", is an analytical fiction. However, it is a serious one, in that the plain is associated with openness, limitlessness, as well as potential and creativity.

The "plateau" I described in Northern Cyprus is similar and yet different. The Mesarya plain is bisected, right through the middle, with a military border which has been in place since 1974. My informants who live [...] on this plain have spoken of feeling confined, entrapped, and suffocated in this slice of territory [...]. Deleuze and Guattari associate the "plateau" with free roaming, movement, multiplicity, and potential, rhizome-style. The thistles, thorns, and bushes I have described [...] may have flourished rhizomatically, shooting off weeds in every direction, crossing over barricades and barbed wire. So has the rust grown on the surfaces of abandoned cars, dumped refrigerators, farming tools, as well as bullets which one finds on the plain, cast aside or left behind some time after the war. Rust is rhizomatic [...].

And yet, I prefer to describe my ethnographic material, these prickly plants and wastelands, in terms of ruins, shards, rubble, and debris (à la Walter Benjamin's imagination), rather than the rhizome. What is the spatial orientation of ruins? Horizontal or vertical? Are ruins about "roots" in Deleuze and Guattari's sense? They may well, partially, be so. My informants "traced" the ruins around them, not just passing them by, but locating them in time and space. "Those bullet holes are from 1963", they would say, "whereas the bullet holes over there are from '74". [...]

The affect discharged by the bullet holes was symbolized, politicized, and interpreted by my informants.

[...]

Rather than casting roots against rhizomes, through my preferred metaphor of "the ruin", I would like to suggest another kind of orientation. We said that the root is vertical, whereas the rhizome is horizontal. The ruin, however, which describes my ethnographic material, is both and neither. A ruin is rhizomatic in the sense that it grows in uncontrollable and unforeseen ways. [...] But a ruin is also about roots, because it is sited as a "trace" of a historical event [...]. The ruin, then, works against Deleuze and Guattari's paradigm setting (or what I have called "ruination"). It is vertical and horizontal at the same time; both root and rhizome.

[...] How would affect be theorized were we to work with the metaphor of the "ruin" rather than the "rhizome"? Are certain affectivities projected onto the ruins by the subjects who make them or who live in their midst? Or do the ruins exude their own affect? Once again, I would argue that both are evident. Paradigm-setting has cast subjectivity against affect, as if one cancels the other and as if one had to choose between camps of theoretical approach: a subject-centred *or* an object-orientated one. But neither the ruin in my ethnography, nor the people who live around it are affective on their own or in their own right, but both produce and transmit affect *relationally*. An environment of ruins discharges an affect of melancholy. At the same time, those who inhabit this space of ruins feel melancholic: they put the ruins into discourse [...].

Melancholic Objects and Spatial Melancholia

In the spirit of what I have proposed, I would like to ask: What would an anthropology of melancholia look like? The reader will see that my material calls for a conceptual merging of affect and subjectivity, object and subject, root and rhizome, verticality and horizontality, asking for three- rather than two-dimensional analysis. Ethnography works against the grain of paradigm-setting; it asks for all scopes of the imagination to be kept on board.

[...] Sovereignty and the making of distinct political communities [...] do not allow for the ritualized mourning of persons lost to the other side of the divide or those of a different political affiliation. The feeling of loss, not cognitively registered, can therefore generate melancholia, a psychical-subjective state where the object of loss is largely unconscious to the identity of the mourner [...].

And yet, [...] I find that this analysis of melancholia which would register it singularly in the field of subjectivity or the psyche is limiting as much as it is enlightening. In its centredness on the subject, or the interior experience of the human being, it misses significant aspects of the relations that generate melancholia and loses out on possibilities of analysis. [...] "[T]he lost object" is not only a person (a Greek-Cypriot). Rather, in this case, the lost object (the person) is present in the life of the melancholic in the form of an actual material (or non-human) object (such as a household item, fields of olive trees, or animals). [...] The affect of that loss experienced by members of the other community (in this case, Greek-Cypriots) lingers uncannily in the spaces and objects which they have left behind. And Turkish-Cypriots inhabit many of these spaces and employ, still, many of these objects. [...] Therefore, we can speak [...] of *melancholic objects*, things which exude an affect of melancholy, and *spatial melancholia*, an environment or atmosphere which discharges such an affect.

The melancholy which the Turkish-Cypriots feel, then, [...] refers neither, exclusively, to affect nor to subjectivity, but to both. [...] But there is also another order of melancholy, having to do with violence done to others by way of appropriating their objects. The melancholy experienced, via the everyday presence of objects belonging to others, in this case, is a loss of a sense of moral integrity. This is articulated and consciously symbolized (put into discourse) by the Turkish-Cypriots, [...] as in my analysis of moral discourses around *ganimet*. In this final interpretation, melancholy is the loss of the self to the self, the loss of a sense of the self as clean and pure. [...] Melancholia, then, is both interior and exterior. It refers to subjectivity and the world of objects at one and the same time. Here, beyond paradigmatic shifts and wars, theories of affect and subjectivity, as well as of objects and symbolization, demand to be merged. Social constructionism and an object-orientated approach, the linguistic and the affective turns may have been posed as antitheses of one another by the philosophers. But ethnography leads us to write against the grain of "ruination" in being anti-, trans-, or multi-paradigmatic.

References

Deleuze, G. & F. Guattari 2004. *A thousand plateaus: capitalism and schizophrenia*. London: Continuum.

Guattari, F. 1996. Ritornellos and existential affects. In *The Guattari reader/Pierre Félix Guattari* (ed.) G. Genosko, 158–71. Oxford: Blackwell.

Henare, A., M. Holbraad & S. Wastell (eds) 2007. *Thinking through things: theorising artefacts ethnographically*. London: Routledge.

Kristeva, J. 1982. *Powers of horror: an essay on abjection*. New York: Columbia University Press.

Latour, B. 1993. *We have never been modern*. Harlow: Pearson Education.

Latour, B. 2005. From *Realpolitik* to *Dingpolitik* or how to make things public. In *Making things public: atmospheres in democracy* (eds) B. Latour & P. Weibel, 14–43. Cambridge, Mass.: MIT Press.

Massumi, B. 2002. *Parables for the virtual: movement, affect, sensation*. Durham, N.C.: Duke University Press.

Thrift, N. 2000. Afterwords. *Environment and Planning D: Society and Space* 18, 213–55.

SECTION 16

Imagining Methodologies
and Meta-things

53

Beyond "Culture": Space, Identity, and the Politics of Difference

Akhil Gupta and James Ferguson

[...] For a subject whose central rite of passage is fieldwork, whose romance has rested on its exploration of the remote ("the *most* other of others" [Hannerz 1986:363]), whose critical function is seen to lie in its juxtaposition of radically different ways of being (located "elsewhere") with that of the anthropologists' own, usually Western, culture, there has been surprisingly little self-consciousness about the issue of space in anthropological theory. (Some notable exceptions are Appadurai [1986, 1988], Hannerz [1987], and Rosaldo [1988, 1989].) [...]

Representations of space in the social sciences are remarkably dependent on images of break, rupture, and disjunction. The distinctiveness of societies, nations, and cultures is based upon a seemingly unproblematic division of space, on the fact that they occupy "naturally" discontinuous spaces. The premise of discontinuity forms the starting point from which to theorize contact, conflict, and contradiction between cultures and societies. For example, the representation of the world as a collection of "countries," as in most world maps, sees it as an inherently fragmented space, divided by different colors into diverse national societies, each

"rooted" in its proper place. [...] It is so taken for granted that each country embodies its own distinctive culture and society that the terms "society" and "culture" are routinely simply appended to the names of nation-states, as when a tourist visits India to understand "Indian culture" and "Indian society," or Thailand to experience "Thai culture," or the United States to get a whiff of "American culture."

Of course, the geographical territories that cultures and societies are believed to map onto do not have to be nations. We do, for example, have ideas about culture-areas that overlap several nation-states, or of multicultural nations. On a smaller scale, perhaps, are our disciplinary assumptions about the association of culturally unitary groups (tribes or peoples) with "their" territories: thus, "the Nuer" live in "Nuerland" and so forth. The clearest illustration of this kind of thinking are the classic "ethnographic maps" that purported to display the spatial distribution of peoples, tribes, and cultures. But in all these cases, space itself becomes a kind of neutral grid on which cultural difference, historical memory, and societal organization are inscribed. It is in this way that space functions as a central organizing principle in the

Anthropology in Theory: Issues in Epistemology, Second Edition. Edited by Henrietta L. Moore and Todd Sanders.
© 2014 John Wiley & Sons, Inc. Published 2014 by John Wiley & Sons, Inc.

social sciences at the same time that it disappears from analytical purview.

This assumed isomorphism of space, place, and culture results in some significant problems. First, there is the issue of those who inhabit the border, that "narrow strip along steep edges" (Anzaldua 1987:3) of national boundaries. The fiction of cultures as discrete, object-like phenomena occupying discrete spaces becomes implausible for those who inhabit the borderlands. Related to border inhabitants are those who live a life of border crossings – migrant workers, nomads, and members of the transnational business and professional elite. What is "the culture" of farm workers who spend half a year in Mexico and half a year in the United States? Finally, there are those who cross borders more or less permanently – immigrants, refugees, exiles, and expatriates. In their case, the disjuncture of place and culture is especially clear: Khmer refugees in the United States take "Khmer culture" with them in the same complicated way that Indian immigrants in England transport "Indian culture" to their new homeland.

A second set of problems raised by the implicit mapping of cultures onto places is to account for cultural differences *within* a locality. "Multiculturalism" is both a feeble acknowledgment of the fact that cultures have lost their moorings in definite places and an attempt to subsume this plurality of cultures within the framework of a national identity. Similarly, the idea of "subcultures" attempts to preserve the idea of distinct "cultures" while acknowledging the relation of different cultures to a dominant culture within the same geographical and territorial space. Conventional accounts of ethnicity, even when used to describe cultural differences in settings where people from different regions live side by side, rely on an unproblematic link between identity and place.[1] Although such concepts are suggestive because they endeavor to stretch the naturalized association of culture with place, they fail to interrogate this assumption in a truly fundamental manner. We need to ask how to deal with cultural difference while abandoning received ideas of (localized) culture.

Third, there is the important question of post-coloniality. To which places do the hybrid cultures of postcoloniality belong? Does the colonial encounter create a "new culture" in both the colonized and colonizing country, or does it destabilize the notion that nations and cultures are isomorphic? As discussed below, postcoloniality further problematizes the relationship between space and culture.

Last, and most important, challenging the ruptured landscape of independent nations and autonomous cultures raises the question of understanding social change and cultural transformation as situated within interconnected spaces. The presumption that spaces are autonomous has enabled the power of topography to conceal successfully the topography of power. The inherently fragmented space assumed in the definition of anthropology as the study of cultures (in the plural) may have been one of the reasons behind the long-standing failure to write anthropology's history as the biography of imperialism. For if one begins with the premise that spaces have *always* been hierarchically interconnected, instead of naturally disconnected, then cultural and social change becomes not a matter of cultural contact and articulation but one of rethinking difference *through* connection.

To illustrate, let us examine one powerful model of cultural change that attempts to relate dialectically the local to larger spatial arenas: articulation. Articulation models, whether they come from Marxist structuralism or from "moral economy," posit a primeval state of autonomy (usually labeled "precapitalist"), which is then violated by global capitalism. The result is that both local and larger spatial arenas are transformed, the local more than the global to be sure, but not necessarily in a predetermined direction. This notion of articulation allows one to explore the richly unintended consequences of, say, colonial capitalism, where loss occurs alongside invention. Yet, by taking a preexisting, localized "community" as a given starting point, it fails to examine sufficiently the processes (such as the structures of feeling that pervade the imagining of community) that go into the construction of space as place or locality in the first instance. In other words, instead of assuming the autonomy of the primeval community, we need to examine how it was formed *as a community* out of the interconnected space that always already existed. Colonialism, then, represents the displacement of one form of interconnection by another. This is not to deny that colonialism, or an expanding capitalism, does indeed have profoundly dislocating effects on existing societies.

But by always foregrounding the spatial distribution of hierarchical power relations, we can better
understand the process whereby a space achieves
a distinctive *identity* as a place. Keeping in mind
that notions of locality or community refer both to
a demarcated physical space *and* to clusters of
interaction, we can see that the identity of a place
emerges by the intersection of its specific involvement in a system of hierarchically organized
spaces with its cultural construction as a
community or locality.

It is for this reason that what Jameson (1984)
has dubbed "postmodern hyperspace" has so fundamentally challenged the convenient fiction that
mapped cultures onto places and peoples. In the
capitalist West, a Fordist regime of accumulation,
emphasizing extremely large production facilities, a relatively stable work force, and the welfare
state, combined to create urban "communities"
whose outlines were most clearly visible in
company towns (Davis 1984; Harvey 1989;
Mandel 1975). The counterpart of this in the
international arena was that multinational corporations, under the leadership of the United States,
steadily exploited the raw materials, primary
goods, and cheap labor of the independent
nation-states of the postcolonial "Third World."
Multilateral agencies and powerful Western states
preached, and where necessary militarily
enforced, the "laws" of the market to encourage
the international flow of capital, while national
immigration policies ensured that there would be
no free (i.e., anarchic, disruptive) flow of labor to
the high-wage islands in the capitalist core.
Fordist patterns of accumulation have now been
replaced by a regime of flexible accumulation –
characterized by small-batch production, rapid
shifts in product lines, extremely fast movements
of capital to exploit the smallest differentials in
labor and raw material costs – built on a more
sophisticated communications and information
network and better means of transporting goods
and people. At the same time, the industrial production of culture, entertainment, and leisure
that first achieved something approaching global
distribution during the Fordist era led, paradoxically, to the invention of new forms of cultural
difference and new forms of imagining
community. Something like a transnational
public sphere has certainly rendered any strictly
bounded sense of community or locality obsolete.
At the same time, it has enabled the creation of

forms of solidarity and identity that do not rest on
an appropriation of space where contiguity and
face-to-face contact are paramount. In the pul-
verized space of postmodernity, space has not
become irrelevant: it has been *re*territorialized in
a way that does not conform to the experience of
space that characterized the era of high modernity. It is this that forces us to reconceptualize
fundamentally the politics of community, solidarity, identity, and cultural difference.

Imagined Communities, Imagined Places

People have undoubtedly always been more mobile and identities less fixed than the static and
typologizing approaches of classical anthropology
would suggest. But today, the rapidly expanding
and quickening mobility of people combines with
the refusal of cultural products and practices to
"stay put" to give a profound sense of a loss of
territorial roots, of an erosion of the cultural distinctiveness of places, and of ferment in anthropological theory. The apparent deterritorialization
of identity that accompanies such processes has
made Clifford's question (1988:275) a key one for
recent anthropological inquiry: "What does it
mean, at the end of the twentieth century, to
speak...of a 'native land'? What processes rather
than essences are involved in present experiences
of cultural identity?"

Such questions are of course not wholly new,
but issues of collective identity today do seem to
take on a special character, when more and more
of us live in what Said (1979:18) has called "a generalized condition of homelessness," a world
where identities are increasingly coming to be, if
not wholly deterritorialized, at least differently
territorialized. Refugees, migrants, displaced and
stateless peoples – these are perhaps the first to
live out these realities in their most complete
form, but the problem is more general. In a world
of diaspora, transnational culture flows, and
mass movements of populations, old-fashioned
attempts to map the globe as a set of culture
regions or homelands are bewildered by a daz-
zling array of postcolonial simulacra, doublings
and redoublings, as India and Pakistan apparently reappear in postcolonial simulation in
London, pre-revolution Tehran rises from the
ashes in Los Angeles, and a thousand similar
cultural dreams are played out in urban and rural

settings all across the globe. In this culture-play of diaspora, familiar lines between "here" and "there," center and periphery, colony and metropole become blurred.

Where "here" and "there" become blurred in this way, the cultural certainties and fixities of the metropole are upset as surely, if not in the same way, as those of the colonized periphery. In this sense, it is not only the displaced who experience a displacement (cf. Bhabha 1989:66). For even people remaining in familiar and ancestral places find the nature of their relation to place ineluctably changed, and the illusion of a natural and essential connection between the place and the culture broken. "Englishness," for instance, in contemporary, internationalized England is just as complicated and nearly as deterritorialized a notion as Palestinian-ness or Armenian-ness, since "England" ("the real England") refers less to a bounded place than to an imagined state of being or moral location. Consider, for instance, the following quote from a young white reggae fan in the ethnically chaotic neighborhood of Balsall Heath in Birmingham:

> there's no such thing as "England" any more...welcome to India brothers! This is the Caribbean!...Nigeria!...There is no England, man. This is what is coming. Balsall Heath is the center of the melting pot, 'cos all I ever see when I go out is half-Arab, half-Pakistani, half-Jamaican, half-Scottish, half-Irish. I know 'cos I am [half Scottish/half Irish]...who am I?...Tell me who I belong to? They criticize me, the good old England. Alright, where do I belong? You know, I was brought up with blacks, Pakistanis, Africans, Asians, everything, you name it...who do I belong to?...I'm just a broad person. The earth is mine...you know we was not born in Jamaica...we was not born in "England." We were born here, man. It's our right. That's the way I see it. That's the way I deal with it. [Hebdige 1987:158–9]

The broad-minded acceptance of cosmopolitanism that seems to be implied here is perhaps more the exception than the rule, but there can be little doubt that the explosion of a culturally stable and unitary "England" into the cut-and-mix "here" of contemporary Balsall Heath is an example of a phenomenon that is real and spreading. It is clear that the erosion of such supposedly natural connections between peoples and places has not led to the modernist specter of global cultural homogenization (Clifford 1988). But "cultures" and "peoples," however persistent they may be, cease to be plausibly identifiable as spots on the map.

The irony of these times, however, is that as actual places and localities become ever more blurred and indeterminate, *ideas* of culturally and ethnically distinct places become perhaps ever more salient. It is here that it becomes most visible how imagined communities (Anderson 1983) come to be attached to imagined places, as displaced peoples cluster around remembered or imagined homelands, places, or communities in a world that seems increasingly to deny such firm territorialized anchors in their actuality. The set of issues surrounding the construction of place and homeland by mobile and displaced people is addressed in different ways. [...]

Remembered places have often served as symbolic anchors of community for dispersed people. This has long been true of immigrants, who (as Leonard [1992] shows vividly) use memory of place to construct imaginatively their new lived world. "Homeland" in this way remains one of the most powerful unifying symbols for mobile and displaced peoples, though the relation to homeland may be very differently constructed in different settings. Moreover, even in more completely deterritorialized times and settings – settings where "home" is not only distant, but also where the very notion of "home" as a durably fixed place is in doubt – aspects of our lives remain highly "localized" in a social sense, as Peters (1992) argues. We need to give up naive ideas of communities as literal entities (cf. Cohen 1985), but remain sensitive to the profound "bifocality" that characterizes locally lived lives in a globally interconnected world, and the powerful role of place in the "near view" of lived experience (Peters 1992).

The partial erosion of spatially bounded social worlds and the growing role of the imagination of places from a distance, however, themselves must be situated within the highly spatialized terms of a global capitalist economy. The special challenge here is to use a focus on the way space is imagined (but not *imaginary*!) as a way to explore the processes through which such conceptual processes of place making meet the changing global economic and political conditions of lived spaces – the relation, we could say, between place and space. As Ferguson [1992] shows, important tensions may arise when places that have been imagined at a distance must become lived spaces. For places are always imagined in the context of political-economic determinations that have a logic of their own. Territoriality is thus reinscribed at just the point it threatens to be erased.

The idea that space is made meaningful is of course a familiar one to anthropologists; indeed, there is hardly an older or better established anthropological truth. East or West, inside or outside, left or right, mound or floodplain – from at least the time of Durkheim, anthropology has known that the experience of space is always socially constructed. The more urgent task [...] is to politicize this uncontestable observation. With meaning making understood as a practice, how are spatial meanings established? Who has the power to make places of spaces? Who contests this? What is at stake?

Such questions are particularly important where the meaningful association of places and peoples is concerned. As Malkki [1992] shows, two naturalisms must be challenged here. First is what we will call the ethnological habit of taking the association of a culturally unitary group (the "tribe" or "people") and "its" territory as natural, which is discussed in the previous section. A second, and closely related, naturalism is what we will call the national habit of taking the association of citizens of states and their territories as natural. Here the exemplary image is of the conventional world map of nation-states, through which school-children are taught such deceptively simple-sounding beliefs as that France is where the French live, America is where the Americans live, and so on. Even a casual observer, of course, knows that not only Americans live in America, and it is clear that the very question of what is a "real American" is largely up for grabs. But even anthropologists still talk of "American culture" with no clear understanding of what that means, because we assume a natural association of a culture ("American culture"), a people ("Americans"), and a place ("the United States of America"). Both the ethnological and the national naturalisms present associations of people and place as solid, commonsensical, and agreed-upon, when they are in fact contested, uncertain, and in flux.

Much recent work in anthropology and related fields has focused on the process through which such reified and naturalized national representations are constructed and maintained by states and national elites. (See, for instance, Anderson 1983; Handler 1988; Herzfeld 1987; Hobsbawn and Ranger 1983; Kapferer 1988; Wright 1985.) Borneman [1992] presents a case where state constructions of national territory are complicated by a very particular sort of displacement, as the territorial division and reformation of Germany following the Second World War made unavailable to the two states the claims to a territorially circumscribed home and culturally delineated nation that are usually so central to establish legitimacy. Neither could their citizens rely on such appeals in constructing their own identities. In forging national identities estranged in this way from both territory and culture, Borneman argues, the postwar German states and their citizens employed oppositional strategies, ultimately resulting in versions of the displaced and decentered identities that mark what is often called the post-modern condition.

Discussions of nationalism make it clear that states play a crucial role in the popular politics of place making and in the creation of naturalized links between places and peoples. But it is important to note that state ideologies are far from being the only point at which the imagination of place is politicized. Oppositional images of place have of course been extremely important in anticolonial nationalist movements, as well as in campaigns for self-determination and sovereignty on the part of ethnic counter-nations such as the Hutu, the Eritreans, and the Armenians. Bisharat (1992) traces some of the ways in which the imagining of place has played into the Palestinian struggle, showing both how specific constructions of "homeland" have changed in response to political circumstances and how a deeply felt relation to "the land" continues to inform and inspire the Palestinian struggle for self-determination. Bisharat's article serves as a useful reminder, in the light of nationalism's often reactionary connotations in the Western world, of how often notions of home and "own place" have been empowering in anticolonial contexts.

Indeed, future observers of 20th-century revolutions will probably be struck by the difficulty of formulating large-scale political movements *without* reference to national homelands. Gupta [1992] discusses the difficulties raised in attempting to rally people around such a nonnational collectivity as the nonaligned movement; and he points out that similar problems are raised by the proletarian internationalist movement, since, "as generations of Marxists after Marx found out, it is one thing to liberate a nation, quite another to liberate the workers of the world" [...]. Class-based internationalism's tendencies to nationalism (as in the history of the Second International, or that of the USSR), and to utopianism imagined in local rather than universal terms (as in Morris's *News from Nowhere* [1970], where "nowhere" [*utopia*] turns out to be a specifically English "somewhere"), show clearly the importance of attaching causes to places and the ubiquity of place making in collective political mobilization.

Such place making, however, need not be national in scale. One example of this is the way idealized notions of "the country" have been used in urban settings to construct critiques of industrial capitalism (cf. in Britain, Williams 1973; for Zambia, Ferguson [1992]). Another case is the reworking of ideas of "home" and "community" by feminists like Martin and Mohanty (1986) and Kaplan (1987). Rofel [1992] gives another example in her treatment of the contested meanings of the spaces and local history of a Chinese factory. Her analysis shows both how specific factory locations acquired meanings over time and how these localized spatial meanings confounded the modernizing, panoptic designs of planners – indeed, how the durability of memory and localized meanings of sites and bodies calls into question the very idea of a universal, undifferentiated "modernity."

It must be noted that such popular politics of place can as easily be conservative as progressive. Often enough, as in the contemporary United States, the association of place with memory, loss, and nostalgia plays directly into the hands of reactionary popular movements. This is true not only of explicitly national images long associated with the Right, but also of imagined locales and nostalgic settings such as "small-town America" or "the frontier," which often play into and complement anti-feminist idealizations of "the home" and "family."[2]

Space, Politics, and Anthropological Representation

Changing our conceptions of the relation between space and cultural difference offers a new perspective on recent debates surrounding issues of anthropological representation and writing. The new attention to representational practices has already led to more sophisticated understandings of processes of objectification and the construction of other-ness in anthropological writing. However, with this said, it also seems to us that recent notions of "cultural critique" (Marcus and Fischer 1986) depend on a spatialized understanding of cultural difference that needs to be problematized.

The foundation of cultural critique – a dialogic relation with an "other" culture that yields a critical viewpoint on "our own culture" – assumes an already-existing world of many different, distinct "cultures," and an unproblematic distinction between "our own society" and an "other" society. As Marcus and Fischer put it, the purpose of cultural critique is "to generate critical questions from one society to probe the other" (1986:117); the goal is "to apply both the substantive results and the epistemological lessons learned from ethnography abroad to a renewal of the critical function of anthropology as it is pursued in ethnographic projects at home" (1986:112).

Marcus and Fischer are sensitive to the fact that cultural difference is present "here at home," too, and that "the other" need not be exotic or far away to be other. But the fundamental conception of cultural critique as a relation between "different societies" ends up, perhaps against the authors' intentions, spatializing cultural difference in familiar ways, as ethnography becomes, as above, a link between an unproblematized "home" and "abroad." The anthropological relation is not simply with people who are different, but with "a different society," "a different culture," and thus, inevitably, a relation between "here" and "there." In all of this, the terms of the opposition ("here" and "there," "us" and "them," "our own" and "other" societies) are taken as received: the problem for anthropologists is to use our encounter with "them," "there," to construct a critique of "our own society," "here."

There are a number of problems with this way of conceptualizing the anthropological project. Perhaps the most obvious is the question of the identity of the "we" that keeps coming up in phrases such as "ourselves" and "our own society." Who is this "we"? If the answer is, as we fear, "the West," then we must ask precisely who is to be included and excluded from this club. Nor is the problem solved simply by substituting for "our own society," "the ethnographer's own society." For ethnographers, as for other natives, the post-colonial world is an interconnected social space; for many anthropologists – and perhaps especially for displaced Third World scholars – the identity of "one's own society" is an open question.

A second problem with the way cultural difference has been conceptualized within the "cultural critique" project is that, once excluded from that privileged domain "our own society," "the other" is subtly nativized – placed in a separate frame of analysis and "spatially incarcerated" (Appadurai 1988) in that "other place" that is proper to an "other culture." Cultural critique assumes an original separation, bridged at the initiation of the anthropological fieldworker. The problematic is one of "contact": communication not within a shared social and economic world, but "across cultures" and "between societies."

As an alternative to this way of thinking about cultural difference, we want to problematize the unity of the "us" and the otherness of the "other," and question the radical separation between the two that makes the opposition possible in the first place. We are interested less in establishing a dialogic relation between geographically distinct societies than in exploring the processes of *production* of difference in a world of culturally, socially, and economically interconnected and interdependent spaces. [...]

The move we are calling for, most generally, is away from seeing cultural difference as the correlate of a world of "peoples" whose separate histories wait to be bridged by the anthropologist and toward seeing it as a product of a shared historical process that differentiates the world as it connects it. For the proponents of "cultural critique," difference is taken as starting point, not as end product. Given a world of "different societies," they ask, how can we use experience in one to comment on another? But if we question a pre-given world of separate and discrete "peoples and cultures," and see instead a difference-producing set of relations, we turn from a project of juxtaposing preexisting differences to one of exploring the construction of differences in historical process.

In this perspective, power does not enter the anthropological picture only at the moment of representation, for the cultural distinctiveness that the anthropologist attempts to represent has always already been produced within a field of power relations. There is thus a politics of otherness that is not reducible to a politics of representation. Textual strategies can call attention to the politics of representation, but the issue of otherness itself is not really addressed by the devices of polyphonic textual construction or collaboration with informant-writers, as writers like Clifford and Crapanzano sometimes seem to suggest.

In addition to (not instead of!) textual experimentation, then, there is a need to address the issue of "the West" and its "others" in a way that acknowledges the extra-textual roots of the problem. For example, the area of immigration and immigration law is one practical area where the politics of space and the politics of otherness link up very directly. Indeed, if the separateness of separate places is not a natural given but an anthropological problem, it is remarkable how little anthropologists have had to say about the contemporary political issues connected with immigration in the United States.[3] If we accept a world of originally separate and culturally distinct places, then the question of immigration policy is just a question of how hard we should try to maintain this original order. In this perspective, immigration prohibitions are a relatively minor matter. Indeed, operating with a spatially naturalized understanding of cultural difference, uncontrolled immigration may even appear as a danger to anthropology, threatening to blur or erase the cultural distinctiveness of places that is our stock in trade. If, on the other hand, it is acknowledged that cultural difference is produced and maintained in a field of power relations in a world always already spatially interconnected, then the restriction of immigration becomes visible as one of the main means through which the disempowered are kept that way.

The enforced "difference" of places becomes, in this perspective, part and parcel of a global system of domination. The anthropological task of de-naturalizing cultural and spatial divisions at this point links up with the political task of combating a very literal "spatial incarceration of the native" (Appadurai 1988) within economic spaces zoned, as it were, for poverty. In this sense, changing the way we think about the relations of culture, power, and space opens the possibility of changing more than our texts. There is room, for instance, for a great deal more anthropological involvement, both theoretical and practical, with the politics of the US/Mexico border, with the political and organizing rights of immigrant workers, and with the appropriation of anthropological concepts of "culture" and "difference" into the repressive ideological apparatus of immigration law and the popular perceptions of "foreigners" and "aliens."

A certain unity of place and people has been long assumed in the anthropological concept of culture. But anthropological representations and immigration laws notwithstanding, "the native" is "spatially incarcerated" only in part. The ability of people to confound the established spatial orders, either through physical movement or through their own conceptual and political acts of reimagination, means that space and place can never be "given," and that the process of their sociopolitical construction must always be considered. An anthropology whose objects are no longer conceived as automatically and naturally anchored in space will need to pay particular attention to the way spaces and places are made, imagined, contested, and enforced. In this sense, it is no paradox to say that questions of space and place are, in this deterritorialized age, more central to anthropological representation than ever. [...]

Notes

1 This is obviously not true of the "new ethnicity" literature, of texts such as Anzaldua (1987) and Radhakrishnan (1987).

2 See also Robertson (1988, 1991) on the politics of nostalgia and "native place-making" in Japan.

3 We are, of course, aware that a considerable amount of recent work in anthropology has centered on immigration. However, it seems to us that too much of this work remains at the level of describing and documenting patterns and trends of migration, often with a policy science focus. Such work is undoubtedly important, and often strategically effective in the formal political arena. Yet there remains the challenge of taking up the specifically *cultural* issues surrounding the mapping of otherness onto space, as we have suggested is necessary. One area where at least some anthropologists have taken such issues seriously is that of Mexican immigration to the United States (e.g., Alvarez 1987; Bustamente 1987; Chavez 1991; Kearney 1986, 1990; Kearney and Nagengast 1989; and Rouse 1991). Another example is Borneman (1986), which is noteworthy for showing the specific links between immigration law and homophobia, nationalism and sexuality, in the case of the Cuban "Marielito" immigrants to the United States.

References

Alvarez, Robert R., Jr. 1987 *Familia: Migration and Adaptation in Baja and Alta California, 1800–1975.* Berkeley: University of California Press.

Anderson, Benedict 1983 *Imagined Communities: Reflections on the Origin and Spread of Nationalism.* London: Verso.

Anzaldua, Gloria 1987 *Borderlands/La Frontera: The New Mestiza.* San Francisco, Calif.: Spinsters/Aunt Lute.

Appadurai, Arjun 1986 Theory in Anthropology: Center and Periphery. *Comparative Studies in Society and History* 28(1):356–61.

Appadurai, Arjun 1988 Putting Hierarchy in its Place. *Cultural Anthropology* 3(1):36–49.

Bhabha, Homi 1989 Location, Intervention, Incommensurability: A Conversation with Homi Bhabha. *Emergences* 1(1):63–88.

Bisharat, George 1992 Transformations in the Political Role and Social Identity of Palestinian Refugees in the West Bank. In *Culture, Power, Place: Explorations in Critical Anthropology.* Roger Rouse, James Ferguson, and Akhil Gupta, eds. Boulder, Colo.: Westview Press.

Borneman, John 1986 Emigrés as Bullets/Immigration as Penetration: Perceptions of the Marielitos. *Journal of Popular Culture* 20(3):73–92.

Borneman, John 1992 State, Territory and Identity Formation in the Postwar Berlins, 1945–1989. *Cultural Anthropology* 7(1):45–62.

Bustamente, Jorge 1987 Mexican Immigration: A Domestic Issue or an International Reality? In *Hispanic Migration and the United States: A Study in Politics.* Gastón Fernández, Beverly Nagel, and León

Narváez, eds. Pp. 13–30. Bristol, Ind.: Wyndham Hall Press.

Chavez, Leo 1991 Outside the Imagined Community: Undocumented Settlers and Experiences of Incorporation. *American Ethnologist* 18(2):257–78.

Clifford, James 1988 *The Predicament of Culture.* Cambridge, Mass.: Harvard University Press.

Cohen, Anthony 1985 *The Symbolic Construction of Community.* New York: Tavistock.

Davis, Mike 1984 The Political Economy of Late-Imperial America. *New Left Review* 143:6–38.

Ferguson, James 1992. The Country and the City on the Copperbelt. *Cultural Anthropology* 7(1):80–92.

Gupta, Akhil 1992. The Song of the Nonaligned World: Transnational Identity and the Reinscription of Space in Late Capitalism. *Cultural Anthropology* 7(1):63–79.

Handler, Richard 1988 *Nationalism and the Politics of Culture in Quebec.* Madison: University of Wisconsin Press.

Hannerz, Ulf 1986 Theory in Anthropology: Small Is Beautiful, the Problem of Complex Cultures. *Comparative Studies in Society and History* 28(2):362–7.

Hannerz, Ulf 1987 The World in Creolization. *Africa* 57(4): 546–59.

Harvey, David 1989 *The Condition of Postmodernity: An Enquiry into the Origins of Cultural Change.* New York: Blackwell.

Hebdige, Dick 1987 *Cut 'n' Mix: Culture, Identity and Caribbean Music.* London: Methuen.

Herzfeld, Michael 1987 *Anthropology Through the Looking-Glass: Critical Ethnography in the Margins of Europe.* New York: Cambridge University Press.

Hobsbawm, Eric and Terrence Ranger, eds. 1983 *The Invention of Tradition.* New York: Cambridge University Press.

Jameson, Fredric 1984 Postmodernism, or the Cultural Logic of Late Capitalism. *New Left Review* 146:53–92.

Kapferer, Bruce 1988 *Legends of People, Myths of State: Violence, Intolerance, and Political Culture in Sri Lanka and Australia.* Washington, DC: Smithsonian Institution Press.

Kaplan, Caren 1987 Deterritorializations: The Rewriting of Home and Exile in Western Feminist Discourse. *Cultural Critique* 6:187–98.

Kearney, Michael 1986 From the Invisible Hand to Visible Feet: Anthropological Studies of Migration and Development. *Annual Review of Anthropology* 15:331–61.

Kearney, Michael 1990 Borders and Boundaries of State and Self at the End of Empire. Department of Anthropology, University of California, Riverside, unpublished MS.

Kearney, Michael, and Carol Nagengast 1989 *Anthropological Perspectives on Transnational Communities in Rural California.* Working Group on Farm Labor and Rural Poverty. Working Paper, 3. Davis, Calif.: California Institute for Rural Studies.

Leonard, Karen 1992 Finding One's Own Place: The Imposition of Asian Landscapes on Rural California. In *Culture, Power, Place: Explorations in Critical Anthropology.* Roger Rouse, James Ferguson, and Akhil Gupta, eds. Boulder, Colo.: Westview Press.

Malkki, Lisa 1992 National Geographic: The Rooting of Peoples and the Territorialization of National Identity Among Scholars and Refugees. *Cultural Anthropology* 7(1):24–44.

Mandel, Ernest 1975 *Late Capitalism.* New York: Verso.

Marcus, George E., and Michael M. J. Fischer 1986 *Anthropology as Cultural Critique: An Experimental Moment in the Human Sciences.* Chicago, Ill.: University of Chicago Press.

Martin, Biddy, and Chandra Talpade Mohanty 1986 Feminist Politics: What's Home Got to Do with It? In *Feminist Studies/Critical Studies.* Teresa de Lauretis, ed. Pp. 191–212. Bloomington: Indiana University Press.

Morris, William 1970 [1890] *News from Nowhere.* London: Routledge.

Peters, John 1992 Near-Sight and Far-Sight: Media, Place, and Culture. In *Culture, Power, Place: Explorations in Critical Anthropology.* Roger Rouse, James Ferguson, and Akhil Gupta, eds. Boulder, Colo.: Westview Press.

Radhakrishnan, R. 1987 Ethnic Identity and Post-Structuralist Difference. *Cultural Critique* 6:199–220.

Robertson, Jennifer 1988 Furusato Japan: The Culture and Politics of Nostalgia. *Politics, Culture, and Society* 1(4):494–518.

Robertson, Jennifer 1991 *Native and Newcomer: Making and Remaking a Japanese City.* Berkeley: University of California Press.

Rofel, Lisa 1992. Rethinking Modernity: Space and Factory Discipline in China. *Cultural Anthropology* 7(1):93–114.

Rosaldo, Renato 1988 Ideology, Place, and People Without Culture. *Cultural Anthropology* 3(1):77–87.

Rosaldo, Renato 1989 *Culture and Truth: The Remaking of Social Analysis.* Boston, Mass.: Beacon Press.

Rouse, Roger 1991 Mexican Migration and the Social Space of Post-Modernism. *Diaspora* 1(1):8–23.

Said, Edward W. 1979 Zionism from the Standpoint of its Victims. *Social Text* 1:7–58.

Williams, Raymond 1973 *The Country and the City.* New York: Oxford University Press.

Wright, Patrick 1985 *On Living in an Old Country: The National Past in Contemporary Britain.* London: Verso.

54

What is at Stake – and is not – in the Idea and Practice of Multi-sited Ethnography

George E. Marcus

[…] The proposal of something as obvious and inevitable as multi-sited ethnography gains its appeal at present from giving expression to an as yet poorly articulated, but distinctly felt, shift in the conditions of the production of anthropological research. The normative and regulative assumptions of social life that grounded conventional fieldwork have been challenged, but their modification into new sets of practices has not yet been clearly articulated. This is not unlike the impact of the "writing culture" critique of the 1980s; the multi-sited proposal might be understood as a second wave, this time initiating a discussion of the ongoing changing conditions of fieldwork.

The paradigm that I want to outline concerns itself with what I think of as the *non-obvious* applications of multi-sited strategies. The obvious cases of multi-sited ethnography – tracking movements of migrants transnationally in diaspora and exile, or the history of the circulation of objects and techniques, or studying the relationships of dispersed communities and networks that define well-designated macro-processes in the global flow of capital and expertise – are the contexts of contemporary ethnographic work. These contexts are challenging traditional norms

of fieldwork in productive ways and are also opening new conduits of exchange with past interdisciplinary partners in other social sciences. Arjun Appadurai's influential "scape" essays of the early 1990s (see Appadurai 1996), for example, are a metaphorical map for this now strong wave of research.

When anthropologists think of multi-sited work, most think of projects like these whose contexts are defined by given lines of macro-social theory and historical narrative. Macro-processes may be changing, but there is nothing particularly problematic or unclear – *untrackable* – about the relationships or connections of peoples or objects ethnographically probed within the framework of these processes, because they retain their commitment to analyzing observable social process.

While certainly related to and overlapping with this work, the kind of multi-sited ethnography that I want to consider here faces somewhat different challenges, and itself poses more radical alternatives to the norms that have traditionally regulated field-work. I am interested in those cases where the metaphors of tracking or following as a material process do not work as well in constituting multi-sited objects of

From *Canberra Anthropology* 22(2) (1999), pp. 6–14 (with cuts). Reprinted with kind permission of the author

Anthropology in Theory: Issues in Epistemology, Second Edition. Edited by Henrietta L. Moore and Todd Sanders.

ethnographic study, where the relationships or connections between sites are indeed not clear, the discovery and discussion of which are, in fact, the main problem of ethnographic analysis. I am interested here in multi-sited strategies that raise the nature of relationships between sites of activity and social locations that are disjunctive, in space or time, and perhaps in terms of social category as well. For example, Fred Myers' recent work on the circulation of Aboriginal art in different global contexts (see for example Myers 1992); Crapanzano's recent analysis of the course of fundamentalist Christian imagery through various media and social institutions (Crapanzano 2000), and in general, those ethnographies in which the social juxtaposition of, say, elites and subalterns, middle-class and poor, experts and non-experts, institutions and communities – these are examples where the social context of interrelation is *not* obvious as given in any framing regulative or normative analysis. This framework may or may not be posed by ethnographic subjects themselves (this is one of the primary questions for determination by fieldwork itself).

A Non-obvious Paradigm for Multi-sited Ethnography

Schematically posed, this paradigm concerns cases where there is very little actual contact or exchange between two sites but where the functioning of one of the sites (the more strategic one?) depends on a very specific imagining of what is going on elsewhere. The complex nature of the relation between disjunctive sites, how they are coordinated, if they are, is the main objective puzzle of this variety of multi-sited ethnography. Fieldwork in an initial site is oriented primarily to explicating a shared world of a set of subjects derived from attention to situated discourse.

It is the social cartography or social referents elsewhere within this *imagined* world of community that become particularly important. It is not the subject of fieldwork as "other" that is of interest here (he or she really is not "other" to the anthropologist, but more complexly, the counterpart), but rather the other that constructs and is constructed by the subject's imaginary.

Literalness, a sort of naive realism, in making this move is, I would argue, both a virtue and provocation of the project. The fieldwork in the second site is often different in nature to the first site. It is perhaps less intensive than work at the first, interested in probing a way of life as well as an imaginary, but always with the first site in mind. The second site is probed for itself, but the nature of its relation to the first site becomes the foremost question. Is there a reciprocal relation at the level of imaginary, or not? Is there a material relation, one of periodic exchange, or is the relation totally virtual?

The project could end with this interpretation of the relation or connection of the two sites across disjunction where the imaginary at one site is juxtaposed to the ethnography of its literal referent, but a third phase of such a multi-sited project would define itself as intervention, presuming that the project is primarily motivated in conception by being oriented toward the regime of power/knowledge, so to speak, that defines the initial site. The project would end with some strategy of bringing back the ethnography at the second site to the first site, as some effort at cultural critique, that would involve re-engagement with one's original subjects from whose imaginaries and regimes of representation the impetus and strategy for moving the project literally elsewhere were derived.

[...]

Here I want to articulate an argument about a traditional limitation of ethnography and how multi-sited work might alleviate it. This is tied to the suspicion that multi-sited ethnography in its very designation threatens to be profligate, unfocused and superficial. Indeed, the paradigm I have suggested proposes just the opposite. Multi-sited-ness is more an imaginary than a specific strategy for designing ethnographic methodology. Multi-sited research involves innovative ways of bounding the potentially unbounded, but also of refusing the more usual non-ethnographic bounding of the intensively probed and usually site-specific ethnographic study. In the way that I have suggested, carefully moving across sites of fieldwork within a multi-sited imaginary gives traditional ethnography a means of extending itself in a disciplined, closely argued way that it never had before when it was operating within the presumed spaces of the traditional archive of culture areas and their thematic tropes that defined and shaped ethnographies within them. The paradigm I have suggested is one way of giving anthropology something it doesn't have as a regulative ideal for fieldwork – the focused, argument-driven experiment, understood as such, in research terrains that anthropologists themselves have not conceptualised as well, except as metaphorical extensions of how they have done ethnography within their traditional archive of peoples and places.

The traditional modality is one which is holistic and relatively unfocused – topics are developed from the ground of an imagined total ethnography which is implicitly encyclopedic. A focused ethnography achieves its goal and constitutes an argument by opening up unknown territory, a contiguous category or topic against the holistic ground, or the encyclopedia. Something new for traditional ethnography emerges by filling in a new piece of the map, an unexamined part of the functionalist whole, a new category to look at. This is fine in a world of peoples and places contained in culture areas, but is far too limited where cultural formations and objects of study are discontinuous, and the product of complex circulations. The paradigm I suggested does not work like the traditional ethnography in making arguments. The argument is rather embedded in the speculative, experimental aspect of ethnographic probing that is not as certain of the contextualising ground or space in which it is working.

[…]

The Loss and Reclamation of the Social in Recent Ethnography

What is most importantly and most generally at stake for anthropology in the emergence of multi-sited ethnography is indeed a reorientation to the very idea of the social in situated cultural analysis inspired by the cultural turn of the past two decades. There is a general feeling among anthropologists today, more or less articulated in professional "corridor talk",

that the interest in all of those things that would be classed under the "social" – social relations, processes, structures, systems, institutions, matters of political economy – have been relatively neglected in favour of attention to, for example, subject positions, identity construction, dialogic exchange and micro-examinations of embedded practices, restricted to the intimate traditional scene of fieldwork. Indeed, it might be argued that this finely wrought preoccupation with the micro-cultural is about the social (à la Anthony Giddens' location of structuration in situated agency, and Pierre Bourdieu's location of what is systemic in the situation in the habitus) – just a different way of constructing it. But there is no doubt that within the production of ethnography the description of the terrain of the macro-social has suffered in its materialities, attention to scale, regimes of exchange, and resulting exposures of and concerns for inequalities. Instead there has been a tendency in ethnography to let the constructs, theories, and work of other kinds of academics (including cultural geographers, political economists, and post-colonial theorists, among others) to stand in, so to speak, for the macro-, patterned sense of the social that contextualises ethnographic work, while it itself probes voice, discourse, subjectivity, and identity as its primary concerns.

In a sense, letting constructs of the social define the ethnographic centre of contemporary anthropological research insulates the interpretation of ethnographic materials from essentially non-ethnographic perspectives. One major aim, then, of trying to theorise the already occurring multi-sited transformation of fieldwork is to encourage this move of a certain nomadic or rhizomic tendency in ethnography into a motivated change in the way that much contemporary ethnography constructs the space of the social as the contexts for its intimate eye and ear. The world of finance, markets, politics, and their institutions are ethnographic objects of study implicated in every fieldwork project these days and cannot be left to other constructions, if anthropology is to be responsible for its own contexts of meaning and the forging of its own arguments from inside the ethnographic process of research itself. This reclamation of the social context of ethnography is for me the most important stake for the current reconstruc- tion of anthropology through multi-sited ethnographic projects. [...]

References

Appadurai, A. 1996 *Modernity at large*. Minneapolis and London: University of Minnesota Press.

Crapanzano, V. 2000 *Serving the word: literalism in America from the pulpit to the Bench*. New York: New Press.

Myers, F. 1992 Representing culture: the production of discourses for Aboriginal acrylic paintings. In G. Marcus (ed.) *Rereading cultural anthropology*, pp. 319–55. Durham, NC: Duke University Press.

55

Grassroots Globalization and the Research Imagination

Arjun Appadurai

Anxieties of the Global

Globalization is certainly a source of anxiety in the US academic world. And the sources of this anxiety are many: Social scientists (especially economists) worry about whether markets and deregulation produce greater wealth at the price of increased inequality. Political scientists worry that their field might vanish along with their favorite object, the nation-state, if globalization truly creates a "world without borders." Cultural theorists, especially cultural Marxists, worry that in spite of its conformity with everything they already knew about capital, there may be some embarrassing new possibilities for equity hidden in its workings. Historians, ever worried about the problem of the new, realize that globalization may not be a member of the familiar archive of large-scale historical shifts. And everyone in the academy is anxious to avoid seeming to be a mere publicist of the gigantic corporate machineries that celebrate globalization. Product differentiation is as important for (and within) the academy as it is for the corporations academics love to hate.

Outside the academy there are quite different worries about globalization that include such questions as: What does globalization mean for labor markets and fair wages? How will it affect chances for real jobs and reliable rewards? What does it mean for the ability of nations to determine the economic futures of their populations? What is the hidden dowry of globalization? Christianity? Cyber-proletarianization? New forms of structural adjustment? Americanization disguised as human rights or as MTV? Such anxieties are to be found in many national public spheres (including that of the United States) and also in the academic debates of scholars in the poorer countries.

Among the poor and their advocates the anxieties are even more specific: What are the great global agencies of aid and development up to? Is the World Bank really committed to incorporating social and cultural values into its developmental agenda? Does Northern aid really allow local communities to set their own agendas? Can large banking interests be trusted to support microcredit? Which parts of the national state are protectors of stakeholding communities and which parts are direct affiliates of global capital? Can the media ever be turned to the interests of the poor?

From *Public Culture* 12(1) (2000), pp. 1–19. Copyright © 2000 by Duke University Press. All rights reserved. Republished by permission of the copyright holder, Duke University Press. www.dukeupress.edu

Anthropology in Theory: Issues in Epistemology, Second Edition. Edited by Henrietta L. Moore and Todd Sanders.
© 2014 John Wiley & Sons, Inc. Published 2014 by John Wiley & Sons, Inc.

In the public spheres of many societies there is concern that policy debates occurring around world trade, copyright, environment, science, and technology set the stage for life-and-death decisions for ordinary farmers, vendors, slum-dwellers, merchants, and urban populations. And running through these debates is the sense that social exclusion is ever more tied to epistemological exclusion and concern that the discourses of expertise that are setting the rules for global transactions, even in the progressive parts of the international system, have left ordinary people outside and behind. The discourse of globalization is itself growing dangerously dispersed, with the language of epistemic communities, the discourse of states and inter-state fora, and the everyday understanding of global forces by the poor growing steadily apart.

There is thus a double apartheid evolving. The academy (especially in the United States) has found in globalization an object around which to conduct its special internal quarrels about such issues as representation, recognition, the "end" of history, the spectres of capital (and of comparison), and a host of others. These debates, which still set the standard of value for the global professoriate, nevertheless have an increasingly parochial quality.

Thus the first form of this apartheid is the growing divorce between these debates and those that characterize vernacular discourses about the global, worldwide, that are typically concerned with how to plausibly protect cultural autonomy and economic survival in some local, national, or regional sphere in the era of "reform" and "openness." The second form of apartheid is that the poor and their advocates find themselves as far from the anxieties of their own national discourses about globalization as they do from the intricacies of the debates in global fora and policy discourses surrounding trade, labor, environment, disease, and warfare.

But a series of social forms has emerged to contest, interrogate, and reverse these developments and to create forms of knowledge transfer and social mobilization that proceed independently of the actions of corporate capital and the nation-state system (and its international affiliates and guarantors). These social forms rely on strategies, visions, and horizons for globalization on behalf of the poor that can be characterized as "grassroots globalization" or, put in a slightly different way, as "globalization from below." This essay is an argument for the significance of this kind of globalization, which strives for a democratic and autonomous standing in respect to the various forms by which global power further seeks to extend its dominion. The idea of an international civil society will have no future outside of the success of these efforts to globalize from below. And in the study of these forms lies an obligation for academic research that, if honored, might make its deliberations more consequential for the poorer 80 percent of the population of the world (now totalling 6 billion) who are socially and fiscally at risk.

To take up this challenge to American academic thought about globalization, this essay moves through three arguments. The first is about the peculiar optical challenges posed by the global. The second is about area studies – the largest institutional epistemology through which the academy in the United States has apprehended much of the world in the last fifty years. The third concerns the very ground from which academics typically and unwittingly speak – the category of "research" itself. These three steps bring me to a conclusion about the relations between pedagogy, activism, and research in the era of globalization.

The Optics of Globalization

Globalization is inextricably linked to the current workings of capital on a global basis; in this regard it extends the earlier logics of empire, trade, and political dominion in many parts of the world. Its most striking feature is the runaway quality of global finance, which appears remarkably independent of traditional constraints of information transfer, national regulation, industrial productivity, or "real" wealth in any particular society, country, or region. The worrisome implications of this chaotic, high velocity, promiscuous movement of financial (especially speculative) capital have been noted by several astute critics (Greider 1997; Rodrik 1997; Soros 1998, among others) so I will not dwell on them here. I am among those analysts who are inclined to see globalization as a definite marker of a new crisis for the sovereignty of nation-states, even if there is no consensus on the core of this crisis or its generality and finality (Appadurai 1996; Rosenau 1997; Ruggie 1993; Sassen 1996).

My concern here is with the conditions of possibility for the democratization of research about globalization in the context of certain dominant forms of critical knowledge, especially as these forms have come to be organized by the social sciences in the West. Here we need to observe some optical peculiarities. The first is that there is a growing disjuncture between the globalization of knowledge and the knowledge of globalization. The second is that there is an inherent temporal lag between the processes of globalization and our efforts to contain them conceptually. The third is that globalization as an uneven economic process creates a fragmented and uneven distribution of just those resources for learning, teaching, and cultural criticism that are most vital for the formation of democratic research communities that could produce a global view of globalization. That is, globalization resists the possibility of just those forms of collaboration that might make it easier to understand or criticise.

In an earlier, more confident epoch in the history of social science – notably in the 1950s and 1960s during the zenith of modernization theory – such epistemological diffidence would have been quickly dismissed, since that was a period when there was a more secure sense of the social in the relationship between theory, method, and scholarly location. Theory and method were seen as naturally metropolitan, modern, and Western. The rest of the world was seen in the idiom of cases, events, examples, and test sites in relation to this stable location for the production or revision of theory. Most varieties of Marxist theory, though sharply critical of the capitalist project behind modernization theory, nevertheless were equally "realist," both in their picture of the architecture of the world system and in their understanding of the relationship between theory and cases. Thus much excellent work in the Marxist tradition had no special interest in problems of voice, perspective, or location in the study of global capitalism. In short, a muscular objectivism united much social science in the three decades after World War II, whatever the politics of the practitioners.

Today, one does not have to be a postmodernist, relativist, or deconstructionist (key words in the culture wars of the Western academic world) to admit that political subjects are not mechanical products of their objective circumstances, that the link between events significantly separated in space and proximate in time is often hard to explain, that the kinds of comparison of social units that relied on their empirical separability cannot be secure, and that the more marginal regions of the world are not simply producers of data for the theory mills of the North.

Flows and Disjunctures

It has now become something of a truism that we are functioning in a world fundamentally characterized by objects in motion. These objects include ideas and ideologies, people and goods, images and messages, technologies and techniques. This is a world of flows (Appadurai 1996). It is also, of course, a world of structures, organizations, and other stable social forms. But the apparent stabilities that we see are, under close examination, usually our devices for handling objects characterized by motion. The greatest of these apparently stable objects is the nation-state, which is today frequently characterized by floating populations, transnational politics within national borders, and mobile configurations of technology and expertise.

But to say that globalization is about a world of things in motion somewhat understates the point. The various flows we see – of objects, persons, images, and discourses – are not coeval, convergent, isomorphic, or spatially consistent. They are in what I have elsewhere called relations of disjuncture. By this I mean that the paths or vectors taken by these kinds of things have different speeds, axes, points of origin and termination, and varied relationships to institutional structures in different regions, nations, or societies. Further, these disjunctures themselves precipitate various kinds of problems and frictions in different local situations. Indeed, it is the disjunctures between the various vectors characterizing this world-in-motion that produce fundamental problems of livelihood, equity, suffering, justice, and governance.

Examples of such disjunctures are phenomena such as the following: Media flows across national boundaries that produce images of well-being that cannot be satisfied by national standards of living and consumer capabilities; flows of discourses of human rights that generate demands from workforces that are repressed by state violence which is itself backed by global arms flows; ideas about gender and modernity that circulate to create large female workforces at the same time that cross-national ideologies of "culture," "authenticity," and national honor put increasing pressure on various communities to morally discipline just these working women who are vital to emerging markets and manufacturing sites. Such examples could be multiplied. What they have in common is the fact that globalization – in this perspective a cover term for a world of disjunctive flows – produces problems that manifest themselves in intensely local forms but have contexts that are anything but local.

If globalization is characterized by disjunctive flows that generate acute problems of social well-being, one positive force that encourages an emancipatory politics of globalization is the role of the imagination in social life (Appadurai 1996). The imagination is no longer a matter of individual genius, escapism from ordinary life, or just a dimension of aesthetics. It is a faculty that informs the daily lives of ordinary people in myriad ways: It allows people to consider migration, resist state violence, seek social redress, and design new forms of civic association and collaboration, often across national boundaries. This view of the role of the imagination as a popular, social, collective fact in the era of globalization recognizes its split character. On the one hand, it is in and through the imagination that modern citizens are disciplined and controlled – by states, markets, and other powerful interests. But is it is also the faculty through which collective patterns of dissent and new designs for collective life emerge. As the imagination as a social force itself works across national lines to produce locality as a spatial fact and as a sensibility (Appadurai 1996), we see the beginnings of social forms without either the predatory mobility of unregulated capital or the predatory stability of many states. Such social forms have barely been named by current social science, and even when named their dynamic qualities are frequently lost. Thus terms like "international civil society" do not entirely capture the mobility and malleability of those creative forms of social life that are

localized transit points for mobile global forms of civic and civil life.

One task of a newly alert social science is to name and analyze these mobile civil forms and to rethink the meaning of research styles and networks appropriate to this mobility. In this effort, it is important to recall that one variety of the imagination as a force in social life – the academic imagination – is part of a wider geography of knowledge created in the dialogue between social science and area studies, particularly as it developed in the United States after World War II. This geography of knowledge invites us to rethink our picture of what "regions" are and to reflect on how research itself is a special practice of the academic imagination. These two tasks are taken up below.

Regional Worlds and Area Studies

As scholars concerned with localities, circulation, and comparison, we need to make a decisive shift away from what we may call "trait" geographies to what we could call "process" geographies. Much traditional thinking about "areas" has been driven by conceptions of geographical, civilizational, and cultural coherence that rely on some sort of trait list – of values, languages, material practices, ecological adaptations, marriage patterns, and the like. However sophisticated these approaches, they all tend to see "areas" as relatively immobile aggregates of traits, with more or less durable historical boundaries and with a unity composed of more or less enduring properties. These assumptions have often been further telescoped backward through the lens of contemporary US security-driven images of the world and, to a lesser extent, through colonial and postcolonial conceptions of national and regional identity.

In contrast, we need an architecture for area studies that is based on process geographies and sees significant areas of human organization as precipitates of various kinds of action, interaction, and motion – trade, travel, pilgrimage, warfare, proselytization, colonization, exile, and the like. These geographies are necessarily large scale and shifting, and their changes highlight variable congeries of language, history, and material life. Put more simply, the large regions that dominate our current maps for area studies are not permanent geographical facts. They are problematic heuristic devices for the study of global geographic and cultural processes. Regions are best viewed as initial contexts for themes that generate variable geographies, rather than as fixed geographies marked by pre-given themes. These themes are equally "real," equally coherent, but are results of our interests and not their causes.

The trouble with much of the paradigm of area studies as it now exists is that it has tended to mistake a particular configuration of apparent stabilities for permanent associations between space, territory, and cultural organization. These apparent stabilities are themselves largely artifacts of the specific trait-based idea of "culture" areas, a recent Western cartography of large civilizational land-masses associated with different relationships to "Europe" (itself a complex historical and cultural emergent), and a Cold War-based geography of fear and competition in which the study of world languages and regions in the United States was legislatively configured for security purposes into a reified map of geographical regions. As happens so often in academic inquiry, the heuristic impulse behind many of these cartographies and the contingent form of many of these spatial configurations was soon forgotten and the current maps of "areas" in "area studies" were enshrined as permanent.

One key to a new architecture for area studies is to recognize that the capability to imagine regions and worlds is now itself a globalized phenomenon. That is, due to the activities of migrants, media, capital, tourism, and so forth the means for imagining areas is now itself globally widely distributed. So, as far as possible, we need to find out how others, in what we still take to be certain areas as we define them, see the rest of the world in regional terms. In short, how does the world look – as a congeries of areas – from other locations (social, cultural, national)?

For example, the Pacific Rim is certainly a better way of thinking about a certain region today, rather than splitting up East Asia and the Western coast of North America. But a further question is: How do people in Taiwan, Korea, or Japan think about the Pacific Rim, if they think in those terms at all? What is their topology of Pacific traffic?

To seriously build an architecture for area studies around the idea that all "areas" also

conceive or produce their own "areas," we need to recognize the centrality of this sort of recursive refraction. In fact this perspective could be infinitely regressive. But we do not have to follow it out indefinitely: One or two moves of this type would lead us a long way from the US Cold War architecture with which we substantially still operate.

Following this principle has a major entailment for understanding the apparatus through which areal worlds are globally produced. This production happens substantially in the public spheres of many societies, and includes many kinds of intellectuals and "symbolic analysts" (including artists, journalists, diplomats, businessmen, and others) as well as academics. In some cases, academics may be only a small part of this world-generating optic. We need to attend to this varied set of public spheres, and the intellectuals who constitute them, to create partnerships in teaching and research so that our picture of areas does not stay confined to our own first-order, necessarily parochial, world pictures. The potential payoff is a critical dialogue between world pictures, a sort of dialectic of areas and regions, built on the axiom that areas are not facts but artifacts of our interests and our fantasies as well as of our needs to know, to remember, and to forget.

But this critical dialogue between world pictures cannot emerge without one more critical act of optical reversal. We need to ask ourselves what it means to internationalize any sort of research before we can apply our understandings to the geography of areas and regions. In essence, this requires a closer look at research as a practice of the imagination.

The Idea of Research

In much recent discussion about the internationalization of research, the problem term is taken to be "internationalization." I propose that we focus first on research, before we worry about its global portability, its funding, and about training people to do it better. The questions I wish to raise here are: What do we mean when we speak today of research? Is the research ethic, whatever it may be, essentially the same thing in the natural sciences, the social sciences, and the humanities? By whatever definition, is there a sufficiently clear understanding of the research ethic in the academic world of North America and Western Europe to justify its central role in current discussions of the internationalization of academic practices?

Such a deliberately naive, anthropological reflection upon the idea of research is difficult. Like other cultural keywords, it is so much part of the ground on which we stand and the air we breathe that it resists conscious scrutiny. In the case of the idea of research, there are two additional problems. First, research is virtually synonymous with our sense of what it means to be scholars and members of the academy, and thus it has the invisibility of the obvious. Second, since research is the optic through which we typically find out about something as scholars today, it is especially hard to use research to understand research.

Partly because of this ubiquitous, taken-for-granted, and axiomatic quality of research, it may be useful to look at it not only historically – as we might be inclined to do – but anthropologically, as a strange and wonderful practice that transformed Western intellectual life perhaps more completely than any other single procedural idea since the Renaissance. What are the cultural presumptions of this idea and thus of its ethic? What does it seem to assume and imply? What special demands does it make upon those who buy into it?

Today, every branch of the university system in the West, but also many branches of government, law, medicine, journalism, marketing, and even the writing of some kinds of fiction and the work of the armed forces must demonstrate their foundation in research in order to command serious public attention or funds. To write the history of this huge transformation of our fundamental protocols about the production of reliable new knowledge is a massive undertaking, better suited to another occasion. For now, let us ask simply what this transformation in our understanding of new knowledge seems to assume and imply.

Consider a naive definition. Research may be defined as the systematic pursuit of the not-yet-known. It is usually taken for granted that the machine that produces new knowledge is research. But the research ethic is obviously not about just any kind of new knowledge. It is about new knowledge that meets certain criteria. It has

to plausibly emerge from some reasonably clear grasp of relevant prior knowledge. The question of whether someone has produced new knowledge, in this sense, requires a community of assessment, usually preexistent, vocational, and specialized. This community is held to be competent to assess not just whether a piece of knowledge is actually new but whether its producer has complied with the protocols of pedigree: the review of the literature, the strategic citation, the delineation of the appropriate universe – neither shapelessly large nor myopically small – of prior, usually disciplinary, knowledge. In addition, legitimate new knowledge must somehow strike its primary audience as interesting. That is, it has to strike them not only as adding something recognizably new to some predefined stock of knowledge but, ideally, as adding something interesting. Of course, boring new knowledge is widely acknowledged to be a legitimate product of research, but the search for the new-and-interesting is always present in professional systems of assessment.

Reliable new knowledge, in this dispensation, cannot come directly out of intuition, revelation, rumor, or mimicry. It has to be a product of some sort of systematic procedure. This is the nub of the strangeness of the research ethic. In the history of many world traditions (including the Western one) of reflection, speculation, argumentation, and ratiocination, there has always been a place for new ideas. In several world traditions (although this is a matter of continuing debate) there has always been a place for discovery, and even for discovery grounded in empirical observations of the world. Even in those classical traditions of intellectual work, such as those of ancient India, where there is some question about whether empirical observation of the natural world was much valued, it is recognized that a high value was placed on careful observation and recording of human activity. Thus, the great grammatical works of Panini (the father of Sanskrit grammar) are filled with observations about good and bad usage that are clearly drawn from the empirical life of speech communities. Still, it would be odd to say that Panini was conducting research on Sanskrit grammar, any more than that Augustine was conducting research on the workings of the will, or Plato on tyranny, or even Aristotle on biological structures or politics. Yet these great thinkers certainly changed the way their readers thought, and their works continue to change the way we think about these important issues. They certainly produced new knowledge and they were even systematic in the way they did it. What makes it seem anachronistic to call them researchers?

The answer lies partly in the link between new knowledge, systematicity, and an organized professional community of criticism. What these great thinkers did not do was to produce new knowledge in relation to a prior citational world and an imagined world of specialized professional readers and researchers. But there is another important difference. The great thinkers, observers, discoverers, inventors, and innovators of the pre-research era invariably had moral, religious, political, or social projects, and their exercises in the production of new knowledge were therefore, by definition, virtuoso exercises. Their protocols could not be replicated, not only for technical reasons but because their questions and frameworks were shot through with their political projects and their moral signatures. Once the age of research (and its specific modern ethic) arrives, these thinkers become necessarily confined to the protohistory of the main disciplines that now claim them or to the footnotes of the histories of the fields into which they are seen as having trespassed. But in no case are they seen as part of the history of research, as such. This is another way to view the much discussed growth of specialized fields of inquiry in the modern research university in the course of the nineteenth and twentieth centuries.

These considerations bring us close to the core of the modern research ethic, to something that underpins the concern with systematicity, prior citational contexts, and specialized modes of inquiry. This is the issue of replicability or, in the aphoristic comment of my colleague George Stocking, the fact that what is involved here is *not search but re-search*. There is of course a vast technical literature in the history and philosophy of science about verifiability, replicability, falsifiability, and the transparency of research protocols. All of these criteria are intended to eliminate the virtuoso technique, the random flash, the generalist's epiphany, and other private sources of confidence. All confidence in this more restricted ethic of new knowledge reposes (at least in principle) in the idea

that results can be repeated, sources can be checked, citations can be verified, calculations can be confirmed by one or many other researchers. Given the vested interest in showing their peers wrong, these other researchers are a sure check against bad protocols or lazy inferences. The fact that such direct cross-checking is relatively rare in the social sciences and the humanities is testimony to the abstract moral sanctions associated with the idea of replicability.

This norm of replicability gives hidden moral force to the idea, famously associated with Max Weber, of the importance of value-free research, especially in the social sciences. Once the norm of value-free research successfully moves from the natural sciences into the social and human sciences (no earlier than the late nineteenth century), we have a sharp line not just between such "ancients" as Aristotle, Plato, and Augustine on the one hand and modern researchers on the other, but also a line between researchers in the strict academic sense and such modern thinkers as Goethe, Kant, and Locke. The importance of value-free research in the modern research ethic assumes its full force with the subtraction of the idea of moral voice or vision and the addition of the idea of replicability. It is not difficult to see the link of these developments to the steady secularization of academic life after the seventeenth century.

Given these characteristics, it follows that there can be no such thing as individual research, in the strict sense, in the modern research ethic, though of course individuals may and do conduct research. Research in the modern, Western sense, is through and through a collective activity, in which new knowledge emerges from a professionally defined field of prior knowledge and is directed toward evaluation by a specialized, usually technical, body of readers and judges who are the first sieve through which any claim to new knowledge must ideally pass. This fact has important implications for the work of "public" intellectuals, especially outside the West, who routinely address nonprofessional publics. I will address this question below. Being first and last defined by specific communities of reference (both prior and prospective), new knowledge in the modern research ethic has one other crucial characteristic that has rarely been explicitly discussed.

For most researchers, the trick is how to choose theories, define frameworks, ask questions, and design methods that are most likely to produce research with a plausible shelf life. Too grand a framework or too large a set of questions and the research is likely not be funded, much less to produce the ideal shelf life. Too myopic a framework, too detailed a set of questions, and the research is likely to be dismissed by funders as trivial, and even when it is funded, to sink without a bubble in the ocean of professional citations. The most elusive characteristic of the research ethos is this peculiar shelf life of any piece of reliable new knowledge. How is it to be produced? More important, how can we produce institutions that can produce this sort of new knowledge predictably, even routinely? How do you train scholars in developing this faculty for the lifelong production of pieces of new knowledge that function briskly but not for too long? Can such training be internationalized?

I have already suggested that there are few walks of modern life, both in the West and in some other advanced industrial societies, in which research is not a more or less explicit requirement of plausible policy or credible argumentation, whether the matter is child abuse or global warming, punctuated equilibrium or consumer debt, lung cancer or affirmative action. Research-produced knowledge is everywhere, doing battle with other kinds of knowledge (produced by personal testimony, opinion, revelation, or rumor) and with other pieces of research-produced knowledge.

Though there are numerous debates and differences about research style among natural scientists, policy makers, social scientists, and humanists, there is also a discernible area of consensus. This consensus is built around the view that the most serious problems are not those to be found at the level of theories or models but those involving method: data gathering, sampling bias, reliability of large numerical data sets, comparability of categories across national data archives, survey design, problems of testimony and recall, and the like. To some extent, this emphasis on method is a reaction to widespread unease about the multiplication of theoretical paradigms and normative visions, especially in the social sciences. Furthermore, in this perspective, method, translated into research design, is taken to be a reliable machine for producing ideas with the appropriate shelf life. This implicit consensus and the differences it seeks to manage take on special importance for any effort to internationalize social science research.

Democracy, Globalization, and Pedagogy

We can return now to a deeper consideration of the relationship between the knowledge of globalization and the globalization of knowledge. I have proposed that globalization is not simply the name for a new epoch in the history of capital or in the biography of the nation-state. It is marked by a new role for the imagination in social life. This role has many contexts: I have focused here on the sphere of knowledge production, especially knowledge associated with systematic academic inquiry. I have suggested that the principal challenge that faces the study of regions and areas is that actors in different regions now have elaborate interests and capabilities in constructing world pictures whose very interaction affects global processes. Thus the world may consist of regions (seen processually), but regions also imagine their own worlds. Area studies must deliberate upon this aspect of the relationship between regions, as must any discipline that takes subjectivity and ideology as something more than ephemera in the saga of capital and empire. Such deliberation is a vital prerequisite for internationalizing academic research, especially when the objects of research themselves have acquired international, transnational, or global dimensions of vital interest to the human sciences.

One aspect of such deliberation involves a recognition of the constitutive peculiarities of the idea of research, which itself has a rather unusual set of cultural diacritics. This ethic, as I have suggested, assumes a commitment to the routinized production of certain kinds of new knowledge, a special sense of the systematics for the production of such knowledge, a quite particular idea of the shelf life of good research results, a definite sense of the specialized community of experts who precede and follow any specific piece of research, and a distinct positive valuation of the need to detach morality and political interest from properly scholarly research.

Such a deparochialization of the research ethic – of the idea of research itself – will require asking the following sorts of questions. Is there a principled way to close the gap between many US scholars, who are suspicious of any form of applied or policy-driven research, and scholars from many other parts of the world who see themselves as profoundly involved in the social transformations sweeping their own societies? Can we retain the methodological rigor of modern social science while restoring some of the prestige and energy of earlier visions of scholarship in which moral and political concerns were central? Can we find ways to legitimately engage scholarship by public intellectuals here and overseas whose work is not primarily conditioned by professional criteria of criticism and dissemination? What are the implications of the growing gap, in many societies, between institutions for technical training in the social sciences and broader traditions of social criticism and debate? Are we prepared to move beyond a model of internationalizing academic research that is mainly concerned with improving how others practice our precepts? Is there something for us to learn from colleagues in other national and cultural settings whose work is not characterized by a sharp line between social scientific and humanistic styles of inquiry? Asking such questions with an open mind is not just a matter of ecumenism or goodwill. It is a way of enriching the answers to questions that increasingly affect the relationship between academic research and its various constituencies here in the United States as well.

If we are serious about building a genuinely international and democratic community of researchers – especially on matters that involve cross-cultural variation and intersocietal comparison – then we have two choices. One is to take the elements that constitute the hidden armature of our research ethic as given and unquestionable and proceed to look around for those who wish to join us. This is what may be called "weak internationalization." The other is to imagine and invite a conversation about research in which, by asking the sorts of questions I have just described, the very elements of this ethic could be subjects of debate. Scholars from other societies and traditions of inquiry could bring to this debate their own ideas about what counts as new knowledge and what communities of judgement and accountability they might judge to be central in the pursuit of such knowledge. This latter option – which might be called strong internationalization – might be more laborious, even

contentious. But it is the surer way to create communities and conventions of research in which membership does not require unquestioned prior adherence to a quite specific research ethic. In the end, the elements I have identified as belonging to our research ethic may well emerge from this dialogue all the more robust for having been exposed to a critical internationalism. In this sense, Western scholarship has nothing to fear and much to gain from principled internationalization.

It maybe objected that this line of reasoning fails to recognize that all research occurs in a wider world of relations characterized by growing disparities between rich and poor countries, by increased violence and terror, by domino economic crises, and by runaway traffic in drugs, arms, and toxins. In a world of such overwhelming material dependencies and distortions, can any new way of envisioning research collaboration make a difference?

Globalization from Below

While global capital and the system of nation-states negotiate the terms of the emergent world order, a worldwide order of institutions has emerged that bears witness to what we may call "grassroots globalization," or "globalization from below." The most easily recognizable of these institutions are NGOs (nongovernmental organizations) concerned with mobilizing highly specific local, national, and regional groups on matters of equity, access, justice, and redistribution. These organizations have complex relations with the state, with the official public sphere, with international civil society initiatives, and with local communities. Sometimes they are uncomfortably complicit with the policies of the nation-state and sometimes they are violently opposed to these policies. Sometimes they have grown wealthy and powerful enough to constitute major political forces in their own right and sometimes they are weak in everything except their transparency and local legitimacy. NGOs have their roots in the progressive movements of the last two centuries in the areas of labor, suffrage, and civil rights. They sometimes have historical links to the socialist internationalism of an earlier era. Some of these NGOs are self-consciously global in their concerns and their strategies, and this subgroup has recently been labelled transnational advocacy networks (here-after, TANs), whose role in transnational politics has only recently become the object of serious study (Keck and Sikkink 1998). Although the sociology of these emergent social forms - part movements, part networks, part organizations – has yet to be developed, there is a considerable progressive consensus that these forms are the crucibles and institutional instruments of most serious efforts to globalize from below.

There is also a growing consensus on what such grassroots efforts to globalize are up against. Globalization (understood as a particular, con-temporary configuration in the relationship between capital and the nation-state) is demon-strably creating increased inequalities both within and across societies, spiraling processes of eco-logical degradation and crisis, and unviable rela-tions between finance and manufacturing capital, as well as between goods and the wealth required to purchase them. The single most forceful account of this process is to be found in the work of William Greider (1997), though his alarming prognostications have not gone unchallenged (Krugman 1998; Rodrik 1997). Nevertheless, in implying that economic globalization is today a runaway horse without a rider, Greider has many distinguished allies (Garten 1997; Soros 1998). This view opens the prospect that successful TANs might offset the most volatile effects of runaway capital.

Global capital in its contemporary form is characterized by strategies of predatory mobility (across both time and space) that have vastly compromised the capacities of actors in single locations even to understand, much less to antic-ipate or resist, these strategies. Though states (and what we may call "state fractions") vary in how and whether they are mere instruments of global capital, they have certainly eroded as sites of political, economic, and cultural sovereignty. This sense of compromised sovereignty – to which I referred earlier – is the subject of intense debate among political theorists and analysts, but a significant number of these theorists concede that momentous changes in the meaning of state sovereignty are underway (Keohane 1995; Rosenau 1997; Ruggie 1993, [...]; Sassen 1998). These changes suggest that successful transna-tional advocacy networks might be useful players in any new architecture of global governance.

But – and here is the challenge to the academy – most TANs suffer from their inability to counter global capital precisely in its global dimensions. They often lack the assets, the vision, the planning, and the brute energy of capital to globalize through the capture of markets, the hijacking of public resources, the erosion of state sover-eignties, and the control of media. The current geographical mobility of capital is unique in its own history and unmatched by other political projects or interests. Again, there is some debate about whether globalization (as measured by the ratio of international trade to GDP) has really increased over the last century [...] but a significant number of observers agree that the scale, penetration, and velocity of global capital have all grown significantly in the last few decades of this century (Castells 1996; Giddens 1996; Held 1995), especially when new information technologies are factored in as measures of integration and interconnectivity.

Thus it is no surprise that most transnational advocacy networks have thus far had only limited success in self-globalization, since there is a ten-dency for stakeholder organizations concerned with bread-and-butter issues to oppose local interests against global alliances. Thus, their greatest comparative advantage with respect to corporations – that they do not need to compete with each other – is underutilized. There are many reasons for this underutilization, ranging from political obstacles and state concerns about sovereignty to lack of information and resources for networking. While the number of nonstate actors has grown monumentally in the last three decades, especially in the areas of human rights and environmental activism (Keck and Sikkink 1998), there is much more confusion about their relative successes in competing with the orga-nized global strategies of states and corporate interests (Matthews 1997).

But one problem stands out. One of the biggest disadvantages faced by activists working for the poor in fora such as the World Bank, the UN system, the WTO, NAFTA, and GATT is their alienation from the vocabulary used by the uni-versity–policy nexus (and, in a different way, by corporate ideologues and strategists) to describe global problems, projects, and policies. A strong effort to compare, describe and theorize "global-ization from below" could help to close this gap.

The single greatest obstacle to grassroots globalization – in relation to the global power of capital – is the lack of a clear picture among their key actors of the political, economic, and pedagogic advantages of counterglobalization. Grassroots organizations that seek to create transnational networks to advance their interests have not yet seen that such counterglobalization might generate the sorts of locational, informational, and political flexibility currently monopolized by global corporations and their national-civic allies.

By providing a complex picture of the relationship between globalization from above (as defined by corporations, major multilateral agencies, policy experts, and national governments) and below, collaborative research on globalization could contribute to new forms of pedagogy (in the sense of Freire 1987) that could level the theoretical playing field for grassroots activists in international fora.

Such an account would belong to a broader effort to understand the variety of projects that fall under the rubric of globalization, and it would also recognize that the word *globalization*, and words like *freedom, choice,* and *justice*, are not inevitably the property of the state–capital nexus. To take up this sort of study involves, for the social sciences, a serious commitment to the study of globalization from below, its institutions, its horizons, and its vocabularies. For those more concerned with the work of culture, it means stepping back from those obsessions and abstractions that constitute our own professional practice to seriously consider the problems of the global everyday. In this exercise, the many existing forms of Marxist critique are a valuable starting point, but they too must be willing to suspend their inner certainty about understanding world histories in advance. In all these instances, academics from the privileged institutions of the West (and the North) must be prepared to reconsider, in the manner I have pointed to, their conventions about world knowledge and about the protocols of inquiry ("research") that they too often take for granted.

There are two grounds for supposing that this sort of exercise is neither idle nor frivolous. The first is that all forms of critique, including the most arcane and abstract, have the potential for changing the world: Surely Marx must have believed this during his many hours in the British Museum doing "research." The second argument concerns collaboration. I have already argued that those critical voices who speak for the poor, the vulnerable, the dispossessed, and the marginalized in the international fora in which global policies are made lack the means to produce a systematic grasp of the complexities of globalization. A new architecture for producing and sharing knowledge about globalization could provide the foundations of a pedagogy that closes this gap and helps to democratize the flow of knowledge about globalization itself. Such a pedagogy would create new forms of dialogue between academics, public intellectuals, activists, and policymakers in different societies. The principles of this pedagogy will require significant innovations. This vision of global collaborative teaching and learning about globalization may not resolve the great antinomies of power that characterize this world, but it might help to even the playing field.

References

Appadurai, Arjun. 1996. *Modernity at large: Cultural dimensions of globalization.* Minneapolis: University of Minnesota Press.

Castells, Manuel. 1996. *The rise of network society.* Cambridge, Mass.: Blackwell Publishers.

Freire, Paolo. 1987. *Pedagogy of the oppressed.* New York: Continuum.

Garten, Jeffrey E. 1997. Can the world survive the triumph of capitalism? *Harvard Business Review* 75: 144.

Giddens, A. 1996. Globalization – A keynote address. *UNRISD News* 15: 4–5.

Greider, William. 1997. *One world, ready or not: The manic logic of global capitalism.* New York: Simon & Schuster.

Held, David. 1995. *Democracy and the global order.* London: Polity Press.

Keck, Margaret E., and Kathryn Sikkink. 1998. *Activists beyond borders: Advocacy networks in international politics.* Ithaca: Cornell University Press.

Keohane, Robert O. 1995. Hobbes's dilemma and institutional change in world politics: sovereignty in international society. In *Whose world order?*, eds. H. Holm and G. Sorensen. Boulder: Westview Press.

Krugman, Paul R. 1998. *The accidental theorist and other dispatches from the dismal science.* New York: Norton Publishers.

Matthews, Jessica T. 1997. Power shift, *foreign Affairs,* January/February, 50–66.

Rodrik, D. 1997. *Has globalization gone too far?* Washington, DC: Institute for International Economics.

Rosenau, James. 1997. *Along the domestic-foreign frontier: Exploring governance in a turbulent world.* Cambridge: Cambridge University Press.

Ruggie, John Gerard. 1993. Territoriality and beyond: Problematizing modernity in international relations. *International Organization* 47: 139–74.

Sassen, Saskia. 1996. *Losing control? Sovereignty in an age of globalization.* New York: Columbia University Press.

Sassen, Saskia. 1998. *Globalization and its discontents.* New York: The New Press.

Soros, George. 1998. Toward a global open society. *Atlantic Monthly,* January, 20–4, 32.

56

The End of Anthropology, Again: On the Future of an In/Discipline

John Comaroff

Few believe any longer that [the] continued existence [of anthropology] depends on the perpetuity of the primitive or the survival of *le savage*. As long as there are human beings living on the planet, we will, in principle at least, have an object of study. And after that, who cares? More seriously, the real question is not external to anthropology. It is internal. [...]

As Clifford Geertz (1988:71) once suggested, we do seem to suffer from a proclivity for the auto-pathological; he referred to it as "epistemological hypochondria." And yet, while we appear to stagger from one self-inflicted crisis to the next, anthropology lives on to tell the tale: it evinces palpably more rigor than mortis. Indeed, it is almost as though we actually require to look disciplinary death in the face to survive. Perhaps, with apologies to vampires and antifunctionalists everywhere, imminent demise is our necessary lifeblood. [...] Perhaps intermittent iterations of the End of Anthropology do not portend oblivion so much as prevent it.
[...]

Triage: Three Symptomatologies of Crisis

Let me deal briefly with just the three most commonly cited [...] symptoms.

The first is that the discipline has lost its brand – I use the commodity metaphor pointedly – in the form of its signature method, ethnography; its root concepts, especially culture; its research terrain, namely, comparative societies, and in particular, non-Western societies; and its paradigmatic theoretical landscape. In respect of method, goes the angst, many sociologists, political scientists, social psychologists, humanists, even some economists, claim these days to "do ... ethnography," the practice constitutive of our discipline (Geertz 1973:5). What is more, ethnographic technique itself – which, like all qualitative methodologies, has long been under siege from the "hard" social sciences – has become more inchoately imagined than it was in generations past, which may be why so many "how to"

From *American Anthropologist* 12(4) (2010), pp. 524–32. Reproduced with permission of the American Anthropological Association. Not for sale or further reproduction.

Anthropology in Theory: Issues in Epistemology, Second Edition. Edited by Henrietta L. Moore and Todd Sanders.
© 2014 John Wiley & Sons, Inc. Published 2014 by John Wiley & Sons, Inc.

manuals are being produced (e.g., Atkinson et al. 2001; Hobbs and Wright 2006) [...].

As with method, so with concepts. "While emblematic of ... the discipline," argues George Marcus (2008:3), echoing many others, culture "is longer viable analytically"; to wit, its use is typically hedged around with caveats about what it is not being taken to signify. Furthermore, as it has become commonplace to point out, the concept has disseminated itself quite promiscuously. Corporate law firms have courses on it. Sports teams invoke it. Nations brand it. But, most of all, "natives" insist on claiming it for themselves, often trademarking it, sometimes even charging scholars who study it (Comaroff and Comaroff 2009). Worse yet, other disciplines have muscled in on it. And, if that were not enough, our research terrain, "society" and its cognates (social order, system, organization), have been eroded from a number of sides. Existentially, for one. "There is no such thing as society," Margaret Thatcher, organic voice of the 80s, said famously to *Woman's Own* magazine (Keay 1987), anticipating Bruno Latour by several years. [...] But even if we leave the existence of society aside, it is impossible, in this epoch of anti-system, of antitotalization and indeterminacy, to envisage any anthropologist believing that she would be taken seriously were she to rest an analysis on the concept. As with everything else, we can use it in its adjectival form to describe a contingent practice or a process but not as an abstract noun – we may speak of the social, not of society, of the cultural, not of culture (cf. Appadurai 1996:13) – which, I shall argue, actually does have a positive point to it. And something to say about a distinctive future for anthropology.

[...]

The second symptom said to prognosticate the End of Anthropology follows closely. It is that, in contrast to other disciplines that retain well-defined empirical terrains, we have no real subject matter of our own any longer. Why can an account of, say, the Indian advertising industry (Mazzarella 2003) not be as authoritatively done in cultural studies? Or one of fraudulent elections in Nigeria (Apter 1999) by a political scientist?[...] Or one of clothing and adornment in Africa (Hendrickson 1996) by an art historian? [...]The answer is that they could be. Some have been, which simply compounds the angst.

Hence the third symptom of crisis: that, having relinquished its object of study – namely, local "societies" or "cultures" – the subject matter of anthropology has diffused itself into anything and everything, anywhere and everywhere, and hence is about nobody or nothing or nowhere in particular. Marshall Sahlins commented recently that anthropology appears to have become little more than the production of "thin" ethnographic accounts of the myriad, dispersed effects of global capitalism. These days, he added, there are forensic journalists who cover the same topics as do we – and often do so more thoroughly, more insightfully. It is true that, in South Africa, the most memorable recent ethnography of prison gangs is the work of one such journalist (Steinberg 2004), who treats their symbolic economy, their iconography, their legal anthropology, and their sociomaterial existence with extraordinary "thinckness."

The point? That, while Sahlins may have exaggerated somewhat to make a rhetorical point, his remark – which arises out of a genuine fear for the extinction of anthropology – packs a powerful punch. Prima facie, a discipline that takes to doing work that could as well be done, and be done as well, by journalists, technicians of ephemera, is indeed one without a distinctive subject, distinctive theoretical concepts, distinctive methods, or a distinctive place in the disciplinary division of labor. A discipline that hardly exists at all, in fact, other than as an institutional trace waiting to be erased.

[...]

Defying Death, or Vigor Mortis

[...] How have anthropologists reacted to talk of the imminent demise of their discipline? Most do not bother with it at all. Like the vast majority of sociologists (Lopreato and Crippin 1999), they treat it as so much background noise. Among those who have chosen to react, however, three primary tendencies are discernible.

The first is a retreat back into the local – often still, although we rarely admit it, the exotic local. This is owed to the fact that, for many anthropologists, the uniqueness of the discipline remains its "ability to get inside and understand small-scale communities, to comprehend [their] systems of knowledge" (Graeber 2002:1222). Herein lies our sense of security, our source of solace in the face of epistemic or ethical uncertainty. This is in spite of the fact that much contemporary anthropological practice deviates far from the foundational fiction of fieldwork: the conceit that, given sufficient time "on the ground," it is possible to comprehend "the totality of relations" of a "society" or the essential workings of "a culture" (cf. Gupta and Ferguson 1997). [...]

One corollary of the fetishism of the local has been a denial of the relevance to anthropological concerns of macrocosmic forces and determinations in the world, forces and determinations referred to, dismissively, under the sign of globalization. This, in turn, is founded on two assertions: one, of the efficacy of indigenous agency against those global forces; the other, of the banal truism that different peoples do things differently. What follows is a species of relativism, and an intractable realism, that repudiates any "general" theory and method grounded in political economy, history, philosophy, whatever; indeed, any form of knowledge that threatens our distinctiveness [...].

[...] [T]he ethnography of the local is being depicted as an endangered art. Englund and Leach (2000:238 [...]), for instance, argue that "it" is engaged in mortal struggle with "generalizing perspectives." In other words, with Theory, upper case: Theory represented by an ensemble of "familiar sociological" – note, sociological – "abstractions," among them, commodification, modernity, disenchantment, neoliberalism; theory that seeks not merely to describe the world but to account for what goes on within it; theory that opens our scholarly patrimony to the encroachment of an ever-more-generic social science. This sort of self-ghettoization, it seems to me, is less likely to stave off the End of Anthropology than to assure its death by descent into an exquisite form of irrelevance.

The second reaction to perceptions of disciplinary crisis complements the first. It is a retreat into fractal empiricism: the description of acts, events, experiences, images, narratives, and objects in the phenomenal world – in all their concrete, fragmentary, unruly manifestations – without reducing them to any more coherence than is required to render them into words, without imposing any authorial order on them, without seeking meaning "beneath" their surfaces, thus to allow them to speak for themselves. [...]

Which raises a problem: Wherein lies the anthropological value-added? Why call this anthropology at all? Why not literary nonfiction? Literary nonfiction of the highest quality, no question. But unless we ask what it is that gives shape to a social world – how it is imaginatively made social in the first instance; how its internal incoherencies and fractiousness are to be understood; who in it can speak or cannot; what is or is not thinkable and actionable within it; how its realities are constructed, negotiated, empowered, embodied; how its materialities materialize – what makes this particular text, any text, specifically anthropological? And how might it serve to sustain the singularity, or the raison d'être, of the discipline?

The same might be asked of contemporary anthropological writing that shares a commitment to the empiricist but eschews the fractal by resorting to ordering metaphors. Metaphors, I stress, not explanations. Network analysis is a case in point. Here the use of the fecund imagery of reticulation, of the assemblage or the ensemble, stands in for theory, the descriptive tool being an alibi for the presentation of the particular as if it might portray something beyond itself. From this vantage, the concrete itself is the highest permissible form of abstraction. But, again, there is nothing anthropological about this. Network analysis might have had one of its points of origin in the Manchester School [...] where, incidentally, it was never mistaken for theory – but it has dispersed itself widely across the social sciences. For all the fact of it being a response to epistemic crisis, in other words, a resort to empiricism does not, even when coupled with a focus on the intimacy of the local, add up to disciplinary distinction.

This brings me to the third response, especially manifest in the United States. It is to return to basics, so to speak: to the concept of culture – albeit hedged about by caveats, albeit transposed into a lexicon of more contemporary vintage, most usually that of semiotics, of image, representation, voice. Or of phenomenology, of experience, belief, being-in-the-world. A vivid instance has been the recent effort to essay something called the "anthropology of Christianity" (see, e.g., Cannell 2005, 2006; Robbins 2003, 2007). [...] Joel Robbins (2007:5f), in making the case for this "new" field of study, asserts that anthropologists [...] have taken pains to make Christianity "disappear" from anthropological discourse, to "airbrush [it] out" of historical ethnographies, largely by writing it into a narrative that embraces such things as its connections to capitalism and, in Africa, its imbrication in colonialism; largely, also, by giving too much weight to the ways in which its message has been indigenized by "native" populations – and too little to its own intrinsic substance and determinations. [...] [For Robbins] what is particular about the anthropology of Christianity is that it treats the faith primarily as culture. [Thus] greatly to diminish its complexity as a world religion. [...] that contained, within its own Euro-ontology, a credo actually called "Christian political economy" [...].

My object is not to squabble over Christianity or its anthropology. It is to argue that a return to cultural accountancy as the signature of a quintessentially anthropological contribution to the understanding of this or any other phenomenon – and hence as a justification for the continued existence of the discipline – is deeply problematic. Not that culture is unimportant. In dialectical engagement with the sociomaterial, and framed in appropriate theoretical terms (Comaroff and Comaroff 1991:19–31, 1992:27–31), it is indeed critical in making sense of the world. But the reduction of a global religion to it, conceived immaterially and ahistorically, is precisely what gives anthropology a bad name. After all, evangelical Christianity has changed the political and economic face of the planet. All manner of conflict is being conducted under its sign. Christian political economy has returned to haunt us. To distill it to culture is to ensure for the discipline not prolonged life but death by trivialization.

If, then, the three major panaceas for disciplinary perpetuity – retreat into the local, resort to the empirical, and return to the cultural – are part of the problem not the solution, is there a way to speak of the future of anthropology in different terms?

Anthropological Futures: First Thoughts, Second Guesses

There is no easy answer to this question, of course. But let me offer a few thoughts. They lead away from received ideas of the discipline toward a sense of indiscipline, a knowledge regime that seeks to rethink the conceptual foundations, the empirical horizons, and the methodological coordinates of anthropology.

To begin with, the claim that we have lost our distinctive subject matter, methods, concepts, theoretical scaffolding – and, with it, our unique place in the disciplinary division of labor – rests on a fallacy of misplaced typification. This has it that anthropology is a species of knowledge defined by its topical reach and received techniques. In sum, we are what we study and how we study it. [...] Historically speaking, we have also tended to typify ourselves largely in these terms. To continue to do so, however, is at once anachronistic and counterproductive; worse yet, it leads to silly wrangles over what is or is not properly anthropology. In this day and age, it seems to me [...] the discipline ought to be understood as a praxis: a mode of producing knowledge based on a few closely interrelated epistemic operations that lay the foundation for its diverse forms of theory work, mandate its research techniques, and chart its empirical coordinates. They belong, I stress, to the domain of Methodology, upper case: the principled practice by which theory and the concrete world are both constituted and brought into discursive relationship with one another. And they are epistemic in that they entail an orientation to the nature of knowledge itself, its philosophical underpinnings and its notions of truth, fact, value. None of them is new, none of them absent from anthropologies past. Together, they underscore the point that our topical horizons ought to be configured by our praxis, not the other way around.

Let me be clear. I am not suggesting that the discipline shares a single episteme. That is patently not so. The contrasts in this respect between, say, anthropological phenomenology and Marxist anthropology, or structuralism and actor-network theory, are all too plain. However, as we shall see, these epistemic operations, because they belong to the domain of Methodology, transect substantive paradigmatic divides: they may as well chart the anthropology of a practice theorist as a structuralist or a Foucauldian. [...]

First among these operations is the critical estrangement of the lived world, itself founded on a double gesture – on the deconstruction of its surfaces and the relativizing of its horizons – thus to pose the perennial question: What is it that actually gives substance to the dominant discourses and conventional practices of that world, to its subject positions and its semiosis, its received categories and their unruly undersides, to the manner in which it is perceived and experienced, fabricated, and contested? This goes way back. Recall Bronislaw Malinowski's (1927) effort to rewrite Sigmund Freud on the Oedipus complex by demonstrating its very different manifestation among the matrilineal Trobriand Islanders. Here boys were said to evince their first love for their sisters (not their mothers) and hostility toward their maternal uncles (not their fathers), a dramatic transposition of affective patterns found in Europe. The corollary? That the phenomenon has less to do with innate human sex drives than with culturally specific relations of authority and their concomitant ambivalences. Whether or not he was right (cf. Spiro 1983), Malinowski's general point was that Western perceptions of family, kinship, sexuality, and desire required critical decentering if they were to be analytically useful, something that only a comparative anthropology might accomplish.

[...]

The second operation involves being-and-becoming: it is the mapping of those processes by which social realities are realized, objects are objectified, materialities materialized, essences essentialized, by which abstractions – biography, community, culture, economy, ethnicity, gender, generation, identity, nationality, race, society – congeal synoptically from the innumerable acts, events, and significations that constitute them. This operation, in other words, is concerned with establishing how it is that verbs of doing become nouns of being – common nouns, collective nouns, abstract nouns, proper nouns – thus to illuminate the pathways by which lived worlds are pragmatically produced, socially construed, and naturalized. Take, for example, Appadurai (1995) on the "production of locality": it is not the received nature of the local, goes his thesis, but its fabrication that is critical in comprehending the salience of place in social life. Appadurai's (1986) "social life of things" evokes the same sensibility: namely, an impulse to situate the "thingness" of objects, their simultaneous materiality and meaning, in the diachrony of their becoming.

[...]

The third operation is the deployment of the contradiction, the counterintuitive, the paradox, the rupture as a source of methodological revelation. [...]

[...][A]nthropologists have continued to return to them – to the unexpected, the counterintuitive, the rupture – to lay bare worlds both familiar and strange. Note-worthy in this respect is Michael Taussig's (1983) celebrated analysis of a Faustian devil compact to elucidate the contradictions of capitalism, and its misperceived magic, for Colombian cane-field workers. So too, a generation later, is Mateo Taussig-Rubbo's (2007) astonishing image of a one-way mirror in a Californian immigration camp, inverted so that the inmates can see the guards but the guards cannot see the inmates; Taussig-Rubbo commissions this image to interrogate the sorts of sovereignty exercised over "illegal" entrants to the United States in recent times – and, thereby, to illuminate the increasingly contrarian nature of its borders, which are at once ever more both open and closed. [...] Patently, recourse to contradiction, rupture, and the counterintuitive as a methodological stratagem is closely related both to critical estrangement and to mapping processes of being-and-becoming. It is often by such means that the other two operations are enabled, that the interiors of the phenomenal world, in space and time, begin to reveal themselves.

Space and time. The phrase itself points to the fourth epistemic operation: the embedding of ethnography in the counterpoint of the here-and-there and the then-and-now – in a word, its spatiotemporalization. In recent times, the notion of situating almost anything in its broader context has, as often as not, been banalized by reduction to the language of the local-and-the-global; just as the historicization of almost everything tends to be translated into the argot of the epochal, into framing terms like *colonialism, empire, modernity, postcoloniality,* and *neoliberalism.* Blunt instruments, all of them. It goes without saying, or should, that neither spatial nor temporal contextualization is given empirically, nor is it an a priori. Context is always a profoundly theoretical matter.

Spatiotemporalization, as I said earlier, is eschewed by many anthropologists, especially those who repudiate explanation with reference to anything much beyond the enclosed edges of the ethnographic gaze. By contrast, I would argue that anthropology at its most productive is anthropology most comprehensively positioned in the here-and-there and the then-and-now – in proportion, of course, to its analytic object. [...]

[...] [The final epistemic operation, in which converge all the others, is] the founding of the discipline on grounded theory, on an imaginative counterpoint between the inductive and the deductive, the concrete and the concept, ethnographic observation and critical ideation; also, in a different register, between the epic and the everyday, the meaningful and the material. This, self-evidently, implies a respect for the real that does not conflate the empirical with empiricism. And a respect for the abstract that does not mistake theory work for theoreticism. In the absence of one half of this counterpoint (the ethnographic, the inductive, the concrete), we risk becoming second-rate philosophers, or worse, ideologues who deploy "facts" purely in defense of a priori positions. Without the other (the deductive, the concept, critical ideation), we limit our horizons to forensic journalism, to bearing witness, to literary nonfiction or the poetics of pure description. [...] [T]he counterpoint between the empirical and the conceptual offers the most productive pathway for the discipline, maybe the only one, between the Scylla of brute descriptivism and the Charybdis of bloodless abstraction.

[...]

Conclusion

Without a principled praxis, I submit, what pretends to be anthropology is not. Without it, the discipline would indeed be nothing in particular. And difficult to distinguish from others. This is true, too, when it conceives of itself in purely topical terms. That way lies anachronism or indistinction at best, extinction at worst. Conversely, if it remains epistemically grounded in the manner I have described, there is little by way of subject matter that anthropologists cannot take on and address in a distinctive manner. [...]

References

Appadurai, Arjun 1995 The Production of Locality. *In* Counterworks: Managing the Diversity of Knowledge. Richard Fardon, ed. Pp. 208–29. London: Routledge.

Appadurai, Arjun 1996 Modernity at Large: Cultural Dimensions of Globalization. Minneapolis: University of Minnesota Press.

Appadurai, Arjun, ed. 1986 The Social Life of Things: Commodities in Cultural Perspective. New York: Cambridge University Press.

Apter, Andrew 1999 IRB = 419: Nigerian Democracy and the Politics of Illusion. *In* Civil Society and the Political Imagination in Africa: Critical Perspectives. John L. Comaroff and Jean Comaroff, eds. Pp. 267–308. Chicago: University of Chicago Press.

Atkinson, Paul, Amanda Coffey, Sara Delamont, John Lofland, and Lyn H. Lofland 2001 Handbook of Ethnography. London: Sage.

Cannell, Fenella 2005 The Christianity of Anthropology. Journal of the Royal Anthropological Institute 11(2): 335–56.

Cannell, Fenella 2006 Introduction. *In* The Anthropology of Christianity. Fenella Cannell, ed. Pp. 1–50. Durham, NC: Duke University Press.

Comaroff, Jean, and John L. Comaroff 1991 Of Revelation and Revolution, vol. 1: Christianity, Colonialism, and Consciousness in South Africa. Chicago: University of Chicago Press.

Comaroff, John L., and Jean Comaroff 1992 Ethnography and the Historical Imagination. Boulder, CO: Westview Press.

Comaroff, John L., and Jean Comaroff 2009 Ethnicity, Inc. Chicago: University of Chicago Press.

Englund, Harri, and James Leach 2000 Ethnography and the Meta-Narratives of Modernity. Current Anthropology 41(2):225–48.

Geertz, Clifford J. 1973 The Interpretation of Cultures. New York: Basic Books.

Geertz, Clifford J. 1988 Works and Lives: The Anthropologist as Author. Stanford: Stanford University Press.

Graeber, David 2002 The Anthropology of Globalization (with Notes on Neomedievalism, and the End of the Chinese Model of the Nation-State). American Anthropologist 104(4):1222–7.

Gupta, Akhil, and James Ferguson 1997 Discipline and Practice: "The Field" as Site, Method, and Location in Anthropology. *In* Anthropological Locations: Boundaries and Grounds of a Field Science. Akhil Gupta and James Ferguson, eds. Pp. 1–46. Berkeley: University of California Press.

Hendrickson, Hildi, ed. 1996 Clothing and Difference: Embodied Identities in Colonial and Post-Colonial Africa. Durham, NC: Duke University Press.

Hobbs, Dick, and Richard Wright 2006 The Sage Handbook of Fieldwork. London: Sage.

Keay, Douglas 1987 Aids, Education, and the Year 2000! [Interview with Margaret Thatcher.] Woman's Own, October 31:8–10.

Lopreato, Joseph, and Timothy Crippin 1999 Crisis in Sociology: The Need for Darwin. New Brunswick, NJ: Transaction.

Malinowski, Bronislaw 1927 Sex and Repression in Savage Society. London: K. Paul, Trench, Trubner.

Marcus, George E. 2008 The End(s) of Ethnography: Social/Cultural Anthropology's Signature Form of Producing Knowledge in Transition. Cultural Anthropology 23(1):1–14.

Mazzarella, William 2003 Shovelling Smoke: Advertising and Globalization in Contemporary India. Durham, NC: Duke University Press.

Robbins, Joel 2003 What Is a Christian? Notes toward an Anthropology of Christianity. Religion 33(3):191–9.

Robbins, Joel 2007 Continuity Thinking and the Problem of Christian Culture: Belief, Time, and the Anthropology of Christianity. Current Anthropology 48(1):5–38.

Spiro, Melford E. 1983 Oedipus in the Trobriands. Chicago: University of Chicago Press.

Steinberg, Jonny 2004 The Number. Cape Town: Jonathan Ball.

Taussig, Michael 1983 The Devil and Commodity Fetishism in South America. Chapel Hill, NC: University of North Carolina Press.

Taussig-Rubbo, Mateo 2007 The Sovereign's Gift: Reciprocity and Invisibility in U.S. Immigration Detention Camps. Ph.D. dissertation, Department of Anthropology, University of Chicago.

SECTION 17

Anthropologizing Ourselves

57

Participant Objectivation

Pierre Bourdieu

[...] I would like, in the manner of an old sorcerer passing on his secrets, to offer a technique, a method, or, more modestly, a "device" that has helped me immensely throughout my experience as a researcher: what I call "participant objectivation". I do mean participant "objectivation" and not "observation", as one says customarily. Participant observation, as I understand it, designates the conduct of an ethnologist who immerses her- or himself in a foreign social universe so as to observe an activity, a ritual, or a ceremony while, ideally, taking part in it. The inherent difficulty of such a posture has often been noted, which presupposes a kind of doubling of consciousness that is arduous to sustain. How can one be both subject and object, the one who acts and the one who, as it were, watches himself acting? What is certain is that one is right to cast doubt on the possibility of truly participating in foreign practices, embedded as they are in the tradition of another society and, as such, presupposing a learning process different from the one of which the observer and her dispositions are the product; and therefore a quite different manner of being and living through the experiences in which she purports to participate.

By "participant objectivation", I mean the *objectivation of the subject of objectivation*, of the analysing subject – in short, of the researcher herself. One might be misled into believing that I am referring here to the practice, made fashionable over a decade ago by certain anthropologists, especially on the other side of the Atlantic, which consists in observing oneself observing, observing the observer in his work of observing or of transcribing his observations, through a return on fieldwork, on the relationship with his informants and, last but not least, on the narrative of all these experiences which lead, more often than not, to the rather disheartening conclusion that all is in the final analysis nothing but discourse, text, or, worse yet, pretext for text.

It will quickly be clear that I have little sympathy with what Clifford Geertz (1988: 89) calls, after Roland Barthes, "the diary disease", an explosion of narcissism sometimes verging on exhibitionism, which came in the wake of, and in reaction to, long years of positivist repression. [...] But it does not suffice either to explicate "lived experience" of the knowing subject, that is, the biographical particularities of the researcher or the *Zeitgeist* that inspires his work [...]. For

From *Journal of the Royal Anthropological Institute* 9(2) (2003), pp. 281–8, 291–4. Reprinted with permission of John Wiley & Sons UK.

Anthropology in Theory: Issues in Epistemology, Second Edition. Edited by Henrietta L. Moore and Todd Sanders.
© 2014 John Wiley & Sons, Inc. Published 2014 by John Wiley & Sons, Inc.

science cannot be reduced to the recording and analysis of the "pre-notions" (in Durkheim's sense) that social agents engage in the construction of social reality; it must also encompass the social conditions of the production of these pre-constructions and of the social agents who produce them.

In short, one does not have to choose between participant observation, a necessarily fictitious immersion in a foreign milieu, and the objectivism of the "gaze from afar" of an observer who remains as remote from himself as from his object. Participant objectivation undertakes to explore not the "lived experience" of the knowing subject but the social conditions of possibility – and therefore the effects and limits – of that experience and, more precisely, of the act of objectivation itself. It aims at objectivizing the subjective relation to the object which, far from leading to a relativistic and more-or-less anti-scientific subjectivism, is one of the conditions of genuine scientific objectivity (Bourdieu 2001).

What needs to be objectivized, then, is not the anthropologist performing the anthropological analysis of a foreign world but the social world that has made both the anthropologist and the conscious or unconscious anthropology that she (or he) engages in her anthropological practice – not only her social origins, her position and trajectory in social space, her social and religious memberships and beliefs, gender, age, nationality, etc., but also, and most importantly, her particular position within the microcosm of anthropologists. It is indeed scientifically attested that her most decisive scientific choices (of topic, method, theory, etc.) depend very closely on the location she (or he) occupies within her professional universe, what I call the "anthropological field", with its national traditions and peculiarities, its habits of thought, [...] its rituals, values, and consecrations, its constraints in matters of publication of findings, its specific censorships, [...] that is, in the collective history of the specialism, and all the unconscious presuppositions built into the (national) categories of scholarly understanding.

The properties brought to light by this reflexive analysis, opposed in every respect to a self-indulgent, intimist return to the singular, private person of the anthropologist, have nothing singular and still less nothing extraordinary about them. As they are, in good measure, common to

entire categories of researchers (such as graduates of the same school or from this or that university), they are not very "exciting" to naive curiosity. [...] [Yet] the fact of discovering these properties and making them public often appears as a sacrilegious transgression inasmuch as it calls into question the charismatic representation that cultural producers have of themselves and their propensity to see themselves as free of all cultural determinations.

That is why *Homo academicus* (1988) is arguably the most controversial, the most "scandalous" of the books I have written, despite its extreme concern for objectivity. For it objectivizes those who ordinarily objectivize; it unveils and divulges, through a transgression that takes on the air of treason, the objective structures of a social microcosm to which the researcher himself belongs, that is, the structures of the space of positions that determine the academic and political stances of the Parisian academics. [...]

[...] I hardly need say that the French university is, in this case, only the *apparent object*, and that what really has to be grasped there is the subject of objectivation (in this instance myself), his position in that relatively autonomous social space that is the academic world, endowed with its own rules, irreducible to those of the surrounding world, and his singular point of view. [...]

[...]

The reflexivity fostered by participant objectivation is not at all the same as that ordinarily advocated and practised by "postmodern" anthropologists or even philosophy and some forms of phenomenology. It applies to the knowing subject the most brutally objectivist tools that anthropology and sociology provide, in particular statistical analysis (usually excluded from the arsenal of anthropological weapons), and aims, as I indicated earlier, to grasp everything that the thinking of the anthropologist (or sociologist) may owe to the fact that she (or he) is inserted in a national scientific field, with its traditions, habits of thought, problematics, shared commonplaces, and so on, and to the fact that she occupies in it a particular position (newcomer who has to prove herself versus consecrated master, etc.), with "interests" of a particular kind which unconsciously orientate her scientific choices (of discipline, method, object, etc.).

In short, scientific objectivation is not complete unless it includes the point of view of the objectivizer and the interests he may have in objectivation (especially when he objectivizes his own universe) but also the historical unconscious that he inevitably engages in his work. By historical, and more precisely academic, unconscious (or "transcendental"), I mean the set of cognitive structures which can be attributed to specifically educational experiences and which is therefore to a large extent common to all the products of the same (national) educational system or, in a more specified form, to all the members of the same discipline at a given time. [...]

To take as one's project the exploration of this academic unconscious (or transcendental) is nothing other than turning anthropology against itself, as it were, and engaging the most remarkable theoretical and methodological discoveries of anthropology in the reflexive analysis of the anthropologists themselves. I have always regretted that those responsible for the most extraordinary advances of cognitive anthropology – I think of Durkheim and Mauss (1976) analysing "primitive forms of classification" or of Lévi–Strauss (1966) dismantling the workings of the "savage mind" – never applied [...] to their own universe some of the scientific insights that they provided about societies remote in space and time. [...]

[...]

It begins to become clear, or so I hope, that objectivation of the subject of objectivation is neither a mere narcissistic entertainment, nor a pure effect of some kind of wholly gratuitous epistemological point of honour, in that it exerts very real scientific effects. This is not only because it can lead one to discover all kinds of "perversions" linked to the position occupied in scientific space, [...] or that kind of fossilization of research and even thought that can ensue from enclosure in a scholarly tradition perpetuated by the logic of academic reproduction. More profoundly, it enables us also to subject to constant critical vigilance all those "first movements" (as the Stoics put it) of thought through which the unthought associated with an epoch, a society, a given state of a (national) anthropological field smuggle themselves into the work of thought, and against which warnings against

ethnocentrism hardly give sufficient protection. I am thinking in particular of what might be called "Lévy-Bruhl's mistake", which consists in creating an insurmountable distance between the anthropologist and those he takes as object, between his thought and "primitive thought", for lack of having gained the necessary distance from his own native thought and practice by objectifying them.

The anthropologist who does not know himself, who does not have an adequate knowledge of his own primary experience of the world, puts the primitive at a distance because he does not recognize the primitive, pre-logical thought within himself. Locked in a scholastic, and thus intellectualist, vision of his own practice, he cannot recognize the *universal logic of practice* in modes of thought and action (such as magical ones) that he describes as pre-logical or primitive. In addition to all the instances of misunderstandings of the logic of practices [...], I could invoke here Ludwig Wittgenstein who suggests, in his "Remarks on Frazer's *Golden bough*" [1993] that it is because Frazer does not know himself that he is unable to recognize in such so-called "primitive" behaviour the equivalent of the behaviours in which he (like all of us) indulges in similar circumstances [...].

[...]

One only has to have once performed these psychologically necessary and totally desperate acts that one accomplishes on the grave of a beloved one to know that Wittgenstein is right to repudiate the very question of the function and even of the meaning and intention of certain ritual or religious acts. [...]

It follows that, while the critique of ethnocentrism (or anachronism) is, at a first level, legitimate to warn against and ward off the uncontrolled projection of the knowing subject onto the object of knowledge, it can, at another level, prevent the anthropologist (as well as the sociologist or the historian) from making rational use of his native – but previously objectivated – experience in order to understand and analyse other people's experiences. Nothing is more false, in my view, than the maxim almost universally accepted in the social sciences according to which the researcher must put nothing of himself into his research (Bourdieu 1996). He should on the contrary refer continually to his own experience but not, as is too often the case, even among the best researchers, in a guilty, unconscious, or uncontrolled manner. Whether I want to understand a woman from Kabylia or a peasant from Béarn, [...] or a writer like Flaubert, a painter like Manet, a philosopher like Heidegger, the most difficult thing, paradoxically, is never to forget that they are all people like me, at least inasmuch as they do not stand before their action – performing an agrarian rite, following a funeral procession, negotiating a contract, taking part in a literary ceremony, painting a picture, giving a conference, attending a birthday party – in the posture of an observer; and that one can say about them that, strictly speaking, they do not know what they are doing (at least in the sense in which I, as observer and analyst, am trying to know it). They do not have in their heads the scientific truth of their practice which I am trying to extract from observation of their practice. What is more, they normally never ask themselves the questions that I would ask myself if I acted towards them as an anthropologist: Why such a ceremony? Why the candles? Why the cake? Why the presents? Why these invitations and these guests, and not others? And so on.

[...]

I would like to close by discussing another effect of reflexivity, more personal but of great importance, in my view, for the progress of scientific research which, I have gradually come to think – as if in spite of myself and contrary to the principles of my primary vision of the world – has something of an initiatory search about it. Each of us, and this is no secret for anyone, is encumbered by a past, his or her own past, and this social past, whatever it is – "working class" or "bourgeois", masculine or feminine, and always closely enmeshed with the past that psychoanalysis explores – is particularly burdensome and obtrusive when one is engaged in social science. I have said, against the methodological orthodoxy sheltered under the authority of Max Weber and his principle of "axiological neutrality" (*Wertfreiheit*), that I believe that the

researcher can and must mobilize his experience, that is, this past, in all his acts of research. But he is entitled to do so only on condition that he submits all these returns of the past to rigorous scientific examination. For what has to be questioned is not only this reactivated past but one's entire relation to this past which, when it acts outside of the controls of consciousness, may be the source of a systematic distortion of evocation and thus of the memories evoked. Only a genuine socio-analysis of this relation, profoundly obscure to itself, can enable us to achieve the kind of reconciliation of the researcher with himself, and his social properties, that a liberating anamnesis produces (Bourdieu 2001).

I know that I run the risk, once again, of appearing at once abstract and arrogant, whereas I have in mind a simple experiment that any researcher can, it seems to me, perform for her- or himself with very great scientific and also personal profit. The reflexive device that I set in motion by carrying out ethnographic research at about the same time in Kabylia and in Béarn, in a far-away colony and in my home village, had the effect of leading me to examine as an anthropologist – that is to say, with the inseparably scientific and ethical respect due to any object of study – my own milieu of origin [...]. And this *conversion of the whole person*, which goes far beyond all the requirements of the most demanding treatises on methodology, was at the basis of a theoretical conversion which enabled me to reappropriate the practical relation to the world more completely than through the still-too-distant analyses of phenomenology. This turn-around was not effected in a day, through a sudden illumination, and the many returns I made to my Béarn fieldwork – I carried out my study of male celibacy thrice over – were necessary both for technical and theoretical reasons but also because the labour of analysis was accompanied each time by a slow and difficult labour of self-analysis (Bourdieu 2002). [...]

References

Bourdieu, P. [1984] 1988. *Homo academicus*. Cambridge: Polity Press.

Bourdieu, P. [1993] 1996. "Understanding". *Theory, Culture, and Society* 13, 13–37.

Bourdieu, P. 2001. *Science de la science et réflexivité.* (Cours et travaux). Paris: Raisons d'agir Editions.

Bourdieu, P. 2002. *Le Bal des célibataires. Crise de la société paysanne en Béarn.* Paris: Seuil/Points.

Durkheim, E. & M. Mauss [1903] 1976. *Primitive forms of classification.* Chicago: The University of Chicago Press.

Geertz, C. 1988. *Works and lives: the anthropologist as author.* Stanford: University Press.

Lévi-Strauss, C. [1963] 1966. *The savage mind.* Chicago: University Press.

Wittgenstein, L. 1993. Remarks on Frazer's *Golden bough.* In *Philosophical occasions, 1912–1951,* L. Wittgenstein, 119–55. Indianapolis: Hackett.

58

Anthropology of Anthropology?
Further Reflections on Reflexivity*

P. Steven Sangren

This article is concerned with reflexivity, understood to mean applying anthropology's methods and insights to the study of anthropology itself, and specifically the need to overcome important institutional inhibitions intrinsic to knowledge production in our discipline in order to achieve this objective. In contrast to 1980s invocations of reflexivity, characterized by a focus on analysis of authority in texts, a more genuinely "anthropological" reflexivity would require broadening the enquiry to include the social processes of anthropological knowledge production, including the informal or offstage conversations, tactics, career trajectories and etiquette that comprise academic life. Such practices, I argue, are unacknowledged in official disciplinary ideologies which implicitly revolve around utopian notions of a free marketplace of ideas.

Calling attention to the operation of such unofficial practices and implicit values, however, risks violating important norms of academic etiquette – etiquette that in turn plays a significant role in sustaining scholarly communication. Viewed institutionally in these terms, anthropology discourages the very reflexivity it claims as a distinguishing disciplinary virtue. I believe that an anthropology of anthropology remains an important project, both epistemologically and ethically, but one fraught with difficulties and requiring considerable politesse.

My thoughts here respond to a growing interest among anthropologists in topics such as the professions, sciences and other arenas of "knowledge production". Beyond the self-evident intrinsic importance of such topics, this trajectory seems motivated in part by the notion that our own discipline needs new objects to study [...]. Especially noteworthy, however, is that this movement might also be viewed as an intensification of anthropology's quite traditional, long-standing promise to bring the lessons learned about cultural processes in exotic locales closer to home. Anthropologists have long claimed relevance, in part on the grounds that our geographical and intellectual pilgrimages to meet the "other" deepen our knowledge of ourselves. "Reflexivity" registers this aspiration, among others.

Efforts to engage our own culture are to be commended, especially where they address the arenas within it most obviously associated with the production of knowledge – including those in which we are ourselves engaged. [...] As a frequently voiced disciplinary slogan has it, we seek not only to show our students how the exotic can

*Editors' note: This is a substantially abridged version of the original article.

From Anthropology Today 23(4) (2007), pp. 13–16. Reprinted with permission of John Wiley & Sons UK.

Anthropology in Theory: Issues in Epistemology, Second Edition. Edited by Henrietta L. Moore and Todd Sanders.
© 2014 John Wiley & Sons, Inc. Published 2014 by John Wiley & Sons, Inc.

be made familiar (or at least intelligible), but also to show how the familiar might be viewed as exotic – that is to say, how we, too, are socially constituted beings; that we cannot suppose that our own taken-for-granted apprehensions of human nature and human realities are unaffected by cultural and social circumstance.

[…] In this endeavour we claim, implicitly, to convey tolerance (of cultural difference), humility (our culture, too, is ethnocentric), and (let us acknowledge) to possess sophistication (especially compared to competing disciplines and to what we sometimes portray as dominant views in our own society). My main point is that despite these claims and aspirations to illuminate Western culture as a whole, there is considerable systemic resistance within anthropology to studying its own knowledge practices.

[…]

The "Objectivity" Conundrum

These observations raise important and contentious issues that have long vexed anthropology. Among them is the recurrent conundrum that anthropology, perhaps more than any other discipline, must face with respect to justifying the status of anthropological knowledge: How can we claim to be expert producers of knowledge if the object of our knowledge – culture – can reasonably be understood as itself an alternative mode of knowledge production? Does not our "expertise" entail a problematic claim to transcend – in a sense, to dominate – "the other" with respect to knowledge? […]

Unlike some, I do not consider this problem to be intractable in philosophical terms, but my confidence in this respect depends on allegiance to what I will characterize below as a utopian ideal of academic discourse – the same sort of ideal that I shall argue complicates attempts to approach anthropology reflexively. This conviction is linked to another – that "knowledge" cannot be comprehended outside a consideration of the role of ideology in social production. This latter claim locates my theoretical understanding of culture in a particular academic tradition – to characterize broadly, practice theory or the Marxian tradition. Although widely affirmed, this understanding is

by no means ubiquitous among anthropologists. Clearly, to outline satisfactorily how ideology figures in social production would require more discussion than I can provide here. However, although the present argument is informed by this perspective, its more general observations do not depend on it.

Arenas of Reflexivity: Textual and Institutional

Dominic Boyer has drawn attention recently to the fact that not only has "reflexivity" long been a conscious dimension of the anthropological enterprise, it has also taken a number of forms (Boyer 2003). The 1980s discussions, for example, focused on the rhetorical construction of authority in ethnographic texts (Marcus 1980, Clifford 1986, Clifford and Marcus 1986, Marcus and Fischer 1986). My response to those discussions was to insist that the vision of culture as interpretable text widely advocated at the time [see Geertz, chapter 16, this volume] was reproduced by defining reflexivity primarily with reference to similarly conceived representational forms – that is to say, texts – rather than with reference to the processes of social production of knowledge (texts being, of course, only one of its elements) (Sangren 1988, 1989, 1995).

Focusing critique mainly on the rhetorical construction of textual or scientific authority mislocates (or at least misleadingly constrains) the relevant social field, including the immediate contexts of academic social life and careers in which the production of anthropological knowledge and authority occurs. A more thoroughly anthropological form of reflexivity, I argued, ought to look beyond representational forms to consider encompassing social processes. Texts or representations are only part of the story; focusing solely on them would constitute a contemporary variant of the idealism that Marx so effectively exposed 170 years ago in The German ideology (Marx and Engels 1970). Moreover, any linking of representation and social action necessarily implicates ideology. Or, to bring the point more provocatively to the present argument, "ideology" indexes the difference between the ideal of the academy as a free marketplace of ideas – a sort of "instituted fantasy" – and the more encompassing social processes of knowledge production.

Etiquette and the Academy as Instituted Fantasy

And on this point, I believe, anthropologists who aspire to investigate either knowledge as practice or the practice of knowledge in our own society face a dilemma. The dilemma I have in mind is not a new one, but raises itself with particular force when the objects of one's research are themselves possessed of high status, power or expertise in our own society – and becomes especially acute when our own disciplinary practices are brought under such scrutiny. In this regard, I speculate that one of the reasons that much-disparaged disciplinary boundaries in the social sciences and humanities nonetheless persist is that boundaries may actually facilitate cross-disciplinary critique. One wonders, for example, how some of our colleagues in economics or neurobiology would respond if they were regularly obliged to confront what cultural anthropologists think (and, of course, vice versa). For an anthropologist to rail against the ideological misrecognitions of, say, sociobiology or even neo-liberal economics – whatever the scientific or philosophical merits – does not place one at nearly the social or professional risk that taking aim at trends in one's own discipline (whether conventional or avant-garde) would do. Indeed, anti-reductive polemics against other disciplinary knowledge forms clearly serve a solidarity- or identity-producing function for anthropology itself. (We all know that identity construction requires construction of others.)

The dilemma I have in mind is, in short, that if one accepts the proposition that ideology is a crucial concept for any attempt to link knowledge to the processes of its production, then any conceivable anthropology of knowledge entails a critique of ideology – that is to say, a critique of the often unspoken premises and linked practices that define anthropology as a *social* as opposed to *conceptual* object. [...] But here is the crux: to critique elements of the thought or practices of one's own professional community as ideological violates deeply instituted norms of etiquette and sociality.

This dilemma is diagnostic of formidable obstacles confronting reflexive study of anthropology's own knowledge practices, but in order to convey what I have in mind, I shall continue anecdotally and self-referentially. In the mid-1980s I began to write about ideology in the academy. I intended to approach neoclassical economic theory, sociobiology and post-modernist thought as variant but linked ideological forms by showing how they reproduce according to institutional logics little connected to the publicly acknowledged values – the idealized community of pure scholarship alluded to above – to which most academics implicitly pledge allegiance. In particular, I had in mind the notion that what we think of as "the academy" operates more or less as a free marketplace of ideas; that in this marketplace innovation, imagination, but most of all analytic or explanatory power in logical or scientific terms determine our professional value as producers of knowledge; that this "market" rewards productivity of explanation understood in terms both quantitative and qualitative. I argued that even though in our gossip [...] and other important practices we are *well aware* that this marketplace is a *utopian fantasy*, nonetheless our "front-stage" or official discourse proceeds *as if* this utopia obtained.

Although few believe that the "academy" operates wholly according to these utopian dictates, we are all nonetheless deeply invested in perpetuating the fantasy, and our etiquette in official or public venues (publications, lectures etc.) both insists and depends upon this ideal. We are, for example, aware that networking, exchanges of favours, bias, narcissism and much worse contaminate this free marketplace of ideas, but this awareness does not usually prevent us from behaving in "official" contexts *as though* things were as the official fantasy imagines. [...]

[...]

Needless to say, my project remains on the back burner. The reasons it has remained there are instructive. In brief, there are important systemic obstacles – simultaneously ethical, institutional and political – that make realization of a reflexive anthropology of anthropological knowledge practices a very daunting task indeed. To put it bluntly, anthropology as a form of knowledge practice – like all forms of knowledge practice – encompasses *systemic defences* against, oddly, an anthropology of itself – that is to say, against anthropological reflexivity. Etiquette is certainly one of the most important of these defences. To justify this claim, however, would require that I accomplish what I have just suggested is all but prevented by the social organization and ethical norms of our profession, so the best I can do is to gesture toward what I have in mind.

Lessons from "Reflexive Sociology"

In this regard, consider the efforts of Pierre Bourdieu, without doubt the social scientist whose project most nearly approaches the type of reflexivity at issue. [...] Bourdieu and Passeron's *The inheritors* [...] reveals [...] an ideology of "giftedness" produced in the implicit exchanges of recognition of talent between professors and students (Bourdieu and Passeron 1979). Yet even Bourdieu's jaundiced view linking avant-garde idealism to the interests of a bourgeois intelligentsia [...] may invest the processes of knowledge production with more dignity – that of class interest – than they deserve. (Bourdieu has much to say about class interests, less about narcissism, careerism and the seamier back-stage operations of academic politics.)

I single out Bourdieu not only as a pioneer of reflexive sociology but also because his career is itself an interesting case in point. Note that his characterization of many luminaries of the French academy as "heresiarchs" may have won him as many enemies as converts (Bourdieu 1988). [...] During a [...] month's visit to the École des Hautes Études en Sciences Sociales in 1999, I found among my French colleagues that admiration for Bourdieu's undeniable achievements was tempered by ironic observations to the effect that his apparent iconoclasm seemed to work very well with respect to his own professional advancement.

My point is that "reflexivity" becomes a difficult resource to control with respect to any sociology/anthropology of anthropological knowledge – it is too easily converted into a weapon against which few are invulnerable [...].

Lest I be misunderstood, I do not propose that the risks associated with reflexivity warrant suspending study of our own knowledge practices.

Indeed, I would argue that etiquette, gossip and careerist strategizing are important elements in the production of knowledge that cannot be overlooked. But just as is the case when the sensitivities of our more exotic objects of analysis might be offended, obviously politesse and humility with respect to one's own motives and interests is essential. In other words, let us be wary of the forces that a genuine reflexivity might unleash.

Curmudgeonry as "Paraethnography"

[...] I emphasize that the task of creating conceptual tools necessary even to conceive, much less to develop, an anthropology of our own knowledge practices is very much continuous with both traditional ethnographic methods and the intellectual legacy of social theory. [...]

[...]

[...] Marcus and Holmes recommend a collaborative approach to research in relation to professionals with sophisticated knowledge, and suggest the term "paraethnography" to designate such an exercise (Holmes and Marcus 2005a [see chapter 60, this volume], 2005b, 2006). The term might be deployed quite differently, however. Anthropologists themselves, I suggest, possess considerable expertise with respect to the processes that characterize our practices, but this expertise is constrained by etiquette to remain largely outside (or "beside") our explicit professional discourse.

Our back-stage talk may, in short, embody a more realistic sociology of anthropology than does our official (if implicit) disciplinary self-representation. And although the risk that genuine reflexivity might devolve into free-for-all denunciation is real, there are important potential gains. Among these might be an enhancement of anthropology's critical authority to address the dangers of reductive thinking and other forms of ideology and their unacknowledged social consequences. As things stand, our effectiveness as social critics is diminished by our own forms of professional ethnocentrism, which manifest in the ways our professional practices forestall precisely the reflexivity that we so proudly announce as one of our defining virtues. [...]

References

Bourdieu, P. 1988. *Homo academicus*. Stanford: Stanford University Press.

Bourdieu, P. and Passeron, J.-C. 1979. *The inheritors: French students and their relation to culture, with a new epilogue*. Chicago: University of Chicago Press.

Boyer, D. 2003. "The dilemma of the anthropology of expertise". Paper read at Annual Meeting of the American Anthropological Association, session on "Knowledge and Practice".

Clifford, J. 1986. Introduction: Partial truths. In: Clifford, J. and Marcus, G. E. (eds.) *Writing culture: The poetics and politics of ethnography*, pp. 1–26. Berkeley: University of California Press.

Clifford, J. and Marcus, G. E. (eds.) 1986. *Writing culture: The poetics and politics of ethnography*. Berkeley: University of California Press.

Holmes, D. R. and Marcus. G. E. 2005a. Cultures of expertise and the management of globalization: Toward the re-functioning of ethnography. In: Ong, A. and Collier, S. J. (eds.) *Global assemblages: Technology, politics and ethics as anthropological problems*, pp. 235–52. London: Blackwell.

Holmes, D. R. and Marcus, G. E. 2005b. Refunctioning ethnography within cultures of expertise. In: Lincoln, Y.

and Denizen, N. (eds.) *Handbook of qualitative research*, pp. 1099–26. Thousand Oaks: Sage Publications.

Holmes, D. R. and Marcus, G. E. 2006. Fast capitalism: Para-ethnography and the rise of the symbolic analyst. In: Holmes, D. R. and Marcus, G. E. (eds.) *Frontiers of capital: Ethnographic reflections on the new economy*, pp. 33–57. Durham, NC: Duke University Press.

Marcus, G. E. 1980. Rhetoric and the ethnographic genre in anthropological research. *Current Anthropology* 21(4): 507–10.

Marcus, G. E. and Fischer, M. M. J. 1986. *Anthropology as cultural critique: An experimental moment in the human sciences*. Chicago: University of Chicago Press.

Marx, K. and Engels, F. 1970. *The German ideology*. New York: International Publishers.

Sangren, P. S. 1988. Rhetoric and the authority of ethnography: "Postmodernism" and the social reproduction of texts. *Current Anthropology* 29: 405–35.

Sangren, P. S. 1989. Comment on "Ethnography without tears" by Paul A. Roth. *Current Anthropology* 30: 564.

Sangren, P. S. 1995. Comment on "Ethnography: Storytelling or science?" by Robert Aunger. *Current Anthropology* 36(1): 121–2.

59

World Anthropologies: Cosmopolitics for a New Global Scenario in Anthropology

Gustavo Lins Ribeiro

I view the issues that anthropologists address, their theoretical preoccupations, contributions to knowledge, dilemmas and mistakes, the heuristic and epistemological capabilities of the discipline, as embedded in certain social, cultural and political dynamics that unfold in contexts which are differently and historically structured by changing power relations. The main sociological and historical forces that traverse anthropology's political and epistemological fields are connected to the dynamics of the world system and to those of the nation-states, especially regarding the changing roles that "otherness" or "alterity" may play in such international and national scenarios.

This article is heavily inspired by a collective movement called the World Anthropologies Network (WAN), of which I am a member (see www.ram-wan.org). The network aims at pluralizing the prevailing visions of anthropology in a juncture where the hegemony of Anglo-Saxon discourses on difference persists. It stems from the realization that, in an age of heightened globalization, anthropologists have failed to discuss consistently the current nature of their practice and its transformations on a global scale. [...]

The "world anthropologies" project wants to contribute to the articulation of a diversified anthropology that is more aware of the social, epistemological, and political conditions of its own production. The network has three main goals: (a) to examine critically the international dissemination of anthropology – as a changing set of Western discourses and practices – within and across national power fields, and the processes through which this dissemination takes place; (b) to contribute to the development of a plural landscape of anthropologies that is both less shaped by metropolitan hegemonies and more open to the heteroglossic potential of globalization; (c) to foster conversations among anthropologists from various regions of the world in order to assess the diversity of relations between regional or national anthropologies and a contested, power-laden, disciplinary discourse. [...] It questions not only the contents but also the terms and the conditions of anthropological conversations. "World Anthropologies" aims at the construction of a polycentric canon, one that [...] calls for a reconceptualization of the relationships among anthropological communities. [...]

From *Critique of Anthropology* 26(4) (2006), pp. 363–86 (with cuts). Copyright © 2006. Reprinted with permission of SAGE.

Cosmopolitics

The notion of cosmopolitics seeks to provide a critical and plural perspective on the possibilities of supra- and transnational articulations. It is based, on the one hand, on the positive evocations historically associated with the notion of cosmopolitism and, on the other hand, on analysis in which power asymmetries are of fundamental importance (on cosmopolitics see Cheah and Robbins, 1998, and Ribeiro, 2003). [...] I am particularly interested in cosmopolitics that are embedded in conflicts regarding the role of difference and diversity in the construction of polities. I view anthropology as a cosmopolitics about the structure of alterity (Krotz, 1997) that pretends to be universal but that, at the same time, is highly sensitive to its own limitations and to the efficacy of other cosmopolitics. We could say that anthropology is a cosmopolitan political discourse about the importance of diversity for humankind.

Looking at anthropology as cosmopolitics means, right from the beginning, that the discipline is not the only discourse on the importance of diversity, in spite of its sophistication. [...]

Another important implication of viewing anthropology as cosmopolitics is the awareness that the history of North-Atlantic academic anthropology is not sufficient to account for the history of the anthropological *knowledge* on a global scale. [...] Mexican anthropologists, for instance, usually locate the beginning of Mexican "anthropology" in the 16th century and refer in particular to the writings of monks such as Bernardino de Sahagún as the founding moment of anthropological thought in that country (Lomnitz, 2002: 132). Ajit K. Danda [1995] rightly considers that it is necessary to distinguish between anthropology as an "academic discipline" and anthropology as a "body of knowledge". [...]

Like other cosmopolitics, anthropology reflects the historical dynamics of the world system, especially those related to the structure of alterity. Some of the most fundamental changes in anthropology in the 20th century were due to changes in the subject position of anthropology's "object" par excellence, native peoples all over the planet.

But I want to show [...] that, currently, there are new agents at play [...]. Such new agency is not made up of leaders of indigenous populations transformed by modernization nor of "exotic" migrants in global cities [...]. What I want to emphasize is that we are also now to see a new force coming from within anthropology itself. [...]

[...]

[...] [C]urrently there is another element which was never duly incorporated by previous critiques and is bound to impact anthropology: the increased importance of the non-hegemonic anthropologists in the production and reproduction of knowledge. [...] I am not so much concerned with the migration of persons and the contributions that many foreign scholars have historically made to the strength of hegemonic centers. My main preoccupation is with what could be called the migration of texts, concepts and theories. The monotony of international cross-fertilization is not an exclusive problem of anthropology. Sociolinguist Rainer Enrique Hamel (2003) considered that "it may be taken as a symptom of English scientific imperialism in itself that ... most authors from English speaking countries and their former colonies who write about the world as a whole do so without quoting a single non-English language text in their vast bibliographies" (p. 20). This problem, however, is particularly interesting when noticed in a discipline that praises diversity so dearly.

Heteroglossia in anthropological production should start with the recognition of an enormous production in different world locales that needs to gain visibility if we take seriously the role of diversity in the construction of denser discourses and in cross-fertilization. Second, it should mean an awareness of the unequal exchanges of information that occur within the world system of anthropology (Kuwayama, 2004) and a deliberate political position that intends to go beyond this situation towards a more egalitarian and hence enriching environment. Finally, it should also mean an intellectual critique, and subsequent critical action, on the mechanisms that sustain such uneven exchanges not only within the academic milieu but also without it, involving other forms of knowledge production, other cosmopolitics about otherness.

[...] Many anthropologies are ready to come to the forefront. Indeed, their greater international visibility is a prerequisite for reaching more complex forms of creating and circulating theory and knowledge on a global level. Much of the improvement of anthropology will depend on how we answer this question: in an era of heightened globalization, and after the intense epistemological and methodological critique of the past 15 years, how can we establish new conditions of academic exchange and regimes of visibility?

[...]

Anthropologies of Empire-Building/ Anthropologies of Nation-Building

[...] The project of developing Latin American post-imperialist cosmopolitics (Ribeiro, 2003, 2005a) points to the existence of post-national and post-imperial anthropologies in which several reversals of power positions are to be sought. Since an important post-imperial quest is to provincialize the United States through the critique, for instance, of its mediascapes and ideascapes (on these notions see Appadurai, 1990), one of the tasks of Latin American researchers would be to generate knowledge through field research on North American subjects, especially on those that powerfully prefigure cosmopolitics and ideologies of power and prestige. At the same time that we need to do research on the subalterns of the South, we need to do research on the elite of the North. Up and North the anthropologist goes. Since hegemony is the art of exerting power silently, let's not only let the subalterns speak, let's make the powerful speak!

[...]

Post-imperial world anthropologies will develop through theoretical critique but also, and perhaps more importantly, through the political activity of those who are interested in such propositions. World anthropologies imply, for instance, the construction of other conditions of conversability, by bringing together in networks anthropologists and, I submit, anthropological institutions to discuss how we can make the heterogenizing forces of globalization work in favor of heteroglossic initiatives. This is the main factor underpinning the existence of the World Anthropologies Network (www.ram-wan.org). [...] [and] the World Council of Anthropological Associations [...] WCAA has as its primary goal to promote more diverse and equal exchanges between anthropologies and anthropologists worldwide (see www.wcaanet.org).

Much more is yet to be done. I considered, in another article, other possible initiatives to enhance cosmopolitanism in the global anthropological scenario. Translation of different anthropological materials into English, for instance, is highly necessary but not enough.

If we want to avoid linguistic monotony, we also need to increase the quantity of heterodox exchanges and translations. German anthropologists should be translated into Japanese, Mexicans into German, Australians into Portuguese, Brazilians into Russian, and so on. National congresses of anthropology could always include sessions and debates on other forms of anthropological knowledge and on how to improve anthropological diversity within the international community of anthropologists. [...] An electronic collection of classics from different countries and a global anthropology e-journal are real possibilities. (Ribeiro 2005b: 5)

Asymmetric Ignorance: Metropolitan Provincialism and Provincial Cosmopolitanism

[...] Two notions are helpful to understand this situation. They refer to what Dipesh Chakrabarty (2000: 28) called asymmetric ignorance and I call a tension between metropolitan provincialism and provincial cosmopolitanism.

Metropolitan provincialism and provincial cosmopolitanism are based on the existing unequal relations in the global symbolic economy. I will give a brief definition of both notions. Metropolitan provincialism means the ignorance that hegemonic centers usually have of the production of non-hegemonic centers. Provincial cosmopolitanism means the knowledge that non-hegemonic centers usually have of the production of hegemonic centers. This asymmetrical ignorance may express itself in such curious albeit common situations as the fact that the history of universal anthropology (i.e. of hegemonic anthropologies) is known and studied by non-hegemonic anthropologists but the reverse is not true. The processes through which these anthropologies without history, to use Krotz's apt expression, became institutionalized and grew are not taught, or at best are seldom taught, even in their own countries. Classics include almost exclusively foreign anthropologists.

In many graduate programs outside the hegemonic core, being able to read at least two languages other than one's own is mandatory. Indeed both metropolitan provincialism and provincial cosmopolitism can be better understood if we consider the language issue, a rather complicated one when transnational communication is at stake. English has been the most expansive language in the past five centuries (Hamel, 2003: 16). [...] [T]he more central a language is in the world market of linguistic goods, the smaller the proportion of texts which are translated into it. In the United States and England, less than 5 percent of the publications are translations, while in France and Germany this number is around 12 percent and in Spain and Italy it is up to 20 percent. Here is an important angle of the sociolinguistic basis from which metropolitan provincialism stems. We may suppose that the opposite is true: the less important a language the more translations there will be. This would be one of the sociolinguistic sources of provincial cosmopolitanism.

[...]

[...] In this sense, if we think of the practice of anthropology on a global scale, we will see a strong potential for cross-fertilization scattered in different "glocales", with a potential for creativity impossible to be found in a single place. There is sociological and linguistic evidence that such a creativity is located in and coming from non-hegemonic locales, since provincial cosmopolitanism allows for a more differentiated vision of the discipline as an international discourse. This is not a call for ignoring the important contributions hegemonic anthropologies have made and continue to make to knowledge. Quite the contrary, I mentioned how closely the history and production of hegemonic anthropology are followed everywhere. But it means a need for other academic practices that include more horizontal exchanges and the recognition that today anthropology is a much more diverse discourse than what most North Atlantic-centric interpretations suppose. It is time to strive for multicentrism in lieu of one or a few kinds of centrism.

Final Comments

[...] Proposing "world anthropologies" is obviously not a resentful claim of authenticity nor a resentful perspective on hegemonic anthropology. The pretension of a nativist perspective has been clearly rejected in this text in favor of an openly dialogical and heteroglossic vision. Furthermore, any idea of a "periphery" that is the essential source of authenticity, pristine otherness or unparalleled creativity and radicalism is doomed to be another sort of Orientalism (see Velho, 2006). [...]

It would be ironic if the project of world anthropologies is seen as the new capacity of the "periphery" to strike back, a simplistic frame of mind akin to some interpretations of the aims of the post-colonial critique regarding former imperial metropolises. I'd rather think that this is a moment for widening the anthropological horizon that will make anthropology a richer academic cosmopolitics, one that is capable of dealing with the new challenges arising in the 21st century. World anthropologies provide a window of opportunities for all those who (a) know that hegemony of a certain universalism is not a natural given; (b) understand that difference is not inequality; and (c) realize that diversity is an asset of humankind.

In this text, I wanted to avoid an intellectualist approach to the problems that theory in anthropology has faced in the past and still faces today. Instead, I chose a sociological perspective in order to suggest that challenges and horizons in anthropological theory are embedded in several historical predicaments. My goal was to show that changing the relationships and flows of information within a yet to be fully developed global community of anthropologists is a powerful way of changing theoretical orientations today. [...]

[...] The many resurrections and reincarnations of anthropology can only be understood if we consider that it is a highly reflexive discipline that projects itself onto and receives feedback from the topics and subjects it studies. As a consequence, anthropology is fine-tuned to the sociological changes that historically occur. In a globalized world we need to have more diverse international voices and perspectives participating in any

570 GUSTAVO LINS RIBEIRO

assessment of the frontiers of anthropological knowledge. Indeed, a globalized world is a perfect scenario for anthropology to thrive since one of our discipline's basic lessons is respect for difference. A discipline that praises plurality and diversity needs to foster these standpoints within its own milieu. The time is ripe for world anthropologies.

References

Appadurai, Arjun (1990) "Disjuncture and Difference in the Global Cultural Economy", in Mike Featherstone (ed.) *Global Culture*, pp. 295–310. London: Sage.

Chakrabarty, Dipesh (2000) *Provincializing Europe: Postcolonial Thought and Historical Difference.* Princeton: Princeton University Press.

Cheah, Pheng and Bruce Robbins (eds) (1998) *Cosmopolitics: Thinking and Feeling Beyond the Nation.* Minneapolis: University of Minnesota Press.

Danda, Ajit K. (1995) *Foundations of Anthropology: India.* New Delhi: Inter-India Publications.

Hamel, Rainer Enrique (2003) *Language Empires, Linguistic Imperialism and the Future of Global Languages.* Universidad Autónoma Metropolitana, México (mimeo).

Krotz, Esteban (1997) "Anthropologies of the South: Their Rising, Their Silencing, Their Characteristics", *Critique of Anthropology* 17(3): 237–51.

Kuwayama, Takami (2004) *Native Anthropology: The Japanese Challenge to Western Academic Hegemony.* Melbourne: Trans Pacific Press.

Lomnitz, Claudio (2002) "A antropologia entre fronteiras: dialética de uma tradição nacional (México)", in Benoît de L'Estoile, Federico Neiburg and Lygia Sigaud (eds.) *Antropologia, impérios e estados nacionais*, pp. 125–58. Rio de Janeiro: Relume Dumará/ FAPERJ.

Ribeiro, Gustavo Lins (2003) *Postimperialismo. Cultura y politica en el mundo contemporáneo.* Barcelona/ Buenos Aires: Gedisa.

Ribeiro, Gustavo Lins (2005a) "Post-imperialism: A Latin American Cosmopolitics", *Série Antropologia no. 375.* Brasília: Universidade de Brasília.

Ribeiro, Gustavo Lins (2005b) "A Different Global Scenario in Anthropology", *Anthropology News* 46(7): 5–6.

Velho, Otávio G. (2006) "The Pictographics of *Tristesse*: An Anthropology of Nation-building in the Tropics and its Aftermath", in Gustavo Lins Ribeiro and Arturo Escobar (eds) *World Anthropologies: Disciplinary Transformations in Systems of Power*, pp. 261–79. Oxford: Berg.

60

Cultures of Expertise and the Management of Globalization: Toward the Re-functioning of Ethnography*

Douglas R. Holmes and George E. Marcus

[…] [I]t might be difficult for cultural and social anthropologists to extend their mode of basic research to the worlds of financial experts, bankers, and bureaucrats, Yet, if they are to engage in an anthropology of the contemporary, and now of a globalizing world, they must do so, as they have already been doing impressively in science and technology studies […]. In our experience, ethnographers trained in the tradition of anthropology do not approach the study of formal institutions such as banks, bureaucracies, corporations, and state agencies with much confidence. These are realms in which the traditional informants of ethnography must be rethought as counterparts rather than "others" – as both subjects and intellectual partners in inquiry. These are technocratic milieus in which […]that which is valued most by ethnographers – "understanding contemporary society from experience" – is most devalued within them.

[…] [R]arely do ethnographers have access to the details of the everyday lives of expert subjects. Working through the complex techniques of experts in various ways tied to the flow of money – "the statistical mode of analysis in context" – is of course one potentially valuable option in undertaking an ethnography of such experts. But we seek to connect this sort of inquiry to more conventionally social and cultural factors that underpinned traditional ethnography. In short, what is the anthropological interest in studies of domains of expertise dominated by particular forms of the statistical mode of knowledge production? And how do we reclaim "experience" as an analytic bridge to these distinctive domains?

[…] Is the point of doing fieldwork among experts to do a conventional ethnography of them? We believe it is highly unlikely that a robust ethnography of "everyday life" can be done within these cultures of expertise, where the public and private spheres are strictly demarked. If we study not only the practice of statistical modes of knowledge-making, then what other kinds of "native points of view" remain to study in the domain of experts? Here we suggest a particular strategy for *re-functioning ethnography* around a research relation in which the ethnographer identifies a para-ethnographic dimension in such domains of expertise […]. Making ethnography from the

*Editors' note: This is a substantially abridged version of the original article.

From A. Ong and S. Collier (eds.), *Global Assemblages* (New York: Blackwell, 2004). pp. 236–41, 243–6, 248–50. Reprinted with permission of John Wiley & Sons UK.

Anthropology in Theory: Issues in Epistemology, Second Edition. Edited by Henrietta L. Moore and Todd Sanders.
© 2014 John Wiley & Sons, Inc. Published 2014 by John Wiley & Sons, Inc.

found para-ethnographic redefines the status of the subject or informant, asks what different accounts one wants from such key figures in the fieldwork process, and indeed questions what the ethnography of experts means within a broad, multi-sited design of research. Crucial to this re-functioning is the status of the construct of the para-ethnographic as a kind of illicit, marginal social thought – in genres such as "the anecdotal," "hype," and "intuition" – within practices dominated by the technocratic ethos [...].

Central Banks

From preliminary investigation, we have chosen to pursue an illustration of the form that the para-ethnographic takes in the work of the personnel of central banks. The para-ethnographic here provides, as we will argue below, a somewhat subversive, yet controlled, access to fugitive social facts in a key contemporary system of technocratic expertise, which conceives and produces the idea of the global as daily practice. Central banks operate not merely under the sway of fast-capitalism; they have played a direct role in creating and mediating it. The lever that a central bank wields, as an agency regulating financial markets, is both strategic and simple: by determining interest rates by which money can be borrowed, it can influence decisively the tempo of activity in an entire economy. But to wield this lever requires the constant monitoring of massively complex representations of the entire economy and its articulations within a world system of markets. [...]

[...] Once there are sustained puzzles or displacements in the models that track and represent the behavior of an entire economy, the opportunity emerges for the influence of ways of knowing that are normally repressed, subordinated, and considered slightly illicit – the ways of knowing relegated in such technocratic organizations to the realm of the anecdotal, of hype, of intuition, of experience. Just as the decision-makers in central banks become more powerful in the public sphere as symbolic and political actors – as broader governing agents – so do para-ethnographic insights on the margins compete with what "the numbers" indicate.
[...]

Elsewhere, we have referred to the cultural formation created by this wide-ranging program of neoliberal reform as fast-capitalism. We have argued that the most distinctive feature of fast-capitalism is its propensity to subvert the science, political economy, and metaphysics of solidarity upon which modernist conceptions of society rest. Indeed, the abiding irony is that the personnel working within central banks must overcome precisely the subversions of the social that they have had a direct hand in creating through their promotion of neoliberal reform. In other words, they must reconstruct a meaningful engagement with society in order to pursue their own knowledge work and expert practice. Para-ethnography is the means by which they recast a semiotics of the social in the face of the corrosive influence of fast-capitalism.
[...]

The Anecdotal Amid Other Genres of the Para-ethnographic: A Glimpse at Alan Greenspan's Practice of the Para-ethnographic

[...] Alan Greenspan [Chairman of the Federal Reserve] was a para-ethnographer extraordinaire, who established his particular persona and reputation at the Fed by frequently countering the methods and modalities of econometrics in relying on the kind of information that those who represent the movements of the economic leviathan through measurement would dismissively characterize as "anecdotal." The following [extracts reveal] how the para-ethnographic engages the "darkly unknowable":

> Over the next months, when Greenspan analyzed data, he saw that the future orders were down in a wide range of businesses. That meant demand for goods was falling and economic growth was slowing. Greenspan tapped into his network of business contacts in New York. [...] Sounding out his long list of contacts took a great deal of time, and Greenspan eventually set up a system in which Fed staff members would formally call a long list of companies each week to get their real-time numbers. [...] He tried not to overschedule himself, making only three or four

appointments or meetings a day. The rest was for study and reading.

Greenspan went to lunches at the Business Council, an organization of business leaders, and listened to the CEOs of America's largest corporations. As soon as they saw he wasn't going to disclose much or press his own conclusions on them but instead wanted to listen, they poured out their anxieties or latest good news. Greenspan insisted that he nearly always learned more from the people who came to hear him speak than they learned from him.

It is the so-called fugitive social facts in the continuously changing contemporary that give rise to the sorts of knowledge-making among experts that can be identified as para-ethnographic by the ethnographer. [...]

Para-ethnography as Method

[...] How do we make ethnography of the para-ethnographic found in the marginal ways of knowing – centrally the anecdotal – within technocratic regimes? When deployed counterculturally and critically, by the most privileged within these regimes such as chairman Greenspan, these genres suggest where ethnography might literally go in fieldwork. [...]

It is regrettable that, in the absence of bridges or alliances between his interest and other kinds of scholarship, Greenspan was left to "go it alone" in his development of an anecdotal critique of the dominant econometric mode of representing the economy. [...] On the other side – the side that would have supported the sociology or ethnography in Greenspan's para-ethnographic insight – there is already a large amount of research – much of it ethnographic and qualitative – about the current state of workers in their own domestic and everyday contexts. [...] Yet, this knowledge simply does not count in Greenspan's world, and there is no bridging contact to make it count; it is as if this relevant research exists in another world. [...] [H]ow to relate what the ethnographer knows to the visceral mediation of the para-ethnographic by Greenspan – in short, how to relate relevant ethnography from something he experiences [physically, e.g. as a "pain in the stomach"] to formally thought out concepts? This

requires a very different presentation of ethnography than one makes to professional peers.
[...]

The Beige Book

Its formal title is *Summary of Commentary on Current Economic Conditions by Federal Reserve District*, and it is [...] published eight times a year, about a week prior to the regularly scheduled FOMC [Federal Open Market Committee] meetings. [...]

This legal authority over the management of monetary policy, exercised primarily through the setting of interest rates, makes the Committee one of the most – if not the most – powerful single institutions governing financial markets. The Beige Book is the Committee's briefing document and a means by which its members assess the current state of the economy. [...]

[...] Jason Bram [is] the analyst who does the research and has written the Beige Book entry for the New York District of the Federal Reserve for the past five years or so. [...]

Mr. Bram solicits accounts from a network of strategically positioned informants. He seeks an acute anecdotal portrayal of the economy under the administrative purview of the New York District. [...] [W]orking with a small staff, begins calling his contacts about a week before the report is due and drafts the actual document at the last possible moment to make it as contemporaneous as possible.

[...] Mr. Bram cultivates highly developed "contacts" with human interlocutors who oversee daily transactions within strategic spheres of the economy. These interlocutors are not employees of the Fed, but informants – bankers, manufacturers, real estate brokers, and retailers – who transact loans, book orders (and cancellations), and track store sales minute-to-minute, hour-to-hour. These interlocutors operate in real time, providing the closest approximation to a contemporaneous engagement with the economy.

[...] By gleaning knowledge from these interlocutors, Mr. Bram gains access to those profound and elusive cultural forces guiding the economy: expectations and sentiments.
[...]

It is not merely that these reports amassed by Mr. Bram provide a means to overcome the inevitable "lag" attendant with quantitative data; rather, it is their inherently social nature that provides these "anecdotal reports" with an agile purchase on the contemporary. And these reports would have little force if it were not for the fact that these informants speak from an intimate, subjective sense of the situated business practices and predicaments that they track anecdotally from day to day. These anecdotes are not just a different kind of supplementary data; rather, they have a distinctive cogency in their own right, legitimized through a socially mediated "native point of view." Thus, what makes these reports persuasive is the experience of the interlocutors, their judgment, their feel. These intricate exchanges that report on the economy in something that approximates "real time" constitute an acute illustration of para-ethnography and its analytic purchase.

[...]

[...] Mr. Bram described his autodidactic method in terms that are familiar to an anthropologist. "It's sort of an art, you have to know the people you are talking to." "I can't put it into a formula, it is very opportunistic." "It is very wide open." "As you do it, I have been doing it for four or five years, you learn. [...] It's a very subjective kind of thing, you have to learn what kinds of questions to ask." [...] Though Mr. Bram's method lacks a formal disciplinary identity, it yields a refined analytic engagement with staggeringly complex economic activity and human behavior.

What is compelling about this approach to cultures of expertise is that it immediately provides a basis of exchange with expert subjects. By marking out the para-ethnographic character of their expert practices, an intricate basis of discussion is opened between the anthropologist and subject. The anthropologist's presence in these domains is thereby legitimized and the basis of meaningful exchange is created. A critical seam is opened up – through a shared ethnographic enterprise – that allows the anthropologist entry into these intriguing cultural domains.

Mr. Bram's research expertise converges with our conceptualization of para-ethnography. His knowledge practices, however, also expose a deeper dimension of the workings of the native

point of view and its engagement with the contemporary. His informants, his interlocutors, and his contacts are themselves engaged in a direct para-ethnography that is so deeply embedded in their consciousness and aligned to their practices as to be virtually invisible. Once these knowledge practices are opened to scrutiny, they reveal how the contemporary is socially reproduced through the cumulative action of multiple and manifold para-ethnographies. Acutely drawn anecdotal material is the fabric of this dynamic contemporary. Mr. Bram's contacts summon para-ethnographies as they act within and upon the contemporary and by so doing give it – the contemporary – social form and cultural content.

[...]

As the political economy of the nation-state is effaced by transnational forces, conventional accounts of society as a discrete construct are increasingly superseded. Class, status, and power no longer cleave merely to the instrumentalities of the state; they are unbound. The overarching interpretive challenge for the ethnographer is to gain access – through para-ethnographic practices of expert subjects – to these emergent formations of political economy. We believe that what is revealed in the cumulative para-ethnographies of experts such as Mr. Bram are crucial ways in which social and economic phenomenon are being reconfigured as global process. More fundamentally, it is through the knowledge work of these experts that society and economy are re-created as analytic constructs and empirical facts.

The Warrant for the Postulation of the Para-ethnographic in Cultures of Expertise

We want merely to stipulate here the interesting debate that might ensue from our postulation of the "para-ethnographic" as a key construct in the design of multi-sited ethnography. This debate might focus on the phenomenological bases of the recognition and accessing of such a dimension of subjects' discourse and actions as the "para-ethnographic"; it would focus on the nature and capacity of the faculty of practical consciousness and whether anything about it could ever be equated with "the scholastic point of view," the domain of distanced reflective reason which we reserve for ourselves as academics. And if one were able to establish such collaborative relations with subjects on this level, what implications would this have for the whole project of ethnography, where certain defining distances are closed between ethnographer and subject, at least in certain reaches of the domain of multi-sited fieldwork? [...]

[...]

In sum, within traditional ethnography one never would have asked for the para-ethnography of the Trobriand islander or the Nuer. The need for radical translation was assumed. The ethnographer wanted modes of thought, systems of belief, ritual performances, and myths as the means to "the native point of view." What does it mean to substitute the "para-ethnographic" for this traditional apparatus of ethnographic knowing? As we have suggested, it means that when we deal with contemporary institutions under the sign of the global symptom, as we have termed it, we presume that we are dealing with counterparts rather than "others" – who differ from us in many ways but who also share broadly the same world of representation with us, and the same curiosity and predicament about constituting the social in our affinities. [...]

Index

Anthropology in Theory: Issues in Epistemology, Second Edition. Edited by Henrietta L. Moore and Todd Sanders.
© 2014 John Wiley & Sons, Inc. Published 2014 by John Wiley & Sons, Inc.

584

INDEX

Irigaray, Luce 390
irrationality 34–5

Jackson, Michael 257, 345, 350, 353
Jackson, Peter 370
Jakobson, Roman 194
Jameson, Fredric 271, 272, 368, 524
jealousy 39
Jefferson, Thomas 295
Johnson, Mark 345, 346, 370
Johnson, Philip 272
Johnson-Laird, Philip 213, 216, 219
Jolly, Margaret 401
Jordaneva, I. J. 272–3
judicial procedure 30
Jung, C. G. 34
Junod, Henri-Alexandre 378

Kachin culture 70–7, 177–8
Kant, Immanuel 339, 430, 442
Kapferer, Bruce 184, 320
Kash, Don E. 271, 273
Katz, Jerrold J. 153
Keat, Russell 255
Kessler, Suzanne J. 453
Keynes, John Maynard 502
kinship systems 85, 86, 116, 117, 154–5, 157, 189, 369
  bilateral systems 408–9
  commodification 400–1, 408
  cutting ties 408–9
  maternal uncles 192–3, 196, 197, 198, 199, 200–1
  moral and biological parameters 276–7, 280
  structural linguistics and 193–202
Klatt, Berthold 24
Klemm, Gustave 22
Kluckhohn, Clyde 34, 166
Knorr Cetina, Karin 505
knowledge 99–101
Kracke, Waud 431
Kristeva, Julia 390, 515
Kroeber, A. L. 78, 81, 82, 85, 86, 195, 255
Krotz, Esteban 568
Krystal, Matthew 371
Kuhn, Thomas 348, 379
Kuranko culture 248–54
Kwakiutl culture 2, 45, 51

La Barre, Weston 431
Laclau, Ernesto 311
Lakoff, George 345, 346
Lamarck, Jean-Baptiste 23
Lamphere, Louise 359
language 3, 4, 9, 29, 318
  cognitive science and 210–19
  connectionism 215–16, 217
  English language 568, 569

grammar 152, 153, 156, 218, 384
hermeneutics 152, 154, 156
heteroglossia 567, 568
mythopoesis 156
non-linguistic knowledge 10, 212–15, 217, 516
objectification 152–3
ordinary language 204–9
sentence-logic model 10, 215, 217
speech-communities 67
see also linguistics
language-based models 10, 11
language-like phenomena 210, 211, 216, 217
langue 8, 151, 302
Lapp culture 145
Laqueur, Thomas 450
Latour, Bruno 402, 403, 404, 405, 427, 436, 510, 515–16, 548
Laud, William 291
Lave, Jean 212, 216
law 44, 68–9, 328, 329
Law, John 404
Law, Sylvia 273
Lazarus, Richard 233–4
Le Wita, Béatrix 484
Leach, E. R. 6, 142–3, 144, 147, 173, 175, 176, 177, 178, 250
Leacock, Eleanor 358
Leander, Kevin 231
learning 212–14, 216, 218, 238
Leenhardt, Maurice 256
legalism 158
Leibniz, G. W. 333, 336, 339, 380, 472
Leonardo da Vinci 38
Lepowsky, Maria 361
Leroi-Gourhan, A. 212
Lesser, Alexander 303
levels of organization 33, 301
Levinas, Emmanuel 416
Lévi-Strauss, Claude 7–8, 73, 156, 158, 160, 186, 238, 260, 345, 347, 357, 360, 462–3, 464, 467, 468, 472, 482, 485, 490, 493, 498, 558
Levy, Marion 136
Lewis, I. M. 143
life forms 476–7
  artificial life 477–8
  astrobiology 479
  marine microbiology 478–9
  three limits biologies 477, 479–80
lineage society 7
linguistic privacy 169, 208
linguistics 152–3, 192–203, 384
Linnaeus, Carl 22
Lipuma, Edward 275
literalists 174
Little, Walter 371
Livingston, Julie 277